THE SIERRA LEONE SPECIAL COURT AND ITS LEGACY

The Special Court for Sierra Leone (SCSL) is the third modern international criminal tribunal supported by the United Nations and the first to be situated where the crimes were committed. This timely, important, and comprehensive book is the first to critically assess the impact and legacy of the SCSL for Africa and international criminal law. The collection, containing thirty-six original chapters from leading scholars and respected practitioners with inside knowledge of the tribunal, analyzes cutting-edge and controversial issues with significant implications for international criminal law and transitional justice. These include joint criminal enterprise; the novel crime against humanity of forced marriage; the war crime prohibiting enlisting and using child soldiers (in the first court to prosecute that offense); the prosecution of the war crime of attacks against UN peacekeepers (in the first tribunal where this offense was prosecuted); the tension between truth commissions and criminal trials (in the first country to simultaneously have the two); and the questions of whether it is permissible under international law for states to unilaterally confer blanket amnesties to local perpetrators of universally condemned international crimes, whether the immunities enjoyed by an incumbent head of a third state bars his prosecution before an ad hoc treaty-based international criminal court, and whether such courts may be funded by donations from states without compromising judicial independence.

CHARLES CHERNOR JALLOH is an Assistant Professor at the University of Pittsburgh School of Law, USA. A graduate of Guelph, McGill, and Oxford universities, he has worked in several international criminal courts, including as the Legal Advisor to the Office of the Principal Defender at the Special Court for Sierra Leone where he also served as interim court-appointed counsel to former Liberian President Charles Taylor. Professor Jalloh, who is the Founding Editor-in-Chief of the *African Journal of Legal Studies*, has published widely on issues of international criminal justice especially as they pertain to Africa in prestigious peer-reviewed journals and books. He is editor of *Consolidated Legal Texts for the Special Court for Sierra Leone* (2007) and the lead editor of the first comprehensive multivolume *Law Reports of the Special Court for Sierra Leone* (2012 and 2013).

Advance Praise

"In this fundamental work, Professor Charles Jalloh, a Sierra Leonean–Canadian scholar who first distinguished himself as an international criminal lawyer in the Charles Taylor Trial at the Sierra Leone Special Court, has assembled a stellar group of experts to comprehensively assess the Court's crucial legacy to Africa and international criminal justice. Covering the full gamut of substantive legal issues of enduring significance to the work of the International Criminal Court and other tribunals charged with the responsibility to prosecute international crimes – ranging from head-of-state immunity to national amnesties for international crimes, child recruitment, the novel crime against humanity of forced marriage, joint criminal enterprise, command responsibility, and the relationship between truth commissions and criminal trials – this outstanding volume is an enormous contribution to the international criminal law and transitional justice literature. This significant achievement of the contributing scholars and the editor, who has quickly become a renowned commentator on issues relating to international justice in Africa, is a must-read for legal and other academics, practitioners, policy makers, students, and anyone else seeking to understand the successes, and limitations, of the second-generation hybrid tribunal model and its place in the global struggle against impunity."

Fatou Bensouda, *Prosecutor, International Criminal Court*

"Over the course of a decade, the Special Court for Sierra Leone demonstrated that a national-international partnership may hold to account persons most responsible for wartime atrocities. Its legacy includes many milestones: the first prosecutions for forced marriage and child soldier recruitment; the first inclusion of a Defense Office within the organs of the Court; and the first conviction since Nuremberg of a former head of state. In this remarkable volume, the foremost experts on the Court analyze all this and more. Their essays examine the past work of the Court with an eye toward the future – toward lessons that may enhance future efforts at accountability and redress. The result is a *vade mecum* for all who work for global justice."

Diane Marie Amann, *Emily and Ernest Woodruff Chair in International Law, University of Georgia*

The Sierra Leone Special Court and Its Legacy

THE IMPACT FOR AFRICA AND INTERNATIONAL CRIMINAL LAW

Edited by

CHARLES CHERNOR JALLOH

University of Pittsburgh
School of Law

CAMBRIDGE
UNIVERSITY PRESS

32 Avenue of the Americas, New York NY 10013-2473, USA

Cambridge University Press is part of the University of Cambridge.

It furthers the University's mission by disseminating knowledge in the pursuit of education, learning and research at the highest international levels of excellence.

www.cambridge.org
Information on this title: www.cambridge.org/9781107546004

© Cambridge University Press 2014

First published 2014
First paperback edition 2015

A catalogue record for this publication is available from the British Library

Library of Congress Cataloguing in Publication data
The Sierra Leone Special Court and its legacy : the impact for Africa and international criminal law / edited by Charles Chernor Jalloh, University of Pittsburgh, School of Law.
    pages   cm
Includes bibliographical references and index.
ISBN 978-1-107-02914-9 (hardback)
1. Special Court for Sierra Leone.   2. International criminal courts – Sierra Leone.   3. International criminal courts – Netherlands.   I. Jalloh, Charles, editor of compilation.
KZ1208.S53A17   2013
341.6'90268–dc23   2013009993

ISBN 978-1-107-02914-9 Hardback
ISBN 978-1-107-54600-4 Paperback

To all the victims of the horrific Sierra Leonean conflict, especially the children and women, who endured the brutal pain, suffering, and other unspeakable horrors that gave birth to the idea of a "special court for Sierra Leone."

Contents

Editor's Biography

Charles Chernor Jalloh is an Assistant Professor at the University of Pittsburgh School of Law, USA, where he teaches Criminal Law, International Law, and International Criminal Law and also holds affiliate faculty appointments in the Graduate School of Public and International Affairs and the African Studies Program. Since joining Pitt Law in 2009, Professor Jalloh has researched, among others, questions of jurisdiction and selectivity in international criminal law especially the tense relationship between Africa and the International Criminal Court (ICC), on which he is a widely recognized expert. A prolific scholar, he has published articles in top scholarly journals on diverse topics. He was previously Counsel in the Crimes Against Humanity and War Crimes Section, Canadian Department of Justice; an Associate Legal Officer assisting Presiding Judge Erik Møse on historic trials involving the 1994 Rwandan genocide at the International Criminal Tribunal for Rwanda; the Legal Advisor to the Defense Office in the Special Court for Sierra Leone, where he was also court-appointed duty counsel to former Liberian President Charles Taylor; and a Visiting Professional at the ICC. A frequently invited speaker, he holds various pro bono positions serving, inter alia, on the Advisory Panel to the President of the International Criminal Tribunal for the Former Yugoslavia; on the Advisory Board of the War Crimes Committee, International Bar Association; and as an elected Co-Chair of the American Society of International Law's International Criminal Law Interest Group. Professor Jalloh is the Founding Editor-in-Chief of the refereed *African Journal of Legal Studies*, an interdisciplinary journal focused on human rights and good governance issues in Africa. His education includes a Bachelor of Arts from the University of Guelph; degrees in common and civil law from McGill University; and a Master's in International Human Rights Law, with distinction, from Oxford University, where he was also a Chevening Scholar.

Biographies of Contributors

Cecile Aptel is an Associate Professor of International Law at the Fletcher School of Law and Diplomacy, Tufts University. Previously, she served at the UN international tribunals for Rwanda and the former Yugoslavia (1995–2005), and helped establish the War Crimes Chamber of the State Court of Bosnia-Herzegovina (2005) and the Special Tribunal for Lebanon (2006). She has participated in international investigations of international crimes and gross human rights violations and terrorism, including at the UN International Independent Investigation Commission in Lebanon. Professor Aptel has advised on rule of law and judicial reform in several countries. She created and directed the International Center for Transitional Justice's program on children (2008–2010) and was awarded the 2010–2011 Jennings Randolph Senior Fellowship by the United States Institute of Peace. She has been the Co-Chair of the International Bar Association's War Crimes Committee since 2008. Her research focuses on international criminal law, transitional justice, and child rights.

Roberta Arnold studied at the Universities of Bern, Nottingham, Sheffield, and Tel Aviv. Between 2002 and 2005, she worked as a legal advisor within the Staff of the Chief of the Armed Forces at the Swiss Department of Defense. She has trained as a barrister and worked as a commissioner in the Special Federal Commission for the Admission of Objectors of Conscience to the Civil Service. Between December 2008 and September 2010, she served in the Swiss Defense Department as a political advisor on Arms Control and Disarmament Policy issues, prior to joining part-time as a lawyer in the Office of the Federal Attorney General (International Judicial Assistance Division and Competence Centre for International Criminal Law). In the Swiss Armed Forces, she holds the rank of specialist officer (Capt.), with the function of examining magistrate of the Swiss Military Justice. Dr. Arnold has published extensively in the areas of international criminal law and international humanitarian law. Her doctoral work at the University of Bern entitled *The ICC as a New Instrument for the Repression of Terrorism* was published by Transnational Publishers (New York). The book was given Honorable Mention by the Francis Lieber Society (ASIL) and awarded the Walther Hug Prize as one of the best doctorates in Switzerland in 2004. She currently serves as the Swiss correspondent of the *Review of the International Society for Military Law and the Law of War*.

Sareta Ashraph specializes in international humanitarian and human rights law. She was most recently the Senior Analyst in the UN Commission of Inquiry into Libya. The

Commission was charged with investigating all violations of international law in Libya, focusing on the period following the rise of the protests there in mid-February 2011. Before her work on Libya, Ms. Ashraph was based in The Hague as the Legal Advisor to the Office of the Public Counsel for Defense in the International Criminal Court, working predominantly on the Kenya post-election violence cases. In 2009, she worked as a Legal Consultant to the UN Fact-Finding Mission on the Gaza Conflict (the Goldstone Inquiry). From 2004 to 2009, Ms. Ashraph was based in Sierra Leone as Co-Counsel on the defense team representing Issa Sesay (interim Leader of the Revolutionary United Front) before the Special Court for Sierra Leone. She is a Deployable Civilian Expert (Justice Sector) with DFID and is also an ad hoc consultant to the Open Society Justice Initiative. Ms. Ashraph is called to the Bar of England and Wales and the Bar of the Republic of Trinidad and Tobago. She is a barrister attached to Garden Court Chambers in London.

Mohamed A. Bangura is a member of the Taylor prosecution team in the Office of the Prosecutor, Special Court for Sierra Leone, The Hague. He was also a prosecutor in the Civil Defense Forces and Revolutionary United Front Cases in Freetown. He holds a Bachelor of Laws (LL.B.) (Hons) from Fourah Bay College, University of Sierra Leone (1991), and qualified as a Barrister and Solicitor (BL) from the Sierra Leone Law School (1992). He holds a Master of Laws (LL.M.) from the University of London (External) (2001) and a Master of Science (M.Sc.) in Property Law from South Bank University London (2001). He is a member of the Sierra Leone Bar.

Ilias Bantekas, LL.B. (Athens), LL.M. (Liverpool), Ph.D. (Liverpool), Dip. Theology (Cambridge), is a Professor of International Law at Brunel University School of Law, United Kingdom, and a Senior Fellow at the Institute of Advanced Legal Studies, University of London. He has held full-time/visiting academic posts at Harvard, Miami, Cleveland State, Trier, the School of Oriental and African Studies, Westminster, and others. He has advised governments, international organizations, NGOs and private clients in most fields of international law and human rights. His publications include *International Criminal Law* (4th edition 2010); *International Human Rights Law* (2012); and *Trust Funds under International Law: Trustee Obligations of the U.N. and International Development Banks* (2009).

Linda E. Carter is a Professor of Law and Co-Director of the Global Center, University of the Pacific, McGeorge School of Law, Sacramento, California. Professor Carter has lectured and researched international criminal law issues in multiple venues. In 2005, she studied the Gacaca trials in Rwanda and conducted a workshop in Cambodia. In 2007, she served as a Visiting Professional in the Appeals Chamber of the International Criminal Court in The Hague and as a Legal Researcher at the International Criminal Tribunal for Rwanda. She was a Fulbright Senior Specialist in Senegal in 2009. Since 2003, she has worked with the Brandeis Institute for International Judges, which convenes meetings of judges from all major international tribunals. Prior to entering academia, Professor Carter litigated civil and criminal cases: from 1978 to 1981, she was an attorney in the Honors Program of the Civil Rights Division of the U.S. Department of Justice in Washington, DC, and from 1981 to 1985, she was an attorney with the Legal Defender Association in Salt Lake City, Utah. She is the author of books and articles on domestic and international criminal law and procedure.

Theresa M. Clark is an Associate Professor at Villanova University School of Law, Pennsylvania, USA, where she has taught since 2007. Professor Clark received her J.D. from Washington University, and through the Fulbright Program, earned a Master's in Human Rights and Democratization jointly from Ruhr-Universitat, Universidad de Duesto, Universita degli studi di Padova, and Universita Ca Foscari. Moreover, as a Legomsky-Dagen Fellow, she studied public international law at The Hague Academy of International Law. Her scholarly interests focus on transitional justice, international criminal law, international human rights, and legal analysis, writing, and oral advocacy.

Vivian Grosswald Curran is a Professor at the University of Pittsburgh, where she specializes in comparative law and founded the Law School's Languages for Lawyers program. She is an elected member of the American Law Institute and the International Academy of Comparative Law and a past Secretary of the American Society of Comparative Law. In 2004, she was appointed by the State Department as the U.S. member of the Austrian General Settlement Fund Committee to adjudicate compensation claims for Nazi-era property expropriations in Austria. The Austrian government decorated her for her work with the *große goldene Ehrenzeichen* in 2007. A native speaker of both French and English, Curran is the author, editor, and/or translator of several books and regularly publishes in English and French in American, French, and Canadian law reviews, journals, and books.

Margaret M. deGuzman teaches criminal law, international criminal law, and transitional justice at the Temple University Beasley School of Law, Pennsylvania. She has authored a number of publications on such issues as the definition of crimes against humanity, the role of case and situational gravity in the legitimacy of the International Criminal Court (ICC), and the theoretical underpinning of selection decisions at the ICC. She is currently participating in an international expert group drafting general rules and principles of international criminal procedure. Professor deGuzman is a graduate of Yale Law School, the Fletcher School of Law & Diplomacy, and Georgetown University's School of Foreign Service. She was a Fulbright Scholar in Senegal and is currently a Ph.D. candidate at the Irish Center for Human Rights of the National University of Ireland. Before joining the Temple faculty, she clerked on the Ninth Circuit Court of Appeals and practiced law in San Francisco for six years, specializing in criminal defense. She also served as a legal advisor to the Senegal delegation at the Rome Conference on the ICC and as a law clerk in the Office of the Prosecutor of the International Criminal Tribunal for the Former Yugoslavia.

Amy E. DiBella currently practices in the area of criminal defense. She holds a B.A. in Latin American Hemispheric Studies (summa cum laude) from George Washington University; a J.D. (cum laude and Order of the Coif) from the University of Pittsburgh Law School, where she was awarded the Faculty Award for Excellence in Legal Scholarship for her paper *The Right to Confrontation: Reconciling the Constitution with International Criminal Proceedings*; and an LL.M. in International Law of Human Rights and Criminal Justice from Utrecht University in the Netherlands. She previously worked as an intern in the Office of Public Counsel for the Defense at the International Criminal Court.

Viviane E. Dittrich is currently a postgraduate researcher in the Department of International Relations at the London School of Economics and Political Science (LSE). Her research focuses on international institutions, specifically international criminal tribunals, and post-conflict justice and peace. She is examining the institutional developments of the ad hoc tribunals toward completion in light of their imminent closure and legacy. Viviane received an M.Sc. in International Relations from the LSE and a Master's degree from Sciences Po Paris (double degree). At present, she is working as a teaching assistant in the Department of International Relations at the LSE; previously she has worked as a temporary staff member at the Institute of International Education in Washington, DC; a teaching assistant at Wellesley College; and a project member of Afric@ction, a development aid project in Niamey (Niger).

Jennifer Easterday is a Ph.D. Researcher for the "_Jus Post Bellum_" project at the Grotius Centre for International Legal Studies, Leiden University in the Netherlands. She is also a consultant trial monitor the for Open Society Justice Initiative, monitoring the Katanga and Ngudjolo trial before the International Criminal Court. She previously worked for International Criminal Law Services, an NGO based in The Hague, on a variety of international criminal law projects including drafting training materials tailored to the Balkans region as part of any OSCE/ODIHR – ICTY legacy project, international criminal law capacity-building projects in Uganda and Rwanda, and other projects related to international criminal justice. She has also worked as a Senior Researcher and Trial Monitor for the UC Berkeley War Crimes Studies Center, researching and monitoring the Special Court for Sierra Leone trial of Charles Taylor and developing projects related to trial monitoring at other international and hybrid tribunals. She has experience at the International Criminal Tribunal for the Former Yugoslavia and with other international criminal law and human rights NGOs in the United States and Latin America. She received her J.D. from the University of California, Berkeley, School of Law, and is a member of the California State Bar.

Stuart Ford's academic interests are in international criminal law and international criminal courts. He has published articles on the International Criminal Court, the responsibility to protect doctrine, crimes against humanity, and genocide. His current work explores the cost and value of international criminal tribunals. He teaches Civil Procedure, International Organizations, and International Criminal Law at the John Marshall Law School in Chicago. Prior to joining John Marshall, Professor Ford worked as an Assistant Prosecutor at the Extraordinary Chambers in the Courts of Cambodia (ECCC), which was jointly established by the Royal Government of Cambodia and the United Nations to prosecute senior leaders of the Khmer Rouge for atrocities committed in Cambodia between 1975 and 1979. He participated in the selection of crime sites and suspects for investigation, conducted preliminary investigations, and participated in the co-investigating judges' investigations. In addition, he represented the Co-Prosecutors during the trial of Kaing Guek Eav, alias "Duch," the first person to be tried by the ECCC.

Micaela Frulli is currently Associate Professor of International Law at the University of Florence, Italy. She received her Ph.D. in International Law from the University "Federico II" of Naples (2000). She was a Jean Monnet Fellow (2001–2002) at the Law Department of the European University Institute (2001–2002). She was also a Marie Curie Fellow (2010) at the EUI, sponsored by the European Union, with a project on the criminalization of attacks against cultural heritage and the impact of international criminal law on the protection of cultural property. Dr. Frulli has done extensive research in public international law, international criminal law, the law of international organizations, and human rights law. In recent years she has focused on the following topics: immunity of state officials suspected of international crimes; state immunity and human rights; private military companies: issues of accountability. She has published books (as author and editor) and essays, articles, and book chapters in Italian, English, and French. Her most recent publications include articles in the *European Journal of International Law, Journal of International Criminal Justice*, and *The Oxford Companion to International Criminal Justice* (edited by A. Cassese).

Kenneth S. Gallant is a Professor of Law at the University of Arkansas at Little Rock. Previously, he was at the University of Idaho, where he directed the clinic and taught on the faculty. Before entering teaching, he served first as a prosecutor and later as Attorney-in-Charge for Special Litigation with the Office of the District Attorney of Philadelphia. He served as a law clerk to the late Judge Samuel J. Roberts of the Supreme Court of Pennsylvania and Judge Louis H. Pollak of the U.S. District Court for the Eastern District of Pennsylvania. Professor Gallant teaches criminal law, international law, conflict of laws, and lawyering skills. He has published extensively in the area of international law. His most recent work is a book, *The Principle of Legality in International and Comparative Criminal Law* (2009).

Lansana Gberie is a Sierra Leonean historian and writer based in New York. He was Senior Researcher with the Africa Conflict Prevention Program of the Institute for Security Studies in Addis Ababa, Ethiopia. Before that, he was Senior Research Fellow at the Kofi Annan International Peacekeeping Training Centre in Accra, Ghana. An academic and journalist, Dr. Gberie is the author of *A Dirty War in West Africa: The RUF and the Destruction of Sierra Leone* (2005). He was awarded the "Outstanding Research Award" by the Canadian government body International Development Research Center in 2002 for his work with Partnership Africa Canada on the Human Security and International Diamond Trade project. He holds a Ph.D. in History from VU University in The Netherlands.

Annie Gell is currently the Sandler Fellow in the International Justice Division of Human Rights Watch. She is a graduate of Columbia College and Columbia University School of Law. She has worked and conducted research in India, Cambodia, Liberia, Sierra Leone, and Haiti. Prior to joining Human Rights Watch, Ms. Gell was the coordinator of the Rape Accountability and Prevention Project at the Bureau des Avocats Internationaux (BAI) in Port au Prince, Haiti.

Charles Chernor Jalloh is an Assistant Professor at the University of Pittsburgh School of Law, USA. A graduate of Guelph, McGill, and Oxford universities, he has worked in several international criminal courts, including as the Legal Advisor to the Office of the Principal Defender at the Special Court for Sierra Leone, where he also served as interim court-appointed counsel to former Liberian President Charles Taylor. Professor Jalloh, who is the Founding Editor-in-Chief of the *African Journal of Legal Studies*, has published widely on issues of international criminal justice, especially as they pertain to Africa in prestigious peer-reviewed journals and books. He is editor of *Consolidated Legal Texts for the Special*

Court for Sierra Leone (2007) and the lead editor of the first comprehensive multivolume *Law Reports of the Special Court for Sierra Leone* (2012 and 2013).

Wayne Jordash specializes in international and humanitarian law, international criminal and human rights law, and related transitional justice issues. He has represented individuals in the United Kingdom, at the International Criminal Tribunal for the Former Yugoslavia (ICTY), the International Criminal Tribunal for Rwanda (ICTR), and the Special Court for Sierra Leone. Clients have included a mayor (Baglishema), a prominent businessman (Bagaragaza), and the interim leader of the Revolutionary United Front (RUF) (Sesay). He has been a consultant at the Extraordinary Chambers in the Courts of Cambodia advising on international law issues relevant to the defense of former Khmer Rouge members of the Pol Pot regime, including the deputy to Pol Pot (Nuon Chea) and the former Minister of Foreign Affairs, Khieu Samphan. He is currently lead counsel at the ICTY defending Jovica Stanišić, the first intelligence chief to be tried by an international criminal tribunal, and a consultant on the appeal in *Prosecutor v. Innocent Sagahutu* at the ICTR. He is also a consultant to the Cambodian Centre for Human Rights, advising on a range of international, criminal, and human rights law issues for the NGO that works to promote democracy and human rights throughout Cambodia. He has published widely in international journals and textbooks.

Sara Kendall is currently based in The Hague at Leiden University's Grotius Centre for International Legal Studies. She received a Ph.D. from the University of California at Berkeley, where her dissertation research examined the politics and jurisdiction of the Special Court for Sierra Leone. Her fieldwork was supported by Berkeley's War Crimes Studies Center, and it included monitoring and weekly reporting on trial proceedings for all four of the Court's cases. She has coauthored publications for the War Crimes Studies Center assessing the practice and jurisprudence of the SCSL in addition to an article on the Court's voluntary funding structure published in the *Leiden Journal of International Law*. She is currently undertaking fieldwork for a multiyear research project assessing the International Criminal Court's interventions in Uganda, Kenya, and the Democratic Republic of Congo.

Alhagi B. M. Marong is Legal Advisor and Deputy Head of the Office of Legal Affairs at the United Nations Assistance Mission (UNAMA) in Kabul, Afghanistan. Before joining UNAMA, he worked as a Legal Officer at the Chambers Support Section of the UN International Criminal Tribunal for Rwanda, and as Senior Legal Officer at the Appeals Chamber of the Special Court for Sierra Leone. Earlier in his career, Dr. Marong served as State Counsel at the Attorney-General's Chambers and Ministry of Justice in The Gambia, taught international law at the American University of Armenia in Yerevan, and served as Staff Attorney and Co-Director for Africa Programs at the Environmental Law Institute in Washington, DC. He obtained his Bachelor of Laws (honors) degree at Fourah Bay College, University of Sierra Leone, before proceeding to McGill University in Montréal, Canada, where he graduated with a Master of Laws with distinction in 1997 and a Doctor of Civil Law in international law in 2003. He was called to the Bar in 1993.

Scott Martin was co-counsel for Mr. Augustine Gbao in the case *Prosecutor v. Sesay et al.* at the Special Court for Sierra Leone. He is currently co-counsel in *Prosecutor v. Stanišić and Simatović* at the International Criminal Tribunal for the Former Yugoslavia (ICTY) and *Prosecutor v. Ndindiliyimana et al.* at the International Criminal Tribunal for Rwanda. He has also worked for the Appeals Chamber at the ICTY. Mr. Martin is a member of the District of Columbia Bar in the United States and graduated from the George Washington University School of Law in Washington, DC.

Simon M. Meisenberg is currently seconded by a German government organization (Gesellschaft für Internationale Zusammenarbeit) as Legal Advisor to the Extraordinary Chambers in the Courts of Cambodia and was formerly a Senior Legal Officer at the Special Court for Sierra Leone. He joined the SCSL in January 2005 following a previous interval in 2003, and he assisted Trial Chamber I and II on the trials and judgments in *Prosecutor v. Brima, Kamara and Kanu; Prosecutor v. Sesay, Kallon and Gbao*; and *Prosecutor v. Charles Taylor*. Before working at the SCSL, he was a legal assistant on a Defense Team at the International Tribunal for the Former Yugoslavia and in a Trial Chamber at the International Criminal Tribunal for Rwanda. He is associated with the Institute for International Law of Peace and Armed Conflict at the Ruhr-University of Bochum, Germany. He is a member of the German Working Group for International Criminal Law, the UN Association of Germany, the European Society of International Law, and the African Law Association. He studied law at the universities in Trier, Bonn (Germany), and Lausanne (Switzerland) and is a qualified lawyer, holding the First and Second Legal State Examination, which makes him eligible for all judicial posts in Germany. Mr. Meisenberg, who has published widely on the Sierra Leone Court, is coeditor of the multi-volume *Law Reports of the Special Court for Sierra Leone* (2012).

Chacha Bhoke Murungu, LL.B (Hons.) (Dar es Salaam), LL.M. and LL.D. (Pretoria), is a Senior Lecturer in Law and Head, Department of Law, University of Dodoma, Tanzania. Dr. Murungu, who is an advocate of the High Court of Tanzania, has conducted research at the Centre for Human Rights in the University of Pretoria, South Africa, and published on aspects of international criminal law relating to Africa in leading peer-reviewed journals such as the *Journal of International Criminal Justice*. He is a coeditor of *Prosecuting International Crimes in Africa* (2011) and coordinator of the African Expert Study Group on International Criminal Justice, a project of Konrad Adenauer Stiftung.

Vincent O. Nmehielle has more than twenty-one years of professional and academic experience. He is currently the Head of the Wits Program in Law, Justice and Development in Africa at the University of the Witwatersrand (Wits) School of Law, Johannesburg, South Africa, where he has taught since February 2002. He is a Barrister and Solicitor of the Supreme Court of Nigeria. Dr. Nmehielle held the Bram Fischer Chair in Human Rights Law at Wits from 2002 to 2004. He was a Professorial Lecturer in Law at the Oxford University and George Washington University Human Rights Program in 2003 and 2004. From 2005 to 2008, Professor Nmehielle served as the Principal Defender of the Special Court for Sierra Leone in Freetown, Sierra Leone. He returned to Wits in June 2008. He holds a Bachelor of Laws degree from the Rivers State University of Science & Technology, Port Harcourt, Nigeria; a Master of Laws degree in International Law from the University of Notre Dame in the United States; and a Doctor of Juridical Science Degree in International and Comparative Law from the George Washington University in Washington, DC. His professional, academic, and research interest is in the theme area of law, governance, justice, and development in Africa.

Noah Benjamin Novogrodsky is a Professor at the University of Wyoming College of Law, and Co-Director of the Center for International Human Rights Law and Advocacy. He teaches international human rights law, immigration law, and civil procedure. He is a Phi Beta Kappa graduate with highest honors from Swarthmore College. He holds a law degree from Yale and an M.Phil. in International Relations from Queens' College at Cambridge University, where he won the Daniel Vincent Prize for the best thesis on the Middle East. After law school, professor Novogrodsky served as law clerk to the Honorable Nancy Gertner of the U.S. District Court for the District of Massachusetts. He was a Robert L. Bernstein Fellow in International Human Rights in Eritrea, Ethiopia, and South Africa; a litigation associate at Howard, Rice, Nemerovski, Canady, Falk & Rabkin in San Francisco; and a founding director of the International Human Rights Clinic at the University of Toronto Faculty of Law (Canada). Professor Novogrodsky has also been a Visiting Professor at Georgetown University Law Center and the University of Connecticut School of Law. His scholarship has focused on the global HIV/AIDS pandemic and international criminal justice.

Valerie Oosterveld joined the University of Western Ontario Faculty of Law (Canada) in 2005, where she teaches courses in international criminal law, international human rights law, international organizations, and public international law. Before joining Western Law, Valerie served in the Legal Affairs Bureau of Canada's Department of Foreign Affairs and International Trade. In this role, she provided legal advice on international criminal accountability for genocide, crimes against humanity, and war crimes, especially with respect to the International Criminal Court (ICC), the Special Court for Sierra Leone (SCSL), the International Criminal Tribunals for the Former Yugoslavia and Rwanda, and other transitional justice mechanisms. During Canada's Security Council tenure in 1999–2000, she was deeply involved in the discussions surrounding the creation of the SCSL and its Management Committee. She was a member of the Canadian delegation to the ICC negotiations, subsequent Assembly of States Parties, and the 2010 Review Conference of the Rome Statute of the ICC. Her research and writing focus on gender issues within international criminal justice and on the closure of the time-limited criminal tribunals, including the SCSL.

Peter Penfold, who retired in 2002, served in the British Diplomatic Service for thirty-eight years. He spent time in Africa and the Caribbean, witnessing several coups, insurrections, civil wars, kidnappings, and hurricanes. Prior to his appointment to Sierra Leone, he was the governor of the British Virgin Islands and the British government's Advisor on drug trafficking in the Caribbean. Her Majesty The Queen awarded him the CMG (1995) and OBE (1986). During his tenure as the British High Commissioner to Sierra Leone (1997–2000), he was closely identified with the country's efforts to embrace democracy and achieve stability and lasting peace. His experiences brought him into face-to-face negotiations with the rebels and contact with local and international humanitarian agencies. He worked closely with the United Nations, the international community, and British and African military forces. In recognition of his efforts he was appointed a Paramount Chief and made a Freeman of the city of Freetown. He has remained involved with Sierra Leone, visiting the country and promoting assistance for the disabled. He appeared before the Special Court for Sierra Leone as a defense witness on behalf of Chief Sam Hinga

Norman. He is the author of *Atrocities, Diamonds and Diplomacy: The Inside Story of the Conflict in Sierra Leone* (2012).

René Provost holds a Bachelor of Laws from the Université de Montréal, a Master of Laws from the University of California at Berkeley, and a D.Phil. from the University of Oxford. He served as law clerk to the Honorable Justice Claire L'Heureux-Dubé at the Supreme Court of Canada in 1988–1989 and taught international law at Lehigh University in Pennsylvania in 1991. He joined the Faculty of Law of McGill University in 1994, first as a Boulton Fellow (1994–1995), then as Assistant Professor (1995–2001) and Associate Professor (from 2001). He was the Associate Dean (Academic) of the Faculty of Law from 2001 to 2003. From 2005 to 2010 he was the founding Director of the McGill Centre for Human Rights and Legal Pluralism. Professor Provost teaches public international law, international human rights law, international humanitarian law, international environmental law, legal anthropology, and various courses in legal theory. He is the author of *International Human Rights and Humanitarian Law* (2002); the editor of *State Responsibility in International Law* (2002), and coeditor of *International Law Chiefly as Applied and Interpreted in Canada* (6th ed., 2006); *Confronting Genocide* (2011), and *Dialogues on Human Rights and Legal Pluralism* (2012). He was the president of the Société québécoise de droit international from 2002 to 2006.

Stephen J. Rapp of Iowa is Ambassador-at-Large, heading the Office of Global Criminal Justice in the U.S. Department of State. Prior to his appointment, Ambassador Rapp served as Prosecutor of the Special Court for Sierra Leone (SCSL) beginning in January 2007. He led the prosecutions of former Liberian president Charles Taylor and other persons alleged to bear the greatest responsibility for the atrocities committed during the civil war in Sierra Leone. During his tenure at the SCSL, his office won the first convictions in history for recruitment and use of child soldiers and for sexual slavery and forced marriage as crimes under international humanitarian law. From 2001 to 2007, Mr. Rapp served as Senior Trial Attorney and Chief of Prosecutions at the International Criminal Tribunal for Rwanda, heading the trial team that achieved convictions of the principals of RTLM radio and *Kangura* newspaper – the first in history for leaders of the mass media for the crime of direct and public incitement to commit genocide. He was the United States Attorney in the Northern District of Iowa between 1993 and 2001.

Leila Nadya Sadat is the Henry H. Oberschelp Professor of Law at Washington University School of Law and Director of the Whitney R. Harris World Law Institute. Professor Sadat is an award-winning and prolific scholar with more than seventy-five articles and several books to her name. She is also the Director of the *Crimes Against Humanity Initiative*, a multiyear project to study the problem of crimes against humanity and draft a comprehensive convention addressing their punishment and prevention. Sadat teaches public international law, international criminal law, and human rights and is considered one of the world's leading experts on the International Criminal Court. From 2001 to 2003, she was appointed by Congress to the nine-member U.S. Commission for International Religious Freedom. She often lectures and teaches abroad, and in 2011 held the Alexis de Tocqueville Distinguished Fulbright Chair in Paris, France. In 2012, Professor Sadat was elected to membership on the Council of Foreign Relations she holds or has held leadership positions in several professional associations and learned societies, including the American Law Institute and the American Society of International Law. Sadat received her B.A. from Douglass College and her J.D. from Tulane Law School (summa cum laude), and she holds graduate degrees from Columbia University School of Law (LL.M., summa cum laude) and the University of Paris I – Sorbonne (*diplôme d'études approfondies*).

Shakiratu Sanusi was most recently a Human Rights Officer with the Commonwealth Secretariat. She is a qualified solicitor with experience in academia, legal practice, and the civil society sector. She worked with a number of NGOs dealing with human rights issues from an international and African regional perspective prior to qualifying as a solicitor in the United Kingdom. In her work as a solicitor, she specialized in civil liberties cases, particularly actions against the police, bringing claimant proceedings against public authorities alleging discrimination, serious wrongdoing, abuse of position or power, and/or significant breaches of human rights as well as housing law and housing-related public law. At the Special Court for Sierra Leone, she worked as Legal Taxing Officer in the Office of the Principal Defender and subsequently as Legal Advisor to the Registrar and as the Senior Legal Advisor to the Registrar. She holds a Ph.D. in international human rights law from the London School of Economics and Political Science with a focus on women's rights, in particular, the omission of race and culture from feminist approaches to international human rights law from an African perspective, her area of special interest.

Michael P. Scharf is the John Deaver Drinko–Baker & Hostetler Professor and Associate Dean for Global Legal Studies at Case Western Reserve University School of Law. During the elder Bush and the Clinton administrations, Scharf served in the Office of the Legal Adviser of the U.S. Department of State, where he held the positions of Attorney-Adviser for Law Enforcement and Intelligence, Attorney-Adviser for United Nations Affairs, and delegate to the United Nations Human Rights Commission. During a sabbatical in 2008, Mr. Scharf served as Special Assistant to the Prosecutor of the Cambodia Genocide Tribunal. He is the author of fourteen books in the field of international criminal law, three of which have received book-of-the-year awards. Mr. Scharf and the Public International Law & Policy Group, an NGO he cofounded and directs, were nominated for the Nobel Peace Prize by the Prosecutor of the Special Court for Sierra Leone for the work they have done to help in the prosecution of major war criminals, including of Charles Taylor.

Alpha Sesay is the Open Society Justice Initiative's (OSJI) Legal Officer for International Justice based in The Hague. From the start of the Charles Taylor trial in The Hague, Mr. Sesay has monitored the proceedings on a full-time basis for the OSJI, writing and posting daily summaries and analysis on a trial-monitoring blog (www.charlestaylortrial.org) and working with civil society and the media in Sierra Leone and Liberia to enhance their involvement in the work of the Special Court for Sierra Leone (SCSL). He previously lectured on human rights at the University of Sierra Leone, worked with the SCSL and with Human Rights Watch in New York, and cofounded and served as National Director of the Sierra Leone Court Monitoring Program. Mr. Sesay also cofounded and served as President of the Fourah Bay College Human Rights Clinic. He is a Sierra Leonean human rights practitioner with an LL.B. (Hons.) from the University of Sierra Leone and an LL.M. in International Human Rights Law from the University of Notre Dame.

Sandesh Sivakumaran is a lecturer in the School of Law and member of the Human Rights Law Centre, University of Nottingham, United Kingdom. He has worked at the International Court of Justice, the Appeals Chamber of the International Criminal Tribunal for the Former Yugoslavia, and the Special Court for Sierra Leone. Mr. Siva has acted as an expert or advisor for a number of states, UN entities, and NGOs. He is the author of *The Law of Non-International Armed Conflict* (2012) and coeditor of *International Human Rights Law* (2010). For his research, he has been awarded the *Journal of International Criminal Justice* Giorgio La Pira Prize and the Antonio Cassese Prize for International Criminal Law Studies.

Alison Smith is the Legal Counsel and Coordinator of the International Criminal Justice Program for No Peace Without Justice, having formerly worked as its Country Director in Sierra Leone. Her experience includes service as the chief legal advisor to the Vice President of Sierra Leone on the Special Court for Sierra Leone and international humanitarian law. She has acted as international legal advisor to a number of clients including the Tibetan Government in Exile and some Kosovar politicians. In 2000, she was a legal advisor to the government of Thailand during the UN Preparatory Commissions for the establishment of an International Criminal Court and during the first sessions of the Assembly of States Parties. Ms. Smith worked in Kosovo as an international legal officer for the International Crisis Group's Humanitarian Law Documentation Project. Before that, she was a researcher at the Kennedy School of Government's Carr Center for Human Rights Policy at Harvard University. Ms. Smith is an Australian barrister and holds a Master's degree in International Law from the Australian National University.

Sidney Thompson is a Crown Counsel with the Public Prosecution Service of Canada. From 2007 through 2010 she was a Legal Officer in Chambers at the Special Court for Sierra Leone on the Armed Forces Revolutionary Council and Charles Taylor Trials. She has also worked with the Office of the Prosecutor at the United Nations International Criminal Tribunal for Rwanda and as a Prosecutor in the Territory of Nunavut in Canada's eastern arctic region. Prior to turning to law, she specialized in gender and development, providing consultancy services in Canada and working with NGOs in Cambodia, Thailand, and Tanzania. She holds a B.A. Hons. (Toronto), LL.B./B.C.L. (McGill), and an LL.M. (Columbia). In 2011, she was granted the John Peters Humphrey Fellowship in International Human Rights Law and Organization by the Canadian Council on International Law.

Harmen van der Wilt is a Professor of International Law at the University of Amsterdam Faculty of Law and the Amsterdam Center for International Law. His research interests lie in the concepts of criminal responsibility in international criminal law; European arrest warrant; ICC: principle of complementarity; harmonization of criminal law in Europe; criminal procedure of international criminal tribunals; legal reaction to terrorism; and cooperation between states and international criminal tribunals. Professor van der Wilt has been involved in professional training programs for judiciary and public prosecutors in Addis Ababa, Ethiopia, and training programs for young staff members of Lobatchevski University of Nijni Novgorod. He has been a member of the Research Council of an EU project on the European Arrest Warrant and is currently a member of the Steering Committee of the EU project DOMAC (Impact of International Procedures on Domestic Criminal Procedures in Mass Atrocity Cases). In 1997 he was honored by the Faculty of Law as "best teacher of the year" and in 1999 he received the Edmond Hustinx prize for excellent research. He has published widely on issues of international criminal law and currently serves on the editorial board of the *Journal of International Criminal Justice.*

Foreword

William A. Schabas, OC MRIA[*]

"We'd forgive most things if we knew the facts," wrote Graham Greene in his novel about the lives of British administrators in Second World War–era Sierra Leone. His remark is an interesting idea full of significance for transitional justice. Greene's great novel *The Heart of the Matter* describes the corruption, depravity, and violence of colonialism in Africa. A progressive man himself, Greene may well have understood the perversity of such a situation, although like many others he might not have anticipated how quickly it would come to an end. Less than two decades after publication of his novel, Sierra Leone was an independent state and a full member of the United Nations. With two nearby West African states, Nigeria and Liberia, it cosponsored the 1961 Monrovia conference at which the Organization of African Unity – now the African Union – was established. At the time, Sierra Leone had a higher standard of living than Singapore. Its university, Fourah Bay College, was renowned throughout the continent. It was a time of great hope and optimism.

The British will claim they brought civilization of a sort to the country, depositing shiploads of freed slaves and giving the name Freetown to its major urban center. In the late eighteenth century, Africans who had sided with them in opposing the revolution were also settled there, after an unsuccessful experiment in Nova Scotia. With independence, Sierra Leone soon became a kind of hell with few equivalents elsewhere in Africa. For complex reasons that neither international courts nor truth and reconciliation commissions will ever be able to explain, the British legacy quickly degenerated into a cycle of despotism and coups d'état. Understandably, young men and women, stung by the hopelessness of their circumstances, turned to rebellion, egged on by revolutionary charlatans such as Mouamar Gaddafy. Civil war began in earnest in 1991. It became apparent that the perverse leadership of those purporting to overthrow a rotten regime was no improvement on those they sought to replace.

The parties fought to a deadlock. Neither side could prevail on the battlefield. In 1999, after the rebels launched a murderous attack on Freetown, intense negotiations resulted in a controversial peace agreement. It was a nasty compromise, integrating the rebel leaders into a power-sharing framework, and promising all parties to the conflict that they would be immune from prosecution, even for the notorious war crimes and crimes against humanity that had been perpetrated during the eight-year conflict. The measure was sugarcoated by the promise that a truth and reconciliation commission would be established, promising a modest degree of accountability for the many unsatisfied victims.

[*] Professor of International Law, Middlesex University, London. Author of more than 20 books and more than 300 articles in international law, Schabas was a member of the Sierra Leone Truth and Reconciliation Commission.

Only the year before, the Rome Statute of the International Criminal Court had been adopted. There was a growing unwillingness to accept impunity of the sort pledged in the Lomé Peace Agreement. Indeed, the United Nations road tested a new policy, welcoming the end of the war in Sierra Leone but frowning mightily on the amnesty that the combatants had been granted, which is to say granted to themselves. In 2000, maneuvering within the unstable new government brought a resurgence of violence. The rebels took up arms again, holding hundreds of UN peacekeepers hostage and killing some of them. With British help, this new rebellion was quickly brought under control and its leaders taken into custody.

In his marvelous memoir *All the Missing Souls*, David Scheffer describes how the proposal for the Special Court for Sierra Leone emerged. There were four main parties in the negotiations: the United States, the United Nations, the United Kingdom, and the government of Sierra Leone. Sierra Leone's President Kabbah preferred a Security Council tribunal modeled on the existing ad hoc institutions for the former Yugoslavia and Rwanda. However, the United Nations was only beginning to realize that the two tribunals it had set up in the 1990s were immensely expensive, difficult to control, and almost impossible to shut down. Something more modest would have to be devised. The British preferred to leave everything with the local courts in Sierra Leone. As Ambassador Scheffer explains, early in the discussions, the United States had begun to push for the sui generis institution that eventually resulted.

The structure of the Court that was finally agreed by the Security Council had a number of curious features. There were some bizarre concessions to the government of Sierra Leone that really had no place in international justice, such as the possible exercise of jurisdiction over juvenile offenders and the inclusion within the subject-matter jurisdiction of some domestic offenses defined in the archaic language of nineteenth-century England. Comprised within the statute, in practice they were completely ignored by the successive prosecutors.

The United Nations and the government of Sierra Leone were to share in the appointment of judges and prosecutors. It is essentially this aspect of the Court that led many to describe it as a "hybrid" institution. Although far from transparent, the appointment process on the UN side was certainly credible enough, and there could be no real complaint capable of impeaching the integrity of those who were named. On the Sierra Leone side, matters were rather more opaque. In hindsight, allowing the government of Sierra Leone to designate judges and a prosecutor was not a very good idea. It may have been a helpful concession in getting the agreement of Sierra Leone, although there would have been other ways of encouraging President Kabbah to compromise.

One of the biggest defects in the architecture of the Court concerned its funding. Unlike the two ad hoc tribunals for the former Yugoslavia and Rwanda, which were financed out of the general budget of the United Nations, the Special Court for Sierra Leone was to operate on the basis of voluntary contributions. That essentially meant wealthy states in Western Europe and North America – and in particular the two big powers who viewed Sierra Leone as in some sense part of their sphere of influence – were to provide the resources. Originally, the Secretary-General insisted on getting all of the money in his bank account before starting the project, but that proved to be unfeasible. The states that were contributing the money preferred to keep it on a drip feed, the better to influence decisions and the behavior of the

Court. But when defense lawyers challenged the funding scheme as being incompatible with an independent and impartial tribunal, their arguments were summarily dismissed by an unsympathetic Appeals Chamber.

While the Court was being established, the United Nations also proceeded with the Truth and Reconciliation Commission that had been promised in the 1999 peace agreement. Although such institutions had already become part of the transitional justice landscape, there was virtually no experience with the simultaneous operation of a truth commission and an international court. Several proposals emerged about how to manage the relationship, reflecting competing visions about the relative importance of criminal prosecution and other forms of accountability. The two bodies became operational at about the same time, in mid-2002. No formal agreement was ever reached between them, although they worked in parallel with relative serenity, aside from a few difficult moments. In its judgments, the Court barely referred to the findings of the Truth and Reconciliation Commission.

Many were taken by surprise when the first indictments were announced by Prosecutor David Crane in March 2003. Charges against leaders of the two rebel factions had been expected, but less predictable was the decision to prosecute the pro-government militia, including its patron, cabinet minister Hinga Norman. The lingering and still-unanswered question is why the president himself escaped indictment, given the presumption that he too was part of a joint criminal enterprise or, at the very least, was liable for conviction under the doctrine of superior responsibility.

The Special Court for Sierra Leone was the first international criminal tribunal since Nuremberg and Tokyo to sit in the place where the crimes were committed. The shortcomings in the outreach activities of the Yugoslavia and Rwanda tribunals were often attributed to their physical remoteness. Locating the Special Court in Freetown held the promise of a much better rapport with the people of the country. There were also dividends expected in terms of building capacity within Sierra Leone's rather dismal criminal justice system. But to the extent that the Court was a shared endeavor of the United Nations and the government of Sierra Leone, the latter's role was increasingly eclipsed as time wore on. By the time Charles Taylor was arrested, the government seemed happy enough for proceedings to move to The Hague. Opinions remain sharply divided among those working within the Court as to whether this was really necessary or advisable.

With the work of the Court now virtually completed, it is time to assess its contribution to international justice. As a model, there are some positive, constructive aspects of the structure and organization, although many lessons about pitfalls have also been learned. It was originally expected that the Court would cost about $50 million, but it probably came in at five or six times that figure. Given the extreme poverty in the country, it is legitimate to ask whether such an expense in order to prosecute a handful of perpetrators is really legitimate when so many other parts of the society desperately cry out for attention.

In Rwanda and the former Yugoslavia, international prosecution was only one element of accountability for criminal behavior during the conflicts. At the national level, there has been a great deal of judicial activity in both jurisdictions, something that is entirely absent in Sierra Leone, where the amnesty remains in force. There have also been a more limited number of universal jurisdiction prosecutions in third states for international offenses perpetrated during the conflicts in Rwanda and the former Yugoslavia. This, too, is missing completely in the case of Sierra Leone. On balance, then, Sierra Leone has not really had very much justice. Has it had enough justice to be of any significance? Or is the contribution of the Court to peace, justice, reconciliation, and all of the other alleged benefits of international prosecution something that is both marginal and ephemeral? As Chinese Premier Chou En-Lai famously remarked to Charles De Gaulle, when asked if the French revolution had been a success: "It's too early to tell."

Sierra Leone has been at peace for nearly fifteen years. Democratic elections have been held in a relatively serene environment and without serious complaint by international monitors. However, it remains mired in poverty and despair, the very factors that were at least partially responsible for the outbreak of the civil war more than two decades ago. A decade ago, the country was once at the absolute bottom of the United Nations' Human Development Index; it has climbed slowly, but not much, and in 2011 was 180th out of 187. On a more symbolic note: the once rather-distinguished City Hotel located at Gloucester and Lightfoot Boston streets in central Freetown, where Graham Greene often stayed while posted in Sierra Leone, and that provided inspiration for *The Heart of the Matter*, gradually deteriorated into a dismal fleabag and finally burned to the ground in 2010.

Professor Charles Chernor Jalloh is one of the most prominent scholars to have studied the Special Court for Sierra Leone. The conference that he hosted at the University of Pittsburgh in 2012 generated most of the chapters in this collection. The authors represent a cross section of specialists, including many who, like Professor Jalloh, have worked at the Court. There is an especially important introductory essay by one of the Court's Prosecutors, Stephen J. Rapp. The contributions have been carefully organized and edited. They cover many features of the institution in a thorough, professional, and often exhaustive manner. This book immediately becomes the authoritative reference on the Special Court for Sierra Leone. There simply is nothing else remotely comparable on the subject. It is and is likely to remain very much the last word on the subject of this fascinating and unprecedented institution.

Preface and Acknowledgments

This book was inspired by the International Conference Assessing the Legacy and Contributions of the Special Court for Sierra Leone to Africa and International Criminal Justice that I convened at the University of Pittsburgh School of Law, Pennsylvania, from April 19 to 21, 2012. The project, which took two years from conception to implementation, was predicated on the assumption that, given the impending closure of the Special Court for Sierra Leone (SCSL) after completion of its last trial involving former Liberian president Charles Taylor, and the Court's scheduled transformation into a residual mechanism, it would be desirable, if not necessary, to engage in at least a preliminary assessment of the SCSL's legacy to Sierra Leoneans, in whose name it was asked to render credible justice, and the international community, whose generous anti-impunity dollars made its work possible.

The primary goal of the conference was to provide a timely forum for the leading experts most familiar with the Sierra Leone Tribunal's work to critically examine its contributions to international criminal law and practice as well as its possible impact on transitional justice in the Mano River Union sub-region of West Africa. While memories are still fresh, and keeping in mind the specific legal basis, mandate, and historic context of its establishment, scholars, practitioners, and scholar-practitioners would convene at Pitt Law to reflect on what appeared to work, and what did not, in Sierra Leone's struggle to mete out justice for atrocity crimes in the aftermath of one of the worst conflicts in recent memory. The mechanism chosen, that is, a sui generis court with a mixed subject-matter jurisdiction and staff composition, quickly became a known entity in international law because of several innovations in its legal mandate, its location in situ, and its subsequent practice. These unique features generated high expectations among Sierra Leoneans as well as international lawyers about what the Court would likely accomplish, some of which with the benefit of hindsight, were not only premature but also unrealistic.

Against this backdrop, the ultimate objective of the Pittsburgh conference, and now this book, was to convene leading minds to discuss and debate the core legal questions of worldwide interest that confronted the SCSL and to capture, for posterity, their years of accumulated wisdom as close participants in and/or observers of the work of international penal courts generally and the Sierra Leone Tribunal in particular.

The stage was set when several prominent legal scholars and practitioners, as well as a cadre of relatively young but rising legal stars, accepted invitations to prepare new academic papers on key assigned topics for this first major attempt to assess the Court's impact and legacy on the development of international criminal law and practice. The authors were to draft their papers and submit them a full month before the conference. Once the drafts were available, they were paired up with expert commentators on their particular topics who then reviewed them and offered detailed comments. The papers were also circulated to all the other conference participants, with the co-panelists particularly encouraged to read their colleagues' papers. Many of them, as well as the others who attended, gave the authors feedback directly or indirectly through the convener. The result was a rigorous peer-review and highly collaborative knowledge-sharing process. So much so that in Pittsburgh, over the course of the three days of the conference, the presenters, discussants, and others could have a highly focused, highly stimulating, and ultimately highly fruitful debate on the legacy of the SCSL. The debate centered on important legal controversies that the Court wrestled with during its trials, most of which were interesting not only because they impacted the processes in Sierra Leone, but because they also held broader implications for other transitional justice situations in Africa and other parts of the world.

Consistent with the Court's so-called hybridity, the conference sought to reflect the dual national and international character and ownership of the SCSL process. This book has retained that same objective. Both have therefore attempted to elicit international as well as African, particularly Sierra Leonean, perspectives on the legacy of the Tribunal, a delicate task that proved to be more challenging than initially envisaged, especially given funding and other practical constraints. Nevertheless, the conference successfully brought together about seventy-five experts, tribunal practitioners, policy makers, and civil society advocates. Many of the participants had unique insights to share because they had worked in, collaborated with, or closely followed the SCSL from its earliest days through to its twilight days.

Ultimately, although the conference emphasized what one might term the international legal legacy of the Tribunal over any national ones that might exist, I am pleased that we succeeded in carving out some space in the conference as well as in this subsequent volume for those that insiders in Freetown referred to as the "internationals" and "nationals" or "locals." About thirteen of the chapter authors come from North America; eight are from Europe; one is from Australia/Oceania; eight are African, and of those, four, including the editor, are Sierra Leoneans. This seems relevant as one of the supposed features of "hybrid courts" generally and the SCSL in particular was the opportunity it apparently offered Sierra Leone to encourage local ownership of the Tribunal by including domestic law in its statute. But, perhaps more significantly, the unique chance that the Court's existence offered for Sierra Leonean lawyers to work side by side with their international counterparts to advance the cause of justice for international crimes. Whether at the end of the day this produced any impact on the few national lawyers who made it into the exclusive halls of the SCSL, or on the wider local bar and the domestic legal system, as is so frequently touted in the literature as a major advantage of the Sierra Leone model, remains an open question that is largely beyond the scope of this book.

It seems noteworthy that, because of deliberate attention to the point by the editor, there was a roughly even gender representation in this group of contributors, with about half of the authors women and the other half men. Although conscious efforts were made to add disciplinary diversity to the conference and book, it will be readily apparent that the lawyers ended up dominating the conversation in the volume. In one way, that might not be too surprising. To begin with, the relative infancy of international criminal law suggests that academic lawyers are perhaps more likely to be interested in assessing the legacies of international penal courts in an attempt to discern possible advances in the law – no matter how incremental those may be. That said, it is a pleasure to note that at least three authors, one of whom is a Sierra Leonean, brought frankly refreshing non-lawyer perspectives to bear on the legacy assessment. One is a political scientist, another a historian/political scientist, while an other was a longtime diplomat. Of course, this is not to imply that anyone anticipated, coming as we do from different disciplines, that the lawyers and the nonlawyers would necessarily agree on the thorny issues under discussion any more than we would expect a consensus among the lawyers in the room.

Furthermore, although admittedly reflecting their particular interests and methodologies rather than by deliberate design, several of the legal academics invoked anthropological and in one case even an empirical approach to their chapters. It is my hope that this book, by bringing together all these diverse perspectives and methodologies, will add richness to the legacy conversation that we have started here as well as help to deepen our understanding of both the perceived contributions, and limitations, of the SCSL.

The second goal of the conference was to analyze the Sierra Leone Tribunal against the backdrop of the rapid rise of human rights in the post–Cold War era that set in motion, among other things, an unprecedented process of building justice institutions, beginning with the UN Security Council's fateful decision to establish the International Criminal Tribunals for the Former Yugoslavia in 1993 and for Rwanda in 1994. Buoyed by those two precedents, as widely known by now, states could thereafter more swiftly agree on a draft statute for the establishment of the permanent International Criminal Court in July 1998 – an eminently sensible idea but one that had been floating on the backburner of international law and relations since at least the adoption of the Convention on the Prevention and Punishment of the Crime of Genocide in 1948.

The thinking was to essentially situate the SCSL within the broader normative context of the international community's search for a viable model of the ad hoc tribunal that is expected to not only be efficient, effective, and cost-effective, but to also at the same time uphold the high fair-trial standards of modern international human rights law. For this reason, it was envisaged that although each post-conflict situation will obviously be different and will therefore require its own solutions, to the extent possible at this early stage, some of the chapters in this collection could start to offer preliminary reflections on best practices and lessons learned from the Sierra Leone Tribunal experiment for other transitional justice situations in Africa and perhaps even other regions of the world. I am pleased that most of the authors succeeded in doing so.

But planning and hosting a large international conference of the kind held at Pitt Law in April 2012, and preparing this sizable volume that now constitutes its main output, could not have been possible without the assistance and generosity of so many individuals and organizations. Their support shaped the conference and ultimately gave rise to this book. I regret that because of space constraints I cannot list everyone here. I do, however, wish to acknowledge and thank a few of them even as I hope that those who I have not mentioned will understand and forgive me for the omission.

First, because without their support the conference and this book would simply not have been possible, I am grateful to all the funders of the international conference within and outside the University of Pittsburgh who enthusiastically endorsed my proposal for an SCSL legacy conference from the inception. At Pitt, I would like to express my profound gratitude for the personal and financial support received from the Office of the Dean of the University of Pittsburgh School of Law, in particular Dean Mary Crossley and her staff in the Development Office; the Center for International Legal Education and its staff, especially Professor Ronald A. Brand and Ms. Gina Huggins; the Ford Institute for Human Security, in particular, its directors Professors Taylor Seybolt and Louis A. Picard and their colleague Ms. Diane Cohen; and the University Center for International Studies (UCIS), especially Dr. Larry Feick, UCIS Director, and Dr. Jennifer Creamer, Associate Director. The last two were at the helm of the Hewlett International Grant Program process that awarded much-needed last-minute funds to supplement the conference finances after my proposal was selected through their university-wide competitive grant application process.

Outside the University of Pittsburgh, I am indebted to the Africa and International Criminal Law Interest Groups of the American Society of International Law (ASIL) as well as The Africa Law Institute (ALawI). In this regard, I thank the cochairs of those ASIL interest groups: Professors James Gathii (Loyola Chicago) and Angela Banks (William and Mary), who as of writing are the current cochairs of the Africa IG; and Professor Shahram Dana (The John Marshall Law School, Chicago), my cochair of the ICL IG, for all their support. I should also acknowledge my ALawI colleagues, Dr. Alhagi Marong (United Nations) and Professor Janewa Osei-Tutu (FIU College of Law), for their endorsement.

Second, this first major academic attempt to evaluate the legacy of the SCSL and its contributions to international criminal law and practice would not have occurred but for the hard work and patience of the dedicated contributing authors. I therefore thank all the friends and colleagues who kindly accepted invitations to write papers for this volume for their insights and engagement, during the conference and afterward. All the participants praised the highly stimulating and lively discussions they had during the conference deliberations. Credit for that must go to everyone present, but especially so to the authors who kindly produced working drafts of their chapters and presented them succinctly to spark immensely rich conversations. I thank them also for cheerfully reworking their chapters subsequently, despite the short deadlines that I often imposed on them. I should note here that several thoughtful pieces were written by authors who could not, for various reasons, present their works at the conference. I thank them too for their additions, which also enrich this book. Regrettably, despite their best efforts, two prosecutors who had initially agreed to contribute papers failed to secure permission from their tribunal bosses to participate in the project. This was regrettable as it meant that there were fewer attorneys representing that perspective at the conference and thus in this book.

Third, the conference benefited tremendously from the capable moderators and equally capable discussants that we were fortunate to have from the first through to the last sessions. That these academic colleagues took their respective roles seriously was reflected in the high quality of the discussions at Pitt and their often detailed comments on the draft chapters assembled in this volume. I wish to acknowledge each of them, for without their help taking up this task, the conference and this book would likely not have been of the same caliber: Professors Dapo Akande (Oxford), Cecile Aptel (The Fletcher School of Law and Diplomacy), Ilias Bantekas (Brunel), Elena Baylis (Pittsburgh), Nancy A. Combs (William and Mary), and Margaret M. deGuzman (Temple); Dr. Mark S. Ellis (International Bar Association); Professors Mark A. Drumbl (Washington and Lee), Kenneth Gallant

(Arkansas at Little Rock), Haider A. Hamoudi (Pittsburgh), David Harris (Pittsburgh), and Bernard Hibbitts (Pittsburgh); Mr. Wayne Jordash (Defense Counsel, International Criminal Tribunals); Dr. Sara Kendall (Leiden); Professor Jules Lobel (Pittsburgh); Dr. Alhagi B. M. Marong (United Nations); Professors Vincent O. Nmehielle (Witwatersrand), Diane Orentlicher (American), and Valerie Oosterveld (Western Ontario), Ambassador Peter Penfold (former British High Commissioner to Sierra Leone); Professor Leila N. Sadat (Washington University in St. Louis); Mr. Alpha Sesay (Open Society Justice Initiative); Professors Taylor Seybolt (Pittsburgh, GSPIA), and Jenia I. Turner (Southern Methodist University); Ms. Penelope Van Tuyl (Berkeley War Crimes Studies Center); and Professor Harmen van der Wilt (Amsterdam). I am especially thankful to those among these participants who accepted invitations to serve as discussants, even though most of them were also presenting their own papers during the conference. Dapo, a generous friend, stayed up late in the U.K. in order to participate as an excellent discussant on the immunity panel via Skype. I am much indebted to him.

Among others, Mr. Robert Petit (Senior Counsel, Crimes Against Humanity and War Crimes Section, Canadian Department of Justice, and former Senior Trial Attorney in the SCSL Office of the Prosecutor), Mr. Joseph Kamara (Commissioner, Sierra Leone Anti-Corruption Commission, and former Acting Prosecutor of the SCSL), and Ms. Melinda Taylor (Legal Counsel, Office of the Public Counsel for the Defense, International Criminal Court) enhanced the conference through provocative but excellent presentations.

I should single out my old classmate and friend from Oxford, Mel, who despite a hectic schedule arising from her now deservedly renowned work fighting for justice in the Libya Situation before the ICC, made time to join us in Pittsburgh just weeks before she traveled to Zintan, where she was unlawfully detained. While I regret that she could not in the end contribute a chapter, understandably because of the more pressing needs of the Saif al- Islam Gaddafi litigation as a court-appointed co-counsel for the defense, her remarks helped to focus the discussion about the institutional autonomy issues relating to the Defense at the SCSL. I am glad that she brought her ICC defense lawyer experience to this academic discussion and continue to admire her courage in fighting for the presumption of innocence and fair-trial rights of even those accused with the worst crimes known to law.

Fourth, I wish to thank the following staff at Pitt Law for all their assistance with different aspects and various stages of the conference: Sarah Barca, Patty Blake, Megan O'Donnell, LuAnn Driscoll, and Matt Kurpiewski. Patty, more than anyone at Pitt Law, went well beyond her job description and worked long hours to help ensure that the conference was a huge success. I cannot thank her enough. Sarah joined Patty and me much later, but displayed superb organizational skills that were crucial as we put the finishing touches to the conference.

In addition, I received excellent help from LaTi Wells and Kirk Knutson, my J.D. student research assistants, who were reliable and always willing to address ad hoc conference issues that came up and that could not have been anticipated. This is probably a good place for me to also acknowledge and thank the following Pitt Law students for assisting, pro bono, with various helpful tasks during the conference, including serving as rapporteurs for the various sessions: Sarah Beaver, Marie Brown, Megan Crouch, Aman Kakar, Leah Merchant, and Mikhail Pappas. Emma Founds, a bright former student and now attorney colleague, enthusiastically volunteered to rapporteur despite a recovering broken leg. She later helped edit and convert footnotes for several of the chapters. I thank her so much and encourage her to pursue her dream of becoming an international criminal lawyer.

Fifth, although I was fully responsible for the preparation, organization, and editing of this manuscript, I could not have done without the additional hands that came on deck in the final phase of this project to help out with some proofreading, footnote conversion, citation checking, formatting, and other important aspects of compiling this large book for the publisher. The folks at the Document Technology Center, who are the true unsung heroines of the Pitt Law staff, again came through for me with their usual dedication, editorial skills, and Bluebook expertise. For their top-notch work, always under tight time lines, Phyllis Gentille, Karen Knochel, Darleen Mocello, and especially Barbara Salopek deserve a huge thank you.

Of course, on a more personal note, I am indebted to my beloved wife, Julia J. Janewa Osei Tutu, for holding down the fort on the family front during the numerous times I was away planning the conference and the many long hours subsequently put into editing this book. I am truly lucky to have had such an adventurous and supportive friend and partner with whom to make many wonderful memories. Although they did not always understand why Daddy had to be away, and would rather have me at home, I am grateful to Salieu (aka "Sal"), Chay, and Kannin, the joys of my life. Their unconditional love inspires and sustains me. And throughout this book's preparation, I never lost sight of the fact that some of the children sadly robbed of a childhood during the war were barely older than Sal and Chay. I hope that the Sierra Leone my boys will grow up to know will be in peace and prosperity instead of the one of the 1990s, renowned for the child soldiers, mass atrocities, and internationally supported prosecutions discussed in this work.

From the moment that we first corresponded, John Berger of Cambridge University Press promptly responded to all my queries. I benefited from his enormous patience and publishing experience as I prepared the proposal for this work, but perhaps more importantly, this manuscript for publication. I thank him, as well as the three anonymous peer reviewers of the proposal for Cambridge who unanimously endorsed the book and made some useful suggestions, which I took on board to the extent possible. I look forward to the opportunity to work with him and his colleagues at Cambridge on other projects in the future.

Last but certainly not least, I wish to thank Professor William A. Schabas for accepting my invitations to write the foreword to this book. Bill, who needs no introduction to anyone working in the international criminal law field, always had a strong interest in what was going in Sierra Leone, Rwanda, and other parts of Africa, even before he was appointed an international commissioner on the Sierra Leone Truth and Reconciliation Commission. And despite his stature as a noted authority on international law, my interactions with him from the moment we first corresponded have always been pleasant, supportive, and inspiring. It is hard to imagine a better person to write the foreword to this particular book, for which I am most grateful.

Abbreviations

ACHPR	African Charter of Human and People's Rights
ACLT	Advisory Committee on Legal Texts, International Criminal Court
ADC-ICTY	Association of Defense Counsel Practicing in the International Criminal Tribunal for the Former Yugoslavia
AFRC	Armed Forces Revolutionary Council
ANCs	Accountability Now Clubs
AP I and II	First and Second Additional Protocols to the 1949 Geneva Conventions
APC	All People's Congress
ASP	Assembly of States Parties of the International Criminal Court
AU	African Union
AZAPO	Azanian Peoples Organization
CCP	Commission for the Consolidation of Peace
CDF	Civil Defense Forces
CEDAW	Convention on the Elimination of All Forms of Discrimination Against Women
CoJA	Coalition for Justice and Accountability
CRC	Convention on the Rights of the Child
CSOs	Civil Society Organizations
DAC	Directive on the Assignment of Counsel
DDR	Disarmament, Demobilization, and Reintegration
DSS	ECCC's Defence Support Section
ECCC	Extraordinary Chambers in the Courts of Cambodia
ECHR	European Convention on Human Rights
ECOMOG	Economic Community of West African States Monitoring Group
ECOWAS	Economic Community of West African States
EIDHR	European Instrument for Democracy and Human Rights
EU	European Union
FoSL	Friends of Sierra Leone
FRY	Federal Republic of Yugoslavia
GC	1949 Geneva Conventions I to IV
GNU	Government of National Unity
GoSL	Government of Sierra Leone
HRW	Human Rights Watch

ICC	International Criminal Court
ICC&Ts	International Criminal Courts and Tribunals
ICCPR	International Covenant on Civil and Political Rights
ICG	International Crisis Group
ICJ	International Court of Justice
ICRC	International Committee of the Red Cross
ICTR	International Criminal Tribunal for Rwanda
ICTY	International Criminal Tribunal for the Former Yugoslavia
IHL	International Humanitarian Law
IMT	International Military Tribunal at Nuremberg
IMTFE	International Military Tribunal for the Far East
IOs	International Organizations
JCE	Joint Criminal Enterprise
LSC	Legal Services Contract
MICT	Mechanism for International Criminal Tribunals
NCDDR	National Commission for Disarmament, Demobilization and Reintegration
NCDHR	National Commission for Democracy and Human Rights
NPFL	National Patriotic Front of Liberia
NPRC	National Provisional Ruling Council
NPWJ	No Peace Without Justice
OAU	Organization of African Unity (later transformed into the African Union)
OHCHR	Office of the High Commissioner for Human Rights
OPCD	Office of Public Counsel for the Defense
OPD	Office of the Principal Defender
OSIWA	Open Society Initiative for West Africa
OTP	Office of the Prosecutor
OTP WMU	Office of the Prosecutor Witness Management Unit
POW	Prisoner of War
PRIDE	Post Conflict Reintegration Initiative for Development and Empowerment
PTC	Pre-Trial Chamber of the International Criminal Court
RPE	Rules of Procedure and Evidence
RSCSL	Residual Special Court for Sierra Leone
RSLMF	Republic of Sierra Leone Military Forces
RUF	Revolutionary United Front
RUF/SL	Revolutionary United Front of Sierra Leone
RUFP	Revolutionary United Front Party
Rules	Rules of Procedure and Evidence
SCSL	Special Court for Sierra Leone
SCWG	Special Court Working Group
SierraLII	Sierra Leone Legal Information Institute
SL	Sierra Leone
SLA	Sierra Leone Army

SLPP	Sierra Leone People's Party
STL	Special Tribunal for Lebanon
TRC	Truth and Reconciliation Commission
UDHR	Universal Declaration of Human Rights
U.K.	United Kingdom
UN	United Nations
UNAMID	United Nations Assistance Mission in Darfur
UNAMIR	United Nations Assistance Mission in Sierra Leone
UNAMSIL	United Nations Assistance Mission for Rwanda
UNICEF	United Nations Children's Fund
UNIOSIL	United Nations Integrated Office in Sierra Leone
UNIPSIL	United Nations Integrated Peacebuilding Office in Sierra Leone
UNMIL	United Nations Mission in Liberia
UNOMSIL	United Nations Observer Mission in Sierra Leone
U.N.S.C.	United Nations Security Council
UNSG	United Nations Secretary-General
UNTAET	UN Transitional Administration in East Timor
U.S.	United States of America
WVS or WVSS	Witness and Victims Section or Witness and Victims Support Section

Introduction

Assessing the Legacy of the Special Court for Sierra Leone

Charles Chernor Jalloh

I. THE CONTEXT

Since the end of the Cold War, various types of ad hoc criminal tribunals have been established in different parts of the world with varying degrees of success. Although the UN Security Council–created International Criminal Tribunals for the Former Yugoslavia (ICTY) and Rwanda (ICTR) were the modern pioneers, and are therefore better known, the Special Court for Sierra Leone (SCSL) followed not long afterward and quickly began to carve out its own place in the edifice of modern international criminal law.

The SCSL, which was created through a bilateral treaty between the United Nations and the government of Sierra Leone in January 2002, was designed to address the perceived shortcomings of the ICTY and ICTR, in particular, their apparently costly nature; the slow pace of their proceedings; their geographic and emotional distance from the local populations in whose names they were asked to render justice; and their seemingly unfocused prosecutions that sometimes included lower-ranking suspects that some deemed more appropriate for trial within national courts rather than before an international penal tribunal.[1] The coercive Chapter VII legal basis of the twin UN tribunals and the consensual[2] treaty-based character of the SCSL therefore differ markedly, reflecting the particular historical and political circumstances of their establishment.

Today, as the ICTY, ICTR, and the SCSL approach the completion of their respective mandates, academics are increasingly turning toward efforts aimed at evaluating the potential impact, and limitations, of these ad hoc courts, using doctrinal, semi-empirical and empirical approaches in an attempt to discern their legacy. Of course, the idea that academic lawyers would be interested in conducting normative and doctrinal assessments of the legacy of the international criminal courts that states have created to prosecute crimes in specific situations is not new. Indeed, the notion of legacy has some historical pedigree

---

[1] See Independent Expert, *Report on the Special Court for Sierra Leone* ¶ 29 (Dec. 12, 2006) (Antonio Cassese).

[2] Admittedly, one should not stretch the consent argument. It seems obvious that even UN member states would have consented to be bound by UN Security Council decisions addressing threats to international peace and security by fiat of their prior consent to the Charter of the United Nations. So, the decisions of the Council to create the twin ad hoc tribunals (which became binding because of their Chapter VII nature and Article 25 of the UN Charter) are to some extent a reflection of indirect consent. For this argument in relation to the distinctive legal basis of the SCSL vis-à-vis the ICTY and ICTR, see Charles C. Jalloh, *The Contribution of the Special Court for Sierra Leone to the Development of International Law*, 15 Afr. J. Int'l. & Comp. L. 165, 207, 187 (2007).

dating at least as far back as the conclusion of the first international trials at the Nuremberg International Military Tribunal (IMT) in 1946.

Although it does not appear that the term "legacy" was in vogue then as much as it is now, no less than Justice Robert Jackson, the chief American prosecutor at Nuremberg, argued only months after the delivery of the final judgment that the success of the IMT could be assessed against whether it had achieved what it set out to do.[3] Even though he conceded that it would otherwise be premature to reflect upon the long-range impact of that tribunal, just months after the completion of the judicial process, Justice Jackson could readily identify at least six legal accomplishments attributable to the trials of the Nazi leadership.[4] To him, although the Allies' conclusion of the London Agreement, which established the IMT and the historic trial that was subsequently carried out would not imply the end of aggressive war or the persecution of minorities or the commission of international crimes, what we would in today's parlance call the Nuremberg Legacy had established new standards of conduct for humanity. He expected that those standards would in the future serve as bulwarks of peace and tolerance by holding individuals accountable for international crimes at the international level. In his characteristic eloquence, he then concluded that this had thus put "International Law squarely on the side of peace as against aggressive warfare, and on the side of humanity as against persecution."[5]

Even though often mentioned in contemporary international criminal law discourse, but not always defined, the term "legacy" as used here should be understood as a narrow and specific reference to the body of legal rules, innovative practices, and norms that the tribunal is expected to hand down to current and future generations of international, internationalized and national courts charged with the responsibility to prosecute the same or similar international crimes. This definition, although perhaps imperfect, is to be distinguished from the arguably overbroad conception of legacy offered by the United Nations in relation to hybrid courts as their "lasting impact on bolstering the rule of law in a particular society, by conducting effective trials to contribute to ending impunity, while also strengthening domestic judicial capacity."[6] My use of the term here does not contemplate the physical infrastructure such as the Court buildings that will be left behind in Freetown or the documents and archives and records of the Tribunal, matters that are more appropriately considered in discussions of the residual mechanism.

It follows that the sense in which I invoke the "L" word is more modest. It is closer to, but distinct from, the definition offered by Richard Steinberg in his equivalent work on the ICTY.[7]

---

[3] ROBERT H. JACKSON, THE NUENBERG CASE, at xiv (1947).

[4] *See* Jackson, *supra* note 3, at xiv to xvii. In addition, on December 11, 1946, just months after the completion of the Nuremberg Trials, the UN General Assembly unanimously adopted Resolution 1(95) in which it affirmed the strength of the "principles of international law recognized by the Charter of the Nuremberg Tribunal and the Judgment of the Tribunal." At the General Assembly's request, about four years later, the International Law Commission formulated the principles of international law recognized at Nuremberg, which were formally endorsed on December 12, 1950.

[5] *Id.* at xvii.

[6] Office of the High Commissioner for Human Rights, *Rule-of-Law Tools for Post-conflict States. Maximizing the Legacy of Hybrid Courts* (2008), *available at* http://www.ohchr.org/Documents/Publications/HybridCourts. pdf (last visited November 2012), at 4–5.

[7] ASSESSING THE LEGACY OF THE ICTY 5–6 (Richard H. Steinberg ed., 2011) (defining "legacy" as including the findings of that tribunal, its legal legacy, records, institutional, regional, and normative legacy).

Legacy thus describes the *corpus juris* of rules, doctrines, and innovative tribunal precedents and institutional practices that the Court may be said to have developed and contributed to the advancement of the emerging body of substantive international criminal law and procedure. This focus seems particularly significant because, as is widely known, after the watershed post–World War II prosecutions at Nuremberg and Tokyo, international criminal law[8] essentially languished in desuetude for several decades until it was at last resuscitated by the United Nations through the creation of the ad hoc Chapter VII tribunals in the early 1990s.

Be that as it may, today, with all but one of its nine trials complete (that involving the former Liberian president Charles Taylor, which is expected to conclude by December 2013), the SCSL will be the first of the modern ad hoc international criminal tribunals[9] to complete all of its cases through to appeals and to symbolically close down its doors even as it transforms into a residual mechanism.[10] Perhaps not surprisingly given that they were the first truly international criminal courts to be established, various scholarly efforts have already been undertaken to assess the legacy and impact of the ICTY,[11] and to a lesser extent, the ICTR.[12] Most of the attempts to evaluate the legacy of the twin

---

[8] "International criminal law" has had a plethora of inconsistent definitions over the years. Here, I endorse the definition by a group of scholars who referred to it as "encompassing not only the law governing genocide, crimes against humanity, war crimes and aggression, but also the principles and procedures governing the international investigation and prosecution of these crimes"; see ROBERT CRYER, HAKAN FRIMAN, DARRYL ROBINSON & ELIZABETH WILMSHURT, AN INTRODUCTION TO INTERNATIONAL CRIMINAL LAW AND PROCEDURE 5 (2d ed. 2010).

[9] The ICTR, which was established by the UN Security Council in 1994, recently symbolically completed its last of seventy-five substantive cases that were prosecuted all the way to trial judgment. On December 20, 2012, the ICTR Trial Chamber issued its judgment in which it unanimously found the former Rwandese Minister of Planning Augustine Ngirabatware guilty of genocide, and direct and public incitement to genocide and rape as a crime against humanity. He was sentenced to thirty-five years' imprisonment. See the *Statement of the Chief Prosecutor of the Tribunal, Justice Hassan B. Jallow* (reflecting on the significance of that moment for the ICTR after eighteen years of work and succinctly summarizing that tribunal's key case accomplishments) at http://www.unictr.org/tabid/155/Default.aspx?id=1336 (last visited December 22, 2012). The Security Council, by Resolution 1966 adopted on December 22, 2010, established the International Residual Mechanism for Criminal Tribunals to continue certain essential functions. The Arusha-based court's component was operationalized on July 1, 2012, whereas the ICTY's is currently scheduled for activation on July 1, 2013.

[10] On the other hand, although the agreement for the establishment of the Residual Special Court for Sierra Leone (RSCSL) was signed by the United Nations and the Sierra Leone government in August 2010, and ratified by Sierra Leone's Parliament in December 2011, the RSCSL will not become operational until issuance of a final judgment in the Charles Taylor appeal. That is expected to take place by December 2013. Even though the SCSL issued its own last trial judgment in that case on April 26, 2012, followed by the sentencing judgment on May 30, 2012, because the case is now on appeal the Court arguably is not the first to technically complete its work. Yet, because it seems that the Ngirabatware case will go on appeal albeit before the Residual Mechanism in Arusha, a strong argument can be made that the SCSL was in fact the first from among those three UN ad hoc courts to complete its work.

[11] For some leading works on the subject, see DIANE F. ORENTLICHER, SHRINKING THE SPACE FOR DENIAL: THE IMPACT OF THE ICTY IN SERBIA (OSJI, May 2008), THE LEGACY OF THE INTERNATIONAL CRIMINAL TRIBUNAL FOR THE FORMER YUGOSLAVIA (Bert Swart, Alexander Zahar & Göran Sluiter eds., 2011), ASSESSING THE LEGACY OF THE ICTY (Richard H. Steinberg ed., 2011).

[12] Although there have been several notable academic works on the legal contributions of the Rwanda tribunal to the development of international criminal law, there is to date no comprehensive book on its "legacy" as such. For examples of works comprehensively addressing the core legal issues during the process, see WILLIAM A. SCHABAS, THE UN INTERNATIONAL CRIMINAL TRIBUNALS: THE FORMER YUGOSLAVIA, RWANDA AND SIERRA LEONE (2006); LARISSA VAN DEN HERIK, THE CONTRIBUTION OF THE RWANDA TRIBUNAL TO

UN tribunals have focused on their pioneering additions to the Nuremberg Legacy and the normative advancement of the concept of individual criminal responsibility at the international level as well as on the elaboration of the substantive content of the various international crimes within their jurisdiction, in particular, genocide, crimes against humanity, and war crimes.

In stark contrast, since the SCSL was established in January 2002, fewer scholarly works have systematically studied that tribunal and its role in post-conflict Sierra Leone or its legacy to international criminal law and practice. Although there now appears to be an exponential growth in literature on the Court, until recently the bulk of the commentary focused on its apparent hybridity compared to the ICTY and ICTR and its possibilities of serving as a leaner and cheaper institutional model for bringing justice to diverse post-conflict situations. Even fewer studies have examined the law and *practice* of the SCSL between the time its first indictments were issued in March 2003 and the near completion of all its trials in 2012 to determine whether it has made, or failed to make, meaningful additions to the broader international criminal justice project.

Yet, because of the near unique fact pattern of the Sierra Leone conflict, the SCSL was often confronted with a range of novel legal issues in the course of its proceedings. This allowed it to develop some interesting jurisprudence on issues of wider significance to international criminal law and practice. The Court was therefore among the first to grapple with some of the more important and recurring legal dilemmas for many modern post-conflict situations. For example, among others, the SCSL was the first international criminal court to try and convict persons for the recruitment and enlistment of children for the purposes of using them in hostilities. It was also the first international tribunal to prosecute the war crime of attacks against UN peacekeepers, the first to recognize the new crime against humanity of forced marriage as an "other inhumane act," and perhaps more notably, the first to indict, fully try, and then convict a former African president for planning and aiding and abetting the commission of international crimes in a neighboring state.

Finally, because of the SCSL's landmark jurisprudential precedents, future legal efforts to hold perpetrators to account may now benefit from greater clarity on, among others, questions such as whether sitting heads of third states in such a tribunal are immune from prosecution for serious international crimes before a bilateral treaty-based international court[13]; whether amnesties granted under domestic law barred the prosecution of universally condemned international crimes before an ad hoc international criminal court[14]; whether alternative accountability mechanisms such as special tribunals and truth commissions can

---

THE DEVELOPMENT OF INTERNATIONAL LAW (2005), and GEORGE MUGWANYA, THE CRIME OF GENOCIDE IN INTERNATIONAL LAW: APPRAISING THE CONTRIBUTION OF THE UN TRIBUNAL FOR RWANDA (2007). Key articles from those involved in the ICTR's work include Erik Møse, *Main Achievements of the ICTR*, 3 J. INT'L CRIM. J. 920–43 (2005) and Hassan B. Jallow, *The Contribution of the United Nations International Criminal Tribunal for Rwanda to the Development of International Criminal Law*, in AFTER GENOCIDE: TRANSITIONAL JUSTICE, POST-CONFLICT RECONSTRUCTION, AND RECONCILIATION IN RWANDA AND BEYOND (Philip Clark & Zachary Kaufmann eds., 2009). There are various other studies in the transitional justice literature examining the impact of the ICTY/ICTR on reconciliation. *See, e.g.*, MY NEIGHBOR, MY ENEMY: JUSTICE AND COMMUNITY IN THE AFTERMATH OF MASS ATROCITY (Harvey M. Weinstein & Eric Stover eds., 2004).

[13] Prosecutor v. Charles Ghankay Taylor, Case No. SCSL-2003–01-I, Decision on Immunity from Jurisdiction, 59 (May 31, 2004).

[14] Prosecutor v. Allieu Kondewa, Case No. SCSL-2004–14-AR72(E), Decision on Lack of Jurisdiction/Abuse of Process: Amnesty Provided by the Lomé Accord 128 (May 25, 2004).

coexist and complement each other where used simultaneously[15]; and whether individual criminal responsibility accrued to recruiters of child soldiers at customary international law by November 30, 1996.[16]

This edited book considers the SCSL's legacy on all these issues as well as many others. It aims to help fill a part of the current gap in the emerging literature on the legacy of ad hoc international criminal courts by offering the first comprehensive doctrinal assessment of the legacy of the Sierra Leone Court. The focus is to analyze the "legal legacy" of the Tribunal, in particular, its judicial opinions, practices, and decisions as well as their possible contributions to the wider corpus of norms for substantive international criminal law and procedure.

To contextualize the Court and the subsequent chapters in this volume, the next part of this Introduction will provide a brief historical overview of the circumstances in Sierra Leone that led to the creation of the SCSL. In the second part, I will discuss key attributes of the SCSL's jurisdiction. As the Court completed only a handful of trials when compared to the twin UN tribunals, partly because of a lack of political will to bankroll another expensive international tribunal and its consequently limited mandate to prosecute only those bearing "greatest responsibility," the third part of the chapter will offer a short summary of its nine cases and their final verdicts and sentences. Finally, in the fourth part, I will describe the contents and organization of the volume before offering concluding remarks. A separate Conclusion at the end of the book highlights the main preliminary lessons from the SCSL experience for the field of international criminal law.

II. A BRIEF OVERVIEW OF THE SIERRA LEONEAN CONFLICT

The Sierra Leone conflict, which started on March 21, 1991 and ended on January 18, 2002, gained notoriety around the world for its brutality and the perpetration of some of the worst atrocities against civilians ever witnessed in a modern conflict.[17] The war, which is estimated to have resulted in the deaths of seventy thousand[18] people, the displacement of about 2.6 of the country's population of 5 million, and the maiming of thousands of others, was characterized by widespread killings, mass amputations, abductions of women and children, recruitment and use of children as combatants, rape, sexual violence against mostly women and underage girls (including their taking as "bush wives"), arson, pillage, looting, burning, and wanton destruction of villages and towns.

[15] Prosecutor v. Samuel Hinga Norman, Case No. SCSL-2003–08-PT, Decision on the Request by the Truth and Reconciliation Commission of Sierra Leone to Conduct a Public Hearing with Sam Hinga Norman 101 (Oct. 29, 2003). *See also* Prosecutor v. Samuel Hinga Norman, Case No. SCSL-2003–08-PT, Decision on Appeal by the Truth and Reconciliation Commission for Sierra Leone and Chief Samuel Hinga Norman JP against the Decision of His Lordship, Mr. Justice Bankole Thompson Delivered on the October 30, 2003 to Deny the TRC's Request to Hold a Public Hearing with Chief Samuel Hinga Norman JP, November 28, 2003, at 122.

[16] Prosecutor v. Samuel Hinga Norman, Case No. SCSL-2004–14-AR72(E), Decision on Preliminary Motion on Lack of Jurisdiction (Child Recruitment) 132 (May 31, 2004).

[17] Several books offer useful accounts on the history of the Sierra Leone conflict. *See, e.g.,* LANSANA GBERIE, A DIRTY WAR IN WEST AFRICA: THE RUF AND THE DESTRUCTION OF SIERRA LEONE (2006), DAVID KEEN, CONFLICT AND COLLUSION IN SIERRA LEONE (2006), and PETER PENFOLD, ATROCITIES, DIAMONDS AND DIPLOMACY (2012). An official history, comprising several volumes, was produced by the Sierra Leone Truth and Reconciliation Commission in 2004. Most of the material in this introduction is drawn from the authoritative TRC Reports.

[18] MARY KALDOR & JAMES VINCENT, UNITED NATIONS DEVELOPMENT PROGRAMME EVALUATION OFFICE CASE STUDY SIERRA LEONE 7 (2006). I have used this number, drawn from this UN Report, in the apparent absence of official statistics on the numbers of people killed during the war.

It was not always so. Indeed, the tragedy of the Sierra Leonean conflict and that country's relatively recent association with signature atrocities, "blood diamonds" and the prosecutions of international crimes through the SCSL, which is the subject of this book, is that it was previously considered a haven of political stability and a renowned center of higher learning in Africa. Sierra Leone, which along with Gambia, Ghana, and Nigeria were the four English colonies in West Africa, secured political independence from Britain on April 27, 1961. Self-government was followed by what seemed to be an auspicious start for democracy with the first peaceful transfer of power to an elected opposition party in an independent African State in 1967.[19] However, the British political legacy, if indeed there was one, proved to have little longevity as the country quickly degenerated down the path of instability with a spate of military coups and countercoups.[20] Ultimately, the civilian All People's Congress (APC) party formed a stable government around 1970.

Unfortunately, the APC government, under the stewardship of then-president Siaka P. Stevens, stifled democracy by transforming itself into a despotic one-party regime and sustaining its stranglehold on the country through massive corruption, nepotism, plunder of public assets, and exacerbation of ethnic, regional, and rural–urban cleavages.[21] In the decade between 1980 and early 1990, bad governance, economic decay, intolerance for dissent, and the shrinking of the democratic space, among other factors, had created sufficient malaise for the outbreak of conflict in the country.[22]

In March 1991, a group of about forty to sixty armed men entered Bomaru Village in Kailahun District, eastern Sierra Leone near the Liberian border. The attack, in which thirteen people, only two of whom were combatants perished, turned out to be one of the first salvoes of the murderous Revolutionary United Front (RUF) rebels. They were apparently led by one Foday Sankoh, a disgruntled former soldier in the Sierra Leone Army (SLA), whose apparent goal was to overthrow the then-government under President Joseph Saidu Momoh.

In a few weeks, the rebels, with human, material, logistical, and other support from Charles Taylor of the National Patriotic Front of Liberia (NPFL),[23] increased the intensity and frequency of their attacks. The ill-equipped and corrupt SLA, which had more experience putting down peaceful pro-democracy student demonstrations than fighting a war, proved unable to contain the unrelenting guerrilla attacks. In a few months, most of Kailahun District in the east and Pujehun District in the south, both not far from the Liberian border, had fallen under rebel control. Given the SLA's inability to combat the war, and the lack of leadership among the Freetown government elite, it was only a matter of time before the war would spread to other parts of the country – with devastating consequences for the local population.

---

[19] John R. Cartwright, Politics in Sierra Leone: 1947–1967, at 4 (1970).

[20] Sierra Leone Truth and Reconciliation Commission, Report of the Commission "Executive Summary," Vol. 2, Ch. 1, *available at* http://www.sierraleonetrc.org (last visited Dec. 22, 2012).

[21] *Id.*

[22] *Id.*

[23] Taylor started a guerrilla war in Liberia in 1989 similar to that led by Sankoh in Sierra Leone. He served as Liberia's president from 1997 to 2003. On the need for accountability for the wartime atrocities in that country, see Chernor Jalloh & Alhagi Marong, *Ending Impunity: The Case for War Crimes Trials in Liberia*, 2 Afr. J. Legal Stud. 53 (2005) (arguing for the expansion of the SCSL's jurisdiction to try those bearing greatest responsibility for serious international crimes committed during the Liberian conflict).

President Momoh lacked a coherent strategy to deal with the nation's security even as his largely undisciplined and inexperienced army continued to suffer terrible losses from the ragtag RUF. The rebels, as they experienced initial military setbacks, resorted more to guerrilla-style hit-and-run tactics, and engaged in barbaric acts aimed at instilling fear in their enemy as well as the local civilian population. Their strategy of terrorizing and then abducting civilians, drugging and enlisting children to fight, burning and looting villages, and raping young girls and women, developed in the early days of the war, were to later become the tragic images associated with the Sierra Leone conflict by those in other parts of the world.

With the army having lost confidence in their commander-in-chief, Momoh was ousted from power in April 1992 by a group of mutinying soldiers led by a twenty-seven-year-old Captain Valentine Strasser, an army paymaster with no political experience. They took over the reins of state in a coup and formed a junta regime styling itself the National Provisional Ruling Council (NPRC). Although very popular at the beginning, especially among the urban youth and students, the NPRC suspended the national constitution, and thereafter, ruled the country by decree. But the inexperienced Strasser, as well as his former deputy (Julius M. Bio)[24] who later overthrew him in a palace coup in January 1996, failed to decisively end the conflict. Partly because of deep mistrust of the army, who locals aptly labeled "sobels" (a coinage from the words *soldier* and *rebels* used to describe the phenomena of soldiers by day and rebels by night), the government turned to hiring mercenaries, first from Nepal and afterward South Africa, to help fight the war in return for generous diamond concessions. The presence of foreign fighters initially offered some respite to the government forces. However, it proved to be only a Band-Aid instead of a permanent solution, temporarily enabling the regime to continue its sovereign control of the mineral-rich mining areas in the east and south of the country.

Under pressure mostly from war-weary Sierra Leoneans clamoring to participate in their country's governance through the ballot box, the junta eventually restored constitutional rule. Long-anticipated democratic elections were finally conducted in 1996. The Sierra Leone People's Party (SLPP) candidate Ahmad Tejan Kabbah, a former UN bureaucrat who had returned home to enter the contest, won the elections. President Kabbah immediately entered into negotiations with the RUF and concluded a peace accord in Ivory Coast in 1996 aimed at ending the conflict. The Abidjan Accord[25] contained, among others, provisions calling for termination of the hostilities, removal of the Executive Outcomes foreign mercenaries from the country within three to six months, and an amnesty under which no judicial action would be taken against the RUF for the crimes perpetrated by them up to the date of signature of the agreement.[26]

Nevertheless, as there did not appear to be good faith on the rebel side to transform itself into a political movement with the rights, privileges, and duties recognized under Sierra

---

[24] Interestingly, in the most recent presidential contest in Sierra Leone on November 17, 2012, Bio, who had long resigned from the army, was the lead opposition Sierra Leone People's Party candidate. He ran against incumbent president Ernest Bai Koroma. Koroma won a second term with 58.7 percent while Bio secured up to 37.4 percent of the vote. *See National Electoral Commission, Statement from the NEC Chairperson on the Conduct and Result of the Presidential Elections,* (Dec. 4, 2012), *available at* http://www.nec-sierraleone.org/.

[25] *See Peace Agreement between the Government of the Republic of Sierra Leone and the Revolutionary United Front of Sierra Leone signed at Abidjan, Ivory Coast* (Nov. 30, 1996), *available at* http://www.usip.org/files/file/resources/collections/peace_agreements/sierra_leone_11301996.pdf

[26] *See id.* at Articles 1, 2, 12, 14.

Leonean law, the Abidjan Accord failed; hostilities resumed; and yet another military coup took place on May 25, 1997, this time by a group known as the Armed Forces Revolutionary Council (AFRC). President Kabbah fled to neighboring Guinea where he essentially set up a government-in-exile in Conakry. The AFRC coupists, who released Major Johnny Paul Koroma who was in jail at the time, installed themselves as the new regime, declared martial law, and invited Sankoh and the RUF leadership to share power.

But the uneasy AFRC–RUF coalition failed to gain international recognition. A massive and unprecedented campaign of civil disobedience from Sierra Leoneans simply fed up with the war effectively shut down the country for periods at a time. As the army was no longer loyal, the desperate Kabbah government designated a civilian militia, the Civil Defense Forces led by Sam Hinga Norman, Kabbah's deputy defense minister, to help fight the rebels. With strong international backing, especially from the regional Economic Community of West African States (ECOWAS), which was committed to restoring the democratically elected government, Kabbah was reinstated to power after ten months on March 10, 1998. In July 1999, the militarily weakened Kabbah government buckled under international pressure and negotiated the comprehensive Lomé Peace Agreement with the RUF in the hope of ending the conflict once and for all.[27] The Lomé package, reflecting the weaknesses of a government teetering on the brink of collapse, tried to placate the rebels through power oversharing, including offering four deputy minister positions, four key minister positions, and even the vice-presidency of the state to the RUF.[28]

In perhaps the worst strategic blunder that could have been made by a Sierra Leonean government dependent on minerals for core revenue, President Kabbah agreed to create a commission that would be solely responsible for the exploitation of the country's immense gold, diamond, and other strategic mineral resource wealth.[29] He ceded the chairmanship of that board to Sankoh, the RUF rebel leader, who could now lawfully take what he previously had to plunder. The parties also agreed to disarmament, rehabilitation, and reintegration of the former combatants into society.[30] The United Nations and ECOWAS undertook to serve as the "moral guarantors" of the peace through the subsequent deployment of peacekeepers to monitor the parties' compliance with the agreement.

Significantly, to avoid any type of criminal accountability for the despicable crimes committed during the conflict, the parties provided for the establishment of a Truth and Reconciliation Commission to purportedly "address impunity, break the cycle of violence, provide a forum for both victims and the perpetrators of human rights violations to tell their story" about the war and to promote national healing.[31] In a controversial move, especially within Sierra Leone, President Kabbah capitulated to the RUF demands and expanded the amnesty concession first included in Article 14 of the Abidjan Accord. However, even the blanket amnesty granting Sankoh personally and all other combatants and collaborators "absolute and free pardon and reprieve"[32] in respect of all their depraved actions between

---

[27] *See* Peace Agreement between the Government of Sierra Leone and the Revolutionary United Front signed at Lomé, Togo (July 7, 1999), *available at* http://www.sierra-leone.org/lomeaccord.html (last visited Dec. 2012).

[28] *See id.* Article V.

[29] *See id.* Article VII.

[30] *See id.* Article XVI.

[31] *See id.* Articles VI(2) and XXVI.

[32] *See id.* Article IX.

the start of the war and the conclusion of the Lomé Peace Agreement proved insufficient to restore peace to Sierra Leone.

Around this time, even though the Sierra Leonean conflict had largely been ignored by most Western media up to that point, the sensational stories of human savagery to fellow humans going on in the small West African nation started generating external interest. The publicity efforts were led by local and international civil society advocacy groups, with Sierra Leonean women's groups, fed up with the war, taking the lead in several mass public protests in Freetown. Human Rights Watch and Amnesty International, for their part, led the international naming and shaming efforts with a series of widely disseminated and shocking reports.[33] The demobilization, reintegration, and rehabilitation programs for the combatants soon began to run into difficulties, and it became evident that some factions of the RUF were bent on undermining the peace. They were not sufficiently invested in winning the peace as much as they were in the continuation of war so as to voluntarily lay down their weapons.

The government, which had cowered in a corner and refused to seriously consider the criminal accountability option, appeared to undergo a significant change of heart when, in May 2000, over five hundred UN peacekeepers were disarmed and held hostage by renegade rebel commanders. Sankoh, it was now evident, had only limited influence and authority over his key battlefield commanders. He was arrested following civilian demonstrations and a shootout at his home in the West End of Freetown. He was thereafter detained at an undisclosed location. The following month, in June 2000, President Kabbah formally declared that his government could no longer tolerate further RUF violations of the key terms in the Lomé Peace Agreement. Consequently, under renewed pressure from the local and international civil society to repudiate the blanket amnesty and to establish some type of criminal accountability mechanism to prosecute the worst offenders, the Kabbah government turned to the United Nations seeking assistance to create a credible court to try the worst offenders, especially the RUF leadership.

III. BRIEF OVERVIEW OF THE ESTABLISHMENT AND JURISDICTION OF THE SPECIAL COURT FOR SIERRA LEONE

On January 16, 2002, representatives of the United Nations and the Sierra Leonean government met in Freetown, the Sierra Leonean capital, to sign the agreement establishing the SCSL.[34] This represented the culmination of the process that President Kabbah had begun when he sent his June 2000 letter to the United Nations Security Council through Secretary-General Kofi Annan requesting the international community's assistance in establishing an independent "special court" that, through prosecution of those leaders who had planned and directed a notoriously brutal conflict characterized by atrocity crimes and the taking of UN peacekeepers as hostages, would help bring justice

---

[33] *See, e.g.*, Human Rights Watch, *Sierra Leone: Getting Away with Murder, Mutilation, Rape* (July 1999, Vol. 11, No. 3A), http://www.hrw.org/reports/1999/sierra/ (documenting, inter alia, shocking victim testimony of RUF atrocities, and calling for the international community to oppose the blanket amnesty for all combatants and accountability for crimes under Sierra Leonean and international law).

[34] *See* Agreement between the United Nations and the Government of Sierra Leone on the Establishment of a Special Court for Sierra Leone, 2178 U.N.T.S. 137 (Jan. 16, 2002).

and ensure a lasting peace.[35] President Kabbah maintained that, but for international support, Sierra Leone would not have the legal, logistical, human, and other resources necessary to prosecute those responsible for the atrocities.[36]

In Resolution 1315, adopted on August 14, 2000, the Security Council formally endorsed President Kabbah's request.[37] Thus it directed Secretary-General Annan to negotiate an agreement with the government of Sierra Leone to establish an independent special tribunal with jurisdiction to prosecute those bearing "greatest responsibility," focusing in particular on those who had threatened the establishment and implementation of the peace process.[38] The subject matter jurisdiction was to include war crimes, crimes against humanity, and other serious violations of international humanitarian law, as well as various offenses under national law.[39] The temporal jurisdiction would cover the crimes committed after November 30, 1996, over the express objections of the Sierra Leonean government that ultimately wanted international support to prosecute crimes that dated back to the beginning of the conflict in March 1991. The geographic jurisdiction was confined to the offenses that actually took place on Sierra Leonean territory. This latter maybe contrasted with the ICTR, which had jurisdiction over certain crimes associated with the 1994 genocide, but that took place on the territory of neighboring states. This could have been done in the Sierra Leone situation, given the intimate connections between the Sierra Leonean and Liberian conflicts.

The Statute of the SCSL, which entered into force on April 12, 2002 after each of the parties had complied with their respective formalities for its implementation, contained many novel features that were intended, among other things, to reflect the specificities of the Sierra Leone war. It was an attempt to create a cheaper and inexpensive institution compared to other tribunals and that was expected to conclude its work in about three years. For these reasons, as well as others more prosaic, the Court scored a series of firsts. It was (1) the first international penal tribunal to be given a narrowly framed personal jurisdiction to prosecute only those deemed to bear the greatest responsibility for the various international and national crimes within its jurisdiction; (2) the first international tribunal since Nuremberg and Tokyo to sit in the *locus commisi delicti* – that is, the place where the crimes were committed; (3) the first to provide scope for the affected state (Sierra Leone) to appoint some of its principal officials, such as a minority of the judges in each of the trial and appeal's chambers and the deputy prosecutor; (4) the first to be funded entirely through donations by UN member states; (5) the first to be overseen by an independent management committee comprised of nonparty states to give it assistance and oversee its operational aspects; and finally, (6) the first court anywhere in the world to operate alongside a truth and reconciliation commission in a post-conflict situation.[40]

---

[35] President of the Republic of Sierra Leone, Annex to the Letter dated Aug. 9, 2000 from the Permanent Representative of Sierra Leone to the United Nations addressed to the President of the Security Council, U.N. Doc. S/2000/786 (Aug. 10, 2000).

[36] *Id. See also* Charles C. Jalloh, *Special Court for Sierra Leone: Achieving Justice?*, 32 Mich. J. Int'l L. 395, 398–99 (2011).

[37] S.C. Res. 1315, U.N. Doc. S/RES/1315 (Aug. 14, 2000).

[38] S.C. Res. 1315, *id.* at para. 3.

[39] Statute of the Special Court for Sierra Leone, Jan. 16, 2002, 2178 U.N.T.S. 145, arts. 2 (crimes against humanity), 3 (war crimes), and 4 (other serious violations of international humanitarian law). Article 5 listed the offenses prosecutable using Sierra Leonean law.

[40] The TRC, as discussed later by several authors in this book, was established pursuant to the government's undertaking in the Lomé Peace Agreement. See, for example, the chapters by Leila Sadat and Alpha Sesay.

Upon its establishment, the SCSL also landed a set of other firsts. Thus, among other things, the Court became the first ad hoc international criminal tribunal to create under its Rules of Procedure and Evidence a semiautonomous Office of the Principal Defender (OPD) within the Registry mandated to specifically "ensure" that the rights and interests of suspects and accused persons are protected; the first to have created a dedicated Outreach Office unprecedented within international criminal courts for its location in situ, depth, scope, and reach; and the first to create a Legacy Phase Working Group, which was comprised of staff from the various sections of the SCSL and entrusted with devising several innovative projects that it was anticipated would help leave a lasting legacy to the people of the host state extending beyond the mere prosecutions of a handful of war criminals.[41]

IV. THE TRIALS CONDUCTED BY THE SPECIAL COURT FOR SIERRA LEONE

Once its treaty entered into force in April 2002, and sufficient funds had been raised for its operations to start, Secretary-General Annan appointed the first Prosecutor (David Crane) and the Registrar (Robin Vincent) on, respectively, April 17, 2002 and June 10, 2002. They both took up their assignments by August 2002. Subsequently, in December 2002, the Judges, who had in the interim been appointed by the United Nations and Sierra Leone, were sworn in.

With record speed for an international court, literally around March 2003, the Prosecutor had carried out some investigations and unveiled applications for thirteen indictments of largely military and political leaders drawn from the three main warring factions in the Sierra Leone armed conflict.[42] These suspects comprised the mutinying elements of the national army known as the Armed Forces Revolutionary Council (AFRC), the Civil Defense Forces (CDF) militia and the Revolutionary United Front (RUF) rebels. Most of the indictees were arrested without difficulty because they were based in Sierra Leone.

The RUF and CDF cases were heard by Trial Chamber I, while the AFRC, and later the Taylor case, were entrusted to Trial Chamber II. In the first of the SCSL cases to conclude were three AFRC commanders, namely Alex Tamba Brima, Brima Bazzy Kamara, and Santigie Borbor Kanu. Between March 7, 2003, and September 16, 2003, Brima, Kamara, and Kanu were separately indicted on seventeen counts of war crimes, crimes against humanity, and other serious violations of international humanitarian law. About a year later, their separate indictments were amended and the charges reduced to fourteen counts. At the Prosecution's request, the Trial Chamber ordered the joint trials of the three men on February 18, 2005. A consolidated Indictment, containing fourteen counts, was later

---

[41] *See* Vincent O. Nmehielle & Charles C. Jalloh, *The Legacy of the Special Court for Sierra Leone*, 30(2) FLETCHER F. WORLD AFF. 107 (2006) (discussing the innovations that the SCSL was developing in its practice in those three areas).

[42] Several additional indictments were issued by the Court for RUF Leader Foday Sankoh, one of his alleged field commanders Sam Bockarie (aka "Mosquito"), and AFRC junta leader Major Johnny Paul Koroma. These will not be discussed here because both Sankoh's and Bockarie's Indictments were withdrawn, following their confirmed deaths. However, as Major Koroma is missing, his Indictment remains valid. He is the only remaining fugitive from the SCSL. Although there was evidence alleging his death presented at the Taylor Trial in The Hague, because that has been deemed inconclusive, provision has been made in the Statute of the Residual Special Court for Sierra Leone for Koroma's trial should he surface at some point in the future.

approved. The trial opened in Freetown a year later (on March 7, 2005), and eight months later, the Prosecution case concluded. On June 5, 2006, the defense case opened and closed around the end of October 2006, after the Accused had called eighty-seven witnesses. Final oral arguments were heard in the first week of December 2006.

On June 20, 2007, the Judges of Trial Chamber II found all three men guilty of eleven out of fourteen counts of war crimes, crimes against humanity, and other serious violations of international humanitarian law. The three were sentenced on July 19, 2007 to prison terms of fifty years each for Brima and Kanu and forty-five years for Kamara. The Appeals Chamber upheld all the sentences on February 22, 2008.

Besides the AFRC cases, the SCSL completed the joint trials of six others from the CDF and RUF groups. Whereas Sam Hinga Norman, a former Deputy Defense Minister in Sierra Leone, was indicted on March 7, 2003, his CDF compatriots Moinina Fofana and Allieu Kondewa were indicted just over three months later on June 26, 2003. The Trial Chamber granted the Prosecution's request for a joint trial on February 28, 2004 and approved a consolidated Indictment not long afterward. The CDF trial opened on June 3, 2004, and on July 14, 2005, the Prosecution closed its case after calling 75 witnesses and was followed by the defense, which called 44 witness, one of whom was Norman. Final arguments did not take place until the end of November 2006 due to disposition of the motion for judgment of acquittal and the alternating schedule of this same group of Judges who were during the intervals also adjudicating the RUF case.

On August 2, 2007, the Trial Chamber rendered the Court's second judgment, finding in respect to Fofana and Kondewa that each was guilty of four counts in the Indictment. The two CDF Accused were convicted by a majority comprised of a Canadian and Cameroonian judge. In an interesting but controversial twist, especially outside Sierra Leone, the lone Sierra Leonean judge on the bench refused to convict. He would have acquitted the defendants because of necessity and their motive for fighting: the restoration of democracy to Sierra Leone. On October 9, 2007, Fofana was sentenced to six years while Kondewa received eight years. However, on appeal, the Appeals Chamber modified some of the grounds for the convictions and rejected the necessity argument by Judge Bankole Thompson. But in perhaps the most significant part of their May 28, 2008 judgment, at least for the defendants, the appeals judges increased the sentences for Fofana to fifteen years while Kondewa was awarded twenty years.

In the meantime, in the period between the close of the CDF case and rendering of trial judgment on August 2, 2007, the first Accused, Norman, had suddenly died in a hospital in Senegal where he had been taken for medical treatment. An internal inquiry was conducted into the circumstances of his death. Unfortunately, to this day, the findings of the investigative judge remain hidden from the public. In May 2007, the Chamber terminated the proceedings against him.

In the RUF group of cases, Issa Sesay and Morris Kallon were indicted on March 7, 2003 on seventeen-counts for war crimes, crimes against humanity, and other serious violations of international humanitarian law. One count was later added to the Indictment. Gbao was indicted on April 16, 2003. On March 5, 2004, the Trial Chamber ordered the joint trials of the three Accused. The RUF case started on July 5, 2004, with seventy-five witnesses testifying for the Prosecution, while eighty-five appeared for the Defense. The parties made closing submissions on August 5, 2008.

The Trial Chamber determined on February 25, 2009 that Sesay and Kallon were guilty on sixteen of the eighteen counts in the Indictment. Gbao, for his part, was found guilty on fourteen counts including for his role in abducting UN peacekeepers as hostages in May 2000. Sesay was sentenced to fifty-two years, Kallon was awarded forty years, while Gbao was condemned to twenty-five years. On October 26, 2009, the Appeals Chamber overturned Gbao's conviction on one of the counts but otherwise generally upheld the other Trial Chamber findings in respect of him and the other RUF commanders, including the sentences.

Charles Taylor, former Liberian president and Sankoh associate, was the only non–Sierra Leonean to be indicted by the Prosecutor. An initial seventeen-count Indictment issued on March 7, 2003 for war crimes, crimes against humanity, and other serious international humanitarian law violations was sealed. The world learned about it on June 4, 2003, when the Prosecution hastily announced its existence, apparently before seeking a judicial order making it a public document, in an attempt to have Taylor arrested in Ghana where he was attending peace talks.[43] He left the talks for Liberia under the escort of an embarrassed Ghanaian government. It took several years, and much diplomatic wrangling between West African and other states, but Taylor was eventually arrested and transferred to the custody of the SCSL on March 29, 2006 where he was arraigned. Some concerns were then expressed about the security conditions in Liberia and Sierra Leone, both of which were emerging from the shadows of devastating internal conflicts. It was speculated that Taylor still had supporters capable of engaging in violence and destabilization of Sierra Leone and Liberia. Thus, in one of the most controversial decisions to ever be taken by the Court, Taylor was transferred to The Hague on June 30, 2006. This was after the UN Security Council gave its imprimatur to the decision and Dutch authorities had indicated a willingness to allow his trial to be conducted on their territory on condition that Britain house him if he were convicted.

A month before the trial opened, on May 29, 2007, his seventeen-count Indictment was reduced to eleven counts. The Taylor case formally opened on June 4, 2007, but the Accused fired his legal team and insisted he would represent himself due to the inadequate time and resources allocated to his provisionally assigned counsel. The Chamber's attempt to appoint Karim Khan as a court-appointed lawyer for the defendant was rebuffed by the defense counsel who said that this would be contrary to the preference of his client. The judges then appointed Charles Jalloh, the Legal Advisor to the Principal Defender based in The Hague, as interim counsel until the replacement counsel could be found for Taylor. The case was put on hold for the evidentiary phase until January 2008 after the Office of the Principal Defender appointed new counsel, in August 2007, who then successfully sought and obtained an adjournment to review the thousands of pages of prosecution disclosure before the witness hearing phase would begin. Once it got underway early in the new year, the trial continued without significant interruptions until close to its conclusion, with Taylor taking the stand and testifying in his own defense for several months. Closing arguments were heard on February 8, 2011 and final briefs were turned in a month later.

The Trial Chamber issued its judgment on April 26, 2012. Taylor was convicted on all eleven counts, as an aider and abettor and a planner of war crimes, crimes against humanity, and other serious humanitarian law violations committed by his RUF subordinates in

---

[43] Evidence came out much later indicating that the American prosecutor had also shared an advance copy of the indictment with the government of his own country. This led to later speculation, during the Taylor Trial, whether the then Prosecutor might have also taken instructions from that government regarding whom to indict. That would be contrary to his express duty not to seek or receive any instructions from any source, in accordance with the prohibitions contained in the Statute.

Sierra Leone. On May 30, 2012, he was sentenced to fifty years imprisonment. He has since appealed his conviction. Appeals hearings will be conducted in The Hague in January 2013. The forecast, at this point, is that the appeals judgment will be rendered before the end of 2013 and likely in the early fall.

The eight AFRC, CDF, and RUF convicts are currently serving their jail terms at a maximum security prison near the Rwandan capital, Kigali, under an enforcement of sentence agreement between the government of Rwanda and the SCSL. They were transferred there in October 2009. In contrast, with respect to Taylor, whose case is currently before the appellate chamber, he would serve his jail term in Britain if indeed his conviction and sentence are upheld. That will mark the completion of a significant and final trial milestone for the SCSL.

Consistent with the UN Security Council–mandated Completion Strategy, the Court has already effectively wound down its main operations at its seat in Freetown. It has retained only the Appeals Chamber judges and essential Registry and other staff required for final disposition of the Taylor case in The Hague, where they now sit, in addition to a few other core personnel engaged in work on the residual mechanism. Even though it was the last to be created of the three ad hoc international criminal courts for the former Yugoslavia, Rwanda, and Sierra Leone, and leaving aside the East Timor trials because of their different legal basis, the SCSL seems set to become the first of the modern ad hoc international criminal courts to finally accomplish its mandate.

V. THE ORGANIZATION AND CONTENTS OF THIS VOLUME

Besides this overview chapter, and the keynote speech delivered at the Pitt Law conference, this book contains thirty-six substantive chapters and the Conclusion. The sheer size of the volume means that its contents can only be briefly summarized below. It is arranged into eight parts corresponding with the major themes discussed in each. The book opens with the remarks by Stephen J. Rapp, former Prosecutor of the SCSL and now U.S. Ambassador-at-Large in the Office of Global Criminal Justice of the State Department, on the topical matter regarding the challenge of case selection in the investigation and prosecution of international crimes. That issue is a timely and important one in international criminal law circles, especially given recent debates about the exercise of prosecutorial discretion in the ad hoc tribunals and at the permanent ICC. Everyone wants to know how prosecutors select cases, and additionally at the ICC, the situations to investigate for the possible commission of international crimes. But, save for the unique ICC prosecutorial practice of providing some explanations as to what criteria are used to make such determinations, no one really knows how such decisions are reached. This has definitely been the case in the ad hoc tribunals, including at the SCSL. This chapter therefore shines much needed light on a topic that has largely escaped serious scholarly scrutiny. Ambassador Rapp's essay, drawing from his extensive experience as both a national prosecutor in the United States and an international prosecutor in the Rwanda and Sierra Leone Tribunals, examines and illuminates the tremendous moral, legal, and practical challenges that international prosecutors face in the process of case selection. In reading his chapter, one is struck with how difficult, even under the best of circumstances, the process of choosing is bound to be, especially given the context of mass atrocities that tend to pervade the commission of international crimes. Yet, the task seems to become even more challenging when the prosecutors have to additionally operate under a severely restricted jurisdictional mandate, as was uniquely the case in the SCSL, to prosecute only those bearing the "greatest responsibility" for the atrocities committed in a given conflict.

Part I, which contextualizes the Court and sets out the main expectations of its key stakeholders, contains three chapters. Vivian Curran situates the Sierra Leone Tribunal in a broader historical perspective, conceiving it as part of a continuing "revolution" in international law, which began when individuals assumed their place as proper subjects instead of just mere objects of international law at Nuremberg, which resonated decades later all the way to The Hague, Arusha, and Freetown. The next two chapters, respectively by Alison Smith and Peter Penfold, two individuals whose association with Sierra Leone began at pivotal moments, remind readers of two broadly defined national and international stakeholder communities and the high expectations of the Court in the period leading up to and immediately after its establishment. These chapters, taken together, offer one general if admittedly indeterminate benchmark on which we can judge the legacy of the SCSL in answer to the question that Justice Jackson asked himself just after the Nuremberg Trial: did the Court do what it was supposed to do?

Part II (Chapters 4 to 9) assesses the SCSL's jurisprudential approach to the determinations of individual criminal responsibility in the AFRC, RUF, CDF, and Taylor cases. The first two chapters focus on the most controversial mode of liability in the SCSL and in international criminal law more generally: the doctrine of Joint Criminal Enterprise (JCE). Simon Meisenberg, a former Legal Officer in both the AFRC and Taylor cases at the SCSL, and Wayne Jordash and Scott Martin, two former defense counsel in the RUF cases in Freetown, bring their insider perspectives to bear by examining the Court's liberal interpretation and application of JCE, especially the so-called extended form (JCE III), in specific cases such as in *Gbao* and *Taylor*. The last four chapters, from respectively Sandesh Sivakumaran (on the duty to take measures to prevent and punish subordinates), Harmen van der Wilt (on the application of the test for command and control to irregular armed groups in Sierra Leone), Ilias Bantekas (on how a context-sensitive anthropological approach to the construction of criminal liabilities can help yield just outcomes) and Réne Provost (on the judicial and other tensions arising from the SCSL's application of rationalist Western doctrines of authority and responsibility in the CDF Trial in which the alleged magical powers of one Accused was invoked as the basis of his criminal liability). All four respected scholars in the international criminal law field focus on command or superior responsibility, the other contested mode of liability within international criminal law dating back to the post–World War II cases, and how it was easily and uneasily adapted to punish the crimes committed in Sierra Leone. Bantekas and Provost usefully draw on interdisciplinary insights to inform the legal literature on the Court.

In Part III (Chapters 10 to 14), the area where the SCSL might well have left its biggest jurisprudential imprint on international law, the authors analyze the Court's approach to and treatment of the substantive international crimes within its jurisdiction. The first two chapters, from Michael Scharf and Sidney Thompson, discuss forced marriage, which was recognized for the first time in international law in the SCSL as part of the residual category of other inhumane acts of crimes against humanity. It was meant to address a particularly nasty feature of the Sierra Leonean conflict under which rebels seized, raped, and enslaved women while deliberately and misleadingly labeling them "bush wives." The two chapters on this topic were not set up as a debate. The first of them was written by a known scholar in the field, and the second by a practitioner who had the vantage point of someone who had worked as a Legal Officer in the Chambers of the Court. However, their different perspectives on the merits of recognizing forced marriage as a new international crime and placement in the book right next to each other have the effect of simulating somewhat of a debate. I have no doubt that their chapters will inform future analyses of this important topic on the SCSL legacy.

The chapter by Valerie Oosterveld, a thoughtful scholar who has written on many gender issues in international criminal law, widens our viewpoint in her assessment of the Court's approach to forced marriage and gender crimes more broadly, highlighting both the Tribunal's important contributions as well as some of its key limitations. The last two chapters in this part, by Roberta Arnold (an IHL expert from the Swiss Armed Forces) and Alhagi Marong (whose work experience include serving as a Senior Legal Officer to the Appeals Chamber in the AFRC Appeal and Judgment Coordinator in the ICTR), assess the SCSL's judicial contribution to our understanding of the prosecution of terrorism as a war crime and the first convictions in an international criminal court of the war crime of attacks against UN peacekeepers.

The five contributions in Part IV (Chapters 15 to 19) examine challenging issues that have bedeviled international criminal lawyers at the SCSL, and that continue to do so in other ad hoc courts and even the ICC. The part opens up with a chapter by a prominent scholar assessing the Court jurisprudence on the live question whether domestic amnesties may bar prosecutions of international crimes before an ad hoc international criminal tribunal (Leila Sadat), followed by an analysis of the always fascinating but equally always divisive issue of head-of-state immunity in the Taylor case (Micaela Frulli), the war crime of forcible enlistment of children for the purposes of using them in hostilities (Cecile Aptel), and the Court's approach to the phenomenon of child soldiers as victims and perpetrators of serious crimes (Noah Novogrodsky). The last piece rounding up this part, on sentencing at the SCSL, takes an early look at one of the most controversial topics in the literature and jurisprudence of the modern ad hoc tribunals (Margaret deGuzman). For some reason, despite the reality that the Sierra Leone court has dished out some of the harshest sentences for the international crimes in its jurisdiction compared to the frankly laconic sentences from her sister ICTY and ICTR for some of the world's worst crimes, sentencing at the SCSL has hardly received any serious scholarly interest. DeGuzman's chapter on sentencing seems to therefore be a welcome break of that trend and a useful addition to the literature on the SCSL. It is hoped that more academics will take up this topic in the future as sentencing is a widely ignored but likely major legacy item that the Court's jurisprudence will bequeath to international criminal law.

In Part V, comprised of six chapters (20–25) written by a mix of academics and practitioners, some of whom also worked in or on the Court as trial monitors, or both, the book turns to important process, funding, and cooperation-related issues. We start with the most controversial institutional aspect of the SCSL: the question of its mode of financing (Sarah Kendall), which divided the UN Secretary-General and the Security Council when the former presciently but unsuccessfully argued that donations were unviable and unsustainable as a means of financing international tribunals such as the Court. The lesson of Sierra Leone appears resoundingly clear that donations should never be used as the primary means of funding the work of an international penal court. Kendall's chapter is followed by several trial-related jurisprudence chapters on the now largely ignored topic of subpoenas in international criminal law (Chacha Murungu), the role of witnesses and protective measures in helping the Court achieve its mandate (Amy DiBella), the consequences of witness payments and the dangers that they pose for the credibility of witnesses and the evidence that they gave during the trials especially in the Taylor case (Jennifer Easterday), the overall smooth and supportive relationship between the SCSL and its host and other states (Shakiratu Sanusi), and last but not least, the complex but generally friendly relationship between the SCSL and the Sierra Leone Truth and Reconciliation Commission when the two briefly operated alongside each other (Alpha Sesay).

On the subjects in respect of which the SCSL is perceived to have already left a significant institutional legacy, readers will find four thoughtful chapters (26–29), on respectively, the SCSL's creation of an outreach section (Stuart Ford), and the Office of the Principal Defender. Ford's chapter adopts a refreshing empirical approach to reach what may be described as the most critical conclusion yet on the supposed impact of the Court's outreach unit. Although some insiders will be wont to dispute its conclusions, perhaps reflexively in the face of years of claims based on untested assumptions, the chapter opens up a legitimate debate about one of the more grandiose assertions that the SCSL has made in its self-evaluation of its outreach program as a huge success.

As to the Defense, Vincent Nmehielle comes to the topic from a more institutional perspective of the Principal Defender, who held office during the core of the SCSL trials and was thrust in the center of internal tribunal battles for adequate facilities to enable fair trials that defense counsel were often not privy to. In contrast Sareta Ashraph, a cocounsel (with Wayne Jordash) in the RUF Sesay case, approaches the issues from the perspective of an independent defense counsel. Nmehielle's and Ashraph's chapters were set up as a debate between two insiders in an attempt to expose the complexities of the defense experience in the SCSL. Although there are many areas of agreement between the two authors, in a face-off that seemed to sometimes reflect the palpable tensions that characterized the work of the OPD vis-à-vis defense counsel during the Freetown trials, the two passionately debate whether the Defence Office was as innovative and as useful as some scholars had claimed it to be. They expose the resource and institutional autonomy issues that sadly drove a wedge in the defense family in Freetown, even among the advocates who shared an unquestionable personal commitment to holding the Court's feet to the fire to help ensure that it would fulfill its statutory promise to fully respect the fair trial rights of the accused persons. While my own assessment of the defense legacy lies somewhere between the middle of the positions that Nmehielle and Ashraph advanced, what has hitherto been glorified in the literature as a resoundingly positive SCSL legacy on defense matters now surely invites further engagement by other scholars and practitioners, especially those of us who have worked in the Court.

The final chapter in Part VI reminds us why we should not allow ourselves to get lost in the trees by failing to see the forest. Kenneth Gallant's thoughtful chapter examines the "democracy deficit" in the lawmaking settings of international penal tribunals where the defense has historically been typically excluded, and when included, wittingly or unwittingly banished to the margins. A big added value of this work is that it relates the Sierra

Leone experience, involving defense counsel in rule making, to the developments at the permanent ICC while building on the SCSL's contribution to advocate for greater defense participation in tribunal law-making.

In Part VII, three chapters (30–32) from Charles Jalloh, Lansana Gberie, and Annie Gell, respectively, take up three special challenges that occupied the SCSL in a major way during its lifetime. Jalloh, who worked in the Court before joining academia, takes up previously uncharted terrain in an early attempt to evaluate the SCSL's jurisprudential legacy regarding the most widely cited but at the same time most widely misunderstood personal jurisdiction over those bearing "greatest responsibility" for the heinous offenses committed in Sierra Leone. The author laments the apparent popularity of that phrase in international criminal law and evaluates the jurisprudential debates about its meaning during the Freetown trials, arguing that its entry into our lexicon masked a crucial signal of a turn toward justice on the cheap by the key sponsors of international criminal justice at the United Nations, which hardly bodes well for the future. When read in conjunction with Rapp's chapter, it becomes evident that the greatest responsibility threshold had a chilling effect on prosecutions of many otherwise culpable middle level and even higher ranked persons who perpetrated international crimes in Sierra Leone. This includes publicly known key figures such as Ibrahim Bah, a Sankoh and Taylor liaison, who is allegedly responsible for gunrunning and supplying many other logistics to the RUF and AFRC that were used to commit crimes during the war.

Gberie, a Sierra Leonean historian, journalist, and academic, gives eloquent intellectual expression to a very popular Sierra Leonean view questioning the wisdom and propriety of the SCSL's indictment and trial of Sam Hinga Norman, Moinina Fofana, and Allieu Kondewa, in the CDF trial, alongside their former enemies in the RUF and the AFRC. The irony was not lost on Gberie that the popular Norman, even though he died before the trial verdict was rendered, spent years in detention sharing the same physical space with the detainees who were found to have orchestrated many of the more devastating atrocities during the Sierra Leone conflict. Though this is not the place to resolve this issue, to any impartial observers of what happened in Sierra Leone and the crucial role the CDF militia played to restore democracy, the moral and legal debate will likely continue regarding the propriety of the international prosecutions of the *Kamajor* leaders even though the two that were convicted clearly committed some excesses during the war. Despite Rapp's compelling response on the issue in his essay, as a former prosecutor who appealed the guilty verdict and sentences, it is certain that for many Sierra Leoneans like Gberie the decision to try the CDF trio, especially Norman, cannot ultimately be divorced from politics and may be the Macbethian ghost that will haunt Sierra Leone into the future.

In the third chapter concluding Part VII, Gell draws on primary materials, extensive interviews, and fieldwork to analyze the impact and implications of the SCSL's most important case – the trial of former Liberian president Charles Taylor, the first former head of state to be fully tried, convicted, and sentenced for war crimes and crimes against humanity in a contemporary international criminal tribunal. That case will no doubt continue to be debated going forward. This is not the least because of some of the legal controversies that came up in the course of the proceedings regarding alleged payments of monies to witnesses in return for their testimony, an issue that Easterday discusses in her chapter, and the still unexplained decision of the alternate judge to enter a "dissenting opinion" following the unanimous Trial Chamber verdict.[44]

In the last section of the book, Part VIII (Chapters 33 to 36), four authors examine various issues categorized as the impact and legacy of the SCSL. Although the theme here is in a way the focus of the book as a whole, this grouping was justified on the basis that these chapters generally focused on the big-picture influence of the Court. Toward that end, Viviane Dittrich assesses the meaning of legacy and the SCSL's attempt to institutionalize its legacy, and argues for plural conceptions of "legacies" and dynamic "legacies in the making" (Chapter 33). For his part, Mohamed Bangura, a Sierra Leonean prosecutor who has been involved in all the Court's trials as a trial attorney in Freetown as well as in The Hague, considers and critiques some of his compatriot's views about how much justice was delivered by the SCSL and whether it could be said to be enough in any sense (Chapter 34). His broad and apparently laudatory chapter covers much ground, and although not deliberately designed to do so, serves as a recapitulation of many of the key achievements and limitations of the Court.

In her insightful chapter, Linda Carter, in one of the first works to ever do so, offers us preliminary thinking about how we might begin to conceptualize a possible framework for transitional justice that draws on the rich experiences gained from the Sierra Leone and Rwanda situations (Chapter 35). This is important as those were the two African countries that not only shared in collective trauma occasioned by the atrocity crimes each experienced in the 1990s, but that are now further symbolically conjoined through the enforcement of sentence agreement between Rwanda and the SCSL.

Finally, in taking up one of the most methodologically difficult questions to answer about the Court, or any international tribunal for that matter, Theresa Clark attempts an early assessment of the SCSL's normative contributions to achieving truth, reconciliation, accountability and reparations in Sierra Leone (Chapter 36). Her chapter raises many big picture questions about the Court's ultimate contributions to Sierra Leone's transition process from conflict to peace. Considering that scholars are divided on whether it is even the job of international penal courts to achieve broader goals that extend beyond their core prosecution mandates, I sincerely hope that additional commentators will seek to answer the preliminary questions posed, using both interdisciplinary, empirical and other methodologies.

VI. CONCLUDING REMARKS

Overall, this early assessment of the legacy and contributions of the SCSL is intended to stimulate interest in, and thinking about, the long-term impact and legacy of the Court. Although not an empirical work, as a glance at the title might at first blush suggest, this doctrinal and normative analysis will hopefully be received in the spirit in which it was offered: that is, as an invitation to current and future researchers and colleagues in international law and beyond to engage in the exploration of what can be said to be the SCSL's substantive contributions to Sierra Leoneans, Africans, and the international community as a whole.

---

[44] See, for more on this, Charles C. Jalloh, *The Verdict(s) in the Charles Taylor Case*, JURIST (May 14, 2012), http://jurist.org/forum/2012/05/charles-jalloh-taylor-verdict.php and *Why the Special Court for Sierra Leone Should Establish an Independent Commission to Address Alternate Judge Sow's Allegation in the Charles Taylor Case*, JURIST (Oct. 1, 2012), http://jurist.org/forum/2012/10/charles-jalloh-sow-scsl.php.

Keynote Address

The Challenge of Choice in the Investigation and Prosecution of International Crimes in Post-Conflict Sierra Leone

Keynote Address delivered by Stephen J. Rapp[*][†]

Thank you, Charles [Jalloh], for the invitation to this conference and for holding this great event. I am sorry that I was not been able to attend from the beginning, though I heard last night about the panels and the intense discussions that have taken place here in the last several days.

It is good to be back here, because as you said, it is not the first time. Indeed, it was one of the earliest invitations that I accepted after I became Ambassador-at-Large for War Crimes Issues, as we called it then, to come to University of Pittsburgh School of Law.

As you may know, I do a lot of traveling in my present job. Last year, it was 222 days on the road, the year before it was 220, and so far I have been to some 47 or 48 countries. I have visited not only the places for which courts are trying those alleged to be responsible for mass atrocities, but also other locations to meet the victims of past or present violations, where the promise of accountability has not yet been met. There the victims invariably ask, "Why has there been no justice for us? Why has the truth not been established in our country?"

When you hear of a person being "at large," it is common to think of someone who is on the run because of the law. So it is with an ambassador-at-large, as I am on the run trying to help meet the rising expectations for accountability and justice that now follows the commission of crimes under international law.

The topic that has been chosen for me today concerns the challenges of investigation and prosecution at the Special Court for Sierra Leone (SCSL). I speak to this topic from my experience as the former Prosecutor of the SCSL. I was nominated for that position by UN Secretary General Annan in early December 2006, went to Freetown for several days around December 15 to meet court officials, returned to take up the office on January 9, 2007, and then held the position for the next thirty-two months.

---

[*] Ambassador-at-Large, Office of Global Criminal Justice (formerly Office of War Crimes Issues), U.S. Department of State, 2009–current; Prosecutor, Special Court for Sierra Leone, 2007–2009; Chief of Prosecutions, 2005–2007, Senior Trial Attorney, 2001–2005, International Criminal Tribunal for Rwanda; United States Attorney, Northern District of Iowa, 1993–2001; B.A., Harvard University, 1971; J.D., Drake University Law School, 1974.

[†] The views expressed in this piece are the author's alone, and do not represent those of the U.S. government. The keynote address was delivered extemporaneously. The transcript of the address was edited by the author for publication. The author gratefully acknowledges the assistance of Diya Rattan on references and footnotes.

The challenge to which I will speak today is one which I know is of considerable interest. Indeed, in the last panel I heard that interest expressed in a question by Wayne Jordash. The challenge is how to exercise the most important power vested in the Office of the Prosecutor, and that is the question of choice.

How do you choose? Whom are you going to investigate, and among those that your investigation shows bear responsibility, how do you choose whom you are going to prosecute? How do you do this in a court like the SCSL that has an explicit mandate to limit its prosecutions,[1] a little similar to that of the Extraordinary Chambers in Courts of Cambodia[2] but certainly much more limited than at the International Tribunal for the former Yugoslavia (ICTY)[3] and the International Criminal Tribunal for Rwanda (ICTR).[4] At the SCSL, only those bearing the greatest responsibility for serious violations of the relevant law were to be prosecuted.[5] The choice of against whom to present charges was at the sole discretion of the Prosecutor.

Now prosecutorial discretion is something with which I was familiar from my own national system. I was a United States Attorney in Iowa for eight years. Iowa is not a place known for lots of crime, but indeed there were thousands of instances of wrongdoing that I could have made into federal cases. In my office we generally chose to prosecute about two hundred cases a year.

I know that in some places of the world, the idea of prosecutors having discretion to throw the weight of the law against one culpable individual and not against another is controversial. This was a topic that we sometimes discussed in our annual Colloquiums of International Prosecutors. The first one of these was hosted by the ICTR Prosecutor in Arusha in November 2004, and the second by the SCSL Prosecutor in Freetown in June 2005. Indeed, that was my first visit to Freetown. The third one was in The Hague in November of 2006, hosted by both the ICTY Prosecutor and the International Criminal Court (ICC) Prosecutor. I remember Luis Moreno Ocampo describing "focused investigations," talking about filing perhaps only one or two cases a year, but of having great impact by casting a "shadow." Where to go and whom to charge was, to him, a matter of discretion.

Carla Del Ponte, the cohost of the conference reacted, "Discretion, discretion. What is this discretion? I prosecute guilty people." Indeed, in the civil law system, it is the rule to investigate all who may be culpable. To exclude somebody in such a system is a violation of the principle of legality.

I saw some of the result of Carla's approach when I joined the ICTR in May 2001, and was parachuted to lead the prosecution as the senior trial attorney in the Media trial that was then in its seventh month. It is fair to say that there were difficulties with the evidence, and lots of things that required additional investigations. But I immediately confronted the reality that our investigative force over in Kigali had been directed to begin thirty new cases every year, and they did not have any time to help strengthen the prosecution in what I thought was one of the most historic cases at the ICTR.

In late 2003, the ICTR came under the mandate from the UN Security Council to begin to limit the number of cases to the more serious offenders and to look at the possibility that

[1] *See* SCSL Statute art 1(1).
[2] *See* ECCC Statute art. 1.
[3] *See* ICTY Statute art. 1.
[4] *See* ICTR Statute art. 1.
[5] SCSL, *supra* note 1.

mid-level or low-level people might be prosecuted at the national level.[6] At that time we had a so-called Gamma list of about two hundred names of persons to investigate and prosecute, and it was eventually necessary to reduce it to about ninety persons. We had to exercise discretion to make those decisions. But, as to how such discretion is exercised, there does not appear to be a lot of understanding outside of prosecutors' offices. I was on a panel not long ago with our good friend, Professor Bill Schabas, who reacted after I answered an audience question about the subject. Bill kind of threw up his hands and said, "Nobody really understands this! This is unexplored territory."

So, let me explore it in the context of Sierra Leone. And first of all, the point needs to be made that the decision on the thirteen people of which indictments were sought, and of which against whom indictments were returned, was made by the first Prosecutor. When I came to the SCSL on December 15, 2006, with my appointment in hand, for all practical purposes the issue was settled. However, I did have investigators who then recommended to me that we prosecute at least one additional person. I weighed that question for some time, but declined to proceed on practical grounds because of the difficulties and time necessary to make an arrest, and the limitation of the Court's resources that made it impossible to ensure, if we pursued that case, that we could complete it. This was based on my view that before you ask that someone's liberty be deprived, and be required to answer serious charges, you must have some confidence that you can complete the job. You must know that the guilt or innocence of the accused can be judged and that justice can be achieved for the victims who will be called to bear witness.

But as for the thirteen that had been indicted, I came to understand during the course of my thirty-two months at the SCSL how the decision had been made, because I had to answer for it across Sierra Leone. In the dozens of outreach sessions where I appeared around the country, there were none that I did not get the questions – "Why not this case? Why this one?" These were questions that I reflected upon as I made other decisions in these cases, and saw to their prosecution as they progressed through trial and appeal.

First of all, the decision of whom to prosecute must be seen in the context of how the Court was created. It is to be remembered that the process began with the communication from President Kabbah,[7] followed by Security Council Resolution 1315 (2000),[8] and was settled in negotiations between the government of Sierra Leone and the United Nations.[9] From the beginning it was clear that prosecution would be limited to the most responsible and that the focus was to be on the leadership of armed groups. This was understandable

---

[6] S.C. Res. 1534, § 4, at 2 (Mar. 26, 2004); S.C. Res. 1503, § 7, at 3 (Aug. 28, 2003).

[7] *Annex to Letter dated August 9, 2000 from the Permanent Representative of Sierra Leone to the United Nations addressed to the President of the Security Council*, S/2000/786, Annex (June 12, 2000), stating that:

> it is [the Sierra Leonean] Government's view that the issue of individual accountability of the leadership of the RUF for such crimes should be addressed immediately and that it is only by bringing the RUF leadership and their collaborators to justice ... that peace and national reconciliation and the strengthening of democracy will be assured in Sierra Leone.

[8] S.C. Res. 1315 (Aug. 14, 2000), recommending that "the special court should have personal jurisdiction over persons who bear the greatest responsibility for the commission of [war] crimes ... including those leaders who, in committing such crimes, have threatened the establishment of and implementation of the peace process in Sierra Leone."

[9] Agreement between the U.N. and the Government of Sierra Leone on the Establishment of a Special Court for Sierra Leone (Jan. 16, 2002), *available at* http://www.sc-sl.org/LinkClick.aspx?fileticket=CLk1rMQtCHg%3D &tabid=176 (last visited June 20, 2012) establishing "a Special Court for Sierra Leone to prosecute persons who

because there had been a brutal armed conflict, and massive violations had been committed by the members of organized armed groups. These violations included murder, rape, and most notoriously mutilation and amputations, most often of hands or arms – "short sleeves" or "long sleeves" – but also of other parts of the body.[10] There was also enslavement, both for sexual purposes and for forced labor, like the digging of diamonds, and the widespread use of child soldiers. These violations were committed, as we charged, as part of an organized campaign of terror, waged by at least one side, and by the other side to some extent, of counterterror, that devastated Sierra Leone and its people. Thousands lost their limbs, tens of thousands lost their lives, and hundreds of thousands suffered.[11]

If you study the report of the Sierra Leone Truth and Reconciliation Commission (TRC) you can see an accounting of the reported violations attributed to the various armed groups. This was published after the SCSL Prosecution began its work, but was similar to information that was within the Prosecution's possession. But it is important to note that the numbers cited by the TRC are not estimations – they represent actual reports of individual victims, who are listed by name for some, by number for those who wished to remain anonymous. The list in small print fills 230 pages.[12] This is probably only a fraction of the victims, as many may have been fearful or did not have access to the TRC. But the report does give us some useful numbers. For the years in which the SCSL had temporal jurisdiction of the crimes, that being the full calendar years of 1997, 1998, 1999, and 2000, one can total the violations attributed to each identified armed group. A total of 7,082 violations are associated with the Revolutionary United Front (RUF), 3,580 violations are associated with the Armed Forces Revolutionary Council (AFRC), and 1,506 associated with the Civil Defense Force (CDF). For other groups active at that time, the numbers tail down to less than a hundred.[13]

That large number attributable to the CDF bears on one of the most controversial decisions made by the SCSL Prosecutor – the decision to charge several leaders of the CDF. I see in the audience former U.K. Ambassador Peter Penfold, who has spoken critically of that decision.[14] I know that decision came as a surprise to many who had supported the creation of the SCSL. This is perhaps a good place to discuss the factors that go into deciding whether to prosecute "both sides" or all sides that have committed culpable conduct in an armed conflict.

We have seen the recent contrast in the approach between the ICTY and ICTR, tribunals that shared a single prosecutor through September 2003. In the former Yugoslavia, the Prosecutor pursued all sides – Serbs in Serbia, Serbs in Bosnia, Serbs in Croatia,

---

bear the greatest responsibility for serious violations of international humanitarian law and Sierra Leonean law."

[10] Sierra Leone Truth & Reconciliation Commission, *Witness to the Truth: Report of the Sierra Leone Truth & Reconciliation Commission*, vol. 3A, at 476 (2004), *available at* http://www.sierra-leone.org/Other-Conflict/TRCVolume3A.pdf (last visited June 20, 2012).

[11] *Id.*, vol. 2, at 39, 273, *available at* http://www.sierra-leone.org/Other-Conflict/TRCVolume2.pdf (last visited June 20, 2012); *id.*, vol. 3A, at 498–06, 509–14.

[12] *Id.* vol. 2, at 273–503.

[13] *Id.* at 39.

[14] Examination of witness for the defense Peter Penfold, Norman, Fofana and Kondewa ("CDF") (SCSL-2004-14-T), Trial Chamber I, at 51 (Aug. 8, 2006), *available at* http://www.sc-sl.org/LinkClick.aspx?fileticket=%2BImW5zHXRUU%3D&tabid=154 (last visited June 20, 2012).

Croatians in Croatia, Croatians in Bosnia, Bosniaks in Bosnia, and Kosovars in Kosovo, even Macedonians. Everybody was prosecuted except the Slovenians, for whom the civil war ended after only ten days in 1991. I suspect that some of these cases resulted from trips taken by the Prosecutor to ask for cooperation from governments whose nationals were being prosecuted. In Carla del Ponte's book, *Madame Prosecutor*, I can recall the accounts of meetings with national leaders where she asked for cooperation and would get the demand: "What about those other guys? They did horrible things." Her response was, "Find me some evidence and I will see if I can build a case against them too."[15]

It was sometimes possible to do that. However, in some cases, this resulted in prosecutions of persons who were not at a significantly high level and hence perhaps not appropriate for an international court. But when there were innocents killed on all sides, there is natural pressure for prosecutions on all sides. Yet in doing so, one should not ignore questions of gravity and scale, and whether the crimes were part of a widespread pattern of conduct. In the civil war in Bosnia, it was estimated that 90 percent of the war crimes were committed by persons of Serb ethnicity.[16] Should a prosecutor then be spending as much time pursuing those of other ethnicities?

The crimes committed by the "other side" may have involved only occasional or individualistic action and may not have been part of the policy of a particular armed group, and it may reflect the fact that a particular armed group may have been highly irregular and may have been facing a massive threat, and its leaders may not have been in effective control. So prosecuting all sides may not be appropriate. But it is certainly warranted when you can see that the other side is committing widespread violations, and when you can see a pattern of criminal conduct.

Of course, we know of tribunals where both sides could not be prosecuted, and yet are still believed to have achieved success. The greatest example is the International Military Tribunal at Nuremberg. Would it have been possible, if all of the evidence had been available at the time of Nuremberg, to have prosecuted the Soviets for the 1940 killing of more than twenty-two thousand imprisoned Poles and those of other nationalities in the Katyn forest?[17] Clearly not.

Has it been possible to prosecute the leaders of the Rwandan Patriotic Front (RPF) at the ICTR? Our late friend, Alison Des Forges, was more responsible than any other human being for the success that the ICTR has achieved in holding key political, military, government, and media officials responsible for the genocide of the Tutsi population of Rwanda – the murder of at least five hundred thousand men, women, and children in a period of a hundred days in 1994.[18] Before her tragic death in a plane crash in February 2009, she was an

---

[15] See reference to conversation with Rwandan President Kagame regarding crimes allegedly committed by the French where Del Ponte responds, "You give me the evidence, and I'm ready to do it." C. DEL PONTE, MADAME PROSECUTOR: CONFRONTATIONS WITH HUMANITY'S WORST CRIMINALS AND THE CULTURE OF IMPUNITY 226 (2009).

[16] R. Cohen, *C.I.A. Report on Bosnia Blames Serbs for 90% of the War Crimes*, N.Y. Times, Mar. 9, 1995, *available at* http://www.nytimes.com/1995/03/09/world/cia-report-on-bosnia-blames-serbs-for-90-of-the-war-crimes.html?pagewanted=all&src=pm (last visited July 10, 2012).

[17] *Russian Parliament Condemns Stalin for Katyn Massacre*, BBC (Nov. 26, 2012), *available at* http://www.bbc.co.uk/news/world-europe-11845315 (last visited June 20, 2012).

[18] A. Des Forges, *Leave None to Tell the Story: Genocide in Rwanda*, HUM. RTS. WATCH (HRW), 17 (Mar. 1, 1999), *available at* http://www.hrw.org/legacy/reports/1999/rwanda/ (last visited June 20, 2012).

essential expert witness in eleven of the ICTR's most important trials. But in the 1999 book that she wrote for Human Rights Watch, *Leave None to Tell the Story*, she also counts at least thirty thousand Hutu victims allegedly killed by the RPF, the rebel force that defeated the extremist Rwanda government in July 1994 and ended the genocide of the Tutsis.[19] There are more well-known allegations of crimes committed by Rwandan forces during the civil wars in the Congo in the late 1990s, but the killings that Des Forges describes in her book were alleged to have occurred in Rwanda in 1994, and could have constituted war crimes or crimes against humanity within the jurisdiction of the ICTR.

But for the ICTR, which was called into being to achieve justice for the genocide, cooperation with the successor government of Rwanda was essential. This was a situation where the successor government had defeated those who committed the genocide. In its view it was not appropriate for a tribunal established by the international community that had turned its back on the Tutsi victims of Rwanda to judge those who had ended the crime against them. In the end, the ICTR did not itself prosecute any of the alleged killings by the RPF.[20]

In Yugoslavia, it was possible to investigate and prosecute "both sides." The states in the former Yugoslavia were not strong, and there had had not been overwhelming victors in any part of the conflict. They needed the support of the international community. They wanted to be admitted to the European Union. And so it was possible to push for and obtain prosecutions of alleged serious violators on all sides. And obviously, in Sierra Leone, given the situation in Sierra Leone in 2003, it was possible. It was risky and difficult, but it was possible.

I arrived in Freetown after the conclusion of the trial of the CDF leaders when a verdict was anxiously awaited. In my third month, the leading Accused, Chief Sam Hinga Norman, died while convalescing from a hip operation that SCSL had arranged for him in Senegal.[21] Up until the arrest of Charles Taylor, he had been the most prominent of those charged by the SCSL, having been the effective Minister of Defense under President Kabbah during the civil war, and up to his arrest by the SCSL in March 2003.[22]

Some months after his death, the Trial Chamber pronounced guilty verdicts against the two surviving accused persons, Moinina Fofana and Allieu Kondewa, and sentenced them respectively to six and eight years, despite adjudging them responsible for multiple murders

---

[19] *Id.* at 558.

[20] The only public action of the ICTR prosecutor regarding allegations against the RPF involved the referral to a Rwandan military tribunal of the Kabgayi case regarding the June 5, 1994 killing of ten Catholic clerics and three bishops. *Statement by Hassan B. Jallow, Prosecutor of the ICTR*, U.N. Doc. S/PV.5904, at 11 (Jan. 1, 2008). Human Rights Watch criticized the subsequent domestic proceedings as a "sham trial that ignored crucial evidence in an apparent attempt to shield senior RPF members from criminal responsibility." L. Haskell & L. Waldorf, *The Impunity Gap of the International Criminal Tribunal for Rwanda: Causes and Consequences*, 34 HASTINGS INT'L & COMP. L. REV. 49, 50 (2011).

[21] Decision on Registrar's Submission of Evidence of Death of Accused Samuel Hinga Norman and Consequential Issues, Norman, Fofana and Kondewa ("CDF") (SCSL-04–14-T), Trial Chamber I, § 18 (May 21, 2007); Press Release, SCSL, Autopsy Shows Sam Hinga Norman Died of Natural Causes (Mar. 28, 2007), *available at* http://www.sc-sl.org/LinkClick.aspx?fileticket=8f7oadhYQBQ%3d&tabid=110 (last visited June 21, 2012).

[22] During the civil war, President Kabbah formally retained the Defense Ministry portfolio himself. Norman was formally the Deputy Minister, but was the official in charge of the Ministry. *See* "Norman, Samuel Hinga," Academic Research (The Hague Justice Portal), *available at* http://www.haguejusticeportal.net/index.php?id=8328 (last visited June 21, 2012).

and atrocities.[23] It fell to me to decide whether to appeal those sentences as too lenient, which I decided to do despite considerable controversy. We won a three-to-two decision in the Appeals Chamber, which increased the sentences respectively to fifteen and twenty years. The majority consisted of the Judges appointed by UN, the minority of the Judges appointed by Sierra Leone government. It did not break on African and non-African lines, as the majority included UN-appointed Judge Emmanuel Olayinka Ayoola of Nigeria.[24]

Was the prosecution of the CDF justified? I mentioned the large number of violations attributed to the CDF by victims who reported to the Truth and Reconciliation Commission. One also saw the pattern of the use of child soldiers that appeared as widespread among the CDF as among the RUF, though the Judges did not find Kondewa and Fofana criminally responsible. There had also been operations of counterterror conducted against villages that were perceived to be supportive of the rebel side. In these villages the targets explicitly included civilians. There was the testimony at trial of a speech by Chief Norman before the attack on the town of Koribondo that directed the CDF soldiers to kill everyone, to leave nothing standing but "the barri, the mosque, and [school]."[25] There was testimony of another witness that Norman had expressed anger when he saw civilians still alive after the attack. The Trial Chamber found that there were horrific killings of women who were wives of soldiers.[26] In the RUF trial, testimony was heard from so-called bush-wives who had been forcibly married to RUF commanders asserting that one of the reasons they did not attempt escape was the prospect of violence and painful death from the *kamajors*, the term used for the CDF soldiers because the members of this traditional hunting society were at its core.[27]

Given these crimes, we also believed that the decision to prosecute CDF leaders was important to ending the cycle of violence in Sierra Leone that had characterized the conflict. The reaction by some element of the CDF to RUF atrocities had been to try to "fight fire with fire."[28] But this could be seen to have led to a further escalation of brutality. After such counterviolence, the other side then reacted to the horrible things that had happened to their families and communities, and believed that they had reason to escalate further. The only way to break that cycle is to insist that no matter how aggrieved you are, no matter how righteous your cause, you do not take it out on the innocent. And I think that was an important message that we sent to the future in Sierra Leone.

I remember in mid-2007, there was an intense presidential election campaign that went through an initial round and then a runoff. In the end the opposition won, and was able to take office. There were some incidents of violence, though none lethal. I followed it closely, in discussions with Sierra Leoneans, and by reading further in the five or six local newspapers that I received each morning. Several of these were not known for their accuracy, a few were outrageous, and the one called *Peep* was always satirical. But I remember a very

---

[23] Sentencing Judgment, Fofana and Kondewa ("CDF") (SCSL-04-14-T), Trial Chamber 1, § 7 (Oct. 9, 2007).

[24] Judgment, Fofana and Kondewa ("CDF") (SCSL-04-14-T), Appeal Chamber, May 28, 2008, § 5.

[25] Examination-in-chief of witness TF2–032, Norman et al. ("CDF") (SCSL-04-14-T) Trial Chamber I, at 62 (Sept. 13, 2004), *available at* http://www.sc-sl.org/LinkClick.aspx?fileticket=HcoTIoo9XbU%3d&tabid=154 (last visited June 21, 2012).

[26] Judgment, Fofana and Kondewa ("CDF") (SCSL-04-14-T), Trial Chamber I, § 423 (Aug. 2, 2007).

[27] Judgment, Sesay, Kallon, and Gbao ("RUF") (SCSL-04-15-T), Trial Chamber I §§ 1212–1213 (Mar. 2, 2009).

[28] L. Gberie, *An Interview with Peter Penfold*, 104 AFR. AFF. 117, 122 (2005).

serious headline during that campaign which read, *"Special Court to Investigate Election Violence."*

At that point my investigation office had been downsized and we had not the capacity do any such investigation, even if our mandate had permitted it. But I did *not* put out a press release denying it. Yet without our direct intervention, something had changed, and there was the perception that even if you were aggrieved by the other side in the struggle for political power and control, violence was not to be tolerated.

You saw the contrast in Kenya, later that same year of 2007, when there was no question that Kalenjins in the Rift Valley had a legitimate grievance against the Kikuyu-led party of President Mwai Kibaki, when the latter was declared the winner suddenly and without a transparent vote count. Violence was directed against innocent Kikuyu in the Rift Valley. In reaction, violence was then directed against innocent Kalenjins in the rest of the country.[29] The violence cost over 1,100 lives and displaced hundreds of thousands.[30] The grievances were legitimate, but the escalation of violence and counterviolence was devastating to the entire society. It was the practice of an eye for an eye, targeting the innocent of opposing groups, that threatened to leave the whole world blind.

So in Sierra Leone, the decision was made to prosecute the most responsible in the three organized groups that had committed the greatest atrocities. But who should they be? Should it be the cruelest, the nastiest, the most venal individual that one can identify? Should it be the person against whom one can tote the greatest number of individual bloody acts? Or, should it be the guy at the top of the organization?

Now, I come from a law enforcement tradition that targets the top. This is certainly the way that federal prosecutors in the U.S. have pursued organized crime. Of course, you recognize that you have hit men and others who are doing brutal acts down on the street, but back somewhere in the shadows, you have "Mr. Big," the mafia boss, the person who is using those brutal individuals to gain and maintain wealth, and power, and control. I always remember those famous lines in C.S. Lewis's *Screwtape Letters*, where he said, "The greatest evil is ... conceived and ordered ... by quiet men with white collars and cut fingernails and smooth-shaven cheeks who do not need to raise their voice."[31]

In the Sierra Leone context, how could you say that the most direct actors were the most responsible? Would you say that the most culpable was the twelve-year old "Dr. Chop Chop" who was interviewed on tape by one of our witnesses shortly after his demobilization? He had become more proficient than any adult in chopping off arms, of hacking through bone, of cutting through flesh, and veins, and muscles, without revulsion or regret.[32] Was he the person responsible for this crime? Even though the amount of blood sent spurting by his acts was greater than that caused by almost any adult? Was it the young soldier who was described by one of our witnesses as having cut the arms and legs from a younger child and

---

[29] ICC Decision Pursuant to Article 15 of the Rome Statute on the Authorization of an Investigation into the Situation in the Republic of Kenya, Situation in Kenya (ICC-01/09), Pre-Trial Chamber II, §§ 111–112 (Mar. 31, 2010).

[30] ICC Request for Authorization of an Investigation Pursuant to Article 15, Situation in Kenya (ICC-01/09), Pre-Trial Chamber II, § 56 (Nov. 29, 2009).

[31] C.S. Lewis, Screwtape Letters and Screwtape Proposes a Toast 23, at xxv (1961).

[32] Pre-trial Brief, Annex 10, Prosecutor v. Taylor (SCSL-03-01-PT), Trial Chamber II, Exh. 1.298, EV0142 (Apr. 4, 2007).

then threw the screaming victim into a latrine? Was it they, or was it those who took them into service, trained them, led them, and kept them in the field?

The approach that we take in my country in the investigation and prosecution of organized criminal activity is to work up the chain. You develop the evidence against the person who is committing the crime at retail, then you confront him, get him an attorney, and attempt to negotiate an agreement requiring him to plead guilty and testify against his superiors and offering the probability that his cooperation may be rewarded by a reduced sentence.

In exceptional cases, the cooperation may require immunity from prosecution. However, in American federal prosecution this is now exceedingly rare. In my experience as a U.S. attorney, I can remember authorizing immunity for only one person. That was for an individual who was a passive accessory to the crime and an absolutely essential witness. Our practice was to insist on prosecution, after a full debriefing, in a practice that took full account of all relevant criminal conduct, and provided for consideration of sentence reduction based on truthful testimony and other cooperation against higher-ups.

I know that in some countries the possibility of a sentence reduction is viewed negatively. Before a jury in my own country, this incentive can be used to attack the credibility of the witness as one who is "telling a story" to please the prosecutor. Before I was a U.S. Attorney, I spent ten years at the defense bar, and there was nothing quite so delicious as the cross-examination of an insider who had flipped and was testifying for the government. One could probe every bad act for which the witness was to suffer little penalty. If he minimized his own conduct you could shatter his credibility. If he admitted to all he had done, he looked far worse than your client. You always had that last line: "Witness, for a deal like this you would have turned against your own mother."

But for the ends of justice, such testimony has great value if it is corroborated and it fits with other evidence. It also gives you an understanding of how the criminal organization really worked. Otherwise, it is just a matter of educated guesswork. Fully explained, the practice withstands public scrutiny, as long as the witness takes responsibility for his own conduct, and has his sentence reduction determined by a judge based on the genuine value of the cooperation. The resulting sentence reduction can be viewed as a recognition of partial rehabilitation that had been evidenced by the cooperation with the system of justice.

Those who come from civil law systems often argue that you should not have to offer such an incentive. When I was at the ICTR, I spent a lot of time with prosecutors and magistrates in European countries who were pursuing cases of Rwandans who had come to live in their countries and were suspected of involvement in the genocide.

It seemed to me that when their suspects were called for interrogation, they never stood on their right to silence. Now, it may be such a right is enshrined in the relevant conventions, and cautions may be given before interrogation, but it does not appear to be exercised in civil law systems. Invariably, persons under investigation can be counted on to talk, and talk, and talk, and during trial proceedings, they are constantly invited to comment on witness testimony, so to a large extent the prosecution gains the benefits of cooperation without having to bargain for it. Perhaps, it is lack of exposure to the old adage that "No man is hanged except by his own words." Or maybe instruction in criminal defense does not begin with the rule to tell your client "Shut up. Do not say a thing. Not a word until we figure out the deal." But in common law countries, and in the tribunals with their common law dominance, the testimony of culpable insiders can be expected only after a full under-standing of its consequences for the witness.

Of course, defense lawyers are righteously indignant about testimony from criminals who have benefited from bargains from the prosecution. Of course, that is until their client is looking for a deal. But it is the process that permits us to work our way up the chain. Indeed, at the Rwanda Tribunal, it was an approach that I attempted. In Arusha it was not easy. There were the negative attitudes about plea bargains on the part of some judges. There was the history of Prime Minister Kambanda pleading guilty as charged and though "the Prosecutor confirm[ed] that Kambanda had extended substantial cooperation and invaluable information to the Prosecutor," he still received a life sentence.[33] It was also very different from my national system because it was hard to assure the protection of such a cooperator. At home when someone pleaded guilty and then cooperated in other cases, I could recommend that he be sent to a prison where he would be in protective custody. I could make sure he was segregated from anybody that was even associated with the group that was antagonistic to him. I could, at the end of his sentence, get him into witness protec-tion under a different name. I could ensure that that witness faced no significant risk.

At the international level, you do not have those kinds of options, and you have the fun-damental problem that at the end of the day, once a person has taken one of these convic-tions, even if they receive a reduced sentence, on release they may not be admissible in any country in the world other than their own where they may face great dangers. So the approach that we began to favor for those who lived in European countries was arrange-ments whereby they would be prosecuted in those countries, thus being separated from those prosecuted in Arusha, and having a better idea of the likely penal consequences and where they would live when their sentence was served. In a few such cases, it was possible to achieve valuable cooperation.

But almost all of the persons who were culpable for the crimes committed in Sierra Leone still lived in the country, and such arrangements, or even classic plea bargains before the SCSL, did not easily fit within the situation. This followed from a mandate that allowed for the prosecution of only those bearing the greatest responsibility. You could not start at the bottom of the chain and charge the lower level offenders and obtain cooperation for pleas of guilty. You could not start with the corporal, unless it was "Corporal" Foday Sankoh, the leader of the RUF who was called such because of his erstwhile rank in the Sierra Leone army. To prosecute anyone at the lower or mid-level, even on a plea bargain, could be viewed as beyond the mandate.

What could you do? You could research the events, map the conflict, benefit from the fact that police investigators who knew the history, the country, its cultures, its dialects. You could talk to lots of participants at the lower levels whom you could credibly assure would not be subject to prosecution to determine where the killings had occurred, the units and groups involved, and the persons in command.

This allowed for development of a list of persons who could be subject to prosecution who sat at the highest levels of the groups that had committed the crimes. The actual list of those to be prosecuted was to be a short one. That was dictated by the limitations and the capacity of the Court. There was only one trial chamber for almost three years, and only

---

[33] ICTR Judgment and Sentence, Kambanda (ICTR-97–23-S), Trial Chamber I, §§ 47, 62 (Sept. 4, 1998).

then a second. As the list would be limited to those at the highest levels, the geographical and temporal breadth of their responsibility would make for big cases, and even if some events and periods might be excluded in the interests of time and efficiency, it might be necessary to cover a lot of ground to show a pattern of conduct – to prove effective control or sufficient participation in a common plan, as well as intent or knowledge. Prosecuting persons at this level, in this manner, meant that there would be little judicial time to prosecute more than a few cases.

But what about culpable insiders whose testimony would be needed to provide evidence of the conduct of top leaders? They were individuals as to whom research and investigation had determined were not at the top and were not to be subject to prosecution. But many had blood on their hands. They had been active in these movements. They knew of the crimes, and how they were committed. They exhibited the mix of human motivations, and almost all tried to minimize their own conduct. But even in the absence of their full cooperation, and even when a decision was made that that one lacked sufficient credibility to be a witness, it did not cause him to land on the list of persons to be prosecuted. It had already been determined that his prosecution was not appropriate under the mandate.

I remember at some point signing a number of letters for witnesses in the Charles Taylor case, which some people were describing as "immunity letters."[34] I said that they could describe them as they wish, but that they were simply letters to a person saying that we were not interested in prosecuting him. The message was effectively: "We were not coming after you the day before we were interested in your testimony, and we are not coming after you the day after you decide whether or not to testify. We do not have a place on the dance card for you. We're not interested in you. You don't have to worry about prosecution by us, maybe by somebody else, but you don't have to worry about it by us."

Regarding this issue of being prosecuted by someone else, I heard a question from Wayne Jordash posed to the last panel, which implied that there were cases where individuals received a pass at the Sierra Leone national system in return for cooperation with the SCSL Prosecutor. First of all, it must be noted that because of the Lomé Amnesty, the Sierra Leone authorities thought they were fundamentally restrained from prosecuting people whose crimes arose before July of 1999, when almost all of the crimes being prosecuted by the SCSL were committed. But national authorities did prosecute those found at the Sankoh home in May 2000 after the shooting of the demonstrators on Spur Road.[35] There were also members of the "West Side Boys" alleged to have committed crimes in the final phases of the conflict who were also prosecuted.[36] Of these individuals who were nationally prosecuted, I recall that we wished to call one as a prosecution witness in the Taylor trial. At the time we required his testimony, he had been in the Pademba Road Prison for at least seven

[34] Trial transcript of defense final submissions, Taylor (SCSL-2003–01-T), Trial Chamber II, at 49, 481 (Mar. 10, 2001), *available at* http://www.sc-sl.org/LinkClick.aspx?fileticket=zilprnMji%2bs%3d&tabid=160 (last visited June 26, 2012).

[35] *See Revolutionary United Front (RUF)* (GlobalSecurity.org), *available at* http://www.globalsecurity.org/military/world/para/ruf.htm (last visited June 26, 2012).

[36] Amnesty International, *Sierra Leone – Amnesty International Report 2007: Human Rights in Republic of Sierra Leone* (2007), *available at* http://www.amnesty.org/en/region/sierra-leone/report-2007 (last visited June 26, 2012); *see also* "Revolutionary United Front (RUF)," (GlobalSecurity.org), *available at* http://www.globalsecurity.org/military/world/para/ruf.htm (last visited June 26, 2012).

years since his arrest with the group following violence at RUF leader Sankoh's house in Freetown in May 2000.

We faced the complex challenge of bringing him to The Hague to testify. We did have the option of using SCSL Rule 90, which allowed the Judges to order the transfer of a prisoner for purposes of testimony, and presumably such an order would be binding on Sierra Leone authorities. But this would require him to be flown to The Hague under guard, and imprisoned by Dutch authorities during his stay in The Hague. We then checked to see how soon the witness would be eligible for release on conclusion of his Sierra Leone sentence, and received information that it would be in about a year. Under the circumstances, we asked the Presidency of Sierra Leone to include him on a list of persons to receive clemency, so that he could be released and transported to The Hague in the same manner as other witnesses. This was made known to the Defense and they were able to use it to question the witness about whether his testimony was motivated by his early release. From our point of view, this had not represented a bargain but merely the most practical way to enable his testimony. To be frank, I was proud that we were able to work out a cooperative resolution of the matter with Sierra Leone authorities and wish that there could have more such witnesses.

This is because it is so essential to have insiders who were present when key events occurred. In an ideal world, one would not rely on the testimony of persons who have blood on their hands. Maybe if you had a hidden camera behind every tree. But, fundamentally, when you need to determine who was ultimately responsible for the crimes committed by armed groups, and when there are no written records, it requires oral testimony. You do not find people who were in the presence of wrongdoers plotting crimes who are themselves wholly innocent.

As to the question of the effect of the mandate on all of this, I would first note that we took the mandate very seriously, and until the issue was finally settled in the AFRC Appeal in February 2008, we were concerned that the Judges could reject a prosecution on the grounds that the Accused did not bear the greatest responsibility.[37] But whatever the role of Judges in the process, we took the words of the mandate as binding, and it affected how we were able to deal with insider witnesses. As a result, I must say that if it were up to me I would not have written the mandate to limit the Prosecution to those with "the greatest responsibility." I might have included language in the preamble of the resolution calling for prosecutions to be focused on those most responsible, but I think that the Prosecutor should have been free to move up the chain and prosecute some below the top. This is because I would prefer to see witnesses who have blood on their hands come to court and say, "I did wrong. I pleaded guilty. I am going to pay a price. Now I am going to talk about someone who was even more responsible."

This is additionally important because many of the insider witnesses were going to have to receive protective measures that could be characterized as a benefit to them. Why? Because unlike even the poor victim witness, they were going to be taking greater risk, and could be seen as traitors to their brethren, to their religion, or to their ethnic group. They could face as great a risk from retribution after their testimony than of attacks before their

---

[37] Judgment, Brima, Kamara, and Kanu ("AFRC") (SCSL-04-16-A), Appeal Chamber, §§ 272–285 (Feb. 22, 2008).

testimony. The violence could also be visited on members of their family.[38] They were going to have to be protected. They are going to have to be in safe houses for a long time. Some might see them as suffering from being uprooted from their former lives and livelihoods, but the Defense was likely to focus on the costs, to payments for transport or lost income, the value of their safe housing and subsistence, and on the life-changing prospect of relocation to a more prosperous country. Of course, if done properly, the witness should be provided with no more than what is necessary to keep him and his family whole and safe. If you have observed our trials, you have seen that these benefits were all disclosed and subject to intense cross-examination. The judges have also consistently rejected the accusation that the witnesses are paid for their testimony.[39] But in the end, I think that it would have been better if the most culpable insiders had also faced charges.

We then reach the question of who was to be selected under the mandate as among those bearing the greatest responsibility? We concluded that the mandate called for prosecution of persons that were leaders over the widest span of time and territory where the crimes were committed. But did this just mean those who sat at the highest levels of the official chains of command?

I recall that in Rwanda during the genocide, there were some colonels that were more powerful than generals, some majors more powerful than colonels. The power of specific individuals depended on their connection to the ruling family, or to its broader clan or region, and this could give them authority above their rank. There was the classic case of General Marcel Gatsinzi who was actually appointed the first chief of staff of the Rwandan army on the morning that the genocide began, as the successor to the chief of staff had died with the president in the plane crash. During the brief period when he held the position, perhaps two hundred thousand people were murdered, some in mass killings in which units of the Rwandan army actively participated. Now, when he was appointed, the extremists were outraged because he was known to be a moderate. He was forced out by the extremists in less than two weeks, and replaced by General Augustin Bizimungu. Bizimungu was prosecuted by the ICTR, convicted of genocide, and sentenced to life in prison. Gatsinzi has never been prosecuted by the ICTR, or by the authorities of Rwanda where he has lived since the genocide. Indeed, he served a long term as Defense Minister under President Kagame, and remains free to this day.

I led the testimony of a similar individual in several trials at the ICTR. He was a highly protected witness, but the public testimony revealed that he was a national officer of the *Interahamwe*, a group that had begun as the youth wing of a political party that during the genocide had been transformed into a militia that was directly responsible for hacking hundreds of thousands of men, women, and children to death. In his public testimony, he

---

[38] *See, e.g.,* Testimony of Witness Claude Bouchard, Nahimana et al. (ICTR 99–52-T), Trial Chamber I (Nov. 30, 2001), Bouchard testified to an investigation report on an alleged breach of detention rules involving a communication from defendant Hassan Ngeze to prospective prosecution witness Omar Serushago, in which Ngeze attempted to dissuade Serushago from testifying against Ngeze. The translation of the communication included the words "We may not meet again in this life, but our children will meet." Exhibit P78.

[39] *See, e.g.,* Judgment, Sesay, Kallon and Gbao ("RUF") (SCSL-04–14-T), Appeals Chamber, §§ 197–201 (Oct. 26, 2009); Judgment, Brima, Kamara and Kanu ("AFRC") (SCSL-2006–16-A), Appeals Chamber, §§ 119, 130–135 (Feb. 22, 2008).

asserted that there was a "parallel committee" within the *Interahamwe* made of persons who had originally been counselors subordinate to the officers but had eventually taken over effective control in the months leading up to the genocide. While every defense team attacked his testimony about a parallel committee as preposterous and self-serving, I do not believe that his credibility on this issue was effectively challenged.[40]

So who was most responsible? At the SCSL it was determined according to a number of factors. Among these were effective control. As in the law of command responsibility, it is a question of who had the capacity to restrain bad conduct, or to punish it. But command responsibility focuses on responsibility for specific criminal acts, and the question here also has to do with who had the power to establish or alter the general course of conduct over months and years. This may not be so clear in a situation like the genocide in Rwanda that was committed in only a hundred days, but when the crimes go on for an extended period, you can see who has been in a position to gain the greatest knowledge of events on the ground, who was promoted to higher rank or received benefits because of what was done, and whose actions were most instrumental in making possible the continuation of the conduct.

Based on such factors, the decision was made at the Special Court for Sierra Leone regarding the RUF to prosecute six persons. I include the separately prosecuted Charles Taylor as the effective leader of this group. Although his case is now on appeal he was convicted on April 26, 2012 and sentenced to fifty years on May 31, 2012. He was the person who enabled the RUF's success, and he was the person hailed as "Chief" by Sam Bockarie on a satellite phone interview with the BBC during the time of the attack on Freetown.[41] After him, there was Foday Sankoh, the formal RUF chief, who was its effective leader during the times he was free, but who died within weeks of his transfer to SCSL custody.[42] Next there was Sam Bockarie, who linked Taylor with the others, but who was to be killed by Taylor's forces shortly after his indictment by the SCSL.[43] Then there were Issa Sesay, Morris Kallon, Augustine Gbao, the surviving commanding officers from the highest levels of the organization, who significantly participated in the criminal enterprise across time and territory.

In the AFRC, it was Alex Tamba Brima, Ibrahim Bazzy Kamara, and Santigie Borbor Kanu. In the case of the CDF, it was Sam Hinga Norman, Moinina Fofana, and Allieu Kondewa.

---

[40] This witness was given a different pseudonym in each trial to protect him during the period before the required disclosure of his identity was made to the defense in each of the trials. However, during his examination in public sessions, it became known that he was the same individual. *See, e.g.,* Testimony of Witness G, Karemera et al. (ICTR 98–44-T), Trial Chamber III (Oct. 10, 2005), *available at* http://www.unictr.org/Portals/0/Case/English/Karemera/minutes/2005/11–051010.pdf (last visited June 24, 2012); Testimony of Witness D, Bizimungu et al. (ICTR-99-50-T), Trial Chamber II (June 15, 2004), *available at* http://www.unictr.org/Portals/0/Case/English/Bizimungu/case%20minutes/040615–79.pdf (last visited June 26, 2012); Testimony of Witness A, Bagasora et al. (ICTR 98–41-T), Trial Chamber I (June 1, 2004), *available at* http://www.unictr.org/Portals/0/Case/English/Bagosora/minutes/2004/040601.pdf (last visited June 25, 2012); Testimony of Witness X, Nahimana et al. (ICTR 99-52-T), Trial Chamber I (Feb. 18, 2002), *available at* http://www.unictr.org/Portals/0/Case/English/Nahimana/case%20minutes/180202.pdf (last visited June 26, 2012).

[41] *See Rebel Commander Sam Bockarie: Not a Breakthrough,* BBC NEWS at .21–.22 seconds, *available at* http://news.bbc.co.uk/olmedia/250000/audio/_250724_bockari.ram (last visited June 26, 2012).

[42] Decision Withdrawing Indictment, Sankoh (SCSL-2003-02-PT), Trial Chamber (Dec. 8, 2003).

[43] Examination-in-chief of Moses Blah, Taylor (SCSL 2003-01-T), at 9987–88 (May 15, 2008).

As with those charged in the RUF case, each was listed by the Truth and Reconciliation Commission at the top ranks of each organization.[44]

For these reasons, I think that we got it right. Could others have decided it differently? Absolutely. But by prosecuting people at these levels in the four trials of the SCSL, it was possible to present evidence that covered the broad range of crimes committed against the people of Sierra Leone during the period from 1996 through 2000.

Thank you very much.

[44] Sierra Leone Truth & Reconciliation Commission, *Witness to the Truth: Report of the Sierra Leone Truth & Reconciliation Commission*, vol. 2, at 48, 54, 64 (2004), *available at* http://www.sierra-leone.org/Other-Conflict/TRCVolume2.pdf (last visited June 24, 2012).

PART I

The Expectations of the Sierra Leone Tribunal

From Nuremberg to Freetown: Historical Antecedents of the Special Court for Sierra Leone

Vivian Grosswald Curran[*]

"The great promise of the coming times: to return some divinity to man." ("La grande promesse des temps à venir, redonner de la divinité à l'homme.")

Antoine de Saint-Exupéry (*Terre des hommes, 1939*)

"Our past failings by the hand of time rarely are erased." ("Nos fautes passées sont par la main du temps rarement effacées.")

Blin de Sainmore (*Orphanis II, 4, 1773*)

The idea behind the Special Court for Sierra Leone was born of a revolution in modern international law often traced to the International Military Tribunal at Nuremberg. This connection was emphasized, among others, in the recent Sixth Chautauqua Declaration, adopted some two weeks before the writing of the present chapter. The Declaration "celebrat[es] the 10th anniversary of the Statute of the Special Court for Sierra Leone, the obtaining of a guilty verdict against Charles Taylor, the first former head of state indicted whilst in office, and recogniz[es] that this is the first such verdict since Nuremberg . . . ."[1]

In his statement for the Prosecution at Nuremberg, Justice Jackson had begun by underscoring the proceedings' novelty. He described the Trial of the Major War Criminals as "the first trial in history for crimes against the peace of the world . . . , wrongs so malignant, and so devastating that civilization cannot tolerate their being ignored, because it cannot survive their being repeated."[2]

Nuremberg was a watershed event in propelling individuals into a role as legal actors and subjects of international law, and of propelling international human rights into a new age. The city selected for the trials had not been chosen randomly. It was the site of the famous Nuremberg rallies, where Hitler had held his annual Nazi party propaganda events from 1923 to 1938, and the city that had lent its name to the numerous laws, known as the

---

[*] Professor and Distinguished Faculty Scholar, University of Pittsburgh. Unless otherwise noted, all translations are the author's.

[1] The Sixth Chautauqua Declaration (Aug. 29, 2012), *available at* http://www.intlawgrrls.com/2012/08/6th-sixth-chautauqua-declaration.html. Its signatories include F. Bensouda, Int'l Crim. Ct.; S. Brammertz, Int'l Crim. Trib. for the former Yugoslavia; H.W.W. Caming, Int'l Mil. Trib. at Nuremberg; A.T. Cayley, Extraordinary Ch., Cts. of Cambodia; D.M. Crane, Sp. Ct. for Sierra Leone; Sir D. de Silva, Sp. Ct. for Sierra Leone; N. Farrell, Sp. Ct. for Lebanon; B.J. Hollis, Sp. Ct. for Sierra Leone; H.B. Jallow, Int'l Trib. for Rwanda and Int'l Residual Mechanism for Criminal Tribs.

[2] 2 TRIAL OF THE MAJOR WAR CRIMINALS BEFORE THE INTERNATIONAL MILITARY TRIBUNAL 98–99 (1995).

Nuremberg Laws, enacted in 1935, and their subsequent, ever-more repressive and finally deadly, amendments that had transposed anti-Semitism into a German law of terror and, finally, mass extermination. One can say that the choice of Nuremberg for the trial was a way of defining memory for the times to come. It was to be the first stone, according to Justice Jackson's opening statement for the Prosecution above, in the edifice of "never again," a term less elegant than his own phrase, but one that was to settle in the vernaculars of the Western world.

The Nuremberg Tribunal's own roots were planted in the views of great international law theorists, some of whom, such as Hersch Lauterpacht, had conferred at length with Justice Jackson before the trials.[3] Their idea was nothing less than interstate, international cooperation and mutual submission to universal norms of fundamental rights. Nor was this their or international law's first effort at "never again." The idea of eradicating barbarity once and for all through internationally recognized legal norms had been the cherished hope of international law scholars after the First World War, a quarter of a century earlier, scholars who, along with many nonlawyer citizens, had fervently hoped and believed that the Great War had been the "war to end all wars."

In a beautiful article, Nathaniel Berman has described this stalwart group of true-believer international law scholars who met all over Europe after the Paris Peace Congress to create and refine those legal norms.[4] They continued to meet right up to the outbreak of the Second World War, seemingly impervious to the world events churning around them. Their last meeting was in a small town in Poland of the name of Oswiecim mere days before the outbreak of war. The town soon was to become famous, in 1940, under its German name: Auschwitz.

And yet the reaction of international lawyers in 1945 in the aftermath of the calamity of the Second World War, as well as the failed post–World War I project, was to engage more fervently than ever in the same undertaking. Hersch Lauterpacht's career spanned this period, as did, perhaps more famously, that of René Cassin. Cassin was to become one of the principal drafters of the Universal Declaration of Human Rights, as well as a Nobel Prize laureate and president of the European Court of Human Rights, after first having been part of the interwar group of "new lawyers" in the 1920s and 1930s.

Has progress finally been made? The line quoted from Saint-Exupéry at the opening of this chapter, written in 1939, testifies to the will to redemption and improvement, or perhaps to the will to hope, whereas that of Blin de Sainmore, written some two centuries earlier, suggests rather the futility of belief in them. On the negative side, we know that massacres have not ended. Some even say that instead of the "never again" that was supposed to be the Holocaust's legacy, what we got in its wake has been an endlessly repeated "ever again."[5] Moreover, although Nuremberg allowed international law to recognize the individual as an international law actor, on the other hand, paradoxically, there has been an extraordinary

---

[3] For Lauterpacht's correspondence with Jackson on the issue of war crimes, see E. LAUTERPACHT, THE LIFE OF HERSCH LAUTERPACHT 272 (2010); for his influence on Britain's Chief Prosecutor, Sir Hartley Shawcross, see MARTTI KOSKENNIEMI, THE GENTLE CIVILIZER OF NATIONS: THE RISE AND FALL OF INTERNATIONAL LAW 1870–1960, at 388–89 (2001).

[4] Nathaniel Berman, *But the Alternative Is to Despair: European Nationalism and the Modern Renewal of International Law*, 106 HARV. L. REV. 1792 (1993).

[5] *See* Mark Osiel, *Ever Again: Legal Remembrance of Administrative Massacre*, 144 U. PA. L. REV. 463 (1995).

growth in war's depersonalization, with military force of a kind that permits killers to be increasingly remote from those they kill, such that on a psychological level de-individual-ization facilitates for the killers the task of killing.

Yet others take a more positive view. The eminent legal figure and political leader Robert Badinter, former French justice minister, an indefatigable defender of human rights, strikes a decidedly more optimistic note as he looks back on a long life and many battles. Minister Badinter is especially well-known as the author of the 1981 French law abolishing the death penalty.[6] Today, he is eighty-four years old and, in a recent talk, despite noting the dehu-manization of contemporary war through the depersonalization that remote killing engen-ders, he commented about the evolution of international law over the last sixty years in enthusiastic terms. In support of his view, he cited as real progress in the international legal order the fact that states today are binding themselves to each other through international treaties in an almost universal movement.[7]

Since Nuremberg, the idea has been that no one, no matter his or her station in public life, may commit crimes of *jus cogens* with impunity. Article 7 of the Nuremberg Charter had specified that "[t]he official position of defendants, whether as Heads of State or responsible officials in Government Departments, shall not be considered as freeing them from respon-sibility or mitigating punishment."[8]

Thus, public office no longer would be deemed sufficient to protect the holder of public office, even if he or she were a head of state, where the commission of grave crimes against humanity was at issue. Articles 7(2) and 6(2) of, respectively, the Statute for the ad-hoc Tribunal on the former Yugoslavia and that of the Special Court for Sierra Leone, contain language to the same effect. This principle accordingly was applied at the trials of Slobodan Milosevic[9] and Charles Taylor.[10] In March 2012, Thomas Lubanga, the former Congolese warlord, who forced children to become soldiers, became the first defendant to receive a guilty verdict in the International Criminal Court's now ten-year history.[11] On July 10, 2012, he was sentenced to fourteen years in prison.[12]

Among the functions of the post-conflict tribunals has been the inscription of memory, the definition of a national narrative, and the giving of a voice to former victims who once had no voices. In the face of crimes of tremendous enormity and horror, justice necessarily becomes more symbolic than actual. Sometimes, as in the case of Nazi wartime criminals who were tried long after Nuremberg, as well as in the case of Lubanga, this is because evi-dentiary problems prevent the defendants from being convicted of anything more than a lamentably small percentage of the crimes they committed. Since even victims who obtain judgments can never be restored to their status quo ante., the necessarily symbolic nature of such trials may seem to trivialize (and worse, occasionally also to subvert) justice. On the

---

[6] *Loi du 9 oct. 1981 portant abolition de la peine de mort.* In 2007, France's Parliament voted to change the French Constitution to adopt Badinter's proposal to make it impossible for capital punishment to become legal in France again. *See* Fr. Const. Title VIII, art. 66–1 ("*nul ne peut être condamné à la peine de mort*" / "no one may be sentenced to death").

[7] Colloque, Collège de France, public session of Apr. 12, 2012, Quai d'Orsay, Paris.

[8] Charter of the International Nuremberg Tribunal, art. 7.

[9] Prosecutor v. Slobodan Milosevic, Case No. IT-02–54-T (June 16, 2004).

[10] Prosecutor v. Charles Ghankay Taylor, Case No. SCSL-03–1-T (Apr. 26, 2012).

[11] Prosecutor v. Thomas Lubanga Dyilo, ICC-01/04–01/06–2842.

[12] *Id.*, ICC-01/04–01/06–2842.

other hand, the alternative of allowing crimes to go legally unnoticed, to fall into the legal amnesia that is amnesty, seems equally amenable to producing a sense of subverted justice. As we know, both alternative and combined solutions have been explored, with mixed results.[13] Truth and Reconciliation hearings have been advocated in order to harness what often is referred to as collective memory, to stand as a memorial in their own right, and to compensate for some of law's inadequacies when it is asked to fulfill extralegal functions.[14] The results have not been without critics.[15]

The international legal order that traced its path from Nuremberg to Freetown has not emerged without its detractors. Nuremberg has been challenged as an example of victor's justice. The concept of "civilized nations" that undergirded the internationalists from the interwar and postwar periods, a phrase we find in use still today in U.S. Alien Tort Statute case law,[16] has given rise to criticisms concerning an alleged lack of true universality of the principles and neutrality of their application. Additionally, one author challenges the *gradation* of norms in modern international law, notably with its recent emphasis on hierarchizing *jus cogens* offenses as having a higher value than others, as a sign of a "pathology [in] the international normative system" that is causing normativity to "becom[e] a question of 'more or less.'"[17]

The Nuremberg Tribunal was the product of powerful countries. The UN Convention on Genocide, by contrast, owes its genesis to an individual, Raphael Lemkin, a Polish-Jewish lawyer, who is credited with having coined the term "genocide," and who, in a remarkable feat, had understood the Nazi genocidal phenomenon before he learned the facts that later substantiated his theory, by a process of deductive reasoning from his study of Nazi jurisprudence.[18] He dedicated his life after the Second World War to its passage.

Individuals today continue to be able to move mountains. In March 2012, the NGO "Invisible Children" put a thirty-minute video on the Internet denouncing alleged Ugandan warlord Joseph Kony.[19] Kony was the first defendant indicted by the International Criminal Court for alleged rape, murder, and forced kidnapping into his army of children. The film depicting the lives of those children was seen by untold millions in a matter of days, with

---

[13] For some short, poignant remarks on this issue, see William A. Schabas, *Foreword, in* MICHAEL R. MARRUS, SOME MEASURE OF JUSTICE: THE HOLOCAUST ERA RESTITUTION CAMPAIGN OF THE 1990S, at ix–xv (2009). Other examinations of these issues under various angles include Vivian Grosswald Curran, *Politicizing the Crime against Humanity: The French Example,* 78 NOTRE DAME L.J. 677 (2003); Jacob Katz Cogan, *International Criminal Courts and Fair Trials: Difficulties and Prospects,* 27 YALE J. INT'L L. 111 (2002). As this essay is being written, an issue of the suppression of a judge's opinion in the Charles Taylor conviction is being discussed. *See* William A. Schabas, *More Mystery about the Charles Taylor Judgment (and Its Appeal),* on Ph.D. Studies in Human Rights (posted Sept. 14, 2012), *at* http://humanrightsdoctorate.blogspot.com/2012/09/more-mystery-about-charles-taylor.html.

[14] *See* Vivian Grosswald Curran, *History, Memory and Law,* 16 ROGER WILLIAMS U. L. Rev. 100 (2011).

[15] *See id.* at 104, *citing* Rosalind Shaw, *Rethinking Truth and Reconciliation Commissions: Lessons from Sierra Leone,* United States Institute of Peace Special Report #130, at 1 (Feb. 2005); William A. Schabas, *The Relationship between Truth Commissions and International Courts: The Case of Sierra Leone,* 25 HUM. RTS. Q. 1035 (2003) (examining the situation of coexisting international prosecution and truth commission for Sierra Leone).

[16] *See, e.g.,* Filartiga v. Pena-Irala, 630 F.2d 876, 881 (2d Cir. 1980).

[17] Prosper Weil, *Towards Relative Normativity in International Law?,* 77 AM. J. INT'L L. 413, 421 (1983).

[18] *See* Michael Ignatieff, *The Danger of a World without Enemies: Lemkin's Word,* NEW REPUBLIC, Feb. 26, 2001, at 25–28.

[19] *E.g.,* Jacques Attali, *Pour ou contre "Kony 2012"?,* L'EXPRESS, Mar. 14, 2012, at 82.

subsequent controversies highlighting the potentials for information and disinformation as modern technology permits instantaneous information dissemination on a global dimension.[20] Within days of the video's posting, a bill was proposed in the U.S. Senate to augment assistance in capturing him.

From the interwar lawyers to Rafael Lemkin to the NGO "Invisible Children," people have been following Browning's precept that "a man's reach should exceed his grasp/Or what's a heaven for?"[21] And that is how the Special Court for Sierra Leone was born.

---

[20] *See* Neil Ungerleider, *Invisible Children's Kony 2012 Video about Uganda Conflict: The Making of a Viral Masterpiece* (Mar. 7, 2012), *at* http://www.fastcompany.com/1823127/invisible-childrens-kony-2012-video-about-uganda-conflict-making-viral-masterpiece.

[21] Robert Browning, "Andrea del Sarto."

2

The Expectations and Role of International and National Civil Society and the SCSL

Alison Smith[*]

I. INTRODUCTION

The role of national and international civil society over the past fifteen years has changed dramatically, especially in relation to the creation and implementation of effective account-ability processes that are responsive to the needs of victims and communities affected by wide-scale crimes under international law (war crimes, crimes against humanity, and geno-cide) and human rights violations. Civil society has come to be recognized as a key part-ner in these efforts, particularly civil society from the countries where these processes are established.

This chapter attempts to chart the role and expectations of international and national civil society with respect to the Special Court for Sierra Leone. My focus will be on the complementary roles played within and outside Sierra Leone, and how civil society sought to ensure the Court would fulfill its expectations regarding the role it could and should play for the West African country.

II. BEFORE THE NEGOTIATIONS FOR THE SPECIAL COURT AGREEMENT (PRE-AUGUST 2000)

Before the year 2000, the main official response to the crimes committed during the conflict in Sierra Leone since 1991 was the establishment of a Truth and Reconciliation Commission (TRC), which was mandated by the Lomé Peace Agreement (Lomé Agreement) of July 7, 1999.[1] For many – including the Sierra Leone government of the day headed by President Ahmad Tejan Kabbah – this seemed like the pragmatic solution to the problems that beset the country. Just six months before the Lomé Agreement, the Revolutionary United Front (RUF) and the mutinying Armed Forces Revolutionary Council (AFRC) managed to cap-ture Freetown, Sierra Leone's capital, and everyone's minds were turned to how to end the conflict, end the killing, and restore peace. There was little appetite for an international criminal tribunal, primarily because of the mounting costs of the International Criminal

---

[*] International Criminal Justice Program Director and Legal Counsel for No Peace Without Justice. She was formerly the Country Director in Sierra Leone for No Peace Without Justice and served as the chief legal adviser to the Vice President of Sierra Leone on the Special Court and international humanitarian law.

[1] This section is based primarily on recollections from the author and discussions with Sierra Leonean civil society and government representatives on these issues.

Tribunals for the former Yugoslavia (ICTY) and for Rwanda (ICTR), and the fear that talk of setting up such a tribunal would prevent the rebels from coming to the peace-negotiating table, if not spurring them on to even greater horrors than those witnessed during the previous eight years. Even those in favor of accountability – which surely was on the mind of the UN Secretary-General when he appended the famous "no amnesty for crimes under international law" disclaimer to the Lomé Agreement – were not willing to push it at that time, not at the expense of further bloodshed.

In Sierra Leone itself, civil society, not to mention government and society in general, was somewhat divided. There were those who were fully behind a TRC as the means to end violence and restore peace, also by providing a form of accountability for the atrocities that had been committed. However, there were those who believed that although a TRC was useful and necessary to help heal the country, it would neither be sufficient to persuade RUF leader Foday Sankoh and others to lay down their arms, nor sufficient by itself to provide the kind of justice and accountability that Sierra Leone needed to overcome the wounds of the past (and, at that time, the present). These non-supporters of the TRC attempted to persuade the government not to include the amnesty in the Lomé Agreement and to leave the door open for criminal prosecutions in the future. Ultimately, although these arguments had some resonance, in an attempt to secure a quick but lasting peace, the decision was made to focus on the TRC and provide an amnesty to all involved in the conflict.

Unfortunately, those who feared the decisions taken in July 1999 would not deter future violence were proved correct. Although fighting – and atrocities – was dampened in the period immediately following the signature of the peace agreement and the return to Sierra Leone of those brokering it, it was not long before it was "business as usual." This time, voices in both Sierra Leone and the international civil society demanding something more be done grew louder and stronger.[2] This continued until June 2000, when the government of Sierra Leone requested the assistance of the United Nations to establish a Special Court to prosecute those responsible for violations committed during the conflict in Sierra Leone. This led to the United Nations Security Council mandating the Secretary-General to negotiate an agreement with the government of Sierra Leone to that end, which began the process that would end some twelve years later with the final case coming to a close before the Special Court for Sierra Leone.

III. DURING THE NEGOTIATIONS AND THE SCSL'S ESTABLISHMENT (AUGUST 2000 TO JULY 2002)

A. Sierra Leone Civil Society

Sierra Leonean civil society was generally favorable to the news about the UN Security Council Resolution, particularly those who had advocated during the Lomé Agreement negotiations against the amnesty and in favor of criminal accountability. They responded

---

[2] *See, e.g.,* Human Rights Watch, *Sierra Leone: US Urged to Support Criminal Tribunal* (May 19, 2000), *available at* http://www.hrw.org/news/2000/05/19/sierra-leone-us-urged-support-criminal-tribunal (last visited Apr. 8, 2012).

enthusiastically to a request for consultations during a visit from the UN Office of Legal Affairs to Freetown in September 2000, as part of the first round of negotiations for the Special Court Agreement. At that time, there were several as-yet unresolved and contentious issues about which civil society wished to express their views. These included the temporal jurisdiction of the Court, which many felt was Freetown-centric and failed to include some of the most notorious incidents during the conflict; the exclusion of peacekeepers from the jurisdiction of the Court, given the behavior of some Economic Community of West African States Monitoring Group (ECOMOG) troops and the complete lack of accountability for their actions; and the inclusion of children over the age of fifteen within the Court's jurisdiction, about which civil society was divided.[3] This last point has been portrayed by many as something suggested (or insisted on) by the Sierra Leone government,[4] or something that was included because it was wanted by civil society as a whole.[5] However, this provision originated from somewhere within the UN and was already included in the first draft of the Special Court Agreement and Statute that was received by the Sierra Leone government and formed the basis of the first negotiations between the two parties, before the UN met with the government or civil society in Freetown during their first visit in September 2000.[6]

All of these points were to be raised again by civil society – and, sometimes insistently, by the Sierra Leone government with the UN, especially the issue of the Court's temporal jurisdiction[7] – but the only change between the original draft and the Agreement and Statute as finally adopted was the dropping of a Juvenile Chamber, which many thought would force the Special Court to prosecute people under the age of eighteen at the time of the alleged commission of the crimes, whether they bore the greatest responsibility for those crimes or not. Ultimately, civil society and the Special Court's first Prosecutor would put paid to this idea and no one under the age of eighteen at the time of the alleged commission of the crimes was ever prosecuted before the Special Court.[8]

B. International Civil Society

In the time immediately after UN Security Council Resolution 1315, adopted on August 10, 2000, international civil society reacted quickly and favorably to the idea of a Special Court for Sierra Leone. Several organizations issued statements welcoming the developments, also

---

[3] *See generally* M. Nicol-Wilson, *Accountability for Human Rights Abuses – The United Nations' Special Court for Sierra Leone*, 2001 AUSTL. INT'L L.J. 159 (2001).

[4] *See, e.g.*, M. Sieff, *A "Special Court" for Sierra Leone's War Crimes* (2001), *available at* http://www.globalpolicy. org/component/content/article/203-sierra-leone/39438.html (visited Apr. 8, 2012).

[5] Rep. of the Secretary-General on the Establishment of a Special Court for Sierra Leone, U.N. DOC. S/2000/195, at 35 (Oct. 4, 2000).

[6] *See* A. Smith, *A Response to a "Special Court" for Sierra Leone's War Crimes* (2001), *available at* http://www. globalpolicy.org/component/content/article/203/39439.html (last visited Apr. 8, 2012).

[7] Eleventh Rep. of the Secretary-General on the United Nations Mission in Sierra Leone, U.N. DOC. S/2001/857, at 48 (Sept. 7, 2001). *See also* P. Mochochoko & G. Tortora, *The Management Committee for the Special Court for Sierra Leone, in* INTERNATIONALIZED CRIMINAL COURTS 152 (C. Romano et al. eds., 2004).

[8] This decision has been criticized. *See, e.g.*, Chapter 17 in this volume by C. Aptel. Another critical opinion is expressed by J.A. Romero in *The Special Court for Sierra Leone and the Juvenile Soldier Dilemma*, 2 Nw. U. J. INT'L HUMAN RTS. (2004).

outlining what the Court should look like and how it should operate, including drawing several lessons from the experiences of the ICTY and ICTR.[9] At that time, the Rome Statute of the International Criminal Court had only recently been adopted (in July 1998), and had not yet entered into force, which made political will in favor of ending impunity at least appear to be more precarious generally speaking than it does now. Also, the negotiations for the Extraordinary Chambers for Cambodia were stalling and many feared that the Special Court Agreement negotiations might head the same way,[10] particularly given the ongoing fighting in Sierra Leone and the fears that justice would be an obstacle to ending the conflict. There were also concerns raised about how the Special Court would interact with the Truth and Reconciliation Commission (TRC) or what impact it would have on the establishment of the TRC, which had yet to happen despite having been mandated the previous year.[11] In addition, many organizations[12] – as well as the UN Secretary-General himself and the Sierra Leone government – expressed concerns regarding the voluntary funding mechanism insisted upon by the UN Security Council, apparently in reaction to the mounting and seemingly endless costs of the ICTY and ICTR.[13]

Another international civil society response to the news that the Special Court Agreement was soon to be negotiated came through a more unusual route, namely the secondment of legal experts to assist the government of Sierra Leone during the negotiations.[14] In 1998, the international NGO No Peace Without Justice (NPWJ) began its Judicial Assistance Program at the Rome Diplomatic Conference for the International Criminal Court. The program was designed to provide technical assistance to smaller delegations for the negotiations by seconding legal advisers to them, both for legal knowledge and to enable delegations to follow the several discussions that were taking place simultaneously. Provided free of charge to the delegations by NPWJ, the seconded legal advisers took instructions from and reported to their heads of delegation. Some thirty-four legal advisers were seconded throughout the six-week conference and, at the request of several delegations, NPWJ

[9] *See, e.g.*, Human Rights Watch, *U.N. Action on Sierra Leone Court Welcomed* (Aug. 15, 2000), *available at* http://www.hrw.org/news/2000/08/14/un-action-sierra-leone-court-welcomed (last visited Apr. 8, 2012).

[10] For a description of the difficulties in negotiating the Agreement on the Extraordinary Chambers for Cambodia, see D. Shraga, *The Second Generation of UN-Based Tribunals: A Diversity of Mixed Jurisdictions, in* INTERNATIONALIZED CRIMINAL COURTS, *supra* note 7, at 15ff.

[11] *See, e.g.*, Amnesty International, *Sierra Leone: Ending Impunity – An Opportunity Not to Be Missed* (July 25, 2000), *available at* http://www.amnesty.org/en/library/asset/AFR51/060/2000/en/60faeca4-de9a-11dd-b378–99b26579b978/afr510602000en.html (last visited Apr. 8, 2012).

[12] *See, e.g.*, Amnesty International, *The UN Security Council Must Make the Special Court Effective and Viable* (Feb. 13, 2001), *available at* http://www.amnesty.org/en/library/asset/AFR51/001/2001/en/23646266-dc3d-11dd-a4f4–6f07ed3e68c6/afr510012001en.html (last visited Apr. 8, 2012).

[13] For a discussion of the cost of international courts and tribunals vis-a-vis their results, see R. Zacklin, *The Failings of Ad Hoc International Tribunals*, 2 J. INT'L CRIM. JUST. 545 (2004). Although written two years after the establishment of the SCSL, Mr. Zacklin expresses many of the thoughts that were prevalent at the time the SCSL Agreement and Statute were negotiated. *See also* David J. Scheffer, Ambassador at Large for War Crimes Issues, Challenges Confronting International Justice Issues, Address Before International Law professors of the Boston area at dinner hosted by the New England Center for International Law and Policy at the New England School of Law (Jan. 14, 1998), *available at* http://www.nesl.edu/userfiles/file/nejicl/vol4/scheffer.pdf (last visited July 6, 2012).

[14] Information in this section from NPWJ Status Reports on Sierra Leone Mission (October 2000 and July and December 2001), *available at* http://www.npwj.org/ICC/Sierra-Leone-Program.html (last visited July 19, 2012).

continued to second legal advisers for the subsequent Preparatory Committees that worked on the ICC's Elements of Crimes and Rules of Procedure and Evidence.

As one of the delegations receiving seconded legal advisers, Sierra Leone had experienced firsthand the boost that countries lacking technical knowledge and human resources could gain from the Judicial Assistance Program. As such, when it was looking likely that the SCSL negotiations would go ahead, Sierra Leone requested NPWJ to extend its Judicial Assistance Program by seconding a full-time adviser to the Mission in New York and two full-time advisers to the Office of the Attorney-General and Minister of Justice in Freetown.[15] The advisers began their work in August 2000 and would continue in that capacity until the end of 2003, thereby covering all the negotiations with the UN, including for the Special Court Planning Mission in January 2002 during which the Special Court Agreement was signed, as well as the Court's establishment and initial operations, including negotiations for the SCSL's Headquarters Agreement.

As with the normal Judicial Assistance Program during the ICC negotiations, the seconded legal advisers took instructions from, worked under, and reported to the Deputy Permanent Representative of Sierra Leone (Ambassador Allieu I. Kanu) in New York and the Attorney-General and Minister of Justice in Freetown (the Honorable Solomon E. Berewa). Nonetheless, although the legal advisers were embedded within government structures, this was a civil society initiative that played a considerable role in facilitating the active involvement of Sierra Leone in the negotiations for the Special Court, in preparing the ground for the Special Court and in liaising with the Special Court once it was established.

C. Sierra Leonean and International Civil Society Working Together

In Sierra Leone itself, international and national civil society came together at the beginning of 2001 to begin the process of readying themselves and society at large for the Special Court's arrival, with the Freetown Conference on Accountability for Violations of International Humanitarian Law, organized by NPWJ at the Lagoonda Conference Centre on February 20–22, 2001.[16] This Conference brought together government and civil society from across the country to discuss Sierra Leone's accountability processes and how the participants would like them to work – encompassing both the Special Court and the TRC and the interaction between those institutions, as well as how traditional or customary justice could be incorporated into or operate alongside those mechanisms. The five working groups were designed around issues common to all accountability mechanisms, including international tribunals, truth and reconciliation commissions, and national courts. The purpose of these sessions was to get to the heart of the problems facing accountability mechanisms in Sierra Leone and to devise concrete solutions for those problems, drawing from solutions adopted for other accountability mechanisms. The Conference's five working groups covered process and penalties; outreach and transparency; documentation and protective measures;

---

[15] See http://www.npwj.org/ICC/Sierra-Leone-Program.html for more information about the program.
[16] Rep. from the Freetown Conference on Accountability for Violations of International Humanitarian Law in Sierra Leone, *available at* http://www.npwj.org/sites/default/files/ressources/File/SLConferenceReport2001.pdf (last visited July 19, 2012).

staffing, appointment of judges and commissioners, and financing; and Paramount Chiefs and traditional or customary justice.

One of the key innovations of this civil society initiative was to bring to the Conference members of the UN Security Council, some of whom would form key members of the Special Court's Management Committee. The purpose of involving these Security Council members was to let them see for themselves the potential impact of the decisions they were taking at UN headquarters in New York. Until then, many of the persons involved with decision making about the Special Court, how it should operate, and its budget had very little firsthand knowledge or experience about post-conflict situations in general and Sierra Leone in particular. By bringing the UN Security Council members to Sierra Leone and having them sit in on the discussions at the conference, both in plenary and in the working groups, they gained an understanding of the true realities on the ground. This arguably served to put them in a better position to evaluate the impact their decisions in New York would have on the people of Sierra Leone.

Another result of the Conference was the recommendation that Sierra Leonean civil society take an active role in the preparations for the Court and the TRC. The Conference participants felt that there was a strong need for ownership by the people of Sierra Leone of the various accountability mechanisms, agreeing that one way of achieving this sense of ownership was to implement an effective outreach program across the whole country to inform the public about the nature and workings of the TRC and the Special Court. Drawing on the lessons learnt of other mechanisms, especially the ICTY, the Conference participants were determined that the Special Court not be beset by the same problems of distance and inaccessibility, the resulting irrelevance of the ICTY to the people of the former Yugoslavia (which was very evident at that time because President Milosevic had yet to be transferred to The Hague), and politicization of the judicial process. They were also keen to ensure that the Special Court and the TRC be presented as an integrated accountability process for the country, to capitalize on the strengths that each mechanism could bring to the overall process.

D. Special Court Working Group

Following on the recommendations from the Lagoonda Conference, from March to June 2001, NPWJ organized a series of Training the Trainers workshops in Freetown, targeting civil society, the legal profession, the media, and others.[17] These workshops were designed to meet two objectives: the first was to begin spreading information about the Special Court to stakeholders and engaging them in the process; the second was to identify interested individuals and organizations to form a national coalition for civil society to undertake outreach on the Special Court themselves, and also to prepare for working with the Special Court once it was established and had people on the ground. Sixteen four-hour seminars were held, attracting a total of 313 participants, with average attendance at each seminar ranging between 15 and 20 people. Participants came from a diverse range of organizations and institutions, including human rights and civil society organizations, journalists, and other

---

[17] Information in this section from NPWJ Status Reports on Sierra Leone Mission (July and December 2001), *available at* http://www.npwj.org/ICC/Sierra-Leone-Program.html (last visited July 19, 2012).

interested individuals, with "special sessions" held for specific target groups, such as the staff and Commissioners of the National Commission for Disarmament, Demobilisation and Reintegration (NCDDR), Commission for the Consolidation of Peace (CCP) and National Commission for Democracy and Human Rights (NCDHR), senior journalists and editors, ex-combatants' representatives, and Paramount Chiefs.

A key result of these workshops, especially the initial training sessions in March 2001, was the establishment of the Special Court Working Group (SCWG), which had been another key recommendation from the Lagoonda Conference. The SCWG held its inaugural meeting on April 7, 2001, with nineteen organizations coming together on a Saturday morning to decide how they would undertake their work. SCWG meetings were held once every two weeks and the number of participants in working group meetings grew to a total of thirty-nine members at the time of the election of the SCWG's National Executive Committee.

From April to June 2001, the SCWG conducted its work through subgroups,[18] dedicated to devising specific messages and methods of outreach for specific target groups, whose work was adopted by the biweekly plenary meetings of the SCWG. During that time, NPWJ acted as the Secretariat for the SCWG until the elections in June 2001 and the formal establishment of the SCWG as a national coalition working toward justice and accountability. Following its formal establishment, NPWJ and the SCWG continued to produce outreach materials, notably the *Special Court Times*, and broadcast a weekly radio show about the Special Court and accountability issues generally, *Special Court Hour* on Radio UNAMSIL, the radio station operated by the UN Mission in Sierra Leone. NPWJ and the SCWG also continued to conduct outreach with specific target groups in Freetown and selected towns in the provinces, especially Bo, Kenema, and Mile 91, the latter because of its proximity to RUF-held territory at the time and the teams' ability, therefore, to broadcast outreach messages directly into that territory. This played an important role in getting accurate and timely information about the SCSL directly to the RUF leaders, who declared that they were ready to face the Special Court, noting only that others should be held to account for their actions as well.[19]

The SCWG would later change its name to the Coalition for Justice and Accountability (CoJA). Although there were some difficulties maintaining the work of the SCWG, and later CoJA, as a coalition per se,[20] both CoJA and original SCWG member organizations continued to play a critical role in SCSL outreach efforts once the Court was established, and in working on broader accountability issues, including the ICC, over the following decade and beyond.[21] Although it is beyond the scope of this chapter to assess everything done by the SCWG and CoJA from early 2001, their existence, and their early and sustained

[18] The subgroups focused on the following areas: children; ex-combatants; the media; civilians and civil society organizations; and security forces. A sixth subgroup was later formed to explore potential sources of funding and devise a budget for the various activities submitted by each of the subgroups and adopted by the SCWG as a whole.

[19] Issa Sesay, June 25, 2001, http://www.sierra-leone.org/Archives/slnews0601.html (last visited Apr. 8, 2012).

[20] The main difficulties included tensions between the TRC Working Group and the Special Court Working Group; challenges in respect of funding for the work of the coalition and its members; and difficulties in the SCWG Secretariat acting as a Secretariat, under the direction of its members, rather than as a separate organization, which is often challenging for civil society coalitions in general.

[21] In addition, several individual founding members of the SCWG later worked at the Court, especially in the Outreach Section, both as Outreach Coordinators and as District Outreach Officers.

interest in the work of the SCSL and in ensuring its responsiveness to Sierra Leone, almost certainly had a positive effect on the Court's work and on the establishment of the Special Court Interactive Forum by the SCSL in its early years.[22]

E. *SCSL Planning Mission: January 2002*

The Planning Mission for the Special Court for Sierra Leone, held from January 7 to 19, 2002, was a visit to Sierra Leone by the UN Office of Legal Affairs, representatives of states making up the SCSL Management Committee,[23] and various experts on international criminal tribunals.[24] The purpose of the Planning Mission was to assess current conditions on the ground in Freetown with a view to making recommendations as to what steps needed to be taken to secure a smooth setup of the Court, to hold consultations on the appointment of judges and senior court officials, and to assess the availability of evidence relating to crimes within the jurisdiction of the Court. The visit of the Planning Mission to Sierra Leone enabled the signature of the Special Court Agreement to take place in Freetown, which provided an important opportunity for publicization of the SCSL within the Sierra Leonean media. It also allowed for the participation of Sierra Leonean civil society in the signing ceremony and in the Planning Mission's work, which was an important part of the SCWG's advocacy work in late 2001, and generally sent an important signal that the Special Court was intended to be an instrument for Sierra Leone in its path toward peace and reconstruction. These two aspects of the signing ceremony both built on civil society's previous engagement with the Court before its establishment and laid the foundation for ongoing engagement with civil society and the general public for the future, once the Court would arrive and begin its work.

The Planning Mission itself also provided an important opportunity for the views and perspectives of both the Sierra Leone government and civil society to be heard during the initial planning stages of the Court. The members of the Planning Mission met directly with several civil society organizations and with a wide variety of other civil society representatives, including the legal profession, the media, traditional leaders, and others, both in Freetown and outside the capital.[25] The visit of the Planning Mission to Bo, Kenema, and Kono, at the urging of the Sierra Leone government, was of critical importance in this respect. Although all parts of Sierra Leone suffered during the conflict, Kono was particularly affected, and the rule of law at the time of the visit had deteriorated to such an extent that illegal digging for diamonds was taking place throughout Kono's main streets. This proved to be a particularly visual representation of the main message the Planning Mission would hear from those it met, namely that expectations were high that the Special Court would help Sierra Leone

---

[22] Special Court for Sierra Leone Annual Report 2002–2003, at 19, *available at* http://www.sc-sl.org/LinkClick. aspx?fileticket=NRhDcbHrcSs%3D&tabid=176 (last visited Apr. 8, 2012).

[23] The Management Committee of the SCSL consists of representatives of states providing political and financial support for the Court, plus representatives of the UN and the Republic of Sierra Leone. Its main function is to provide financial support for the Court and policy oversight and direction on the Court's nonjudicial functions. For more information, see Mochochoko & Tortora, *supra* note 7.

[24] *See* Letter Dated Mar. 6, 2002 from the Secretary-General addressed to the President of the Security Council, U.N. Doc. S/2002/246, Annex I, *Report of the Planning Mission on the Establishment of the Special Court for Sierra Leone* [hereinafter *Report of the Planning Mission*].

[25] *Report of the Planning Mission, supra* note 24, at para. 4.

restore the rule of law. As such, the decision to visit Kono was particularly significant, also because most Planning Mission members had never visited a country such as Sierra Leone before, which was the poorest country in the world and ranked the lowest on the Human Development Index, nor had they met victims of crimes under international law before.[26] Therefore, not only did the trip up-country provide an opportunity for civil society unable to travel to Freetown to present their views to the Planning Mission, it also deepened the understanding of the Planning Mission members about the challenges the Court would face and the high expectations of the Court throughout the country.

In addition to meetings with the Planning Mission, Sierra Leonean civil society continued the work they had begun the previous year on ensuring the Court would be effective and responsive to the needs of Sierra Leoneans. In the lead-up to the visit of the Planning Mission, and throughout their stay in Sierra Leone, the Special Court Working Group played a key role in ensuring information about the Planning Mission for the Special Court and the Special Court itself was transmitted to the public.[27] To facilitate this effort, the SCWG with support from NPWJ established a Special Court Information Centre at their offices, which proved useful for the local media and others, and did a number of public radio broadcasts concerning both the work of the Planning Mission and the Special Court itself. The participation of the then–Attorney-General and Minister of Justice Solomon Berewa and members of the Planning Mission in a call-in radio show that was broadcast across the country also provided much-needed firsthand information to the general public and helped further embed the idea – and future demands – that the SCSL should be and would be responsive to the people of Sierra Leone. International civil society also took the opportunity provided by the Planning Mission, and the release of its report in March 2002, to restate their policy priorities and concerns about the SCSL, including in particular its relationship with the TRC, its funding mechanism, and its independence.[28]

IV. THE ESTABLISHMENT OF THE SCSL

The Special Court for Sierra Leone was officially established on January 16, 2002, when the SCSL Agreement was signed in Freetown by Hans Corell, representing the UN, and Solomon Berewa, representing the Republic of Sierra Leone. The first Prosecutor, David

---

[26] This continues to be a challenge for international criminal justice, for example in the International Criminal Court, the representatives of whose Assembly of States Parties – which performs similar conceptual functions as the SCSL Management Committee – have little to no firsthand knowledge of the expectations and challenges of victims and communities affected by crimes within the jurisdiction of the ICC. Again, it is the urgings of situation countries and initiatives by civil society that seek to overcome these challenges; *see, e.g.,* NPWJ's ICC Review Conference Public Engagement Initiative, 2009–2010 in Uganda, *available at* http://npwj.org/ICC/Uganda-ICC-Review-Conference-Public-Engagement-Initiative-2009–2010.html-0 (last visited Apr. 8, 2012).

[27] Information in this section from NPWJ Status Report on the SCSL Planning Mission February 2002, *available at* http://www.npwj.org/ICC/Sierra-Leone-Program.html.

[28] *See, e.g.,* Amnesty International, *Sierra Leone: An Independent Prosecution Policy Must Be Assured* (Jan. 21, 2002), *available at* http://www.amnesty.org/en/library/asset/AFR51/001/2002/en/4c4a4bad-d89f-11dd-ad8c-f3d4445c118e/afr510012002en.html (last visited Apr. 8, 2012); *see also* Human Rights Watch, *Sierra Leone: Establish Special Court Quickly* (Mar. 21, 2002), *available at* http://www.hrw.org/news/2002/03/20/sierra-leone-establish-special-court-quickly (last visited Apr. 8, 2012).

Crane, was appointed on April 17, 2002, and the first Registrar, the late Robin Vincent, was appointed on June 10, 2002, enabling the Court to open its doors officially on July 1, 2002, with both principals and a skeleton staff arriving shortly thereafter.[29] The reaction of international civil society was somewhat muted, as most organizations had already issued public statements welcoming the establishment of the Court earlier in the year and providing their policy recommendations for how the Court should conduct its work. Nonetheless, expectations were running high about the Court both within international and national civil society, and a number of initiatives were carried out in Sierra Leone to help ensure that the Court would live up to the expectations of it being embedded in and responsive to Sierra Leonean needs and perspectives.

A. Working with Sierra Leone's Legal Profession

Among the many outward expressions of the SCSL's commitment to being a Court for Sierra Leoneans, an early issue arose in relation to the Special Court and the Sierra Leone legal profession. The Special Court initially recruited lawyers from abroad to work at the Court, particularly those with experience and expertise on international humanitarian and criminal law. From a practical perspective, this was a logical choice, because although the Sierra Leone legal profession was (and is) a vibrant one, most lawyers lacked specific skills and expertise on international law in general and substantive and procedural international criminal law in particular. Nonetheless, the fact that few Sierra Leonean lawyers were included among the Court staff during the first rounds of hiring both raised concerns and criticisms among the legal profession and was seen as a lost opportunity to transfer useful skills and knowledge that could then be used to good effect in Sierra Leone's own courts.[30] It also lost a useful opportunity to capitalize on the benefits that could be brought during those early stages by Sierra Leonean staff, particularly in terms of knowledge of local laws, language, and customs, enabling them to take into account factors that might escape international personnel.[31]

In an attempt to address this situation, NPWJ and the Sierra Leone Bar Association organized a seminar in December 2002 on the SCSL Rules of Procedure and Evidence between the newly sworn-in Judges of the Special Court and members of the Sierra Leone legal profession.[32] The purpose of the seminar was to introduce the Special Court Judges to the Sierra Leone legal community and to initiate a dialogue regarding the Court's relationship with the Sierra Leone legal system and the legacy that it would leave for that system. Following the seminar, the Sierra Leonean facilitators for each part of the Rules prepared written submissions, which were provided to the SCSL Judges before their plenary meeting to adopt

---

[29] First Annual Report of the Special Court for Sierra Leone, at 5, *available at* http://www.sc-sl.org/LinkClick.as px?fileticket=NRhDcbHrcSs%3d&tabid=176 (last visited Apr. 8, 2012).

[30] Author's personal recollection. *See also* S. Gupta, *The Not So Special Court for Sierra Leone*, New Internationalist Mag., Issue 427, *available at* http://www.newint.org/columns/essays/2009/11/01/special-court-sierra-leone/ (last visited Apr. 8, 2012).

[31] A. Cassese, *The Role of Internationalized Courts and Tribunals in the Fight against International Criminality*, *in* Internationalized Criminal Courts, *supra* note 7.

[32] Much of the information for this section comes from the NPWJ Status Report 2002, *available at* http://www. npwj.org/ICC/Sierra-Leone-Program.html (last visited July 19, 2012).

the Rules in March 2003.[33] NPWJ together with the U.K. Bar Human Rights Committee and in collaboration with the Special Court also held training sessions on international humanitarian law for interested Sierra Leonean lawyers, many of whom would later go on to join the SCSL as prosecution or defense counsel before taking up positions either within Sierra Leonean institutions or for international courts and tribunals abroad. Although most of the credit for this positive state of affairs rests with Sierra Leone's lawyers themselves, who simply insisted on not being left out or left aside, the early enthusiasm of the Special Court's first Registrar to include Sierra Leoneans in the Court's work, and the initial receptiveness of the first SCSL Judges to engage with their Sierra Leonean counterparts facilitated what would turn out to be a positive situation for everyone involved.

B. *Conflict Mapping and Engaging Sierra Leoneans in Their Accountability Process*

Another joint international-national civil society initiative that helped spread the word about the Special Court and engage Sierra Leoneans in their accountability process was NPWJ's Conflict Mapping Program.[34] Mapping the conflict directly addresses consequences of conflict by establishing a record of the truth of what happened during that conflict. The chronological and geographical mapping of the conflict, including reconstructing the order of battle and chain of command, serves to prevent denial of those events. An analysis of events according to international law establishes prima facie accountability for violations of international humanitarian law. In so doing, it both serves to strengthen the rule of law and to promote and defend human rights by publicizing the price for violating them. In addition, establishing the chain of command within the armed forces operating in Sierra Leone and assembling these disparate pieces of information to create the bigger picture of the decade-long conflict in Sierra Leone facilitated the crucial phase of establishing who appeared to bear direct and command responsibility for atrocities committed during that conflict. This was intended both to provide a factual and legal analysis of events in Sierra Leone and to facilitate the people of Sierra Leone establishing who should be held accountable for the atrocities committed in Sierra Leone, thereby both avoiding the trap of blaming a group or segment of society and promoting peaceful conciliation.

From 2002 to 2004, NPWJ worked with civil society from around the country to gather information about what happened during the conflict both temporally and geographically, that is, from 1991 to 2002, and in virtually every one of Sierra Leone's 149 chiefdoms. The Conflict Mapping Program identified civil society actors from around the country, called Conflict Mapping Recorders, who were trained in interviewing key persons, namely those people with a good oversight about what happened in their chiefdom during the conflict, as well as in interviewing direct victims and witnesses of events during the conflict. By the end of the project, the information gathered by Conflict Mapping Recorders from key persons comprised over 400 records, each containing an average of 30 pages, with a total of approximately 5,500 separate incidents, that is, instances of an alleged violation of international

---

[33] First Annual Report of the Special Court for Sierra Leone, *supra* note 29, at 7. *See also* NPWJ's Report from the Rules Seminar, *available at* http://www.npwj.org/sites/default/files/ressources/File/Final%20Rules%20Seminar%20Report.pdf (last visited July 19, 2012).

[34] *See Sierra Leone Conflict Mapping, available at* http://www.npwj.org/ICC/Sierra-Leone-Conflict-Mapping.html (last visited Apr. 8, 2012).

humanitarian law or key strategic or other information contained in a record. This information together with open source material was inputted into a secure database, which was subjected to rigorous checking to ensure its accuracy; this provided the analytical tool to put together the factual analysis of what happened across the whole territory of Sierra Leone. The factual analysis enabled the legal analysis of events according to the substantive law of the Special Court, resulting in a report of several thousands of pages covering, as much as possible, each chiefdom and each time period between 1991 and 2002. The final report was both presented to the Truth and Reconciliation Commission and submitted into evidence at the Special Court for Sierra Leone, where it helped provide useful background information, especially for events that were relevant to but fell outside of the SCSL's temporal jurisdiction.[35]

Most important, the Conflict Mapping Program and its resulting report were intended to be complementary to the Special Court itself and to bolster its work. One aim was to provide some form of acknowledgment of people's suffering prior to the commencement of the SCSL's temporal jurisdiction on November 30, 1996, which – as noted earlier – had proved to be one of the most contentious issues about the Court and its setup. Another aim was to involve Sierra Leoneans in the accountability work for their country, both to expand the number of people touched by the Special Court, even if tangentially, and to foster a sense of empowerment by providing an avenue through which they could actually do something tangible.

C. Cementing the Special Court's Place in Sierra Leone, Liberia, and Beyond

Throughout the immediate phase of the Court's establishment and the decade since then, civil society in Sierra Leone has continued to play a key role in the Court's outreach work, which would expand later to civil society in Liberia as the Court began to undertake outreach work there. During its initial months of operations, the Special Court, Sierra Leone civil society, and No Peace Without Justice worked together closely on the Court's outreach work, both in its conceptualization and in its implementation. This was designed to ensure the sustainability of the work already done on outreach in Sierra Leone prior to the Court's establishment and to maximize the utility of lessons already learned and innovative measures that had proved successful, such as the Right Players, a drama group that toured Freetown's markets putting on short skits and singing songs about the SCSL and related issues. It was also designed to help ensure that Sierra Leone's civil society would continue to play an important role in the life of the Court and that they would hold the SCSL itself accountable for putting into practice the vision of the Court as a court for Sierra Leoneans, a role welcomed by all involved.

Over the following decade, both national and international civil society continued to monitor the work of the Court and to work closely with it on its nonjudicial functions, including outreach, legacy, and victims issues. This was done through a mixture of close partnerships between the Court's outreach section and both Sierra Leonean and Liberian civil society, in-country workshops and conferences facilitated by outside actors, and advocacy relating

---

[35] *See, e.g.*, Trial Chamber I's Decision on Prosecution's Request to Admit into Evidence Certain Documents Pursuant to Rules 92bis and 89(C), of July 14, 2005, in *Prosecutor v. Sam Hinga Norman, Moinina Fofana and Allieu Kondewa*, Case No. SCSL-04-14-T.

to the Court's funding, as well as through critical analyses and policy recommendations throughout the different phases of the Court's life, including, for example, in relation to the location of the trial of former Liberian president Charles Taylor.[36] Civil society will also play an important role in the completion of the Court's life, with a survey of the Special Court's impact and legacy due to be conducted (following the issuance of the Court's final judgment in the Taylor case) by NPWJ, Manifesto 99, the Coalition for Justice and Accountability, the Sierra Leone Institute for International Law, and the Liberian NGO Network.[37] Sierra Leonean civil society also plans to continue playing a critical role in relation to the SCSL Residual Mechanism, both through consultations on its design and directly vis-á-vis the Residual Court when it is established.[38]

V. CONCLUSION

Although not always finding agreement on all issues, the role played by national and international civil society and the responsiveness of the SCSL from its earliest days until now has resulted in an accountability mechanism that is more attuned to the needs of the people it was established to serve than any other court or tribunal to date. Much of this was a result of the outreach work carried out by the Court and by civil society, which not only helped inform the people of Sierra Leone and Liberia about the Court, but which also created a vital conduit for needs and expectations to be channeled back to the Court itself.[39]

This role of civil society in relation to the Special Court has both been supported by and helped to strengthen the role of civil society in other international justice efforts, notably in relation to the ICC.[40] Civil society – be it national or international – is no longer content to sit on the margins and be a passive player in the face of monumental developments to end impunity and promote peace such as the Special Court for Sierra Leone. In Tunisia, for example, civil society is playing a leading role in promoting transitional justice efforts for that country, through the establishment of a Transitional Justice Academy, to reinforce key actors and civil society to advocate effectively at the political level and to play a dynamic

---

[36] NPWJ, Statement by No Peace Without Justice on the transfer of Charles Taylor to The Hague (Apr. 5, 2006), *available at* http://www.npwj.org/ICC/Statement-No-Peace-Without-Justice-transfer-Charles-Taylor-Hague. html (last visited Apr. 8, 2012). *See also, e.g.*, Amnesty International, *Special Court Ruling – No Immunity for Former Liberian President Charles Taylor* (June 2, 2004), *available at* http://www.amnesty.org/en/library/ asset/AFR44/018/2004/en/a26ea0ac-d5c7-11dd-bb24-1fb85fe8fa05/afr440182004en.html (visited Apr. 8, 2012); Human Rights Watch, *Report: Justice in Motion, the Trial Phase of the Special Court for Sierra Leone* (Nov. 3, 2005), *available at* http://www.hrw.org/en/reports/2005/11/02/justice-motion (last visited Apr. 8, 2012); ICTJ *Report and Proposals for the Implementation of Reparations in Sierra Leone* (Dec. 2009), *available at* http://ictj.org/sites/default/files/ICTJ-SierraLeone-Reparations-Report-2009-English.pdf (last visited Apr. 8, 2012); and Open Society Justice Initiative, *Legacy: Completing the Work of the Special Court for Sierra Leone* (Nov. 1, 2011), *available at* http://www.soros.org/initiatives/justice/articles_publications/publications/ scsl-legacy-20111101/legacy-scsl-20111101.pdf (last visited Apr. 8, 2012).

[37] *See Sierra Leone: NPWJ Meets with Key Stakeholders to Discuss SCSL Impact and Foster Adoption of ICC Implementing Legislation* (Feb. 24, 2012), *available at* http://www.npwj.org/ICC/Sierra-Leone-NPWJ-meets-with-key-stakeholders-discuss-SCSL-impact-and-foster-adoption-ICC-Implem (last visited Apr. 8, 2012).

[38] Discussions in Freetown with SCSL officials and Sierra Leonean civil society, May 2011.

[39] *See, e.g.*, J. Stromseth, *Strengthening Demand for the Rule of Law in Post-Conflict Societies*, 18 MINN. J. INTL. L. 415, 422–23 (2009).

[40] *See, e.g.*, W. Pace & J. Schense, *The Role of Non-Governmental Organizations, in* THE ROME STATUTE OF THE INTERNATIONAL CRIMINAL COURT: A COMMENTARY-VOLUME 1, ch. 2.5 (A. Cassese et al. eds., 2002).

role in supporting transitional justice processes and help create momentum for the establishment of a National Commission on transitional justice to address violations under previous authoritarian regimes.[41]

With the Special Court expected to close its doors forever in 2013, there is a great deal of focus on its legacy, both for reestablishment of the rule of law and the impact it has had within Sierra Leone and the legacy it will leave for other courts and tribunals, notably for the ICC. One aspect of this legacy is surely an empowered civil society within and outside Sierra Leone, which is prepared to make its voice heard and to continue fighting for accountability efforts that are responsive to the needs of the people. In the end, this is a major achievement of which the Special Court and all those involved in its creation can be proud.

[41] NPWJ, *Tunisia: Launch of the Transitional Justice Academy to Support Building a Future Based on Accountability* (Dec. 14, 2011), *available at* http://www.npwj.org/ICC/Tunisia-launch-Transitional-Justice-Academy-support-building-a-future-based-accountability.html-0 (last visited Apr. 8, 2012).

3

International Community Expectations of the Sierra
Leone Special Court

Peter Penfold[*]

I have been asked to focus this chapter on the international community's expectations of the Special Court of Sierra Leone (SCSL). In so doing, I must stress that although I served as the British High Commissioner (ambassador) to Sierra Leone at the time, I no longer speak on behalf of the British government, or indeed the United Nations, and thus my remarks should not be taken as *official policy*.

I guess that I must be one of the very few nonlegal and nonacademic authors here, and I feel somewhat out of my depth among such legal and academic luminaries. However, I also suspect that I am one of the few authors who was actually in Sierra Leone at the time of the conflict and witnessed at firsthand some of the atrocities that led to the establishment of the SCSL. I was closely involved in trying to resolve the conflict and helping to ensure that there would be no repetition of the terrible times that the beautiful and blessed country of Sierra Leone has endured. I may also be one of the few authors who appeared before the Court as a Defense witness (on behalf of Chief Sam Hinga Norman). My approach to the SCSL is framed from all these experiences.

If one is to examine the international community's expectations of the SCSL, one should first consider the background to setting it up in the first place. As is by now widely known, especially among international lawyers, the decision to establish the Court was as a result of President Ahmed Tejan Kabbah of Sierra Leone's famous letter to the UN Secretary-General, Kofi Anan.[1] But, to my mind, there is no doubt that the impetus to establish the Court came about as much as a result of international pressure from outside rather than from pressure from within the country. Indeed, although Sierra Leone civil society, fed up with a savage war, had oscillated back and forth on the accountability question, back in October 1997, in a speech in London when President Kabbah was addressing the conference *Restoring Sierra Leone to Democracy*, he had dismissed suggestions that the junta that had removed him and his government earlier that year, comprising both the Armed Forces Revolutionary Council (AFRC) and the Revolutionary United Front (RUF), should be treated as *war criminals*. It was in that speech that Kabbah appeared to have first floated the idea of establishing a Truth and Reconciliation Commission:

> I have instead (of setting up a war crimes court) been giving some thought to the establishment of a Truth and Reconciliation Commission following the example of South Africa.

---

[*] Former British High Commissioner to Sierra Leone.
[1] President Kabbah's letter to UNSG dated June 12, 2000.

The merit of adopting this latter course can be easily discerned. This is an idea I intend to pursue so that genuine and lasting reconciliation can take place on the return of my government.[2]

International pressure to establish the SCSL stemmed from the caveat that the UNSG's special representative, Francis Okelo, was instructed to add at the signing of the Lomé Peace Agreement in July 1999. The UN, along with the Economic Community of West African States (ECOWAS), the Organization of African Unity (OAU), as the present day African Union (AU) was known back then, and the Commonwealth Secretariat, were identified as *moral guarantors* of the Agreement, and their representatives in Lomé appended their signatures to the document. However, before adding his, Okelo was instructed to disassociate the UN from the blanket amnesty in Article IX of the Agreement, which stated:

1. In order to bring lasting peace to Sierra Leone, the Government of Sierra Leone shall take appropriate legal steps to grant Corporal Foday Sankoh absolute and free pardon.

2. After the signing of the present Agreement, the Government of Sierra Leone shall also grant absolute and free pardon and reprieve to all combatants and collaborators in respect of anything done by them in pursuit of their objectives, up to the time of the signing of the present Agreement.

3. To consolidate the peace and promote the cause of national reconciliation, the Government of Sierra Leone shall ensure that no official or judicial action is taken against any member of the RUF/SL, ex-AFRC, ex-SLA or CDF in respect of anything done by them in pursuit of their objectives as members of those organisations, since March 1991, up to the signing of the present Agreement ....

To those of us who were around at the time, the UN caveat came as something of a surprise, not least – it seemed – to Okelo himself, who was somewhat embarrassed by the last-minute directive from New York.

Why this was surprising was that the Abidjan Peace Accord, which Kabbah had signed with Sankoh of the RUF in October 1996, and for which the UN had also acted as a *moral guarantor*, had contained similar provisions for a blanket amnesty. But on that occasion there had been no last-minute caveats from the UN. There were also similar amnesty provisions in the Conakry Peace Plan of December 1998, which the international community also supported. Why did they do so at the time of Lomé while not doing so at the time of the Abidjan and Conakry Accords?

There are several reasons, in my view, only the key ones of which I can highlight here. The Lomé Agreement came in the wake of the publication of the Human Rights Watch Report *Getting Away with Murder, Mutilation and Rape*, which had documented the widespread atrocities.[3] This had received extensive publicity. It was closely followed by the visit to Sierra Leone by Mary Robinson, the UN Human Rights Commissioner. During her visit she had described the atrocities as "war crimes" and "crimes against humanity." This had a significant impact in the corridors of New York and especially with members of the UN Security Council.

---

[2] Extract from speech delivered by President Kabbah at the Royal Over-Seas League on Oct. 20, 1997.
[3] 11 Hum. Rts. Watch, No. 3(A), June 1999.

There were fearful echoes of Rwanda. The UN in general, and countries such as the United States, Britain, and France in particular, were still feeling embarrassed that they had not done enough to prevent the Rwandese genocide in 1994. It also had a particular resonance for the UN Secretary-General, Kofi Anan, who had been in charge of UN peacekeeping at the time. Western governments were also reacting to accusations that the West cared more for the plight of Kosovo than Sierra Leone.

Even though Kabbah had officially requested the setting up of the Court, he clearly did not envisage its remit being expanded in the way it was. In his autobiography published in December 2010, Kabbah said that he had "approached the U.N. and requested the setting up of a Special Court to try Foday Sankoh, other senior members of the RUF and their collaborators for crimes against the people of Sierra Leone and for the taking of United Nations peacekeepers as hostage."[4] Kabbah's change of heart over a war crimes court came about out of frustration with Sankoh's actions in May 2000 when the latter demonstrated what so many of us on the ground at the time had been saying all along, that Sankoh could not be trusted to adhere to the provisions of the peace agreement. Kabbah's letter to Kofi Anan came in the wake of the incidents around Sankoh's house in Freetown and the kidnappings of UN peacekeepers by the RUF.

Kabbah's frustration was matched by the annoyance and embarrassment of those who had been promoting the Lomé Agreement. They had insisted on pushing through the power-sharing arrangement, against the stated wishes of the people and the Sierra Leone Parliament, an agreement that made Sankoh de facto Vice President and, in effect, put him in charge of the diamonds. Scarcely two years later, countries that had been promoting the Lomé Agreement, such as the United States and the United Kingdom, were advocating that Sankoh be tried as a war criminal.

Sankoh's actions and the initial disappointing response by the UN led to the deployment of British troops. Buoyed by this successful British military involvement, which led to Sierra Leone being viewed by many as a foreign policy success for Prime Minister Tony Blair, the British government threw its full support behind the SCSL.

As a signatory to the Rome Statute establishing the International Criminal Court, Britain would have preferred to use the ICC, but the Treaty had at that time not received sufficient number of ratifications to bring it into force[5] and therefore, in response to President Kabbah's letter to the UNSG, the United Kingdom went along with the U.S. proposal to establish a Special Court similar to what had been established for Rwanda and Yugoslavia. The other members of the Security Council agreed. (The United States, of course, was boycotting the ICC, as they continue to do today.) For Britain, as with others, the stated policy was that people should not get away with such abhorrent crimes with impunity. "We see it as essential that the perpetrators of the worst atrocities in recent times be brought to justice."[6] In another statement, the British authorities stated: "We are keen to see those responsible for some of the worst atrocities in recent times brought to justice. We firmly believe that the Special Court will achieve this aim."[7]

---

[4] AHMAD TEJAN KABBAH, COMING BACK FROM THE BRINK IN SIERRA LEONE (EPP Books Services 2010).
[5] The Rome Treaty establishing the ICC entered into force on July 1, 2002.
[6] In letter from Foreign Secretary, Jack Straw, to Cabinet colleague, dated Oct. 29, 2003.
[7] In letter from Foreign Office Minister, Chris Mullin, dated Oct. 28, 2003.

As major funders of the Court, the United States and United Kingdom had a big say in its establishment. I was led to believe at the time that originally it had been hoped to find someone from the Commonwealth, preferably an African, to take on the important role of Chief Prosecutor. When it appeared that no suitable candidate could be found, the U.S. government proposed David Crane, a lawyer from the U.S. Department of Defense. Crane did not have a strong human rights background. He had served most recently as senior Inspector-General at the U.S. Department of Defense. Prior to that he had been an Assistant General Counsel in the Defense Intelligence Agency and a professor of international law at the U.S. Army Judge Advocate General's School. Crane brought in a number of American ex-military personnel to serve as investigators, which gave the Office of the Prosecutor a distinct American military aura.

Under the terms of Article 15 of the Sierra Leone Statute establishing the Court, it was deemed that "the Prosecutor shall be assisted by a Sierra Leonean Deputy Prosecutor." However, an amendment to the Statute was rushed through the Sierra Leone Parliament[8] to allow for the appointment of a British QC, Desmond Da Silva. Da Silva had worked with President Kabbah in his younger days when the latter had been practicing law. Da Silva had been admitted to the Bar in Sierra Leone in 1968 to act as the defense in the country's first treason trial. He would later take over from Crane as the Court's Chief Prosecutor before being succeeded by Stephen J. Rapp, our distinguished fellow author and key-note speaker at the conference underlying this book. The British presence in the Court was further strengthened with the appointment of another Brit, Robin Vincent, as the Registrar of the Court.

All the senior positions in the Court were filled by expatriates, which said little for one of the stated intentions of the Court to strengthen the Sierra Leonean judicial process, as noted in UNSC Resolution 1593 and the UNSG's report of October 2000 on the establishment of the Special Court. This was taken by some as showing a lack of respect toward the indigenous population and a lack of recognition in terms of qualified Sierra Leoneans. It totally ignored, for example, that Foday Sankoh had already been found guilty of treason in the Sierra Leone courts, a trial that had been monitored by representatives of the International Bar Association. In his book *Conflict and Collusion in Sierra Leone* David Keen commented: "The Special Court does not trust Sierra Leone to administer justice. If they are not trusted to administer justice, how can they be expected to accept it?"[9] David Crane defended his position by pointing out that 50 percent of his team were African and that 38 percent were Sierra Leonean.[10]

Although the Court's first distinguished President, Geoffrey Robertson, had said that the success of the SCSL would be measured by the fairness with which it carried out its trials, it often appeared that for the international community, success would be determined not by its establishment but by the achievement of successful convictions. An indication of this determination was shown when Ralph Zacklin, the UN Assistant Secretary in the Office of Legal Affairs (OLA), who was charged with the responsibility of working out the mechanics with the Sierra Leone government of establishing the Court, advised that there should be

---

[8] The Special Court Agreement 2002 (Ratification) (Amendment) Act 2002, July 15, 2002.
[9] DAVID KEEN, CONFLICT AND COLLUSION IN SIERRA LEONE (2005).
[10] David Crane addressing a Friends of Sierra Leone (FOSL) meeting in Washington, May 27, 2003.

a change in the UN mandate for the Court. The OLA advised that the phrase "those that bear the greatest responsibility" (for the crimes) should be changed to "those most responsible," as Charles Jalloh discusses in Chapter 30 of this volume. This proposal was rejected by the UN Security Council. In a subsequent note to all the Defense counsel, after the Court was created, the Principal Defender suggested an interesting interpretation: "According to Zacklin's reasoning, even if your clients are the most responsible, they should be acquitted if they are not those that bear the greatest responsibility, which requires a much greater threshold of proof and which is also limited to the most narrow class of offenders."[11]

However, things did not go as planned. Of the nine persons originally indicted by David Crane, both Sankoh and his notorious henchman, Sam Bockarie, alias *Mosquito*, died before the RUF trial got underway – Sankoh while in detention and Bockarie fighting in Liberia. They were allegedly the two persons "most responsible" for the worst of the atrocities. Equally, Johnny Paul Koroma, leader of the AFRC junta, had fled the country and disappeared.[12]

With Sankoh's and Bockarie's deaths there were calls for the Court to be disbanded (including from myself), but these were ignored. The remaining indictees were far lesser figures. The only person of note was Chief Sam Hinga Norman, one of Kabbah's ministers, whom many regarded as a national hero and one of those most responsible for restoring peace and stability to Sierra Leone. Norman's death in 2007 while still in detention and before the conclusion of the CDF trial led to further controversy; indeed it contributed significantly to Kabbah's replacement losing the election later that year.

One of the expectations of the international community was that the activities of the Special Court would help create an environment in which democratic, free, and fair elections could take place. Kabbah had deferred the elections due in 2001 until the following year. The 2002 elections were democratic and were free and fair. However, it remains debatable how much credit is due the Special Court for them taking place so peacefully.

Another expectation was that the Special Court would help promote reconciliation. Again there are mixed views on this, partly depending from which region of the country the views were sought. People in the Western area were generally supportive of the Court; elsewhere, particularly in the south of Sierra Leone, from where the CDF indictees came, they were hostile. More credit was given to the TRC for promoting reconciliation, but the relationship between the TRC and the Special Court could have been better. The TRC Report noted that the relationship "could have been immeasurably stronger had the two institutions shared something of a common vision of the basic goals of post conflict justice."[13]

Yet another expectation of the international community for the SCSL was that it would discourage the abuse of human rights and make it easier to resolve conflicts elsewhere. This is a lofty goal, and the jury is still out. In the past decade in Africa we have continued to see conflicts in places such as the Ivory Coast, Sudan, Egypt, Tunisia, Congo, Nigeria, and most recently Mali, but it could be argued that the human rights violations in these conflicts have not reached the scale of those witnessed earlier in Rwanda, Mozambique, and Sierra Leone. Africa remains the target for international justice but resolving conflicts on the continent

---

[11] Simone Monasebian, SCSL, dated June 3, 2005.
[12] It is widely believed that Koroma died in the Ivory Coast.
[13] TRC Report.

does not appear to have become any easier as a result. This emphasis on Africa by the international community as promoted by the ICC has not endeared itself to African leaders at the AU who continue to view the cause of international justice, as promoted by Western governments, with suspicion and mistrust.[14]

As time has dragged on, the enthusiasm from the international community for the Special Court has somewhat waned, especially in the face of the constant demands for more funding. Nowadays it would appear that there is a greater concern for tackling the problems of corruption and drugs in Sierra Leone than promoting international justice.

Media interest in the Charles Taylor trial has arisen from time to time (e.g., supermodel Naomi Campbell's testimony about receiving "dirty-looking stones" from Taylor), but generally the international community is probably looking forward to the day when the Sierra Leone Special Court has completed its business. The hopes that at least it would leave behind a complex of fine buildings for the country to use were somewhat dashed when the Sierra Leone government realized that it would cost around $400,000 per year to pay for the costs of running the complex.

Hopes for the Court being viewed as a real success were enhanced with the conviction of Charles Taylor. This has been a fairly tortuous path. Crane had set about Taylor's indictment with almost messianic fervor. The unveiling of his Indictment in June 2003 nearly derailed the delicate peace negotiations taking place in Accra to resolve the Liberian conflict, and for a long time President Obasanjo of Nigeria refused to hand him over in spite of the intense pressure from the international community.[15] Indeed the U.S. government went so far as to offer a reward of $2 million to anyone who would help remove Taylor to Sierra Leone to face trial, although this was part of its Rewards for Justice international fugitive tracking program. Taylor, after he was convicted, insisted that his trial was politically motivated and that it was an example of Western powers such as the United States witch-hunting African leaders.

However, the point has been made that no one is above the law—even heads of state can be brought to justice. This is seen as a significant success, although some such as Jalloh had argued that if Taylor, why not President Blaise Compare of Burkina Faso, or Muammar Gadhafi of Libya, both of whom were allegedly said to be as much involved in the Sierra Leone conflict.[16] Indeed, there were even calls for President Kabbah to be indicted given that he was nominally the head of the CDF forces. However, it seems that the SCSL has no stomach to go after heads of state other than Taylor. This may give a measure of credit to his claim that he was selectively prosecuted, although of course, one could also see that as the self-interested argument of a convicted war criminal. Also, the claim that no one was "above the law" was not strictly true, as in establishing the Court a waiver was granted toward "peacekeepers and related personnel."[17] This was inserted for the sake of ECOMOG, who,

---

[14] *See* Charles C. Jalloh, *Regionalizing International Criminal Law?*, 9 INT. CRIM. L. REV. 449 (2009) and Charles C. Jalloh, *Universal Jurisdiction, Universal Prescription? A Preliminary Assessment of the African Union Perspective on Universal Jurisdiction*, 21 CRIM. L. FOR. 1 (2010).

[15] Obasanjo finally handed Taylor over to President Johnson-Sirleaf of Liberia on her election. She immediately passed him on to the Special Court.

[16] Charles C. Jalloh, *Special Court for Sierra Leone: Achieving Justice?* 33 MICH. J. INT'L L. 395, 422–23 (2011).

[17] SCSL Statute art. 1.2.

according to the TRC, had committed about 1 percent of the atrocities and human rights violations.[18]

So have the international community's expectations for the SCSL been realized? The UN and the leading governments who supported the SCSL would probably say yes, if for no other reason than to justify the vast amount of money expended on the Court. (Each convicted indictee currently sitting in prison in Rwanda has cost around $23 million, and the figure for Charles Taylor will be far in excess.)

My fellow authors in this volume have argued the case for the Sierra Leone authorities and the local and international NGOs. But what about the victims themselves? The Rome Statute establishing the ICC talked of acting "in the interests of the victims" and "in the interests of justice," and the SCSL should be seen in a similar vein. In my experience, seen from this prospective, the jury is still out!

---

[18] According to the TRC Report the RUF had committed 60.5 percent of the atrocities, the AFRC/SLA 16.6 percent, the CDF 6 percent, and Ecomog 1 percent.

PART II

Approach to Individual Criminal Responsibility

4

Joint Criminal Enterprise at the Special Court for Sierra Leone

Simon M. Meisenberg[*]

I. INTRODUCTION

The Prosecution of the Special Court for Sierra Leone (SCSL or Court) overwhelmingly relied on the doctrine of Joint Criminal Enterprise (JCE). All initial Indictments at the SCSL charged the Accused on the basis of this mode of liability. In the Charles Taylor case, it has been argued that JCE liability was "the backbone" of the trial.[1] Inevitably, the SCSL had to address this controversial mode of liability. This chapter analyzes the contribution of the SCSL with regards to this doctrine, tracing the course of SCSL jurisprudence from the pleadings through to appellate stages of trials. It argues that despite correctly articulating the legal elements and applicable law thereto, in its application of the JCE doctrine, the Court widened it beyond acceptability and in disregard of fundamental principles of criminal law.

I will first analyze the pleading principles and practice employed by the SCSL, to demonstrate that the acceptance of vague pleadings aggravated an accurate examination of the JCE doctrine. The gravity of this shortcoming became apparent during the first final verdict of the Court where the trial judges rejected the JCE pleading as defective for not alleging a common purpose that amounted to a statutory crime. This decision was overturned on appeal, broadening the concept of JCE and thereby breeding an unseen and misguided conviction of a defendant in a subsequent trial. Through exploring these decisions and their consequences, this chapter contends that the SCSL missed an important opportunity to limit and strengthen the JCE doctrine. The Court's jurisprudence highlights the dangers of JCE being misapprehended or misapplied.

[*] Legal Advisor at the Extraordinary Chambers in the Courts of Cambodia (since 2011); former Senior Legal Officer, and Legal Officer, Trial Chamber II, Special Court for Sierra Leone (2005–2011). Opinions are expressed in a private capacity and are not attributable to the ECCC and SCSL. The author thanks Kathryn Smyth and participants of the Pittsburgh SCSL Legacy Conference for comments on an earlier draft. Any errors remaining are his. This chapter, in particular Section IV, is a revised and expanded version of a forthcoming chapter *in* PUBLIC INTERNATIONAL LAW, INTERNATIONAL CRIMINAL LAW & INTERNATIONAL HUMAN RIGHTS LAW: A CRITICAL EVALUATION OF THE SCHOLARSHIP OF PROFESSOR WILLIAM SCHABAS (K. Cavanaugh & J. Castellino eds., 2014).

[1] Transcript Oral Rule 98 Decision, *Taylor* (SCSL-03–01-T), Trial Chamber, 24204 (May 4, 2009), *available at* http://www.sc-sl.org/CASES/ProsecutorvsCharlesTaylor/Transcripts/tabid/160/Default.aspx (visited June 30, 2012).

II. THE JCE DOCTRINE AND JCE PLEADINGS BEFORE THE SCSL

The Tadić Appeals Chamber Judgment of the International Criminal Tribunal for the former Yugoslavia (ICTY) stated that customary international law provides for a mode of attribution known as JCE.[2] Unlike other hybrid courts, such as the Extraordinary Chambers in the Courts of Cambodia and the Special Tribunal for Lebanon, this doctrine was not challenged or narrowed by the SCSL.[3] Considering Article 20 of the SCSL Statute,[4] there would have been only a minimal possibility to contradict any finding of the ICTY on the customary status of the doctrine. Therefore, and even though not expressly mentioned in the SCSL Statute, all three forms of JCE liability were found to be a mode of attribution pursuant to Article 6(1) of the SCSL Statute.[5]

Before I turn to the SCSL jurisprudence, I briefly summarize the legal elements required to establish JCE liability as follows: All members of the JCE may be found criminally liable for all crimes committed that fall within the common purpose (JCE I and II). The extended form, or JCE III, involves criminal acts that fall outside the criminal purpose. An accused who intends to participate in a common purpose may be found guilty of acts outside that purpose if such acts are a natural and foreseeable consequence of the effecting of that criminal purpose.[6] All three forms of JCE therefore require the following *actus reus*: (1) a plurality of persons; (2) the existence of a common plan amounting to or involving the commission of a crime; and (3) the participation of the defendant in the common plan.[7]

The three forms differ only with regards to the mental elements (*mens rea*). The second or systemic form of JCE shall not be part of the analysis in this chapter, as it did not play a substantial role in the SCSL trials.[8] The basic form requires that the defendant (1) must intend to take part in and contribute to the common plan to commit the crime; (2) must intend the commission of the crime or underlying offense, and (3) must share this intent with the other members of the JCE (shared intent).[9]

---

[2] Judgment, *Tadić* (IT-94-1-A), Appeals Chamber, §§ 188–193 (July 15, 1999) [hereinafter Tadić Appeal Judgment].

[3] Decision on the Application of Joint Criminal Enterprise, *Nuon, Ieng, Samphan, Ieng* (002/19-09-2007/ECCC/TC), Trial Chamber (Sept. 12, 2011); Decision on the Appeals against the Co-Investigative Judges Order on Joint Criminal Enterprise (JCE), *Nuon, Ieng, Samphan, Ieng* (002/19-09-2007-ECCC-OCIJ), Pre-Trial Chamber (May 20, 2010); *see also* K. Gustafson, *ECCC Tackles JCE. An Appraisal of Recent Decisions*, 8 J. INT'L CRIM. JUST. 1323–32 (2010); Interlocutory Decision on the Applicable Law: Terrorism, Conspiracy, Homicide, Perpetration, Cumulative Charging (STL-11-01/I/AC/R176bis), §§ 248–249 (Feb. 16, 2011).

[4] Article 20(3) SCSL Statute provides that the judges of the SCSL Appeals Chamber "shall be guided by the decisions of the Appeals Chamber of the International Tribunals for the Former Yugoslavia and for Rwanda."

[5] Judgment, *Brima, Kamara and Kanu* (SCSL-04-16-A), Appeals Chamber, § 73 (Feb. 22, 2008) [hereinafter Brima or AFRC Appeal Judgment].

[6] Tadić Appeal Judgment, *supra* note 2, § 204. Contrary to the Tadić Appeal Judgment, the SCSL Appeals Chamber uses a "reasonably" foreseeable standard rather than "natural" foreseeable standard. *See* RUF Appeal Judgment, *infra* note 8, § 475.

[7] Tadić Appeal Judgment, *supra* note 2, § 227; AFRC Appeal Judgment, *supra* note 5, § 75; Judgment, *Taylor* (SCSL-03-01-T), Trial Chamber, § 457 (May 2, 2012) [hereinafter Taylor Trial Judgment].

[8] Judgment, *Sesay, Kallon and Gbao* (SCSL-04-15-T-1234), Trial Chamber, §§ 382–385 (Mar. 2, 2009) [hereinafter Sesay or RUF Trial Judgment]; *see also* Partially dissenting and concurring opinion of Justice Shireen Avis Fisher, Judgment, *Sesay, Kallon and Gbao* (SCSL-04-15-A-1321), Appeals Chamber, § 8 (Oct. 26, 2009) [hereinafter Sesay or RUF Appeal Judgment].

[9] Judgment, *Brdanin* (IT-99-36-A), Appeals Chamber, § 365 (Apr. 3, 2007) [hereinafter Brdanin Appeal Judgment]; Taylor Trial Judgment, *supra* note 7, § 465.

In contrast, the mental element for the extended form requires that the defendant (1) must intend to take part in and contribute to the common plan; (2) must have sufficient knowledge that the *additional* crime was a foreseeable consequence to him in particular[10]; (3) must be aware that the crime *falling outside* of the common purpose might be perpetrated by a member of the group; and (4) must willingly take the risk that the crime might occur by joining or continuing to participate in the enterprise.[11]

JCE III has undergone considerable criticism and rejection in both academic literature[12] and jurisprudence.[13] In that respect it is argued that as a form of "commission," the extended form violates the principle of culpability as the perpetrator who merely foresees the crime or assumes the risk in the criminal conduct does not have the same intent as the principal perpetrator. It is further argued that the foreseeability standard is not sufficiently precise and therefore the concept violates the principle of *lex stricta* (i.e., that crimes be narrowly defined).[14] These loud voices of concern faded or, it appears, were simply ignored by the SCSL.

The SCSL Prosecution relied on this mode of attribution in each and every Indictment before the SCSL.[15] One may compartmentalize the Indictments into two categories: One,

---

[10] Judgment, *Martić* (IT-95-11-A), Appeals Chamber, § 83 (Oct. 8, 2008) [hereinafter Martić Appeal Judgment]; Judgment, *Kvočka, Kos, Radić, Žigić and Prcać* (IT-98-30/1-A), Appeals Chamber, § 86 (Feb. 28 2005) [hereinafter Kvočka Appeal Judgment]; Judgment, *Milutinović, Šainović and Ojdanić* (IT-05-87-T), Trial Chamber, § 111 (Feb. 26, 2009) [hereinafter Milutinović Trial Judgment].

[11] Kvočka Appeal Judgment, *supra* note 10, § 86; Brđanin Appeal Judgment, *supra* note 9, § 411; *see also* RUF Appeal Judgment, *supra* note 8, § 475.

[12] *See only* G. Fletcher, *New Court, Old Dogmatik*, 9 J. INT'L CRIM. JUST. 179 (2011); M. Damaška, *What is the Point of International Criminal Justice?*, 83 CHI.-KENT L. REV. 329 (2008); J. Ohlin, *Three Conceptual Problems with the Doctrine of Joint Criminal Enterprise*, 5 J. INT'L CRIM. JUST. 69 (2007); J. Ohlin, *Joint Intentions to Commit International Crimes*, 11 CHI. J. INT'L L. 693 (2011); H. van der Wilt, *Joint Criminal Enterprise: Possibilities and Limitations*, 5 J. INT'L CRIM. JUST. 91, 97 (2007); K. Ambos, *Joint Criminal Enterprise and Command Responsibility*, 5 J. INT'L CRIM. JUST. 159 (2007); K. Ambos, *Amicus Curiae Brief in the Matter of the Co-Prosecutors' Appeal of the Closing Order against Kaing Guek Eav "Duch" Dated 8 August 2008*, 20 CRIM. L. FORUM 353 (2009); M. Badar, *Participation in Crimes in the Jurisprudence of the ICTY and ICTR*, in ROUTLEDGE HANDBOOK OF INTERNATIONAL CRIMINAL LAW 255–57 (W. Shabas & N. Bernaz eds., 2011); M. Badar, *"Just Convict Everyone!" – Joint Perpetration: From Tadić to Stakić and Back Again*, 6 INT'L CRIM. L. REV. 293 (2006); H. Olasolo, *Reflections on the Treatment of the Notions of Control of the Crime and Joint Criminal Enterprise in the Stakić Appeal Judgement*, 7 INT'L CRIM. L. REV. 143, 157 (2007); A. Bogdan, *Individual Criminal Responsibility in the Execution of a "Joint Criminal Enterprise" in the Jurisprudence of the Ad Hoc International Tribunal for the Former Yugoslavia*, 6 INT'L CRIM. L. REV. 63, 108 (2006).

[13] Decision on the Application of Joint Criminal Enterprise, *Nuon, Ieng, Khieu, Ieng* (002/19-09-2007/ECCC/TC), Trial Chamber (Sept. 12, 2011); Decision on the Appeals against the Co-Investigative Judges Order on Joint Criminal Enterprise (JCE), *Nuon, Ieng, Khieu, Ieng* (002/19-09-2007-ECCC-OCIJ), Pre-Trial Chamber (May 20, 2010); Interlocutory Decision on the Applicable Law: Terrorism, Conspiracy, Homicide, Perpetration, Cumulative Charging (STL-11-01/I/AC/R176bis), §§ 248–249 (Feb. 16, 2011); *see also* Separate Opinion of Judge Schomburg on the Individual Criminal Responsibility of Milan Martić, Martić Judgment, *supra* note 10, § 7, stating that "... the current shifting definition of the third category of JCE has all the potential of leading to a system, which would impute guilt solely by association."

[14] Ambos, *supra* note 12; Ohlin, *supra* note 12.

[15] Indictment, *Taylor* (SCSL 2003-03-I), §§ 20, 23 (Mar. 7, 2003); Indictment, *Sankoh* (SCSL 2003-02-I), § 27 (Mar. 7, 2003); Indictment, *Sesay* (SCSL 2003-5-I), § 23 (Mar. 7, 2003); Indictment, *Koroma* (SCSL 2003-3-I), § 24 (Mar. 7, 2003); Indictment, *Brima* (SCSL 2003-6-I), § 23 (Mar. 7, 2003); Further Amended Indictment, *Brima, Kamara, Kanu* (SCSL-04-16-PT), §§ 33, 34 (Feb. 5, 2004) [hereinafter AFRC Indictment]; Corrected Amended Consolidated Indictment, *Sesay, Kallon, Gbao* (SCSL-04-15-PT), §§ 36, 37 (Aug. 2, 2006) [hereinafter RUF Indictment]; Indictment, *Norman, Fofana and Kondewa* (SCSL-2004-14), § 19 (Feb. 5, 2004).

the Indictments against participants of the JCE that belonged to the group of renegade soldiers (i.e., AFRC members) and members of an armed opposition group (RUF members and later also AFRC members) and any alleged supporters of these groups or participants (i.e., Taylor).[16] Two, the Indictments against member of the pro-government militias, the so-called Civil Defense Forces (CDF), who fought for the restoration of the democratically elected government of President Ahmed Tejan Kabbah. This chapter will not analyze in detail the Indictments and Judgment in the case of the *Prosecutor v. Norman, Fofana and Kondewa* (the CDF case) with respect to JCE, as the CDF Judgment found that the Prosecution had not proven beyond reasonable doubt that a common purpose had been agreed upon by the alleged participants belonging to the CDF faction in the civil war.[17] This finding was not challenged on appeal.

In the cases against RUF and AFRC members, as in the initial Indictment in the Taylor case, the Prosecution alleged that the defendants:

> shared a common plan, purpose or design (joint criminal enterprise) which was to take any actions necessary to gain and exercise political power and control over the territory of Sierra Leone, in particular the diamond mining areas.[18]

The first observation is that such a purpose does not allege a crime within the Court's jurisdiction. Even though the SCSL has jurisdiction over certain national crimes, treason is not a crime within the SCSL's jurisdiction and is not an offense known under international law.[19] This was confirmed by the SCSL Appeals Chamber in a separate matter, when considering the validity of amnesties in international law. The SCSL Appeals Chamber stated that the current state of international law does not prohibit overthrowing a government through an internal armed opposition group or dissident armed force within a state.[20] Therefore

---

[16]　The Initial Indictment in the Taylor case alleged a similar common purpose as in the RUF and AFRC cases, and that he and members of those two factions were participants in a JCE. However, in the Taylor case the common purpose was modified to the "terrorization of the civilian population of the Republic of Sierra Leone" (see Decision on Urgent Defense Motion regarding a Fatal Defect in the Prosecution's Second Amended Indictment relating to the Pleading of JCE, *Taylor* (SCSL-03-01-T), §§ 70–76 (Feb. 27, 2009) [hereinafter Taylor Trial Chamber JCE Decision] upheld on appeal by Decision on Defense Notice of Appeal and Submissions regarding the Majority Decision concerning the Pleading of JCE in the Second Amended Indictment, *Taylor* (SCSL-03-01-T-775), § 21 (May 1, 2009) [hereinafter Taylor Appeals Chamber JCE Decision]). The present analysis will therefore focus on the common purpose pleading of the AFRC and RUF cases, but will nevertheless make reference to the Initial Indictment in the Taylor case where appropriate.

[17]　Judgment, *Fofana and Kondewa* (SCSL-04-14-T), Trial Chamber, §§ 732, 744, 770, 803, 814, 850, 858, 865, 907, 914, 939, 949 (Aug. 2, 2007) [hereinafter Fofana or CDF Trial Judgment].

[18]　*See only* Indictment, *Sankoh* (SCSL 2003-02-I), § 27 (Mar. 7, 2003); Indictment, *Sesay* (SCSL-2003-5-I), § 23 (Mar. 7, 2003); Indictment, *Koroma* (SCSL 2003-3-I), § 24 (Mar. 7, 2003); Indictment, *Brima* (SCSL 2003-6-I), § 23 (Mar. 7, 2003); AFRC Indictment, *supra* note 15; RUF Indictment, *supra* note 15, §§ 20, 23, 36, 37; Indictment, *Taylor* (SCSL 2003-03-I), §§ 20, 23 (Mar. 7, 2003).

[19]　Article 5 SCSL Statute provides jurisdiction over the following domestic crimes: (1) offenses relating to the abuse of girls under the Prevention of Cruelty to Children Act, 1926, and (2) offenses relating to the wanton destruction of property under the Malicious Damage Act, 1861.

[20]　Decisions on Challenge to Jurisdiction: Lomé Accord Amnesty, *Kallon and Kamara* (SCSL-2004-15-AR72(E)/SCSL-2004-16-AR72(E)), Appeals Chamber, § 20 (Mar. 13, 2004), referring to M.N. Shaw, International Law 1040 (2003), which states that "[w]hether to prosecute the perpetrators of rebellion for their act of rebellion and challenge to the constituted authority of the State as a matter of internal law is for the state authority to decide. There is no rule against rebellion in international law." For comments, see S.M. Meisenberg, *Legality of Amnesties in International Humanitarian Law: The Lomé Amnesty Decision of the Special Court for Sierra Leone*, 856 Int'l Rev. Red Cross 837 (2004).

international law does not provide for a prohibition or individual criminal responsibility for an act of rebellion within the territory of a state.

For a proper understanding of the JCE pleading, the surrounding paragraphs in the Indictment have to be considered as well. The Indictments allege:

> The joint criminal enterprise included gaining and exercising control over the population of Sierra Leone in order to prevent or minimize resistance to their geographical control, and to use members of the population to provide support to the members of the joint criminal enterprise. The crimes alleged [unlawful killings, abductions, forced labour, physical and sexual violence, use of child soldiers, looting and burning of civilian structures], were either actions within the joint criminal enterprise or were a reasonably foreseeable consequence of the joint criminal enterprise.[21]

This passage clarifies which categories of JCE are alleged. The wording "within" identifies the basic form of JCE, whereas the phrase "a reasonably foreseeable consequence," despite its nuanced difference to the ICTY practice,[22] identifies the third form. It is evident from the pleading of the basic form that underlying offenses, such as crimes against humanity and war crimes, were articulated *within* the common purpose. To that end, the participants of the JCE formulated a plan that was supposed to achieve a noncriminal purpose (i.e., a rebellion) with criminal means (i.e., the commission of crimes against humanity or war crimes against the civilian population). Such a pleading is permissible as it is well-established jurisprudence of the ICTY that a JCE may "involve or amount to crimes" within the jurisdiction of a court. The Indictments provide that the common purpose *involved* crimes.[23] As will be discussed in more detail in Section IV below the pleading of such a common purpose is nevertheless contentious, in particular with respect to JCE III.

A textual and structural reading of the Indictments leads to the conclusion that they refer only to one JCE and do not identify a fluctuation in the JCE, such as a termination and resurrection at different times during the Indictment period. In fact, as the pleadings identify the participants of the JCE as AFRC and RUF members, logically the inception date of the JCE could have only been at the time when the RUF joined the mutinying government soldiers (i.e., AFRC) in May 1997, as before that date they rather had an opposite purpose, being adverse belligerent forces. Given this rather stagnant approach, the judges were unable to look into a JCE exclusively among RUF or AFRC members.[24]

As will be discussed in the next section, the pleading in the Indictments provides little detail and is overly broad. It portrays a view of the armed conflict and of the different warring factions and groups as a static conflict, as if the armed conflict in Sierra Leone was fought in the trenches of Verdun, rather than guerrilla warfare or an asymmetrical armed conflict. Looking at the facts of the AFRC and RUF trial judgments it is clear that the armed conflict experienced many profound changes that affected the dynamics of any purposes and objectives of the warring factions: new participants emerged; former friends became

---

[21] AFRC Indictment, *supra* note 15, § 34; RUF Indictment, *supra* note 15, § 37; *see also* Indictment, *Taylor* (SCSL-03–01–I), § 24 (Mar. 7, 2003).

[22] At the ICTY the accepted standard has been "natural and foreseeable consequences"; *see* Tadić Appeal Judgment, *supra* note 2, § 204. The "reasonably foreseeable standard" was confirmed by the SCSL Appeals Chamber; *see* RUF Appeal Judgment, *supra* note 8, § 475.

[23] For a more detailed analysis see Section IV.

[24] RUF Trial Judgment, *supra* note 8, §§ 2076, 2184.

foes; objectives changed and had multiple layers of purposes.[25] The Prosecution ignored all of these important features that have an effect on the finding of a common purpose and on a participation therein.[26] Instead, the Prosecution portrayed a one-dimensional view, painting a black-and-white picture.[27] That issues were more complex is evident, as, despite the brevity of the Indictments, the AFRC and RUF Judgment ran more than 700 pages.

III. THE SPECIFICITY OF JCE PLEADINGS

The SCSL Prosecution did not follow settled ICTY jurisprudence when drafting the Indictments. When compared to ICTY and ICTR Indictments, SCSL Indictments lack detail and specificity.[28] They provide some personal background about the defendant and rudimentary information about the crimes committed, but do not provide any detailed information about the actual criminal conduct of the defendants in relation to the underlying offenses for which they were charged. According to the former Prosecutor this was purposely done, attempting to improve and simplify the pleading requirements at the SCSL.[29] This deficiency with respect to JCE was accepted by the Trial and Appeals Chamber. Before looking at the specific pleadings in the SCSL Indictments, in particular the pretrial decisions on the JCE pleading,[30] the requirements for such a JCE pleading will be set out first.

A. *JCE Pleading Requirements*

With regards to the pleading of modes of liability in general, there is ample jurisprudence stating that the nature of the alleged responsibility of a defendant has to be pleaded unambiguously.[31] The case law on the pleading principles for JCE liability had been settled at the time of the confirmation of indictments in the SCSL cases.[32] As for pleadings regarding JCE liability, four requirements have to be satisfied:

---

[25] *See only* RUF Trial Judgment, *supra* note 8, §§ 817–820.

[26] RUF Trial Judgment, *supra* note 8, §§ 2073–2076, finding a major rift between AFRC and RUF members ended the JCE among the participants of the enterprise.

[27] *See also* Claire de Silva, THE HYBRID EXPERIENCE OF THE SPECIAL COURT FOR SIERRA LEONE, *in* RESEARCH HANDBOOK ON INTERNATIONAL CRIMINAL LAW 248 (B.S. Brown ed., 2011).

[28] W. Jordash & J. Coughlan, *The Right to Be Informed of the Nature and Cause of the Charges: A Potentially Formidable Jurisprudential Legacy*, *in* JUDICIAL CREATIVITY AT THE INTERNATIONAL CRIMINAL TRIBUNALS 286, 310 (S. Darcy & J. Powderly eds., 2010).

[29] *See* W. Jordash & S. Martin, *Due Process and Fair Trial Rights at the Special Court: How the Desire for Accountability Outweighed the Demand of Justice at the Special Court for Sierra Leone*, 23 LEIDEN J. INT'L L. 585, 590 (2010). That work, as updated to reflect the developments in the Charles Taylor case, is Chapter 5 in this volume.

[30] For example, Preliminary Motion for Defects in the Form of the Indictment, *Sesay* (SCSL-2003–05-PT), Trial Chamber, § 22 (June 23, 2003), wherein the Defense argued that the Indictment failed to plead with sufficient particularity the nature of the Accused's participation in the criminal enterprise.

[31] *See, e.g.*, Judgment, *Furundzija* (IT-95-17/1-A), Appeals Chamber, § 147 (July 21, 2000); Judgment, *Blaskić* (IT-95-14-A), Appeals Chamber, § 215 (Dec. 29, 2004) [hereinafter *Blaskić* Appeal Judgment]; Judgment, *Kordić and Čerkez* (IT-95-14/2-A), Appeals Chamber § 129 (Dec. 17, 2004); Judgment, *Rutaganda* (ICTR-96-3-A), Appeals Chamber, § 303 (May 26, 2003).

[32] H. OLÁSOLO, *The Criminal Responsibility of Senior Political and Military Leaders as Principals to International Crimes* 250 (2009).

(1) the nature or purpose of the joint criminal enterprise;
(2) the time at which, or the period over which, the enterprise is said to have existed;
(3) the identity of those engaged in the enterprise, as far as their identity is known, but at least by reference to their category as a group; and
(4) the nature of the participation by the accused in that enterprise.[33]

Moreover, the jurisprudence of the ICTR and ICTY requires that the Prosecution distinguish between each of the different forms of the JCE. Specifically, with regard to the extended form, more stringent requirements have been placed on the Prosecution. Chambers have refused to rely on this variant in the absence of an express reference to it in the Indictment.[34]

In addition to these four elements, the jurisprudence requires the Prosecution to provide notice of the fact that a common purpose changed over time, altering the original purpose. In such a scenario, the Prosecution is required to notify the defendant of such an altered purpose and has to identify the nature and participants of the JCE.[35] Moreover, the criminal purpose may transform at a later stage if the leading members of the JCE are informed of subsequent crimes that were not contemplated in the original purpose, but did not prevent the recurrence of such additional crimes and continued with the implementation of the original criminal purpose. In such a scenario the Prosecution has to provide notice and identify when such additional crimes became an integral part of the initial common purpose.[36] Finally, if crimes were perpetrated by nonmembers of the JCE, the Prosecution should plead that the commission of the crime by nonmembers of the JCE formed part of the common purpose or were a natural and foreseeable consequence of it.[37] None of those additional pleading requirements were met in the SCSL Indictments.

B. Form of the Indictment Decisions

The point of departure for accepting the vague pleading practice is the Sesay Decision.[38] This was the first decision that looked into a request of the Defense to order, inter alia, a clarification of the Indictment. This motion was addressed pursuant to Rule 72(B)(ii) SCSL RPE and was decided by a single judge. This chapter argues that this decision aggravated many of the problems that the court struggled with respect to JCE. A procedural obstacle compounded the problem, as any trial decision on the form of the Indictment was not open to interlocutory appeal pursuant to Rule 72(D) SCSL RPE.[39] Consequently a potential defective

---

[33] RUF Appeal Judgment, *supra* note 8, § 99; Taylor Appeals Chamber JCE Decision, *supra* note 16, § 15.

[34] Judgment, *Simić* (IT-95-9-T), Trial Chamber, § 146 (Oct. 17, 2003).

[35] Judgment, *Blagojević and Jokić* (IT-02-60-T), Trial Chamber, § 700 (Jan. 17, 2005).

[36] Judgment, *Krajišnik* (IT-00-39-A), Appeals Chamber, § 171 (Mar. 17, 2009) [hereinafter Krajišnik Appeal Judgment].

[37] Martić Appeal Judgment, *supra* note 10, § 171.

[38] Decision and Order on Defense Preliminary Motion for Defects in the Form of the Indictment, *Sesay* (SCSL-2003–05-PT), Trial Chamber (Oct. 13, 2003) [hereinafter Sesay Decision].

[39] Only the Taylor Trial Chamber JCE Decision, *supra* note 16, was granted leave to appeal. The Trial Chamber applied the leave to appeal test of Rule 73(B) SCSL RPE and stated that it was "in the interests of justice that leave to appeal be granted notwithstanding the provisions of Rules 72(A) and (D) [SCSL RPE]"; see Decision on Defense Application for Leave to Appeal the Decision on Urgent Defense Motion Regarding a Fatal Defect in the Prosecution's Second Amended Indictment Relating to the Pleading of JCE, *Taylor* (SCSL-03-01-T), Trial Chamber (Mar. 18, 2009).

indictment was carried to the final appeals stage. This is an unwise procedural rule, as for all participants legal certainty on such fundamental issues is desirable. Challenges on the form of the Indictment were, however, dismissed by the Appeals Chamber on appeal.[40]

The Sesay Defense complained about the JCE pleading, arguing that the prosecution should be ordered to provide additional detail regarding the nature or purpose of the common plan.[41] The Sesay Decision makes a rather general assertion that "[t]he law on this issue where it is alleged (as in the instant Indictment) that the specific international crimes with which an accused is charged involves numerous perpetrators acting in concert, is that the degree of particularity required in pleading underlying facts is not as high as in case of domestic criminal courts."[42] Academic commentators have suggested that the decision conflated several issues regarding the need for specificity, in particular that at the "international level" it was permissible to plead indictments more vaguely given the "sheer scale" of the crimes.[43] The reference to paragraph 6–45 of the commentary *Archbold International Criminal Courts*, and not to international jurisprudence, was misapprehended as a carte blanche for a vague pleading practice. A closer look at this reference demonstrates that the Kvočka Decision, which the *Archbold* refers to, did indeed accept a broader pleading practice with respect to certain aspect of material facts because of the massive scale of the crimes and the number of perpetrators involved when dealing with mass atrocities. This however should not be misunderstood that vagueness may reign international criminal trials. The next paragraph in the *Archbold* then notably adds that an indictment must nevertheless contain a "concise statement of the facts"[44] and must be "sufficiently clear to enable the accused to understand the nature and cause of the charges brought against him."[45]

The Sesay Decision miscomprehends the "sheer scale" argument, as it only provides an exemption of specific detail regarding information on the underlying crimes, such as the identity of the victim and/or perpetrator and the exact date of crime. Still, this cannot be understood as a dilution of specificity when it comes to the participation and the acts and conduct of the defendant. The SCSL Indictments, however, provide only for a technical legal term as notice to the accused regarding the participation in the alleged crimes. Pleading the participation by mere reference to the individual modes of responsibility causes ambiguity and should be avoided.[46] It is preferable that an indictment indicates in relation to each individual count the particular participation in the JCE.[47]

The Sesay Decision identifies the four JCE pleading requirements mentioned in Section III(A). However, the requirements are applied liberally, accepting skeletal information. Moreover, at times the Indictment is read out of context, creating an appearance that the

---

[40] *See* RUF Appeal Judgment, *supra* note 8, §§ 99–111, 116–118.

[41] Sesay Decision, *supra* note 38, § 26.

[42] *Id.* referring to R. Dixon & K. Khan, Archbold International Criminal Courts § 6–45 (2003).

[43] R. Haveman, *Commentary, in* Annotated Leading Cases of International Criminal Tribunals, The Special Court for Sierra Leone 2003–2004, at 277, 278 (A. Klip & G. Sluiter eds., 2006).

[44] Dixon & Khan, *supra* note 42, § 6–46.

[45] *Id.*

[46] Decision on Preliminary Motion on Form of Amended Indictment, *Krnojelac* (IT-97–25), Trial Chamber, § 60 (Feb. 11, 2000).

[47] *Id.; see also* G. Boas, J.L. Bischoff & N.L. Reid, 1 International Criminal Law Practitioner Library: Forms of Responsibility in International Criminal Law 383 (2007); Jordash & Martin, *supra* note 29, at 590–92.

requirements are satisfied. The Sesay Decision identifies the purpose of the enterprise and holds that the nature of the Indictment was set out with much particularity, identifying it as "to take actions necessary to gain and exercise political power and control over the territory of Sierra Leone, in particular the diamond areas."[48] The fact that this purpose is not criminal in nature was not noticed. With respect to the requirement of the "identity of those engaged in the enterprise," it is held that this requirement has been sufficiently pleaded, referring to four paragraphs in that respect. Those references, however, do not name the identity of the JCE participants.[49] Paragraph 8 of the Sesay Decision, which is found under the heading of "general allegations" states:

> Shortly after the AFRC seized power, at the invitation of Johnny Paul Koroma, and upon the order of Foday Saybana Sankoh, leader of the RUF, the RUF joined with the AFRC. The AFRC and the RUF acted jointly thereafter.

Nothing in this paragraph can be understood as identifying the participants in a JCE. All this paragraph states is that the leader of a mutinous and dissident armed group invited the leader of a rebel group into a joint government and that they "acted jointly thereafter." This passage does not refer to the defendant Sesay, alleging that he was part of the decision-making process or agreement to establish a joint government between the RUF and AFRC. Therefore it is difficult to argue that this provides him with notice of a "concise statement of facts" regarding the JCE allegations. Paragraph 20 that was referred to as well, simply states that following Sankoh's arrest in 2000, three years after the alleged inception of the JCE, Sesay directed the activities of the RUF. Can this statement be understood as a participation in a JCE? Last, paragraph 22 of the Sesay Decision was identified in order to provide notice regarding the participants in the JCE. Indeed this paragraph mentions Sesay and five other high-level commanders of the RUF and AFRC. However, it merely states that Sesay, through his positions, individually "or in concert" with Sankoh, Bockarie, Kallon, Koroma, and Brima and other unidentified superiors "exercised authority, command and control over all subordinate members of the RUF, Junta and AFRC/RUF forces."[50] This paragraph can only be understood as a statement relating to command responsibility, despite the wording "in concert," but hardly as an identification of the co-perpetrators in the JCE,[51] unless one accepts that the mere fact that the RUF and AFRC were fighting a democratically elected government is "evil" and as such constitutes the criminal enterprise.[52] The wording "in concert" is insufficient to provide notice of a JCE, especially as the paragraphs that expressly refer to this mode of attribution are only found two paragraphs further below.

---

[48] Sesay Decision, *supra* note 38, § 27.

[49] *Id.* referring to §§ 8, 20, 21, 22.

[50] *Sesay* Indictment, *supra* note 18, § 21.

[51] *See also* Judgment, *Gacumbitsi* (ICTR-2001–64-T), Trial Chamber, § 25 (June 14, 2004).

[52] The Sesay Defense suggested an appearance of bias of Judge Thompson through his expressions in his dissenting opinion in the CDF Trial Judgment, *supra* note 17, § 80, where he held that the CDF Accused fought for the democratically elected government and acted in necessity, similar to the U.S. doctrine of "choice-of-evil" Defense. The request for disqualification was rejected; *see* Decision on Sesay and Gbao Motion Voluntary Withdrawal or Disqualification of Hon. Justice Bankole Thompson from the RUF Case, *Sesay, Kallon and Gbao* (SCSL-04–15-T), Trial Chamber (Dec. 6, 2007); upheld on appeal, see Decision on Sesay, Kallon and Gbao Appeal against Decision on Sesay and Gbao Motion Voluntary Withdrawal or Disqualification of Hon. Justice Bankole Thompson from the RUF Case, *Sesay, Kallon and Gbao* (SCSL-04–15-T), Appeals Chamber (Jan. 24, 2008).

The Sesay Decision then turns to the crimes and states that paragraph 24 alleged that crimes were "within" the scope of the JCE. Interestingly it does not state which crimes were beyond the intended purpose and only a foreseeable consequence of the JCE.[53] With respect to the requirement of the nature of the accused participation, the decision refers to paragraphs 17 to 23 of the Sesay Indictment, which are found in the section addressing the "individual criminal responsibility." A closer look entails yet another revelation. Paragraphs 17 to 21 refer only to certain positions held by Sesay. These paragraphs do not refer to Sesay's participation in a JCE, expressly or impliedly, and they do not suggest that Sesay's participation in the JCE was by the mere fact that he held superior authority or a superior position. Even if this would have been the allegation, then a more specific articulation of this allegation may have been necessary to comprehend the charges. Paragraph 22 states only that Sesay "acted in concert with" Charles Taylor, but does not provide any detail of the specific participation or how they acted in concert. The last paragraph referred to is paragraph 23, which refers to the common purpose, but fails to provide any detail of Sesay's participation. The requirement of identifying a time period of the JCE in the Indictment was not addressed at all, despite the fact that this was considered to be one of the pleading requirements.[54]

In conclusion, the Sesay Indictment provided only one element out of four pleading requirements (i.e., the nature of the JCE). All other elements were not identified with sufficient precision. The Indictment was eventually joined with other indictments and amended before it proceeded to trial. However, the articulations and paragraphs regarding the JCE did not substantively change in the operative indictment against Sesay and the other RUF members standing trial.

The Sesay Decision served as a precedent for all the other pretrial decisions regarding the form of the indictment. The Kanu Decision is worth additional detailed reflection, as, despite the similar language of the Indictment, a slightly different interpretation of the participation of Kanu in the JCE emerged. According to that decision, paragraph 25 of the Kanu Indictment, which is a reference to all applicable modes of liability under the SCSL Statute, provides notice that Kanu participated in the JCE by ordering, instigating, aiding and abetting, planning, or committing the underlying crimes.[55] A textual reading and the coordinating conjunction "or" would suggest otherwise. This reading was disregarded by all Trial Chambers when deciding on the modes of attribution in the final judgments as the different heads of responsibility were understood to stand independently and not to form part of the participation in the JCE.

The third decision with respect to pleading principles on JCE, the Kondewa Decision, largely followed the articulation as the other two decisions in order to preserve logical

---

[53] It is notable that many decisions assessing the form of the indictment regarding JCE neglect a specific analysis of the adequacy of the pleading of JCE III; *see* AFRC Appeal Judgment, *supra* note 5, § 573–87; Decision on Urgent Defense Motion regarding a Fatal Defect in the Prosecution's Second Amended Indictment relating to the Pleading of JCE, *Taylor* (SCSL-03–01-T), Trial Chamber (Feb. 27, 2009); Decision on Defense Notice of Appeal and Submissions regarding the Majority Decision Concerning the Pleading of JCE in the Second Amended Indictment, *Taylor* (SCSL-03–01-T), Appeals Chamber (May 1, 2009).

[54] Sesay Decision, *supra* note 38, § 30, referring to Decision on Form of Second Amended Indictment, *Krnojelac* (IT-97–25), Trial Chamber (May 11, 2000).

[55] Decision and Order on Defense Preliminary Motion for Defects in the Form of the Indictment, *Kanu* (SCSL-2003–13-PT), Trial Chamber, § 12 (Nov. 19, 2003).

coherence and consistency.[56] The fourth decision, the Kamara Decision, similarly rejected the Defense claims that the JCE was not sufficiently pleaded, stating that the Defense claims were "ill-conceived."[57] This decision, which was the first to be decided by the entire Trial Chamber and not by a single judge, adds yet another spurious argument, holding that some of the pleading requirements were "evidentiary matters" and therefore did not need to be specified in the Indictment.[58] With this line of reasoning the Trial Chamber dismissed the claim that the Prosecution is obliged to identify persons associated with the JCE.[59]

Trial Chamber II, seized of the trial and judgment of the defendant Kamara, revisited and reconsidered the Kamara Decision in the AFRC Trial Judgment and rejected the JCE pleading.[60] Trial Chamber II reasoned that the pleading did not provide for a time period of the JCE and that the purpose was not criminal in nature, and with respect to JCE III therefore had to be rejected.[61] The substance and reasoning of this decision will be discussed in Section IV, as the specific question of a noncriminal purpose fundamentally concerns the understanding of the JCE doctrine and the jurisdiction of the Court.

C. Discussion

Despite the generous reference to ICTY jurisprudence demanding more specificity, the decisions cited in previous sections ignore such a call for detailed notice. Rather, the Indictments are read in their broadest sense, saving the Prosecution from rephrasing them. The Defense in its motions did request to quash the Indictments, but this would not really have been an appropriate and reasonable remedy. Instead the Prosecution should have been ordered to add more specificity to its charges. This would have benefited everyone, not only the Defense. The trial proceedings demonstrated that the lack of specificity and vagueness of the Indictment slowed down the trial and raised unnecessary objections and legal questions that could have been prevented with more detailed Indictments.

For example, much evidence was not relied on in the AFRC case, as it simply did not relate to locations pleaded in the Indictment. The Trial Chamber stated that it used the evidence for the *chapeau* requirements instead, but given the documentary evidence and witness testimony this would have not been entirely necessary to prove those elements.[62] Furthermore, and as will be evident through the discussion of the trial and appeal judgments, many of the difficulties surrounding the application of JCE originate from the vagueness of the Indictment, as the judges were left with an unclear articulation of the charges when applying them to facts. From the facts established by the Trial Chambers there was no doubt about the criminal activity of the defendants. However, what the Chambers generally

---

[56] Decision and Order on Defense Preliminary Motion for Defects in the Form of the Indictment, *Kondewa* (SCSL-2003–12-PT), Trial Chamber, § 5 (Nov. 27, 2003).

[57] Decision and Order on Defense Preliminary Motion on Defects in the Form of the Indictment, *Brima, Kamara, Kanu* (SCSL-04–16-PT), § 53 (Apr. 1, 2004) [hereinafter Kamara Form of the Indictment Decision].

[58] *Id.* § 53.

[59] *Id.*

[60] Judgment, *Brima, Kamara and Kanu* (SCSL-04–16-T), Trial Chamber, §§ 67, 85 (June 20, 2007) [hereinafter Brima or AFRC Trial Judgment].

[61] *Id.* §§ 74–76 (JCE I), § 71 et seq. (JCE III).

[62] *Id.* § 37.

struggled with was to fit those facts under the vague and contradictory articulations of the Prosecution.

The only explanation for Trial Chamber I's overly broad interpretation is, as acknowledged, a misapprehension of principles concerning the public's right to speedy trial and fair trial rights of the defendants.[63] As noted above, under expeditiousness considerations, this may have been counterproductive.

IV. THE *AFRC* APPEAL JUDGMENT: THE APPROVAL OF A NONCRIMINAL PURPOSE

One of the most controversial questions regarding JCE before the SCSL was whether the common purpose had to be criminal. Even though this was discussed as a pleading question, it is in fact a jurisdictional one that concerns the scope and understanding of JCE.[64] The Appeals Chamber ultimately decided that a noncriminal or innocent purpose was permissible, but it appears that this finding was made only with regards to JCE I. Following a detailed analysis of the AFRC Trial and Appeal Judgments, it will be argued that a noncriminal purpose is impermissible in relation to JCE III, as it violates the core understanding of the mode of liability and fundamental principles of international criminal law.

A. AFRC Trial Judgment

In most comments and discussions on the AFRC Trial Judgment, the dismissal of JCE is being summarized in the following way: JCE was dismissed as the prosecution did not plead a *criminal* purpose constituting a statutory crime.[65] This is not entirely correct and simplifies the reasoning of Trial Chamber II. It is correct that the Trial Chamber notes that the common purpose does not constitute a crime under the SCSL Statute or under the current state of international law, by referring to an Appeals Chamber decision that noted a rebellion is not a crime under international law.[66] Following this significant conclusion, the Trial Chamber engages in a comparison of other Indictments at the ICTY in order to demonstrate that a *criminal* common purpose is the pleading norm,[67] and emphasizes the need of a criminal common purpose with the rationale behind JCE.[68] Thereafter, the Trial Chamber criticizes and holds impermissible the alternative pleading of the basic and extended forms

---

[63] The permissibility of the admissibility of a lower level of specificity was admitted by the SCSL itself, stating that the "fact that the investigations and trials were intended to proceed as expeditiously as possible in an immediate post-conflict environment is particularly relevant," RUF Trial Judgment, *supra* note 8, § 330; RUF Appeal Judgment, *supra* note 8, § 60; *see also* Cecily Rose, *Troubled Indictments at the Special Court for Sierra Leone: The Pleading of Joint Criminal Enterprise and Sex-Based Crimes,* 7 J. INT'L. CRIM. JUST. 353–72, 353–54 (2009).

[64] Opinion of Prof. W. Schabas, Annex A to the Public Urgent Defense Motion Regarding a Fatal Defect in the Prosecution's Second Amended Indictment Relating to the Pleading of JCE, *Taylor* (SCSL-03–01-T-378), § 2 (Dec. 14, 2007).

[65] *See only* N. COMBS, FACT-FINDING WITHOUT FACTS: THE UNCERTAIN EVIDENTIARY FOUNDATIONS OF INTERNATIONAL CRIMINAL CONVICTIONS 328 (2010); K. Gustafson, *Joint Criminal Enterprise, in* THE OXFORD COMPANION TO INTERNATIONAL CRIMINAL JUSTICE 394 (Antonio Cassese ed., 2009).

[66] AFRC Trial Judgment, *supra* note 60, § 67.

[67] *Id.* §§ 68–69.

[68] *Id.* § 70.

of JCE, stating that if "the charged crimes are allegedly within the common purpose, they can logically no longer be a reasonably foreseeable consequence of the same purpose and *vice versa*."[69] It is important to note that the Trial Chamber did not hold that the practice *per se* is impermissible, but rather the alternative pleading that *all* crimes charged were a foreseeable consequence of the JCE. The only reasonable understanding of this holding can be that the Trial Chamber demanded an identification of the *additional* crimes in excess of the common purpose. The pleading in the AFRC case did not identify such excess crimes in the Indictment.[70]

What follows are the most important articulations of the Trial Judgment as to why a noncriminal enterprise is rejected. In an unorthodox approach the Trial Chamber begins by first addressing the extended form.[71] It holds that a noncriminal purpose is particularly troublesome when joined with the concepts of the extended form of JCE, as it blurs the concept between the international humanitarian law principles of *jus ad bellum* and *jus in bello* and therefore rejected the pleading of the extended JCE.[72] This line of argument was not addressed on appeal.

Thereafter, the Trial Chamber addresses the pleading of the basic form of JCE. The Trial Chamber did not merely dismiss the basic form for the reason that it was noncriminal in nature. This is demonstrated by the fact that the Trial Chamber considered evidence adduced at trial in order to assess whether the crimes committed were intended by the participants at the inception of the enterprise. Following this analysis, the Trial Chamber dismissed the "pleading," even though it actually made a finding of fact that no criminal purpose was agreed upon as alleged. This is worth additional reflection: As the participants, according to the factual finding, did not intend any of the crimes at the inception of the JCE, logically all the crimes charged in the Indictment could only have been a foreseeable consequence of such an innocent plan. Given this factual finding, the judgment could have only considered the extended form, which had already been dismissed for the reasons stated previously. An additional purpose that might have subsequently emerged was not pleaded and therefore could not have been considered by the Trial Chamber.[73]

This finding is even more important in light of the Appeals Chamber criticism of the approach of making a factual finding in a section dealing with the form of the Indictment. The Appeals Chamber stated that the question of whether the Prosecution properly pleaded a crime must be determined on whether all the material facts are pleaded in the Indictment, not on whether evidence supported the allegations.[74] This holding, that a premature finding

---

[69] *Id.* § 71 et seq.

[70] *See also* J. Easterday, *Obscuring Joint Criminal Enterprise Liability: The Conviction of Augustine Gbao by the Special Court for Sierra Leone*, 3 Berkeley J. Int'l L. 36, 43 (2009). The Prosecution only specifically identified excess crimes following the AFRC Trial Judgment in June 2007 in the Taylor case and the RUF case. At that time the Taylor case was already at the trial stage and the RUF case was hearing the Defense cases. *See also* Amended Case Summary, *Taylor* (SCSL-03–01–1), §§ 43.1 and 43.2 (Aug. 3, 2007) alleging specific excess crimes only in the alternative; Prosecution Notice concerning Joint Criminal Enterprise and Raising Defects in the Indictment, *Sesay, Kallon, Gbao* (SCSL-04–15-T), §§ 6–8 (Aug. 3, 2007), alleging specific excess crimes only in the alternative.

[71] AFRC Trial Judgment, *supra* note 60, § 72.

[72] *Id.*

[73] On the requirement that any additional JCE that may emerge must be identified in the indictment, see Krajišnik Appeal Judgment, *supra* note 36, § 184.

[74] AFRC Appeal Judgment, *supra* note 5, § 84.

of fact is not permissible, is debatable, as this was done at the judgment stage, considering all the available evidence. Such an approach would have been impermissible if made at the pretrial stage, where an evidentiary assessment is not possible.[75] Within its prerogative as a trier of fact at the judgment stage, the Trial Chamber simply made a factual finding, albeit in a section that typically deals with legal questions. Given the broad nature of the AFRC case this approach appeared sensible, as the dismissal of the JCE at this early juncture of the judgment allowed the judges to substantially narrow the scope of factual findings that it otherwise would have had to make.

The Trial Chamber also considered whether a different common purpose that might have evolved at a later stage was pleaded, but rejected such a possibility.[76] Last, the judges considered whether there was any prejudice to the Prosecution, as the dismissal of the JCE pleading was effectively a reconsideration of previous decisions.[77] The Trial Chamber concluded that the Indictment was defectively pleaded, and therefore did not consider JCE as a mode of criminal responsibility.[78] The conclusion of the Trial Chamber, that the common purpose has to be criminal, is overwhelmingly supported by academic scholarship.[79] The defendants were nevertheless all held responsible for physically committing crimes or planning, instigating, ordering, and aiding and abetting the charged crimes. In addition, as the Trial Chamber found that all three defendants were superiors of an armed group and had effective command authority over perpetrators of crimes; thus the defendants were held responsible for their failure to prevent and punish crimes.

B. AFRC Appeal Judgment

The Appeals Chamber did not agree with the Trial Chamber ruling and regrettably added much confusion. It first deals with general matters, such as that JCE is an accepted mode of attribution under customary international law and, even though not explicitly mentioned in the SCSL Statute, applicable in the SCSL setting.[80] It is important to note that the Appeals Chamber does not mention the different *mens rea* requirements of the basic and extended

---

[75] Decision on Motion to Dismiss Indictment, *Brdanin* (IT-99–36), Trial Chamber, § 15 (Oct. 5, 1999); Decision concerning Preliminary Motion on the Form of the Indictment, *Krajišnik* (IT-00–39 & 40), Trial Chamber, § 8 (Aug. 1, 2000).

[76] AFRC Trial Judgment, *supra* note 60, §§ 77–82.

[77] *Id.* § 84.

[78] *Id.* § 85.

[79] *See only* W. Schabas, The United Nations Criminal Tribunals: The Former Yugoslavia, Rwanda and Sierra Leone 312 (2006); Opinion of Prof. W. Schabas, Annex A to the Public Urgent Defense Motion Regarding a Fatal Defect in the Prosecution's Second Amended Indictment Relating to the Pleading of JCE, *Taylor* (SCSL-03–01-T-378), Dec. 14, 2007, at 7; M. Sassòli, *Taking Armed Groups Seriously: Ways to Improve Their Compliance with International Humanitarian Law*, 1 Int'l Humanitarian Legal Studies 5, 44 (2010); E. Sliedregt, Individual Criminal Responsibility in International Law 144 (2012); V . Haan, Joint Criminal Enterprise: Die Entwicklung einer mittäterschaftlichen Zurechnungsfigur im Völkerstrafrecht 244 (2008); Boas et al., *supra* note 47, at 132, 133; J. R.W.D Jones et al., *The Special Court for Sierra Leone: A Defense Perspective*, 2 J. Int'l Crim. Just. 225 (2004); Gustafson, *supra* note 65, at 394; M. Milanovic, *An Odd Couple, Domestic Crimes and International Responsibility in the Special Tribunal for Lebanon*, 5 J. Int'l Crim. Just. 1139, 1147 (2007); N. Gilbert & T. Blumenstock, *The First Judgement of the Special Court for Sierra Leone: A Missed Opportunity?*, 6 The Law and Practice of International Courts and Tribunals 367 (2007).

[80] AFRC Appeal Judgment, *supra* note 5, § 73.

form of JCE, but only the common *actus reus* requirements. This, in the author's view, demonstrates (and as will be argued in more detail below) that the Appeals Chamber simply did not address the adequacy of the pleading with regards to the extended form. The Appeals Chamber continues with a general reflection that:

> the criminal purpose underlying JCE can derive not only from its ultimate objective, but also from the means *contemplated* to achieve that objective. The objective and means to achieve the objective constitute the common design or plan. (Emphasis added)[81]

The Appeals Chamber then turns to several pleadings at the ICTY in order to demonstrate that its pleading practice allows for a noncriminal enterprise. Specifically the Appeals Chamber refers to the Kvočka Appeal Judgment and the Indictments in the Martić and Haradinaj cases.[82] This analysis was done in order to counter the Trial Chamber's reasoning that the ICTY's pleading practice always included a criminal purpose.[83] The Appeals Chamber then refers to Article 25(3) of the Statute of the International Criminal Court (ICC) stating that this provision does not require that a joint criminal enterprise has a common purpose that "amounts" to a crime within the ICC jurisdiction.[84] On this very point the reasoning of the Appeals Chamber is misguided, as the case law of the ICC, with one precedent available at the time of the AFRC Appeal Judgment, suggests the exact opposite. In the Lubanga, and Katanga and Ngudjolo cases, the systemic and extended form had been rejected by the Pre-Trial Chambers.[85] In addition, it is far from settled whether Article 25(3)(d)(i) of the ICC Statute addresses conduct in which a crime not originally contemplated by a group of persons, but nevertheless foreseeable, is committed.[86]

With that brief analysis (i.e., referring to three cases at the ICTY and the reference to Article 25(3) of the ICC Statute), the Appeals Chamber overturned the Trial Chamber ruling, concluding:

> that the requirement that the common plan, design or purpose of a joint criminal enterprise is inherently criminal means that it must either have as its objective a crime within the Statute, or contemplate crimes within the Statute as the means of achieving its objective.[87]

Based on this holding, the Appeals Chamber continued to determine that the Indictment, read as a whole, provided sufficient notice to the defendants that, even though the common purpose did not amount to a crime, the actions contemplated as a means to achieve

---

[81] *Id.* § 76; *see also* Taylor Appeals Chamber JCE Decision, *supra* note 16, § 15, stating "the 'purpose of the enterprise' comprises both the objective of the JCE and the means contemplated to achieve that objective."
[82] AFRC Appeal Judgment, *supra* note 5, §§ 77, 78.
[83] AFRC Trial Judgment, *supra* note 60, §§ 68, 69.
[84] AFRC Appeal Judgment, *supra* note 5, § 79.
[85] Decision on the Confirmation of Charges, *Lubanga Dyilo* (ICC-01/04–01/06–803-tEN), Pre-Trial Chamber, §§ 326–329 (Jan. 29, 2007) [hereinafter *Lubanga* Confirmation of Charges Decision]; Decision on the Confirmation of Charges, *Katanga and Chui* (ICC-01/04–01/07–717), Pre-Trial Chamber, § 480 *et seq.* (Sept. 30, 2008); *see also* Ambos, *supra* note 12, at 359.
[86] Boas et al., *supra* note 47, at 128; J.D. Ohlin, *Joint Criminal Confusion*, 12 New Crim. L. Rev. 406, 414 (2009), arguing that JCE III would be inconsistent with the ICC Statute's intent requirements, which do not – contrary to JCE III – cover the *dolus eventualis* standard.
[87] AFRC Appeal Judgment, *supra* note 5, § 80. In another decision the Appeals Chamber stated that means contemplated do not have to be pleaded in an indictment; see *Taylor* Appeals Chamber JCE Decision, *supra* note 16, § 25.

that objective were statutory crimes.[88] It stated that the Trial Chamber took an erroneously narrow view reading by one paragraph of the Indictment in isolation.[89] Nevertheless, and despite the correction of the Trial Chamber's finding, the Appeals Chamber "in the interest of justice" did not see any need to make further factual findings regarding the JCE or to remit the case to the Trial Chamber for that purpose.[90]

C. Discussion

The Appeals Chamber has chosen a wording – that is, "contemplate" – which is highly ambiguous. "Contemplate" could simply refer to "involve" or "include." This understanding would not be a departure of the ICTY jurisprudence and the Tadić Appeal Judgment. However, it could also be understood more broadly, as having a possible result in mind,[91] thereby referring to a subjective element within an *actus reus* requirement. Such an interpretation would conflate the notions between the basic and the extended forms of JCE. As a result of the Appeals Chamber articulation it is only necessary to share the intent concerning a lawful conduct and a *contemplation* that as a consequence of this lawful conduct a crime may be committed in furtherance of the objective.[92] In the RUF Appeal Judgment, however, the Appeals Chamber appears to have provided some clarification:

> [T]he criminal nature of a common purpose can derive from the means contemplated to achieve the objective of the common purpose. That was also the basis for the holding of *Brima et al.* that the Trial Chamber relied on, which stated that a common purpose can be inherently criminal where it "contemplate[s] crimes within the Statute as the means of achieving its objective." In such cases, the objective and the means to achieve the objective constitute the common criminal purpose.[93]

The Appeals Chamber therefore is of the view that the criminal means render the entire common purpose criminal, whether criminal or innocent. This is illustrated in the following graph below (Figure 4.1).

In the Milutinović case the ICTY accepted a noncriminal purpose if its implementation is intended through criminal means.[94] The above clarification nevertheless reinforces the interpretation that the Appeals Chamber addressed only the basic and not the extended form of JCE. The reasoning ignores the Trial Chamber's articulation regarding the extended form of JCE and its cautionary remarks concerning blurring the distinction between *jus ad bellum* and *jus in bello*.

Apart from this silence on the extended form, the reasoning of the Appeals Chamber is disconcerting. The Appeals Chamber references to the cases of *Kvočka, Haradinaj*, and

---

[88] AFRC Appeal Judgment, *supra* note 5, §§ 82–84.

[89] *Id.* § 84.

[90] *Id.* § 87.

[91] *See also* Rose, *supra* note 63, at 362.

[92] W. Jordash & P. van Tuyl, *Failure to Carry the Burden of Proof: How Joint Criminal Enterprise Lost Its Way at the Special Court for Sierra Leone*, 8 J. Int'l Crim. Just. 591, 603, 604 (2010).

[93] RUF Appeal Judgment, *supra* note 8, at para. 295.

[94] Judgment, *Milutinović, Šainović and Ojdanić* (IT-05-87-T), Trial Chamber, vol. 3, § 95 (Feb. 26, 2009), finding that "the common purpose of the joint criminal enterprise was to ensure continued control by the FRY and Serbian authorities over Kosovo and that it was to be achieved by criminal means." *See also* Martić Trial Judgment, *supra* note 10, § 442.

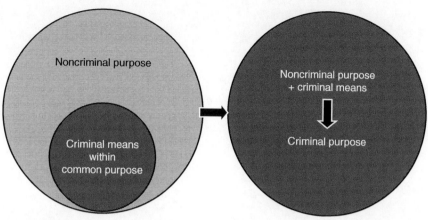

Figure 4.1 Graph 1.

Martić are inaccurate and do not demonstrate that the ICTY has accepted a pleading of a legitimate purpose, in particular with respect to the extended form. First, the Appeals Chamber referred to a version of an indictment in *Haradinaj* that by the time of the AFRC Appeal Judgment had been amended several times.[95] In *Haradinaj* the prosecution alleged that the objective of the JCE was "to consolidate the total control of the KLA over the Dukagjin Operational Zone by the unlawful removal and mistreatment of Serbian civilians and by the mistreatment of Kosovar Albanian and Kosovar Roma/Egyptian civilians, and other civilians, who were, or were perceived to have been, collaborators with the Serbian Forces or otherwise not supporting the KLA."[96] Therefore, the common purpose *involved* the commission of crimes. Moreover, the extended form pleaded in that Indictment, unlike the AFRC Indictment, states that "to the extent that *some* of the crimes charged did not fall within the JCE, they were the natural and foreseeable consequences of the JCE and each Accused was aware that these crimes were the natural and foreseeable consequences of the execution of the JCE." [97] (Emphasis added) A closer look at *Martić* reveals a similar approach.[98] The ICTY pleadings, even where a noncriminal objective is identified, couple the common purpose directly and unequivocally with crimes that are involved within the achievement of the said objective.[99] If an extended form is pleaded, the Indictment indicates that this variant covers *additional* crimes to those originally agreed to. This approach is illustrated in the graph below (Figure 4.2).

Moreover, looking at the wealth of detail and precision of the Haradinaj and Martić Indictments, when compared to the sparseness of the SCSL Indictments, it is rather paradoxical that ICTY Indictments served as an example.

---

[95] The Appeals Chamber in n.136 referred to an indictment in the Haradinaj case dated April 26, 2006. This indictment was amended by Decision on Motion to Amend the Indictment and on Challenges to the Form of the Amended Indictment, *Haradinaj, Balaj, Brahimaj* (IT-04–84-PT) (Oct. 25, 2006).

[96] Revised Second Amended Indictment, *Haradinaj, Balaj, Brahimaj* (IT-04–84-PT), § 26 (Nov. 10, 2006) [hereinafter *Haradinaj* Indictment], confirmed by Decision on Motion to Amend the Amended Indictment, *Haradinaj, Balaj, Brahimaj* (IT-04–84-PT) (Jan. 12, 2007).

[97] *Id.* § 25.

[98] Amended Indictment, *Martić* (IT-95–11), Dec. 9, 2005, § 4.

[99] Rose, *supra* note 63, at 360–61.

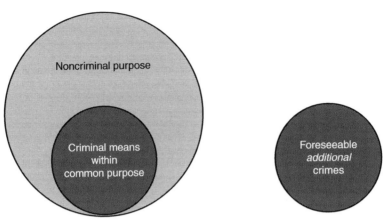

Figure 4.2 Graph 2.

With respect to the pleading requirements of the basic form of JCE, the jurisprudence is clear that the common plan must itself be criminal or at least *involve* crimes, as the shared intent of the participants of the common plan must agree and share the intent to commit crimes.[100] In relation to the pleading of the basic form in the AFRC Indictment it can be reasonably argued that the criminal means to achieve the common purpose render the purpose itself criminal, as illustrated in Figure 4.1 above. This is a sensible interpretation that would not involve any mind twisting. However, the same reasoning and reading of the Indictment cannot be applied to the extended form of JCE, as it cannot be argued that the means (i.e., killing, sexual violence, mutilations, enslavement, recruitment of children, pillage) were part of the agreement between the JCE participants. Rather, these "means" would only be foreseeable from the common purpose. The SCSL Indictments do not, however, specify a *criminal* purpose and do not state which *additional* crimes were foreseeable.[101] This feature of the JCE is visualized in the following graph below (Figure 4.3).

Given the lacking overlap between the innocent purpose and the foreseeable crimes it is difficult to argue, as demonstrated in the first graph, that the entire purpose is rendered criminal. Therefore, the SCSL Appeals Chamber has widened the scope of the extended form to a criminalization of "neutral conduct" if it may be "contemplated" that such neutral acts result in statutory crimes.

Even though the Lubanga Confirmation of Charges Decision has accepted that Article 25(3)(a) of the ICC Statute, which defines joint criminality of co-perpetrators, does not necessarily require a "criminal plan," this conclusion is not applicable to JCE liability for the following reasons. According to the Pre-Trial Chamber the common plan "must include an element of criminality, although it does not need to be specifically directed at the commission of the crime."[102] The Pre-Trial Chamber specified that "[it] suffices: (1) that the co-perpetrators have agreed (a) to start the implementation of the common plan to achieve *a non-criminal goal*, and (b) to only commit the crime if certain conditions are met, or (2) that

---

[100] Boas et al., *supra* note 47, at 132.
[101] The Prosecution only distinguished such excess crimes in the Case Summary of the Taylor case and in a notice in the RUF case that was filed well after the Prosecution case; *see* note 70 *supra*.
[102] Lubanga Confirmation of Charges Decision, *supra* note 85, § 344.

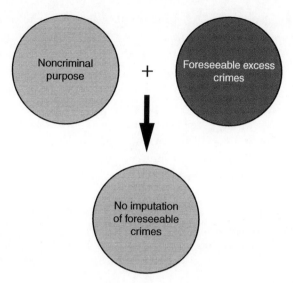

Figure 4.3 Graph 3.

the co-perpetrator are aware (a) of the risk that implementing the common plan (which is specifically directed at the achievement of *a non-criminal goal*) will result in the commission of the crime and (b) accept such an outcome."[103] Even though the ICC accepts a noncriminal plan with regard to vicarious liability, the following factor has to be taken into account. The ICC model of co-perpetration according to Article 25(3)(a) ICC Statute has a stricter *mens rea* standard than JCE liability. In particular the *dolus eventualis* standard does not apply to Article 30 of the ICC Statute, which defines the *mens rea* standard.[104] This is an important consideration, as a co-perpetrator of a noncriminal plan at the least has to be aware that an undesired consequence of the noncriminal plan will occur in the ordinary course of events. A co-perpetrator must therefore have the awareness that his acts or omission *will* cause an undesired consequence that is not covered by the noncriminal plan. JCE III liability, how-ever, accepts a *dolus eventualis* standard, and it is sufficient that the perpetrator willingly accepts a risk that crimes *might* occur.[105] The *dolus eventualis* of JCE III is often conflated with recklessness or even negligence. However, not demanding a criminal purpose effec-tively dilutes the *mens rea* standard of JCE III to such a lower negligence standard. Such a standard, coupled with a noncriminal objective, is in particular troublesome when applied in situations of armed conflict, where crimes may be an inevitable consequence. As will be discussed below, any hostilities – whether legitimate or not – may therefore be criminalized if they result in unintended crimes.

---

[103] *Id.*

[104] Decision Pursuant to Article 61(7)(a) and (b) of the Rome Statute on the Charges of the Prosecutor Against Jean-Pierre Bemba Gombo, *Bemba* (ICC-01/05-01/08-424), Pre-Trial Chamber, §§ 360–369 (June 15, 2009); for comments see K. Ambos, *Critical Issues in the Bemba Confirmation Decision*, 22 Leiden J. Int'l L. 715–18 (2009); *see also* Judgment Pursuant to Article 74 of the Statute, *Lubanga Dyilo* (ICC-01/04-01/06-2842), Trial Chamber, § 1011 (Mar. 14, 2012).

[105] Kvočka Appeal Judgment, *supra* note 10, § 86; Brđanin Appeal Judgment, *supra* note 9, § 411; *see also* RUF Appeal Judgment, *supra* note 8, § 475.

Moreover, the extended form of JCE has come under close scrutiny, and it is argued in academic opinions and jurisprudence that it is not a form of attribution under customary international law.[106] Others do not go that far, but prefer to place certain limitations on this mode of liability.[107] With the exception of the Extraordinary Chambers in the Courts of Cambodia,[108] international tribunals continue to apply this mode of liability.[109] Given the substantive and serious opposition of courts and academics a more reasoned judgment by the Appeals Chamber would have been necessary, in particular when broadening such a controversial doctrine. It appears that the Appeals Chamber, without any justification or reasoning, created a new mode of attribution, akin to organizational responsibility. As will be discussed below, this notion became apparent in the controversial conviction of the defendant Gbao in the RUF case.[110]

The question arises whether the articulation of such a broad understanding of JCE finds support in customary international law. According to the principle of legality, a defendant of a crime may be convicted only if the conduct was in violation of customary international law at the time of its commission.[111] This question will be addressed below, looking at four different considerations.

First, the question arises whether the extended form of JCE as identified in *Tadić* was ever meant to cover an innocent purpose that was not intended, but resulted in criminal conduct that was a natural and foreseeable consequence. A perusal of the case law up to the issuance of the SCSL Indictments and judgments supports the view that the extended form is applicable only to cases where members of a common plan agree to commit certain *criminal* acts and that as a result of this conduct *additional* natural and foreseeable crimes were committed in excess of the original agreement.[112] The ICTY Indictments referred to by the Appeals Chamber demonstrate that the extended form of JCE charged refers to crimes in excess and outside the original agreed purpose.[113] This was not the case in the AFRC Indictment. Here the pleading could only be understood to mean that the crimes referred to were *all* in excess of the noncriminal purpose and a reasonable foreseeable consequence thereof.[114] Moreover,

---

[106] *See supra* notes 12 and 13.

[107] A. Cassese, International Criminal Law 205 (2008); A. Cassese, *The Proper Limits of Individual Responsibility under the Doctrine of Joint Criminal Enterprise*, 5 J. Int'l Crim. Just. 109, 121 (2007). *See also* Interlocutory Decision on the Applicable Law: Terrorism, Conspiracy, Homicide, Perpetration, Cumulative Charging (STL-11-01/I/AC/R176bis), § 248 (Feb. 16, 2011).

[108] Decision on the Application of Joint Criminal Enterprise, *Nuon, Ieng, Samphan, Ieng* (002/19-09-2007/ ECCC/TC), Trial Chamber (Sept. 12, 2011).

[109] So far there have been only four final convictions based on the extended form of JCE; see Tadić Appeal Judgment, *supra* note 2, §§ 230–234; Prosecutor v. Krstić, Appeal Judgment, IT-98-33-A, §§ 147–151 (Apr. 19, 2004); Prosecutor v. Stakić, Appeal Judgment, IT-97-24-A, §§ 91–98 (Mar. 22, 2006); Martić Appeal Judgment, *supra* note 10, §§ 187, 195, 205–06, 210. The conviction of Karemera based on the extended form of JCE at the ICTR is on appeal.

[110] *Infra* Section V.B.

[111] RUF Trial Judgment, *supra* note 8, § 48; Blaskić Appeal Judgment, *supra* note 31, §§ 140–141.

[112] *See only* Tadić Appeal Judgment, *supra* note 2, § 228; this is even acknowledged by the SCSL Appeals Chamber in the RUF Appeal Judgment, *supra* note 8, § 475, stating that "before an accused person can incur JCE 3 liability, he must be shown to have possessed 'the *intention* to participate in and further the criminal activity of the criminal purpose of a group.'" (emphasis original).

[113] *See* Haradinaj Indictment, *supra* note 96, § 25, stating that, "to the extent that some of the crimes charged did not fall within the JCE, they were a natural and foreseeable consequence of the JCE."

[114] Boas et al., *supra* note 47, at 133.

extending JCE III liability to crimes resulting from noncriminal conduct does not find any support in the World War II cases cited in *Tadić* to prove that JCE III was an established mode of attribution in international law. Even if it is accepted that these cases serve as precedent for the extended form of JCE,[115] all deal with a common plan among the participants that involved *criminal* conduct. Neither the Essen Lynching nor the Borkum Island cases deal with noncriminal conduct contemplating crimes.[116] These cases rather deal with mob justice and the question whether excess crimes can be attributed to all the participants of the mob violence.

Second, and turning to one of the main points of the AFRC Trial Judgment, it also appears that an acceptance of such a broad notion of joint criminal enterprise would violate fundamental notions and principles of international humanitarian law. The Trial Chamber argued that the acceptance of an innocent purpose convolutes the distinction between *jus in bello* and *jus ad bellum*.[117] The Appeals Chamber unfortunately remained silent with respect to this line of reasoning. International humanitarian law disregards the causes and motivations for violent acts and focuses on the protections of civilians and other persons, regardless of the party to which they belong. To ensure such a protection, the laws of war must remain independent from the laws on the use of force. Similar opinions have been expressed by John R. W. D. Jones[118]; Karim Khan, in his capacity as defense lawyer for Charles Taylor[119]; and Marco Sassòli.[120] Sassòli is of the view that the mere fact of participating in an armed conflict should not suffice as a criminal enterprise giving rise to criminal responsibility for international humanitarian law.[121] These words of caution became apparent when looking at the RUF Trial Judgment where the Trial Chamber considered that noncriminal conduct furthered the noncriminal purpose, and took into account actions that are permissible under international humanitarian law, such as the overall planning of a military operation or setting of ambushes against belligerent forces.[122] Sassòli rightly warns that such an expansion of the concept of individual criminal responsibility bears inherent risks that this notion could potentially lead to all combatants of an armed force or group being held accountable

---

[115] Decision on the Application of Joint Criminal Enterprise, *Nuon, Ieng, Samphan, Ieng* (002/19–09–2007/ECCC/TC), § 31 (Sept. 12, 2011), holding that the inference drawn by the *Tadić* Appeal Judgment that the conviction in those cases was based on the extended form of JCE was not the only possible conclusion.

[116] Review Judgment, United States v. Haesiker, 12–489–1 (Oct. 16, 1947) (Borkum Island Case); British Military Court of the Trial of War Criminals, Trial of Erich Heyer and Six Others, Dec. 18–19 and 21–22, 1945, UNWCC vol. 1 (1949) (Essen Lynching Case).

[117] AFRC Trial Judgment, *supra* note 60, § 72.

[118] *See* Jones et al., *supra* note 79, at 225.

[119] Taylor Defense Pre-Trial Brief, *Taylor* (SCSL-2003–01-PT), § 53 (Apr. 26, 2006), stating that the Prosecutor's additional contention that "A common plan to control a country by any means necessary, including criminal means, in order to exploit the natural resources of that country may be considered to *amount* to the commission of crimes within the jurisdiction of the court[,]" is also mistaken in law. First, the common plan is one element. Second, the intent of the common plan must be criminal, and not merely the implementation. Having access to the oil in the Middle East is not a criminal purpose in itself, and thus controlling resources in another country by noncriminal means does not constitute the requisite criminal intent, unless the plan was to control such resources unlawfully. Thus, if the common plan alleged by the Prosecutor is not criminal in its inception, and it is not alleged that the plan was amended to become a criminal one, the foundation element for JCE is not met. (Footnotes omitted).

[120] Sassòli, *supra* note 79, at 44.

[121] *Id.*

[122] RUF Trial Judgment, *supra* note 8, §§ 2083, 2094.

as soon as it is foreseeable that crimes are being committed, which according to him is often the case.[123] The SCSL's expansion of JCE therefore becomes guilt by association and criminalizes the waging of war in non-international armed conflict.

Third, the pleading of a noncriminal purpose poses additional concerns regarding fundamental principles of criminal law, such as the *nullum crimen sine lege* and *lex stricta* principles. As an innocent or neutral purpose may result in the foreseeable commission of international crimes the question arises whether an ex post facto view on such events may arbitrarily criminalize conduct that may be open to misuse. Haan is of the opinion that the limits of JCE are reached where the common purpose does not involve or amount to an international crime as it would be impossible for the participant in the common purpose to anticipate the criminal results of such participation.[124] In her view, this would also be the case in a pursuit of an "establishment of an independent State with criminal means."[125]

Last, not requiring a criminal purpose violates the *principle of culpability*. This principle requires the defendant's knowledge of the circumstances of the crime. It has been recognized by the ad hoc tribunals and in particular the *Tadić* Appeal Judgment stating that "nobody may be held criminally responsible for acts or transactions in which he has not personally engaged or in some other way participated (*nulla poena sine culpa*)."[126] If a participant to a neutral act under international law is held accountable for the mere *contemplation* of a crime, without requiring actual knowledge or awareness, such an attribution of responsibility would violate the principles of culpability. Sliedregt states that "JCE enables the attribution of liability for crimes committed by another person because of a common criminal purpose; the common criminal objective is the basis of the attribution of liability."[127] She therefore equally concludes that the Appeals Chamber decision violates the culpability principle.

Therefore and in conclusion, the SCSL Appeals Chamber, by accepting a noncriminal purpose, expanded the notions of JCE beyond its original construction and without any legal precedent or basis in customary international law.[128] Not demanding a *criminal* purpose is contrary to the very rationale of JCE.[129]

V. THE RUF JUDGMENTS: THE JUDICIAL MELTDOWN OF JCE DOCTRINE

The RUF case was the first judgment that convicted defendants on the basis of JCE liability before the SCSL. Two main aspects of the Judgment will be considered below. First, which conduct was considered to make a significant contribution furthering the common purpose? Second, the conviction of the defendant Gbao and the reasoning of the Trial and

---

[123] Sassòli, *supra* note 79, at 44.
[124] HAAN, *supra* note 79, at 244.
[125] *Id.* at 243.
[126] Tadić Appeal Judgment, *supra* note 2, § 186; Martić Appeal Judgment, *supra* note 10, § 82.
[127] SLIEDREGT, *supra* note 79, at 144.
[128] *Id.*
[129] SCHABAS, *supra* note 79, at 311, stating that "obviously [there can] be no criminal liability imposed upon an individual for the acts of members of a group with which he or she is associated if the purpose itself is innocent"; SLIEDREGT, *supra* note 79, at 144; *see also* Jones et al., *supra* note 79, at 225; AFRC Trial Judgment, *supra* note 60, § 70.

Appeals Chamber will be scrutinized. Those aspects of the Judgment will be considered in turn.

A. Noncriminal Purpose and Conduct Misapplied

The dangers of the Appeals Chamber decision to accept a noncriminal purpose were revealed in the RUF Judgment. The RUF Trial Chamber noted with respect to the noncriminal purpose pleading in the RUF Indictment

> that such an objective in and of itself is not criminal and therefore does not amount to a common purpose within the meaning of the law of joint criminal enterprise .... However, where the taking of power and control over State territory is intended to be implemented through the commission of crimes within the Statute, this may amount to a common criminal purpose.[130]

This holding complied with the AFRC Appeal Judgment, but when applied, it exposed rather odd attributions of criminal responsibility. For example the Trial Chamber considered noncriminal conduct permissible under international humanitarian law doctrine such as the overall planning of a military operation, setting of ambushes against belligerent forces, maintaining order with the fighting forces, and organizing foodstuff, in order to find that the defendants significantly contributed and furthered the common purpose.[131]

As mentioned above, this highlights the dangers of accepting a noncriminal purpose within the JCE doctrine as it, coupled with a noncriminal contribution, criminalizes conduct that in of itself is innocent under international law. An expansion of criminal responsibility bears the inherent risks that combatants of an armed group will be held accountable as soon as it is foreseeable that crimes are being committed.[132] The reality of that danger culminated in the conviction of Gbao, as will be explained below. The fundamental distinction between *jus ad bellum* and *jus in bello* must be respected by international criminal law doctrine. Moreover a lacunae is not created as a more precise attribution of crimes would be the knowledge standard of aiding and abetting. A limitation of the JCE liability by excluding the *dolus eventualis* standard from application to cases of noncriminal purposes could have been a reasonable alternative to limit an overly broad and impermissible construction of JCE.

B. The Case of Gbao: Joint Criminal Confusion

The second issue to be mentioned is the misapplication of the JCE doctrine that resulted in the conviction of the defendant Gbao. The Trial Chamber by majority, Justice Boutet dissenting, found that, even though Gbao did not share the intent to commit the crimes charged in all but one district,[133] he contributed to the furtherance of the JCE in his role as ideology trainer for the RUF. The majority concluded that this was a significant contribution to the JCE, because the leadership of the RUF relied on the RUF ideology to ensure and

---

[130] RUF Trial Judgment, *supra* note 8, § 1979.

[131] *Id.* §§ 2083, 2094, 2039.

[132] Sassòli, *supra* note 79, at 44.

[133] RUF Trial Judgment, *supra* note 8, § 2040.

to enforce the discipline and obedience of its forces to the RUF hierarchy and its orders.[134] The majority held that holding a revolutionary idea or an ideology to change a system does not per se amount to or constitute a crime.[135] However, where there is a "criminal nexus" between such an ideology and the crimes, the perpetrators of those crimes should be held criminally accountable under JCE.[136] The Trial Chamber was satisfied that the evidence allowed the "inference" that the ideology of the RUF significantly contributed to the commission of the crimes.[137] A different standard is being introduced here, as the Trial Chamber majority appears to hold that a "criminal nexus," rather than foreseeability or assuming the risk, is the appropriate standard. This could be understood as a requirement of causality, but the majority understanding in that regard remains unclear. It appears that the majority judges refer to an out-of-context pronouncement in *Tadić*, which held that although the defendant's involvement in the criminal acts must form a link in the chain of causation, it is not necessary that this participation be a sine qua non of the form of responsibility.[138] It is remarkable, however, that the Trial Chamber did not see a need to establish a nexus between the persons "indoctrinated" and the actual perpetrator of the crimes. What is further puzzling is that apart from the fact that Gbao was an ideology instructor in 1995 (i.e., before the SCSL's jurisdiction),[139] the judges did not attempt to make any factual findings that Gbao in fact taught the ideology as articulated in the ideology books tendered at trial, thereby even to their own standard failing to establish a "criminal nexus."[140] Therefore it appears that Gbao's conduct was one of upholding and assisting a system rather than directly furthering the means and objective of the common purpose. This would however move Gbao's responsibility near the systemic form or JCE II, rather than responsibility according to JCE I or III as pleaded in the Indictment.

In addition to the ideology, the majority of the Trial Chamber was satisfied that Gbao's role in maintaining order in the fighting force as RUF Internal Defense Unit commander and his assistance in producing foodstuff for the fighters significantly contributed to the *strength and cohesiveness* of the RUF fighting force.[141] This finding is worth additional reflection, as the Trial Chamber appears to have abandoned the need of the requirement that the significant contribution has to "further the common purpose," but here reveals its true reasoning and understanding that contributing to the *strength and cohesiveness* of a fighting force is sufficient. Given this finding, one has to consider the following three factors: First, the pronouncement of the majority that:

> [i]t indeed goes without saying [...] that resorting to arms to secure a total redemption and using them to topple a government which the RUF characterized as corrupt necessarily

---

[134] *Id.* § 2014.

[135] *Id.* § 2013.

[136] RUF Trial Judgment, *supra* note 8, §§ 2013, 2014; *but see* RUF Appeal Judgment, *supra* note 8, § 182, where the Appeals Chamber overturns the Trial Chamber and disallowed the finding of Gbao's significant contribution to the JCE through his role as an ideology expert and instructor for the reasons that this allegation was not contained in the indictment.

[137] RUF Trial Judgment, *supra* note 8, § 2032.

[138] *Tadić* Appeal Judgment, *supra* note 2, § 199.

[139] *See* Dissenting Opinion of Justice Boutet, RUF Trial Judgment, *supra* note 8, § 5.

[140] *Id.*

[141] RUF Trial Judgment, *supra* note 8, § 2039.

implies the resolve and determination to shed blood and commit the crimes for which the Accused are indicted.[142]

Second, that the common purpose pleaded was noncriminal in nature. And third, that it failed to find the shared intent for nearly all the crimes. Hence Gbao did not share the intent that criminal means were to be employed to achieve the common purpose. Therefore, logically, a conviction could have, if at all, only been based on JCE III. Given these three considerations the majority squarely found Gbao guilty for his membership within the RUF.

This error was not corrected by the Appeals Chamber. To the contrary, even though it rejected the conviction of Gbao based on his contribution as an ideology teacher,[143] it nevertheless upheld his conviction without providing reasons how he contributed to the crimes that were within the JCE.[144] That his conviction is based on guilt by association is simply demonstrated by the following articulation of the Appeals Chamber:

> … Gbao "shared the intent for the crimes to be committed in Kailahun District, so he was a participant in the joint criminal enterprise." Gbao it must be recalled was at all material times the *senior RUF Commander* stationed in Kailahun. It follows that, *since Gbao was a member of the JCE,* so long as it was reasonably foreseeable that some of the members of the JCE or persons under their control would commit crimes, Gbao would be criminally liable for the commission of those crimes. As the Trial Chamber found that the crimes in Bo, Kenema and Kono Districts, which were within the Common Criminal Purpose, were reasonably foreseeable, it follows that the Trial Chamber did not err.[145] (Emphasis added)

The obvious conflation of JCE I and JCE III has to be highlighted. Crimes in three districts of Sierra Leone were "within" the common purpose (i.e., means to achieve the purpose), and in addition foreseeable. This appears to be judicial nonsense. It appears the Appeals Chamber misunderstood the exclusionary relationship of the basic and extended form of JCE. The fears expressed by Judge Schomburg that "the third category of JCE has all the potential of leading to a system, which would impute guilt solely by association" came to realization in the RUF Appeal Judgment.[146]

Judge Fisher, in her dissenting opinion, was more critical of the acceptance of accountability through the participation in a noncriminal objective, pursued by means that the defendant Gbao did not intend. In her view the majority collapsed the distinction between the basic and extended forms of JCE. She holds:

> In affirming Gbao's convictions under JCE, the Majority adopts the Trial Chamber's circular reasoning, but compounds the Trial Chamber's error by collapsing the distinction between JCE 1 and JCE 3. The Majority reasons that it was sufficient for the Trial Chamber to conclude that Gbao was a "participant" in the JCE and therefore shared the Common Criminal Purpose. By virtue of that conclusion, the Majority reasons, he is responsible for all crimes by members of the JCE that either he intended or were reasonably foreseeable. Therefore, according to the Majority's reasoning, it matters not whether Gbao intended the

---

[142] *Id.* § 2016.

[143] RUF Appeal Judgment, *supra* note 8, § 182.

[144] RUF Appeal Judgment, *supra* note 8, § 493.

[145] *Id.* § 493.

[146] Separate Opinion of Judge Schomburg on the Individual Criminal Responsibility of Milan Martić, Martić Appeal Judgment, *supra* note 10, § 7.

crimes in Bo, Kenema and Kono; given that he was "a member of the JCE," he was liable for the commission of "the crimes in Bo, Kenema and Kono Districts, which were within the Common Criminal Purpose," so long as it was "reasonably foreseeable that some of the members of the JCE or persons under their control would commit crimes."[147]

Consequently, in Judge Fisher's opinion, Gbao was convicted of crimes which he did not intend, to which he did not significantly contribute, and which were not a reasonably foreseeable consequence of the crimes he did intend.[148] It is worthy of note that Justice Fisher limits her opinion to the "foreseeable consequences of *crimes* he did intend." This is surprising, given the pleading of a noncriminal objective. But as an *argumentum a contrario* one would need to state that if the crimes that were committed by others were not a foreseeable consequence from those he intended, then logically they could have not been foreseeable from the noncriminal purpose that he engaged in.

The error breed in the AFRC Appeal Judgment by accepting a noncriminal purpose was inconsequential to the Accused in that case, but reached its judicial meltdown in the subsequent judgment and conviction of Gbao. His conviction exposes the dangers of a JCE doctrine that does not demand a clearly identified *criminal* purpose. Serendipitously, the RUF Appeals Judgment cannot serve as a precedent on this questionable articulation as there was no majority reasoning on JCE with respect to the conviction of Gbao. The majority judges – Kamanda, King, and Ayoola – came to the same conclusion, but Ayoola appended a separate opinion that offered a different rationale for arriving at a conviction of Gbao.[149] According to the principle of plurality opinion, the RUF Appeal Judgment therefore may not serve as a precedent.

VI. CONCLUDING REMARKS

Did the SCSL jurisprudence contribute to international criminal law through its use and application of the JCE doctrine? The analysis above demonstrates that it did not or, if at all, it added a high degree of confusion. First, the SCSL has not contributed to the doctrine with regards to the pleading requirements for JCE. The articulations of the pleading requirements as such are unremarkable as they recite the case law of the ICTY. What is remarkable, however, is the reasoning of the SCSL: defending the scarcity of the information provided, thereby misapplying the case law of the sister tribunal to a detrimental effect of fair trial rights. A correction of the pleading at the early pretrial stage would have saved much confusion and controversy regarding the application of the JCE doctrine to the facts and charges. Furthermore, voices demanding a cautious and narrow approach of the JCE doctrine were ignored in Freetown. By accepting a noncriminal purpose, the SCSL expanded the notions of JCE beyond its original construction. This expansion has no basis in customary international law and violates fundamental principles and the very rationale of JCE.

---

[147] Partially dissenting and concurring opinion of Justice Shireen Avis Fisher, RUF Appeal Judgment, *supra* note 8, § 17.

[148] *Id.* § 45.

[149] Separate Opinion of Justice Emmanuel Ayoola in Respect of Gbao's Sub-Ground 8(j) and 8(k), *RUF* Appeal Judgment, *supra* note 8, § 57.

These shortfalls were of no major consequence up to the RUF Trial Judgment, as until that point no defendant had been convicted on the basis of JCE liability. This however changed with the conviction of Gbao. His conviction portrays and signifies all the dangers of JCE III when coupled with a poor pleading and the acceptance of a noncriminal purpose. All calls for a more cautious approach toward JCE were ignored by the SCSL, which through its jurisprudence expanded the scope of JCE, in fact creating a new, unfounded form of JCE. The Appeals Chamber dangerously widened the scope of JCE, allowing a conviction of a defendant who did not intend and did not significantly contribute to the crimes and to whom the additional crimes were not a reasonably foreseeable consequence. This is a notion that goes beyond any fears of JCE antagonists. It can be accurately described as the judicial meltdown of all the fears expressed about JCE. The *RUF* Appeal Judgment and Gbao's conviction is of particular concern, not only to the defendant, but to the international justice system as a whole. The strength of international justice derives from its credibility and adherence to fundamental principles of international criminal law. Sound and reasonable decisions are the bedrock for such credibility. The conviction of Gbao undermines the credibility and trust in international justice.

5

How the Approach to JCE in *Taylor* and the RUF Case Undermined the Demands of Justice at the Special Court for Sierra Leone

Wayne Jordash[*] and Scott Martin[**]

I. INTRODUCTION

The mandate of the Special Court for Sierra Leone (SCSL) was from conception premised upon the completion of fair trials in accordance with international standards of justice. As recognized on August 14, 2000, with the adoption by the United Nations (UN) Security Council of Resolution 1315 as a step toward the creation of the Special Court, it was critical to the process of national reconciliation and the maintenance of peace in Sierra Leone that the SCSL be a "strong and credible court" operating in accordance with "international standards of justice, fairness and due process of law."[1] Having commenced its trials in 2004 the SCSL could draw upon ten years of international criminal jurisprudence from its sister tribunals, the International Criminal Tribunal for the former Yugoslavia (ICTY), and the International Criminal Tribunal for Rwanda (ICTR). Presumably it was this jurisprudence, alongside that reflecting human rights principles as understood in national jurisdictions, which the UN Security Council and the drafters of the Court's founding instruments had in mind as defining international standards, reflecting an expectation that the trials would produce just verdicts, where justice was done and seen to be done.

This chapter assesses the fulfillment of this mandate by examining the application of JCE in the trials of Charles Taylor and the ex-members of the Revolutionary United Front (RUF). It focuses on two principal issues: (1) the approach taken by the Trial and Appeals Chamber to Joint Criminal Enterprise (JCE), in particular in assessing the evidential links between the RUF Accused and the crimes pursuant to the mode of liability; and (2) the approach taken by Trial Chamber II to JCE in the Taylor trial. The authors, previous Defense counsel for the first and third Accused (Issa Hassan Sesay and Augustine Gbao), conclude that the judicial approach to these issues in the RUF trial abandoned the safeguards contained in the jurisprudence developed at the ICTY and ICTR, giving rise to a trial that failed to adhere to international standards of justice, fairness, and due process, leading to manifestly unjust

---

[*] Wayne Jordash specializes in international and humanitarian law, international criminal and human rights law and related transitional justice issues. He has represented individuals in the U.K., at the International Criminal Tribunal for the former Yugoslavia (ICTY), the International Criminal Tribunal for Rwanda (ICTR) and the Special Court for Sierra Leone (SCSL).

[**] Scott Martin was co-counsel for Mr. Augustine Gbao in the case *Prosecutor v. Sesay* et al. at the SCSL. He is currently co-counsel in *Prosecutor v. Stanišić & Simatović* at the ICTY and *Prosecutor v. Ndindiliyimana* et al. at the ICTR.

[1] U.N. S.C. Res. 1315, U.N. Doc. S/RES/1315 (Aug. 14, 2000).

convictions. Despite, at the Judgment stage, declining to assess Taylor's guilt through the JCE mode of liability, the approach taken by the Taylor Trial Chamber to JCE through the proceedings undermined the fairness of the trial through a disregard of the notice requirements that ensure an accused is promptly and in detail informed of the nature and cause of the charges. That is not to assert that the errors made in the Taylor case are comparable with the egregious flaws and results in the RUF case, but, by the approach taken to the JCE pleading in the Indictment and the subsequent failure to clarify for the Accused the nature of the JCE case, there can be little doubt that the Taylor Defense was hamstrung from the outset.

The challenge of trying Taylor and the ex-RUF members alleged to bear the "greatest responsibility"[2] (which jurisdiction Jalloh discusses in Chapter 30) for crimes committed during the civil war in Sierra Leone ought not to be underestimated, as the rebellion was long; crimes were widespread and took place in areas with limited contact to the rest of the country, much less the world. Conducting an eleven-year campaign from 1991 to 2002 to overthrow a succession of governments, the RUF had deservedly attracted the reputation as a brutal organization preoccupied with committing horrendous crimes against civilians, ranging from senseless murder, sexual violence, and disfiguring physical violence to mass enslavement and the use of child soldiers. Its membership was widely despised and vilified in the national and international media, and the perception was that, as a consequence of what was known about the RUF as an organization, the high-ranking commanders must bear the greatest responsibility for these crimes. Therefore, the trial of these crimes and individuals in this war-torn and underdeveloped country or, in the case of Taylor, thousands of kilometers away in the spotlight of The Hague, so soon after the end of the conflict, presented the most significant logistical and legal challenges for an international or hybrid court.

However, if trials were to be convened against those individuals alleged to be most responsible, it was critical that the SCSL honor its obligation to provide fair trials for all Accused. Unfortunately, an examination of the way in which JCE was interpreted and used in the RUF and Taylor trial and the issues that will be examined in this chapter shows that both the Trial and Appeal Chambers abandoned international standards of due process – thus undermining the Accuseds' right to a fair trial, at least in the RUF case – in pursuit of broader criminal justice policy objectives.

The first section of this chapter will discuss Trial Chamber I's approach to the right to be informed of the nature and cause of the charges and will examine the principal decisions that deprived the RUF Accused of proper notice of a majority of the charges and the evidence in support. The authors conclude that the approach abandoned the cornerstone principles contained within the ICTY and ICTR jurisprudence, effectively removing the fundamental right and depriving the Accused of the opportunity to mount an effective defense.

The second section will discuss the RUF Trial and Appeal Chamber's approach to the evidential links necessary to convict pursuant to the JCE mode of liability that largely removed the Prosecution's obligation to prove a link between the Accused and the crimes as a basis

---

[2] Statute of the Special Court for Sierra Leone, annexed to the Agreement between the United Nations and the Government of Sierra Leone on the Establishment of a Special Court for Sierra Leone, United Nations and Sierra Leone, art. I., Jan. 16, 2002 [hereinafter SCSL Statute].

for the imputation of criminal liability. Although the discussion will (inevitably) critique the SCSL's approach to the Prosecution's pleading of a JCE without an unambiguously criminal objective, the discussion will focus on the trial and appellate approach to assessing the criminal responsibility of the JCE members for crimes committed by non-JCE members. In many instances the Chambers found the Accused responsible for crimes without requiring the establishment of a link showing that the non-JCE members were "used" to commit the crimes by JCE members in pursuit of their shared common purpose.

The third section will discuss the Trial Chamber's approach to JCE in the Taylor case. Despite making the requisite factual findings that amply justified convicting Taylor on all counts pursuant to the SCSL's interpretation of JCE, the Trial Chamber declined to take that route, instead finding responsibility mainly through aiding and abetting, a secondary mode of participation. However, this abandonment of JCE did not take place until the judgment stage. Instead, the trial was allowed to proceed on the basis of the most expansive internationally based JCE allegation known to international criminal law without the required clarification of its essential elements, effectively misleading the Accused into the futility of wasting valuable forensic resources to contest a nebulous liability that ought to have been abandoned at the outset or soon thereafter. The SCSL's approach to Taylor's right to be informed of the charges was remarkably lax by international standards, leading to a trial conducted through the prism of the vaguest of JCE allegations, lacking clarity and certainty that are the very cornerstone of a fair criminal trial.

The authors conclude that the RUF trial process as a result of the approach taken to these critical procedural and evidential safeguards undermined or in many instances removed any reasonable opportunity to effectively contest the majority of the charges, resulting in convictions that violated the culpability principle, the principle of legality, and the fair trial rights of the Accused. Although the effects of the errors arising in the Taylor case were much less egregious, nonetheless, the Chamber's failure to insist on a clear and detailed indictment, alleging a precisely defined JCE, undermined the fairness of the trial. Putting aside the fundamental errors made by the Appeal Chamber in the RUF case, its novel interpretation of JCE, and its inevitable taint of any JCE conviction in the Taylor case, after the thousands of pages of evidence had cascaded through the courtroom without any obvious place in the JCE pleading for it to cleave, the Taylor Trial Chamber was left with an adequate understanding of the JCE pleading and how to use the liability to process the evidence. Had the pleading of the JCE been properly resolved at an early stage of the proceeding, leading to its inevitable dismissal, this might have been avoided for the betterment of the process, the safeguarding of the Accused's rights, and the conducting of a fair trial.

The authors caution that the legitimacy of international criminal trials rests at least in part on the understanding that the critical objectives underpinning international trials – national reconciliation and the maintenance of peace – depend as much on justice being done and seen to be done, as it does on the final tally of convictions. In light of this the RUF trial is a worthy subject for the examination of the risks inherent in any international criminal process. It stands as a salutary reminder of the challenges presented by international criminal trials in situ and the temptation to adapt or remove procedural safeguards to meet these challenges. This is particularly so when the hopes for a court rest decisively upon the successful prosecution of a mere trio of high-profile accused, as they did in the RUF and Taylor trials. It is in these circumstances that a strict adherence to procedural safeguards is essential to ensure that the presumption of innocence and the Prosecution's duty to prove guilt beyond a reasonable doubt are rigorously maintained.

II. DENIAL OF THE RUF ACCUSED'S RIGHT TO BE INFORMED OF THE CHARGES

A. *International Standards: Prompt and Detailed Notice*

The right to be promptly and in detail informed of the nature and cause of the charges is one of the most fundamental procedural rights of a person facing criminal prosecution. The right is closely linked to and perhaps a corollary of the presumption of innocence, requiring that the Prosecution inform the Accused of the charges, so that he is able to prepare and present his defense.[3] Accordingly the Statutes of the SCSL, the ICTY and ICTR mirror the major human rights instruments in providing for this guarantee, recognizing the fundamental nature of this right to the maintenance of an effective defense and a fair trial.[4]

As recognized by prevailing international standards, the notification of the charges must be prompt, intelligible, and formulated with adequate precision.[5] The duty to notify is an active, rather than passive one, and remains the Prosecution's continuous duty throughout the course of a trial.[6] An Accused must be made aware of the cause (the material facts alleged) and their nature (the legal qualification of those acts) of the charges in the Indictment.[7] The "provision of full, *detailed* information to the defendant concerning the charges against him – and consequently the legal characterisation that the court might adopt in the matter – is an essential prerequisite for ensuring that the proceedings are fair."[8]

The modern jurisprudence at the ICTY and ICTR has moved decidedly away from the minimalist pleading standards adopted in the early cases such as *Tadić*[9] and *Delalić*[10] and toward a more demanding approach. The general principles today dictate that the indictment must be the "primary accusatory instrument" and plead with "sufficient detail the essential aspect of the Prosecution case."[11] The fundamental role of the indictment is to identify each

---

[3] Babera, Messegue and Jabardo v. Spain, Series A, No. 146 (App. Nos. 10588/83; 10589/83;10590/83), ECHR Dec. 6, 1988 (1989), 11 EHRR 360, at para. 77.

[4] SCSL Statute, *supra* note 2, at art. 17(4)(a); Updated Statute of the International Tribunal for the Prosecution of Persons Responsible for Serious Violations of International Humanitarian Law Committed in the Territory of the Former Yugoslavia since 1991, U.N. S.C. Res. 1660 (2006), at art. 21(4)(a); Statute of the International Criminal Tribunal for the Prosecution of Persons Responsible for Genocide and Other Serious Violations of International Humanitarian Law Committed in the Territory of Rwanda and Other Such Violations Committed in the Territory of Neighbouring States, U.N. S.C. Res. 955, art. 20(4)(a) (1994).

[5] *See, e.g.,* Brozicek v. Italy (1989), 12 EHRR 371; Mattoccia v. Italy (2003), 36 EHRR 47.

[6] D. Monguya Mbenge et al. v. Zaire, Communication No. 16/1977 (views adopted on Mar. 25, 1983), *in* U.N. Doc. GAOR, A/38/40; Mattoccia v. Italy (App. No. 23969/94) ECHR July 25, 2000, at para. 65.

[7] I.H. and Others v. Austria (App. No. 42780/98), ECHR Apr. 20, 2006, at para. 30; Mattoccia v. Italy (App. No. 23969/94), ECHR July 25, 2000, at para. 59; and Kamasinski v. Austria (App. No. 9783/82), ECHR Dec. 19, 1989, at para.79.

[8] Soering v. U.K. (App. No. 14038/88) ECHR July 7, 1989, at para. 113 (emphasis added); *see also, e.g.*: Einhorn v. France (App. No. 71555/01) ECHR Oct. 16, 2001.

[9] Prosecutor v. Tadić D., Case No. IT-94-1-A, Judgment (July 15, 1999) [hereinafter Tadić Appeal Judgment].

[10] Prosecutor v. Delalić et al., Case No. IT-96-21-T, Decision on the Accused Mućić's Motion for Particulars (June 26, 1996).

[11] Prosecutor v. Kupreškić et al., Case No. IT-95-16-A, Appeal Judgment, para. 114 (Oct. 23, 2001) [hereinafter Kupreškić Appeal Judgment].

of the essential factual ingredients of the offenses.[12] This requires the Prosecution to state the material facts underpinning the charges in the indictment, but not the evidence by which such material facts are to be proven.[13] An Accused must be able to reasonably identify the crime and conduct specified in each paragraph of the indictment.[14] The materiality of a fact depends upon the nature of the case at hand[15] (i.e., the form of participation alleged in the indictment and the proximity of the Accused to the underlying crime).[16]

Where the Prosecution alleges that the Accused carried out the act(s) in question (personal responsibility), the jurisprudence requires the Prosecution to set out the identity of the victim, the place and approximate date of the alleged criminal act(s), and the means by which they were committed "with the greatest precision."[17] In cases where the Accused is not alleged to have carried out the acts underlying the crimes charged but may have planned, instigated, ordered, or otherwise aided and abetted in the planning, preparation, or execution of a crime or where superior responsibility is charged, the jurisprudence of the ICTY and ICTR allows for a lower standard of specificity.[18] In principle, the Prosecution has an obligation to identify the "particular acts" or "the particular course of conduct" of the Accused which has given rise to the charges in the indictment.[19] The fundamental question in determining whether an indictment is pled with sufficient particularity is whether the accused persons have enough detail to prepare their defense.[20] It is, accordingly, not permissible to delay disclosure of the factual ingredients of the offence(s) until the disclosure of the Prosecution's Pre-trial brief or the service of the evidence.[21]

Finally, of particular relevance to the RUF trial process, the ICTY and ICTR pleading standards require that additional material facts that create a basis for conviction "factually and/or legally distinct from any already alleged in the indictment" must be considered to be a new charge and therefore before forming part of the case against the Accused must be subject to an application to amend the indictment.[22]

---

[12] Prosecutor v. Krnolejac, Case No. IT-97–25-PT, Decision on the Defense Preliminary Motion on the Form of the Indictment, para. 12 n.19 (Feb. 24, 1999).

[13] Kupreškić Appeal Judgment, *supra* note 11, at para. 88.

[14] Prosecutor v. Hadžihasanović, Case No. IT-01–47-T, Decision on Motion of the Accused Hadžihasanović Regarding the Prosecution's Examination of Witnesses on Alleged Violations Not Covered by the Indictment, at 4 (Mar. 16, 2004).

[15] Prosecutor v. Rutaganda, Case No. ICTR-96–3-A, Appeal Judgment, para. 301 (May 26, 2003) [hereinafter Rutaganda Appeal Judgment]; Prosecutor v. Ntagerura, Case No. ICTR-99–46-T, Trial Judgment, para. 31 (Feb. 25, 2004).

[16] Kupreškić Appeal Judgment, *supra* note 11, at para. 89; Prosecutor v. Karemera, Case No. ICTR-98–44-R72, Decision on Defects in the Form of the Indictment, ICTR Trial Chamber III, para. 17 (Aug. 5, 2005).

[17] Prosecutor v. Blaškić, Case No. IT-95–14-A, Judgment, para. 213 (July 29, 2004) [hereinafter Blaškić Appeal Judgment]; Kupreškić Appeal Judgment, *supra* note 11, at para. 89.

[18] Blaškić Appeal Judgment, *supra* note 17, at para. 211; Rutaganda Appeal Judgment, *supra* note 15, at para. 301.

[19] Blaškić Appeal Judgment, *supra* note 17, at para. 213.

[20] Kupreškić Appeal Judgment, *supra* note 11, at para. 88.

[21] Prosecutor v. Brđanin and Talić, Case No. IT-99–36-PT, Decision on Objections by Radoslav Brđanin to the Form of the Amended Indictment, para. 9 (Feb. 23, 2001); *see also* Prosecutor v. Zigiranyirazo, Decision on Defense Urgent Motion to Exclude some parts of the Prosecution Pre-Trial Brief, Case No. ICTR-2001–73-PT30, para. 2 (Sept. 30, 2005).

[22] Prosecutor v. Halilović, Case No. IT-01–48-PT, Decision on Prosecutor's Motion Seeking Leave to Amend the Indictment, para. 30 (Dec. 17, 2004); *see also* Prosecutor v. Prlić et al., Case No. IT-04–74-PT, Decision on Prosecution Application for Leave to Amend the Indictment and on Defense Complaints on Form of Proposed Amended Indictment, para. 13 (Oct. 18, 2005) [hereinafter Prlić Decision].

B. *The RUF Trial and the Right to Be Informed – Departure from International Standards*

1. The RUF Indictment

The Indictments at the SCSL were not intended to accord with the modern pleading standards at the ICTY and ICTR. A comparison of the Indictments with those at the ICTY shows that the degree of particularization of the charges and the specification of material facts was markedly less than those authorized in the very early cases at the ICTY, such as *Tadić*[23] and *Delalić*.[24] David Crane, the original Chief Prosecutor at the SCSL, described the Indictments as a form of "notice pleading,"[25] whereby he intentionally provided fewer details than the prevailing standard at the ICTY and ICTR. Crane proffered the following justification for that departure:

> Early on in the prosecution plan, I wanted to change the way persons accused of international crimes are charged. My review of indictments coming out of the other tribunals showed that those indictments were too long, inaccurate, and fraught with potential legal land mines. This had to change. What I finally decided was to make the indictment simple and direct. As a prosecutor in the United States, I firmly believe in the principle that if you plead it, you have to prove it. Thus we did something that had never been done before – notice pleading. The indictments are shorter, tighter, and cleaner, yet give the indictees the degree of notice required for them to understand the crimes they committed, where they committed them, and when ... I firmly believe that this is the appropriate direction that the drafting of indictments needs to take.[26]

The RUF Indictment alleged that the three Accused (Sesay, Kallon, and Gbao) were responsible pursuant to all forms of responsibility (including participation in crimes pursuant to a JCE) for eighteen counts of crimes against humanity, war crimes, and other serious violations of international law in seven different provinces of Sierra Leone over a period of five years.[27] The following is a representative sample of the pleading standards referred to by Crane and characteristic of the RUF Indictment. Regarding Count 13: enslavement as a crime against humanity, the Indictment alleged the following against Sesay, the first accused in the RUF trial:

> Between about April 1997 and December 1999, ISSA HASSAN SESAY held the position of the Battle Group Commander, subordinate only to the RUF Battle Field Commander, SAM BOCKARIE ... [ ] ..., the leader of the RUF, FODAY SAYBANA SANKOH and the leader of the AFRC, JOHNNY PAUL KOROMA. During the Junta regime, ISSA HASSAN SESAY was a member of the Junta governing body. From early 2000 to about August 2000, ISSA HASSAN SESAY served as the Battle Field Commander of the RUF, subordinate only to the

---

[23] Prosecutor v. Tadić D., Indictment (amended), Case No. IT-94-1-I (Dec. 14, 1995).

[24] Prosecutor v. Delalić, Decision on the Accused Mucic's Motion for Particulars, Case No. IT-96-21-T (June 26, 1996).

[25] D. Crane, Symposium: *International Criminal Tribunals in the 21st Century: Terrorists, Warlords, and Thugs*, 21 AM. U. INT'L L. REV. 505 (2006); *see also* T. Cruvellier & M. Wierda, *The Special Court for Sierra Leone: The First Eighteen Months*, 5 INTERNATIONAL CENTER FOR TRANSITIONAL JUSTICE (ICTJ) CASE STUDY SERIES (Mar. 2004), *available at* www.ictj.org/images/content/1/0/104.pdf (last visited Apr. 20, 2010).

[26] Crane, *supra* note 25.

[27] Prosecutor v. Sesay, Kallon and Gbao, SCSL-04-15-PT, Corrected Amended Consolidated Indictment (Aug. 2, 2006) [hereinafter RUF Indictment].

leader of the RUF, FODAY SAYBANA SANKOH and the leader of the AFRC, JOHNNY PAUL KOROMA.[28]

ISSA HASSAN SESAY, [....] ... by [his] acts and omissions, [is] individually criminally responsible pursuant to Article 6.1 of the Statute for the crimes referred to in Articles 2, 3, and 4 of the Statute as alleged in this indictment which crimes ... [he] ... planned, instigated, ordered, committed, or in whose planning, preparation, or execution ... [he] ..., otherwise aided and abetted, or which crimes were within a joint criminal enterprise in which each Accused participated or were a reasonably foreseeable consequence of the joint criminal enterprise in which each Accused participated.[29]

Count 13: Abductions and Forced Labour

At all times relevant to this Indictment, AFRC/RUF engaged in widespread and large scale abductions of civilians and use of civilians as forced labour. Forced labour included domestic labour and use as diamond miners. The abductions and forced labour included the following[30]:

Kailahun District: At all times [November 1996 to 2001] relevant to this Indictment, captured civilian men, women and children were brought to various locations within the District and used as forced labour.[31]

By their acts or omissions in relation to these events [the accused], pursuant to Article 6.1 ... [ ] ... are individually responsible for the crimes alleged below:Count 13: Enslavement, a CRIME AGAINST HUMANITY, punishable under Article 2.c of the Statute.[32]

This form of pleading was replicated throughout the Indictment with each count, as above, consisting of a formulaic legal categorization alongside an equally formulaic iteration that the Accused was individually criminally responsible or responsible as a superior under Article 6(1) and 6(3) of the Court's statute. Crucially, the Indictment failed to adhere to the requirement that the material facts of the Accused's alleged conduct (his acts and omissions) or those alleged to have committed the crimes be specified, even where a course of conduct is alleged.[33] Instead, the counts consisted of generalized paragraphs listing the crimes committed by the combined forces of two rebel armies (the RUF and AFRC) on specified towns and villages. The material facts particularized failed to explain the proximity of the Accused to the underlying crimes, other than describing the Accused's de jure status in one of the armies. There was nothing to situate the Accused in relation to the events, whether through the particularization of behavior in relation to the respective army or their approximate location at the time of the generalized criminal events. The Indictment failed to provide any detail concerning the manner in which the attacks on the named towns and villages had allegedly taken place – whether through the enunciation of any narrative of the alleged factual events; a description of an identifiable subgroup; an approximation of the numbers participating in the crimes; or the names of *any* direct perpetrators, subordinate commanders, or victims.

---

[28] *Id.* at paras. 21 and 22.
[29] *Id.* at para. 38.
[30] *Id.* at para. 69.
[31] *Id.* at para. 74.
[32] *Id.* at para. 76.
[33] Kupreškić Appeal Judgment, *supra* note 11, at para. 98.

As is plain from an examination of the pleading of Count 13 (the example provided above), the outline of mass enslavement alleged to have been committed pursuant to every mode of criminal responsibility over thousands of square kilometers during a period of almost five years, without the particularization of the Accused's or his subordinate's acts, could not satisfy the requirement that the indictment allow for the effective preparation of the defense.

Although the Prosecution could have remedied some of the deficiencies in the Indictment by providing the required specificity in its pretrial brief, the problem was instead exacerbated. The pretrial brief contained only a small fraction of the charges pursued and these were particularized as broad, generalized descriptions of alleged criminal conduct by unknown members of the two armies, again without the alleged proximity of the Accused to the underlying crimes or their actual conduct being specified, except in a minority of the crimes alleged. For example, the further particularization of the Accused's responsibility for crimes under Count 13 in Kailahun (see example above) was limited to the following additional facts: (1) the forced labor of two hundred civilians in Pendembu; (2) the abduction and detention of 500 civilians in Kailahun District; (3) the forcing of civilians to carry loads; (4) the forcing of civilians to work on Bockarie and Kallon's rice farms; and (5) the forcing of civilians to carry out domestic labor.[34]

A full appreciation of the extent of the deficient notice to the Accused can be obtained from a comparison of the combined notice provided in Count 13 with the convictions entered against the three RUF Accused in relation to the Kailahun District. In relation to Count 13, enslavement, as a crime against humanity, the charges found proven included, inter alia, enslavement of: (1) 300 civilians on two farms in 1996 and 1998 in Giema; (2) civilians on a farm located between Benduma and Beudu after February 1998; (3) civilians on a farm from December 1999 to 2001; (4) civilians on a farm owned by Sesay and one owned by Gbao in Giema from 1996 to 2001; (5) civilians in 1996, 1997, and 2001 in all ten districts of the Luawa Chiefdom in Kailahun District forced to subscribe farm products and fish for the rebel army and to carry subscribed goods from Giema to Kailahun town; (6) 500 civilians regularly forced to trade for the rebels between 1996 to 2001 in Kailahun province; (7) civilians forced to mine for diamonds from 1998 to 1999 in Giema, Yandawahun, in Mafindo (Mafindor), Nyandehun, Jojoima, Yenga, Jabama, and Golahun; and (8) civilians forced to undergo military training at the Bayama Training base and at the Bunumbu Training Base (Camp Lion).[35]

As is clear, a multitude of new and factually distinct charges (including those listed above, such as forced military training and forced fishing) and the material facts (underpinning the charges) were added after the Prosecution case commenced. The new charges – signifi-

---

[34] Prosecutor v. Sesay, Kallon and Gbao, Case No. SCSL-04-15-PT, Prosecution's Pre-Trial Brief Pursuant to Order for Filing Pre-Trial Briefs (Under Rules 54 and 73*bis*) of Feb. 13, 2004 (Mar. 1, 2004); *see also* Prosecutor v. Sesay, Kallon and Gbao, Case No. SCSL-04-15-PT, Prosecution Supplemental Pre-Trial Brief Pursuant to Order to the Prosecution to File a Supplemental Pre-Trial Brief of Mar. 30, 2004 as Amended by Order to Extend the Time for Filing of the Prosecution Supplemental Pre-Trial Brief of Apr. 2, 2004, para. 8 (Apr. 21, 2004).

[35] Prosecutor v. Sesay, Kallon and Gbao, Doc. No. SCSL-04-15-T-1234, Judgment, paras. 1417–1443 (Mar. 2, 2009) [hereinafter RUF Trial Judgment].

cantly transforming the previously notified case – were notified to the Accused through the Prosecution's disclosure of evidence.

This pattern was replicated across the 18 counts of the Indictment, leading to conviction of the three Accused on more than 250 additional charges, none of which had been particularized in the Indictment, in the Prosecution Pre-trial Brief, or in the Prosecution's opening statement.[36] These charges included a variety of modes of liability (including personal or direct commission) and an extensive range of crimes (including acts of terror, collective punishment, unlawful killing, physical violence (including amputations), sexual violence, pillage, and the use of child soldiers) alleged to have been committed in previously notified locations, as well as new towns and villages throughout Sierra Leone. Further, this abandonment of international pleading standards – allowing the vast majority of the charges and material facts to be disclosed for the first time in the evidence, rather than the Indictment – was compounded by a judicial acceptance that this evidence could be disclosed *at any time* during the two-year Prosecution case.

This unprecedented departure from international standards was the result of an erroneous approach to two legal standards: first, the narrow exception to the specificity requirements at the ICTY and ICTR, allowing nonessential information to be omitted in cases of mass criminality (such as the identity of victims); and, second, the requirement that evidence in support of the charges be disclosed promptly and prior to the commencement of the case. The reinterpretation of these requirements created a process that allowed charges and material facts to be disclosed in supplemental witness statements just before being adduced in the courtroom, without any judicial enquiry into the potential prejudice arising from the late disclosure. These two errors will be discussed below.

2. The SCSL's New "Exceptions" to the Indictment Specificity Requirements

The prosecutorial license to omit charges and evidence from the Indictment was born at an early stage in the RUF proceedings. At the pretrial stage of the proceedings, the RUF Trial Chamber laid the foundation for the departure from international standards by ruling that the RUF Indictment[37] was valid as to form, despite the fact that it deprived the Defense of an opportunity to conduct effective Defense preparation.[38] In response to Defense arguments that the indictment was vague and failed to adequately particularize the charges and material facts, the Trial Chamber reinterpreted the salient jurisprudence from the ICTY and ICTR, leading to an approach that allowed the prosecution to omit charges and material facts in cases involving "mass criminality."

In articulating a narrow case-by-case exception to the specificity requirements of international indictments, the Ntakirutimana case at the ICTR stated that "there *may be* instances where the sheer scale of the alleged crimes 'makes it impracticable to require a high degree of specificity in such matters as *the identity of the victims and the dates* for the commission

---

[36] Prosecutor v. Sesay, Kallon and Gbao, SCSL-04–15-PT, Sesay Final Trial Brief, Annex A1–A3 (Aug. 1, 2008) for comprehensive listing of the pretrial notice and the additional and amended charges.

[37] The indictments of the three Accused were subsequently joined together.

[38] *See generally* Prosecutor v. Sesay, Doc. No. SCSL-2003–05-PT, Decision and Order on Defense Preliminary Motion for Defects in the Form of the Indictment (Oct. 13, 2003).

of the crimes.'"[39] This exception is narrow and allows nonessential information such as the names of victims and the precise date of the crime in incidents of mass criminality to be omitted from the indictment.

Purporting to rely upon the Trial Chamber in *Prosecutor v. Ntakirutimana*, the RUF Trial Chamber stated that the "sheer scale of the alleged crimes *made* it impracticable to require a high degree of specificity in such matters as the identity of the victims and the time *and place* of the events."[40] This blanket articulation and widening of the exception to the specificity requirements was employed to hold the Indictment valid as to form, even though its contents provided no meaningful insight into the scale of the distinct criminal events or the impracticability that prevented the Prosecution from being able to provide a single name of any perpetrator or victim; the specific location of any crime within a named village or town, or indeed any time frame of any crime other than measured in months. Compounding the problem at the final judgment stage, the Trial Chamber, instead of conducting an analysis of the timing of the disclosure of the additional 250 charges (and an equal number of associated material facts) declined to address the prejudice to the Accused, ruling again that the Indictment remained valid as to form.[41] The Trial Chamber ruled that in addition to the "criminogenic setting" of the alleged crimes (the Chamber's presumed exception to the specificity requirements), it had also taken into account "the particular context in which the RUF trial unfolded," namely the "the fact that the investigations and trials were intended to proceed as expeditiously as possible in an immediate post-conflict environment."[42] Endorsing this approach, the Appeals Chamber upheld this further exception, noting that the Trial Chamber had, nonetheless, stated that the Indictment must still be sufficiently detailed to allow the Accused to fully prepare his defense and that the Prosecution "may not rely on weaknesses of its own investigation to justify its failure to plead material facts in an Indictment" and therefore no error of law arose in taking this additional factor into consideration.[43]

The Appeal Chamber failed to appreciate, however, that to allow the omission of charges and material facts from an indictment on the basis of a "need" to start the trials in a post-conflict environment is tantamount to an invitation for the prosecution to rely upon its own investigative weaknesses. Worse, it sacrifices an Accused's defense to those considerations.

Thus, neither the Trial Chamber nor the Appeals Chamber dealt with the critical issue: the obvious contradiction between the admonishment that the Accused must be able to fully prepare his defense and the prejudice to that entitlement arising from a Kafkaesque-like situation whereby the majority of the hundreds of charges and material facts remain hidden until partway through the Prosecution case. Neither did either Chamber seek to explain how the civil war in Sierra Leone differed in terms of its "mass criminality" from the genocide in Rwanda or the war in the former Yugoslavia, both of which also required

---

[39] Prosecutor v. Ntakirutimana, ICTR-96–10 and 96–17-T, Judgment, para. 89 (Feb. 21, 2003) [hereinafter Ntakirutimana Trial Judgment]; *see also* Kupreškić Appeal Judgment, *supra* note 11, at para. 89, and Prosecutor v. Sesay, Kallon and Gbao, Case No. SCSL-04–15-A, Appeal Judgment, para. 52 (Oct. 26, 2009) [hereinafter RUF Appeal Judgment].

[40] *Id.* at para. 7(xi) (internal citations omitted, emphasis added).

[41] RUF Trial Judgment, *supra* note 35, at paras. 471, 472.

[42] *Id.* at para. 330.

[43] RUF Appeal Judgment, *supra* note 39, at para. 60.

investigations in the aftermath of a destructive war. In fact, the first indictment at the ICTY was issued in November 1994, while the conflict was still ongoing.[44] Nevertheless, the international standards employed in these institutions mandate that the Prosecution provide the Accused with the essential aspects of its case (the charges and the material facts) prior to its commencement, irrespective of the undoubted investigative difficulties.

3. The RUF Test for the Admissibility of New Evidence

The notice requirements at the ICTY and the ICTR mandate that evidence in support of the charges be disclosed within a reasonable time, and before the trial commences.[45] Further, an Accused is entitled to proceed upon the basis that the Pre-Trial Brief contains a count-by-count summary of the evidence, and this is the only case that he has to meet in relation to the offense(s) charged. If the prosecution intends to elicit evidence in relation to a particular count additional to that summarized in its Pre-Trial Brief, specific notice must be given to the Accused.[46] As determined by the ICTY and ICTR, this is essential to ensure adequate notice and the validity and legitimacy of the liability assessments required, and to enable the essential task of ensuring that the charges are supported by evidence beyond reasonable doubt before finding the Accused guilty of serious violations of international law.[47]

Instead of abiding by these essential prerequisites, Trial Chamber I in the RUF trial created an innovative test to permit all new evidence produced by Prosecution investigations to be admissible at any time during the Prosecution case. The comparative assessment conducted at the ICTY and ICTR and underpinning the disclosure provisions, designed to assess whether evidence disclosed during trial and sought to be relied upon by the Prosecution is new, was abandoned. This assessment required the Chamber to conduct an examination of the evidence and the notice provided in the Prosecution disclosure, including a comparative analysis of the previous notice provided through the Indictment, the pretrial brief, and previous witness statements. The allegedly new evidence had to be assessed to ascertain the extent to which it altered "the incriminating quality of the evidence of which the Defense already had notice."[48] In the event that the evidentiary material was found to be new, the Chamber had to determine what period of notice was adequate to give the Defense time to prepare.[49] In the event that the new material was determined to constitute a new charge, the Prosecution should have been prohibited from relying upon it, or required to apply to amend the Indictment, allowing the question of any resulting prejudice to the Defense to be assessed before it formed part of the case.[50]

---

[44] Case of Dragan Nikolic. *See* ICTY Website "ICTY Timeline" at http://www.icty.org/action/timeline/254. The conflict in Rwanda ended in July 1994, and the first indictment was issued in February 1996. Prosecutor v. Akayesu, Case No. ICTR-96-4-PT, Indictment (Feb. 12, 1996).

[45] *See, e.g.,* Prosecutor v. Nyiramusuhuko, Case No. ICTR-97-21-T, Decision on Defense Motion for Disclosure of Evidence, paras. 38–39 (Nov. 1, 2000).

[46] Prosecutor v. Brđanin, Case No. IT-99-36-T, Decision on Form of Further Amended Indictment and Prosecution Application to Amend, para. 62 (June 26, 2001) (emphasis added).

[47] Prosecutor v. Brdanin, Case No. IT-99-36-A, Judgment, para. 424 (Apr. 3, 2007) (internal citations omitted) [hereinafter Brdanin Appeal Judgment].

[48] *See, e.g.,* Prosecutor v. Bagosora et al., ICTR-98-41-T, Decision on Admissibility of Evidence of Witness DP, para. 6 (Nov. 18, 2003).

[49] *Id.*

[50] Prosecutor v. Halilović, Case No. IT-01-48-PT, Decision on Prosecutor's Motion Seeking Leave to Amend the Indictment, para. 30 (Dec. 17, 2004); *see also* Prosecutor v. Prlić, Case No. IT-04-74-PT, Decision on

Instead of abiding by these essential safeguards the RUF Trial Chamber created a novel admissibility test that allowed all evidence, whether constituting a new charge, new material, or merely supplementary facts to be defined as *not new* and therefore automatically admissible. Purporting to rely upon the ICTY and ICTR jurisprudence, Trial Chamber I decided that evidence that constituted a "building block constituting an integral part of, and connected with, the same *res gestae* forming the factual substratum of the charges in the Indictment"[51] was "not new."[52] The precise meaning of this test or its jurisprudential origins remained unexplained throughout the RUF trial process, although the consequences of dividing "charges" into "building blocks" and the "*res gestae* forming the factual substratum" became abundantly clear. This threshold test had the effect of inviting the prosecution to reinvestigate the case and allowed all the resulting charges and material facts (omitted from the indictment) to be incrementally disclosed to the Accused, often just days before each of the ninety Prosecution witnesses were called to testify. In short, provided that the additional evidence constituted crimes committed in Sierra Leone during the five-year temporal framework of the Indictment, the Chamber's self-fulfilling test deemed it automatically admissible.[53] The implicit invitation by the RUF Trial Chamber to the Prosecution to remedy their pretrial investigations, which no doubt had suffered because of a difficult post-conflict environment, was taken up with a degree of enthusiasm leading to the admission of 250 new charges and vast swathes of fresh evidence in support. Notwithstanding the addition of this volume of new charges, material facts and evidence (including new allegations of direct and indirect liability for, inter alia, unlawful killings, sexual violence, amputations, enslavement, pillage, and the use of child soldiers) and the overwhelming transformation of the original case disclosed prior to the Prosecution's opening all was deemed admissible. Accordingly there was no proper notice to the Accused of these charges or the evidence in the RUF trial. Neither was there any moment in the case when the allegations stopped and the Accused could commence answering in full knowledge of the case to be met.[54]

As noted the Trial Chamber consistently ruled that the evidence was admissible. It defended this decision, in part, by arguing that the new charges and evidence in support did not "significantly alter the incriminatory quality of the evidence" already disclosed to the Defense.[55] This curious claim was maintained by both the Prosecution and the Trial

Prosecution Application for Leave to Amend the Indictment and on Defense Complaints on Form of Proposed Amended Indictment, para. 13 (Oct. 18, 2005): "[i]f a new allegation does not expose an Accused to an additional risk of conviction, then it cannot be considered a new charge."

[51] *See, e.g.,* Prosecutor v. Sesay, Kallon, and Gbao, Case No. SCSL-04-15-T, Decision on the Defense Motion for the Exclusion of Evidence Arising from the Supplemental Statements of Witnesses TF1–113, TF1–108, TF1–330, TF1–041 and TF1–288, para. 10 (Mar. 20, 2006); *see also* Prosecutor v. Sesay, Kallon and Gbao, Case No. SCSL-04-15-T, Decision on Defense Motion Requesting the Exclusion of Evidence Arising from the Supplemental Statements of Witnesses TF1–168, TF1–165 and TF1–041, paras. 11, 13 (Feb. 27, 2006).

[52] *See, e.g.,* Prosecutor v. Sesay, Kallon and Gbao, Doc. No. SCSL-04-15-T-396, Ruling on Application for the Exclusion of Certain Supplemental Statements of Witness TF1–361 and Witness TF1–122, paras. 28 (iv), 29 (vi) (June 1, 2005).

[53] *See, e.g.,* Prosecutor v. Sesay, Kallon and Gbao, Doc. No. SCSL-04-15-T-339, Decision Regarding the Prosecution's Further Renewed Witness List (Apr. 5, 2005).

[54] Prosecutor v. Delalic, Case No. IT-96-21-T, Decision on the Prosecution's Alternative Request to Reopen the Prosecution's Case, para. 20 (Aug. 19, 1998).

[55] *See, e.g.,* Prosecutor v. Sesay, Kallon and Gbao, Doc. No. SCSL-04-15-T-396, Ruling on Application for the Exclusion of Certain Supplemental Statements of Witness TF1–361 and Witness TF1–122, paras. 28(iv), 29(vi) (June 1, 2005).

Chamber until the three Accused attended their sentencing hearing wherein the 250 new charges (and corresponding convictions) formed a principal justification for lengthy sentences of imprisonment.[56] Evidence that the Prosecution and Trial Chamber at one point argued did not "alter the incriminatory quality" of the evidence suddenly formed the foundation for Prosecutorial requests for severe sentences ranging from forty to sixty years imprisonment.

On appeal, the Appeals Chamber declined to interfere with the Trial Chamber's approach that led to this obvious unfairness. Instead of addressing the novel pleading and admissibility threshold invented by the Trial Chamber, the Chamber struck out the Defense complaint on a technicality – ruling that a fifty-page annex describing the 250 new charges and evidence was outside the page limit allowed for appeal.[57]

C. Conclusion: Denial of a Fair Opportunity to Defend the Charges

The final tally of new charges introduced into the RUF case was in excess of 250 with a corresponding number of new material facts underpinning the new and the previously notified charges, as well as reams of new evidence in support, adduced piecemeal throughout a two-year prosecution case. This incremental disclosure was matched by a correspondingly large number of lost opportunities for the Accused to mount an effective defense. Given the Prosecution and Chamber's illogical claim that the material was not new and did not alter the incriminatory quality of the evidence already disclosed, any Defense complaint was foreclosed and any remedial action (e.g., the recalling of witnesses) impossible. The right to be informed of the charges through the indictment and the evidence is a fundamental guarantee that enables an accused to prepare his defense under conditions that do not provide the prosecution with an unfair advantage. The approach of the Trial and Appellate Chamber in the RUF case, by apparent design, handed the Prosecution, whose investigation had perhaps been hampered by the immediate post-conflict environment, the opportunity to continuously bolster its case with new charges, material facts, and evidence, and mold it around the case as it unfolded in the courtroom. In these conditions an Accused cannot have a fair trial as there is no real opportunity to prepare an effective defense or any reasonable prospect of rebutting the charges.

III. IMPUTATION OF CRIMES TO THE RUF ACCUSED: ASSESSING THE EVIDENTIAL LINKS BETWEEN THE ACCUSED AND THE CRIMES PURSUANT TO THE JOINT CRIMINAL ENTERPRISE (JCE) MODE OF LIABILITY

The approach taken by the SCSL judiciary to the assessment of individual liability and the attribution of responsibility through the JCE mode of liability was critical to the RUF judgment and its voluminous convictions. The overwhelming majority of the crimes found

---

[56] *See* Prosecutor v. Sesay, Kallon and Gbao, Sentencing Judgment, Doc. No. SCSL-04–15-T-1251 (Apr. 8, 2009).
[57] RUF Appeal Judgment, *supra* note 39, at para. 44; *also see* Prosecutor v. Issa Hassan Sesay, Morris Kallon and Augustine Gbao, Case No. SCSL-04–15-A, Public Corrected Redacted Grounds of Appeal, Annexes A1–A3 (June 15, 2009); Practice Direction on Filing Documents before the Special Court for Sierra Leone, as amended Jan. 16, 2008, at art. 6(f), which states that "[a]ny appendices or authorities do not count towards the page limit."

proven were those found committed pursuant to the JCE mode of liability, including acts of terror, collective punishments, unlawful killings, sexual and physical violence, pillage, and enslavement. The Trial Chamber found that during the junta regime, high-ranking AFRC (a group of former Sierra Leone military who overthrew the government) and RUF members formed a JCE by sharing a common plan that commenced on May 25, 1997, which was to take any action necessary to gain and exercise political power and control over the territory of Sierra Leone, in particular the diamond mining areas and that the "crimes [within fourteen counts in the indictment] were contemplated by the participants of the joint criminal enterprise to be within the common purpose."[58]

This section will discuss the trial and appellate approach to the assessment of evidence in support of the alleged JCE and the attribution of crimes without proof of the required link between the crime or criminal perpetrator and the Accused. This discussion will inevitably address the SCSL's approach to the pleading of a JCE without a criminal objective but its principal focus is an examination of the finding of individual criminal responsibility of JCE members for crimes committed by non-JCE members. It will explore how the various JCE holdings on this critical attribution issue led to convictions in flagrant breach of the culpability principle.

A. Abandonment of the ICTY and ICTR Approach to JCE: The Attribution of "Contemplated" Crimes to the Accused

The SCSL adopted an unprecedented approach to JCE pleading by approving indictments that failed to articulate a "common purpose" with an essential shared criminal intent at the core of the alleged enterprise. Although JCE doctrine requires that the Prosecution plead, as a material fact, a common purpose that "amounts to or involves" a crime within the statute of the Court, none of the Special Court Indictments pled any crime or criminal intent as a *necessary* part of the common purpose.[59] In the RUF case, the purpose was the noncriminal act of participating in a rebellion: "to take any actions necessary to gain and exercise political power and control over the territory of Sierra Leone, in particular the diamond mining areas."[60] In the paragraph following the articulation of this noncriminal objective,[61] the Indictments stated that: "[t]he crimes alleged in this indictment, including unlawful killings, abductions, forced labour, physical and sexual violence, use of child soldiers, looting

---

[58] RUF Trial Judgment, *supra* note 35, at para. 1985.

[59] W. Jordash & P. Van Tuyl, *Failure to Carry the Burden of Proof: How Joint Criminal Enterprise Lost Its Way at the Special Court for Sierra Leone*, J. INT'L CRIM. JUST. 1 of 23 (2010); *see also* Prosecutor v. Brima, Kamara and Kanu, Case No. SCSL-04-16-I, Further Amended Consolidated Indictment, para. 34 (Feb. 18, 2005) [hereinafter AFRC Indictment]; RUF Indictment, *supra* note 27; Prosecutor v. Norman, Fofana and Kondewa, Case No. SCSL-03-14-I, Consolidated Indictment, para. 19 (Feb. 5, 2004) [hereinafter CDF Indictment]; Prosecutor v. Taylor, Case No. SCSL-03-01-I, Second Amended Indictment, para. 33 (May 29, 2007) [hereinafter Taylor Indictment].

[60] AFRC Indictment, *supra* note 59, at paras. 33–34; RUF Indictment, *supra* note 27, at para. 36; Original Taylor Indictment, *supra* note 59, at para. 23.

[61] M.N. SHAW, INTERNATIONAL LAW 1040 (5th ed. 2003), which stated that "[w]hether to prosecute the perpetrators of rebellion for their act of rebellion and challenge to the constituted authority of the State as a matter of internal law is for the state authority to decide. There is no rule against rebellion in international law."

and burning of civilian structures, were *either* actions within the joint criminal enterprise *or* were a reasonably foreseeable consequence of the joint criminal enterprise."[62]

The Indictment thereby pled all crimes as either within or outside the noncriminal objective, rather than as a necessary part of it. The obvious consequence of this approach is that the common purpose pled the alleged criminality of the joint enterprise as optional or, alternatively, wholly absent, and therefore failed to articulate any definitive criminal intent: that is, a common purpose that alternatively *either* involved crimes within the Statute of the Court *or* did not.

Rather than rectify these defective pleadings, the SCSL judiciary adopted a new interpretation of "common purpose" that appeared to require for a finding that an Accused was a JCE member only proof of participation in a rebellion, a noncriminal pursuit under international criminal law. The Appeal Chamber, reversing a finding by the AFRC Trial Chamber that such a pleading failed to articulate an unambiguous criminal purpose, determined that there was no requirement that a JCE alleges and a trier of fact finds a "necessary relationship between the objective of a common purpose and its criminal means." It is sufficient that the "latter are contemplated to achieve the former."[63]

One effect of the pleading and the Appeal Chamber's "innovation" was that they removed the Prosecution's obligation to prove the foundational elements of a JCE, namely whether a plurality acted together in the implementation of a criminal objective.[64] This question concerns the assessment and identification of specific material elements that demonstrate the existence of an objectively punishable criminal act, precisely determined in time and space.[65] This analysis requires that the trier of fact assess whether the crimes were the product of concerted action – that is, pursuant to the alleged plan – or whether there was another explanation for their commission. This is a necessary step to the next question: whether the Accused had carried out acts that significantly contributed to the furtherance of this criminal purpose, with the knowledge that his acts or omissions facilitated the crimes committed as part of the enterprise.[66]

Conversely the SCSL's JCE allowed a trier of fact to find the existence of a JCE through the identification of mere concerted action in pursuit of a noncriminal objective (taking power over the country through armed rebellion) while contemplating crimes to achieve this objective. Under this interpretation, the RUF Accused could be found responsible for crimes as part of a plurality engaged in concerted action in furtherance of the crimes and contributing to them *or* being part of a plurality engaged in furtherance of a rebellion and contributing solely to that noncriminal objective. This meant that a JCE could be found to exist without a nexus between the JCE member's concerted action and a crime – other than the crimes he contemplated. Logically, in a bloody civil war awash with crimes, the

---

[62] AFRC Indictment, *supra* note 59, at para. 35; RUF Indictment, *supra* note 27, at para. 37; Original Taylor Indictment, *supra* note 59, at para. 24 (emphasis added).

[63] RUF Appeal Judgment, *supra* note 39, at para. 296, *quoting* Prosecutor v. Brima, Kamara and Kanu, Case No. SCSL-04–16–675-A, Judgment, paras. 76, 80 (Feb. 22, 2008) (internal citations omitted).

[64] Brdanin Appeal Judgment, *supra* note 47, at paras. 410, 430.

[65] Prosecutor v. Sagahutu et al., Case No. ICTR-00–56-T, Decision on Sagahutu's Preliminary, Provisional Release and Severage Motions, para. 39 (Sept. 25, 2002).

[66] Prosecutor v. Kvocka et al., Case No. IT-98–30/1-T, Trial Judgment, para. 312 (Nov. 2, 2001); Prosecutor v. Kvocka et al., Case No. IT-98–30/1-A, Appeal Judgment, paras. 99, 263 (Feb. 28, 2005); Prosecutor v. Brdanin, *supra* note 47, at para. 427.

contemplation nexus – that is, the thinking about or being aware of the commission of crimes – is automatically satisfied and impossible to disprove.

In this manifestation of a JCE the trier of fact need not examine concerted action in furtherance of crime (including the pattern of crimes) before being satisfied about the existence of a JCE and before attributing crimes within the JCE. It is sufficient that a plurality engaged in rebellion was prepared to employ the criminal means if the need arose, or even less, that they thought about them ("contemplated it") but rejected the idea upon further contemplation. All crime that the trier of fact considers reasonably foreseeable, that is, contemplated, can be attributed to the shared purpose and to the JCE members.

Further, given Trial Chamber I's explicit presumption in the RUF case that JCE members acted with criminal intent in seeking to take power and control over the country of Sierra Leone, the requirement of a finding that they contemplated crimes may have been superfluous, as the finding of JCE liability was a foregone conclusion. As stated by the Trial Chamber:

> [i]t indeed goes without saying and the Chamber so concludes that resorting to arms to secure a total redemption and using them to topple a government which the RUF characterised as corrupt *necessarily* implies the resolve and determination to shed blood and commit the crimes for which the Accused are indicted.[67]

The Trial Chamber provided no explanation as to the exact meaning of this judicial presumption, and the Appeal Chamber declined to comment upon it or rule upon on its legal validity in light of the presumption of innocence and the burden of proof. However, given that the Trial Chamber assessed individual liability pursuant to a theory of JCE that required only a showing of action in pursuit of the seizure of power in Sierra Leone while contemplating crimes,[68] the attribution of the crimes to the Accused *in light of such a presumption* must have been little other than a foregone conclusion.

B. *The Culpability Principle: Imputing the Crimes of Non-JCE Members to the Accused*

To hold an accused responsible for the criminal conduct of another person requires the finding of a link between the accused and the crime as a legal basis for the imputation of criminal liability.[69] As far as the basic form of JCE is concerned (a common criminal purpose shared by a plurality of persons acting in concert), an essential prerequisite is that the crime in question *forms part of the common criminal purpose.*[70]

The ICTY has made clear that

> to hold a member of a JCE responsible for crimes committed by non-members of the enterprise, it has to be shown that the crime can be imputed to one member of the joint criminal enterprise, and that this member – when using a principal perpetrator – acted in accordance with the common plan. The existence of this link is a matter to be assessed on a case-by-case basis.[71]

---

[67] RUF Trial Judgment, *supra* note 35, at para. 2016 (emphasis added).
[68] RUF Trial Judgment, *supra* note 35, at para. 1985.
[69] Brđanin Appeal Judgment, *supra* note 47, at para. 412.
[70] *Id.* at para. 418.
[71] *Id.* at para. 413 (emphasis added).

In assessing this connection, the factors indicative of a sufficient link "include evidence that the JCE member explicitly or implicitly requested the non-JCE member to commit such a crime or instigated, ordered, encouraged, or otherwise availed himself of the non-JCE member to commit the crime."[72]

Attributing responsibility for the crimes of a non-JCE member to an Accused who is a JCE member, therefore, creates a dual requirement. First, the Trial Chamber must evaluate the evidence to assess whether a JCE member procured a non-JCE member to commit a particular crime. In its most simple construction, if a JCE member explicitly or implicitly requested, ordered, instigated, or otherwise encouraged rebel forces to kill innocent civilians, he cannot escape individual criminal responsibility because he did not personally commit the crime. Second, the JCE member must be using that non-JCE member to further the shared criminal purpose of the JCE. JCE members should not be individually criminally responsible for the crimes committed by non-JCE members (having been procured by another JCE member) for personal reasons such as revenge, personal financial gain, or otherwise.[73] If a JCE member procures a non-JCE member to steal money for his family's personal use, for example, he would not likely be acting in furtherance of the JCE's common criminal objective and the crime therefore ought not to be determined to form part of the common criminal purpose.

As discussed above, in the RUF case the three Accused – Sesay, Kallon, and Gbao – were found individually criminally responsible, inter alia, as members of a JCE whose objective was "to take any action necessary to gain and exercise political power and control over the country of Sierra Leone, in particular the diamond mining areas."[74] It was found that, although this objective was not inherently criminal, it became criminal because the implementation of this goal involved contemplating the commission of crimes.[75] The Chamber found that the crimes for which the RUF were convicted pursuant to the JCE (Counts 1–14 in the Indictment) were *within* the JCE and intended to further the common purpose to take power and control over Sierra Leone; thus, they were all basic-form JCE crimes.[76]

The vast majority of the several hundred charges that led to individual criminal responsibility pursuant to the JCE were committed by non-JCE members. The evaluation of the relationship between the principal perpetrators of crimes and the JCE members and the circumstances that gave rise to the crime was, therefore, crucial to a fair assessment of the individual culpability of each Accused.

1. The SCSL's Departure from International Standards

In deciding whether crimes committed by non-JCE members could be attributed to JCE members, the Trial Chamber explicitly accepted that the jurisprudence (as pronounced in the Brđanin case[77]) required the Trial Chamber to find, on a crime-by-crime basis, that one

---

[72] Prosecutor v. Krajišnik, Case No. IT-00-39-A, Appeal Judgment, para. 226 (Mar. 17, 2009) [hereinafter Krajišnik Appeal Judgment].

[73] Of course, a JCE member may be acting for multiple purposes, in which case the crime could be part of the JCE.

[74] RUF Trial Judgment, *supra* note 35, at para. 1985.

[75] *Id.* at paras. 1979–1985.

[76] *Id.* at paras. 1982, 1985.

[77] RUF Trial Judgment, *supra* note 35, at para. 263, *citing* Brđanin Appeal Judgment, *supra* note 47, at paras. 413, 430.

of the JCE members[78] procured the principal perpetrator of a crime to take actions in furtherance of the common criminal purpose.

Nonetheless, it is plain that the Trial and Appeal Chamber failed to apply this legal requirement. The analysis employed to attribute crimes within the common purpose, or to uphold such findings, was deficient in two distinct ways, each offending the culpability principle and the fair trial rights of the accused.

2. Employment of an Incorrect Evaluative Standard

First, both Chambers appeared to misunderstand the analysis required before crimes committed by non-JCE members might be found to be within the common purpose of a JCE and attributed to the Accused. The Trial Chamber should have assessed whether each crime was committed at the behest of a JCE member in furtherance of the common criminal purpose. Instead, the Trial Chamber in a sweeping, catch-all paragraph incorporating the attribution of hundreds of such crimes to the Accused, held that:

> The Chamber is satisfied that the [principal perpetrators of crimes] were used by said members of the joint criminal enterprise to commit crimes that were *either* intended by the members to further the common purpose, *or* were a natural and foreseeable consequence of the implementation of the common purpose.[79]

The Appeal Chamber reiterated the finding without comment or critique, disregarding the convicted person's complaint and this manifest error of law.[80] Having previously found that the criminal means (Counts 1–14) were crimes "within," and therefore intended by JCE members to further their common criminal purpose,[81] the question of the extended form of JCE and the foreseeability of crimes did not arise for the Trial Chamber's consideration. As a consequence of that finding, JCE responsibility for the RUF Accused was restricted to the crimes found to have been intended by the JCE members to further their common criminal purpose. This legal enunciation evinced a critical misconception that allowed crimes to be attributed to the Accused pursuant to the basic form of JCE without any actual showing that they were intended by any JCE member in furtherance of the common criminal purpose, as required by the JCE doctrine; instead, a mere finding of the crime being foreseeable was sufficient.

As discussed earlier in the chapter, the analysis required to assess crimes committed by non-JCE members as within or intended by JCE members to further the common criminal purpose was that outlined in *Brđanin*; the imputation of crimes to a JCE member relies upon establishing that the member – when using the principal perpetrator – acted in accordance with the common plan. Putting aside the tortuous logic of the notion of a JCE member using a non-JCE member to commit a crime that is only foreseen, crimes only foreseen by a JCE member cannot be found to form part of the common criminal purpose and, therefore, could not be attributed to the Accused pursuant to the basic form. Unintended crimes, that are a natural and foreseeable consequence of the implementation of the common purpose, are by definition outside the common purpose.

---

[78] *See* RUF Trial Judgment, *supra* note 35, at para. 1990, for a list of JCE members in the RUF case.
[79] RUF Trial Judgment, *supra* note 35, at para. 1992 (emphasis added).
[80] RUF Appeal Judgment, *supra* note 39, at paras. 405, 407, 411.
[81] RUF Trial Judgment, *supra* note 35, at para. 1985.

The full ramifications of this judicial misstep are impossible to know – the judgment was largely silent on how the hundreds of specific crimes were *in fact* found to be linked to a JCE member (see discussion later in the chapter). It is, nonetheless, plain that this misconception had significant consequences, allowing a multitude of the gravest of crimes to be attributed to the Accused without being intended by any JCE member in violation of the culpability principle. For example, the Trial Chamber explicitly attributed all the crimes committed by four non-JCE members (individuals nicknamed Rocky, Rambo, Savage, and Staff Alhaji), undoubtedly among the worst perpetrators of crimes in the civil war, on the cursory basis that they were "directly subordinate to and used by members of the joint criminal enterprise to commit crimes that were *either* intended by the members to further the common design, *or* which were a reasonably foreseeable consequence of the common purpose."[82] The crimes attributed to the Accused on this basis included, inter alia, the execution of about 200 civilians, an act of terror, collective punishment, and murder[83]; the killing by Savage of an unknown number of civilians by burning them alive in a house in March 1998, found to be acts of terror and murder[84]; the killing of 29 civilians in Penduma on the orders of AFRC Staff Alhaji, found to be acts of terror and murder[85]; and the killing of 47 civilians by Savage in February/March 1998, found to be acts of terror and murder.[86]

It follows that if the crimes committed by these individuals were only a reasonably foreseeable consequence of the common purpose, the three RUF accused were wrongly convicted for these crimes.

As will be argued in the following subsection, equally problematic was that, other than noting these direct perpetrators' general subordination to one or more JCE members, the Trial Chamber made no findings to link these specific crimes to any action by a JCE member. These showings were required before finding that the JCE member explicitly or implicitly procured the non-JCE member or instigated, ordered, encouraged, or otherwise availed himself of the non-JCE member to commit the crime *in furtherance of the common purpose*. Therefore, even in the instances where the Trial Chamber may have purported to apply the first part of its two-pronged disjunctive test (involving a search for intention), it appears not to have grasped the required analysis and findings demanded by the ICTY jurisprudence that it had explicitly adopted.

3. Failure to Link Crimes to a JCE Member

The Appeal Chamber's approach to the convicted persons' complaint on these issues is noteworthy. It upheld the lower Chamber's factual findings by holding that, although the latter had failed to provide sufficient findings in linking the crimes to JCE members, the hundreds of crimes were clearly committed in furtherance of the JCE's common criminal purpose. Having ignored the ramifications of the erroneous test employed by the Trial Chamber,

---

[82] RUF Trial Judgment, *supra* note 35, at para. 2080 (emphasis added).

[83] *See generally* RUF Trial Judgment, *supra* note 35, at paras. 1165–1169, 1369, 2063; *also see* RUF Appeal Judgment, *supra* note 39, at paras. 429–431.

[84] RUF Trial Judgment, *supra* note 35, at paras. 1167, 1273, 2063; *also see* RUF Appeal Judgment, *supra* note 39, at paras. 429–435.

[85] RUF Trial Judgment, *supra* note 35, at paras. 1192, 1195, 1196, 1278, 2063; *also see* RUF Appeal Judgment, *supra* note 39, at paras. 429–435.

[86] RUF Trial Judgment, *supra* note 35, at paras. 1165, 1274, 2063; *also see* RUF Appeal Judgment, *supra* note 39, at paras. 429–435.

the Appeal Chamber enumerated the approach demanded by *Brđanin*,[87] and purported to conduct the missing analysis, providing ostensible connections between the crimes and the JCE's common criminal purpose.[88]

However, as regards the assessments made by the Trial and Appeal Chambers of the existence of a sufficient nexus between one of the JCE members and crimes committed by non-JCE members, in 30 of the findings (involving approximately 510 civilian deaths) all found to be within the common purpose, there was no mention of a JCE member at all.[89] The higher Chamber's approach was creative – having appreciated that the Trial Chamber's findings on the specific crimes committed by non-JCE members were made largely without reference to a JCE member – it reframed its analysis. The Appeals Chamber abandoned the essential threshold enquiry, instead restricting its appellate analysis to the question of whether the crimes committed were sufficiently widespread or similar to other crimes by JCE members such that all should be considered to be part of the same endeavor.

For example, the Trial Chamber found on more than eight occasions that AFRC and RUF fighters (all non-JCE members) had committed acts of sexual violence in Kono District.[90] Although the *existence* of the crimes had not been challenged by the Defense, none of these crimes were found linked to a named JCE member. The Trial Chamber simply omitted analysis of whether a JCE member procured the perpetrators to commit crimes to further their common criminal purpose. In assessing the correctness of this approach, the Appeal Chamber ruled, inter alia, that the crimes of sexual violence were committed to "break the will of the population and ensure their submission to AFRC/RUF control" and therefore the crimes were within the common purpose that had been found to include such crimes.[91] However, no JCE member was cited as causing or wanting those *specific* crimes to occur. There was nothing in the findings that could be said to have distinguished the crimes as JCE crimes, rather than crimes arising from other criminal enterprises or random criminality by subordinate members of the rebel groups.

An identical approach was taken by the Trial and Appeal Chamber to a large portion of the crimes in other districts, including Bo District. In Bo, the Trial Chamber found that eight different criminal events were committed and were within the common purpose.[92]

---

[87] RUF Appeal Judgment, *supra* note 39, at para. 414.

[88] *See, e.g.*, RUF Appeal Judgment, *supra* note 39, at paras. 416–418.

[89] According to paragraph 1990 of the RUF Trial Chamber Judgment, JCE members included Foday Sankoh, Sam Bockarie, Issa Sesay, Morris Kallon, Superman, Eldred Collins, Mike Lamin, Isaac Mongor, Gibril Massaquoi, Augustine Gbao, and other unnamed RUF Commanders, as well as the following AFRC: Johnny Paul Koroma, Gullit, Bazzy, Five-Five, SAJ Musa, Zagalo, Eddie Kanneh, and others to hold power in Sierra Leone on or shortly after the May 25, 1997. *See* RUF Trial Judgment, *supra* note 35, at para. 1990.

[90] This includes unnamed AFRC/RUF rebels raping TF1–218 in Bumpeh. *See* RUF Trial Judgment, *supra* note 35, at paras. 1206, 1290, 1299, 2063; rape by a man named Staff Alhaji in Tombodu. *See id.*, *supra* note 35, at paras. 1171, 1288, 1299, 2063; rape of TF1–217's wife, as well as an unknown number of other women in Penduma by AFRC/RUF rebels. *See id.*, *supra* note 35, at paras. 1193–1195, 1290, 1299, 2063; AFRC/RUF rebels rape of an unidentified female in Bomboafuidu. *See id.*, *supra* note 35, at paras. 1208, 1289, 1290, 1299, 2063; AFRC/RUF rebels forcing twenty people to have sex with each other in Bomboafuidu. *See id.*, *supra* note 35, at paras. 1207, 1309, 2063; AFRC/RUF rebels using knives to slit genitals in Bomboafuidu. *See id.*, *supra* note 35, at paras. 1208, 2063; AFRC/RUF rebels raping TF1–195 five times and five other women in Sawao. *See id.*, *supra* note 35, at paras. 1181, 1185, 1290, 1299, 2063; AFRC/RUF rebels forcibly marrying an unknown number of women at Wendedu. *See id.*, *supra* note 35, at paras. 1178–1179, 1294, 1297, 1299, 2063.

[91] RUF Appeal Judgment, *supra* note 39, at para. 440.

[92] RUF Trial Judgment, *supra* note 35, at paras. 991–1041.

In six of the eight no JCE member was linked to the crimes.[93] The six included a finding of unnamed AFRC/RUF rebels killing more than 200 civilians in Tikonko village, attributed to the Accused as members of the JCE. There were no findings made to identify the perpetrators (by name, de jure role, or subgroup) or any link to a JCE member established, other than being members of the same rebellion.[94] The Appeal Chamber found that there was sufficient evidence to justify the Trial Chamber's imputation of the crimes to "one or more JCE members" on the basis of two facts: (1) that the crimes had been committed by (non-JCE) members of the AFRC/RUF rebel group; and (2) that the killings followed a similar modus operandi and fitted into the "widespread and systematic nature of the crimes" committed by the RUF/AFRC.[95] The Appeal Chamber could not identify the JCE member alleged to have been involved in the events (or even retrospectively aware of the commission of the crimes) or in any other manner indicate how *those* specific attacks had been procured by a JCE member in furtherance of the common purpose. The crimes were attributed to the JCE without any nexus other than the perpetrators being identified as members of the same two rebel armies, consisting of over ten thousand combatants.

Clearly, pursuant to the culpability principle that allows the attribution of crimes committed by non-JCE members to JCE members and thereafter to the Accused, there must be at least one JCE member associated with a particular crime to allow it to be attributed to the JCE. If a connection cannot be established, the crime cannot be attributed to the JCE, even if the act could legitimately be linked to the JCE member's common criminal purpose. A shared common criminal objective in itself is not enough to demonstrate that a plurality of persons acted in concert with each other to further that objective. Different groups, for example, may share the same goals and commit similar crimes in furtherance of those goals.[96]

Putting aside the Appeal Chamber's failure to comment on the erroneous test employed by the Trial Chamber, the approach it took to the facts in ascertaining the required evidential links from the Trial Chamber's findings was remarkably similar to a standard implied by the latter's own foreseeability test. It had little in common with the Brđanin requirement of a demonstration that a JCE member intentionally used a non-JCE member to commit crimes in furtherance of the common purpose. In the absence of findings focused on named JCE members, the Chamber's almost total reliance on contextual evidence such as that demonstrating a "permissive environment created by control exercised by AFRC and RUF where fighters could commit crimes with impunity"[97] and the findings that crimes were widespread and systematic,[98] although not wrong in principle, was only a fraction of the analysis required. These factors were a poor substitute for a comprehensive and careful analysis (by a trier of fact) that the crimes could be imputed to at least one member of the JCE and that

---

[93] RUF Appeal Judgment, *supra* note 39, at paras. 417–418. In regards to the other two crimes, the Trial Chamber found that Sam Bockarie, a JCE member, was one of the principal perpetrators. *See* RUF Trial Judgment, *supra* note 35, at paras. 1007, 1023, 1029, 1974.

[94] RUF Trial Judgment, *supra* note 35, at paras. 995–1005, 1974–1975, 1984 for findings on crimes committed in Tikonko Junction in Bo District.

[95] RUF Appeal Judgment, *supra* note 39, at paras. 417, 418.

[96] Prosecutor v. Haradinaj, Balaj and Brahimaj, Case No. IT-04–84-T, Appeal Judgment, para. 139 (Apr. 3, 2008); Prosecutor v. Krajišnik, Case No. IT-00–39-T, Trial Judgment, para. 884 (Sept. 27, 2006).

[97] RUF Appeal Judgment, *supra* note 39, at paras. 421–422.

[98] *Id.* at paras. 424, 440, 449.

this member – when using the non-JCE member – acted in accordance with the common plan. This test makes it abundantly clear: if a JCE member in the RUF case is not shown to be linked to crimes committed by non-JCE members, then the crimes cannot be imputed to the Accused pursuant to the JCE.

IV. VIOLATION OF TAYLOR'S RIGHT TO BE INFORMED OF THE CHARGES

As discussed above, the Special Court adopted an unprecedented approach to JCE pleading by approving Indictments that failed to articulate a "common purpose" with an essential shared criminal intent at the core of the alleged enterprise. Although JCE doctrine requires that the Prosecution plead, as a material fact, a common purpose that "amounts to or involves" a crime within the statute of the Court, none of the Special Court Indictments pled any crime as a necessary part of the common purpose, and in the Taylor case, the SCSL upheld an indictment that failed to explicitly plead any common purpose at all, criminal or otherwise.[99]

In May 2007, the second amended indictment in the Taylor case departed even further from established ICTY pleading practices by deleting all references to "joint criminal enterprise" and removing the paragraph in the original Indictment that described the common purpose of the JCE as a plan to "to take any actions necessary to gain and exercise political power and control over the territory of Sierra Leone, in particular the diamond mining areas."[100] The Taylor Indictment that formed the basis of the trial simply alleges that the Accused was responsible, pursuant to Article 6.1 of the Statute, for crimes that "amounted to or were involved within a common plan, design or purpose in which the Accused participated, or were a reasonably foreseeable consequence of such common plan, design or purpose."[101] This pleading failed to articulate an objective – criminal or otherwise – at the core of the alleged common purpose, and furthermore, like the other SCSL indictments, failed to plead criminal intent as a necessary part of the common purpose. Instead, the specific alleged crimes are pled in the alternative, as either within or outside some unspecified common purpose.[102]

By pleading intended crimes as a necessary part of the noncriminal objective, the ICTY approach produces inherently criminal common purposes, which satisfy the threshold requirement that the common criminal purpose of a JCE "amounts to or involves" a crime within the Statute of the Court. The SCSL approach circumvents this requirement, permitting the prosecutor to plead crimes as alternatively either within or outside the noncriminal objective, rather than as a necessary part of it. The obvious consequence of this approach is that the common purposes failed to articulate any definitive criminal intent,

---

[99] *See* AFRC Indictment, *supra* note 59; RUF Indictment, *supra* note 27, at para. 36; CDF Indictment, *supra* note 59; Prosecutor v. Taylor, Case No. SCSL-03–01-I, Second Amended Indictment, para. 33 (May 29, 2007) [hereinafter Amended Taylor Indictment]. As will be discussed in further detail later in this chapter, the Prosecution amended the original Taylor Indictment to omit the common purpose pleading that originally mirrored those in the RUF and AFRC Indictments. *See* Prosecutor v. Taylor, Case No. SCSL-03–01-I, Indictment, para. 23 (Mar. 7, 2003) [hereinafter Original Taylor Indictment].

[100] *See* Original Taylor Indictment, *supra* note 99, at paras. 23–24; *cf.* Amended Taylor Indictment, *supra* note 99, at para. 33.

[101] Amended Taylor Indictment, *supra* note 99, at para. 33.

[102] *Id.*

and therefore pled the alleged criminality of the joint enterprise as optional or, alternatively, wholly absent. The second amended Taylor Indictment took this deviation one step further, failing to describe any specific common purpose at all, let alone particularize criminal means as a necessary part of the shared objective.[103]

In response to an urgent Defense motion regarding defects in the indictment,[104] Trial Chamber II upheld the form of the JCE alleged in *Taylor*,[105] despite the fact that the Second Amended Taylor Indictment departed further than other SCSL indictments from well-established ICTY pleading standards by failing to specifically articulate any common purpose at all, criminal or otherwise.[106]

With neither objective nor means definitively pled as part of a common criminal purpose in the Taylor indictment, a two-judge Trial Chamber majority extrapolated a common purpose from a "holistic" interpretation of nine disparate paragraphs scattered throughout the Second Amended Indictment.[107] From these paragraphs, Trial Chamber II concluded that the Prosecution must have intended to allege the common purpose, design, or plan as a "campaign to terrorize the civilian population" of Sierra Leone, with the underlying crimes in Counts 2 through 11 being either within or a foreseeable consequence of that campaign.[108]

Unsurprisingly, the majority justices in Trial Chamber II relied upon the AFRC Appeal Judgment to justify adopting such a loose standard for specificity of pleading. In dissent, Justice Richard Lussick rejected this erosion of pleading standards:

> I do not interpret the Appeals Chamber decision as meaning that the Appeals Chamber has adopted pleading principles which are any less stringent than those of other international courts nor, in particular, that it has departed from well-established pleading principles by deciding that the common purpose of a joint criminal enterprise need not be clearly specified in an Indictment. Such an interpretation would obviously be an infringement on the statutory rights of the Accused to be informed clearly of the charges against him so that he may prepare a defence.[109]

Unwilling to compensate for Prosecution pleading deficiencies, Justice Lussick maintained that an accused person should not be required to undergo the "brain-twisting exercise" of

---

[103] Notwithstanding this blatant omission, a 2–1 Trial Chamber majority (affirmed on interlocutory appeal) declined to find the pleading defective. *See* Prosecutor v. Taylor, Case No. SCSL-03–1-T, Decision on Urgent Defense Motion Regarding a Fatal Defect in the Prosecution's Second Amended Indictment Relating to the Pleading of JCE (Feb. 27, 2009) [hereinafter Taylor JCE Decision].

[104] Prosecutor v. Taylor, Case No. SCSL-03–01-T-378, Urgent Defense Motion Regarding a Fatal Defect in the Prosecution's Second Amended Indictment Relating to the Pleading of JCE, Dec. 14, 2007 [hereinafter Taylor, Second Amended Indictment].

[105] *See* Taylor JCE Decision.

[106] *See* Taylor, Second Amended Indictment, *supra* note 104, at para. 33. As noted, the Indictment simply alleges that the Accused is responsible, pursuant to Article 6.1 of the Statute, for crimes that "amounted to or were involved within a common plan, design or purpose in which the Accused participated, or were a reasonably foreseeable consequence of such common plan, design or purpose."

[107] Taylor JCE Decision, *supra* note 103, at paras. 69–70 (where the majority of the Court interprets paragraphs 5, 33, 34, 9, 14, 22, 23, and 48 as being "taken together … [to] fulfil the requirements for pleading JCE.").

[108] *Id.* at para. 71.

[109] Prosecutor v. Taylor, Case No. SCSL-03–1-T, Dissenting Opinion of Justice Richard Lussick to the Decision on Urgent Defense Motion Regarding a Fatal Defect in the Prosecution's Second Amended Indictment Relating to the Pleading of JCE, para. 14 (Feb. 27, 2009).

reading disparate paragraphs of the indictment to "fathom what liability facts are most likely to form the basis for his alleged joint criminal enterprise. An indictment which requires an accused to do so is obviously defective in that it fails to clearly inform the accused of the case he is required to meet."[110]

Unfortunately, the Appeals Chamber subsequently confirmed that it was prepared to accept substantially less-stringent pleading requirements than those at the ICTY. Ignoring serious concerns raised in the dissent, the Chamber concluded that "[I]t is clear from a holistic reading of the Second Amended Indictment that the allegations in paragraph 5 complement the allegations in paragraph 33 ... [enough to] sufficiently plead the alleged common purpose of the JCE."[111]

Although the majority decision appeared to provide the Prosecution in the Taylor case with an inherently criminal common purpose at the core of its JCE, this interpretation of the pleading is curious, to say the least, as it was inconsistent with the common purpose described in the Amended Case Summary,[112] as well as Prosecution submissions in response to the Defense motion, which advanced an entirely different objective, arguing that "the 'common purpose' of the JCE alleged in this trial has always been 'to take any actions necessary to gain and exercise control of Sierra Leone, particularly the diamond mining areas.'"[113] Neither the Trial majority nor the four Appellate justices who upheld the decision on interlocutory appeal[114] took these inconsistencies into account.

It is worthwhile reflecting further on the effect of these cumulative decisions from the perspective of the right to be informed of the charges. First, the timing of the decisions was of critical concern. The Taylor Trial Chamber was seized of the Defense urgent motion in December 2007 alleging a defect in the JCE pleadings. The Taylor trial commenced the presentation of evidence in January 2008, and the Prosecution case rested one year later in February 2009. The Trial Chamber did not rule on the application until February 2009, after the close of the Prosecution case.

Putting aside the intractable problems of principle and practice that arose from the novel appellate law that must have weighed against a careful and precise understanding of the nature of the *actus reus* and *mens rea* alleged as constituting the fundamentals of the JCE, the trial advanced during the Prosecution case with an alleged common purpose "to take any actions necessary to gain and exercise control of Sierra Leone, particularly the diamond mining areas." At the close of that case, and as the Defense were completing their final preparations, the Accused was notified by the Trial Chamber that the common purpose,

---

[110] *Id.* at para. 15.

[111] Prosecutor v. Taylor, Case No. SCSL-03-1-T, Decision on Defense Notice of Appeal and Submissions Regarding the Majority Decision Concerning the Pleading of JCE in the Second Amended Indictment, Appeals Chamber, para. 21 (May 1, 2009).

[112] *See* Prosecutor v. Taylor, Case No. SCSL-03–01-T-327, Prosecution Notification of Filing of Amended Case Summary, paras. 42–44, 69–70 (Aug. 3, 2007).

[113] Taylor JCE Decision, *supra* note 103, at para. 34. Incidentally, this language articulates the same noncriminal objective the Prosecution chose to delete from the allegations when they amended the original Taylor Indictment. It remains a mystery why they chose to delete the language, but continued to rely upon the common purpose construction.

[114] The interlocutory decision on the Taylor JCE motion was issued May 1, 2009 by a four-judge Appeals Chamber. The chamber was short one member because Justice Fernando passed away in November 2008, and his replacement, Justice Fisher, was not sworn in until May 4, 2009.

design, or plan alleged was a "campaign to terrorize the civilian population" of Sierra Leone, with the underlying crimes in Counts 2 through 11 being either within or a foreseeable consequence of that campaign. In other words, the Accused had advanced a case to attempt to rebut the Prosecution's common purpose, only to be informed at the end of the Prosecution case that he had aimed at the wrong one.

As argued by the Defense in their closing brief, and noted by the Trial Chamber, there were several forms of prejudice that resulted from this unreasonable delay, namely: (1) the Accused could not conduct meaningful pretrial investigation into the alleged common purpose and the nature of the Accused's participation in it; (2) effective cross-examination of Prosecution witnesses regarding the common purpose of the JCE and the Accused's participation in it was severely undermined and hindered by the unresolved legal ambiguities surrounding the Indictment; (3) preparation for the Defense case during the currency of the Prosecution's case was fractured and impossible to progress due to uncertainty regarding which JCE allegations to defend; and (4) the very fact of a majority opinion on the JCE Motion serves to confirm that reasonable minds, including those of the judges, differed in their understanding of what the common purpose of the alleged JCE was.[115]

These were demonstrably reasonable arguments that are consistent with the pleadings standards that are the cornerstone of the jurisprudence at the ICTY and ICTR.[116] As argued earlier in this chapter, this requires that the Accused receives consistent notice concerning the charges and the material facts underpinning them. That is not to argue that the JCE pleading rules at the ICTY and ICTR are anything other than minimal, if not inadequate.

Historically, the Appeal Chamber at both the ICTY and the ICTR has been more than a little sanguine about upholding indictments (and convictions for JCE) without any pleading of a common purpose or with only vaguely defined common purposes.[117] The most obvious example of this is the Tadić case.[118] Clearly, as JCE did not yet exist, there was no pleading of a well-defined common purpose. Nonetheless, having read the JCE liability into Article 7(1) of the ICTY Statute, the Appeals Chamber went on to find the Accused responsible pursuant to a JCE.[119] Similarly Krstić, who at the time of the Srebrenica crimes was the Commander of the Drina Corps,[120] was convicted pursuant to Article 7(1) for participation in two JCEs, despite no JCE being pled.[121] The Trial Chamber considered it within its discretion to "convict the Accused under the appropriate head within the limits of the indictment and fair notice of the charges and insofar as the evidence permits."[122] It claimed that the Defense had been put on notice of this mode of liability through the Prosecutor's

---

[115] Prosecutor v. Taylor, Case No. SCSL-03-01-T, Judgment, para. 142, *citing* Defense Final Trial Brief, para. 54.

[116] *See* Wayne Jordash & John Coughlan, *The Right to Be Informed of the Nature and Cause of the Charges: A Potentially Formidable Jurisprudential Legacy*, in JUDICIAL CREATIVITY AT THE INTERNATIONAL CRIMINAL TRIBUNALS (Shane Darcy & Joseph Powderly eds., 2010), which discusses the development of more human rights law–compliant standards at the ICTR and ICTY in the last fifteen years.

[117] Prosecutor v. Krnojelac, Case No. IT-97-25-T, Judgment, paras. 84–86 (Mar. 15, 2002); *see also* Prosecutor v. Krnojelac, Case No. IT-97-25-A, Judgment, para. 138 (Sept. 17, 2003).

[118] *See, e.g.*, Prosecutor v. Tadić, Second Amended Indictment, Case No. IT-94-1-1, paras. 4.2, 4.5 (Dec. 14, 1995).

[119] Prosecutor v. D. Tadić, Case No. IT-94-1-T, paras. 366–376 (May 7, 1997); Prosecutor v. D. Tadić, Case No. IT-94-1-A, Judgment, para. 232 (July 15, 1999).

[120] The Drina Corps was a formation of the Bosnian Serb Army.

[121] Prosecutor v. Krstić, Case No. IT-98-33-T, Judgment (Aug. 2, 2001) [hereinafter Krstić Trial Judgment].

[122] *Id.* at para. 602.

Pre-Trial Brief, which "discussed this form of liability, specifically in the context of ethnic cleansing."[123] However, the sole reference to this mode of liability in the Prosecution's brief were the following remarks: "A theory of co-perpetration can also apply to a participation in ethnic cleansing," followed by the observation that this theory had previously been applied in the Kupreškić case at the ICTY, and one of the Accused had been found guilty "because he adhered to a common plan for the execution of the cleansing campaign in the village, which by necessity was a highly coordinated effort and required full prior knowledge of the intended activities and subordination to a common plan of action."[124] Notwithstanding these wholly tangential comments, the Appeals Chamber upheld Krstić's conviction pursuant to one of the JCE's found by the Trial Chamber.[125]

The same is true of the Kvočka case.[126] The Trial Chamber rejected the Defense's contention that the absence of JCE pleading precluded it from consideration by the Trial Chamber. It noted that the charges in the Amended Indictment that the accused "instigated, committed or otherwise aided and abetted" crimes may include responsibility for participating in a JCE designed to accomplish such crimes, and stated that "[a]lthough greater specificity in drafting indictments is desirable, failure to identify expressly the exact mode of participation is not necessarily fatal to an indictment if it nevertheless makes clear to the accused the 'nature and cause of the charge against him.'"[127] Again, the Trial Chamber considered it within its discretion to characterize the form of participation of the Accused, if any, according to the theory of responsibility it deemed most appropriate, within the limits of the Amended Indictment and insofar as the evidence permitted.[128] The Appeal Chamber agreed with this approach. Even though the Prosecution had failed to plead the category of JCE, let alone the basic elements of the JCE (such as the purpose of the enterprise, the identity of the participants, and the nature of the Accused's participation in the enterprise),[129] and the common purpose pled in the pretrial brief was a common purpose to persecute Muslims and Croats in the whole of Prijedor,[130] it nonetheless decided that the Accused had received sufficient notice of a common purpose limited to one detention center within the municipality.[131]

Indeed, lest the authors of this chapter appear to suggest otherwise, a close review of the body of jurisprudence defining JCE pleading standards even at the ICTY and ICTR shows that the rule determining the specificity of the pleading of *all* the constituent elements of JCE are less than demanding. The Prosecution has to plead the purpose of the enterprise, the identity of the participants, the nature of the Accused's participation in the enterprise, and his *mens rea*.[132] Astonishingly, apart from the requirement that these basic elements are

---

[123] *Id.*

[124] Prosecutor v. Krstić, Case No. IT-98-33-PT, Prosecution's Pre-Trial Brief (Feb. 25, 2000).

[125] Prosecutor v. Krstić, Case No. IT-98-33-A, Judgment (Apr. 19, 2004).

[126] Prosecutor v. Kvočka et al., Case No. IT-98-30/1-T, Judgment (Nov. 2, 2001) [hereinafter Kvočka Trial Judgment]; *see also* Prosecutor v. Zoran Kupreškić et al., Case No. IT-95-16-T, Judgment (Jan. 14, 2000) [hereinafter Kupreškić Trial Judgment].

[127] Kvočka Trial Judgment, *supra* note 126, at para. 247 (internal quotations omitted).

[128] *Id.* at para. 248. (internal quotations omitted).

[129] Prosecutor v. Kvočka et al., Case No. IT-98-30/1-A, Judgment, para. 42 (Feb. 28, 2002) [hereinafter Kvočka Appeal Judgment].

[130] Prosecutor v. Kvočka, Case No. IT-98-30/1-T, Prosecution Pre-Trial Brief, para. 216 (Feb. 14, 2000).

[131] Kvočka Appeal Judgment, *supra* note 129, at paras. 39, 44, 45, 196, 198, 246, and others.

[132] *Id.* at para. 28.

mentioned in the Indictment, the jurisprudence says little else. There are no other specific requirements concerning the details required to effectively describe the contours of the criminal purpose. There is no requirement that the Indictment pleads precisely the conduct of the JCE members said to demonstrate the shared intent at the heart of the JCE.[133] As concerns the pleading of the Accused's contribution to the JCE, the Prosecution is not required to be precise. Despite the fact that JCE liability is classified as a form of Article 7(1) commission, the Prosecution is allowed to circumvent the usual requirements that the Accused's role in a course of conduct has to be described so that the constituent acts are particularized.[134] Instead, Indictments are permitted to particularize a précis of the alleged conduct in the broadest of generic terms (e.g., training, supplying, supporting, authorizing, facilitating, failing, etc.)[135] It is permissible to particularize a course of conduct that is sufficiently vague to include anything (and exclude nothing) that might emerge from hundreds of witnesses and tens of thousands of pages of evidence over the years of a trial.

However, the problem was hugely exacerbated for Taylor. First, as noted previously, the Indictments at the SCSL were based on a notion that the Prosecution termed "notice pleading." They provided substantially less notice of the charges than at the other tribunals. In the words of the then-Chief Prosecutor of the SCSL, the indictments were supposed to be "shorter, tighter, and cleaner." The label "notice pleading" and this collection of synonyms in reality connotes nothing more than an approach that omitted most of the charges, material facts, and detail of the modes of responsibility that fifteen years of jurisprudence at the ICTY and ICTR had accepted as being essential for a fair trial of this size and complexity. Taylor and the other Accused at the SCSL were therefore tried on Indictments that would not have been accepted at the ICTR and ICTY because they violated the fundamental right to be informed promptly and in detail of the charges.

Therefore, even without the unfortunate delay in the Trial Chamber's decision clarifying the majority's view of the nature of the criminal purpose, the Accused was confronted with an Indictment that provided him with less of an opportunity to prepare an effective defense and an increased risk that the Prosecution case would change as it progressed, given that there was less by way of particularization of the case to prevent the inevitable shift in the evidence from impacting upon the overall parameters of the case.

Second, not only was the Taylor Defense handicapped by this lack of information and the increased flexibility provided to the Prosecution, but they were misled into accepting a criminal purpose that proved to be the wrong one. Although Justice Lussick was correct

---

[133] A recent ICTR Appeals Chamber Decision appears to suggest that the ICTR might be prepared to find this a requirement if the pleading inconsistently describes the conduct of some of the JCE members, but not others. That is, the Chamber took the view in the specific circumstances of that Indictment that the inclusion of incomplete details created ambiguity. It does not appear to create a general rule that all indictments must from thereinafter particularize the conduct of the JCE members: *see* Prosecutor v. Uwinkindi, Case No. ICTR-01–75-AR72(C), Decision on Defense Appeal against the Decision Denying Motion Alleging Defects in the Indictment, para. 14 (Nov. 16, 2011) [hereinafter Uwinkindi Decision of Nov. 16, 2011].

[134] For example, when the Prosecution pleads a case of "instigation," it must precisely describe the instigating acts and the instigated persons or groups of persons. *See, e.g.,* Prosecutor v. Blaškić, Case No. IT-95-14-A, Judgment, Oct. 22, 2001, paras. 213, 226; Uwinkindi Decision of Nov. 16, 2011, *supra* note 133, at para. 36.

[135] *See, e.g.,* Prosecutor v. Martić, Case No. IT-95–11, Amended Indictment (Sept. 9, 2003) [hereinafter Martić Amended Indictment]; Prosecutor v. Brdanin, Case No. IT-99–36-I, Sixth Amended Indictment (Dec. 9, 2003); Prosecutor v. Krajišnik, Case No. IT-00–39, Consolidated Amended Indictment (Mar. 7, 2002); Prosecutor v. Karadžić, Case No. IT-95–5/18–1, Third Amended Indictment (Feb. 27, 2009).

to caution against an approach that effectively required an accused person to interpret the indictment or, worse, guess at the criminal purpose from different parts of an indictment,[136] the more overriding problem in the case (following the ruling of the majority) was that the criminal purpose alleged by the Prosecution – set out with a degree of clarity in the Case Summary – presumably the blueprint for the trial in the first half, was no longer deemed to be operative in the second half of the trial.

Putting aside the fact that the majority in the Trial Chamber appeared to have assumed the role of Prosecutor by deciding on the most appropriate formulation of the JCE (or, put another way, by replacing the Prosecution's view of their own indictment with the Chamber's view, presumably based, at least in part, on the latter's view of what would best fit the facts as they had emerged in the courtroom), this meant that both parties must have progressed into the second half of the trial on a different basis than the first with real consequences for the preparation of an effective defense both during and after the Prosecution case. The Taylor Defense had investigated, cross-examined (or chosen not to) ninety-four witnesses (three experts, fifty-nine crime base, and thirty-two linkage witnesses), interviewed prospective witnesses, filed a Defense case summary, and advanced dismissal submissions (at the close of the Prosecution case) on a manifestly false premise.

The Trial Chamber dealt with this change in the common purpose in the final judgment by studiously ignoring it. The Trial Chamber noted "the Accused was on notice from May 29, 2007, when the second Amended Indictment was filed, of the common purpose of the JCE. As the Trial Chamber found that the pleading was not defective (a finding that was upheld by the Appeals Chamber), the Defense did not suffer any prejudice resulting from the fact that the JCE Decision was rendered only at the close of the Prosecution case."[137]

In Chapter 32 of this volume, Annie Gell, who authored the Human Rights Watch (HRW) report entitled "Even a 'Big Man' Must Face Justice,"[138] providing an assessment of the progress and achievements of the Taylor trial process, also declined to offer any meaningful criticism of the Taylor Indictment or the impact upon the Accused of the delay in ruling upon the Defense Motion. On the contrary, the report omitted any discussion of the impact of the fluctuating nature of the criminal purpose and downgraded the impact of the delay of the decision on the pleading of the JCE to an impotent warning that the Defense "allegations of prejudice to the accused might have been avoided if the Trial Chamber had rendered its decision in a more reasonable time."[139]

Concerning the overall nature of the pleading in the indictment, the HRW position was equally untroubled by the abandonment of pleading standards designed to make manifest the Accused's right to be informed of the charges. Conversely, the report noted, inter alia:

> The Taylor prosecution employed a different approach than that of Milošević, using a technique called "notice pleading" – a short and plain statement of the charges to give the defendant notice, while omitting substantial detail. The indictment, and accompanying

---

[136] Prosecutor v. Taylor, Case No. SCSL-03–1-T, Dissenting Opinion of Justice Richard Lussick to the Decision on Urgent Defense Motion Regarding a Fatal Defect in the Prosecution's Second Amended Indictment Relating to the Pleading of JCE, paras. 14, 15 (Feb. 27, 2009).

[137] Taylor Trial Judgment, para. 147.

[138] Human Rights Watch, *Even a "Big Man" Must Face Justice: Lessons from the Trial of Charles Taylor* (July 25, 2012), http://www.hrw.org/reports/2012/07/25/even-big-man-must-face-justice (last visited Sept. 12, 2012).

[139] *Id.* at 26 (internal quotations omitted).

case summary, provides more general geographic areas and time periods of crimes rather than specific crime scenes and identification of individual victims. The Taylor indictment also includes a limited list of charges – 11 in all.[140]

The prosecutor's efforts to provide an indictment in the Taylor case unencumbered by excessive details with a limited number of counts alleged appear to have contributed to avoiding some of the pitfalls of the Milošević trial.[141]

Crafting indictments that are representative of the crimes committed but not burdened by an unmanageable number of charges or excessive detail is desirable. However, achieving expeditious and fair proceedings will necessitate carefully balancing considerations of efficiency and manageability with the imperative of providing sufficient information to ensure adequate notice to the accused.[142]

Gell's and HRW's approach is characteristic of a general malaise in international criminal trials to an Accused's right to be informed promptly and in detail of the charges. Despite the oft-stated importance of this right to the overall fairness of a criminal trial, in the main, the need to ensure that this right is given reality through common-sense and practical-based pleadings and particularization of the case is not only underappreciated but often misunderstood, or worse, pointedly disregarded. Of course, no one can disagree with HRW's admonishment that "[c]rafting indictments that are representative of the crimes committed but not burdened by an unmanageable number of charges" is desirable. However, delivering the "imperative of providing sufficient information to ensure adequate notice to the accused" requires a firm application of principles in the trial setting. It must mean something practically, if it is not to become a meaningless mantra.

HRW's analysis on the issue suffers from the same misconceptions concerning the importance of disclosure to an Accused that must have underpinned the Taylor Trial Chamber's failure to rule on the JCE issue until after the close of the Prosecution case and that plagued the RUF Trial Chamber's treatment of the right. As the RUF Trial Chamber failed to grasp the definition or the legal significance of a charge, and the Taylor Trial Chamber failed to understand the need for a settled view of the JCE alleged, HRW's analysis failed to appreciate the difference between charges and counts and the importance of each to the management of the trial. The Taylor Indictment did not include a limited list of eleven charges in all[143]; rather it contained eleven counts. Critically, the trial involved several hundred charges – that is several hundred distinct bases for conviction – most of them not particularized in the indictment or Case Summary and most of them alleged pursuant to the wrong criminal purpose.

HRW's claim that the SCSL's approach to indictments (less particularization of charges and less detail all around) avoided some of the delays encountered in the Milošević case must therefore be viewed through this analytical error. Rather than the case management or speed of a trial being foremost dependent upon the number of counts or excessive detail, it is in fact the number of charges that remains the paramount consideration. The delays in the Milošević case were largely the result of an overambitious indictment, which contained

---

[140] *Id.* at 23 (internal quotations omitted).
[141] *Id.*
[142] *Id.*
[143] *Id.*

too many counts, too many crime bases, *and* too many charges. It is not excessive details that slow a trial down: what matters are the volume of crime scenes and number of charges arising from them. A one-count trial pleaded without any detail in the indictment may be as forensically heavy as a ten-count trial, depending upon these critical criteria.

If we put these misconceptions aside, HRW was right to suggest that "[c]rafting indictments that are representative of the crimes committed but not burdened by an unmanageable number of charges" is of paramount importance.[144] An accused facing an indictment containing only eleven charges *may* not, depending on the circumstances, be unduly hindered in the preparation of his defense by notice pleading, or by a failure to particularize the charges in the indictment (provided they appear in some accusatory documentation early enough in the proceedings) or even by delay in the clarification of the precise form of the liabilities alleged. However, this is not the position of most international accused, and certainly not Taylor. In sum, it is not the detail that is pled to explain the charges that is the problem. Nor is it a solution to omit the charges from the indictment or case summary but, nonetheless, allow them to be adduced through the witness testimony. This approach is akin to pretending that the charges are not part of the case, until they flood the Chamber causing confusion and delay as the Prosecution struggles to claim that they were always part of their case, the Accused clogs the courtroom with ongoing complaints about disclosure, and the Trial Chamber struggles to inculcate the changes into an ever-growing evidential case. Such an approach does nothing other than cause case management problems, as well as undermine the fairness of the trial by rising roughshod over an accused's right to be informed of the case.

The Milošević trial was hundreds of charges heavier and tens of thousands of pages of evidence larger than the Taylor trial. It was this excess that led to the delays, not the detailed particularization of the charges in the Indictment, which could only have enhanced the certainty required to conduct the criminal trial. It is this certainty that ought to be at the forefront of the right to be informed of the charges. It is essential to stop cumbersome international trials being undermined by shifting goalposts and unclear aims and objectives. Only then may the accused, generally suffering from a lack of resources (although this may well not be true of the Taylor case, which eventually received healthy funding), be prevented from being overwhelmed by hundreds of charges that may fall within the four posts of a broad indictment but are allowed to cascade into the courtroom without being tethered to an indictment pleading, a settled view of the law, or a consistent view of the liabilities.

A. Conclusion: Punishment for Membership in the RUF, the Imputation of Crimes, and the Hamstringing of the Taylor Defense

Most of the convictions entered against the three Accused as JCE members were based on the actions of others, particularly non-JCE members. As outlined above: in terms of unlawful killings, approximately 510 deaths were attributed to the Accused without any showing that the non-JCE members implicated were connected in the Brđanin/Krajišnik sense to at least one member of the JCE.

---

[144] *Id.*

Regarding the hundreds of criminal acts of sexual and physical violence, the overwhelming majority were found perpetrated by non-JCE members. The Appeals Chamber upheld these convictions without a Brđanin/Krajišnik showing.[145] By failing to apply the correct and complete test, the Court held the Accused responsible for most of the crimes committed by AFRC and RUF fighters regardless of whether any JCE member could be said to have "used" a non-JCE member to commit a crime in furtherance of the JCE's common criminal purpose. The RUF trial's judicial failure to connect most of the crimes to a JCE member is precisely the type of "open-ended concept that permits convictions based on guilt by association,"[146] which the Appeal Chamber in *Brđanin*, the leading JCE case at the ICTY and ICTR, repeatedly emphasized was an unacceptable perversion of the JCE doctrine. Attributing crimes without this essential nexus – a common feature of the RUF trial and appellate judgments – is to return guilty verdicts for hundreds of the gravest of crimes in clear contravention of the culpability principle.[147]

Moreover, attributing criminal responsibility to the Accused for crimes committed by all members of their group, JCE member or otherwise, in these circumstances, punished them for being an RUF member. Whether the Appeals Chamber believed the RUF to be a criminal organization or not, membership in a criminal organization is not prohibited under international criminal law,[148] and to de facto attribute criminal liability for this membership was a flagrant infringement of the principle *nullum crimen sine lege*.

For Taylor, the situation was less egregious, but still a trial without the certainty of liabilities and charges will be to a greater or lesser degree unfair. The Trial Chamber's treatment of the issue, first to rewrite the criminal purpose from the one notified by the Prosecutor in its case summary, before disregarding the change or its impact on the preparation of an effective defense in the final trial judgment[149] was a curious approach to the Defense complaint. The summary dismissal of the complaint at one time or another by the Trial and the Appeal Chamber said more about the motives to ensure a smooth trial than a serious attempt to protect Taylor's right to prompt, consistent, and detailed notice of the charges, including the associated liabilities.

B. Conclusion: Trials Lacking Due Process

Premised upon these fundamental procedural and evidential deficiencies in the trial and appellate process, the RUF trial failed to adhere to international standards of justice, fairness, and due process. The volume of late charges and evidence and the corresponding prejudice are unprecedented in modern international criminal law. While the ICTY and ICTR Appeal Chambers grapple with appellant complaints of a handful of late charges and material facts, the prosecution of the RUF Accused involved hundreds.

---

[145] *Id.*

[146] Brđanin Appeal Judgment, *supra* note 47, at para. 428.

[147] Prosecutor v. Sesay et al., Doc. No. SCSL-04–15-A-279, Appeal Brief for Augustine Gbao, June 1, 2009, Annex I, for a full description of the crimes committed by non-JCE members that were left unconnected to a JCE member.

[148] Prosecutor v. Milutinovic et al., Case No. IT-99-37-AR72, Decision on Dragoljub Ojdanic's Motion Challenging Jurisdiction – Joint Criminal Enterprise, para. 25 (May 21, 2003).

[149] Taylor Trial Judgment, para. 147.

Although avoiding such manifest unfairness, largely by returning convictions on other liabilities, the Taylor trial nonetheless failed to provide the Accused with a clear under-standing of either the charges alleged or the criminal purpose at the heart of the JCE. It is this information that is most essential for an accused in the context of an international criminal trial, especially one that predicates the prosecution on the back of an expansive JCE stretching across multiple countries.

There can be no justification for such processes, and the relevant SCSL Trial or Appeal Chambers that felt constrained to comment proffered nothing but avoidance instead of explanation. A trial in manifest breach of a right to be informed of the charges and evidence ceases to be a trial; rather it is a process of attrition with no end to the allegations and the evidence and no real chance of an effective defense. This is demonstrably not an application of the presumption of innocence, which involves the maintenance of a process that allows a reasonable opportunity to present a defense to every allegation made.

That the SCSL Appeal Chamber struck out the RUF complaint on these matters on a technicality, arguing that the Appellant had breached a page limit rule (when there were no novel arguments in the annex, and its length corresponded to the number of new charges and material facts pled through the evidence),[150] and that the Taylor Trial Chamber simply ignored the issue, is perhaps an eloquent demonstration of the policy objectives at play in the trials and the sacrifice of fairness in pursuit of them.

Equally, imputing criminal liability to JCE members for crimes committed by non-JCE members (part of the same AFRC/RUF rebel group) without providing an evidentiary nexus between the crimes, the non-JCE, and the JCE member, is a clear demonstration of a breach of the culpability principle and the principle of legality. This is precisely what occurred for hundreds of crimes in the RUF case. Such findings hold the three Accused responsible for the acts of all the RUF, independent of whether the crimes were committed to further the JCE's common criminal purpose or not and irrespective of whether the Accused intended or even foresaw the crimes. It is the attribution of guilt without fault, akin to collective pun-ishment by an international court.

Consequently the RUF trial remains a worthy object for study and reflection. It ought to be soberly examined by those entrusted with the law. It is a reminder of the need to hold tight to basic due process principles and to build upon – not ignore – the jurispruden-tial lessons from the ICTY and ICTR. The types of demonstrably unsafe convictions may well satisfy those focused only on the immediate policy objectives defined by the need to bring accountability in war-torn countries. Nonetheless, it should also be recalled that the long-term legitimacy of international criminal law rests at least in part on the understand-ing that these critical objectives – national reconciliation and the maintenance of peace – depend as much upon justice being done and seen to be done, as it does on the final tally of convictions.

---

[150] *See* Prosecutor v. Sesay, Kallon and Gbao, SCSL-04-15-PT, Sesay Final Trial Brief, Annex A1–A3 (Aug. 1, 2008) for a comprehensive listing of the pretrial notice and the additional and amended charges.

6

Command Responsibility in the Sierra Leonean Conflict: The Duty to Take Measures to Prevent Crimes and Punish the Perpetrators

Sandesh Sivakumaran[*]

I. INTRODUCTION

The Special Court for Sierra Leone (Special Court or SCSL) has made a number of important contributions to the elucidation and development of international humanitarian law and international criminal law. In the interest of clarifying the law and developing it further, this chapter analyzes one area that was largely neglected by the Special Court despite the need for it to have been considered.

In certain situations, commanders of armed forces may be held criminally responsible for crimes that were committed by their subordinates. As is well-known, there are essentially three elements of command responsibility[1]: a superior/subordinate relationship between the person accused of command responsibility and the perpetrator of the crime; a certain knowledge on the part of the superior that the subordinate was about to, or had committed, a crime; and a failure of the superior to take reasonable measures to prevent and punish the crime.[2]

Command responsibility applies in both international armed conflicts and non-international armed conflicts and in regular armed forces and irregular military organizations. The manner in which the three elements play out, however, differ as between state armed forces and irregular forces such as paramilitary groups and non-state armed groups. The Special Court had to consider the issue of command responsibility in three irregular forces – the Civil Defense Forces (CDF), the Armed Forces Revolutionary Council (AFRC), and the Revolutionary United Front (RUF) – a pro-government armed group, a dissident force, and a non-state armed group respectively. Accordingly, it is instructive to analyze the jurisprudence of the Special Court in this regard.

The SCSL made important pronouncements on the superior–subordinate element and the notion of effective control in irregular forces.[3] In particular, the indicia it set out in this regard are valuable. This contribution explores the element that was largely neglected by Trial and Appeal Chambers of the Special Court, namely the failure to take necessary and

[*] Associate Professor and Reader in Public International Law, University of Nottingham. This is a developed- and Special Court for Sierra Leone–focused version of *Command Responsibility in Irregular Groups*, which appeared in 10 JICJ 1129 (2012).
[1] The term "command responsibility" will be used interchangeably with "superior responsibility."
[2] The three elements may, of course, be broken down further. For the International Criminal Court, causation constitutes a fourth element.
[3] *See* Harmen van der Wilt's Chapter 7 in this volume.

reasonable measures to prevent and punish the offense. It considers the specificities of the obligation and how it is applied in the context of irregular forces.

II. DUTY TO TAKE MEASURES TO PREVENT AND PUNISH

The third limb of command responsibility is that the superior in question failed to take necessary and reasonable measures to prevent the crime and punish the perpetrators of the crime. As the jurisprudence of the international criminal tribunals have stressed, this is more a matter of evidence than substantive law.[4] Nonetheless, a few general points on the law are in order. In particular, as command responsibility is an omission-based mode of liability, several questions follow. First, is a preexisting legal duty required? If so, second, where does the duty come from? Third, what is the substantive content of the duty? These questions will be considered in turn.

A. Is a Duty Required?

As to the first question, the SCSL has consistently held that a preexisting duty on the part of the superior is required. The *AFRC* Trial Chamber indicated that liability is for an omission (i.e., for the failure to perform an act required by international law).[5] The *CDF* and *RUF* Trial Chambers were even clearer on this point, providing that:

> the nature of responsibility pursuant to Article 6(3) is based upon the duty of a superior to act, which consists of a duty to prevent and a duty to punish criminal acts of his subordinates. It is thus a failure to act when under a duty to do so which is the essence of this form of responsibility. It is responsibility for an omission where a superior may be held criminally responsible when he fails to take the necessary and reasonable measures to prevent the criminal act or punish the offender.[6]

Thus, in the view of the Special Court, responsibility lies in the failure to perform a preexisting duty. This is an important clarification as, in the early jurisprudence of the ICTY, it was not altogether clear whether a preexisting duty was required. Although the word "duty" was often mentioned, there was little, if any, discussion on the nature of the duty.

B. Locating the Duty

More difficult, and largely missing from the judgments of the SCSL, is from where the preexisting duty emanates. The majority of cases before the Special Court – and before the ICTY – skip over this important issue leaving the matter untouched; only in an occasional case is the matter given any attention.

---

[4] *See, e.g.,* Prosecutor v. Halilović, IT-01–48-T, Judgment, para. 74 (Nov. 16, 2005) [hereinafter *Halilović* Trial Judgment].

[5] Prosecutor v. Brima, Kamara and Kanu, SCSL-04–16-T, Judgment, para. 783 (June 20, 2007) [hereinafter *AFRC* Trial Judgment]. *See also* Prosecutor v. Fofana and Kondewa, SCSL-04–14-T, Judgment, para. 249 (Aug. 2, 2007) [hereinafter *CDF* Trial Judgment], both referring to ICTY jurisprudence.

[6] *CDF* Trial Judgment, *supra* note 5, at para. 234; Prosecutor v. Sesay, Kallon and Gbao, SCSL-04–15-T, Judgment, para. 283 (Mar. 2, 2009) [hereinafter *RUF* Trial Judgment], both referring to ICTY jurisprudence.

The *AFRC* Trial Chamber indicated that liability stems from "the failure to perform an act required by international law."[7] Likewise, the *Halilović* Trial Chamber held that "international law imposes an affirmative duty on superiors to prevent and punish crimes committed by their subordinates."[8] The question then arises as to which part of international law creates such a duty. It is submitted that the duty is inherent in the notion of a responsible command. This is the consequence of the *Hadžihasanović* Decision on Command Responsibility. Implicit in the holding that command responsibility is derived from the responsible command is the idea that there is a duty on commanders to take measures to ensure compliance with international humanitarian law. Indeed, at one point in the Decision, the Appeals Chamber explicitly refers to the idea that "the concept of responsible command looks to the duties comprised in the idea of command."[9]

Throughout history, obligations have been placed on commanders to ensure respect for the law on the part of subordinates.[10] The idea has even been traced back to the trial of Peter von Hagenbach.[11] The principle can also be found in the conventional instruments. For example, the 1899 Hague Regulations reference "[t]he laws, rights, and duties of war apply[ing] not only to armies, but also to militia and volunteer corps fulfilling the following conditions: 1. To be commanded by a person responsible for his subordinates."[12] For its part, the 1929 Geneva Convention on the Wounded and Sick provides that "[t]he Commanders-in-Chief of belligerent armies shall arrange the details for carrying out the preceding articles."[13] Other conventions also provide for obligations on the part of commanders.[14] Thus, the idea that commanders have certain obligations insofar as compliance with the law is concerned has a long history.

The obligation is by no means limited to commanders involved in international armed conflicts. The principle also has a long history in situations of non-international armed conflict and in respect of regular forces and irregular forces alike. Prior to, and during, the U.S. war of independence, the American Articles of War provided that:

> Every officer commanding, in quarters or on a march, shall keep good order, and, to the utmost of his power, redress all such abuses or disorders which may be committed by any officer or soldier under his command: If upon any complaint [being] made to him, of officers or soldiers beating, or otherwise ill-treating any person, or committing any kind of riot, to the disquieting of the inhabitants of this Continent; he, the said commander, who shall refuse or omit to see justice done on the offender or offenders, and reparation made to the party or parties injured, as far as the offender's wages shall enable him or them, shall, upon due proof thereof, be punished, as ordered by a general court-martial, in such manner as if he himself had committed the crimes or disorders complained of.[15]

---

[7] *AFRC* Trial Judgment, *supra* note 5, at para. 783. *See also CDF* Trial Judgment, *supra* note 5, at para. 249, both referring to ICTY jurisprudence.

[8] Para. 54.

[9] Para. 22. *See also Halilović* Trial Judgment, *supra* note 4, at paras. 39–40.

[10] *See*, tracing the history, W.H. Parks, *Command Responsibility for War Crimes*, 62 MIL. L. REV. 1 (1973).

[11] *Id.* at 4–5. On the trial, see G. SCHWARZENBERGER, THE LAW OF ARMED CONFLICT 462 (1968).

[12] Hague Regulations art. 1. *See also* 1907 Hague Regulations art. 1.

[13] *Id.* art. 26.

[14] *See, e.g.*, 1907 Hague Regulations art. 43.

[15] American Articles of War, June 30, 1775, art. XII, *reproduced in* 2 JOURNALS OF THE CONTINENTAL CONGRESS 1774–1779, at 111, 114 (1905). A largely similar provision was adopted in the American Articles of War, Sept. 20, 1776, sec. IX, *reproduced in* 5 JOURNALS OF THE CONTINENTAL CONGRESS 1774–1779, at 777, 794.

The Articles demonstrate that certain obligations are vested in commanders.

During the American–Philippines war (1899–1902), various individuals were tried before a U.S. military commission in respect of (what today would be described as) command responsibility for violations of the law of war. The individuals in question included members of the Philippine non-state armed group.[16] The cases are important precedents. A majority of the U.S. Supreme Court would refer to them in *Yamashita* in support of the observation that "officers have been held liable where they knew that a crime was to be committed, had the power to prevent it and failed to exercise that power."[17] Importantly for the purposes of this chapter, the cases stand out in their applicability of command responsibility to non-international armed conflicts and to commanders of non-state armed groups. Thus, even in the law of non-international armed conflict, commanders are vested with an obligation to take certain measures to ensure observance with international humanitarian law on the part of subordinates. This is true of commanders of regular armed forces and irregular military organizations.

The principle is also reflected in the domestic law of various states. Very many states provide for a legal duty on the part of commanders to prevent and punish crimes in certain circumstances.[18] National military manuals provide likewise.[19] A number of armed groups also have provisions on the subject.[20]

The consequence of all this is that, aside from certain classes of persons who have their own duties, such as persons controlling occupied territory and supervisors of prisoners of war and other detention camps,[21] the superior in question must be part of the responsible command of the group in order to have the requisite duty. The precise status of the individuals is unimportant; they may be part of the de jure command structure or part of the de facto command, a military commander or a civilian acting as a commander. Nonetheless, they must be part of the command structure.

All organized armed groups have some form of responsible command. Otherwise they would not constitute a "group" for the purposes of international humanitarian law; instead, they would comprise a loose band of individuals. In the case of a non-state armed group party to a non-international conflict, the group is required to be organized, and an aspect of organization is responsible command.[22] If the group is not organized, the situation will not amount to a non-international armed conflict. Thus, responsible command is an element of each and every non-state armed group fighting in a non-international armed conflict. Likewise, responsible command is an element of paramilitary groups. As indicated above,

---

[16] General Orders No. 130, Headquarters Division of the Philippines, June 19, 1901, *reproduced in* CHARGES OF CRUELTY, ETC, TO THE NATIVES OF THE PHILIPPINES, 57th Cong. 1, S. DOC. No. 205, Part 2, 85–6; General Orders No. 264, Sept. 9, 1901, *reproduced in id.* at 364.

[17] 327 U.S. 1, 39–40 (1946).

[18] *See generally* J.-M. HENCKAERTS & L. DOSWALD-BECK, CUSTOMARY INTERNATIONAL HUMANITARIAN LAW, VOLUME II: PRACTICE 3745–51 (2005).

[19] *See generally id.* at 3738–45.

[20] *See, e.g.*, Chin National Front's Guidelines on the Code of War art. 33 (undated). The Article is entitled "Responsibilities of Officials" and is located in a Part on the "Prevention of War Crimes and Responsibilities."

[21] On which, see I. BANTEKAS, PRINCIPLES OF DIRECT AND SUPERIOR RESPONSIBILITY IN INTERNATIONAL HUMANITARIAN LAW 102–08 (2002); E. VAN SLIEDREGT, THE CRIMINAL RESPONSIBILITY OF INDIVIDUALS FOR VIOLATIONS OF INTERNATIONAL HUMANITARIAN LAW 147–48 (2003).

[22] *See* S. SIVAKUMARAN, THE LAW OF NON-INTERNATIONAL ARMED CONFLICT 164–65, 174 (2012).

as far back as 1899, The Hague Regulations referred to "[t]he laws, rights, and duties of war apply[ing] not only to armies, but also to militia and volunteer corps" inter alia with a responsible command.[23] The situation in Sierra Leone provides a useful example. The RUF, despite being something of a ragtag armed group, had a responsible command. So too did the AFRC, the classic example of a dissident force, as indeed did the CDF, a pro-government armed group.[24]

Responsible command in regular armed forces may not look the same as that in irregular forces. The very notion of the de facto commander and the test of effective control testify to this. In particular, certain armed groups will not utilize a pyramidal system of organization; instead, they will utilize a more horizontal form of organization. However, this does not mean that the group is not organized. To require a pyramidal system of organization is to transform the model of organization in regular forces into the only acceptable notion of organization.

III. CONTENT OF THE DUTY

A. *General Remarks*

Before analyzing the content of the duty, one general remark is in order. Although the obligation to take measures to prevent and punish together comprise the third limb, and are related, they comprise two distinct duties. This has long been recognized with the *RUF* Trial Chamber noting that "they are not alternative obligations" and supporting the ICTY statement that a superior's "obligations to prevent will not be met by simply waiting and punishing afterwards."[25] Yet the consequences of this point have not been followed through and, all too often, the two issues are conflated in the jurisprudence. For example, the *AFRC* Trial Chamber found:

> on the basis of the evidence examined … that the Accused Kamara had the ability to issue orders which were followed; that he took over authority for promoting AFRC soldiers after JPK left Kono District; and that generally, the AFRC troops maintained an effective day-to-day chain of command and regularly mustered, *that therefore* it was within the Accused's material ability to prevent crimes committed by his subordinates or to punish subordinates for committing crimes.[26]

The ability to issue orders and to promote fighters may well go to the ability to prevent crimes, although much will turn on the nature of the orders and the like. However, it has far less to do with the ability to punish crimes. It is critical to keep the two obligations separate as different evidence will go to each. Just because a superior has the ability to order a particular action does not mean that the same superior has the ability to punish individuals, and vice versa. The relevant functions may well vest in different persons. Furthermore, the time at which the knowledge is to be judged differs for the obligation to prevent a crime and

---

[23] Regulations art. 1. *See also* 1907 Regulations art. 1.

[24] *See* the contribution of Harmen van der Wilt (Chapter 7 of this volume).

[25] *RUF* Trial Judgment, *supra* note 6, at para. 314; Prosecutor v. Limaj, IT-03–66-T, Judgment, para. 527 (Nov. 30, 2005) [hereinafter *Limaj* Trial Judgment].

[26] *AFRC* Trial Judgment, *supra* note 5, at para. 1891 (emphasis added).

the obligation to punish that crime. Thus, although the elements of prevent and punish are related, they are not at all the same, and need to be judged separately from one another.

B. Measures Taken to Prevent

Insofar as taking measures to prevent a crime of a subordinate is concerned, the general rule is that "the kind and extent of measures to be taken depend on the degree of effective control exercised by the superior at the relevant time, and on the severity and imminence of the crimes that are about to be committed."[27] In this regard, the *Halilović* Trial Chamber distinguished between a general obligation to prevent and a specific obligation to prevent, the latter of which alone could result in criminal responsibility.[28] The general obligation includes such things as ensuring subordinates are aware of their international humanitarian law obligations, to train subordinates, and to ensure discipline.[29] The specific obligation includes such things as securing reports that military actions were carried out in accordance with international law, issuing orders aimed at bringing relevant practices in accord with international humanitarian law, protesting against or criticizing criminal action, taking disciplinary measures to prevent commission of atrocities by subordinates, and insisting before a superior authority that immediate action be taken.[30] The Special Court referred to these latter indicia.[31]

However, this is not the best way to understand the duty to prevent.[32] The measures to be taken in this regard are not of two classes, one of which may result in liability and the other not; rather, the measures form a spectrum. The obligation to take measures to prevent the crime arises when the superior knows or has reason to know that a crime is about to be committed. Thus, instruction, training, and the like that should have been undertaken prior to the gleaning of knowledge cannot go to the liability of the commander. That being said, the lack of instruction and training on international humanitarian law are precisely some of the indicia that may put the commander on notice that there is a risk that crimes are about to be committed.[33] The chances of a crime being committed are far higher because no general orders to comply with international humanitarian law were issued. A climate in which violations are more likely to be committed is thus being fostered. More has to be done in order to satisfy the obligations of the superior.

So, what are the measures that could be taken to prevent the commission of a crime on the part of a subordinate once the superior possesses the relevant knowledge or is on notice, bearing in mind both the superior and subordinate are part of an irregular force? The measures are of various sorts. A first category of measures are orders not to undertake certain actions, (re-)issuing orders to comply with international humanitarian law, reminding

---

[27] *AFRC* Trial Judgment, *supra* note 5, at para. 798, referring to Prosecutor v. Orić, IT-03–68-T, Judgment, para. 329 (June 30, 2006) [hereinafter *Orić* Trial Judgment].

[28] *Halilović* Trial Judgment, *supra* note 4, at para. 80. *See also Orić* Trial Judgment, *supra* note 27, at para. 330.

[29] *Halilović* Trial Judgment, *supra* note 4, at paras. 81–88.

[30] *Id.* at para. 89; Prosecutor v. Strugar, IT-01–42-T, Judgment, para. 374 (Jan. 31, 2005) [hereinafter *Strugar* Trial Judgment], referring in turn to post-WWII jurisprudence.

[31] *CDF* Trial Judgment, *supra* note 5, at para. 248; *RUF* Trial Judgment, *supra* note 6, at para. 315.

[32] *See also* Prosecutor v. Halilović, IT-01–48-A, Judgment, para. 64 (Oct. 16, 2007).

[33] *AFRC* Trial Judgment, *supra* note 5, at paras. 794, 1730 and 1732; *RUF* Trial Judgment, *supra* note 6, at para. 311.

subordinates of internal regulations of the group that contain an obligation to abide by the law, and undertaking (further) training on international humanitarian law. The orders should not simply be of the routine sort and must be conveyed to all the necessary individuals.[34] The formal terminology of international humanitarian law does not have to be used; language understood by fighters could – indeed should – be used instead, for example "do not take liberty from women," to use the wording of the RUF regulations, rather than "do not rape," assuming this is indeed the language understood by fighters. A second category of measures involves making clear the disapproval of the intended action, instituting disciplinary proceedings if the planning of the crime has gone beyond a certain stage, and even arresting or interning individuals if commission of the crime is imminent. It would include recalling particular individuals from the area if they are known to be planning a crime, redeploying troops, or adding a further level of monitoring and oversight. Should the superior in question be unable to take any such actions, it may consist of reporting the intended acts up the chain of command or referring the matter to persons who do have the authority to forestall the action.[35]

There is also a progressive element to the issue. If the superior sought to prevent the commission of a crime, for example, through the issuance of an order, but that order failed to prevent the violation, next time the mere issuance of an order will not suffice. The superior will have to go a step further, again, provided it is within his ability to go a step further. Merely repeating what was done earlier, and which failed, will not suffice. Should there by a history of unlawful conduct or a systematic practice of unlawful conduct, the duty to punish (earlier) crimes of subordinates will also form part of the component of the measures to be taken to prevent (future) crimes.

If the violations are of a systematic nature and the superior has the material ability to do so – usually when the person is at the highest levels of the group – he or she may be expected to introduce more systematic policies. To take a concrete example, during the Chinese civil war, pillage, looting, and the like was commonplace. Accordingly, the Eight Points for Attention, one of the Chinese People's Liberation Army's internal regulations, contained no fewer than four norms on the subject.[36] This was done in order to seek to put an end to such violations and maintain good relations with the people.[37] The adoption of an internal rule would constitute one of the measures that superiors may be expected when on notice of systematic violations, in order to seek to prevent future violations of a similar sort. Mere adoption, of course, would be insufficient; the rule would also have to be enforced. Thus, although the RUF adopted its Eight Codes of Conduct, which was largely the same as the Eight Points of the CPLA,[38] it was rarely enforced. Indeed, on the contrary, at one

---

[34] Prosecutor v. Bemba Gombo, ICC-01/05–01/08, Decision Pursuant to Article 61(7)(a) and (b) of the Rome Statute on the Charges of the Prosecutor Against Jean-Pierre Bemba Gombo, para. 496 (June 15, 2009); *Orić* Trial Judgment, *supra* note 27, at para. 331.

[35] For a range of measures, see *Strugar* Trial Judgment, *supra* note 30, at para. 374; *Orić* Trial Judgment, *supra* note 27, at para. 331.

[36] These were: Pay fairly for what you buy; Return everything you borrow; Pay for anything you damage; Do not damage crops.

[37] O. Bangerter, *Reasons Why Armed Groups Choose to Respect International Humanitarian Law or Not*, 93 IRRC 353, 363 (2011).

[38] *Reproduced at* RUF Trial Judgment, *supra* note 6, at para. 705.

point in time, the RUF instituted "Operation Pay Yourself" by which fighters were to pay themselves by looting civilian property.[39]

Ultimately, as noted above, precisely what measures will be undertaken will depend on the material abilities of the superior. The obligation is only engaged as the superior in question has been established as having effective control over the relevant subordinate. The indicia pointing to this effective control will thus have an impact on the measures that were within the superior's powers. For example, usually, effective control is demonstrated through the issuance of orders on the part of the superior and the orders being followed on the part of the subordinates.[40] In such a case, the superior may be expected to issue an order prohibiting the commission of the relevant acts. However, even in this respect, much will turn on the nature and subject of the orders in question. A superior may have the authority to order the deployment of fighters but not to control the methods of combat used. Likewise, a superior may have the authority to order the release or transfer of prisoners,[41] or to promote; however, this does not mean that he has the ability to order the movement of subordinates. The specificities, in addition to the generalities, are important.

Should the superior be involved in the commission of the crime, encourage it, or provide support for it, this goes against all notions of the obligation to take the necessary and reasonable measures. In such a situation, it will be easy to demonstrate that the necessary and reasonable measures were not taken. Indeed, in such a case, the accused may better be charged under a different mode of liability. Command responsibility was sometimes treated by the Office of the Prosecutor as if it were a default mode of liability where no other mode of liability captures the relevant conduct. However, that is not how command responsibility should operate. It is a specific mode of liability in its own right with particular elements needing to be proven.

In considering the measures to be taken, a number of points must be kept in mind. First, in many an irregular group, the superior will likely have "less control over his troops than a commander would have over highly disciplined troops in a regular army."[42] Thus, the measures to be taken within the two groups may not be exactly the same. Second, the obligation is not one of result – the superior was not obligated to prevent the unlawful act. Rather, the obligation is one of conduct – the superior was under an obligation to take the necessary and reasonable measures to seek to prevent the unlawful act.[43] Third, the particular measures to be taken must have been within the power of the superior, and this is an element that needs to be proven rather than assumed. It does not follow from the mere fact of effective control that the particular measures x, y, and z could have been taken. Fourth, there should be a focus on measures that were capable of effectively preventing the underlying crime rather than measures of a broader level of generality. Finally, if the superior took some measures that were within his power but not others, it may be that, in an appropriate situation, it is held that, on balance, the superior has taken the necessary measures to satisfy his obligations even if the underlying crime results.

---

[39] *Id.* at paras. 782–86.

[40] *See, e.g., id.* at para. 292; *AFRC* Trial Judgment, *supra* note 5, at para. 785.

[41] *RUF* Trial Judgment, *supra* note 6, at para. 292.

[42] *AFRC* Trial Judgment, *supra* note 5, at para. 140.

[43] *Cf. CDF* Trial Judgment, *supra* note 5, at para. 880, slightly overstating the obligation.

All too often, a Chamber of the Special Court held that a superior did not take any measures to prevent a crime or to punish the perpetrators,[44] and thus found the Accused responsible on this basis. However, such a holding is insufficient in and of itself, as well as being potentially misleading. The Prosecution has to establish, and the Trial Chamber to determine, that there were measures that could have been taken and that were not. To hold otherwise is to suggest that there is an absolute obligation to prevent a crime and to punish a crime. This stems, in part, from the language used by Chambers. The phrase "failure to prevent and punish" tends to be used as shorthand for the actual element, namely that the superior failed to take necessary and reasonable measures to prevent the crime or punish the perpetrators of the crime.[45] Thus the element is not one of result; rather it is one of conduct. Yet this is not captured in the shorthand, which suggests precisely an element of result. This is unfortunate.

C. *Measures Taken to Punish*

The general rule, insofar as measures taken to punish the perpetrators of a crime is concerned, is that "[a] superior is bound to conduct a meaningful investigation with a view to establish the facts, order or execute appropriate sanctions, or report the perpetrators to the competent authorities in case the superior lacks sanctioning power."[46] Thus the obligation may be satisfied if the superior himself undertakes certain measures, such as conducting an investigation or imposing sanctions on the perpetrator, or if the superior refers the matter to the competent authorities for the competent authorities to investigate or impose sanctions. Thus, the *RUF* Appeals Chamber indicated that "it need not be the superior who undertakes the actual investigation or institutes the punishment; however, the superior must at least ensure the matter is in fact investigated. This may be established through referral of the matter to the competent authorities."[47]

1. Punishment by the Superior

The relevant investigation may be conducted, or the sanction imposed, by the superior himself. Indeed, the *AFRC* Trial Chamber was of the view that the ability of a superior to take disciplinary measures was one of the "key traditional indicia of effective control."[48] Whether an individual superior is able to investigate or administer the sanctions himself will largely depend on whether or not the relevant superior has the authority and power to sanction wrongful conduct. In many cases, particularly those concerning high-level leaders, this will be the case. However, in other instances, particularly insofar as lower-level superiors are

---

[44] *See, e.g., AFRC* Trial Judgment, *supra* note 5, at paras. 1949, 2079; *RUF* Trial Judgment, *supra* note 6, at paras. 2132, 2150, 2291.

[45] *See, e.g., RUF* Trial Judgment, *supra* note 6, subheadings before paras. 2132, 2150, 2291.

[46] *AFRC* Trial Judgment, *supra* note 5, at para. 799, referring to *Limaj* Trial Judgment, *supra* note 25, at para. 529; *Orić* Trial Judgment, *supra* note 27, at para. 336; *Strugar* Trial Judgment, *supra* note 30, at para. 376. *See also CDF* Trial Judgment, *supra* note 5, at para. 250. *RUF* Trial Judgment, *supra* note 6, at para. 317.

[47] Prosecutor v. Sesay, Kallon and Gbao, SCSL-04–15-A, Judgment, para. 505 (Oct. 26, 2009). *See generally Halilović* Trial Judgment, *supra* note 4, at paras. 97–100.

[48] *AFRC* Trial Judgment, *supra* note 5, at para. 789. On which, see the contribution by Harmen van der Wilt (Chapter 7 of this volume).

concerned, such individuals may not have the authority to investigate or administer a sanction; rather, they will have to refer the matter higher up the chain of command or to a separate body internal to the group. Much will depend on the structure and workings of the group and the level of the superior.

(a) Sanctions

Insofar as the actual sanctions to be administered are concerned, these may take a variety of forms. Sanctions utilized by irregular forces, particularly armed groups, tend to be of five sorts: disciplinary sanctions, including reprimands, warnings, confiscation of weapons, demotion, and dismissal from the group; financial sanctions, including fines, suspension of pay, and compensation to victims; curtailing of movement, ranging from detention to house arrest; corporal sanction, such as drill exercises or beatings; and criminal sanctions, including capital punishment.[49]

The RUF operated along similar lines. Not infrequently, RUF fighters who failed to obey orders were executed.[50] Other sanctions administered by the RUF included flogging, reassignment of areas, detention, deployments, and sending for further training.[51] For its part, the AFRC put to death fighters who raped other fighters' 'wives'.[52] Accordingly, it is evident that sanctions are utilized by irregular groups. However, they tend to be more brutal in their nature.

What is crucial is that the sanctions adopted be necessary and reasonable. The issue is often judged by reference to the nature of the control exercised by the superior.[53] Although this is undoubtedly important – only feasible measures that are within the power of the superior can be expected to be taken – it is not the only pertinent element. Whether the measures taken were necessary and reasonable will also depend on the nature of the underlying unlawful acts being punished. In the case of regular forces, the ICTY Appeals Chamber noted:

> It cannot be excluded that, in the circumstances of a case, the use of disciplinary measures will be sufficient to discharge a superior of his duty to punish crimes under Article 7(3) of the Statute. In other words, whether the measures taken were solely of a disciplinary nature, criminal, or a combination of both, cannot in itself be determinative of whether a superior discharged his duty to prevent or punish under Article 7(3) of the Statute.[54]

The language "[i]t cannot be excluded that . . .," however, suggests that it will be relatively rare that disciplinary measures alone will suffice. Indeed, later on in the judgment, the Appeals Chamber indicated that a disciplinary sanction of detention for a maximum of sixty days could not be acceptable punishment given the gravity of the offences, namely murder and cruel treatment.[55] For its part, the Trial Chamber had held that disciplinary measures may

---

[49] *See* SIVAKUMARAN, *supra* note 22, at 446.

[50] *RUF* Trial Judgment, *supra* note 6, at para. 706 and n.1333.

[51] *RUF*, Transcript, May 22, 2007 at 113 (Sesay).

[52] *AFRC* Trial Judgment, *supra* note 5, at paras. 1739 and 1741.

[53] R. CRYER ET AL., AN INTRODUCTION TO INTERNATIONAL CRIMINAL LAW AND PROCEDURE 395 (2010).

[54] Prosecutor v. Hadžihasanović, IT-01-47-A, Judgment, para. 33 (Apr. 22, 2008).

[55] *Id.* at para. 152.

be sufficient to punish crimes such as plunder but could never suffice to punish crimes such as murder and cruel treatment.[56]

The point is an important one – there must be a certain degree of proportionality, in the sense of sufficiency or adequacy, between the wrong that is the subject of the sanction and the punishment administered. It would obviously be insufficient for a series of murders or rapes to be punished by a reprimand. However, adequacy may also be difficult to judge, particularly in the case of irregular forces. What may seem a strong sanction from the outside may not be seen that way by members of the group. For example, Che Guevara indicated that:

> [t]he punishment of putting a soldier in jail for ten days constitutes for the guerrilla fighter a magnificent period of rest; ten days with nothing to do but eat, no marching, no work, no standing the customary guards, sleeping at will, resting, reading, etc. From this it can be deduced that deprivation of liberty ought not to be the only punishment available in the guerrilla situation ... deprivation of his right to be armed can constitute a true punishment for the individual and provoke a positive reaction.[57]

Thus, when judging adequacy, regard must be had for how it is viewed from within the group, not from the outside. Furthermore, adequacy should be judged as not clearly disproportionate rather than a strict proportionality. It should also be borne in mind that sanctions administered by irregular forces will likely be crude, even barbaric. When perpetrators are held accountable by armed groups, the principal form of accountability tends to be corporal punishment or capital punishment.[58] Thus, a certain care needs to be taken so as not to encourage capital punishment or corporal punishment without due process and thus commission of another crime.

Furthermore, certain sanctions may be difficult to enforce. It may not be possible for certain armed groups to sentence a fighter for a lengthy term of imprisonment if, for example, the group is unable to house detainees because of limited control over territory. In some situations, groups will release captives of the other side after confiscating their weapons, or will execute them, because they are unable to detain them.[59] Accordingly, a lengthy period of detention may not prove possible and would thus not constitute a *reasonable* measure to be expected of the commander. However, this does not mean that, in such situations, an appropriate sanction will not prove forthcoming. In such an instance, expulsion from the group may well constitute a punishment of similar, even greater, severity than detention. For other groups, detention may be perfectly possible, and such concerns do not arise. Regard must thus be had for the specificities of a particular group and the particular conditions in which they operate.

Oftentimes, instead of sanctioning wrongful conduct, subordinates may have been ordered to undertake the practice in the first place. Alternatively, they may be commended for their wrongful conduct, often given some sort of reward for so acting. Rewards tend to be of the same sorts as the sanctions themselves: disciplinary rewards, including such things

---

[56] Prosecutor v. Hadžihasanović and Kubura, IT-01-47-T, Judgment (Mar. 15, 2006). *Cf.* paras. 893, 899 and 2056–58, *with* paras. 1776–77.

[57] C. Guevara, Guerrilla Warfare 117–18 (1969).

[58] *See, e.g., RUF* Trial Judgment, *supra* note 6, at para. 706.

[59] Sivakumaran, *supra* note 22, at 296–97, 300–01.

as promotion, praise, and the awarding of medals; financial rewards, including monetary awards, salary increase, or license to plunder; extra leave; and tasks that are associated with a more senior position.[60] From the perspective of the fighter, rewards may be viewed as important as sanctions as this too incentivizes compliance and encourages the fighter to continue along the same lines as that for which he was rewarded. In such cases, it will be easier to demonstrate that the necessary and reasonable measures to punish were not taken because the exact opposite was in fact done.

2. Referral to the Competent Authorities

A frequent statement in the jurisprudence is that, if a superior does not have the authority to sanction the relevant perpetrator, then the superior must refer the matter to the competent authorities.[61] This works well insofar as state armed forces are concerned. The matter can be referred to the military disciplinary system – courts-martial and the like – or to the national criminal system. However, whether and how this works in irregular groups is an altogether different question, as the identity of the competent authorities may be unclear, and it may be difficult to apply in the case of splinter groups. Indeed, although in its section on the applicable law, the *AFRC* Trial Chamber recited the same position, in its section on the facts, the *AFRC* Trial Chamber went so far as to say that "[i]t is not useful to inquire whether the Accused Brima adopted measures commonly cited in the jurisprudence, such as reporting the perpetrators to competent authorities or commencing formal investigations."[62] Seemingly, the *AFRC* Trial Chamber took the view that such possibilities did not exist in the case of irregular groups in general or the AFRC in particular. However, this rather sweeping proposition was not followed by other Chambers or by the Appeals Chamber in the *RUF* case.

There are a number of competent authorities that ought to be considered in this regard, although many of them will prove impractical. The first is the competent authorities of the state against which the group is in conflict. Although this is canvassed from time to time, it is entirely unrealistic to suggest that the armed group should hand over those alleged to have committed violations to the state for the state to investigate and prosecute. This possibility may, however, be useful where the group in question is a paramilitary group with links to the state. The second is the competent authorities of a third state. Again, this possibility is occasionally canvassed[63]; however, it presumes the willingness of a third state to so investigate and prosecute. It also presumes that an armed group will have good relations with a third state so as to transfer the alleged violators to the state and to be sure that they will not be extradited to the state against which they are in conflict. In general terms, then, this possibility would also be ruled out in practice. A third possibility sometimes suggested is that the armed group should refer the matter to the Prosecutor of the International Criminal Court.[64] However, for jurisdictional and capacity reasons, this will

---

[60] Bangerter, *supra* note 37, at 207.

[61] *See, e.g.,* AFRC Trial Judgment, *supra* note 5, at para. 799.

[62] *AFRC* Trial Judgment, *supra* note 5, at para. 1738.

[63] Amicus Curiae Observations on Superior Responsibility submitted pursuant to Rule 103 of the Rules of Procedure and Evidence, *Prosecutor v. Jean-Pierre Bemba Gombo*, ICC-01/05–01/08–406, Pre-Trial Chamber II, para. 25 (Apr. 20, 2009).

[64] *Id.*

not always prove realistic. Furthermore, it is hardly to be encouraged that the armed group should refer the matter to the Prosecutor in order to escape command responsibility, knowing full well that the Prosecutor will not take the matter further. Accordingly, the competent authorities in question are essentially going to be those of the group itself.

(a) Disciplinary Body

What we are concerned with, then, are the authorities within the group that are able to administer sanctions. In practice, all groups have some form of disciplinary procedure, be they de jure according to the law of the armed group or de facto, vested in one entity or in each and every commander, systematic or ad hoc. In the absence of such a procedure, groups are unable to maintain order internally within the group. In this regard, Che Guevara noted that:

> [o]ne of the most important features of military organization is disciplinary punishment. Discipline must be one of the bases of action of the guerrilla forces (this must be repeated again and again).... it should spring from a carefully reasoned internal conviction; this produces an individual with inner discipline. When this discipline is violated, it is necessary always to punish the offender, whatever his rank, and to punish him drastically in a way that hurts.[65]

In particular, there will be authorities within the group that are able to sanction noncompliance with orders of superiors or violation of internal regulations of the group. Thus, the *RUF* Trial Chamber found that "[t]he importance of discipline and obedience of orders issued by superior officers was instilled in RUF fighters as part of their training and formed a pillar of the RUF military ideology."[66] The *RUF* Trial Chamber also found that:

> the RUF's disciplinary system was critical to maintaining its operation as a cohesive military organisation, particularly as the force grew with the addition of captured civilians trained as fighters. There is evidence of radio messages sent from Sankoh periodically to reiterate the importance of discipline, respect for the chain of command and of obeying RUF rules. Fighters who failed to obey orders were liable to be executed.[67]

The *RUF* Trial Judgment went on to note that:

> the RUF disciplinary system functioned essentially to allow the leadership to maintain control over all the RUF fighters and impose and maintain order in RUF-held territory. It failed to systematically deter or regularly and effectively punish crimes against civilians or persons *hors de combat*. The disciplinary process was fundamentally a means of keeping control over their own fighters and was not a system to punish for the commission of crimes. However, some crimes were punished in areas under RUF control and where no hostilities were then taking place in order to appease the population who reacted to a particular situation.[68]

This latter holding confirms that the disciplinary structure was not intended to punish crimes of subordinates routinely and systematically; rather, it punished them when it was

---

[65] GUEVARA, *supra* note 57, at 117.
[66] *RUF* Trial Judgment, *supra* note 6, at para. 704.
[67] *Id.* at para. 706.
[68] *Id.* at para. 712.

in the interests of the group to do so. The same was true of the AFRC, which appointed a Provost Marshal whose task it was to ensure "jungle justice." An aspect of this was capital punishment for fighters who raped other fighters' "wives."[69] As the Trial Chamber remarked, this was not a case of punishment for the crime of rape, rather, it was for the fact that the victim "belonged" to another fighter.[70] However, the fact that the disciplinary system of both the AFRC and RUF were selective in their application and applied on an ad hoc basis is unimportant for these purposes as this aspect of command responsibility concerns the ability to punish wrongful conduct and not the willingness to do so.

In respect of the AFRC, the Trial Chamber indicated that:

> the AFRC faction had a functioning disciplinary system in Bombali District. The Trial Chamber accepts that this system was not advanced in the sense of being properly codified and formally sanctioned by competent authorities. Nevertheless, the Trial Chamber finds that this disciplinary system could have been employed by the Accused Brima. Instead, there is no evidence that the Accused Brima took measures to punish subordinates for the commission of crimes. To the contrary, witnesses testified that on occasion the Accused Brima commended offending subordinates.[71]

Indeed, the presence of a disciplinary system was the only point canvassed by the Trial Chamber insofar as the punishment aspect of command responsibility was concerned. Failure to refer a matter to the disciplinary organ, when the individual has the power to do so, will often be critical in determining that a superior did not take the necessary and reasonable measures to punish a subordinate perpetrator. As the quote makes clear, the disciplinary system in question may be a de facto one. It may not have been "properly codified" or "formally sanctioned." However, if such a system is present, it may have to be utilized, in an appropriate case, to sanction noncompliance with the law.

To date, outside of the Special Court, little emphasis has been placed on how superiors of the group sanction failure to comply with orders or violation of internal regulations. Although the modalities of sanctioning noncompliance with orders may not be the same as those for sanctioning violations of international humanitarian law, an understanding of the former will be useful in understanding obligations associated with the latter. In this way, the measures that were within the power of the superior become far more apparent. Greater attention ought to be paid to this aspect of group procedures than is currently the case.

Close attention will thus have to be paid to the operation of such authorities within the group and to who may refer matters to them. For example, it may be that each and every superior has the ability to sanction noncompliance with an order on the part of subordinates. If this is the case, and an order has been issued to carry out an operation in compliance with international humanitarian law, for example, then the superior will be able to sanction violations of international humanitarian law. Likewise, if an internal regulation or code of conduct of an armed group contains norms associated with international humanitarian law – for example the Eight Codes of Conduct of the RUF provided inter alia "[d]o

---

[69] *AFRC* Trial Judgment, *supra* note 5, at paras. 1739 and 1741.
[70] *Id.* at para. 1739.
[71] *Id.*

not take liberty from women" and "[d]o not ill-treat captives"[72] – then the superior may well be able to punish violations of the code.

In other situations, the superior himself may not have the ability to sanction noncompliance with an order or violation of internal regulations but will have to refer the matter to the appropriate authority. Likewise, low-level superiors may not have the power to refer the matter to a disciplinary or judicial body of the group but will have to refer the matter up the chain of command to persons who do have that authority. For example, in the case of the RUF, a Joint Security Board of Investigations (JSBI) was established. The JSBI:

> was essentially an investigating panel convened on an *ad hoc* basis to investigate serious cases of misconduct, such as rape or murder....
>
> If a fighter admitted to wrongdoing, he would be punished and a JSBI would not be required. However, if a fighter disputed culpability, the Brigade IDU Commander would inform the Brigade Commander of the allegation. The High Command had the exclusive power to initiate a JSBI investigation.[73]

Thus, in the case of the *RUF*, not every commander could initiate a JSBI investigation. The matter had to go through the relevant processes. In such a situation, all a low-level commander may be able to do is refer the matter up the chain of command. This will satisfy his relevant obligations as a commander.

(b) Judicial Body

As indicated above, with respect to certain classes of conduct, criminal sanctions will be warranted. How does this play out insofar as referral to the competent authorities of irregular groups is concerned? In such a situation, a superior of an irregular group may be obliged to refer the matter to a judicial organ of the group rather than a disciplinary organ assuming it is within his power to do so and assuming that such an organ exists. In practice, as with disciplinary organs more generally, the vast majority of armed groups operate some sort of court or tribunal.[74] The RUF, for example, recounted:

> A few RUF fighters in the bush went on the rampage and as their own way of stating their objection to the planned elections, they proceeded on a campaign to cut off the hands of innocent villagers as a message that no voting should occur. This was how the amputation of hands started in Sierra Leone by desperate RUF men ... Pa Foday Sankoh, the RUF leader was especially chagrined at the actions taken by these few RUF fighters. Our leader is aware that in war, atrocities occur especially when young disenfranchised men are revolting against an oppressive system. However, Pa Sankoh has never condoned acts of violence against civilians by RUF fighters. Pa Foday Sankoh immediately set up a special investigative Tribunal. This Tribunal was set up by the RUF War & Peace Council to look into the actions of and subsequently discipline the RUF fighters who performed these amputations. After the tribunal, all those fighters found guilty of this were publicly executed.[75]

---

[72] *RUF* Trial Judgment, *supra* note 6, at para. 705.
[73] *Id.* at paras. 701–02 (emphasis added).
[74] For examples, see SIVAKUMARAN, *supra* note 22, at 549–55.
[75] RUF Political Leadership-Kailahun District, *RUF Calls for Independent Investigations*, Jan. 15, 1999.

The same sorts of considerations as considered above apply also in respect of judicial bodies of armed groups.

This raises a more general point. As is well known, whether a situation of violence amounts to a non-international armed conflict is judged by reference to the intensity of the violence and the organization of the armed group. One of the indicia of the organization of the armed group relates to the presence of an internal disciplinary structure.[76] This need not be particularly developed. However, as the presence of an internal disciplinary structure is going to be crucial insofar as command responsibility is concerned, it should be an important aspect of judging whether an armed group can be said to be organized for the purposes of the existence of an armed conflict.

IV. CONCLUSION

The jurisprudence of the Special Court has established that command responsibility operates in irregular military organizations just as it does regular armed forces. However, it has been altogether less clear on the third element of command responsibility, namely the duty to take the necessary and reasonable measures to prevent and punish crimes of subordinates. To be fair to the Special Court, this is also true of the other ad hoc international criminal tribunals.

This chapter has sought to locate that duty and analyze its content through a consideration of the irregular groups that were involved in the conflict in Sierra Leone. In particular, it serves to remind us that the workings and capabilities of irregular forces will differ from those of regular forces. These differences do not render the obligation to take measures illusory; rather, they illustrate that the particular measures to be taken and the manner in which they are taken will not be the same as measures adopted by armed forces of the state. For example, the cases of the AFRC and the RUF confirm that, insofar as the obligation to take measures to punish crimes is concerned, irregular forces institute sanctions and utilize disciplinary and judicial bodies. The operation of these bodies is different from the operation of bodies maintained by regular forces, but they are present in, and used by, irregular groups nonetheless.

Ultimately, the structure and workings of each irregular group will have to be analyzed in order to assess how the third element of command responsibility plays out. However, the jurisprudence of the Special Court should put to rest any argument that the principle cannot operate outside of regular armed forces.

---

[76] *See e.g.*, *Limaj* Trial Judgment, *supra* note 25, at paras. 113–17; Prosecutor v. Haradinaj, Balaj and Brahimaj, IT-04-84-T, Judgment, para. 60 (Apr. 3, 2008); Prosecutor v. Boškoski and Tarčulovski, IT-04-82-T, Judgment, paras. 274–75 (July 10, 2008).

7

Command Responsibility in the Jungle: Some Reflections on the Elements of Effective Command and Control

Harmen van der Wilt[*]

I. INTRODUCTION

Like the Statutes of the International Criminal Tribunals for the Former Yugoslavia (ICTY) and Rwanda (ICTR), the Statute of the Special Court for Sierra Leone (SCSL) provides for criminal responsibility for the superior who has failed to exercise proper control over his subordinates who have committed international crimes.[1] And indeed, with the initial exception of Augustine Gbao and more recently Charles Taylor, all the Accused standing trial before the SCSL have also been convicted on the charge of superior responsibility.

Whether superior responsibility could serve as a proper basis for conviction in internal armed conflicts had been a matter of some debate. Defense counsel in the case *Prosecutor v. Sam Hinga Norman* contested the jurisdiction of the Special Court in this respect, arguing that "the principle of command responsibility is not a basis for liability in internal armed conflicts and was not part of international humanitarian law at the time relevant to the Indictment."[2] The motion was not likely to succeed, as the issue had been a foregone conclusion. In the *Hadžihasanović* case, the Appeals Chamber of the ICTY had already found that:

> The applicability of command responsibility to internal armed conflicts is not disputed in the cases of the tribunal established for Rwanda, Sierra Leone and East Timor. It is said that these tribunals were established after the ICTY. However, in the view of the Appeals Chamber, the establishment of these bodies was consistent with the proposition that customary international law previously included the principle that command responsibility applied in respect of an internal armed conflict.[3]

The SCSL Trial Chamber had no trouble following the opinion of the ICTY's Appeals Chamber.[4] Indeed, it would have been rather strange had the Chamber reached another

---

[*] Professor of International Criminal Law, Faculty of Law, University of Amsterdam.

[1] Article 6(3) of the Statute of the Special Court reads virtually the same as Article 6(3) of the Statute of the ICTR and Article 7(3) of the Statute of the ICTY.

[2] Prosecutor v. Norman, Decision on the Defense Preliminary Motion on Lack of Jurisdiction: Command Responsibility, Case No. SCSL-2003–08-PT, § 1 (Oct. 15, 2003) [hereinafter *Prosecutor v. Norman*].

[3] Prosecutor v. Hadžihasanović, Alagić and Kubura, Decision on Interlocutory Appeal Challenging Jurisdiction in Relation to Command Responsibility, Case No. IT-01–47–1AR72, § 26 (July 16, 2003).

[4] *Prosecutor v. Norman, supra* note 2, § 24.

conclusion. After all, the status of *lawful combatant*, both in international and internal armed conflicts, is predicated on the requirement that the forces are subordinated to *responsible command* and that they conduct their activities in accordance with the laws and customs of warfare.[5] Read in conjunction, these requirements suggest that the observance of the law of armed conflict can only be accomplished if the soldiers operate in obedience to their commanders and that the commanders are to blame if they fail to exercise control over their subordinates.

Nonetheless, the issue whether the doctrine of superior responsibility is applicable in internal armed conflicts conceals a deeper problem that might not so easily be resolved. The doctrine of superior responsibility is, at least originally, strongly wedded to the concept of military hierarchy. Its crucial element, *effective control*, presupposes a streamlined organization, with adequate channels of information, clear-cut patterns of hierarchy, and unquestioned obedience, which functions even (or should we rather say: in particular?) in the heat of fighting. Such an archetypical model begs the question whether the doctrine can be applied at all to *irregular groups*, which do not meet the organizational standards of traditional armies.[6] The assumption of those who put this into question is that, absent such an organizational framework, it would be unfair to hold *superiors* responsible, because they would lack the proper tools to steer their subordinates.

It requires little imagination to understand that the issue surfaced in the case law of the Sierra Leone Court, which had to disentangle cluttered power relations and makeshift command structures in order to attribute criminal responsibility for heinous crimes. The Court has contributed interesting case law on the topic, shedding light on the proper limits of "effective command and control." In this chapter, I intend to focus on superior responsibility in respect of irregular forces, as divulged in the case law of the Sierra Leone Court.[7] I will especially explore whether the Special Court has maintained a rigorous standard in respect of the "chain of command," deriving from traditional military organizations, or whether it has been inclined to apply more flexible standards, taking into account more loosely structured forces. At this point it is useful to explain my point of view on the conjunctive "effective command and control," encapsulating the superior–subordinate relationship. In my opinion, effective command subsumes effective control, whereas the reverse is not necessarily the case. As will transpire in the following text, the Sierra Leone Court ascribes much importance to "effective command" and therefore the focus in this chapter will be on this concept.

---

[5] These requirements had been stipulated in the Hague Convention (II) on the Laws and Customs of War on Land of 1899 and the Hague Convention (IV) respecting the Laws and Customs of War on Land of 1907. They reappear in Article 4A, section 2 of the Third Geneva Convention on the Protection of Prisoners of War (1949).

[6] For a sceptical view, see G.J.A. Knoops, *The Transposition of Superior Responsibility onto Guerrilla Warfare under the Laws of the International Criminal Tribunals*, 7 INT'L CRIM. L. REV. 505, 529 (2007) ("It is questionable whether this concept (of superior responsibility) is suitable when it concerns the prosecution of members of irregular forces.").

[7] In a previous publication I have merely used this case law as an illustration to contrast it with command responsibility in traditional military hierarchies; *see* Harmen van der Wilt, Commentary on Prosecutor v. Halilović, *Judgment*, Case No. IT-01-48-T, T. Ch. I (Nov. 16, 2005), *in* 27 ANNOTATED LEADING CASES OF INTERNATIONAL CRIMINAL TRIBUNALS; THE INTERNATIONAL CRIMINAL TRIBUNAL FOR THE FORMER YUGOSLAVIA 2005, at 694–700 (André Klip & Göran Sluiter eds., 2011).

I will start with shortly expounding the constituent elements of the doctrine of superior responsibility, focusing on the aspect of "effective command and control" (Part II). Next, I will analyse the relevant case law of the SCSL, which has been confronted with the accused wielding (some measure of) control over several organizations, exhibiting distinct structural features. I will demonstrate that the Court, in spite of its readiness to expand the application of the concept of superior responsibility beyond the scope of traditional military organizations, is still strongly inclined to search for parameters that more loosely structured "irregular forces" have in common with the accepted paradigm (Part III). And finally I will ponder on the normative implications of these findings, discussing whether the doctrine of superior responsibility is best served by such a rather rigid interpretation (Part IV).

II. CONSTITUENT ELEMENTS OF SUPERIOR RESPONSIBILITY

Under the legal regime of the ad hoc international criminal tribunals and the SCSL, a superior incurs responsibility in respect of international crimes committed by his subordinates if he knew or had reason to know that the subordinates were about to commit such acts, or had done so and the superior had failed to take the necessary and reasonable measures to prevent such acts or to punish the perpetrators thereof. The concept of superior responsibility thus consists of a power element ("effective command and control"), which the superior exerts over his subordinates by virtue of the hierarchical relationship between them, a required *mens rea* (actual knowledge or constructive knowledge), and an omission (failure to prevent or punish), which actually triggers the criminal responsibility. I will leave the *mens rea* aside and concentrate my attention on the concept of "effective command and control," which has been defined as "the material ability to prevent and punish criminal conduct."[8] In this way, a direct and meaningful link is forged between the first and third elements of the doctrine.[9]

Simultaneously, by defining the element of "effective control" in terms of a counterfactual event – what the superior presumably would be capable of doing but obviously had failed to accomplish – the tribunals have not been very helpful in illuminating the content of the power to exercise control. What does this power exactly entail? International criminal tribunals agree that "effective control" may emerge from a de jure or de facto superior–subordinate relationship.[10] In the military context, de jure power serves as point of departure. That position was at least defended by the Trial Chamber in the Kordič-case: "Military positions will usually be strictly defined and the existence of a clear chain of command, based on strict hierarchy, easier to demonstrate."[11] The Appeals Chamber in *Delalič*, however, while concurring with the Trial Chamber in *Kordič* that de jure powers offered an

---

[8] Prosecutor v. Delalič et al., Judgment of the Appeals Chamber, Case No. IT-96-21-A, A. Ch., § 256 (Feb. 20, 2001) [hereinafter *Prosecutor v. Delalič et al.*]; Prosecutor v. Blaskič, Judgment, Case No. IT-95-14-A, A. Ch., § 69 (July 29, 2004).

[9] *Compare* Prosecutor v. Strugar, Judgment, Case No. IT-01-42-T, § 371 (Jan. 31, 2005): "The question of whether a superior has failed to take all necessary and reasonable measures to prevent the commission of an offence or to punish the perpetrators is intrinsically connected to the question of that superior's position of power."

[10] *See Prosecutor v. Delalič et al.* (Appeals Chamber), *supra* note 8, § 192 and Prosecutor v. Gacumbitsi, Judgment of the Appeals Chamber, Case No. ICTR-01-64-A, A. Ch. (July 7, 2006).

[11] Prosecutor v. Kordič and Čerkez, Judgment, Case No. IT-95-14/2-T, T. Ch., § 419 (Feb. 26, 2001) [hereinafter *Prosecutor v. Kordič and Čerkez*].

important prima facie indication, reversed the order by holding that the factual assessment of superior authority should prevail over the legal evaluation:

> [...] whereas formal appointment is an important aspect of command authority or superior authority, the actual exercise of authority in the absence of a formal appointment is sufficient for the purpose of incurring criminal responsibility. Accordingly, the factor critical to the exercise of command responsibility is the actual possession, or non-possession, of powers of control over the actions of the subordinates.[12]

The predominance of factual indications of effective command and control over de jure authority may especially be relevant in the context of paramilitary groups and guerrilla movements, as has expressly been acknowledged by the Appeals Chamber in *Delalič*.[13]

The emphasis on factual assessment of superior responsibility, to the apparent detriment of de jure command powers, requires some qualification. For one thing, it may have been introduced to enable the application of the doctrine to civilian authorities, which by definition lack the rigid hierarchical framework tying them to their subordinates. By contrast, the international tribunals may still be inclined to adhere to the formal chain of command when dealing with military superiors. There are some strong indications for this proposition. As is well-known, Article 28 of the Rome Statute differentiates between the responsibility of military and civilian superiors.[14] Whereas the Statutes of the international criminal tribunals make no such distinction, it is generally acknowledged that both military and civilian superiors can incur criminal responsibility on the basis of the doctrine.[15] Although the "effective control" test applies equally to military commanders and civilian superiors, that concept need not necessarily be established and assessed in the same way.[16] Censuring the approach of the Trial Chamber, which had searched for de jure or de jure–like relationships between the Accused and his supposed subordinates, in an attempt to determine whether the Accused's authority – a civilian superior – was comparable to that exercised in a military context, the Appeals Chamber in *Bagilishema* suggested that the application of

---

[12] *Prosecutor v. Delalič et al.* (Appeals Chamber), *supra* note 10, § 736.

[13] *Id.* § 193: "The power of authority to prevent or punish does not solely arise from *de jure* authority conferred through official appointment. In many contemporary conflicts, there may be only *de facto*, self-proclaimed governments and therefore *de facto* armies and paramilitary groups subordinate thereto. Command structure, organized hastily, may well be in disorder and primitive."

For a similar view, see I. Bantekas, *The Contemporary Law of Superior Responsibility*, 93 AM. J. INT'L L. No. 2, 584 (1999): In the majority of civil wars de jure command paints only half the picture. In such situations the traditional communal leaders are customarily endowed with powers far above those initially granted them by virtue of their office. In these cases both de jure and de facto command are sought in order to assess the accused's precise quantity of authority.

[14] In the Bemba decision, the ICC Pre-Trial Chamber rather bluntly assumed that there was sufficient evidence to pursue criminal proceedings against the Accused on the basis of military command responsibility; Decision Pursuant to Art. 61(7)(a) and (b) of the Rome Statute on the Charges of the Prosecutor against Jean-Pierre Bemba Gombo, *Bemba* (ICC-01/05–01/08), Pre-Trial Chamber II (June 15, 2009). In an interesting contribution, Nora Karsten criticizes the Pre-Trial Chamber's decision for insufficiently elaborating on the question whether Bemba would qualify as a military commander, a person "effectively acting as a military commander" or a civilian superior, Nora Karsten, *Distinguishing Military and Non-Military Superiors*, 7 J. INT'L CRIM. JUSTICE 983–1004 (2009).

[15] *See, e.g.*, Prosecutor v. Aleksovski, Judgment by the Appeals Chamber, Case No. IT-95–14/1-A, § 76 (Mar. 24, 2000).

[16] Prosecutor v. Bagilishema, Judgment by the Appeals Chamber, Case No. ICTR-95–1A-A, § 52 (July 3, 2002).

such rigid standards would be inappropriate outside the scope of the military-style chain of command.[17]

For military commanders, the relevance of formal hierarchy and corresponding legal powers is more pronounced. The entity in which the military commander operates offers the necessary framework to exercise his control and is therefore an indispensable prerequisite for command responsibility. In *Aleksovski*, the Trial Chamber held that a superior must have the possibility to transmit reports *through his position in the hierarchy*.[18] (emphasis added) Most explicitly, the Trial Chamber in *Kordić* held that "superiors can only incur criminal responsibility if they are *clearly part of a chain of command*."[19] (emphasis added) Mere power, by virtue of psychological preponderance, to control or punish other people does not suffice.[20]

The interesting question is whether the requirement that the superior should occupy some position in a hierarchical organization only applies to military commanders of traditional armies, or would also be a necessary element in case of irregular troops or even for civilian superiors. Nora Karsten appears to embrace the latter position. She rightly censures the sweeping and unsubstantiated opinion of Roberta Arnold, who argues that "everyone holding *de facto* authority over someone guilty of war crimes is subject to this doctrine, independently from affiliation to a regular or irregular armed group."[21] For her part, Karsten favors application of the "entity-related approach," both for military and civilian superiors, although she candidly avows that this approach will not resolve the quandary of assessing the difference in effective control for military and civilian superiors respectively, as this would depend on the question-begging nature of the entity.[22] Karsten's view seems to be corroborated by the Judgment of the Trial Chamber in *Kordić*, which does not distinguish between de jure or de facto leaders, or between military and civilian leaders, as to the requirement that they should be part of the *chain of command*. In other words: the organizational context, providing them with the necessary tools, is a legal requirement for the criminal responsibility of all superiors. The next section intends to demonstrate how this requirement worked out in the specific situation of Sierra Leone.

III. THE SIERRA LEONE COURT AND SUPERIOR RESPONSIBILITY

Confronted with Accused wielding power over armies and military groups displaying rather distinct levels of organization, the SCSL has made earnest efforts to identify the proper indicia for superior responsibility, trying to reconcile an eye for the particular circumstances of the case with the need to uphold the normative framework. In the next three subsections I address the context and findings of the Special Court in the three large joint-accused cases.

---

[17] *Id.* § 55.

[18] Prosecutor v. Aleksovski, Judgment, Case No. IT-95-14/1-T, § 281 (June 25, 1999).

[19] *Prosecutor v. Kordić and Čerkez, supra* note 11, § 416.

[20] Prosecutor v. Bikindi, Judgment by the Appeals Chamber, Case No. ICTR-01-72-A, A. Ch., § 213 (Dec. 2, 2008).

[21] R. Arnold & O. Triffterer, *Article 28, in* COMMENTARY ON THE ROME STATUTE OF THE INTERNATIONAL CRIMINAL COURT: ARTICLE BY ARTICLE 829 (O. Triffterer ed., 3d ed. 2008).

[22] Karsten, *supra* note 14, at 994–95.

A. The AFRC-Case

The most explicit acknowledgement of the need to adapt the interpretation of the doctrine of superior responsibility, at least partially, to the particular context of the situation, was made in the Judgment of the Trial Chamber in the so-called Armed Forces Revolutionary Council (AFRC) case against Brima, Kamara, and Kanu.[23] After having identified a number of parameters that would be indicative of "effective control," the Trial Chamber held that:

> In a conflict characterised by the participation of irregular armies or rebel groups, the traditional indicia of effective control provided in the jurisprudence may not be appropriate or useful. As the Trial Chamber has observed, the formality of an organisation's structure is relevant to, but not determinative of, the question of the effective control of its leaders. The less developed the structure, the more important it becomes to focus on the nature of the superior's authority rather than his or her formal designation.[24]

Next, the Trial Chamber mentioned a number of indicia that, in the absence of formal power relations, might still point at the existence of "effective control":

> The Trial Chamber considers that indicia which may be useful to assess the ability of superiors in such irregular armies to exercise effective control over their subordinates, include that the superior had first entitlement to the profits of war, such as looted property and natural resources; exercised control over the fate of vulnerable persons such as women and children; the superior had independent access to and/or control of the means to wage war, including arms and ammunition and communications equipment; the superior rewarded himself or herself with positions of power and influence; the superior had the capacity to intimidate subordinates into compliance and was willing to do so; the superior was protected by personal security guards, loyal to him or her, akin to a modern praetorian guard; the superior fuels or represents the ideology of the movement to which the subordinates adhere; and the superior interacts with external bodies or individuals on behalf of the group.[25]

Obviously, these parameters did not come out of the blue. They were strongly engrafted upon the evidence available to the Chamber and could be considered as anticipating the Chamber's conviction on the charge of superior responsibility. Simultaneously, one may wonder whether, by applying these indicia, the Chamber did not run the risk of drifting from the original concept of superior responsibility. After all, the leader's prime share in the booty or his representation of the group in relation to others may well testify to his privileged position within the group, but does not necessarily imply that he wields effective control over his subordinates.

Surprisingly, however, the Trial Chamber qualified its bold interpretation to a large extent in the following paragraph:

> Nonetheless, the key traditional indicia of effective control remain central, although they may be more loosely defined. For example the power of the superior to issue orders is crucial, although these orders may be criminal in nature. Similarly, the superior must be

---

[23] Prosecutor v. Brima, Kamara and Kanu, Judgment, Case No. SCSL-04-16-T (June 20, 2007).
[24] *Id.* § 787.
[25] *Id.* § 788.

capable of taking disciplinary action, even though the measures taken may be more brutal and arbitrarily utilized.[26]

I have chosen to quote these passages from the judgment in toto because they perfectly reflect the quandary of the Court. Essentially, while acknowledging that the rebel forces in Sierra Leone did not match the rigid hierarchy of traditional armies and that some interpretative flexibility was necessary if the doctrine of superior responsibility were to be applied successfully at all, the Court still wished to assess the command structure of those irregular armies against the ideal type of traditional military organizations. The careful deliberations of the Trial Chamber in *Brima* testify to this approach.

The Trial Chamber admitted that the AFRC "was not a traditional military organisation" and that "it is likely that the Accused Brima had less control over his troops than a commander would have over highly disciplined troops in a regular army."[27] The Chamber closely followed Brima's career within the ranks of the AFRC. Initially, he had been a member of the AFRC Supreme Council in which capacity he supervised and monitored various government ministries. Obviously, such a position alone did not confer upon him any power and control over subordinates: "Membership of the Supreme Council and attendance at meetings *per se*, does not suffice to prove beyond reasonable doubt that Brima was in a superior–subordinate relationship with the perpetrators of the offences committed in Bo, Kenema and Kailahun Districts during the relevant Indictment period."[28] Gradually, however, as the armed conflict evolved, Brima moved to occupy military positions. He had been the overall commander of the AFRC forces that committed the crimes in Bombali District in 1998. Consequently, the Trial Chamber discussed the quality of the organization at his disposal: "It has been established that the AFRC in this period had a functioning chain of command, planning and orders process, and disciplinary system. Structures were therefore in place to facilitate the effective control by the Accused Brima of his subordinates."[29]

The next step to be taken by the Trial Chamber was to investigate whether the Accused could indeed reap the benefits of this tight organization. The Chamber had no qualms that he could: "There is ample unchallenged evidence that the Accused Brima's orders were obeyed. (…) The Trial Chamber is satisfied that the Accused Brima's exercise of effective control was not sporadic, but constant. His orders remained effective and applicable to incidents that occurred some time after their issuance."[30] Of special relevance in this context was the existence of a system of "Jungle Justice" that included a law prohibiting rapes during operations: any fighter who raped another fighter's wife would be put to death.[31] However, the Trial Chamber was not satisfied that this system would absolve the Accused from responsibility "as the soldier in such cases was not being punished for committing the crime of rape, but for the fact that his victim 'belonged' to another perpetrator."[32] Obviously, the Trial Chamber insinuated that the "Jungle Justice" corroborated the potential of Brima

[26] *Id.* § 789.
[27] *Id.* § 1738 and § 1740 respectively.
[28] *Id.* § 1657.
[29] *Id.* § 1723.
[30] *Id.* §§ 1724–1725.
[31] *Id.* § 1741.
[32] *Id.* § 1740.

and his co-accused to discipline his subordinates, a factual determination that only added to his liability as a superior.[33]

Of particular interest are the Trial Chamber's deliberations on the responsibility for crimes committed in the wake of the attack on Freetown, because they shed a light on the limits of superior responsibility within an army in disarray. In the beginning of 1999, the tide had turned against the forces of the AFRC under Brima's overall command. He had been forced to retreat, and there were witnesses who testified that Brima no longer wielded control over his troops who, dispirited and disorganized, had ravaged and looted the surroundings of Freetown, Sierra Leone's capital. The Trial Chamber, however, did not accept the representation of a fully disrupted force, but rather embraced the opinion of a military expert who had contended that "although the battalion structure had completely broken down, the AFRC fighting force retained cohesion in retreat," adding that "commanders were still able to make sound decisions and the command structure was effective enough to be able to conduct a relatively complex manoeuvre."[34] The implication is obvious: if military commanders have sufficient power and authority over their subordinates to make them perform difficult military operations, they certainly possess the power to prevent them from committing heinous crimes.

On the other hand, one might wonder whether the Trial Chamber did not take the military expert's opinions too easily at face value. The initial capacity to steer complex military operations does not automatically imply that irregular forces, panic-struck and confronted with increasing chaos, will not relapse into their former anarchic attitude. As the Trial Chamber simply adopted the views of the military expert and did not elucidate its own reasoning, it missed the opportunity to clarify the jurisprudence on the application of the superior responsibility doctrine to irregular forces.

B. The RUF Case

In the RUF case, the SCSL had to grapple with a complex organization, displaying several functional layers that were not strictly hierarchically structured.[35] The Trial Chamber meticulously investigated the RUF's Operational Command Structure and noticed that the apex consisted of a triumvirate, featuring the Leader, the Battlefield Commander, and the Battle Group Commander who wielded authority over the military units of the RUF. Nonetheless, all different kinds of other functionaries, although outside the "chain of command," interacted with the military units and appeared to be important for the war effort. The Chamber found that individual assignment, rather than formal rank or status, was the most important distinction.[36]

Despite its rather cluttered appearance, the RUF revealed many features of a well-trained and efficiently structured army. The Trial Chamber considered that "the RUF's disciplinary

---

[33] The Appeals Chamber found the appeal of Brima without merit and corroborated the Trial Chamber's findings on superior responsibility, Prosecutor v. Brima et al., Appeal Judgment, Case No. SCSL-2004–16-A, § 229 (Mar. 3, 2008).

[34] *Id.* § 1805.

[35] Prosecutor v. Sesay, Kallon and Gbao, Judgment, Case No. SCSL-04–15-T (Mar. 2, 2009) [hereinafter *Prosecutor v. Sesay, Kallon and Gbao*].

[36] *Id.* § 673.

system was critical to maintaining its operation as a cohesive military organisation, particularly as the force grew with the addition of captured civilians trained as fighters."[37] Nonetheless, and as was the case with the AFRC, the Trial Chamber observed that the RUF disciplinary system was notorious for its highly selective application: "We therefore find that the RUF disciplinary system functioned essentially to allow the leadership to maintain control over all the RUF fighters and impose and maintain order in RUF-held territory. It failed to systematically deter or regularly and effectively punish crimes against civilians or persons *hors de combat*."[38]

A crucial element in the preservation of effective control is of course communication. The Trial Chamber recognized the potential hurdles for guerrilla groups operating in vast areas with poor infrastructure and concluded that the "radio system permitted RUF Commanders to maintain regular and adequate communication between all operational levels throughout the entire Indictment period," confirming that "the communications system was thus integral to the successful operation of the chain of command within the RUF military hierarchy."[39]

The Trial Chamber summarized its findings by holding that

> from the foregoing analysis, the Chamber finds that throughout the Indictment period the RUF organisation operated pursuant to an organized hierarchical command structure with assignment, status and rank constituting recognised sources of seniority and authority. This command structure was enforced by an elaborate disciplinary system operated by the various RUF security units.[40]

After the Trial Chamber had determined the well-organized chain of command within the RUF, it had to address the position of the Accused within that framework.[41] The Trial Chamber's findings were rather short and straightforward. The assessment of their superior responsibility in respect of the assaults on the United Nations Mission in Sierra Leone (UNAMSIL) peacekeeping personnel serves as a good illustration. As Battle Field Commander, Sesay was effectively the overall military Commander of the RUF on the ground. Sesay transmitted orders to RUF fighters, *many of which pertained to UNAMSIL*

---

[37] *Id.* § 706.

[38] *Id.* § 712.

[39] *Id.* §§ 719–720.

[40] *Id.* § 941. One may question whether the qualification "elaborate" is not an exaggeration, in view of earlier findings of the Trial Chamber that the disciplinary system was not applied systematically and consistently. Probably, the Trial Chamber intended to convey that the RUF had such a disciplinary system at its disposal, but did not apply it when needed most.

[41] It is interesting to contrast the findings of the Trial Chamber with the conclusions of the Sierra Leonean Truth and Reconciliation Commission (*Witness to Truth; Report of Sierra Leone Truth & Reconciliation Commission*, vol. 2), *available at* http://www.Sierra-leone.org/other-conflict/TRCVolume2.pdf (last visited June 20, 2012). There are some striking differences in the assessment of the structural dimensions of the RUF. In general terms, the TRC concluded that "the RUF became a totally amorphous movement after the arrest of its leader Foday Sankoh in Nigeria in March 1997. Its command structure was decapitated and it opened the way for opportunists to assert their leadership in his place." (§ 123). The TRC focused on the responsibility of lower rank "Ground Commanders" (§§ 145–149), but acknowledged that the hostilities against UNAMSIL peacekeepers (which culminated in their abductions) had been initiated and commanded at the instance of Morris Kallon and Augustine Bao (sic) (§ 164). In respect of the RUF leadership, the TRC found that "while certain individuals held effective command responsibility at certain times over certain combatants, the Commission found it difficult to discern any consistent and centralized vertical structure of leadership." (§ 171).

personnel. He was a strict disciplinarian and a respected Commander whose subordinates were highly loyal to him. In relation to an attack on UNAMSIL peacekeepers, Sesay had ordered the destruction of a road linking and if possible attack and capture.[42] On the basis of these facts, the Trial Chamber had no difficulty in finding Sesay in effective control over the perpetrators of the attacks against UNAMSIL peacekeeping forces. The relationship between Kallon, at the time a Battle Group Commander, and the Battalion Commanders was even more tight and direct. Those commanders, including an RUF Commander who had been directly involved in the May 9th attacks on UNAMSIL peacekeepers, reported to Kallon and had sought instructions from him.[43] Gbao, on the other hand, did not incur superior responsibility, because the Prosecutor failed to prove in what manner he was integrated into the RUF command structure at this point in time and also had not indicated the effects of his new functions on his ability to control RUF fighters.[44]

C. Fofana and Kondewa

Although the Special Court could recognize with relative ease the structural elements deriving from traditional armies in the AFRC and the RUF, the real test came with the Civil Defense Forces (CDF) case.[45] The CDF was an outgrowth of Kamajor society, a tribe of hunters that were deployed by the government as vigilantes to protect the country against the rebels. Hinga Norman, an Accused who stood trial at the SCSL together with Fofana and Kondewa, but who passed away in February 2007 before the Trial Chamber reached its final judgment, had been appointed Chairman of the Kamajors.

In 1997, the civil strife flared up, and after a coup, sitting president Kabbah was ousted from office. From his exile in Conakry, he founded the CDF, appointing Norman as its National Coordinator. Norman's major assignment was to coordinate the activities of the civil defense/Kamajors in supporting the military operations of the Economic Community of West African States Monitoring Group (ECOMOG), a West African multilateral armed force, established by the Economic Community of West African States (ECOWAS), to reinstate the government of President Kabbah.[46] The operational ties between ECOMOG, CDF, and the Kamajors were therefore close and lasting.

Norman, Fofana, and Kondewa were the unquestioned leaders of Kamajor society.[47] Whereas the Kamajors had engaged in unthinkable atrocities against civilians who were

---

[42] *Prosecutor v. Sesay, Kallon and Gbao, supra* note 35, §§ 2268, 2270 and 2278.

[43] *Id.* § 2286.

[44] *Id.* § 2297. The findings of the Trial Chamber were largely corroborated on appeal. In respect of Kallon's challenge of his superior responsibility in relation to Kono District, the Appeals Chamber held that "the Trial Chamber reasonably concluded (…) that not only was Kallon able to issue orders to RUF troops and Commanders, but that those orders were actually followed and that he had the power to punish RUF perpetrators of alleged criminal conduct in Kono District." Prosecutor v. Sesay, Kallon and Gbao, Appeal Judgment, Case No. SCSL-04-15-A, § 848 (Oct. 26, 2009).

[45] Prosecutor v. Fofana and Kondewa, Judgment, Case No. SCSL-04-14-T (Aug. 2, 2007) [hereinafter *Prosecutor v. Fofana and Kondewa*].

[46] *Id.* § 81.

[47] *Id.* § 337: The three of them were the key and essential components of the leadership structure of the organization and were the executive of the Kamajor society. They were the ones actually making the decisions, and nobody could make a decision in their absence. Whatever happened, they would come together because they were the leaders and the Kamajors looked up to them.

suspected of siding with the rebels, the Court obviously had to address the question whether they would incur direct individual criminal responsibility or superior responsibility for their failure to prevent or suppress those crimes. The problem was that the leadership, consisting of the three men dubbed the Holy Trinity, had strong psychological and even spiritual or mystical overtones, but lacked perhaps the more practical, down-to-earth ability to steer operations of war. Moreover, local Kamajor leaders enjoyed a large degree of autonomy and were not accustomed to receiving and following orders: "Since the formation of the Kamajor society in 1991, the Kamajors were organised essentially as a group of native hunters who responded to the directives of the chiefs and chiefdom authorities when being requested to protect people from the rebels and to defend their chiefdoms."[48] It was precisely the mission of Norman to forge these unruly elements into a more organized and disciplined unity who could equal and surpass the rebels on the battlefield: "Upon his arrival at Base Zero, Norman attempted to synchronise the command structure, so that everyone could abide by the centralised commands coming from Base Zero. At that time the Kamajors were still operating in different groups according to which chiefdom they hailed from. (…) Norman introduced some military terminology and concept into the organisation of the CDF, such as, division of the Kamajors on the basis of sections, squads, platoons and companies, varying in size from three to 75–100 men."

The appointment of Fofana as Director of War squared with Norman's attempts to build a hierarchically structured and smoothly functioning war machine. Fofana's main task was to plan and execute the strategies for war operations. He served as a go-between, linking Norman with the commanders in the field. For his part, Fofana was assisted by a certain Albert Nallo, a secondary though pivotal figure who frequently features in the factual assessments of Fofana's superior responsibility. Nallo, in charge of commanders in the Southern Region, was a typical errand boy, who, in implementing commands, "did not distinguish between lawful and unlawful ones and did not recognise that he had discretion to not implement them."[49] As Nallo wielded command over his subordinates and presumably might have been prosecuted on the charge of superior responsibility himself, the construction is a good example of so-called multiple superior responsibility that has previously been accepted by the ICTY in the Blagojević and Orić rulings.[50]

In this layered construction, Fofana's criminal liability obviously depended on the question whether his subordinate Nallo exercised effective control over *his* subordinates. The Trial Chamber, although not questioning the power and authority Fofana had over Nallo, was not convinced that the latter always exercised the required degree of control over local commanders: "By Nallo's own admission, he could not exercise full or strict control over all of the Kamajors in the Southern Region due to their large numbers."[51] Nallo's

---

[48] *Prosecutor v. Fofana and Kondewa, supra* note 45, § 354.

[49] *Id.* § 352.

[50] *Prosecutor v. Blagojević*, Judgment by the Appeals Chamber, Case No. IT-02-60-A, §§ 277–285 (May 9, 2007) and *Prosecutor v. Orić*, Judgment by the Appeals Chamber, Case No. IT-03-68-A, § 21 (July 3, 2008). For a critical assessment, see Elies van Sliedregt, *Command Responsibility at the ICTY – Three Generations of Case-Law and Still Ambiguity, in* THE LEGACY OF THE INTERNATIONAL CRIMINAL TRIBUNAL FOR THE FORMER YUGOSLAVIA 387 (A. Zahar, G.K. Sluiter & A.H.J. Swart eds., 2011).

[51] *Prosecutor v. Fofana and Kondewa, supra* note 45, § 819.

predicament illustrated the extant difficulties of turning the free-roaming Kamajors into an efficient and disciplined armed force. On a more general note, the Trial Chamber observed that:

> Although the CDF was regarded as a cohesive force under one central command, there were some fighters who acted on their own without knowledge of the central command because their area of operation was so wide. Commanders' authority to discipline their men on the ground was entirely their own. The CDF also did not keep records of its members like a conventional army would.[52]

Parallel to the CDF, which gradually displayed the features of a well-organized armed force, more ephemeral and spiritual spheres of influence still persisted, epitomized in the person of Kondewa, the High Priest of the entire CDF organization (whose role as a magician is further discussed in René Provost's Chapter 8 in this volume).

> He was the head of all the CDF initiators initiating the Kamajors into the Kamajor society in Sierra Leone. His job was to prepare herbs which the Kamajors smeared on their bodies to protect them against bullets. Kondewa was not a fighter, he himself never went to the war front or into active combat, but whenever a Kamajor was going to war, he would go to Kondewa for advice and blessing. (...) The Kamajors believed in the mystical powers of the initiators, especially Kondewa, and that the process of the initiation and immunisation would make them "bullet-proof." The Kamajors looked up to Kondewa and admired the man with such powers. (...) Because of the mystical powers Kondewa possessed, he had command over the Kamajors from every part of the country.[53]

The use of the term "command" is slightly misleading in this context and should at least not be taken literally, in the sense of *"military* command." His mystical powers and authority did not suffice to sustain Kondewa's superior responsibility;

> The Chamber noted that Kondewa's de jure status as High Priest of the CDF gave him the authority over all the initiators in the country as well as put him in charge of the initiations. This authority did not give him the power to decide who should be deployed to go to the war front. He also never went to the war front himself.[54]

With regards to another event – the harassment of the citizens of Bonthe Town, which had been sieged by Kamajors – Kondewa's exercise of factual powers were sufficient to tip the balance in favor of the Trial Chamber's conclusion that he exercised effective control:

> By virtue of his *de jure* status as High Priest and his *de facto* status as a superior to these Kamajors in that (Bonthe) District, Kondewa exercised effective control over them. Kondewa had the legal and material ability to issue orders to Kamara, both by reason of the leadership role at Base Zero, *being part of the CDF High Command,* and the authority he enjoyed in his position as High Priest in Sierra Leone and particularly so in Bonthe District.[55] (Emphasis added)

[52] *Id.* § 358.
[53] *Id.* §§ 344–346.
[54] *Id.* § 806.
[55] *Id.* § 686.

Apparently, Kondewa's powers and authority as a military (-like) commander had lain dormant and could serve as an adequate legal basis sustaining a superior–subordinate relationship whenever he decided to seize the opportunity.[56]

IV. SOME FINAL REFLECTIONS

The previous analysis of the SCSL's case law on the topic of superior responsibility makes it abundantly clear that its Trial Chambers, even (or should we rather say in particular?) in the irregular setting of civil wars are inclined to look for familiar command structures. Moreover – and in line with the opinion of the ICTY, as expressed in the Kordić case – they explicitly required that a superior, be it a military or a civilian, belong to the "chain of command." Mere "psychological" or spiritual power over people will not suffice to sustain a finding of criminal liability, even if this power would be so strong as to enable the power holder in question to prevent people from committing (international) crimes by threatening them with severe punishment. Kondewa only incurred criminal responsibility as a superior when his mystical powers over the Kamajors solidified in a more concrete capacity to issue orders by virtue of his being integrated in the chain of command. This contrasts with the findings of the ICTR Trial Chamber in the Musema case, who already deduced Musema's legal and financial control over his employees from his power to appoint or remove them from their positions at the Tea Factory of which he was the owner.[57] In view of the more demanding requirements of the ICTY and the SCSL, as expounded earlier in this chapter, the Musema Trial Chamber's opinion is probably in need of legal correction.[58]

In the opinion of the present author, the requirement that the superior be part and parcel of the chain of command has a double function. First of all, it simply corroborates the social fact that military organizations are predicated on principles of unquestionable command and strict obedience that enable those higher in the military hierarchy to steer the conduct of their subordinates. But that is obviously not its only meaning, as it would allow evidence of other methods to exercise "effective control" over other people, making the condition perhaps not redundant as a useful indication, but not indispensable. The requirement must therefore have a normative connotation as well, and in that capacity it serves to compensate the far-ranging criminal responsibility of the doctrine.

From a criminal law perspective the *mens rea* and its character as a crime of omission are the most conspicuous and most contested elements of the concept of superior responsibility. Combining these features, one may be justifiably surprised to learn that someone can be held responsible, simply by failing to act, for the most heinous crimes, of which he may not have been aware and which occurrence he did not intend. Trial Chambers of the ICTY

---

[56] Kondewa's appeal, challenging the findings of the Trial Chamber, was of no avail. The Appeals Chamber confirmed the Trial Chamber's conclusion: "The Appeals Chamber therefore finds that Kondewa has failed to show that no reasonable trier of fact could have reached the conclusion that a superior–subordinate relationship existed between him and his alleged subordinates in Bonthe District." Prosecutor v. Fofana and Kondewa, Case No. SCSL-04–14-A, § 188 (May 28, 2008).

[57] Prosecutor v. Musema, Judgment, Case No. ICTR-96–13-T, T. Ch., § 880 (Jan. 27, 2000).

[58] Also critical is G. METTRAUX, THE LAW OF COMMAND RESPONSIBILITY 166 (2009), who comments that "the view of the *Musema* Chamber appears to lower the standard of – effective – control necessary to a point where it means no more than a contractual relationship."

have suggested the consideration of superior responsibility as a separate crime of omission, based on a dereliction of duty, rather than as a form of participation in the very crimes, in order to downplay the degree of "guilt" and correspondingly to justify a lower sentence.[59] This proposition has been widely discussed and endorsed in legal literature.[60] Indeed the idea is certainly attractive, but it does not resolve all problems. This is especially so with respect to the issue of the legal basis for criminal liability pertinent to omissions. Crimes of omission by definition require a legal obligation to act, and Alexander Zahar has correctly pointed out that this duty has been neglected in the case law of the ad hoc tribunals.[61] He argues that this legal duty is simply presumed to derive from the existence of a superior–subordinate responsibility, without the Chambers having paid much heed to the nature of that relationship.

It is my contention that the insertion of the requirement that the superior must be part of the chain of command meets the objections of Zahar, provided that the features of this chain of command are further elucidated. The normative point of departure is, as indicated previously, the military hierarchical organization. The essential element of this organization is the power to issue orders. Concomitant characteristics are an institutionalized confidence that those orders are obeyed and an adequate reporting mechanism to check whether that confidence is warranted. Since time immemorial this stratified structure has not only served to increase the efficiency of military organizations in light of their demanding tasks, but has also been considered as a guarantee to reduce the risk of mayhem and mischief as much as possible. Military commanders have both the capacity and the obligation to exercise effective control over their subordinates, because if they fail to do so, things will seriously go awry, in view of the inherently dangerous affairs in which they engage.

The normative embedment of the doctrine of superior responsibility in military culture has two consequences. First of all, it implies that superior responsibility for civilians is essentially problematic.[62] Civilian superiors should only incur criminal responsibility if their relationship vis-à-vis their subordinates mirrors the military example. This strict interpretation seems to be corroborated by the Trial Chamber in *Delalić* when it expressed agreement with the opinion of the International Law Commission, holding that "the doctrine of superior responsibility extends to civilian superiors only to the extent that they

---

[59] For the first time in Prosecutor v. Hadžihasanović, Decision on Interlocutory Appeal Challenging Jurisdiction in Relation to Command Responsibility, Case No. IT-01-47-AR72 (July 16); Partial Dissenting Opinion of Judge Shahabuddeen, § 32; Separate and partially Dissenting Opinion of Judge Hunt, § 13. *See* furthermore and explicitly the Appeals Chamber's opinion in Prosecutor v. Krnojelac, Judgment of the Appeals Chamber, Case No. IT-97-25-A, A. Ch., § 171 (Sept. 17, 2003): "(...) it cannot be overemphasized that, where superior responsibility is concerned, an accused is not charged with the crimes of his subordinates but with the failure to carry out his duty as a superior to exercise control." In a similar vein: Prosecutor v. Halilović, Judgment, Case No. IT-01-48-T, § 54 (Nov. 16, 2005) and Prosecutor v. Orić, Judgment, Case No. IT-03-68-T, § 782 (June 30, 2006).

[60] Compare for instance Bing Bing Jia, *The Doctrine of Command Responsibility Revisited*, 3 CHINESE J. INT'L L. 1–42 (2004); C. Meloni, *Command Responsibility – Mode of Liability for the Crimes of Subordinates or Separate Offense of the Subordinate?*, 5 J. INT'L CRIM. JUSTICE 619 (2007); V. Nerlich, *Superior Responsibility under Article 28 ICC Statute: For What Exactly Is the Superior Held Responsible?*, 5 J. INT'L CRIM. JUSTICE 665 (2007); M. Damaška, *The Shadow Side of Command Responsibility*, 49 AM. J. COMP. L. 455 (2001); and Harmen van der Wilt, *Why International Criminal Lawyers Should Read Mirjan Damaška*, in FUTURE PERSPECTIVES ON INTERNATIONAL CRIMINAL JUSTICE 44–57 (Carsten Stahn & Larissa van den Herik eds., 2010).

[61] ALEXANDER ZAHAR & GÖRAN SLUITER, INTERNATIONAL CRIMINAL LAW 258–61 (2008).

[62] For a similar point of view, ZAHAR & SLUITER, *supra* note 61, at 260.

exercise a degree of control over their subordinates which is similar to that of the military commanders."[63]

Secondly, leaders of *irregular* armed forces can only be tried and convicted on the basis of the doctrine of superior responsibility if those forces display a chain of command, akin to traditional military organizations, and the accused effectively is part of that structure. This chapter has demonstrated that the SCSL, after shortly having strayed from this rigid interpretation and having toyed with the idea of harboring a broader view, has consequently applied this standard. In the view of the present author, this approach guards against unjust results.

---

[63] *Prosecutor v. Delalić*, § 378. The Trial Chamber elucidated its point of view by indicating that "*de facto* authority should be accompanied by the trappings of the exercise of *de jure* authority. By this the Trial Chamber means the perpetrator of the underlying offence must be the subordinate of the person of higher rank and under his direct or indirect control." *Prosecutor v. Delalić*, § 646.

8

Authority, Responsibility, and Witchcraft: From *Tintin* to the SCSL

René Provost[*]

When tribunals developed the doctrine that military superiors ought to be held responsible for crimes of their subordinates not only when they had ordered such crimes, but also in situations in which the superior had been in a position to prevent their occurrence or punish the perpetrator, the tribunals offered a narrative about moral accountability and social structures. Violence, if it is ever to be lawful, must be under the control of the state or similar institutions. Command responsibility jurisprudence paints a picture of what a legitimate structure to control violence must look like. This is primarily a military model built on hierarchy and discipline that tribunals rely upon as an ideal-type, which for a time forestalled a more profound questioning of the basis of this doctrine. When international criminal law enlarged beyond the military the scope of those who might be caught in the net of accountability because of the authority they wielded over the direct authors of international crimes, it raised in a new way the question of the nature of the authority that might justify criminal responsibility on that basis.

Deprived of an idealized military model, courts are forced to confront the endless variety of social relations and question why some relations of authority might be said to carry responsibility, and others not. Why the war criminal's commander, but not his mother who actually might have held more sway? The matter becomes even more fraught if there is a transcultural dimension to this process of social mapping, when it is carried out by an institution the structure, membership, and foundations of which are all linked to societies different from the one under examination. In such a context, the narrative of authority and accountability created by the court ineluctably becomes as well a narrative of difference, a statement of the court's own identity.

These are the issues at the heart of the decision of the Special Court for Sierra Leone in the CDF Trial, in which the Court was asked to apply the doctrine of command responsibility to a relationship based on magical powers, far removed from the usual idea of a military chain of command (as discussed by Harmen van der Wilt and Sandesh Sivakumaran). The

[*] Professor and Director, Centre for Human Rights and Legal Pluralism, McGill University. This chapter is a revised version of a text first published in 2012 in *Law, Text, Culture*, whose editors I thank for granting permission to reprint it here. The essay was originally written in French and presented at a conference at the Université libre de Bruxelles. I thank my research assistant, Caylee Hong, for her enormous help in the preparation of the initial essay. The translation was done by Neesha Rao, whom I thank as well. This is part of a broader interdisciplinary team project titled "Centaur Jurisprudence," exploring the intersection of law and culture, funded by the Canadian Social Sciences and Humanities Research Council.

various judgments in that case offer a fascinating dialogue not only on the legal recognition of magical powers, but also on the uneasy negotiations of identity for an international tribunal operating in a cultural setting very different from the one that inspired the creation of the international criminal law regime. Such transcultural consideration of the nature and significance of magic and authority is also at the heart of a very different narrative, *Tintin au Congo*, written by Hergé in 1930 during the Belgian colonial period. In describing the adventures of a young white European in Africa, Hergé also engaged in a social mapping of sorts, a projection of what he imagined to be the place of magic and power in that culture. A parallel between these two narratives separated by time, form, and purpose highlights the constructed nature of command responsibility and the need for a deeper consideration of its foundations in international criminal law.

I. MYSTICISM, MODERNITY, AND AUTHORITY IN *TINTIN AU CONGO*

The portrayal of Africa as completely permeated by colonialism in *Tintin au Congo*[1] explains why that work regularly has been condemned as racist. The purpose of this chapter is not to revisit the description of Africans as unable to speak correctly ("me so tired"), convinced of the physical and intellectual superiority of Westerners ("Them say, in Europe all young white men is like Tintin"), unable to understand foreign objects (the Babaoro'm king who uses a rolling pin as a scepter), and wanting nothing more than to conserve their subaltern colonial status (teaching school children: "Today, children, I will tell you about your country: Belgium!"). Beyond this discourse, which seeks to highlight for the presumed amusement of the reader the enormous cultural gap between Tintin and the Congolese, Hergé also evokes, on various occasions, magic as a symbol of the backward nature of African society. We can identify three variants of this encounter between magic and modernity in three separate episodes of *Tintin au Congo*: magic as a lie used by local elites to control indigenous people, magic as a tool to further colonial domination, and magic as a barrier beyond which lays unattainable modernity. As we will see, the interaction between mysticism and modernity in *Tintin* is not without striking parallels to that in the jurisprudence of the SCSL regarding the nature of authority in an armed insurgent group.

The first evocation presents magic as a false belief and as a tool in the hands of elites that allows them to manipulate a gullible population. We see this with Tintin's arrival in the Babaoro'm tribe: Tintin is welcomed by the king, who disappears for the rest of the story and is replaced as an authority figure in the tribe by the witch doctor, Muganga. This linking of power with mysticism is also present in twentieth century anthropological literature on African societies. As seen in classic texts by authors such as Max Gluckman[2] and Edward

---

[1] References to *Tintin au Congo* throughout the article come from the original edition of the story, published in 1930 in the newspaper *Le Petit XXe*. This version was reproduced in *Archives Hergé*, vol. 1 (1973); Casterman 185–293, presented with no irony as the "version primitive, en noir et en blanc"! Quotations in English are taken from the translation by LESLIE LONSDALE-COOPER & MICHAEL TURNER, *Tintin in the Congo* (London, Egmont 2010). See JEAN-LOUIS DONNADIEU, *Colonisation – l'Afrique de l'homme blanc, in* LES PERSONNAGES DE TINTIN DANS L'HISTOIRE: LES ÉVÉNEMENTS DE 1930 À 1944 QUI ONT INSPIRÉ L'ŒUVRE D'HERGÉ 32–37 (2011).

[2] M. GLUCKMAN, CUSTOM AND CONFLICT IN AFRICA (1955).

Evans-Pritchard,[3] occult power intersects with and is necessary for political power; witch-craft constitutes an important, if not the most important, vector of social ordering. That said, magic is not reduced to power: the king might disappear from the story, but the sorcerer never becomes king himself; his power is other.

In Hergé's story, the witch doctor is displeased by Tintin's arrival in his tribe. Tintin managed, bare-handed, to tame a lion that had scared away all the warriors. This threatens the sorcerer's control of the tribe because Tintin's powers are not connected to the occult. Muganga, who has allied himself with Tom, an evil white man who wants to get rid of Tintin, decides to use his "magic" to unjustly accuse Tintin of having defiled the tribe's fetish, leading to Tintin's capture. This accusation effectively writes Tintin's death sentence. Hergé, thus, presents magic as trickery, diverted from its usual function in the tribe in order to serve the personal interests of the sorcerer and the evil white man, and used to manipulate the natives. Tintin nevertheless succeeds in escaping his captors, and overhears a conversation between the witch doctor and the evil white man in which they boast of having planned everything. ("And I, witch-doctor of Babaoro'm, can keep they ignorant and stupid people in my power....").[4] Fortunately, Tintin had brought a video camera and a phonograph with him, allowing him to film everything and later show it to the Babaoro'm warriors. The recording makes it clear that the witch doctor himself does not believe in the magic he claims to control ("Ha! Ha! Ha! .... If they only knew.... How I make fun of they and their stupid fetish! ....").[5]

Modernity, as represented by the Western scientific tools that permit objective access to the truth (the camera, the phonograph), defeats the supposed magic, an obscurantism hijacked by elites to enslave the ignorant population. The warriors feel foolish for having been tricked by Muganga, and chase him away under a rain of projectiles. This illustrates the collective nature of magical power: as noted by Marcel Mauss, an individual can never be seen as a lone recipient of magical power—it is necessarily produced dialectically by the community in question.[6] Witchcraft and the witch doctor are not rejected by the tribe. Rather, the apparent abuse was sanctioned by the community, allowing Muganga to go on as witch doctor in the rest of the story. That said, traditional authority finds itself replaced by a new, white, and modern authority in the person of Tintin, whom the warriors proclaim the new Chief of the Babaoro'm. This modernity is translated as a source of wisdom (Tintin makes a Solomonic judgment to put an end to a dispute by splitting a hat in half) and of quasi-miraculous scientific powers (Tintin used quinine to instantly heal and chase what the sick man's wife calls "bad juju come to live inside him").[7] We could also read this last vignette as a metaphor in which mystical beliefs are an illness for which science and knowledge are the remedy.[8] In short, European reason defeats African obscurantism, making all better off.

---

[3] E. Evans-Pritchard, Witchcraft, Oracle and Magic among the Azande (1937).
[4] Hergé, Tintin in the Congo (2010).
[5] *Id.* at 26.
[6] M. Mauss, *Esquisse d'une théorie générale de la magie' Année sociologique* 10–11 (1903), http://classiques.uqac.ca/classiques/mauss_marcel/socio_et_anthropo/1_esquisse_magie/esquisse_magie.pdf.
[7] Hergé, *supra* note 4, at 28.
[8] P.N. Ndong, *La sorcellerie est une maladie*, Afrik.com: l'actualité de l'Afrique noir (2005), http://www.afrik.com/article8371.html (last visited Oct. 28, 2011).

A second episode in *Tintin au Congo* also invokes magic, but in a very different way because this time it is Tintin who uses the Africans' risible beliefs in supernatural powers. In this case, modernity exploits mysticism to serve its own ends, identifying it as a source of power that can entrench Western authority in the tribe and supplant the power traditionally held by witch doctors.

Following their expulsion, Muganga, the witch doctor, and Tom, the evil white man, use deception to provoke a war between the Babaoro'm and a neighboring tribe, the 'M Hatuvu. The king of the 'M Hatuvu is confident that he will be able to easily defeat his enemy thanks to his army "trained and equipped like a European army,"[9] which is visibly rendered by the army's bearskin hats and blunderbuss on wheels ("heavy artillery"). Tintin positions himself in the open so as to provoke the enemy, who shoot multiple arrows and yet never manage to hit him. The arrows are all redirected toward a tree behind which Tintin has hidden a powerful electromagnet: this is the magic of modernity, which provides the warrior Tintin with an invincibility against the weapons of the enemy, doing so in a manner that is invisible and incomprehensible to his enemy.

Witchcraft is a recurring theme in the context of armed conflict in Africa and, as we will see, a theme that is also present in the jurisprudence of the SCSL.[10] More generally, we find in colonialism the practice of appropriating mystical and far-fetched beliefs for the purpose of serving Western interests. For example, "white" tribunals made indigenous witnesses swear on potions that indigenous peoples believed had supernatural powers. In Sierra Leone, at the beginning of the twentieth century, a British court prepared a mixture of salt, pepper, ashes, and water every Monday; witnesses drank this potion while promising to tell the truth or risk sudden death by snakebite, drowning, or similar misfortune.[11]

In Hergé's story, faced with the impossibility of hitting Tintin with bow and arrow, the 'M Hatuvu attempt to shoot him with the help of the "heavy artillery": the blunderbuss. Despite using a technique modeled in the European instructions (one positions the instrument at precisely a range of 43.5 meters), the blunderbuss explodes on the shooters instead of reaching Tintin. This completes the metaphor of modernity, which is not only incomprehensible to the indigenous people, but also beyond their reach. Any attempt to appropriate modernity and use it against the colonial power is doomed to fail and ultimately harm the indigenous population. Sure enough, defeated by the magical powers of civilization, the 'M Hatuvu fall prostrate before Tintin ("you great juju man") and proclaim him king of their tribe. They leave the scene singing, happy in their subjugation. It is interesting to note that, in both tribes, the recognition of Tintins's superior "magical" powers do not lead him to become the new sorcerer, but rather the chief. In resisting and co-opting African ideas about power, modern Western thought refuses to engage it on its own terms but, rather, renders it according to its own grammar of power.

The third and final episode related to witchcraft in *Tintin au Congo* demonstrates the unattainable nature of modernity; the magical powers of the Africans are no match for modernity, and in fact ultimately reinforce their inferiority. In the story, following the

---

[9] HERGÉ, *supra* note 4, at 29.

[10] N. WLODARCZYK, MAGIC AND WARFARE: APPEARANCE AND REALITY IN CONTEMPORARY AFRICAN CONFLICTS (2009).

[11] Sir K.J. BEATTY, SPECIAL COMMISSION COURT, HUMAN LEOPARDS: AN ACCOUNT OF THE TRIALS OF HUMAN LEOPARDS BEFORE THE SPECIAL COMMISSION COURT 25–26 (1915).

thwarting of their attempt to provoke a war between the two tribes, Muganga the witch doctor and his white stooge learn that Tintin plans to spend a night on the outskirts of the village, on the lookout for a leopard. The witch doctor then reveals that he is a member of a secret society, the Aniotas, assassins who dress as leopards in order to kill their victim. The Aniotas disguise themselves by attaching iron claws to their hands, covering their body in leopard skin, and using a stick whose carved end leaves the paw-prints of the animal. In fact, leopard-men and, to a lesser extent, crocodile-men and monkey-men, terrorized a region of Africa at the end of the nineteenth and the beginning of the twentieth centuries. Often associated with the fear of cannibalism, this practice for decades camouflaged murders thought to be the work of wild animals. Colonial officials in the Belgian Congo, Sierra Leone, and other colonies reacted to the rise of these assassins at the beginning of the previous century by a campaign to eradicate the leopard-men, whose activities destabilized the territory and thereby threatened colonial authority.[12] In *Tintin au Congo*, the phenomenon of the leopard-men is reduced to another attempt by indigenous elites to exploit the naïve beliefs of the general population to "fight the white man's civilizing influence" and also to solidify their hold on power.[13] Unsurprisingly, Tintin easily thwarts the plot hatched against him to unmask – figuratively and literally – the witch doctor, and, in the process, actually saves the life of the witch doctor, who declares himself Tintin's slave.

It is important to highlight the extent to which, during the last century and a half, the fear of leopard-men occupied a central place in African mysticism. Beyond the brotherhood of assassins wearing leopard skin, as evoked by Hergé, we also see a widespread belief that some witch doctors were able to project their spirit into the body of a real leopard in order to control it and use it to kill people. In the popular imagination, there is not necessarily a stark difference or marked boundary between these two versions of the leopard-men phenomenon. Whereas Hergé's narrative is one of trickery, a native reading of the same events may well have underscored the opacity and complexity of witchcraft to demur from the quick judgment Hergé calls for. The truth of magic reflects beliefs that are not vulnerable to contrary demonstrations.[14] Leopard-men targeted not only leaders who had been won over to the cause of colonialism, but also anyone whom the sorcerers wanted to get rid of or whose death would undermine or increase the authority of a local chief. The ritual of murder by the leopard-man would bring power and riches to its sponsor. Anthropological studies have linked these beliefs to the disappearance of the Atlantic slave trade, which indigenous people widely associated with a Western cannibalism in which the captives were taken overseas to be eaten.[15]

Many have suggested that murder by the leopard-men constituted another form of consumption, because the word "to eat" in many dialects evokes more generally the ritualistic appropriation of the power contained in the body of another person.[16] Mystical beliefs were

---

[12] M. KALOUS, CANNIBALS AND TONGO PLAYERS OF SIERRA LEONE (1974); BEATTY, *supra* note 11; P. JOSET, LES SOCIÉTÉS SECRÈTES DES HOMMES-LÉOPARDS EN AFRIQUE NOIRE (1955).

[13] Hergé, 1930 *Tintin au Congo*, in ARCHIVES HERGÉ, vol. 1, 185, 236 (1973).

[14] J. Siegel, *The Truth of Sorcery*, 18 CULTURAL ANTHROPOLOGY 135, 139 (2003).

[15] R. Shaw, *The Politician and the Diviner: Divination and the Consumption of Power in Sierra Leone*, 26/1 J. RELIGION AFR. 30, 48 (1996).

[16] R. SHAW, CANNIBAL TRANSFORMATIONS: COLONIALISM AND COMMODIFICATION IN THE SIERRA LEONE HINTERLAND 50–70 (Henrietta L. Moore & Todd Sanders eds., 2001).

used as evidence of the primitive nature of African society at the time, serving to justify colonial expansion. Colonialism was thus aimed at civilizing the population and also at liberating Africa from the yoke of false beliefs. In *Tintin au Congo*, colonialism is needed as the new truth, symbolized by the last image in the book where a warrior comes to kneel before fetishes in the image of Tintin and Milou, who have replaced the magic fetish that the tribe had venerated before. Tintin the chief can no longer be physically present to exert authority, but his power has come to occupy the mystical sphere as well: modernity has entirely displaced mysticism.

The encounter between mysticism and modernity in *Tintin au Congo* marks a well-defined line between these two universes, a clear distinction between the type of power that each corresponds to. This line affirms ontological distinctions between fact and non-fact, truth and fantasy, real and occult, civilization and barbarism. One could say that the famous "clear line" developed by Hergé to structure his illustrations is meaningful not only formally but also conceptually. In this reading, the line dividing witchcraft and modernity is equally clear; the two cannot coexist. One effect of modernity's rational discourse is to make any consultation of the occult illegitimate; relying on the occult is like relying on a lie and evidences gullibility, if not madness. We would expect therefore that the juridical discourse at the heart of international criminal law would subscribe to this dominance of rational thinking. Instead, as we see in the judgments of the SCSL in *Fofana and Kondewa*, it is not always as easy as Hergé makes it seem in *Tintin au Congo* to draw a fine line between mysticism and modernity.

II. THE LIMITS OF RATIONAL DISCOURSE IN THE CDF TRIAL

Allieu Kondewa was one of the defendants in the trial of the leaders of the Civil Defense Forces (CDF) before the SCSL. He was accused of eight counts of war crimes, crimes against humanity, and other serious violations of international humanitarian law.[17] The charges against Kondewa are unique because he never personally committed any of the crimes of which he is accused. Attributing international criminal responsibility on the basis of the responsibility of superiors or commanders, or through application of the doctrine of aiding and abetting, is not uncommon; in this case, however, Kondewa did not hold a political or military role of the type that normally attracts responsibility for the act of another. Kondewa was instead the witch doctor for the CDF, officiating initiation ceremonies for new fighters in the Kamajors secret society and administering lotions and potions to make fighters invisible and invincible to bullets. The SCSL was therefore called to pronounce upon the legal implications of occult magical rituals in international criminal law. This exercise provoked a lively debate among the judges regarding the place of magic in the law. This debate reflects the ambiguous character of the interaction of legal discourse, an emblem of modernity, and certain mystical beliefs that remain present in Africa. We see here one of the themes that inspired Hergé in *Tintin au Congo*: the encounter between the universalizing West and black Africa. Contrary to *Tintin*, which was a monologue by Hergé, the judgments of the SCSL in the CDF Trial are a dialogue between authors with contrasting perspectives. Thus, the jurisprudence of the SCSL offers a real site of encounter, where differing visions of the nature

---

[17] *Prosecutor v. Moinina Fofana and Allieu Kondewa Trial Chamber* [hereinafter *CDF Trial*].

of law and its conjugation in different cultures are articulated. After briefly presenting the foundations of the jurisdiction of the SCSL, we will highlight how the Trial Chamber and the majority of the Appeals Chamber reduce facts through law. We will then contrast this with the sensational dissent by the Sierra Leonean president of the Appeals Chamber, for whom the law must separate itself entirely from a discourse based on false beliefs.

A. General Context

The civil war that raged in Sierra Leone during the 1990s implicated, on both sides of the conflict, diverse armed groups that committed large-scale abuses of all kinds. The rebel groups Revolutionary United Front (RUF) and Armed Forces Revolutionary Council (AFRC) are generally blamed for the worst abuses, including countless civilian executions, sexual violence and slavery, amputations, kidnappings, forced marriages, theft, and destruction of property. Groups allied with the government of Sierra Leone, such as the Civil Defense Forces (CDF), also committed grave violations such as the recruitment and use of child soldiers and torture. Even the force sent by the regional economic organization, ECOWAS, has faced serious accusations of having committed extrajudicial executions of suspects.[18] In general, the conflict was portrayed in the media and in reports of international observers as marked by extreme, unrestrained, even irrational violence in the hands of children and irregular fighters acting under the influence of diverse drugs. More specifically, the media's representation revealed a Western fascination for the profoundly bizarre superposition of modern warfare with ancestral practices and beliefs: the image of a cannibal warrior covered in talismans, fighting with an AK-47, evokes an ahistorical primitivism that is incompatible with modernity.[19]

After multiple twists and many failed attempts to end the conflict, the government and the insurgents signed a peace agreement in Lomé in 1999, the terms of which required the insurgents to turn over their weapons in exchange for a role in the government and an amnesty for all crimes committed during the civil war. The agreement called for the creation of a Truth and Reconciliation Commission, which required the presence of a large contingent of international peacekeepers. It became rapidly clear to representatives of the international community that the amnesty declared by the Lomé Agreement was an obstacle preventing them from addressing the root causes of the conflict in Sierra Leone, thereby threatening the peace that had been so difficult to achieve. Following negotiations between the government of Sierra Leone and the United Nations, as well as resolution 1315 of the Security Council, the Special Court for Sierra Leone was created in order to try the leaders who were most responsible for the crimes committed during the civil war in the country after November 30, 1996.[20] According to the governing statute of the SCSL, these crimes

---

[18] L.A. HORVITZ & C. CATHERWOOD, ENCYCLOPEDIA OF WAR CRIMES AND GENOCIDE 136–37 (2006).

[19] R. SHAW, *Robert Kaplan and "Juju Journalism"* in *Sierra Leone's Rebel War: The Primitivizing of an African Conflict* 81, 82 in B. Meyer & P. Pels (eds.), MAGIC AND MODERNITY: INTERFACES OF REVELATION AND CONCEALMENT (Stanford University Press, 2002), 81; G. Anders, *Testifying about "Uncivilized Events": Problematic Representations of Africa in the Trial against Charles Taylor*, 24 LEIDEN J. INT'L L. 937, 940 (2011).

[20] U.N. Security Council, Security Council Resolution 1315 (2000) [on establishment of a Special Court for Sierra Leone] (Aug. 14, 2000), S/RES/1315 (2000), http://www.unhcr.org/cgi-bin/texis/vtx/refworld/rwmain?docid=3b00f27814 (last visited June 18, 2012).

could be violations of international norms prohibiting crimes against humanity, war crimes or other violations of international humanitarian law, or other acts criminal under Sierra-Leonean laws on abuse against girls and wanton destruction of property.[21] In practice, the SCSL functions essentially as an international criminal tribunal, and its analysis is almost exclusively situated in jurisprudence and texts relevant to international law.[22] Although the SCSL is a hybrid institution with a mixed jurisdiction, it produces international law lacking much reference to the local legal context. The CDF Trial and the issue of Allieu Kondewa's responsibility as a superior highlight the necessary vernaculization of international justice in the jurisprudence of the SCSL and challenge the normative possibility of isolating international criminal law from the context in which it is applied.[23]

The Civil Defense Forces were a paramilitary group created in 1997 to protect the elected government of Sierra Leone against other groups who had usurped power in the country.[24] Kamajors, members of a traditional hunting society that ensured the security of villages against all threats, both physical and metaphysical, constituted the nucleus of the CDF. Historically, the main task of the Kamajors ("hunters" in the Mende language) was to gather meat for the village. After the coup d'état, and the outbreak of a new civil war in Sierra Leone, the government decided to co-opt the Kamajors in order to make them the spearhead of the effort to regain power. The fallen president of Sierra Leone named the man who would become the guiding spirit of the CDF, Samuel Hinga Norman, as its "national coordinator." Norman was also one of the three original co-accused in the trial of the CDF. He directed the CDF along with Moinina Fofana, "Director of War," and Allieu Kondewa, "High Priest."

An expert at the Trial Chamber of the SCSL described these three men as the Holy Trinity of the CDF: Norman, Father God; Fofana, the Son; and, Kondewa, the Holy Ghost.[25] Each member of the triumvirate exercised functions distinct from those of the others, but no important decision was reached without the agreement of all three. As to Kondewa, his role as High Priest meant that he presided over all initiation ceremonies of new members to the Kamajors society, using potions and ceremonies he had created. He prepared a mix of magical herbs that fighters would rub on themselves in order to become invincible to bullets. For each new battle, the Kamajors would line up before Kondewa to receive his benediction, and Kondewa would read their fortunes and decide who was fated to fight on that particular day. No Kamajors would dare participate in a battle without the blessing of their High Priest.[26] Kondewa never personally went to the battle sites and, most importantly, never gave orders of an operational or strategic nature. With one exception, he was not charged with

[21] U.N. Security Council, Statute of the Special Court for Sierra Leone (Jan. 16, 2002), http://www.unhcr.org/refworld/type,INTINSTRUMENT,3dda29f94,0.html (last visited June 18, 2012).

[22] C. Jalloh, *Special Court for Sierra Leone: Achieving Justice*, 32 Mich. J. Int'l L. 395–460 (2010).

[23] S.E. Merry, Human Rights and Gender Violence: Translating International Law into Local Justice (2009).

[24] M. Ferme & D. Hoffman, *Hunter Militias and the International Human Rights Discourse in Sierra Leone and Beyond*, 50 Afr. Today 73 (2004); D. Hoffman, *The Meaning of a Militia: Understanding the Civil Defence Forces of Sierra Leone*, 106 Afr. Aff. 639 (2007).

[25] *CDF Trial Transcripts*, para. 337 (Nov. 30, 2006), http://www.sc-sl.org/CASES/ProsecutorvsFofanaandKondewaCDFCase/Transcripts/tabid/154/Default.aspx (last visited June 18, 2012).

[26] *Id.* at paras. 344–347.

having directly committed a single international crime.[27] As mentioned above, Kondewa is indicted with crimes based on his criminal responsibility for the acts of others.[28]

In terms of the legal issues in the case, the Appeals Chamber and the Trial Chamber of the SCSL adopt a very standard approach to the issue of imputing responsibility to Kondewa for the actions of others. In fact, the Prosecutor and the Defense agreed on the major tenets of the doctrine of superior responsibility and on the doctrine of aiding and abetting, the two modes of participation by which the Prosecutor sought to link Kondewa to the actual facts and actions that were direct violations of international criminal law. Importantly, as we have already seen, Kondewa was not charged with having personally committed any reprehensible act. With respect to his responsibility as a superior, the facts implicate Kondewa through short speeches and benedictions given during parades prior to the start of missions during which others committed acts that violate international law. Kondewa's responsibility is also based on the fact that he presided over initiation ceremonies for child soldiers and rituals that were meant to make fighters invincible (bulletproofing). With respect to aiding and abetting, Kondewa's role as one of the three directors of the CDF, who had to approve all operations undertaken by the group, was invoked. Application of the doctrine of aiding and abetting in the judgments again turns on the legal effect of some allocutions delivered by Kondewa as well as his position in the CDF structure.

The articulation of the doctrine of superior responsibility is now well recognized in international criminal law, primarily because of the jurisprudence of the International Criminal Tribunals for the former Yugoslavia and for Rwanda. As agreed by all sides in the CDF Trial, a defendant can be held responsible for the act of another if he exercised, at the time of the event, "effective control" over this other person or group. In order for this to be the case, the existence of a relationship of authority between the accused and the direct author of the crime must be proven in a manner that would permit the former to issue orders to the latter, to prevent the committing of international crimes, or to punish the commission of the crimes.[29] This relationship could be one of authority de jure, based on the position of the accused in the hierarchy of a group, taking into consideration the nature of the group and its rules and structure. It could also be one of de facto authority, perhaps through some dominion exercised by an individual over others in particular circumstances, even if this dynamic is not recognized on an institutional level. A relationship of authority calling for criminal responsibility can exist as much in a military framework as in a civilian context. In the case at hand, with respect to applying this doctrine to Kondewa, all judges agreed that any differences between the positions of the Prosecution and that of the Defense were factual and not substantive.[30] But it was precisely a factual issue that revealed a fracture between the four judges constituting the majority of the Appeals Chamber and the dissenter, Judge George Gelaga King. This divide reflects diverging visions of the nature of international criminal law, the type of authority that can sustain the application of the

---

[27] The sole exception related to an extrajudicial execution, which the SCSL deemed not proven beyond reasonable doubt.

[28] D. Hoffman, THE WAR MACHINES: YOUNG MEN AND VIOLENCE IN SIERRA LEONE AND LIBERIA 233–38 (2011).

[29] *Prosecutor v. Moinina Fofana and Allieu Kondewa Appeal Chamber*, para. 161 [hereinafter *CDF Appeal*].

[30] *Id.* at para. 171.

doctrine of command responsibility, and, more generally, the identity of the legal discourse of a tribunal such as the SCSL.

B. *The Trial Chamber and the Majority of the Appeals Chamber*

For the majority of judges in the CDF Trial, both at the trial and appeal levels, Kondewa's legal responsibility as a superior comes from the fact that the fighters believed that Kondewa had effective control over them. Thus, the factual analysis turns on whether this belief actually existed, not on whether the powers claimed by Kondewa are real. We can divide this question posed by the majority into two parts: first, did this belief exist in the minds of the fighters who committed international crimes, and, second, was this belief of a nature to confer on Kondewa the level of control required in order for him to be charged with these crimes, in the name of superior responsibility?

In the Trial Chamber of the SCSL, the judges described how the fighters perceived Kondewa in the following terms:

> The Kamajors believed in mystical powers of the initiators, especially Kondewa, and that the process of the initiation and immunization would make them "bullet-proof." The Kamajors looked up to Kondewa and admired the man with such powers. They believed that he was capable of transferring his powers to them to protect them. By virtue of these powers Kondewa had command over the Kamajors in the country. He never went to the war front himself, but whenever a Kamajor was going to war, Kondewa would give his advice and blessings, as well as the medicine which the Kamajors believed would protect them against bullets. No Kamajor would go to war without Kondewa's blessings.[31]

In this lengthy trial level judgment, we find multiple references to Kondewa's mystical status in the eyes of the fighters. These passages have the same vague formulation as the above quote.[32] For the Court, Kondewa's role as High Priest gave him a de jure status within the CDF, an official role that completes the operational and strategic command roles held by the two other Accused, Norman and Fofana. That said, despite its repeated emphasis on Kondewa's influence over the fighters, the Trial Chamber concluded that it was not proven beyond a reasonable doubt that this power was of a nature to prevent or punish violations of international law. Without this type of effective control, the simple role of High Priest is insufficient to charge Kondewa with command responsibility.[33] Similarly, the mere fact that

---

[31] *Id.* at para. 721(vii).

[32] For example, *CDF Trial, supra* note 17, at para. 765: "Kondewa gave his blessing and the medicines which would make the fighters fearless if they did not spoil the law. He also said that all of his power had been transferred to them to protect them, so that no cutlass would strike them and that they should not be afraid."

[33] *CDF Trial, supra* note 17, at para. 853: "Although he possessed command over all the Kamajors from every part of the country, this was, however, limited to the Kamajors' belief in mystical powers which Kondewa allegedly possessed. This evidence is inconclusive, however, to establish beyond reasonable doubt that Kondewa had effective control over the Kamajors, in a sense that he had the material ability to prevent or punish them for their criminal acts. The Chamber noted that Kondewa's *de jure* status as High Priest of the CDF gave him the authority over all the initiators in the country as well as put him in charge of all the initiations. This authority did not give him the power to decide who should be deployed to go to the war front. He also never went to the war front himself. The evidence adduced, therefore, has not established beyond reasonable doubt that Kondewa had any superior–subordinate relationship with the Kamajors who operated in Bo District."

The same passage, word for word, is reproduced at paragraphs 806 and 916.

in 1998 Kondewa reviewed the fighters, blessing them and giving them potions to make them bulletproof, was not sufficient for the SCSL to find him to have aided and abetted in the commission of the crimes by the fighters.[34]

That said, the judges at trial did not find that the Kamajors' belief in Kondewa's mystical powers was without any legal effect. Thus, in another troop review in 1997, Kondewa was found to have aided and abetted in the crimes of Samuel Norman because he had encouraged the Kamajors to follow Norman's exhortation to take no prisoners. The Trial Chamber explained the impact of Kondewa's speeches and blessings by referring to the belief of the Kamajors in the High Priest's mystical powers.[35] Similarly, the court concluded that in one particular district, Bonthe, Kondewa had a special relationship with the local commander that went beyond his relationship with the Kamajors in the rest of the country: in Bonthe, for reasons that are not clear from the facts, the operational commander of the Kamajors battalion, a Mr. Kamara, considered himself under Kondewa's authority, giving Kondewa effective control of a nature that permitted him to prevent or punish crimes committed by fighters; Kondewa could issue written and oral orders, and threatened to punish by "a terrible death" anyone who lied to him.[36] The Trial Chamber treated the exact foundation of this authority with a degree of vagueness:

> By virtue of his *de jure* status as High Priest Kondewa [sic] and his *de facto* status as a superior to these Kamajors in that District, Kondewa exercised effective control over them. Kondewa had the legal and material ability to issue orders to Kamara, both by reason of his leadership role at Base Zero, being part of the CDF High Command, and the authority he enjoyed in his position as High Priest in Sierra Leone and particularly so in Bonthe District.[37]

It is significant that in this passage Kondewa is described by the SCSL as a High Priest of Sierra Leone in general and of the Bonthe district in particular: we have moved beyond the distinct belief in the minds of those who committed the violations in order to evoke Kondewa's objective status within the country as a whole. Despite what might be the reassuring use of the legal categories of de jure and de facto to classify the nature of Kondewa's authority, it seems futile to try to disentangle what, in this particular context, would belong to one category as opposed to the other. It is clear that Kondewa's magical powers are inseparable from the other sources of his authority, and contribute simultaneously to his de jure and de facto statuses. The taxonomic inclination of law, which longs to define, identify, interpret, and classify facts and norms, finds itself challenged by the multivalent nature of mysticism, which is difficult to reconcile with known legal categories.

It is often noted that the ontological distinction between fact and law reflects a peculiarly Western evolution in legal thinking.[38] As in the case at hand, separating facts and law evokes a violent, often arbitrary, dislocation of reality as it is perceived by the actors involved. In a context concerning the activities of a witch doctor within a secret society that is part of an

---

[34] *CDF Trial, supra* note 17, at paras. 765 and 800.

[35] *Id.* at paras. 735–739.

[36] *Id.* at para. 869.

[37] *CDF Trial, supra* note 17, at para. 868. "Base Zero" was the CDF base camp, where the three Accused were normally found.

[38] H.P. GLENN, LEGAL TRADITIONS OF THE WORLD 149 (4th ed. 2010).

armed conflict in Africa, the discourse of international criminal law struggles to make that separation. In this case, the Trial Chamber approaches the legal classification of Kondewa's magical powers with some caution, recognizing that they could have a real impact on the application of international criminal law; the Court, however, refrains from clearly articulating the precise nature of those implications.

If the decision of the Trial Chamber is marked by caution bordering on vagueness, the majority of the Appeals Chamber opted for an evasive maneuver to marginalize mysticism. With respect to the question of whether the Trial Chamber committed an error of fact on the issue of Kondewa's involvement in the 1997 Passing Out parade, the Defense and Prosecution agreed that the applicable standard was that of "substantial effect."[39] The majority on appeal limited itself to essentially describing the reasoning of the Trial Chamber, without adding to it. Similarly, the Appeals Chamber adopted the conclusion of the trial court that the mere fact that Kondewa had given medicine to the Kamajors in order to make them bulletproof during another passing out parade in 1998 did not constitute aiding and abetting in the acts committed at the hands of the fighters.[40]

Conversely, on the issue of Kondewa's responsibility as a superior, a difference of opinion appeared between the Trial and Appeals Chambers with respect to the legal significance of Kondewa's mystical role in the CDF. Here, again, the parties agreed that the applicable test in order to determine the existence of a superior/subordinate relationship is whether there was "effective control."[41] The Defense stressed the inconsistency, even the incoherence, of the analysis of the Trial Chamber, which, on the one hand, denied that Kondewa's role as High Priest and his mystical powers could by themselves give him effective control over the Kamajors but, on the other hand, found that those same mystical powers and role contributed to his effective control in the Bonthe district. The majority of the Appeals Chamber recognized that this presented a tension, and concluded that Kondewa's role as High Priest and his mystical powers were not relevant. Effective control could be found despite these facts by concentrating solely on the factual authority of Kondewa over the Kamajor commanders in the Bonthe district.[42]

Using the same logic, the majority at appeal overturned a conviction for looting in the Moyamba district, because a declaration that the role and mystical powers of Kondewa are irrelevant did not leave a sufficient base to find effective control in that region.[43] As noted by Bantekas in his contribution to this volume, this begs the question of the nature of a person's authority and capacity, which meets the requirement for imposing command responsibility. If the actor Chuck Norris is taken by many fighters as the legendary embodiment of the warrior ethos, could we argue that he should be held accountable if he had the material capacity to stop a crime from being committed by broadcasting a message to that effect? The likely negative answer suggests that there is something more to authority than

---

[39] *CDF Appeal, supra* note 29, at paras. 70–75.

[40] *Id.* at paras. 89 and 110.

[41] *Id.* at para. 174. The Appeals Chamber rejects a Defense argument that the standard is different according to whether the superior is a civilian or a military commander: para. 175.

[42] *CDF Appeal, supra* note 29, at para. 179; N.A. Combs, Fact-Finding without Facts – The Uncertain Evidentiary Foundations of International Criminal Convictions 212–14 (2010).

[43] *CDF Appeal, supra* note 29, at paras. 212–215.

the capacity to influence. What exactly this mysterious (should we say "magic"?) ingredient might be is left unarticulated in the analysis of the majority in the CDF Appeals and in the jurisprudence on command responsibility generally.

Already in the Trial Chamber, magic was treated with caution and discussed elliptically, making its legal implications ambiguous. The decision of the majority of the Appeals Chamber marks an even greater disengagement from the issue of magic, demonstrated by its willingness to reject the relevance of Kondewa's mystical role.[44] This makes Judge King's thunderous dissent in the appeal decision, which we will soon turn to, even more startling.

The judgments of the SCSL in the CDF Case that we have just described constitute a narrative where rational, Western, civilized modernity is confronted with mysticism, a symbol of precolonial African primitivism. How can we understand the dynamic of the interaction between these two discourses? In the interaction between modernity and mysticism in the judgments at first instance and on appeal, we find the same three dynamics that we identified earlier in *Tintin au Congo*. Seen in this light, the narrative of the majority in the CDF Appeals Judgment can be viewed as furthering the myth of savagery evoked by Hergé in his story of the adventures of Tintin in the Congo.

First, like the manipulation of the Babaoro'm by the witch doctor Muganga in *Tintin au Congo*, we can understand the magic possessed by Kondewa as a tool that permits him to control the Kamajors by exploiting their gullibility and ignorance. By leveraging the desperate desire of young fighters to survive a vicious war, the Accused manipulated a system of traditional beliefs to serve their own ends. There are, not only in the judgments but also in the examination of witnesses and final arguments, allusions by the lawyers to the fact that such beliefs seem absurd.[45]

By highlighting the absurdity of believing that smearing oneself in herbs and lotions could make one bulletproof, the lawyers signaled to the judges their membership in the rational world of law. This is a world distinct from mysticism, for which mysticism is in fact an "other" whose rejection shapes law's identity. Unlike Tintin, who demonstrated to the Congolese the falsity of their beliefs through objects of modernity (the video and sound recorders), the Defense invited the judges to abstain from pronouncing on the values and beliefs of the Kamajors: "The Kamajors should not be patronized or judged more harshly for using means that seem less advanced or more .... or more unbelievable to others."[46] It is an invitation to abstain from imposing an external perspective on beliefs that, as we saw, the Trial Chamber and the majority at appeal for the most part heeded. This charitable suspension of incredulousness corresponds to the "rituals of distanciation," an expression used to describe and criticize the attitude of English historians with respect to witchcraft: by reducing mystical belief to an abnormality or pathology, it becomes justifiable to explain nothing but the causes of the belief and ignore its

---

[44] This is clearly articulated by Judge Winter in her partial dissent, which is otherwise not relevant to the issues under consideration in this chapter: "Not being a domestic court, it cannot also accept any cultural consideration as excuses for criminal conduct. The principle of individual criminal responsibility requires that an accused be held responsible for his acts or omissions, whatever his status. In the case where concrete acts or omissions of an accused have an impact on the commission of the crime in question, it is irrelevant, for instance, if this accused believes that he has supernatural powers or if he uses the cultural superstitions of people involved." *CDF Appeal*, *supra* note 29, Justice Winter Dissent, para. 4.

[45] *CDF Trial Transcripts*, *supra* note 25, at para. 36.

[46] *Id.* at 37.

structure and content.[47] With respect to the legal discourse, this "ritual of distanciation" leads the judges away from examining the merits or content of supernatural beliefs. Instead, the judges reduce these beliefs to facts, the legal implications of which must be determined.

In *Tintin au Congo*, a second interaction between modernity and mysticism appears in the form of modernity's appropriation of mysticism: Tintin uses an electromagnet to deflect arrows away from him and also persuades the tribesmen that he possesses magic powers that make him invincible. In the analysis of the SCSL there is also a hijacking of mystical beliefs by the legal discourse to serve its own ends, in this case the administration of international criminal responsibility. Even though the Trial Chamber was not interested in the content of the Kamajors' belief that Kondewa possessed the power to project his spirit to make them brave and to prepare medicine to render them bulletproof, the court still attached consequences to this belief. The fact as interpreted by the law is thus emptied of its content; the system of beliefs and traditional practices is reduced to a category defined entirely by international law. The customary cosmology of Sierra Leone is kidnapped by the cosmology of international law, which consumes it, saving only the parts that serve its own purposes. It is a conjuring that operates thanks to the magic of international law. Starting with a factual setting, law can create a narrative that depicts a reality very different from that perceived by its principal participants.

In a detailed anthropological study of the CDF militia, Danny Hoffman suggests that the group can hardly be reduced to a fighting unit mirroring the state's armed forces, within which Kondewa would have occupied a command position in the military hierarchy. He argues that the CDF "was the militarization of complex and poorly understood logics of patronage, wealth and values"[48] within which power flowed along different axes. Kondewa is reported as having behaved in ways that did not always conform to the objectives and methods of the CDF as a fighting unit, leading to his eventual removal by its leaders.[49] As highlighted by Clifford Geertz, legal representation of fact is normative from the start.[50] The image of the process by which facts are construed or even created by the SCSL suggests a disengagement of international criminal law from the process of vernacularizing justice, despite the stated ambition to contribute to the post-conflict reconstruction of society in Sierra Leone. Far from vernacularizing, the legal narrative thus created affirms its own modernity by distancing itself from a mythical other.[51]

The final vignette of the interaction between modernity and mysticism suggests that Tintin, as a symbol of Western civilization, cannot be undermined by the baleful power of the African leopard-man. We could suggest a parallel with the impact that engagement with magic, of the kind we see in the CDF case, would have on the jurisprudence of the SCSL, particularly on its credibility. One could believe that recognition by the tribunal of

---

[47] D. Purkiss, The Witch in History: Early Modern and Twentieth Century Representations 61 (1996); *as cited in* P. Geschiere, *Sorcellerie et modernité: les enjeux des nouveaux procès de sorcellerie au Cameroun – approches anthropologiques et historiques*, 53/6 Annales. Histoire, Sciences Sociales: 1251–79 (1998).

[48] Hoffman, *supra* note 28, at 129.

[49] *Id.* at 237.

[50] C. Geertz, Local Knowledge: Further Essays in Interpretive Anthropology (1983).

[51] P. Fitzpatrick, The Mythology of Modern Law 21 (1992).

the existence of Kondewa's magical powers distorts the logic of international criminal law because of the dyspeptic nature of such irrational thinking – thinking that is incompatible with legal reasoning. But, as we have seen, the approach of the SCSL eludes this pitfall by completely emptying the belief of its content, such that the only content left is that required for Kondewa to have the necessary control to find him guilty on the grounds of superior responsibility.

The Defense, however, made an effort to use the content of the belief for its own purposes. Thus, the Defense argued that during the magical initiations and ceremonies over which Kondewa presided, he transferred not only his spirit to the fighters to give them courage and invincibility, but he also gave them "the law." The Defense relied on witnesses from both the Defense and the Prosecution to the effect that Kamajors had an obligation to respect the elderly, not to steal the property of civilians, not to kill innocents, and not to harass civilians. In fact, according to the Defense, the Kamajors had an obligation to protect these people.[52] Further, Kondewa said that any violation of these laws would have the effect of canceling out the invincibility that had been conferred, leading to the fighter's death in battle. These laws were shared by all Kamajor initiators, often laced with religious references to the Koran or the Bible.[53] "What more deterrent against atrocities on civilians can anybody ask for?," asked Kondewa's lawyer.[54] The Defense thus sought to bring the SCSL to the conclusions of its own logic and to force it to recognize the effects of giving Kondewa's magical powers legal meaning in the context of criminal responsibility.

We could in the same sense imagine a defense resting on the exception of duress, recognized inter alia in article 31(1)(d) of the Statute of the International Criminal Court, if the accused committed a crime under the threat of a curse pronounced by a witch doctor. The court would then be asked to determine if the belief of the accused in danger was "real," or, in other words, whether the existence of this danger should be evaluated in an objective manner ("would a reasonable person have believed in the threat?") or in a subjective manner ("did the accused honestly feel threatened?"). In African legal systems, it is required in general that the belief be reasonable in order for an effect to stem from it, whereas under the ICC Statute the threat must be "real."[55] That said, legal effect has occasionally been given to such beliefs. Thus, in a South African case where the accused killed a child with an axe under the belief that it was an evil bat, Judge Richard Goldstone commented:

> Objectively speaking, the reasonable man so often postulated in our law does not believe in witchcraft. However, a subjective belief in witchcraft may be a factor which may, depending on the circumstances, have a material bearing upon the accused's blameworthiness. As such it may be a relevant mitigating factor to be taken into account in the determination of an appropriate sentence.[56]

In a general sense, the rationality at the heart of the international criminal law – and of Western law – necessarily reduces the causes and consequences of an illegal act to a fact that

---

[52] *CDF Trial Transcripts, supra* note 25, at paras. 33–34.
[53] HOFFMAN, *supra* note 28, at 236.
[54] *CDF Trial Transcripts, supra* note 25, at para. 37.
[55] S. Yeo, *Compulsion and Necessity in African Law*, 53/1 J. AFR. L. 90, 95–96 (2009).
[56] The State v. Netshiavha, (366/87) [1990] ZASCA 101. In that case, in consideration of these beliefs, the Court reduced the sentence from ten to four years' imprisonment.

is empirically verifiable; a divergent cultural belief is reduced to a factual error or to a lack of reason.[57] In the CDF Case, Kondewa's argument regarding his positive influence against the commission of war crimes and crimes against humanity was reduced to nothing: the SCSL ignored it altogether.

We can close this analysis of the discourse of the Trial Chamber and of the majority of the Appeals Chamber by asking: who is the audience constructed by this discourse? From what we have discussed, we can see that the SCSL projects first and foremost a dialogue with the international community, more precisely with the segment of that community engaged in prosecuting war crimes, crimes against humanity, and genocide. The narrative is entirely internal to law, it produces its own truth as required by the imperatives of justice, and it corresponds to a culture of legality that is self-sufficient and all encompassing. This narrative is offered as universal and capable of transcending all cultural differences in beliefs, practices, values, and norms.[58] The majority attempts to stay neutral or agnostic vis-à-vis mystical beliefs held by Kamajor fighters, essentially by remaining as silent as it could while still carrying out the required legal analysis. For this dissenter, however, no such neutrality is possible, and the majority's silence throws shadows linking this narrative to colonial discourse.

C. Judge Gelaga King's Dissent in the Appeals Chamber

The partial dissent of Judge George Gelaga King, native of Sierra Leone, takes an entirely different color. From the outset, Judge King gives a determinative importance to the fact that the Civil Defense Forces were fighting for the return to power of Sierra Leone's democratically elected government, against groups that had taken power through a coup d'état. Conversely, the majority of the Appeals Chamber concluded that this factor was irrelevant in determining the international criminal responsibility of those accused of war crimes and crimes against humanity. This highlights the importance of the political context for the dissenting judge.

Judge King then attacks in an exceptionally virulent manner the application of the doctrine of superior responsibility by the majority of the Appeals Chamber and the Trial Chamber. He emphatically rejects the title of "High Priest" given to Kondewa. Citing the *Oxford English Dictionary*, the judge denies that the Accused is a member of the clergy or a religious minister of any type: not being a priest, he can hardly be given the designation of "High Priest!" In the eyes of the dissenter, Kondewa was more "a 'juju man' or 'medicine man' or in local parlance 'meresin man'; he was a 'masked dancer' or in local parlance 'deble dancer,' a 'gorboi' dancer."[59] Even though the Defense had compared Kondewa to a military chaplain, as military chaplains are not usually blamed for the crimes committed by the

[57] J.L. Comaroff & J. Comaroff, *Criminal Justice, Cultural Justice: The Limits of Liberalism and the Pragmatics of Difference in South Africa*, 31/2 AM. ETHNOLOGIST 188 (2004).

[58] Despite exceptional efforts to plant the work of the SCSL within Sierra Leone, including visits to the most reclusive locations, in order to explain the role of the court, it appears that the Court remains largely viewed as a Western imposition. *See* Stuart Ford, *How Special Is the Special Court's Outreach Section?* (2012), *available at* ssrn.com/abstract=2021370; Lydia Apori Nkansah, *Justice within the Arrangement of the Special Court for Sierra Leone versus Local Perceptions of Justice: A Contradiction or Harmonious?* (2011), APSA 2011 Annual Meeting Paper, *available at* ssrn.com/abstract=1901113.

[59] *CDF Appeal*, *supra* note 29; Judge King's Dissent, para. 68.

soldiers they bless, Judge King rejects this analogy, denying that Kondewa had any *official* role whatsoever.[60] From there, with striking passion, he sharply criticizes the majority for having seen in Kondewa's powers sufficient authority to underpin the application of command responsibility:

> It boggles the imagination to think that on the basis of purporting to have occult powers, on the basis of his fanciful mystical prowess, Kondewa could be said to qualify as a "commander" in a superior/subordinate relationship. Without remarking on the novelty of its finding, the Appeals Chamber Majority Opinion, for the first time in the history of international criminal law has concluded that a civilian Sierra Leonean juju man or witch doctor, who practised fetish, had never been a soldier, had never before been engaged in combat, but was a farmer and a so-called herbalist, who had never before smelt military service ("he never went to the war front himself") can be held to be a commander of subordinates in a bush and guerrilla conflict in Sierra Leone, "by virtue" of his reputed superstitious, mystical, supernatural and suchlike fictional and fantasy powers![61]

We see in this passage multiple words that evoke the unreal and the irrational: "occult", "fanciful", "mystical" (twice), "fetish", "superstitious", "supernatural", "fictional", "fantasy". The dissent highlights the incompatibility of these elements with the legal reasoning that an international court, based on rationality and a symbol of modernity, is meant to use. To make his point even more clearly, and without the kind of restraint that defines the very legal tradition he claims to defend, Judge King hammers:

> In my opinion, the roles found to have been performed by Kondewa as "High Priest," are so ridiculous, preposterous and unreal as to be laughable and not worthy of serious consideration by right-thinking persons in civilized society. If the Kamajors believe in the mystical power of Kondewa as an initiator, his imaginary immunisation powers (as if it was scientific), do the Chambers of the Special Court also believe that Kondewa could make Kamajors "bullet-proof" and that Kondewa's "blessings" would make them impervious to machine-gun bullets? And on that basis find him to be a commander? Obviously not.[62]

The intellectual framework for the dissent could not be clearer: the rational thinking of civilization. This leads him to reject that magic could be a real fact that can be recognized by a court; on the contrary, it stands as a system of thought with which legal discourse cannot interact. Anthropologists conducting research on the occult in Africa have highlighted that terminology itself poses problems: the word "*sorcellerie*" in French or "witchcraft" in English reflects a very particular, Western historical construction, which marks those words as baleful and diabolical.[63] The words used in African languages refer to a more diverse and nuanced set of ideas. Magic can be both good and bad, depending on who uses it under what circumstances, and there is a vast vocabulary that reflects this diversity.[64] But, far from seeking to introduce a more nuanced reading of magic into the reasoning of the SCSL, one that is perhaps more faithful to reality as perceived by the Kamajors, Judge King links magic

---

[60] *CDF Trial Transcripts, supra* note 25, at 38.

[61] *CDF Appeal, supra* note 29; Judge King's Dissent, para. 69.

[62] *CDF Appeal, supra* note 29; Judge King's Dissent, para. 70.

[63] Geschiere, *supra* note 47, at 1253.

[64] Éric de Rosny, *Justice et sorcellerie en Afrique*, 42 Études – Revue de culture contemporaine 171, 172–73 (2005).

to the ridiculous, the absurd, and the untrue, all of which are the opposite of civilized rationality.[65] According to this vision, no engagement is possible between legal discourse and mystical belief; we should resist any dissolution of the border between magic and modernity as incompatible with secular law's rejection of transcendence.[66]

Judge King's approach in his dissent identifies the SCSL as a site where a discourse of African modernity can be elaborated. To better understand the context and scope of his position, one must understand the paradoxical role of witchcraft in many African countries today. On one level, governments and elites often condemn mystical beliefs as absurd and primitive. Magic is construed as a fabrication to which an educated person would never subscribe, a relic of a precolonial past that contemporary African states, in the wake of colonial authorities, should try to eliminate. This vision is inspired by liberal philosophy and is anchored in legality, relying on an individualistic humanism "formulated in a grammar or rights and legal privileges."[67] Legal discourse, which emanates from and affirms the sovereignty of the state, is at the heart of this vision.

At the same time, we find in these same African societies popular belief that embraces mysticism daily and without pause. Thus, a governmental commission of inquiry into the phenomenon of violence linked to witchcraft in South Africa reported that in 1996 there were ten thousand healers in Johannesburg and that 85 percent of black households in the city used their services from time to time.[68] More dramatically, the non-negligible number of murders of people suspected of being witches highlights both the prevalence and gravity of mystical beliefs. Anthropological literature suggests that the widespread prevalence of witchcraft reflects an ancestral heritage that colonialism never succeeded in eliminating, as well as a common disenchantment in Africa with the discourse of development, whose promises are now widely seen as empty.[69] For communities in the grip of poverty, illness, and insecurity, witchcraft brings real and immediate responses, whereas the long-term solutions of modernity rarely seem concrete.[70] Seen in this light, magic is both true and real.

The paradox of witchcraft in Africa today goes even further. Indeed, mystical beliefs and practices are not the preserve of undereducated populations who are denied access to the benefits of modernity. On the contrary, the same elites who publicly reject witchcraft as irrational and unreal often use it themselves in private. It is important to understand that there exists a very strong association in the popular imagination between power and witchcraft: if a person is powerful, she must enjoy considerable magical power. In a country such as Sierra Leone, it is expected that a "Big Man" – a government minister, a businessman, a judge – will discretely consult his witchdoctor from time to time to maintain or increase his

---

[65] Thus, Judge Gelaga King calls the reasoning of the Trial Chamber an error of fact: CDF Trial, Dissenting Opinion of Judge Gelaga King, para. 73.

[66] FITZPATRICK, *supra* note 51, at 10; SHAW, *supra* note 19, at 92.

[67] C. TAYLOR, SOURCES OF THE SELF 11–12 (1989), *cited in* Comaroff & Comaroff, *supra* note 57, at 192.

[68] N.V. RALUSHAI, REPORT OF THE COMMISSION OF INQUIRY INTO WITCHCRAFT VIOLENCE AND RITUAL MURDERS IN THE NORTHERN PROVINCE OF THE REPUBLIC OF SOUTH AFRICA 47 (Ministry of Safety and Security Northern Province RSA 1996).

[69] P. Geschiere, *Witchcraft and the State: Cameroon and South Africa. Ambiguities of "Reality" and "Superstition"*, 3 PAST & PRESENT SUPPLEMENT 313, 314–35 (2008).

[70] I. Niehaus, *Witchcraft in the New South Africa: From Colonial Superstition to Postcolonial Reality?* 184, 200 in Moore & Sanders (eds.), MAGICAL INTERPRETATIONS, MATERIAL REALITIES: MODERNITY, WITCHCRAFT AND THE OCCULT IN POSTCOLONIAL AFRICA (2001).

status.[71] What is more, a certain postcolonial current seeks to openly recover witchcraft as a symbol of an Afro-modernity that does not disown its ancestral traditions. By rejecting the civilizing, colonial categorization of magic as antimodern, one affirms that magic can, to the contrary, permit the understanding and anchoring of a modernity that belongs to the African continent.[72] The crisscrossing discourses of witchcraft and modernity in Africa are thus contested terrains of identity and politics. It is with this in mind that we should read Judge King's dissent in the CDF case.

If we ask of Judge King's dissent the same question that we raised for the majority decisions (what is the audience for whom it is intended?), we can recognize the ambiguity of his position. On one level, the audience imagined by the dissent is the same as that of the majority, but with a separate objective. He addresses not only the community of international criminal institutions, of which the SCSL is a part, but more generally the international community as a whole, to protest against the image of Sierra Leone as a land of savages who still believe in magic. In the language of the postcolonialists, the subaltern speaks to resist the image of Africa as drowning in superstition, an image that for a long time has served to justify colonial policies and the Western civilizing mission.[73] To do this, the dissenting judge links the mystical beliefs of the Kamajors to the factual conclusion made by the majority, suggesting that the reasoning of the majority can stand only if the judges of the SCSL themselves believe in Kondewa's magical powers. According to this evident distortion of the majority's logic, if one is false, then the other must be as well. By denying that these beliefs could really exist in a manner that justifies their legal recognition as fact, Judge King responds to the media's representation of the conflict in Sierra Leone, which portrayed the bulletproofing and invisibility rituals as symbols of an ahistorical primitivism that is irreconcilable with modernity.[74] Judge King responds to Hergé to reject the image of Africans as uncultivated and irrational.

On another level, the dissent belongs to a different dialogue, one of African modernity. The audience for this discourse are African elites, marked, as we saw, by ambiguous and contradictory positions regarding mysticism. Law occupies a central place in the dialogue surrounding afro-modernity, as it does for modernity in general. The end of colonialism in countries such as Sierra Leone did not mark the return to a status quo ante, to a precolonial reality excluding all changes stemming from colonialism. On the contrary, after the rupture of colonialism came the rupture of decolonization, producing a fragmented society the governance of which required a new force capable of maintaining cohesion. This force was, more often than not, legal discourse, a sort of new fetish whose neutral rationality was presented as capable of overcoming societal divides.[75] The connection with power is

---

[71] Shaw, *supra* note 15, at 35–41; Greshiere, *supra* note 47, at 1273; P. Geschiere, The Modernity of Witchcraft – Politics and the Occult in Postcolonial Africa 97–130 (1997).

[72] Niehaus, *supra* note 70, at 185.

[73] Shaw, *supra* note 16, at 50.

[74] Shaw, *supra* note 19, at 82.

[75] Comaroff & Comaroff, *supra* note 57, at 192: "But why this fetishism of the law? In policultural nation-states, the language of legality affords an ostensibly neutral medium for people of difference to make claims on each other and on the state, to transact unlike values, to enter into contractual relations, and to deal with their conflicts. In so doing, it produces an impression of consonance amidst contrast: of the existence of universal standards that, like money, facilitate the negotiation of incommensurables across otherwise intransitive boundaries."

furthermore maintained because the law in question is uniquely that of the state, reflecting a positivist reading of legal normativity.

Conversely, magic is considered subversive, fuelling threats to state sovereignty and delaying economic development, and disrupting social structures.[76] Interestingly, ethnographic studies of Cameroon have found that witchcraft is often portrayed as subversive in the official discourse of state representatives, often in the mouths of judges presiding over trials dealing with occult practices; that said, witchcraft is broadly not seen as subversive by the individuals directly involved in those practices.[77] On the contrary, interviews with villagers suggest that, for them, magic remains an essentially local and social issue.[78] In Sierra Leone, this subversive reading of magic was highlighted in the repression of an attempted coup d'état in 1992: seventeen people were accused of having used black magic, and on that basis executed.[79]

In many African countries, accusing someone of witchcraft (which often provokes lynching) and practicing witchcraft ("if it is susceptible of breaching public peace, or harming individuals or property") are both punishable offenses.[80] Far from being a relic of an obsolete colonial past, cases involving witchcraft can comprise a significant part of judicial activity in a given jurisdiction, leading to possible imprisonment and non-negligible financial sanctions.[81] By offering law as a response to witchcraft, and by using legal institutions in order to eliminate mysticism and impose rational thinking, law and magic are forced to interact in a way that transforms them both. How is it possible to condemn a person for a crime the reality of which we seek first and foremost to deny? Witchcraft, thus, remains a crime without statutory or jurisprudential definition, a normative obscurity cleverly maintained by legal actors.

Furthermore, in witchcraft cases, law invites magic to invade its own territory. As remarked by a judge from the Central African Republic, "one must be a witch in order to know who is a witch!"[82] Judges refuse to characterize themselves as witch doctors – the contradiction would be too extreme. Instead, judges have developed a widespread practice of inviting witch doctors to testify as experts regarding the identity of an accused as a witch, the occult nature of certain practices, or the evil effects of certain objects. Far from denying the reality of magic, legal discourse ends up instead proclaiming its merits. This legal legitimation of the powers of witch doctors has a modernizing effect on witchcraft; in general, these "expert" testimonies are given by a new generation of witch doctors who mix ancient

---

[76] B. Kapferer, The Feast of the Sorcerer: Practices of Consciousness and Power 285 (1997).

[77] P. Geschiere, *Witchcraft and the Limits of the Law* in J. Comaroff & J. Comaroff eds., Law and Disorder in the Postcolony (2006) 219, 277.

[78] Geschiere, *supra* note 47, at 1266.

[79] Shaw, *supra* note 15, at 33.

[80] Article 251, Code pénal du Cameroun ("*si elle est susceptible de troubler l'ordre ou la tranquillité publics, ou de porter atteinte aux personnes, aux biens ou à la fortune d'autrui.*"). There are variations of this provision in the criminal law of many French-speaking African countries. In English-speaking Africa, there are many statutes inspired by the 1899 Witchcraft Suppression Act (e.g., in Zimbabwe, http://www.parlzim.gov.zw/attachments/article/95/WITCHCRAFT_SUPPRESSION_ACT_9_19.pdf). See Mounyol À. Mboussi, Sorcellerie en justice au Cameroun (2004).

[81] It is reported that between 1970 and 1980, 40 percent of trials in the criminal court of Bangui, the capital of the Central African Republic, related to witchcraft! *See* Rosny, *supra* note 64, at 174.

[82] Rosny, *supra* note 64, at 175.

customs with the symbols of Western modernity, for example by using the title "doctor" or by suggesting European medical training.[83]

The image of mysticism that emerges from the interaction of justice and witchcraft in multiple African countries rejects the caricature of witchcraft as an absurd and obsolete belief, as represented by Judge Gelaga King in his dissent in the CDF Trial. Furthermore, magic is not open to being reduced to a simple fact construed entirely according to the logic of law and emptied of all content, as suggested by the majority's analysis in the Appeals Chamber in the same case. What the application of the doctrine of command responsibility in the CDF Trial called for was a recognition that witchcraft speaks to truths that remain otherwise hidden and reflects relations of authority that do not follow the military taxonomy reflected in international criminal law. The combination of mysticism and modernity conjure a more complex, uniquely African, modernity.

III. CONCLUSION

It is reported that the SCSL Registrar, Robin Vincent, in an effort to make prisoners responsible, wanted them to clean their own cells. He therefore ordered that brooms be distributed to the prisoners so they could clean. This provoked a strong reaction from the guards in charge of watching the prisoners, all of whom were local employees of the Court. The guards objected that brooms were well-known magical objects, and that the prisoners would use them to escape from the prison. The project therefore had to be abandoned.[84] This anecdote illustrates the difficulty modernity faces in constructing reality for its own ends. Even if law, as in the approach of the majority in the CDF Case, seeks to instrumentalize the factual context in order to reduce the culture to a coherent whole that can be inserted into the rational reasoning of legal discourse, culture escapes all attempts at subjugation and continues to operate on its own terms. It is here that the magic of *Tintin au Congo* truly appears: in Hergé's own world, the author has unlimited power to imagine a reality in which rational modernity triumphs entirely over African mysticism. On the last page, the old fetish has been replaced by effigies of Tintin and Milou. It is tempting to see in the majority opinion in the CDF Appeals Judgment a belief in a similar magical power for law.

What divides the majority and the dissent is not necessarily or not merely conflicting views about the existence and meaning of magic in African societies, but a wider construction of what it means to be modern. In the majority opinion, we see reflected an idea of modernity that reflects the progressive construction of the individual as a purely rational autonomous self, buffered from the external world by his or her rational powers.[85] The mystical is discarded as a way of experiencing the world. Seen in this light, the post-Enlightenment disenchanted self can make sense of believing in things such as magical bulletproofing as a psychological reflex of young men afraid to die in combat. Likewise, leaders such as Kondewa reasonably turn to mystical practices if it can solidify their authority on fighters

---

[83] C. Fisiy & P. Geschiere, *Judges and Witches, or How Is the State to Deal with Witchcraft? Examples from Southeast Cameroon*, 30/118: CAHIERS D'ÉTUDES AFRICAINES 135, 146–47 (1990); Geschiere, *supra* note 69, at 327.

[84] Interview by the Author of Luc Côté, former Chief of Prosecutions of the SCSL (Nov. 2011).

[85] C. TAYLOR, WESTERN SECULARITY 31, 39–40 (Craig Calhoun et al. eds., 2011).

in their group. The great subterfuge performed by law is that it imposes this perspective as the only legitimate, sensible one.

For the dissenter, however, modernity does not necessarily correspond to this disenchanted self, produced by several centuries of intellectual evolution in the West. In Judge King's reasons, we can discern a different modernity that reconciles a rational self with acceptance that there is no firm boundary between self and the cosmos, between inner and outer, between the rational and the spiritual. Magic moves back and forth across these otherwise impenetrable boundaries. We can read the dissenter's anger as a reaction against an imposition by the majority of a certain idea of modernity as the only one that can be truly modern, all alternatives falling into the primitive. In daily life, between the vernaculization of norms and the globalization of culture, legal discourse and mystical beliefs are two among many sites for the elaboration of modernity, with none able to claim primacy over the others. What is at play in the construction of practices such as bulletproofing is not the establishment of truth but more accurately the articulation of relations to truth: who can tell the truth, for whom, and for what purpose. Mysticism and modernity, each in its own way, attempts to give us a paradigm that explains why things are the way they are. The challenge that is posed by the dissent is whether modernity and in its wake law need be monolithic, or whether we can imagine a plural idea of modernity and law that can reconcile rational thinking with other forms of beliefs.

9

Legal Anthropology and the Construction of Complex Liabilities

Ilias Bantekas[*]

There is something common among international trials that have involved the use of command responsibility, in that the boundaries of fault in some cases were not at all clear. Here, I distinguish between *material fault* and *liability*. Material fault is impossible in the absence of a preexisting criminal conduct, which in turn gives rise to liability. This liability may further be distinguished twofold: first, in terms of satisfying the mental and factual elements of the offense in question (which may be termed *legal fault*), and second, in terms of categorizing the perpetrator's overall participation in the crime (i.e., as principal, accessory, co-perpetrator, or other). Thus, it follows that fault is circumscribed and dependent on the particular forms of liability pertinent to each offense.

By way of illustration, liability for unlawful homicide lies with the direct perpetrator, as well as possible accessories. Quite clearly, fault and liability are ascribed to the same actors. This pattern is pretty much consistent in domestic criminal laws, no doubt because domestic crimes in their majority do not involve complex organizations and multiple victims. In international law, the aforementioned fault-liability paradigm has been severed not only because of the obvious complexity underlying international crimes such as genocide and crimes against humanity, but more importantly because it is recognized that the concept of legal and material *fault* is incapable of fully encompassing the complexities of *justice lato sensu*. The liability associated with the responsibility of persons in authority and effective control over others seems at first glance to satisfy the dictates of justice. However, as the authors writing on command responsibility in this volume have rightly identified (see the foregoing chapters by Sandesh Sivakumaran, Harmen van der Wilt, and Réne Provost), as well as those writing before them, when one departs from the fault-liability paradigm, one has to justify this expansion of fault. If this is not done convincingly it will lack legitimacy and will therefore undo the very justice it was originally set up to serve.[1]

What is also a common thread behind international criminal trials since the ICTY, and which has a direct bearing on command responsibility, is the fact that the donors, through the collective facade of "international community," expect convictions rather than justice more generally. This is exemplified by numerous accounts, but I will simply state a few. Of particular importance are: (1) the constructions of complex liabilities, such as joint criminal

[*] Professor of International Law, Brunel Law School, United Kingdom.

[1] This lack of legitimacy has been a constant criticism of JCE. *See* M.E. Badar, *Just Convict Everyone! Joint Perpetration: From Tadic to Stakic and Back Again*, 6 INT'L CRIM. L. REV. 293 (2006).

enterprise (JCE) and command responsibility in the absence of other liabilities that facilitate conviction; (2) the attraction of donors through the semantics of convictions and the subsequent success of the various prosecutors on this basis; as well as (3) the absence of any meaningful dialogue with the victimized communities in order to assess their needs and desires with respect to transitional justice and development.

Ethnographic studies on the SCSL's outreach program in the heartlands of Sierra Leone, for example, demonstrate that the people were simply informed of the international community's decision and effort to establish the Special Court, but were not meaningfully consulted on any alternatives or asked to express their own desires and aspirations – a claim that I qualify somewhat given the chapters by Alison Smith and Stuart Ford in this volume. Ultimately, and in any event, it seems that the majority of the local population were not simply highly suspicious of the Special Court, but more important their primary concerns centered around the fulfillment of fundamental human needs and development rather than meting out expensive justice to a handful of individuals.[2] Hence, it is not clear whether the formulation of complex liabilities beyond the fault-liability paradigm is the product of donor expectations for convictions or the direct result of justice gaps identified by the judges of international tribunals that are freed from the procedural and constitutional limitations inherent in domestic systems. The truth must necessarily lie somewhere in the middle.

The current status of command responsibility under international law is well settled, at least in most respects.[3] It would probably be more accurate to say that there is widespread agreement as regards its boundaries, because there is still fierce debate as to how we should approach knowledge and effective control, among others. What I propose to do in the remainder of this chapter is to assess the evolution and difficulties in applying the doctrine, as elaborated thus far in scholarly opinion and the jurisprudence of courts and tribunals, from the point of view of the anthropological realities of Africa and Sierra Leone.

I. ANTHROPOLOGY AS A TOOL FOR ASSESSING COMPLEX LIABILITIES

Anthropology and law seem at first glance to have nothing in common. The first seeks to elucidate collective human behavior and understand its cultural underpinnings whereas the second is concerned with rules and order. It is evident that as rules and order are not produced in a void but rather with a view to regulating human relations, it follows that law is a necessary component of culture in the same manner as work, leisure, art, religion, and others.[4] Law need not necessarily be formal, as is the case with legislation that is promulgated under strict constitutional procedures, but it may just as well be informal without the sanction of government. This informal law does not only exist in past and present rural societies in the heartlands of Africa and Asia, but also in the very midst of industrialized Western

---

[2] G. Anders, *Juridification, Transitional Justice and Reaching out to the Public in Sierra Leone, in* LAW AGAINST THE STATE: ETHNOGRAPHIC FORAYS INTO LAW'S TRANSFORMATIONS 94, at 100, 108 (J. Eckert, B. Donahoe, C. Strümpell & Z.O. Biner eds., 2012); *see also* Charles C. Jalloh, *Special Court for Sierra Leone: Achieving Justice?*, 32 MICH. J. INT'L L. 457, 395–460 (2011) and Mohamed Bangura's Chapter 34 in this volume.

[3] *See* G. METTRAUX, THE LAW OF COMMAND RESPONSIBILITY (2009), who paints an accurate and holistic picture of the boundaries and controversies surrounding the concept.

[4] For a general overview, see J.M. Conley & W.M. O'Barr, *Legal Anthropology Comes Home: A Brief History of the Ethnographic Study of Law*, 27 LOY. L.A. L. REV. 41 (1993).

societies. The so-called *lex mercatoria* and the pursuit of self-regulation by particular indus-tries, as is indeed the very concept of contract and party autonomy thereto,[5] is evidence of man's desire to regulate in certain cases human interaction by means of informal, but no less binding, prescriptions. Besides regulating human relations, both formal and informal law, particularly the latter, provides evidence of social relations, status, and social interaction within a given community.

By way of illustration, the village chief is typically the judge and the recognized authority in the interpretation of customary law, and as such is regarded as a revered figure. Equally, the male warriors of the tribe, whose authority to hunt is recognized as a customary entitle-ment, may enjoy first rights to the tribe's game. Social status and the existence of complex roles and rules are also evident in the internal sphere of criminal gangs operating in indus-trialized settings.[6] In Islamic law, too, the *social* from the *legal* is inseparable in countries strictly adhering to classical shariah. For example, the inferior status ascribed to women in terms of entitlements (e.g., the right to be elected, weight of testimony etc.) also determines their social status.

At a very basic level and in relation to our study of command responsibility, anthro-pology can assist us to ascertain those elusive de facto indicia that are necessary for con-structing authority, power, and ultimately effective control. It also allows us to understand whether the "subordinates" that committed the crimes were under sufficient compulsion or control by their superior, such that justifies the latter's conviction despite the absence of direct fault. Before we go on, however, it is important to make a significant observation that relates to semantics. If anthropology is viewed as a method by which to draw conclusions pertinent to the fault–liability paradigm or complex liabilities, then this method requires an appropriate language in order to communicate concepts and ideas into the sphere of law.[7] Communication is crucial not only because certain words are not translatable from one language to another, but also because wholesale concepts and ideas themselves are alien from one culture to another.[8]

A very poignant example is necessary in order to better illustrate the point. In the case against Charles Taylor, a prosecution witnesses named "ZigZag" Marzah was quite clearly unfamiliar with the Western idiom of remorse and conscience.[9] He also claimed that he was involved in cannibalism of enemy corpses, arguing that this was something expected of all

---

[5] According to Teubner, the ultimate validation of *lex mercatoria* rests on the fact that not all legal orders are created by the nation-state and accordingly that private orders of regulation can create law. G. Teubner, *Global Bukowina: Legal Pluralism in the World Society, in* GLOBAL LAW WITHOUT A STATE 15 (G. Teubner ed., 1997).

[6] *See* J.D. Vigil, *Urban Violence and Street Gangs,* 32 ANN. REV. ANTHROPOLOGY 225 (2003); D. LAMM WEISEL, CONTEMPORARY GANGS: AN ORGANISATIONAL ANALYSIS (2002).

[7] *See* E. Mertz, *Language, Law and Social Meanings: Linguistic/Anthropological Contributions to the Study of Law,* 26 LAW & SOC'Y REV. 413 (1992).

[8] *See* M. VAN HOECKE, LAW AS COMMUNICATION (2002), in which the author's central thesis is that all legal relations are to be understood in terms of dialogue, conversation, and communicative processes, rather than as traditional command–obedience structures. Legal anthropologists such a Bohannan argued that Western legal terms and categories should not be employed to study the organization and order of non-Western soci-eties. He believed that such a methodology prevented a comprehensive understanding of other cultures and argued in favor of using native legal terms whose meaning would become evident within an ethnographic context. P. BOHANNAN, JUSTICE AND JUDGMENT AMONG THE TIV (1957).

[9] G. Anders, *Testifying about Uncivilised Events: Problematic Representations of Africa in the Trial against Charles Taylor,* 24 LEIDEN J. INT'L LAW 937, at 944–45 (2011).

warriors battling on the side of Charles Taylor.[10] Whether or not this statement is true, it certainly stirs a wealth of emotions in the Western psyche and reinforces myths and stereotypes associated with primitive Africa. In fact, anthropological research reveals that cannibalism was historically unknown in African societies. Anders recalls the Human Leopards case investigated by a Special Commission Court set up by British colonial authorities in early twentieth century Sierra Leone. There, and without any corroborating forensic evidence, the court was convinced that members of a secret society dressing up in leopard skins went about ritual cannibalism. The basic story was described by insider witnesses whose communication with their colonizers must have been agonizing through language that was fraught with significant misunderstanding and symbolism and that was moreover read through two very different sociocultural perspectives. Anders accurately captures this as follows:

> In Sierra Leone and Liberia, as in many parts of Africa, social relationships and personal development are framed in a rich language of eating and consumption. Initiation into secret societies such as the *poro* is also expressed in an idiom of being eaten or devoured by the bush spirits in order to be reborn as a full member of the community.... The political sphere, in particular, is conceptualized as a potentially dangerous terrain where powerful people "eat" each other in order to grow "big." This has been famously coined by Bayart as the politics of the belly, who describes the consumption of the State's resources by politicians and bureaucrats. In Sierra Leone, corrupt politicians are referred to as *bobor bele* – literally, guys with a belly eating the State's resources. Therefore, the frequent cannibalism accusations in West Africa must not always be read literally. They should rather be interpreted in terms of a highly symbolic political language and critique of existing injustices [as is the case with Sierra Leone].[11]

To a Western audience it seems implausible that anyone can genuinely confuse symbolism with reality, or to put it bluntly, to confuse actual cannibalism with its metaphors. How can you say one thing and, without lying, actually mean something completely different? How is it that symbolism can so easily be transformed into action? This is not the time or place to expand fully on these issues, and I am not sure I have the requisite knowledge to do so; thus I will simply make reference to two case studies from the recent past. A significant part of the Rwandan genocide was predicated on a myth or symbolism reiterated and spread by the Hutu that the Tutsi were cockroaches and inferior beings. Whereas no Hutu would typically act on this myth unilaterally, it was the seed for future events when animosity was stirred through artificial means and channels and in which case an illiterate and highly polarized populace was unable to separate myth from reality. Anthropological research on the Rwandan genocide tends to show that one of the principal cultural metaphors in Rwanda, the "flow," may shed some light on some of the methods for killing and torturing used by the Hutu. Flow in general represents something healthy, as is the case with our blood stream or the transformation of food into feces and insemination into childbirth. Blockage of flow is associated with disease and death. The impalement of victims from the anus to the mouth as well as mass killings at checkpoints, in addition to other motives, symbolizes

---

[10] *Id.* at 948–49.
[11] *Id.* at 956.

the end of flow.[12] To a Western audience it may to some degree explain certain acts of sheer cruelty (although certainly not fully), as well as concretize genocidal patterns amounting to *systematic*.

The second example is very similar, despite the fact that it took place more than fifty years earlier and fueled the psyche of a much more literate and "civilized" population. I am referring to Nazi propaganda well prior to the commencement of World War II in 1939 through a process of dehumanizing its enemies, such as Slavs, communists, and Jews. The rest of the story is well-known.

In the context of the ICTR's investigation, legal anthropology played a significant part in the reconstruction of liability for genocide. It will be recalled that in its first case, that of Jean Paul Akayesu, the Tribunal was reluctant to apply the exact terms of Article II of the Genocide Convention, which required that the crime could only be committed against members of another ethnic, national, religious, or racial group. Forensic evidence demonstrated that the Hutu and the Tutsi were not ethnically or racially distinct—quite the opposite. Their respective designations had been engineered by their Belgian colonizers, and these had subsequently matured into distinctions of class or social status. The Tribunal therefore turned to legal anthropology in order to construct a more objective theory of victimhood for the purposes of the Genocide Convention. It held that beyond external characteristics such as race and ethnic origin, membership of a group may also come about by the personal belief of a group's members as to their distinctiveness.[13] This personal self-distinction and self-categorization is sanctioned only if it is validated by anthropological evidence; that is, if the group members have actually distinguished themselves, and in addition other groups perceive them as being distinct. For the purposes of command responsibility, the conclusion is that such groups cannot, without evidence to the contrary, be presumed to be under the de facto control of non-group members.

II. ELUSIVE EFFECTIVE CONTROL

One of the issues identified in the chapters dealing with command responsibility is the degree to which one may assume effective control in respect of jungle-based armies and militias. This is by no means a new theme, given that it has troubled lawmakers and courts since command responsibility was first punctuated on the legal map with the Yamashita case.[14] There, it was controversially held that Yamashita retained effective control over Japanese troops that went on the rampage against civilians in Manila, even though he had split the Japanese forces on the Philippines into four distinct groups, with all communication between them having been severed by their adversaries. The tribunal maintained that

---

[12] C.C. Taylor, THE CULTURAL FACE OF TERROR IN THE RWANDAN GENOCIDE, *in* ANNIHILATING DIFFERENCE: THE ANTHROPOLOGY OF GENOCIDE 137–38 (A.L. Hinton ed., 2002).

[13] ICTR Prosecutor v. Akayesu, Trial Chamber Judgment, para. 702 (Sept. 2, 1998). In *ICC Prosecutor v. Al-Bashir*, Decision on the Prosecution's Application for a Warrant of Arrest against Omar Al-Bashir, para. 137 (Mar. 4, 2009) [hereinafter *Al-Bashir Warrant Decision*], an ICC Pre-Trial Chamber claimed that three Sudanese tribal groups living in the same area, namely the Fur, the Masalit, and the Zaghawa, constitute distinct ethnic groups because each possesses its own language, tribal customs, and traditional links to its lands. Without realizing it, the Pre-Trial Chamber made an anthropological observation with legal significance.

[14] *Trial of General Tomoyuki Yamashita*, 4 LAW REPORTS OF TRIALS OF WAR CRIMINALS 1 (1945).

the atrocities were so widespread that Yamashita must have known about them and could have prevented them, despite the argument of the accused that he had given strict instructions to the Manila-based commander to evacuate the island and return to Japan. Clearly, in the absence of any direct orders the tribunal could not have constructed Yamashita's command liability had it not arbitrarily assumed that he enjoyed effective control of all Japanese forces on the island.

Whatever the actual facts on the ground, a retrospective examination of effective control would no doubt be illumined by reference to anthropological data. Again, it is not my intention to go into any significant detail, but given that the case hung on whether Yamashita's subordinates had in fact disobeyed his orders to evacuate and to avoid harming civilians, it is worth investigating Japanese military culture at the time. With the adoption of Shinto as the country's official state religion in 1890 an emperor cult was established whereby the emperor's divinity was based on his descent from the Goddess Amaterasu. This meant that the emperor's commands, and by implication those of his representatives, were to be obeyed without objection. This unswerving loyalty to the emperor as the basis of the Japanese State (known as *kokutai*, which may be translated manifold, particularly as "sovereign" or "national essence") had earlier been institutionalized by the introduction of universal conscription, which resulted in the indoctrination of the country's youth and which continued through subsequent generations.[15]

This cultural dimension, coupled undoubtedly with fear and other elements, accounts for the acceptance of brutality within the ranks of the Japanese army and its members' loyalty-to-the-death. As a result, it would have been characteristically untypical and out of all logic for the forces under Yamashita's de jure command to disobey their commander's direct orders. By logical implication, no distinction can be made between de jure and de facto command in respect of Japanese military organization during World War II because even if separated from their commanders, units and subunits therefore, would always religiously adhere to their superiors' original orders – unless of course there were no other available orders. This observation also suggests that in this particular socio-military context the absence of material capacity to prevent or punish is irrelevant in establishing de facto or de jure command because the conduct of subordinates is uniform irrespective of the person under command.

In the Rwanda conflict, de facto command and control became a central issue because, unlike the military-styled paramilitary groups on the territory of the former Yugoslavia, a significant amount of authority was exercised on the basis of traditional socioeconomic structures. Rwandan society, like most of Africa, is tribal and class-based, with authority and privileges typically belonging to the elite in each tribe or clan.[16] As a result, authority and wealth go hand-in-hand, with the elite also being the richest and better educated among the tribe. Until the creation of the ICTR the construction of command responsibility had been applied to regular armies and, at worst, to tightly structured paramilitary units,

---

[15] In fact, *kokutai* was introduced as a fundamental building block in Article 4 of Japan's 1890 Constitution, also known as the Meiji Constitution, on account of the Tenno dynasty, which assumed power through the 1868 Meiji restoration, remaining in power until 1945. *See* G.M. Beckmann, The Making of the Meiji Constitution: The Oligarchs and the Constitutional Development of Japan, 1868–1891 (1957).

[16] For an excellent anthropological account, see R. Lemarchand, *Power and Stratification in Rwanda: A Reconsideration*, 6 Cahiers d'etudes Africaines 592 (1996).

which however resembled regular armies principally because they were formed and run by ex-military personnel, as was the case with indictments before the ICTY. The most complex cases had been those dealt with by subsequent WWII military tribunals in respect of civilians, particularly industrial and political leaders.[17]

The ICTR paid particular attention to these distinct anthropological features in its construction of hierarchies and authority in Rwandan society. In the Akayesu case the accused was the burgomaster of Taba commune, a position akin to that of mayor in Western parlance. Whereas Western mayors enjoy no other authority than to enact peripheral bylaws and set the municipality's economic agenda on the basis of municipal taxes and other income, in Rwanda the burgomaster enjoyed far greater authority. His powers were found to be much wider than his de jure authority.[18] In fact, he was perceived as the "father" of the people, whose every order was to be obeyed without question or deviation.[19] Clearly, informal law and power arrangements, whether explicit or implicit, played an important role in ascertaining the enjoyment of effective control over the actions of civilian populations acting as mobs, random groups, or under a self-perceived identity. The existence of such effective control is further reinforced by class and education. This African case study exemplifies the tribunal's desire to construct (or expand) complex liabilities on the basis of anthropological observations in order to reach a just conclusion; in the case at hand to establish the liability of an influential figure urging those under his circle of influence to commit genocide.

III. THE ROLE AND ORIGIN OF INFLUENCE IN SIERRA LEONE'S ARMED GROUPS

The jurisprudence of the SCSL has revealed two broad types of military authority. The first is consistent with that found in regular armies and rebel forces, on the basis of a strict or not-so-strict hierarchical structure. This seems to be the case with the AFRC and the RUF. The second type of authority depends less on formal hierarchies and is instead entrenched in symbolism and mythology. This much is true with respect to the Kamajors and their Civil Defense Forces (CDF). No doubt, elements of both types of authority are found in all groups in one form or another.

That mythology, mysticism, and symbolism played a role in the military organization of Sierra Leone's factions comes as no surprise if one has followed the observations made in earlier sections of this chapter. This was further facilitated by the fact that although the country is host to approximately twenty African groups (the largest of which are the Mende and the Temne) it is multireligious and the war did not start along ethnic or religious lines. Rebel groups and militias were thus ethnically and religiously diverse, a phenomenon already reflected in membership to the country's secret societies, particularly the *poro* and the *bondo*.

---

[17] *See* Government Commissioner of the General Tribunal of the Military Government for the French Zone of Occupation in Germany v. Roechling, 14 Trials of War Criminals before the Nuremberg Military Tribunals [Trials] 1097; USA v. Flick, 6 Trials 1187; and USA v. von Weizsaecker [*Ministries* case], 14 Trials 308. Once again, although no direct anthropological questions were asked by these tribunals, it was deemed implicit that those to whom powers were delegated by the Nazi regime enjoyed sufficient control over persons committing particular crimes. This was a direct consequence of Nazi culture that permeated all elements of the Reich's socioeconomic raison d'etre.

[18] *Akayesu* Trial Judgment, *supra* note 13, at para. 57.

[19] *Id.* at paras. 55, 74.

Exceptionally, the composition of the Kamajors was Mende-based, albeit their aim was not necessarily to engage in inter-ethnic rivalries.[20] That the Special Court made a serious effort to explain the mythology and mysticism underlying the organization of the Kamajors is evidence of the fact that socio-anthropological phenomena are of acute relevance in ascribing the attributes of authority in order to construct complex liabilities (even though, as René Provost suggests in his chapter in this book, that attempt only goes so far). Still, it will be recalled that the ICTY largely rejected or, at least, ignored such factors, on the assumption that factions in the territory of Bosnia were neatly divided along ethnic/religious lines, and as a result there was no need to inquire into other shared traits between members of the groups.

I will draw on one element here that is intriguing and that, although rejected by the ICTY, should have found a place in the jurisprudence of the Special Court. I am referring to the power or authority to "influence" as an indication or evidence of effective control. Indeed, in the Čelebići case the accused Delalić was found to be a highly influential figure in the Bosniac army. He possessed authority to sign contracts and release orders in a POW camp and liaise with the highest echelons of the Bosnian Muslim authorities; yet, he did not possess formal authority over other subordinates, especially those in the POW camp. The Tribunal did not consider that this highly influential individual, in the absence of any direct subordinates, yielded sufficient control over those running the POW camp such that would have allowed him to intervene in the commission of crimes against the prisoners.[21] This conclusion was drawn at a time when the construction of the complex liability of command responsibility did not warrant open-ended expansion. It was enough for the Tribunal that only persons exercising effective control over subordinates were subject to the doctrine. It rightly felt that if everyone yielding influence could also be encompassed the floodgates would be open to convict persons who were not at fault.[22]

The key word here is *fault*. If D, a boy-scout leader, has exerted and continues to exert significant influence over a group of boy scouts who are recruited as minors by a rebel group, it cannot be seriously claimed that he possesses sufficient control over all their future actions, particularly when they are spatially and geographically removed from him. D clearly lacks fault for failing to use his powers of influence to dissuade the youths. However, if D was in proximity to the minors and was an influential figure in the broader echelons of the group, he possesses the material capacity to employ his influence over the minors, even if he does not enjoy effective control by reason of direct subordination. In this latter scenario D is at material fault, although it will depend on the particular circumstances of each situation as to whether this fault may substantiate command responsibility. These particular circumstances are none other than D's material capacity to act.[23] It defies logic and the dictates of

---

[20] K. Dupuy & H.M. Binningsbø, *Power-Sharing and Peace-Building in Sierra Leone* 3–4 (CSCW Papers 2007).

[21] ICTY Prosecutor v. Delalić et al., Trial Chamber Judgment, paras. 266, 653–56 (Nov. 16, 1998) [Čelebići case].

[22] This is particularly reflected in its pronouncements in *ICTY Prosecutor v. Brdjanin and Talić*, Trial Chamber Judgment, paras. 276, 281 (Sept. 1, 2004), and *ICTY Prosecutor v. Naletilić and Martinović, Trial Chamber Judgment*, para. 68 (Mar. 21, 2003). These judgments certainly influenced the decision of the State Court of Bosnia and Herzegovina in *Prosecutor v. Alić*, Trial Chamber Judgment, Case No. X-KR-06/294, at 46 (Apr. 11, 2008).

[23] This is why Mettraux, *supra* note 3, sides with the Judgments of the ICTY to reject influence as establishing de facto control.

justice to assert that a person with the direct capacity to save hundreds of lives by simply averting the would-be perpetrators bears no liability simply because he was not incumbent with a preexisting duty to act. This is not merely an iteration or transplantation of the duty to save strangers typically associated with civil law jurisdictions. It goes to the very heart of material fault and all that it stands for.

It is not clear whether the SCSL shares this conviction given that it has not expressly rejected or upheld this thesis.[24] It is certain that the Special Court was unaware of the scholarly literature suggesting that power of influence is possible even in the absence of authority over one's target audience.[25] Imagine if influence and authority are merged into a single entity. Had the Special Court been cognizant of these arguments it might have taken up the proposition that in situations where the power relations and social status between several individuals is chaotic, direct subordination is not necessary in order for the more influential person to establish effective control merely by his or her powers of influence.[26] This chaotic power gap certainly existed in the context of the military factions engaged in Sierra Leone's bloody wars. The spiritual leader of the Kamajors, Kondewa, is an interesting case study. The Kamajors were originally organized as a group of Mende hunters who responded to the directives of their various chiefs to protect people from the rebels.[27] As a result, its members did not possess the military skills and discipline of a regular or rebel army. They were in need of organization and guidance in order to become an organized fighting unit.[28] This guidance came both from military as well as spiritual leaders. Kondewa was of the latter kind. The Chamber described his role as follows:

> He was the head of all the CDF initiators initiating the Kamajors into the Kamajor society in Sierra Leone. His job was to prepare herbs which the Kamajors smeared on their bodies to protect them against bullets. Kondewa was not a fighter, he himself never went to the war front or into active combat, but whenever a Kamajor was going to war, he would go to Kondewa for advice and blessing. (....) The Kamajors believed in the mystical powers of the initiators, especially Kondewa, and that the process of the initiation and immunisation would make them bullet-proof. The Kamajors looked up to Kondewa and admired the man with such powers. (....) Because of the mystical powers Kondewa possessed, he had command over the Kamajors from every part of the country.[29]

The Special Court opined that Kondewa's mystical powers did not automatically confer upon him military authority over the recruits and their operations.[30] On the contrary, it

---

[24] In *SCSL Prosecutor v. Brima, Kamara and Kanu*, Judgment, para. 788 (June 20, 2007), the Special Court referred to a number of indicia as evidence of effective control. These may implicitly be read – although one could argue otherwise – as encompassing cases of significant and overpowering influence.

[25] *See* L.A. HILL, EXERCISING INFLUENCE WITHOUT FORMAL AUTHORITY: HOW NEW MANAGERS CAN BUILD POWER AND INFLUENCE (2008); A.R. COHEN & D.L. BRADFORD, INFLUENCE WITHOUT AUTHORITY (2005). The motto of Hill, a pioneer on this topic, is that "all influential managers have power but not all powerful managers have influence."

[26] *Influence* is probably not the appropriate term here, and this certainly explains why the ad hoc tribunals have rejected influence-based effective control out-of-hand. It should be understood as possessing the material and mental power to compel another to do or abstain from doing something.

[27] SCSL Prosecutor v. Fofana and Kondewa, Judgment, para. 354 (Aug. 2, 2007).

[28] Even so, universal discipline remained problematic because some fighters "acted on their own without knowledge of central command because their area of operation was so wide." *Id.* at para. 358.

[29] *Id.* at paras. 344–346.

[30] *Id.* at para. 806.

was his de jure position of High Priest of the CDF that granted him some degree of effective control in certain situations, and it was in respect of these that he was found to enjoy effective control.[31]

The Special Court missed a golden opportunity to defy the Čelebići myth by expressly stipulating that under certain circumstances the yielding of influence between asymmetric actors can give rise to effective control irrespective of the military, civilian, or other context in which it is exercised. If a person can persuade another that in following a ritual he will be unaffected by his adversaries' weapons, it is absurd to claim that this person does not possess powers akin, if not far superior, to those enjoyed in a superior–subordinate relationship. Such powers of influence are no doubt rare, but in Sierra Leone – where the mystical and the symbolic coincide with the real and the brutal – the anthropological basis of the relevant relationships should have been given much more prominence. Just like the results of one anthropological study cannot be transplanted into another – although some general observations may be possible – in the same manner the findings of the Special Court need not necessarily have to be accepted as immutable truths applicable in all future conflicts. I am not convinced by the argument that influence can never give rise to effective control-type situations. This position is sustainable of course as long as it is proven that the person in question had the material capacity to prevent or punish the crimes committed by those persons over whom he enjoyed significant influence. I can only hope that the jurisprudence of current or future international criminal courts confronted with these questions will take anthropological evidence into consideration and finally move toward this direction.

---

[31] *Id.* at para. 686.

PART III

Approach to Substantive International Crimes

10

Forced Marriage as a Separate Crime against Humanity

Michael P. Scharf[*]

I. INTRODUCTION

At the height of the fighting in Sierra Leone's civil war, thousands of women were abducted and forced to "marry" their captors against their will. These women were made to assume all the obligations of a wife while simultaneously rendered unable to acquire any of the rights or privileges traditionally and legally given to a spouse. They were raped repeatedly; made to cook, clean, and care for their captor-husbands; beaten, branded, and cut; and many became pregnant and were forced to bear and then rear the children. But forced marriage is far more than just the sum of its parts. These forced marriages demean and distort the institution of marriage itself. Victims not only endure the egregious constituent acts of rape, sexual slavery, forced pregnancy, enslavement, and torture but they are indefinably and inexorably bound, "married," to the men who victimize them.

Although the constituent acts have previously been recognized as crimes against humanity, forced marriage had never been recognized or even identified as a separate crime against humanity before 2004 when the Special Court for Sierra Leone (SCSL) became the first ever war crimes tribunal to charge defendants in the Revolutionary United Front (RUF) and the Armed Forces Revolutionary Council (AFRC) cases with the crime of forced marriage. The SCSL Trial Chamber in the RUF Case upheld the charge,[1] but the SCSL Trial Chamber in the AFRC case dismissed the "forced marriage" count on grounds of redundancy, concluding that the crime was subsumed in "sexual slavery."[2] The decisions produced strongly worded dissents. Ultimately, the SCSL Appeals Chamber reversed the AFRC Trial Chamber and upheld the charges of forced marriage as a separate crime against humanity.[3] But the

---

[*] Associate Dean for Global Legal Studies and John Deaver Drinko – Baker & Hostetler Professor of Law at Case Western Reserve University School of Law. This is an updated and expanded version of a chapter published in Volume 3 of the Africa Legal Aid's Special Book Series, entitled *African Perspectives on International Criminal Justice* (2005) (with Suzanne Mattler).

[1] Judgment, Prosecutor v. Sesay, Kallon and Gbao, SCSL, Trial Chamber, para. 168 (Mar. 2, 2009) [hereinafter RUF Trial Judgment].

[2] Judgment, Prosecutor v. Brima, Kamara and Kanu, SCSL, Trial Chamber, para. 714 (June 20, 2007) [hereinafter AFRC Trial Judgment].

[3] Judgment, Prosecutor v. Brima, Kamara and Kanu, SCSL, Appeals Chamber, para. 195 (Feb. 22, 2008) [hereinafter AFRC Appeals Judgment]:[b]ased on the evidence on record, the Appeals Chamber finds that no tribunal could reasonably have found that forced marriage was subsumed in the crime against humanity of sexual slavery. While forced marriage shares certain elements with sexual slavery such as non-consensual sex and deprivation of liberty, there are also distinguishable factors. First, forced marriage involves a perpetrator

soundness of the Appeals Chamber's decision was subsequently questioned in the 2012 Charles Taylor Judgment, in which the Trial Chamber went out of its way to assert in dicta that forced marriage was not a specifically indictable crime against humanity.[4]

What the victims of Sierra Leone's forced marriages must have suffered is unfathomable; the Special Court's attempt to punish those responsible is commendable. However, international tribunals must operate within the bounds of their statutes and international law. Unless the offense of forced marriage is deemed to conform to both international law and the statutes of these tribunals, and unless it can be distinguished as a unique crime against humanity, the tribunals will be compelled to rule that the specific offense of forced marriage is outside of its prosecutorial reach.

This chapter explores whether international criminal tribunals can validly pursue forced marriage as a separate crime against humanity under their statutes and international law. It begins with a brief recounting of the history of the Sierra Leone civil war, a summary of typical marriage practices in Sierra Leone, and a description of forced marriage during the conflict. The next section addresses prosecuting forced marriage as a crime against humanity under current international law. This section not only addresses the reach of crimes against humanity, but also the international community's understanding of marriage – its purpose, the rights and responsibilities of spouses, what makes a marriage valid, and how the crime of forced marriage differs from the custom of arranged marriage. Following this discussion of international law, the chapter turns to the Statute of the Special Court for Sierra Leone to examine how forced marriage fits into the Special Court's statutory framework and functions in conjunction with the existing crimes against humanity. Next, based on the case law of the SCSL, the chapter sets forth and defines the elements of the crime against humanity of forced marriage. This analysis of the history of forced marriage in Sierra Leone, the customary international law of crimes against humanity and marriage, and the Statute of the Special Court, leads to the conclusion that forced marriage is a valid and viable category of crime against humanity, triable by the SCSL and other war crimes tribunals.

II. MARRIAGE, WAR, AND CRIMES AGAINST HUMANITY IN SIERRA LEONE

A. *The Conflict in Sierra Leone*

In March 1991, small groups of armed men calling themselves the RUF began attacking villages along the eastern Sierra Leone–Liberia border, fighting against then-head of state Major

---

compelling a person by force or threat of force [...] into a conjugal association with another person resulting in great suffering or serious physical or mental injury on the part of the victim. Second, unlike sexual slavery, forced marriage implies a relationship of exclusivity between the "husband" and "wife," which could lead to disciplinary consequences for breach of this exclusive relationship. These distinctions imply that forced marriage is not predominantly a sexual crime.

[4] Prosecutor v. Charles Ghankay Taylor, Judgment, SCSL-03–01-T, at paras. 422, 425, 426, 427, and 429 (May 18, 2012). Taylor was not indicted for the offense of "forced marriage," but the Trial Chamber felt compelled to discuss the legitimacy of such an offense because of the "extensive testimony by women and girls [during the Taylor trial] regarding forced conjugal association to which they were subjected." *Id.* at para. 422.

General Joseph Saidu Momoh.[5] Throughout the early 1990s, the RUF steadily advanced, seizing control of more and more of the nation.[6] In 1997, after being pushed back to the eastern border by government-hired mercenaries, the RUF was invited to join the government by Major Johnny Paul Koroma, who had overthrown President Ahmad Tejan Kabbah.

The RUF's grip on political power was to be short-lived, however; ten months later they were ousted and President Kabbah was reinstated.[7] Less than a year later, the RUF regrouped and again tried to seize Sierra Leone. A violent campaign began on January 6, 1999, with the fighting reaching all the way west to the capital Freetown. Thousands were killed before the RUF was again driven back.[8] On July 7, 1999, the Lomé Peace Agreement between President Kabbah and RUF leader Foday Sankoh established a cease-fire. Both sides agreed to allow international peacekeeping forces (Nigerian ECOMOG and UN forces) to assist in disarming and stabilizing the country.[9] Eventually, the Nigerian forces withdrew and peacekeeping duties were assumed wholly by the United Nations Mission in Sierra Leone (UNAMSIL). The RUF violated the terms of the peace agreement almost immediately, raiding supply lines and taking hundreds of UNAMSIL personnel hostage. Sporadic fighting and unrest continued throughout the country for the next three years despite the signing of a second cease-fire agreement in November 2000.[10] The civil war was finally declared officially over on January 18, 2002.[11]

B. Marriage in Sierra Leone

There are three types of marriage recognized in Sierra Leone: customary, religious (Islamic or Christian), and civil ceremonies. The three types are not as clearly delineated, however, as that simple statement may lead one to believe.[12] Rather, marriage in Sierra Leone is often a complex amalgam of customary rites and religious and civil ceremonies.[12] Customary rites of marriage derive from indigenous tribal traditions and involve many intermediate steps and ceremonies, rather than one defining event as in a civil, Islamic, or Christian marriage.[13] More than just a union between two individuals, customary marriage is viewed as a union between the two families.[13] The relatives of the intending spouses, especially the bride's family, are heavily involved in all steps of a customary marriage, and an intending

---

[5] U.S. Department of State, Bureau of African Affairs, Background Note: Sierra Leone (Nov. 2003), *at* http://www.state.gov/r/pa/ei/bgn/5475pf.htm.

[6] *Id.*

[7] *Id.*

[8] *Id.*

[9] Peace Agreement between the Government of Sierra Leone and the Revolutionary United Front of Sierra Leone (July 7, 1999).

[10] Abuja Ceasefire Agreement between the Government of Sierra Leone and the Revolutionary United Front (Nov. 10, 2000).

[11] President Alhaji Dr. Ahmad Tejan Kabbah, Speech at the Ceremony Marking the Conclusion of Disarmament and the Destruction of Weapons, Lungi (Jan. 18, 2002), Transcript, *available at* http://www.sierraleone.org/kabbah011802.html.

[12] Anastasia J. Gage & Caroline Bledsoe, *The Effects of Education and Social Stratification on Marriage and the Transition to Parenthood in Freetown, Sierra Leone, in* Nuptuality in Sub-Saharan Africa: Contemporary Anthropological and Demographic Perspectives 150 (Caroline Bledsoe & Gilles Pison eds., 1994).

[13] Mariane C. Ferme, The Underneath of Things: Violence, History, and the Everyday in Sierra Leone 88 (2001).

husband usually needs the consent of the family of the bride before the couple can wed.[14] Because the formalization of transition from the unwed to wedded state is gradual rather than defined by a single event, the customary marriage process may begin when the bride-to-be is still a young child, far earlier than the age at which an individual could be wed in a civil or religious ceremony under Sierra Leonean marriage laws.[15] Two intending spouses may have completed several steps toward the progression to marriage – for example, through the giving of gifts to the woman and her family, first sexual relations, cohabitation, and childbearing – but their relationship may still fall well short of a recognized entrance into the marital state and its attendant rights and responsibilities.[16] Increasingly, in modern Sierra Leone, the customary rites are combined with either a civil or religious ceremony. The intending spouses may participate in the ceremonies of a customary marriage as part of an "engagement" period before a religious or civil marriage, they may undertake a full customary marriage first and then a civil or religious marriage, or they may have a civil or religious marriage first and then complete the customary rites.[17] Both spouses are equally capable of dissolving the marriage under Sierra Leonean law, but under customary marriages, the woman's ability to dissolve the marriage is highly dependent on the consent of her relatives.[18]

C. Forced Marriage in the Sierra Leonean Civil War

Amid the other atrocities committed during the ten-year civil war, thousands of women were abducted and forced to become the sexual partners of their captors, remaining with their abductors for years.[19] Although no formal marriage took place, these women were considered "wives" of their captors, known locally as "bush wives," and were coerced, usually by force or threat of violence, to undertake all of the duties normally expected of a wife. They were raped by their captors and their captors' associates, cooked for them, cleaned for them, and bore and raised their captors' children.[20] The exact number of women who were "wed" under these circumstances is difficult to establish. Only a small percentage of these "marriages" were ever formalized in a ceremony, although it is clear that the women who were "wed" to their abductors without a military official pronouncing it so were just as bound to their "husbands" as those who were married in official ceremonies. In fact,

---

[14] *Id.* at 90.

[15] Gage & Bledso, *supra* note 12, at 151.

[16] *Id.* To try to put it into comparable Western terms, if a man takes a woman out on a date, it is assumed to show his intention of courtship. The couple may then progress to a stage where they agree to see each other describe the exclusively and their status changes to "dating." After that, they may cohabitate and the relationship because "serious." If all goes well there, then there may be a proposal, the couple is considered "engaged." These are the steps a Western couple generally undertakes prior to marriage, but they are not considered to be married after or during any of those steps. In customary African marriage the status of the couple similarly evolves, and the individual steps may be more ceremonial, but there is no final, culminating event that marks the couple as married.

[17] *Id.* at 152.

[18] FERME, *supra* note 13, at 104.

[19] Human Rights Watch, *Human Rights Watch Report 2001: Sexual Violence within the Sierra Leone Conflict* (Feb. 26, 2001), *at* http://www.hrw.org/backgrounder/africa/sl-bck0226.htm.

[20] Jennifer Swallow, *Brutalized Legacy; Jennifer Swallow Reports from Sierra Leone on the Continuing Civil War*, MORNING STAR, July 10, 2004, at 9.

many "bush wives" currently remain with their spouses even though the conflict has long ended.[21]

These forced marriages were a stark departure from marriage as it was typically understood under the laws and customs of Sierra Leone. The few official ceremonies that were performed did not conform to any recognized religious or civil union; they occurred in the absence of consent by the "wife" or her family, in violation of the requirements and forms of such marriages. These forced marriages were also anomalous in the context of customary marriages. The consent of the woman's family was not obtained, nor, in many cases, was the family a party to the proceedings or paid "bridewealth" – typically a substantial element of the customary marriage and generally considered one of the main bases of the marriage's legitimacy.[22] Additionally, the woman's transition from the unwed to wedded state was accomplished by one defining act, namely the perpetrating spouse declaring the woman his "wife."

III. FORCED MARRIAGE AND INTERNATIONAL LAW

Any prosecution of a previously unidentified crime against humanity must be guided first by the principle of *nullum crimen sine lege*.[23] This principle functions to protect the fundamental rights of the accused from infringement by capricious or arbitrary prosecution for acts that were not recognized as crimes when they were committed.[24] To prosecute an individual for a previously unrecognized crime against humanity, but still pay proper heed to the principle, one must study established customary international law to see if it speaks to the crime.[25] If the perpetrator's conduct is clearly criminal under existing customary international law, then it can be assumed that the perpetrator indeed had knowledge that his conduct was criminal, and should have an expectation of punishment for that conduct.[26] The conduct does not have to be recognized as criminal in the state in which it is perpetrated to be considered a crime against humanity under customary international law.[27]

Related to the *nullum crimen sine lege* principle is the general prohibition of ex post facto law: the retroactive application of criminal penalties to acts that were not criminalized at the time they were committed.[28] Freedom from retroactive punishment has been established in various human rights treaties and has gained acceptance as a fundamental human right.[29] This does not, however, prevent courts from refining, elaborating on, or clarifying existing rules; nor does it prevent courts from relying on judicial precedent from other jurisdictions.[30]

---

[21] Fourth Report of the Secretary-General on the United Nations Mission in Sierra Leone, U.N. Doc. S/2000/455 (May 19, 2000).

[22] Iman Ngondo A. Pitshandenge, *Marriage Law in Sub-Saharan Africa, in* Nuptuality in Sub-Saharan Africa: Contemporary Anthropological and Demographic Perspectives 118 (Caroline Bledsoe & Gilles Pison eds., 1994).

[23] Antonio Cassese, International Criminal Law § 7.2 at 145 (2003).

[24] *Id.*

[25] *Id.* at § 7.4.3.

[26] Cassese, *supra* note 23, § 7.4.2.

[27] The Allied Control Council Law No. 10, art. 2(1)(c) (Dec. 10, 1945).

[28] Cassese, *supra* note 23, § 7.4.2.

[29] *Id.*

[30] *Id.*

The crimes enumerated in the Statute of the Special Court of Sierra Leone all properly recognize the principle of *nullum crimen sine lege*.[31] The enumerated crimes against humanity, including "other inhumane acts," have all been culled directly from earlier tribunals – the International Criminal Tribunal for Yugoslavia (ICTY) and the international Criminal Tribunal for Rwanda (ICTR) – and have thus passed into customary international law entailing individual criminal responsibility.[32] The "other inhumane acts" category enjoys a particularly strong assurance of compliance with *nullum crimen sine lege*, as it has been a crime against humanity since its incorporation into the Nuremberg Charter in 1945.[33] Since its inception, the "other inhumane acts" category has existed as a "catch-all" category to ensure prosecution of those crimes against humanity not previously envisioned and specifically enumerated, in effect safeguarding against human ingenuity.[34] The concept of an "other inhumane act" has passed into customary international law, but the acts constituting "other inhumane acts" have to the present remained vague and purposefully ill-defined.[35] As recognized in the judgments of previous war crimes tribunals, other inhumane acts have included economic discrimination, confiscation, pillage, and plunder of Jewish property;[36] beatings and general inhumane treatment;[37] and sexual violence in the form of forced public nudity.[38] Recent decisions have identified causing a third party to witness torture as an "other inhumane act."[39] What constitutes an "other inhumane act" is to be determined on a case-by-case basis.

To date, no specific act identified in an indictment before a war crimes tribunal as a crime against humanity under the "other inhumane acts" category has been successfully challenged on the grounds that it violated *nullum crimen sine lege* as it has long been established that the general category conforms to the principle. Though it is a catchall category, "other inhumane acts" is not to be used to prosecute obscure or minor offenses. Acts prosecuted under "other inhumane acts" must be comparable to the enumerated crimes against humanity.[40] Examining past precedent and customary international law, then, is an effective way to ensure that the act of forced marriage is viewed as comparable to the other crimes against humanity in the eyes of the international community and to head off any possible *nullum crimen sine lege* challenges.

The act of forced marriage does withstand *nullum crimen sine lege* scrutiny. The subject matter jurisdiction of the Special Court of Sierra Leone includes "persons who bear the greatest responsibility for serious violations of international humanitarian law and Sierra Leonean Law...."[41] During the formation of the ICTY in 1993, the Secretary-General limited

---

[31] Report of the Secretary-General on the Establishment of a Special Court for Sierra Leone, at para. 12, U.N. Doc. S/2000/915 (Oct. 4, 2000).

[32] *Id.* at para. 14.

[33] Charter of the International Military Tribunal, 59 Stat. 1544, 82 U.N.T.S. 284, 288 (Aug. 8, 1945), *available at* http://www.yale.edu/lawweb/avalon/imt/proc/imtconst.htm [hereinafter Nuremburg Charter].

[34] Prosecutor v. Kupreškic, IT-95-16-T, Judgment, at para. 563 (Jan. 14, 2000) [hereinafter *Kupreškic*].

[35] *Id.*

[36] Matthew Lippman, *International Law and Human Rights Edition: Crimes against Humanity*, 17 B.C. Third World L.J. 171, 201 (1997).

[37] Prosecutor v. Tadic, IT-94-1-T, Judgment, at para. 730 (May 7, 1997) [hereinafter *Tadic*].

[38] Prosecutor v. Akayesu, ICTR-96-4-T, Judgment, at para. 697 (Sept. 2, 1998) [hereinafter *Akayesu*].

[39] Prosecutor v. Kayishema, ITCR-95-1-A, Judgment, at para. 151 (June 1, 2001) [hereinafter *Kayishema*].

[40] Elements of Crimes, art. 7(1)(k) (Sept. 3–10, 2002), U.N. Doc. ICC-ASP/1/3.

[41] SCSL Statute art. (1)(1), *available at* http://www.sc-sl.org/scsl-statute.html (last visited: April 2, 2013).

the tribunal to the application of rules that were beyond doubt part of customary international law.[42] The Secretary-General then limited what qualified as customary international law to the law embodied in the Geneva Conventions, the 1907 Hague Conventions, the Conventions on the Prevention and Punishment of the Crime of Genocide, and the Charter of the Nuremberg Tribunal.[43] The next tribunal to be established, the ICTR in 1994, was given a more expansive definition of applicable international law. The Security Council did away with the enumerated instruments and described customary international law as encompassing international instruments "regardless of whether they were considered part of customary international law or whether they have customarily entailed the individual criminal responsibility of the perpetrator of the crime."[44] Under the more expansive approach set forth for the ICTR, customary international law is clear on the subject of forced marriage – the practice is an affront to long-established and well-documented human rights doctrines, as well as a degradation of the institution of marriage, which the international community has expressed an interest in protecting and preserving.

A. *The International Community Has Long Recognized the Constitutive Physical Acts Perpetrated against the Victimized Spouse of a Forced Marriage as Crimes against Humanity*

The crime against humanity of forced marriage is more complex than a crime such as murder, where there is only one act (the unlawful taking of a human life). It is not simply the single act of forcing someone to take a vow of marriage or designating that person as a "spouse"; forced marriage covers a multitude of sins. It comprises multiple constituent acts, some or all of which are perpetrated upon the victim within the confines of the forced marriage: rape, torture, enslavement, sexual slavery, and forced pregnancy.[45] All of these constituent acts are already recognized as crimes against humanity in their own right.[46] Moreover, the horrors inflicted upon women in forced marriage have a long history of vigorous prosecution as crimes against humanity; anyone committing them has an expectation of punishment.[47] The constituent acts remain just as grave when subsumed under the label of forced marriage. It is inconceivable that they cause any less suffering or are any less

---

[42] Report of the Secretary-General Pursuant to Paragraph 2 of Security Council Resolution 808, at para. 34, U.N. Doc. S/25704 (May 3, 1993) ("In the view of the Secretary-General, the application of the principle *nullum crimen sine lege* requires that the international tribunal should apply rules of international humanitarian law which are beyond any doubt part of customary international law so that the problem of adherence of some but not all States to specific conventions does not arise. This would appear to be particularly important in the context of an international tribunal prosecuting persons responsible for serious violations of international humanitarian law.").

[43] *Id.* at para. 35.

[44] Report of the Secretary-General Pursuant to Paragraph 5 of Security Council Resolution 955, at para. 12, U.N. Doc. S/1995/134 (Feb. 13, 1995).

[45] Monika Satya Kalra, *Forced Marriage: Rwanda's Secret Revealed*, 7 U.C. Davis J. Int'l L. & Pol'y 197, 205 (2001).

[46] SCSL Statute, *supra* note 41, art. 3.

[47] Allied Control Council No. 10, *supra* note 27, Article II(3)(c) lists rape, enslavement, and torture as crimes against humanity. Geneva Convention Relative to the Protection of Civilian Persons in Time of War, at 75 U.N.T.S. 287 (Aug. 12, 1949). Article 27 prohibits rape; Article 32 prohibits torture; Article 40 prohibits forced labor. The Rome Statute of the International Criminal Court, art. 7(1)(g) (July 17, 1998), U.N. Doc. A/Conf. 183/9 (1998) [hereinafter Rome Statute] recognizes sexual slavery and forced pregnancy as crimes against humanity.

serious breaches of human rights or international humanitarian law simply because they were perpetuated repeatedly upon a woman under the guise of a "marriage."[48]

B. *The International Community Has a Vested Interest in Protecting the Family and the Institution of Marriage*

The international community recognizes the family as the most basic unit of society.[49] It also recognizes the necessity of protecting and encouraging the stability of the family.[50] Marriage has long been viewed in both the secular and ecclesiastical realms as the foundation of the family. It is through the joining of the two spouses in marriage that a family is initially formed. Marriage is the most common means by which a family is established and its attendant rights and responsibilities are conferred upon its members. The international community, then, has a vested interest in protecting the institution of marriage as a means of protecting the family. Forced marriage undermines marriage by using the institution to justify the egregious crimes of rape, torture, enslavement, sexual slavery, and forced pregnancy, and to entrap the victim for an indefinite period of time via the rights and status attaching to a spouse. A marriage under these conditions does not serve to protect and foster a stable, healthy family or a stable, healthy base for society as a whole.

A fundamental part of the institution of marriage is the change in social and legal status of the spouses and the attendant rights and privileges that flow from marriage. This includes both the intrinsic rights and obligations shared between the spouses in the marriage and the extrinsic rights and obligations conferred by state and ecclesiastical authorities upon a married couple. The matrimonial state is more than simply an identification of the spouses as "married"; the spouses are afforded certain rights and obligations to each other within the marriage that they do not share with other members of society, such as monogamy, shared responsibility for children, or expectations of privilege and confidentiality.

A married couple is afforded certain rights and obligations by state and religious bodies as well. The marital status of two individuals has a significant impact on how they are treated by religious institutions and will affect how laws pertaining to inheritance, taxes, health care, child welfare, and even criminal liability[51] affect them. In some states, a married woman is legally a minor and is dependent upon her husband, who may gain rights over her property, assets, or even welfare.[52] Beyond the legal realm, society as a whole has certain expectations and rules of comportment for married individuals, whose societal status differs from unmarried individuals.

The changes in the societal, legal, and religious status of a married couple are meant to protect the marriage and respect the autonomy and privacy of the married couple within the family sphere. Marriage enjoys a favored and often protected status in the law and in

---

[48] Kalra, *supra* note 45, at 203–04.

[49] "The family is the natural and fundamental group unit of society and is entitled to protection by society and the State." International Covenant on Civil and Political Rights, art. 23(3) (Mar. 23, 1976) [hereinafter ICCPR], *available at* http://www.unhchr.ch/html/menu3/b/a_ccpr.htm, Universal Declaration of Human Rights, art. 16 (Dec. 10, 1948) [hereinafter UDHR], *available at* http://www.un.org/Overview/rights.html.

[50] *Id.*

[51] Both the United States and Sierra Leone recognize spousal privilege. George Fisher, Evidence 841 (2002) and Criminal Procedures Act § 83(3) (1963) (Sierra Leone).

[52] Pitshandenge, *supra* note 22, at 124.

public policy.[53] Religious and social taboos regarding adultery exist to protect the marital relationship from infidelity in a manner not afforded to nonmarital relationships. However, in a forced marriage, changes in status are used to trap the nonconsenting spouse within the forced marriage. As discussed above, for a woman to dissolve her customary marriage, she needs the permission of her relatives, to whom a victim of forced marriage rarely has access. By virtue of attaching the rights of a spouse to her, her "husband" traps her within the forced marriage through cultural and social mores in place to protect valid marriages. For example, in Sierra Leone, strong taboos exist regarding victims of rape.[54] A woman who has been raped may be seen as unfit for marriage, but if she is "married" to her rapist, then the sexual violence is deemed merely a part of the marital relationship and the woman is spared censure. The difference in cultural status between a wife and a rape victim compels the victim to stay in her forced marriage. The institution of marriage enjoys protected status because it facilitates the betterment of the individual and of society, objectives that cannot be met in a forced marriage. The international community, therefore, has a clear interest in sending a strong message that forced marriage is an unacceptable perversion of a protected and valued institution, and it, and the threat it poses to the family, will not be tolerated.

C. All Marriages Require the Consent of Both Parties to Be Valid

The international community has a vested interest in protecting valid marriages because it is through valid marriages that families are formed. But, as was briefly illustrated in the discussion of marital custom in Sierra Leone in Section II(B), there are many types of marriage: religious, regional customary, and civil – all of which are considered equally valid and all of which are equally deserving of the protections afforded to marriages by the state. The state is generally reticent to intrude into the private family sphere out of deference to the marriage, but in the case of forced marriage, the state must pry into the "marriage." It is clear that a forced marriage is not a valid marriage and therefore not entitled to the protected deferential status that valid marital unions enjoy. Before any prosecution of forced marriage can commence, *forced* marriages must be distinguished from *valid* marriages.

The fundamental element in a valid marriage is consent: a marriage is not valid unless entered into with the full and free consent of both spouses. This holds true in secular law as well as in ecclesiastical law.[55] Clearly, no such consent is given in the case of a forced marriage. The women in forced marriages in Sierra Leone do not enter into them of their own volition; instead they are compelled by violence or coerced through exploitation of

---

[53] 52 Am. Jur. 2d *Marriage* § 2.

[54] *Qualitative Comments and Testimonies of Women and Girls, in* Physicians for Human Rights, War-Related Sexual Violence in Sierra Leone: A Population-Based Assessment 78–79 (2002), *available at* http://www.phrusa.org/research/sierra_leone/pdf_files/04_qualitative.pdf [hereinafter Physicians for Human Rights].

[55] ICCPR and UDHR, *supra* note 49. The Catholic Church maintains that "[a] marriage is brought into being by the lawfully manifested consent of persons who are legally capable. This consent cannot be supplied by any human power." Codex Iuris Canonici 1983 CODE c. 1057 § 1. Islam also requires the full and free consent of both parties for a valid marriage. Mashood A. Baderin, International Human Rights and Islamic Law 133 (2003). Although Hinduism has recognized forced marriages in the past, the Hindu Marriage Act of 1955 also requires that both intending spouses give valid consent to the marriage. Hindu Marriage Act, § 5(ii) (1955) (India) (amended 1976).

the vulnerable position in which they, like all civilians, find themselves during conflict. Therefore, a forced marriage is not a valid marriage and does not warrant the deference usually afforded to marriage.

D. The Crime of "Forced Marriage" Is Distinct from an Arranged Marriage

If marriage requires consent to be valid, it necessarily raises the question: how can forced marriage be deemed a crime against humanity while arranged marriage is viewed as an acceptable practice under the principle of cultural relativism? There are two bases upon which the distinction between the crime against humanity of forced marriage and the practice of arranged marriage can be made. First, there is still consent in an arranged marriage. Whereas intending spouses, or at least their fiduciaries, consent to the marriage itself in an arranged marriage, no such consent is present in a forced marriage. Second, to be prosecuted as a crime against humanity, forced marriage must be a part of a widespread and systematic attack upon a civilian population. The practice of arranged marriage in no way constitutes an attack on a civilian population.

An arranged marriage can be understood as the intending spouses delegating the selection process to their family members rather than finding a spouse on their own. Granted, they may be consenting to cast their lot with someone whom they have never met before the ceremony, but recognized international law does not require that both spouses know each other well or at all, just that they consent to be wed to one another.[56] The spouses in an arranged marriage still consent to the marriage.

Although it is easy to draw such technical distinctions between arranged marriages and forced marriages, the reality of arranged marriages is often closer in spirit to a forced marriage than the description of the practice earlier in this section might indicate. In some cases, betrothals are made when the intending spouses are still legal minors. The "consent" of a woman entering into an arranged marriage may be less a product of her own will than pressure from her family. It is growing increasingly difficult to accept such unions in the face of modern human rights law.[57] In fact, if the marriage is made in exchange for monetary

---

[56] The relevant portion of the UDHR reads:

   1. Men and women of full age, without any limitation due to race, nationality or religion, have the right to marry and to found a family. They are entitled to equal rights during marriage and at its dissolution.
   2. Marriage shall be entered into only with the free and full consent of the intending parties.
   3. The family is the natural and fundamental group unit of society and is entitled to protection by society and the State.

   Supra note 49.
   The ICCPR reads:

   1. The family is the natural and fundamental group unit of society and is entitled to protection by society and the State.
   2. The right of men and women of marriageable age to marry and found a family shall be recognized.
   3. No marriage shall be entered into without the free and full consent of the intending parties.

   4. State Parties to the present Covenant shall take appropriate steps to ensure equality of rights and responsibilities of spouses as to marriage, during marriage and at its dissolution. In the case of dissolution, provisions should be made for the necessary protection of any children.

   Supra note 49.

[57] Convention on the Elimination of All Forms of Discrimination against Women, art. 16 (Dec. 18, 1979), *available at* http://www.un.org/womenwatch/daw/cedaw/econvention.htm [hereinafter CEDAW].

or similar consideration, the "marriage" is considered slavery, and under customary international law could be subject to prosecution by any state at any time.[58] Even if one were to accept such arranged marriages as valid although one or both of the intending spouses have not consented to the marriage, one can still distinguish between these family-imposed arranged marriages and forced marriage. In an arranged marriage, the woman's family or guardian still must consent to the union to make the marriage valid.

Someone in a fiduciary relationship with the woman, theoretically looking out for her best interests, is the ultimate arbiter of the union in an arranged marriage. In a forced marriage, consent is obtained neither from the forced spouse nor anyone with a fiduciary relationship to her.

Distinguishing arranged marriage from forced marriage based upon the legal foundations of the marriages can be difficult, especially in those cases of arranged marriage in which the intending spouses have no ability to object to the marriage. These types of arranged marriages are becoming increasingly disfavored among customary international human rights instruments that emphasize consent between the intending spouses alone.[59] Even so, the practice of arranged marriage does not and cannot rise to the level of a crime against humanity as forced marriage does, because arranged marriage is not a systematic and widespread attack on a civilian population; it is not an "attack" at all. To "attack" is to "affect or act upon injuriously."[60] Those cultures that practice arranged marriage do so to *assist* the civilian population. Parents arrange marriages for their children to protect their children's welfare; assist them in the difficult and vital process of selecting a mate; and ensure the perpetuation of social, cultural, and religious values. The practice of arranged marriage is not injurious to the groups that practice it in intent or result. Forced marriage, in contrast, has no basis in the benevolent parental objectives to assist children or to perpetuate important values, and it is highly injurious to its victims.

IV. *Forced Marriage and the Statute for the Special Court for Sierra Leone*

Article 2 of the Statute of the Special Court of Sierra Leone vests the Court with the power to prosecute crimes against humanity.[61] Forced marriage is not enumerated as a crime against humanity in the Statute. For it to be legitimately prosecuted, it must be done under the broad category of "other inhumane acts." Crimes eligible for prosecution under this category are those in which:

1. The perpetrator inflicted great suffering, serious injury to body or mental or physical health by means of an inhumane act; such act was of a character similar to any other crime against humanity;[62]

---

[58] Supplementary Convention on the Abolition of Slavery, and the Slave Trade, and Institutions and Practices Similar to Slavery, art. 1(c)(i) (Sept. 7, 1956), *available at* http://www.unhchr.ch/html/menu3/b/30.htm.

[59] UDHR, *supra* note 49; ICCPR, *supra* note 49; CEDAW, *supra* note 57.

[60] MERRIAM-WEBSTER ON-LINE DICTIONARY (2004), *at* http://m-w.com/cgi-bin/dictionary?book=Dictionary &va=attack. "Attack.(v.) 1. To set upon or work against forcefully. 2. To assail with unfriendly or bitter words. 3. To begin to affect or to act on injuriously. 4. To set to work on. 5. To threaten (a piece in chess) with immediate capture."

[61] SCSL Statute, *supra* note 41, art 2.

[62] *Id.* This would include the crimes against humanity of murder, extermination, enslavement, deportation, imprisonment, torture, rape, sexual slavery, enforced prostitution, forced pregnancy, any other form of sexual violence, and persecution on political, racial, ethnic, or religious grounds.

2. The perpetrator was aware of the factual circumstances that established the character of the act;

3. The conduct was committed as part of a widespread or systematic attack directed against a civilian population; and

4. The perpetrator knew that the conduct was part of or intended the conduct to be part of a widespread or systematic attack directed against a civilian population.[63]

This category of crimes against humanity is intended as a "catch-all" for atrocities that were not specifically contemplated by the Statute's drafters. The category of "other inhumane acts" is therefore purposefully vague to free the prosecution from unnecessary constraints when confronted by such crimes.[64] The ICTY Trial Chamber in *Kupreškic et al.* sought to provide a practical definition of "other inhumane acts," which the Chamber defined as acts that, under the proper circumstances, are grave and serious violations of standard international human rights.[65] The standard international human rights can be extrapolated through a study of various international human rights instruments.[66] The previous section amply demonstrates how forced marriage violates many human rights as they are enumerated in multiple international instruments. For forced marriage to be a crime valid for prosecution as a specifically recognized crime against humanity, then, it must be (1) a source of great suffering for its victim; (2) of a character similar to the other listed crimes against humanity, and (3) part of a widespread and systematic attack against the civilian population – qualifications that it most emphatically meets.

A. *Perpetrators of Forced Marriage Inflict Great Suffering, and Serious Injury to Body or Mental or Physical Health by Means of an Inhumane Act upon Their Victims*

"Great suffering," in the context of crimes against humanity falling into the category of other inhumane acts, is judged upon an *ejusdem generis* standard; that is, the suffering of the victim of the "other inhumane act" must be of comparable gravity and severity to suffering of victims of the crimes against humanity specifically enumerated in the Statute.[67] There must also be a "nexus" between the inhumane act and the victim's suffering.[68] There can be no doubt of the gravity of the suffering endured by the victims of forced marriages during the armed conflict in Sierra Leone or the connection between their suffering and the forced marriage.

Survivor accounts more than adequately demonstrate that the depth of their suffering is comparable with that of other victims of crimes against humanity. According to these accounts, women were taken, usually during raids of villages after witnessing the rape, maiming, and murder of friends and family by rebel forces.[69] Girls as young as thirteen[70]

---

[63] Elements of Crimes, *supra* note 40, art. 7(1)(k).

[64] CASSESE, *supra* note 23, § 4.3.10.

[65] *Kupreškic, supra* note 34, at para. 566.

[66] *Id.*

[67] *Id.*

[68] *Kayishema, supra* note 39, at para. 146.

[69] PHYSICIANS FOR HUMAN RIGHTS, *supra* note 54, at 64–73.

[70] *Id.* at 68.

were often kidnapped and forced into circumstances where their captors informed them that they were now the wives of the men who had taken them. Now "married," they were raped repeatedly.[71] These rapes often resulted in pregnancy[72] and sexually transmitted diseases.[73] Women were given narcotics by their "husbands" to keep them compliant and as a means of compelling them to commit other crimes.[74] Captor husbands carved the letters "RUF" into their "wives'" bodies[75] or branded them.[76] The women were often beaten and forced into labor for their "husbands."[77] The suffering of women subjected to such treatment is certainly comparable to the suffering of victims of other crimes against humanity, including rape, sexual slavery, torture, forced pregnancy, and enslavement.

B. Forced Marriage Is an Act of a Similar Character to the Other Enumerated Crimes against Humanity because it Is Composed of Constitutive Acts That Are Crimes against Humanity in Their Own Right

To qualify for prosecution under the designation "other inhumane acts," the objective act or acts that define the crime must be comparable to the objective acts that comprise the other enumerated crimes against humanity. The gravity of the objective elements of the crime, the *actus reus*, is judged based upon the same *ejusdem generis* standard as the suffering of the victims.[78]

Unlike murder or torture, forced marriage is not composed of only one *actus reus*. Rather, it encompasses multiple constituent acts: rape, torture, enslavement, sexual slavery, and forced pregnancy. Each of these constituent acts is already recognized separately as a crime against humanity.[79] In fact, some constituent acts, namely; enslavement, torture, and arguably rape, rise to the level of *jus cogens* norm violations.[80] Rights protected by *jus cogens* norms are nonderogable, are binding on all states at all times, cannot be preempted by treaty, and can be prosecuted against anyone at any time.[81] It follows, then, that just as the suffering of a victim of forced marriage compares to that of victims of the enumerated crimes against humanity, forced marriage is sufficiently similar to the other enumerated crimes against humanity to fall into the "other inhumane acts" category because it encompasses those other enumerated crimes against humanity. It defies reason that combining these crimes and perpetrating them repeatedly, or by perpetrating the crimes under the

---

[71] *Id.* at 66, 70.

[72] *Id.* at 67–68, 70.

[73] *Id.* at 68.

[74] *Id.* at 66, 68.

[75] *Id.* at 68.

[76] Swallow, *supra* note 20.

[77] Fifth Report of the Secretary-General on the United Nations Mission in Sierra Leone, U.N. Doc. S/2000/751 (July 31, 2000).

[78] *Kupreškic, supra* note 34, at para. 564.

[79] SCSL Statute, *supra* note 41, art. 2, and Rome Statute, *supra* note 47, art. 7.

[80] Kelly D. Askin, *Stefan A. Riensenfeld Symposium 2002: Prosecuting Wartime Rape and Other Gender-Related Crimes under International Law: Extraordinary Advances, Enduring Obstacles*, 21 BERKELEY J. INT'L L. 288, 349 (2003).

[81] 45 AM. JUR. 2D *International Law* § 1.

guise of "marriage," diminishes their severity or renders them any less "odious an attack on human dignity."[82]

C. Forced Marriage Was Part of a Widespread and Systematic Attack against the Civilian Population of Sierra Leone

The widespread or systematic nature of an attack, and the fact that it is conducted against a civilian population, defines a crime against humanity.[83] These qualifications distinguish it both from mere acts of random violence and war crimes. A particular act does not need to be committed in a widespread and systematic manner to meet this qualification, but it must be part of a widespread and systematic attack.[84] The ICTR Trial Chamber in *Akayesu* defined "widespread" as "massive, frequent, large scale action, carried out collectively with considerable seriousness and directed against a multiplicity of victims,"[85] and "systematic" as "thoroughly organized and following a regular pattern on the basis of a common policy involving substantial public or private resources."[86] The policy is not required to be official state policy, but "some kind of preconceived plan or policy must exist."[87]

After a decade of incredibly bloody civil war, stretching from the eastern border of the country, there can be no doubt that a widespread attack was carried out in Sierra Leone. From the accounts of the survivors, civilian women and girls abducted from their homes during raids and forced to marry the rebel soldiers who abducted them, it is also clear that forced marriage was a part of that widespread attack, which was carried out against the civilian population.

D. Forced Marriage Is More than the Sum of Its Constituent Acts and Should Be Prosecuted as a Separate Crime in Order to Appropriately Recognize Its Gravity, Prevent Future Instances, and Properly Recognize the Suffering of the Victims

As all of the constituent acts that comprise a forced marriage are already recognized as crimes against humanity by the Statute of the Special Court of Sierra Leone,[88] some consideration must be given to the need for creating a new category of crime. If the incidents of rape, sexual slavery, enslavement, torture, and forced pregnancy that take place within a forced marriage can all be sufficiently punished under existing international humanitarian law, formulating a new offense of "forced marriage" is unnecessary. Arguably, it would be redundant and a waste of judicial resources to pursue a new crime if the perpetrators can be adequately punished under existing law. If "forced marriage" were simply the sum of its parts, as heinous as those parts may be, a new offense would not advance the interests of justice, the victims would receive no additional vindication, and there would be no need

---

[82] CASSESE, *supra* note 23, § 4.1.1. One of the defining features of crimes against humanity is that "[t]hey are particularly odious offenses in that they constitute a serious attack on human dignity or a grave humiliation or degradation of one or more human beings."

[83] *Id.*

[84] Prosecutor v. Kunarac, IT-96-23-T, at para. 419 (Feb. 22, 2001).

[85] *Akayesu*, *supra* note 38, at para. 580.

[86] *Id.*

[87] *Id.*

[88] SCSL Statute, *supra* note 41, art. 2.

to take additional steps to prevent a recurrence of these crimes. But forced marriage is far more than its constituent elements – it is inescapable rape, sexual slavery, torture, forced pregnancy, and enslavement on a continuing basis as well as the degradation of an internationally valued social and spiritual institution.

A useful paradigm for recognizing forced marriage as a crime against humanity can be found in the recent recognition of sexual slavery as a crime against humanity. Sexual slavery was first recognized as a distinct crime against humanity in 1998 when it was enumerated in the Rome Statute of the International Criminal Court (ICC).[89] Before this, conduct that would have constituted sexual slavery was prosecuted as other crimes against humanity, usually enforced prostitution or enslavement. Like forced marriage, sexual slavery is composed of multiple constituent acts, namely enslavement and rape, which were both previously recognized individually as crimes against humanity. However, the drafters of the Rome Statute recognized that sexual slavery is more than enslavement and more than rape.[90] Rape properly describes the sexual violence inherent in the conduct, but not the loss of individual liberty. Enslavement properly describes the deprivation of personal liberty, but enslavement alone does not include the element of sexual violence that is vital to the crime. Because sexual slavery is more than slavery and more than rape, the victim of sexual slavery suffers differently from the victims of other crimes against humanity.[91] International human rights law recognizes that the enslavement for the purposes of forcing the victim to perform sexual acts is a particularly egregious form of enslavement deserving of specific recognition.[92] Rome Statute drafters and commentators endorsed the new classification of crime because it more accurately described the conduct than enslavement or rape does.

The existing category of crime against humanity of enforced prostitution was similarly deemed insufficient to properly prosecute incidences of sexual slavery. Enforced prostitution arguably conveyed a more accurate description of the complete *actus reus* of sexual slavery – that is, women detained and forcibly compelled to perform acts of sexual nature – but it did not fully convey the profound deprivation of personal liberty that accompanies the deprivation of the victim's sexual autonomy.[93] The deprivation of personal liberty that rises to the level of "slavery" may not be present in all types of enforced prostitution.[94] The term "enforced prostitution" was further unsuitable because it labels the victim a "prostitute." This term carries a certain stigma, connoting a certain degree of volunteerism from the victim, and conceals the violence inherent in the crime.[95] "Slavery" has far fewer negative connotations in that it does not carry the presumption of volunteerism, which makes it a more sensitive and more accurate characterization of the conduct.[96]

Forced marriage parallels sexual slavery in that the conduct comprising forced marriage is a unique violation of human rights and international human rights law that is not fully captured by current enumerated crimes against humanity. None of the other crimes against

---

[89] Rome Statute, *supra* note 47, arts. 7(1)(g), 8(2)(b)(xxii), 8(2)(e)(vi).
[90] Valerie Oosterveld, *Sexual Slavery and the International Criminal Court: Advancing International Law*, 25 MICH. J. INT'L L. 605 (2004).
[91] *Id.*
[92] *Id.* at 623.
[93] *Id.* at 622.
[94] *Id.*
[95] *Id.* at 618–19.
[96] *Id.* at 620.

humanity that comprise forced marriage describe the *totality* of the perpetrator's conduct or the victim's experience. Enslavement describes the loss of personal freedom, but obscures the sexual violence inherent in the crime.[97] Sexual slavery describes the loss of personal freedom and the sexual violence, but does not speak to the forced domestic labor, childbearing, child rearing, and degradation of the institution of marriage.[98] Torture, rape, and forced pregnancy do not address the victim's loss of personal liberty and individually may not be present in all cases of forced marriage.[99] Forced marriage is a profound deprivation of individual autonomy. None of the enumerated crimes against humanity recognize a crime where the victim is denied her personal liberty, and is forced into sexual acts, domestic labor, childbearing, and child rearing through the denigration of an important and protected social and spiritual institution. Therefore, it is appropriate for war crimes tribunals to now apply a new category of crimes against humanity that recognizes the entirety of the conduct.

E. *Forced Marriage Is a Unique Crime and It Would Not Be Duplicitous to Proceed with Charges of Forced Marriage in Light of the Existence of Similar Crimes against Humanity of Enslavement and Sexual Slavery*

As discussed in the previous section, one of the difficulties that arose in describing and defining the crime of sexual slavery was in differentiating it from other, already established crimes against humanity, namely enforced prostitution and enslavement. The constitutive acts that made up the different crimes were undeniably similar; it would have been a waste of judicial time and resources, as well as an affront to the principle of due process, to pursue different charges if they were tantamount to the exact same crime. Although sexual slavery shared some subjective elements with enforced prostitution and enslavement, the international community recognized that neither one encompassed all of the subjective elements, and the differences between them were significant enough to classify sexual slavery as a separate crime.

The same concern for judicial resources and the formulation of duplicitous crimes applies when evaluating the viability of forced marriage as a crime against humanity. At first blush, sexual slavery appears strikingly similar to the crime of forced marriage. However, as in the case of comparing sexual slavery to enforced prostitution and enslavement, as one compares the essential elements of forced marriage with sexual slavery, substantial differences between the crimes quickly appear.

As defined by the Rome Statute the elements of sexual slavery are:

1. The perpetrator exercised any or all of the powers attaching to the right of ownership over one or more persons, such as by purchasing, selling, lending or bartering such a person or persons, or by imposing on them a similar deprivation of liberty.
2. The perpetrator caused such person or persons to engage in one or more acts of a sexual nature.

---

[97] Elements of Crimes, *supra* note 40, art. 7(1)(c).
[98] *Id.* at art. 7(1)(g)-2.
[99] *Id.* at arts. 7(1)(f), 7(1)(g)-1, and 7(1)(g)-4.

3. The conduct was committed as part of a widespread or systematic attack directed against a civilian population.
4. The perpetrator knew that the conduct was part of or intended the conduct to be part of a widespread or systematic attack directed against a civilian population.[100]

Sexual slavery and forced marriage share elements 3 and 4 as these define them as crimes against humanity.[101] However, further examination of the two crimes shows them disparate with respect to the first two elements.

The defining element that makes sexual slavery "slavery" is the perpetrator's attaching the right of ownership to the victim. This deprivation of the victim's liberty and personal autonomy distinguishes sexual slavery from other sexually based crimes against humanity.[102] The personal liberty of a "wife" in a forced marriage is similarly constrained in a forced marriage, but the constraint is accomplished not through attachment of right of ownership, but through the enforced, nonconsensual attachment of the rights and privileges of marriage. Wives compelled into forced marriages are not "owned" as the victims of sexual slavery are, but are still inextricably bound to their captors by the ties of matrimony and the obligations flowing from it that the perpetrator foists upon the victim.

As discussed above, marriage changes the rights and duties owed to the individuals within the marital relationship as well as their rights and duties in the eyes of extrinsic institutions. In a forced marriage, the perpetrator extracts the privileges normally expected within a marital relationship – sexual congress, labor, childbearing, child rearing, fidelity, obedience, and more – from "wives," who never consented to be so bound. There is also no equality of rights in these relationships. Even though the roles of each spouse in a marriage may differ, both spouses should have equal rights within the marriage at all times.[103] This is not true of a forced marriage, within which the perpetrator holds all the power. The attachment of the rights of spouse to the victim drastically changes how she is perceived by social, state, and religious entities. Depending on the victim's religious convictions, it may change her responsibilities and rights within the faith, and it may also change her rights in certain situations under secular law even though the victim has never consented to such a status change. Laws and customs about the transfer of property, the bearing and rearing of children, or the ability of the victim to contract for other marriages, which were meant to protect spouses, now entrap the victimized spouse. Whereas a victim of sexual slavery is bound intrinsically by her captor and his ability to restrain her movement, a victim of forced marriage is bound both intrinsically by her captor and extrinsically by the bonds placed upon a married couple by religion, society, and state.

The second element of sexual slavery, which states that "[t]he perpetrator caused such person or persons to engage in one or more acts of a sexual nature," underscores the violation of the victim's sexual autonomy and the sexual violence that inheres in the crime. Here again, a distinction can be drawn between sexual slavery and forced marriage. Sexual

---

[100] Elements of Crimes, *supra* note 40, art. 7(1)(g)-2.
[101] CASSESE, *supra* note 23, § 4.1.2.
[102] Elements of Crimes, *supra* note 40, art. 7(1)(g)1–6. None of the other sexually based crimes against humanity have deprivation of liberty listed in the elements.
[103] ICCPR, *supra* note 49; UDHR, *supra* note 49, and European Convention on Human Rights, art. 6 (Nov. 4, 1950).

violence is a serious and substantial element of forced marriage. Sexual intimacy is an important element to marriage, as the most cursory review of religious and legal views of adultery makes abundantly clear. One of the hallmarks of forced marriage is that the victim is forced to become her captor's sexual partner and is repeatedly raped as her captor extracts the marital privilege of sexual congress from his victim.[104] This is especially significant in Sierra Leone, where there is no recognition of marital rape.[105] The theory is that a woman who has entered into a marriage has given implied consent to sexual intercourse at all times within the marriage, and a husband may resort to force if his sexual overtures are rebuffed.[106]

But there are more obligations owed between husband and wife than simply sexual relations. Marriage also includes shared duties of fidelity, childbearing, child rearing, and the physical labor necessary to run a household. As these additional obligations are assumed to attach to the victim under the rubric of marriage, they too should be recognized as part of the crime of forced marriage. Because the duties attaching under right of a spouse include more than sexual congress, the crime of forced marriage necessarily encompasses these additional violations of the victim's autonomy as well. Forced marriage is not just a violation of the victim's sexual autonomy: it is impressment into domestic labor, it is denial of the victim's reproductive autonomy, and it prevents the victim from contracting for marriage with someone of her or her family's choice. Reflecting only the sexual elements, sexual slavery does not adequately address these other aspects of the crime: defining such far-reaching conduct as sexual slavery is far too narrow and fails to address the other substantial, nonsexual elements of the crime. Forced marriage, then, should be distinguished from sexual slavery so as to capture these other elements.

If sexual slavery is insufficient to describe the conduct that constitutes forced marriage, then enslavement is similarly ill-equipped to accurately and concisely characterize the crime that is forced marriage. The only distinguishing element of the crime against humanity of enslavement is "[t]he perpetrator exercised any or all of the powers attaching to the right of ownership over one or more persons, such as by purchasing, selling, lending or bartering such a person or persons, or by imposing on them a similar deprivation of liberty."[107] It is broader than sexual slavery and can be construed as encompassing both the sexual and nonsexual elements of the crime, but to classify these crimes as "enslavement" alone is an inexact description of the crime at best and misleading at worst. In the crime of enslavement, as in sexual slavery, the perpetrator's control over the victim comes from attaching of the right of ownership to the victim, whereas in forced marriages the perpetrator obtains control over the victim by attaching the obligations of a spouse to the victim. The victim of forced marriage is bound not only by the force exerted over her by the perpetrator but by the shift in legal, social, and religious rights and status arising from marriage.

Additionally, enslavement is silent on the sexual violence and forced labor aspects of the crime. Although the sexual element should not be emphasized to the exclusion of all

---

[104] Human Rights Watch, *supra* note 19.

[105] Note by Secretary-General, Report of the United Nations High Commissioner for Human Rights on assistance to Sierra Leone in the field of human rights, U.N. Doc. A/59/340 at para. 30 (Sept. 9, 2004).

[106] *Id.*

[107] Elements of Crimes, *supra* note 40, art. 7(1)(c).

other elements of the crime, as it would be in sexual slavery, the sexual violence inherent in the crime makes it particularly offensive to human dignity and should be acknowledged accordingly along with forced labor, forced pregnancy, and the other acts that constitute forced marriage. Enslavement lacks the specificity necessary to accurately describe the crime of forced marriage and would inevitably lead to confusion as to how the perpetrator maintained control over the victim.

V. DEFINING FORCED MARRIAGE – ELEMENTS FOR A NEW CRIME AGAINST HUMANITY

Thus far, the crime of forced marriage has been described in terms of international custom and other crimes against humanity. It has been distinguished from valid marriage, including arranged marriage. The constituent acts of the conduct have been examined with respect to other crimes against humanity to prove that forced marriage is comparable, both in the nature of the conduct and the degree of suffering inflicted upon the victims, to the other crimes against humanity listed in the Statute of the Special Court of Sierra Leone. It has been distinguished from the similar crime against humanity of sexual slavery and enslavement to prove that forced marriage is sufficiently different to warrant independent prosecution. The previous analysis has thus focused on what forced marriage is *not*, but in order to prosecute the crime, one must define it for what it *is*.

In its 2008 AFRC decision, the SCSL Appeals Chamber defined forced marriage as "a situation in which the perpetrator through his words or conduct, or those of someone for whose actions he is responsible, compels a person by force, threat of force, or coercion to serve as a conjugal partner resulting in severe suffering, or physical, mental or psychological injury to the victim."[108] Although it captures the essence of the offense, this definition has several shortcomings. First, perhaps in an effort to avoid the circularity of using the term in its own definition, the Appeals Chamber employs the term "conjugal partner" to describe the victim's status. But this phrase does not fully reflect the harm inflicted by perversion of the institution of marriage. And second, the Appeals Chamber definition requires specific proof of severe suffering – something that is not required for other crimes against humanity such as slavery or enforced prostitution, where the suffering is inherent in the imposed status of the victim.

As an alternative approach, the previous analysis indicates that the crime of "forced marriage" should be defined in terms of the following five elements:

1. The perpetrator imposed the status of "spouse" on one or more persons without the individual's consent by threat of force or coercion, such as that caused by fear of violence, duress, detention, psychological oppression or abuse of power, against such person or persons or another person, or by taking advantage of a coercive environment or such person's or persons' incapacity to give genuine consent;

2. In conjunction with the victim's status as "spouse," the perpetrator caused such person or persons to engage in one or more acts of a sexual nature, and/or forced domestic labor, childbearing, or child rearing;

---

[108] AFRC Appeals Judgment, *supra* note 3, at para. 196.

3. The perpetrator makes it so that the victim is unable to dissolve the marriage until the war ends and the victim has access to relief;

4. The conduct was committed as part of a widespread or systematic attack directed against a civilian population; and

5. The perpetrator knew that the conduct was part of or intended the conduct to be part of a widespread or systematic attack directed against a civilian population.

The first element of the crime is distinct when compared to the other sexually based crimes against humanity.[109] Unlike sexual slavery, where there is a similar imposing of a status on the victim by the perpetrator, forced marriage requires that the status of "wife" be conferred without the consent of the victim. The consent element is the first distinction between forced marriage and enslavement or sexual slavery, and it distinguishes a valid marriage from a forced marriage. As no one can consent to slavery, individual autonomy being a nonderogable right, consent is a moot point in cases of slavery. However, individuals can consent to marriage, and as discussed above, that consent is what validates the marriage. The lack of valid consent through force or coercion, then, is an integral part of what makes imposing the status of marriage a grievous violation of the victim's autonomy and abhorrent to human rights.

It is also vital that the status imposed on the victim by the perpetrator be classified as the *right of marriage* or the *right of a spouse* rather than the *right of ownership*, which attaches in cases of enslavement or sexual slavery. First, this highlights the fact that forced marriage is a perversion of the protected institution of marriage which is one of the reasons it is repugnant to international law and custom. Second, there are conceivably situations where an individual could be forced into a marriage and unable to escape the perpetrating spouse because of the obligations and duties placed upon that person by marriage, but where the perpetrator has not attached the right of ownership to the spouse. Without this distinction, there is a substantial risk that the perpetrators of forced marriage will be able to avoid prosecution for their conduct under the enslavement crimes because they "married" their victims, which does not rise to the depravation of liberty required for enslavement.

The second element of the crime recognizes, in a manner not available under any of the enumerated crimes against humanity, that there is more to the crime of forced marriage than the sexual crimes committed against the victim during the forced marriage. The second element is constructed this way for several reasons. It acknowledges the range of constituent acts that may be present in a forced marriage and that those constituent acts may extend beyond sexual acts alone. Forced marriage can properly be defined as a sexually based crime against humanity. However, as was discussed with respect to the first element, for the crime to constitute forced marriage, the perpetrator must have imposed the status of spouse upon the victim. The rights owed to a spouse within a marriage encompass more than conjugal duties; they also include all acts necessary to establish and maintain a family, such as domestic labor, childbearing, and child rearing. This necessitates adding forced labor, childbearing, and child rearing to the list of constituent acts that define forced marriage.

---

[109] *See* Elements of Crimes, *supra* note 40, art. 7(1)(a)–(i).

Including these other acts does not diminish the severity and gravity of the sexual violence suffered by the victims of forced marriage, nor does it suggest that forced acts of a sexual nature are insufficient alone to constitute a crime meeting the other three criteria to the status of forced marriage. It is simply meant to recognize that because the rights of a spouse extend beyond sexual intercourse, the range of acts the victim of forced marriage may suffer extends beyond sexual acts. This construction also broadens the reach of forced marriage to situations where the perpetrator has imposed the status of marriage on a victim, the victim has the social and legal status of a spouse, and the victim is forced into domestic labor and child rearing, but there is no sexual element.

Moreover, it puts the proper emphasis on *all* of the constituent acts that make up forced marriage. When forced marriage was compared previously with sexual slavery and enslavement, difficulties arose regarding how much importance to place on the sexual violence inherent in the crime. With the enumerated crimes against humanity, it was an all-or-nothing situation; either the sexual element of the crime was not addressed in the elements of the crime, or it was the only aspect of the crime addressed. Neither of these extremes is appropriate in the case of forced marriage. This construction finds a suitable middle ground by acknowledging the sexual violence that is integral to the crime of forced marriage while simultaneously recognizing that the sexual acts are not the *only* constituent acts and that there is more to forced marriage than sexual violence alone.

It also bears mentioning that the list is not meant to be exhaustive, but merely illustrative of some of the traditionally recognized duties of one spouse to another. Different cultures define those duties and rights owed between spouses within a marriage differently. The expected duties of a spouse should always be considered within the cultural context of the situation.

The third element is included to acknowledge the inequity of the rights of the "spouses" within the forced marriage and to emphasize the fact that the victimized spouse suffers a severe deprivation of liberty. According to some of the major international human rights instruments, both spouses should have equal rights within the marriage as well as to the dissolution of the marriage. Within a forced marriage, however, no such equality exists; the recourses normally available to a spouse in a situation of marital inequality, sexual violence, physical violence, and forced labor, namely dissolution of the marital state, are lost to the victim of forced marriage, effectively trapping her with the perpetrating spouse.

The fourth and fifth elements of forced marriage are shared with all crimes against humanity. The fourth distinguishes the conduct as a crime against humanity.[110] Crimes against humanity do not encompass acts committed against enemy combatants; those crimes are relegated to the area of war crimes. It is the systematic and widespread nature of the conduct that elevates it to the status of a crime against humanity and brings it within the jurisdiction of the Special Court rather than the jurisdiction of the state courts. To be a crime against humanity, the crime must be of such a magnitude that it constitutes an attack on *humanity* and not simply a sporadic event. The fifth element is the subjective *mens rea*, element of all crimes against humanity. The intent element extends beyond the criminal intent (recklessness) of the underlying crime and also requires that the perpetrator know the offense is part of a broader system or policy of widespread abuse. It is not necessary that the perpetrator

---

[110] CASSESE, *supra* note 23, § 4.1.

anticipate all the consequences of the conduct, only that he is aware of the risk that the conduct will yield grave consequences. It is also not necessary for the perpetrator to know that his conduct is part of a broader policy, just that there is an attack on a civilian population and that he is a part of that attack. This element also helps to distinguish crimes against humanity from war crimes.

VI. CONCLUSION

The mandate of the Special Court for Sierra Leone was to "prosecute persons who bear the greatest responsibility for serious violations of international humanitarian law and Sierra Leonean law committed in the territory of Sierra Leone since 30 November 1996."[111] Recognizing forced marriage as a crime against humanity under the categorization of "other inhumane acts" was a significant legal development that assisted the Special Court in carrying out that mandate. Thousands of women were abducted during the conflict and forced into marriage with men who had murdered their friends and families. Trapped in these marriages, women endured unimaginable suffering as their most fundamental human rights were stripped away though rape, violence, torture, forced pregnancy, and forced labor. The perpetrators used the rights and privileges attached to a protected institution to bind their victims to them, to the extent that many victims of forced marriage remain "married" to their captor-husbands today. Forced marriage is unique and distinct from the other crimes against humanity, which are inadequate to capture all of the conduct that constitutes a forced marriage. The offense properly describes the conduct that does comprise a forced marriage, or characterize the experiences of the victims. The most efficient way, then, for the court to address these violations of humanitarian and international law is to recognize and prosecute forced marriage as the unique crime that it is.

Unfortunately, the crime of forced marriage has not been confined to the situation in Sierra Leone. The defendants in Case 002 currently pending before the Extraordinary Chambers in the Courts of Cambodia were charged with forced marriage as a crime against humanity.[112] The Closing Order issued in 2010 by the investigative judges of the Cambodia Tribunal indicated that the Khmer Rouge would perform group ceremonies, forcing twenty to thirty couples at a time with the threat of execution to marry partners drawn from a hat.[113] The elements of the crime of forced marriage developed above could apply to the Cambodia Tribunal proceedings as well.

Throughout this chapter, the crime of forced marriage is discussed as a crime against women, and it is assumed that the forced spouse is the wife. It is for the sake of clarity that this assumption is made. This chapter addresses the crime of forced marriage within the context of the conflict in Sierra Leone, and in that conflict the victimized spouse was always the "wife." But it is important that forced marriage should be universally condemned regardless of the victimized spouse's gender. Thus in the Cambodia context, both spouses could be viewed as the victims of the crime against humanity of forced marriage.

---

[111] Agreement between the United Nations and the Government of Sierra Leone on the Establishment of a Special Court for Sierra Leone, at 1(1) (Jan. 16, 2002), *available at* http://www.sc-sl.org/scsl-agreement.html.

[112] Closing Order, Prosecutor v. Nuon, Ieng, Khieu and Ieng, ECCC, Office of the Co-Investigating Judges, at paras. 1442–1447 (Sept. 15, 2010).

[113] *Id.* at para. 842.

11

Forced Marriage at the Special Court for Sierra Leone: Questions of Jurisdiction, Legality, Specificity, and Consistency

Sidney Thompson[*]

I. INTRODUCTION

In recent decades, international criminal law has seen a slow and uneven but nevertheless grow-ing recognition of the need to fully account for the nature of sexual violence suffered by victims during times of conflict. The crime of forced marriage, charged and adjudicated for the first time at the international level by the Special Court for Sierra Leone (SCSL), advanced the state of the law in this area and was just one aspect of what was on balance a progressive and robust prose-cutorial commitment to the investigation and prosecution of crimes of a sexual nature.

However, the value of the SCSL's jurisprudence on forced marriage as a precedent in international criminal law is unfortunately diminished by a lack of precision in the plead-ings, procedural concerns, and variation in the legal findings relating to the nature of the alleged criminal conduct both within each of the Trial Chamber's own jurisprudence as well as between the Trial Chambers and the Appeals Chamber. This variation extended not only to the finer details of the constituent acts of the crime, but also to fundamental con-siderations such as whether forced marriage was in fact a sexual crime at all. That such core issues remained unsettled during the course of the Armed Forces Revolutionary Council (AFRC) and Revolutionary United Front (RUF) trials raises concerns related to the *nul-lum crimen sine lege* principle and whether the accused persons can be said to have been on adequate notice of the nature of the charge. Insofar as this also opens up the findings to criticism on the legitimacy of the process, it weakens the quality of the justice provided to the victims of the conflict in Sierra Leone.

II. QUESTIONS OF JURISDICTION, LEGALITY, AND LIMITED SPECIFICITY IN PLEADING

A. Addition of Forced Marriage to the Indictments

In February 2004, approximately one year after the first Indictments were filed against the six individuals charged from the AFRC and RUF forces, the Prosecution filed new Indictments

[*] B.A. (Hons.), LL.B., B.C.L., LL.M.; Crown Counsel with the Public Prosecution Service of Canada. From 2007 through 2010, she was a Legal Officer in Chambers at the Special Court for Sierra Leone on the *Armed Forces Revolutionary Council* and *Charles Taylor* Trials. She has also worked with the Office of the Prosecutor at the U.N. International Criminal Tribunal for Rwanda and as a Prosecutor in the Territory of Nunavut in Canada's eastern arctic region.

joining the charges against the three Accused aligned with the RUF[1] and the charges against the three Accused aligned with the AFRC,[2] thereby streamlining the cases into two trials. The sexual crimes pled in these joint Indictments were rape, sexual slavery and any other form of sexual violence, and outrages on personal dignity.[3] Four days after filing the joined Indictments, and about five months before the start of the RUF trial[4] and eleven months before the AFRC trial,[5] the Prosecution requested leave to amend the Indictments.[6] It moved to add "Count 8: Other Inhumane Act, a Crime Against Humanity, punishable under 2.i. of the Statute"[7] as well as the following particulars to every paragraph relating to the sexual crimes alleged to have occurred in the various districts of Sierra Leone:

> [...] members of the AFRC/RUF raped hundreds of women and girls at various locations throughout the District [...] An unknown number of women and girls were abducted from various locations within the District and used as sex slaves *and/or forced into "marriages." The "wives" were forced to perform a number of conjugal duties under coercion by their "husbands."*[8] (Amended particulars in italics)

The Prosecution did not propose to disclose fresh evidence to support the count.[9] Rather, it argued that the additional charge was merely a new legal characterization of facts already disclosed.[10]

Only three of the accused persons in the AFRC and RUF cases, Augustine Gbao, Issa Sesay, and Santigie Borbor Kanu, objected to the Prosecution's motions to amend the Indictments.[11] Among other lines of argument, the accused persons complained that the proposed charge was too vague,[12] imprecisely defined,[13] did not comply with the principles of specificity[14] or legality,[15] and that the addition of the proposed charge would violate Rule 47 of the Rules of Procedure and Evidence (RPE), which requires a judge to be satisfied that an indictment charges a suspect with a crime within the jurisdiction of the court and that

---

[1] Indictment, Sesay et al. (SCSL-04–15-PT-005) (Feb. 5, 2004).

[2] Indictment, Brima et al. (SCSL-04–14-PT-006) (Feb. 5, 2004).

[3] The trials against the three Accused affiliated with the CDF were also joined, but no sexual crimes were charged. The Prosecution later sought to amend the joined Indictment to include sexual crimes, but this was rejected by Trial Chamber I. This issue is discussed further later in the chapter.

[4] The RUF trial opened on July 5, 2004.

[5] The AFRC trial opened on March 7, 2005.

[6] At this point in time, Trial Chamber II, which would later take carriage of the AFRC trial, had not yet been convened; Request to Amend the Indictment, Sesay et al. (SCSL-04–15-PT-007) (Feb. 9, 2004); Request for Leave to Amend the Indictment, Brima et al. (SCSL-04–16-PT-011) (Feb. 9, 2004).

[7] *Id.* at para. 11.

[8] *Id.*

[9] *Id.* at para. 12.

[10] It argued "[t]he factual allegations underlying the new count are the same factual allegations contained in the current Consolidated indictment against the accused [...] which support the sexual violence charges in Counts 6–8 [...]." *Id.* at para. 10 (both motions).

[11] Kallon did not respond directly to this motion, but brought a related motion requesting that the Indictment against him be quashed in its entirety.

[12] Response to Prosecution's Motion to Amend the Indictment, Sesay et al. (SCSL-2004–15-PT-020), Gbao, para. 13 (Feb. 19, 2004) [hereinafter Gbao Response].

[13] *Id.*

[14] Kanu Defense Response to Prosecution's Request for Leave to Amend the Indictment, Brima et al. (SCSL-04–16-PT-021), para. 5 (Feb. 17, 2004) [hereinafter Kanu Response].

[15] Response to Prosecution's Motion to Amend the Indictment, Sesay et al. (SCSL-2004–15-PT-021), Sesay, para. 4 (Feb. 19, 2004) [hereinafter Sesay Response].

the charges contain sufficient particulars.[16] Both the Prosecution and Defense also made extensive arguments about the timing of the motions and the potential prejudice to the accused persons.[17]

In nearly identical decisions deciding the motions in favor of the Prosecution in both cases, the majority of Trial Chamber I focused almost exclusively on the timing and prejudice arguments raised.[18] It remarked upon the need for international criminal justice to recognize the importance of bringing alleged perpetrators of sexual crimes to justice, observing that the Prosecution should exercise "vigilance, diligence, and attention" in its investigations so as to bring evidence of such crimes before the court.[19] The Trial Chamber found that the Prosecution had properly gathered such evidence during its investigations, as demonstrated by the inclusion of the other sexual crimes in the Indictments, and concluded that as the material facts of the new charge had long been disclosed to the Defense, the amendment of the Indictments would not unduly prejudice the accused persons.[20]

Notably, however, the Trial Chamber did not make any direct findings with regard to the Defense complaints that the charge of forced marriage lacked specificity and that it violated the principle of legality. Nor did the Trial Chamber cite or address Rule 47. In permitting the charge of forced marriage to be added to the Indictments without responding to these complaints, the Trial Chamber not only missed an opportunity to provide much-needed clarity that could have given greater focus to the trials and judgments, but arguably committed a procedural error in permitting a charge to be laid against the accused persons that was vaguely articulated and over which the Court had not affirmatively established having jurisdiction.

B. *Jurisdiction and Other Inhumane Acts*

As a hybrid tribunal, the Statute of the SCSL establishes the Court's jurisdiction over international crimes such as crimes against humanity, violations of common Article 3 to the

---

[16] Kanu Response, *supra* note 14, at paras. 3–4.

[17] The defense teams also argued that the speciality principle prohibited the prosecution of the Accused on charges other than those on which he was previously arrested (see Kanu Response, *supra* note 14, at para. 9); that the Prosecution failed to disclose the new charge promptly (see Kanu Response, *supra* note 14, at para. 9; Gbao Response, *supra* note 12, at paras. 3, 9–11, 14; Sesay Response, *supra* note 15, at para. 5); and that the amendment would require additional investigations to be undertaken very near to the start of the trial causing prejudice to the Accused and an unjustified delay in the trials (see Gbao Response, *supra* note 12, at paras. 11–13, 15; Sesay Response, *supra* note 15, at paras. 6, 9–11). The Prosecution countered that the count did not violate the principle of specificity as it was not charged as "forced marriage" per se, but as an "other inhumane act" the elements of which are clear and unambiguous, see Kanu Response, *supra* note 14, at para. 13. It also argued that forced marriage amounted to a crime against humanity as it was an act of comparable seriousness and met the requirements of an "other inhumane act." It did not specifically address Rule 47, but submitted that in order for a determination to be made as to whether forced marriage constituted a crime against humanity, the charge must be alleged in the Indictment so it could be considered at trial. See Kanu Response, *supra* note 14, at paras. 4–12.

[18] Decision on Prosecution Request for Leave to Amend the Indictment, Sesay et al. (SCSL-2004–15-PT-108), Trial Chamber, para. 27 (May 6, 2004); Note that oral arguments were also heard during a status conference on March 2 and 3, 2004; however, the transcripts of these have not been published on the SCSL website.

[19] *Id.* at para. 34.

[20] *Id.* at para. 51. In his Dissenting Opinion, Thompson J. mirrored the focus of the majority on the potential prejudice to the accused persons. Given the potential for additional delay in granting leave to amend and in consideration of the right of the Accused to a fair and expeditious trial, Thompson J. would have denied the motion. *Id.*, Dissenting Opinion of Judge Bankole Thompson.

Geneva Conventions and Additional Protocol II, and other serious violations of international humanitarian law, as well as domestic Sierra Leonean crimes such as offenses relating to the abuse of girls and wanton destruction of property.[21] An element of jurisdiction that is not explicitly set out by the Statute, but that is implied by the principle of legality, also known as *nullum crimen sine lege*, is that an accused may not be held criminally responsible for an act that did not constitute a crime at the time he or she is alleged to have committed it. This is a fundamental principle of criminal law and is recognized as being part of international customary law.[22]

The SCSL Statute, adopted by Sierra Leone and the United Nations following Security Council Resolution 1315,[23] codifies existing international and domestic crimes but it has no legislative authority and cannot, in and of itself, create new crimes. Thus, it is not correct to conclude that an alleged crime does not violate the *nullum crimen sine lege* principle simply because it appears in the Statute. Rather, it must be established that the alleged crime was in existence either as a matter of domestic Sierra Leonean law or as customary international law during the temporal jurisdiction of the court, namely as of November 30, 1996.[24]

For most of the crimes set out in the SCSL Statute there is little need to assess jurisdiction as the Statute codifies conduct that was clearly criminalized in domestic Sierra Leonean law or in customary international law prior to the conflict in Sierra Leone. However, this cannot be said unequivocally when it comes to the charge of other inhumane acts. Although there is no question of the customary international law status of other inhumane acts itself,[25] the reference is not in fact to a single known crime, but rather to a residual *category* of crimes against humanity.[26] Put simply, "[t]here is no crime labeled 'other inhumane acts' under any source of international or national law."[27] By its very definition "other inhumane acts" cannot be exhaustively set out and defined.[28] Rather, alleged conduct may be found to amount to an other inhumane act where it satisfies the requisite elements, including that the act resulted in great suffering or serious injury to body, mental, or physical health and that the act is of a similar gravity to the other crimes against humanity set out in the Statute.[29] Thus,

---

[21] SCSL Statute arts. 3–5.

[22] Thus, for example, Article 22(1) of the Rome Statute states that "[a] person shall not be criminally responsible [...] unless the conduct in question constitutes, at the time it takes place, a crime within the jurisdiction of the Court."

[23] SCSL Statute, Preamble. The Statute was adopted following Security Council Resolution 1315 (2000) of August 14, 2000.

[24] SCSL Statute art. 1.

[25] Notably, other inhumane acts were included among the list of crimes against humanity set out in Article 6(c) of the Charter of the International Military Tribunal at Nuremberg. Other inhumane acts also appear in the definition of Crimes Against Humanity in Article II of Law No. 10 of the Control Council for Germany.

[26] *See* Commentary of the International Law Commission, which states with reference to other inhumane acts that "this *category* of acts is intended to include only additional acts that are similar in gravity to those listed in the preceding subparagraphs." I.L.C. Draft Code of Crimes Against the Peace and Security of Mankind, *Report of the International Law Commission on the Work of Its Forty-Eighth Session*, May 6–July 26, 1996, G.A.O.R., 51st Sess., Supp. No. 10, 30, U.N. Doc. A/51/10.

[27] M. Cherif Bassiouni, Crimes against Humanity: Historical Evolution and Contemporary Application 405 (2011).

[28] *See, e.g.*, Judgment, Kayishema and Ruzindana, Trial Chamber, para. 150 (May 21, 1999).

[29] Judgment, Brima et al. (SCSL-04–16-T-613), Trial Chamber, para. 698 (June 20, 2007) adopting the Rome Statute, Elements of Crimes, art. 7(l)(k).

other inhumane acts are in some respects best understood as a threshold test of allegedly criminal conduct.[30]

When forced marriage was charged in the AFRC and RUF Indictments as an other inhumane act under Article 2.i. of the Statute, it was not presumptively evident that the alleged conduct fell within the court's jurisdiction. Rather, the conduct alleged would fall within the jurisdiction of the court only *if* it met the threshold requirements of other inhumane acts.[31] This was an especially pertinent consideration given that forced marriage had never previously been litigated before any international tribunal and thus the question of whether the conduct alleged met the threshold requirements of other inhumane acts had never previously been examined.

C. *Judicial Oversight of the Court's Jurisdiction*

In arguing for leave to amend the Indictments to include forced marriage, the Prosecution submitted that the status of the charge as a crime against humanity should be evaluated at trial.[32] However, there is a good argument to be made that this assessment could and should have been undertaken *before* such leave was granted. In the first place, it is consistent with the fundamental principles of *nullem crimen sine lege* in that an accused person should not be required to defend against a charge that does not amount to a crime at the time he or she was alleged to have committed it.[33] Judicial oversight in this respect is an important limitation on prosecutorial discretion. Additionally, it serves to ensure that the court's time and resources are not diverted to hearing evidence and argument throughout the course of a trial in proof of a charge that may in any event be found to be moot.

Moreover, Rules 47 and 50 of the SCSL RPE specifically require such judicial oversight. At the SCSL, as at the ad hoc tribunals for the former Yugoslavia and Rwanda, following investigations and when first submitted by a Prosecutor, indictments are subject to approval, also known as confirmation, by a Designated Judge. SCSL Rule 47 (B) specifies that the Prosecutor must be satisfied that the crimes of which the accused is suspected fall within the jurisdiction of the Court and only then can the Prosecutor prepare and submit an indictment for approval by the Designated Judge.[34] Thereafter, according to Rule 47(E), the Designated Judge must review the proposed indictment, together with the accompanying material provided by the Prosecutor, and may approve it only if he or she is satisfied that "the indictment charges the suspect with a crime or crimes *within the jurisdiction* of the Special Court."[35]

---

[30] For a consideration of forced marriage in relation to the elements of other inhumane acts, see M. Scharf & S. Mattler, *Forced Marriage: Exploring the Viability of the Special Court for Sierra Leone's New Crime against Humanity*, Case Research Paper Series in Legal Studies, Working Paper 05–35 (Oct. 2005), *available at* http://ssrn.com/abstract=824291 (last visited June 10, 2012).

[31] *See* N. Goodfellow, *The Miscategorization of "Forced Marriage" as a Crime against Humanity by the Special Court for Sierra Leone*, 11 INT'L CRIM. L. REV. 5, 831–67 (2011).

[32] Reply to Defense Response to Prosecution Request for Leave to Amend the Indictment, Brima et al. (SCSL-2004–16-PT-023), Kanu, paras. 4–12 (Feb. 20, 2004).

[33] J. Lincoln, *Nullum Crimen Sine Lege in International Criminal Tribunal Jurisprudence: The Problem of the Residual Category of Crime*, 7 EYES ON THE ICC 137 (2010–2011).

[34] Rule 47, SCSL RPE (emphasis added).

[35] Rule 47(E)(i), SCSL RPE (emphasis added). It is interesting to note that the corresponding Rule 47 in the RPE of the ICTY and ICTR does not explicitly contain a jurisdictional review requirement although the powers

Whereas Rule 47 governs the initial approval of indictments, Rule 50 governs any subsequent amendments. It specifies that once an Accused has had his or her initial appearance, leave of the Trial Chamber is required before any further amendment can be made. In granting leave to amend, Rule 50 does not specifically demand that the Trial Chamber satisfy itself that the requirements of Rule 47 including the jurisdictional requirement have been met. However, as a matter of procedural equity, the Prosecution should not be able to evade satisfaction of the jurisdictional requirement when a charge is laid subsequently as an amendment to the indictment rather than being included within the initial set of charges. Indeed, Rules 47 and 50 taken together suggest that the Trial Chamber should have satisfied itself that forced marriage was in fact a crime within the jurisdiction of the Court before granting leave for the charge to be added to the RUF and AFRC Indictments. This is consistent with the gatekeeping role of the Designated Judge under Rule 47 or the Trial Chamber under Rule 50.

Where a Designated Judge is satisfied that all the charges relate to crimes within the jurisdiction of the Court and confirms an indictment, it nevertheless remains open to the Defense to contest that indictment including questions of jurisdiction, especially during the pretrial phase. Similarly, the Defense may raise questions of jurisdiction where the Prosecution in a later course of trial seeks leave to amend an indictment. Although such arguments were made by the Defense when the Prosecution sought leave to amend the AFRC and RUF Indictments, they were not addressed by Trial Chamber I. As is discussed further later in the chapter, in fact, the determination of whether forced marriage constituted a crime against humanity was not explicitly undertaken until Trial Chamber II rendered its Final Judgment in the AFRC case.

D. *Limited Specificity in the Pleading of Forced Marriage*

One of the core rights of an accused person is the right to know the case against him or her. Article 17(4)(a) of the SCSL Statute, which is a verbatim recitation of Article 14(3)(a) of the International Covenant on Civil and Political Rights,[36] affords an accused as a "minimum guarantee" the right "to be informed promptly and in detail [...] of the nature and cause of the charge against him or her."[37] The provision of detailed information about the "nature" and "cause" of the charge are two distinct components of the right. According to the jurisprudence of the ad hoc tribunals, an indictment is sufficiently clear only if it enables the accused to "fully understand" both of these components.[38] The "nature of the charges" has been interpreted to mean "the precise legal qualifications of the offence," and the "cause of the charge" has been interpreted to mean the facts underlying it.[39] The key issue at play is notice: an indictment must contain all the material facts and inform the accused of the charges against him or her with sufficient detail that he or she may properly prepare his or her defense.

---

and responsibilities of the reviewing Judge under those rules are more extensive and implicitly extend to this level of review. ICTR and ICTY Rule 47 also incorporates by reference Article 19 of the Statutes of the ICTY.

[36] ICCPR, art. 14(3)(a).

[37] SCSL Statute art. 17(4)(a).

[38] V. Tochilovsky, Indictment, Disclosure, Admissibility of Evidence: Jurisprudence of the ICTY and ICTR 2 (2004).

[39] *Id.* at 3.

As with the judicial oversight of the Court's jurisdiction detailed above, the SCSL RPE also provides for judicial oversight of the sufficiency of particulars in an indictment. Rule 47 (E)(ii) states that a judge may only approve the indictment if satisfied that "the allegations in the prosecution's case summary would, if proven, amount to the crime or crimes as particularized in the indictment." This logically requires that to be approved, an indictment must contain sufficient particulars to make out the crime.

Generally, an indictment need not specify the precise elements of each alleged crime;[40] however, this poses some difficulties when a charge is pled as an other inhumane act because unlike other crimes, the precise criminal conduct alleged cannot be incorporated by reference to the recognized elements of the crime.[41] That is to say that reference to the established elements of other inhumane acts is of little guidance in determining the particular alleged criminal conduct. Where a specific other inhumane act has previously been adjudicated upon, an accepted articulation of the nature of the criminalized conduct may exist that can be adopted by reference. However, this was not the case when forced marriage was added to the AFRC and RUF Indictments.

The Trial Chamber in the Kupreskic case at the ICTY dealt directly with challenges to the principle of specificity posed by other inhumane acts. It expressed concern that "this category lacks precision and is too general to provide a safe yardstick for the work of the Tribunal and hence, that it is contrary to the principle of the 'specificity' of criminal law."[42] It suggested that the *ejusdem generis* rule of interpretation, that is expressions that cover actions similar to those specifically provided for, is not of great assistance[43] and that a better indication of the legal standards that would allow the Tribunal to identify the prohibited inhumane acts could be found, for example, in international standards on human rights such as those laid down in the Universal Declaration and the two United Nations Covenants on Human Rights.[44]

The Kupreskic Trial Chamber's reference to *ejusedem generis* in its analysis of specificity reinforces the fact that it is intertwined with the principle of legality. In short, if interpretation by way of *ejusedem generis* is not "carefully circumscribed," it may be deemed a violation of the principles of legality.[45] Similarly, Article 22(2) of the Rome Statute states:

[t]he definition of a crime shall be strictly construed and shall not be extended by analogy. In case of ambiguity, the definition shall be interpreted in favour of the person being investigated, prosecuted or convicted.[46]

Indictments at the ad hoc tribunals tend to contain fewer particulars than those in most domestic jurisdictions.[47] In large part, this is recognition of the practical difficulties inherent

---

[40] *Id.* at 4.

[41] A similar concern arises with regard to the pleading of outrages on personal dignity, a violation of Common Article 3 of the Geneva Conventions and Additional Protocol II.

[42] Judgment, Kupreskic (IT-95-16-T), Trial Chamber, para. 563 (Jan. 14, 2000).

[43] *Id.* at para. 564.

[44] *Id.* at paras. 565–566.

[45] Bassiouni, *supra* note 27.

[46] Rome Statute, art. 22(2).

[47] SCSL RPE Rule 47(C) as well as the corresponding Rule 47(C) in the RPE of the ICTY and ICTR requires that an indictment contain [...] the name and particulars of the suspect, a statement of each specific offense of which the named suspect is charged and a short description of the particulars of the offense.

in capturing in detail the nature of crimes that are alleged to have occurred on an immense scale such as during the conflicts in the former Yugoslavia and Rwanda.[48] A similar justification can be offered at the SCSL given the scale of the crimes committed during the war in Sierra Leone. However, even taking this into consideration, the indictments before the SCSL are notably more abbreviated than even those at the ICTY and ICTR.

The rationale for such particularly abbreviated indictments at the SCSL lies in the philosophy adopted when the Court was first established. It was designed to be a more efficient and less costly tribunal than the ICTR and ICTY.[49] Indictments were brought only against a limited number of individuals believed to bear the greatest responsibility for the crimes committed during the conflict, and it was originally predicted that trials could be completed in as little as three years.[50] The initial burst of activity on the part of the Office of the Prosecutor and its investigators was remarkable. Within only seven months of operation in-country, the Prosecution was able to present eight Indictments for confirmation,[51] and the remaining five were confirmed within the year. Yet, such extraordinary speed may have occasioned a reduction in detail when it came to the pleading of the Indictments. For example, not only did they tend to contain fewer charges than those at the ICTR, they also utilized a brief form of pleading known as "notice pleading."[52] Thus, although the Indictments contained fewer charges, they covered a "great breadth but little depth" of alleged criminal conduct.[53]

The particulars added to the AFRC and RUF Indictments in relation to forced marriage were skeletal. Following the allegations that an unknown number of women and girls were raped, abducted, and used as sex slaves by members of the AFRC/RUF in the various districts of Sierra Leone, the Prosecution inserted the following words: "and/or forced into 'marriages.' The wives were forced to perform a number of conjugal duties under coercion by their 'husbands.'"

This brief manner of pleading invites a substantial amount of interpretation and arguably, was insufficient to inform the accused persons before the SCSL in detail of the nature and cause of the charge against them as required by Article 17(4)(a). To illustrate, the particulars do not in and of themselves[54] establish whether the Prosecution understood forced marriage to include the crimes of rape and sexual slavery as constituent elements or whether it

---

[48] R. May & M. Wierda, International Criminal Evidence para. 2.60 (2002); H. Klann, *Vagueness of Indictment: Rules to Safeguard the Rights of the Accused*, in From Human Rights to International Criminal Law: Studies in Honour of an African Jurist, the Late Judge Laïty Kama 111 (Emmanuel Decaux, Adama Dieng & Malik Sow, eds. 2007).

[49] A. Cassese (Independent Expert), *Report on the Special Court for Sierra Leone*, at 1 (Dec. 12, 2006).

[50] T. Cruveillier & M. Wierda, *The Special Court for Sierra Leone: The First Eighteen Months*, International Center for Transitional Justice, Case Study Series, Mar. 2004, at 1, *available at* http://ictj.org/publication/special-court-sierra-leone-first-eighteen-months (last visited Mar. 30, 2011).

[51] *Id.* at 4.

[52] *Id.*

[53] *See* C. Rose, *Troubled Indictments at the Special Court for Sierra Leone: The Pleading of Joint Criminal Enterprise and Sex-Based Crimes*, 7 J. Int'l Crim. Just. 353–72 (2009).

[54] As is detailed below, in its submissions on the motions to amend the Indictments and in other documents before the court, the Prosecution laid out more details on its conception of the crime of forced marriage. It also established its intention to plead the crimes cumulatively. Where an indictment is found to be defective, these articulations may help to determine whether the accused was nevertheless on notice of the charge. They may not, however, be read into the indictment or be used to determine whether the indictment was sufficient in the first place.

understood forced marriage to be a stand-alone crime made-up of the act of forcing a victim into "marriage" and the forced performance of conjugal duties. Moreover, the particulars provide no guidance as to what specific acts were being alleged as "conjugal duties" – a term that even in its plain meaning is incapable of precision. The particulars do not indicate whether the "marriages" contemplated were unions recognized as binding and legitimate under custom or law or alternatively, whether the term "marriage" was invoked as an expedient description of the relationship between the perpetrator and the victim that mimics but also perverts customary or legal understandings of the term. Nor do the particulars explain whether the "marriages" were understood to be exclusive relationships between the perpetrator and the victim.

Given the potential scope of interpretation arising from the skeletal pleading of forced marriage, a question can be raised as to the degree to which the accused persons can realistically be said to have been on proper notice of the nature and cause of the crime with which they had been charged. As is set out in the following section, this was compounded by varying articulations of the constituent elements of forced marriage made by the Prosecution and the Trial Chambers over the course of the AFRC and RUF trials. A comprehensive description of the alleged criminal conduct encompassed by the charge of forced marriage was not provided by the Prosecution until it submitted its Final Trial Brief in the AFRC case, and the final judicial adoption of a definition of forced marriage and its constituent acts came only with the delivery of the AFRC Appeals Judgment, approximately four years after the charge was first pled.

III. SHIFTING PROSECUTORIAL ARTICULATIONS AND VARIED JUDICIAL FINDINGS

A. Forced Marriage Added to the Indictments as a Crime of a Sexual Nature

The first indication of the specific acts or criminal conduct the Prosecution intended to be encompassed in its allegations of forced marriage was provided in an investigator's statement annexed to the Prosecution motions to amend the Indictments in the AFRC and RUF cases. The investigator attested as follows:

> I have found that the acts of sexual violence committed against women and girls within the temporal jurisdiction of the Special Court was not limited to rape and the use of women as sex slaves but also includes the abduction and forcing of women into conjugal-like relationships or forced "marriages" by the AFRC/RUF leadership and their subordinates. These women were commonly referred to as "bush wives" and often kept for the exclusive use of their captors.
>
> [...]
>
> In the instances where the women were taken as "bush wives," they were confined and prevented from escaping through various forms of coercion, usually through the use or threat of serious physical harm. The "wives" were forced not only to provide sexual services but also perform a range of conjugal duties including domestic chores, in some cases having children and taking care of the family – including their rebel "husbands." As a result of the stigma attached to their association with members women are still "married" to their captors.[55]

---

[55] Request to Amend the Indictment, Annex B, Sesay et al. (SCSL-04–15-PT-007), paras. 5–7 (Feb. 9, 2004).

At its most inclusive interpretation, this description suggests that forced marriage might encompass (1) rape or other types of sexual violence ("sexual services"); (2) sexual slavery; (3) abduction; (4) forcing women and girls into "conjugal-like relationships"; (5) assertion of the status of "bush wife" over the victim; (6) exclusivity of the relationship; (7) captivity; (8) threat of nonsexual physical harm; (9) forced performance of "conjugal duties" defined as including domestic chores, child rearing and taking care of the "husband"; (10) pregnancy; and (11) a relationship that continues after the end of hostilities. The use of the term "conjugal-like relationships" and the quotations inserted around the words "marriage," "bush wives," "wives," "husbands", and "married" suggests that at this point the Prosecution did not intend to allege that the relationships between the perpetrators and victims involved the attempt to forcibly establish formal marriages recognized in law or by custom.

In a subsequent submission during the amendment of the Indictments phase, the Prosecution described the crime slightly differently, arguing that forced marriage encompassed coercion, sexual violence, and enslavement and that enslavement itself is *indicated* by some of the acts enumerated above, including forced labor and sex.[56] In this same submission, the Prosecution also clarified that forced marriage was being charged cumulatively to rape and sexual slavery, and by inference confirmed its understanding that forced marriage may be inclusive of the constituent acts of rape and sexual slavery.[57]

The Prosecution's Pre-Trial Brief in the RUF case was filed on March 1, 2004[58] and in the AFRC case on March 5, 2004,[59] both just weeks after the motions for leave to amend the Indictments to add the charge of forced marriage had been filed. In terms of their articulations related to forced marriage, the briefs were similar. In them, the Prosecution stated that women and girls were raped, abducted, forcibly married, and forced to carry out conjugal duties and domestic chores.[60] The Pre-Trial Briefs slightly expanded upon

---

[56] It stated "[...] the act of "forced marriage" encompasses elements of coercion, sexual violence and enslavement. [... it] results in serious mental and physical suffering or injury. The Kunarac Judgment defined enslavement in terms of control and ownership of an individual, restriction or control of an individual's autonomy and freedom of choice or movement, often accruing some gain to the perpetrator. According to the Tribunal, other indications of enslavement include exploitation, citing the example of forced labor, prostitution and sex. Indeed, the act of "forced marriage" may encompass some of these indicators, but the Prosecution believes that it goes beyond that, making it a distinct form of inhumane act." Reply to Defense Response to Prosecution Request for Leave to Amend the Indictment, Brima et al. (SCSL-2004-16-PT-023), para. 9 (Feb. 20, 2004).

[57] *Id.* at para. 8.

[58] Prosecution's Pre-Trial Brief Pursuant to Order for Filing Pre-Trial Briefs (Under Rules 54 and 73*bis*) of Feb. 13, 2004, Sesay et al. (SCSL-2004-15-PT-39) (Mar. 1, 2004) [hereinafter RUF Pre-Trial Brief].

[59] Prosecution's Pre-Trial Brief Pursuant to Order for Filing Pre-Trial Briefs (Under Rules 54 and 73*bis*) of Feb. 13, 2004, Brima et al. (SCSL-2004-16-PT) (Mar. 5, 2004).

[60] Some examples are illustrative: The Prosecution submitted that at the time of the Freetown invasion, sexual violence against women and girls was "often marked by accompanying physical violence, abduction, sexual slavery and forced marriage. Women and young girls were raped during or after an attack, abducted and later forcibly married to AFRC/RUF members. Once 'married,' civilian women were expected to carry out conjugal duties in addition to other forced labour, such as carrying loads." RUF Pre-Trial Brief, *supra* note 58, at para. 65. In describing its allegations in Koinadugu District, the Prosecution stated, "[t]ypically, women and young girls were raped during or after an attack, abducted and later forcibly 'married' to AFRC/RUF members. Once 'married,' civilian women became known as 'bush wives' where they were expected to carry out domestic/conjugal duties in addition to other forced labour, such as carrying loads during troop movements." *Id.* at para. 82.

the Prosecution's prior articulations by suggesting that actual nonsexual physical violence (rather than the threat thereof) might also be involved in forced marriage and that the conjugal duties envisaged included carrying loads.[61] The Prosecution also alleged that in Kono District, "wives" were subjected to rapes from rebels other than their "bush husbands,"[62] which contrasted with the investigator's statement, attached to the motions for leave to amend the Indictments, that the forced marriage relationships were mostly exclusive.

Trial Chamber I's decision granting leave to amend the AFRC and RUF Indictments was handed down two months later on May 6, 2004. In it, the Trial Chamber described forced marriage as being in essence a sexual offense, opining that it "is as much a sexual, indeed, a gender offence as those that were included in the initial individual indictments and that feature in the current consolidated indictment on which this application to amend is based" and could be classified as a "'kindred offence' to those in the consolidated indictment in the view of the commonality of the ingredients needed to prove offences of this nature."[63] It was in large part because of this commonality of elements that the Trial Chamber found that "the amendment sought is not a novelty that should necessitate fresh investigations" and therefore the addition of the new charge would not cause an undue delay of the trial or breach the fair trial rights of the Accused.[64]

In his opening statement in the RUF case a month later, Prosecutor David Crane grouped forced marriage together with other sexual crimes. He indicated the Prosecution's intention to prove that during attacks against civilians by the AFRC/RUF, captured women and girls were raped, abducted, and used as sex slaves and in forced marriage arrangements.[65] He suggested the evidence would show that:

> [w]omen were especially singled out for over a decade; degraded, enslaved, mutilated, assaulted, sodomised and forced to live a life in the bush. We will show that this condition, these forced marriage arrangements, were and are inhumane acts and should forever be recognized as a crime against humanity. Sadly, even today, there are women and girls still in the bush out there in these forced marriage arrangements.[66]

B. Trial Chamber I Indirectly Reverses Itself

Although Trial Chamber I had categorized forced marriage as a sexual or gender crime pled under Article 2(i) of the Statute when it granted leave to amend the Indictments, it indirectly reversed itself in a ruling in the CDF case a year later.

---

[61] "Carrying loads" in the evidence before the SCSL tended to involve victims being forced to carry food, military equipment, looted property or the personal goods of the perpetrator as the troops moved from one location in the bush to another.

[62] "In addition to domestic chores, scores of abducted women and girls were routinely raped and paired with 'rebel husbands' throughout the District. During captivity, many were also subjected to rapes from rebels other than their 'bush husbands.'" RUF Pre-Trial Brief, *supra* note 58, at para. 99.

[63] Decision on Prosecution Request for Leave to Amend the Indictment, Sesay et al. (SCSL-2004–15-PT-108), para. 50 (May 6, 2004).

[64] *Id.* at para. 51.

[65] Transcript, Sesay et al. (SCSL-04–15-T), at 26 (July 5, 2004).

[66] *Id.* at 27.

In the CDF case, the Prosecution did not include charges relating to sexual crimes in the initial Indictments and sought leave to do so during the pretrial phase. Trial Chamber I, with Boutet J. in vigorous dissent, denied leave to amend. Thereafter, the Prosecution attempted to bring evidence of sexual crimes under Counts 3 and 4 of the Indictment relating to physical violence as an other inhumane act under Article 2(i) of the Statute.

However, in an oral ruling on May 24, 2005, with reasons following a month later on June 23, 2005,[67] Trial Chamber I refused to hear any evidence of a sexual nature in the CDF trial, even where such evidence went to proof of other elements of the Prosecution's case. It found that as there were no specific factual allegations of sexual violence under Counts 3 and 4, evidence of sexual violence could not now be introduced thereunder. Both the decision denying leave to amend the Indictment and the decision to exclude evidence of sexual crimes have been roundly criticized for silencing victims of sexual violence by CDF forces and for having perverse effects on the ability of witnesses to testify fully and coherently to the events that occurred.[68]

Beyond these criticisms, however, the decision to exclude evidence of sexual crimes also had a knock-on effect that would open up an interpretation of forced marriage as a *nonsexual* crime. This is because in the same decision, Trial Chamber I declared that no crimes of a sexual nature could be pled under Article 2(i) of the Statute. In what can be fairly described as obiter dicta[69] it found:

> in the light of the separate and distinct residual category of sexual offences under Article 2(g), it is *impermissible* to allege acts of sexual violence (other than rape, sexual slavery, enforced prostitution, forced pregnancy) under Article 2(i) since "*other inhumane acts*," even if residual, must logically be restrictively interpreted as covering only acts of a nonsexual nature amounting to an affront to human dignity.[70]

Although it did not address the contradiction suggesting that the reversal may have been inadvertent, this left Trial Chamber I in the seemingly untenable position of having explicitly permitted a sexual crime (i.e., forced marriage) to be added to the AFRC and RUF Indictments under Article 2(i) of the Statute, but then having expressly denied that this was permissible in the CDF case. Short of a reconsideration of this finding, one of two implications was possible: either forced marriage had been improperly pled and improperly added to the Indictments, or forced marriage was a nonsexual crime.

---

[67] Reasoned Majority Decision on Prosecution Motion for a Ruling on the Admissibility of Evidence, Norman et al. (SCSL-04-14-PT), para. 19 (May 24, 2005) (issued on June 23, 2005).

[68] For a detailed critique of the Court's treatment of gender crimes, see Valerie Oosterveld's Chapter 12 in this volume. Additional articles include S. Kendall & M. Staggs, *Silencing Sexual Violence: Recent Developments in the CDF Case at the Special Court for Sierra Leone* (Berkeley, U.C. Berkeley War Crimes Studies Center, 2005); M. Staggs-Kelsall & S. Stepakoff, *"When We Wanted to Talk about Rape": Silencing Sexual Violence at the Special Court for Sierra Leone*, 1 INT'L J. TRANSNAT'L JUST. 355–74 (2007).

[69] The Trial Chamber did not provide any references to support this conclusion. Nor was it strictly necessary for the Chamber to make this finding. They had already held that the evidence was inadmissible because it did not correspond with the particulars in the Indictment related to the Counts under which the Prosecution sought to bring it.

[70] Reasoned Majority Decision on Prosecution Motion for a Ruling on the Admissibility of Evidence, Norman et al. (SCSL-04-14-PT), para. 19 (May 24, 2005) (issued June 23, 2005).

C. Trial Chamber II Contemplates Forced Marriage as a Nonsexual Crime

On January 17, 2005, a second bench of judges, Trial Chamber II, was sworn in and was assigned to hear the AFRC Trial.[71]

The Prosecution continued in the AFRC case to describe forced marriage as a sexual crime with similar constituent acts as described at the start of the RUF case. Thus, in his opening statement on March 7, 2005, Prosecutor David Crane described the Prosecution's intention to bring evidence of women and girls who had been abducted, coerced into marriages, and forced to cater to the sexual and domestic needs of their rebel husbands.[72] Throughout the AFRC case-in-chief, the Prosecution led evidence of women and girls who were abducted, held in captivity, repeatedly raped, and forced to perform labor such as washing dishes and doing laundry, and who were referred to as "wives."

At the end of the Prosecution's case, the Defense teams brought motions for acquittal under Rule 98 *bis* requesting the Trial Chamber to review the evidentiary record and to acquit the Accused on any aspects of the Indictment for which the Prosecution had not established a prima facie case. In its March 31, 2006 decision on the Rule 98 *bis* motion, Trial Chamber II explicitly extended Trial Chamber I's opinion regarding the impermissibility of charging sexual crimes under Article 2(i) to forced marriage.[73]

Indeed, contrary to all the articulations of the Prosecution up until that point of the AFRC and RUF trials that forced marriage was a sexual crime, and despite the specific finding of Trial Chamber I to this effect when forced marriage was added to the Indictments, Trial Chamber II suggested that forced marriage could be considered as a *nonsexual* crime made up of abduction, submission to marital relationships, and performance of conjugal duties. It held:

> there is evidence which falls within that category relating to the abductions of women and girls and forcing them to submit to "marital" relationships and to perform various conjugal duties. [...] We find that upon such evidence a reasonable tribunal of fact could be satisfied beyond reasonable doubt of the guilt of each of the Accused Brima, Kamara and Kanu for

---

[71] Press Release, SCSL Press and Public Affairs Office, Judges of Second Trial Chamber Sworn In (2005), *available at* http://www.sc-sl.org/PRESSROOM/RegistryPressReleases/2005/tabid/112/Default.aspx (last visited Feb. 15, 2012).

[72] He submitted, "the AFRC/RUF routinely captured and abducted members of the civilian population. Captured women and girls were raped, and many of them were abducted and used as sex slaves and in forced marriages." Transcript, Brima et al. (SCSL-04-16-T), at 27 (Mar. 7, 2005); Following the Freetown invasion, "many of the girls abducted from Freetown were subjected to repeated rapes. The girls were not released until months afterwards. Many were coerced into forced marriages with the rebels and left with no choice but to cater to the sexual and domestic needs of their rebel husbands," *id.* at 33; In Yiffin, in April 1998, "women and girls were routinely captured by the AFRC/RUF troops and shared amongst themselves for their use as wives. Those who were not abducted and given off as wives, were raped," *id.* at 35; Similarly, in Kailahun, the AFRC/RUF "brought with them the women whom they had abducted from various parts of the country and continued to use these women as wives for their domestic and sexual purposes" and "continued to abduct women and girls and forcibly make them their wives, using them to satisfy their various needs, sexual, domestic and other." *Id.* at 38. Following an attack on Karina, "[t]he rebels abducted about 30 women. They forced the women to strip naked. They marched them off. And, like the pieces of property they had looted, they distributed the women as wives amongst themselves." *Id.* at 39.

[73] Decision on Defense Motions for Judgment of Acquittal Pursuant to Rule 98, Brima et al. (SCSL-04-16-T-469), para. 165 (Mar. 31, 2006).

the crime of other inhumane acts as a crime against humanity pursuant to Art. 2.i. of the Statute.[74]

D. Sexual or Nonsexual? Trial Chamber I Does Not Commit

Following the completion of the Prosecution's case-in-chief in the RUF case in September 2006, the RUF Defense teams also filed motions of acquittal under Rule 98 *bis*. The forced marriage charge was hotly contested. The Gbao Defense argued forced marriage did not exist in international law either as a crime against humanity under Count 8 or as a war crime, under Count 9, Outrages on Personal Dignity.[75] The Kallon Defense contested the existence of forced marriage under customary law, and argued that in any event, insufficient evidence had been adduced to prove it.[76] The Sesay Defense took note of Trial Chamber II's findings in its Rule 98 *bis* decision on the impermissibility of pleading forced marriage under Article 2(i) of the Statute and argued that the count ought to be dismissed.[77]

In response, the Prosecution appeared to adapt to Trial Chamber II's findings, altering its prior articulation of forced marriage and arguing that it might or might not include sexual acts. It submitted:

> [e]vidence has been lead of "bush wives" and of women and girls captured by combatants and forced to carry out domestic work and other tasks associated with marital relationships, which may include sexual relations.[78]

In subsequent oral arguments, the Sesay Defense characterized this shift as "trial by ambush" and one that "contradicts completely the *bona fide* submissions [the prosecution] made when trying to amend the Indictment to add Count 8 to it." The Sesay Defense argued it could not be properly on notice in relation to that count.[79]

Trial Chamber I delivered its decisions on the motions for acquittal in the RUF case as an oral ruling two weeks later, on October 25, 2006. It made no reference to its prior findings that it was impermissible to plead sexual crimes under Article 2(i) of the Statute and skirted the issue of whether forced marriage was a crime of a sexual nature. It found that Count 8 "relates generally to sexual violence,"[80] reiterated that the charge was made up of the

---

[74] *Id.* at paras. 165–166.
[75] The Gbao defense submitted:

> There is no separate crime of forced marriage under customary international law. It simply does not exist. In terms of the way in which the prosecution expert defines the concept it cannot be an inhumane act in the form of sexual violence, sexual slavery or other form of violence, an outrage upon personal dignity as a war crime and as a category of sexual violence. Whether sexual violence and mistreatment of a woman falls into the category inhumane act, sexual slavery, other forms of sexual violence is a question of fact in association with the elements of each crime. Forced marriage as a concept adds nothing to the legal evaluation of the guilt or innocence of the accused [sic] should therefore be the subject of a finding of no case to answer.
> Skeletal Argument for Oral Submission Under Rule 98, Sesay et al. (SCSL-2004-15-T-644), Gbao, para. 29 (Sept. 25, 2006).

[76] Revised Skeleton Motion for Judgment of Acquittal of the Second Accused Morris Kallon, Sesay et al. (SCSL-04–15-T-648) (Sept. 27, 2006).
[77] *Id.* at para. 48.
[78] Consolidated Prosecution Skeleton Response to the Rule 98 Motions by the Three Accused, Sesay et al. (SCSL-04–15-T-650), para. 16 (Oct. 6, 2006).
[79] Transcript, Sesay et al. (SCSL-04–15-T), at 15–18 (Oct. 16, 2006).
[80] Transcript, Sesay et al. (SCSL-04–15-T), at 21 (Oct. 23, 2006).

elements of other inhumane acts,[81] and dismissed the Defense arguments as "[going] to the root of the form of the Indictment." As such, they could not "be examined at this stage of trial as to its merits." It invited the Defense to raise the issues in their final closing arguments.[82] It concluded there was evidence capable of supporting a conviction under Count 8.[83]

E. AFRC Prosecution Final Trial Brief – The First Comprehensive Definition of Forced Marriage

The Prosecution's Final Trial Brief in the AFRC case provided the first concrete definition of the crime of forced marriage before the SCSL. It submitted that forced marriage:

> consists of words or other conduct intended to confer a status of marriage by force or threat of force or coercion, such as that caused by fear of violence, duress, detention, psychological oppression or abuse of power against the victim, or by taking advantage of a coercive environment, with the intention of conferring the status of marriage.[84]

The Prosecution also provided a comprehensive description of the nature of the crime, noting that "some of the factual elements which go to define the allegation of 'forced marriage' include sexual slavery in a marital-type union where the abducted are labeled as 'wife' and the conjugal status is imposed by coercion or threat."[85] It submitted that the women could not leave for fear of threat of death, had no capacity to give genuine consent given the coercive war environment, were forced to perform domestic chores such as cooking and laundering as well as other forms of forced labor, and were reduced into servile status, and that victims often bore children fathered by their captors.[86] It concluded:

> [i]t is the case of the Prosecution, that there is evidence to prove beyond a reasonable doubt that members of the AFRC (SLA)/RUF engaged in sexual slavery and/or forced "marriages" or other forms of sexual violence by exercising ownership over women and girls, battering them, depriving them of liberty and causing their engagement in acts of a sexual nature by use of force, threat of force, coercion or by taking advantage of a coercive environment or the victim's incapacity to give genuine consent in the circumstances.[87]

The Prosecution also clarified that no marriage transactions or ceremonies were actually held,[88] that the use of the term "wife" was a label of ownership,[89] and that the relationships were not legal marriages. It argued: "[i]t is the captors who gave the label of 'wife' to the girls they captured. And these terminologies are nothing more than descriptive of the relationships that existed. It does not mean that formal marriages took place between the abducted girls and the AFRC/RUF ...."[90] Finally, the Prosecution distinguished its allegations of

---

[81] *Id.* at 22–23.
[82] *Id.* at 8.
[83] *Id.* at 26.
[84] Prosecution Final Trial Brief, Brima et al. (SCSL-04–16-T-601), paras. 1009–1012.
[85] *Id.* at para. 1869.
[86] *Id.* at para. 1870.
[87] *Id.* at para. 1872.
[88] *Id.*
[89] *Id.* at para. 1874.
[90] *Id.* at para. 1876.

forced marriage as a crime against humanity from customary arranged marriage practiced in Sierra Leone.[91]

F. AFRC Trial Judgment – Forced Marriage Is Only Nonsexual

On June 20, 2007, Trial Chamber II handed down its judgment in the AFRC trial. It was significant in two ways. First, the majority confirmed that according to the logic of the Statute, other inhumane acts under Article 2(i), must be restrictively interpreted to apply only to acts of a nonsexual nature.[92] In so doing, it further entrenched its Rule *98 bis* findings, namely that forced marriage is a nonsexual crime. Second, it held that all of the acts pled by the Prosecution as evidence of forced marriage – abduction and forcible detention of girls and women, imposition of the label "wife," extraction of labor, and control of the victim's sexuality – were completely subsumed by the crime of sexual slavery.[93] It found that there was no lacuna in the law that would necessitate a separate crime of forced marriage as an other inhumane act under Article 2(i).[94] The Trial Chamber stated:

> the use of the term wife by the perpetrator in reference to the victim is indicative of the intent of the perpetrator to exercise ownership over the victim, and not an intent to assume a marital or quasi-marital status with the victim in the sense of establishing mutual obligations inherent in a husband wife relationship.[95]

It also found that forced marriage as a nonsexual crime would not have amounted to a crime against humanity under Article 2(i):

> [t]he Prosecution evidence in the present case does not point to even one instance of a woman or girl having had a bogus marriage forced upon her in circumstances which did not amount to sexual slavery. Not one of the victims of sexual slavery gave evidence that the mere fact that a rebel had declared her to be his wife had caused her any particular trauma, whether physical or mental. Moreover, in the opinion of the Trial Chamber, had there been such evidence, it would not have by itself amounted to a crime against humanity, since it would not have been of similar gravity to the acts referred to in Article 2(a) to (h) of the Statute.[96]

Sebutinde J. appended a Concurring Option in which she elaborated upon the findings of the majority. Doherty J. appended a Dissent in which she argued that forced marriage is not necessarily a sexual crime, although the presence of rape may go to proof of the lack of consent of the victim. She opined, "[t]he crime is concerned primarily with the mental and moral suffering of the victim"[97] and that the "crucial element of 'forced marriage' is the

---

[91] *Id.* at para. 1884.
[92] Judgment, Brima et al. (SCSL-04–16-T-613), para. 697 (June 20, 2007). The majority also dismissed Count 7, Sexual Slavery and Any Other Form of Sexual Violence, as being bad for duplicity, Doherty J., dissenting, and in the interest of justice the Trial Chamber then considered the evidence of forced marriage/sexual slavery as a war crime under Count 9, Outrages on Personal Dignity. *See* para. 713.
[93] *Id.* at para. 711.
[94] *Id.* at para. 713.
[95] *Id.* at para. 711.
[96] *Id.* at para. 710.
[97] *Id.*, Partly Dissenting Opinion of Justice Doherty, para. 52.

imposition, by threat or by physical force arising from the perpetrator's words or other conduct, of a forced conjugal association by the perpetrator over the victim."[98]

G. AFRC Appeals Judgment – Forced Marriage Is "Predominantly" Nonsexual

The findings of the majority in the AFRC Trial judgment were overturned on appeal on February 22, 2008.[99] Notably, in framing its grounds for appeal, the Prosecution adopted a characterization of forced marriage as "not predominantly sexual."[100] It argued that the imposition of a forced conjugal association alone was sufficiently grave to meet the threshold of an other inhumane act and that the distinguishing element of forced marriage is a "forced conjugal association by the perpetrator over the victim. It represents forcing a person into the appearance, the veneer of a conduct (*i.e.* marriage), by threat, physical assault or other coercion."[101] Moving away from its characterizations of forced marriage during the pretrial and trial phases, the Prosecution submitted that although acts of forced marriage may in certain circumstances amount to sexual slavery, they do not always involve the victim being subjected to nonconsensual sex or even forced domestic labor.[102]

In its judgment, the Appeals Chamber noted that "the Prosecution may have misled the Trial Chamber by the manner in which forced marriage appeared to have been classified in the Indictment"[103] but refrained from extending this point to considerations of the degree to which this may also have misled the accused persons in the preparation of their defense. It concluded that the Trial Chamber had erred in finding that Article 2(i) of the Statute excludes sexual crimes,[104] but ultimately agreed with the Prosecution's submissions on appeal, concluding that forced marriage was predominantly nonsexual in nature and that it was not subsumed by sexual slavery. It held that:

> no tribunal could reasonably have found that forced marriage was subsumed in the crime against humanity of sexual slavery. While forced marriage shares certain elements with sexual slavery such as non-consensual sex and deprivation of liberty, there are also distinguishing factors. First, forced marriage involves a perpetrator compelling a person by force or threat of force, through the words or conduct of the perpetrator or those associated with him, into a forced conjugal association with a another person resulting in great suffering, or serious physical or mental injury on the part of the victim. Second, unlike sexual slavery, forced marriage implies a relationship of exclusivity between the "husband" and "wife," which could lead to disciplinary consequences for breach of this exclusive arrangement. These distinctions imply that forced marriage is not predominantly a sexual crime.[105]

The Appeals Chamber found that acts of forced marriage were of similar gravity to other crimes against humanity in the Statute and therefore met the threshold requirement of other inhumane acts.[106]

---

[98] *Id.* at para. 53.
[99] Judgment, Brima et al. (SCSL-04–16-A), Appeals Chamber (Feb. 22, 2008).
[100] *Id.* at para. 178.
[101] *Id.*
[102] *Id.* at para. 189.
[103] *Id.* at para. 181.
[104] *Id.* at para. 186.
[105] *Id.* at para. 195.
[106] *Id.* at para. 200.

H. The RUF Trial Judgment – Forced Marriage Confirmed

The RUF Trial judgment was handed down on March 2, 2009.[107] Trial Chamber I held that forced marriage relates to women and girls being forced into "marriages" and being forced to perform a number of conjugal duties under coercion by their "husbands."[108] It took into consideration evidence that the RUF had distributed female captives among themselves, with each rebel claiming a woman or girl as his "wife," as well as evidence that victims performed domestic chores and were repeatedly raped by the perpetrators.[109] It consequently found all three accused persons guilty of sexual slavery and forced marriage,[110] concluding that convictions on both sexual slavery and forced marriage were permissible as the former was not subsumed by the latter, which contains the distinct element of a "forced conjugal association based on exclusivity between the perpetrator and victim."[111]

Neither the Prosecution nor the Defense appealed the Trial Chamber's findings in relation to the nature and cause of the crime of forced marriage.[112]

I. The Charles Taylor Trial – Forced Marriage Is Withdrawn

It is notable that in the Charles Taylor trial, the last of the cases to be held before the SCSL, the Prosecution dropped all references to forced marriage from the Indictment.[113] However, as both Valerie Oosterveld and Michael Scharf discuss in their chapters in this volume, Trial Chamber II in its April 26, 2012 Judgment in the Taylor case nevertheless went on to make several further observations about forced marriage, including that in its view the Court had been misled by the Prosecution's erroneous pleading of forced marriage as an Other Inhumane Act under Article 2(i) of the Statute and that both sexual and nonsexual acts should be considered as inseparable and integral to the concept forced conjugal association.

IV. CONCLUSION

From the time the Indictments in the AFRC and RUF cases were amended to include the charge of forced marriage until the time it was finally defined by the Appeals Chamber, there was notable fluidity in the articulation of its central nature as either a sexual or nonsexual crime, as well as inconsistency in terms of the specific content of its constituent acts. This was, in turn, compounded or perhaps even driven by a significant degree of variation of legal findings both within and between the Trial Chambers and the Appeals Chamber.

---

[107] Judgment, Sesay et al. (SCSL-05-15-T-1234) (Mar. 2, 2009) [hereinafter RUF Trial Judgment].

[108] *Id.* at para. 164.

[109] *Id.* at paras. 1212–1214, 1409–1413.

[110] For an evaluation of the RUF Trial Judgment and its jurisprudence on forced marriage see V. Oosterveld, *The Gender Jurisprudence of the Special Court for Sierra Leone: Progress in the Revolutionary United Front Judgments*, 44 Cornell Int'l L.J. 49–74 (2011).

[111] RUF Trial Judgment, *supra* note 107, at para. 2307.

[112] Judgment, Sesay et al. (SCSL-04-15-A), Appeals Chamber (Oct. 26, 2009). Note that Kallon appealed his conviction under superior responsibility for forced marriage (see p. 298), and Gbao appealed the Trial Chamber's finding that sexual slavery and forced marriage were acts of terror (see p. 393).

[113] Indictment, Taylor (SCSL-03-01-PT-263) (May 29, 2007).

Taken together, these issues suggest an adaptive approach to elucidating the contours of forced marriage rather than a proactive one. It also gives rise to concern as to whether the *nullum crimen sine lege* principle was offended, and whether in the circumstances the accused persons can be said to have been properly on notice of the nature of their alleged criminal conduct.

It also leads to another uneasy implication: the procedural concerns highlighted above must be taken into consideration in any balanced evaluation of the weight of the jurisprudence of the SCSL on the crime of forced marriage. This is not just an issue to be considered by international criminal law academics and practitioners. The victims of the conflict in Sierra Leone suffered tremendously. Sexual violence was used to demean, to subdue, to humiliate, and to destroy these victims and their communities. There is no question that they deserved justice for the crimes that were committed against them and that such justice should, as much as possible, account for the full range of their experience of criminal violence. Unfortunately, to the extent that the problems of procedure and shifting interpretations of forced marriage diminish the legitimacy of the process and engender criticism with regard to fair trial rights, it also undermines the value of the project itself and therefore weakens the quality of the justice provided to these victims.

12

Evaluating the Special Court for Sierra Leone's Gender Jurisprudence

Valerie Oosterveld[*]

I. INTRODUCTION

The Special Court for Sierra Leone (SCSL) has a very interesting, though somewhat mixed, record in addressing gender-based violence, including sexual violence, in the context of the cases it has considered regarding the armed conflict in Sierra Leone. There are aspects of the SCSL's jurisprudence that are groundbreaking and potentially precedent-setting, such as the Court's consideration of the role of sexual violence in the war strategy of the Revolutionary United Front (RUF) and Armed Forces Revolutionary Council (AFRC) in the Sesay, Kallon and Gbao (or RUF) case and in the Taylor trial judgment.[1] There are other aspects that are similarly positive and confirmatory, demonstrating how gender-based crimes can and do intersect in crucial ways with each other and with seemingly gender-neutral crimes. This is seen, for example, in the observations in Brima, Kamara and Kanu (AFRC case) of how rape was often accompanied by other forms of physical and psychological brutality.[2] Other examples are found in the discussions of forced marriage in the AFRC, RUF and Taylor cases, in which the Court grapples with the interrelationship of forced marriage with rape, sexual slavery, and enslavement (specifically forced domestic labor).[3]

And yet, there are other, more unfortunate aspects of the SCSL's jurisprudence – most notably, the complete silence in the Fofana and Kondewa trial judgment on gender-based violence in areas held by the Civil Defense Forces (the CDF case).[4]

This chapter begins by exploring how the SCSL has addressed four specific types of gender-based violence: the crimes against humanity of rape, sexual slavery and inhumane acts (forced marriage), and the war crime of outrages upon personal dignity. Unlike the two specific contributions on forced marriage by Michael Scharf and Sidney Thompson in this volume, it examines how the Court considered all these prohibited acts from a factual and

---

[*] Associate Professor, University of Western Ontario Faculty of Law (Canada). I wish to thank the Social Sciences and Humanities Research Council of Canada for its support of my research.

[1] Prosecutor v. Sesay, Kallon and Gbao, Case No. SCSL-04-15-T, Judgment, paras. 1347–1356 (Special Court for Sierra Leone, Trial Chamber I, Mar. 2, 2009) [hereinafter RUF Trial Judgment]; Prosecutor v. Taylor, Case No. SCSL-03-01-T, Judgment, paras. 2034–2036 (Special Court for Sierra Leone, Trial Chamber II, May 18, 2012) [hereinafter Taylor Trial Judgment].

[2] Prosecutor v. Brima, Kamara and Kanu, Case No. SCSL-04-16-T, Judgment, paras. 989–1009 (Special Court for Sierra Leone, Trial Chamber II, June 20, 2007) [hereinafter AFRC Trial Judgment].

[3] See discussion in Section II(C) infra.

[4] Prosecutor v. Fofana and Kondewa, Case No. SCSL-04-14-T, Judgment (Special Court for Sierra Leone, Trial Chamber I, August 2, 2007) [hereinafter CDF Trial Judgment].

legal perspective, and concludes that the SCSL played a crucial role in naming these as serious violations. The benefit of such labeling should not be underestimated: naming is a key expressive tool of the law, authoritatively transforming a legally unacknowledged experience into an acknowledged wrong requiring legal redress.[5] In other words, these experiences of (largely) women and girls were not just collateral damage of the war, as they have sometimes wrongly been considered historically, they were *crimes*.

The chapter then turns to subtler – and yet just as important – ways that the SCSL has advanced gender jurisprudence within international criminal law. The Court has explored the intersectionality of gender-based violence with the war crime of committing acts of terror. It has also recognized both sexual and nonsexual gender-based violence directed at men and boys, helping to shed light on these often overlooked crimes. Finally, the chapter turns to the negative consequences of rulings at the trial level in the CDF case, forever denying female victims of the CDF the chance to tell their stories of gender-based violence to the SCSL.

The conflict in Sierra Leone was marked by various – and often brutal – forms of gender-based violence, including rape, sexual slavery, and forced marriage.[6] Gender-based violence during the Sierra Leone civil war essentially brought the armed conflict onto, and into, the bodies of women and girls, men and boys. The SCSL has achieved an important measure of success in recording this in its jurisprudence, but, at the same time, has missed certain opportunities to do so clearly and with an eye to gender justice.

II. THE SCSL'S JURISPRUDENCE ON SPECIFIC TYPES OF GENDER-BASED VIOLENCE

A. Rape

The SCSL has explored the widespread nature of rape in the Sierra Leone conflict, first in the AFRC case (heard by Trial Chamber II), then in the RUF case (heard by Trial Chamber I), and finally in the Taylor case (also heard by Trial Chamber II). Although the consecutive nature of the judgments seemed to provide the opportunity for a sort of unified analysis of the crime against humanity of rape, with one case building on the insights of the other, the actual result was quite different. At the trial level, all three cases adopted helpful factual findings on the types and locations of rape, but they came to somewhat contradictory conclusions on the reasons behind the use of rape. Similarly, all of the cases carefully examined the legal parameters of the prohibited act of rape, but adopted differing elements of crime with varying reach.

With respect to the factual findings, Trial Chamber II in the AFRC judgment concluded that the AFRC had committed a range of violations against women and girls, such as gang rape.[7] In the RUF case, Trial Chamber I also concluded that rape was commonplace in RUF-

---

[5] R. Cook & S. Cusack, Gender Stereotyping: Transnational Legal Perspectives 39 (2010).

[6] Gender-based violence is violence that is directed against an individual because of socially constructed norms of maleness or femaleness. One example of gender-based violence is sexual violence (such as rape). On gender-based violence during the Sierra Leone conflict, see Human Rights Watch, *"We'll Kill You if You Cry"*: Sexual Violence in the Sierra Leone Conflict 26–27 (2003), *available at* http://www.hrw.org/en/reports/2003/01/15/well-kill-you-if-you-cry. *See also* Physicians for Human Rights, *War-Related Sexual Violence in Sierra Leone: A Population-Based Assessment* (2002), *available at* http://physiciansforhumanrights.org/library/reports/war-related-sexual-violence-sierra-leone-2002.html.

[7] AFRC Trial Judgment, *supra* note 2, at paras. 1031–1035, 1728, 1926–1927, 2040, and 2043.

controlled areas, taking different forms such as gang rape, multiple rapes, rape with weapons and other objects, rape in public, rape in which family members are forced to watch, and rape in which civilians or family members are forced to rape each other.[8] Trial Chamber II, in the Taylor trial judgment, confirmed that both the RUF and AFRC (as well as other affiliated fighters) were responsible for the rape of civilian girls and women.[9] The rape victims were often abducted and held captive, and some witnessed the killing or beating of other family members who tried to intercede.[10] No one was safe from rape: young girls, breastfeeding mothers and older women were all targeted, although girls were especially at risk.[11] Some victims were gang-raped; raped in public or in the midst of other captives; beaten before, after, or while being raped (including on the genitals); or sexually mutilated with sticks.[12]

In all three cases, the Court usefully noted the intersection of rape with other forms of atrocity, finding that rape by the AFRC and the RUF was often accompanied by other forms of harm, such as abduction, forced labor, forced nudity, murder, mutilation (including sexual mutilation), forced marriage, and physical assault.[13] The Court also highlighted that rape within AFRC- and RUF-held territory was not accidental. The AFRC trial judges concluded that rape was tolerated and institutionalized within the AFRC.[14] The RUF Trial Chamber similarly found that "[t]he deliberate and concerted campaign to rape women constitutes an extension of the battlefield to women's bodies."[15] The Taylor trial judgment put it somewhat differently, concluding that the crimes committed by the AFRC and RUF, including rape, were inextricably linked to how these groups achieved their political and military objectives.[16] However, the RUF and Taylor judgments went further than did the AFRC judgment, identifying rape by the RUF and AFRC as an important contributor to the war crime of committing acts of terror.[17] This conclusion can be directly contrasted with the conclusion of the AFRC Trial Chamber that sexual violence such as rape was not used to spread terror among civilians, but "rather was committed by the AFRC troops to take advantage of the spoils of war, by treating women as property and using them to satisfy their sexual desires and to fulfill other conjugal needs."[18] Although rape can be committed during an armed conflict for many reasons, ranging from opportunistic to strategic,[19] and these reasons can overlap and change over time, it is somewhat surprising to see such different

---

[8] RUF Trial Judgment, *supra* note 1, at paras. 1181, 1185, 1193–1194, 1205–1207, and 1289.

[9] *E.g.*, Taylor Trial Judgment, *supra* note 1, at paras. 893–894, 897, 904–905; 913–914; 919; 930; 931–932; 939; 961; 966; 970–972; 980; 984; 989; 992; 999; 1007; 1015 and 1016.

[10] *Id.* at paras. 889, 894, 895, 898, 904, 919, 930, 961, 967, 983, 984, 995, and 1002.

[11] *Id.* at paras. 891, 894, 903, 905, 977, 980, 981, 983, 989, 992, 995, and 1008.

[12] *Id.* at paras. 895, 898, 903, 927, 989, and 992.

[13] RUF Trial Judgment, *supra* note 1, at paras. 1180, 1182, 1195, 1205, 1208, 1212–1213, 1290–1297, 1302, and 1406; AFRC Trial Judgment, *supra* note 2, at paras. 989–1009; Taylor Trial Judgment, *supra* note 1, at paras. 889–890, 896–897, 901, 903, 907, 912, 918, 923–928, 941, 959, 965, 967–968, 979, 981–982, 994–996, 1002, 1004, and 1008–1014.

[14] AFRC Trial Judgment, *supra* note 2, at para. 1741.

[15] RUF Trial Judgment, *supra* note 1, at para. 1602.

[16] Taylor Trial Judgment, *supra* note 1, at paras. 6797 and 6799.

[17] This is explored further in Section III.

[18] AFRC Trial Judgment, *supra* note 2, at para. 1459.

[19] X. Agirre Aranburu, *Sexual Violence beyond Reasonable Doubt: Using Pattern Evidence and Analysis for International Cases*, 23 LEIDEN J. INT'L L. 609, 613–14, 622 (2010).

explanations given by Trial Chamber II in the AFRC and Taylor cases. Nevertheless, given the more detailed examination of the RUF–AFRC collaboration in Taylor, the explanation of rape in that judgment seems to supersede the approach in the AFRC judgment.

On the legal side, there are also differences – albeit smaller, with more points of agreement than disagreement – between the conclusions of the AFRC, RUF, and Taylor cases. The AFRC Trial Chamber adopted these elements (in addition to the general elements required for all crimes against humanity) for the prohibited act of rape:

1. The non-consensual penetration, however, slight, of the vagina or anus of the victim by the penis of the perpetrator or any other object used by the perpetrator, or of the mouth of the victim by the penis of the perpetrator; and
2. The intent to effect this sexual penetration, and the knowledge that it occurs without the consent of the victim.[20]

These elements were taken from the Kunarac appeals judgment in the International Criminal Tribunal for the Former Yugoslavia (ICTY).[21] The Taylor trial judgment reiterated these elements.[22] The RUF Trial Chamber adopted slightly different, and somewhat more detailed, elements:

1. The Accused invaded the body of a person by conduct resulting in penetration, however slight, of any part of the body of the victim or of the Accused with a sexual organ, or of the anal or genital opening of the victim with any object or any other part of the body;
2. The invasion was committed by force, or by threat of force or coercion, such as that caused by fear of violence, duress, detention, psychological oppression or abuse of power against such person or another person or by taking advantage of a coercive environment, or the invasion was committed against a person incapable of giving genuine consent;
3. The Accused intended to effect the sexual penetration or acted in the reasonable knowledge that this was likely to occur; and
4. The Accused knew or had reason to know that the victim did not consent.[23]

The etymology of these RUF elements is mixed. The first two elements, denoting the *actus reus*, are taken from the International Criminal Court's (ICC's) elements of crime for rape.[24] The RUF Trial Chamber noted that the first element is meant to define the type of invasion of the body required to constitute the offense of rape: genital, anal or oral penetration by a

---

[20] AFRC Trial Judgment, *supra* note 2, at para. 693.

[21] *Id.* at para. 693 (citing Prosecutor v. Kunarac et al., Case No. IT-96-23 & 23/1), Judgment para. 127 (Int'l Crim. Trib. for the Former Yugoslavia, Appeals Chamber, June 12, 2002) [hereinafter Kunarac Appeals Judgment].

[22] Taylor Trial Judgment, *supra* note 1, at para. 415.

[23] RUF Trial Judgment, *supra* note 1, at para. 145 (replicating the approach taken by the Trial Chamber in Transcript of Oral Rule 98 Decision, RUF, paras. 21–22 (Oct. 25, 2006)). The transcript of the RUF Oral Rule 98 Decision does not include any explanation as to why the RUF Trial Chamber chose this particular approach to the elements of rape.

[24] Elements of Crimes arts 7(1)(g)-1, 8(2)(b)(xxii)-2 and 8(2)(e)(vi)-1. The Trial Chamber made some inconsequential changes, changing the ICC's word "perpetrator" to the Chamber's preferred word "accused." As well, the SCSL did not replicate the ICC's footnote after the term "genuine consent" in its elements, but the SCSL referred to the content of that footnote within a footnote. RUF Trial Judgment, *supra* note 1, at 51 n.293.

sexual organ or something other than a sexual organ, such as an object.[25] The RUF approach to this element covers more penetration scenarios than does the AFRC/Taylor approach. Both sets of elements cover vaginal, anal and oral penetration of the victim by the perpetrator. The RUF approach additionally covers situations in which a male victim is forced to use his penis for vaginal, anal or oral penetration of a perpetrator, whether male or female.[26] In addition, the RUF approach would cover penetration by a finger, whereas it is not clear that the AFRC/Taylor approach would cover this type of penetration.[27]

The second element set out by the RUF Trial Chamber "refers to the circumstances which would render the sexual act in the first element criminal" – "those circumstances in which the person could not be said to have voluntarily and genuinely consented to the act."[28] The Chamber also accepted, following the jurisprudence of the ICTY, that the circumstances prevailing in cases in which crimes against humanity or war crimes are charged "will be almost universally coercive."[29] The final clause of the element covers situations where, "even in the absence of force or coercion, a person cannot be said to have genuinely consented to the act," due to age, illness, disability, or being under the influence of a substance.[30]

Both the RUF and AFRC Trial Chambers agreed, in relation to the *actus reus* elements, that "the very specific circumstances of an armed conflict where rapes on a large scale are alleged to have occurred, coupled with the social stigma which is borne by victims of rape in certain societies' may require reliance on circumstantial evidence."[31] This approach was confirmed in Taylor.[32]

The second element set out by the AFRC and Taylor Trial Chambers, and the third and fourth elements set out by the RUF Trial Chamber, address the *mens rea* and introduce the concept of non-consent of the victim. It is interesting to note that, although the RUF Trial Chamber adopted its first two elements from the ICC's Elements of Crimes document, it did not follow the ICC's elements for the *mens rea* component. The ICC's elements deliberately do not contain a non-consent aspect, reflecting the view that "non-consent was not an element of the crime of rape where coercive circumstances are involved."[33]

In contrast, like Trial Chamber II in both the AFRC and Taylor cases, the RUF Trial Chamber followed the approach of the ICTY in the Kunarac judgment.[34] The evolution in

---

[25] RUF Trial Judgment, *supra* note 1, at para. 146.

[26] *Id.* at para. 145.

[27] In the AFRC element, it is not clear that the word "object" would include a body part such as a finger, whereas the RUF approach refers specifically to "any other part of the body."

[28] RUF Trial Judgment, *supra* note 1, at para. 147.

[29] *Id.* (citing Kunarac Appeals Judgment, *supra* note 21, at para. 130). The AFRC Trial Judgment contains the same observation, AFRC Trial Judgment, *supra* note 2, at para. 694.

[30] RUF Trial Judgment, *supra* note 1, at para. 148. The Taylor Trial Judgment contains the same observation. *See* Taylor Trial Judgment, *supra* note 1, at para. 416.

[31] RUF Trial Judgment, *supra* note 1, at para. 149. Trial Chamber II made the same observations: AFRC Trial Judgment, *supra* note 2, at para. 695. Both Trial Chambers followed the standard approach found in the ICTY and International Criminal Tribunal for Rwanda (ICTR) cases, which reiterate these points. For example, Prosecutor v. Muhimana, Case No. ICTR-95–1B-A, Judgment para. 49 (Int'l Crim. Trib. for Rwanda, Appeals Chamber, May 21, 2007).

[32] Taylor Trial Judgment, *supra* note 1, at para. 416.

[33] E. La Haye, *Article 8(2)(b)(xxii) – Rape, Sexual Slavery, Enforced Prostitution, Forced Pregnancy, Enforced Sterilization, and Sexual Violence, in* The International Criminal Court: Elements of Crimes and Rules of Procedure and Evidence 181, at 184 and 189 (R.S. Lee & Hakan Friman eds., 2001).

[34] Kunarac Appeals Judgment, *supra* note 21, at para. 127.

international criminal jurisprudence from an initial approach similar to that of the ICC, to the current (except for the ICC) non-consent-based approach, has generated controversy within international criminal legal circles.[35] It therefore would have been helpful if the RUF Trial Chamber explained its reasons for following the ICC's elements with respect to the *actus reus*, but then switching to the Kunarac approach with respect to non-consent. Indeed, as Eriksson notes, the fact that the two Trial Chambers adopted two differing sets of elements "without an analysis [in the RUF case] as to the reasons for the departure from the first definition" is "perplexing."[36] Although this might be explained by the fact that one Trial Chamber is not bound by the decisions of the other Trial Chamber, given that the AFRC judgment preceded the RUF judgment, it simply makes sense for the subsequent Trial Chamber to at least reference the approach of the preceding Trial Chamber and indicate why it chose a different one. Similarly, the Taylor trial judgment would have benefited from a reference to the elements of crime adopted in the RUF trial judgment (and not only the AFRC trial judgment).[37]

As can be seen, the legal elements set out by the two Trial Chambers contain many similarities, and some small differences. Both definitions define the *actus reus* in gender-neutral terms, in order to capture the rape of both females and males.[38] Both use broad language to cover different forms of penetration, although the RUF approach captures additional forms of penetration not covered by the AFRC/Taylor approach. The RUF approach is detailed as to the methods through which the rape can occur (for example, force, threat of force, or coercion) whereas the AFRC/Taylor approach is silent in this respect. Both Trial Chambers adopt a requirement that the perpetrator knows (or, in the RUF element, had reason to know) that the victim did not consent to the penetration. This general agreement on legal modalities helps to (somewhat) clarify international law on the elements of rape, and can be contrasted with the very different conclusions of the trial judgments as to the role played by rape (the view of rape as opportunistic versus a deliberate tool used to effect social control over civilians).

B. Sexual Slavery

The first-ever international convictions for the crime against humanity of sexual slavery took place in the RUF case, followed by the Taylor trial judgment.[39] In addition, sexual slavery was discussed in the AFRC trial judgment.[40] These exciting developments represent

---

[35] Eriksson discusses this controversy: M. Eriksson, Defining Rape: Emerging Obligations for States under International Law? 390–93 (2011).

[36] *Id.* at 402. *See also* V. Oosterveld, *The Gender Jurisprudence of the Special Court for Sierra Leone: Progress in the Revolutionary United Front Judgments*, 44 Cornell Int'l L.J. 49, 57–59 (2011).

[37] Taylor Trial Judgment, *supra* note 1, at paras. 415–416. The Trial Chamber did refer to the RUF Appeal Judgment, Prosecutor v. Sesay, Kallon and Gbao, Case No. SCSL 04-15-A, Appeals Judgment (Oct. 26, 2009) [hereinafter RUF Appeals Judgment]. *See* Taylor Trial Judgment, *supra* note 1, at n.1027 (on coercion and no need for "continuous resistance") and the RUF Trial Judgment, *supra* note 1, at n.1028 (on consent and capacity because of age, etc.).

[38] This was noted by the RUF Trial Judgment, *supra* note 1, at para. 146.

[39] Press Release, SCSL, Prosecutor Welcomes Convictions in RUF Appeals Judgment (Oct. 26, 2009), *available at* http://www.sc-sl.org/LinkClick.aspx?fileticket=ITUGDfogLfQ%3d&tabid=196 (last visited Apr.4, 2012); Taylor Trial Judgment, *supra* note 1, at paras. 7000(i)(v) and 7000(ii)(v).

[40] AFRC Trial Judgment, *supra* note 2, at paras. 696–714.

important progress, given that sexual slavery was not even specifically named as a prohibited act until the adoption of the Rome Statute of the International Criminal Court (ICC) in 1998[41] and the Statute of the Special Court for Sierra Leone in 2002.[42]

Unlike in their discussions of rape, the AFRC, RUF, and Taylor Trial Chambers adopted similar approaches to sexual slavery, helping to clarify and solidify international criminal law in this regard. The Court's unified approach to the *mens rea* and *actus reus* elements of sexual slavery is explored in detail later in this chapter. However, first it is important to note that Trial Chamber II, in both the AFRC and Taylor cases, classified sexual slavery as a continuing crime.[43] This recognition of the continuous nature of sexual slavery is crucial because it captures the fact that sexual slavery does not comprise one discrete event: it is composed of a number of actions, sometimes over a period of time and over a changing geographical space. In the context of the Sierra Leone conflict, perpetrators were often on the move between villages and districts over a significant period of time, taking their sexual slaves with them.[44] Thus, the Trial Chamber concluded that it was not practical for the Prosecutor to plead specific locations for this crime.[45]

The AFRC, RUF, and Taylor trial judgments identified the elements of sexual slavery that must be proven by the Prosecutor:

1. The Accused exercised any or all of the powers attaching to the right of ownership over one or more persons, such as by purchasing, selling, lending or bartering such a person or persons, or by imposing on them a similar deprivation of liberty;
2. The Accused caused such a person or persons to engage in one or more acts of a sexual nature; and
3. The Accused intended to exercise the act of sexual slavery or acted in the reasonable knowledge that this was likely to occur.[46]

The first two elements, which focus on the *actus reus*, are taken from the ICC's Elements of Crimes document,[47] with the slight change of the term "perpetrator" to "accused" (except for Taylor, which maintained the reference to "perpetrator").[48] The third element sets out the required *mens rea*, and was articulated in a similar fashion in all three cases.[49]

---

[41] For more on this, *see* V. Oosterveld, *Sexual Slavery and the International Criminal Court: Advancing International Law*, 25(3) Mich. J. Int'l L.605 (2004).

[42] SCSL Statute art. 2(g).

[43] AFRC Trial Judgment, *supra* note 2, at paras. 39–40; Taylor Trial Judgment, *supra* note 1, at paras. 119 and 1018.

[44] Taylor Trial Judgment, *supra* note 1, at para. 119.

[45] *Id.* at paras. 119 and 1018.

[46] RUF Trial Judgment, *supra* note 1, at para. 158; AFRC Trial Judgment, *supra* note 2, at para. 708; Taylor Trial Judgment, *supra* note 1, at para. 418. Note that Taylor used slightly different wording in the third element: "The perpetrator intended to engage in the act of sexual slavery or acted with the reasonable knowledge that this was likely to occur." Note also that, unlike in the discussion of the elements of rape, the Taylor Trial Judgment did reference both the RUF and AFRC trial judgments. *Id.* at n.1030.

[47] ICC Elements of Crimes arts. 7(1)(g)-2, 8(2)(b)(xxii)-2 and 8(2)(e)(vi)-2. Neither the AFRC nor the RUF trial judgments replicated the ICC's footnote explaining "deprivation of liberty," which links trafficking in women and children to sexual slavery. *Id.* at 13 n.18; 34 n.53; and 44 n.65.

[48] Taylor Trial Judgment, *supra* note 1, at para. 418.

[49] The wording is slightly different between the three trial judgments, but has the same meaning: RUF Trial Judgment, *supra* note 1, at para. 158; AFRC Trial Judgment, *supra* note 2, at para. 708; Taylor Trial Judgment, *supra* note 1, at para. 418.

The AFRC, RUF, and Taylor trial judgments jointly help to provide the contours of the *actus reus* requirement. There are two aspects: first, that the Accused exercised any or all of the powers attaching to the right of ownership over a person or persons; and, second, that the enslavement involved sexual acts.[50] With respect to the first aspect, two Trial Chambers found that the list of ways in which powers attaching to the right of ownership might be exercised (purchasing, selling, lending, or bartering) is not exhaustive.[51] The AFRC and Taylor trial judgments also noted that payment or exchange (for example, of money) is not required to establish the exercise of ownership.[52] All three trial judgments also found that the exercise of powers attaching to the right of ownership does not require that victims be physically confined; they may remain under the control of their captors because they have nowhere else to go and fear for their lives.[53] The Taylor trial judgment gave an example: witness TF1–189 described how she was permitted to shop for food items with a female rebel. She did not attempt to escape because she had been warned that, if she tried to do so, "it would not be good for her."[54] In order to determine whether the *actus reus* requirement had been met, the RUF and Taylor trial judgments replicated the list of indicia of enslavement from the ICTY's Kunarac judgment: "control of someone's movement, control of physical environment, psychological control, measures taken to prevent or deter escape, force, threat of force or coercion, duration, assertion of exclusivity, subjection to cruel treatment and abuse, control of sexuality and forced labor."[55]

Just as the issue of non-consent arose in the Trial Chambers' discussion of the *actus reus* required for proof of rape, it also came up in their consideration of sexual slavery. However, both Trial Chambers agreed that consent or free will of the victim is not present in conditions of enslavement, and the RUF Trial Chamber explicitly noted that

> the lack of consent of the victim of enslavement or to the sexual acts is *not* an element to be proved by the Prosecution, although whether or not there was consent may be relevant from an evidentiary perspective in establishing whether or not the Accused exercised any of the powers attaching to the right of ownership (emphasis added).[56]

The RUF Trial Chamber also accepted the view, originally put forward by the ICTY, that "circumstances which render it impossible to express consent may be sufficient to presume the absence of consent."[57] Even so, the Trial Chamber explicitly found that the atmosphere of extreme violence and terror in RUF-controlled areas provided evidence that the perpetrators had knowledge that the women did not consent to sexual slavery.[58] On appeal,

---

[50] RUF Trial Judgment, *supra* note 1, at para. 159. The Taylor Trial Judgment was very careful to clearly set out its findings first on the enslavement aspect, and then, second, on the sexual aspect. *E.g.*, Taylor Trial Judgment, *supra* note 1, at paras. 1132 and 1163.

[51] RUF Trial Judgment, *supra* note 1, at para. 160; AFRC Trial Judgment, *supra* note 2, at para. 709.

[52] AFRC Trial Judgment, *supra* note 2, at para. 709; Taylor Trial Judgment, *supra* note 1, at para. 420.

[53] AFRC Trial Judgment, *supra* note 2, at para. 709; RUF Trial Judgment, *supra* note 1, at para. 161; Taylor Trial Judgment, *supra* note 1, at para. 420.

[54] Taylor Trial Judgment, *supra* note 1, at para. 1069.

[55] RUF Trial Judgment, *supra* note 1, at para. 160, citing Prosecutor v. Kunarac, Case No. IT 96–23-T& 23/1 T, Judgment para. 543 (Int'l Crim. Trib. for the Former Yugoslavia, Trial Chamber, Feb.22. 2001); Taylor Trial Judgment, *supra* note 1, at para. 420.

[56] RUF Trial Judgment, *supra* note 1, at para. 163.

[57] *Id.* (citing Kunarac Appeals Judgment, *supra* note 21, at para. 120).

[58] RUF Trial Judgment, *supra* note 1, at paras. 1466 and 1470–1471. *See also id.* at para. 1581.

Sesay tried to make use of the Trial Chamber's (and ICTY's) view, arguing that the Trial Chamber had erred by creating an incorrect presumption of absence of genuine consent.[59] The Appeals Chamber made several findings to counter Sesay's claim: first, consent to sexual slavery is impossible and is not a relevant consideration;[60] second, that captivity alone can vitiate consent;[61] and third, that the Trial Chamber had actually found, rather than presumed, an absence of consent.[62]

The Taylor Trial Chamber recited strong evidence of the forceful (and therefore inherently nonconsensual) nature of sexual slavery in the Sierra Leone conflict: "the women were forced by their captors to have sex if the women did not want to die."[63] The Chamber rejected the suggestion of a Defense witness that female civilians were not coerced: "the Trial Chamber finds the witness' statements that abducted women were treated with 'love' and not forced to have sexual relations[] to be contrary to the overwhelming volume of evidence and to be disingenuous and unreliable."[64] The Trial Chamber also noted evidence that the RUF did not mete out discipline for fighters engaged in sexual slavery; rather, the evidence instead showed that RUF commanders would seek out RUF officials to ask that their sex slaves be disciplined when they had "overlooked the commanders" (i.e., been disrespectful).[65] The evidence also recorded that the sex slaves were punished by their captors for refusing to submit to sexual intercourse: the Taylor Trial Chamber described evidence of one commander who stripped a girl down to her underwear and lashed her fifty times with a long cable made from a vehicle tire.[66]

The *mens rea* requirement was discussed at some length in the Taylor trial judgment, in the context of a prosecutorial argument relating to the wider issue of slavery, but is also applicable to the subset of sexual slavery. In that case, the Prosecutor argued that the *mens rea* required is that the accused "either intended enslavement or acted in the reasonable knowledge that it was likely to occur."[67] The Trial Chamber found that this amounted to an expansion of the required *mens rea* "as it is difficult to envisage what the requirement of 'acting in the reasonable knowledge that enslavement was likely to occur' would entail in the context of enslavement where the *actus reus* requires exercising powers of ownership."[68] This approach conforms strictly to the elements adopted (which say "the perpetrator exercised these powers intentionally")[69] and ICTY jurisprudence.[70] However, the Prosecutor's approach conforms to that of the ICC.[71] This illustrates an interesting tension

---

[59] RUF Appeals Judgment, *supra* note 37, at paras. 729–730.

[60] *Id.* at paras. 734 and 736.

[61] *Id.* at para. 736.

[62] *Id.* at paras. 734 and 737.

[63] Taylor Trial Judgment, *supra* note 1, at para. 1058 (footnotes omitted).

[64] *Id.* at para. 1038.

[65] *Id.* at para. 1063.

[66] *Id.* at para. 1064.

[67] *Id.* at para. 449.

[68] *Id.* at para. 450.

[69] *Id.* at para. 446.

[70] Kunarac Appeals Judgment, *supra* note 21, cited in Taylor Trial Judgment, *supra* note 1, at n.1076.

[71] Prosecutor v. Katanga and Chui, Case No. ICC-01/04–01/07, Decision on the Confirmation of Charges, para. 346 (Sept. 30, 2008), which states that the subjective elements of sexual slavery includes *dolus directus* of the second degree (in which the perpetrator was aware that in the ordinary course of events the objective elements of the crime would occur as a consequence of his or her actions or omissions) [hereinafter Katanga, Confirmation of Charges].

in the SCSL: although the crime against humanity of sexual slavery was first introduced in the ICC's Rome Statute and therefore it has chosen to follow the ICC's lead in some respects, in other respects it prefers to follow the jurisprudence of the ICTY and other time-limited tribunals.

Although the Trial Chambers' views on the crime against humanity of sexual slavery were largely uniform, and therefore helped to solidify international criminal law in this regard, the Chambers diverged on two issues. The first issue relates to whether cumulative convictions are permitted for the crimes against humanity of sexual slavery and rape. Both Trial Chambers agreed that the offense of rape and the offense of sexual slavery contain distinct elements: the offense of rape requires sexual penetration, whereas sexual slavery requires the exercise of powers attaching to the right of ownership and acts of a sexual nature, which do not necessarily require sexual penetration.[72] However, Trial Chamber I in the RUF trial judgment, concluded from this that "[w]here the commission of sexual slavery, however, entails acts of rape, the Chamber finds that the act of rape is subsumed by the act of sexual slavery. In such a case, a conviction on the same conduct is not permissible for rape and sexual slavery."[73] In contrast, Trial Chamber II in the Taylor trial judgment, held that, as each offense contains a distinct element not required by the other, it is legally permissible to enter convictions on both counts.[74] It also concluded that it is not bound to follow the finding in the RUF trial judgment.[75]

The second issue on which the Trial Chambers diverged relates to the way in which sexual slavery was charged in the AFRC and RUF cases. In both cases, the Prosecutor had charged the Accused with "sexual slavery and any other form of sexual violence,"[76] which the judges in both cases found was two offenses impermissibly charged under the same count.[77] This decision was not surprising, as the Prosecution had been warned early in the AFRC case that the charge was duplicative, and it had not taken steps to cure the defect.[78] What was surprising, however, is that a majority of the AFRC Trial Chamber chose to cure this duplicity by taking the radical step of dismissing the charge in its entirety, rather than simply striking out the portion of the charge referring to "any other form of sexual

---

[72] RUF Trial Judgment, *supra* note 1, at para. 2305; Taylor Trial Judgment, *supra* note 1, at para. 6995.

[73] RUF Trial Judgment, *supra* note 1, at para. 2305.

[74] Taylor Trial Judgment, *supra* note 1, at para. 6995. Similarly, it also found that it is permissible to enter cumulative convictions for the war crimes of committing acts of terror and committing outrages upon personal dignity because the former requires the intent to spread fear and the latter requires humiliating or degrading treatment. *Id.* at para. 6996.

[75] Taylor Trial Judgment, *supra* note 1, at n.15602.

[76] Prosecutor v. Brima, Kamara and Kanu ("AFRC"), Case No. SCSL-04–16-PT, Further Amended Consolidated Indictment, Count 7 (Special Court for Sierra Leone, Feb.5, 2004) [hereinafter AFRC Indictment]; Prosecutor v. Sesay, Kallon and Gbao ("RUF"), Case No. SCSL-04-15-PT, Corrected Amended Consolidated Indictment, Count 7 (Special Court for Sierra Leone, Aug. 2, 2006) [hereinafter RUF Indictment]. The Prosecutor had fixed this problem by the time of the Taylor Indictment, Prosecutor v. Taylor, Case No. SCSL-03–01-PT, Prosecution's Second Amended Indictment, Count 5 (Special Court for Sierra Leone, May 29, 2007) [hereinafter Taylor Indictment].

[77] AFRC Trial Judgment, *supra* note 2, at paras. 92–95; RUF Trial Judgment, *supra* note 1, at para. 458.

[78] Prosecutor v. Brima, Kamara and Kanu ("AFRC"), Case No. SCSL-04–16-T, Decision on Defense Motions for Judgment of Acquittal Pursuant to Rule 98, para. 9 (Special Court for Sierra Leone, Trial Chamber II, Mar. 31, 2006), in which Justice Sebutinde noted in her Separate Concurring Opinion that "the defect could be cured by an amendment pursuant to Rule 50 of the Rules that splits offences into two separate counts" [hereinafter AFRC Rule 98]. It is not clear why the Prosecutor did not pursue this amendment.

violence."[79] This is especially so given that one of the majority judges had earlier noted the lack of prejudice to the accused persons of splitting the charges.[80] The end result was that, in the AFRC case, the sexual slavery charges were dismissed in their entirety, and evidence of sexual slavery was considered instead under the war crime of outrages upon personal dignity.[81] In addressing the same issue, the SCSL's Appeals Chamber, and the RUF Trial Chamber, concluded that the fairer remedy was to proceed on the basis of the sexual slavery charge and to strike out the charge of "any other form of sexual violence."[82]

The SCSL's two Trial Chambers have expressed a mostly unified view of the crime against humanity of sexual slavery, which provides significant clarity to international criminal law on this prohibited act. The ICC has also charged individuals with sexual slavery, and will undoubtedly consider the SCSL's approach when determining its own way forward.[83]

C. Forced Marriage/Conjugal Slavery

The SCSL's contribution to international criminal law's gender jurisprudence is perhaps most striking when considering forced marriage (as Scharf and Thompson show with their chapters). Although previous international courts had considered factual scenarios involving forced marriage,[84] the SCSL was the first international criminal tribunal to consider individual criminal accountability and to convict individuals for forced marriage as an inhumane act or as two forms of enslavement.[85] The groundbreaking jurisprudence of the SCSL on forced marriage began when the Prosecutor brought charges for forced marriage in the RUF and AFRC cases.[86] As the SCSL Statute does not specifically list forced

---

[79] This latter course of action was persuasively argued on dissent by Justice Doherty. AFRC Trial Judgment, *supra* note 2, at Partially Dissenting Opinion of Justice Doherty on Count 7 (Sexual Slavery) and Count 8 (Forced Marriage), para. 12. The Appeals Chamber agreed with Justice Doherty on the remedy. *See* Prosecutor v. Brima, Kamara and Kanu ("AFRC"), Case No. SCSL-04-16-A, Trial Judgment, para. 109 (Special Court for Sierra Leone, Trial Chamber II, Feb. 22, 2008) [hereinafter AFRC Appeals Judgment]. Even so, it held that it was not necessary for it to substitute a conviction for sexual slavery because the Trial Chamber had considered the evidence of sexual slavery under the war crimes charge of outrages upon personal dignity. *Id.* at para. 110.

[80] AFRC Rule 98, *supra* note 78, at Separate Concurring Opinion of Justice Sebutinde, para. 9: "In my opinion, the defect could be cured by an amendment pursuant to Rule 50 of the Rules that splits the offences into two separate counts. In my view, such a procedure would not unduly delay the trial, nor would it prejudice the accused persons since it would not necessitate the introduction of any new evidence of which they are not already aware and would in fact be in the interests of justice."

[81] AFRC Trial Judgment, *supra* note 2, at para. 714. For a critique of that outcome, see V. Oosterveld, *The Special Court for Sierra Leone's Consideration of Gender-Based Violence: Contributing to Transitional Justice?*, 10 Hum. Rts. Rev. 73, 82–84 (2009).

[82] AFRC Appeals Judgment, *supra* note 79, at para. 109; RUF Trial Judgment, *supra* note 1, at para. 458.

[83] This has already occurred: Katanga Confirmation of Charges, *supra* note 71, at paras. 340 and 428.

[84] For example, Prosecutor v. Gacumbitsi, Case No. ICTR–01–64–T, Judgment and Sentence, para. 204 (Int'l Crim. Trib. for Rwanda, Trial Chamber, June 17, 2004); and Prosecutor v. Muhimana, Case No. ICTR-95–1B-T, Judgment and Sentence paras. 307–323 (Int'l Crim. Trib. for Rwanda, Trial Chamber, Apr. 28, 2005).

[85] Press Release, SCSL, Prosecutor Welcomes Arraignment of RUF and AFRC Indictees on Charges Related to Forced Marriage (May 17, 2004), *available at* http://www.sc-sl.org/LinkClick.aspx?fileticket=76Mb8Cd2aPU%3d&tabid=196; Press Release, SCSL, Special Court Prosecutor Hails RUF Convictions (Feb. 25, 2009), *available at* http://www.sc-sl.org/LinkClick.aspx?fileticket=dupqs76CgyU%3d&tabid=196; and SCSL Press Release, *supra* note 39; Taylor Trial Judgment, *supra* note 1, at paras. 7000(i)(v) and (x) and 7000(ii)(v) and (x).

[86] RUF Indictment, *supra* note 76, at para. 60; and AFRC Indictment, *supra* note 76, at para. 57. The Prosecutor was unsuccessful in bringing similar charges in the CDF case – discussed *infra* in Section V of this chapter.

marriage as a prohibited act within the crime against humanity provision, the Prosecutor chose to categorize forced marriage as the crime against humanity of "other inhumane acts," and to rely on evidence of forced marriage to support the war crimes charge of "outrages upon personal dignity" and, in the RUF case, the war crime of committing acts of terror.[87] He brought evidence demonstrating that girls and women – often captured or abducted civilians – were forcibly assigned as "wives" to rebel commanders or soldiers.[88] These "wives" were expected to undertake sexual intercourse on demand and to provide domestic services to the "husband," including cooking, cleaning, childbearing, and childrearing.[89] The lives of these "wives" were often punctuated by extreme violence.[90] The Sierra Leonean civil war was therefore brought directly into the living spaces, and even the bodies, of these "wives."

The first Trial Chamber to consider forced marriage struggled to understand its exact contours. Conceptually, it was easy for the Court to understand that there were girls and women forced to be "bush wives" during the conflict.[91] However, in order to convict individuals for forced marriage, the Trial Chamber needed to determine the elements of this particular prohibited act. The case history demonstrates divergent opinions on what the term "forced marriage" encompasses and the exact harm meant to be addressed by the term.

The Prosecutor described forced marriage to the Court as a prohibited act in which the victim is forced into taking on multifaceted roles, for example, as a sex slave, cook, launderer, childcare provider, etc.[92] He defined the crime as:

> consist[ing] of words or other conduct intended to confer a status of marriage by force or threat of force or coercion, such as that caused by fear of violence, duress, detention, psychological oppression or abuse of power against the victim, or by taking advantage of a coercive environment, with the intention of conferring the status of marriage.[93]

He argued that the act of forced marriage is separate from sexual slavery and that it has its own distinctive features: victims of forced marriage are literally forced to take on the duties of "wives" whereas sexual slaves are not necessarily obliged to pretend to be perpetrators' "wives," and victims of sexual slavery may not necessarily be forced to perform tasks attached to "marriage," unlike victims of forced marriage.[94]

It appears that the Prosecutor had a twofold view of the harms captured under the term "forced marriage." First, there is harm caused by the nonconsensual conferral of the status of "marriage" and the resulting physical and psychological damage stemming from that

---

[87] RUF Indictment, *supra* note 76, at para. 60; AFRC Indictment, *supra* note 76, at para. 57; RUF Trial Judgment, *supra* note 1, at paras. 1300–1301 and 1493; AFRC Trial Judgment, *supra* note 2, at para. 717.

[88] AFRC Trial Judgment, *supra* note 2, at Partly Dissenting Opinion of Justice Doherty on Count 7 (Sexual Slavery) and Count 8 ("Forced Marriages"), para. 46 [hereinafter AFRC Doherty Dissent].

[89] AFRC Appeals Judgment, *supra* note 79, at para. 190.

[90] *Id.* at paras. 191–192.

[91] The term "bush wife" was widely used during the conflict: for example, see AFRC Doherty Dissent, *supra* note 88, at para. 31.

[92] Prosecutor v. Brima, Kamara and Kanu ("AFRC"), Case No. SCSL-04-16-T, Prosecutor Trial Brief, paras. 1868–1918 (Special Court for Sierra Leone, Trial Chamber II, Dec. 6, 2006) [hereinafter AFRC Prosecutor Trial Brief].

[93] AFRC Trial Judgment, *supra* note 2, at para. 701.

[94] *Id.* at para. 701.

conferral, especially societal stigmatization.[95] Second, there are physical and psychological harms caused by the forced duties associated with being a "wife."[96] Yet, even while he argued for the recognition of a specific harm to be named as forced marriage, he also – for unclear reasons – focused strongly on the sexual violence suffered by the victims of forced marriage.[97] For example, the Prosecutor categorized forced marriage in the AFRC indictment under the heading "Sexual Violence"[98] and, in the Final Trial Brief, listed both of the crimes against humanity charges of sexual slavery and forced marriage together as "sexual slavery and/or forced marriage."[99]

The Prosecutor's somewhat mixed signals were replicated by the Trial Chamber. This was evident as early as the Chamber's decision on the Defense motion for acquittal following the close of the prosecution case. In that decision, Justice Sebutinde found that forced marriage was a form of sexual slavery: "This is because the sexual elements inherent in these acts tend[] to dominate the other elements therein such as forced labor and other forced conjugal duties."[100] Clearly, at that time, she viewed the sexual aspects of the forced marriage evidence to be more important than the nonsexual aspects. Her view became the dominant view in the AFRC trial judgment, in which a majority dismissed the forced marriage charges for redundancy because the Prosecution's evidence of forced marriage was "completely subsumed" by the crime of sexual slavery.[101]

In the majority view, there was no distinct harm that needed to be named as "forced marriage": "there is no lacuna in the law which would necessitate a separate crime of 'forced marriage' as an 'other inhumane act.'"[102] More specifically, the majority judges rejected the Prosecutor's view of forced marriage as encompassing a distinct prohibited act encompassing two types of harm. It found no evidence of harm stemming from the forced conferral of the status of "marriage": "Not one of the victims of sexual slavery gave evidence that the mere fact that a rebel had declared her to be his wife had caused her any particular trauma, whether physical or mental."[103] And, in the opinion of the Trial Chamber, "had there been such evidence, it would not by itself have amounted to a crime against humanity, since it would not have been of a similar gravity to the [other crimes against humanity in the SCSL Statute]."[104] Thus, the majority judges took a very different approach to that of the Prosecutor.

Although the Prosecutor used the term "marriage" to indicate that a girl or woman was forced into a subordinate role,[105] the majority used it to indicate a situation that "establish[es]

---

[95] *Id.*

[96] AFRC Prosecutor Trial Brief, *supra* note 92, at paras. 1868–1918.

[97] It could be that the Prosecutor focused on the sexual aspects because he felt that they best illustrated the violations endured by victims, although this is not clear from the transcripts or briefs filed.

[98] AFRC Indictment, *supra* note 76, at para. 12.

[99] AFRC Prosecutor Trial Brief, *supra* note 92, at paras. 1868–1918.

[100] AFRC Rule 98, *supra* note 78, at para. 14.

[101] AFRC Trial Judgment, *supra* note 2, at paras. 713–714.

[102] *Id.* at para. 713.

[103] *Id.* at para. 710. The Court did have expert evidence before it relating to the stigmatization of "bush wives" within Sierra Leonean society: *id.* at Separate Concurring Opinion of the Hon. Justice Julia Sebutinde Appended to Judgment Pursuant to Rule 88(C), para. 13. This comment illustrates that the Prosecutor should have more clearly drawn this evidence of harm from the victim-witnesses.

[104] AFRC Trial Judgment, *supra* note 2, at para. 710.

[105] *Id.* at para. 701.

mutual obligations inherent in a husband[–]wife relationship."[106] This might indicate confusion between using the term as a social versus legal construct, but it also explains to some extent why the majority judges viewed the evidence, and therefore the harm, as amounting to sexual slavery. According to the majority judges, if marriage involves mutuality, then the evidence does not fit as it shows "wives" under the complete control of their "husbands."[107] This view of mutuality as defining marriage, however, did not take into account the actual subordinate situation of most women and girls in Sierra Leone before and during the conflict.[108] It also does not explain the complete focus of the majority on the sexual aspects of the "husband's" control, to the exclusion of the many non-sexual roles which undoubtedly occupied most of the victim's time as a "wife."

In dissent, Justice Doherty took a different approach, viewing forced marriage as "concerned with the mental and physical trauma of being forced unwillingly into a marital arrangement, the stigma associated with being labeled a rebel 'wife' and the corresponding rejection by the community."[109] She differentiates between marriage as a "relationship founded on the mutual consent of both spouses and forced marriage, in which the perpetrator subsumes the victim's will and undermines her exercise of self-determination."[110] She seems to focus exclusively on the first harm identified by the Prosecutor, and is not convinced that the second type of harm falls within the term, finding that "the conduct contemplated as 'forced marriage' does not necessarily involve elements of physical violence such as abduction, enslavement or rape, although the presence of these elements may go to prove the lack of consent of the victim."[111]

The Appeals Chamber strongly disagreed with the approach of the majority judges of the Trial Chamber: "no tribunal could reasonably have found that forced marriage was subsumed in the crime against humanity of sexual slavery."[112] It defined forced marriage in a similar, yet slightly different, manner than did the Prosecutor or Justice Doherty. According to the Appeals Chamber, forced marriage:

> describes a situation in which the perpetrator[,] through his words or conduct, or those of someone for whose actions he is responsible, compels a person by force, threat of force, or coercion to serve as a conjugal partner resulting in severe suffering, or physical, mental or psychological injury to the victim.[113]

In its descriptions, the Appeals Chamber appears to agree with the Prosecutor's description of the twofold harm underlying forced marriage, identifying injuries related to the imposition of the label of "wife" and its resultant stigmatization, and violations related to living as a "wife" (including those resulting from sexual, physical, and psychological abuse).[114]

---

[106] *Id.* at para. 711.

[107] *Id.*

[108] K. Belair, *Unearthing the Customary Law Foundations of "Forced Marriages" during Sierra Leone's Civil War: The Possible Impact of International Criminal Law on Customary Marriage and Women's Rights in Post-Conflict Sierra Leone*, 15 COLUM. J. GENDER & L. 551, 567–77 (2006).

[109] AFRC Doherty Dissent, *supra* note 88, at para. 42.

[110] *Id.* at para. 69.

[111] *Id.* at para. 70.

[112] AFRC Appeals Judgment, *supra* note 79, at para. 195.

[113] *Id.* at para. 196.

[114] *Id.* at paras. 190–193 and 199–200.

Interestingly, the Appeals Chamber highlighted the fact that there was systematicity in the forced marriages occurring in AFRC-held territory: "these forced conjugal associations were often organized and supervised by members of the AFRC or civilians assigned by them to such tasks."[115] As well, the victims of forced marriage were among the most vulnerable civilians in the conflict – abducted girls.[116] In sum, the Chamber concluded that forced marriage definitely qualifies as the crime against humanity of other inhumane acts, though it declined to enter fresh convictions against those particular defendants.[117]

The RUF Trial Judgment also considered charges relating to forced marriage, again charged as the crime against humanity of other inhumane acts. It concluded that there was a "pattern of conduct" undertaken by the RUF, under which women and girls were abducted or captured, assigned to RUF commanders or soldiers as "wives" regardless of their preexisting marital status, and then expected to behave in a certain way.[118] These "wives" were expected to submit to sex on demand (rape); maintain an exclusive sexual relationship with the "husband"; live in the "husband's" house; serve the "husband" by cooking, cleaning, and carrying out other domestic duties for him; carry the "husband's" possessions or looted supplies from camp to camp; bear and rear any children resulting from the "marriage"; and always show strict loyalty to the "husband."[119] If the "wife" did not live up to these expectations, she could expect to be violently punished or killed, or to be sent to fight on the front lines.[120] The RUF Trial Chamber also explicitly considered the "lasting social stigma" carried by victims of forced marriage, acknowledging that this stigmatization "hampers their recovery and reintegration into society."[121]

Very interestingly, the RUF Trial Chamber delved into the role played by forced marriage within the overall goals of the RUF. It concluded that "the use of the term 'wife' by the rebels was deliberate and strategic, with the aim of enslaving and psychologically manipulating the women and with the purpose of treating them like possessions."[122] Forced marriage satisfied two aims of the RUF at the same time, providing free domestic and sexual services to members of the RUF, and demonstrating RUF control over civilians in the area. It is for this reason that the Trial Chamber concluded that acts of forced marriage and sexual violence committed by the RUF "were not intended merely for personal satisfaction or a means of sexual gratification for the fighter"; they were a way to "effectively disempower[] the civilian population" and to "instill[] fear on entire communities."[123] All of the RUF Accused were convicted on the forced marriage charges, which were upheld on appeal.[124]

---

[115] *Id.* at paras. 191 and 201.

[116] *Id.* at para. 200.

[117] *Id.* at paras. 199–202. The Appeals Chamber did not enter fresh convictions because it was convinced that society's disapproval of the forceful abduction and use of women and girls as forced conjugal partners as part of a widespread or systematic attack against the civilian population is adequately reflected by recognizing that such conduct is criminal and that it constitutes an "Other Inhumane Act" capable of incurring individual criminal responsibility in international law. *Id.* at para. 202.

[118] RUF Trial Judgment, *supra* note 1, at paras. 1154, 1155, 1211–1213, 1293, 1295, 1412, 1413, and 1466–1472.

[119] *Id.*

[120] *Id.*

[121] *Id.* at para. 1296.

[122] *Id.* at para. 1466.

[123] *Id.* at para. 1348.

[124] *Id.* Disposition at paras. 678 (Sesay), 682 (Kallon), and 685 (Gbao, Justice Boutet dissenting); RUF Appeals Judgment, *supra* note 38, at paras. 740 (Sesay), 861 (Kallon), and 972 (Gbao).

Although Charles Taylor was not charged with forced marriage as an inhumane act, the Prosecutor did introduce extensive evidence of RUF, AFRC, and other affiliated fighters forcibly taking "bush wives."[125] In so doing, the Trial Chamber added even more detail to the record on this phenomenon. For example, the judges emphasized the young age of many of the "bush wives": there was evidence that the age range of bush wives was eight to twenty years, with members of the Small Boys Unit (of boy fighters) taking the eight- to ten-year-old girls to cook, launder, and pound rice.[126] There was also evidence that "wives" could be lent out as laborers to others by their commanders.[127] Despite the fact that forced marriage was not specifically charged in the Taylor case, Trial Chamber II took the opportunity to opine again on the issue of forced marriage, including on issues not directly related to his case.

The Trial Chamber began by stating that the Prosecutor erred in the AFRC and RUF cases in charging forced marriage under the category of inhumane acts.[128] The Trial Chamber stated that the term is a misnomer because there is no actual marriage: "The Trial Chamber does not consider the nomenclature of 'marriage' to be helpful in describing what happened to the victims of this forced conjugal association and finds it inappropriate to refer to their perpetrators as 'husbands.'"[129] In its view, the offense meant to be captured – forced conjugal association – has two main aspects: sexual slavery and forced labor in the form of domestic work (such as cooking and cleaning).[130] Thus, what has otherwise been incorrectly termed "forced marriage" is actually two different forms of enslavement imposed through forced conjugal association, which it refers to as "conjugal slavery."[131] The Trial Chamber felt that it is therefore incorrect to refer to conjugal slavery as a new crime.[132]

There are positive aspects of the Court's various discussions of forced marriage or conjugal slavery in the AFRC, RUF, and Taylor judgments, as well as key questions still left unanswered. These discussions helped to name as a crime a certain form of gender-based violence that was commonplace within areas under AFRC and RUF control in the Sierra

---

[125] Taylor Trial Judgment, *supra* note 1, at para. 422.

[126] *Id.* at para. 1101.

[127] *Id.* at para. 1700.

[128] *Id.* at para. 424.

[129] *Id.* at para. 426; *see also* para. 425.

[130] *Id.* at paras. 424–425.

[131] *Id.* at paras. 427–428. The Trial Chamber views conjugal slavery as composed of both sexual and nonsexual aspects, all of which are enslavement. *Id.* at para. 427. There is no differentiation between the sexual and nonsexual acts, and they are not limited to sexual slavery. *Id.* at para. 428. That said, the Trial Chamber then confuses its discussion somewhat by referring to the forced labor aspect of conjugal slavery as "a descriptive component of a distinctive form of sexual slavery" [as opposed to enslavement]. *Id.* at para. 429. The Judgment states, "[i]t is not a definitional element of a new crime, in the same way that gang rape is a distinctive form of rape, yet nevertheless falls within the scope of rape." *Id.* The Trial Chamber may have felt that it needed to say this because it was considering the forced marriage evidence under the charge of sexual slavery, and it did not want to be seen as stepping outside of the dictates of the indictment. However, in reality, its application of the evidence was to divide the forced marriage evidence into evidence applicable to sexual slavery, and the evidence applicable to enslavement (forced labor). This approach makes sense, as the Chamber had categorized both aspects of forced marriage as forms of enslavement in para. 427, so it is not clear why the analysis mentioned above in para. 429 was necessary.

[132] *Id.* at para. 430. This was in response to some commentators referring to the "new" crime of forced marriage: *see, e.g.*, M. Frulli, *Advancing International Criminal Law: The Special Court for Sierra Leone Recognizes Forced Marriage as a "New" Crime against Humanity*, 6 J. INT'L CRIM. JUST. 1033 (2008).

Leone conflict. Naming is an important expressive tool of the law, and the recognition of forced marriage or conjugal slavery as prohibited acts within crimes against humanity authoritatively transformed a previously legally unacknowledged experience into acknowledged wrongs.[133] The "wives" or victims suffered a unique harm caused by being affiliated in an intimate way with members of the warring parties and are therefore viewed by many within Sierra Leonean society as collaborators.[134] This naming helps to legitimize the experiences of the victims, and identifies these experiences as crimes.

That said, the discussions raise some important questions. The analysis outlined above shows that there is still no agreement about what to call this crime – forced marriage or conjugal slavery? – or how exactly to define or categorize it. On the issue of what to call the prohibited act or collection of acts, there are arguments both for and against using the term "forced marriage." The argument in favor of the term is that it reflects the language used by victims to describe the subjugation as a "bush wife" by their "husbands." It is important for victims to be able to self-identify with the crimes charged.

The main argument against the term is that, at least in the context of Sierra Leone, no actual marriage took place as it is understood either in international human rights law or domestic Sierra Leonean law.[135] Thus, the "marriage" in "forced marriage" must always be understood as a perversion of the term[136] (this appears to be why the Appeals Chamber chose a definition focusing on conjugality). It is for this reason that Patricia Sellers believes that "forced marriage" is a descriptive rather than a legal phrase and argues that the term represents "linguistic camouflage."[137]

There are also arguments for and against the term proposed by the Taylor Trial Chamber, "conjugal slavery." A strong argument for the term is that "slavery" seems to more precisely capture the totality of the experiences of the victims, with the term "conjugal" meant to describe the rape and forced domestic labor aspects of the slavery. In Sellers' view, the term "slavery" is more accurate than that of "forced marriage."[138] It is not entirely clear, however, whether a reference to slavery fully captures the twofold harms outlined by the Prosecutor when defining the harm of forced marriage. The term "conjugal" also causes concern. The SCSL Appeals Chamber explained the differing roles expected in the conjugal relationship as follows: the "wife" was expected to provide sex on demand, domestic labor, childbearing and childcare, whereas the "husband" was to provide food, clothing, and protection (including protection from rape by other men).[139]

---

[133] Cook & Cusack, *supra* note 5, at 39. On the importance of the SCSL recognizing forced marriage, see A. Palmer, *An Evolutionary Analysis of Gender-Based War Crimes and the Continued Tolerance of "Forced Marriage,"* 7(1) Nw. J. Int'l Hum. Rts. 133, 134 (2008).

[134] B. Van Schaack, *Atrocity Crimes Litigation: 2008 Year-In-Review*, 7(2) Nw. J. Int'l Hum. Rts. 170, 205 (2009); B. Nowrojee, *Making the Invisible War Crime Visible: Post-Conflict Justice for Sierra Leone's Rape Victims*, 18 Harv. Hum. Rts. L.J. 85, 102 (2005); Hon. T. Doherty, *Developments in the Prosecution of Gender-Related Crimes – The Special Court for Sierra Leone Experience*, 17(2) Am. U.J. Gender Soc. Pol'y & L.327, 331 (2009).

[135] J. Gong-Gershowitz, *Forced Marriage: A "New" Crime against Humanity?*, 8(1) Nw. J. Int'l Hum. Rts. 53, 66 (2009).

[136] Note that Kelsall argues differently: T. Kelsall, Culture under Cross-Examination: International Justice and the Special Court for Sierra Leone 243–55 (2009).

[137] *See* P. Viseur Sellers, *Wartime Female Slavery: Enslavement?*, 44(1) Cornell Int'l L. Rev. 115, 137, 142 (2011).

[138] For a more detailed discussion, see V. Oosterveld, *Forced Marriage and the Special Court for Sierra Leone: Legal Advances and Conceptual Difficulties*, 2 J. Int'l Humanitarian Legal Stud. 127, 152–53 (2011).

[139] AFRC Appeals Judgment, *supra* note 79, at para. 190.

These are highly gendered roles. It would be very worrisome if this patriarchal under-standing of conjugality became the only understanding of conjugality in international criminal law.[140] This concern has caused some commentators to warn that forced mar-riage must be able to be applied in a gender-neutral manner, so as to capture situations where both the "wife" and the "husband" are forcibly married, as in Cambodia during the Khmer Rouge period;[141] where two women or two men are forcibly married; where both the victim and the perpetrator are the same sex; or where the perpetrator is female and the victim is male.[142] On the other hand, these concerns might be addressed if, in each circumstance of conjugal slavery explored, the judges made clear that the nature of the "conjugality" associated with the slavery is determined not only by the social mores of the society being examined, but also by a consideration of the ways in which that "conjugal-ity" violates the victim's international human rights.

The SCSL's consideration of forced marriage/conjugal slavery raises the question of how best to categorize the prohibited act(s). The AFRC and RUF trial and appeals judgments considered forced marriage as a subcategory of the crime against humanity of "other inhu-mane acts."[143] The Taylor trial judgment instead classified the acts previously described as forced marriage as conjugal slavery, considering the evidence of sexual violence under the crime against humanity of sexual slavery and the forced labor evidence under the crime against humanity of enslavement.[144] These different forms of categorization seem to capture different harms.

In the AFRC case, the Prosecutor and the Appeals Chamber appeared to agree that there were two kinds of harm – namely, harm caused by the nonconsensual conferral of the sta-tus of "marriage" and the resulting physical and psychological damage stemming from that conferral, especially societal stigmatization, and the physical and psychological harms caused by the forced duties associated with being a "wife."[145] This approach has been praised by some as capturing, in one term, a constellation of harms that other international crim-inal law terms, such as sexual slavery, rape, and forced labor do not adequately cover.[146] In other words, forced marriage is not simply a name given to a compound crime (for exam-ple, rape plus enslavement); it represents a distinct harm that equals more than the sum of

---

[140] Nowrojee, *supra* note 134, at 102.

[141] Prosecutor v. Nuon, Ieng, Khieu and Ieng, Case No. 002/19–09–2007-ECCC/TC, Closing Order, paras. 842, 845, 848 and 1442–1447 (Extraordinary Chambers in the Court of Cambodia, Office of the Co-Investigating Judges, Sept. 15, 2010) [hereinafter ECCC Closing Order]. The Extraordinary Chambers in the Court of Cambodia (ECCC) have similarly described forced marriage as a situation in which the victims were forced to enter into conjugal relationships in coercive circumstances. *Id.* at paras. 1442–1447.

[142] B.A. Toy-Cronin, *What Is Forced Marriage? Toward a Definition of Forced Marriage as a Crime against Humanity*, 19(2) COLUM. J. GENDER & L. 539, 579–81 (2010); Nowrojee, *supra* note 135, at 102; Oosterveld, *supra* note 138, at 155; and M.P. Scharf & S. Mattler, *Forced Marriage: Exploring the Viability of the Special Court for Sierra Leone's New Crime against Humanity* 23 (Case Research Paper in Legal Studies, Working Paper 05-35, 2005).

[143] AFRC Trial Judgment, *supra* note 2, at paras. 703–707; AFRC Appeals Judgment, *supra* note 79, at paras. 197–201; and RUF Trial Judgment, *supra* note 1, at paras. 1283–1297.

[144] Taylor Trial Judgment, *supra* note 1, at, *e.g.*, paras. 1066, 1072–1075, 1094, 1098, 1108, 1144–1146, 1828, and 1833.

[145] AFRC Trial Judgment, *supra* note 2, at para. 701; AFRC Prosecutor Trial Brief, *supra* note 92, at paras. 1868–1918; AFRC Appeals Judgment, *supra* note 79, at paras. 190–193 and 199–200.

[146] Van Schaack, *supra* note 134, at 205. *See also* Oosterveld, *supra* note 138, at 144–45.

its parts.[147] However, there are others who question whether both harms can or should be captured within the term "forced marriage." They believe that forced marriage should be narrowly understood as the forced conferral of the status of "marriage" and that the harm relates specifically to the ongoing effects of the "marriage" status on victims.[148] In this way, it would be a continuing crime, just like sexual slavery.[149] These commentators feel that other harms suffered by the victim within the forced marriage should be charged as separate offenses, such as rape, sexual slavery, or enslavement.[150] They argue that the AFRC Appeals Chamber's approach is unclear as to exactly which harms are included under the duties associated with being a "wife," and therefore raises issues of *nullum crimen sine lege*.[151] The Appeals Chamber seems to answer this by pointing out that the constellation of acts satisfying the second type of harm are illegal in and of themselves.[152]

Although the acts captured by the term "forced marriage" are undoubtedly inhumane, Sellers believes that a much more straightforward approach would be to consider the forced marriage acts under the crime against humanity of enslavement.[153] She argues – convincingly – that all of the aspects of forced marriage, whether defined narrowly or broadly, fit within the definition of enslavement.[154] The Taylor trial judgment came close to this approach by considering the evidence under two different charges: the sexual violence evidence under sexual slavery,[155] and the forced labor evidence under the crime against humanity of enslavement.[156] Sellers' approach of classifying all of the acts inherent in forced marriage as the crime against humanity of enslavement, and the Taylor approach of splitting the classification between sexual slavery and enslavement, are attractive not least because they both avoid issues of *nullum crimen sine lege*. Although the classification of enslavement or conjugal slavery is also attractive because it accurately and precisely includes the sexual violence and forced labor aspects of serving as a "bush wife," it does raise questions of whether the stigmatization harm identified as specific to "bush wives" is captured within enslavement, and whether victims would self-identify as slaves.[157] Thus, it is not absolutely clear that naming and classifying forced marriage as a form of enslavement is necessarily the perfect route.

Forced marriage or conjugal slavery clearly require further consideration within international criminal legal circles, but the SCSL has made a very good start in bringing this

---

[147] N. Jain, *Forced Marriage as a Crime against Humanity: Problems of Definition and Prosecution*, 6 J. Int'l Crim. Just. 1013, 1031 (2008).

[148] Toy-Cronin, *supra* note 142, at 576.

[149] AFRC Trial Judgment, *supra* note 2, at paras. 39–40; Taylor Trial Judgment, *supra* note 1, at paras. 119 and 1018.

[150] *Id.* at para. 576; K. Carlson & D. Mazurana, *Forced Marriage within the Lord's Resistance Army, Uganda* 64 (May 2008), *available at* http://sites.tufts.edu/feinstein/2008/forced-marriage-within-the-lra-uganda.

[151] Toy-Cronin, *supra* note 142, at 578–79; N.A. Goodfellow, The Miscategorization of "Forced Marriage" as a Crime against Humanity by the Special Court for Sierra Leone, 11 Int'l Crim. L. Rev. 831, 848–53 (2011).

[152] AFRC Appeals Judgment, *supra* note 79, at para. 201. *See also* S. Wharton, *The Evolution of International Criminal Law: Prosecuting "New" Crimes before the Special Court for Sierra Leone*, 11 Int'l Crim. L. Rev. 217, 232 (2011), and Frulli, *supra* note 132, at 1033.

[153] Sellers, *supra* note 137, at 135.

[154] *Id.*

[155] Taylor Trial Judgment, *supra* note 1, paras. 1072–1075, 1094, 1098, 1108, 1132, 1144–1146, and 1163.

[156] *Id.* at paras. 1828 and 1833 for an example of how this evidence was considered separately.

[157] For a more detailed discussion, see Oosterveld, *supra* note 138, at 152–53.

violation to the attention of the international and Sierra Leonean community. It will undoubtedly be developed further by other tribunals, including the ECCC and the ICC.[158]

D. *Outrages on Personal Dignity*

The SCSL again played a confirmatory role, thereby helping to solidify international criminal law's gender jurisprudence, in its consideration of the war crime of outrages against personal dignity. The AFRC, RUF and Taylor Trial Chambers adopted similar elements of crime, based on the ICC's elements of crime:[159]

1. The perpetrator humiliated, degraded or otherwise violated the personal dignity of the victim;
2. The humiliation, degradation or other violation was so serious as to be generally considered an outrage upon personal dignity;
3. The perpetrator intentionally committed or participated in an act or omission which would be generally considered to cause serious humiliation, degradation or otherwise be a serious attack on human dignity; and
4. The perpetrator knew that the act or omission could have such an effect.[160]

The RUF trial judgment noted that the *actus reus* of the offense "is that there was an act or omission that caused serious humiliation, degradation or otherwise violated the personal dignity of the victim," and this determination is based on an objective assessment.[161] It also confirmed that the act need not cause lasting suffering to the victim.[162] Such acts include rape and sexual slavery.[163] The *mens rea* of the offense requires that the act or omission be done intentionally and that the Accused must have known that his or her act could cause serious humiliation or degradation, or otherwise be a serious attack on human dignity.[164] The Chamber noted that the Prosecutor need only prove that the Accused knew of the possible consequences of the act, and not that he or she knew of the actual consequences.[165] As well, the Accused need not have a discriminatory intent or motive.[166]

Of the three cases, the Taylor trial judgment appeared to add the most nuance to international criminal law's consideration of outrages upon personal dignity. It considered that acts that would normally be recognized as outrages upon personal dignity could be aggravated

---

[158] For example, in the trial judgment relating to Case 002 (see ECCC Closing Order, *supra* note 141, at paras. 1442–1447). Forced marriage is not charged as such by the ICC, but does arise in the facts. *See* Prosecutor v. Katanga and Chui, Case No. ICC-01/04-01/07, Prosecution's Submission of Public Version of Document Containing the Charges Annex 1, § 89 (Apr.24, 2008), stating "Some women, who were captured at Bogoro and spared because they hid their ethnicity, were raped and forcibly taken to military camps. Once there, they were sometimes given as a 'wife' to their captors or kept in the camp's prison, which was a hole dug in the ground."

[159] International Criminal Court Elements of Crimes art. 8(2)(b)(xxi).

[160] Taylor Trial Judgment, *supra* note 1, at para. 431; AFRC Trial Judgment, *supra* note 2, at para. 716; RUF Trial Judgment, *supra* note 1, at para. 175.

[161] RUF Trial Judgment, *supra* note 1, at para. 176.

[162] *Id.*

[163] AFRC Trial Judgment, *supra* note 2, at paras. 718 and 719; Taylor Trial Judgment, *supra* note 1, at para. 432.

[164] RUF Trial Judgment, *supra* note 1, at para. 177.

[165] *Id.*

[166] *Id.*

by adding a public or additionally humiliating or degrading aspect to the commission of the prohibited act. Therefore, it found that acts such as sexual mutilation through insertion of objects into a victim's vagina, such as wood; forced undressing as a prelude to rape; and public humiliation combined with rape, such as rape in public, where neighbors, community members, or husbands, children, or other family members are forced to watch, are forms of aggravated outrages upon personal dignity.[167] In Taylor, the Trial Chamber took a strict interpretation of the indictment, which charged "outrages upon personal dignity, including rape and sexual slavery," and considered only evidence of rape and sexual slavery under the charge.[168] The Trial Chamber found that the Prosecutor did not provide notice to the Accused of any other forms of sexual violence.[169]

The SCSL's consideration of the war crime of outrages upon personal dignity was largely supportive of already-existing law on the matter.[170] It did provide helpful additional detail by finding that the specific act of sexual slavery amounted to an outrage upon personal dignity, and that an outrage upon personal dignity could be aggravated by the addition of a public element, such as rape in front of family members; or an extra-humiliating element, such as forced undressing prior to rape; or insertion of an object into the victim's vagina following rape.

III. RELATION OF GENDER-BASED CRIMES TO OTHER CRIMES: INTERSECTIONALITY

Gender-based violence taking place during conflict is usually part of a broader picture of complex victimization. For example, sexual violence of one type, such as rape, may occur side by side with other types of sexual violence, such as sexual slavery or sexual mutilation, or gendered violence, such as forced marriage or forced domestic labor. In the conflict in Sierra Leone, sexual slavery commonly intersected with forced marriage: the RUF Trial Chamber noted that "it was common practice for rebels to keep captured women subject to their control as sex slaves and to force conjugal relationships on women who unwillingly became their 'wives.'"[171] [Note, however, that under the Taylor analysis, sexual slavery and the sexual portion of forced marriage are not overlapping, but are considered to be the same conduct.][172] Sexual violence may also occur alongside, or be used to facilitate, other types of prohibited acts such as murder, torture, and enslavement. One excellent example of this intersectionality is found in the RUF and Taylor trial judgments. In the RUF judgment, the Trial Chamber characterized the gender-based violence inflicted by the RUF as intimately linked to the larger strategy of the RUF. The "acts were not intended merely for the personal satisfaction or a means of sexual gratification for the fighter."[173] Rather, they were intended to terrorize civilians into submission to the RUF.[174] In order to achieve this goal, the RUF created "an atmosphere

---

[167] Taylor Trial Judgment, *supra* note 1, at para. 1196; *see also* para. 1200(iii) for an example of a victim raped in front of her child and other captured persons.

[168] *Id.* at para. 1194.

[169] *Id.*

[170] *E.g.*, Kunarac Appeal Judgment, *supra* note 21, at para. 163.

[171] RUF Trial Judgment, *supra* note 1, at para. 1465.

[172] Taylor Trial Judgment, *supra* note 1, at para. 427.

[173] RUF Trial Judgment, *supra* note 1, at para. 1348.

[174] *Id.* at para. 1348.

in which violence, oppression and lawlessness prevailed."[175] They then adopted a "calculated and concerted pattern" of sexual violence.[176] This pattern included "perverse methods of sexual violence against women and men of all ages," such as "brutal gang rapes, the insertion of various objects into victims' genitalia, the raping of pregnant women and forced sexual intercourse between male and female civilian abductees."[177] It also included forcing girls and women to serve as "wives" to RUF commanders and fighters.[178] The result of this gender-based violence was powerful: it "effectively disempowered the civilian population and had a direct effect of instilling fear on entire communities."[179] The RUF did this by abusing, debasing and isolating the individual victim, therefore "deliberately destroy[ing] the existing family nucleus" by relying on the stigma attached to sexual violence within Sierra Leonean society.[180] This meant that "[v]ictims of sexual violence were ostracized, husbands left their wives, and daughters and young girls were unable to marry within their community."[181] This pattern of gender-based violence resulted in the unraveling of "cultural values and relationships which held the societies together."[182] The Trial Chamber found that this demonstrated a specific intent to terrorize the civilian population, a view which was upheld on appeal.[183]

Similarly, in the Taylor trial judgment, the Trial Chamber held that sexual violence committed by the RUF, AFRC, and affiliated fighting forces had the primary purpose of spreading terror, and was "deliberately aimed at destroying the traditional family nucleus, thus undermining the cultural values and relationships which held society together."[184] It also found that sexual violence was committed in public as a deliberate tactic on the part of the perpetrators to spread terror among the civilian population, and was not merely a means of sexual gratification.[185]

The war crime of committing acts of terror is not normally understood as a gendered crime. However, the analysis of the RUF and Taylor Trial Chambers has shed crucial light on just how critical gender-based violence was in the rebels' quest to control the civilian population. This sets important precedent for the consideration of this and other seemingly gender-neutral crimes by other courts: it shows how such crimes can be carried out in gender-specific ways or may have gendered outcomes.[186] By considering the interrelationships among crimes and their constituent prohibited acts, the RUF and Taylor Trial Chambers demonstrated both the serious nature of the sexual violence committed by the rebels, and the gendered nature of the seemingly gender-neutral war crime of committing acts of terror. This conscious contextualization allows for a more nuanced understanding of the role played by gender within armed conflicts.

---

[175] *Id.* at para. 1347.
[176] *Id.*
[177] *Id.* at para. 1347 (footnotes omitted).
[178] *Id.* at para. 1351.
[179] *Id.* at paras. 1348 and 1351.
[180] *Id.* at paras. 1348–1349.
[181] *Id.* at para. 1349.
[182] *Id.*
[183] *Id.* at paras. 1352 and 1356; RUF Appeals Judgment, *supra* note 37, at para. 990.
[184] Taylor Trial Judgment, *supra* note 1, at para. 2034; *see also* paras. 2037, 2051–2052, 2175, and 2177.
[185] *Id.* at para. 2036.
[186] Oosterveld, *supra* note 36, at 71.

IV. ACTS OF GENDER-BASED VIOLENCE DIRECTED AGAINST MEN AND BOYS

Another positive development within the SCSL's RUF jurisprudence was that attention was brought to gender-based violence directed against men and boys. It is interesting to compare the different approaches in this respect between the AFRC and the RUF Trial Chambers. In the AFRC, RUF, and Taylor cases, the Prosecutor restricted the pleading on the specific counts related to sexual violence as being directed at women.[187] In the AFRC case, the Trial Chamber therefore restricted its consideration of sexual violence crimes to those committed against women and girls.[188] Similarly, in the Taylor case, the same Trial Chamber found that the Indictment's reference to "women and girls" cannot be considered inherently corrected to include men and boys because the Prosecutor did not provide the Accused with subsequent timely, clear, and consistent notice that the criminal acts include sexual violence directed against men and boys.[189]

The RUF Trial Chamber, in contrast, found that, although the Prosecutor had indeed restricted his pleadings in the Indictment to crimes committed against women and girls, the subsequent clear, timely, and consistent notice provided by the Prosecutor on crimes directed against men and boys cured this defect in the Indictment.[190] Thus, the Court considered numerous instances of gender-based violence, including sexual violence, directed against men and boys "of all ages."[191] For example, in Bomboafuidu, male and female civilians captured by the RUF were paired up and ordered to have sex with each other.[192] The rebels then sexually mutilated the victims, slitting the sexual organs of both the male and female captives.[193] The Trial Chamber also recounted evidence in which rebels in Bumpeh ordered a couple to have sexual intercourse in the presence of their daughter and other captured civilians and, after the rape, they forced the man's daughter to wash her father's penis.[194] The Chamber found that these acts severely humiliated both members of the couple and their daughter.[195]

Additionally, the Chamber seemed to recognize the psychological harm caused to a husband who was forced by RUF fighters to count as eight rebels consecutively raped his wife, and then watched her die at the hands of the same rebels.[196] The Chamber recognized that the effect of these acts was to disempower the male members of the community, by demonstrating that they "were unable to protect their own wives, daughters, mothers and sisters."[197]

---

[187] AFRC Indictment, *supra* note 76, at para. 51; RUF Indictment, *supra* note 76, at paras. 54–60; Taylor Indictment, *supra* note 7, at paras. 14–17.

[188] AFRC Trial Judgment, *supra* note 2, at paras. 969–1068.

[189] Taylor Trial Judgment, *supra* note 1, at paras. 124–134. This meant that sexual violence directed against men and boys was rarely mentioned, although there are references such as that found in *id.* at para. 1699, about a man who tried to escape who had his testicles lacerated, then civilians were forced to kill him.

[190] RUF Trial Judgment, *supra* note 1, at paras. 1303–1304. Although this discussion occurs in the section discussing outrages upon personal dignity, it appears to apply more broadly.

[191] *Id.* at para. 1347.

[192] *Id.* at paras. 1207, 1208, and 1307.

[193] *Id.*

[194] *Id.* at para. 1302.

[195] *Id.* at para. 1305.

[196] *Id.* at para. 1347.

[197] *Id.* at para. 1350.

The Chamber also noted nonsexual but gendered targeting of men and boys. In Tomandu, the RUF divided the male and female civilians into two groups, with the men subjected to having "RUF" carved into their backs and arms.[198] In Penduma, the rape of women was accompanied by the killing or limb amputation of men.[199] In examining the widespread phenomenon of recruitment of child soldiers, the Chamber noted that the RUF specifically recruited and used young boys as soldiers because of their ability to effectively conduct hazardous activities, their loyalty to the movement, and their lack of fear in killing human beings.[200] Even though the analysis of gender-based crimes directed against men and boys could have been even more extensive, this recognition is still welcome and groundbreaking.[201]

V. CREATING SILENCE ON GENDER-BASED CRIMES: THE CDF CASE

This chapter has, to this point, highlighted the gender jurisprudence of the SCSL by examining the AFRC, RUF, and Taylor decisions and judgments. Unfortunately, there is another aspect of the SCSL's jurisprudence seen in the CDF case: that of silence on gender matters. The Prosecutor had intended that the CDF case also address crimes of gender-based violence. Four months before the start of the CDF trial, he requested leave to amend the CDF Indictment to add four new counts: rape as a crime against humanity, sexual slavery and other forms of sexual violence as a crime against humanity, forced marriage as the crime against humanity of other inhumane acts, and the war crime of outrages upon personal dignity.[202] In his request, the Prosecutor explained that the reason he was requesting leave to amend the Indictment was because he had only recently obtained evidence strong enough to bring these charges.[203] Four months later and just prior to the start of the CDF trial, a majority of the Trial Chamber rejected the Prosecutor's request. It found that granting the amendment would prejudice the rights of the Accused to a fair and expeditious trial.[204] It interpreted the Prosecutor's amendment motion as a request for an exception for "gender offences and offenders" to the general rule on timeliness.[205] The Prosecutor sought leave to appeal. He explained that collection of evidence of gender-based crimes was more difficult in the CDF case than in other cases because of the risks to victims created by ongoing popular support for the CDF.[206] His request was denied by the Trial Chamber majority.[207]

---

[198] *Id.* at para. 1210.

[199] *Id.* at para. 1354.

[200] *Id.* at para. 1616.

[201] See Sivakumaran's plea for more attention to gender-based violence directed against men and boys in S. Sivakumaran, *Lost in Translation: UN Responses to Sexual Violence against Men and Boys in Situations of Armed Conflict*, 92 INT'L REV. RED CROSS 259, 276–77 (2010); and S. Sivakumaran, *Sexual Violence against Men in Armed Conflict*, 18 EUR. J. INT'L L. 253 (2007).

[202] Prosecutor v. Norman, Fofana and Kondewa, Case No. SCSL-04–14-PT, Prosecution Request to Amend the Indictment (Special Court for Sierra Leone, Feb. 9, 2004).

[203] Prosecutor v. Norman, Fofana and Kondewa, Case No. SCSL-04–14-PT, Decision on Prosecution Request for Leave to Amend the Indictment para. 10(c) (Special Court for Sierra Leone, May 20, 2004).

[204] *Id.* at para. 86.

[205] *Id.* at para. 84.

[206] Prosecutor v. Norman, Fofana and Kondewa, Case No. SCSL-04–14-T, Majority Decision on the Prosecution's Application for Leave to File an Interlocutory Appeal against the Decision on the Prosecution's Request for Leave to Amend the Indictment, para. 8 (Special Court for Sierra Leone, Aug. 8, 2004).

[207] *Id.* at paras. 37–38.

Subsequently, the Prosecutor was denied, by the same majority, the opportunity to introduce evidence of gender-based violence to substantiate existing charges of the crime against
humanity of inhumane acts and the war crime of cruel treatment.[208] The reasoning for this
decision was contrary to the existing trend within the International Criminal Tribunals for
the Former Yugoslavia and Rwanda.[209] The majority denied the admission of sexual violence evidence using regressive – indeed, alarming – reasoning. For example, Justice Itoe
implied that evidence of gender-based crimes is much more likely to impugn the reputation
of the Accused than any other kind of evidence and therefore make it difficult for the judges
to fairly evaluate the case.[210] Staggs Kelsall and Stepakoff studied the effects on victim-witnesses of these decisions, and found that the active silencing of the victims' sexual violence
evidence by two of the Trial Chamber judges had a negative psychological impact.[211]

Although a majority of the Appeals Chamber decided not to revisit the majority Trial
Chamber's decision on the amendment of the Indictment, the Chamber did find that the
second decision – not to allow evidence of gender-based crimes to prove the crime against
humanity of inhumane acts or the war crime of cruel treatment – was incorrect.[212] The
Appeals Chamber also strongly (and correctly) criticized Justice Itoe, by observing that
the right to a fair trial "cannot be violated by the introduction of evidence relevant to any
allegation in the trial proceedings, regardless of the nature or severity of the evidence."[213]
However, the Appeals Chamber did not reopen the trial judgment, choosing instead to view
its comments as providing "guidance to the Trial Chamber."[214] Thus, the history of rape and
other forms of sexual violence committed by the CDF against women and girls will never
be recorded by the SCSL.[215]

VI. CONCLUSION

This chapter has explored developments within the SCSL with respect to four specific types
of gender-based violence: rape, sexual slavery, forced marriage (or conjugal slavery), and
outrages upon personal dignity. In many respects, the Court's consideration of these prohibited acts served either to reaffirm existing international law (on rape and outrages upon

---

[208] Prosecutor v. Norman, Fofana and Kondewa, Case No. SCSL-04–14-T, Reasoned Majority Decision on
   Prosecution Motion for a Ruling on Admissibility of Evidence para. 20 (Special Court for Sierra Leone, May
   24, 2005). For critiques of the majority Trial Chamber decisions, see M. Staggs Kelsall & S. Stepakoff, *When
   We Wanted to Talk About Rape: Silencing Sexual Violence at the Special Court for Sierra Leone*, 1(3) INT'L J.
   TRANSITIONAL JUST. 355 (2007), and V. Oosterveld, *The Special Court for Sierra Leone, Child Soldiers, and
   Forced Marriage: Providing Clarity or Confusion?*, 45 CANADIAN Y.B. INT'L L. 131, 159–68 (2007).
[209] This was pointed out on appeal: Prosecutor v. Fofana and Kondewa ("CDF"), Case No. SCSL-04–14-A,
   Judgment nn.855–56 (Special Court for Sierra Leone, Appeals Chamber, May 28, 2008) [hereinafter CDF
   Appeals Judgment].
[210] Prosecutor v. Norman, Fofana and Kondewa, Case No. SCSL-04–14-T, Separate Concurring Opinion of Hon.
   Justice Benjamin Mutanga Itoe, Presiding Judge, on the Chamber Majority Decision on Prosecution Motion
   for a Ruling on the Admissibility of Evidence paras. 64 and 78(vi) (Special Court for Sierra Leone, May 24,
   2005).
[211] Staggs Kelsall & Stepakoff, *supra* note 208, at 373–74.
[212] CDF Appeals Judgment, *supra* note 209, at paras. 426–427, 441, 443, 446, 450.
[213] *Id.* at para. 446.
[214] *Id.* at para. 451.
[215] The CDF Trial Judgment did note some instances of sexual violence directed against men. *See* CDF Trial
   Judgment, *supra* note 4, at paras. 496 and 520.

personal dignity) or went further and helped to develop international law (on sexual slavery and forced marriage/conjugal slavery). Given the groundbreaking nature of its discussion of the latter two prohibited acts, it is not surprising that some of the Court's conclusions on forced marriage/conjugal slavery raise more questions than they answer. However, it can be said that one of the Court's major successes has been expressive in nature. By labeling the gender-based violence suffered by women and girls as forced marriage/conjugal slavery and sexual slavery, and by naming the rape that was carried out against women, girls, men, and boys as criminal, these violations were publicly and internationally acknowledged as wrongs.

Although much attention has been focused on the SCSL's addition of forced marriage to international criminal law's gender lexicon, it is important to recognize that the Court's contributions to gender-sensitive jurisprudence do not stop there. This chapter also examines the Court's nuanced understanding of how gender-based crimes intersect with other crimes, thereby allowing for a deeper understanding of the complexity of victimization during the conflict. The Court also focused on the targeting of men and boys for gender-based violence, including rape, thereby bringing much-needed attention to this form of victimization. Unfortunately, the SCSL's gender jurisprudence is marred by serious mistakes made in the CDF case, resulting in the exclusion of gender-based crimes from consideration in the trial judgment. The CDF case must serve as a cautionary tale: although international criminal jurisprudence is becoming increasingly gender-sensitive, this sensitivity can be very fragile as it depends on the gender knowledge of the Court officials.

13

The Judicial Contribution of the Special Court for Sierra Leone to the Prosecution of Terrorism

Roberta Arnold[*]

I. INTRODUCTION

September 11, 2001 marked a radical change in the qualification of terrorism: traditionally considered as a criminal offense to be fought with law enforcement and judicial assistance mechanisms,[1] in the aftermath of the attacks in New York and Washington, it developed into a phenomenon to be addressed, according to some, with military force.[2] A decade after the U.S.-led invasion and occupation of Afghanistan, which was accused of hosting terrorist movements, alleged key players such as Osama Bin Laden have departed, but the world is still left with the heavy inheritance to discover the formula for its eradication.

None of the methods adopted so far seems to have been particularly successful. The first approach probably depends too much on domestic prosecution and international cooperation, whereas the second is too heavily reliant on tools (the military), which were not conceived and trained to fight an (invisible) adversary who does not follow traditional (and lawful) rules of warfare. At the same time, while the reflectors of the international scene were focused on the "war on terror" in Afghanistan, backstage the international legal community has been working on the improvement of international judicial mechanisms as an alternative tool. The main merit of the international criminal tribunals[3] that have been

---

[*] PhD (Bern), LLM (Nottingham), Legal Assistant within the Federal Attorney General's Office, Competence Centre for International Criminal Law, Bern, Switzerland. The views represented here are the author's only and do not necessarily correspond with the views of the Federal Attorney General's office.

[1] In the 1960s–1980s the preferred method was the adoption of domestic criminal law provisions via the implementation of international treaties such as the 1963 Tokyo Convention on Offenses and Certain Other Acts Committed on Board Aircraft, the 1979 U.N. International Convention against the Taking of Hostages, or the 1988 Convention for the Suppression of Unlawful Acts against the Safety of Maritime Navigation.

[2] U.N. Security Council: Letter dated October 7, 2001 from the Permanent Representative of the United States of America to the United Nations Security Council Addressed to the President of the Security Council, U.N. Doc. S/2001/946 (Oct. 7, 2001); Letter dated October 7, 2001 from the Chargé d'affaires a.i. of the Permanent Mission of the United Kingdom of Great Britain and Northern Ireland to the United Nations addressed to the President of the Security Council, U.N. Doc. S/2001/947; W. Lietzau, *Old Laws, New Wars: Jus Ad Bellum in an Age of Terrorism*, 8 U.N. Y.B. 8, 383; *contra* MYRA WILLIAMSON, TERRORISM, WAR AND INTERNATIONAL LAW: THE LEGALITY OF THE USE OF FORCE AGAINST AFGHANISTAN IN 2001 (2009); James A. Green, Book Review, *Myra Williamson Terrorism, War and International Law: The Legality of the Use of Force against Afghanistan in 2001* (Aldershot, Ashgate 2009), 80(1) BRITISH Y.B. INT'L L. 439–42 (2009).

[3] I.e., the International Criminal Tribunal for Rwanda, ICTR (1994), the International Criminal Tribunal for the Former Yugoslavia, ICTY (1996), the Special Court for Sierra Leone, SCSL (2000), and the International Criminal Court, ICC (2002).

created since the early 1990s, along with their presumed contribution to international peace and reconciliation, is their identification of old criminal phenomena – such as terrorism – and their qualification, sometimes in an innovative fashion,[4] as international crimes subject to universal jurisdiction.

The images of terrified civilians during the conflicts in the former Yugoslavia, Rwanda, and Sierra Leone proved that acts of terrorism are often resorted to as an (unlawful) warfare strategy in armed conflicts. By qualifying them as war crimes, the International Criminal Tribunal for the former Yugoslavia (ICTY) was the first[5] to restate their prohibition under international humanitarian law and to assert that breaches thereof entail individual criminal responsibility pursuant to customary law.[6]

This chapter examines the judicial contributions of the Special Court of Sierra Leone (SCSL) on this issue in the wake of the ICTY's jurisprudence. After this brief introduction, Section II will illustrate the ban on *acts of terrorism* under the Laws of Armed Conflict (LOAC). Section III will examine some of the ICTY's leading cases on this subject and the way in which they may have paved the way for the works of the SCSL, so that a thorough analysis will be undertaken, allowing for a comparison between the two. Section IV will focus on the jurisprudential contributions of the SCSL to this topic, whereas Part V will draw the conclusions.

II. THE BAN OF ACT OF TERRORISM UNDER THE LOAC

A. *The Notion of Acts of Terrorism in Warfare*

No international consensus has been reached yet on a comprehensive legal definition of terrorism, partly because this has often been considered as a subjective notion. So far, the international legal community has adopted a piecemeal approach by targeting specific sub-forms thereof, eligible for a legal definition. As a consequence, different facets of terrorism are now addressed in a long catalog of conventions; when addressing the phenomenon on this basis, reference is generally made to terrorism as a treaty (based) crime. These generally refer to what the author defines as acts of terrorism in peacetime (i.e., acts taking place beyond the framework of an armed conflict).

This chapter focuses on acts of *terrorism in wartime*[7] – those adopted by one or more parties to a conflict as a means of warfare. Unlike treaty-based acts of terrorism, these are subject to the LOAC, which prohibit them in several provisions of the Geneva Conventions of 1949 (GCs) and their two Additional Protocols of 1977 (APs), under given conditions.[8]

---

[4] E.g., by extending the notion of war crimes to non-international armed conflicts. *Cf.* R. ARNOLD, *The Development of the Notion of Terrorism in Non-International Conflicts through the Jurisprudence of the U.N. Ad Hoc Tribunals*, 2002 (3) HUMANITÄRES VÖLKERRECHT – INFORMATIONSSCHRIFTEN 134; ICTR Statute art. 4.

[5] Terrorism has been on the international agenda since 1934, when the League of Nations discussed a draft convention for the prevention and punishment of terrorism, which was adopted in 1937 but which never came into force.

[6] Galić, IT-98–29-T, Judgment, para. 133, Trial Chamber (Dec. 5, 2003) (hereinafter *Galić TJ*); Blagojević and Jokić, IT-02–60-T, Judgment, para. 589, Trial Chamber (Jan. 17, 2005) (herinafter *Blagojević TJ*).

[7] For a definition, *cf.* R. ARNOLD, THE ICC AS A NEW INSTRUMENT FOR REPRESSING TERRORISM 5 (2005).

[8] Art. 33 IV GC, art. 51(2) AP I, art. 4 AP I, and art. 13 AP II.

Prosecution on this basis, as *international crimes*, presents several advantages: (1) the GCs and most provisions of the APs are universally binding, either on a conventional or customary law basis;[9] (2) they apply indistinctively, (3) and regardless of their political motivation, to all the parties to a conflict; (4) serious breaches thereof entail individual criminal responsibility subject to the principle of universal jurisdiction. Depending on the context, however, the very same conduct may not necessarily fall under the LOAC and/or qualify as a terrorist act: much depends on the context, which will have to be assessed ad hoc. Accordingly, three categories of acts of terrorism can be identified:

1. acts of terrorism in wartime;
2. acts of terrorism in wartime, but out of theater; and
3. acts of terrorism in peacetime.

The first covers acts occurring during an armed conflict, such as the intimidation of civilian prisoners. The second refers to acts related to an armed conflict, but taking place beyond the territorial boundaries of the parties, such as the hijacking of the Italian cruise ship *Achille Lauro* in 1985.[10] The last category includes acts taking place beyond the framework of an armed conflict, such as those perpetrated in the 1970s by the Red Brigades in Italy.[11]

B. *Difficulties Related to the Scope of Application of the LOAC*

The use of terrorist acts as a means of warfare is explicitly addressed in the following provisions of the LOAC:

- Art. 33 IV GC (individual responsibility, collective penalties, pillage, reprisals)

  No protected person may be punished for an offence he or she has not personally committed. Collective penalties and likewise all measures of intimidation or of terrorism are prohibited.

  Pillage is prohibited.

  Reprisals against protected persons and their property are prohibited.

- Art. 51(2) AP I (Protection of the civilian population)

  The civilian population as such, as well as individual civilians, shall not be the object of attack. Acts or threats of violence the primary purpose of which is to spread terror among the civilian population are prohibited.

- Art. 4 (2)(d) AP II (fundamental guarantees)

  1. All persons who do not take a direct part or who have ceased to take part in hostilities, whether or not their liberty has been restricted, are entitled to respect for their person,

---

[9] While the Geneva Conventions have been universally ratified, there are 171 States party to Additional Protocol I, 166 to Additional Protocol II and 59 to Additional Protocol III. See the Treaties and Documents website of the ICRC.

[10] The hijacking was led by the Palestine Liberation Front (PLO) in retaliation to Israel's attack on the Palestinian Liberation's Front's headquarters in Tunis a week earlier. Notwithstanding its nexus to the Israeli–Palestinian conflict, the attack took place on an Italian ship (i.e., on Italian territory). See ARNOLD, *supra* note 7, at 156–57.

[11] *Id.* at 20ss; Richard Drake, *Red Brigades, in* THE INTERNATIONAL ENCYCLOPEDIA OF TERRORISM 578 (1997).

honour and convictions and religious practices. They shall in all circumstances be treated humanely, without any adverse distinction. It is prohibited to order that there shall be no survivors.

2. Without prejudice to the generality of the foregoing, the following acts against the persons referred to in paragraph 1 are and shall remain prohibited at any time and in any place whatsoever:

[…]

(d) acts of terrorism

- Art. 13(2) AP II (protection of the civilian population)

  1. The civilian population and individual civilians shall enjoy general protection against the dangers arising from military operations. To give effect to this protection, the following rules shall be observed in all circumstances.

  2. The civilian population as such, as well as individual civilians, shall not be the object of attack. Acts or threats of violence the primary purpose of which is to spread terror among the civilian population are prohibited

[…]

The first difficulty in prosecuting acts of terrorism *in wartime* pursuant to the LOAC lies in the assessment whether the criteria of their material and personal scope are met. The first prerequisite is the existence of an armed conflict. Moreover, Articles 33 IV GC and 51(2) AP I require this to be *international* (i.e., taking place between two or more High Contracting Parties to the Conventions).[12] Articles 4 and 13 AP II, instead, only apply to *non-international* conflicts, which need to take place "in the territory of a High Contracting Party between its armed forces and dissident armed forces or other organized armed groups which, under responsible command, exercise such control over a part of its territory as to enable them to carry out sustained and concerted military operations and to implement this Protocol."[13] AP II's threshold, thus, is higher than that of common Article 3 to the GCs (fundamental guarantees), which applies indistinctively to all non-international armed conflicts, as long as the situation does not amount to internal disturbances and tensions, such as riots, isolated and sporadic acts of violence, and other acts of a similar nature.[14] Thus, the first hurdle is the qualification of the context.

Another difficulty lies in the personal scope of application of the LOAC.[15] The doctrine is divided on their active personal scope of application and the question whether the war crimes provisions should apply only to (regular) combatants under Article 4(A)(2) III GC, to the exclusion of civilians who have no nexus to any party to the conflict and who should

---

[12] *See* art. 1 AP I and U.N. GA Resolution 3103 (XXVIII) (Dec. 12, 1973); A. BOUVIER & M. SASSOLI, HOW DOES LAW PROTECT IN WAR? 109 (1st ed. 1999). The AP I additionally applies also to occupations and so-called self-determination wars but, unlike the IV GC, it has not been ratified universally, even though its main provisions are considered to be part of customary law.

[13] Art. 1 AP II.

[14] *Cf.* art. 2 AP II.

[15] GC I and II address sick and wounded combatants, GC III addresses prisoners of war, whereas GC IV addresses civilians, as special categories of protected persons (passive personal scope of application).

rather be prosecuted under ordinary criminal law.[16] Jurisprudence shows a trend toward the extension of these provisions to everyone, irrespective of status.[17] The issue is not without relevance, as a terrorist suspect may accordingly have to face trial pursuant to the LOAC, as opposed to treaty-based antiterrorism legislation, thus possibly under different jurisdictions (military/civilian) and procedural guarantees,[18] in particular if emergency laws are in place.

On the other hand, the LOAC's antiterrorism provisions primarily refer to civilians as protected persons. Other vulnerable categories, such as combatants hors de combat appear to be able to invoke protection merely under Article 4 AP II (fundamental guarantees), a provision originally thought for non-international conflicts. Thus, it is questionable whether prisoners of war (POWs), a category known only in international conflicts (GC III), may also invoke protection under this provision, possibly on the basis of customary law. These aspects will be clarified later, during the analysis of the jurisprudence.

The geographical and temporal scope of application requirements do not present particular difficulties; therefore they are not going to be dealt with any further.

In addition to the general scope of application requirements of the LOAC (which are reflected in their antiterrorism provisions) the conduct-specific elements also need to be proven in order for the provisions to apply. For example, the concepts of *terror* and *terrorism* used therein seem to refer only to acts that are *primarily* aimed at spreading fear among the civilian population (or, as long as AP II applies, also among people hors de combat). On the other hand, acts that may have the same effect but which lack this primary aim may be legitimate, under the LOAC, as long as they abide by the other general principles of the LOAC (i.e. military necessity, proportionality, and limitation).[19] To illustrate, the attack on a legitimate military target that may have, as a side effect, the terrorization of civilians living in the neighborhood would not fall under the anti-terrorism provisions.[20] These aspects will also be clarified during the analysis of the existing jurisprudence.

---

[16] The dilemma is recalled by Bouvier & Sassoli, *supra* note 12, at 215:The most delicate case is that of individuals who can not be considered as connected to one party, but nevertheless commit acts of violence contributing to the armed conflict for reasons connected with the conflict. If such individuals are not considered as addresses of IHL, most acts committed in anarchic conflicts would neither be covered by IHL nor consequently punishable as violations of IHL.However, these conclusions were drawn before the *Akayesu AJ* of 2001, *infra*, paras. 439–44, which ruled that the TC had erred in requiring a link of the perpetrators to a party to the conflict. A nexus with the conflict was sufficient.

[17] *Cf.* R. Arnold, *The Liability of Civilians under International Humanitarian Law's War Crimes Provisions*, 5 Y.B. Int'l Humanitarian L. 344–59 (2002); Arnold, *supra* note 7, at 125ss., 139, 195ss. and 338–39, with reference to L.C. Green, The Contemporary Law of Armed Conflict 276 (1993); Tadic, Case IT-94-1.T, Decision on the Defense Motion on Jurisdiction, para. 61 (Oct. 19, 1995); Akayesu, ICTR-96-4, Judgment, paras. 444–445, Appeals Chamber (June 1, 2001).

[18] A good example is the situation of so-called unlawful combatants detained in Guantanamo. These are considered as combatants for purposes of detention, so that this may be extended until the end of the hostilities, on the basis of GC III. At the same time, however, as they do not meet the criteria of regular combatants, they are denied the privileges of prisoner of war (POW) status. They are not considered as civilians, either, so that they cannot rely on the procedural guarantees that normally apply to regular detainees suspected of a specific crime. Unlawful combatants, thus, are a sort of hybrid category, which can neither enjoy the privileges of civilian or POW status nor the privileges of ordinary criminal procedural law. Due to their detention in relation to a conflict, the assumption is that they can be detained for security reasons, as it is normally the case with POWs, until the end of the hostilities. *See* R. Arnold, *Human Rights in Times of Terrorism*, 66 Heidelberg J. Int'l L. 297 (2006).

[19] Arnold, *supra* note 7, at 339.

[20] *Id.* at 51 and 78.

III. ACTS OF TERRORISM "IN WARTIME" AND INDIVIDUAL CRIMINAL RESPONSIBILITY

The conclusion that specific acts of terrorism are banned under the LOAC does not imply their qualification as war crimes[21] (i.e., as serious breaches entailing individual criminal responsibility). This needs to be assessed on the basis of the jurisprudence.

A. Post–World War II Jurisprudence

Already the International Military Tribunal of Nuremberg (IMT) suggested that the use of terrorism as a means of warfare is in serious breach of the LOAC. In the Judgment for the Trial of German Major War Criminals, it held that the use of protective arrests, collective punishments, taking and killing of hostages, mass murders, and torture, aimed at terrorizing the population, in particular in furtherance of the Night and Fog Decree,[22] along with the creation of concentration camps for political opponents, constituted war crimes.[23] Likewise in the Rosenberg Judgment it concluded that the use of terror was a serious breach of the Hague Rules of Land Warfare of 1907 and, thus, a war crime, amounting moreover to customary law.[24] The IMT paved the way for the developments that took place at the end of the twenty-first century, in particular with the creation of the two UN ad hoc tribunals and the SCSL, and their clarification of the contours of the war crime of terrorism.

B. The Position of the UN Ad Hoc Tribunals

Unlike the ICTR Statute (Article 4(d)), the ICTY Statute does not enlist terrorism in its war crimes catalog (Article 3). Nonetheless, the ICTY, in its jurisprudence, confirms the IMT's view that the use of acts of terrorism as a means of warfare may amount to a serious breach entailing individual criminal responsibility. Two lines of thought can be identified: according to the first, followed in *Aleksovski*,[25] one of the ICTY's first cases on this topic, acts of terrorism can be generally considered as a *violation of the laws or customs of war*, whenever the elements of other war crimes provisions (e.g., murder or torture) are met. According to the second, adopted in the *Galic Judgment*,[26] acts of terrorism are instead emancipated to a specific war crime, with its own elements. The jurisprudence of the SCSL needs to be

---

[21] For instance, they are not listed under the grave breaches provisions of the GCs and the APs.

[22] *Nacht und Nebel Erlass*: Under this decree, persons who had committed offenses against the Reich or the German forces in occupied territories, except where the death sentence was certain, were to be taken secretly to Germany and handed over for trial or punishment in Germany, with the purpose of intimidating the population in an efficient and enduring way. See the *Judgment of the IMT for the Trial of German Major War Criminals* (IMT Judgment), section "Judgment on War Crimes and Crimes against Humanity," Sept. 30 and Oct. 1, 1946, Nuremberg, *available at* http://elsinore.cis.yale.edu/lawweb/avalon/imt/proc/judwarcr.htm.

[23] IMT Judgment, Count Three, IMT Judgment, Indictment, Count Three (Oct. 1945), *available at* http://www.yale.edu/lawweb/avalon/imt/proc/count3.htm. For a review see ARNOLD, *supra* note 7, at 91ss.; R. Arnold, *The New War on Terror: Legal Implications under International Humanitarian Law*, *in* SUSAN C. BREAU & AGNIESZKA JACHEC-NEALE, TESTING THE BOUNDARIES OF INTERNATIONAL HUMANITARIAN LAW (2006).

[24] *Rosenberg Judgment*, *at* http://www.yale.edu/lawweb/avalon/imt/proc/judrosen.htm. For a detailed analysis, see ARNOLD, *supra* note 7, at 91ss.

[25] Aleksovski, IT-95–14/1-T, Judgment, Trial Chamber (June 25, 1999) (hereinafter *Aleksovski TJ*).

[26] *Galić TJ*.

examined in the wake of this latter trend, which also paved the way for the adoption of Article 3(d) SCSL Statute.

In *Aleksovski*,[27] the Trial Chamber of the ICTY found the former commander of the Kaonik prison[28] responsible (1) for aiding and abetting the mistreatment of detainees by his being present during such mistreatment and not objecting it; (2) for ordering, instigating, and aiding and abetting violence on two detainees, who were beaten regularly during their detention, occasionally in his presence or otherwise near his office; (3) for aiding and abetting the mistreatment of the detainees during their interrogation after the escape of a detainee; (4) for aiding and abetting psychological terror, such as the playing of screams over the loudspeaker at night[29]; and (5) for aiding and abetting the use of detainees as human shields and trench digging.[30] The Trial Chamber observed that conduct amounting to terrorism could be inferred, inter alia, by the use of screams played over loudspeakers[31]; the use of psychological violence, including direct[32] or repetitive threats[33]; and the uncertainty weighing on the minds of the detainees as to whether they would be dispatched to dig trenches or whether they would be released.[34] In sum, the judges concluded that:

> the violence in question constitutes an outrage upon personal dignity and, in particular, degrading or humiliating treatment within the meaning of Common Article 3 of the Conventions and therefore constitutes a violation of the laws or customs of war within the meaning of Article 3 of the Statute for which the accused must be held responsible under Articles 7(1) and 7(3) of the Tribunal's Statute.[35]

Aleksovski was convicted and sentenced to two-and-a-half years' imprisonment,[36] but on appeal, the Prosecutor argued[37] that the sentence was manifestly disproportionate.[38] The Appeals Chamber allowed this argument[39] by concluding that:

> [...] the Trial Chamber erred in not having sufficient regard to the *gravity of the conduct* of the Appellant for the following reasons. His offences were not trivial. Instead of preventing it, the Appellant as a superior involved himself in violence against those whom he should have been protecting, and allowed them to be subjected to psychological terror. He also failed to punish those responsible. Most seriously, the Appellant, by participating in the selection of detainees to be used as human shields and for trench digging, as he must have known, was putting at risk the lives of those entrusted to his custody. With his direct participation as a commander he provided additional encouragement to his subordinates to

---

[27] *Aleksovski TJ.*

[28] Aleksovski, IT-95–14/1-A, Judgment, para. 174, Appeals Chamber (Mar. 24, 2000) (hereinafter *Aleksovski AJ*).

[29] *Id.* at para. 175, with reference to *Aleksovski TJ*, paras. 187 and 203.

[30] *Aleksovski AJ*, para. 175.

[31] *Aleksovski TJ*, para. 224.

[32] Holders of military identity papers were threatened with death.

[33] Men entering cells at night; screams played over a loudspeaker.

[34] *Aleksovski TJ*, para. 226.

[35] *Aleksovski TJ*, para. 228.

[36] Count 10 of the Indictment, see *Aleksovski TJ*, para. 230.

[37] Third ground of appeal.

[38] *Aleksovski AJ*, para. 179.

[39] *Id.* at para. 187.

commit similar acts. The combination of these factors should, therefore, have resulted in a longer sentence and should certainly not have provided grounds for mitigation.[40]

Likewise in the Čelebići case,[41] which addressed events that had occurred in 1992 at a detention facility in a village in Bosnia and Herzegovina, the four Accused – Delalic, Mucic, Delic, and Landzo – were charged with grave breaches of the GCs (Article 2 ICTY Statute) and violations of the laws and customs of war (Article 3 ICTY Statute)[42] for the mistreatment of detainees.[43] Landzo, who worked as a guard, was found guilty[44] of torture as a grave breach (Article 2(b) ICTY Statute)[45] and as a violation of the laws and customs of war (Article 3(1)(a) ICTY Statute)[46] for the mistreatment of Momir Kuljanin, a detainee who was repeatedly and severely beaten with shovels, kicked to unconsciousness, and suffocated, and who had a cross burned on his hand and unknown corrosive powder applied to his body. The Trial Chamber ruled that:

> The actions of Mr. Landzo are clearly of a cruel nature, inflicted with the intent of causing severe pain and suffering to Mr. Kuljanin, and for the purposes of punishing and intimidating him, as well as contributing to the atmosphere of terror reigning in the camp and designed to intimidate all of the detainees.[47]

The same conclusion was reached with regard to the mistreatment of two other detainees,[48] which was additionally considered as a contributing factor to the *climate of terror* reigning in the camp. The Trial Chamber thus recognized that specific acts amounting to torture or inhumane acts, and that could be prosecuted as grave breaches or serious violations of the laws of war under Articles 2 and 3 ICTY Statute,[49] could additionally be considered as forming part of a campaign of intimidation and terrorization:

> [...] the detainees in crowded conditions of detention were obliged to helplessly observe the horrific injuries and suffering caused by this mistreatment, as well as the bodies of detainees who had died from the abuse to which they were subjected [....] by their exposure to these conditions, the detainees were compelled to live with the ever-present fear of being killed or subjected to physical abuse. This psychological terror was compounded by the fact that many of the detainees were selected for mistreatment in an apparently arbitrary manner, thereby creating an atmosphere of constant uncertainty.[50]

---

[40] *Id.* at paras. 183 and 188. In considering the sentence to be inadequate, the TC also referred to Art. 142 SFRY Criminal Code, which bans the "use of measures of intimidation and terror and the unlawful taking to concentration camps and other unlawful confinement."

[41] Mucić, Delić, Landžo & Delalić, T-96–21-T*bis*-R117, Judgment, Trial Chamber (Oct. 9, 2001) (hereinafter *Čelebići TJ*; Mucić, Delić, Landžo & Delalić, IT-96–21-A*bis*, Judgment, Appeals Chamber (Apr. 8, 2003) (hereinafter *Čelebići AJ*).

[42] *Čelebići TJ*, para. 3.

[43] *Id.* at para. 4.

[44] *Cf.* Counts 15–16 of the Indictment.

[45] Count 15.

[46] Count 16.

[47] *Čelebići TJ*, para. 923; *Čelebići AJ*, para. 35.

[48] Mr. Spasoje Miljevic and Mr. Mirko Dordic, *Čelebići TJ*, paras. 976 and 998.

[49] See Count 46: A Grave Breach punishable under Article 2(c) (willfully causing great suffering) of the Statute of the Tribunal; and Count 47: A Violation of the Laws or Customs of War punishable under Article 3 of the Statute of the Tribunal and recognized by Article 3(1)(a) (cruel treatment) of the Geneva Conventions. *Čelebići TJ*, para. 1073.

[50] *Id.* at para. 1087.

The Chamber added that arbitrary mistreatment, along with threats to be killed, aggravated the detainees' sense of physical insecurity and fear, thereby demonstrating the existence of an enduring and constant psychological torment, giving rise to an *all-pervasive atmosphere of terror*,[51] which was further corroborated by the detainees' fear about reporting or complaining:

> the detainees in the Čelebići prison-camp were exposed to conditions in which they lived in constant anguish and fear of being subjected to physical abuse. Through the frequent cruel and violent deeds committed in the prison-camp, aggravated by the random nature of these acts and the threats made by guards, the detainees were thus subjected to an immense psychological pressure which may accurately be characterised as "an atmosphere of terror."[52]

Mucić,[53] Delic,[54] and Landzo[55] were found guilty of grave breaches of the GCs (Article 2 ICTY Statute) for willfully causing great suffering or serious injury to body or health by contributing to the inhumane conditions in the camp,[56] in particular by creating an *atmosphere of terror*:

> Hazim Delic is guilty of contributing to the atmosphere of terror that prevailed in the prison camp as a result of the foregoing acts. He deliberately contributed to conditions where detainees were compelled to live with the ever present fear of being killed or subjected to physical abuse. Further, Hazim Delic contributed to this atmosphere by threatening the detainees. For example, Witness R stated that, when Mr. Delic was confronted by a request for medical care by a detainee he responded with the statement "sit down, you have to die anyway, whether you are given medical assistance or not."[57]

Mucić[58] was additionally convicted for having failed, as commander, to prevent his subordinates from committing violent acts and subjecting the detainees to an atmosphere of terror.[59]

The ICTY took a different approach in *Galić*,[60] which considered the events surrounding the military encirclement of Sarajevo in 1992 by Bosnian Serb forces and the role of Maj. Gen. Stanislav Galić, one of the three officers in command of the units of the Bosnian-Serb Army (VRS) operating in the area.[61] As the Trial Chamber observed, this was the first time that the use of terror was considered as a specific crime in a Tribunal judgment, even though the terrorization of civilians had been factored into convictions on other charges in the past.[62] Galić was charged with individual and superior criminal

---

[51] *Id.* at para. 1116.
[52] *Id.* at para. 1091.
[53] *Id.* at para. 1086*ff*.
[54] *Id.* At paras. 1121, 1253, and 1266.
[55] *Id.* at paras. 1122 and 1276, Counts 46–47.
[56] *See* Count 46.
[57] *Čelebići TJ*, para. 1266.
[58] *Id.* At paras. 1123 and 1237.
[59] *Id.* At para. 1123; *Čelebići AJ*, para. 35.
[60] *Galić TJ*.
[61] I.e., the Sarajevo Romanija Corps (SRK).
[62] *Galić TJ*, para. 66, with ref. to *Čelebići TJ*, paras. 976, 1056, 1086–91 and 1119, in which acts of intimidation creating an *atmosphere of terror* in prison camps were punished as grave breaches of the GCs (torture or inhuman treatment) and as violations of Art. 3 common to the GCs (torture or cruel treatment); Blaškić,

responsibility[63] for acts and omissions in relation to the crime of terror committed through a protracted campaign of sniping and shelling against civilians.[64] The Court first examined the prerequisites of Article 3 ICTY Statute (violation of the laws and customs of the war), that is whether a state of armed conflict existed at the time of the alleged crime and whether the two were *closely related*. After answering in the affirmative,[65] it then examined the *conditions* set forth in the Tadic jurisdiction decision,[66] in particular whether the alleged breach (*in casu* the use of terrorist acts)[67] was serious enough and criminally punishable. Following the conclusion that Article 51(2) AP I applied on a conventional basis,[68] the Chamber referred to the Motomura et al. case.[69] This judgment, delivered in 1947 by a court martial sitting in the Makassar (Netherlands East-Indies), was referred to as being the first conviction for the use of systematic terrorism against a civilian population, in particular by the use of "repeated, regular and lengthy torture and/or ill-treatment, the seizing of men and women on the grounds of wild rumours, repeatedly striking them ... the aforesaid acts having led or at least contributed to the death, severe physical and mental suffering of many."[70] The Chamber referred further to the consideration of *systematic terrorism* in the London Conference for the creation of the IMT[71] and its inclusion as a specific prohibition in Article 33 IV GC[72] and *numerous* states' domestic legislations.[73]

IT-95-14-T, Judgment, paras. 695, 700, 732–33, Trial Chamber (Mar. 3, 2000), in which the Accused was convicted for the grave breach of inhuman treatment and the war crime of cruel treatment, because of "the atmosphere of terror reigning in the detention facilities." Blaškić was additionally convicted for unlawful attack on civilians partly on the basis that soldiers terrorized the civilians by intensive shelling, murders, and sheer violence (paras. 630, 505, and 511). In Krstić, IT-98-33-T, Judgment, para. 533, Trial Chamber (Aug. 2, 2001), the TC characterized the crimes of terror and the forcible transfer of the women, children, and elderly at Potočari as constituting persecution and inhumane acts.

[63] Direct and command responsibility.

[64] *Galić TJ*, paras. 3–4, Count 1 of the Indictment.

[65] *Galić TJ*, para. 9.

[66] *Galić TJ*, paras. 10–11. Prosecutor v. Dusko Tadic, Decision on the Defense Motion for Interlocutory Appeal on Jurisdiction, para. 94 (Oct. 2, 1995), *available at* http://www.icty.org/x/cases/tadic/acdec/en/51002.htm. The four conditions are as follows:

(i) the violation must constitute an infringement of a rule of international humanitarian law;

(ii) the rule must be customary in nature or, if it belongs to treaty law, the required conditions must be met;

(iii) the violation must be "serious," that is to say, it must constitute a breach of a rule protecting important values, and the breach must involve grave consequences for the victim;

(iv) the violation of the rule must entail, under customary or conventional law, the individual criminal responsibility of the person breaching the rule.

On the applicability of the fourth condition, see Robert Cryer, Prosecutor v. Galič *and the War Crime of Terror Bombing*, 2 ISRAEL DEFENSE FORCES L. REV. 75, at 82*ss*. (2005–2006).

[67] *Galić TJ*, para. 65.

[68] *Galić TJ*, para. 68. The TC concluded that it did, irrespective of the character of the conflict, following to the signing by the parties to the conflict of the *22th May Agreement* (1992) (i.e., an agreement under the auspices of the International Committee of the Red Cross (ICRC) in order to protect the civilian population, aimed at bringing into force, inter alia, Articles 35 through 42, and 48 through 58 AP I). See on this B. Don Taylor II, *Crimes against Humanity in the Former Yugoslavia, in* INTERNATIONAL CRIMINAL JUSTICE: LAW AND PRACTICE FROM THE ROME STATUTE TO ITS REVIEW 306 (Roberto Bellelli ed., 2010).

[69] *Trial of Shigeki Motomura and 15 Others*, 13 LAW R. TRIALS WAR CRIM. 138 (hereinafter *Motomura*).

[70] *Galić TJ*, paras. 114–15.

[71] *Galić TJ*, para. 117.

[72] For a critique, see Cryer, *supra* note 66.

[73] *Galić TJ*, para. 95.

With regard to the personal scope of application of Article 33 IV GC, the judges observed that notwithstanding its reference to persons *in the hands of a party to the conflict*,[74] following the adoption of Article 51(2) AP I in 1977, which contains a similar ban, its protection was extended to civilians.[75] In support of this view, the judges further cited a judgment rendered in 1995 by the County Court of Split (Croatia) on the use of terrorism against civilians as a prohibited method of warfare.[76] Thus, they concluded that breaches of this prohibition are serious and that they entail individual criminal responsibility, so that the ICTY retains jurisdiction over this offense. They then examined whether such conduct fulfilled both the elements common to the offenses falling under Article 3 ICTY Statute and those specific to the war crime of terrorist acts, which were defined as follows[77]:

1. Acts of violence directed against the civilian population or individual civilians not taking direct part in hostilities causing death or serious injury to body or health within the civilian population.
2. The offender wilfully made the civilian population or individual civilians not taking direct part in hostilities the object of those acts of violence.
3. The above offence was committed with the primary purpose of spreading terror among the civilian population.

Interestingly, the Trial Chamber held that the *causing of death or serious harm to body or health* is required, whereas the actual infliction of *terror* is not,[78] as no support can be found in either the wording or the *travaux préparatoires* of Article 51(2).[79] The fact that the civilian population suffered and experienced terror during an armed conflict may, however, serve as corroboration of the intent.

The Trial Chamber further interpreted several terms: "civilian population" was read as "the majority of the population, or at least a large segment of it"; "terror" was understood as "extreme fear"[80]; "acts of violence" were considered as not including "legitimate attacks against combatants" but only unlawful attacks against civilians; and "primary purpose" signified the *mens rea* of the crime and had to be understood as "excluding dolus eventualis or recklessness from the intentional state specific to terror." In this judgment the ICTY qualified for the first time the use of terrorist acts related to armed conflicts as a specific-intent crime.[81] The AC upheld this, by specifying that[82]:

---

[74] *Galić TJ*, para. 119.

[75] *Galić TJ*, para. 120ss.

[76] Radulović and other members of the army of Republika Srpska were convicted pursuant to provisions including Article 33 GC IV, Article 51 AP I, and Article 13 AP II, for, inter alia, "a plan of terrorising and mistreating the civilians," and "carrying out the orders of their commanders with the goal to terrorise," which included opening random fire against civilian areas and threatening to demolish, and indeed proceeding to demolish, a dam with the intention of drowning the approximately thirty thousand people living downstream. *See Galić TJ*, para. 126.

[77] *Galić TJ*, para. 133.

[78] For a critique, see Cryer, *supra* note 66, at 93.

[79] *Galić TJ*, para. 134.

[80] *Galić TJ*, paras. 74 and 137.

[81] *Galić TJ*, para. 135.

[82] Galić, IT-98–29-A, Judgment, para. 454, Appeals Chamber (Nov. 30, 2006) (hereinafter *Galić AJ*), with ref. to *Galić TJ*, para. 764.

The gravity of the offences committed by General Galić is established by their scale, pattern and virtually continuous repetition, almost daily, over many months. Inhabitants of Sarajevo – men, women, children and elderly persons – were terrorized and hundreds of civilians were killed and thousands wounded during daily activities such as attending funerals, tending vegetable plots, fetching water, shopping, going to hospital, commuting within the city, or while at home. The Majority of the Trial Chamber also takes into consideration the physical and psychological suffering inflicted on the victims. Sarajevo was not a city where occasional random acts of violence against civilians occurred or where living conditions were simply hard. This was an anguishing environment in which, at a minimum hundreds of men, women, children, and elderly people were killed, and thousands were wounded and more generally terrorized.

With regard to the recognition of this offense as customary law, Judge Shahabuddeen clarified that "by taking up that position, the Appeals Chamber is not suggesting that a comprehensive definition of terror is known to customary international law but rather speaking of a core concept. This refers to a 'core or predominant meaning of 'terror' for which there was individual criminal responsibility at the material times.'"[83] Judge Meron observed that this could be inferred from the ban on declaring that no quarter will be given, contained in the 1907 Fourth Hague Convention on the Laws and Customs of War (IV HC): "if threats that no quarter will be given are crimes, then surely threats that a party will not respect other foundational principles of international law – such as the prohibition against targeting civilians – are also crimes. The terrorization at issue here is exactly such a threat."[84]

This (majority) view was criticized by Judge Schomburg,[85] in whose opinion this ban does not only differ from the prohibition of acts of terrorism in its content, but also with regard to its passive personal scope of application (enemy combatants as opposed to civilians).[86] In his view, moreover:

> there is no basis to find that this prohibited conduct as such was penalized beyond any doubt under customary international criminal law at the time relevant to the Indictment. Rather, I would have overturned Galić's conviction under Count 1 and convicted him under Counts 4 and 7 [violations of the laws or customs of war; attack on civilians] for the same underlying criminal conduct, taking into account the acts of terrorization against a civilian population as an aggravating factor in sentencing, thus arriving at the same adjusted sentence.[87]

According to Judge Schomburg, the recognition, under customary law, that breach of a provision entails criminal responsibility cannot be inferred from the customary character of the prohibition itself.[88] In his opinion, thus, it would have been preferable to follow precedents of the ICTY and prosecute such breaches under other war crimes headings.

---

[83] *Galić AJ*, separate opinion of Judge Shahabuddeen, para. 3.
[84] *Galić AJ*, separate opinion of Judge Meron, para. 2.
[85] *Galić AJ*, separate opinion of Judge Schomburg, para. 17, at 217.
[86] *Id.*
[87] *Id.* at para. 2.
[88] *Id.* at para. 7, at 214. This position is correct, as not all prohibitions under the LOAC, in fact, amount to war crimes entailing this kind of responsibility.

He questions in particular the accuracy of the statement that *numerous* states have criminalized acts of terrorism in their domestic legislation in a similar fashion to the LOAC[89] and claims that the Appeals Chamber could establish with certainty only that "an extraordinarily limited number of states at the time" followed this norm,[90] so that established state practice could not be proven.[91] Moreover, in his view, both the Norwegian Penal Code and the Swiss Military Criminal Code (MCC), both of which had been cited by the majority, only made a *general* reference to breaches of the AP, without specifically banning the use of terror.[92] This position, however, can be rebutted with the argument that Article 109 MCC was a general and abstract provision referring in generic terms to all violations of the LOAC, without enlisting in detail any war crimes or grave breaches provisions[93] (Article 109 MCC has now been replaced by a war crimes catalog[94]).

Judge Schomburg further mentioned states that have explicitly chosen not to pass legislation in this regard,[95] remarking that neither the IMT or the IMTFE[96] Charters, nor Control Council Law No. 10 penalized the terrorization of the civilian population.[97] However, his view disregards the fact that several IMT judgments contained conclusions about the illegality of the use of terrorism as a warfare strategy against civilians, under the LOAC,[98] and that these trials were conducted on the basis of LOAC principles common to the Allies, following the 1943 Moscow Declaration and the 1945 London Agreement.[99] After the IMT's

---

[89] *Id.* at para. 8, at 214, with ref. to *Galić TJ*, para. 95.

[90] Côte D'Ivoire, the then-Czechoslovakia, Ethiopia, the Netherlands, Norway, and Switzerland.

[91] *Galić AJ*, separate opinion of Judge Schomburg, para. 10, at 214–15.

[92] *Id.* at 215.

[93] This would have permitted a direct application, via this provision, of the ban contained in Art. 33 IV GC, for example. The advantage of a broad and general provision is exactly the possibility of encompassing different situations, as opposed to specific provisions. However, in order to avoid conflicting situations with the principle of legality, following the ratification of the Rome Statute, an amended version of the Swiss Criminal Code and the MCC entered into force on January 1, 2011. Art. 109 MCC reads as follows:

1. Wer den Vorschriften internationaler Abkommen über Kriegführung sowie über den Schutz von Personen und Gütern zuwiderhandelt, wer andere anerkannte Gesetze und Gebräuche des Krieges verletzt, wird, sofern nicht schärfere Strafbestimmungen zur Anwendung gelangen, mit Gefängnis, in schweren Fällen mit Zuchthaus bestraft.

2. In leichten Fällen erfolgt disziplinarische Bestrafung.

[94] Article 109 MCC was replaced by a set of new provisions addressing specific war crimes, which, unfortunately, do not encompass the ban on terrorism set forth by art. 51(2) AP I, art. 4, and 14 AP II and art. 33 IV GC. But breach therefore may be still prosecuted on the basis of art. 264j MCC, which, like art. 3 ICTY Statute, addresses "other violations of international humanitarian law." At the same time, the jurisdiction over this type of offenses was split between the Military and the Ordinary Criminal Justice; the Swiss Military Justice should retain jurisdiction only where the actor or the victim are members of the Swiss armed forces or if the offense was committed within the framework of an armed conflict to which Switzerland is a party. In all other situations, the competence to investigate and prosecute such crimes lies with the Federal Attorney General's Office. See Article 23(1)(g) new Swiss Criminal Code of Procedure (on the Federal jurisdiction) in conjunction with Article 264bss of the Swiss Criminal Code, and Article 2 of the new Swiss Military Criminal Code of Procedure. On the military provisions, see R. Arnold & S. Wehrenberg, *Kommentar zu Art. 264k StGB, in* KOMMENTAR ZU DEN VÖLKERSTRAFRECHTSBESTIMMUNGEN DES StGB (H. Vest et al. eds., forthcoming); *see also* R. Arnold, *Military Criminal Procedures and Judicial Guarantees – The Example of Switzerland*, (3)3 J. INT'L CRIM. JUST. 749–77 (2005).

[95] The United States, the U.K., Australia, Germany, Italy, and Belgium.

[96] International Military Tribunal for the Far East.

[97] *Galić AJ*, separate opinion of Judge Schomburg, para. 14, at 216.

[98] For a detailed analysis, see ARNOLD, *supra* note 7, at 91.

[99] The legitimacy of the IMT itself was based on the argument that together, the Allied Powers were allowed to do what any of them could have done singly. Thus the competences of the single national criminal jurisdictions

condemnation of such practices, it could be argued that their criminalization *was* indeed recognized by the Allies as a common principle, or else they would not have applied in the IMT. Finally, Judge Schomburg concludes that:

> In addition, and even though I am fully aware of Article 10 of the Statute of the International Criminal Court, it must be pointed out that the Rome Statute does not have a provision referring to terrorization against a civilian population. If indeed this crime was beyond doubt part of customary international law, in 1998 (!) states would undoubtedly have included it in the relevant provisions of the Statute or in their domestic legislation implementing the Statute.[100]

Although this view is probably correct, it could be counterargued that the Rome Statute was the result of a political compromise and that *several* customary law prohibitions, such as the ban on chemical or biological weapons, failed to be included. As noted in Article 10 ICC Statute, nothing in Part Two of the ICC Statute (jurisdiction, admissibility, and applicable law) should be interpreted as limiting or prejudicing in any way existing or developing rules of international law for purposes other than the ICC Statute.

In sum, the Galić case set the precedent establishing that the use or threat of use of acts primarily aimed at terrorizing the civilian population within the framework of an armed conflict is a serious specific-intent war crime under customary law. The specific intent may be inferred from circumstantial evidence:

> The evidence, especially in relation to the nature of the civilian activities targeted, the manner in which the attacks on civilians were carried out and the timing and duration of the attacks on civilians, consistently shows that the aim of the campaign of sniping and shelling in Sarajevo was to terrorise the civilian population of the city.[101]

During the sniping and shelling of Sarajevo, for instance, civilians were targeted during funerals, in ambulances, in hospitals, on trams, on buses, when driving or cycling, at home, and while tending gardens or fires or clearing rubbish in the city (i.e., while doing routine activities and at public sites known to be frequented by civilians).[102] The acts need to be targeted at a majority of the population, but the actual infliction of terror is not a condition, so that causality does not need to be proven. On the basis of the definition provided in Article 49(1) AP I, acts of violence (i.e., also acts of terrorism) "can comprise attacks or threats of attacks against the civilian population."[103] Also the circumstances may provide evidence about the real intent of the military conduct:

> The attacks on civilians had no discernible significance in military terms ... very clearly the message which they carried was that no Sarajevo civilian was safe anywhere, at any time of day or night ... the SRK attacked civilians ... in particular while engaged in typical civilian

---

(the United States, the USSR, France, and the U.K.) were converted into an international-quadripartite one, embodied by the IMT. *Agreement for the Prosecution and Punishment of the Major War Criminals of the European Axis, August 8, 1945, in* Y. BEIGBEDER, JUDGING WAR CRIMINALS: THE POLITICS OF INTERNATIONAL JUSTICE 32 (1999).

[100] *Galić AJ*, separate opinion of Judge Schomburg, para. 20, at 218.

[101] *Galić TJ*, para. 592.

[102] *Galić TJ*, para. 582*ss*.

[103] *Galić AJ*, para. 102. *See* Milošević, IT-98–29/1-A, Restatement in Judgment, para. 15, Appeals Chamber (Nov. 12, 2009) (hereinafter *Milošević AJ*).

activities or where expected to be found, in a similar pattern of conduct throughout the city of Sarajevo ... the only reasonable conclusion ... is that the primary purpose of the campaign was to instill in the civilian population a state of extreme fear.[104]

The Trial Chamber thus concluded that the campaign of sniping and shelling against the civilian population of Sarajevo was conducted with the primary purpose of spreading terror. These events were also the subject of *Milošević*.[105] In that case, the judges determined that "throughout the siege, the civilian population was subjected to conditions of extreme fear and insecurity", which, combined with the inability to leave the city, resulted in "deep and irremovable mental scars on that population as a whole"[106] and held that in these circumstances, *every incident* of sniping and shelling by the SRK had been deliberately conducted with the intent to terrorize the civilian population, thereby qualifying as unlawful attacks against civilians under Article 3 ICTY Statute.[107] Milošević's orders to target civilians in Sarajevo were considered as forming part of the "continuous strategy of sniping and shelling of civilians commenced under Galić's command" and the Trial Chamber "was satisfied that he planned and ordered those attacks with the intent to spread terror among the population." Milošević, thus, was found personally responsible of the crime of terror under Article 3(d) ICTY Statute.[108]

On appeal he contended that the Chamber had failed "to articulate the indicia from which the specific intent to spread terror could be inferred, notably the nature of the civilian activities targeted, as well as the manner, timing, and duration of the attacks."[109] He argued that all the activities of the SRK were lawful military action and that terror was not the primary purpose of the attacks.[110] The Appeals Chamber reversed the finding made by the TC in *Galić*, pursuant to which "actual infliction of death or serious harm to body or health is a required element of the crime of terror," stating that this represents *only one* of the possible modes of commission of the crime; it is not an element of the offense *per se*. What is required is that the victims suffered grave consequences resulting from the acts or threats of violence, which may include, but are not limited to, death or serious injury to body or health.[111] It also held that indiscriminate attacks may also contribute to the climate of terror, even though the *actual infliction* of terror is not an element.[112]

In general, the Milošević appeals judgment concurred with the Galić findings on the elements and interpretation thereof, additionally clarifying that on the basis of Article 50 AP I, the term "civilian population" generally refers to a population that is *predominantly* civilian and whose civilian status "may change due to the flow of civilians and combatants."[113] The Court then recalled that the protection from attacks under Article 51(2) AP I is suspended

---

[104] *Galić TJ*, para. 593.

[105] *Milošević AJ*, para. 2*ss*. (under Count 1 of the Indictment).

[106] *Id*.

[107] *Milošević AJ*, para. 4, with ref. to *Milošević* TJ, para. 910.

[108] On the basis of Count 1 of the Indictment. See *Milošević AJ*, para. 5, with ref. to *Milošević* TJ, para. 928 and para. 1006.

[109] *Milošević AJ*, para. 25.

[110] *Id*.

[111] *Milošević AJ*, para. 33.

[112] *Id*. At paras. 36 and 38. See also para. 66, which states that the indiscriminate character of attack can be indicative of the fact that the attack was directed against the civilian population.

[113] *Id*. at paras. 50–51.

when and for such time as the civilians directly participate in hostilities (Article 51(3) AP I). Accordingly, to establish that the crimes of terror and unlawful attacks against civilians have been committed, the Court is required to find beyond reasonable doubt that the victims of individual crimes were civilians *and* that they were not participating directly in the hostilities.[114] With regard to the *mens rea*, by reference to the Strugar case, the Appeals Chamber recalled that:

> the intent to target civilians can be proved through inferences from direct or circumstantial evidence. There is no requirement of the intent to attack particular civilians; rather it is prohibited to make the civilian population as such, as well as individual civilians, the object of an attack. The determination of whether civilians were targeted is a case-by-case analysis, based on a variety of factors, including the means and method used in the course of the attack, the distance between the victims and the source of fire, the ongoing combat activity at the time and location of the incident, the presence of military activities or facilities in the vicinity of the incident, the status of the victims as well as their appearance, and the nature of the crimes committed in the course of the attack.[115]

In conclusion, the Court found Milošević guilty of the crime of terror (Articles 3(d) and 7(3) ICTY Statute)[116] for failing to prevent and punish the crimes committed by the SRK troops in the context of the sniping and shelling of the civilian population of Sarajevo.[117] In his dissenting opinion, Judge Liu Daqun contested the customary law status of the offense, along the lines of Judge Schomburg's dissenting opinion in *Galić*.[118]

In the Blagojević *Case*,[119] instead, the "terrorising of Bosnian Muslim civilians in Srebrenica and at Potočari" was considered under the heading of persecution as a crime against humanity.[120] The Prosecution asserted that terrorization, as set out in this case, was the denial of fundamental rights, including the right to security of person,[121] and that this "involves establishing, through unlawful acts, physical and psychological conditions designed to create an atmosphere of terror or panic among a civilian population." He contended that such conditions may include acts of "beating, torture, rape and murder, as well as verbal abuse, threats and intimidation; shelling and shooting in and around the population centre; separation of family members; deprivation of the population's basic needs such as food, water and medical treatment; burning of homes and other property around the population centre" and that the "use of terrorisation as a form of persecutions is distinct from the charged offence of terrorisation in the Galić case."[122] The Trial Chamber concluded that although this act is not to be found as such in the ICTY Statute, its content is similar to the one prohibited under Articles 51(2) AP I and 13(2) AP II, which is punishable under

---

[114] *Id.* at para. 57.
[115] *Id.* at para. 66.
[116] *Id.* at para. 116.
[117] *Id.* at paras. 281–282, and 295.
[118] *Milošević AJ*, ch. VIV, para. 1.
[119] *Blagojević AJ*, Judgment, Appeals Chamber (May 9, 2007).
[120] Count 5 of the Indictment, *Blagojević TJ* (Jan. 17, 2005), paras. 8 and 588.
[121] Prosecution Final Brief, para. 565, referred to in *Blagojević TJ*, para. 1946.
[122] *Blagojević TJ*, para. 588.

Article 3 ICTY Statute, and that it constitutes a denial of the fundamental (customary) right to security of persons under Article 9 ICCPR and Article 5 ECHR.[123]

It concurred with *Galić* on the elements and the interpretation of *terror* as *extreme fear*[124] and held that the Prosecution only needed to prove that such acts or threats thereof were carried out to create an atmosphere of extreme fear "or uncertainty of being subjected to violence among the civilian population."[125] Moreover, the infliction of terror had to be the primary, but not necessarily the only objective of the acts.[126] On the facts, the Trial Chamber concluded that the United Nations compound in Srebrenica had been shelled while thousands of Bosnian Muslim refugees were seeking protection there and that the aim was to cause fear and panic and force them to flee the enclave. Those seeking shelter in Potočari "were continuously subjected to terrifying threats and physical attacks," especially during the *night of horror* on July 12, 2004, when "the refugees suffered from extreme fear." The taking of the Bosnian Muslim men to a place called the White House and the order to leave their personal belongings, wallets, and documents outside the building were considered by the chamber to be "intended to terrify the men as it suggested that their fate – death – had been sealed." The Chamber therefore found that such conduct was carried out with the primary purpose to create an atmosphere of extreme fear among the population[127] and that the widespread or systematic attack against the civilian population of Srebrenica had been carried out with a discriminatory intent, so that the elements of persecution as a crime against humanity were satisfied.[128]

The judges further concluded that members of the Bratunac Brigade had given practical assistance to the terrorizing of the civilian population,[129] particularly by guarding the detained Bosnian Muslim men,[130] and thus found Blagojević, as their commander, guilty of aiding and abetting persecutions as a crime against humanity.[131]

On appeal[132] Blagojević submitted that the TC had erred in fact in finding that he was aware of the discriminatory intent of the perpetrators and the discriminatory context in which the underlying crimes were committed,[133] and that any act of the Bratunac Brigade had substantially contributed to the crimes. This ground of appeal was dismissed.[134]

It is interesting to note, that notwithstanding the existence of precedents such as *Galić*, in which acts of terrorism were clearly identified as specific intent-war crimes under the

---

[123] *Blagojević TJ*, para. 592. U.N. International Convention on Civil and Political Rights (ICCPR) and European Convention on Human Rights (ECHR).

[124] *Blagojević TJ*, paras. 589–590.

[125] *Id.* at para. 590.

[126] *Id.* at para. 591.

[127] *Id.* at para. 613.

[128] *Id.* at paras. 620 and 752. *See* para. 619: "The circumstances accompanying the terrorising and the cruel and inhumane treatment of the Bosnian Muslim civilians, the subsequent forcible transfer of the women and children and the organised executions of the men substantiate the existence of a discriminatory intent on racial, religious or political grounds of the perpetrators."

[129] *Blagojević AJ*, para. 132.

[130] *Blagojević AJ*, para. 289, with reference to *Blagojević TJ*, paras. 213, 214, and 734.

[131] *Blagojević TJ*, paras. 759ss. and 797.

[132] Fifth ground of appeal, *Blagojević AJ*, para. 114.

[133] *Blagojević AJ*, para. 114.

[134] *Blagojević AJ*, at 137 (disposition).

LOAC and customary law, in *Blagojević* the Prosecution opted for the charge under crimes against humanity, which posed more difficulties, as it required proof of widespread and systematic attack with discriminatory intent. A charge under Article 3 ICTY Statute (violations of the laws and customs of war) would have been easier, as neither the existence of an armed conflict in the former Yugoslavia nor the nexus of the underlying acts to the armed conflict were at debate.

On the criminalization of acts of terrorism *in wartime*, the ICTR goes a step further by specifically addressing them in Article 4(d) ICTR Statute, which concerns violations of Article 3 common to the GCs and of AP II. Unfortunately its jurisprudence in this regard is not particularly significant, largely because the focus of that prosecution and consequently the cases tried by the tribunal has been on genocide.

One of the aims of next paragraph is to examine if, and to what extent, the SCSL has developed the ICTY's understanding of acts of terrorism as a specific war crime, when committed within the framework of an armed conflict.

IV. THE SCSL JURISPRUDENCE ON ACTS OF TERRORISM "IN WARTIME"

Pursuant to its Statute, the SCSL had the power to prosecute war crimes constituting serious violations of Article 3 common to the four GCs and of AP II (Article 3 SCSL Statute) and other serious violations of international humanitarian law (IHL),[135] such as intentional attacks against the civilian population or child recruitment (Article 4 SCSL). Unlike in the ICTY Statute, grave breaches are not listed as a specific category, as these are applicable only to armed conflicts of an international character (which was not the case in Sierra Leone).

One of the distinguishing features is the inclusion of acts of terrorism as a serious violation of the LOAC applicable to non-international armed conflicts in Article 3(d) of the SCSL Statute.[136] Breaches thereof have been charged in several cases, including *Koroma*[137] and *Sankoh*,[138] which dealt with the role of two former leaders of the Armed Forces Revolutionary Council (AFRC) and the AFRC/Revolutionary United Front (RUF) in the commission of acts of violence as part of a terrorist campaign against the civilian population. However, following their alleged death,[139] in the Sankoh case the Indictment was withdrawn,[140] whereas in the Koroma case it is yet to be withdrawn.[141]

---

[135] IHL in this chapter is used as a synonym of LOAC.

[136] Prosecutor v. Moinina Fofana & Allieu Kondewa, SCSL-04-14-T, Judgment, para. 168, Trial Chamber I, (Aug. 2, 2007) (hereinafter *CDF TJ*); Prosecutor v. Moinina Fofana, Case No. SCSL-2004-14-AR72(E), Decision on Preliminary Motion for Lack of Jurisdiction Materiae: Nature of the Armed Conflict, para. 17, Appeals Chamber (May 25, 2004).

[137] Koroma, SCSL-2003.03.I, Indictment, para. 32 (Mar. 7, 2003).

[138] Sankoh, SCSL-03-02-I-001, Indictment, para. 35, Count 1 (Mar. 7, 2003).

[139] Tanu Jalloh, *Johnny Paul's Dead Body Found in Liberia*, CONCORD TIMES, FREETOWN (ALLAFRICA.COM) (Sept. 11, 2008) (last visited Mar. 1, 2012); *Is Ex-Sierra Leone Junta Leader Johnny Paul Koroma Dead Or Alive?*, DEMOCRAT (Oct. 25, 2010), *available at* http://allafrica.com/stories/201010260617.html.

[140] Sankoh Case, Doc. SCSL-03-02-PT-054, Withdrawal of Indictment (Dec. 8, 2003).

[141] See the website of the SCSL: http://www.sc-sl.org/CASES/JohnnyPaulKoroma/tabid/188/Default.aspx.

In the CDF[142] and in the Brima (AFRC)[143] cases, analogous charges have seen instead a successful end. In the former,[144] the Court clarified that Article 3(d) SCSL Statute stems from Article 4(2) AP II and that this provision, itself based on Article 33 IV GC,[145] encompasses Article 13(2) AP II[146] and is complemented by Article 51(2) AP I.[147] The SCSL, therefore, seems to adopt a broad interpretation of Article 3(d) SCSL Statute as covering all the antiterrorism provisions contained in the GCs and their APs. This conclusion, however, has to be read in the light of the specific context of the conflict in Sierra Leone, which was non-international and subject to both the APs on a conventional basis, thus making the qualification of the conflict irrelevant for the application of Article 3(d) SCSL Statute.[148] It should not be understood, though, as meaning that such qualification may be also superfluous to establish the application of Article 4(2) AP II to other cases, or that the LOAC's antiterrorism provisions may apply interchangeably.

In the Brima (AFRC) case, contrary to *Galić*, the acts were considered as a specific breach of the *fundamental guarantee* of humane treatment (Article 4 AP II[149]) and not as *other serious violations of IHL*[150] (Article 4 SCSL Statute)[151] (e.g., as an unlawful attack against the civilian population).[152] The focus, thus, was on terrorism as a breach of the so-called Geneva Law.[153]

Prior to analyzing the crime-specific elements, in the CDF case the Trial Chamber defined its jurisdiction, holding that this was limited to cases: (1) concerning persons who bear the greatest responsibility[154]; (2) for serious violations of IHL and Sierra Leonean law; (3) committed in the territory of Sierra Leone; (4) since November 30, 1996.[155] Because the Indictment did not contain charges under Sierra Leonean law, the Trial Chamber concluded that the acts of terrorism referred to therein were not contemplated as a crime by the country's domestic law, but held that their ban under Article 4(2) AP II amounted to customary

---

[142] Prosecutor v. Moinina Fofana & Allieu Kondewa, TJ, Case No. SCSL-04–14-T (Aug. 2, 2007) (hereinafter *CDF TJ*) and Prosecutor v. Moinina Fofana & Allieu Kondewa, AJ, Case No. SCSL-04–14-A (May 28, 2008) (hereinafter *CDF AJ*).

[143] Brima, SCSL-04–16-T, Judgment, Trial Chamber (June 20, 2007) (hereinafter *Brima TJ*).

[144] *CDF TJ*, para. 167, Count 6 of the Indictment.

[145] Which prohibits "all measures of intimidation or of terrorism" of or against protected persons (civilians).

[146] *CDF AJ*, para. 346.

[147] *CDF TJ*, para. 168; *Brima TJ*, para. 661. Articles 51(2) AP I and 13 AP II refer to only acts *directed against* civilians. However, unlike Article 33 IV GC, a typical Geneva Law provision aimed at protecting human rights, these provisions only ban acts or threats of violence whose *primary purpose* is to spread terror. This is because they stem from the 1907 *Hague Rules and Methods of Warfare*, so that they are actually focused on the principle of military necessity, rather than on the principle of distinction. On this see ARNOLD, *supra* note 7, at 75.

[148] *CDF TJ*, paras. 99 and 102, with reference to *Čelebići AJ*, para. 150.

[149] By virtue of its customary law status. *See also Brima TJ*, para. 660ss.

[150] International humanitarian law, which is used as a synonym in this chapter of the laws of armed conflict (LOAC).

[151] ICTY Statute art. 3 and SCSL Statute art. 4.

[152] Which are addressed in Art. 4 AP II and Art. 33 IV GC.

[153] As opposed to the Hague Law. *See* F. Bugnion, *Law of Geneva and Law of the Hague*, INT'L REV. OF THE RED CROSS 884 (2001). R. Cryer argues that in general, prosecuting Hague law crimes is extremely difficult, reason for which the vast majority of war crimes prosecutions before the ICTY and ICTR have related to Geneva law. The Galić Judgment represents one of the few exceptions. *See* Cryer, *supra* note 66, at 76.

[154] *CDF TJ*, para. 92.

[155] *Id.* at para. 89.

law[156] and that breaches thereof, in accordance with the ICTY ruling, entailed individual criminal responsibility.[157] *Serious violations* were defined as cases "where a rule protecting 'important values' is breached, resulting in 'grave consequences' for the victim,"[158] including acts of terrorism.[159] It then held the general requirements that must be proved to show the commission of war crimes pursuant to Article 3 SCSL Statute are that: (1) an armed conflict existed at the time of the alleged violations; (2) there existed a nexus between the alleged violation and the armed conflict; (3) the victim was a person not taking direct part in the hostilities at the time of the alleged violations; and (4) the accused knew or had reason to know that the person was not taking a direct part in the hostilities at the time of the act or omission.[160] It concluded that unless a nexus could be proven between the acts and the armed conflict , these were to be prosecuted as an ordinary offense.

In assessing this, the Trial Chamber referred to the following indicia:

> the fact that the [Accused] is a combatant; the fact that the victim is a non-combatant; the fact that the victim is a member of the opposing party; the fact that the act may be said to serve the ultimate goal of a military campaign; and the fact that the crime is committed as part or in the context of the [Accused's] official duties.[161]

This requirement is particularly important with regard to acts of terrorism, which are often perpetrated in borderline scenarios between armed conflicts subject to the LOAC and simple uprisings and sporadic acts of violence. This was discussed in *Kunarac*[162] and *Akayesu*. In *Akayesu*, the ICTR's Appeals Chamber concluded that common Article 3 to the GCs does not set specific limitations on its active personal scope of application and that everyone can be liable for war crimes, as long as they acted in furtherance of an armed conflict.[163] Thus, the nexus criterion only requires a link between the *acts* and the armed conflict, not between the *perpetrator* and a High Contracting Party thereto.[164] This is very important, as often so-called terrorist groups lack any nexus to a High Contracting Party to the GCs, thereby forfeiting their right to combatant status under Article 4(A)(2) III GC. Accordingly, these persons shall be prosecuted as civilians who have unlawfully taken up arms in breach of ordinary criminal law rather than the LOAC.[165] It is beyond the scope of this chapter to venture into this doctrinal debate, because international jurisprudence seems to support an extensive active personal scope of application. However, the reader should be aware of the risk implicit in this extension of ending up operating double standards[166] and granting official recognition to civilians who unlawfully engage in hostilities.

---

[156] *Id.* at para. 96.

[157] *Id.* at paras. 88–89.

[158] *Id.* at para. 94, with reference to Tadić, IT-94–1, Decision on the Defense Motion for Interlocutory Appeal on Jurisdiction, para. 94, Appeals Chamber (Oct. 2, 1995) (hereinafter *Tadić Appeal Decision on Jurisdiction*).

[159] *CDF TJ*, para. 106.

[160] *Id.* at para. 122.

[161] *Id.* At paras. 129–130. *Cf.* ARNOLD, *supra* note 7, at 119.

[162] Kunarac et al., IT-96–23 and IT-96–23/1, Judgment, para. 407, Trial Chamber (Feb. 22, 2001).

[163] Akayesu, ICTR-96–4, Judgment, paras. 435–437, Appeals Chamber (June 1, 2001) (hereinafter *Akayesu AJ*).

[164] *Id.* at paras. 439 and 444.

[165] *Cf.* Arnold, *supra* note 7.

[166] The recognition that irregular (terrorist) groups not qualifying for combatant status (i.e., civilians), who unlawfully engage in hostilities, shall be subject to IHL for purposes of incrimination, raises in fact the ques-

Interestingly, though, in concurrence with the ICTY, in the CDF case, the SCSL Trial Chamber concludes that civilians can only be granted protection from terrorist acts as long as it is proven that they did *not* participate in the hostilities.[167] In doing so, it reads *e contrario* Article 4(2)(d) AP II, which simply states that "All persons who do not take a direct part or who have ceased to take part in hostilities, whether or not their liberty has been restricted, are entitled to respect for their person, honour and convictions and religious practices." This provision was meant to *extend* the protection of fundamental guarantees to *all* persons who are no longer engaged in hostilities, including military personnel "hors de combat,"[168] who unfortunately do not enjoy a similar protection under Article 33 IV GC or Article 51(2) AP I.[169] In the CDF case, however, the Trial Chamber *narrows* such protection by excluding civilians who participate in the hostilities. This is the logical consequence of the fact that combatants, and likewise civilians who take up arms, become legitimate military targets. A question that arises, though, is why only persons hors de combat should enjoy the protection of their core, fundamental guarantees. The strategy behind terrorist acts in wartime is to destroy the morale of the adverse party's troops by targeting their families back at home, thereby making the combatants feel unable to fulfill their task, as males and combatants, to protect them. Gross violations of core fundamental rights, such as mutilations, rapes, murders, aimed at being displayed in public in order to terrify the enemy, cannot and should not be justified by military necessity: they shall be considered disproportionate and in breach of the principle of unnecessary suffering and, thus, outlawed irrespective of the character of the target, be this a person in or hors de combat. Obviously it cannot be expected to outlaw acts that terrorize combatants, as the instillation of fear is implicit in war. Nonetheless, acts that are inhumane in nature should be prohibited regardless of the qualification of the target. In this case, thus, the question is whether combatants should be given the right to claim victims' status, too, for compensation purposes, where they have been the ultimate target of an attack launched against their family members, especially where these family members are deceased and are no longer capable of claiming their rights.

This approach, however, raises the problem of the borderline between human rights and international humanitarian law. Combatants who are not wounded, not sick, and not held captive have no specific rights under the laws of war, except maybe for protection from the use of certain weapons considered to be in breach of the principle of unnecessary suffering.[170] The question that one may ask is whether a fifth Geneva Convention should be possibly introduced, specifying the rights to be enjoyed by combatants, too, including for example the principles governing the laws on weapons and the core and fundamental human rights applicable at all times, under all circumstances. It is not to be understood, for instance, why protection from the use of (psychological) torture shall be enjoyed by persons "hors de combat" only. There are some conducts, such as perfidy, which are forbidden

---

tion whether they shall not be subject to IHL also for purposes of privileged status in case of capture. *Cf.* Arnold, *supra* 7 at 165.

[167] *CDF TJ*, para. 132.

[168] That is, the sick or wounded, or those detained by the adverse party.

[169] These provisions only address civilians as protected persons.

[170] See the St. Petersburg's Declaration Renouncing the Use, in Time of War, of Explosive Projectiles under 400 Grammes Weight, Nov. 29/Dec. 11, 1868 and Article 23(e) of the Hague Regulations on Land Warfare of 1899 and 1907.

at all times, no matter against whom they are perpetrated. It is thus to be questioned why combatants should be unable to invoke victims' status when their relatives have been intentionally targeted in a strategy to destroy their morale. This approach, however, would probably require the rethinking of the structure of the Geneva Conventions, which is not the topic of the present chapter.

In the Court's view, "the question whether civilians have participated directly in hostilities has to be decided on the specific facts of the case and there must be a sufficient causal relationship between the act of participation and its immediate consequences."[171] More in particular "direct participation should be understood to mean 'acts which by their nature and purpose, are intended to cause actual harm to the enemy personnel and material.'"[172] Intervention in legitimate self-defense, thus, shall not fall under the concept of direct participation. By reference to the ICTY's Rule 98 Decision in *Galić*, the Trial Chamber observed, however, that the prohibition extends to attacks against installations that would cause the same effect.[173] The Court, thus, identified the following elements of the crime:

(i)   Acts or threats of violence directed against persons or property;
(ii) The Accused intended to make persons or property the object of those acts and threats of violence or acted in the reasonable knowledge that this would likely occur; and
(iii) The acts or threats of violence were committed with the primary purpose of spreading terror among persons.[174]

It confirmed the ICTY jurisprudence holding that threats[175] are also encompassed and that this is a specific-intent crime, meaning that only the intention *to create an extreme sense of fear* in the targets of the attack under (iii) must be specific, whereas the level of intent to make persons or property the object of acts of violence under (ii) may amount to recklessness (*dolus eventualis*).[176] The *mens rea*, thus, needs to be proven on two levels (i.e., with regard to the acts of violence *and* the terrorization). By accepting recklessness as a sufficient *mens rea* level, it can be said that the SCSL goes a step further than the ICC Statute.[177]

Both Accused were acquitted from the charge of acts of terrorism under Count 6, on the basis that "it was not proved beyond reasonable doubt that either possessed the requisite *mens rea*."[178] Moreover, the Court introduced a double threshold[179] by holding that "*only those acts for which the Accused have been found to bear criminal responsibility under another count of the Indictment may form the basis of criminal responsibility for acts of terrorism.*"

---

[171] *CDF TJ*, para. 134.
[172] *Id.* at para. 135.
[173] *Id.* at para. 173.
[174] *Id* at para. 170.
[175] *Id.* at para. 171.
[176] In the sense of the subjective disregard of an objectively substantial and unjustifiable risk. For a comparison between Anglo-Saxon and German-Roman terminology, see ARNOLD, *supra* note 7, at 171. *See also Galić AJ*, para. 54.
[177] For a comparison, in this regard with the ICC Statute, see Cryer, *supra* note 66, at 81, and ARNOLD, *supra* note 7, at 171–72. In drafting Article 30 ICC Statute there was the deliberate intention not to accept liability based on recklessness.
[178] *CDF AJ*, para. 323.
[179] *Id.* at paras. 324 and 327; *CDF TJ*, paras. 49, 167, and 900.

This line of thinking was challenged on appeal. The Prosecutor argued that by adopting a limited interpretation of Count 6, the Trial Chamber "had added a prerequisite to the elements of the offence which resulted in it erroneously disregarding acts of violence charged in the Indictment, such as the burning of houses."[180] The Appeals Chamber concluded that this charge clearly referred to Article 13(2) AP II, which bans *"acts or threats of violence the primary purpose of which is to spread terror among the civilian population"* and the elements of which had been identified in *Galić* by the ICTY[181] as requiring:

i)   acts or threats of violence;
ii)   that the offender willfully made the civilian population or individual civilians not taking part in hostilities the object of those acts or threats of violence, and
iii) the acts or threats of violence were carried out with the specific intent of spreading terror among the civilian population.

It then observed that "acts or threats of violence are also not limited to direct attacks against civilians or threats thereof but include indiscriminate attacks or disproportionate attacks or threats,"[182] and that it was not necessary to prove that such conduct satisfied the elements of any other specific crime. Therefore, acts of burning may also constitute acts of terrorism, even though they do not satisfy the elements of pillage.[183] The Appeals Chamber further remarked, however, that "whilst actual terrorization of the civilian population is not an element of the crime, the acts or threats of violence alleged must, nonetheless, be such that are at the very least capable of spreading terror."[184] This is to be assessed in each case by taking into consideration the context and establishing whether the act was capable of causing extreme fear in the victims.[185]

With regard to the *mens rea*, the Appeals Chamber restated the Trial Chamber's conclusions by interpreting the term "wilfully" in the sense of Article 85 AP I (ban on attacks wilfully directed against the civilian population and individuals) as requiring that the Accused acted consciously and with intent or recklessness; negligence is not enough.[186] Only the intent to spread terror among the civilian population needs to be specific, although this need not be the *only* purpose. The specific intent is also to be determined in each single case and *"it may be inferred from the circumstances, the nature of the acts or threats and the manner, timing or duration"* thereof.[187]

In the Brima (AFRC) case, the Accused were charged under Article 3(d) SCSL Statute[188] as being responsible directly and as superiors[189] for acts of terrorism committed by the AFRC between May 25, 1997 and January 2000.[190] In determining jurisdiction and the applicability of Article 3(d) SCSL Statute, the Trial Chamber restated the criteria set forth in the CDF

---

[180] *CDF AJ*, paras. 325–326.
[181] *Id.* at para. 350.
[182] *Id.* at para. 351, with reference to *Galić AJ*, para. 102.
[183] *CDF AJ*, para. 359.
[184] *Id.* at para. 352.
[185] *Id.* at para. 352, with reference to *Galić AJ*, para. 104.
[186] *CDF AJ*, para. 35, and 5, with reference to *Galić TJ*, para. 54.
[187] *Id.* at para. 357.
[188] As a violation of Art. 3 Common to the GCs and of AP II.
[189] *Brima TJ*, para. 18.
[190] *Id.* at paras. 14 and 240.

case, including the nexus requirement[191]: "The rationale of the said requirement is to protect the victims of internal armed conflicts, but not from crimes unrelated to the conflict. The nexus is satisfied where the perpetrator acted in furtherance of or under the guise of the armed conflict."[192]

It also confirmed that a state of armed conflict existed in Sierra Leone and that as "the characterisation of the armed conflict in Sierra Leone was not canvassed at trial and no submissions were made on it by the parties," Articles 3 and 4 SCSL Statute applied to the present case, irrespective of the nature of the conflict,[193] even though the conflict in Sierra Leone was non-international.[194] This shows the Court's recognition of the different regimes applicable to international and non-international armed conflicts, but its intention not to consider it in the specific case since it was not raised by the parties.

The Court concurred with the findings of the CDF case that Article 3(d) SCSL Statute reproduces Article 4(2)(d) AP II[195] (which is itself tied to Article 13(2) AP II[196]), and concurred with *Galić* in concluding that this prohibition amounts to customary law.[197] It recalled that it "was first explicitly evoked after the First World War, when a deliberate use of a 'system of general terrorisation' of the population to secure control of a region was found to be contrary to the rules of civilised warfare" and that it was later introduced in several conventions[198] and military manuals. It argued that although terrorism as such was not explicitly criminalized by the IMT Charter, evidence of terror violence was considered in the context of the murder and mistreatment of the civilian population and that post—World War II domestic tribunals incorporated the crimes of *systematic terrorism* and *systematic terror* in their statutes.[199] Reference was made also to the adoption of the anti-terrorism provisions in the GCs and the APs, along with Article 4(2) ICTR Statute and several ICTY judgments adjudicating the infliction of terror as a war crime.[200] The elements of the offense were drawn from the Galić case,[201] a judgment with which the Trial Chamber concurred with regard to the view that threats are also encompassed; that the aim of terrorizing needs to be the primary, but not the only one objective; and that the ambit of acts of terrorism "extends beyond acts or threats of violence committed against protected persons to acts directed against installations which would cause victims terror as a side-effect."[202]

---

[191] *Id.* at para. 246*ss.*

[192] *Id.* At para. 246, with reference to ICTY and ICTR jurisprudence.

[193] *Brima TJ*, para. 250.

[194] *Id.* At para. 251.

[195] Which prohibits acts of terrorism.

[196] Which provides that "[a]cts or threats of violence the primary purpose of which is to spread terror among the civilian population are prohibited." *Brima TJ*, para. 661.

[197] *Id.* at para. 662.

[198] *Id.* at para. 662, with reference to the Draft Convention for the Protection of Civilian Populations against New Engines of War, Amsterdam, 1938; Declaration of Minimum Humanitarian Standards, *reprinted in* Report of the Sub-Commission on Prevention of Discrimination and Protection of Minorities on its 46th Sess., Commission on Human Rights, 51st Sess., Provisional Agenda Item 19, at 4, U.N. Doc. E/CN.4/1995/116 (1995).

[199] *Brima TJ*, para. 663.

[200] *Id.* at para. 665.

[201] *Id.* at paras. 668–669.

[202] *Id.* at para. 671; Motions for Judgment of Acquittal Pursuant to Rule 98, Oct. 21, 2005, para. 112. *See also* Prosecution Final Trial Brief, para. 978.

The Indictment alleged that members of the RUF,[203] AFRC,[204] Junta, and/or AFRC/RUF forces (AFRC/RUF), subordinate to and/or acting in concert with the three Accused, conducted armed attacks throughout Sierra Leone directed at, inter alia, civilians, primarily in order to terrorize them but also to punish them for failing to provide support to the AFRC/RUF, or for allegedly providing support to the Kabbah government or to pro-government forces. Such attacks included unlawful killings, physical and sexual violence, abductions, looting, and destruction of civilian property. Many civilians saw these crimes committed, whereas others returned to their homes to find dead bodies, mutilated victims, and looted and burned property.[205] The campaign of terror and punishment of the AFRC/RUF included the routine capture and abduction of members of the civilian population: women and girls were raped or abducted and used as sex slaves and as forced labor, whereas men and boys were also used as forced labor; many boys and girls were used in active fighting. It was also alleged that AFRC/RUF mutilated people by amputating their hands or feet or carving "AFRC" and "RUF" on their bodies.[206] Brima, Kamara, and Kanu were charged with unlawful killings, sexual and physical violence, use of child soldiers, abductions and forced labor, looting, and burning, as part of a campaign to terrorize the civilian population of Sierra Leone, which did terrorize that population.[207]

This approach is innovative, as it suggests that various conducts, if perpetrated with the specific intent of terrorizing the civilian population, may be prosecuted under the heading of *acts of terrorism*; this may, thus, be used as a kind of "default" war crime provision, applicable whenever the underlying acts fail to meet more specific elements of other war crimes. A difficulty lies in the proof of the specific intent, which may nonetheless be inferred from the circumstances. This aspect becomes particularly relevant when assessing gender-based crimes, an aspect that will be looked at next, and which may present an intersection with the war crime of terrorism.

In evaluating the evidence, the Trial Chamber held that although certain acts of violence were of such a nature "that the primary purpose can only be reasonably inferred to be to spread terror among the civilian population regardless of the context in which they were committed," it could not be inferred that all acts of violence, even when committed in the context of other acts of violence the primary purpose of which may be to terrorize the civilian population, were committed in furtherance of such a campaign.[208] For instance, it concluded that the "primary purpose of the conscription and use of child soldiers by the AFRC during the conflict in Sierra Leone, was not to spread terror among the civilian population, but rather was primarily military in nature."[209] Likewise, the primary purpose of sexual slavery was the taking "of advantage of the spoils of war, by treating women as property and using them to satisfy their sexual desires and to fulfil other conjugal needs,"[210] whereas the purpose behind the abductions and forced labor was "primarily utilitarian or military

---

[203] Revolutionary United Front.
[204] Armed Forces Revolutionary Council.
[205] *Brima TJ*, para. 1431.
[206] *Id.* at para. 1432.
[207] *Id.* at para. 1434.
[208] *Id.* at paras. 1445–1446.
[209] *Id.* at para. 1450
[210] *Id.* at para. 1459.

in nature."[211] Although "the abduction and detention of persons from their homes and their subjection to forced labour under conditions of violence spread terror among the civilian population," this is a side effect that, as such, was not sufficient to establish the specific intent of terror with regards to these acts.[212] On the contrary, the chamber was satisfied that many of the amputations that were carried out "were used by the AFRC with the primary purpose to spread terror among the civilian population."[213] With regard to the sustained attacks of the AFRC/RUF forces in the Kenema District following the AFRC coup in May 1997 on positions held by the CDF or Kamajors,[214] the Trial Chamber concluded that in consideration of the deliberate and sustained duration of the attacks and their particularly brutal nature, including the burning of civilians in a house and the grotesque public display of a mutilated body, it was satisfied that the primary purpose thereof was to spread terror among the civilian population.[215] It reached the same conclusion with regard to (similar) acts that took place in other areas,[216] including Freetown.[217]

The three Accused were found guilty for acts of terrorism pursuant to Article 3(d) SCSL.[218] The Prosecutor's contention on appeal that the recruitment of child soldiers, the abductions and forced labor, and the sexual slavery (the three "enslavement crimes") should have also been included under this heading was dismissed by the Appeals Chamber on the ground that "the Prosecution's attempt to search for further acts of terrorism by adding the three enslavement crimes to this list is an unnecessary exercise since the Appellants have already been convicted of acts of terrorism and an adequate sentence has been imposed."[219] This judgment, however, should not be read as excluding enslavement crimes as such from the list of sub-offenses that may contribute to a campaign of terrorism. In this case, the exclusion was based on the lack of a specific intent, in that the enslavements purported a different aim than terrorization (military effort).[220] It does not mean, however, that under different circumstances they may not constitute terrorist attacks.

With regard to the intersection of the war crime of terror and gender-based violence, Professor Oosterveld, in her contribution in this volume, remarks that although in the CDF case the SCSL fully missed the opportunity to examine the topic, in the RUF case the Trial Chamber's judgment noted that the rebels acted egregiously by concluding that in Sierra Leone the "acts were not intended merely for the personal satisfaction or a means of sexual gratification for the fighter,"[221] and they were "intended to terrorize civilians into submission

---

[211] *Id.* at paras. 1454 and 1468.

[212] *Id.* at para. 1453.

[213] *Id.* at para. 1462.

[214] As defined in *Brima TJ*, para. 2, these were "traditional hunters, normally serving in the employ of local chiefs to defend villages in the rural parts of the country."

[215] *Brima TJ*, para. 1475.

[216] Tikonko, Gerihun (*Brima TJ*, para. 1495); Koidu Town, Tombudu (*Brima TJ*, para. 1525) Kabala Town (*Brima TJ*, para. 1538) Bornoya, Mateboi, Mandaya, Karina, Gebendembu, Rosos (*Brima TJ*, para. 1571).

[217] *Brima TJ*, para. 1610.

[218] *Id.* At paras. 2113, 2117, and 2121; para. 2 of Annex A to the *AJ* Judgment (procedural history). See Count 1 of the Indictment.

[219] *Brima AJ*, para. 172.

[220] *Brima TJ*, paras. 1454 and 1468; *Brima AJ*, para. 170ss.

[221] Sesay, Kallon and Gbao (RUF), SCSL-04-15-T, Judgment, para. 1348, Trial Chamber I (Mar. 2, 2009) [hereinafter RUF Trial Judgment].

to the *RUF*."[222] To do so, the RUF created "an atmosphere in which violence, oppression and lawlessness prevailed,"[223] based on perverse methods of sexual violence, including the forcing of girls into enforced marriages with the fighters, resulting in the effective disempowerment of the civilian population and in the unraveling of the cultural values that kept the societies together.[224] In her view, therefore, because gender-based acts of violence may be committed with the ultimate goal of terrorizing the population, this heading may also encompass this type of offenses.

As previously mentioned, however, this was well-accepted in the Brima (AFRC) case,[225] according to which there is no need to prove that the sub-conduct amounted to an offense, as long as the specific intent is proven. In this case, the ban on terrorist acts may be considered as a kind of default rule, applicable whenever the elements of a more-specific (war) crime are not met. Likewise, gender-based crimes and/or acts of sexual violence, including those that do not meet the criteria of any specific sexual offense, may be prosecuted under this heading, as long as these requirements are met. One may ask whether this is the best approach, in terms of prevention, as it is only during the last decades has it been accepted that sexual offenses may be perpetrated in furtherance of an armed conflict and, thus, qualify as war crimes. Their prosecution under the (general) heading of the war crime of terrorism may weaken the stigmatization that has been eventually attached to them by prosecuting them as specific war crimes. The heading on terrorism could therefore be a valid alternative or concurrent applicable provision, but it should not be considered as the first provision to apply. This may play an important difference also for the victims. A rape victim probably needs to see her/his case addressed in its specificity, as a single important episode, which should not be overshadowed by the vast scale of analogous (sad) episodes. Prosecution under the broader heading of acts of terrorism would probably mean that the victim, Ms. X, may end up being "swallowed" up in the collectivity of victims addressed in a prosecution based on the heading of the war crime of terrorism. In this case, the victim's individuality needs to step back for the well-being of the collectivity. This approach may not be the best suited in the case of gender-based violence, which violated the most intimate sphere of a person, who probably needs recognition of her/his individuality and identification of the perpetrator.

Alternatively, the heading on crimes against terrorism may play an important subsidiary role whenever prosecution under a more-specific heading is impaired (for instance because one of the elements is missing or difficult to prove). In sum, one of the main innovations brought by the SCSL is its recognition that acts of terrorism may qualify as a war crime irrespective of the qualification of the sub-conduct. This means that as long as a specific act, be this sexual harassment, rape, or a form of psychological duress, falls short of the elements required by a specific war crime provision, it may by default be prosecuted under the heading of terrorism. But as long as conduct such as rape may be prosecuted under a specific heading, stigmatizing it as such, its additional enlistment in the indictment as the war crime of terror should be ancillary or concurrent, not prevailing.

---

[222] See Valerie Oosterveld's chapter in this volume.
[223] RUF Trial Judgment, para. 1347.
[224] Oosterveld, *supra* note 222.
[225] *Brima TJ*, para. 1434.

An analogous argument may arise with regard to prosecution under the heading of persecution as a crime against humanity, along the lines of terrorism in the Blagojević case. However, neither in the CDF nor in the Brima cases were acts of terrorism considered under this heading.

V. CONCLUSIONS

The qualification of so-called acts of *terrorism in wartime* as a war crime has undergone major developments since its first appearances in the IMT trials. Since its original meaning as the breach of LOAC conventional rules applicable to international armed conflicts only, aimed at protecting the civilian population from indiscriminate attacks of the adverse party primarily aimed at terrorizing them, it has developed into a customary law prohibition applicable to *all* types of armed conflicts and binding on *all* the parties thereto. From its roots in The Hague Law,[226] which was aimed at regulating the conduct of hostilities, the prohibition is now understood as protecting fundamental guarantees rooted in the Geneva Law, in particular Article 4(2) AP II.

The ICTY, in particular with the Galić case, defined for the first time in clear terms the elements of the offense, establishing that this had to be committed in relation to an armed conflict and with the primary, but not exclusive, aim to raise an extreme sense of fear in individual civilians or members of the civilian population. Protection, however, is granted only to civilians not participating in the hostilities, thereby excluding other categories of protected persons (e.g., prisoners of war, sick and wounded combatants). The war crime of *acts of terrorism* was qualified as a specific-intent crime. The acts need only to have the potential to instigate terror: neither infliction of terrorism nor, thus, causality are required elements. The Galić case paved the way for the qualification of acts of terrorism in wartime as an independent, specific war crime. In the wake of the ICTY's jurisprudence and the inclusion of this offense in the ICTR Statute, the SCSL also included the prohibition of acts of terrorism in Article 3(d) of its Statute, qualifying it as a serious violation of common Article 3 to the GCs and AP II.

In the CDF and Brima trials, the SCSL corroborated the precedents set by the ICTY in *Galić* and *Blagojević* and developed the list of underlying offenses that may constitute acts of terrorism. It clarified that these need not be criminal offenses, so that there is no necessity to prove the meeting of specific elements of a crime. For example, the burning of a house committed with the primary aim to terrorize the civilian population does not need to meet the criteria of the war crime of looting. The SCSL then restated the principle that only civilians who do not take part in the hostilities are protected. This approach is questionable, as the concept of direct participation in hostilities is not clear and as on this basis a party may claim that also civilians working for the war industry (e.g., in ammunition factories or similar firms) by contributing to the hostilities may be made the target of terrorist acts. It is to be hoped that future jurisprudence, instead of restricting the passive scope of application of the anti-terrorism provisions to civilians who do not participate in hostilities, will expand

---

[226] In particular the 1923 *Hague Rules on Warfare* and the 1938 *Draft Convention for the Protection of Civilian Populations against New Engines of War* expressly prohibited "[a]erial bombardment for the purpose of terrorising the civilian population." See *Galić AJ*, para. 88.

it in order to cover, in a first step, all persons hors de combat, including prisoners of war, wounded and sick combatants, or those lost at sea. Ideally, an even better outcome would be its extension to all parties engaged in a conflict.

From an ethical point of view, it is questionable whether the use of terrorist attacks as a warfare strategy is compatible with the principles of proportionality and the prohibition of unnecessary suffering. If the passive personal scope of application of these provisions were extended to combatants, too, conduct such as mass rapes or the looting of the civilians left back at home, aimed at defeating the morale of the adverse party, particularly of the male relatives engaged in combat, could be prosecuted under this heading. This approach would have the advantage to better protect combatants from the exposure to unnecessary suffering, particularly in the era of asymmetric warfare, where they are often confronted with an adverse party not abiding by the LOAC. The SCSL, by highlighting the fact that indiscriminate attack with no apparent military necessity such as amputations of vast scales of the civilian population, may have opened the gate to this approach. One of its major merits is the recognition that acts of terrorism in wartime constitute a specific category of war crimes, the specific intent of which may be inferred from circumstantial evidence, which needs to be examined in each single case. What has to be kept in mind, however, is that the SCSL was created on a special basis and with regard to the peculiar context of the non-international armed conflict that took place in Sierra Leone. Some of its conclusions with regard to the crime of acts of terrorism, such as its possibility to apply the anti-terrorism provisions of IHL regardless of the qualification of the conflict or of the status of the parties thereto, are to be considered in light of these particular circumstances and not necessarily be transposed to other scenarios, where the dichotomy of the IHL regimes applicable to international as opposed to non-international armed conflicts may be still relevant.

14

Fleshing Out the Contours of the Crime of Attacks against United Nations Peacekeepers – The Contribution of the Special Court for Sierra Leone

Alhagi B. M. Marong[*]

I. INTRODUCTION

In March 2009, Trial Chamber I of the Special Court for Sierra Leone (SCSL) convicted Issa Hassan Sesay, Morris Kallon, and Augustine Gbao for war crimes including attacking, killing, and taking UN peacekeepers as hostages.[1] Sesay, Kallon, and Gbao were, until the time of their arrest and detention, senior commanders of the Revolutionary United Front (RUF), the rebel group that fought an eleven-year civil war against the government of the Republic of Sierra Leone.

The Judgment of the SCSL in the RUF case represented the first time an international criminal tribunal considered the international crime of attacks against UN peacekeepers.[2] Sesay, Kallon, and Gbao therefore became the first persons to be tried and convicted for such a crime at international law. This Judgment of the Special Court is historic, as it was the first time following a full trial that an international judicial institution convicted anyone for attacking UN peacekeepers. The crime of attacking UN peacekeepers is not a new offense as it forms part of the general prohibition in customary international law against attacks on civilians.[3] In the history of modern international criminal law, the offense of attacks against UN peacekeepers was first introduced in the Statute of the International Criminal Court, and the matter has come up in some preliminary motions in that court;[4] however, no one has been tried for the offense at the ICC.

---

[*] Legal Adviser, UNAMA and former Senior Legal Officer, Appeals Chamber, Special Court for Sierra Leone, and Legal Officer and Judgment Coordinator, U.N. International Criminal Tribunal for Rwanda.

[1] The Prosecutor v. Issa Hassan Sesay, Morris Kallon, and Augustine Gbao (Judgment), SCSL-2009 Case. No. SCSL-04–15-T (Mar. 2, 2009) [hereinafter RUF Trial Judgment].

[2] Sandesh Sivakumaran, *War Crimes before the Special Court for Sierra Leone: Child Soldiers, Hostages, Peacekeepers and Collective Punishments*, 8 J. INT'L CRIM. JUST. 1009, 1024 (2010); Alice Gadler, *The Protection of Peacekeepers and International Criminal Law: Legal Challenges and Broader Protection*, 11 GERMAN L.J. 585, 600 (2010). *See also* RUF Trial Judgment, *supra* note 1, at para. 214.

[3] RUF Trial Judgment, *supra* note 1, at para. 215, citing with approval the Report of Secretary-General on the Establishment of the Special Court, para. 16, that the international crime of attacks against peacekeepers was first included in the Rome Statute of the ICC, but that it was not considered a new crime. Rather, given that peacekeeping personnel were protected to the extent that they are entitled to protection recognized under international law to civilians in armed conflict, the prohibition in Article 4(b) of the SCSL Statute "is a specification of a targeted group within the generally protected group of civilians which because of its humanitarian or peacekeeping mission deserves special protection."

[4] *The Prosecutor v. Abu Garda, infra* note 39 and accompanying text.

This chapter discusses the jurisprudence of the Special Court on the crime of attacks against UN peacekeepers and argues that the RUF Trial Judgment has made several significant contributions to international criminal law. As the first reasoned judicial pronouncement on the crime of attacks against UN peacekeepers, the Court has clarified the elements of the crime and added meaning and substance to the provision. Such clarity is important not only for judges, practitioners, and scholars of international criminal law, but also for policy makers at the UN Department of Peacekeeping Operations (DPKO). Equally important is the fact that clarity regarding the elements of the crime will give accused persons good notice of the allegations they face and permit them to prepare a full defense.

Second, by affirming United Nations Mission in Sierra Leone (UNAMSIL)'s status as a UN peacekeeping force operating under Chapter VI of the UN Charter, the Court gave judicial approval to the principle that such forces enjoy the same status and protection as civilians or noncombatants under international humanitarian law. Given the upsurge in attacks on UN peacekeepers, especially during various internal armed conflicts in the 1990s, this holding will likely enhance the legal protection afforded to such peacekeepers. Greater protection for peacekeepers in turn will advance the policy and practice of peacekeeping as a tool of global collective security at the disposal of the UN Security Council and other regional organizations.[5] The attacks against peacekeepers in such places as Bosnia-Herzegovina and Rwanda in the 1990s, coupled with the weak material and legal capacity of such forces to respond to or otherwise defend themselves against such attacks, has produced great reluctance on the part of member states to contribute troops for peacekeeping duty. Hence, greater legal protection for peacekeepers will likely address what has until now been a deficit in state willingness to contribute forces to UN peace operations.

Third, given that Article 4(b) of the Special Court Statute is *ipsissima verba* with Article 8(b)(iii) and 8(e)(iii) of the Rome Statute, the Special Court's Judgment in the RUF case will likely influence the ICC's interpretation in future cases and contribute to the progressive development of international law in this area. We have already seen the ICC Trial Chamber rely on the SCSL case law in other areas – for example, when fleshing out the elements of the war crime of child recruitment in their March 14, 2012 judgment in the Thomas Lubanga case, as Cecile Aptel discusses in Chapter 17 of this volume.

Finally, by holding that the crime of attacks against UN peacekeepers is not a new crime but a reflection of the general prohibition against attacks on civilians or noncombatants during armed conflict, the Special Court Judgment is likely to influence future judicial interpretation of the Geneva Conventions on the protection of civilians in times of conflict.

The remainder of this chapter is organized as follows: in Section II, I briefly discuss the normative foundations of UN peacekeeping as contained in the Charter of the United Nations. Section III discusses the international humanitarian law norms that prohibit attacks against civilians or noncombatants, including the Geneva Conventions and their Additional Protocols, which reflect customary international law; the provisions of the Rome

---

[5] The legal authority for peacekeeping operations is conferred by Chapters VI, VII, and VIII of the Charter of the United Nations, which deal, respectively, with pacific settlement of disputes, actions with respect to threats to the peace, breaches of the peace and acts of aggression, and regional arrangements. In West Africa, an example of a regional peace operation was the intervention in Liberia by forces of the sub-regional economic grouping ECOWAS in the early 1990s. That intervention force, the ECOWAS Monitoring Group (ECOMOG), was authorized under the ECOWAS Treaty and endorsed by the UN Security Council.

Statute and SCSL Court Statute that prohibit attacks against UN peacekeepers; and the 1994 Convention on the Safety of United Nations and Associated Personnel that represents a sui generis legal regime requiring Parties to criminalize and prosecute or extradite for prosecution persons who commit crimes against UN peacekeepers.

Section IV argues that based on a review of the UN Security Council Resolutions establishing UNAMSIL, its rules of engagement, and other factual circumstances that governed its operations, the UNAMSIL troops were a peacekeeping force. This proposition is true despite the fact that their initial mandate had evolved from one of traditional peacekeeping to one that permitted the robust use of force in certain circumstances, including for the protection of civilians under imminent threat of attack. Section V of the chapter discusses the reasoning and conclusions of the SCSL in the RUF case and identifies the Court's contributions to international criminal law. Section VI offers a few concluding remarks.

II. NORMATIVE FOUNDATIONS FOR UN PEACEKEEPING

Peacekeeping operations have been an important instrument of global collective security in the practice of the United Nations. The United Nations was established at the end of the Second World War as a manifestation of a global commitment "to save succeeding generations from the scourge of war."[6] In order to do this, the Organization aimed, inter alia, to work for the maintenance of international peace and security. In particular, the Security Council was authorized to take collective measures to prevent or remove threats to the peace, acts of aggression, and breaches of the peace.[7] The Organization can also resort to measures for the peaceful settlement of disputes in a manner consistent with the principles of justice and international law.[8]

In carrying out its mandate for the maintenance of international peace and security, the United Nations Charter provides that the Security Council established under Article 23 shall have primary, but not exclusive, jurisdiction to act on behalf of member states.[9] In doing so, the Council is empowered to employ both peaceful, and where appropriate, coercive measures to maintain or restore international peace and security.[10] One implication of this power is that international law distinguishes between peacekeeping and peace-enforcement. Peacekeepers enjoy protections under the international law of armed conflict and are generally deemed to have the same status as civilians. On the other hand, peace-enforcement troops, which enjoy the authority to use offensive force in implementing their mandate, are deemed to be combatants under international law and can therefore be legitimate targets during hostilities. As discussed more fully later on, although the SCSL Trial

---

[6] U.N. Charter, June 26, 1945, pmbl.

[7] U.N. Charter art. 1(1).

[8] *Id.*

[9] U.N. Charter, June 26, 1945, 59 Stat. 1031, art. 24. In *Certain Expenses of the United Nations*, ICJ Rep. 151 (1962), the International Court of Justice held that the Security Council had primary, but not exclusive, responsibility for the maintenance of international peace and security. The Court noted that the General Assembly also has a role in matters of international peace and security and can make recommendations to the Security Council or to member states, except that pursuant to Article 12 of the Charter, the UN General Assembly cannot make recommendations on matters that are being dealt with by the Security Council.

[10] U.N. Charter, Chapters VI and VII deal, respectively, with the pacific settlement of disputes and coercive measures to address breaches of the peace.

Chamber did not lose sight of this distinction in the RUF Judgment, the Court missed an opportunity to express support for even more robust legal protection for peacekeepers irrespective of whether they operate under Chapter VI or VII of the UN Charter.

The normative framework for maintenance of international peace and security consists of a variety of measures under Chapters VI and VII of the Charter ranging from pacific settlement to economic sanctions and military intervention. The first formal peacekeeping operation, which was to lay down some of the operative principles of UN peacekeeping, was established in 1948 to supervise the Arab–Israeli ceasefire over the Palestinian conflict.[11] The UN Truce Supervision Organization (UNSTO) laid down impartiality, prohibition on the use of force, and consent of the parties as bedrock principles upon which UN peacekeeping forces operated.[12] These principles now enjoy a firm place in UN peacekeeping doctrine. However, the use of force principle has in practice shifted from its traditional incarnation to a situation where peacekeepers now need to project such force as is necessary to credibly protect themselves and their mandate.[13] As discussed later, the internal armed conflict in Sierra Leone demonstrated one of those situations in which the ability of peacekeeping troops to project deterrent force against would-be spoilers was sorely tested.

III. INTERNATIONAL LAW PROHIBITING ATTACKS ON UN PEACEKEEPERS

No international legal instrument specifically prohibited attacks on UN peacekeepers prior to 1994. Peacekeeper protection norms were therefore implied from the general provisions of the UN Charter such as Article 105, which requires member states to grant the United Nations such privileges and immunities as are necessary to fulfill the organization's purposes.[14] Protection of UN peacekeepers was also implied from customary international law norms prohibiting attacks on civilians and civilian objects under the Geneva Conventions and their Additional Protocols. According to Professor Greenwood,

> it is possible to infer certain protections for non-party U.N. peacekeepers from [the law of armed conflict] … the parties to the conflict have a duty to respect and protect U.N personnel engaged in relief operations. More generally, because U.N. peacekeeping units, the civilian personnel attached to them, their buildings, vehicles, and equipment would not constitute military objectives under Articles 48 and 50–52 of Protocol I, attacks upon them by a party to an international armed conflict are unlawful.[15]

---

[11] U.N. S.C. Res. 50, May 29, 1948, which called for a ceasefire between Israel and its Arab neighbors, and set up an Observer Mission to supervise the truce.

[12] James Sloan, *The Use of Force in U.N. Peacekeeping: A Cycle of Boom and Bust?*, 30 HASTINGS INT'L & COMP. L. REV. 385, 386 (2007), referring to consent, impartiality, and nonuse of force except in self-defense as "the holy trinity" of UN peacekeeping.

[13] United Nations, *An Agenda for Peace* (A/47/277 S/24111) and its 1995 Supplement to an Agenda for Peace (A/50/60/S), which recognized consent, impartiality, and the nonuse of force except in self-defense as essential principles of UN peacekeeping. *See also* United Nations, *Comprehensive Review of the Whole Question of Peacekeeping Operations in All Their Aspects* (2000) "Brahimi Report," A/55/305 S/2000/809, which endorses a paradigm shift from traditional peacekeeping to complex, multi-dimensional peace operations that require a review of peacekeeping mandates, especially as they relate to the use of force.

[14] U.N. Charter art. 105.

[15] Christopher Greenwood, *Protection of Peacekeepers: The Legal Regime*, 7 DUKE J. COMP. & INT'L L. 185, 190 (1996).

Conversely, where UN forces become combatants, as in enforcement actions under Chapter VII of the Charter, they are subject to the law of armed conflict and enjoy protections extended to other combatants.[16] Professor Walter Gary Sharp, however, argues that existing international law could at times be viewed as weakening legal protections for UN peacekeepers because such protections apply only so long as the peacekeepers do not engage in offensive military operations. As a result, forces operating under Chapter VII of the Charter are not only excluded from the protections extended to noncombatants but could become legitimate targets of war under existing international law.[17] During the 1990s, attacks on UN peacekeepers in Somalia, the former Yugoslavia, and Rwanda led to the adoption of several resolutions by the Security Council calling upon member states to protect peacekeepers.[18] The resolutions, however, proved largely ineffective, leading to increased reluctance on the part of UN member states to commit troops to peacekeeping duties. Given this reluctance, New Zealand and Ukraine proposed the adoption of a multilateral convention to enhance protection for peacekeeping personnel.[19] The result was the 1994 Convention on the Safety of United Nations and Associated Personnel.[20]

For the purposes of this chapter, I will highlight three critical provisions of the Convention: (1) it specifically prohibits attacks on UN and associated personnel involved in a peacekeeping operation[21]; (2) it requires state parties to criminalize and prosecute or extradite those accused of crimes against peacekeepers[22]; and (3) it preserves the application of international humanitarian law to combat situations in UN peace enforcement as opposed to peacekeeping operations.[23]

The adoption of the Convention was an important development in international law as it was the first legal instrument to specifically prohibit attacks on UN peacekeeping personnel.[24] The Convention applies to "United Nations operations" defined as "an operation established by the competent organ of the United Nations in accordance with the Charter ... and conducted under United Nations authority and control."[25] On the face of it, this

---

[16] *Id.* at 189.

[17] Walter Gary Sharp, Sr., *Protecting the Avatars of International Peace and Security*, 7 DUKE J. COMP. & INT'L L. 93, 126–27 (1996).

[18] Evan T. Bloom, *Protecting Peacekeepers: The Convention on the Safety of United Nations and Associated Personnel*, 89 AM. J. INT'L L. 621, 622 (1995). *See, e.g.*, U.N. S.C. Res. 733 (1992), para. 8, which called on "all parties to take all the necessary measures to ensure the safety of personnel sent to provide humanitarian assistance, to assist them in their tasks and to ensure full respect for the rules and principles of international law regarding the protection of civilian populations."

[19] Bloom *supra*.

[20] Convention on the Safety of United Nations and Associated Personnel, 34 ILM 482 (1995).

[21] Article 9 of the Convention prohibits the intentional commission of murder, kidnapping, or other attack on the person or liberty of the United Nations or associated personnel; violent attacks on UN premises, accommodation, or means of transport; and attempts or threats to commit any such attack.

[22] Articles 10 and 14 respectively, which require each state party to take measures to establish jurisdiction over these crimes, and where the alleged offender is present on its territory, to prosecute or extradite such person for prosecution by another state party.

[23] Article 2(2) provides that the Convention shall not apply to UN operations authorized by the Security Council as enforcement action under Chapter VII of the Charter.

[24] Siobhan Wills, *The Need for Effective Protection of United Nations Peacekeepers: The Convention on the Safety of United Nations and Associated Personnel*, 10 WTR HUM. RTS. 26 (2003).

[25] Art. 1.

appears to extend to all such operations authorized by the Security Council either under Chapter VI or Chapter VII of the Charter.

Article 2(2) specifically states that the Convention does not apply where the Security Council authorizes enforcement action under Chapter VII in order to avoid undermining the Geneva Conventions of 1949 and to ensure that peacekeepers are protected either under international humanitarian law or the Convention. This caveat is for good reason as international humanitarian law operates on the basis of the principle of equal application. In other words, the humane treatment provisions of the law of war bind all parties at all times during an armed conflict. Therefore, when the United Nations authorizes the use of military force as an enforcement action, these forces become combatants – implying that they can be legitimate military targets.

Sir Hersch Lauterpacht argues that the principle of equal application is important because it provides incentives for both parties in an armed conflict to respect the rules of war.[26] Greenwood has additionally argued that criminalizing attacks on UN combat forces will undermine the equal application principle, produce adverse incentives on the part of opposing forces to respect the *jus in bello*, and consequently expose UN troops to greater danger.[27] Other scholars maintain that there should be no distinction between belligerent and nonbelligerent peacekeepers and that both categories should enjoy full protection under international law.[28] This argument is informed by the significance these scholars attach to the sacrifices peacekeepers make in placing themselves in harm's way in furtherance of international collective security. The argument goes that if it is necessary for peacekeepers under Chapter VII of the UN Charter to use deadly force in support of their mandate or for civilian protection, they should also enjoy those protections under the international law of armed conflict that equally recognize their higher role as defenders of the collective interest. Such an approach would not affect the equal application principle because protecting Chapter VII peacekeepers from attack by other organized armed forces or groups would not imply that such peacekeepers should themselves not adhere to the rules of the *jus in bello*.

By contrast, the Safety Convention is intended to protect noncombatant peacekeeping forces who form a distinct category of civilians deserving legal protection during war. Although this proposition can be simply stated, its application in practice raises difficult interpretive problems. There is little doubt that traditional, unarmed peace observers or lightly armed peacekeepers and civilian members of a peacekeeping mission fall squarely under the protective regime of the Convention. The hard questions relate to contemporary peacekeeping forces, in vogue since the 1990s, to whom the Security Council has granted

---

[26] H. Lauterpacht, *The Limits of the Operation of the Laws of War*, 30 Brit. Y.B. Int'l L. 206, 212 (1953), *cited in* Greenwood, *supra* note 15, at 205.

[27] Greenwood, *supra* note 15, at 206. *But see* Sharp, *supra* note 17, at 93, who argues that the law of armed conflict should not apply to the United Nations, and that the Safety Convention should be extended to Chapter VII enforcement actions so as to criminalize all manner of attack on UN forces.

[28] Sharp, *supra* note 17, at 163: "existing international law must be changed to protect all military personnel who serve in U.N. forces, combatants and non-combatants alike." He further suggests that until international law is so changed, all future UN resolutions authorizing the deployment of peacekeeping troops, whether under Chapter IV, VI, or VII, "should declare that the members of the force are not combatants so long as their use of force is within the mandate, and that all attacks on the force constitute an international crime."

robust mandates and significant authority to use "all necessary means" to defend themselves or their mandates.[29]

Peacekeeping troops have also been authorized to protect civilian populations[30] and facilitate the delivery of humanitarian assistance[31] to needy populations. If in carrying out such mandates these forces become embroiled in armed conflict, then the question becomes "at what point do they cross the threshold from noncombatant to combatant status so as to lose protection under the Convention?" As established by the jurisprudence of the Special Court for Sierra Leone[32] and argued by some commentators,[33] the fact that the United Nations has adopted an expansive interpretation of the self-defense principle in contemporary peacekeeping to include defense of the mandate and civilian protection does not per se take peacekeeping forces outside the purview of the Safety Convention.

It is clear that the Convention does not apply to peace-enforcement forces authorized by the Security Council under Chapter VII, because such forces are deemed to be combatants under international humanitarian law and hence their operations are governed by the rules governing the conduct of hostilities under the Geneva Conventions.[34] Another important innovation of the Safety Convention is that it distinguishes between detained or captured UN peacekeepers on the one hand and prisoners of war on the other. The Convention requires that detained or captured peacekeepers must be promptly released to the United Nations as soon as their identity has been established, whereas under international humanitarian law, prisoners of war can be held until the cessation of hostilities. The captured peacekeepers during the course of their detention must be treated according to universally recognized human rights standards, as well as the principles and spirit of the 1949 Geneva Conventions.[35]

The Safety Convention marks an important effort to establish an international protective regime for peacekeepers as it is the first multilateral agreement to outlaw attacks on personnel and installations involved in UN peace operations, and to provide for universal jurisdiction in case of such attacks. Its effectiveness, however, is potentially limited because of its reliance on domestic prosecution and the reality that most states on whose territory such attacks take place (such as Sierra Leone, Rwanda, Somalia or the former Yugoslavia) are in conflict or have recently emerged from conflict. Legal and judicial institutions in

---

[29] James Sloan, *The Use of Offensive Force in U.N. Peacekeeping: A Cycle of Boom and Bust*, 30 Hastings Int'l & Comp. L. Rev. 385 (2007).

[30] *See, e.g.*, U.N. S.C. Res. 1270 (1999) and 1313 (2000), which authorize UNAMSIL to use all necessary means to defend civilians under imminent threat of physical violence.

[31] This was the case for UNPROFOR during the Balkan Conflict.

[32] *The Prosecutor v. Sesay, Kallon & Gbao*, Judgment, TC I, at para. 233, "… the use of force by peacekeepers in self-defence in the discharge of their mandate, … would not alter or diminish the protection afforded to peacekeepers." *See also* para. 1911, "… the fact that the peacekeepers were empowered under Chapter VII to use force in certain exceptional and restricted circumstances does not alter the fundamental nature of the UNAMSIL mission as a peacekeeping, and not a peace enforcement, mission."

[33] Greenwood, *supra* note 15, at 198; Bloom, *supra* note 18, at 625; *contra* A. Gadler, *The Protection of Peacekeepers and International Criminal Law: Legal Challenges and Broader Protection*, 11 German L.J. 585, 591 (2010) (arguing that the use of force in self-defense by peacekeepers should be limited to self-defense under international humanitarian law, and that the latter does not include the use of force in defense of the mandate).

[34] *See* art. 2(2) of the Convention.

[35] Art. 8, Safety Convention. *See also* Wills, *supra* note 24, at 27, noting that the Safety Convention was the first to extend Geneva Convention protections to UN peacekeepers.

such countries as a consequence have collapsed or are largely dysfunctional.[36] Despite these shortcomings, the Convention marks an important development in international law that has influenced the introduction of similar prohibitions both under the Statute of the International Criminal Court and the Special Court for Sierra Leone. To that end, it is safe to state that the real impact of the Safety Convention is that it signaled international resolve to combat impunity for attacks against the "avatars of international peace and security."[37]

The influence of the Safety Convention is evident from the fact that four years after its adoption, negotiators of the Rome Statute agreed that it was a war crime in international and internal armed conflicts to intentionally direct attacks against personnel, installations, material, units, or vehicles involved in a peacekeeping or humanitarian assistance mission.[38] Although no one has been tried at the ICC for this offense, a Pre-Trial Chamber of the Court has had occasion, in the Abu Garda case, to consider the scope and application of the provision in Article 8(2)(e)(iii) of the Rome Statute.[39] The Accused was charged with individual criminal responsibility for the attack on September 29, 2007, against an African Union Mission in Sudan (AMIS) base in Darfur, which led to the death of at least twelve peacekeepers. In discussing the meaning of "attack" under the Statute, the Court referred to Article 49 of Additional Protocol I, holding that the term signified "an act of violence against the adversary, whether in offence or defence."[40] Critically, the Court also held that the perpetration of such an act of violence was sufficient to establish individual criminal responsibility as there was no requirement that the attack must create a material result or harmful impact.[41] This Decision marked an important point in the process of legal clarification of the elements of the offense under consideration because the Special Court for Sierra Leone in deciding the RUF case reached the same conclusion as the ICC Pre-Trial Chamber – a position that was in direct opposition to the view of the ICTY on a similar point of law.[42]

Influenced by the Safety Convention and the ICC Statute, the Statute of the Special Court for Sierra Leone also criminalized intentional attacks against UN personnel and installations as being another serious violation of international law.[43] As discussed in detail below, Article 4(b) was one of the provisions for which Sesay, Kallon, and Gbao were tried and convicted by the Special Court for Sierra Leone. This chapter highlights the Special Court's

---

[36] Wills, *supra* note 24, at 27, "… the law enforcement capabilities of a state requiring outside forces for internal stability are generally insufficient to investigate, try, and prosecute persons for such crimes."

[37] Sharp, *supra* note 17.

[38] For international armed conflicts, see art. 8(2)(b)(iii) of the ICC Statute, and art. 8(2)(e)(iii) for non-international armed conflicts.

[39] The Prosecutor v. Bahr Idriss Abu Garda, Decision on the Confirmation of Charges – Public Redacted Version, Feb. 8, 2010, ICC-02/05–02/09–243-Red, Pre-Trial Chamber I.

[40] *Id.* at para. 65.

[41] *Id.* According to the Pre-Trial Chamber, "… article 8(2)(e)(iii) of the Statute does not require any material result or harmful impact on the personnel, installations, material, units or vehicles involved in the peacekeeping mission which are being targeted by the attack."

[42] The Prosecutor v. Kordic & Cerkez, Judgment of the Appeals Chamber, Dec. 17, 2004, paras. 55–68, holding that the war crime of attacks against civilians is a result crime. In other words, "the attacks must be shown to have caused deaths and/or serious bodily injuries or extensive damage to civilian objects." *See also* The Prosecutor v. Strugar et al., Decision on Defense Preliminary Motion Challenging Jurisdiction, June 17, 2002, paras. 17–23, on the more general point that customary international law supported the existence of a war crime of attacks against civilians and civilian objects.

[43] SCSL Statute art. 4(b).

contribution to international law governing the protection of peacekeepers by analyzing the reasoning and conclusions of the Trial Chamber in the RUF case. In order to place the ensuing discussion in its proper context, I will briefly discuss the establishment of the UN Mission in Sierra Leone (UNAMSIL) and argue that a review of UNAMSIL's constitutive instruments as well as the mandate and rules of engagement of its forces shows that it was a peacekeeping mission with a robust mandate. The Trial Chamber therefore correctly held that UNAMSIL peacekeepers were legitimately entitled to the protection accorded to civilians under the Geneva Conventions and the 1994 Safety Convention.

IV. UNAMSIL AS A PEACEKEEPING MISSION

Under the leadership of President Ahmed Tejan Kabbah, the government of Sierra Leone signed a peace agreement with rebels of the Revolutionary United Front (RUF) on July 7, 1999, in Lomé, Togo. The Agreement brought to an end a violent over-a-decade-long internal armed conflict that wracked the country and led to massive deaths, the displacement of thousands of people, and life-long physical and psychological scars to thousands more. The Economic Community of West African States (ECOWAS), then under the chairmanship of the president of Togo, General Gnassingbé Eyadéma, negotiated the Lomé Peace Agreement. The Agreement provided for a complete cessation of hostilities between the warring parties, power-sharing between the government and rebels, disarmament, demobilization, and reintegration of former combatants, as well as amnesty for RUF leader Foday Sankoh, among others (as Charles Jalloh discusses in the introductory chapter of this volume).

In a statement appended to the Lomé Accord, the representative of the UN Secretary General at the peace talks noted the United Nations' understanding that the amnesty provisions do not apply to serious international crimes, including genocide, war crimes, and crimes against humanity.[44] It is also important to note for the purposes of this chapter that the Lomé Agreement specifically provided for the continued role of UN and ECOMOG troops as well as civilian personnel in the implementation of the peace agreement. Furthermore, it called on the United Nations to review UNOMSIL's[45] mandate to enable it to undertake the activities envisaged under the Agreement.

The Agreement also specifically guaranteed the "safety, security and freedom of movement" of UN and other peacekeeping personnel and offered them "unimpeded access" to any part of Sierra Leone in carrying out their activities. The Lomé Peace Agreement therefore signified one of the key principles for deployment of a peacekeeping force – that is, consent of the parties.[46] This is important in the Sierra Leone context, which was an

---

[44] *See* U.N. S.C. Res. 1315 (2000), pmbl. *See also* art. 10 of the SCSL Statute, which provides that an amnesty granted to any person in respect of international crimes under the jurisdiction of the Court shall not be a bar to prosecution before the Court. In the *Prosecutor v. Kallon & Kamara*, Decision on Challenge to Jurisdiction: Lomé Accord Amnesty, Mar. 13, 2004, the SCSL Appeals Chamber held that the amnesty granted under Article IX of the Lomé Peace Agreement could not operate to prevent the prosecution of crimes before an international criminal court such as the Special Court for Sierra Leone, and that such amnesties were valid only within the domestic legal system of the state that granted them.

[45] UNOMSIL (the United Nations Observer Mission in Sierra Leone), was the predecessor of UNAMSIL.

[46] See art. 2(7) of the U.N. Charter prohibiting intervention in matters that are within the domestic jurisdiction of member states.

internal armed conflict characterized by multiple warring factions with differentiated loyalties.[47] Having signed up to the Agreement, both the government of Sierra Leone and the RUF expressed their consent to the continued presence of UN troops in the country, including that these troops would be actively engaged in the implementation of the peace process.

The UN Security Council, having determined that the situation in Sierra Leone continued to constitute a threat to international peace and security, established UNAMSIL in October 1999 with a mandate to cooperate with the government of Sierra Leone and other parties in the implementation of the peace agreement.[48] The Security Council also authorized UNAMSIL "to encourage" the parties to create confidence-building mechanisms, to facilitate humanitarian assistance and to support the work of the Special Representative of the Secretary General and other civilian members of the mission.[49] UNAMSIL was further authorized under Chapter VII of the Charter to "take the necessary action ... to ensure the security and freedom of movement of its personnel and ... to afford protection to civilians under imminent threat of physical violence."[50] This provision of Resolution 1270 therefore marked the starting point of UNAMSIL's evolving mandate from one of traditional peacekeeping to one with increasing authority and capacity to use force in clearly delineated circumstances.

A few months later, the UN Security Council noted that there was "limited and sporadic participation in the [DDR][51] programme ... and continued hostage taking and attacks on humanitarian personnel" in Sierra Leone. It revised UNAMSIL's mandate, and now authorized it to "take the necessary action" to discharge that mandate.[52] This marked another important development, as by authorizing UNAMSIL to "take the necessary action," the Security Council implicitly recognized that the force must act more decisively and assert its authority more effectively against those who might want to disrupt the peace process. This circumstance was placed beyond doubt with the adoption of U.N. Security Council Resolution 1313 on August 4, 2000, which condemned the RUF's armed attacks against and detention of UN personnel and authorized UNAMSIL to "decisively counter the threat of

---

[47] In addition to the RUF, the other groups engaged in the Sierra Leone conflict at various points in time included the Armed Forces Revolutionary Council, a group of ex-servicemen from the Sierra Leone Army who staged a successful military takeover in January 1997 under the leadership of Major Johnny Paul Koroma; the Civil Defense Forces (CDF), a pro-government militia made up of traditional hunters and warriors under the leadership of Chief Hinga Norman. There are conflicting reports about the fate of Major Koroma. There is some anecdotal evidence to suggest that he died in exile in Liberia, whereas others still maintain he is on the run. Chief Hinga Norman was charged by the SCSL Prosecutor for war crimes and crimes against humanity, but died before the conclusion of his trial. His colleagues in the CDF, Kondewa and Fofanna, were convicted and sentenced to various terms of imprisonment.

[48] Given the Parties' consent to UNAMSIL's deployment, the legal basis, under the Charter, for the Security Council's action becomes less significant. *See, e.g.*, RUF Trial Judgment, *supra* note 1, at para. 222, noting the view of commentators that "the legal basis for peacekeeping missions is of no practical significance as peacekeeping missions are deployed with the consent of the parties and their legitimacy is no longer questioned."

[49] U.N. S.C. Res. 1270 (1999), para. 8.

[50] *Id.* at para. 14.

[51] DDR stands for "Disarmament, Demobilization and Reintegration." It is one of the processes by which the international community implements peace agreements following internal armed conflict.

[52] U.N. S.C. Res. 1289 (2000), para. 10(e).

RUF attack by responding robustly to any hostile actions or threat of imminent and direct use of force."[53]

A close reading of the above resolutions suggests that in creating UNAMSIL, the Security Council envisaged a peacekeeping mission that was deployed with the full consent of the parties, that was authorized to use force in limited circumstances, and that would act as an impartial interlocutor in the implementation of the peace process. The fact that UNAMSIL was composed of unarmed observers and lightly armed troops, who could use force only as a last resort in clearly defined circumstances, meant that UNAMSIL never lost its initial legal status as a peacekeeping entity. For these reasons, UNAMSIL was entitled to the protective guarantees stipulated under the Lomé Peace Agreement.

UNAMSIL personnel were also entitled to the protections extended to civilians under the international law of armed conflict. Although UNAMSIL's initial traditional peacekeeping mandate was revised over time and became more robust, the revisions were necessitated by the belligerence of the RUF, the need for civilian protection, and the imperative to maintain the mission's integrity. It is in this context that the Security Council's limited resort to Chapter VII powers in Resolutions 1270 and 1289 must be understood. In the circumstances, the UN Security Council's reference to Chapter VII powers and UNAMSIL's use of force in self-defense did not change its essential peacekeeping character, nor was it transformed into a peace enforcement mission. UNAMSIL remained a peacekeeping mission throughout the period for which the attacks by the RUF unfolded. As such, UNAMSIL personnel enjoyed the same status as civilians under international humanitarian law. Any attacks on them constituted violations of the laws of war and of the SCSL Statute, and as the Special Court for Sierra Leone held, were punishable as such. I will now discuss the jurisprudence of the SCSL in the RUF case.

V. THE JUDGMENT OF THE SPECIAL COURT IN THE RUF CASE

After a trial lasting about four years, Trial Chamber I of the Special Court for Sierra Leone rendered its reasoned, written judgment in the case of the *Prosecutor v. Issa Hassan Sesay, Morris Kallon and Augustine Gbao* on March 2, 2009.[54] The three Accused were senior leaders of the RUF rebel group who were charged with individual criminal responsibility for eight counts of crimes against humanity, eight counts of violations of the laws of war, and two counts of other serious violations of international humanitarian law.[55] Although the Trial Chamber entered convictions against all three accused persons for various war crimes,

---

[53] U.N. S.C. Res. 1313 (2000), para. 3(b). The resolution also affirmed UNAMSIL's mandate to protect civilians under imminent threat of physical violence, as well as to ensure freedom of movement and facilitate the provision of humanitarian assistance. In order to achieve these objectives, para. 6 of the Resolution recognized that UNAMSIL would need to be fully equipped with the required capabilities and adequate resources to implement its mandate in full.

[54] The Prosecutor v. Sesay, Kallon, & Gbao, Trial Judgment, Mar. 2, 2009. The Chamber delivered an oral summary of its Judgment on Feb. 25, 2009. The evidential phase of the trial lasted from July 5, 2004 to Aug. 5, 2008.

[55] The Prosecutor v. Sesay, Kallon, & Gbao, Case No. SCSL-2004–15-PT, Corrected Amended Consolidated Indictment, Aug. 2, 2006 [hereinafter Corrected Indictment].

this chapter focuses on the reasoning and findings of the Chamber regarding attacks on UN peacekeepers as another serious violation of international humanitarian law.[56]

The Indictment alleged that between April 15, 2000 and September 15, 2000, AFRC/RUF rebels engaged in widespread attacks – killings, abductions, and hostage taking – against UNAMSIL peacekeepers and humanitarian assistance workers within the Republic of Sierra Leone. The Trial Chamber found that between May and June 2000, the RUF directed a total of fourteen attacks against UNAMSIL personnel working in Sierra Leone, leading to the death of at least 4 peacekeepers and the abduction and detention of up to 150 others.[57] The Chamber found that these attacks constituted serious violations of international humanitarian law pursuant to Article 4 of the Court's Statute. Although the evidence also showed that the attacks were perpetrated against UNAMSIL installations, materials, and vehicles, the Court did not make any legal findings on this evidence as the Prosecution did not charge the Accused with attacks on installations or equipment.[58] This omission may be considered a missed opportunity because although the SCSL Statute prohibits attacks on civilians in general, it does not explicitly criminalize attacks on civilian objects in non-international armed conflicts.[59] As the SCSL Prosecutor did not charge the RUF for attacks against UNAMSIL equipment, vehicles, and installations, the Court did not have an opportunity to consider and make pronouncements on the elements of this offense, which could have been another important contribution to international law.

Compared to the war crimes charge, the Chamber dismissed the crimes against humanity charge on the ground that the attacks on the peacekeepers did not form part of a widespread or systematic attack against the civilian population of Sierra Leone.[60] The Chamber's reasoning and conclusions on this matter are noteworthy. First, the Chamber made no secret of its finding that the RUF/AFRC committed widespread or systematic attacks against the civilian population of Sierra Leone, and that the hallmarks of these attacks included the "indiscriminate targeting of civilians ... the commission of crimes against large groups of civilians ... the sustained terrorisation of civilians by raping, killing and amputations ... the mass enslavement of civilians; and the targeting and punishment of civilians for perceived support for the [rebels'] adversaries."[61]

Second, the Chamber found that the peacekeepers were entitled to the same protection guaranteed to civilians under the law of armed conflict.[62] It reasoned, however, that for the attacks to qualify as crimes against humanity, the UN peacekeepers must have been targeted "as part of" the civilian population of Sierra Leone. The Chamber concluded that because "the nature and purpose of the killings bears none of the hallmarks of the crimes committed

---

[56] Corrected Indictment, *supra* note 55, at Count 15, which charges the three Accused for "intentionally directing attacks against personnel involved in a humanitarian assistance or peacekeeping mission as an 'other serious violation of international humanitarian law,' punishable under Article 4.b of the Statute."

[57] The Chamber did not make any factual or legal findings regarding attacks on humanitarian workers because the Prosecution had conceded during proceedings for judgment of acquittal under Rule 98 that it adduced no evidence with respect to humanitarian workers. RUF Trial Judgment, *supra* note 1, at para. 1885, and Transcript of Oct, 25, 2006, Oral Decision on Rule 98, at 39–41.

[58] RUF Trial Judgment, *supra* note 1, at para. 1886.

[59] Sivakumaran, *supra* note 2, at 1024.

[60] RUF Trial Judgment, *supra* note 1, at para. 1956.

[61] *Id.* at para. 1947.

[62] *Id.* at para. 1949.

as part of the widespread or systematic attack on the civilian population of Sierra Leone [and] were geographically and temporally removed from the crimes against civilians,"[63] a reasonable doubt existed as to whether there was a sufficient nexus between the attacks on UN personnel and the widespread or systematic attacks on the civilian population.

It is interesting to note that the Chamber entered an acquittal in respect of the crimes against humanity charge despite its findings on the war crimes charge of "other serious violations of international humanitarian law" for which it found the Accused guilty. With respect to the latter, the Chamber found that the chapeau elements of war crimes (i.e., that an armed conflict existed at the time of the offense and that there was a nexus between the alleged offense and the armed conflict) had been proved beyond a reasonable doubt. For that reason, it found that the attacks against UN peacekeepers were proved beyond reasonable doubt as violations of Article 4(b) of the Statute. Given that the crimes against humanity charges were based on the same temporal period and largely based on the same factual allegations,[64] it is difficult to see how the Chamber could have held that a nexus existed between the armed conflict and the attacks on UN peacekeepers for the purpose of the war crimes charge, but that widespread or systematic attacks against the civilian population had ceased at the time of the attacks on UNAMSIL peacekeepers, for the purpose of the crimes against humanity charge.

Perhaps the Chamber's decision could have been better grounded on an interpretation of the term "as part of." Using this approach, the Chamber might have been able to reason that although the peacekeepers enjoyed the same protections extended to civilians under international law of armed conflict, they were not targeted "as part of" that civilian population. The peacekeepers, under this line of reasoning, were targeted as representatives of the international community in order to disrupt the implementation of the peace process in Sierra Leone.[65] The Judges perhaps were simply reluctant to enter convictions for both war crimes and crimes against humanity on the basis of the same facts and allegations as opposed to there being any compelling legal distinction, given the inconsistency in the Chamber's findings.

The Chamber also dismissed the charge of hostage taking on the ground that the prosecution failed to prove an essential element of the crime – the use of a threat against the detainees so as to obtain a concession or gain an advantage. The Trial Chamber specifically found that the offense of hostage taking requires the threat to be communicated to a third party with the intent of compelling that third party to act or refrain from acting as a condition for the safety or release of the hostages.[66] This holding was reversed by the Appeals

---

[63] *Id.* at para. 1952.

[64] The Chapeau to Counts 15–18 of the Corrected Indictment, which supports both the war crimes and crimes against humanity charges, states, inter alia, that the AFRC/RUF fighters engaged in widespread attacks against UNAMSIL personnel and humanitarian assistance workers in various parts of Sierra Leone. In addition the Corrected Indictment states in paragraphs 5 and 6 that[A]t all times relevant to this Indictment, a state of armed conflict existed within Sierra Leone.... A nexus existed between the armed conflict and all acts and omissions charged as violations of Article 3 common to the Geneva Conventions and Additional Protocol II and as Other Serious Violations of International Humanitarian Law.

[65] *See, e.g.*, U.N. S.C. Res. 1313 (2000), in which the Security Council condemned in the strongest terms attacks against and detention of UN personnel; also Statute of the Special Court for Sierra Leone, art. 1(1), which specifically confers competence on the Court to try persons who, in committing crimes, threatened the peace process in Sierra Leone.

[66] RUF Trial Judgment, *supra* note 1, at paras. 1967–1969.

Chamber, which reviewed the *Hostages Convention*, the Elements of Crime of the Rome Statute, the jurisprudence of the ICTY, and certain national court decisions to come to the conclusion that there was no requirement that the threat must have been communicated to a third party. The Appeals Chamber, as a result, held that the Trial Chamber erred in law by introducing communication as a new element of the crime of hostage taking.[67]

In its consideration of the international legal status of the offense in Article 4(b) of the SCSL Statute, the Trial Chamber closely analyzed state practice, the practice of international organizations, international conventions, and juristic opinions to affirm that the prohibition of attacks against UN peacekeepers is not a new crime but rather a "particularization of the general and fundamental prohibition in international humanitarian law against attacks on civilians and civilian objects."[68] UN peacekeepers under this reasoning are protected under international law only to the extent that they are "entitled to the protection given to civilians or civilian objects under international law of armed conflict."[69] This is an important qualification for it implies that like civilians under international humanitarian law, UN peacekeepers are protected only to the extent that they do not actively engage in hostilities. In other words, UN forces operating under a "peace enforcement," rather than a peacekeeping mandate, are viewed as combatants, and hence do not enjoy the same protections extended to civilians or persons placed hors de combat under international law.

The Chamber further held that customary international law supported individual criminal responsibility for the offense of intentionally directing attacks against UN peacekeepers in both international and non-international armed conflicts.[70] This finding is particularly significant given that the principle *nullum crimen sine lege* prohibits convictions for acts that did not constitute a crime at the time of their perpetration. By holding that there was a customary international law offense of intentionally directing attacks against UN peacekeepers, the Chamber ensured that the acts of the RUF against personnel of the UNAMSIL force during the internal armed conflict in Sierra Leone constituted violations of extant international criminal norms for which they could be legitimately tried and punished.

Even though the Special Court's affirmation that attacks against UN personnel constituted crimes under customary international law was historic in the sense that it was the first time any international criminal tribunal held as such, the Court's key contributions are to be found in its articulation of the elements of the offense. The end result was that the SCSL was the first, and remains the only international criminal tribunal to flesh out the contours of this offense by clarifying the elements that must be proved in order to establish individual criminal responsibility.

According to the Court, the offense requires the following elements[71]:

(i)   That the accused directed an attack against personnel, installations, material or units involved in a U.N peacekeeping operation;

(ii) The accused intended such personnel, installations, etc., to be the object of the attack;

---

[67] RUF Appeal Judgment, *infra* note 73, at paras. 575–586.
[68] RUF Trial Judgment, *supra* note 1, at para. 215.
[69] *Id.*
[70] *Id.* at para. 218.
[71] *Id.* at para. 219.

(iii) The personnel, installations, etc., were entitled to the protection given to civilians or civilian objects under international law of armed conflict;

(iv) The accused knew or had reason to know that the personnel, installations, etc., were protected.

In discussing the term "attack," the Trial Chamber referred to Article 49(1) of Additional Protocol I to the Geneva Conventions, which defined "attack" as an "act of violence" and held that the term had the same meaning in both international and non-international armed conflicts.[72] It noted that although the prosecution was not legally required to prove actual physical injury or damage as a result of the attack, threats alone would not suffice to establish legal liability for the offense. The Court stated the need to adopt an expansive interpretation of the term "attack," in order to fully protect UN peacekeepers, noting that "an act of violence ... requires a forceful interference which endangers the person or impinges upon the liberty of the peacekeeper."[73]

This interpretation is evidence of the influence of the Safety Convention on the Trial Chamber's reasoning. Article 9(1)(a) of that Convention criminalized "murder, kidnapping or other attack upon the person or liberty of any United Nations or associated personnel." The SCSL's deliberate departure from the view that an attack is limited to "the rifle shot and the exploding bomb, not the act of taking someone prisoner"[74] is particularly important in the law's application to peacekeeping operations. In conflicts in the former Yugoslavia and Sierra Leone, attacks against peacekeepers very often took the form of abduction, disarming, and detention of peacekeeping personnel without necessarily killing or otherwise injuring them.[75] If international law is to effectively protect peacekeepers, it must prohibit and punish such deprivations of liberty, which interfere with the mandate of peacekeeping missions.

The expansive interpretation of the term "attack" is consistent with the SCSL Trial Chamber's avowed intention to give full effect to the fundamental protections to which peacekeepers are entitled, thereby enhancing the protection of UN peacekeepers during armed conflict. Prior to 2009, the ICTY had held that attacks on civilians or civilian objects must lead to death or serious injury in order for legal liability to ensue.[76]

The Special Court's interpretation is likely to influence future judicial determinations regarding the protection of peacekeepers as well as civilians or noncombatants in armed conflict, given that peacekeepers are a distinct group within the larger category of protected civilians. This influence is likely to be seen in the specific context of the work of the ICC,

---

[72] *Id.* at para. 220.

[73] RUF Trial Judgment, *supra* note 1, at paras. 220 and 1889. *See also* The Prosecutor v. Issa Sesay, Morris Kallon and Augustine Gbao (Judgment), Appeals Chamber, SCSL-04-15-A (Oct. 26, 2009), para. 500 [hereinafter RUF Appeal Judgment].

[74] Gadler, *supra* note 33, at 595, *citing* FRITS KALSHOVEN & LIESBETH ZEGVELD, CONSTRAINTS ON THE WAGING OF WAR – AN INTRODUCTION TO INTERNATIONAL HUMANITARIAN LAW 97 (3d ed. 2001).

[75] *See* RUF Trial Judgment, *supra* note 1, at para. 1891, where the Trial Chamber noted that "deprivation of [UNAMSIL peacekeepers'] liberty is itself an act of violence which endured until such time as their release was secured.... [Similarly, the fact that] RUF kept the peacekeepers under constant armed guard and threatened them with their weapons ... [was] no less effective than physical restraint ... and must be regarded as a forceful interference which endangered the person and impinged on the liberty of the UNAMSIL personnel."

[76] Kordic & Cerkez, Appeals Judgment, paras. 55–67; Kordic & Cerkez, Trial Judgment, para. 328; Blaskic Trial Judgment, para. 180. *See also* Sivakumaran, *supra* note 2, at 1025.

because as discussed earlier, although the Special Court was the first international tribunal to consider and apply this crime in a specific case, the Rome Statute was the first to provide for international criminal responsibility for perpetrators of attacks against personnel or objects involved in a humanitarian assistance or peacekeeping mission.[77]

As evidenced in the Abu Garda case, the ICC has begun to show signs of influence by the SCSL jurisprudence. In that case, a Pre-Trial Chamber of the ICC interpreted "attack" against African Union peacekeeping personnel to require proof that the Accused committed an act of violence, without necessarily causing injury or material loss or damage.[78] The Pre-Trial Chamber of the ICC in the Katanga case has addressed the more general question of attacks on civilians. It held that such an attack "does not require any harmful impact on the civilian population or on individual civilians not taking direct part in hostilities who have not fallen yet into the hands of the attacking party."[79] These rulings of the ICC Pre-Trial Chamber, when considered alongside the Elements of Crimes for attacks against civilians, humanitarian assistance, or peacekeeping personnel, foreshadow a more robust protective regime for these categories of noncombatants. The approach of the SCSL and ICC, when applied consistently in the future, could enhance judicial protection of civilians and noncombatants in armed conflict and greatly increase the chances of successful prosecution of such offenses.

The Special Court clarified the second element to mean that the offense under consideration requires specific intent – that is, that the accused intended the personnel, installations, materials, or units involved in a peacekeeping mission to be the primary object of the attack.[80]

The Trial Chamber noted the conceptual difference between peacekeeping and peace enforcement. It observed that although the UN Security Council has never specifically mentioned Chapter VI in establishing peacekeeping missions, it has in recent times resorted to the use of Chapter VII powers to grant more robust mandates to peacekeepers, especially in non-international armed conflicts.[81] However, the Court hastened to add that a robust mandate by itself does not change a mission from one of peacekeeping to one of peace enforcement as "the use of force by peacekeepers in self-defen[s]e in the discharge of their mandate ... would not alter or diminish the protection afforded to peacekeepers."[82]

The distinction between peacekeeping and peace enforcement noted by the Court has an important bearing on the legal protection of peacekeepers. Therefore in considering the third element, the Chamber observed that like civilians, peacekeepers who take an active part in hostilities – subject to the exception of the limited use of force in self-defense – lose their protective status, become combatants under international law of armed conflict, and

---

[77] Article 8(2)(b)(iii) of the ICC Statute, which makes it a war crime to carry out such attacks.

[78] *See also* Rome Statute, Elements of Crimes, arts. 8(2)(b)(iii) and 8(2)(e)(iii) listing seven elements of the war crime of attacking personnel or objects involved in a humanitarian assistance or peacekeeping mission. These elements do not include injury or damage as a result of the attack.

[79] The Prosecutor v. Germain Katanga, Decision on the Evidence and Information provided by the Prosecution for Issuance of a Warrant of Arrest for Germain Katanga (ICC-01/04-01/07-55), Pre-Trial Chamber, Nov. 5, 2007, at para. 37; and Decision on the Confirmation of Charges, Sept. 30, 2008 (ICC-01/04-01/07-717), Pre-Trial Chamber, paras. 264–274.

[80] RUF Trial Judgment, *supra* note 1, at para. 232.

[81] *Id.* at paras. 222 and 223.

[82] *Id.* at para. 233.

can be legitimate targets during war.[83] The Chamber noted that in determining whether peacekeepers enjoy the status of civilians or whether they have lost such status and become combatants, it must consider the totality of the circumstances existing at the time of the offense. These circumstances include the relevant UN Security Council resolutions establishing the mission, the specific operational mandates, rules of engagement and operational orders, the equipment and arms available to the peacekeeping force, the circumstances surrounding incidents of the use of force during the peacekeeping operation, and the conduct of the alleged victim(s) and other personnel.[84]

This is an important judicial pronouncement on the legal protection for peacekeepers. The question though remains whether by placing UN peacekeepers on the same legal footing as civilians or other persons who cross the noncombatant threshold, the Court went far enough in recognizing the special role of peacekeepers as persons who put their own lives at risk in pursuit of a higher goal – peace and security for international society. Although I will not go as far as Professor Sharp to suggest that the principle of equal application in international humanitarian law should be abolished in respect of UN peacekeepers, I do share his concern that international peacekeeping runs a great risk of being undermined unless the rules of the game are changed to enhance protections for those who make priceless sacrifices in the service of peace and security for humankind. Judges facing this question in the future can greatly enhance the protective regime for peacekeepers by invoking evidentiary presumptions that these troops enjoy international legal protection, unless specific circumstances before the Court clearly demonstrate that they were in fact combat forces.

In deciding whether UNAMSIL was a peacekeeping force, the SCSL Trial Chamber closely examined the various UN Security Council resolutions under which UNAMSIL operated, its rules of engagement and operational orders, and the nature of UNAMSIL's arms and equipment, as well as its practice and interactions with the RUF. On the latter, the Chamber made it a point to observe that prior to May 1, 2000, UNAMSIL forces did not engage in any hostilities with the RUF or any other group, that the peacekeepers were only lightly armed, and that the military observers were not armed at all.[85] It was also noted that in several situations the peacekeepers exercised restraint and did not use force even when attacked.[86]

Based on this analysis, the Court concluded that UNAMSIL was a Chapter VI mission deployed with the consent of the parties to act as an impartial facilitator in the implementation of the Lomé Peace Agreement.[87] Significant in this analysis is the Chamber's holding that although UNAMSIL was authorized to take "necessary action" to ensure the security of its personnel and to protect civilians under threat of physical violence, this served only as a "trigger" permitting UNAMSIL personnel to use force in specific and defined circumstances.[88] The Chamber also considered it relevant that UNAMSIL was not mandated to engage in hostilities, but rather to preserve the ceasefire agreed in Lomé

---

[83] *Id.* at para. 233.
[84] *Id.* at para. 234. *See also* RUF Appeal Judgment, *supra* note 73, at para. 529.
[85] RUF Trial Judgment, *supra* note 1, at paras. 1918–1924.
[86] *Id.* at paras. 1926–1927, 1931.
[87] *Id.* at para. 1907.
[88] RUF Trial Judgment, *supra* note 1, at para. 1908.

through cooperation, negotiation, and peaceful dispute resolution.[89] In conclusion, it was the Chamber's view that the mere fact that UNAMSIL was empowered under Chapter VII of the Charter to use force in certain exceptional and restricted circumstances did not alter its fundamental nature from a peacekeeping to a peace-enforcement mission. "Instead," added the Court, "the reference to Chapter VII merely reinforces the right of the peacekeepers to use force in self-defence by grounding it in the binding powers of the Security Council."[90]

The SCSL Chamber's reasoning and conclusions on this matter again bear import because they potentially lay to rest the uncertainty surrounding the permissible scope of the use of force in self-defense. Prior to 2009, some commentators had questioned whether an expansive interpretation of the principle of use of force in self-defense so as to include protection of civilians or fulfillment of the mandate did not cross the noncombatant threshold under international humanitarian law.[91] Self-defense for these authors should be limited to individual self-defense, including defense of oneself, of others, and of property. Similar questions have arisen in the past over whether if a part of a peacekeeping force engages in combat this will transform the remainder of the force into combatants. The SCSL's Judgment rightly shows that these questions cannot be answered in isolation. Rather, the fact that part of the forces have engaged in combat operations is only one circumstance to be considered alongside other factors including the mission mandate, rules of engagement, prior conduct of the peacekeeping forces, and conduct of the victims or other parties with whom the peacekeepers were dealing. It is important that the Judges liberally interpret the rules in favor of a presumption of peacekeeper protection in order to ensure the maximum protection for peacekeepers.

With regards to *mens rea*, the Chamber held that the Accused must have known or had reason to know that the personnel, installations, etc. were protected. This does not require proof of actual legal knowledge of their protective status, but rather that the Accused was aware of the factual basis of the protection.[92]

In addition to its pronouncements on the elements of the war crime of directing attacks against peacekeeping personnel, the Court also expressed judicial approval for the view that consent of the parties, impartiality, and nonuse of force except in self-defense and defense of the mandate are the necessary foundation for a peacekeeping operation.[93] Significantly, with regard to the application of the self-defense principle, the Court observed that the notion of the use of force in self-defense has evolved in contemporary peacekeeping practice to include the "right to resist attempts by forceful means to prevent the peacekeeping operation from discharging its duties under the mandate of the Security Council."[94] However,

---

[89] *Id.* at para. 1910.

[90] *Id.* at para. 1911. *See also* RUF Appeal Judgment, para. 531, where the Appeals Chamber notes that "it is settled law that peacekeepers – like civilians – are entitled to use force in self-defence; such use does not constitute taking a direct part in hostilities."

[91] Gadler, *supra* note 15, at 597, *citing* Michael Cottier, *Article 8 Para. 2(b)(iii)*, *in* COMMENTARY ON THE ROME STATUTE OF THE INTERNATIONAL CRIMINAL COURT. OBSERVER'S NOTES, ARTICLE BY ARTICLE 336 (O. Triffterer ed., 2008).

[92] RUF Trial Judgment, *supra* note 1, at para. 235.

[93] *Id.* at para. 225.

[94] *Id.* at para. 228, *citing* U.N. DPKO, *United Nations Peacekeeping Operations: Principles and Guidelines* 34 (U.N. New York 2008).

such use of force must be employed only as a measure of last resort when other means have failed or proved ineffective.[95]

VI. CONCLUSION

The SCSL was established by agreement of the United Nations and the government of Sierra Leone to hold accountable those "bearing the greatest responsibility" for the grave crimes committed during the 1990s in a decade of internal armed conflict in Sierra Leone. Although scholars and practitioners will continue to debate whether and how to measure the SCSL's success in the realization of its mandate to prosecute those bearing the greatest responsibility for these heinous crimes, no one can question the Court's many and varied contributions to the development of international law and the advancement of the fight against impunity for serious international crimes. This chapter discusses and highlights the Court's contribution in one area of international law – the prohibition of attacks against UN peacekeepers. I have argued that the SCSL Judgment in the RUF case marks an important milestone in the development of international law, as the first international criminal tribunal to try and convict anyone for this crime. The Court has affirmed that the prohibition against such attacks enjoyed support under customary international law as part of the broader prohibition of attacks against civilians; it clarified the elements of the offense for the benefit of future prosecutors, judges, scholars and policy makers; and its reasoning and conclusions are likely to influence the work of future international courts, especially the ICC as the Rome Statute contains a similar provision to Article 4(b) of the Special Court Statute. As we have discussed above, the ICC Pre-Trial Chamber decision in the Abu Garda case illustrates how that Court is already benefitting from the SCSL jurisprudence.

I have argued in the chapter that the weak legal protection for peacekeepers has traditionally been an impediment to the willingness of UN member states to contribute troops for peacekeeping duties. By adopting an expansive interpretation of the prohibition against attacks on UN peacekeepers to include deprivations of liberty, alongside physical injury or death, the SCSL significantly enhances the legal framework for protecting peacekeeping forces. Similarly, the Court ensures continued legal protection for peacekeepers by holding that the recent evolution of peacekeeping mandates to include more robust use of force in specific circumstances, such as protection of civilians, does not per se convert peacekeepers into peace-enforcers. Consequently, the SCSL's judgment in the RUF case not only challenges impunity for serious international crimes, but also gives impetus to the international community's collective security agenda, of which peacekeeping is an important pillar.

---

[95] RUF Trial Judgment, *supra* note 1, at para. 228.

PART IV

Approach to Challenging Issues in International Criminal Law

15

The Lomé Amnesty Decision of the Special Court for Sierra Leone

Leila Nadya Sadat[*]

In this volume dedicated to the legacy of the Special Court for Sierra Leone (SCSL or "the Court"), it is appropriate to highlight the important contribution of the SCSL to the emerging understanding of the relationship between justice and peace during and following periods of violent conflict. This chapter addresses the questions raised by the Lomé Agreement of 1999 with respect to the ability of the Court to proceed to trial regarding the Accused claiming to be exempted from the SCSL's jurisdiction because of the amnesty provisions of that agreement. It will then offer some reflections on the significance of the Court's decision in light of evolving state and international practice on amnesties, and finally, briefly consider the status and effect of the Lomé amnesty in Sierra Leone itself.

I. THE CONFLICT IN SIERRA LEONE, AMNESTY, AND THE LOMÉ AGREEMENT

Sierra Leone is a small country located in West Africa, situated between Liberia to the South, Guinea to the North and East, and the North Atlantic Ocean to the West. From 1991 onward, the country experienced a brutal civil war as a rebel group known as the Revolutionary United Front (RUF) fought against three successive governments. The war ravaged the country and resulted in thousands of deaths and millions of displaced persons; it was "unique in the scale and grotesque nature of attacks on civilian populations."[1] Mutilations, rape, sexual slavery, murder, pillage and looting traumatized a helpless civilian population while negotiators, both inside and external to Sierra Leone, endeavored to bring the conflict to a close. As the peace process faltered, frustration and anger grew at the criminal behavior of the participants in the fighting.

The conflict began in 1991 when the RUF, headed by Corporal Foday Sankoh, entered Sierra Leone from Liberia and tried to bring down the government.[2] The Abidjan Peace

---

[*] Henry H. Oberschelp Professor of Law, Washington University in St. Louis, and Director, Whitney R. Harris World Law Institute.

[1] Terhi Lehtinen & Nosakhare Ogumbor, *"Diamonds, Mercenaries and Civilian Targets" – the Brutal War in Sierra Leone. See also* Owen Fiss, *Within Reach of the State: Prosecuting Atrocities in Africa*, 31 HUM. RTS. Q. 59 (2009); Okechukwu Oko, *The Challenges of International Criminal Prosecutions in Africa*, 31 FORDHAM INT'L L.J. 343 (2007–2008); Comment, *Constructing Durable Peace: Lessons from Sierra Leone*, 38 CAL. W. INT'L L.J. 117 (2007–2008).

[2] Prosecutor v. Kallon & Kamara, *Decision on Challenge to Jurisdiction: Lomé Accord Amnesty*, Case Nos. SCSL-2004–15-AR72(E), SCSL-2004–16-AR72(E), para. 3 (SCSL App. ch., Mar. 13, 2004) [hereinafter *Kallon & Kamara*].

Accord, signed in 1996, offered amnesty to all RUF fighters,[3] but fighting broke out soon after it was signed.[4] It persisted until 1999 when another peace deal was brokered. This second accord, known as the Lomé Peace Agreement, was signed between the government of Sierra Leone and the RUF, the parties having met in Lomé, Togo, from May to July 7, 1999 and negotiated under the auspices of the Chairman of the Economic Community of West African States (ECOWAS) at the time.

Article IX of the Lomé Agreement, entitled "Pardon and Amnesty" is worth setting forth in relevant part as it created significant difficulties for the Court in its early years, and forms the basis of the discussion in this chapter. In addition to granting "absolute and free pardon" to RUF leader Sankoh, it provided:

[2.] After the signing of the present Agreement, the Government of Sierra Leone shall also grant absolute and free pardon and reprieve to all combatants and collaborators in respect of anything done by them in pursuit of their objectives, up to the time of the signing of the present Agreement.

[3.] To consolidate the peace and promote the cause of national reconciliation, the Government of Sierra Leone shall ensure that no official or judicial action is taken against any member of the RUF/SL, ex-AFRC, ex-SLA, or CDF in respect of anything done by them in pursuit of their objectives as members of these organizations since March 1991, up to the signing of the present Agreement.[5]

Following signature of the Lomé Agreement, it was announced that the Special Representative of the UN Secretary General, Francis Okello, had entered a disclaimer to the text of Article IX, prior to appending his signature to the document, to the effect that the United Nations did not recognize the validity of the amnesty in Article IX to war crimes, crimes against humanity, and genocide.[6] The Parliament of Sierra Leone ratified the Lomé Agreement on July 15, 1999, thereby incorporating its provisions into national law.[7]

II. THE DECISION OF THE SPECIAL COURT FOR SIERRA LEONE ON THE EFFECTIVENESS OF THE AMNESTY PROVISIONS OF THE LOMÉ AGREEMENT

Like the Abidjan Accord, the Lomé Agreement did not produce the peaceful settlement of the conflict that the people of Sierra Leone yearned for. Instead, following the accord, the RUF continued their killings and mutilations of civilians, and maintained their control over the diamond areas, which provided them with funds to continue operations. Yet the act that

---

[3] DAVID SCHEFFER, ALL THE MISSING SOULS 306 (2011).

[4] RUF leader Foday Sankoh repudiated it five days after it was signed. *Id.*

[5] Peace Agreement between the Government of Sierra Leone and the Revolutionary United Front of Sierra Leone (RUF/SL), Lomé, July 7, 1999 [hereinafter Lomé Agreement]. The Agreement was negotiated between the government of Sierra Leone and the Revolutionary United Front (RUF). Although a representative of the Secretary-General of the United Nations and outside governments (Togo, the United Nations, the OAU, ECOWAS and the Commonwealth of Nations, and the United States) signed as "moral guarantors" of the agreement, *id.*, art. 34, only two factions of Sierra Leoneans were parties thereto: President Kabbah, who signed on behalf of the Sierra Leone government, and Corporal Sankoh on behalf of the RUF.

[6] *Kallon & Kamara, supra* note 2, at para. 26; *see also* SCHEFFER, *supra* note 3, at 312–13. *See also* the excellent chapter of Alpha Sesay in this volume on this issue.

[7] *Kallon & Kamara, supra* note 2, at para. 25.

finally goaded the international community into action was the RUF abduction of more than five hundred UN peacekeepers, in an operation in which they seized their weapons, arms, and uniforms and even murdered several.[8] Following these incidents, and responding to a letter from President Kabbah requesting the establishment of a "strong and credible court" to prosecute the crimes, the Security Council adopted a resolution empowering the United Nations to enter into negotiations with the government of Sierra Leone to establish a court, which became the Special Court for Sierra Leone.[9]

The agreement was difficult to negotiate; however, the SCSL was established on January 16, 2002, with the signature of a bilateral treaty between the United Nations and the government of Sierra Leone.[10] The jurisdiction *ratione materiae* of the Court was set forth in Article 2–5 of the SCSL Statute, and included crimes against humanity (Article 2); violations of common Article 3 and additional Protocol II (Article 3); other serious violations of international humanitarian law, including attacks on civilians, attacks on humanitarian missions, and conscripting, enlisting, and using child soldiers (Article 4), as well as several domestic crimes under Sierra Leonean law (Article 5). Article 10 of the Court's Statute specifically addressed the issue of amnesty, providing:

> An amnesty to any person falling within the jurisdiction of the Special Court in respect of crimes referred to in Articles 2 to 4 of the present Statute [excluding the domestic crimes] shall not be a bar to prosecution.[11]

In an opinion on the question of amnesties for international crimes, dated March 14, 2004, the SCSL Appeals Chamber considered the appeals of two defendants, Morris Kallon and Brima Bazzy Kamara, who argued that the amnesty provisions of the Lomé Agreement precluded their trial before the Court. The defendants asserted that, notwithstanding the international nature of the crimes, the SCSL was bound to respect the amnesty granted by the Lomé Agreement because it was an international treaty, having been signed by other states and a number of international organizations, including the RUF. The Appeals Chamber disagreed, holding that [t]he role of the United Nations as a mediator of peace, the presence of a peacekeeping force that generally is by consent of the state, and the mediation efforts of the Secretary-General cannot add up to a source of obligation to the international community to perform an agreement to which the United Nations is not a party.[12] Instead, the Court found although there were other states signatories to the agreement, they had signed as "moral guarantors," and that the Agreement could not be characterized as an international instrument given that the RUF had no international legal personality. To the extent that the amnesty may have been lawful, a point I shall refer to later in this chapter, the SCSL therefore characterized it as a domestic amnesty, and appeared to at least entertain the possibility that it would apply in the courts of Sierra Leone.[13]

---

[8] SCHEFFER, *supra* note 3, at 315.

[9] S.C. Res. 1315 (Aug. 14, 2000).

[10] Agreement between the United Nations and the Government of Sierra Leone on the Establishment of a Special Court for Sierra Leone (Jan. 16, 2002) [hereinafter SCSL Statute]. The Statute is appended to the Report of the Secretary-General on the Establishment of a Special Court for Sierra Leone, U.N. Doc. S/2000/915 (Oct. 4, 2000).

[11] SCSL Statute, *supra* note 10, at art. 10.

[12] *Kallon & Kamara, supra* note 2, at para. 39.

[13] *Id.* at paras. 34, 42.

Conversely, it essentially held that the SCSL was an international court, having been established by an international treaty. The Appeals Chamber reasoned that Article 10 of the Court's Statute, forbidding the tribunal from taking into consideration an amnesty granted to any person falling within the jurisdiction of the SCSL in respect of [international] crimes [within the Court's jurisdiction] shall not be a bar to prosecution. Therefore, any amnesty granted to the Accused for international crimes within the SCSL Statute had no effect. In the words of the Appeals Chamber:

> Where jurisdiction is universal, a State cannot deprive another State of its jurisdiction to prosecute the offender by the grant of amnesty. It is for this reason unrealistic to regard as universally effective the grant of amnesty by a State in regard to grave international crimes in which there exists universal jurisdiction. A State cannot bring into oblivion and forgetfulness a crime, such as a crime against international law, which other States are entitled to keep alive and remember.[14]

The SCSL concluded that the crimes within its jurisdiction – crimes against humanity and war crimes committed in internal armed conflict – are the subject of universal jurisdiction under international law. Going beyond many prior national court decisions, which found that states were entitled to exercise jurisdiction over such crimes,[15] and citing the Eichmann case as well as more recent international precedent,[16] the Court suggested that the prosecution of such crimes was perhaps required, given that the obligation to protect human dignity is a peremptory norm and has assumed the nature of an obligation *erga omnes*.[17]

III. UNIVERSAL JURISDICTION CRIMES

A fundamental contribution of the Kallon & Kamara amnesty decision was the specific linkage made between the universal nature of the international crimes within the SCSL Statute and the ineffectiveness of amnesties therefor. Many discussions of amnesties avoid the question of the legal status of the crimes in question. Yet one cannot discuss the matter without at least determining in advance which international crimes are so uniformly accepted by the international community that both the exercise of universal jurisdiction by states, as well as the exercise of universal jurisdiction by the international community as a whole, are generally accepted. The theory of *jus cogens* has been the subject of much

---

[14] *Kallon & Kamara, supra* note 2, at para. 67.
[15] Leila Nadya Sadat, *Exile, Amnesty, and International Law*, 81 NOTRE DAME L. REV. 955, 999–1013 (2006).
[16] This decision followed the opinion of the ICTY in *Furundzija* to the same effect, Prosecutor v. Anto Furundzija, Judgment, Case No., IT-95-17/1-T (T. ch. II, Dec. 10, 1998) [hereinafter *Furundzija*], and was cited with approval by a recent UN report on impunity. *Promotion and Protection of Human Rights: Impunity*, Commission on Human Rights, 61st Sess., U.N. DOC. E/CN.4/2005/102 (Feb. 18, 2005) (Professor Diane Orentlicher, Independent Expert) [hereinafter *Orentlicher Impunity Study*].
[17] *Kallon & Kamara, supra* note 2, at para. 71. The SCSL reaffirmed *Kallon & Kramer* a few months later in Prosecutor v. Allieu Kondewa, Decision on Lack of Jurisdiction/Abuse of Process: Amnesty Provided by the Lomé Accord, Case No. 14-AR72(E) (SCSL App. ch., May 25, 2004). In *Kondewa*, Justice Robertson authored a special opinion arguing that the amnesty had become ineffective, not because of the international nature of the crimes, but because it had been forfeited by the resurgence of the conflict. *Id., Separate Opinion of Justice Robertson*, para. 28.

dispute and scholarly commentary.[18] However, the near-universal acceptance of the notion of peremptory or *jus cogens* norms[19] as set out in the Vienna Convention on the Law of Treaties[20] suggests that modern international criminal law, both explicitly and implicitly, embodies within its prescriptions certain nonderogable principles of peremptory application.[21] Although not all international criminal law scholars address the question of peremptory norms (indeed, the concept does not even figure in the otherwise excellent monograph of Antonio Cassese),[22] fundamental to the notion of a duty to prosecute international crimes, a duty incumbent upon all states, is the nonderogability of the norms at issue.[23] Amnesties are problematic because they contradict this fundamental principle. Perhaps this is why not one jurisdiction has, to date, accepted the juridical validity of a foreign amnesty decree for the commission of human rights atrocities. As the International Criminal Tribunal for the Former Yugoslavia opined in *Prosecutor v. Furundzija*, a case cited by the Court in *Kallon & Kamara*, regarding the crime of torture:

> While the *erga omnes* nature [of the crime] appertains to the area of international enforcement (*lato sensu*), the other major feature of the principle proscribing torture relates to the hierarchy of rules in the international normative order. Because of the importance of the values it protects, this principle has evolved into a peremptory norm of *jus cogens*, that is, a norm that enjoys a higher rank in the international hierarchy than treaty law and even "ordinary customary rules." [24]

Even if one agrees, however, on the status of *jus cogens* crimes in principle, determining which offenses are entitled to that status is challenging. I have addressed this issue in earlier writings,[25] but it seems relatively clear – and the SCSL appears to confirm – that the list includes war crimes, genocide, and crimes against humanity. The *Princeton Principles* categorize these as serious crimes under international law, adding to the list piracy, slavery,

---

[18] *See, e.g.,* Anthony D'Amato, *It's a Bird, It's a Plane, It's* Jus Cogens, 6 CONN. J. INT'L L. 1 (1990); Gennady M. Danilenko, *International* Jus Cogens: *Issues of Law-Making*, 2 EUR. J. INT'L L. 42 (1991).

[19] *See, e.g.,* Alain Pellet, *Internationalized Courts: Better than Nothing …, in* INTERNATIONALIZED CRIMINAL COURTS 444 (Cesare P.R. Romano, André Nollkaemper & Jann K. Kleffner eds., 2004) (stating that all states, "even … France," accept the notion of peremptory norms of international law).

[20] Vienna Convention on the Law of Treaties, art. 53, 1155 U.N.T.S. 331 (May 23, 1969).

[21] In its report on what became Article 53 of the Vienna Convention, the International Law Commission gave as examples of treaties that would violate a peremptory norm of international law a treaty contemplating an unlawful use of force, a treaty contemplating an act criminal under international law, and a treaty conniving or contemplating slave trading, piracy, or genocide. The Commission also mentioned as possibilities treaties violating human rights, the equality of states, and the principle of self-determination. II YEARBOOK OF THE INTERNATIONAL LAW COMMISSION 248 (1966).

[22] *See* ANTONIO CASSESE, INTERNATIONAL CRIMINAL LAW (2003).

[23] *Accord* M. Cherif Bassiouni, *Universal Jurisdiction for International Crimes: Historical Perspectives and Contemporary Practice*, 42 VA. J. INT'L L. 104 (2001); Kristin Henrard, *The Viability of National Amnesties in View of the Increasing Recognition of Individual Criminal Responsibility at International Law*, 8 MSU-DCL J. INT'L L. 595, 645 (1999); Natalino Ronzitti, *Use of Force,* Jus Cogens *and State Consent, in* THE CURRENT LEGAL REGULATION OF THE USE OF FORCE 147 (Antonio Cassese ed., 1986). *Cf.* Claudia Annacker, *The Legal Régime of* Erga Omnes *Obligations in International Law*, 46 AUSTRIAN J. PUBL. INT'L L. 131, 135 (1993).

[24] *Furundzija, supra* note 16, at para. 153. This holding is arguably dicta. *See* William Schabas, *Commentary on* Prosecutor v. Furundzija, *in* III ANNOTATED LEADING CASES OF INTERNATIONAL CRIMINAL TRIBUNALS 755 (André Klip & Göran Sluiter eds., 1999).

[25] Sadat, *supra* note 15.

crimes against peace, and torture.[26] The International Law Commission, in its 1996 draft regarding Crimes against the Peace and Security of Mankind, included aggression, genocide, crimes against humanity, crimes against United Nations and associated personnel, and war crimes.[27] Finally, the U.S. Restatement on Foreign Relations takes the position that universal jurisdiction crimes (or *jus cogens* offenses) include piracy, the slave trade, attacks on or hijackings of aircraft, genocide, war crimes, and perhaps certain acts of terrorism.[28]

The Restatement's omission of aggression and torture is problematic given the relatively widespread acceptance of these crimes (although this may simply be a function of the fact that it is almost twenty years old). Conversely, its addition of terrorism may be appropriate in light of the Security Council Resolutions issued following the attacks of September 11, 2001, particularly Resolution 1373.[29] Among other things, Resolution 1373 provides that all states have a duty to enact legislation criminalizing certain acts of terrorism,[30] suggesting that amnesties, either de facto or de jure, for such crimes would contravene international law. Indeed, Resolution 1373 suggests that these are crimes over which the exercise of universal jurisdiction would be appropriate, and even mandatory, as a matter of customary international law.[31]

IV. THE SCSL AS AN INTERNATIONAL COURT

In its amnesty decision, the SCSL assumed that the set of *jus cogens* crimes is coterminous with the set of crimes over which states may exercise universal jurisdiction,[32] at least as regards crimes against humanity and war crimes. This assumption seems to be correct. It also differentiated between the ability of the Accused to raise the amnesty they believed

---

[26] PRINCETON PROJECT ON UNIVERSAL JURISDICTION, THE PRINCETON PRINCIPLES ON UNIVERSAL JURISDICTION 2004, principle 2 [hereinafter PRINCETON PRINCIPLES].

[27] International Law Commission Articles on the Draft Code of Crimes against the Peace and Security of Mankind (1996). For a recent discussion of the universal jurisdiction nature of the crime of aggression, see Michael P. Scharf, *Universal Jurisdiction and the Crime of Aggression*, 43 HARV. INT'L L.J. 358 (2012).

[28] RESTATEMENT (THIRD) OF THE LAW OF FOREIGN RELATIONS § 404 (1987).

[29] S.C. Res. 1373, para. 1, U.N. DOC. S/RES/1373 (Sept. 28, 2001).

[30] *Id.*, art. 2(e). According to the *Princeton Principles*, terrorism is not a crime of universal jurisdiction. *See* PRINCETON PRINCIPLES 2(1), *supra* note 26. However, Resolution 1373, which "decides" that every state must punish and prevent terrorism, suggests that it is the Council's belief that this crime is now a crime for which universal jurisdiction exists and for which a duty to punish is present. Therefore, in the Council's view, presumably any amnesties granted to terrorists would be illegal.

[31] *See* Leila Nadya Sadat, *Terrorism and the Rule of Law*, 3 WASH. U. GLOBAL STUD. L. REV. 135, 150 (2004). The Resolution requires all states to "ensure that any person who participates in the financing, planning, preparation or perpetration of terrorist acts" is brought to justice. S.C. Res. 1373, *supra* note 30, at art. 2. Given that the Security Council presumably has no power to create international law, the question remains whether Security Council Resolution 1373 is the codification of custom or a new form of Security Council "legislation." *See generally* Paul C. Szasz, *The Security Council Starts Legislating*, 96 AM. J. INT'L L. 901 (2002).

[32] Obviously, there are contrary views that have been expressed about the set of "universal jurisdiction crimes." See, for example, the separate opinion of Judge Guillaume in the Yerodia case, where he stated categorically that "international law knows only one true case of universal jurisdiction: piracy." Case concerning the Arrest Warrant of April 11, 2000 (Democratic Republic of the Congo v. Belgium), Separate Opinion of Judge Guillaume, 2002 I.C.J. 121, para. 12 [hereinafter *Congo v. Belgium*]. Moreover, even in cases where universal jurisdiction is accepted *in principle* regarding certain crimes, a court may nevertheless refuse the exercise of universal jurisdiction in a particular case as a matter of comity or for lack of resources. See the discussion of the Spanish jurisprudence on this question in Sadat, *supra* note 15, at 1010–14.

they were entitled to before Sierra Leonean courts as opposed to an international court such as the Court, or a third state. In its decision on amnesty, it did not need to reach the question whether it was an international court or something else, but the opinion nonetheless suggests the SCSL was leaning in that direction. The Court did not provide an extensive conceptual framework supporting its conclusions, but its opinion clearly states that domestic amnesties, even if valid in one state, have no application before international courts and tribunals or even third states. Regarding cases involving third states, or what I have elsewhere referred to as the "inter-state" application of universal jurisdiction,[33] states seeking to exercise universal jurisdiction over the perpetrator of a *jus cogens* crime are employing their own legislative authority to prescribe as regards an international law norm. They sit, in such a case, as if they were a court of the international community, as the former president of the Criminal Chamber of the French Court of Cassation, Christian LeGunehec, noted in his role as *rapporteur* for the Barbie case nearly thirty years ago.[34]

The situation before an international court or tribunal, however, is quite different. The vertical relationship between international and national law, and at least as regards *jus cogens* crimes, extant as a function of the basic principles of international law, is quite different from the horizontal perspective apparent in cases of universal inter-state jurisdiction. As the International Military Tribunal at Nuremberg declared, individuals have international duties that transcend the national obligations of obedience imposed by the individual state.[35] Standing alone, this statement neither created a rule or custom, nor, importantly, did it imply that international courts necessarily have primacy over national courts, although the Tribunal itself asserted that its adjudicative power was based upon the fact that the signatories to the London Charter were merely "do[ing] together what any one of them might have done singly." Instead, what this statement suggests is that international *law* (as a matter of prescriptive content) may sometimes prime national law, and that international courts may, in appropriate circumstances, exercise adjudicative jurisdiction in questions involving international legal obligations.

Although some commentators have argued that international courts such as the SCSL are exercising jurisdiction delegated to them by states,[36] this argument is probably overstated. As the Appeals Chamber of the ICTY held in the Blaskic case, the grant of authority to the ICTY by the UN Security Council created a vertical relationship between the ICTY and states, not only as to the international law involved, but with regard to the judicial and injunctory powers of the ICTY.[37] Of course, the SCSL was not created but was authorized by the Security Council, but, like the Nuremberg Tribunal itself, by an international agreement, albeit one entered into with the United Nations, and not just an agreement between

[33] Leila Nadya Sadat, *The New International Criminal Court: An Uneasy Revolution*, 88 Geo. L. Rev. 381, 406 (2000); Leila Nadya Sadat, *Redefining Universal Jurisdiction*, 35 New Eng. L. Rev. 241, 244 (2001).

[34] Judgment of January 26, 1984, Cass. Crime., 1984 J.C.P. II G, No. 20,197, J.D.I. 308 (1984) (Report of Counselor Le Gunehec). The Barbie case and this line of French jurisprudence is discussed in Leila Sadat Wexler, *The Application of the Nuremberg Principles by the French Court of Cassation: From Touvier to Barbie and Back Again*, 32 Colum. J. Transnat'l L. 289 (1994).

[35] International Military Tribunal (Nuremberg), *Judgment and Sentences*, 41 Am. J. Int'l L. 172 (Oct. 1, 1946).

[36] Madeline Morris, *The United States and the International Criminal Court: High Crimes and Misconceptions: The ICC and Non-Party States*, 64 L. & Contemp. Prob. 13 (2001).

[37] Prosecutor v. Tihomir Blaskic, Case No. IT-95–14-A, Judgment on the Request of the Republic of Croatia for Review of the Decision of Trial Chamber II of July 18, 1997, para. 47 (App. ch., Oct. 29, 1997).

states. Thus, it seems logical that in the Lomé Amnesty decision, the Appeals Chamber would at least implicitly determine the international nature of its own jurisdiction.

In *Congo v. Belgium*, the International Court of Justice (ICJ) held that a sitting foreign minister was immune from criminal jurisdiction by virtue of his status as such. However, perhaps to meet the critique that its decision could promote impunity for international crimes, the ICJ stated that several fora would nonetheless be available for his prosecution – that is, his immunity before the courts of Belgium was not tantamount to *impunity* for the commission of crimes under international law.[38] In particular, he could be tried before the courts of his own state, or in a foreign state if either his state waived its immunity or after his tenure in office ceased,[39] and that finally, an incumbent or former foreign minister for Foreign Affairs may be subject to criminal proceedings before certain international criminal courts, where they have jurisdiction. The ICJ referred specifically in this paragraph to the ICC, and the ad hoc Tribunals for Rwanda and the former Yugoslavia, but did not foreclose other international courts from relying upon this holding in support of their own jurisdiction.

Two months after its decision on the effectiveness of the Lomé Amnesty, the SCSL squarely confronted the question whether it was an international court (or something else) in opining on the question of immunity for a sitting head of state, Charles Taylor. In a fascinating opinion, the Court rejected Taylor's immunity claims on the grounds that it was an international, not a domestic court.[40] The SCSL, while admitting that it was not immediately evident why national and international courts could differ as to their treatment of immunities under international law, suggested that: *first*, the principle of the sovereignty of states was inapplicable, given the Court's status as an international organ; and *second*, as a matter of policy, states have considered the collective judgment of the international community to provide a vital safeguard against the potential destabilizing effect of unilateral judgment in this area.[41] Of course, as alluded to above, there is another explanation of the difference between the jurisdiction of national and international courts in this area, *which is that they are not exercising the same form of universal jurisdiction at all.*

The crimes committed in Sierra Leone from 1991 to 1999 shocked the conscience of humanity,[42] in terms of their seriousness and their pernicious effect on peace and security in West Africa. The preamble to the Rome Statute suggests that crimes of this magnitude threaten two separate sets of core values: the value of community; and the value of peace, security, and public order. Embodied in this conceptualization is the notion of a world or

---

[38] *Congo v. Belgium, supra* note 32, at para. 60.

[39] Here, however, the court has created significant confusion as to what acts may be chargeable, stating that he may be charged with acts subsequent to his period of office "as well as in respect of acts committed during that period of office in a private capacity." *Id.* at para. 61.

[40] Prosecutor v. Charles Ghankay Taylor, Case No. SCSL-2003–01–1, Decision on Immunity from Jurisdiction (SCSL App. ch., May 1, 2004). For a discussion of that decision, see Micaela Frulli's chapter in this volume. *See also* Charles Chernor Jalloh, *The Contribution of the Special Court for Sierra Leone to the Development of International Law*, AFR. J. INT'L & COMP. L. 165–207, 197 (2007).

[41] *Id.* at para. 51 (*citing* Amicus Brief of Professor Diane Orentlicher, at 15).

[42] *Rome Statute of the International Criminal Court*, United Nations Diplomatic Conference of Plenipotentiaries on the Establishment of an International Criminal Court, July 17, 1998, Annex II, U.N. DOC. A/CONF. 183/9 (1998), pmbl., cl. 2 [hereinafter *Rome Statute*]. *See also generally* THEODOR MERON, HUMAN RIGHTS AND HUMANITARIAN NORMS AS CUSTOMARY LAW (1989).

global community in which the peoples of the world are united by common bonds whose cultures are pieced together like the tiles in a delicate mosaic.[43] Implicit in the metaphor of the mosaic is the notion that if tiles are removed from the picture, the image captured therein may no longer be recognizable, and that humanity will become crippled, shattered, and even destroyed through the elimination of its separate components. The idea of the mosaic also suggests that if some of the tiles are removed, others will be loosened, leading eventually to the degradation of the whole. The development of norms prohibiting the commission of *jus cogens* crimes has evolved out of a sense of urgency that the crimes under consideration represent such an extraordinary threat to human society that turning a blind eye to their prevention and punishment is a luxury that modern society can no longer afford. The Lomé Amnesty decision of the SCSL fits into this paradigm.

V. THE LEGALITY OF AMNESTIES FOR JUS COGENS CRIMES UNDER INTERNATIONAL LAW

The Court left open the question whether the amnesty provided by the Lomé Agreement was acceptable under international law. It noted the trend away from the legality of amnesties, but refrained from opining whether a norm against the legality of amnesties for international crimes had definitively crystallized under international law. This would be consistent with principle 7(1) of the Princeton Principles on Universal Jurisdiction, which provides that amnesties are generally inconsistent with the obligation of states to provide accountability for serious crimes under international law, suggesting the undesirability, but perhaps not a per se prohibition, on all domestic amnesties for *jus cogens* crimes under international law. The view taken by the drafters of the Principles in 2001 has been strengthened by recent state and international practice, and my research to date has not uncovered any *recent* case in which a foreign or international court has respected a national amnesty with respect to a *jus cogens* crime. Nonetheless, even if courts are unwilling to consider amnesties for *jus cogens* crimes as having any extraterritorial effect (or any effect before international courts), they are still hesitant to declare them unlawful per se. For example, the amnesty opinion of the SCSL held (perhaps as dictum), that although the Lomé amnesty was inapplicable before it, there was no general obligation for states to refrain from amnesty laws on these [*jus cogens*] crimes. Consequently, if a state passes any such law, it does not breach a customary rule.[44]

As regards war crimes, most authorities distinguish between amnesties that might be given for crimes committed in international and non-international armed conflict.[45] The grave breaches regime of the four Geneva Conventions of 1949 mandates the exercise of universal jurisdiction over those crimes.[46] Although it is certainly possible that only the

---

[43] *Rome Statute*, *supra* note 42, pmbl., cl. 1.

[44] *Kallon & Kamara*, *supra* note 2, at para. 71.

[45] Although amnesty clauses for war crimes committed in international armed conflict were generally incorporated in peace agreements prior to World War I, they were vigorously rejected thereafter. Fania Domb, *Treatment of War Crimes in Peace Settlements – Prosecution or Amnesty?*, 24 ISR. Y.B. HUM. RTS. 253, 256–57 (1994).

[46] This obligation was expanded on in the 1977 Protocol Additional to the Geneva Conventions of 12 August 1949 Relating to the Protection of Victims of International Armed Conflicts (Protocol I), 1125 U.N.T.S. 3 (June

substantive provisions of the Conventions and not their procedural provisions have risen to the level of custom, most commentators have accepted that, at least with respect to war crimes committed in international armed conflict that fall within the grave breaches regime, a fair (but not watertight) case can be made not only for the existence of a customary international law duty to prosecute or extradite the offender, but, as a corollary,[47] for a rule prohibiting blanket amnesties.[48]

As regards non-international armed conflicts, an argument can be made that general amnesties are not only permitted, but are encouraged by existing law.[49] This view relies upon Article 6(5) of Protocol II relating to the Protection of Victims of Non-International Armed Conflict, which provides: At the end of hostilities, the authorities in power shall endeavor to grant the broadest possible amnesty to persons who have participated in the armed conflict, or those deprived of their liberty for reasons related to the armed conflict, whether they are interned or detained.[50]

This provision was relied upon by the South African Constitutional Court in confirming the validity, under international law, of the amnesties granted by the TRC.[51] Yet this decision failed to analyze the crimes committed (apartheid) as crimes against humanity, and did not consider whether there exists any customary international law duty to punish offenders of a prior regime for such crimes.[52] The ICRC takes the position that Article 6(5) may not be invoked in favor of impunity of war criminals, as it applied only to prosecution for the sole participation in hostilities.[53] Thus although soldiers may benefit from a general amnesty for

---

8, 1977). Domb, *supra* note 45, at 261; Michael Bothe, *War-Crimes in Non-International Armed Conflicts*, 24 Isr. Y.B. Hum. Rts. 241 (1994).

[47] There are two related, yet distinct, issues raised by the question of amnesties. First, whether states have a duty to punish and prosecute (or extradite) those who commit crimes falling under universal jurisdiction. Second, even if no such duty to punish exists, whether international law recognizes the legality of amnesties for such offenses. The two questions are often conflated, but they are distinct. One can answer the first question in the negative, for example, but still recognize that the absence of an affirmative obligation to prosecute does not permit states carte blanche in their reaction to the commission of mass atrocities. On the other hand, an affirmative duty to prosecute or extradite would appear to rule out the legality of amnesties.

[48] Scholars are divided on this question. Professor Meron argues that every state has a duty to try or extradite those guilty of grave breaches, and has "the right, although probably not the duty, to prosecute [other] serious violations of the Geneva Conventions." Theodor Meron, *Is International Law Moving towards Criminalization*, 9 Eur. J. Int'l L. 18, 23 (1998). On the other hand, states have generally not complied with this obligation, thereby undermining its claim as custom. Antonio Cassese, *On the Current Trends towards Criminal Prosecution and Punishment of Breaches of International Humanitarian Law*, 9 Eur. J. Int'l L. 2, 5 (1998); M. Cherif Bassiouni & Edward M. Wise, Aut Dedere Aut Judicare: The Duty to Extradite or Prosecute in International Law 44–46 (1995).

[49] Domb, *supra* note 45, at 266–67.

[50] Protocol Additional to the Geneva Conventions of 12 August 1949, and Relating to the Protection of Victims of Non-International Armed Conflicts, art. 6(5), 1125 U.N.T.S. 609, 614 (June 8, 1977) [hereinafter Protocol II].

[51] Azanian Peoples Organization (AZAPO) v. The President of the Republic of South Africa, 1996 (4) S.A.L.R. 671, para. 30 (South African Const. Ct.).

[52] John Dugard, *Reconciliation and Justice: The South African Experience*, 8 Transnat'l L. & Contemp. Probs. 277, 302 (1998). This criticism is consistent with the notion that there may be an international legal obligation to punish at least the worst offenders after a civil war as a necessary corollary of the need to protect human rights. Bothe, *supra* note 46, at 248 (arguing that principles of state responsibility may require prosecution). Nonetheless, although the distinction between international and non-international armed conflict may be disappearing, it has not done so yet.

[53] II Customary International Humanitarian Law: Practice 4043 (Jean-Marie Henckaerts & Louise Doswald-Beck, ICRC 2005).

combatants, the ICRC takes the position that they may not receive immunity for the com-mission of atrocities during a conflict.[54]

With respect to crimes against humanity and genocide, some commentators have asserted the existence of a duty to investigate and punish human rights violations committed under a prior regime.[55] Certainly, the Genocide Convention and the Torture Convention sug-gest that a duty is assumed by state parties to those conventions to pursue and punish (or extradite, in the case of the Torture Convention) those who violate the Conventions' pro-hibitions.[56] The International Court of Justice recently reaffirmed this obligation under the Torture Convention.[57]

As to a generalized customary international law rule requiring punishment, although the human rights instruments that guarantee a right to bodily integrity and freedom from torture and other abuses do not typically, by their terms, require states to investigate and prosecute abuses of rights,[58] regional human rights courts and international human rights monitoring bodies have been unanimous in imposing an affirmative obligation on states to investigate human rights abuse.[59] Additionally, in 2001, the Inter-American Court rendered

---

[54] *Id.*

[55] Diane F. Orentlicher, *Settling Accounts: The Duty to Prosecute Human Rights Violations of a Prior Regime*, 100 YALE L.J. 2537, 2546–48 (1991).

[56] Article 3 of the Genocide Convention, provides that "genocide ... is a crime under international law which they undertake to prevent and to punish." The convention is not based on a principle of universal jurisdiction, but of territorial jurisdiction; that is, pursuant to article 6 of the Convention, those charged with genocide or similar acts "shall be tried by a competent tribunal of the State in the territory of which the act was commit-ted, or by [an international penal tribunal]." Convention on the Prevention and Punishment of the Crime of Genocide, adopted Dec. 9, 1948, G.A. Res. 260A(II), 78 U.N.T.S. 227, entered into force Jan. 12, 1951. Similarly, Article 4 of the Torture Convention requires state parties to "ensure that all acts of torture are offences under [their] criminal law" and article 7 requires them to either extradite or prosecute alleged torturers. Convention against Torture or Other Cruel, Inhuman or Degrading Treatment or Punishment, G.A. Res. 39/46, 39 U.N. GAOR Supp. (No. 51) at 197, U.N. DOC. A/39/51 (1984).

[57] Questions relating to the Obligation to Prosecute or Extradite (Belgium v. Senegal), 2012 I.C.J. para. (July 2012).

[58] Naomi Roht-Arrizia, *Sources in International Treaties of an Obligation to Investigate, Prosecute and Provide Redress, in* IMPUNITY AND HUMAN RIGHTS IN INTERNATIONAL LAW AND PRACTICE 28 (Naomi Roht-Arrizia ed., 1995).

[59] The leading case is Velásquez Rodríguez, Inter-Am. Ct. H.R. (Ser. C) No. 4 (1988) (July 29, 1988). *Velásquez* has been followed by the Inter-American Human Rights commission to find that Chile's amnesty laws vio-lated the right to judicial protection in the Convention, as well as the state's duty to "prevent, investigate and punish" any violations of the rights found in the Convention. Garay Hermosilla et al. v. Chile, Inter-Am. C.H.R., Report No. 36/96, para. 73 (Oct. 15, 1996). *See also* Inter-American Commission on Human Rights (Case No. 133/99), Report No. 133/99, paras. 102–107. The European Court of Human Rights has, similarly, suggested that states may have affirmative obligations to prevent and remedy breaches of the Convention in certain circumstances, suggesting in one case that criminal prosecution could be required as part of that obli-gation. In the Case of X and Y v. The Netherlands (ECHR Feb. 27, 1985), para. 27 (holding that the Netherlands was required to adopt criminal-law provisions to remedy sexual abuse of a mentally handicapped individual living in a home for mentally handicapped children because "the protection afforded by the civil law in [this] case is ... insufficient. This is a case where fundamental values and essential aspects of private life are at stake. Effective deterrence is indispensable in this area and it can be achieved only by criminal-law provisions."). *See also* Selçuk & Asker v. Turkey, para. 96 (ECHR Apr. 24, 1998). The Human Rights Committee has reached a similar conclusion, finding that criminal prosecutions may sometimes be required. *Orentlicher Impunity Study, supra* note 16, at para. 37 n.48 (cases cited). Finally, the African Commission on Human and Peoples Rights has concluded that governments have not only negative obligations, but affirmative duties to pro-tect their citizens. SERAC & CESR v. Nigeria, Communication 155/96, 15th Annual Activity Report, para. 57 (2001–2002).

its first judgment on the merits of an amnesty, finding in the Barrios-Altos case Peru's amnesty laws incompatible with international law.

The Human Rights Committee, regional human rights courts, the ICJ and the ICTY have consistently held that amnesties for *jus cogens* crimes are inconsistent with international law and without effect outside the country in which they were issued. As noted above, in *Prosecutor v. Furundzija*, the ICTY held that not only was the prohibition on torture *jus cogens*, but that any amnesty therefore would be inconsistent with international law. The discussion of amnesties was not necessary to the resolution of the case, as the problem of amnesties was not raised during the proceedings; however, the Trial Chamber cited with approval a Comment from the Human Rights Committee that amnesties are generally incompatible with the duty of states to investigate torture.[60] Moreover, the Trial Chamber noted that even in the light of an amnesty, a prosecution could be instituted either before a foreign court, an international tribunal, or in their own country under a subsequent regime.[61]

These decisions are highly significant, particularly when viewed in light of emerging state practice. Although one still finds examples of blanket amnesties being issued by governments seeking to quell rebel movements or pacify armed insurgents, such as the amnesties offered by Uganda in recent years, they appear less and less frequent, and are increasingly limited to certain segments of a population and conditioned upon certain benchmarks being achieved. Although some countries have granted amnesties to the perpetrators of atrocities under a prior regime – amnesties that in some instances have been sustained by higher courts[62] – this practice appears to be changing, certainly in countries where democratic institutions have come to replace dictatorships or military regimes, as the examples of Chile and Argentina seem to suggest.[63] Indeed, it may be that amnesties are acceptable within a society only so long as they are needed to provide stability, after which time their beneficiaries need to repay the liberty they received under duress. The international decisions suggest that a prohibition against the grant of blanket amnesties for the commission of *jus cogens* crimes may now have crystallized as a matter of general customary international law.[64]

The ICC Statute is explicit on certain challenges to accountability such as superior orders,[65] head of state immunity,[66] and statute of limitations,[67] but is silent both as to any duty to prosecute and with regard to amnesties.[68] Although the issue was raised during the Rome Conference at which the Statute was adopted, no clear consensus developed among the delegates as to how the question should be resolved. This suggests that customary

---

[60] *Furundzija, supra* note 16, at para. 153 n.170.

[61] *Id.* at para. 155.

[62] *See, e.g.,* Garay Hermosilla case, para. 7 (Oct. 15, 1996) (describing decision of Supreme Court of Chile in 1990 to uphold a self-amnesty).

[63] Sadat, *supra* note 15 (passim).

[64] Orentlicher, *supra* note 55, at 2568–81; Geoffrey Robertson, Crimes against Humanity: The Struggle for Global Justice 248–53 (2000).

[65] *Rome Statute, supra* note 42, at 24.

[66] *Id.* art. 27.

[67] *Id.* art. 29.

[68] For a good discussion of some of the issues raised by the Statute, see Michael P. Scharf, *The Amnesty Exception to the Jurisdiction of the International Criminal Court,* 32 Cornell Int'l L.J. 507, 523–25 (1999).

international law had perhaps not crystallized on this point in 1998. According to the Chair of the Conference's Committee of the Whole, the question was purposely left open by the drafters: although the Statute does not condone the use of amnesties by its terms, presumably the Prosecutor has the power to accept them if doing so would be "in the interests of justice."[69]

VI. CONCLUSION

The Sierra Leone amnesty decision has been important and internationally influential. Because of the confusion surrounding the Lomé amnesty issue, UN representatives are now very clear that in international peace negotiations, amnesties are off the table for genocide, war crimes, and crimes against humanity. As stated by the UN Secretary-General in his 2000 report on the establishment of the SCSL:

> While recognizing that amnesty is an accepted legal concept and a gesture of peace and reconciliation at the end of a civil war or an internal armed conflict, the United Nations has consistently maintained the position that amnesty cannot be granted in respect of international crimes, such as genocide, crimes against humanity or other serious violations of international humanitarian law.[70]

Stephen Mathias, the UN Assistant Secretary-General for Legal Affairs, made this point clearly at a recent conference discussing the possibility of amnesty for Bashir al Assad to entice him to leave Syria.[71] Both as a political matter and as a matter of law, the granting of blanket amnesties for atrocity crimes even in times of crisis appears unacceptable, as was demonstrated recently during the unrest of the Arab Spring, as accountability of former leaders was insisted upon by both local and international stakeholders in Egypt, Tunisia, and Libya. The Sierra Leone experience has contributed to this understanding, and the Lomé Amnesty decision also provides further evidence that a norm prohibiting amnesties for *jus cogens* crimes has crystallized in customary international law, not only as regards their enforceability before international courts and tribunals, but third-state domestic courts as well. The recent case of *Belgium v. Senegal* before the International Court of Justice appears to align itself with this view in finding that the obligation imposed by the torture convention to try or prosecute alleged torturers has an *erga omnes* character.[72] Yet, if it is clear that the Lomé Amnesty has no extraterritorial effect, it seems that it has been respected within Sierra Leone, as no prosecutions other than those before the Court have occurred.

This raises a separate question: has Sierra Leone benefitted from the Lomé amnesty as a domestic matter? This chapter cannot fully answer that question, and perhaps it is too

---

[69] *Rome Statute, supra* note 42, at art. 53(1)(c). The delegates were largely unable to achieve consensus on the issues of pardons, commutations, and amnesties. *See* John T. Holmes, *The Principle of Complementarity, in* THE INTERNATIONAL CRIMINAL COURT: THE MAKING OF THE ROME STATUTE (Roy S. Lee ed., 1999).

[70] *Report of the Secretary-General on the Establishment of a Special Court for Sierra Leone*, S/2000/915, para. 22 (Oct. 4, 2000). *See also Report of the Secretary-General on the Rule of Law and Transitional Justice in Conflict and Post Conflict Societies*, U.N. Doc. S/2004/16, paras. 6, 7, 18 (Aug. 23, 2004).

[71] Remarks of Stephen Mathias, U.N. Ass't Sec'y-General for Legal Affairs, Annual Meeting of the American Society of International Law (Apr. 2012).

[72] Questions relating to the Obligation to Prosecute or Extradite (Belgium v. Senegal), 2012 I.C.J. para. 103 (July 2012).

soon to do so, but I will nonetheless venture a few observations. Unlike Rwanda, which conducted extensive domestic proceedings in the form of the Gacaca trials,[73] or South Africa, which coupled its conditional amnesty provisos with both prosecutions and a Truth and Reconciliation Commission, Sierra Leone has largely simply moved on, meaning that accountability has essentially only been undertaken with respect to the very few Accused tried by the Court.[74] Certainly, the immediate experience of the Abidjan and Lomé amnesties were that they were completely ineffective in stopping the violence perpetrated by the RUF and other fighting groups in Sierra Leone. Indeed, it would seem that the efforts by international negotiators to swap amnesty for peace appear to offer little more than a temporary respite for those leading the fighting to regroup before restarting their attacks. To this extent, the example of Sierra Leone suggests that our intuitions about amnesties for the commission of atrocities may be correct that they promote a culture of impunity in which violence remains the norm rather than the exception.

Longer term, Sierra Leone is now "at peace," the war having ended in 2002. There have been many reports suggesting that the trials conducted by the Court, all of which, except for the Charles Taylor case, took place in situ, were generally well received by the people of that country. Indeed, the location of the SCSL in Freetown meant that Sierra Leoneans could witness firsthand and participate in the work of the Tribunal. Yet ethnic tensions remain high, and it is not clear that the ethnic tensions that contributed to the civil war have abated. There remain many human rights challenges in the country,[75] and the UN Development index places it eighth from the bottom, at 180 out of 187 countries measured.[76] In 2008, the International Crisis Group referred to the presence of "social and economic time bombs," in the country,[77] difficulties that remain today. Just as Sierra Leone argued that it did not have the infrastructure to conduct trials itself in 2000, it continues to struggle with poverty, corruption, disease, and the difficulty of providing basic services such as healthcare and education to its population. These problems are no doubt more pressing than the question of accountability, which may have to wait as the country continues to rebuild from the devastation wrought by over ten years of civil war.[78] Meanwhile, as others have suggested, it may be more important – or at least more practical – to implement the recommendations of the Sierra Leone Truth and Reconciliation Commission to promote the truth about what happened, treat the victims of atrocity crimes, and promote anticorruption measures and increased political accountability and transparency than to pursue criminal accountability for perpetrators of atrocities committed in the past. Hopefully, the trials conducted by the SCSL have helped make the country safer and more peaceful so that it can accomplish these objectives.

---

[73] See the excellent paper of Linda Carter in this volume; *see also* Leila Sadat, *Transjudicial Dialogue and the Rwandan Genocide: Aspects of Antagonism and Complementarity*, 22 Leiden J. Int'l L. 543 (2009).

[74] Charles C. Jalloh, *Special Court for Sierra Leone: Achieving Justice?*, 32 Mich. J. Int'l L. 420, 395–460 (2011) (arguing that the SCSL's failure to prosecute more than a handful of perpetrators has undermined its legacy to the people of Sierra Leone).

[75] 2010 Country Reports on Human Rights, Sierra Leone, *available at* www.state.gov.

[76] United Nations Human Development Index, *available at* http://hdr.undp.org/en/statistics/.

[77] Sierra Leone: A New Era of Reform? International Crisis Group (2008), *available at* http://www.crisisgroup.org/en/regions/africa/west-africa/sierra-leone/143-sierra-leone-a-new-era-of-reform.aspx.

[78] In anticipation of the November elections, the Security Council renewed the mandate of the UN Integrated Peace building Office in Sierra Leone until March 31, 2013, and stressed the importance of the elections as a "benchmark" of the country's political maturity. S.C. Res. 2065 (Sept. 12, 2012).

16

Piercing the Veil of Head-of-State Immunity: The Taylor Trial and Beyond

Micaela Frulli[*]

I. INTRODUCTION

In the Taylor case before the Special Court for Sierra Leone (SCSL), the issue of head-of-state immunity was settled at a very preliminary stage, with the *Decision on Immunity from Jurisdiction* issued in May 2004, after the motion to quash the Indictment introduced by Taylor's defense team.[1] The question was not further discussed during trial: the judges took the view that the immunity issue had already been disposed of, and there was no need to further elaborate on it. Consistent with this viewpoint, the issue was not dealt with in the judgment.[2] This attitude is certainly also because at the time of his arrest, Taylor had already relinquished his position and could no longer claim to enjoy head-of-state immunity.[3]

Nonetheless the whole Taylor case, from the initial arrest warrant against a serving head of state to the circumstances of his arrest and surrender to UN forces, which took him into custody and brought him to the SCSL and finally to the completion of trial, sets an important precedent for actual or potential head-of-state cases before the International Criminal Court (ICC) and marks one of the important legacies of the SCSL, which is interesting to discuss.[4]

---

[*] Associate Professor of International Law, University of Florence, Italy. She received her PhD in International Law at the University "Federico II" of Naples (2000).

[1] SCSL, Decision on Immunity from Jurisdiction, Prosecutor v. Charles Ghankay Taylor, Case No. SCSL-03-1-T, Appeals Chamber (May 31, 2004) [hereinafter *Decision on Immunity*]. This decision and all relevant documents are available on the website of the SCSL, http://www.sc-sl.org.

[2] See the transcript of April 3, 2006 (Initial Appearance of Taylor before the SCSL) where Trial Chamber II confirmed its jurisdiction over the Accused and referred to the previous decision on immunity (at pp. 14–15), http://www.sc-sl.org/LinkClick.aspx?fileticket=fXnh5O5uoAg%3d&tabid=160). *See also* Annex B to the Judgment (Prosecutor v. Taylor, Case No. SCSL-03-1-T, Trial Chamber II, Judgment (May 18, 2012), *available at* http://www.sierra-leone.org/SCSL-03–01-T-1283.pdf) containing the Procedural History of the case (para. 7, at 2485–86).

[3] Former heads of state may only invoke functional immunity to avoid being tried by a foreign court. However, it is universally acknowledged that functional immunity may not be invoked by state officials, not even by heads of state who are accused of having committed international crimes. *See* A. CASSESE, INTERNATIONAL CRIMINAL LAW 305 *ff.* (2008).

[4] It is interesting to note that Taylor was sentenced to fifty years imprisonment, and that one of the aggravating factors in sentencing was his position as head of state. As noted by Mark Drumbl, who speaks of fetishization of head of state status:

The crimes were truly horrific, but the 50 year sentence derives in material part from the fact that Taylor was a Head of State. The sentencing judgment is redolent with cues in this regard – the crescendo of references to Taylor's uniqueness in that he is a Head of State (paras. 97, 103), his "special

II. HEAD OF STATE IMMUNITY BEFORE INTERNATIONAL CRIMINAL
COURTS: THE STATE OF THE ART

The arrest warrant issued by the SCSL against Charles Taylor in 2003, when he held office as president of Liberia, was not the first one of its kind. A few years before, the International Criminal Tribunal for the former Yugoslavia (ICTY) had issued an Indictment and an arrest warrant against the then-president of the Federal Republic of Yugoslavia (FRY), Slobodan Milošević.[5] However, the defense team representing Taylor was indeed the first one to challenge the Indictment and the arrest warrant on the basis of the argument that a serving head of state may neither be arrested nor surrendered by a foreign state, not even to face trial for charges of international crimes.[6] This is an argument that Milošević never used to challenge the legality of the ICTY arrest warrant. Taylor's defense lawyers took the view that the SCSL was in fact obliged to respect the personal immunities accruing to incumbent heads of state under international law, and introduced a motion to quash the Indictment. The SCSL issued a decision that rejected the motion, and had the opportunity to discuss head-of-state immunity in depth.[7] It is therefore important to recollect the content and meaning of this decision and to assess its impact on (a quite troubled) current practice.

It is widely shared that, under customary international law, incumbent heads of state are entitled to personal immunity from arrest and criminal prosecution in the territory of foreign states when facing charges of international crimes before a domestic court.[8] Recent case law supports the existence of this rule,[9] which was also authoritatively upheld by the

---

status" (paras. 97, 100), how he is in a "class of his own" (para. 101), and how he himself told the judges: "I was President of Liberia [...] not some petty trader on the streets of Monrovia" (para. 97).

See M. Drumbl, *The Charles Taylor Sentence and Traditional International Law* (June 11, 2012), OPINIO JURIS BLOG, http://opiniojuris.org/2012/06/11/charles-taylor-sentencing-the-taylor-sentence-and-traditional-international-law/.

[5] For a summary of the review of the indictment against Slobodan Milosević and the issuance by Judge Hunt of the consequential orders, including the warrant of arrest against Milosević, see the website of the ICTY at www.icty.org/ (home page). Judge Hunt held that UN member states are bound to comply with an order for the arrest and detention of a person by the ICTY, by virtue of Article 29(2) of the Statute.

[6] It is interesting to note that after the indictment and the arrest warrant issued by the SCSL, the Republic of Liberia sought to file a complaint before the International Court of Justice (ICJ) against Sierra Leone for the alleged violation of the rules on head-of-state immunity (Application filed on Aug. 4, 2003. Press Release 2003/26, *available at* http://www.icj-cij.org/presscom/index.php?pr=1027&pt=1&p1=6&p2=1&PHPSESSID=5c407). However, Sierra Leone did not accept the jurisdiction of the ICJ to settle the dispute.

[7] *See Decision on Immunity, supra* note 1.

[8] Under international law, state officials are entitled to different types of immunity from foreign jurisdiction. Generally, two categories of immunities are identified: the so-called functional immunity (or *ratione materiae*), and personal immunities (or *ratione personae*). Functional immunity from the jurisdiction of foreign states cover activities performed by various state officials in the exercise of their functions, and it survives the end of office. The rationale behind this rule is that official activities are performed by state organs on behalf of their state and, in principle, must be attributed to the state itself. Personal immunities, which only accrue to some categories of state organs because of the crucial relevance of their official position (diplomatic agents, heads of state, heads of government, and ministers of foreign affairs), cover every act performed by those who benefit from these rules, but they last only until the organs concerned remain in office. *See* CASSESE, *supra* note 3, at 302ff. M. Frulli, *Immunities of Persons from Jurisdiction, in* THE OXFORD COMPANION TO INTERNATIONAL CRIMINAL JUSTICE 368ff. (A. Cassese ed. 2009).

[9] For an overview of the most important cases, including recent ones, see International Law Commission, *Immunity of State Officials from Foreign Criminal Jurisdiction. Memorandum prepared by the Secretariat*, Mar. 31, 2008, A/CN.4/596, § 146.

International Court of Justice (ICJ) in the well-known Arrest Warrant case in 2002.[10] On the contrary, it is generally affirmed that personal immunities do not constitute a bar to the exercise of criminal jurisdiction by international criminal courts, as was again incidentally confirmed by the ICJ. In this respect, the Arrest Warrant judgment left a number of questions open, and it was precisely starting from there and trying to answer some of these questions that the SCSL contributed to the debate. The merits and pitfalls of the SCSL decision on immunity have been extensively discussed elsewhere,[11] so this chapter will try to focus only on the most important points of the decision itself with a view to putting them in perspective. The SCSL maintained that the rules on personal immunities have no bearing whatsoever on the exercise of jurisdiction by international criminal courts.[12] Hence, the first step to take for the Court was to establish itself as an international tribunal. The Appeals Chamber admittedly mixed up different issues while addressing this crucial question. In particular, it endeavored to show that the SCSL was endowed with Chapter VII powers deriving from the UN Charter and left aside both the problem of its treaty-nature and the question whether Article 6(2) of the SCSL Statute[13] – which was interpreted as removing personal immunities – could be applied to third-states' officials. The decision has then been thoroughly criticized for the line of reasoning chosen and especially for the attempt to fit the SCSL into the Chapter VII category. Indeed the SCSL followed a tortuous path to reach the conclusion that it may be classed among international criminal tribunals, but that conclusion is the correct one.[14] The discussion about this decision helped in outlining the features that characterize an international criminal tribunal and distinguish it from a domestic one.[15]

---

[10] ICJ, Case concerning the Arrest Warrant of 11 April 2000 (Democratic Republic of Congo v. Belgium) (Feb. 14, 2002), ICJ Reports (2002). The ICJ found that the issuance of the arrest warrant by Belgium against the serving Minister of Foreign Affairs of the Democratic Republic of the Congo (and a fortiori this applies to incumbent heads of state) breached the international customary rules on personal immunities accruing to high-level state officials. The Court also ruled the international circulation of the arrest warrant constitutes a violation by Belgium of the rules on personal immunities because the international circulation of the warrant could have resulted in the arrest of the person entitled to immunities in a country other than Belgium.

[11] M. Frulli, *The Question of Charles Taylor's Immunity. Still in Search of a Balanced Application of Personal Immunities?*, 2 JICJ 1118–29 (2004); V. Klingberg, *(Former) Heads of State before International(ized) Criminal Courts: The Case of Charles Taylor before the Special Court for Sierra Leone*, 46 GERMAN Y.B. INT'L L. 537–64 (2004); Z. Deen-Racsmány, *Prosecutor v. Taylor: The Status of the Special Court of Sierra Leone and Its Implications for Immunity*, 18 LJIL 299–322 (2005); S. Nouwen, *The Special Court for Sierra Leone and the Immunity of Taylor: The Arrest Warrant Case Continued*, 18 LJIL 645–69 (2005); C. Ragni, *Immunity of Heads of State: Some Critical Remarks on the Decision of the Special Court for Sierra Leone in the Charles Taylor Case*, 18 ITALIAN Y.B. INT'L L. 372–88 (2005).

[12] See *Decision on Immunity*, supra note 1, § 51.

[13] Article 6(2) of the SCSL Statute reads: "The official position of any accused persons, whether as Head of State or Government or as a responsible government official, shall not relieve such person of criminal responsibility nor mitigate punishment."

[14] As another commentator said: "(…) that conclusion has been undermined by the methodology it adopted to elucidate its legal character and some of the weak justifications offered to support it."; C.C. Jalloh, *The Contribution of the Special Court for Sierra Leone to the Development of International Law*, 15 AFR. J. INT'L & COMP. L. 165, 192 (2007). See also the authors quoted supra note 11.

[15] The nature of the Special Court as an international criminal tribunal may be proved by relying on the characteristics of the SCSL, which are in fact those of an international organization. It was established by way of an international agreement, it is vested with the specific competence to prosecute persons who bear the greatest responsibility for the most serious international crimes committed in the territory of Sierra Leone since November 30, 1996, and it is endowed with the necessary autonomy to pursue this objective. The SCSL may enter into agreements with states and other international legal subjects and enjoys privileges and immunity. In addition, its composition is mixed, but international judges appointed by the UN Secretary-General

However, the most important aspect of this decision – if one looks at it in light of subsequent practice – is that it laid down an important stone that helped consolidate an emerging trend. It may be contended that there is an emerging customary rule that establishes an exception to personal immunities accruing to incumbent heads of states as far as the jurisdiction of an international criminal tribunal is concerned, irrespective of its treaty-nature.[16] The crucial question to be answered in order to decide on the international nature of a tribunal is whether such a tribunal has an international legal personality and may act independently from the states and/or other actors that created it.

Admittedly, it is also decisive to determine whether it has direct support or at least an indirect backing by the United Nations, in order to avoid the "4 States" dilemma.[17] It does not suffice that two or more states sign a treaty to create a new tribunal – with whatever subject-matter and personal jurisdiction – give it independence of action and legal personality to have an international criminal tribunal before which head-of-state or personal immunity does not constitute a procedural bar to prosecution. Two other characteristics seem to be necessary.

In the first place the tribunal created by way of an international agreement must be competent over the most serious crimes under international law for which states are entitled to exercise universal jurisdiction: for these crimes states may well decide to delegate their jurisdictional competence to an international body that offer a greater degree of independence and impartiality. Second, in order to establish the degree of support for an international criminal tribunal in the international community, it is crucial to evaluate the role played by the United Nations in its establishment and functioning. UN direct action, as in the case of the ICTY and ICTR established by the Security Council, or more indirect backing – such as for the SCSL and even more for the ICC – crucially show the will of the most important intergovernmental organization with universal membership to act as a guarantor of the genuine objective of prosecuting the most serious crimes under international law pursued by international criminal tribunals (if necessary under the framework of Chapter VII of the UN Charter), and again of their independence and impartiality. If these assumptions are correct, the SCSL is an international criminal tribunal,[18] and so is the

---

represent the majority both in Trial and Appeals Chambers (SCSL Statute art. 12). The SCSL is financed by voluntary contributions by the members of the international community. Finally, it is worth mentioning that the Sierra Leonean Special Court Agreement 2002 Ratification Act 2002 expressly provides that the SCSL is not part of the judiciary of Sierra Leone and that offenses prosecuted before the SCSL are not prosecuted in the name of the Republic of Sierra Leone.

[16] *See* CASSESE, *supra* note 3, at 311–12; P. Gaeta, *Does President Al Bashir Enjoy Immunity from Arrest?*, 7 JICJ 315–32 (2009); S. Papillon, *Has the United Nations Security Council Implicitly Removed Al Bashir's Immunity?*, 10 INT'L CRIM. L. REV. 275–88 (2010). It is interesting to quote also Article 11, para. 3 of the Resolution on Immunities from Jurisdiction and Execution of Heads of State and of Government in International Law, adopted in 2001 by the *Institut de droit international* (IDI): "Nothing in this Resolution implies nor can be taken to mean that a Head of State enjoys an immunity before an international tribunal with universal or regional jurisdiction." The resolution is available on the website of the IDI at http://www.idi-iil.org/idiE/resolutionsE/2001_van_02_en.PDF.

[17] I owe the outline of the "4 States" dilemma to the comments of Professor Diane Orentlicher, whom I warmly thank.

[18] For the SCSL it would be more correct, in my view, to speak of a dual nature, but it may be contended that these organs act as international organs when they exercise their jurisdiction to prosecute international crimes.

ICC,[19] which was already confronted with the issue of immunity of serving heads of states and is now facing various problems with the consequences deriving from the removal of personal immunities.

Are there sufficient elements supporting the emergence of such a rule? In the Taylor case, as already with Milošević, no state protested the issuance of an arrest warrant against an incumbent head of state. And the same holds true for the Indictment and arrest warrant of the president of Sudan, Omar Al-Bashir, which is posing major problems not because of the exercise of jurisdiction by the ICC, but because of the lack of cooperation by states (even state parties to the ICC Statute) in enforcing the warrant.[20] In fact, it seems that most states support the existence of such a rule as far as the exercise of jurisdiction by international courts is concerned, including most African states that were among the strongest supporters of the ICC Statute.[21] In addition, the contention that personal immunities do not constitute an obstacle to proceedings before an international criminal court was made by a large number of scholars who affirmed – along different lines of reasoning – that personal immunities may not be invoked before an international criminal tribunal, not even by officials of states that are third parties with respect to a treaty-based tribunal.[22] The ICC Pre-Trial Chamber has also adopted this point of view, albeit its decisions on the issue were harshly criticized for their allegedly inadequate legal reasoning.[23]

There are also strong logical arguments that lie beneath the emergence of such an exception. The rules of customary international law providing for personal immunities (which include inviolability or immunity from arrest and detention, and immunity from the criminal jurisdiction of foreign courts) for heads of states and for other specific classes of high-level state officials originally stemmed from the necessity to protect officials representing

---

[19] In referring a situation to the ICC, the SC clearly exercises a power conferred upon it by the SC, but it also acts under Chapter VII of the UN Charter.

[20] See *infra* next paragraph.

[21] The position of the African Union, on which I will come back to in paragraph 3, does not seem to be in contrast with the exercise of ICC jurisdiction over sitting high state officials. See on this point, for instance, the joint Report: AU-EU Expert Report on the Principle of Universal Jurisdiction, COE, 8672/1/09, Rev. 1, para. 31 (Apr. 16, 2009). The AU casts doubts on the obligation of states to enforce the arrest warrant issued against a serving head of state of a state that is not a party to the ICC; see *infra* next paragraph.

[22] *See* Gaeta, *supra* note 16; D. Akande, *The Legal Nature of Security Council Referrals to the ICC and Its Impact on Al Bashir's Immunities*, 7 JCIC 333, at 340–42 (2009); M. Milanovic, *ICC Prosecutor Charges the President of Sudan with Genocide, Crimes against Humanity and War Crimes in Darfur*, 12 ASIL INSIGHT (July 28, 2008), *available at* http://www.asil.org/insights080728.cfm. However some distinguished commentator argued that: "In principle, the Rome Statute can only bind member states. Art. 27(2) removes immunities from heads of state. This only applies to heads of state of States Parties and cannot be invoked against heads of state of non-party States."; W. Schabas, *Obama, Medvedev and Hu Jintao May Be Prosecuted by International Criminal Court, Pre-Trial Chamber Concludes* (Dec. 15, 2011), *available at* http://humanrightsdoctorate.blogspot.com/2011/12/obama-medvedev-and-hu-jintao-may-be.html.

[23] See Decision on the Prosecution's Application for a Warrant of Arrest against Omar Hassan Ahmad Al Bashir, ICC-02/05–01/09–3 (Mar. 4, 2009), in which PTC I held: "the current position of Omar Al Bashir as Head of a state which is not a party to the Statute, has no effect on the Court's jurisdiction over the present case" (para. 41). *See also* Decision on the "Prosecutor's Application Pursuant to Article 58 as to MuammarMohammed Abu Minyar Gaddafi, Saif Al-Islam Gaddafi and Abdullah Al Senussi," ICC-01/11, para. 9 (June 27, 2011). These decisions were criticized because they did not dwell on the obligations of states to enforce the warrant and on the relationship between Article 27(2) and Article 98(1) of the ICC Statute. Only recently the ICC PTC issued two decisions discussing whether Omar Al Bashir is immune from arrest in ICC State parties, holding that Malawi and Chad breached their obligations of cooperation with the Court by not arresting Bashir when he visited those countries in 2011. See *infra* next paragraph.

foreign states abroad from any possible abuse of authority.[24] It essentially originated as a tool to foster smooth diplomatic inter-state relations among states. In fact, personal immunities accrue only to certain categories of state officials, namely those organs that are entrusted to represent their state in the territory of foreign states and, more generally, to represent their state at the international level. Indeed, diplomats enjoy personal immunities so long as they remain in office. It is also universally acknowledged that acting heads of states, heads of governments, and ministers of foreign affairs enjoy personal – that is to say absolute – inviolability and immunity from the criminal jurisdiction of foreign courts as long as they hold office.[25] The principle underlying these rules is commonly identified as "functional necessity," and often expressed with the Latin formula *ne impediatur legatio* or *ne impediatur officium*: certain state officials must be free to exercise sovereign functions abroad without any risk of interference for politically motivated reasons.

In striking the balance between different values at stake – that is to say the prosecution of international crimes and the rules on personal immunities – international law gives precedence, up until now, to immunities, with a view to ensuring the smooth functioning of inter-state relations. For this reason, personal immunities apply before domestic courts irrespective of the gravity of the crime allegedly committed by any state official enjoying this kind of immunity. On the other hand, this rationale fades into the background when a state official is indicted by an international criminal tribunal. International criminal tribunals that are truly international in nature, as highlighted above, do not act as organs of a group of states, but as independent legal subjects that have been created – with some differences the one from the other – precisely with the objective to prosecute the most serious international crimes with all the guarantees of fairness and impartiality that domestic courts may not always offer. Whereas at the "horizontal" level – a level of relation among equals – the need to protect foreign state officials from the possible abuse of jurisdiction by other states prevails, at the "vertical" level things change completely, because the exercise of jurisdiction by international criminal tribunals may not be assimilated to an exercise of authority of a state upon that of another state, and fulfilment of the task entrusted to these tribunals (i.e., the repression of the most serious crimes under international law), overcomes any immunity issue.[26] In addition, international criminal courts act to protect fundamental values on behalf of the international community, and they offer guarantees of impartiality and independence that certainly avoid the danger of political abuse.[27] All these factors deprive personal immunities of their very *raison d'être* and tip the scales in favor of prosecution of serving heads of state by international criminal tribunals.

The decision of the SCSL was the first issued by an international criminal tribunal to duly stress the reasons for this removal, and as such it represents a precious precedent, which,

---

[24] Head-of-state immunity also originated from the will to ensure respect for the principle of sovereign equality of states, a rationale that however progressively lost importance with respect to personal immunities.

[25] In its decision in the Arrest Warrant case (Arrest Warrant of Apr. 11, 2000 (Democratic Republic of the Congo v. Belgium), Judgment (Feb. 14, 2002)), the ICJ held that the rationale of personal immunity accruing to incumbent ministers of foreign affairs is to "protect the individual concerned against any act of authority of another State which would hinder him or her in the performance of his or her duties" (para. 54).

[26] For further interesting elaboration on the topic of "verticality," see F. Mégret, *In Search of the "Vertical": An Exploration of What Makes International Criminal Tribunals Different (and Why)*, in C. Stahn & L. Herik, Future Perspectives on International Criminal Justice 182 *ff.* (2010).

[27] *See* Cassese, *supra* note 3, at 312.

one could reasonably argue, paved the way for the development of the customary exception and, indirectly, for the indictments and arrest warrants later issued by the ICC against serving heads of state as Al-Bashir and Gaddafi.

From the theoretical perspective, one may recall the work of René-Jean Dupuy, who depicted two different categories of customary rules: the wise custom (*coutume sage*) and the wild custom (*coutume sauvage*).[28] Wild customs develop over a short period of time and emerge on the wave of the strong will of a large number of states to impose the protection of certain values or interests. In these cases the *opinio juris* element prevails over the repetition in time (*usus*) and allows a rapid process of consolidation of a new customary rule. The customary exception to personal immunities before international criminal tribunals could perfectly fit into the category of wild customs.

III. THE ENFORCEMENT OF ARREST WARRANTS ISSUED AGAINST THIRD-STATE OFFICIALS BY TREATY-BASED INTERNATIONAL CRIMINAL TRIBUNALS

The existence of a customary exception to the rules on personal immunities whenever jurisdiction is exercised by an international criminal court – irrespective of its treaty-based nature – must be differentiated from the question of whether all states may lawfully set aside those rules in order to comply with a request for arrest and surrender issued by that court. International criminal courts do not have enforcement powers, and they have to rely on the cooperation of national authorities in order to get their warrants enforced. However, when states enforce an arrest warrant by an international criminal court against the state official of another state, they act at the "horizontal" level and they do exercise their sovereign authority over a foreign state official. Therefore, it cannot be assumed that they are obliged to cooperate with international criminal tribunals and that they can automatically disregard personal immunities.

In the case of the execution of Taylor's arrest warrant, for instance, one may contend that Ghana – where Taylor found himself when the arrest warrant was disclosed and circulated – would have violated international rules on personal immunity accruing to serving head of states had it enforced the warrant. Neither Ghana nor other states are in fact obliged to cooperate with the SCSL, which was established by means of a bilateral treaty between Sierra Leone and the United Nations, whereas they are bound by customary rules on personal immunities. In this respect, the position of the SCSL and of other treaty-based tribunals, as the ICC, differs from that of the ad hoc criminal tribunals created by the UN Security Council.

With regard to the ICTY and ICTR, it is generally acknowledged that there is an obligation incumbent on all UN member states to cooperate with those tribunals by virtue of the fact they were established through binding resolutions of the Security Council adopted on the basis of Chapter VII. The obligation to cooperate inserted in the ICTY and ICTR Statutes – which certainly includes the obligation to enforce arrest warrants or any other order or request issued by the tribunals – rests on the authority of the Security Council. These obligations override other international obligations incumbent upon UN member

---

[28] R-J. Dupuy, *Coutume sage et coutume sauvage*, *in* MÉLANGES ROUSSEAU. LA COMMUNAUTÉ INTERNATIONALE 75–87 (C. Rousseau ed., 1974).

states by virtue of Article 103 of the UN Charter.[29] A similar case never materialized before the ad hoc tribunals, but one may contend that a state enforcing an arrest warrant issued by the ICTY or ICTR against a serving head of state or any other official enjoying personal immunity would not incur international responsibility because that state would act to implement prevailing obligations deriving from the UN Charter.[30]

On the other hand, the SCSL was not established by means of a UN Security Council resolution, and there is no obligation on third states deriving directly from the UN Charter. Hence, the issue of the role that the Security Council may play through Chapter VII becomes a crucial one.[31] The Taylor case may be very useful again to draw a hypothetical scenario: it may be argued that a binding resolution by the UN Security Council based on Chapter VII could have compelled UN member states to cooperate with the SCSL and, more specifically, could have expressly authorized them to disregard Taylor's personal immunity from arrest.[32] In such a scenario, the SCSL would have come closer to the ICTY and to the ICTR: the obligation to cooperate would not spring directly from the SCSL Statute, but from a binding resolution establishing an obligation for UN member states to cooperate with the SCSL.[33] In the case at hand, as it is well-known, there was no need for a similar resolution as Taylor stepped down from the presidency a few months after the Indictment and thus stopped enjoying personal immunities.

The question of a potential conflict between different sets of obligations is still one of actual relevance. and it has extensively been debated with regard to the indictment and arrest warrant issued by the ICC against the sitting president of Sudan, Omar Al-Bashir.[34] With respect to the ICC, as it was established through a multilateral treaty and not through a bilateral one as the SCSL, it is necessary to evaluate the different position of state parties to its Statute and third states with respect to the obligation to cooperate with the ICC in general and, more specifically, with respect to the possibility to arrest and surrender a state official enjoying personal immunity. The most difficult position is that of state parties to the ICC with respect to a warrant-of-arrest issue against serving officials of third states. This is

---

[29] According to Article 103 of the UN Charter: "In the event of a conflict between the obligations of the Members of the United Nations under the present Charter and their obligations under any other international agreement, their obligations under the present Charter shall prevail."

[30] Actually, had the conflict arisen in the Milošević *affaire* there could have been problems, as in any other case where the official enjoying personal immunities belong to a state that is not a UN member state. At the time of the indictment of Milošević, when he was an acting head of state, the question of the membership of the FRY in the United Nations was still an open one.

[31] In fact the SCSL in the Decision on Immunity focused on trying to show it was endowed with Chapter VII powers more than on other aspects.

[32] The UN Security Council has a wide margin of appreciation in determining the existence of a threat to the peace (Article 39) and to adopt measures not including the use of force (Article 41) in order to contribute to the maintenance of peace and security.

[33] One could also argue that a simple recommendation to cooperate with the SCSL, adopted on the basis of Chapter VII by the Security Council, could have sufficed to avoid the commission of an international wrongful act by the state that decided to enforce the arrest warrant. *See* B. Conforti, *Le rôle de l'accord dans le système des Nations Unies*, 142 RDC (1974-II), 262–65.

[34] Press Release, ICC Office of the Prosecutor, ICC Issues a Warrant of Arrest for Omar Al Bashir, President of Sudan (Mar. 4, 2009); Situation in Darfur, Sudan (ICC-02/05–157), Public Redacted Version of Prosecutor's Application under Article 58 filed on July 28, 2008, Pre-Trial Chamber (Sept. 12, 2008); Prosecutor v. Omar Al Bashir (ICC-02/05–157), Decision on the Prosecution's Application for a Warrant of Arrest against Omar Hassan Ahmad Al Bashir, Pre-Trial Chamber I (Mar. 4, 2009) and Warrant of Arrest for Omar Hassan Ahmad Al Bashir, Pre-Trial Chamber I (Mar. 4, 2009).

precisely the crux of the matter in the Al-Bashir case, and it has been the object of two decisions issued by the ICC Pre-Trial Chamber (PTC) in December 2011 about noncompliance
by state parties in the enforcement of arrest warrants,[35] and of a number of AU decisions
calling on AU member states not to cooperate with the ICC.[36] It is interesting to develop
some reflections on the actual bone of contention to see whether useful hints to finding a
suitable solution for the ICC may be drawn from the Taylor case.

First, most commentators agree that Sudan, although not a party to the ICC Statute, is
obliged to cooperate with the ICC by virtue of UN Security Council Resolution 1593, which
referred the situation in Darfur to the ICC.[37] This is also the position held by the ICC PTC.
The Chamber, however, did not initially deal with the issue of the necessary coordination
of Article 27(2), removing personal immunities, and Article 98(1) relating to cooperation
for the enforcement of arrest warrants and providing that the Court may not proceed with
a request for surrender or assistance that would require the requested state to act inconsistently with its obligations under international law with respect to the state or diplomatic
immunity of a person or property of a third state, unless the Court can first obtain the cooperation of that third state for the waiver of the immunity. The PTC pronounced on this issue
only in its decisions mentioned earlier, admittedly a little bit too late. In these decisions,
the Court took the view that Malawi and Chad failed to comply with the Statute. It simply
argued that because heads of states of nonparties to the ICC Statute may not invoke personal immunity from the jurisdiction of the ICC, states enforcing an arrest warrant and sur-
rendering an indicted head of state to the Court would not violate their obligations under
international law. In other words the Court's Judges took the view that "article 98(1) of the
Statute does not apply."[38] But they did not explain why and how the lack of immunity in
the vertical relationship among the ICC and states automatically extend to the horizontal

---

[35] Decision Pursuant to Article 87(7) of the Rome Statute on the Failure by the Republic of Malawi to Comply
with the Cooperation Requests Issued by the Court with Respect to the Arrest and Surrender of Omar
Hassan Ahmad Al Bashir (ICC-02/05–01/09) (Dec. 12, 2011) [hereinafter *Decision Pursuant to Article 87(7)*]
and Décision rendue en application de l'article 87–7 du Statut de Rome concernant le refus de la République
du Tchad d'accéder aux demandes de coopération délivrées par la Cour concernant l'arrestation et la remise
d'Omar Hassan Ahmad Al Bashir (ICC-02/05–01/09) (Dec. 13, 2011), *available at* www.ICC-CPI.int.

[36] The AU Assembly has adopted a number of decisions regarding cases at the ICC. In one of the latest meetings
(Jan. 2012) the AU Assembly reiterated its request that the UN Security Council defer the proceedings against
Sudanese president Bashir in accordance with Article 16 of the ICC Statute. It also "urge[d] all [AU] Member
States to comply with [AU] Assembly Decisions on the warrants of arrest issued by the ICC against President
Bashir of the Sudan pursuant to Article 23(2) of the [AU] Constitutive Act and Article 98 of the Rome Statute
of the ICC." Those decisions called on African states, even state parties to the ICC statute, not to comply with
the request by the ICC for the arrest and surrender of Bashir. See the AU Press Release of Jan. 9, 2012, *available at* http://www.au.int/en/sites/default/files/PR-%20002-%20ICC%20English.pdf. See also the decisions of
the AU on the ICC, *available at* http://au.int/en/summit/sites/default/files/ASSEMBLY%20AU%20DEC%20
391%20-%20415%20%28XVIII%29%20_e_0.pdf.

[37] *See* Gaeta, *supra* note 16; A. Ciampi, *The Obligation to Cooperate, in* 2 THE ROME STATUTE OF THE
INTERNATIONAL CRIMINAL COURT: A COMMENTARY 1621 (A. Cassese, P. Gaeta & J.R.W.D. Jones eds., 2002);
Akande, *supra* note 22, at 333–52.

[38] Chamber finds that customary international law creates an exception to head-of-state immunity when international courts seek a head of state's arrest for the commission of international crimes. There is no conflict
between Malawi's obligations toward the Court and its obligations under customary international law; therefore, article 98(1) of the Statute does not apply. *Decision Pursuant to Article 87(7), supra* note 35, at para. 43.
The PTC also says that "the unavailability of immunities with respect to prosecutions by international courts
applies to any act of cooperation by states which forms an integral part of those prosecutions." (Para. 44).

level. The poor legal reasoning of the PTC decisions on such sensitive issues did not help in defusing the tension with African states, and even prompted the AU to consider requesting to the ICJ to deliver an advisory opinion "regarding the immunities of State Officials under international law."[39] Most recently, however, the Republic of Malawi withdrew the offer to host the 19th AU Summit meetings initially scheduled in Lilongwe from July 9 to 16, 2012 (now transferred to Addis Ababa) because of the insistence on inviting all African leaders, including Al-Bashir.[40]

In legal scholarship these decision have been severely criticized.[41] In any case, well before these decisions by the ICC PTC, there were several studies tackling this topic, with scholars expressing three main positions. According to the first, the treaty establishing the ICC derogates from the rules of customary international law on personal immunities with respect to the exercise of jurisdiction by national authorities, including the execution of an arrest warrant issued by the ICC, but only with respect to the relationship among contracting states. Article 98 recognizes that state parties are obliged to respect international rules on personal immunities accruing to officials of states that are not parties to the ICC Statute.[42] Therefore state parties are not compelled to execute the ICC request for surrender of President Al-Bashir – who belongs to a third state – and can lawfully decide not to comply with it. On the contrary, among state parties personal immunities may be disregarded when a foreign state official is indicted and searched for arrest by the ICC. The arrest and surrender of a serving head of state of a state party by the authorities of another state party would not, under Article 98(1), violate obligations under international law.[43] According to a different position, it may be contended that the referral to the ICC of the situation of Sudan by the UN Security Council would have rendered the ICC Statute applicable to Sudan as if it were a state party. As a consequence, not only Sudan is obliged to cooperate with the Court and to arrest Al-Bashir, but the same holds true for all state parties to the ICC Statute. In addition, by virtue of the referral, third states are allowed to cooperate with the ICC for the enforcement of the arrest warrant without incurring international responsibility, but they have no obligation to do so.[44]

---

[39] Assembly of the AU, Decision on the Progress Report of the Commission on the Implementation of the Assembly Decisions on the International Criminal Court (ICC), Doc. EX.CL/710(xx) (Feb. 9, 2012), *available on the website of the African Union at* http://au.int/en/summit/sites/default/files/ASSEMBLY%20AU%20DEC%20391%20-%20415%20%28XVIII%29%20_e_0.pdf.

[40] See the ICC Press Release of June 12, 2012, President of the Assembly on Malawi's decision regarding cooperation with the ICC, ICC-ASP-20120612-PR806, *available at* http://www.icc-cpi.int/menus/asp/press%20releases/press%20releases%202012/pr806.

[41] See the critical remarks by D. Akande, *ICC Issues Detailed Decision on Bashir's Immunity (… At Long Last …) But Gets the Law Wrong*, EJIL Talk! (Dec. 15, 2001), *available at* http://www.ejiltalk.org/icc-issues-detailed-decision-on-bashir%E2%80%99s-immunity-at-long-last-but-gets-the-law-wrong/. *See also* G. Sluiter, *ICC's Decision on Malawi's Failure to Arrest Al Bashir Damages the Authority of the Court and Relations with the African Union*, iLAWYER Blog (Mar. 6, 2012), http://ilawyerblog.com/iccs-decision-on-malawis-failure-to-arrest-al-bashir-damages-the-authority-of-the-court-and-relations-with-the-african-union/.

[42] K. Prost & A. Schlunck, *Article 98*, in Commentary on the Rome Statute of the International Criminal Court. Observers' Notes, Article by Article 1131 (O. Triffterer ed., 1999).

[43] *See* Gaeta, *supra* note 16.

[44] *See* Akande, *supra* note 22. There is also a slightly different position according to which Security Council Resolution 1593 implicitly removed personal immunities. *See* Papillon, *supra* note 16; Milanovic, *supra* note 22.

According to the third position personal immunities of officials of third states are simply not removed by the ICC Statute and a fortiori have to be respected by state parties.

The first position seems to be the correct one. In fact, the referral does not seem to automatically make the Statute binding on third states and indeed, as it has been noted, the language of Resolution 1593 is quite clear in this respect: Sudan is obliged to cooperate with the ICC, but other states are simply urged to cooperate.[45] In addition, it does not seem that the said resolution has implicitly removed personal immunities accruing to Sudanese officials.[46]

However, it could be argued that all the various positions expressed may be reconciled through the adoption of a specific binding resolution by the Security Council, adopted on the basis of Chapter VII, and requesting states to cooperate with the ICC in order to enforce specific orders or warrants – such as that issued against Al-Bashir – as described in the hypothetical scenario for the Taylor case drawn above.

It would not be the first time that the UN Security Council would have called upon states to assist in the apprehension and prosecution of alleged criminals. It would also not be the first time that the Council would have determined that the lack of cooperation in prosecuting individuals suspected of serious crimes represents a threat to the peace. In 2002, the Security Council urged Libya to extradite to the United Kingdom or to the United States those suspected of being involved in the Lockerbie terrorist attack, and later determined that the failure of Libya to cooperate and to extradite the alleged offenders was a threat to the peace and security,[47] and imposed sanctions under Article 41 in order to compel Libya to comply with a number of requests. including the surrender of suspected terrorists. With regard to the Taylor case, the Security Council moved a step further when it passed Resolution 1638 (2005), in which it determined that Taylor's "return to Liberia would constitute an impediment to stability and a threat to the peace of Liberia and to international peace and security in the region" and extended the mandate of the UN Mission in Liberia (UNMIL) to include the detention and transfer of Taylor to the SCSL in the event of his return to Liberia.

In the Al-Bashir case, the Security Council, which referred the Darfur situation to the ICC (and which up until now refuses to decide in favour of a deferral of proceedings as requested by the African Union),[48] would be entitled to follow up on that situation with a view to exercising its powers to maintain peace. The UN Security Council has a wide discretionary power in ascertaining threats to the peace under Article 39 of the UN Charter,[49] and it could well determine that the failure to cooperate with the ICC by Sudan violates Resolution 1593 and amounts to a threat to the peace and security, opening the possibility

---

[45] *See* Gaeta, *supra* note 16.

[46] On this point, see also C.C. Jalloh, *Regionalizing International Criminal Law?*, 9 INT'L CRIM. L. REV. 445, 484 (2009).

[47] S.C. Res. 731 (Jan. 21, 1992) and S.C. Res. 748 (Mar. 31, 1992).

[48] *See* C.C. Jalloh, D. Akande & M. Du Plessis, *Assessing the African Union Concerns about Article 16 of the Rome State of the International Criminal Court*, 4 AFR. J. LEGAL STUD. 5–50 (2011), in which the authors seek to articulate a clearer picture of the law and politics of deferrals within the context of the AU's repeated calls to the UN Security Council (U.N. S.C., or the Council) to invoke Article 16 to suspend the processes initiated by the ICC against President Omar Al Bashir of Sudan.

[49] *See* ICTY, Prosecutor v. Tadić, Decision on the Defense Motion for Interlocutory Appeal on Jurisdiction, para. 28, Appeals Chamber (Oct. 2, 1995).

of adopting binding measures under Chapter VII. The Security Council could then pass a resolution expressly authorizing or even imposing cooperation with the ICC on UN member states: these would be measures not involving the use of force falling under Article 41. After all the Security Council has been given by the Statute a discretionary power to refer a situation, and it would be logical that, at a later stage, it may follow up – according to the role in peace maintenance designed in Chapter VII – and monitor the situation with a view to adopting, if need be, measures to foster cooperation with the court. As has already been said, it would not be the first time that a direct link is made between the maintenance of peace and security and the prosecution of those alleged to have committed serious crimes.

In this hypothetical case as imagined for the SCSL, the ICC would come closer to the ICTY and ICTR, and the legal basis of the obligation of all UN member states to cooperate with the ICC would be a binding decision of the Security Council. Ultimately, states would be compelled to give precedence to the enforcement of the warrant and to disregard personal immunity by virtue of Article 103 of the UN Charter. This of course would be a legal but not necessarily a viable political solution available for the near future.[50]

IV. THE ARREST OF TAYLOR BY U.N. FORCES: PAVING THE ROAD TO FOLLOW?

There is also another possibility suggested by the Taylor case. Resolution 1638 mentioned in Section III and the material arrest of Taylor by the UN Forces could pave the way for a possible road to follow in the future.

With Resolution 1638 the Security Council included in the mandate of UNMIL the apprehension and detention of former president Charles Taylor, in the event of his return to Liberia. The resolution also provided for Taylor's transfer to Sierra Leone for prosecution before the SCSL, where he was facing an indictment for war crimes and crimes against humanity.[51] Taylor was already a former head of state, but a similar solution could be envisaged, *mutatis mutandis*, for a sitting head of state. Indeed, the precedent established with Taylor's arrest by UN forces could be another precious legacy left by the SCSL experience and one to be kept in mind to build up an option for the ICC.

As I have already argued elsewhere,[52] Resolution 1638 may be seen against the background of the Security Council's tendency to increasingly resort to international criminal justice as a tool to face situations threatening international peace and security where large-scale atrocities were committed. This trend began with establishment of ICTY and ICTR on the basis of reports provided by two international commissions of inquiry, which had previously been charged by the Security Council with the task of establishing whether grave international

---

[50] On the dangers of the African States perceiving the ICC as having a biased or politicized attitude only toward one single region of the world, see Jalloh, *supra* note 46.

[51] The crucial paragraph reads that the Council: "*Decides* that the mandate of the United Nations Mission in Liberia (UNMIL) shall include the following additional element: to apprehend and detain former President Charles Taylor in the event of a return to Liberia and to transfer him or facilitate his transfer to Sierra Leone for prosecution before the Special Court for Sierra Leone and to keep the Liberian Government, the Sierra Leonean Government and the Council fully informed." It is worth noting that Resolution 1638 was adopted unanimously. Only Brazil and Argentina wished to make statements in explanation of their vote, and they both underlined the importance of the Security Council's action in combating impunity.

[52] M. Frulli, *A Turning Point in International Efforts to Apprehend War Criminals: The UN Mandates Taylor's Arrest in Liberia*, 4 JICJ 351–61 (2006).

crimes had been committed in the former Yugoslavia and Rwanda.[53] The ad hoc tribunals also had a strong impact on the establishment of transitional justice mechanisms such as the SCSL. The SCSL was not directly created by the Security Council, but nonetheless it was established by means of a bilateral agreement between the United Nations and the government of Sierra Leone, which was negotiated by the Secretary-General at the explicit request of the Security Council.[54] To give a few other examples: the "Special Panels with jurisdiction over Serious Criminal Offences" within the District and the Appeal Courts in Dili were established by the UN Transitional Administration in East Timor (UNTAET),[55] created by Resolution 1272 (1999) of the Security Council; the International Commission of Inquiry on Darfur was tasked by the Security Council in 2005 with determining whether genocide and other crimes had taken place, as well as identifying the perpetrators of major international crimes committed in Darfur with a view to holding them accountable.[56] And it is precisely on the basis of the Commission's report and of its recommendations[57] that the Security Council decided, for the first time, to refer the situation to the Prosecutor of the ICC.[58] A similar pattern was then followed by the Security Council for the referral of the Libyan situation.

In the Taylor case, the Security Council took advantage of politically favorable circumstances to push for stronger cooperation with an international criminal tribunal by providing it with the means for exercising its judicial function. Thus it moved a step further in the effort to prosecute those accountable for the most serious crimes under international law. By imposing an obligation to cooperate with the SCSL on UN peacekeepers, the Security Council succeeded in skillfully solving both a diplomatic and a legal problem because it secured Taylor's arrest and transfer to the SCSL. While commending Nigeria for its efforts to bring peace and stability in Liberia and in the region,[59] the Security Council referred to

---

[53] The two international commissions of experts were respectively established on the basis of S.C. Res. 780, October 6, 1992, and of S.C. Res. 935, July 1, 2004. It is also worth mentioning S.C. Res. 1012, August 28, 2005, on the establishment of an international commission of inquiry with the mandate, inter alia: "To establish the facts relating to the assassination of the President of Burundi on October 21, 1993, the massacres and other related serious acts of violence which followed."

[54] S.C. Res. 1315 (Aug. 14, 2000).

[55] *See* UNTAET Regulation 2000/15 (June 6, 2000). There have also been a mixed tribunal for Cambodia, proposed under a national law specially promulgated in accordance with a treaty; a court within a court in the form of a Special Chamber in the State Court of Bosnia and Herzegovina; and the use of international judges and prosecutors in the courts of Kosovo, pursuant to regulations of the UN Interim Administration Mission in Kosovo (established by the Security Council).

[56] By Resolution 1564, adopted on September 18, 2004, the Security Council requested the Secretary-General to establish an international, independent commission of inquiry "to investigate violations of international humanitarian law and human rights law in Darfur by all parties, to determine also whether or not acts of genocide have occurred, and to identify the perpetrators of such violations with a view to ensuring that those responsible are held accountable" (§ 12).

[57] *See* Report of the International Commission of Inquiry on Darfur to the Secretary General Pursuant to S.C. Res. 1564, Annex to Letter dated Jan. 31, 2005 from the Secretary-General addressed to the President of the Security Council, §§ 489–522, U.N. Doc. S/2005/60 (Feb. 1, 2005).

[58] S.C. Res. 1593 (Mar. 31, 2005). For a series of critical comments on the creation of the Commission and on its Report, see the *Symposium* published on 3 JICJ 539 *ff* (2005).

[59] The Nigerian president reportedly announced to be ready to surrender Taylor at the request of a regularly elected Liberian government, and it is worth noting that the Security Council seems to acknowledge this possibility in the preamble of the resolution.

the *temporary stay* of Taylor in that country.[60] Neither Nigeria nor Liberia found themselves in the potentially difficult position of having to surrender Taylor to the SCSL.

If such a solution was legally feasible to secure Taylor's arrest, why should it not be possible to foster cooperation with the ICC for the enforcement of the Al-Bashir arrest warrant?

For political reasons, this avenue is not likely to be taken in the near future. There is a high degree of controversy surrounding the case, and it is very unlikely that the Security Council may find an agreement to expand the mandate of the peacekeeping operation currently stationed in Darfur without transforming it into a coercive operation, not relying anymore on the consent of the host state. In the case of UNMIL, which eventually took Taylor in custody and transferred him to the SCSL in Freetown, the extension of the mandate of the peacekeeping force was approved by the new Liberian government, and UNMIL maintained a consensual basis and could rely on cooperation with the host state authorities.

There is a precedent in which the Security Council authorized a peacekeeping force to arrest suspected war criminals – who were not even indicted by any tribunal – without relying on the consent of the host state and of the other parties involved. UNOSOM II, which was established and deployed in Somalia in 1993[61] (and which was a peace-enforcement operation from its inception) was authorized, under Resolution 837, to take all necessary measures against those responsible for serious armed attacks against peacekeepers and for publicly inciting their commission,[62] "including [to secure] the investigation of their actions their arrest and detention for prosecution, trial and punishment."[63] Unfortunately however, UNOSOM II ended up in failure. After the adoption of Resolution 837, UN peacekeepers engaged a military offensive against Somali militia positions. UN troops opened fire, notwithstanding the fact that Somali militia used human shields: there were several civilian victims, including women and children. The situation grew out of control, and it became evident that UNOSOM II could not fulfill its ambitious mandate. On February 4, 1994, the Security Council revised UNOSOM II's mandate to exclude the use of coercive methods.[64] The most-wanted Somali was the war lord, General Aidid, who was never arrested, let alone brought to trial. Needless to say this is an example not to be followed: the lack of consent and cooperation rendered the mandate to arrest war criminals not only unattainable, but also dangerous to fulfill.

In the case of the UN Assistance Mission in Darfur (UNAMID)[65] in Sudan – besides the fact that its current mandate includes the task "to assist in promoting the rule of law, including through institution-building, and strengthening local capacities to combat impunity"; and "to ensure an adequate human rights and gender presence capacity, and expertise in Darfur in order to contribute to efforts to protect and promote human rights in Darfur,

---

[60] The preamble reads: "*Expressing* its appreciation to Nigeria and its President, Olusegun Obasanjo, for their contributions to restoring stability in Liberia and the West African subregion, and acknowledging that Nigeria acted with broad international support when it decided to provide for the temporary stay of former President Charles Taylor in Nigeria."

[61] UNOSOM II (Second United Nations Operation in Somalia) was established by S.C. Res. 814, Mar. 26, 1993.

[62] In a series of armed attacks against UNOSOM II troops throughout south Mogadishu by Somali militia apparently belonging to General Aidid's faction, twenty-five Pakistani soldiers were killed, ten were reported missing, and fifty-four wounded, in total disregard of any rule of international humanitarian law.

[63] S.C. Res. 837, § 5 (June 6, 1993).

[64] S.C. Res. 897 (Feb. 4, 2004).

[65] Established with S.C. Res. 1769 (July 31, 2007).

with particular attention to vulnerable groups"[66] – it does seem likely that the government may agree on an extension of the mandate to include the enforcement of the arrest warrant against Al-Bashir.[67] It must also be recalled that UNAMID is a hybrid UN-AU operation, and that the AU has repeatedly affirmed that AU member states shall not enforce the arrest warrant against Al-Bashir. This solution envisaged for Taylor's arrest – albeit unlikely to be realized in the nearest future for the ICC – should not be completely set aside.

Ultimately, I would argue that this is an important contribution of practice that emerged with respect to the SCSL that will be of potential benefit for the international community in future cases involving sitting heads of state. One could imagine, for instance, that a peace-keeping force deployed in a state other than Sudan (most likely a state party to the Statute, for instance a state that has already made clear that it could enforce the warrant, such as Kenya[68]) could be tasked to arrest Al-Bashir. In case he travels to that country, the Security Council could authorize such a force, with the agreement of the host state, to enforce the warrant without taking into account the Sudanese president's personal immunity. The lack of cooperation by Sudan and the free traveling of an indicted senior state official could be equated with a threat to the peace and pave the way for an authorization to peacekeepers to arrest him. Such an authorization would avoid state parties finding themselves having to choose between conflicting obligations, and at least Al-Bashir's freedom of movement would be seriously undermined.

---

[66] UNAMID has the protection of civilians as its core mandate, but is also tasked with contributing to security for humanitarian assistance, monitoring and verifying implementation of agreements, assisting an inclusive political process, contributing to the promotion of human rights and the rule of law, and monitoring and reporting on the situation along the borders with Chad and the Central African Republic.

[67] In its most recent resolution 2003 of July 29, 2011, the Security Council underlined the need for UNAMID to make full use of its capabilities and prioritize the protection of civilians and safe, timely and unhindered humanitarian access; and to complement efforts to promote the peace as well as the political process negoti-ated in Doha, Qatar. It demanded that all parties to the conflict, including all armed movements, immediately end the violence and make every effort to reach a permanent ceasefire and a comprehensive settlement under the Doha Document.

[68] Following the failure of the Kenyan government to arrest President Al-Bashir when he visited the country for the promulgation ceremony of Kenya's new constitution in 2010, the Kenya Chapter of the International Commission of Jurists filed an application for a provisional arrest warrant to be issued against Al-Bashir the next time he sets foot in the country. Kenya's High Court ruled in November 2011 that President Omar Al-Bashir be arrested if he sets foot in the nation. The Kenyan government however said the warrant issued by the High Court is unenforceable, and filed an appeal seeking to overturn the ruling.

17

Unpunished Crimes: The Special Court for Sierra Leone and Children

Cecile Aptel[*]

When you are there, you would have no way of escaping because if you were caught attempting to escape, they would kill you. Or if you risk it and you escape, if you landed in the hands of a Kamajor and they find that you are from a rebel zone, then they would kill you and eat up your flesh.

-Testimony of a child formerly associated with the Revolutionary United
Front, Special Court for Sierra Leone.[1]

I. INTRODUCTION

The Special Court for Sierra Leone (SCSL or "Court") is well-known and lauded for its important contribution to the recognition and clarification of the international crime of "child soldiering."[2] As the very first international or hybrid court to have tried and convicted individuals for recruiting or using children in hostilities, it has been praised for paying attention to the crimes endured by these children and for bringing them to the public attention.

This chapter critically reviews the groundbreaking findings of the SCSL pertaining to the recruitment and use of children. The Court was the first international or internationalized court to acknowledge this "child-specific offence," the victims of which are exclusively children.[3] The chapter traces how this offence came under the jurisdiction of the SCSL, and analyzes the customary nature of this crime, revisiting the Court's important 2004 interlocutory appeal on this issue. It contends that the definition by the SCSL of the term "use to participate actively in hostilities," probably influenced by a human-rights and child-right approach, provided too broad an understanding of which activities are deemed to qualify as "use to participate actively in hostilities." The approach had an influence on the recent Lubanga trial judgment rendered by the International Criminal Court (ICC). This chapter argues that rather than adopting a broad understanding of the terms, justice would have

---

[*] Associate Professor of International Law, the Fletcher School of Law and Diplomacy, Tufts University. I am grateful to Mark Drumbl and Charles Jalloh for their thoughtful comments, and thank Suparva Narasimhaiah and Sarah Marie Miano for their outstanding research assistance.

[1] Testimony of TF1–314, RUF Trial Transcript, Trial Chamber I, TF1–314, at 43 (Nov. 2, 2005).

[2] In this chapter, the terms "child soldier" and "child associated with armed forces or armed groups" are used interchangeably. The use of these terms is not meant to confer any legitimacy on these appalling crimes.

[3] The distinction between "child-specific offences" as distinct from other "generic" offenses is useful to qualify the specificity of the former crimes. *See* Cecile Aptel, *International Criminal Justice and Child Protection, in* CHILDREN AND TRANSITIONAL JUSTICE: TRUTH TELLING, ACCOUNTABILITY AND RECONCILIATION 67–114 (Sharanjeet Parmar, Mindy Jane Roseman, Saudamini Siegrist & Theo Sowa eds., 2010).

been better served had the prosecutors and judges considered not only the crime of recruitment and use of child soldiers in hostilities, but also the other crimes committed against these children, such as enslavement, torture, sexual slavery, and rape, which are equally important and deserving of punishment and remedy for the victims.

The chapter also analyzes the challenging mandate given to the SCSL to prosecute juveniles through Article 7 of its Statute.[4] It assesses the prosecutorial decision not to exercise this part of the mandate vis-à-vis the compelling circumstances that led to the inclusion of Article 7 in the Statute. It finds that the decision of the Prosecutor of the SCSL to focus on those responsible for recruitment, instead of investigating juveniles, was well-founded in a context of very limited resources, where only a few cases could actually be put forward. It nevertheless questions the missed opportunity to make the young offenders of Sierra Leone acknowledge their crimes, notably as a way to facilitate their reintegration.

Although acknowledging the achievements of the SCSL in the recognition of some crimes against children, this chapter submits that the Court has made only a limited contribution in documenting the many other international crimes endured by the children in Sierra Leone.[5] It contends that the SCSL has concentrated its focus on the "child-specific" offenses of "child-soldiering," and to a lesser extent on the girl-victims of rape, sexual violence, sexual slavery, and so-called forced marriages. The focus on these two highly visible categories of crimes and their victims appears to have been made to the detriment of other crimes against children. Indeed, the SCSL has been less diligent in prosecuting "generic" crimes[6]: those in which the children of Sierra Leone were victimized alongside adults, such as maiming and killing. These latter undocumented and unpunished crimes, and the untold stories of the tens of thousands of child-survivors of atrocities, sometimes handicapped for life, are yet to be acknowledged.

II. CONSCRIPTING OR ENLISTING CHILDREN UNDER THE AGE OF 15 YEARS INTO ARMED FORCES OR GROUPS OR USING THEM TO PARTICIPATE ACTIVELY IN HOSTILITIES AS A WAR CRIME

Well, the children who were captured, they started giving them training, and myself up and my companions called them SBUs [Small Boys' Unit].[7]

A. The Inclusion of the Crime in the Jurisdiction of the SCSL

As a result of the widespread recruitment and use of children, estimated to include 10,000–15,000 children, by most, if not all, armed groups and forces in Sierra Leone, and at the insistence of a large caucus of child rights advocates,[8] the drafters of the Statute included in

---

[4] ICTR Statute, Article 7 is titled "Jurisdiction over persons of 15 years of age." See Section 3 of this chapter.

[5] This chapter does not review the modalities of the participation of children in proceedings before the Court, or the broader interaction of the Court with children, for instance as part of its outreach efforts toward children.

[6] Aptel, *supra* note 3.

[7] Testimony of TF1–334, AFRC Trial Transcript, Trial Chamber II, TF1–334, at 6 (May 20, 2005).

[8] Ilene Cohn, *The Protection of Children and the Quest for Truth and Justice in Sierra Leone*, 55 No. 1 J. INT'L AFF. 1–34, 19 (Fall 2001).

its material jurisdiction, under Article 4(c), qualified as a serious violation of international humanitarian law, or a war crime, the "[c]onscripting or enlisting children under the age of 15 years into armed forces or groups or using them to participate actively in hostilities" (the crime of "recruitment and use").

Rather than adopting the language of Article 8 of the ICC Statute, out of concern that it had possibly gone beyond codified international law,[9] the initial formulation of the SCSL Statute instead referred to: "abduction and forced recruitment of children under the age of 15 years into armed forces or groups for the purpose of using them to participate actively in hostilities."[10] This formulation was fiercely contested by a number of states and entities, notably those supportive of the ICC, and the provision was subsequently amended to reflect the ICC Statute.[11]

B. Early Focus on Those Responsible

Although these crimes had been introduced in the ICC Statute before the SCSL Statute, it is in fact the SCSL that first prosecuted for them. In 2003, the first Prosecutor, David Crane, declared that "[t]wo of the most egregious uses of children are sexual slavery and conscription of children into armed conflicts. Sierra Leone's conflict was characterized by both, and we hope to establish a strong precedent that these abuses must end."[12] Crane proceeded to charge thirteen individuals with the crime of recruitment and use, in addition to other charges.[13]

C. The Customary Nature of the Crime

In one of the first appeals before the SCSL, Sam Hinga Norman filed an interlocutory appeal contesting the validity of the charges and the jurisdiction of the SCSL.[14] He argued that the Court lacked jurisdiction over him because the crime did not form part of international customary law, and was in violation of the principle of legality, in particular the rules against nonretroactivity and specificity.[15]

---

[9] Report of the Secretary-General on the Establishment of a Special Court for Sierra Leone, U.N. Doc. S/2000/915, Oct. 4, 2000, para. 18, at 4 [hereinafter *Report of the Secretary-General*].

[10] Cohn, *supra* note 8, at 20. *See also* Separate and Dissenting Opinion of Justice Robertson, Decision on Preliminary Motion Based on Lack of Jurisdiction (Child Recruitment), Prosecutor v. Sam Hinga Norman (SCSL-2004–14-AR 72(E)), SCSL Appeals Chamber, para. 4 (Oct. 4, 2000) [hereinafter Justice Robertson Dissenting Opinion].

[11] Cohn, *supra* note 8.

[12] Press Release, SCSL, Honouring the Inaugural World Day against Child Labour (June 12, 2003), *available at* http://www.sc-sl.org/LinkClick.aspx?fileticket=YWu2kyIoImM%3D&tabid=196 (last visited Mar. 30, 2012).

[13] Indicted on March 7, 2003 (Brima, Koroma, Norman, Sankoh, Bockarie, Sesay, Kallon, and Taylor), Mar. 28, 2003 (Kamara), Apr. 16, 2003 (Gbao), June 26, 2003 (Fofana and Kondewa) and Sept. 16, 2003 (Kanu).

[14] Decision on Preliminary Motion Based on Lack of Jurisdiction (Child Recruitment), Sam Hinga Norman (SCSL-2004–14-AR 72(E)), SCSL Appeals Chamber, paras. 1 & 3 (May 31, 2004) [hereinafter Norman case].

[15] *Id.* at para. 1. Additionally, Norman had sought a clarification that if the court were to hold the recruitment of child soldiers had indeed been codified into customary international law, then when and at what point of time had the crystallization taken place?

In May 2004, the SCSL Appeals Chamber issued one of its most cited rulings, declaring, in a majority decision, that the prohibition on unlawful recruitment and use of children under the age of fifteen had crystallized into a norm of customary international law between 1994 and November 1996, with both the element of state practice and *opinio juris* fulfilled.[16] It further declared that the crime attracted individual criminal responsibility at least from November 1996 onward.[17] However, in a dissenting opinion, Judge Robertson found no common state practice of explicitly criminalizing non-forcible enlistment prior to the adoption of the ICC Statute.[18] He indicated that the enlistment of child-volunteers to perform noncombatant tasks, away from the battlefield, in particular, was not criminalized.[19]

The customary nature of the prohibition to recruit and use children to participate in hostilities had certainly crystallized by 1996, and more likely earlier: shortly after the adoption of the two Additional Protocols to the Geneva Convention in 1977. But there is a major leap from prohibition to criminalization, and the customary nature of the former does not necessarily imply or even lead to the customary nature of the latter. Yet, the jump from prohibition to criminalization of the recruitment and use of children under fifteen by both armed groups and armed forces did not apparently create any disagreement when the Statute of the ICC was negotiated.[20]

Since the 2004 ruling of the SCSL Appeals Chamber, the criminalization of the conscription, enlistment, and use to participate in hostilities of those children under fifteen has certainly gained further recognition. The use of children under fifteen in various non-international armed conflicts has been repeatedly and vigorously condemned by the international community, including by the UN Security Council.[21] In retrospect, it would be appropriate to conclude that the 2004 SCSL interlocutory appeals in fact, through its finding of the customary nature of the *criminalization* of the conscription, enlistment, and use of children to participate actively in hostilities contributed to the further entrenchment of this customary norm.

D. Convictions and Precedent

Having clarified the legality of the charge of recruitment and use of children, the trials proceeded, resulting in the very first convictions for this crime in 2007. Three leaders of the Armed Forces Revolutionary Council (AFRC) were found guilty of conscripting children

---

[16] Norman case, *supra* note 14, at paras. 52–53.

[17] *Id.* at para. 32.

[18] *Id.* at paras. 48–50. He noted that Norman had initially been indicted for conscripting or enlisting children, but that the conscription had been dropped. *See also* Justice Robertson Dissenting Opinion, *supra* note 10; Noah B. Novogrodsky, *Litigating Child Recruitment before the Special Court for Sierra Leone,* 7 San Diego Int'l L.J. 421–59, 422–25 (2005–2006).

[19] Justice Robertson Dissenting Opinion, *supra* note 10, at para. 9.

[20] *See* Jean-Marie Henckaerts & Louise Doswald-Beck, 1 Customary International Humanitarian Law 584: Rules, ch. 44: Rule 156(ii) – Other Serious Violations of International Humanitarian Law Committed during an International Armed Conflict (continued) (reprint 2005 ed., 2009).

[21] *See, e.g.,* U.N. S.C. Res. 1071, para. 9 (Aug. 30, 1996); U.N. S.C. Res. 1083, para. 6 (Nov. 27, 1996); U.N. S.C. Res. 1261, para. 2 (Aug. 25, 1999); U.N. S.C. Res. 1314 (Aug. 11, 2000); U.N. S.C. Res. 1379 (Nov. 20, 2001); U.N. S.C. Res. 1460 (Jan. 30, 2003); U.N. S.C. Res. 1539 (Apr. 22, 2004); U.N. S.C. Res. 1612 (July 26, 2005); U.N. S.C. Res. 1882 (Aug. 4, 2009); U.N. S.C. Res. 1998 (July 12, 2011).

under the age of fifteen into armed groups and forces, or using them to participate actively in hostilities and other serious violations of International Humanitarian Law (IHL), pursuant to Article 4(c) of the Statute.[22] The three men were convicted for conscripting, enlisting, and/or using boys and girls under the age of fifteen to participate in active hostilities. It was notably found that children were most often abducted and then enlisted into the armed forces,[23] and routinely abducted and recruited for military purposes by the AFRC fighting forces[24] during the AFRC government period.

This judgment was swiftly followed by another conviction for the same crime, this time of the Civil Defense Forces (CDF) leadership.[25] One of the prominent members of the CDF leadership was convicted by the Trial Chambers for enlisting children under the age of fifteen into an armed force or group, while the other was acquitted. [26] However, on appeal, the conviction was also overturned. [27] In the CDF case, the discussion on the issue of crimes against child soldiers had been limited to the question of initiation of just one child soldier.

Subsequently in 2009, in the Revolutionary United Front (RUF) case, two of the most prominent RUF leaders viz. Issa Hassan Sesay and Morris Kallon, were convicted of the offense of conscription and use of children under fifteen years to actively participate in hostilities.[28] Only the third leader, Augustine Gbao, who was also indicted and prosecuted for this offense, was acquitted.[29]

Most recently, on April 26, 2012, the SCSL also convicted another individual for this crime, Charles Taylor, the former Liberian president, on grounds of conscripting and enlisting children under the age of fifteen into armed groups and using them to participate actively in the hostilities.[30] The appeals are pending.

Crane rightly predicted that the jurisprudence of the SCSL would "certainly assist in the advancement of jurisprudence in the area of child recruitment," and that future international tribunals would "look upon the groundbreaking work of the Special Court for Sierra Leone as a cornerstone."[31] In the first-ever ICC judgment, the case of Thomas Lubanga Dyilo ("Lubanga") proceeded solely on three counts of war crimes for enlisting and conscripting

---

[22] Judgment, Brima, Kamara and Kanu (AFRC) (SCSL-04-16-T), Trial Chamber II (June 20, 2007 [hereinafter AFRC case]; Judgment, Brima, Kamara and Kanu (AFRC) (SCSL-2004-16-A), Appeals Chamber (Feb. 22, 2008) [hereinafter AFRC case – Appeals]. A fourth Accused, John Paul Koroma, was never arrested, and was presumed dead in 2003.

[23] AFRC case, *supra* note 22, at paras. 1244–76.

[24] *Id.* at paras. 1276–1277.

[25] Judgment, Fofana and Kondewa (CDF) (SCSL-04-14-T), Trial Chamber I (Aug. 2, 2007) [hereinafter CDF case].

[26] Judgment, Fofana and Kondewa (CDF) (SCSL-04-14-A), Appeals Chamber (May 28, 2008) [hereinafter CDF case – Appeals].

[27] *Id.* at paras. 142–145.

[28] Judgment, Sesay, Kallon and Gbao (RUF) (SCSL-04-15-T), Trial Chamber – I, paras. 2223–2234 (Feb. 25, 2009) [hereinafter RUF case].

[29] *Id.* at paras. 2235–2237.

[30] Judgment, Charles Ghankay Taylor (SCSL-03-01-T), Trial Chamber – II (Apr. 26, 2012) [hereinafter Charles Taylor case].

[31] David Crane, *Strike Terror No More: Prosecuting the Use of Children in Times of Conflict – The West African Extreme, in* INTERNATIONAL CRIMINAL ACCOUNTABILITY AND THE RIGHTS OF CHILDREN 131 (K. Arts & V. Popovski eds., 2006).

children under the age of fifteen in the Democratic Republic of the Congo and using them to participate actively in hostilities.[32] The ICC noted:

> The jurisprudence of the SCSL has been considered by the Trial Chamber. Although the decisions of other international courts and tribunals are not part of the directly applicable law under Article 21 of the Statute, the wording of the provision criminalizing the conscription, enlistment and use of children under the age of 15 within the Statute of the SCSL is identical to Article 8(e) (vii) of the Rome Statute, and they were self-evidently directed at the same objective. The SCSL's case law therefore potentially assists in the interpretation of the relevant provisions of the Rome Statute.[33]

E. Use of Children to Participate Actively in Hostilities

It would be beyond the scope of this chapter to review extensively the jurisprudence of the SCSL on Article 4(c) of its Statute, which has in any case been already extensively reviewed.[34] Analysis, for instance on the important distinction between conscription and enlistment, can be found elsewhere.[35] Against this background, the following focuses on a single aspect of the SCSL case law, the "use to participate actively in hostilities," under Article 4(c), because it is particularly problematic, yet insufficiently analyzed at this stage.[36]

The expression "use to participate actively in hostilities" is historically related to the better-known concept of "direct participation in hostilities," familiar to international humanitarian lawyers and other specialists of the law of armed conflict. Article 77(2) of Additional Protocol I to the Geneva Conventions stipulates:

> "The parties to the conflict shall take all feasible measures in order that children who have not attained the age of fifteen years do not take a *direct* part in hostilities [...]" (emphasis added), and Article 4(3) (c) of Additional Protocol II that: "children who have not attained the age of fifteen years shall [not be] allowed to take part in hostilities."

This international humanitarian legal taxonomy was incorporated in the subsequent 1989 Convention on the Rights of the Child, its Article 38(2) requesting state parties to "take all feasible measures to ensure that persons who have not attained the age of fifteen years do not take a *direct* part in hostilities" (emphasis added).

The historical root of the expression "use to participate actively in hostilities" in the body of international humanitarian law is important because it refers to the fundamental principle of distinction, and to the protection of civilians during armed conflict. Civilians should never be targeted, and only those who "directly participate in hostilities" lose their

---

[32] Judgment, Thomas Lubanga Dyilo (Situation in Democratic Republic of the Congo) (ICC-01/04–01/06), Trial Chamber I (Lubanga case) (Mar. 14, 2012). The convicted was tried for the crimes committed from July 1, 2002 to December 31, 2003: enlisting or conscripting children into the FPLC (the military wing of the Union des Patriotes Congolais) and using these children to participate actively in hostilities.

[33] *Id.* at para. 603.

[34] *See notably* Sandesh Sivakumaran, *War Crimes before the Special Court for Sierra Leone: Child Soldiers, Hostages, Peacekeepers and Collective Punishments*, 8 J. Int'l Crim. Justice 1009–34 (2010); Novogrodsky, *supra* note 18; and Alison Smith, *Child Recruitment and the SCSL*, 2 J. Int'l Crim. Justice 1141–53 (2004).

[35] *See* Aptel, *supra* note 3, at 77 *et seq.*

[36] In this regard, it is important to note that the SCSL and several observers have pondered whether there are in fact two or possibly three different crimes subsumed under "conscripting or enlisting children or using them to participate actively in hostilities." *See, e.g.,* Aptel, *supra* note 3, at 79.

protection and become legitimate targets for such time as they directly participate in hostilities.[37] The origin of the prohibition for children under fifteen years "to take a direct part in hostilities" is obviously directly connected with the principle of distinction: children should not take a direct part in hostilities because they otherwise become a legitimate target during the conflict, and can be killed by other combatants. This is the essence of the prohibition and criminalization of "recruiting and using children": to hold accountable those responsible for putting the lives of children in danger and exposing them to great risks.

Whether children are victims of a war crime because they were recruited or because they were used is irrelevant at this point: these children become legitimate targets when – but only when – they directly participate in hostilities. From this perspective, children are best protected when a very narrow, restrictive understanding of who "directly participate[s] in hostilities" or is "used to participate actively in hostilities" is adopted, so that children cannot be construed as legitimate targets.

Such legal understanding was captured in the earlier formulation of what became Article 4(c) of the SCSL, when it mentioned the "transformation of the child into, and its use as, among other degrading uses, as a 'child-combatant.'"[38] The term "child-combatant" again directly referred to the taxonomy of international humanitarian law. But the inclusion of the phrase "other degrading uses" indicated a paradigmatic shift because it referred to the terminology of international human rights law.

Indeed, with the development of child-rights and of their corollaries, child protection agencies, a different logic began to inform the understanding of the category "use to participate actively in hostilities." This approach aspired to broaden the category as much as possible so as to embrace all the children associated with armed forces and groups, notably the girls, who were often exploited, but less frequently carried weapons or participated directly in hostilities. Because they were previously overlooked as part of this category, girls, as well as younger boys who were used, for example, as cooks, were denied access to ill-conceived disarmament, demobilization, and reintegration programs, which focused on disarmament, and therefore on those children who had once been equipped with a weapon.

It is this human-rights and child-rights logic that led Graça Machel, in her pivotal report on the impact of armed conflict on children, to define "child soldier" as "any child – boy or girl – under the age of 18, who is compulsorily, forcibly or voluntarily recruited or used in hostilities by armed forces, paramilitaries, civil defense units or other armed groups. Child soldiers are used for forced sexual services, as combatants, messengers, porters and cooks."[39]

This logic also inspired the formulation of the Paris Principles, which state that "children associated with armed forces or groups" do not refer only to those who are taking or have taken a direct part in hostilities. The Paris Principles and Guidelines on Children Associated with Armed Forces or Armed Groups defines "child associated with an armed force or group" as: any person below the age of 18 who is or has been recruited or used by an armed force or armed group in any capacity, including children, both boys and girls, as

---

[37] On the concept of direct participation in hostilities, see Nils Melzer, *Interpretive Guidance on the Notion of Direct Participation in Hostilities under International Humanitarian Law*, ICRC (May 2009).

[38] *Report of the Secretary-General, supra* note 9, at para. 18.

[39] Graça Machel, The Impact of War on Children: A Review of Progress since the 1996 United Nations Report on the Impact of Armed Conflict on Children 7 (2001).

fighters, cooks, porters, messengers or spies, or for sexual purposes. In fact, the definition in the Paris Principles explicitly underlines that children associated with armed forces or groups are not only those who are taking or have taken a direct part in hostilities.[40]

Against this background, concomitantly with the elaboration of the Paris Principles and Guidelines, the SCSL defined the terms "use to participate actively," finding that "[u]sing children to 'participate actively in the hostilities' encompasses putting their lives directly at risk in combat" and that "[a]ny labour or support that gives effect to, or helps maintain, operations in a conflict constitutes active participation."[41] Broadening active participation to mean more than just participating in hostilities also considerably expanded the category of victims of this crime.

This aspect of the SCSL jurisprudence has largely influenced the subsequent case law at the ICC, in the Lubanga case. The Pre-Trial Chamber in this matter noted the evolution of the terminology, observing that the phrase "participate actively in hostilities," found in the ICC Statute, was broader and therefore more encompassing than the language "take a direct part in hostilities" used in other international legal instruments.[42] The ICC Trial judges disagreed on the sensitive question of the definition of "use to participate actively in hostilities," leading to a separate and dissenting opinion by Judge Odio-Benito, who argued for the inclusion of "[...] sexual violence within the legal concept of 'use to participate actively in the hostilities'" (para. 17) and found that: "[...] Sexual violence is an intrinsic element of the criminal conduct of 'use to participate actively in the hostilities.'[...]"[43]

Judge Odio-Benito's findings appeared to have been directly inspired by the submission and expert testimony of the UN Special Representative of the Secretary General for Children in Armed Conflict, who, in her submissions to the ICC, warned the Court against attempting to determine specific activities qualifying under the term "participate actively," which would risk excluding a great number of child soldiers, particularly girls. She recommended that the ICC adopt a case-by-case approach, relying on the appreciation of "whether the child's participation served an essential support function to the armed force or armed group during the period of conflict."[44] She asked that the ICC consider all children, including girls, as child-soldiers, regardless of whether they engaged in direct combat functions during conflict.[45] She further advocated for a broadening of the reach of who is deemed to "participate actively in hostilities" to "deliberately include any sexual acts perpetrated, in particular

---

[40] The Paris Principles: The Principles and Guidelines on Children Associated with Armed Forces or Armed Groups (The Paris Principles), para. 2.1 (Feb. 2007).

[41] AFRC case, *supra* note 22, at paras. 736–737.

[42] Decision on the Confirmation of Charges, Thomas Lubanga Dyilo (Situation in Democratic Republic of the Congo) (ICC-01/04–01/06), Pre-Trial Chamber I, para. 261 (Jan. 29, 2007).

[43] Separate opinion by Judge Odio-Benito, Lubanga case, *supra* note 32, para. 20.

[44] Annex A, Amicus curiae brief of the United Nations Special Representative of the Secretary-General on Children and Armed Conflict, Thomas Lubanga Dyilo (ICC-01/04–01/06–1229-AnxA), para. 22 (Mar. 18, 2008).

[45] Official Court Transcripts, Thomas Lubanga Dyilo (ICC-01/04–01/06-T-223-ENG), 15–16 (Jan. 7, 2010). The SRSG was appearing before the ICC as an expert witness in the case. She declared: when girl children are abducted or enlisted or enrolled, even as sexual slaves, that it be regarded as enlistment or conscription from the day they entered the camp, because they play – they will play multiple roles in those camps. [...] it would just be impossible [to determine] on these days she is a combatant and on these days she is a domestic aid [...]. *Id.* at 36.

against girls, within its understanding of the 'using' crime," underscoring that the "use" of girls in armed conflict includes sexual violence.[46]

The dilemma faced when defining "use to participate actively in hostilities' highlights the difficulty of balancing the victims' right to be protected, which often demands a progressive and more encompassing construction of the law, with the rights of the defendants and the principle of legality, a fundamental principle that calls for the law to be specific and clear, and not to apply retroactively. In these circumstances, so as to criminalize the full extent of reprehensible conduct and render justice to all child victims while respecting the fundamental rights of the defendants, I argue that prosecutors and judges should refrain from unduly broadening an offense, and should rather use their entire legal arsenal to charge those responsible not only – or not necessarily – for the recruitment and use of child soldiers, but also for the other crimes committed against the child-victims, such as enslavement, torture, sexual slavery, and rape, which are equally important and separately criminalized.

Is subsuming sexual crimes under the category of "the use to participate actively in hostilities" the optimal solution to highlight the plight of the children victims of these crimes? Is this the best manner to demonstrate the tragic and long-lasting suffering caused to the victims of sexual violence, rape, sexual slavery, and forced pregnancies, too often suffered by the girls associated with armed groups? As all and each of these crimes constitute separate offenses, duly recognized and criminalized, I argue that they are worthy of separate consideration, as a way to fully acknowledge their existence and the particular harm suffered by the victims, *in addition to* the harm caused by their recruitment or use by armed groups/forces and it is not clear why this was not done.

It seems that this possibility of cumulative charges was not sufficiently exploited at the SCSL, and that this same approach was unfortunately replicated and even aggravated at the ICC, limiting the visibility given to the totality of the suffering experienced by the girls and boys associated with armed forces and groups, in all of its forms.

III. JUVENILE OFFENDERS

Well, these children who stayed with the various commanders, when it came to amputation, these children were used to amputate people in Kono.
Witness TF1–334.[47]

A. *The Inclusion of Juvenile Offenders in the Mandate*

From the inception of the talks between the United Nations and the government of Sierra Leone, a contentious issue was the alleged criminal responsibility of juveniles, notably those recruited by armed groups and armed forces. Opposing views emerged, with some insisting on accountability for the crimes committed by those under eighteen and others opposed to the prosecution of children. Among those insisting on accountability and refusing to exclude children from the jurisdiction of the SCSL were the government and representatives of Sierra Leone civil society.[48]

---

[46] *Id.* at para. 25.

[47] Testimony of Witness TF1–334, AFRC Trial Transcript, Trial Chamber II, TF1–334, at 6 (May 20, 2005).

[48] *Report of the Secretary-General, supra* note 9, para. 36, at 7.

This led the UN Secretary-General, in his report on the establishment of the Court, to recognize that "[t]he possible prosecution of children for crimes against humanity and war crimes presents a difficult moral dilemma."[49] Indeed, many in Sierra Leone, especially the victims, believed that the children who committed grave crimes should fall within the mandate of the Court.[50] The demands for justice were rife, and many victims of the gruesome crimes in which children participated did not look kindly upon clemency based on the proclaimed "innocence" of their tormentors. Some of the children associated with the armed groups had participated in terrible atrocities. Mariatu Kamara, the Sierra Leonean author, describes how, as a child, she became a double amputee at the hands of other children:

> Two boys steadied me as my body began to sway. As the machete came down, things went silent. I closed my eyes tightly, but then they popped open and I saw everything. It took the boy two attempts to cut off my right hand. The first swipe didn't get through the bones, which I saw sticking out in all different shapes and sizes.[51]

Even within the United Nations there were different views. On the one hand, UNICEF was strongly opposed to children being subjected to criminal prosecutions. On the other hand, the UN Special Representative for Children and Armed Conflict had commented positively on the possibility of the SCSL prosecuting children aged fifteen to eighteen.[52]

The UN Special Representative, Olara Otunnu, on the basis of his own upbringing in Uganda, had firsthand experience of the impact of crimes committed by children on themselves and on their communities.[53] He insisted upon the provision of legal and other assistance and the ordering of protective measures to ensure the privacy of the juveniles within the proceedings. The penalty of imprisonment was sought to be excluded in the case of a juvenile offender, and a number of alternative options of correctional or educational nature were suggested instead.[54] The provisions aimed to respect the best interests of the child, and prioritize the rehabilitation, recovery, and reintegration of the juvenile offenders, in conformity with the CRC.[55] The UN Special Representative recommended the creation within the SCSL of a juvenile chamber overseen by a judge with juvenile justice expertise, and the supervision of the implementation of sentences. Human rights and child protection organizations disagreed on the proposal. Some of these organizations, notably Human Rights Watch, argued that juvenile justice should be handled by the national courts, and possibly the Truth Commission of Sierra Leone, and not by the SCSL.[56] Other organizations, such as the International League for Human Rights and Amnesty International, supported the prosecution of juveniles, insofar as it conformed to international guidelines and standards.[57] Ultimately, the proposal of the UN Special Representative was endorsed by the

---

[49] *Id.* at para. 32.
[50] Diane Marie Amann, *Calling Children to Account: The Proposal for a Juvenile Chamber in the Special Court for Sierra Leone,* 29 Pepp. L. Rev. 167, at 174 (2001), *available at* http://digitalcommons.law.uga.edu/fac_artchop/660 (last viewed on Apr. 15, 2012).
[51] Mariatu Kamara with Susan McClelland, The Bite of the Mango 40–41 (2008).
[52] Cohn, *supra* note 8.
[53] Interview with the author (Mar. 2012).
[54] *Report of the Secretary-General, supra* note 9, para. 37, at 8.
[55] Convention of the Rights of the Child (1989), arts. 39 and 40.
[56] *See* Cohn, *supra* note 8, at 10.
[57] *Id.* at 6.

UN Secretary-General, who proposed the inclusion of Article 7 in the Statute of the SCSL, thereby granting jurisdiction to the Court to handle proceedings for crimes committed by those between fifteen and eighteen.[58]

Peculiarly, while proposing the inclusion of Article 7 in the Statute, the Secretary-General declared that "ultimately, it will be for the Prosecutor to decide if, all things considered, action should be taken against a juvenile offender in any individual case."[59] The President of the UN Security Council also apparently declared that the provisions on juvenile trials were mere guidelines for the prosecutor of the SCSL, who would ultimately decide whether or not to prosecute a juvenile.[60]

B. *The Use of Prosecutorial Discretion against the Prosecution of Juvenile Offenders: A Missed Opportunity?*

Mindful of these statements emanating from the highest UN authorities, as well as of the debates that had surrounded the inclusion of juvenile offenders in the mandate of the SCSL, the first Prosecutor, David Crane, decided early in his tenure that he would not indict children.[61] In 2002, he publicly declared that, instead, he would prosecute those "who forced thousands of children to commit unspeakable crimes."[62]

His argument was based on the postulation that children were not among those most responsible for the crimes committed in Sierra Leone, that they had not risen very high through the ranks, and therefore were not among those "who bear the greatest responsibility for the commission of the crimes," the envisaged focus of the SCSL.[63] Based as it was on an understanding of what constitutes "the greatest responsibility," which is inherently subjective and value-driven, and has led to many controversies at the SCSL,[64] this decision was nevertheless justified. Indeed, in a context of very limited resources, where only a few cases could actually be investigated and prosecuted, the decision to focus on those responsible for recruitment instead of investigating juveniles did indeed make sense.

However, bearing in mind that this prosecutorial decision was made as early as 2002, one pertinent question is whether it was based on an actual review and assessment of the available information and evidence, or whether this was a mere assumption based on personal

---

[58] Amman, *supra* note 50, at 174 (quoting Kofi Annan).

[59] *Report of the Secretary-General*, *supra* note 9, para. 38, at 8.

[60] Cohn, *supra* note 8, at 17.

[61] Press Release, SCSL, Special Court Prosecutor Says He Will Not Prosecute Children (Nov. 2, 2002), *available at* http://www.sc-sl.org/LinkClick.aspx?fileticket=XRwCUe%2BaVhw%3D&tabid=196 (last visited Apr. 21, 2012) [hereinafter SCSL Press Release].

[62] *Id.*

[63] *Report of the Secretary-General*, *supra* note 9:

> In accordance with the U.N. S.C. Res. 1315 (2000) the personal jurisdiction of the Special Court should extend to those "who bear the greatest responsibility for the commission of the crimes," which is understood as an indication of a limitation on the number of accused by reference to their command authority and the gravity and scale of the crime.

[64] This issue has been repeatedly debated, with many arguing that among those bearing the greatest responsibility are not only those individuals holding high-ranking positions, but also those whose actions were particularly atrocious in terms of gravity and scale. One view is that both terms focus on hierarchy and formal rank or official position of the concerned person, another view is that the gravity of the crimes and their egregious nature should be considered, and a third view is that only those individuals who both held high-ranking positions and committed particularly heinous crimes should be deemed among those holding the greatest responsibility. For more on this, see Chapter 30 of this volume where Charles Jalloh discusses this issue.

and cultural values and informed by a conception of children being primarily victims, rather than perpetrators.[65] As underlined by Mark Drumbl, the "legal fiction" that considers children primarily as victims rather than as perpetrators appears widely diffused, especially among child-rights advocates and international actors.[66] It seems clear that these views, probably more reflective of the values of international actors than of local stakeholders, informed David Crane's decision, as shown by his choice of words when he referred to the children who were "forced" to commit crimes.[67]

Even when embracing the views that children associated with armed forces and groups should be treated primarily as victims rather than as perpetrators, as envisaged in the 2007 Paris Commitments,[68] and assuming that the circumstances in which these children act are inherently coercive,[69] it remains that this does not automatically and systematically exclude each of these children from all and any forms of accountability. Having established that the Court could not be realistically expected to deal with juvenile offenders, especially as they did not fall within the category of those bearing the greatest responsibility, the moral and policy issues pertaining to the treatment of the children who had allegedly participated in atrocities remained. Should they have been tried domestically? Should they have had access to other fora, such as other transitional justice mechanisms, to acknowledge their crimes? Should they have been officially pardoned?

Answering these questions certainly goes beyond the scope of this chapter, which will limit itself to a few considerations. First, it is important to consider and respect not only the rights of every child, including child perpetrators, but also the rights and demands of the victims, including the victims of crimes that may have been committed by children. Victims of such gross human rights abuses or international crimes also have fundamental rights, including the right to a remedy.[70] Has the right balance been struck between their respective competing rights? This is a difficult question, especially considering the fact that many of the victims were children themselves, as in the case of Mariatu Kamara, cited above – a girl whose hands were cut off by two boys.

Second, consideration of the right of victims to a remedy and of how best to deal with juvenile offenders brings to the fore the situation of prevailing impunity in Sierra Leone, where the work of the SCSL has offered the only – and limited – avenue for criminal account-ability.[71] This context and its perverse consequences cannot be attributed to the Court itself,

---

[65] These views were later incorporated in the 2007 Paris Commitments at para. 11.

[66] MARK A. DRUMBL, REIMAGINING CHILD SOLDIERS IN INTERNATIONAL LAW AND POLICY (2012).

[67] SCSL Press Release, *supra* note 61.

[68] Paris Commitments, *supra* note 65. These views correspond to the accepted position of child-protection agencies considering that children should primarily be treated as victims rather than perpetrators of crimes.

[69] Aptel, *supra* note 3, at 107 *et seq.*

[70] Notably through the work of the Commission on Human Rights and its Sub-Commission three sets of Draft principles and guidelines have been adopted viz. the Van Boven Principles on the Basic Principles and Guidelines on the Right to Reparation for Victims of Gross Violations of Human Rights and Humanitarian Law, 1996; the Joinet Principles on the Set of Principles for the Protection and Promotion of Human Rights through Action to Combat Impunity, 1997 and the Bassiouni Principles on the Basic Principles and Guidelines on the Right to a Remedy and Reparation for Victims of International Human Rights and Humanitarian Law, 2000, which have all enumerated the three basic rights of victims as (1) the victims' right to know; (2) the victims' right to justice; and (3) the victims' right to reparations.

[71] On whether the Lomé agreement precluded prosecutions in domestic courts for the crimes committed prior to July 1999, see notably, Antonio Cassese, *The Special Court and International Law: The Decision Concerning the Lomé Agreement Amnesty*, J. INT'L CRIM. JUSTICE 1130–40 (2004).

which could certainly not be – and never was – expected to replace an entire insufficient domestic criminal justice system.

Third, any answer to the above questions should take into consideration first and foremost the best interests of the child, as provided by the Convention on the Rights of the Child. What would have been in the best interests of the children concerned, over the short-term but also over the medium to long-term, especially as many of them had only very limited access to rehabilitative programs? How have those children who were involved in horrendous crimes dealt with their own transgressions?[72] Do they even conceive of them as transgressions, and, if not, what does that indicate of their moral and mental states?

Fourth, the best interests of the child can seldom be strictly separated from the views and expectations of the child's communities. The questions on acknowledgement of crimes and accountability are not only individual, but also inherently collective, as they concern the restoration of societal links. In a context such as Sierra Leone, where many children, especially the older boys, had not been abducted, but rather had joined armed groups voluntarily, questioning their involvement in atrocities may perhaps have facilitated their reintegration. If children were perceived as perpetrators, and if they were to be effectively reconciled into the society, they needed to have undergone objective standards of evaluation to fully realize the nature of their acts, and recognize them as crimes and as morally abhorrent, in the hope that this process would not only promote their reintegration, but also prevent threat of future relapses.

Fifth, at the global level, the deliberate exclusion of juvenile offenders may have contributed to reinforcing the generally accepted dichotomy between, on the one hand, adults as active perpetrators of atrocities, and, on the other, children as passive and innocent victims.[73] Assuming that children were all manipulated into committing crimes and were therefore merely instrumentalized by adults denies their individual agency.

Finally, although far from conclusive, it seems that, in Sierra Leone as in other contexts, it may well be in the best interests of children to be encouraged to acknowledge their crimes and face up to their responsibility, as long as this is done under protective conditions.[74] Alternative forms of accountability within the arsenal of transitional justice mechanisms that are more rehabilitative than criminal prosecutions, such as truth commissions and traditional ceremonies, may facilitate the reintegration of children.

On this note, it is useful to note that the Sierra Leonean Truth and Reconciliation Commission, with a purpose and modalities obviously very different from the SCSL, has documented the role of children in the perpetration of crimes, placing these crimes within their contexts.[75] The Commission sought to understand the complex and evolving roles of

---

[72] Anecdotal but interesting evidence was recorded by Richard Maclure and Myriam Denov, who argue that observers note that many children considered their violent acts as laudable rather than shameful. *See* Richard Maclure & Myriam Denov, *I Didn't Want to Die so I Joined Them: Structuration and the Process of Becoming Boy Soldiers in Sierra Leone*, 18 Terrorism & Political Violence 119, 126 (2006).

[73] Drumbl, *supra* note 66, at 23. *See also* Children and Youth on the Front Line: Ethnography, Armed Conflict and Displacement (Studies in Forced Migration) xv (Jo Boyden & Joanna De Berry eds., 2004).

[74] *See* Aptel, *supra* note 3. *See also* Drumbl, *supra* note 66.

[75] *See notably* Philip Cook & Cheryl Heykoop, *Child Participation in the Sierra Leonean Truth and Reconciliation Commission*, *in* Children and Transitional Justice, *supra* note 3.

children as *both* victims and perpetrators, noting that the most heinous crimes committed by children were carried out while under the influence of drugs, and bringing to the fore the issue of a child's diminished capacity to distinguish right from wrong.[76] It documented how child soldiers, through coercion and under the influence of narcotics,[77] were often forced to commit heinous atrocities, including carrying out the killing, amputation, or rape of a loved one or community member.[78] It is unlikely that any criminal prosecution could have managed to set such a complete picture of the complexity of the situation for both the adults and the children involved.

IV. THE MANY OTHER CRIMES ENDURED BY CHILDREN IN SIERRA LEONE

Yes, the three of them had guns with them and I was forced to have sexual intercourse with them.(Testimony of Witness TF1–314)[79]

To what an extent has the SCSL considered crimes against children other than the recruitment and use of child soldiers? This section aims to answer this question by briefly reviewing the efforts of the SCSL in documenting, first, the other violations suffered by "child-soldiers" in addition to being recruited or used, notably the sexual crimes and forced marriage committed against "girl-soldiers"; and, second, the crimes perpetrated against the other Sierra Leonean children.

By considering the achievement of the SCSL against the larger backdrop of the universe of crimes committed against the children of Sierra Leone, this section indicates how much more it could have done. Indeed, while it focused on child soldiering, on sexual violence, and on the crime of forced marriage, the Court did not highlight the full extent of crimes suffered by children in Sierra Leone. Apart from those crimes committed against child-soldiers, none of the four cases tried by the Court focused on the plight of the Sierra Leonean children: the widespread killings of children, their maiming, abductions, and the child-victims of slavery or forced labor. Although the judgments contain some references to isolated cases of child-victims of such crimes, very few were highlighted, and the children were generally subsumed under the broader category of "civilians," as if their age and particular vulnerability did not matter.

A. *Additional Crimes Committed against "Child-Soldiers"*

While it concentrated on the crime of recruitment and use of children, the Court did not thoroughly document the many other violations suffered by these children. Indeed, even when additional crimes within the jurisdiction of the SCSL were mentioned in Court or in the judgments as having been committed against the child-victims of recruitment or use, these other crimes were usually not separately charged, and consequently did not result in

---

[76] *Id.* at 280.
[77] *Id.*
[78] *Id.* at 263.
[79] Witness Testimony of TF1–314, RUF Trial Transcript, Trial Chamber I, TF1–314, at 26 (Nov. 2, 2005).

convictions – with some exceptions, notably for sexual violence and the so-called forced marriage.

The so-called military training of "child-soldiers" was repeatedly described in court in ways that indicate that such "training" may in fact have constituted separate war crimes or crimes against humanity, and could have been charged as such, either separately or at least cumulatively.[80] A witness described that, as a child soldier with the AFRC, he had been repeatedly flogged and was threatened with amputation, and only narrowly escaped that happening.[81] In the RUF judgment, the Court noted that, in several so-called training camps, children were required to crawl on the ground with their hands crossed on their backs, while being beaten with canes by the instructors.[82] Children were also required to walk over "monkey bridges," and those who lost balance and fell landed on barbed wires and were also at times shot.[83] "Recruits who were unable to endure the training regime would be shot and killed."[84]

Several children who had been associated with either the RUF or the AFRC testified about how they had been forced or incited to take harmful drugs. A witness in the AFRC case recounted how, as part of the so-called military training, he had been repeatedly flogged and subjected to injections and tablets of drugs that he believed to be cocaine.[85] All children recruited by the RUF were habitually drugged before and after combat, apparently in order to become fearless and participate in atrocities.[86] A child soldier who refused to take drugs would be beaten and might, in some cases, be killed.[87] The children were also sometimes cut with blades on their bodies and legs as a means to administer the drug and ensure that it would be absorbed by their system. These cuts were also meant to physically mark their allegiance to the "RUF," such marks often being carved on their chests.[88] Clearly, such abhorrent

---

[80] Some of these acts may have been qualified as "war crimes" – or violations of art. 3 common to the Geneva Convention – under art. 3(a) of the SCSL Statute (Violence to Life, Health and Physical or Mental Well-Being of Persons, in Particular Murder as well as Cruel Treatment Such as Torture, Mutilation or Any Form of Corporal Punishment) – or under art. 3(e) of the Statute (Outrages upon Personal Dignity, in Particular Humiliating and Degrading Treatment, Rape, Enforced Prostitution and Any Form of Indecent Assault). Some of these acts may also have been constitutive of crimes against humanity, in particular as murder, under art. 2(a) of the Statute; as imprisonment, under art. 2(e) of the Statute; as torture, under art. 2(f) of the Statute; or as "other inhumane acts," under art. 2(i). In the AFRC case, the forced military training of children and their abductions was also considered under Count 1 and 2 Acts of Terrorism and Collective Punishments. Count 10 (Violence to Life, Health and Physical and Mental Well-Being of Persons, in Particular Mutilation) and Count 11 (Other Inhumane Acts) dealt more with the attack against the civilian population and mutilations of the civilians. Children subjected to gruesome training and mutilations in the course of the forced military trainings were referred to under the crime of conscription and use of child soldiers (Count 12). In, the RUF case, the gruesome treatment meted out to children was subsumed within the crime of conscription, enlistment, and use of children under the age of fifteen years. There is also a small mention of the forced military trainings under Count 13 Abductions and Forced Labor where reference has been made to the other civilians who were also subject to gruesome military trainings, and to some extent under the broad umbrella of Count 1: Acts of Terrorism.

[81] AFRC case, *supra* note 22, at para. 1254.

[82] RUF case, *supra* note 28, at para. 1640. The court relies on the testimony of TF1–141.

[83] *Id.*

[84] *Id.* at para. 1641. The court relies on the testimony of TF1–141.

[85] AFRC case, *supra* note 22, at 1254.

[86] RUF case, *supra* note 28, at para. 1623.

[87] *Id.*

[88] *Id.* at paras. 1623–1624.

crimes cannot be – and should not have been – simply subsumed under the "recruitment and use" of child soldiers or referred generally under other counts as they do constitute separate international crimes, qualifying as war crimes or crimes against humanity.[89]

Among the crimes committed against child soldiers, as already noted, an important difference in the practice of the SCSL concerned sexual crimes, and the so-called forced marriage. Many girl soldiers suffered from these crimes, and those who resisted were often executed.

B. Forced Marriage and Sexual Crimes against Girls

Although many girl soldiers suffered from sexual violence, slavery, rape, and forced marriage, they were not the only victims of these abhorrent crimes. The SCSL adequately prosecuted these offenses as separate from the recruitment and use of child soldiers. Noting the scholarship already existing on this part of the SCSL jurisprudence, including three excellent chapters in this book,[90] this section only briefly considers these crimes insofar as they victimized children. In this regard, a striking ambiguity is found in the formulation of the charges for these crimes, and of the resulting convictions, referring to the victims as "civilian women *and girls*" (emphasis added).[91] Presuming that the term "girl" applies to female children,[92] this formulation does not specify how many girls were concerned, or the percentage of children among the victims. Yet, there are many reasons to believe that these crimes disproportionally affected younger victims. The Court itself heard evidence to that effect in the context of the RUF trial. First, an expert witness known as TF1–369, the author of an Expert Report on Forced Marriage,[93] testified that many of the victims of forced marriages and sexual slavery were schoolchildren and petty traders who had been abducted from various districts.[94] Second, a medical expert, witness TF1–081, had testified that "*of 1,168 patients examined between March and December 1999, 99% had been abducted following the 6 January 1999 invasion. … Out of these patients, … 200 (17.1%) were pregnant, over 80% of whom were girls between the ages of 14 and 18.*"[95]

---

[89] Some of these acts may have qualified as "war crimes" – or violations of Article 3 common to the Geneva Convention – under Article 3(a) of the Statute (Violence to Life, Health and Physical or Mental Well-Being of Persons, in Particular Murder as well as Cruel Treatment Such as Torture, Mutilation or Any Form of Corporal Punishment) – or under Article 3(e) of the Statute (Outrages upon Personal Dignity, in Particular Humiliating and Degrading Treatment, Rape, Enforced Prostitution and Any Form of Indecent Assault). Some of these acts may also have been constitutive of crimes against humanity, in particular as torture, under Article 2(f) of the Statute, or as "other inhumane acts," under Article 2(i).

[90] On the SCSL's treatment of gender crimes, see Chapter 12 by Valerie Oosterveld in this volume.

[91] See, e.g., Prosecution's Second Amended Indictment, Charles Ghankay Taylor (SCSL-03–01-PT), Trial Chamber II, at 4–5 (May 29, 2007) where the charge reads, inter alia, "the accused committed widespread acts of sexual violence against civilian women and girls."

[92] No definition of the term "girl" is given.

[93] This report was exhibit 138 in the RUF case, *supra* note 28.

[94] RUF case, *supra* note 28, at para. 1409.

[95] *Id.* at para. 1520: citing from Exhibit 104B, Exhibit P25 from AFRC Trial Witness's Report, at 6319–20:

> Expert Witness TF1–081 testified that of 1,168 patients examined between March and December 1999, 99% had been abducted following the 6 Jan. 1999 invasion, the "vast majority" of whom originated from Freetown. Out of these patients, 274 (23.4%) had been beaten for refusing to engage in sexual relations or carry heavy looted goods; 648 (58.5%) of the abductees had been subjected to rape, some by more than two and up to 30 men; 281 (24.1%) complained of vaginal discharge and 327 (27.9%)

Crucially, the ambiguity of the above formulation "women and girls" also deprives the child-victims of the recognition of the particularly brutal impact such crimes may have had on them. Indeed, although all of the victims suffered tragically, it is evident that the impact of forced marriage and sexual crimes is even worst on the younger victims, both in physical and psychological terms, and that their suffering, again measured in both physical and psychological terms, may also be greater. In addition, within the sociocultural context of Sierra Leone, the stigma associated with rape, sexual violence, sexual slavery, and the so-called forced marriage are also probably greater on child-victims than on adults. A SCSL Trial Chamber noted, in the context of the RUF trial, that the "[v]ictims of sexual violence were ostracized, husbands left their wives, and daughters and young girls were unable to marry within their community,"[96] finding that these crimes resulted in the unraveling of "cultural values and relationships which held the societies together."[97] In this context, the long-term consequences for the young victims can be dire, as illustrated by a victim, TF1–314, who testified in the RUF trial that she had been abducted and raped at the age of ten, and forcefully "married" to a rebel commander, undertaking domestic chores and being repeatedly raped by him.[98]

The ambiguity regarding the age and status of the victims, and the lumping together of "women and girls" is possibly one of the reasons that the SCSL never exercised its jurisdiction over the "[o]ffences relating to the abuse of girls under the Prevention of Cruelty to Children Act, 1926" which prohibits (1) abusing a girl under thirteen years of age, contrary to section 6; (2) abusing a girl between thirteen and fourteen years of age, contrary to section 7; and (3) abduction of a girl for immoral purposes, contrary to section 12, under Article 5(a) of the Statute.[99] This is very unfortunate, because this offense constitutes the only other "child-specific" offense contained in the SCSL Statute, in addition to the crime of "recruitment and use of children."[100]

Is the failure to exercise this part of the SCSL jurisdiction and the ambiguous categorization of "women and girls" a reflection of the evidential difficulties met when attempting to establish the age of each individual victim? This argument, which was never explicitly made

had pelvic inflammatory disease, both of which are transmitted through sexual intercourse; and 200 (17.1%) were pregnant, over 80% of whom were girls between the ages of 14 and 18.

In addition the Special Representative of the Secretary General for Children and Armed Conflict had stated that "It is estimated that around 60 per cent of children kidnapped during the January 1999 incursion were girls; 9 out of 10 abducted girls are believed to have been sexually abused." *See also* Office of the Special Representative of the Secretary General for Children and Armed Conflict, *Action to Assist War-Affected Children in Sierra Leone Proposed by Special Representative for Children and Armed Conflict* (Sept. 14, 1999) (HR/4432), *available at* http://www.un.org/children/conflict/english/pr/1999–09–1478.html (last viewed June 30, 2012).

[96] *Id.* at paras. 1347–1349. The Trial Chamber cites: "According to TF1–369, fear of discrimination and stigmatisation remains an enormous barrier to the effective reintegration of victims and their families, which prevented the victims from returning to their communities, those who have been reintegrated struggle with psychological trauma and most live in denial along with their families," Exhibit 138, Expert Report Forced Marriage, at 12088.

[97] *Id.*

[98] *Id.* at paras. 1460–1461 and also paras. 1407–1408. The witness referred to other girls between the ages of ten and fifteen, who had had the same experience.

[99] This is done in references to Cap. 31 of Sierra Leonean law.

[100] *See* Aptel, *supra* note 3.

by the SCSL, would in any case not hold in light of the prosecution for recruitment and use of child soldiers, which had to establish that the victims were under the age of fifteen at the time of the offense. If the latter were possible, why would it not be possible to establish the age of the victims of rape, sexual violence, sexual slavery, and forced marriage?

Turning to the offense of "forced marriage," the SCSL has often been lauded for inno-vatively recognizing this offense and defining it as a crime against humanity.[101] Yet, the use of the term "marriage" in this new offense is not unequivocal. This term normally refers to a freely accepted contractual relationship, which obviously does not match the reality of abduction. On this basis, "forced marriage" is an oxymoron. Yet, in a context such as Sierra Leone, where the practice of "early marriage" remains prevalent and is a concern for child rights' advocates, it would have been a major contribution of the SCSL had its SCSL case law helped change attitudes toward the abuse of young girls, formally "married" against their will, whether in times of war or peace.

Finally, the focus on sexual violence and forced marriage is extremely important to bring visibility to the crimes and denounce them, but it also carries the risk of projecting an image of girls as powerless victims, undermining their agency. An Michels, a psychologist who worked for the SCSL in its early years noted that "It is striking that the choice of wit-nesses generally reflects a typical gender division: boys are called to testify about being a child ex-combatant, women and girls testify about sexual violence."[102] In Sierra Leone, as in other places, girls participated in the hostilities and boys were sexually abused.[103] By calling as witnesses mostly male victims with regard to the crime of recruitment and use in hostili-ties, and girls as victims of sexual crimes and slavery, the prosecutors of the SCSL may have inadvertently contributed to a skewed understanding of the respective experience of boys and girls during conflicts.

C. Other Crimes against Other Children

The focus and determination of the Prosecution in investigating and prosecuting the crimes committed against children (as discussed in the previous sections), primarily their recruit-ment and use as child soldiers, and also the sexual crimes and forced marriages suffered by many girls, is certainly impressive. It is also to be noted that, in sentencing, the SCSL considered the vulnerability and the young age of some of the victims as an aggravating factor, focusing in particular on the fact that sexual violence, mutilation, torture, murder, and other crimes had been committed against children of tender age.[104] Nevertheless, these major developments have polarized the attention on these specific crimes, and away from

---

[101] See, in this volume, the contributions by Michael Scharf (Chapter 10) and Sydney Thompson (Chapter 11) on the topic of forced marriage.

[102] A. Michels, *As If It Was Happening Again: Supporting Especially Vulnerable Witnesses, in Particular Women and Children, at the Special Court for Sierra Leone, in* INTERNATIONAL CRIMINAL ACCOUNTABILITY AND THE RIGHTS OF CHILDREN 135 (2006).

[103] S.J. Park, *Other Inhumane Acts': Forced Marriage, Girl Soldiers and the Special Court for Sierra Leone*, 15(3) SOCIAL AND LEGAL STUDIES 321 (2006).

[104] Sentencing Judgment, RUF (SCSL-04–14- T) at para 128, see also Sentencing Judgment, AFRC (SCSL-04–16-T) at para 19 and 34; Sentencing judgment, CDF (SCSL-04–14-T) at para 14; Sentencing Judgment, Charles Ghankay Taylor (SCSL-03–01-T) at para 20.

the other tens of thousands of child-victims[105]: those who were killed, maimed, persecuted, deprived of access to basic services essential to their survival, or suffered from other crimes falling within the Court's mandate. This point is particularly salient, because several sources have documented the extent and gravity of the many crimes committed in Sierra Leone, and noted that children not only were not spared, but in fact may have been particularly victimized in the campaign of terror that unraveled there.

Certain specific crimes known to have a particularly grave impact on children, such as deportation or forced displacement,[106] which too often cause the separation of a family with dire consequences for children (including nutritional problems) were not the focus of any prosecutions at the SCSL.

When crimes against children are mentioned in the SCSL judgments, children are merely cited among the civilian casualties, as they are for instance in the AFRC and RUF cases.

The AFRC judgment refers to a dead child who had been shot in the chest, found among other persons killed or severely injured after an attack in Tikonko.[107] The Court also recorded that many little children were killed by being thrown into burning houses, for instance during a mass attack on the village of Karina,[108] and noted a specific instance when one of the Accused in the "Kamamra" case, had, with others, locked five young girls into a house, set the house on fire, and burned them to death.[109] Much evidence of the widespread amputations and mutilations of civilians was heard and accepted, with a witness specifically referring to an instance when the rebels cut off the hand of a child.[110] Similarly, the RUF judgment contains some references to children killed. One witness, TF1–235, lost seven of his children, who were killed by the rebels.[111] Other dreadful accounts include how a rebel leader cleaved a six-year-old in two with a machete,[112] how the rebels performed amputations on a fifteen-year-old boy, cutting his hands from his wrists and his legs from his ankles before throwing him into a pit latrine.[113]

Citing children among other civilian casualties may be logical when prosecuting some crimes, especially to demonstrate their widespread or systematic character, or that civilians

---

[105] Office of the Special Representative of the Secretary General for Children and Armed Conflict, *supra* note 95. The then- Special Representative, Mr. Olara A. Otunnu, states:

> The children of Sierra Leone have suffered beyond belief in this war: many children have been deliberately maimed, with their limbs brutally cut off; in the month of January 1999 alone, over 4,000 children were abducted during the Revolutionary United Front (RUF)/Armed Forces Revolutionary Council (AFRC) incursion into Freetown; 60 percent of abducted children were girls, the vast majority of whom have been sexually abused; more than 10,000 children have been serving as child soldiers in various fighting groups; over 60 percent of the 3 million Sierra Leoneans who have been displaced by war within and outside their country are children; and many children are suffering from serious psychological trauma.

[106] *Id.* It would also be pertinent to note that deportation as a Crime against Humanity under art. 2(d) of the SCSL statute was neither charged nor used in any conviction in the three cases.

[107] AFRC case, *supra* note 22, para. 814 (Testimony of witness TF 1–004).

[108] *Id.* at paras. 887–889. The court relies on the testimony of TF1–334, Court Transcripts, May 23, 2005, at 65–67.

[109] *Id.* at para. 887 (Testimony of witness TF1–334).

[110] *Id.* at para. 1242 (Testimony of witness TF1–085).

[111] RUF case, *supra* note 28, at para. 1534.

[112] *Id.* at para. 1536 (Testimony of witness TF1–331).

[113] *Id.* at paras. 1149–1150 (Testimony of witness TF1–015).

were targeted. It is also the regular way to proceed when crimes were clearly perpetrated as part of a broader attack, as they often were. An example would be the crimes described by witness TF1–209 in the AFRC case, who recounted her ordeal when both her six-year-old son and her husband were killed by rebels who then sexually assaulted and abducted her.[114]

Nevertheless, although recognizing that the limited number of cases that the Court could take necessarily limited the scope of its prosecutions, it remains deplorable that not a single case focused on the suffering of children. This would have drawn greater attention to these crimes, including their scope and impact, thereby giving recognition to the suffering experienced by many of the children of Sierra Leone, who account for not less than a third of the entire population.[115]

V. CONCLUSION

In sum, the SCSL made some crucial advances in fostering accountability for the crimes committed against children, but it also fell short in documenting the broader suffering of children in armed conflict, and missed opportunities to further advance the cause of child-victims. But at least, although far from perfect, the Court made a dent in the impunity of the perpetrators of crimes against children.

The SCSL has often been referred to as a model for initiating the fight against impunity for grave crimes against children, and it rightly deserves to be lauded for this. It broke new ground by focusing on the recruitment of children under the age of fifteen and their use to participate actively in hostilities, contributing to the stigmatization of those responsible for these abhorrent crimes. It has powerfully shown that crimes against children are as significant as those against older individuals. It demonstrated that even high-ranking leaders can be held criminally responsible for such crimes.

But the decision by the SCSL to prosecute the child-specific offenses of recruitment and use of children to participate in hostilities may have been to the detriment of the prosecution of more generic crimes perpetrated against children. Although the Court prosecuted rapes, sexual violence, and sexual slavery, and innovated by recognizing the crime of "forced marriage," it did not exercise its jurisdiction over Article 5(a) of the Statute, which would have enabled the prosecutions of specific sexual crimes against girls. Furthermore, crimes against children were not the object of specific prosecutions for other more generic crimes, such as being killed, maimed, persecuted, deprived of access to basic services essential to their survival, etc. Although limited by the number of cases the Court could take up, which curtailed the scope of its prosecutions, it is nonetheless disappointing that there has not been a single case focusing on the suffering of children, who make up about a third of Sierra Leone's population.

The SCSL also failed to clarify whether and how children between the age of fifteen and eighteen should be held accountable if they allegedly participate in international crimes, despite the deliberate inclusion of those in that age bracket within the mandate of the

---

[114] AFRC case, *supra* note 22, at para. 868.
[115] CIA World Factbook, Sierra Leone, *available at* https://www.cia.gov/library/publications/the-world-fact-book/geos/sl.html (last viewed July 15, 2012). Children in the age group 0–14 years constitute 41.8 percent of the population of Sierra Leone.

Court. The decision of the first Prosecutor, sustained by his successors, to concentrate on the crimes committed against children rather than by children, is perfectly legitimate in light of the very limited resources of the Court and the few cases it could actually pursue. Yet, this decision led to a missed opportunity to better understand why, how, and to what extent children between fifteen and eighteen were involved in committing atrocities.

Although international – or hybrid – criminal jurisdictions can try only a very few selected cases, these cases are highly symbolic. In this context, the priority given to specific crimes against children to the exclusion of others is understandable – and again it is a welcome and important start – but it also fell short of identifying much wider patterns of victimization of children.

In a statement to the Truth and Reconciliation Commission of Sierra Leone, a group of children declared:

> Every child in this country has got a story to tell: a heartbreaking one. Unfortunately, only a handful of these stories will be told and made known to the world. But the devastating impact lingers and endures all the time. It continues to linger in the minds and hearts of young people.[116]

This certainly applied with even more acuity to the Court: it made very important contributions indeed, not only legally but also by contributing to the stabilization of the country, and its work on the war crime of recruiting and using children will continue to be cited, but ultimately, only a handful of stories were told and retained, very few children appeared, and too few crimes against children were documented and recognized.

---

[116] 3b The Final Report of the Truth and Reconciliation Commission of Sierra Leone, Children and the Armed Conflict in Sierra Leone, ch. 4, at para. 124, at 260 (2004).

18

After the Horror: Child Soldiers and the Special Court for Sierra Leone

Noah Benjamin Novogrodsky[*]

I. INTRODUCTION

The Special Court for Sierra Leone (SCSL), like the war that preceded it, may well be defined by its treatment of child soldiering. The phenomenon of pressing children into warfare is known by many names – abduction, employment, conscription, enlistment, and recruitment – but the core activity remains the same: the use of children in war and all that the idea connotes for legal norms and society writ large. One of the unique contributions of the SCSL has been to call the practice a crime. In a cluster of powerful cases, the SCSL has held individual commanders criminally responsible for the offense of recruiting child soldiers into armed conflict.

The first such decision was the jurisdictional ruling in *Prosecutor v. Sam Hinga Norman, Moinina Fofana and Allieu Kondewa* (hereinafter *Norman*), which held that Norman and his co-defendants could be prosecuted for the crime of enlisting children under the age of fifteen into armed forces or groups, and of using them to participate actively in hostilities.[1] Norman was the one-time leader of the Civil Defense Forces (CDF), a pro-government militia group comprised predominantly of traditional hunters known as *Kamajors*. The indictment issued against Norman accused him of systematically forcing small boys into armed combat. Norman challenged the Court's subject matter jurisdiction on the grounds that enlisting child soldiers was not a crime under customary international law at the times relevant to the indictment (between 1996 and 2001). He argued that although international instruments, such as Additional Protocol II to the Geneva Conventions and the Convention on the Rights of the Child, may have prohibited the recruitment of child soldiers, these instruments did not affix specific criminal responsibility to the activity. If child recruitment amounts to an international crime, Norman insisted, it only became so after the drafting of the Rome Statute of the International Criminal Court in 1998 – not before.

The Court rejected Norman's preliminary motion, holding that the offense does not violate the international legal prohibition on retroactive criminal liability (*nullum crimen sine lege*), and that Norman was properly charged with a grave breach of humanitarian law. The Appeals Chamber found that the prohibition against recruiting child soldiers had

[*] Professor of Law, University of Wyoming College of Law. The author is grateful for the research assistance of Felicia Resor and Mary Freeman, and for the editing suggestions of Mark Drumbl.
[1] Decision on Preliminary Motion Based on Lack of Jurisdiction, Prosecutor v. Norman (SCSL-2004–14-AR72(E)), Appeals Chamber (May 31, 2004).

crystallized into a crime under customary international law before November 1996, and that, accordingly, individuals bearing the greatest responsibility could be prosecuted for this offense at any time under the temporal jurisdiction of the Special Court. In the process, the SCSL opened the gates to a more sustained and developed understanding of the international criminal law covering child soldiering than any other single institution.[2]

This chapter examines the Court's legacy on the subject with respect to three audiences: victims, perpetrators, and bystanders. Of course, these artificial groupings are both interesting and problematic as identities are fluid, particularly in armed conflict. The same person can occupy all three roles such that an individual could be victim, victimizer, and/or observer. In addition, it is crucial to note that our ability to develop a capacious understanding of child soldiering is impeded by rigid categories. But even a cursory review of the case law demonstrates that international criminal law relies heavily on distinct labels that separate wrongdoers from sufferers and an almost reflexive discomfort with multiple identities.

For the purposes of this chapter, I discuss the impact of the Court's jurisprudence in reverse order of human consequence. By examining bystanders first, I argue that the Court has achieved considerable success as an institution built largely by, of, and for the international community. The jurisprudential accomplishment of the Court's docket has consolidated international criminal law norms, generated expressive values, and produced meaningful educational effects that have inspired other prosecutions and facilitated accountability efforts well beyond Sierra Leone. The legacy of the Court is less apparent in the treatment of the next category of affected persons: perpetrators. The Court has managed to try representative adult defendants even as it draws lines to eschew the possibility of charging child soldiers themselves, but it has also generated the inevitable charge of arbitrariness. Caught in the prosecutorial grip of a widespread sociological phenomenon, are these defendants the most culpable individuals? And will the next generation of recruiters be deterred by the Court's work? Last, I consider the most important group, the victims whose voices have been quieted and in whose name the Court purports to operate. With respect to victims, this chapter argues that the Court has adopted a monochromatic view of child soldiers that may ultimately limit its participatory and remedial functions.

II. BYSTANDERS

It is beyond dispute that the same international community that has prosecuted Sierra Leonean actors responsible for child soldiering after the fact did precious little to prevent the abuse and exploitation of a generation of young people in the first place. I use the term "bystander" intentionally, but it refers to more than passive witnesses; in the context of the Sierra Leonean civil war, the word describes the universe of those who could have

---

[2] The crime of recruiting child soldiers is at once overinclusive and underinclusive. It is overinclusive because it attaches equal criminal responsibility to the military commander who accepts an underage volunteer as it does to the abductor who forces young people to fight with his forces. It is underinclusive for the reasons that Cecile Aptel outlines in this volume, namely the way in which the moniker of recruitment masks the very real crimes of sustained sexual violence that so many girls were subjected to and romanticizes the fighting qualities of a phenomenon that was frequently characterized by involuntary servitude.

intervened but did not, and those who watched atrocities committed by and against children from near and far. Who were the bystanders?

That group is comprised of diplomats who attempted to broker peace in the Abidjan Accord in 1996 and again in the calamitous Lomé Agreement of 1999. It includes foreign troops, mercenary armies, and UN peacekeepers organized as UNAMSIL. The most influential group of bystanders was the legion of journalists and the expansive NGO community whose consistent reporting brought accounts of the unfolding tragedy to a wider audience.[3] From a position in Freetown, the capital, aid workers watched in horror as the RUF and other groups attacked UN peacekeepers and took nearly 500 foreign troops hostage.[4] Everywhere there were armed children, often wearing Leonardo DiCaprio Titanic T-shirts and bandanas printed with gang colors and Western brand insignia, the informal uniform of a ragtag army carrying outsized automatic weapons. British Special Forces intervened in 2000 and were shocked to find so many children carrying weapons, a juvenile force capable of terrorizing the community, but helpless against a modern army.[5]

Representatives of international organizations in the country attempted to mobilize outrage, even as they became professional witnesses to anguish on a massive scale. The master images they circulated told a story of the absence of governance, humanity, and law.[6] In this environment, children were depicted (not always inaccurately) as orphans, abused waifs, and members of drug addled–militias responsible for amputations, sexual slavery, and brutal initiation rites. As Mark Drumbl has noted, this picture relies on and disseminates a narrative through which Sierra Leone is seen as violent and anarchic, and a place where children are disconnected from the ties of family. Children and youth vacillate among representations of passive victims, irreparably damaged goods, and demons or bandits.[7]

For better and for worse, the manifold depictions of children as participants in war lodged in the popular global imagination. By the time the SCSL was being considered in 2001 and 2002, to the outside world Sierra Leone had become synonymous with child soldiering. Extensive newspaper and television coverage of Sierra Leonean child soldiers was soon joined by a growing literature and awareness that children were at the center of the conflict. From Dave Eggers's *What Is the What*,[8] the semi-fictional account of Valentino Achak Deng, to Ishamel Beah's *A Long Way Gone: Memoirs of a Boy Soldier*,[9] a best-selling autobiographical account of a Sierra Leonean child soldier, to Romeo Dallaire's *They Fight Like Solders, They Die Like Children*,[10] to Gulu Walk and the Kony 2012 campaign, diverse and influential voices have equated African youth with child soldiering.

---

[3] *See, e.g.,* Human Rights Watch, *Sowing Terror: Atrocities against Civilians in Sierra Leone* (1998), *available at* http://www.hrw.org./reports98/sierra/ (last visited July 11, 2012).

[4] Laura R. Hall & Nahal Kazemi, *Prospects for Justice and Reconciliation in Sierra Leone*, 44 HARV. INT'L L.J. 287, 289 (2003).

[5] Noah B. Novogrodsky, *Speaking to Africa – The Early Success of the Special Court for Sierra Leone*, 5 SANTA CLARA J. INT'L L. 194, 197 (2006).

[6] Consciously or not, many of these accounts analogized Sierra Leone to the unmoored violence at the heart of William Golding's *Lord of the Flies. See, e.g.,* Steve Coll, *The Other War*, WASH. POST MAG., Jan. 9, 2000.

[7] MARK A. DRUMBL, REIMAGINING CHILD SOLDIERS IN INTERNATIONAL LAW AND POLICY 7–9 (2012).

[8] DAVE EGGERS, WHAT IS THE WHAT: THE AUTOBIOGRAPHY OF VALENTINO ACHAK DENG (2006).

[9] ISHAMEL BEAH, A LONG WAY GONE: MEMOIRS OF A BOY SOLDIER (2008).

[10] ROMEO DALLAIRE, THEY FIGHT LIKE SOLDERS, THEY DIE LIKE CHILDREN (2011).

Enter the Court, the culmination of extensive international legal and political negotiations, which immediately recognized the existence of child soldiers as an unmitigated disaster. Article 4(c) of SCSL statute criminalizes the act of "[c]onscripting or enlisting children under the age of 15 years into armed forces or groups using them to participate actively in hostilities ("child recruitment")."[11] In that, the SCSL Statute provides that penal responsibility attaches only to the recruitment of persons under the age of fifteen.[12] The Court's statute also addresses the question of whether children may appear as defendants by providing that the SCSL can exercise jurisdiction over children between the ages of fifteen and eighteen, but requires that juvenile offenders be treated differently than adults.[13] Plainly, the provision related to juvenile offenders was retained to provide the Prosecutor with flexibility to determine who should be prosecuted. Because of the large number of child soldiers who actively participated in the conflict in Sierra Leone, provisions relating to how those children were to be treated were required, in the case – however unlikely – that the Prosecutor ultimately decided to prosecute them.

For a collection of bystanders – conceived broadly – the prosecution of individuals accused of stealing the innocence of Sierra Leone's children is a way for the international community to express its opprobrium through law. Financed almost entirely by non-Sierra Leonean sources, the Court represents a form of targeted institution-building. However, the SCSL alone is unlikely to bring peace or promote economic development. What it can do is consolidate international criminal law norms, generate expressive values, and produce meaningful educational effects. Nowhere is that clearer than in the focus on the crime of recruiting child soldiers common to each of the Court's four cases.

Beginning with the jurisdictional ruling in *Norman*, the Court has consistently invoked the Nuremburg precedent through which the International Military Tribunal found that:

> The law of war is to be found not only in treaties, but in the customs and practices of states which gradually obtained universal recognition, and from general principles of justice applied by jurists, and practiced by military courts. This law is not static, but by continual adaptation follows the needs of a changing world.[14]

Applied to child soldiering, the Nuremberg logic permits *Norman* and its progeny to bridge several gulfs: the gap between violations of humanitarian and human rights law and individual criminal responsibility, the space between customary international law and penal sanctions, and the divide that has separated international from domestic law.

---

[11] SCSL Statute art. 4(c).

[12] It is significant that the Court fixes the prohibited age at fifteen rather than eighteen, the age of majority used in many other international law instruments. *See, e.g.*, Convention on the Rights of the Child General Assembly: GA Res. 44/25, 20 (Nov. 1989) (Convention on the Rights of the Child).

[13] Graça Machel, The Impact of War on Children: A Review of Progress since the 1996 United Nations Report on the Impact of Armed Conflict on Children 7 (2001) (defining a child soldier as "any child – boy or girl – under the age of 18, who is compulsorily, forcibly or voluntarily recruited or used in hostilities by armed forces, paramilitaries, civil defence unites or other armed groups. Child soldiers are used for sexual services, as combatants, messengers, porters and cooks.").

[14] *See* Judgment and Sentence, *Trial of German Major War Criminals (Goering et al.)*, International Military Tribunal (Nuremberg) Sept. 30 and Oct. 1, 1946 (Cmd. 6964, HMSO, London); *Judgment of the Nuremberg International Military Tribunal, 1946*, 41 Am. J. Int'l L. 172 (1947).

In the first of these cases to reach trial, three former military leaders of the Armed Forces Revolutionary Council (AFRC) were convicted of crimes related to child soldiering.[15] The trial of defendants Brima, Kamara, and Kanu focused on abduction, which is the compelled participation of children in fighting forces. The guilty verdict and lengthy sentences of each of the AFRC defendants were confirmed on appeal, thus rooting the decision in the universal domestic prohibition against kidnapping and assigning blame to adult parties for a crime committed against children. The AFRC Sentencing Judgment summarizes the Court's view of the tragedy:

> Children were forcibly taken away from their families, often drugged and used as child soldiers who were trained to kill and commit other brutal crimes against the civilian population. Those child soldiers who survived the war were robbed of a childhood and most of them lost the chance of an education.[16]

The second trial involved CDF leaders Moinina Fofana and Allieu Kondewa (Sam Hinga Norman, who was the first Accused, died in 2007).[17] The Trial Chamber acquitted Fofana of the charge of enlisting children under the age of fifteen into an armed force, reasoning that Fofana's presence at a base where child soldiers were present was insufficient to establish criminal responsibility. Kondewa was convicted of crimes related to the use of child soldiers although, on appeal, his conviction for initiating recruits into the CDF was overturned on the ground that performing an initiation ritual does not equal enlistment.[18]

The third case centered on the surviving leaders of the Revolutionary United Front (RUF): Issa Hasan Sesay, Morris Kallon, and Augustine Gbao. At trial, Sesay and Kallon were convicted of planning the forcible recruitment of children into active hostilities.[19] The RUF trial detailed the conscription and use of children, some of them shockingly young, for use in fighting forces as well as non-combat roles; both of the RUF convictions were upheld on appeal.[20] In the fourth and final case, Charles Taylor, the former president of Liberia, was convicted under a theory of command responsibility related to the RUF's and AFRC's use of children to actively participate in hostilities.[21]

Collectively, the recruitment cases represent a concerted *ex post* effort to capture the widespread and systematic use of child soldiers in Sierra Leone and to elucidate the criminalization of the practice. This quartet of cases also exemplifies the development of humanitarian law norms:

> It mirrors the shift from negotiated reciprocal restraints on the methods of warfare to a norm that protects human dignity, and in particular, increases the scope of protections for civilians in times of armed conflict and civil strife. ... This phenomenon stands to increase

---

[15] Trial Judgment, Prosecutor v. Brima, Kamara, and Kanu (SCSL-04–16-T), Trial Chamber (June 20, 2007).

[16] Sentencing Judgment, Prosecutor v. Brima, Kamara, and Kanu (SCSL-04–16-T), Trial Chamber § 34 (June 20, 2007).

[17] Trial Judgment, Prosecutor v. Fofana and Kondewa (SCSL-04–14-T), Trial Chamber (Aug. 2, 2007).

[18] Appeals Judgment, Prosecutor v. Fofana and Kondewa (SCSL-04–14-A), Appeals Chamber (May 28, 2008). The CDF Appeal Judgment included as a mental element of the crime of conscription that the Accused "knew or should have known that such person or persons ... may be trained for or used in combat." *Id.*

[19] Trial Judgment, Prosecutor v. Sesay, Kallon, and Gbao (SCSL-04–15-T), Trial Chamber (Mar. 2, 2009). The third Accused, Gbao, was acquitted of charges related to enlisting child soldiers. *Id.*

[20] Appeals Judgment, Prosecutor v. Sesay, Kallon, and Gbao (SCSL-04–15-A) (Oct. 26, 2009).

[21] The Prosecutor vs. Charles Ghankay Taylor (SCSL-03–01-T), Trial Chamber II (May 18, 2012).

as humanitarian law expands to encompass internal wars and crimes committed outside armed conflicts.[22]

No longer an uncodified wrong, the crime of child recruitment now represents a full-fledged war crime founded on a host of human rights instruments.

The SCSL's case law also provides critical details that serve to distinguish criminal from non-criminal behavior. *Kondewa*, for example, demonstrates that, without more, initiation rituals do not qualify as conscription. However, the Trial Chamber's decision in *Taylor* holds that portering and food-finding missions in support of armed forces constitute acts of child soldiering.[23] Additionally, the SCSL jurisprudence demonstrates the ability of courts to assign varying degrees of blame to diverse actors bearing responsibility for the crime of child recruitment.

At the level of denunciation too, the child soldier cases perform an important expressive function. In meting out legalized retribution, the Court has identified conduct that is criminal (abduction, for example), and linked the offense to other war crimes and crimes against humanity – the destruction of family units, forced pregnancy, and enforced prostitution, for example – that have a disproportionate effect on children. The expressive value of these cases defines the place of criminal sanctions bounded by the rule of law and within an emerging tradition of transitional justice.[24] For bystanders, the articulation of an unqualified legal wrong may have particular resonance as it communicates that children have universal and inalienable rights and that context, confusion, and the fallibility of judgment have no bearing on the criminal act of involving youth in war.

In addition to declaring certain conduct beyond the pale of human relations, the expansion of international criminal law in this field represents a reactive ordering to domestic chaos – what Professor Ruti Teitel calls bringing the Messiah through law.[25] Here, international law joins the tattered shell of domestic law in a redemptive enterprise, aiming to strengthen municipal law and imbue it with a sense of justice and proportionality.[26] Having failed to protect Sierra Leone's children or prevent the outbreak of atrocities,[27] the unambig-

---

[22] Noah B. Novogrodsky, *Litigating Child Recruitment before the Special Court for Sierra Leone*, 7 San Diego Int'l L.J. 421, 425 (2006).

[23] The Prosecutor vs. Charles Ghankay Taylor (SCSL-03-01-T), Trial Chamber II, §§ 1546 and 1523 (May 18, 2012).

[24] For more on the expressive function of law, see Cass R. Sunstein, *On the Expressive Function of Law*, 144 U. Pa. L. Rev. 2021, at 2023 (1996); *see also* Ruti G. Teitel, Transitional Justice 28–30 (2000) (acknowledging that conventional understandings of punishment and individual accountability are adapted in transitional circumstances and often hinge on selective and largely symbolic prosecutions of individuals); Robert Sloane, *The Expressive Capacity of International Punishment: The Limits of the National Law Analogy and the Potential of International Criminal Law*, 43 Stan J. Int'l L. 39 (2007). Margaret M. deGuzman, *Choosing to Prosecute: Expressive Selection at the International Criminal Court*, 33 Mich. J. Int'l L. 265 (2012).

[25] Ruti G. Teitel, *Bringing the Messiah through the Law*, in Human Rights in Political Transitions: Gettysburg to Bosnia 339–42 (C. Hesse & R. Post eds., 1999).

[26] Article 5 of the Special Court's statute imports the 1926 Sierra Leonean law on sexual assault, creating three categories of offenses corresponding to the age of the victim. SCSL Statute art. 5.

[27] The horrors of Sierra Leone and the relatively successful intervention by British Special Forces were very much on the minds of the drafters of the Responsibility to Protect (R2P) doctrine. International Commission on Intervention and State Sovereignty, *Responsibility to Protect Report* (Dec. 2001), *available at* http://responsibilitytoprotect.org/ICISS%20Report.pdf (last visited July 11, 2012). Of course, the R2P doctrine did not exist at the time the Court was created.

uous condemnation of criminal activity serves as a clear rule on individual culpability and a return to relevance for international law and the family of nations.

Third, the child soldier cases have provided an opportunity to educate Sierra Leoneans and the international community alike about the wrongfulness of recruitment. Trials strengthen the rule of law by teaching all segments of society that the appropriate means of resolving conflict is through impartial justice. Of course, trust in law and ordered punishment is not automatic, and the conditions necessary to promote a system of criminal justice require myriad cultural stakeholders to accept the basic premise that the enterprise is both fair and better than the alternative. Traumatized or corrupt societies tend to perpetuate cycles of violence or turn inward in favor of self-help and private security; legal norms are fragile, and education is integral to the acceptance of the applicability of law after a rupture in the societal fabric.[28] In this regard, the SCSL's exhaustive outreach efforts were particularly appropriate.[29] From the Court, an authoritative interpretation of what happened, who was at fault, and how the crimes occurred may even have begun to shift the burden of knowledge from privately held information to the arena of public acknowledgment.

As the instantiation of a global community of concerned bystanders, the SCSL has fulfilled its purpose. If success is defined as establishing a mechanism to prosecute and punish some of the worst abusers of children in modern history, then the Court has achieved its primary goal. Tempting as it is to ask whether witnesses to atrocities could have done more at an earlier stage, and why judicial accountability became the principal contribution of the international community, the SCSL remains a principled and enduring response to the phenomenon of child soldiering.

III. PERPETRATORS

The principal benefit of the Court's work on perpetrators has been the clarity it has brought to the question of who may be charged. In unequivocal terms, the Court has disfavored the prosecution of child soldiers for their warlike acts, and it recognizes age-defined combatants as victims, not perpetrators. The SCSL's consistent interpretation of international criminal law is that children may not be prosecuted unless the exercise of criminal jurisdiction is intended to serve a rehabilitative function. This is particularly true for child soldiers who were unlawfully recruited and whom international law categorizes as victims, requiring them to be treated in such a manner as to promote their rehabilitation and reintegration into society. In sum, the Court's decisions hold that children illegally recruited into armed conflict are deemed to have served involuntarily and are therefore unprosecutable. In most cases, children recruited into armed conflict are treated as victims of a war crime; in all cases, they are viewed as victims of human rights violations.

The effect of this work for international criminal law generally is paradoxical: by limiting the categories of potential defendants, the Court has actually facilitated the prosecution of adults who have conscripted or employed children in armed conflict. Insofar as the SCSL's

---

[28] *See* William Finnegan, *The Kingpins: The Fight for Guadalajara*, NEW YORKER, July 2, 2102, at 40 (describing the loss of faith in law enforcement that Mexicans have experienced in the narcowars).

[29] Noah B. Novogrodsky, *Redressing Human Rights Abuses in Sierra Leone*, NEXUS MAG., June 9, 2003 (relating how SCSL Office of the Prosecutor staff made use of the culturally appropriate term *"kakatua"* (big birds) to explain the limited pool of defendants to the local populace).

attention to the phenomenon of child soldiering has spurred judicial interest from other tribunals, the Court has had an outsized impact. The judicialization of recruitment before the SCSL offers a template for other international criminal bodies and emboldens prosecutions of alleged war criminals in diverse contexts. It is no exaggeration to say that the law on the prohibition of child soldiers is fast becoming a Special Court export. The focus on the subject, coupled with the *Norman* decision on jurisdiction, resonates for other global conflicts where the enlistment of child soldiers was or is prevalent: Colombia, Burma, the DRC, Uganda, Mozambique, Angola, Liberia, Rwanda, Somalia, and Sudan. It may be premature to declare a cascade effect of prosecutions, but in 2010, Colombian authorities reported that more than 1,000 investigations had begun related to the unlawful recruitment and use of child soldiers.[30] That same year, Chadian authorities arrested a group of Sudanese men for attempting to recruit children as young as twelve into the Sudanese Liberation Army from the Goz Amer refugee camp.[31]

Nowhere are the consequences of the SCSL's work on child soldiers clearer than at the International Criminal Court (ICC). The first Indictments of suspected LRA leaders included the charge of forcibly recruiting child soldiers; the first arrest, the first trial, and the first conviction before the ICC in the *Lubanga* case involved the question of recruiting child soldiers.[32] The charge of child soldiering is also central to the second ICC case to go to trial, *Prosecutor v. Germain Katanga and Mathieu Ngudjolo Chui.*[33] Katanga and Chui, former commanders of Congolese militias, are being jointly prosecuted for crimes against humanity and for war crimes, including the use of child soldiers during the Ituri conflict in the Eastern DRC. The Court heard closing arguments in the case in May 2012.

Lubanga owes much of its normative inspiration and legal architecture to the SCSL's treatment of child soldiers. Lubanga was ultimately tried and convicted solely on three counts of war crimes for enlisting and conscripting children under the age of fifteen in the DRC and using them to participate actively in hostilities. At sentencing, Presiding Judge Adrian Fulford echoed the reasoning of the SCSL in his declaration that "The vulnerability of children means they need to be afforded particular protection."[34] Indeed, throughout the Trial Chamber's decision, the ICC referred to SCSL jurisprudence as instrumental in its interpretation of Article 8(e)(vii) of the Rome Statute.[35] If *Lubanga* is a harbinger of future reliance, the SCSL's body of judgments is already providing guidance to the ICC on the interpretation of the elements of crimes for conscription, enlistment, and use of child soldiers. The ICC will have an opportunity to elaborate on questions the SCSL has not definitively resolved – for

---

[30] U.S. Department of State, Bureau of Democracy, Human Rights, and Labor, 2010 Human Rights Reports: Colombia, 4, *available at* http://www.state.gov/documents/organization/160452.pdf (last visited last July 11, 2012).

[31] Children and Armed Conflict: Report of the Secretary-General, U.N. Doc. A/65/820-S/2011/250 (Apr. 23, 2011).

[32] In 2006, the ICC Chief Prosecutor issued a warrant for Thomas Lubanga Dyilo's arrest in connection with his alleged responsibility for the war crime of conscripting, enlisting, and using child soldiers under the age of fifteen to further the war in the DRC's Ituri district during 2002 and 2003.

[33] ICC, *Situation in the Democratic Republic of the Congo*, Case Information Sheet, *Prosecutor v. Germain Katanga and Mathieu Ngudjolo Chui*, May 14, 2012, http://www.icc-cpi.int/iccdocs/PIDS/publications/KatangaChuiEng.pdf.

[34] *Congolese Warlord Sentenced in the Hague*, N.Y. Times, July 10, 2012.

[35] ICC, *The Prosecutor v. Thomas Lubanga Dyilo*, Case Information Sheet, September 13, 2012, http://www.icc-cpi.int/iccdocs/PIDS/publications/LubangaENG.pdf/.

example, what the legal linkage is between abductions and child soldier recruitment, and how to distinguish between active and non-active participation of children under fifteen in hostilities – but the foundation has been set. Notwithstanding potentially troubling contextual and conflict-location differences, *Lubanga* demonstrates that perpetrators well beyond Sierra Leone now face the possibility of criminal sanctions for their actions within a tested framework for individual culpability.

For the actual perpetrators of child recruitment in Sierra Leone, the Court represents selective or exemplary prosecution. On one level, there is comfort in the positive law quality of the prohibition on the use and recruitment of child soldiers. The SCSL's interpretation of the enlistment and use of children soldiers has effectively converted the offense into a strict liability crime, not unlike statutory rape. On another level, however, the prosecution of the defendants – with the notable exception of Charles Taylor – appears arbitrary. The Gbao acquittal demonstrates that the defendants were not uniquely situated; they were instead leaders of forces that embraced recruitment as a systemic practice. Moreover, the criminal jurisdiction of the Special Court is circumscribed in ways that justifies the claim that prosecution is selective or abjectly politicized. The Court's statute prevents temporal jurisdiction over offenses committed prior to November 30, 1996, Article 1 largely immunizes UNAMSIL or other foreign peacekeepers from prosecution, and balanced numbers of defendants were chosen as representatives of the three major fighting forces, not because their crimes were especially heinous.[36]

Accordingly, there would appear to be little deterrent value in the particular prosecutions. The literature on the deterrent effect of selective international criminal prosecutions questions whether subsequent actors will desist from specific actions based on the existence of an authorized tribunal.[37] In West Africa alone, the use of mass rape in Guinea, which borders Sierra Leone; the prevalence of child diamond miners in Liberia, another of Sierra Leone's neighbors; and a recent eruption of teenage combatants in Cote D'Ivoire suggests that the threat of prosecution has not curtailed the use and recruitment of child soldiers.

IV. VICTIMS

Law tells stories of right and wrong, heroes and villains. For the SCSL, there is only one script for child soldiers: they are the victims of adult depredations.[38] Because the Court

---

[36] See Article 1 SCSL Statute, para. 2, which provides that:Any transgressions by peacekeepers and related personnel present in Sierra Leone pursuant to the Status of Mission Agreement in force between the United Nations and the Government of Sierra Leone or agreements between Sierra Leone and other Governments or regional organizations, or, in the absence of such agreement, provided that the peacekeeping operations were undertaken with the consent of the Government of Sierra Leone, shall be within the primary jurisdiction of the sending State.

[37] See Julian Ku & Jide Ndzelibe, *Do International Criminal Tribunals Deter or Exacerbate Humanitarian Atrocities?*, 84 WASH. U. L.Q. (2007) (using certainty and severity of punishment to examine whether anyone is in fact deterred from committing atrocities, and concluding that with very exceptions they are not); *but see* Payam Ahkavan, *Beyond Impunity: Can International Criminal Justice Prevent Future Atrocities?*, 95 AM. J. INT'L L. 7–31 (2001) (arguing that some categories of potential offenders, including mid-level commanders, may be deterred by the existence of a functioning criminal tribunal).

[38] See, e.g., Sentencing Judgment, Prosecutor v. Sesay, Kallon, and Gbao (SCSL-04-15-T), Trial Chamber, § 182 (Apr. 8, 2009). "The Chamber takes the view that the exceptionally young age of those who were abducted and

exists to try those who bear the greatest responsibility for atrocity crimes committed in Sierra Leone, a tension emerges in evaluating the legacy of a defendant-focused criminal tribunal on the relevant community of victims.

To be sure, the Court includes a Witness and Victims Support Section, and has sought to link its work with broader reconstruction, demobilization, and rehabilitation efforts. But the Court is not primarily about the combatants themselves, the needs of young people, or even the future of Sierra Leone. It is focused instead on exemplary prosecutions for the purpose of exacting a measure of symbolic justice. This particular drama requires that the defendants be legally responsible adults and that children be consigned to the role of casualties, survivors, or pained witnesses, often disembodied, damaged, and, all too often, the object of brutal amputations. Consistent with this narrative, the Court's first Prosecutor, David Crane, announced that he would not charge anyone for crimes committed while the Accused was under the age of eighteen, and no such charges were brought. [39]

The problem with treating child soldiers as infantilized victims is the oversimplification of complex and dynamic identities. Almost all accounts of the war confirm that Sierra Leonean children were victims and victimizers, observers and willing participants, as well as the subjects of kidnapping and many forms of abuse. As anthropologist Danny Hoffman explains, Sierra Leonean "youth constitute[d] a demographic of those excluded, a populace in which childhood and alienation become synonymous."[40] Mounting violence and the militarization of youth in Sierra Leone surely exacerbated the exploitation of minors. At the same time, many of the worst atrocities were committed by children against other young people.

The Court's inability to recognize multiple realities creates both legal and sociological problems. If criminal responsibility is conferred only for the recruitment of persons under the age of fifteen, and individuals will be tried only if they are eighteen or older at the time of the commission of offenses, commanders may be incentivized to recruit fifteen-, sixteen-, and seventeen- year-olds. Additionally, the SCSL has been predisposed to discount certain voices in evidence; for example, the Trial Chamber has occasionally found the testimony of child survivors to be unreliable and susceptible to improper influences. Other children may have been re-traumatized in the process of testifying.

By removing the threat of prosecution, the Court has attempted to destigmatize individuals, many of whom are now ostracized from their home communities. And yet an overly simplistic view of child soldiers may limit the participation of former combatants in truth-seeking exercises and while setting them up for limited forms of rehabilitation.[41] Beginning with Disarmament, Demobilization, and Reintegration (DDR) campaigns in 2001, Sierra

---

conscripted rendered them vulnerable. Children as young as 8 or 9 years old were forcibly taken for military training, some barely able to lift the guns they were to shoot." *Id.*

[39] Press Release, SCSL, Special Court Prosecutor Says He Will Not Prosecute Children (Nov. 2, 2002), *available at* http://www.sc-sl.org/LinkClick.aspx?fileticket=XRwCUe%2baVhw%3d&tabid=196 (last visited July 11, 2012).

[40] Danny Hoffman, *Like Beasts in the Bush: Synonyms of Childhood and Youth in Sierra Leone*, 6 POSTCOLONIAL STUD. 297 n.3 (2003).

[41] Romeo Dallaire describes how postwar rehabilitation in Sierra Leone meant that thousands of former child soldiers were trained as mechanics in a country with very few cars. DALLAIRE, *supra* note 10.

Leone's child soldiers were instructed that they were not to blame for their actions. The truth is more nuanced for the thousands of combatants who began fighting while under the age of fifteen (or eighteen), but continued committing abuses into adulthood. To the extent that the Court regards youth only as faultless victims, it absolves them of responsibility for their actions, while simultaneously assigning the full measure of accountability to persons who had reached the somewhat arbitrary age of eighteen.

Institutionally too, the Court's approach is mismatched with the experience of companion organizations. The task of societal restoration and individual rehabilitation falls largely outside the purview of the SCSL, but in this domain, NGOs engaged in psychological counseling; development agencies and the Sierra Leonean Truth Commission have all found that the bright-line rules embraced by the SCSL have little applicability to the experience of most war-affected persons. The age of the offender matters less for reintegration purposes than whether the individual has a family to return to, whether the child combatant voluntarily participated in hostilities, whether the community pushed the individual to take up arms (as in the case of many CDF fighters), or whether the former child soldier committed atrocities in his or her home village. Against this backdrop, the refrain that "it's not your fault" and the related assumption that children do not have the capacity to exercise agency is at odds with perceptions of wartime reality and engrained community norms.[42] A one-dimensional representation of youth in law may also undermine future efforts to assist traumatized young people. Personal responsibility is not an on/off switch, and blanket legal exculpations are difficult to reconcile with the predictable difficulties the generation of child soldiers will have as they reach adulthood.

It is similarly unclear that the designation of victim in law is helpful to former child soldiers themselves. Do child victims want to tell their story before the Court, and do they have a sense that their experiences matter? Does calling one-time commanders to account for their conduct assist former child soldiers in finding a sense of equilibrium? Do children of this generation have a notion that the SCSL contributes to the rule of law and good governance in a shattered state? Can the Court contribute to developmental understandings of right and wrong for children who came of age in this environment? To date, there is scant evidence that the tribunal-generated label of "victim" produces catharsis, forgiveness, or renewal.

In the end, whether former child soldiers are liberated or redeemed by the SCSL's legacy will depend less on jurisprudential achievements and more on the content of broader reconstruction efforts. The Court is but one part of that process; for victims, the non-penal transitional justice modes of the Truth Commission and community-level reintegration programs are likely to play a larger role in the creation of civil society and functional interpersonal relations.

V. CONCLUSION

The SCSL can be justifiably proud of its contributions to the jurisprudence on child soldiers. The purity of positions articulated by the Court and the codification of custom will endure

---

[42] DRUMBL, *supra* note 7; TIM KELSALL, CULTURE UNDER CROSS-EXAMINATION: INTERNATIONAL JUSTICE AND THE SPECIAL COURT FOR SIERRA LEONE 158 (2009).

as a legacy of the tribunal. Yet ironically, the SCSL is likely to do more to clarify criminal responsibility for future conflicts than it can for Sierra Leone. This is ultimately a form of bystander justice in which neutral outsiders develop an authoritative history of the conflict and assign preordained roles to victims and perpetrators alike.

19

The Sentencing Legacy of the Special Court for Sierra Leone

Margaret M. deGuzman[*]

I. INTRODUCTION

This chapter examines the legacy that the Special Court for Sierra Leone (SCSL) leaves through its sentencing practice. The SCSL was established by agreement between the government of Sierra Leone and the United Nations to try "persons who bear the greatest responsibility"[1] for the serious international crimes committed during the country's long civil war. The SCSL conducted four trials of nine individuals, convicting each of them and imposing sentences ranging from fifteen to fifty-two years.[2] The first three trials addressed the crimes of the leaders of the three main armed groups in the conflict: the Revolutionary United Front (RUF), the Armed Forces Revolutionary Council (AFRC), and the Civil Defense Forces (CDF).[3] The fourth trial involved a single defendant, former Liberian president Charles Taylor, and resulted in the first international conviction of a head of state.[4]

In its sentencing judgments in these cases, the SCSL developed international sentencing law by identifying and prioritizing the goals of sentencing, articulating the considerations relevant to sentence allocations, determining the appropriate weight to be accorded to various factors, and ultimately handing down sentences. Through these decisions, the SCSL has left a sentencing legacy that will likely influence international and national courts for the foreseeable future. Indeed, the SCSL's sentencing legacy is particularly important because international sentencing law and theory remain highly underdeveloped.[5]

For purposes of this analysis, the word "legacy" requires deconstruction. In recent years, a number of ad hoc international courts and tribunals have completed their work or started the process of winding down. Scholars and practitioners have reacted to the imminent

---

[*] Associate Professor, Temple University Beasley School of Law, USA. Thanks to Charles Jalloh for very helpful comments and to Keith Greenwald for excellent research assistance.
[1] SCSL Statute art. 1(1).
[2] The Court also conducted a contempt hearing, which is excluded from this analysis.
[3] Sentencing Judgment, Sesay, Kallon, and Gbao (RUF) (SCSL-04-15-T), Trial Chamber I (Apr. 8, 2009) [hereinafter *RUF Sentencing*]; Sentencing Judgment, Brima, Kamara, Kanu (AFRC) (SCSL-04-16-T), Trial Chamber II (July 19, 2007) [hereinafter *AFRC Sentencing*]; Sentencing Judgment, Fofana and Kondewa (CDF) (SCSL-04-14-T), Trial Chamber I (Oct. 9, 2007) [hereinafter *CDF Sentencing*].
[4] Sentencing Judgment, Taylor (SCSL-03-01-T), Trial Chamber II (May 30, 2012) [hereinafter *Taylor Sentencing*].
[5] See, e.g., R. Henham, *The Philosophical Foundations of International Sentencing*, 1 J. INT'L CRIM. JUST. 64, 64 (2003); R.D. Sloane, *The Expressive Capacity of International Punishment: The Limits of the National Law Analogy and the Potential of International Criminal Law*, 43 STAN. J. INT'L STUD. 39, 39 (2007).

closures by seeking to identify the "legacies" of these institutions.[6] Few of these writers have explained in any detail what they mean by the term "legacy," however. Instead, the term tends to be used loosely, conflating concepts that are importantly distinct.[7]

In this chapter, I examine three types of sentencing legacies.[8] First, as a descriptive matter, the SCSL developed law relevant to sentencing. Although not binding on any other court, the SCSL's statements regarding the appropriate goals of sentencing, the factors relevant to sentencing, and the weight to be given to these considerations will inform other international and perhaps national courts sentencing perpetrators of international crimes. I call this law the Court's "legal legacy." Second, the Court's legal holdings can be assessed normatively. Did the SCSL identify the right goals of sentencing and apply them appropriately? This can be termed the Court's "normative legacy." Finally, an important aspect of the SCSL's legacy – perhaps the most important – is the perceptions of relevant audiences about whether the Court's sentencing practice was appropriate. This is the Court's "sociological legacy." The chapter examines each of these aspects of the SCSL's sentencing legacy and concludes that although it is too soon to reach definitive conclusions, the legal legacy will likely be important and lasting while the normative and sociological legacies remain ambiguous and contested.

II. LEGAL LEGACY

Authors who write about the legacies of international courts often have primarily in mind the courts' major legal holdings. For example, the Honorable Teresa Doherty, Justice of the SCSL, identifies as the legacy of the SCSL its "landmark decisions in International Law."[9] The Court's legal decisions help to build the body of international criminal law that future courts reference in adjudicating cases. Thus, as the late Professor Antonio Cassese wrote, the legacy includes "something useful" that the Court leaves behind.[10] The legal legacy of the SCSL with regard to sentencing includes all of the Court's holdings that are generalizable and thus potentially instructive to other courts. In light of space constraints, this section will highlight only a few of the holdings that are likely to have a significant impact on the future development of international sentencing practice. These include the SCSL's decisions regarding the goals of sentencing as well as the factors relevant to particular sentencing decisions and the priorities among them.

---

[6] *See, e.g.*, J. Cockayne, *The Fraying Shoestring: Rethinking Hybrid War Crimes Tribunals*, 28 FORDHAM INT'L L.J. 616 (2005); S.J. Rapp, *Achieving Accountability for the Greatest Crimes – The Legacy of the International Tribunals*, 55 DRAKE L. REV. 259(2007) [hereinafter Rapp, *Achieving Accountability*]; R. Kerr & J. Lincoln, *The SCSL for Sierra Leone: Outreach, Legacy and Impact, Final Report*, War Crimes Research Group, Department of War Studies, King's College London, University of London (Feb. 2008), *available at* https://www.kcl.ac.uk/sspp/departments/warstudies/research/groups/wc/slfinalreport.pdf (last visited July 12, 2012).

[7] *See, e.g.*, Rapp, *supra* note 6 (discussing the "legacies" of international tribunals from both legal and normative perspectives).

[8] My deconstruction of "legacy" is inspired by Richard Fallon's tripartite analysis of the concept of legitimacy. R.H. Fallon, Jr., *Legitimacy and the Constitution*, 118 HARV. L. REV. 1787, 1789 (2005).

[9] Hon. T. Doherty, *Developments in the Prosecution of Gender-Based Crimes – The SCSL for Sierra Leone Experience*, 17 AM. U. J. GENDER, SOC. POL'Y & L. 327, 328 (2009).

[10] Antonio Cassese, *Report on the SCSL for Sierra Leone*, Report of Independent Expert on 12 December 2006 (SCSL), para. 276, *available at* http://www.sc-sl.org/LinkClick.aspx?fileticket=VTDHyrHasLc=& (last visited July 12, 2012).

With regard to the goals of sentencing, the SCSL's legacy is not entirely clear. The Court's statute, like those of the other international tribunals, does not specify goals of sentencing but rather leaves their elaboration up to the judges. The SCSL has two trial chambers and an appeals chamber, each of which has made statements about the goals of sentencing in its judgments. Moreover, the various statements are not entirely consistent.[11] Nonetheless, an important theme runs through the sentencing judgments: that the SCSL is an *international* court and, as such, should give priority to international goals in sentencing. This view was expressed particularly strongly in the appellate judgment in the CDF case where the judges declared the SCSL to be "an international court with responsibility to protect and promote the norms and values of the international community."[12] The Court thus deemed its "paramount" concerns to be the "international interests in protecting humanity."[13]

This international orientation is also reflected in the sources the SCSL judges used to identify the goals of sentencing. Rather than look primarily to the goals of sentencing in the laws of Sierra Leone, the judges turned to the jurisprudence of the International Criminal Tribunals for the former Yugoslavia (ICTY) and Rwanda (ICTR). Indeed, in the AFRC sentencing judgment the Trial Chamber declined to consider Sierra Leonean law on the grounds that no national crimes were charged.[14] Yet the SCSL statute allows the trial chamber recourse to the sentencing practice of both the ICTR and national courts "as appropriate."[15] Nothing in the statute indicates that reference to national sentencing practice is appropriate only when national crimes are charged. Moreover, as Justice King opined in his dissenting opinion in the CDF case, the statute's failure to mention ICTY jurisprudence as a source of law for the trial chambers arguably made their references to ICTY case law inappropriate.[16]

The SCSL's international orientation had significant consequences for the sentences it handed down. In the CDF case, for example, the Appeals Chambers justified increasing the defendants' sentences largely on the basis of a professed need to send a strong message about the international norm being upheld.[17] The Court thus seemed to give priority to the goal of international norm expression rather than focusing on retributive proportionality, or the needs for specific and general deterrence, or even individual and social rehabilitation, including reconciliation. In other judgments, however, the international emphasis led the SCSL to give priority to the goals of retribution and deterrence over individual and societal rehabilitation.[18] Indeed, in several decisions, the SCSL explicitly noted that the Court's international nature requires a de-emphasis on rehabilitation.[19] Although the discussion of

---

[11] *Compare CDF Sentencing, supra* note 3, para. 26 (Trial Chamber I claiming that "the primary objectives of sentencing are retribution, deterrence and rehabilitation"), *with Taylor Sentencing, supra* note 4, para. 15 (Trial Chamber II deciding that "the primary objectives must be retribution and deterrence").

[12] Judgment, CDF (SCSL-04-14-A), Appeals Chamber, para. 561 (May 28, 2008) [hereinafter *CDF Appeals*].

[13] *Id.* at para. 563.

[14] *See, e.g., AFRC Sentencing, supra* note 3, at paras. 32–33.

[15] SCSL Statute art. 19(1).

[16] *See, e.g., CDF Appeals, supra* note 12, Dissenting Opinion of Justice Gelaga King as to Sentence, paras. 112–113.

[17] *CDF Appeals, supra* note 12, paras. 530–533.

[18] In fact, despite emphasizing norm expression in justifying its sentences, the CDF appeals judgment declared that the most important goals of sentencing are retribution and deterrence. (*Id.* at para. 532.)

[19] *CDF Sentencing, supra* note 3, at para. 28; *AFRC Sentencing, supra* note 3, at para. 17; *Taylor Sentencing, supra* note 4, at para. 15; *RUF Sentencing, supra* note 3, at para. 16.

rehabilitation in the judgments focuses largely on individual rehabilitation, the judgments also pay little attention to the possibility of using sentencing to foster societal rehabilitation, including reconciliation.[20] This is noteworthy in light of the SCSL's overall purpose of fostering peace and reconciliation in Sierra Leone.[21]

The SCSL followed international jurisprudence not only in identifying sentencing goals but also in determining the factors relevant to allocating particular sentences.[22] The SCSL's statute, like those of the other ad hoc tribunals, requires the judges to consider "such factors as the gravity of the offence and the individual circumstances of the convicted person."[23] The SCSL adopted the views of the ICTY and ICTR with regard to what "gravity" means, as well as which "individual circumstances" should be taken into account, and in what ways.[24] Thus, the SCSL held that determining the gravity of a crime includes consideration of a number of factors, including the nature of the conduct, the impact on the victims, the vulnerability of the victims, and the degree of participation of the Accused.[25] Like the other ad hoc tribunals, the Court sometimes considered the mode of liability under which the Accused was convicted as part of the gravity analysis.[26] The SCSL was also careful to follow the ICTY rules that factors considered in determining culpability should not also be counted in determining gravity,[27] and that factors counted under gravity should not also be included as aggravating circumstances.[28]

Finally, the SCSL drew on the jurisprudence of the ICTY and ICTR in identifying relevant aggravating and mitigating factors.[29] In sum, because the SCSL considered itself "international," an important aspect of its legal legacy is that it served to reinforce the sentencing legacies of the international tribunals that preceded it: the ICTY and ICTR.

At the same time, the SCSL made some important legal innovations of its own in its sentencing jurisprudence. For example, with regard to aggravating factors, the Trial Chamber in the Charles Taylor case invoked the novel idea that the extraterritorial nature of the criminal conduct constitutes an aggravating factor.[30] The Court drew on the ICJ holding that the type of assistance that Taylor provided to facilitate crimes in Sierra Leone constitutes a

---

[20] *But see CDF Sentencing, supra* note 3, at para. 95, *overturned* on appeal (justifying a relatively low sentence for the defendants because "a manifestly repressive sentence … will neither be consonant with nor … in the overall interests … of justice, peace, and reconciliation that this Court is mandated by U.N. Security Council Resolution 1315, to achieve").

[21] *See* S.C. Res. 1315 pmbl (2000).

[22] *See, e.g., AFRC Sentencing, supra* note 3, at paras. 19–25 nn.32–52 (citing the ICTY fifty-one times, the ICTR four times, and the SCSL's Rules two times, but not citing Sierra Leonean or any other national system's practices).

[23] SCSL Statute art. 19(2).

[24] *See, e.g., Taylor Sentencing, supra* note 4, at paras. 19–23.

[25] *See, e.g., id.* at paras. 19–21.

[26] *See, e.g., CDF Sentencing, supra* note 3, at para. 34.

[27] *See, e.g.,* Judgment, RUF (SCSL-04-15-A), Appeals Chamber, paras. 1234–1237 (Oct. 26, 2009) [hereinafter *RUF Appeals*].

[28] *See AFRC Sentencing, supra* note 3, at para. 23 nn.46 and 47.

[29] *See, e.g., id.* at paras. 21–25 nn.43–52.

[30] *Taylor Sentencing, supra* note 4, at paras. 27 and 98. Mark Drumbl has noted that this amounts to an invocation of the crime of aggression, which is not within the Court's jurisdiction, to enhance Taylor's sentence. *See* M. Drumbl, *The Charles Taylor Sentence and Traditional International Law,* Opinio Juris Blog (June 11, 2012), http://opiniojuris.org/2012/06/11/charles-taylor-sentencing-the-taylor-sentence-and-traditional-international-law.

violation of the principles of nonintervention and nonuse of force.[31] Here again, the SCSL seems to be seeking to promote an international norm rather than focusing on retribution or deterrence in rendering Taylor's sentence.

The Taylor sentencing decision also represents an important holding on the roles that leadership position and modes of liability play in sentence allocation. The trial chamber convicted Taylor of planning, and aiding and abetting various crimes against humanity and war crimes, but acquitted him of joint criminal enterprise, instigating, ordering, and superior responsibility for those crimes.[32] In many legal systems, aiding and abetting is considered a less serious form of liability that merits a lower sentence than direct commission or ordering. In Sierra Leone, however, as the Trial Chamber notes, an accessory "may be ... punished in all respects as if he were a principal felon."[33] Nonetheless, on the grounds that Taylor was not a principal participant, the Trial Chamber rejected the government's request for an eighty-year sentence.[34] The Trial Chamber thus revealed again the Court's international orientation.

At the same time, the Trial Chamber awarded Taylor the relatively high sentence of fifty years' imprisonment.[35] That sentence is significantly higher than sentences awarded at the ICTY and ICTR for aiding and abetting crimes.[36] The Trial Chamber justified this sentence largely on the grounds of Taylor's position of authority as the president of Liberia and as a regional political leader.[37] According to the Trial Chamber, these roles put Taylor "in a class of his own."[38] As the Trial Chamber took many factors into account in explaining Taylor's sentence, it is difficult to isolate the importance of any particular factor. Nonetheless, the Trial Chamber seems to have placed greater emphasis on Taylor's leadership position than on the mode of liability of which he was convicted.[39] This holding may well influence future courts, particularly those adjudicating the crimes of heads of state.

Another important sentencing decision the SCSL made is that mitigation should not be granted based on the "just cause" for which a defendant fought.[40] The CDF case was

---

[31] *Id.*

[32] Judgment, Taylor (SCSL-03-01-T), Trial Chamber II, paras. 6900, 6953, 6971, 6972, 6973 and 6986 (May 18, 2012).

[33] *Taylor Sentencing, supra* note 4, at para. 37.

[34] *Id.* at para. 94.

[35] *Id.* at para. 40.

[36] *See, e.g.,* Judgment, Đorđević (IT-05-87/1-T), Trial Chamber II, paras. 2193–2194 and 2230–2231 (Feb. 23, 2011) (twenty-seven years for aiding and abetting and joint criminal enterprise liability for the crimes against humanity of deportation, murder, and persecution and the war crimes of forcible transfer and murder); Judgment, Aleksovski (IT-95-14/1-A), Appeals Chamber, paras. 1–2, 36 and 191 (Mar. 24, 2000) (seven years for aiding and abetting and superior responsibility for the war crime of outrages upon personal dignity); *see also, e.g.,* Judgment Summary, Gacumbtsi (ICTR-2001-64-T), Trial Chamber III, paras. 33, 40, 52, 54 and 72 (June 17, 2004) (thirty years for aiding and abetting and other modes of liability for genocide).

[37] *Taylor Sentencing, supra* note 4, at paras. 96–103.

[38] *Id.* at para. 101.

[39] *Id.* at paras. 97 and 102 (explaining that his leadership position was a position of public trust, which he violated by participating in the crimes, and this betrayal "outweighs the distinctions that might otherwise pertain to the modes liability"). Wayne Jordash has argued that JCE was proven at the Taylor trial, but the Court chose not to convict on that basis to avoid having to apply the SCSL's expansive interpretation of JCE, which has been attacked as a violation of *nullum crimen sine lege. See* W. Jordash, *Charles Taylor, JCE and Letting Sleeping Dogs Lie,* iLAWYER: A BLOG ON INTERNATIONAL JUSTICE (June 27, 2012), http://ilawyerblog.com/charles-taylor-jce-and-letting-sleeping-dogs-lie.

[40] *CDF Appeals, supra* note 12, at paras. 529–534.

controversial because the CDF had fought to restore the democratically elected government of Sierra Leone. Some observers thus argued that the CDF leaders should not be prosecuted at all and, once they were convicted, argued that their sentences should be lenient in light of the laudable goal they pursued.[41] Following this logic, the Trial Chamber granted CDF leaders Moinina Fofana and Allieu Kondewa "significant" mitigation based on the purpose for which they fought and the sense of "civic duty" that motivated their participation in the cause.[42] The Trial Chamber awarded Fofana a sentence of six years' imprisonment for aiding and abetting and superior responsibility for the war crimes of murder, cruel treatment, pillage, and collective punishment.[43] Kondewa received eight years for aiding and abetting, superior responsibility, and committing the war crimes of murder, cruel treatment, pillage, collective punishment, and recruiting child soldiers.[44] These sentences were significantly lower than those the SCSL awarded to other defendants convicted of similar crimes.[45]

The Appeals Chamber reversed.[46] It held that although motives may generally be considered in mitigation, "just cause," civic duty, and other political motives do not mitigate punishment for international crimes.[47] The Chamber reasoned that international humanitarian law is founded on the distinction between *jus ad bellum* and *jus in bello* and that "[t]he political motivations of a combatant do not alter the demands on that combatant to ensure their conduct complies with the law."[48] It further opined that for a court to consider political motives in mitigation of sentence, even when "meritorious ... provides implicit legitimacy to conduct that unequivocally violates the law."[49] Finding that the Trial Chamber had taken "just cause" into account, the Appeals Chamber increased Fofana's sentence to fifteen years and Kondewa's to twenty years.[50]

---

[41] *See, e.g.*, L. Fofana, *Putting People on Trial May Ignite Fresh Conflict*, INTER PRESS SERVICE NEWS AGENCY (Mar. 11, 2004), *available at* www.ipsnews.net/2004/03/rights-sierra-leone-putting-people-on-trial-may-ignite-fresh-conflict (last visited July 16, 2012) (explaining that there were protests surrounding the CDF trial because the defendants fought for the restoration of the democratically elected government); *see also, e.g.*, C. Timberg, *Sierra Leone SCSL's Narrow Focus: Well-Funded but Selective War Crimes Probe Draws Resentment of Impoverished Victims*, WASH. POST (Mar. 26, 2008), *available at* www.washingtonpost.com/wp-dyn/content/article/2008/03/25/AR2008032503156.html (last visited July 16, 2012) (stressing that the Court sits in Freetown and that "many in Freetown [regard the CDF] as valiant defenders of their city against vicious rebels"); *see also, e.g.*, C.C. Jalloh, *SCSL for Sierra Leone: Achieving Justice?*, 32 MICH. J. INT'L L. 395, 424–25 (2011) (arguing that the prosecution and jailing of CDF members, seen as heroes to many Sierra Leoneans, was "too daring for the delicate political balance necessary in the post-conflict society").

[42] *CDF Sentencing, supra* note 3, at paras. 91 and 94.

[43] *CDF Sentencing, supra* note 3, at 33 (The Court awarded Kondewa eight years for murder, eight years for cruel treatment, five years for pillage, six years for collective punishment, and seven years for child soldier crimes.).

[44] *Id.* at 34.

[45] *See, e.g.*, *RUF Sentencing, supra* note 3, at paras. 93–98 (awarding defendants, variously, forty-five years for collective punishment, fifty years for child soldier crimes, fifteen years for pillage, and fifteen years for murder).

[46] *CDF Appeals, supra* note 12, at paras. 559–560.

[47] *Id.* at paras. 528–531.

[48] *Id.* at para. 530.

[49] *Id.* at para. 534. Many commentators have criticized this decision. *See, e.g.*, L. Gberie, "The Civil Defense Forces Trial: Limit to International Justice?," Chapter 31 in this volume; Jalloh, *supra* note 41, at 425.

[50] *CDF Appeals, supra* note 12, at paras. 560–565. Justice Gelaga King dissented, arguing that the Trial Chamber had not mitigated based on "just cause." *Id.*, Dissenting Opinion of Justice Gelaga King as to Sentence, paras. 107–110.

The significance of these and other SCSL legal holdings regarding sentencing remains to be seen. The most important determinant of the impact of the SCSL's sentencing legacy will probably be the extent to which the permanent International Criminal Court (ICC) follows the SCSL's holdings or uses the Court's jurisprudence to inform ICC sentencing decisions. As the SCSL is a "hybrid" court comprised of both international and national judges, prosecutors, and laws, the ICC is perhaps less likely to follow its precedents than those of the more strictly international ICTY and ICTR. Nonetheless, particularly on issues about which no purely international court has spoken, the ICC may well take into consideration the rulings of the SCSL. In fact, the ICC has done so already in its first sentencing decision. In sentencing Thomas Lubanga for conscripting and using child soldiers, the ICC discussed SCSL sentencing jurisprudence, noting that the SCSL is the only other international court to have convicted defendants of those crimes.[51] The Lubanga judgment notes the rather high sentences awarded to two SCSL defendants convicted of child soldier offenses and seems to distinguish those cases from Lubanga's based on the number of counts of which the SCSL defendants were convicted.[52] Although the Lubanga judgment gives little indication of the extent to which the SCSL sentences influenced Lubanga's sentence, it is significant that the ICC found them worthy of consideration.

Another important determinant of the impact of the SCSL's legal legacy will be the extent to which Sierra Leonean courts adjudicate international crimes that took place in the civil war or that take place in the future.[53] If the courts of Sierra Leone consider the SCSL's approach to adjudicating international crimes relevant to their own work, the Court's legal legacy will have a lasting impact. Indeed, other national courts, particularly in Africa, may make use of the SCSL's precedents in reaching sentencing decisions for international crimes. Finally, the SCSL's sentencing legacy may well influence the work of future hybrid courts, which continue to be established even after the creation of the permanent ICC.

III. NORMATIVE LEGACY

Authors discussing the legacies of international courts often extend their understanding of the term "legacy" beyond a description of the courts' important legal holdings to the question of whether those holdings, as well as the court's practices more generally, were right or wrong, good or bad. Charles Jalloh, the editor of this volume, and Vincent Nmehielle suggest that a court's legacy can be understood, at least in part, in terms of the extent to which it met its stated goals.[54] Similarly, Stephen Rapp, one of the SCSL's chief prosecutors, has written about the legacy of international courts in terms of their successes

---

[51] Decision on Sentence Pursuant to Article 76 of the Statute, Lubanga (ICC-01/04–01/06–2901), Trial Chamber I, paras. 12–15 (July 10, 2012).

[52] *Id.* at para. 14.

[53] Although many of the civil war crimes are covered by a national amnesty, Sierra Leonean courts have tried some defendants for crimes that took place after the amnesty was passed. However, these were tried as "ordinary" crimes, not war crimes, because Sierra Leonean law does not include international crimes. *See* S. Horovitz, *Sierra Leone: Interaction between International and National Responses to the Mass Atrocities*, DOMAC 26–29, 52 (Dec. 2009), *available at* www.domac.is/media/domac/DOMAC3-SH-corr.pdf (last visited July 19, 2012).

[54] *See, e.g.,* V.O. Nmehielle & C.C. Jalloh, *International Criminal Justice: The Legacy of the SCSL for Sierra Leone*, 30 FLETCHER F. WORLD AFF. 107, 120 (2006).

and shortcomings – the former are to be emulated and the latter avoided in the work of future courts.[55] James Cockayne, who worked in the SCSL's Defense Office, has analyzed the extent to which the Court has left a "positive legacy" by meeting performance standards.[56] These authors thus employ the term "legacy" to include a normative evaluation of a court's work.

There are multiple ways to perform a normative assessment of a court's work. One possibility is to evaluate that work in relation to the norms in place prior to the court's establishment. Thus, for example, if the norm in a given community were to sentence defendants purely with an eye to their rehabilitation, a court that failed to consider a defendant's prospects for rehabilitation would leave a negative legacy in that regard. Another possibility is to evaluate a court's work in terms of identified moral principles. One could argue, for instance, that sentencing a defendant more harshly than he or she deserves violates the principle of retributive proportionality. In this short chapter, I do not seek to draw such conclusions about the SCSL's normative legacy, however. Instead, my argument is that the SCSL missed an opportunity to promote its normative vision by failing adequately to address the tension created by its hybridity. The SCSL thus left itself open to charges that by privileging international justice objectives it was insufficiently attentive to justice in Sierra Leone.

As discussed above, in its sentencing judgments, the SCSL adopted a distinctly international vision of the Court's role with little discussion of the justifications for this approach.[57] Yet, as a "hybrid" or "quasi-international" court, it is far from clear that the Court should orient its sentencing decisions around such international objectives. As the SCSL is among only a small number of hybrid tribunals created in recent years, there is no preexisting norm against which to evaluate the SCSL's work in this regard. Instead, the Court's normative legacy must be considered in terms of the norms that it helped to create for future courts.

A debate has evolved in the literature about the extent to which hybrid courts should consider themselves international.[58] According to one view, hybrid courts are essentially international courts to which national governments have consented for particular situations.[59] Their goals should thus largely mirror those of courts created entirely under international

---

[55] Rapp, *supra* note 6, at 267–85.

[56] Cockayne, *supra* note 6, at 622–25 and 660 (listing the performance standards and noting that "a positive legacy is not a self-fulfilling prophecy, but must be carefully designed and produced.").

[57] The CDF and Taylor judgments are especially notable in this regard because the Court speaks explicitly in those decisions about its role as a disseminator of international norms. *See, e.g., CDF Sentencing, supra* note 3, at para. 79 (stating that recognizing "necessity" as a defense "would negate the resolve and determination of the International Community to combat these crimes which [harm] innocent victims or … the civilian population that it intends to protect"); *Taylor Sentencing, supra* note 4, at para. 14 (explaining that the SCSL, as an international court, must issue a sentence that would "make plain the condemnation of the international community … and show that the international community is not ready to tolerate serious violations of international humanitarian law and human rights").

[58] *See, e.g.,* R. Cryer et al., An Introduction to International Criminal Law and Procedure 183 (2d ed. 2010) (explaining that the Court controversially declared itself international, and by doing so could circumvent head-of-state immunity).

[59] *See, e.g.,* S. Morrison, *Extraordinary Language in the Courts of Cambodia: Interpreting the Limiting Language and Personal Jurisdiction of the Cambodian Tribunal,* 37 Cap. U. L. Rev. 583, 583 (2009) (referring, throughout the piece, to hybrid courts as international courts, and explaining that they are formed by agreements between a state and the United Nations for the purpose of trying war crimes, genocide, and crimes against humanity).

law and with uniformly international staffing.[60] Another perspective, however, holds that hybrid courts are more appropriately considered stand-ins for ill-equipped or nonfunctioning national courts and thus should primarily adopt national goals.[61] The debate is complicated by the fact that there is no standard mold for hybrid courts. Instead, each court has a different mix of national and international personnel, laws, and procedures.[62]

By simply pronouncing itself "international" for purposes of sentencing goals, the SCSL missed an opportunity to promote its normative vision by engaging this important debate about the nature of hybrid courts. Indeed, the Court missed this opportunity in other areas of its legal legacy as well. For example, in deciding to disregard a national amnesty, the judges declared the SCSL to be "international" without meaningfully engaging with the Court's hybrid character.[63] The Court employed a similar approach to explain why then-Liberian president Charles Taylor was not entitled to immunity.[64]

Yet it is not self-evident that the SCSL should be considered international, at least for purposes of elaborating sentencing goals. Although the goals of sentencing are not coextensive with the overall objectives of a criminal court, the two are importantly related. A court established to deter crime in a particular community, for example, should consider such deterrence to be one of its most important sentencing goals. In determining which sentencing goals to pursue therefore, the SCSL should consider the purposes for which it was established as an important source of norms.

To determine the purposes for which the SCSL was created, it is useful to reflect on the express motivations of its creators. The impetus for the creation of the SCSL was a request by Sierra Leone's then-president Kabbah for international support to establish a court to prosecute "the RUF leadership and their collaborators."[65] The primary purpose of such prosecution according to President Kabbah was to bring peace and national reconciliation to the country.[66] International assistance was needed, according to President Kabbah, because Sierra Leone did not have the capacity to perform the prosecutions itself.[67] In response, the Security Council adopted a resolution requesting the Secretary-General to negotiate an agreement with the government to set up a court.[68] The resolution noted both

---

[60] *See, e.g., id.* at 587–88 (explaining that hybrids are popular because they are developed for dispensing international justice, like the ad hoc tribunals, but the international community prefers them because they are cheaper than the ad hoc tribunals).

[61] *See, e.g.,* R.F. Carolan, *An Examination of the Role of Hybrid International Tribunals in Prosecuting War Crimes and Developing Independent Domestic Court Systems: The Kosovo Experiment*, 17 TRANSNAT'L L. & CONTEMP. PROBS. 9, 13–14 (2008) (explaining that the Kosovo hybrid courts were established because the Kosovo court system was essentially destroyed and that the new courts would follow existing Kosovo law, as long as it did not violate international standards).

[62] For example, in contrast to the SCSL, at the Extraordinary Chambers in the Courts of Cambodia a majority of the judges must be Cambodian nationals. Law on the Establishment of Extraordinary Chambers in the Courts of Cambodia for the Prosecution of Crimes Committed during the Period of Democratic Kampuchea, arts. 9, 10, 11, NS/RKM/1004/006 (Oct. 27, 2004).

[63] Decision on Challenge to Jurisdiction: Lomé Accord Amnesty, Kallon and Kamara (SCSL-2004-16-AR72(E)) and (SCSL-2004-15-AR72(E)), Appeals Chamber (Mar. 13, 2004) (in a decision of approximately thirty-six pages, three paragraphs were devoted to the international/national nature of the Court).

[64] Decision on Immunity from Jurisdiction, Taylor (SCSL-2003-01-AR72(E)), Appeals Chamber, paras. 37–40 (May 31, 2004).

[65] Jalloh, *supra* note 41, at 398–99.

[66] *Id.* at 399.

[67] *Id.*

[68] S.C. Res. 1315, § 1 (2000).

the international community's interest in ensuring accountability for serious violations of international humanitarian law and Sierra Leone's interest in a court that "would end impunity and would contribute to the process of national reconciliation and to the restoration and maintenance of peace."[69] The resolution further noted "the pressing need for international cooperation to assist in strengthening the judicial system of Sierra Leone."[70] As Charles Jalloh has pointed out, the preference in Sierra Leone was for a national court with international participation and funding, whereas the United Nations preferred an international court with strong national participation.[71] The result was something in between with a majority of judges appointed by the UN Secretary-General and a minority by the government of Sierra Leone, the prosecutor and registrar appointed by the Secretary-General, and the deputy prosecutor appointed by the government.[72] Importantly, and unlike the ICTY and ICTR, the SCSL was located in Sierra Leone and had the ability to adjudicate crimes under Sierra Leonean law as well as international law.[73]

The SCSL was thus created to pursue a mix of international and national goals, with no clear priorities among them. The legislative history and composition of the SCSL at least arguably suggest that the Court's primary orientation should have been toward the national community rather than the international community.[74] According to its creators, the primary purposes of the SCSL were to deter crimes in Sierra Leone, to contribute to peace and reconciliation in that country, and to help strengthen the national judiciary.[75] As such, perhaps the SCSL's sentencing practice should have been aimed less at promoting international norms and more at implementing national sentencing norms. Rather than looking to the ICTY and ICTR for guidance on the goals of sentencing, perhaps the Court should have followed Sierra Leonean sentencing law and practice, as it was permitted to do under the statute.[76]

It is beyond the purview of this chapter to explore in depth whether a more national orientation would have resulted in different sentencing outcomes. It seems likely, however, that at least some of the sentences would have been different. The most obvious example is the CDF case. There the Appeals Chamber seems to have focused largely on the need to promote the norms of international humanitarian law in increasing the defendants' sentences well beyond those allocated by the Trial Chamber.[77] Had the appellate judgment instead centered on the retributive desert of the defendants, or the need to deter them or others

---

[69] *Id.* at pmbl.

[70] *Id.*

[71] *Id. at* 401.

[72] Agreement between the United Nations and the Government of Sierra Leone on the Establishment of a Special Court for Sierra Leone, arts. 2(2)(a),(c), 3(1),(2) and 4(1) 2178, U.N.T.S. 137 (Jan. 16, 2002).

[73] SCSL Statute art. 1(1).

[74] *See, e.g.,* N.J. Udombana, *Globalization of Justice and the Special Court for Sierra Leone's War Crimes,* 17 EMORY INT'L L. REV. 55, 83–87 (2003) (discussing the nature of the Special Court and explaining that it is not international in the sense that the ICJ and ad hoc courts are because the Special Court is formed through an agreement between the United Nations *and* Sierra Leone, "it lacks the power of the ICTY and ICTR to assert primacy over national courts of third States or to order the surrender of an accused located in any third State," it must have Sierra Leonean personnel, and "the Court is not an international court of a universal character with general jurisdiction like the International Court of Justice.")

[75] *See* S.C. Res. 1315 pmbl. (2000).

[76] SCSL Statute art. 19.

[77] *CDF Appeals, supra* note 12, at paras. 561–567.

like them in Sierra Leone from committing future crimes, or even the goal of promoting national reconciliation, the result might well have been lower sentences.

In sum, the SCSL's normative legacy remains ambiguous because the Court failed to address adequately a critical question facing hybrid courts: whether to be principally guided by national or international norms.

IV. SOCIOLOGICAL LEGACY

A third sense in which the term "legacy" is sometimes used is to denote the extent to which a court's work comports with the expectations of relevant communities. For example, Charles Jalloh has suggested that a court's legacy includes an assessment of the extent to which it met the expectations of the community for which it worked.[78] Applying the notion of sociological legacy to the SCSL is complicated by the question raised above: what is the primary "community" for the purposes of evaluating the Court's work? Many commentators seem to assume that the community that matters most is the national community of Sierra Leone.[79] The Court on the other hand seems to have been significantly concerned with the perceptions of the international community.[80] Indeed, the SCSL's president, Ernest Bai Koroma, noted that "[i]n school [sic] and universities around the world, students study the laws that we have created at the SCSL."[81] In light of the Court's international orientation, it is perhaps not surprising that its sociological legacy appears more positive when viewed through the eyes of the international community than through those of the national community.

Although no systematic study has been conducted concerning the Sierra Leonean public's perceptions of the SCSL's sentencing practice, some anecdotal evidence exists, largely in the news media. Some of these sources reveal criticism of SCSL sentences within Sierra Leone.[82] In particular, there was dissatisfaction with the high sentences awarded to the CDF defendants.[83] Moreover, in addition to the sentences themselves, Sierra Leoneans have criticized the Court for allowing defendants to serve their sentences in the relative comfort of foreign jails while the country's broader population suffers from extreme poverty.[84] Some

---

[78] Jalloh, *supra* note 41, at 444.

[79] *See, e.g., id.*; J. Ramji-Nogales, *Designing Bespoke Transitional Justice: A Pluralist Process Approach*, 32 MICH. J. INT'L L. 1, 2–4 (2010).

[80] *See CDF Appeals, supra* note 12, at paras. 561 and 564 (stating that the Court is international "with a responsibility to protect and promote the norms and values of the international community [, and a] paramount [consideration] in the sentencing … is the revulsion of mankind, represented by the international community").

[81] *Quoted in* P. Sama, *President Koroma Wishes … "SCSL Leaves a Magnificent & Imposing Legacy,"* AWOKO NEWSPAPER (July 27, 2010), *available at* www.awoko.org/2010/07/27/president-koroma-wishes%e2%80%a6-%e2%80%9cspecial-court-leaves-a-magnificent-imposing-legacy%e2%80%9d (last visited July 16, 2012).

[82] *See* Nina DeVries, *Mixed Reaction to Sentencing of Liberia's Charles Taylor*, VOICE OF AMERICA (May 30, 2012), *available at* http://www.voanews.com/content/mixed_reaction_sentencing_of_liberia_charles_taylor/1145285.html (some criticized the sentence as too heavy, others as too weak, and others were satisfied).

[83] *See, e.g.,* Jalloh, *supra* note 41, at 424–25 (noting that many Sierra Leoneans viewed the CDF defendants as national heroes).

[84] *Id.* at 456–57 (pointing out that the SCSL sentences were served in prisons "providing humane conditions," whereas in Sierra Leone "gross indignities such as use of force or torture … are not unheard of," [and] "the [SCSL] convicts were spared the ultimate punishment of death, which still applies in Sierra Leone"); *see also, e.g.,* J. Sandefur, *Was the Charles Taylor Trial Worth the Price Tag?*, GLOBAL DEVELOPMENT: VIEWS FROM THE CENTER: BLOG FOR THE CENTER FOR GLOBAL DEVELOPMENT (May 31, 2012), http://blogs.cgdev.org/globaldevelopment/2012/05/was-the-charles-taylor-trial-worth-the-price-tag.php (last visited July 16, 2012) (comparing the poor Sierra Leone population and the difficult conditions of Sierra Leonean prisons

Sierra Leoneans interviewed after the AFRC judgment also indicated dissatisfaction with those sentences,[85] although others were more positive.[86] The international community's reactions to the SCSL sentences have been largely positive.[87]

V. CONCLUSION

The SCSL's legal legacy with regard to sentencing is likely to be lasting and important. Other international courts will reference the SCSL's sentencing jurisprudence in rendering their sentences, and national courts may do so as well. The extent of the SCSL's influence on future sentencing jurisprudence will depend significantly, however, on whether the ICC considers the SCSL sufficiently "international" to be relevant to its work, and whether national courts view it as adequately reflecting national sentencing goals. The SCSL's normative legacy is also complicated by this underlying question of identity. The SCSL adopted a strongly international orientation in its sentencing jurisprudence. Whether or not this was the right approach, the SCSL missed an opportunity to explore the tensions inherent in its hybrid structure and to justify fully its international focus. Finally, the sociological legacy of the SCSL's sentencing practices remains largely unexplored, but current indications point to a high level of acceptance among international audiences and a more mixed reception in Sierra Leone.

---

with the "expensive venue[, high-priced] defense attorneys[,] … conjugal visits …, fancy Dutch food … [,] internet access, and … rabbinical visits to indulge [Taylor's] new interest in Judaism [associated with Charles Taylor's prosecution and incarceration]").

[85] *See, e.g.,* J. Hollett, *Rebels Jailed for "Heinous" Crimes; Sierra Leone Court Gives Trio 40–50 Years for Atrocities Committed during Brutal Civil War,* Toronto Star, July 20, 2007 (quoting various Sierra Leonean's reactions immediately following the AFRC sentencing decision, including criticisms that the sentences did not go far enough).

[86] *See, e.g., id.* (quoting one man as saying, "All of us are victims of this war. The judges were fair.").

[87] *See, e.g.,* M. Aksenova, *Guest Post: Why 50 Years of Imprisonment Is an Adequate Sentence for Charles Taylor,* Opinio Juris Blog (June 4, 2012), http://opiniojuris.org/2012/06/04/guest-post-why-50-years-of-imprisonment-is-an-adequate-sentence-for-charles-taylor (crediting the SCSL with upholding international sentencing norms when it sentenced Taylor to fifty years of jail time); Clair MacDougall, *Taylor's 50-Year Sentence Draws Mixed Reactions in Liberia,* Christian Sci. Monitor, http://www.csmonitor.com/World/Africa/2012/0530/ Taylor-s-50-year-sentence-draws-mixed-reactions-in-Liberia-video (last visited July 26, 2012) (indicating a positive reaction to the Taylor sentence by international groups such as Amnesty International and Global Witness); *but see* K.J. Heller, *Taylor Sentenced to 50 Years Imprisonment,* Opinio Juris Blog (May 30, 2012), http://opiniojuris.org/2012/05/30/taylor-sentenced-to-50-years-imprisonment (last visited July 26, 2012) (criticizing Taylor sentence as too high).

PART V

Funding, Process, and Cooperation

20

Marketing Accountability at the Special Court for Sierra Leone

Sara Kendall[*]

I. INTRODUCTION: ON "DONORS' JUSTICE"

There are a number of possible approaches for assessing the legacy of the Special Court for Sierra Leone (SCSL or the Court). In the field of international criminal law, the SCSL will likely be remembered for pioneering the criminalization of the use of child soldiers and the crime of forced marriage, two contested legal developments for the field that may be invoked by other international or internationalized criminal courts.[1] It will certainly be remembered as the first tribunal to bring a trial against a sitting head of state through to its conclusion.[2] Institutionally, the Court has offered a different model for conceptualizing international criminal accountability, with its "hybrid" structural elements and the establishment of an independent defense office (the SCSL's "fourth pillar"). It developed an extensive outreach program that has been an inspiration for subsequent courts and tribunals,[3] and it began to consider the significant issues of legacy and closure relatively early in its lifespan.[4] Such aspects of the Court's work constitute important parts of its legacy, but this chapter takes up a more neglected dimension of its practices, namely the SCSL's voluntary funding structure and its political and institutional effects.[5]

As the Court's own official documents reveal, there is much to be said about the constraints of the voluntary funding mechanism and how it bears upon institutional practice. The fact that the Committee on Budget and Finance of the International Criminal Court (ICC) was considering funding some aspects of the ICC's work through a mixture of assessed and voluntary contributions should give the international legal community pause.[6] What lessons

---

[*] PhD (Berkeley); Researcher, Grotius Centre for International Legal Studies, LeidenUniversity.

[1] On the court's treatment of forced marriage, in this volume see the chapters by Michael Scharf, Sidney Thompson, and Valerie Oosterveld. For analyses of the treatment of child recruitment, see the chapters by Cecile Aptel and Noah Novogdrosky.

[2] See, on the question of head of state immunity and trial, the chapters by Micaela Frulli and Annie Gell.

[3] See Stuart Ford's chapter in this volume.

[4] For a discussion of the legacy issue, see Viviane Dittrich's chapter in this volume. *See also* Vincent Nmehielle & Charles Jalloh, *The Legacy of the Special Court for Sierra Leone*, 30 FLETCHER FORUM OF WORLD AFFAIRS 107 (2006).

[5] This chapter has drawn upon material from within S. Kendall, *Donors' Justice: Recasting Criminal Accountability*, 24 LEIDEN J. INT'L L. 585–606 (2011), © The Foundation for the Leiden Journal of International Law, published by Cambridge University Press, published with permission.

[6] Report of the Committee on Budget and Finance on the Work of Its Seventeenth Session, ICC-ASP/10/15, para. 25 (Nov.18, 2011): "There may well be other areas of current Court activity that could benefit from a mixed financing system of assessed and voluntary contributions, such as outreach and public information."

might be drawn from the SCSL's experience with voluntary funding, and to what extent did it shape the Court's institutional legacy? This challenging aspect of the SCSL's structure has received little more than passing attention in much of the scholarly literature on the Court. This chapter argues that the SCSL's novel funding structure is central to its institutional legacy: the constraints produced through what I refer to as "donors' justice" have shaped the institution's practices throughout the Court's lifespan as well as its broader contribution to the field of international criminal justice.

By virtue of its funding structure, marketing its work to a donor audience has featured prominently among the SCSL's activities. At first glance this appears to be the pragmatic outcome of a structural feature of the Court: because it does not have a guaranteed budget, it must engage in fund-raising much like a civil society organization approaching grant-making bodies. Yet here I would like to pause and interrogate this "economy of justice" or "investment" in international criminal accountability. What does it mean to conceive of international justice as a kind of product on a market that states might be persuaded to fund?

I have written about this elsewhere, where I argued that the voluntary contributions model is a symptom of a general neoliberal approach to justice.[7] By "neoliberal" here, following social theorist Michel Foucault, I mean the tendency to subject traditionally non-market areas of social life – such as criminal accountability – to market-based rationalities. For Foucault, one of the consequences of neoliberalism is that "analysis in terms of the market economy or, in other words, of supply and demand, can function as a schema which is applicable to nonmarket domains."[8] A revealing example of this neoliberal tendency can be found in a speech by then-ICTY prosecutor Carla Del Ponte to Goldman Sachs: "International justice is cheap … Our annual budget is well under 10% of Goldman Sachs' profit during our last quarter. See, I can offer you high dividends for a low investment."[9] Here international justice is presented as one possible foreign policy "investment" for wealthy states (predominantly from the global North), and as presented by Del Ponte in this instance, for wealthy corporations as well.

The SCSL has also been described in neoliberal terms, and specifically concerning its reliance upon voluntary contributions to fund its budget. Addressing an audience at a U.S. law school in 2007, then-prosecutor of the SCSL Stephen Rapp explained:

> Rather than being financed by United Nations dues, this Special Court would be supported by voluntary contributions from individual countries. Those involved with the court would essentially put together a plan and go to world capitals saying, "This is what we want to do. If you think it is important, contribute your tax money to this cause. Here is our budget for

---

Article 116 of the ICC Statute provides that "the Court may receive and utilize, as additional funds, voluntary contributions from Governments, international organizations, individuals, corporations, and other entities, in accordance with relevant criteria adopted by the ASP." The danger of this shift is that the closest tangible entity we may have to an "international community" is the United Nations, and without UN-assessed contributions, the ad hoc donor-driven form of funding international accountability projects appears more partial, selective, and in line with the interests of strong states who can afford to fund it.

[7] Kendall, *supra* note 5.

[8] M. Foucault, The Birth of Biopolitics: Lectures at the College de France, 1978–1979, at 243 (2008).

[9] C. Del Ponte, *The Dividends of International Criminal Justice* (Oct.6, 2005), *available at* www.icty.org/x/file/Press/PR_attachments/cdp-goldmansachs-050610-e.htm.

this year, next year, and the following year. If you provide us with contributions to meet this budget, you will see this quantity of justice."[10]

This statement by Prosecutor Rapp captures many dimensions of what I want to examine in greater detail in this chapter, and it is thus worth unpacking this statement to consider its various claims. For one, the Court's funding structure is presented here as a reaction to the expense of the United Nations–backed ad hoc tribunals for Rwanda and the former Yugoslavia. Prosecutor Rapp comments that "[t]hese tribunals were supported by mandatory contributions from all 192 countries of the United Nations, but it seems that they were not accomplishing enough for what was being expended."[11] The mandatory or "assessed" contributions model had generated bureaucratic, UN-style institutions that were slow to deliver verdicts and were consuming substantial percentages of the UN budget.[12] The SCSL was thus presented as a new, "compact" model, as the title of Prosecutor Rapp's speech suggests; yet this approach also appears to suggest the need for this new model to demonstrate tangible results to stakeholders who are quite literally investing in its work.

Who are these stakeholders? As noted above, the Court's funding would be drawn from individual states that would elect to support the SCSL's budget. Material support for the Court is thus on a voluntary – and indeed *contingent* – basis, which makes it necessary for SCSL actors to "put together a plan and go to world capitals" to essentially "sell" their "product." The audience of this "sale" is states, who are told (in Prosecutor Rapp's hypothetical pitch), "If you think it is important, contribute your tax money to this cause." This characterization captures another element of what I have been calling "donors' justice" – states have to be persuaded to think of justice (and the institutions through which it is performed) as an investment that will generate some kind of return. What exactly is the return? We are not told, but we are given the impression that there is some sort of proportional relationship between the amount of funding and the amount of justice that will be achieved: "If you provide us with contributions to meet this budget, you will see this quantity of justice." Is the "quantity" of justice linked to the number of indictments (and possible convictions), or does it refer to something else? The nature of this form of justice is also left ambiguous. Who are its beneficiaries – conflict-affected populations, regional governments, and/ or donor states?

Although Prosecutor Rapp's statement is a hypothetical rather than an actual effort to obtain funding from a donor, it demonstrates the different elements of this "new model" of tribunal. For one, it is a reaction to – or shift away from – the assessed contributions model previously used for the ad hoc tribunals. As a result of this shift from mandatory budgetary support to voluntary contributions, court actors are tasked with an additional activity: they must generate capital to support the institution and include fund-raising among their many

---

[10] S. Rapp, *The Compact Model in International Criminal Justice: The Special Court for Sierra Leone*, 57 DRAKE L. REV. 11–48, 21 (2008–2009).

[11] *Id.*

[12] According to then-U.N. Secretary-General, as of 2004 the ad hoc tribunals for Rwanda and the former Yugoslavia were consuming roughly 15 percent of the UN budget; *see* the U.N. S.C., *The Rule of Law and Transitional Justice in Conflict and Post-Conflict Societies, Report of the Secretary-General*, U.N. DOC. S/2004/616 (2004).

other administrative responsibilities.[13] Furthermore, the addressee of their fund-raising will be states – states who will need to consider whether a criminal tribunal is a sufficiently important investment in line with their security or development objectives.

Elsewhere I have defined "donors' justice" as "third-party financial support for the work of international criminal justice institutions, where funders are technically not a party to the conflict that the court was set up to adjudicate."[14] The third-party or external funding dimension is significant because most prosecutions for international crimes take place domestically;[15] prosecutions in international or internationalized/hybrid courts are exceptional, and when they do occur it begs the question of why third-party states regard them as a worthwhile use of resources that might be delegated to other security or development initiatives. "Donors' justice" operates on multiple levels: discursively, or in how the work of international criminal justice is increasingly described as an investment (as shown in Del Ponte and Rapp's language above); politically, where third-party states may conceive of tribunals as vehicles for their own foreign policy objectives; and economically, where tribunals are presented as commodities on a market with other competing social goods. With the "donors' justice" analytic in the background, the following section tracks the emergence of the Court's voluntary funding structure and the development of a "Management Committee" as its oversight body. This now-settled funding structure was contested at the time of its creation, as the following section shows.

II. ESTABLISHING THE COURT'S VOLUNTARY FUNDING STRUCTURE

Following the Sierra Leonean president's request to the United Nations to assist in setting up a court, the inevitable question of how to materially support it was raised by the various parties involved in the SCSL's establishment. In the mid-1990s, observers were already noting that members of the Security Council were complaining of "tribunal fatigue."[16] The UN Security Council and the UN Secretary-General advanced different perspectives on the funding issue, with the Security Council pushing for voluntary contributions and the Secretary-General expressing concern about what this might entail in practice. UN Security Council Resolution 1315 (2000) states that the Court should be supported through the voluntary contributions of funds, equipment, and services from states, and intergovernmental and nongovernmental organizations.

By contrast, Secretary-General Kofi Annan expressed reservations with this approach in a 2000 report on the SCSL's establishment:

---

[13] The UN-funded ad hoc courts were not without their own funding challenges; David Scheffer noted that in the mid-1990s funding issues threatened the "viability" of the ICTY and ICTR, both of which sought to obtain voluntary contributions in addition to the UN-assessed contributions. The U.S. government made large voluntary contributions to the tribunals. *See* D. Scheffer, *International Judicial Intervention*, 102 FOREIGN POLICY 34, 45 (1996).

[14] Kendall, *supra* note 5, at 587. Arguably some of these states may have nevertheless intervened in Sierra Leone, directly or indirectly, as was the case with the United Kingdom and Nigeria (through ECOMOG). In this broader interpretation of a state's role as a party to the conflict, it would seem that these states may be both parties *and* donors.

[15] K. SIKKINK, THE JUSTICE CASCADE: HOW HUMAN RIGHTS PROSECUTIONS ARE CHANGING WORLD POLITICS 5 (2011).

[16] Scheffer, *supra* note 13, at 48.

[T]he risks associated with the establishment of an operation of this kind with insufficient funds, or without long-term assurances of continuous availability of funds, are very high, in terms of both moral responsibility and loss of credibility of the Organization, and its exposure to legal liability.[17]

Annan concluded that a court based on voluntary contributions "would be neither viable nor sustainable."[18] Despite the Secretary-General's concerns, the Court's founding agreement codified the voluntary contributions arrangement suggested by the UN Security Council resolution. Article 6 of the Special Court's 2002 founding Agreement stipulates that:

The expenses of the Special Court shall be borne by voluntary contributions from the international community [...] the Secretary-General will continue to seek contributions equal to the anticipated expenses of the Court beyond its first three years of operation. Should voluntary contributions be insufficient for the Court to implement its mandate, the Secretary-General and the Security Council shall explore alternate means of financing the Special Court.

Similar funding structures were eventually established for Cambodia (Extraordinary Chambers in the Courts of Cambodia – ECCC) and Lebanon (Special Tribunal for Lebanon – STL), supporting Prosecutor Rapp's claim that the SCSL was indeed a new paradigm for criminal tribunals. Even the permanent ICC, which is funded through assessed contributions from its states parties, includes provisions in its founding statute that provides a secondary funding mechanism for voluntary contributions.[19]

III. THE MANAGEMENT COMMITTEE

In addition to developing a new mechanism for funding tribunals through voluntary contributions, the founders of the SCSL also pioneered a new administrative form.[20] Early in the Court negotiations, members of the UN Security Council suggested establishing what they termed a "management committee" in a letter from the President of the Security Council to the Secretary-General:

In order to assist the court on questions of funding and administration, it is suggested that the arrangements between the Government of Sierra Leone and the United Nations provide for a management or oversight committee which could include representatives of Sierra Leone, the Secretary General of the United Nations, the Court and interested voluntary contributors. The management committee would assist the court in obtaining

---

[17] *Report of the Secretary General on the Establishment of a Special Court for Sierra Leone*, para. 70, U.N. Doc. S/2000/915 (Oct.4, 2000).

[18] *Id.*

[19] *See supra* note 6. The Assembly of States Parties issued a resolution requesting governments and other organizations to declare that voluntary contributions under Article 116 are "not intended to affect the independence of the Court" and requesting the Registrar to "assure himself/herself" that any offered contributions will not affect the ICC's independence. Resolution ICC-ASP/1/Res.11, "Relevant criteria for voluntary contributions to the International Criminal Court" (Sept.3, 2002).

[20] For an argument that the SCSL Management Committee may serve as a new model, see Phakiso Mochochoko & Giorgia Totora, The Management Committee for the Special Court for Sierra Leone, *in* Internationalized Courts and Tribunals: Sierra Leone, East Timor, Kosovo, and Cambodia (Cesare Romano, Andre Nollkaemper & Jan Kleffner eds., 2004).

adequate funding, provide advice on matters of Court administration and be available as appropriate to consult on other non-judicial matters.[21]

As with the Security Council suggestion to fund the Court through voluntary contributions, this suggestion for an oversight body was also codified in the Special Court Agreement. Article 7 of the Agreement addresses the role of the Management Committee, which states that:

> interested States will establish a management committee to assist the Secretary-General in obtaining adequate funding, and provide adequate advice and policy direction on all non-judicial aspects of the operation of the Court, including questions of efficiency, and to perform other functions as agreed by interested States. The management committee shall consist of important contributors to the Special Court. The Government of Sierra Leone and the Secretary-General will also participate in the Management Committee.[22]

The Management Committee is mentioned in the Court's founding Agreement as well as in its Rules of Procedure (briefly in the beginning definitional section), but it does not appear in the Court's governing Statute. There is very little guidance in these documents defining the role of the Committee and its relationship to Court practice, with vague references to activities such as providing advice and policy direction on nonjudicial matters. Indeed, the Committee's terms of reference notes that it is "an *informal arrangement* open to important contributors to the Special Court."[23] Furthermore, the language in Article 7 states that the Committee will be empowered to "perform other functions as agreed by interested States," but offers no guidance concerning what these "other functions" might be.

With a name that seems more suggestive of a corporate board than of a tribunal oversight body, it is unsurprising that reservations have been expressed about the ambiguity of the Committee's role both within and outside the Court. Some staff members have noted that the role of the Management Committee has not been clarified legally; all of the Court's bodies should be regulated by rules and practice directions, yet no such guidance exists for the Committee, nor are the meetings of its minutes accessible to the general public. Questions thus remain as to the degree of discretion that the Committee exercises, particularly concerning the SCSL's budget and its oversight of high-level Court personnel. This oversight is perhaps unsurprising within the "donors' justice" frame, where donor states are naturally concerned about the performance of their investments, but it also reveals the SCSL's structural vulnerability. If donor states think of their contributions as performance-based – and, in particular, based on the performance of key personnel – the institution as a whole may suffer from reduced contributions, with implications for fair trial rights of the accused, the job security of staff (particularly at the national level), and the security of witnesses.

Throughout the Court's lifespan, commentators have raised questions about the mandate and practice of the Committee. In a report released after the start of the first trials in 2004, Human Rights Watch noted that:

---

[21] *Letter dated 22 December 2000 from the President of the Security Council addressed to the Secretary-General*, U.N. Doc. S/2000/1234 (Dec.22, 2000).

[22] *Special Court Agreement, 2002 (Ratification) Act, 2002* [Sierra Leone], No. 9 of 2002 (Apr.25, 2002).

[23] "Terms of Reference for the Management Committee for the Special Court for Sierra Leone," Appendix III of the *Letter dated 6 March 2002 from the Secretary-General addressed to the President of the Security Council*, U.N. Doc. S/2002/46 (Mar.8, 2002) (emphasis added).

Special Court staff expressed frustration that the Management Committee has tended to focus its attention more on where to cut budgets proposed by the Registry than on zealously advocating with governments and the United Nations as to why additional funding is necessary to ensure that the court can function fairly and effectively.[24]

In a 2006 report for the International Center for Transitional Justice, Tom Perriello and Marieke Wierda pointed out that "questions of cost and efficiency" dominate Management Committee discussions while "other important criteria are often neglected."[25] Nevertheless, annual reports generated by the Court consistently note the Committee's critical role in providing fund-raising support.[26]

Empowering a vaguely defined oversight body – an admittedly "informal arrangement" – comprised of representatives of key donor states at an international organization may provide further support for claims of state influence. The STL has a management committee modeled after the SCSL, with indications that some donors preferred to use this form rather than the United Nations Trust Fund model, where the United Nations would have retained control over contributions and the Fund would have been guided by UN financial regulations.[27] Donors apparently preferred the SCSL Management Committee model because it would allow them to retain budgetary oversight. This begs the question of the degree of influence afforded by such a structure, and whether it indicates a shift toward more corporate modes of governance in international institutional forms. Whereas efficiency and flexibility reflect the values of the private sector, these values should be balanced by the public norms of transparency and accountability; otherwise, international institutions could slip into what might be interpreted as neoliberal forms of governance, or as new avenues for strong state influence.

IV. DONORS' JUSTICE IN PRACTICE

The donors have paid for a court; all they can expect is that it will do justice to every defendant according to law.[28]

Who are the third parties who make "donors' justice" possible? Over the course of the Court's lifespan, roughly fifty countries have contributed to funding its budget, with four countries – the United States, the United Kingdom, the Netherlands, and Canada – providing

---

[24] *Bringing Justice: The Special Court for Sierra Leone*, HUM. RTS. WATCH, at IX (B) (Sept. 2004).

[25] T. Perriello & M. Wierda, *The Special Court for Sierra Leone under Scrutiny*, INT'L CENTER FOR TRANSITIONAL JUSTICE PROSECUTION CASE STUDIES SERIES (Mar. 2006).

[26] For example, the Court's most recent annual report notes that "It was only the extraordinary efforts of the Court's Management Committee members that averted a financial crisis." Special Court for Sierra Leone, *Eighth Annual Report of the President of the Special Court for Sierra Leone*, at 38 (2011).

[27] The U.N. Secretariat created a Trust Fund to receive contributions for the Special Tribunal for Lebanon in 2007. At the end of the year states unanimously agreed that the tribunal's budget should be managed directly by the tribunal rather than the UN Trust Fund, and a Management Committee was established in early 2008. Leaked diplomatic cables noted that some donors preferred this model because it would allow them to retain oversight of the budget, whereas the UN Trust Fund model would limit the role of donor states to providing policy advice.

[28] Prosecutor v. Sam Hinga Norman, Case No. SCSL-2003–08-PT, Preliminary Motion based on Lack of Jurisdiction: Judicial Independence, para. 24 (June 26, 2003); Separate Opinion of Justice Geoffrey Robertson.

two-thirds of the court's support for its first year of operations. All four countries have maintained positions on the SCSL's Management Committee. Overall, the top three contributors to the SCSL have been the United States, the United Kingdom, and the Netherlands. The United States is the largest donor: Stuart Ford has noted that between 2007 and 2009, the United States has contributed nearly 30 percent of the Court's budget,[29] and by November 2010 it had contributed over $80 million.[30] In 2008, the SCSL's external consultant on residual issues (and subsequently Deputy Registrar) noted that since its inception, the funding of the Court had been "a controversial matter," remarking that "[u]ltimately, the survival of the SCSL has been based on a reliance on a small group of key donors."[31] Yet as Periello and Wierda point out, "reliance upon a small group of key donors may have reduced the court's independence."[32]

A jurisdictional challenge was brought in the early stages of the court along these lines, wherein counsel for Sam Hinga Norman in the CDF case argued that the Court's funding arrangements "create a legitimate fear of political interference by economic manipulation."[33] The Appeals Chamber rejected this claim, though Justice Robertson's separate opinion continues with a kind of donor logic:

> The interest of donor states is that the Court they pay for will be successful – but "success" cannot be judged by its conviction rate … Although states all have foreign policy objectives, their purpose in funding an international criminal court cannot be assumed to include the obtaining of convictions against all or even most indictees.[34]

Although Justice Robinson does not accept the defense claim that obtaining convictions are among the objectives of donor states, he acknowledges that states route foreign policy objectives through the SCSL. Although this may be unsurprising from the perspective of political realism, it suggests that we may need to rethink the ways in which we describe the work of international criminal justice and in whose name it is carried out. As William Schabas points out, voluntary contributions make tribunals "more vulnerable to inappropriate influences and even manipulation, something incompatible with judicial bodies. Neither Prosecutor nor judges should be forced to contemplate the consequences for the Tribunal should they proceed with investigations and indictments that affect, even indirectly, the interests of a major donor state."[35] Donors and "their purpose in funding an international criminal court"

---

[29] S. Ford, *How Leadership in International Criminal Law Is Shifting from the United States to Europe and Asia: An Analysis of Spending on and Contributions to International Criminal Courts*, 55(3) St. Louis U. L.J. 977 (Spring 2011).

[30] Press Release, U.S. Department of State, The US Provides $4.5 Million to Fund Special Court for Sierra Leone Trial of Charles Taylor (Nov. 23, 2010), *available at* www.state.gov/r/pa/prs/ps/2010/11/151810.htm.

[31] F. Donlon, *Report on the Residual Functions and Residual Institution Options of the Special Court for Sierra Leone* 12 (Dec. 16, 2008).

[32] Periello & Wierda, *supra* note 25, at 32.

[33] Prosecutor v. Sam Hinga Norman, Case No. SCSL-2003–08-PT, Preliminary Motion Based on Lack of Jurisdiction: Judicial Independence, para. 2 (June 26, 2003).

[34] Prosecutor v. Sam Hinga Norman, Case No. SCSL-2003–08-PT, Preliminary Motion Based on Lack of Jurisdiction: Judicial Independence, para. 24 (June 26, 2003); Separate Opinion of Justice Geoffrey Robertson.

[35] W. Schabas, *The U.N. International Criminal Tribunals: The Former Yugoslavia, Rwanda and Sierra Leone* 623 (2006).

should thus figure more centrally in our analyses of the field – their interests form one of the key conditions of possibility of international criminal justice in our time.

It would be difficult to authoritatively demonstrate the causal link between donor funding and donor influence in restricting the Court's independence, but it is certainly the case that donor funding affected the composition of staff – that is, those who participated in the production of justice at the Court. The Management Committee's terms of reference stipulate that it would assist in "identifying nominees for the positions of Registrar, prosecutor and judges."[36] With the exception of one Chief Prosecutor from the United Kingdom, all Chief Prosecutors at the SCSL have been from the United States, the Court's largest donor. Having previously worked for the Pentagon, the Court's first Prosecutor had ties to the U.S. government. Prosecutor Crane's efforts were not always backed by U.S. policy, as in the case of U.S. involvement in brokering Taylor's exile in Nigeria, and the degree of U.S. interest in the Court has varied over time. Yet U.S. nationals have been arguably overrepresented in the Office of the Prosecutor, a fact not lost on Charles Taylor in his final statement to the Trial Chamber at his sentencing hearing.[37] Visits by Court personnel to lobby U.S. politicians at both the executive and legislative levels appear to have been more common than other lobbying efforts, as the following section will show. As with the two ad hoc tribunals, the United States assumed a key role in the SCSL's establishment,[38] and the Court was seen as an avenue for pursuing U.S. foreign policy objectives connected to the "war on terror."[39] Whether the United States' role as primary donor affected the independence of the Court remains a contested and perhaps irresolvable question because of the dearth of publicly available information, though it is well established that the state played a significant role in bringing the SCSL into being and in staffing some of its key positions.

---

[36] "Terms of Reference for the Management Committee for the Special Court for Sierra Leone," Appendix III of the *Letter dated 6 March 2002 from the Secretary-General addressed to the President of the Security Council*, U.N. Doc. S/2002/46 (Mar.8, 2002).

[37] Taylor argued that the Prosecution was a "U.S.-based attack pack led by Lieutenant-Colonel David Crane, defense intelligence 30 years, prosecutor ... The rest of the operational team are Colonel Brenda Hollis, Defence intelligence, CIA, U.S. Air Force, senior trial counsel, and now Prosecutor. James C. Johnson, U.S. Army, expert 20 years on conventional and special operations, chief of prosecutions for the SCSL. Allen White, 30 years Defence intelligence, recalled from retirement to head up investigations at the Special Court for Sierra Leone. Stephen J. Rapp came on board as Chief Prosecutor for a short time with experience from Capitol Hill where he served on a Senate Judiciary Subcommittee sometime before."
The Prosecutor of the Special Court v. Charles Ghankay Taylor, Case No. SCSL-2003–01-T, Sentencing Hearing Transcript at 50, lines 9–23 (May 16, 2012).

[38] J. Cerone, *Dynamic Equilibrium: The Evolution of U.S. Attitudes toward International Criminal Courts and Tribunals*, 18 EUR. J. INT'L L. 277 (2007). Thierry Cruvellier points out that "some have argued that the United States is deliberately promoting the Special Court as an alternative to the International Criminal Court," INTERNATIONAL CENTER FOR TRANSITIONAL JUSTICE, THE SPECIAL COURT FOR SIERRA LEONE: THE FIRST EIGHTEEN MONTHS 7 (2004). The Special Court was established around the time that the ICC's Rome Statute came into effect. On the ad hoc tribunals, David Scheffer argued in 1996 that the United States "was at the forefront in creating both tribunals and continues to be their leading source of political, financial, personnel, logistical, and information-sharing support." *See* Scheffer, *supra* note 13, at 38.

[39] A report marked "Confidential" from the SCSL Office of the Prosecutor detailing links between al-Qaeda operatives and Charles Taylor as well as cooperation between SCSL investigations and CIA operations is available at journalist Douglas Farah's website: see *Special Court for Sierra Leone Report on al Qaeda Ties to the Diamond Trade, available at* www.douglasfarah.com/materials/php under the "Related Materials'" tab (last visited June 16, 2012). The Special Court's third Prosecutor suggested a relationship between the crimes the Court was set up to address and the global problem of terrorism; see Rapp, *supra* note 10, at 11.

V. SCSL ANNUAL REPORTS: NARRATING BUDGETARY CHALLENGES

The reservations expressed by Kofi Annan in 2000 about the vulnerabilities of the voluntary contributions system proved prescient, and the SCSL's own reporting practices illustrate his concerns about the viability and sustainability of such a funding structure. Under Article 25 of the SCSL Statute, the President of the Special Court is required to submit annual reports to the UN Secretary-General and the government of Sierra Leone. Although the reports are meant to discuss the Court's operations and activities, this section illustrates how they also capture another dimension of its institutional life. As the official narrative presented by the SCSL to the general public, they reveal the Court's ongoing budgetary struggles as well as the proliferation of fund-raising as a main activity of senior officials.

From the very first year of the SCSL's operation, the challenges posed by the voluntary structure were apparent to Court actors and publicly acknowledged in its annual report (December 2002–December 2003):

> Overall, as will be mentioned elsewhere in this report, the Court's major challenge, which continues to be ongoing, has been the securing of funding past its first full financial year. The Court remains grateful to those States who have made and, in many cases, have continued to make contributions, and it is to be hoped that the remaining period of the Court's life will see a more settled pattern in terms of funding.[40]

The report's language indicated the severity of the funding issue during the Court's first year, noting that budgetary insecurity had been "a dominant feature of the Court during the period"[41] that "seriously threatened the capacity of the Court to meet its mandate in all respects."[42] External auditors "expressed concern about the SCSL's 'precarious funding position.'"[43] Funding for the second year required drawing upon pledged contributions for the Court's third year, essentially borrowing off of its future in the hope that additional funding would be forthcoming.

The second annual report (January 2004–January 2005) describes how it required additional budgetary support from the United Nations through a subvention grant, which was regarded at the time as a one-off event although Court officials returned to the UN for budgetary support again in 2010. During the second year of its operations the SCSL was already bringing in private funding from the Ford Foundation to hire a fund-raising consultant "who will seek funding to ensure the continuing operations of the Court beyond December 2005, and funds to meet the Court's residual costs beyond completion of its mandate."[44] The third annual report (January 2005–January 2006) recounts a flurry of fund-raising activities undertaken by court personnel and the consultant, including briefings for foundations hosted by philanthropic and civil society organizations. The Registry convened a pledging conference with UN member states to raise funds for the following year of core operations.

---

[40] Special Court for Sierra Leone, *First Annual Report of the President of the Special Court for Sierra Leone* 6 (2003). This and subsequent reports mentioned below are available at www.sc-sl.org.

[41] *Id.* at 20.

[42] *Id.* at 31.

[43] *Id.* at 29.

[44] Special Court for Sierra Leone, *Second Annual Report of the President of the Special Court for Sierra Leone* 6 (2004).

A mid-year event in New York with North American foundations "sought to raise the pro-file of the Special Court within the American donor community," and an event at the end of the year in Brussels "was organized to raise the profile of the Special Court and attract the interest of potential donors to fund its legacy projects."[45]

Although the first three reports treat fund-raising in an ad hoc fashion, subsequent reports add subsections or even full sections devoted to addressing the Court's budget and its efforts to obtain additional funding. The fourth and fifth annual reports contain a Registry subsection entitled "External Relations and Fundraising," and the sixth, seventh, and eighth reports include whole "Fundraising and Diplomatic Relations" sections. These last three reports also include an annex entitled "Significant fundraising and diplomatic meetings held during the reporting period," with lists of states that Court actors have met during the period under review. As they become more detailed and professionalized over the years, these annual reports appear increasingly as efforts to document the extent of international lobbying undertaken to fund Court activities.

For example, the fourth report (January 2006–May 2007) recounts the "extensive dip-lomatic and fundraising initiatives abroad" to the U.S. Congress and members of the State Department as well as to European states and organizations in Brussels. This report iden-tifies the fund-raising consultant for the first time and describes how, together with the consultant, the Court's "New York Office assisted the SCSL in its efforts to raise funds from private sources."[46] The fifth report (June 2007–May 2008) announces that fund-raising remains a priority of the Registry, and notes that "[i]n the year ahead, the Special Court faces renewed challenges in raising the necessary voluntary contributions that fund the Special Court's 'core' operations."[47] It documents the extensive travels of the Registrar as well as fund-raising visits by the Prosecutor to European and North American capitals.[48] Although commendable for its transparency in documenting where funds were sought, the report reveals how fund-raising consumed a significant amount of time, energy, and resources of key Court personnel.

The sixth annual report (June 2008–May 2009) adopts a more strained tone than previ-ous reports in its introduction, noting that it "proved to be a very difficult year": the Court continued to "struggle" with fund-raising activities, particularly in the wake of the global financial crisis, and it sought assistance from the United Nations to help raise funds.[49] The seventh report (June 2009–May 2010) explains how the Court's President and Prosecutor

---

[45] Special Court for Sierra Leone, *Third Annual Report of the President of the Special Court for Sierra Leone* 25 (2006).

[46] The website of Development Resources Inc., the Court's fund-raising consultant, presents a strikingly neolib-eral account of its work:

> Non-profit and philanthropic organizations are as complex as any commercial enterprise. To success-fully achieve their mission, they must have a solid vision, a sound corporate culture, clear operating procedures and effective tactics. In addition, today's donors are savvy and well-informed. They expect more from the organizations they support, and demand solid results from their investment.... To nav-igate this new environment, philanthropic organizations must understand – as never before – that they are a business, and must be savvier, strategic, sustainable and ethical.

> *See* http://driconsulting.com/index.cfm?fa=main.bcsOverview (last visited June16, 2012).

[47] Special Court for Sierra Leone, *Fifth Annual Report of the President of the Special Court for Sierra Leone* 11 (2008).

[48] *Id.* at 36.

[49] Special Court for Sierra Leone, *Sixth Annual Report of the President of the Special Court for Sierra Leone* (2009).

jointly addressed the UN Security Council on its financial structure, requesting the Security Council to grant earmarked contributions from UN member states for the remainder of the tribunal's lifespan.[50] It overtly attributes the SCSL's existential struggles to its budgetary structure:

> In spite of significant budgetary reductions by the Court, the Court continues to experience serious difficulties in securing adequate funding to complete its mandate. This is due to the funding mechanism, which relies solely on the voluntary contributions of the international community.[51]

The eighth report (June 2010–May 2011) recounts how Court officials needed to approach the United Nations for a second subvention grant after failing to secure enough voluntary contributions to fund its 2010 operations.[52] Through requiring access to these subvention funds of unallocated assessed contributions from the UN in order to stay afloat, the Court demonstrates that the voluntary funding mechanism is "neither viable nor sustainable," as Kofi Annan had presciently warned as far back as October 2000.

The annual reports considered here work simultaneously as accounts of the Court's progress, and marketing brochures to current and prospective donors reflecting the values of an increasingly market-driven global justice culture. Meanwhile, these marketing activities draw resources away from core operations, as noted by former ICTY and STL judge Antonio Cassese in his commissioned evaluation of the Court's work:

> The annual reports of the Special Court are professionally reproduced in a glossy colour pamphlet, suitable for distribution to potential donors. In contrast, the reports of the ICTR and ICTY are printed on plain paper and distributed electronically. These fundraising activities are expensive and require additional staffing.[53]

This raises questions about what constitutes the "core activities" of the Court: has fund-raising become a central activity along with supporting the judicial process? It also suggests an additional understanding of outreach apart from the recognized task of informing affected communities of the Court's work; the seventh annual report notes that:

> [d]ue to the continuing difficulties the Court faces to secure funding, the Office of the President, the Office of the Prosecutor and the Office of the Registrar worked closely together to honour all invitations to speak before institutions, entities, media and governments in order to disseminate information about the work of the Special Court and to keep the interest of the donor community focused on its activities.[54]

The audience of Court outreach is thus at least double: outreach activities are directed toward the people of the region to foster greater comprehension of the trials and the Court's

---

[50] Special Court for Sierra Leone, *Seventh Annual Report of the President of the Special Court for Sierra Leone* 11 (2010).

[51] *Id.* at 40.

[52] The UN General Assembly approved a subvention grant in the amount of $9.9 million, with the possibility of a second subvention for 2012.

[53] A. Cassese, *Report on the Special Court for Sierra Leone* (2008), *available at* www.sc-sl.org/DOCUMENTS/tabid/176/Default.aspx.

[54] Special Court for Sierra Leone, *supra* note 50, at 11.

legacy, but substantial operations are also directed to the donor community "investing" in the SCSL's work.

Commentators have noted the considerable amount of time spent by key Court actors on fund-raising activities throughout the SCSL's lifespan and have pointed out the "immediately apparent weakness"[55] of using voluntary contributions as a material basis for international criminal justice. Human Rights Watch observed in 2004 that "[i]nsufficient and insecure funding has undermined the court's operations. Court officials have needed to devote extensive time to raising funds."[56] A consultant hired to consider the residual functions of the Special Court (and now Deputy Registrar) agreed with this assessment in a 2008 report.[57] In the same year, the prosecutor explained how the uncertain framework of voluntary contributions "sometimes left the court within only days of insufficient funding," which he alleged threatened the ongoing detention of defendants.[58] Judges with experience at other international criminal tribunals have pointed out these consequences as well: a former ICTY judge observed that the SCSL "has not been able to overcome entirely the persistent problems of volatile out-of-country financing,"[59] and Judge Cassese listed "the financial insecurity resulting from funding based on voluntary contributions" as the first of three reasons the SCSL has not lived up to its original expectations.[60]

VI. EFFECTS ON COURT PRACTICE

As the previous section showed, courts with voluntary funding arrangements are particularly vulnerable to the vicissitudes of the global market and shifting state interests. As one critic points out, voluntary contributions "are by their very nature highly volatile and unreliable," with the consequence that "[t]hey run fast and easily into donor fatigue."[61] More institutional energy and resources are expended in securing funding through various activities, including hiring private fund-raising consultants and deploying key staff on fund-raising "missions." Even the United Nations has noted the extensive fund-raising activity undertaken by Court staff as a result of the funding structure:

> [S]ince 2009, 174 fund-raising meetings have been held by the [Special Court] across capitals and diplomatic missions, and 225 fund-raising appeal letters have been sent to capitals and diplomatic missions. Despite these efforts it has proved impossible to secure voluntary contributions sufficient to complete the mandate of the Special Court.[62]

---

[55] C.L. SRIRAM, GLOBALIZING JUSTICE FOR MASS ATROCITY: A REVOLUTION IN ACCOUNTABILITY 97 (2005). *See also* C.L. Sriram, *Wrong-Sizing International Justice? The Hybrid Tribunal in Sierra Leone*, 29 FORDHAM INT'L L.J. (2006).

[56] *Bringing Justice, supra* note 24.

[57] Donlon, *supra* note 31, at 13.

[58] Rapp, *supra* note 10, at 31.

[59] P. Wald, *International Criminal Courts: Some Kudos and Concerns*, 150 PROCEEDINGS OF THE AMERICAN PHILOSOPHICAL ASSOCIATION 241, 254 (2006).

[60] Cassese, *supra* note 53, at 2.

[61] C. Romano, *The Price of International Justice*, 4 LAW & PRACTICE INT'L COURTS & TRIBS. 281, 309 (2005).

[62] Report of the U.N. Secretary-General, *Request for a Subvention to the Special Court for Sierra Leone*, U.N. DOC. A/65/570, 65 Sess. of the United Nations General Assembly, Agenda Item 129, Programme Budget for the Biennium 2010–2011 (2010).

An evident effect of this funding arrangement on the Court's work in practice is thus to transform SCSL administrators – and even to some extent the Court prosecutor[63] – into marketing agents for the "product" of accountability.

Within the donors' justice framework, even the contentious movement of the Charles Taylor trial from Freetown to The Hague was reframed in terms of its consequences for funding.[64] Despite the clear advantages of locating the tribunal in situ, the SCSL president took an administrative decision to relocate the Taylor trial to The Hague in 2006 because of alleged security concerns (and perhaps because of higher security costs had the trial proceeded in Freetown). Representatives of Sierra Leonean civil society groups challenged the move, arguing that it "to a large extent dissipates the hybrid nature of the Court and would likely reduce the impact of the legacy of the Court to the people of West Africa in particular."[65] Yet as then-prosecutor Stephen Rapp noted, "[f]ortunately, with the Taylor trial occurring in The Hague and this case being viewed as a test of international justice, there has been support from some countries at greater levels than would have been offered for proceedings in Freetown."[66] This statement is particularly remarkable given that the Court's location in Freetown was originally conceived as one of the advantages of the Court's "hybrid" form – an advantage that Rapp points out in the same speech.[67] Why donors would view a Hague-based court more favorably is not explained, although the funding implications suggest that the site of international justice production has been further consolidated in the global North, and specifically in The Hague, rendering conflict-affected countries increasingly peripheral as sites of tribunal-based accountability.

Former prosecutor Rapp's statement shows that the geographical location of judicial proceedings appears to carry consequences for the Court's funding – a quality that should be arbitrary from an ethical standpoint. Put another way, accountability for Charles Taylor's crimes should in theory be equally valuable to a donor state regardless of whether his trial takes place in The Hague or in Freetown, but Rapp's statement about the increased funding that accompanied the trial's move to The Hague suggests that donors do care about where trials take place. Indeed, the tribunal's establishment of a Hague "sub-office" and its use of space at the ICC and the STL suggest a kind of symbiotic relationship between tribunals and further consolidates The Hague as the locality of international criminal justice – an identity that the Dutch government, one of the Court's key donors, actively invests in.

I have argued thus far that the "donors' justice" framework affects the nature of the work of the SCSL's high-level staff, who must not only work as diplomats but also as marketing

---

[63] Rapp, *supra* note 10, at 31: "the prosecutor takes it as part of his mission to ensure the necessary resources are available. Since appointment, this has involved visits to ten capitals, meetings with diplomatic representatives of almost one hundred nations, and scores of public presentations."

[64] Charles Jalloh addresses the financial dimensions of this move in *The Contribution of the Special Court for Sierra Leone to the Development of International Law*, 15(2) AFR. J. INT'L & COMP. L. 165 (2007).

[65] Prosecutor v. Taylor, "Civil Society *Amicus Curiae* Brief Regarding Change of Venue of Taylor Trial Back to Freetown," Case No. SCSL-2003-01-PT, T.Ch. II, para. 5 (Mar. 9, 2007).

[66] Rapp, *supra* note 10, at 31.

[67] Rapp, *supra* note 10, at 21:

> the court would be sited in Sierra Leone rather than away from the scene of the crimes. This would facilitate hearing witnesses and make it possible for the people of Sierra Leone to better understand the charges, evidence and judgments. The public would not need to follow reports from distant locations on the radio or in the newspapers because citizens could actually go to the court building and watch the testimony themselves or at least see coverage of the trials by the local media.

agents for the Court. I will briefly highlight two additional areas where the donors' justice framework and its implications for financing the Court bears upon the SCSL in practice: first, the problem of limited indictments, and second, the implications on staffing and labor practices.

As is noted elsewhere in this volume, the Court was established with a limited mandate to try those "bearing the greatest responsibility" for grave crimes committed in Sierra Leone during the period of the Court's temporal jurisdiction. Under this mandate the Special Court's first Prosecutor indicted thirteen individuals, ten of whom were brought to trial, despite earlier estimates of a larger number of potential indictees. Charles Jalloh has argued that the Prosecutor's narrow interpretation of his mandate "seemed to have been driven by concerns about the limited funding available to the Court."[68] According to the International Crisis Group (ICG), the mandate of the SCSL "to handle only a limited number of cases is tied directly to the desire of all states that supported its creation to keep it much smaller and less costly."[69] Indeed, in his keynote address at a SCSL legacy conference that led to this volume, former prosecutor Rapp noted that when he began his tenure at the Court, investigators suggested that he prosecute at least one other person; he determined not to do this for "practical reasons," including concerns about an ongoing ability to fund the case.[70]

Issues of the interpretation of the Court's mandate in light of resource constraints surfaced in SCSL jurisprudence in a dispute over whether "the greatest responsibility" was a jurisdictional requirement or merely a guide to the exercise of prosecutorial discretion.[71] Convicted AFRC member Santigie Borbor Kanu took up this issue on appeal, arguing that the Trial Chamber had failed to establish that he was not one of those individuals bearing the greatest responsibility. Kanu claimed that the Statute drafters were aware that the Court would have only limited time and resources, and as a consequence they deliberately circumscribed the SCSL's personal jurisdiction through establishing the "greatest responsibility" threshold as a requirement rather than treating it as a guide to prosecutorial strategy. Agreeing with the Prosecution's claims that "greatest responsibility" was a discretionary guide rather than a jurisdictional requirement, the Appeals Chamber determined that "it is inconceivable that after a *long and expensive trial*" the Court could conclude that despite establishing Kanu's commission of grave crimes, the Indictment against him should be struck because he was not proven to have been one of those bearing the greatest responsibility.[72] This determination is of interest both for its emphasis on financial considerations – the expense of the trial – as well as for its deference to prosecutorial discretion.

The restricted number of Indictments at the Court is thus one of the consequences of the SCSL's voluntary funding structure. Even though prosecuting fewer people might bring great gains in terms of efficiency and cost, one of the unintended consequences of this "new model" has been the heavy reliance on insider witnesses who might have been indicted

---

[68] Charles Jalloh, *Special Court for Sierra Leone: Achieving Justice?*, 32 MICH. J. INT'L L. 395 (2011). Jalloh notes that key actors in the Court's establishment envisioned at least double the number of indictments.

[69] INTERNATIONAL CRISIS GROUP, THE SPECIAL COURT FOR SIERRA LEONE: PROMISES AND PITFALLS OF A "NEW MODEL" (2003), *available at* www.unhcr.org/refworld/docid/3f5218d64.html.

[70] Keynote address of Ambassador Stephen J. Rapp at *Assessing the Contributions and Legacy of the Special Court for Sierra Leone to Africa and International Criminal Justice*, Apr. 21, 2012, in this volume.

[71] For more on this debate, see Charles Jalloh's article on greatest responsibility in this volume (Chapter 30).

[72] Prosecutor against Alex Tamba Brima, Brima Bazzy Kamara, and Santigie Borbor Kanu, SCSL-2004–16-A, Appeals Judgment, para. 283 (Feb. 22, 2008) (emphasis added).

under a slightly wider interpretation of the Court's mandate. Many high-level commanders who were involved in planning and ordering operations and who were directly implicated in crimes under the Court's Statute were able to escape accountability because of the small number of Indictments issued, as domestic criminal trials have been restricted by an amnesty agreement and by lack of political will.[73] The pressures of constraining the Tribunal's operating costs and restricting the timeline of its proceedings thus produced an impunity gap, where a number of individuals who testified about committing or ordering the commission of serious crimes were relocated or offered assistance from the Court. This product of the limited mandate – itself a product of "the desire of all states that supported its creation," according to ICG – has certainly affected how the SCSL is perceived in Sierra Leone and the broader West African region, with implications for its legacy.

The vulnerability of the Court's funding structure has also affected its operations concerning its staffing and labor practices. Its financial struggles were public knowledge and were noted regularly in its own annual reports, and Court employees were frequently reminded of the imminent insolvency of their employer. Staff attrition has been high, as noted by the SCSL president in 2009, who claimed that the Court's work was "affected by the unfortunate but understandable departure of many valuable and well-trained staff members, who have accepted longer-lasting and better paid work at other courts and international institutions."[74] Although not limited to the SCSL, these staffing issues have been compounded by the insecure funding arising from the voluntary contributions model.

This problem became even more acute as the Court neared the completion of its trial phase. In 2011, shortly before the Charles Taylor judgment was due to be delivered, staff members "with critical institutional knowledge" left for "more secure jobs in other institutions."[75] Meanwhile, throughout the perennial budgetary crises of the Court the division between national and international staff became further entrenched and inequitable. Disparity in pay between national and international staff appears to be a broader reality of the UN system that was replicated within the SCSL, but other dimensions may have further deepened the divide. With the Taylor trial's movement to The Hague, Sierra Leonean staff on national staff contracts working in The Hague did not have their flights from Freetown paid while international staff continued to fly business class at the Court's expense.[76] Although donor states' funding decisions substantially affect the SCSL's operations, "donors' justice" has its limits: donors are unable to intervene to manage the judicial pace of proceedings.

---

[73] Defense counsel for some of the Accused claimed that the Prosecution had effectively offered amnesty to individuals who had committed similar offenses as those allegedly committed by defense counsel's clients, speculating that those individuals may have been offered immunity as a result of working as witnesses for the Prosecution. *See* Prosecutor v. Kallon and Kamara, *Decision on Challenge to Jurisdiction: Lomé Accord Amnesty*, Case No. SCSL-2004–15-AR72 (E) and SCSL-2004–16-AR72 (E), A.Ch., para. 59 (Mar. 13, 2004). Indeed, former prosecutor Rapp noted that he had signed letters for insider witnesses in the case against Charles Taylor that some commentators referred to as "immunity letters"; Rapp, *supra* note 10.

[74] Special Court for Sierra Leone, *supra* note 45, at 5.

[75] Special Court for Sierra Leone, *supra* note 22, at 7.

[76] A Staff Appeals judge adjudicated several contract disputes with national staff following the move of the Taylor trial to The Hague and its implications for national staff contracts. National staff had to apply for the coveted positions in The Hague, which paid ten times the salary as equivalent Freetown-based jobs. In order to spread this financial advantage more equitably among national staff members, the Court rotated staff between Freetown and The Hague, yet this may have violated staff contracts by unilaterally changing the employee's duty station.

This has generated significant delay at great cost while expensive judicial salaries continue to be paid, as was particularly the case with the belated delivery of the Taylor judgment.[77] At the same time, in light of its budgetary struggles and the implementation of its "completion strategy," the Court needed to cut staff positions and costs. It appears that the SCSL may have been attempting to save money largely at the expense of national staff, who are institutionally more expendable than higher-level and more costly international staff at the Under Secretary-General and Assistant Secretary-General levels.

There does appear to be one limited advantage to the more ad hoc voluntary contributions model: the Court's outreach budget is not restricted by its overall budget and can be supplemented with private funding. One outreach staff member with experience at both the SCSL and at the ICC noted that the Special Court model provided greater flexibility: the Court could receive earmarked funds from the European Commission and civil society organizations such as the Open Society Initiative for West Africa, whereas the ICC budget is controlled by its Assembly of States Parties and cannot be supplemented with outside funding for outreach activities.[78] States and private foundations have prioritized funding outreach as one of the Court's main legacy contributions. Nevertheless, even this apparent advantage is subjected to the vicissitudes of state interests and the programming priorities of philanthropic foundations.

VII. CONCLUSION

What kind of legacy is left by the Court's funding structure – the material conditions that make its work possible? What are some of the challenges the SCSL model may pose for the future of international (criminal) justice? This chapter has shown how the Court faced struggles in securing funding throughout its lifespan, a reality noted by actors and scholarly commentators alike. The voluntary contributions structure has also furthered neoliberal dimensions of international criminal justice: it creates the need for constant fund-raising activities and "marketing" of the Court's work; it produces novel institutional forms such as the Management Committee, which emulate corporate practice; and it requires its high-level staff to effectively double as fund-raisers. Other Court employees live in a state of relative insecurity as administrators threaten that the SCSL's work may come to a halt in the absence of additional funding. The language of "targets" and "milestones" permeates Court discourse, and concerns with efficiency have accompanied the work of the SCSL since its inception.

This new institutional paradigm was originally designed with a three-year mandate in response to the lengthy proceedings at the ICTY and ICTR, although at the time of this writing the SCSL is in its tenth year of operations. As the Court's former Chief of Investigations noted in 2002, before trials began, "If you are a donor and are getting assessed for these

---

[77] The judgment delivery, anticipated for September 2011, was delayed until April 2012. Meanwhile, the fully reasoned judgment was not available for several weeks after the oral judgment was pronounced. One possible interpretation of this gap between the oral summary judgment and the publication of the full reasoned judgment is that the Court felt pressure to meet the "benchmark" of judgment delivery even though the final product was not ready.

[78] Author's interview with Maria Kamara, ICC Public Information and Documentation Section staff member, Nairobi, Kenya (Jan.16, 2012).

kinds of tribunals it can be rather disconcerting when you don't see the results you expect to be achieved in a shorter amount of time."[79] Yet the practice of international criminal justice unfolds according to its own timeline, and with competing values such as fair trial rights that must be balanced against the values of efficiency and expediency. Administrative nudges only go so far: as the Court's most recent annual report noted, "As a result of unforeseen developments in the [Charles Taylor] trial the milestones were not met."[80] International criminal justice's legalist framework thus does not conform well to the production of "deliverables" and the meeting of "milestones," and donors need to be persuaded that their financial support will contribute to broader objectives than individual convictions.

International criminal tribunals are therefore portrayed as broader security and development/"rule of law" initiatives that will aid in producing peaceful social outcomes. For example, while appearing before members of the U.S. Congress in 2006 to advocate for pressuring Nigeria to turn Charles Taylor over to the SCSL (and calling for the establishment of a hybrid tribunal in Liberia), the Special Court's first Prosecutor suggested a kind of "equation" – truth plus justice leads to a lasting peace in post-conflict contexts:

> To have a sustainable peace in Liberia, you must have truth and justice under the mantle of the rule of law and good governance. It is a simple A+B = C proposition. Truth plus justice equals a sustainable peace. Certainly, with this equation, Congress could be more assured that any funding and political capital expended would not be flushed down the drain.[81]

Justice within this framework is understood as international criminal accountability, not as distributive or restorative forms of justice. The problem with such calculations is that donor funding is zero-sum: as some scholars have argued, "tribunal funding is simply another form of aid," and thus "tribunals must compete with other assistance categories to obtain resources necessary to apprehend, to try, and to deliver justice."[82] Funding tribunals may thus come at the expense of other justice efforts that may be more in line with the desires of conflict-affected populations.[83] As Gerry Simpson notes, "we might ask what is *not* done when we are busy spending moral capital or political energy on using law to punish evil."[84]

This raises the broader question of the constituencies of international criminal tribunals such as the SCSL. Moving beyond the rhetorical gesture of justice carried out in the name of conflict-affected populations, who are the addressees of this particular form of justice as

---

[79] As quoted by Charles Cobb Jr. in *Sierra Leone's Special Court: Will It Hinder or Help?*, and interview with Alan White for Allafrica.com (Nov.21, 2022), *available at* http://allafrica.com/stories/200211210289.html (last visited June16, 2012).

[80] Special Court for Sierra Leone, *supra* note 22, at 34.

[81] *The Impact of Liberia's Election on West Africa: Hearing Before the Subcommittee on Africa, Global Human Rights and International Operations of the Committee on International Relations*, 109th Cong. 76, 2d Sess. (Feb. 8, 2006).

[82] S. Roper & L. Barria, *Gatekeeping versus Allocating in Foreign Assistance: Donor Motivations and Contributions to War Crimes Tribunals*, 51 J. CONFLICT RESOL. 285, 300–01 (2007).

[83] For example, a press release from the Human Rights Commission of Sierra Leone expressed concern over the privileging of criminal accountability over reparations: "HRCSL notes that while over $82 million has been spent so far on the Charles Taylor trial, as at June 30, 2010, less than U.S. $45,000 has actually been paid into the Sierra Leone War Victims Fund, almost all of it by Sierra Leoneans and their Government." Press Release No. 21, The Human Rights Commission of Sierra Leone, Transfer of "Blood Diamonds" to War Victims Fund in Sierra Leone (Aug. 10, 2010).

[84] G. SIMPSON, LAW, WAR & CRIME: WAR CRIMES, TRIALS, AND THE REINVENTION OF INTERNATIONAL LAW 10 (2007).

international criminal accountability? As much as the Court attempts to address its efforts toward the people of Sierra Leone and the broader West African region, the SCSL also appears to be equally oriented toward the donor community as a matter of existential necessity. This donors' market is increasingly characterized by blurred boundaries among justice, security, and development objectives, and recipient states are the beneficiaries of funding that aligns with donor states' foreign policy objectives.

James Goldston of the Open Society Justice Initiative argues "rule of law priorities are, to a great extent, shaped by those donor governments who dominate the 'international community' and its rule of law expert fellow travelers."[85] Meanwhile, there is an expanding field of professional knowledge accompanied by a market-driven demand for teaching, training, and practice, as well as the indirect effects that this profession has on state and local economies, whether in Freetown, Phnom Penh, or The Hague. The extent to which the "fair trial" paradigm the Court has modeled will affect domestic legal practice is an open question for legacy studies and empirical research, but one clear effect of the SCSL's work has been to contribute more personnel to the ever-growing professional elite specializing in the field of international criminal justice. Whether it equally benefits the people of Sierra Leone and the region remains to be seen.

---

[85] J. Goldston, *The Rule of Law at Home and Abroad*, 1 HAGUE J. RULE L. 41 (2009).

21

Subpoena Ad Testificandum and Duces Tecum: An Examination of the Jurisprudence of the Special Court for Sierra Leone

Chacha Bhoke Murungu[*]

I. INTRODUCTION

This chapter discusses the issue of subpoenas in international law, particularly as found in the jurisprudence of the Special Court for Sierra Leone (SCSL). The purpose here is to show the peculiar contribution and sometimes confusion by the SCSL on the issue of subpoenas in international law. Although the focus is essentially on the Court, as appropriate, this chapter will account for the jurisprudence of other international criminal tribunals on subpoenas.

The chapter is divided into five sections. Section I gives an introduction and clarification on the concept of subpoenas to testify and adduce evidence in international courts. Section II traces the legal basis for subpoenas under international law, whereas Section III sets out the requirements for the issuance of subpoenas. Such requirements are found and firmly established in the statutes, rules of procedure, and evidence as well as jurisprudence of international courts or tribunals. Section IV of the chapter is devoted to the discussion on the jurisprudence of the SCSL on the issue of subpoenas, indicating both the contribution and confusion created by the Court in this field of law. Section V concludes regarding the mixed approaches adopted by the SCSL on subpoenas and tries to give recommendations that international courts consider issuing subpoenas to all persons, regardless of their political or social positions in their countries. It is argued that this will assist international courts reach fair decisions, better enabling them to establish the truth about the international crimes committed in a specific armed conflict and to apportion individual criminal responsibility to the perpetrators.

A. Definitional Issues

A subpoena is an order of a court, which seeks to instruct and compel a person to appear before it. A "subpoena ad testificandum" is an order to appear in court and testify before the court for the purpose of a trial (an order to testify before a court). This may be issued by the

[*] Senior Lecturer in Law and Head, Department of Law, University of Dodoma. Much of the research for this chapter was conducted at the Centre for Human Rights, University of Pretoria during my doctoral studies. I am particularly grateful to the Faculty of Law, University of Pretoria for the bursary award. I am also thankful to Prof. Charles Jalloh for his guidance and useful comments on the draft of this chapter. Caveats as to contents and liability apply.

court itself or at the request of the accused person or the prosecutor by filing a motion for the issuance of a subpoena ad testificandum

A subpoena duces tecum is a court order issued against a person to produce or bring before the court documents or other items and materials that are required as evidence for the purpose of conducting a trial. Thus, "a subpoena is a due process compelling alternative which the court has recourse to as a last resort, after necessary and traditional ways of securing a witness have been utilised but in vain."[1] A subpoena is therefore a compelling and coercive remedy sought by a person who seeks to rely on it. Normally, courts are reluctant to issue this form of remedy, or they issue it very cautiously in extreme cases, perhaps because of its inherent punitive nature if a witness fails to comply with it. Failure to comply with a subpoena issued by the court constitutes contempt of court, punishable by a fine or imprisonment.[2] Subpoenas can also be ordered by judges, *proprio motu*, or upon request for subpoenas necessary for the investigation, preparation, or conduct of trials.

B. Outline of the Chapter and Arguments

This chapter addresses the issue of subpoenas, which is largely scant in the academic writings, particularly at the international level. Only the subpoena to testify (ad testificandum) and the subpoena to adduce evidence or submit documents in court (duces tecum) is the main focus of this chapter. Although the chapter discusses subpoenas per se, it is important to briefly highlight some other ways to ensure the appearance of persons in courts.

There are various ways to ensure the appearance of suspects of international crimes or attendance of witnesses before international courts. The Statute of the International Criminal Court (ICC Statute) lists warrants of arrest and summons to appear before the Pre-Trial Chamber of the ICC as ways to secure attendance of persons before the ICC.[3] The Trial Chamber of the ICC may require the attendance and testimony of witnesses and production of documents and other evidence by obtaining, if necessary, the assistance of states.[4] From the provision of Article 64(6) of the ICC Statute, the Trial Chamber of the ICC may seek state cooperation in obtaining evidence and testimony of individuals. This means that, where necessary, state officials, may also be required to cooperate with the ICC or accused persons during the conduct of trial or pretrial interviews by the Prosecutor or the defense counsel for accused persons.

Voluntary surrender, appearance, or attendance of an individual before an international court is another way. The voluntary appearance is usually done through a summons to appear issued by an international court.[5] A voluntary appearance signifies that a suspect or

---

[1] Prosecutor v. Sesay, Kallon and Gbao, Case No. SCSL-04–15-T, Trial Chamber I (June 30, 2008), A Separate Concurring Opinion of Hon. Justice Benjamin Mutanga Itoe on the Chamber's Unanimous Written Reasoned Decision on the Motion for the Issuance of a Subpoena to H.E. Dr. Ahmad Tejan Kabbah, former President of the Republic of Sierra Leone, § 13.

[2] *See* Rule 77(i), (iii) and (g) SCSL RPE; Rule 77 ICTY RPE ("inspection of material"); Prosecutor v. Brdanin and Talić, Case No. IT-99–36-AR73.9, Decision on Interlocutory Appeal, § 31 (Dec. 11, 2002). Prosecutor v. Milosevic, Decision on Assigned Counsel Application for Interview and Testimony of Tony Blair and Gerhard Schroder, § 35 (Dec. 9, 2005).

[3] ICC Statute art. 58(1) and (7).

[4] ICC Statute art. 64(6).

[5] ICC Statute art. 58(7).

potential witness is cooperating with the court, and respects its order requiring him or her to appear before it.

In principle, witnesses appear to testify at the request of the party seeking to rely on their evidence. Where a witness has been invited by the party seeking to rely on the person's evidence, and refuses to testify, this could lead to an application to the Court for the issuance of a subpoena to compel him or her to appear and testify.[6] If a person fails to attend voluntarily before the court to serve as a witness either for the Prosecutor or the Accused (defense), or fails to produce documents to be used as evidence in court, the court may order issuance of a subpoena to compel such person to appear and testify, or to produce evidence before the court. Any failure to attend or produce evidence will be deemed contempt of court and may render such person vulnerable to imprisonment or fine.

The focus here is on the coercive legal measures to compel persons to appear and testify before international courts, or to produce documents or other evidence in such courts. This is discussed in the context of the jurisprudence of the SCSL, but before we deal with the jurisprudence on subpoenas, it is necessary to establish the basis and conditions for the issuance of subpoenas.

II. LEGAL BASIS FOR SUBPOENAS IN INTERNATIONAL LAW

Subpoenas are governed by the Rules of Procedure and Evidence, as well as statutes of the international penal courts. For example, Rule 54 of the Rules of Procedure and Evidence (RPE) of the International Criminal Tribunal for the former Yugoslavia (ICTY) and International Criminal Tribunal for Rwanda (ICTR) respectively, empowers judges to issue, on request or *proprio motu*, subpoenas that are "necessary" for an investigation or for the preparation or conduct of a trial. Article 64(6)(b) of the ICC Statute empowers the Trial Chamber of the ICC to require the attendance and testimony of witnesses and production of documents and other forms of evidence by obtaining, if necessary, the assistance of states. Rule 84 of the Internal Rules of the Extraordinary Chambers in the Courts of Cambodia allows witnesses to be called to appear before the Trial Chambers to testify. In the SCSL, Rule 54 of the SCSL RPE, which is based on the ICTR Rules *mutatis mutandis*,[7] gives a Judge or a Trial Chamber the power to issue "such orders, summons, subpoenas, warrants and transfer orders as may be necessary for the purposes of an investigation or for the preparation or conduct of the trial." Such orders clearly include issuance of a subpoena ad testificandum or duces tecum, although those terms are not included in Rule 2, which contains definitions of key terms in the SCSL RPE.

Besides being governed by the RPE of international courts as such,[8] subpoenas also find a basis in international human rights law as well. For example, Article 17(4)(e) of the Statute of the SCSL requires that the accused shall be entitled to examine, or have examined the witnesses against him or her, and to obtain the attendance and examination of witnesses on his or her behalf under the same conditions as witnesses against him or her. This is also echoed in the Separate Concurring Opinion of Judge Benjamin Mutanga Itoe in *Prosecutor v. Issa*

---

[6] *Prosecutor v. Sesay, Kallon and Gbao, supra* note 1, §§ 3–4.
[7] *See* SCSL Statute art. 14(1).
[8] Rule 54 SCSL RPE.

Hassan Sesay, Morris Kallon and Augustine Gbao.[9] International human rights law therefore also allows room for the accused persons to seek subpoenas, by for example, according right to the accused person "to examine, or to have examined, the witnesses against him and to obtain the attendance and examination of witnesses on his behalf under the same conditions as witnesses against him."[10] The object here would seem to be giving a right for the accused to fair trial and equality of arms in trial proceedings.

III. CONDITIONS FOR THE ISSUANCE OF SUBPOENAS

From the jurisprudence of international criminal tribunals, particularly the ICTY, ICTR, and SCSL,[11] several conditions have to be satisfied before a court can issue subpoenas ad testificandum or duces tecum against a prospective witness, which would certainly include serving state officials. In *Prosecutor v. Bagosora, Kabiligi, Ntabakuze and Nsengiyumva*,[12] the Trial Chamber of ICTR stated the principles governing the issuance of subpoenas in the following way:

> The applicant for a subpoena requiring a person to give testimony or submit to an interview must show that three conditions are satisfied: (i) reasonable attempts have been made to obtain the voluntary cooperation of witnesses; (ii) the prospective witness has information which can materially assist the applicant in respect of clearly identified issues relevant to the trial; and (iii) the witness's testimony must be necessary and appropriate for the conduct and fairness of the trial.[13]

Further, the Trial Chamber stated that "subpoenas should not be issued lightly" and that a Chamber must consider "not only the usefulness of the information to the applicant but … its overall necessity in ensuring that the trial is informed and fair."[14] The Trial Chamber of ICTR went on to refer to the decision rendered by the Appeals Chamber n *Prosecutor v. Halilović* that:

---

[9] *Prosecutor v. Sesay, Kallon and Gbao, supra* note 1, § 12.

[10] ICCPR art. 14(e).

[11] *See, e.g.*, Prosecutor v. Sesay, Kallon and Gbao, Case No. SCSL-04–15-T, Written Reasoned Decision on Motion for Issuance of a Subpoena to H.E. Dr. Ahmad Tejan Kabbah, Former President of the Republic of Sierra Leone, Trial Chamber I, §§ 15–17 (June 30, 2008) and cases cited therein.

[12] *See* Prosecutor v. Bagosora, Gratien Kabiligi, Aloys Ntabakuze and Nsengiyumva, Case No. ICTR-98–41-T, Decision on Request for Subpoenas of United Nations Officials, "Request for Subpoenas of Kofi Annan, Iqbal Riza, Shaharyar Khan and Michel Hourigan Pursuant to Rule 54" of Aug. 25, 2006, Trial Chamber I (Decision of Oct. 6, 2006) (Judge Erik Møse, Presiding; Jai Ram Reddy; Sergei Alekseevich Egorov, Judges).

[13] *See Prosecutors v. Bagosora, Gratien Kabiligi, Aloys Ntabakuze and Nsengiyumva, id.*, § 3; Prosecutor v. Krštić, Case No. IT-98–33-A, Decision on Application for Subpoenas, Appeals Chamber of ICTY, § 10 (July 1, 2003); Prosecutor v. Halilović, Case No. IT-01–48-AR73, Decision on the Issuance of Subpoenas, Appeals Chamber of ICTY, § 7 (June 21, 2004); Prosecutor v. Bagosora et al., Decision on Request for a Subpoena, Trial Chamber of ICTR, § 5 (Sept. 11, 2006); Prosecutor v. Karemera et al., Case No. ICTR-98–44-T, Decision on Defense Motion for Issuance of Subpoena to Witness T, Trial Chamber of ICTR, § 4 (Feb. 8, 2006); Prosecutor v. Bagosora et al., Case No. ICTR-98–41-T, Decision on Ntabakuze Motion for Information from the UNHCR and a Meeting with One of Its Officials, Trial Chamber I, §§ 6 and 9 and accompanying text in nn.7 and 8 of § 6 thereof (Oct. 6, 2006); Prosecutor v. Bagosora et al., Case No. ICTR-98–41-T, Decision on Request for Cooperation of the Government of France, Trial Chamber I, § 2 (Oct. 6, 2006).

[14] *See* Prosecutor v. Halilović, Case No. IT-01–48-AR73, Decision on the Issuance of Subpoenas, Appeals Chamber of ICTY, § 7 (June 21, 2004).

The applicant seeking a subpoena must make a certain evidentiary showing of the need for the subpoena. In particular, he must demonstrate a reasonable basis for his belief that the prospective witness is likely to give information that will materially assist the applicant with respect to clearly identified issues in the forthcoming trial. To satisfy this requirement, the applicant may need to present information about such factors as the position held by the prospective witness in relation to the events in question, any relation the witness may have had with the accused which is relevant to the charges, any opportunity the witness may have had to observe or learn about those events, and any statements the witness made to the Prosecution or others in relation to them. The Trial Chamber is vested with discretion in determining whether the applicant succeeded in making the required showing, this discretion being necessary to ensure that compulsive mechanism of the subpoena is not abused. As the Appeals Chamber has emphasized, Subpoenas should not be issued lightly, for they involve the use of coercive powers and may lead to the imposition of a criminal sanction.[15]

In addition, the Chamber observed that "Chambers have considered factors such as the specificity with which the prospective testimony is identified and whether the information can be obtained other than through the prospective witness."[16] Further, it is generally accepted that, for a subpoena to be issued, there must be a "directness of a witness's observation of events as opposed to being an eye witness to whom a subpoena is sought."[17] However,

---

[15] *Prosecutor v. Halilović, id.* at para. 6; on the same conditions stated, *see also* Prosecutor v. Bagosora and Others, Case No. ICTR-98-41-T, Decision on Request for a Subpoena, Trial Chamber I, § 5 (Sept. 11, 2006); Prosecutor v. Bagosora, Case No. ICTR-98-41-T, ICTR Trial Chamber, Decision on Request for a Subpoena for Major J. Biot, § 2.

[16] Prosecutors v. Bagosora et al., Decision on Request for a Subpoena, Trial Chamber of ICTR, § 6 (Sept. 11, 2006); Prosecutor v. Karemera et al., Decision on Nzirorera's *Ex Parte* Motion for Order for Interview of Defense Witnesses NZ1, NZ2, Trial Chamber of ICTR, § 12 (July 12, 2006); Prosecutor v. Milošević, Case No. IT-02-54-T, Decision on Assigned Counsel Application for Interview and Testimony of Tony Blair and Gerhard Schroder, Trial Chamber of ICTY, §§ 30 and 33 (Dec. 9, 2005), *but see also* para. 9 referring to *Rule 54bis* of the Rules of Procedure and Evidence of the ICTY.

[17] Prosecutor v. Bagosora et al., Case No. ICTR-98-41-T, Decision on Request for Subpoena of Ami R. Mpungwe, Trial Chamber I, § 2 (Oct. 19, 2006) (referring to: "Prosecutor v. Krštić, Case No. IT-98-33-A, Decision on Application for Subpoenas, Appeals Chamber of ICTY, July 1, 2003, § 10; Prosecutor v. Halilović, Case No. IT-01-48-AR73, Decision on the Issuance of Subpoenas, Appeals Chamber of ICTY, June 21, 2004, § 7; Prosecutor v. Bagosora et al., Case No. ICTR-98-41-T, Decision on Request for Subpoenas of United Nations Officials, Trial Chamber, Oct. 6, 2006, § 3; Prosecutor v. Bagosora et al., Decision on Request for a Subpoena, Trial Chamber, Sept. 11, 2006, § 5; Prosecutor v. Karemera et al., Decision on Defense Motion for Issuance of Subpoena to Witness T, Trial Chamber, Feb. 8, 2006, § 4"); Prosecutor v. Bagosora et al., Case No. ICTR-98-41-T, Decision on Request for a Subpoena, Trial Chamber of ICTR (Sept. 11, 2006) (General Marcel Gatsinzi, former Chief of Staff of Rwandan Army); Prosecutor v. Bagosora et al., Case No. ICTR-98-41-T, Decision on Request for Subpoenas of United Nations Officials, Trial Chamber, § 3 (Oct. 6, 2006); Prosecutor v. Bagosora et al., Case No. ICTR-98-41-T, Decision on Ntabakuze Motion for Reconsideration of Denial of Issuance of Subpoena to a United Nations Official, Trial Chamber I, §§ 2–4 (Dec. 12, 2006); Prosecutor v. Bagosora et al., Decision on Request for a Subpoena Compelling Witness DAN to Attend for Defense Cross-Examination, Trial Chamber of ICTR (Aug. 31, 2006) (eyewitness of conduct by soldiers allegedly under the command of the Accused); Prosecutor v. Bagosora et al., Decision on Request for a Subpoena for Major Jacques Biot, Trial Chamber of ICTR (July 14, 2006) (military observer present in Gisenyi April 6–13, 1994); Prosecutor v. Bagosora et al., Decision on Motion Requesting Subpoenas to Compel the Attendance of Defense Witnesses DK 32, DK 39, DK 51, DK 52, DK 311 and DM 24, Trial Chamber of ICTR (Apr. 26, 2005); Prosecutor v. Bagosora et al., Decision on Defense's Request for a Subpoena regarding Mamadou Kane, Trial Chamber of ICTR (Oct. 22, 2004) (political advice to the Special Representative of the Secretary-General in Rwanda from December 1993 until May 1994); Prosecutor v. Bagosora et al., Decision on Prosecutor's Request for a Subpoena Regarding Witness BT, Trial Chamber (Aug. 25, 2004) (witness allegedly overheard

where a state and witness are willing and cooperative with the court, no subpoena may be issued.

In summary, the jurisprudence of the international courts demonstrates that a person applying for a subpoena to be issued must fulfill the following conditions: (1) such person must show that he or she has exhausted reasonable attempts to obtain the voluntary cooperation of the witness intended to be subpoenaed; (2) the applicant must show "legitimate forensic purpose," that is to say, a reasonable basis for the belief that there is a good chance that the prospective witness will be able to give information that will materially assist the applicant in proving his or her case; (3) the information requested must be convenient to be obtained and helpful for the preparation of the trial; (4) such information to be sought from the prospective witness must be of considerable and substantial assistance to a clearly identified issue that is relevant to the trial; (5) the applicant must demonstrate a nexus between such information and the case against the accused person[18]; (6) sometimes, a subpoena can be issued on the basis that it is the "last resort."[19]

Although courts have generally considered those conditions as imposing stringent requirements before they can grant applications for subpoenas, it is argued that such requirements are basically beyond what is prescribed by the statutes and RPE.[20] The rules only empower courts to issue orders and subpoenas in such cases where compulsory procedure is necessary for the purpose of the prosecution's investigation or either side's preparation for or conduct of the trial. As Justice Robertson observed,

> [Rule 54 of the SCSL Rules of Procedure and Evidence] says nothing about the nature of the evidence to be elicited from witnesses or document custodians to whom the orders may be directed, and it sets out no "requirements" … before it can be activated. It simply enables the court, of its own or upon application by either party, to order that valuable evidence must be brought into the courtroom: it will be necessary to make the order if the witness likely to give such evidenc refuses to attend or surrender documents.[21]

Equally, save for what has been said in the jurisprudence of the courts, there is no presumption in the statutes and RPE that applications for subpoenas shall be granted only "sparingly"[22] or after the defense has exhausted all the steps as outlined by courts in their

---

statement made by one of the Accused); Prosecutor v. Bagosora et al., Decision on Request for Subpoena of Major General Yaache and Cooperation of the Republic of Ghana, Trial Chamber (June 23, 2004) (subpoena to sector commander of UNAMIR).

[18] *See, e.g.,* Prosecutor v. Norman, Fofana and Kondewa, Case No. SCSL-04-14-T, Decision on Motions by Moinina Fofana and Sam Hinga Norman for the Issuance of a Subpoena Ad Testificandum to H.E. Alhaji Dr. Ahmad Tejan Kabbah, President of the Republic of Sierra Leone, Trial Chamber I, §§ 57–180 (June 13, 2006); Prosecutor v. Milošević, Case No. IT-02-54-T, Trial Chamber of the ICTY, Decision on Assigned Counsel Application for Interview and Testimony of Tony Blair and Gerhard Schroder (Dec. 9, 2005); Prosecutor v. Halilović, Case No. IT-01-48-AR73, Appeals Chamber of ICTY (Decision of June 21, 2004).

[19] Prosecutor v. Milošević, Case No. IT-02-54-T, Trial Chamber of the ICTY, Decision on Assigned Counsel Application for Interview and Testimony of Tony Blair and Gerhard Schroder (Dec. 9, 2005). *See also* F. Gayner, *Subpoenas, in* THE OXFORD COMPANION TO INTERNATIONAL CRIMINAL JUSTICE 524–25 (A Cassese ed., 2009).

[20] SCSL Statute art. 17(4)(e); Rule 54 SCSL RPE; art. 64(6)(b) ICC Statute; Rule 54 ICTY RPE; arts. 20(4)(e) and 28 ICTR Statute; Rule 54 ICTR RPE.

[21] Prosecutor v. Norman, Fofana and Kondewa, Case No. SCSL-04-14-T, Dissenting Opinion of Hon. Justice Robertson on Decision on Interlocutory Appeals against Trial Chamber Decision Refusing to Subpoena the President of Sierra Leone, § 3 (Sept. 11, 2006) (emphasis added).

[22] *Id.* § 4.

jurisprudence on the proper interpretation of Rule 54 of the RPE of the SCSL, ICTR, and ICTY. According to Justice Robertson, what the courts have done in interpreting Rule 54 is simply "to adopt what are no more than considerations or factors which are relevant to deciding whether evidence is likely to be material, and to fashion them into a complicated test which requires subpoena applicants to satisfy 'purpose' requirements and 'necessity' requirements."[23]

Thus, the purpose of Rule 54 of the SCSL RPE (similar to ICTY and ICTR) is expansive: "it provides that a compulsory order may be issued wherever the court is satisfied that it is 'necessary', in the sense that relevant evidence will not otherwise be brought to court. That is all Rule 54 says, and all that Rule 54 means."[24] Truly, this rule applies only to evidence that is likely to be material and that is the only relevant evidence to be brought to court for the preparation of or, conduct of the trial. Once a court is satisfied that a person is likely to give evidence that is likely to be useful and material, or that a person is likely to produce any document likely to be material, and that such person will not voluntarily attend as a witness or will not voluntarily produce the document, then the court should issue a subpoena.

Rejections of subpoena applications on the ground that they are merely "tactical" do not hold substance in interpreting the rules of procedure and evidence particularly on subpoenas. Subpoenas can be issued on the strength of the applications, fair trial rights, and equality of arms in the preparation or conduct of trials. Applicants for a subpoena only rely on information provided or statements made by potential witnesses and their roles and positions in the past, with a view that such statements or information can materially assist the applicant and the court in establishing the truth about criminal responsibility of the accused person.

Thus, the jurisprudence of courts regarding conditions for issuing subpoenas should be considered with caution as some of the cases, especially those of *Milošević*[25] and *Blaškić*[26] were decided based on the cooperation of states with international courts – where it was not necessary to issue subpoenas against state officials. However, this position was later changed by the same court in 2003 in *Krštić*[27] when the ICTY realized that its orders could be issued to states and its subpoenas could be directed to individuals, including state officials, in order to provide cooperation in adducing evidence in court. Moreover, the jurisprudence of international courts on issues of subpoenas is not consistent and should be considered on a case-by-case basis. Whereas in some cases courts have been open to issuing subpoenas for state officials to testify, in some other cases, the same courts have declined to issue subpoenas against state officials on grounds, based on grounds that arguably defeat the purpose of full fair trial rights to accused persons.[28]

---

[23] *Id.*

[24] *Id.*

[25] Prosecutor v. Milošević, Case No. IT-02-54-T, Decision on Assigned Counsel Application for Interview and Testimony of Tony Blair and Gerhard Schröder, §§ 1–69 (Dec. 9, 2005).

[26] Prosecutor v. Blaškić, Case No. IT-95-14, Judgment on the Request of the Republic of Croatia for Review of the Decision of Trial Chamber II of July 18, 1997 (Oct. 29, 1997), Appeals Chamber, § 25 (July 18, 1997).

[27] Prosecutor v. Krštić, Case No. IT-98-33-A, Decision on Application for Subpoenas, Appeals Chamber of ICTY, § 29 (July 1, 2003).

[28] *Cf.* Prosecutor v. Karadžić, Case No. IT-95-5/18-T, Decision on Motion for Subpoena to Interview President Karolos Papoulias, §§ 12–14 (Mar. 20, 2012) (while denying the Motion, the Trial Chamber avoided considering whether the serving head of state of Greece enjoys immunity from being subpoenaed by the ICTY – which

Based on the preceding discussion, it seems appropriate to reject the stringent steps adopted by courts regarding applications for subpoenas as they go beyond the plain requirements set by the statutes and RPE. Consequently, applications for subpoenas should be granted on a three-stage approach, as rightly propounded by Justice Robertson, namely:

(i) Does the named witness have immunity (in which case the court may not proceed further) or a testamentary privilege?

(ii) Is the potential evidence likely to be material to an issue in the trial – in particular to a legitimate defence?

(iii) Are the court's compulsory powers really necessary to bring that relevant evidence to court, or may it be delivered by some other means?[29]

In addition to the three listed questions, courts should be guided by the principles of fair trial, particularly that "no potential witness, however high and mighty, in possession of information that might determine the outcome, can be spared from the public duty of divulging it,"[30] and that "no accused person, however demonized and otherwise disempowered, should be denied access to the court's compulsory machinery if that is necessary to bring such evidence into the courtroom."[31] These principles can be reflected in the statutes of international courts and international human rights treaties as discussed in Section II.[32] It must be emphasized that fair trial rights are expressly recognized in the statutes of international courts,[33] and as such, the rights create negative obligations on all potential witnesses, whether they are willing to appear in court to testify or not.[34]

I think was an abdication of its functions and powers – bearing in mind the Appeals Chamber's prevailing decision in *Krštić*, in 2003 (*supra* note 27, § 29 – that state officials can be subpoenaed by the ICTY!)); *Prosecutor v. Karadžić*, Case No. IT-95-5/18-T, Decision on Accused's Motion for Subpoena to Interview Vladimir Zagorec, §§ 1–15 (Mar. 12, 2012) (granting the Motion whereby the Trial Chamber issued a subpoena to General Vladimir Zagorec, former defense minister of the Republic of Croatia, compelling him to submit to an interview with the Accused's legal advisor. If we go by this unchallenged precedent, it is likely that the ICTY Trial Chamber will issue a subpoena to former U.S. president Bill Clinton compelling him to submit to an interview with Karadžić's legal advisor, Peter Robinson, *Prosecutor v. Karadžić*, Case No. IT-95-5/18-T, Motion for Subpoena to Interview President Bill Clinton, at 1–34, §§ 1–37 (June 1, 2012), with Annexes A, B, and C; *see Karadzic Files Motion for ICTY to Subpoena President Clinton*, *available at* http://www.scribd.com/doc/97871707/Karadzic-Files-Motion-for-ICTY-to-Subpoena-President-Clinton-1-Jun-12 (last visited July 15, 2012)); *Prosecutor v. Krštić*, *supra* note 27 (granting the Motion), as opposed to *Prosecutor v. Milošević*, *supra* note 25 (denying the Motion); *see further Prosecutor v. Issa Hassan Sesay, Morris Kallon, Augustine Gbao*, *infra* note 35 (granting the Motion); and *Prosecutor v. Norman, Fofana and Kondewa*, *infra* note 35 (denying the Motion).

[29] *Supra* note 21, § 1.

[30] *Id.* § 1.

[31] *Id.* § 1.

[32] See Section II of this chapter.

[33] See. for example, SCSL Statute art. 17(4)(e), which provides that:

> In determination of any charge against the accused pursuant to the present Statute, he or she shall be entitled to the following minimum guarantees, in full equality …
> (e) To examine, or have examined, the witnesses against him or her, to obtain attendance and examination of witnesses on his or her behalf under the same conditions as witnesses against him or her …

[34] *Supra* note 21, § 2 (where Justice Robertson reasoned that art. 17(4)(e) of the SCSL Statute "expressly guarantees that a mechanism will be available to the accused to obtain the attendance and the examination of witnesses, whether they are willing or not. That mechanism, available to the prosecution and defense alike, is provided by Rule 54 of the Rules of Procedure and Evidence.").

IV. THE QUESTION OF SUBPOENAS BEFORE THE SPECIAL
COURT FOR SIERRA LEONE

The Trial Chamber of the SCSL has dealt with the question of subpoenas in several cases.[35] Two cases decided in 2006 and 2008 respectively have touched on the subpoena against the serving or former president of Sierra Leone, Ahmad Tejan Kabbah, and one case decided in 2010 is about a subpoena to British model Naomi Campbell. Issues surrounding immunity of the head of state were raised in the first two subpoena cases and used as a basis to deny the subpoena application, but it was then decided by the Court in 2008 that former president Tejan Kabbah could testify before the SCSL.

The chapter turns to examine the jurisprudence of the SCSL on these cases. The first subpoena decision of 2006 calls for a deeper analysis. The two Accused persons, Moinina Fofana and Samuel Hinga Norman, had applied for the issuance of a subpoena ad testificandum of the then-sitting president of Sierra Leone, Ahmad Tejan Kabbah. They wanted him to appear and testify on their behalf before the Trial Chamber of the SCSL. They believed that President Kabbah had refused to heed their repeated requests for him to appear and testify on their behalf such that a subpoena was necessary as a last resort.

Norman and Fofana, who had filed joint submissions for the subpoenas on December 15, 2005, contended that as their Civil Defense Forces (CDF) leader, President Kabbah knew that they did not bear the "greatest responsibility"[36] for such crimes. They further argued that President Kabbah was commanding and materially supporting and communicating with the leadership of the CDF, which they had been heading. On the basis of his communication, command, and support to them, President Kabbah also bore the greatest responsibility for the crimes that Norman and Fofana were charged with, as they contended that the president was responsible both politically and militarily. Further, Norman and Fofana contended that President Kabbah had issued commands and communications, and materially supported them both during his exile in Conakry in Guinea and from his presidential palace in Freetown, Sierra Leone. As such, they submitted that President Kabbah "may himself have been among a group or, at the very least, that he was in a position to give evidence regarding the relative culpability of the three accused persons."[37]

The Trial Chamber declined the application for the subpoena because the requirements set out in Rule 54 of the *SCSL Rules of Procedure and Evidence* (the necessity and legitimate forensic purpose) had not been satisfied. It stated categorically that:

> The President is as well the Head of State and finds himself at the top of the State machinery.... President Tejan Kabbah is not an ordinary Sierra Leonean but also, ... the current,

---

[35] *See* Prosecutor v. Norman, Fofana and Kondewa, Case No. SCSL-04-14-T, Decision on Motions by Moinina Fofana and Sam Hinga Norman for the Issuance of a Subpoena Ad Testificandum to H.E. Alhaji Dr. Ahmad Tejan Kabbah, President of the Republic of Sierra Leone, Trial Chamber I, June 13, 2006; see the Separate Concurring Opinion of Hon. Justice Benjamin Mutanga Itoe on the Chamber Majority Decision on Motions, especially §§ 57–58, 83–93, and 94–180; Prosecutor v. Taylor, Case No. SCSL-03-1-T, Decision on Prosecution Motion for the Issuance of a Subpoena to Naomi Campbell, 1–7 (June 30, 2010); Prosecutor v. Issa Hassan Sesay, Morris Kallon, Augustine Gbao, Case No. SCSL-04-15-T, Written Reasoned Decision on Motion for Issuance of a Subpoena to H.E. Dr. Ahmad Tejan Kabbah, former President of the Republic of Sierra Leone, 1–9 (June 30, 2008).

[36] SCSL Statute art. 1(1).

[37] *See* Prosecutor v. Norman, Fofana and Kondewa, SCSL-04-14-T, Fofana Motion for Issuance of a Subpoena Ad Testificandum to President Ahmad Tejan Kabbah, § 13 (Dec. 15, 2005).

sitting in, and incumbent President and Sovereign Head of State of the Republic of Sierra Leone.... The President belongs to a different category and regime of immunities.... In fact, his immunity under Section 48(4) of the Constitution [of Sierra Leone] should ordinarily include, not only immunity against criminal and civil actions, but also against Subpoenas, other Court processes, or even being compelled to appear in court as a factual witness unless he, President Kabbah on his own volition, voluntarily accepts and decides to so testify in these proceedings.[38]

This holding appears to have reaffirmed immunity of the head of state under Section 48(4) of the Constitution of Sierra Leone, based on the concepts of recognizing the dignity of the head of state, the need for convenience in any testifying, and the avoidance of interference with the head of state. This has an implication that the court applied a domestic legal provision to protect an incumbent head of state from testifying before an international court. Although the SCSL in *Norman, Fofana, and Kondewa* had the benefit of the existing jurisprudence of ICTY on subpoenas (some of which it applied), it failed to recognize and apply the precedent found in the Krštić case whereby the ICTY Appeals Chamber provided a strong authority that subpoenas ad testificandum can be issued to serving state officials to submit for an interview with the Accused's counsel, or to appear and testify in court whether or not such agents witnessed the relevant facts in their official capacity.[39] Further, the SCSL Trial Chamber failed to appreciate the importance of the powers conferred on international courts with respect to subpoenas. Contrary to the SCSL, the ICTY has recognized expressly that even state officials are subject to the orders of an international tribunal. It said this in the following manner:

In conclusion, the fact that a person identified by the International Tribunal as being in possession of important documents is an official of State does not preclude the issuance of a *subpoena duces tecum* addressed to him or her directly.... It has been established that binding orders may be issued by the International Tribunal addressed to both States and individuals and there is, therefore, no reason why a person exercising State functions, who has been identified as the relevant person for the purposes of the documents required, should not similarly be under an obligation to comply with a specific order of which he or she is the subject.[40]

This is an appropriate approach that should have been taken by the SCSL in its application for subpoenas. The SCSL decision suggests that state officials cannot be compelled to testify in court. The chamber acted as if it were a party to the proceeding, arguing as if it were the State of Sierra Leone, which had its head of state being required to appear. Such position is common to most states, particularly where their state officials are required to appear in court. We now look at some of the most surprising arguments advanced by states.

In the *Milošević* case at the ICTY, Germany and the United Kingdom argued that "calling Mr. Blair and Mr. Schröder as witnesses serve[d] no legitimate forensic purpose and that the official capacity of the prospective witnesses entitle[d] them to certain immunities which

---

[38] *Prosecutor v. Norman, Fofana and Kondewa, id.*, §§ 58, 98–100 and see the Separate Concurring Opinion of Hon. Justice Benjamin Mutanga Itoe on the Chamber Majority Decision on Motions, especially § 132.

[39] *Prosecutor v. Krštić*, Case No. IT-98-33-A, ICTY Appeal Chamber, Decision on Application for Subpoenas decision, § 27 (July 1, 2003).

[40] *Prosecutor v. Blaškić, supra* note 26, § 69.

may prevent the issuance of a subpoena against them."[41] Likewise, Greece submitted before the ICTY that a subpoena for an interview was unknown to the Greek legal system and that it would "raise considerable problems of a legal and practical nature," and essentially, that sitting heads of state should fall into a category of certain officials protected by law, and that "issuing subpoenas would constitute a disproportionate measure and unnecessary intrusion of the dignity of the state President's office."[42] In such cases, the ICTY declined to consider issues of immunity, based on grounds that the requirements for subpoenas had not been met.[43]

However, it is argued here that immunity does not arise as to subpoenas issued by international courts because international courts have inherent powers to issue binding orders and subpoenas to states and individuals. Hence, courts should not be hesitant in issuing subpoenas, and they must not refrain from granting subpoena applications on the ground that state officials might be harassed or humiliated, or that their dignity would be compromised. The ICTY has cautioned that:

> As States can act only through their officials, a high government official who is subpoenaed in his official capacity to carry out obligations on behalf of a State would not be taking part in the proceedings as a private person but as an agent of the State (...) – the fear of harassment of diplomatic officials – is not valid for an international criminal tribunal established by the Security Council.[44]

Back to the decision of the SCSL, Judge Thompson in his dissenting opinion offered a different approach to a subpoena against President Kabbah. He said:

> There is nothing, I reckon, problematic about statutory powers to issue Subpoenas, nationally or internationally.... I take for granted that, *if a priori there is no entitlement to immunity from international criminal prosecution reserved to a Head of State or government or any responsible government official under international law as regards the perpetration of international crimes, a fortiori international law does not confer any like immunity on such officials from testifying as witnesses in international criminal tribunals(...) Specifically, therefore, in the context of the Special Court, no such immunity is expressly or impliedly provided for in the constitutive instruments or subordinate legislation of the tribunal....* On this view, the President cannot claim immunity from subpoena as a logical derivative from his explicit immunity from prosecution since it is waived vis-à-vis the [SCSL]. Therefore, while the President enjoys immunity under the domestic law of Sierra Leone from prosecution by reason of Section 48(4) of the *Sierra Leone Constitution Act No. 6 of 1991*, no immunity to appear as witness before the domestic court is granted. *No immunity to appear as a witness before the international criminal tribunals, likewise, exists.*[45]

The dissenting opinion of Judge Thompson against the majority decision of the Trial Chamber has a very strong position that the law allowed the SCSL to issue subpoena ad

[41] *Prosecutor v. Milošević, supra* note 25, § 2.

[42] *Prosecutor v. Karadžić, supra* note 28, § 4.

[43] *Prosecutor v. Milošević, supra* note 25, § 67; *Prosecutor v. Karadžić, supra* note 28, § 13.

[44] Prosecutor v. Blaškić, Case No. IT-95-14-PT, Decision on the Objection of the Republic of Croatia to the Issuance of Subpoenae Duces Tecum, Trial Chamber II, § 89 (July 18, 1997).

[45] *See* Dissenting Opinion of Hon. Justice Bankole Thompson on Decisions on Motions by Moinina Fofana and Sam Hinga Norman for the Issuance of a Subpoena Ad Testificandum to H.E. Alhaji Dr Ahmed Tejan Kabbah, President of the Republic of Sierra Leone (Case No. SCSL-04-14-T), §§ 8, 15 and 16.

testificandum to President Kabbah to testify before the court.[46] Because of the serious differences between the Judges on the interpretation of Rule 54, the Defense applied for leave to appeal against the majority decision. Leave was granted.[47] The majority in the Appeals Chamber of the SCSL confirmed the decision of the Trial Chamber.[48] In this author's view, the majority decisions both by the Trial and Appeals Chambers of the SCSL were wrong. The correct position is that which is stated in the Dissenting Opinion of Judge Thompson (Trial Chamber) and Dissenting Opinion of Justice Robertson (Appeals Chamber). Justice Robertson's Dissenting Opinion against the majority decision of the Appeals Chamber is echoed along the same lines with the reasoning of the Dissenting Opinion of Judge Thompson.[49] Justice Robertson provided useful guidance on subpoenas against state officials. He said,

> The public … has a right to every man's evidence, including evidence in possession of the Head of State. …. It is, after all, a court set up with plenary power to indict anyone, including President Kabbah himself, and that power to indict must, a *fortiori*, include a power to direct that he should testify.[50]

It is argued that President Kabbah should have been called to testify by whatever means appropriate, including by way of a subpoena, because he might have had information that could have materially assisted the accused persons in refuting certain allegations contained in the charges against them, or that his evidence could support the legitimate defense case. For example, it would seem, the information that was being sought by Fofana from President Kabbah was that based on the chain of command. It is doubtful if this information could have been given by anyone else other than President Kabbah, who was at the top of the chain of command in Sierra Leone as the country's commander in chief.[51]

Taking on the issue of immunity of President Kabbah, Justice Robertson reasoned that although national law of Sierra Leone accords immunity to the president, such immunity does not apply to an international court such as the SCSL.[52] It is well-recognized that the official position of an individual whether as a head of state or government official does not exonerate such person from criminal responsibility for international crimes. This extends to issues for subpoenas in respect of international crimes, as rightly observed by Justice Robertson in his dissenting opinion.[53] More important, the ICTY Appeals Chamber gave a very decisive position regarding immunity of state officials in the following strong words:

> The Appeals Chamber did not say that the functional immunity enjoyed by the State officials provided immunity against being compelled to give evidence of what the official saw or heard in the course of exercising his official functions. Nothing which was said by

---

[46] *Id.* §§ 14–30.

[47] *See* Prosecutor v. Norman, Fofana, and Kondewa, Case No. SCSL-04-14-T, Decision on Motions by the First and Second Accused for Leave to Appeal the Chamber's Decision on Their Motions for the Issuance of a Subpoena to the President of the Republic of Sierra Leone (June 29, 2006).

[48] Prosecutor v. Norman, Fofana and Kondewa, SCSL Appeals Chamber, §§ 8–39 (majority decision).

[49] *See* Dissenting Opinion of Judge Geoffrey Robertson against the decision of the Appeals Chamber of SCSL, §§ 10–50.

[50] *Supra* note 21, § 16.

[51] *Supra* note 21, § 34.

[52] *Supra* note 21, § 38.

[53] *Supra* note 21, §§ 41–47.

the Appeals Chamber in the Blaskic Subpoena Decision should be interpreted as giving such immunity to officials of the nature whose testimony is sought in the present case. No authority for such a proposition has been produced by the prosecution, and none has been found. Such an immunity does not exist.[54]

Had the SCSL subpoenaed President Kabbah, he would have complied with the order (as he did in another subpoena application to be discussed later in the chapter) because the court was established at his request, and the court's decisions are binding even as to the officials of the government of Sierra Leone, which had the legal obligation to cooperate with the court.[55]

It is imperative in the positions stated by Judge Thompson and Justice Robertson in their Dissenting Opinions that immunity does not apply to issuance of a *subpoena ad testificandum and subpoena duces tecum* when the international criminal courts deal with international crimes. In this regard, it is clear that like other individuals, heads of state are not immune from the subpoenas issued by international criminal tribunals. This position is arguably in line with contemporary international criminal law. Further, even if the Appeals Chamber and the Trial Chamber were correct in exercising their discretion under Rule 54 of the SCSL RPE, such discretion is not absolutely free. Accordingly, exercising discretion should have been in conformity with Articles 17(4)(e) of the Statute of SCSL and 14(e) of the International Covenant on Civil and Political Rights, 1966, and settled jurisprudence on subpoena matters.[56]

However, on June 30, 2008, the Trial Chamber of the SCSL, having perhaps recognized the errors it had made in the first subpoena decision in the case of *Norman, Fofana and Kondewa* above, changed its position, albeit too late, and in respect of a former president (not the sitting president), Ahmad Tejan Kabbah of Sierra Leone. This time the Trial Chamber of the SCSL held boldly that "the [d]efence has met the prescribed standard for the issuance of a subpoena under Rule 54 thereby justifying the exercise by the Chamber of its discretion to grant the orders sought."[57] After this finding, the Chamber granted the application by Counsel for Issa Hassan Sesay for the issuance of a subpoena to Ahmad Tejan Kabbah, former president of Sierra Leone, for a pre-testimony interview and for testimony at the trial. The Chamber thus ordered Ahmad Tejan Kabbah to testify, if called as a defense witness, which order was complied with.

The Chamber did so under the purported pretext that the present application was different from that of *Norman, Fofana and Kondewa*. Judge Benjamin Mutanga Itoe revealed the differences, which may not necessarily be genuine differences at all. The Judge observed that whereas in the first subpoena application the Accused sought evidence of President Tejan Kabbah, contending that he also bore the greatest responsibility for the crimes they were charged with (which also showed that they wanted the president to be charged with

---

[54] *Prosecutor v. Krštić, supra* note 39, at para. 27.

[55] Rule 8(A) SCSL RPE; SCSL Statute art. 17.

[56] *See* Prosecutor v. Kordić and Mario Cerkeć, Case No. IT-95-14/2, Decision on Appeal Regarding Statement of a Deceased Witness, Appeals Chamber, ICTY, § 20 (July 21, 2000).

[57] Prosecutor v. Sesay, Kallon and Gbao, Case No. SCSL-04-15-T, Written Reasoned Decision on Motion for Issuance of a Subpoena to H.E. Dr. Ahmad Tejan Kabbah, Former President of the Republic of Sierra Leone, Trial Chamber I, § 21 (June 30, 2008).

the same crimes), in the second subpoena application, the accused persons "did not conceal their intention." Instead,

> the objective of their application was for Ex-President Kabbah to appear in Court to testify on their behalf to the effect that they did not, as stipulated in the Agreement and in the Statute of [the] Court, bear the greatest responsibility for the crimes committed during the conflict to have warranted their prosecution.[58]

The Judge observed further that in the initial subpoena application, the Accused had wanted to ridicule and embarrass President Tejan Kabbah by exposing his involvement and conduct in the conflict as the CDF boss, who would ultimately bear criminal responsibility.[59]

An observation in the second subpoena decision by the Trial Chamber of the SCSL is that the court clearly lacks consistency in the way it treats state officials in relation to prosecution and subpoenas in respect of international crimes. Although it is a position stated in the first subpoena decision in *Norman, Fofana and Kondewa* on June 13, 2006 that President Kabbah – then–serving president – enjoyed immunity from testifying before the Trial Chamber of the SCSL, in the second case decided on June 30, 2008, the Trial Chamber drastically deviated from its own weak position it had stated in 2006. A further observation is on the way Judge Benjamin Mutanga Itoe himself came to agree that there was no immunity for President Tejan Kabbah from testifying before the SCSL. The Judge's inconsistency was also obvious when he stated that:

> Even though the earlier motion was denied on the basis of the same criteria on which this one is granted, it is my finding that these two applications, even though identical in their subject matter and in the objective they seek to achieve, are distinguishable and that the verdict or stand adopted by This Chamber, in the earlier one, does not necessarily bind it to come to a similar conclusion based on similar reasons, in the later case given the configuration and divergence of the facts on which the two applications were made and canvassed.[60]

The above paragraph proves a self-contradicting position adopted by Judge Benjamin Mutanga Itoe and the Trial Chamber of the SCSL generally. It calls for the question: whether the position of the SCSL regarding immunity is that there is no immunity for state officials from testifying before it. This is true, and more so, when the reality is revealed that at the time the second subpoena application was made, President Tejan Kabbah had ceased to be a president, whereas the SCSL had refused to grant an application for a subpoena against him when he was still in office as president. Would the testimony of President Tejan Kabbah really not have assisted the accused persons, Norman, Fofana, and Kondewa in 2006? Why did the SCSL change its position to say that the evidence of former president Tejan Kabbah would materially assist the Accused in *Sesay, Kallon and Gbao*? Is there any significant difference between the two subpoena applications?

---

[58] Prosecutor v. Sesay, Kallon and Gbao, Case No. SCSL-04–15-T, Trial Chamber I, June 30, 2008, A Separate Concurring Opinion of Hon. Justice Benjamin Mutanga Itoe on the Chamber's Unanimous Written Reasoned Decision on the Motion for Issuance of a Subpoena to H.E. Dr. Ahmad Tejan Kabbah, Former President of the Republic of Sierra Leone, § 22.

[59] *Id.* § 31.

[60] *Supra* note 58, § 34.

There seems to be no difference between the two subpoena applications, save for the parties to the case. Rather, there are more similarities than differences. All involve the same conflict, time, circumstances, crimes committed, and potential witness, and were before the same court. In this respect, one would have expected the court to treat same circumstances and similar cases alike. Arguably, President Kabbah was probably "uniquely placed to testify about those issues." By refusing to allow President Kabbah to testify in the first subpoena application, the SCSL denied the Accused their right to call a witness to support their case, as per Article 17(4)(e) of the Statute of the SCSL, as well as to ensure fair trial and equality of arms. It could have been true that Kabbah ordered and communicated with the CDF leadership in Sierra Leone during the armed conflict.

Commenting on the inconsistency in the jurisprudence of the SCSL on the issue of subpoenas, Patrick Hassan-Morlai has rightly observed that the jurisprudence of the court is highly inconsistent on this point, and that "it is doubtful whether the subpoena decision has created a precedent or made a positive contribution to existing jurisprudence in this area of law."[61] Hassan-Morlai seriously challenged the court's first subpoena decision in that it substantially failed to follow and appreciate the jurisprudence of the ICTY and ICTR on subpoenas. It appears from the jurisprudence of the SCSL that, so far, it has been a position of that court *not* to recognize immunity of former state officials from testifying before it. This is observed above in the second subpoena decision where former president Kabbah was ordered to testify for the Accused, Issa Hassan Sesay.

Another example is when a different trial chamber of the SCSL allowed the Prosecution's motion for the issuance of a subpoena against former vice-president of Liberia, Moses Blah, to testify against Charles Taylor. On May 14, 2008, former vice-president Blah was called in to testify for the Prosecution, but he turned into a hostile witness and chose to testify for Taylor. This could have been influenced by the fact that he was a subordinate of Taylor, and Taylor had handed power to him when Taylor left for asylum in Nigeria in 2003. The SCSL has only been faced with one real challenge involving the then serving president, Tejan Kabbah. Nevertheless, the practice on granting subpoenas has apparently developed with ease before the SCSL.[62]

It can be contended that state officials have a duty to assist international criminal tribunals or courts, especially when dealing with international crimes. Arguably, such state officials should not be accorded immunity from testifying. It is argued that such immunity does not extend to issues of a subpoena ad testificandum or duces tecum as long as there are circumstances linking such senior state officials to the commission of international crimes. The idea is that state officials are to be treated like other individuals and must not go unsummoned before international courts when such persons possess certain information or material relevant to the expeditious conduct of a trial. However, it must be understood that courts may face certain difficulties in getting serving state officials to testify before international courts. These, as was argued by Greece, Germany and the United Kingdom in different cases discussed earlier in the chapter, involve technicalities caused

---

[61] P.M. Hassan-Morlai, *Evidence in International Criminal Trials: Lessons and Contributions from the Special Court for Sierra Leone*, 3 AFR. J. LEGAL STUD. 96–118, 108 (2009).

[62] *See, e.g., Prosecutor v. Taylor, Case No. SCSL-03-1-T, Decision on Public with Confidential Annexes A and B Prosecution Motion to Call Three Additional Witnesses, Trial Chamber, §§ 1–22, especially § 21 (June 29, 2010).*

by domestic laws (which should not principally preempt international courts from issuing subpoenas), practical considerations, issues of the dignity of the head of state, humiliation and harassment of the head of state, sovereign immunity, and national security concerns. Although these problems should not prevent the courts from issuing subpoenas, they have nevertheless been considered as obstacles in ensuring cooperation with the international courts, particularly when state officials are called to testify or submit documents to be used as evidence in court.

Where states fail to cooperate with the courts, the matter can be brought to the attention of the UN Security Council, which established some of these international criminal tribunals. Here the Security Council could take actions against the particular state that is not cooperating. This is so because international courts cannot operate without the cooperation of states, including state officials in particular cases. It is argued that when subpoenas are issued for the appearance of state officials, states should not and do not have the discretion or power to choose who should testify. Instead, they must ensure there is smooth cooperation with international courts. Court orders from international courts must be complied with by states, as well as by state officials.[63]

V. CONCLUSION

The Appeals Chambers of the SCSL surprisingly held that a head of state could not be subpoenaed in order to testify or appear for interview or submit important documents to be used as evidence before the Court. The decision in the Norman and Moinina Fofana case is an example to that effect. This position has created a state of "confusion" and "controversy" on subpoenas in international law. It is important to understand the dissenting opinions expressed by Judges Bankole Thompson and Geoffrey Robertson in opposition to that position as stated by the SCSL in the Norman and Fofana case. The dissenting opinions are to the effect that no state official enjoys immunity from being subpoenaed to testify or produce important documents that may be used as evidence in international criminal tribunals.

Clearly, the jurisprudence of the SCSL on the question of subpoena is inconsistent and confusing. The inconsistency is observed in the way the Trial Chamber of the SCSL later came to accept the fact that a former president can testify before it and thus granted subpoena applications for President Kabbah to testify as a defense witness in *Sesay, Kallon and Gbao* on June 30, 2008. The same goes for the court's position in allowing former vice-president of Liberia Blah to testify against Charles Taylor in May 2008. Hence, although this might be explained by the reality that the latter decision was taken by a different trial chamber, there is a notable inconsistency and contradiction, especially in the decisions of Trial Chamber I of the SCSL.

It is therefore important to treat state officials like other individuals in respect of testifying before international courts. This requirement is quite important for all trials before international tribunals, and perhaps presently, the International Criminal Court (ICC) might benefit from the SCSL's jurisprudence for its future work.

As the ICC is a permanent court dealing with international crimes, it should adopt as persuasive authorities (although it is not legally bound to follow the decisions of other courts)

---

[63] *Prosecutor v. Blaškić, supra* note 26, § 13.

the good decisions on subpoenas by the Trial Chamber of the SCSL and the Dissenting Opinions of Judges Bankole Thompson and Geoffrey Robertson in the subpoena decisions before the Trial Chamber and Appeals Chamber of the SCSL in *Norman and Fofana*, and the decision of the Trial Chamber of SCSL in *Sesay, Kallon and Gbao* respectively. These decisions are important regarding the treatment of state officials, particularly on issues of subpoenas. Similarly, the ICC can benefit from the rich and progressive jurisprudence on subpoenas as found in the Krštić and Karadžić decision of March 12, 2012 regarding General Vladimir Zagorec, former defense minister of Croatia. Equally, the court could benefit from the Bagosora[64] subpoena decisions discussed in this chapter.

These decisions could be relevant for the ICC to interpret and apply the provisions of Article 64(6)(b) of the ICC Statute in a more progressive way. Like the SCSL, the ICC should not shy away from compelling state officials to appear before it, or to testify and produce important documents before it for the purpose of fair preparation or conduct of trials. It is the view of this author that state officials enjoy no immunity from the normal legal processes to compel them to testify or give evidence before the ICC and international criminal tribunals. This is particularly so because such leaders have a duty to assist the ICC and the international criminal tribunals, especially when dealing with international crimes.

Compelling such state officials to appear for an interview, or to testify, inevitably renders equality of arms in proceedings and a fair trial for the accused in the courts, especially when conditions for the issuance of subpoenas have been met and efforts to secure the voluntary attendance of these officials have failed. Further, because of their position in their governments, state officials may possess important information or evidence for the purpose of conducting or preparing for trials. From the practice at the SCSL, state officials should not be accorded immunity from subpoenas ad testificandum or duces tecum as long as there are circumstances linking such senior state official to the commission of international crimes.

This suggestion, however, recognizes the complications and worries related to state officials being summoned to appear and testify in court. Such worries are evident in the jurisprudence of the courts, particularly as expressed in the submissions by Greece in the Karadžić subpoena decision of March 20, 2012; the arguments submitted by Germany and the United Kingdom in *Milošević*; and of course the fear expressed by Justice Mutanga Itoe in his Concurring Opinion on the subpoena decision protecting the dignity of President Tejan Kabbah in *Norman, Fofana and Kondewa* as discussed above. Nevertheless, international courts have inherent powers to exercise their functions, particularly by issuing binding orders to states and subpoenas to individuals, including state officials. Immunities have no place in contemporary international criminal justice relevant to the prosecution of international crimes.

With regard to discussions on applications for subpoenas involving state officials, the correct approach that should be taken is the three-step one advanced by Justice Robertson in his dissenting opinion in *Norman, Fofana and Kondewa*,[65] asking basically whether such state officials enjoy immunities from subpoenas issued by international courts, and whether it is necessary to issue subpoenas where other means can be used to obtain evidence from state officials.

---

[64] *Supra* note 16.
[65] *Supra* notes 21 and 29, § 1.

22

Witnessing History: Protective Measures at the Special Court for Sierra Leone

Amy E. DiBella[*]

I. INTRODUCTION INTO WITNESS AND VICTIM PROTECTION AND SUPPORT

Witness protection is a fundamental concern of international criminal justice.[1] Without providing adequate protective measures to guarantee the safety and support of witnesses and victims, it is very likely that these courts could not exist, at least certainly not as they do today. For instance, the Special Court for Sierra Leone (SCSL or "the Court") might not be able to be located in Sierra Leone, or the Court might have been forced to depend less on the in-court live presentation of evidence.[2]

The concept behind this book (and the accompanying conference hosting the numerous authors and other legal scholars and practitioners with special insight into the Court) is to assess the "SCSL's contribution and legacy both to Sierra Leoneans, in whose name it was asked to render impartial justice, and the international community, whose generous anti-impunity dollars made its work possible."[3] It seeks to provide a forum to "critically assess and reflect on [the Court's] contribution to Sierra Leone and to international criminal law and justice"[4] and ultimately, to "make a valuable contribution to existing knowledge regarding the potential, and limits, of one of the more significant internationally supported anti-impunity initiatives in post–Cold War era Africa."[5]

With those aims in mind, this chapter considers the SCSL's mechanisms to coordinate support and protection for witnesses, whether these mechanisms have affected the success of the Court, and if so, how. The critical analysis contemplates the implementation of wit-

---

[*] Amy DiBella, Esquire, currently practices in the area of criminal defense in Pittsburgh, Pennsylvania, USA.

[1] UNHRC, Twelfth Session Annual Report of the United Nations High Commissioner for Human Rights and Reports of the Office of the High Commissioner and the Secretary General – Right to the Truth, para. 42 U.N. DOC. A/HRC/12/19 (Aug. 21, 2009) (explaining how increasingly the attention of international and human rights bodies is devoted to the protection of victims and witnesses) and para. 33 (listing numerous manuals of best practices for witness protection) [hereinafter UNHRC].

[2] Phoebe Knowles, *The Power to Prosecute: The Special Court for Sierra Leone from a Defence Perspective*, 6 INT. C.L.R. 387 (2006) (explaining how "the Court's seat and associated security concerns for witnesses" affect the ability of the Court to provide public trials).

[3] Charles C. Jalloh, Assessing the Contributions and Legacy of the Special Court for Sierra Leone to Africa and International Criminal Justice, Concept Note, at 3, *available at* http://www.law.pitt.edu/events/2012/04/assessing-the-contributions-and-legacy-of-the-special-court-for-sierra-leone-to-afric (last visited Oct. 27, 2012).

[4] *Id.* at 3.

[5] *Id.* at 5.

ness protection measures in furtherance of the goals of the SCSL in light of the locus of the tribunal in situ and its statutory framework.

Following this introduction, I present my underlying argument that the goals – and thus, the success – of the SCSL are inextricably intertwined with witness protection. Next, structural arguments will be considered. First, how designating the seat of the Court directly in Sierra Leone, which had not even emerged from conflict by the time of the signing of the agreement to establish the tribunal, impacted the type of witness support and protection offered, and second, how the organizational structure of the tribunal impacted witness support and protection matters. Finally, each of these sections will analyze how well the SCSL addressed witness issues, and whether and how that might have contributed to a more or less credible Court.

II. THE SCSL'S GOALS RELATE TO WITNESS PROTECTION ISSUES

Rather than theorize about how best to measure the successes at the Court with regard to witness protection,[6] this inquiry is anchored by two goals that were well-established and publicized, and whose achievement is directly dependent on witness testimony, protection, and support. The UN Security Council, the Secretary-General, and the government of Sierra Leone enunciated the plans for the creation of the SCSL through numerous reports, resolutions, letters, and other documents. Those documents provide insight into the reason for the creation of the Court and the initial goals that it aimed to achieve.[7] Because those documents set out countless ideals, only some of which are relevant to witness protection, I narrow the inquiry to two goals that are closely related to witness issues. First, the Court's ability to deliver credible justice[8] is one of the most useful benchmarks for evaluating the SCSL's achievements.

A. Credible Justice

From its inception, the SCSL was envisioned as a forum for "credible" justice for Sierra Leone. In fact, when Sierra Leonean President Alhaji Ahmad Tejan Kabbah wrote to the Security Council requesting UN and international support for the creation of a "special court for Sierra Leone,"[9] he referred three times to the necessity of "credible justice."[10] He sought to create a "strong and credible court that will meet the objectives of bringing justice

---

[6] James Cockayne, *The Fraying Shoestring: Rethinking Hybrid War Crimes Tribunals*, 28 FORDHAM INT'L L.J. 616, 620–22 (2005) (assessing the direction of the SCSL using an impressive "rudimentary" model that identifies the stakeholders, the responsibility of the Court to those stakeholders, and the minimum performance standards as discerned from the legal texts that provide the foundation for the Special Court. His aim was to "better understand whether the Special Court is meeting the high expectations placed on it.").

[7] Charles Chernor Jalloh, *Special Court for Sierra Leone: Achieving Justice?*, 32 MICH. J. INT'L L. 395, 398 (2011) ("The role of the SCSL is best discerned through examination of the original objectives of those who created it.").

[8] Along similar lines, Cockayne, *supra* note 6, at 622–23, identifies five key responsibilities owed by the Special Court to the "Affected population," among which are "Security and reconciliation" and "Generation of an accurate and impartial historical record."

[9] Letter from the President of the Republic of Sierra Leone to the President of the Security Council, at 2, U.N. DOC. S/2000/786 (Aug. 10, 2000) [hereinafter Kabbah Letter].

[10] *Id.* at 2–3.

and ensuring lasting peace."[11] He asked for international support and efforts similar to those provided with regard to Rwanda and the former Yugoslavia,[12] and he sought "effective, secure, fair and credible justice" for the people of Sierra Leone and the UN peacekeepers who had been victimized in the crisis.[13]

In August 2000, the Security Council responded with Resolution 1315, in which it recognized the need for a "credible system of justice and accountability"[14] and the desire of the government of Sierra Leone for a "strong and credible court that will meet the objectives of bringing justice and ensuring lasting peace."[15] Resolution 1315 called on the Secretary-General to negotiate an agreement with the government of Sierra Leone and emphasized "the importance of ensuring the impartiality, independence and credibility of the process, in particular with regard to the status of the judges and the prosecutors."[16] Following those negotiations, the Secretary-General reported back and also referred to the creation of a "credible system of justice."[17] Scholars, too, emphasized the importance of credibility. In his 2011 article considering whether the SCSL was "achieving justice," Charles Jalloh argued that "dispensing *credible justice* on behalf of Sierra Leonean victims of conflict is a noble goal that was the *raison d'être* for the SCSL's creation."[18]

At a superficial level within trial and appeal decisions, credibility is a question of the admissibility, reliability, and weight given to witness testimony. The Trial Chamber elucidated the considerations in evaluating witness testimony in the Taylor Judgment:[19]

> When evaluating the credibility of witnesses who gave evidence viva voce, the Trial Chamber has taken into account a variety of factors, including their demeanour, conduct and character (where possible), their knowledge of the facts to which they testified, their proximity to the events described, the plausibility and clarity of their testimony, their impartiality, the lapse of time between the events and the testimony, their possible involvement in the events and the risk of self-incrimination, inconsistencies in their testimony and their ability to explain such inconsistencies, any motivations to lie, and their relationship with the accused.

However, credibility means much more than that with regard to the Court's provision of protection, support and security to witnesses. Credible, according to Merriam-Webster's dictionary, means "offering reasonable grounds for being believed." Following that definition, the credibility of the SCSL depends on whether Sierra Leoneans and other interested persons – not just the judges or court personnel – have been provided enough information

---

[11] *Id.* at 2.

[12] *Id.*

[13] *Id.* at 3.

[14] U.N. S.C. Res. 1315 (Aug. 14, 2000), U.N. Doc. S/RES/1315, preambulatory para. 7.

[15] *Id.* at preambulatory para. 9; *see also* Wayne Jordash & Scott Martin, *Due Process and Fair Trial Rights at the Special Court: How the Desire for Accountability Outweighed the Demands of Justice at the Special Court for Sierra Leone*, 23 L.J.I.L. 585, 585–86 (2010).

[16] U.N. Doc. S/RES/1315, *supra* note 14, at para. 4.

[17] Report of the Secretary-General on the Establishment of a Special Court for Sierra Leone, para. 74, U.N. Doc. S/2000/915 (Oct. 4, 2000).

[18] Jalloh, *supra* note 7, at 396–97; *see also* Cockayne, *supra* note 6, at 644; *and* Jordash & Martin, *supra* note 15, at 585–86.

[19] Prosecutor v. Charles Ghankay Taylor, SCSL-03–01-T-1283, Judgment, para. 165 (May 18, 2012) (internal citations omitted) [hereinafter Taylor Judgment].

to believe in the Court. Put another way, the mosaic of evidence presented *to the public* must support and be seen to support the indictments, decisions, verdicts, and other actions of the Court. In that sense, the credibility of the SCSL is undoubtedly dependent on the publicity and transparency of its processes. Former chief prosecutor Stephen Rapp stated that the Court has placed "the highest priority on outreach.... For as important as it is to do justice, for all those that the Court intends to serve it is also important that justice be seen to be done."[20] In addition to activities outside of the courtroom, for justice to be done and seen to be done, inside of the courtroom evidence must be delivered and evaluated in an open and impartial court to enable the public to engage in the process.[21]

B. Overarching Concerns for Security

In addition to credible justice, safety and security were also paramount concerns from the inception of the SCSL, concerns that certainly relate to witness protection. When contemplating, planning, and developing the SCSL's framework and structure, the Secretary-General, the Security Council, and the government of Sierra Leone expressed numerous intentions for establishing the Court, but consistently referred to the importance of security. The Court was first established out of necessity amid the failure of the Lomé Peace Accord to bring calm to the region.[22] Indeed, its initial purpose was to be to contribute to lasting peace and justice in a country that had been experiencing one of the worst civil conflicts in history.[23] Thus, it is no surprise that the immediate focus of the Court was to create security.

In July 2000, the Secretary-General reported that he had begun taking steps toward the creation of a court.[24] He explained that "[t]he security of the court, its premises, equipment, personnel and that of the accused, is the Government's main concern."[25] That main concern undoubtedly also encompasses the security of witnesses without whom justice is impossible. By September 2000, the negotiations between the government of Sierra Leone and the Secretary-General were well underway, and the framework for the Court (i.e., the Agreement between the United Nations and Sierra Leone, and the Statute) was practically in place.[26] In October 2000, the Secretary-General reported back to the Security Council

---

[20] Prosecutor Rapp made a statement while briefing the Security Council. U.N. S.C. Verbatim Record, U.N. Doc. S/PV.6163 (July 16, 2009).

[21] Jordash & Martin, *supra* note 15, at 586 (expectation that trials must meet international standards reflects "an expectation that trials would produce verdicts, where justice was done and see to be done."); and Cockayne, *supra* note 6, at 654 (referring to the importance of the creation of an "Accurate and Impartial Record").

[22] Peace Agreement between the Government of Sierra Leone and the Revolutionary United Front of Sierra Leone, U.N. Doc. S/1999/777/Annex (July 12, 1999); Priscilla Hayner, Center for Human Dialogue, *Negotiating Peace in Sierra Leone: Confronting the Justice Challenge* 23–25 (Dec. 2007), http://www.hdcentre.org/files/Sierra%20Leone%20Report.pdf (last visited Apr. 14, 2012) (describing how by May 2000 peace had begun breaking down). That accord, especially its controversial amnesty provision, was discussed in depth by Leila Sadat in Chapter 15 of this volume.

[23] Kabbah Letter, *supra* note 9, at 2.

[24] Fifth Report of the Secretary-General on the United Nations Mission in Sierra Leone, paras. 9–11, U.N. Doc. S/2000/751 (July 31, 2000).

[25] *Id.* at para. 11.

[26] U.N. Doc. S/2000/915, *supra* note 17, at paras. 5–6 (first stage of negotiations was held at the UN Headquarters from September 12 to September 14, 2000, and focused on the establishment of two "constitutive instruments establishing the Special Court," the Agreement between the United Nations and the government of Sierra

regarding numerous issues, giving extra attention to concerns of the location of the Court and how that could impact witnesses and collection of evidence.[27] That report placed special emphasis on security:[28]

> As the Security Council itself has recognized, in the past circumstances of Sierra Leone, a credible system of justice and accountability for the very serious crimes committed there would end impunity and would contribute to the process of national reconciliation and to the restoration and maintenance of peace in that country ... the Security Council should bear in mind the expectations that have been created and the state of urgency that permeates all discussions of the problem of impunity in Sierra Leone.

The goal was clear: the SCSL was to contribute to peace and security and that goal would be contemplated at every step along the way. As Prosecutor David Crane reflected, his strategy would affect the security of the region and "[m]istakes could cost lives and disrupt the transition process from conflict to peace."[29] International law scholars have also focused on security and reconciliation as guiding purposes of the Court.[30]

The abstract principles of security and reconciliation have evolved into slightly more tangible concerns for witness safety and support. When budgetary pressures arose, for instance, they were met with sympathetic calls for support for "witness protection" programs, which undeniably offer a relatively less uncontroversial fund-raising focus. For instance, Prosecutor Rapp sought support from the international community by urging: "There is no substitute for programmes such as victim and witness protection until the last sentence has been served."[31]

The Court's obligation to take appropriate measures to protect witnesses from potential retaliation or intimidation and to provide support for witnesses[32] was established in the SCSL's principal documents. It can be found in the Statute of the Special Court for Sierra Leone and the Rules of Procedure and Evidence. Article 16 paragraph 4 of the Statute of the SCSL establishes the legal basis for the Registrar to create the Witness and Victims Support Section (WVS) and provides[33]:

> The Registrar shall set up a Victims and Witnesses Unit within the Registry. This Unit shall provide, in consultation with the Office of the Prosecutor, protective measures and security arrangements, counseling and other appropriate assistance for witnesses, victims who appear before the Court and others who are at risk on account of testimony given by such witnesses. The Unit personnel shall include experts in trauma, including trauma related to crimes of sexual violence and violence against children.

Leone, and the Statute of the Special Court. The second, held September 18–20 in Sierra Leone, involved discussion of legal issues, location of the court, and other logistics).

[27] *Id.* at paras. 51–54 (discussing how relocation might be necessary for safety reasons, but that it might have a negative impact on witnesses).

[28] *Id.* at para. 74.

[29] David M. Crane, *Dancing with the Devil: Prosecuting West Africa's Warlords: Building Initial Prosecutorial Strategy for an International Tribunal after Third World Armed Conflicts* 37 Case W. Res. J. Int'l L. 1, 8 (2005).

[30] Cockayne, *supra* note 6, at 644–45.

[31] U.N. Doc. S/PV.6163, *supra* note 20, at 15.

[32] UNHRC, *supra* note 1, at para. 39.

[33] SCSL Statute art. 16(4).

Moreover, under the Statute, the Office of the Prosecutor has the power to question witnesses,[34] and the Accused has the right to examine or have examined witnesses against him and obtain witnesses on his behalf.[35] Although the Statute references consultation for witness protection only *with regard to the Prosecution*, Rule 34 of the Rules of Procedure and Evidence states that the Witness and Victims' Section (WVS) should consult with the Defense Office as well for the protection of defense witnesses.[36]

That Rule sets out the "functions" of the WVS. With regard to *all* witnesses and victims who appear before the Special Court, and others who are at risk on account of testimony given by witnesses, the WVS must (1) recommend protective and security measures; (2) provide "adequate protective measures and security arrangements and develop long-term and short-term plans for their protection and support"; and (3) ensure those persons "receive relevant support, counseling and other appropriate assistance, including medical assistance, physical and psychological rehabilitation, especially in cases of rape, sexual assault and crimes against children."[37]

The obligation also extends to the Chambers. As enunciated in Rule 26*bis*, the Trial and Appeals Chambers shall ensure that trial is fair and expeditious, and "conducted in accordance with the Agreement, the Statute and the Rules, with full respect for the rights of the accused and *due regard for the protection of victims and witnesses*."[38] Based on the foregoing analysis it is clear that the SCSL from the beginning was tied to the goals of bringing credible justice, and more immediately, developing security and maintaining peace in the region. Those initial goals were enunciated again in the Statute and Rules – as laid out previously and discussed further later in the chapter – and tested through the practice and jurisprudence of the Court.

Protective measures, when successfully implemented, could enable the truth to come to light in circumstances where it otherwise might have been hidden.[39] Herman von Hebel, the Registrar for the SCSL, explained[40]:

> The protection and support of witnesses and victims is of seminal importance to the functioning of the Special Court for Sierra Leone. As with any judicial process that relies on witness testimony, ensuring that witnesses' security and wellbeing are well catered for is a priority: a witness who is uncomfortable with what is being asked of them undermines the delivery of justice.

As the UN High Commissioner of Human Rights' Report on the Right to Truth explains, the protection of witnesses is not just essential to the effectiveness of the court and delivery of testimony, but is also a uniquely important human rights concern. "[T]he failure to provide protection to witnesses can severely affect fundamental rights, such as the right

---

[34] SCSL Statute art. 15(2).
[35] SCSL Statute art. 17(4)(e).
[36] Rule 34, RPE.
[37] Rule 34, RPE.
[38] Rule 26*bis*, RPE.
[39] Special Court for Sierra Leone, Best-Practice Recommendations for the Protection & Support of Witnesses; An Evaluation of the Witness and Victims Section at the Special Court for Sierra Leone (2008), "Foreword" [hereinafter Best-Practice Report] 5 (explaining that the success of the Court is dependent on those who testify).
[40] *Id.*, at "Foreword."

to justice and the right to the truth."[41] The 2008 "Best-Practice Recommendations for the Protection & Support of Witnesses," published by the SCSL, stated that the effectiveness of the Court depends on the witness experience.[42] However, when used improperly – that is, when protective measures create a meaningful interference with the transparency of the process and the rights of the accused – protective measures may undermine the credibility and effectiveness of justice.[43]

C. Commitment to the Live Delivery of Testimony

Witness protection and support is particularly important at the SCSL because the Court has emphasized and prioritized the *live* delivery of justice.[44] The live commitment is clear: during the Taylor trial alone, a total of 115 witnesses, 94 called by the Prosecution and 21 by the Defense, gave viva voce testimony.[45] The Statute provides that the accused "shall be entitled to a fair and **public** hearing," thus expressing commitment to the core value afforded and required under international human rights law.[46] The guarantee is strong, but not absolute. The second half of the sentence qualifies the first and explains that the accused's entitlement to a fair and public hearing is "subject to matters ordered by the Special Court for the protection of victims and witnesses."[47]

As noted in the Eighth Annual SCSL Report, the theoretical commitment to public trials as promulgated in the Statute was implemented in practice: "The Court's trials have relied heavily on witness testimonies for evidence."[48] In fact, the trials at the SCSL relied primarily on eyewitness testimony rather than documentary evidence.[49]

On the one hand, it seems only natural that trials relating to the Sierra Leonean conflict would be heavily reliant on oral, rather than written, evidence. Witness testimony is more likely to be found than other types of evidence in contexts such as Sierra Leone. On the other, the Court's efforts and commitments to the fair and public trial have been a point of discussion, if not contention, among scholars and practitioners who suggest that orality is overvalued at the expense of justice. It has been suggested that the SCSL's method of hearing testimonial evidence in open court is more time-consuming and costly than would be the presentation of documentary evidence in its stead, if done in appropriate circumstances.

For instance, in his independent expert report, Cassese identified the adversarial principle of orality as one possible culprit of prolonged proceedings: "Proving an international crime requires an immense amount of evidence that must be presented through testimony

---

[41] UNHRC, *supra* note 1, at para. 32.

[42] Best-Practice Report, *supra* note 39, at 5–6.

[43] Knowles, *supra* note 2, at 417 ("security concerns prompting excessive protective measures, closed sessions and witness payments limit the realization of the model's aim to provide a truly fair and impartial justice that is also seen to be both fair and impartial.").

[44] Best-Practice Report, *supra* note 39.

[45] Taylor Judgment, *supra* note 19, at para. 163.

[46] SCSL Statute art. 17(2).

[47] *Id.*

[48] President of the Special Court for Sierra Leone, Eighth Annual Report of the President of the Special Court for Sierra Leone (June 1, 2010 to May 31, 2011), 30 [hereinafter SCSL Eighth Annual Report].

[49] Best-Practice Report, *supra* note 39, at 5.

of witnesses or the oral presentation of documentary or physical evidence."[50] Cassese suggested "incorporating some basic elements of the inquisitorial system into the adversarial
model" in order to enhance the efficiency of the proceedings to make them "less cumbersome and time consuming."[51] He presented the option of "[s]peeding up the evaluation of
evidence by admitting written evidence whenever appropriate" as under Rules 92*bis*, and
Rules 92*ter*[52] and 92*quater*.[53] In order to reduce the burdensome and time-consuming process of oral examination of witnesses,[54] Cassese suggested to the Plenary[55]:

> I suggested the addition of Rules 92*ter* and *quater* which would allow Judges to forgo oral
> examination in appropriate circumstances, particularly when the evidence is duplicative or
> general in nature and does not affect the fairness of the proceedings.

The Plenary accepted modifications of Rule 92*ter*, which, according to Cassese, gave
Judges more options to admit written evidence.[56] However, it must be noted that under the

---

[50] Independent Expert (Antonio Cassese), Report on the Special Court for Sierra Leone (Dec. 12, 2006), para.
76 [hereinafter Cassese].

[51] *Id.* at para. 99.

[52] *Id.* Annex A, which proposes Rule 92*ter*, entitled Admission of Written Statements and Transcripts in Lieu of
Oral Testimony, provides that "(A) A Trial Chamber may dispense with the attendance of a witness in person,
and instead admit, in whole or in part, the evidence of a witness in the form of a written statement or a transcript of evidence, which was given by a witness in proceedings before the Tribunal, in lieu of oral testimony
which goes to proof of a matter other than the acts and conduct of the accused as charged in the indictment."
In so doing, the Chamber should look to numerous factors (i), such as whether such evidence (a) is cumulative; (b) relates to the historical, political or military background; (c) is a general or statistical analysis of the
population's ethnic composition; or (d) "concerns the impact of crimes upon victims." That proposal goes on
to list, in subsection (ii), "Factors against admitting evidence in the form of a written statement or transcript,"
such as if there is (a) "an overriding public interest" in oral presentation of evidence; (b) a party who objects
and demonstrates that the evidence is unreliable, or that the probative value of the evidence is outweighed by
prejudicial effect; or (c) if there are other factors which make the witnesses in person attendance more appropriate. Subsection (B) and (C) of that proposed rule provide as follows:(B) If the Trial Chamber decides to
dispense with the attendance of a witness, a written statement under this Rule shall be admissible if it attaches
a declaration by the person making the written statement that the contents of the statement are true and
correct to the best of that person's knowledge and belief and (i) the declaration is witnessed by: (a) a person
authorised to witness such a declaration in accordance with the law and procedure of a State; (b) a Presiding
Officer appointed by the Registrar of the Tribunal for that purpose; and (ii) the person witnessing the declaration verifies in writing: (a) that the person making the statement is the person identified in the said statement;
(b) that the person making the statement stated that the contents of the written statement are, to the best of
that person's knowledge and belief, true and correct; (c) that the person making the statement was informed
that if the content of the written statement is not true then he or she may be subject to proceedings for giving
false testimony; and (d) the date and place of the declaration. The declaration shall be attached to the written statement presented to the Trial Chamber.(C) The Trial Chamber shall decide, after hearing the parties,
whether to require the witness to appear in person. If the Trial Chamber so determines, it may nevertheless
decide to admit the witness' statement in lieu of the examination-in-chief and to permit cross-examination
pursuant to Rule 92*quater*.

[53] Rule 92*quater*: Other Admission of Written Statements and Transcripts (A) A Trial Chamber may admit, in
whole or in part, the evidence of a witness in the form of a written statement or transcript of evidence given
by a witness in proceedings before the Tribunal, under the following conditions: *(i) the witness is present in
court; (ii) the witness is available for cross-examination and any questioning by the Judges; and (iii) the witness
attests that the written statement or transcript accurately reflects that witness' declaration and what the witness
would say if examined. (B) Evidence admitted under paragraph (A) may include evidence that goes to proof of
the acts and conduct of the accused as charged in the indictment;* *Id.* at para. 100.

[54] *Id.* at para. 106.

[55] *Id.* at para. 107.

[56] *Id.* at para. 108.

independent expert's proposed Rules, Judges could exercise their discretion to admit written evidence only "when this does not affect the fairness of the proceedings."[57] Moreover, if the Bench opted to hear the witness in person, it could admit the statement in lieu of examination-in-chief, but the witness would have to be available for cross-examination and questioning by the bench, pursuant to Rule 92*quater*.[58]

Although Cassese's vision of the Statute and its implementation may not have come to fruition in the exact form he proposed, the experience of the Taylor trial shows that documentary evidence was frequently used in lieu of oral testimony at the SCSL. The Prosecution initially requested that witnesses be permitted to testify via closed-circuit video, not for efficiency of the proceedings, but instead "to avoid difficult, stressful, and costly travel,"[59] and later, requested prior testimony be admitted "in order to prevent the stress of testifying and make the trial more expeditious" under Rule 92*bis*.[60] The Berkeley War Crimes Study Center reported that in October 2008, nearly half of all witnesses to testify were Rule 92*bis* witnesses[61]:

> Nearly half of the [32 prosecution] witnesses testified under Rule 92*bis*, which allowed them to submit prior written statements in lieu of undergoing direct examination. Pursuant to court order, however, the Defense was granted the right to cross-examine any 92*bis* witness it wished to question in open court. After Defense made clear that it intended to call all proposed 92*bis* witnesses to The Hague for cross-examination, the Prosecution reduced the total number of witnesses it intends to call from 144 (72 *viva voce* and 72 via Rule 92*bis*), to about 95, nearly 50 witnesses fewer than originally slated.

In light of the commitment to live delivery of justice, it is not surprising that the Court has consistently upheld the accused's inherent right to have produced and cross-examine every witness.[62] This has thus led to a situation where certain witnesses were never led by Prosecution through examination-in-chief but instead, started right off with cross-examination.[63] Under those circumstances it came to be that the Prosecution, perhaps begrudgingly, decided it would call certain witnesses live who it did not apparently intend to call live in the beginning; and it opted not to call certain witnesses on whose written testimony it sought to rely initially.[64] Nonetheless, this awkward situation seems much preferable to the fate often complained of at the ad hoc tribunals that the defense rights would be overshadowed, or that the trial would become overridden with excessive documentary evidence.[65]

The Court's strong commitment to public trials and the oral delivery of evidence might have led to greater concern for witness safety and contributed to the perception that

---

[57] *Id.*, Annex A, proposed Rule 92*ter* Reasons.

[58] *Id.*, Annex A proposed Rule 92*quater* and Reasons.

[59] U.C. Berkeley War Crimes Studies Center, *Charles Taylor Trial Report* 7 (Oct. 1–Oct 31, 2008) [hereinafter October 2008 Taylor Trial Report]. The initial request was made under Rule 85(D).

[60] *Id.* at 7.

[61] *Id.* at 3.

[62] *See* Prosecutor v. Taylor, Case No. SCSL 03–01-T-556, Decision on Prosecution Notice under Rule 92*bis* for the Admission of Evidence Related to *Inter Alia* Kenema District and on Prosecution Notice under Rule 92*bis* for the Admission of Prior Testimony of TF1–036 into Evidence (July 15, 2008).

[63] October 2008 Taylor Trial Report, *supra* note 60, at 8.

[64] *Id.* at 1.

[65] Stephanos Bibas & William W. Burke-White, *International Idealism Meets Domestic-Criminal-Procedure Realism*, 59 DUKE L.J. 637, 699 (2010).

witnesses were undergoing stress and facing potential risks. However, as noted previously and discussed in greater detail later in the chapter, the fair and public trial promised to the accused is qualified by the protection ordered for victims and witnesses,[66] which is fleshed out in greater detail by consideration of the Rules of Procedure and Evidence.

There is some indication that witness protective measures were used with greater regularity at the SCSL than at other international tribunals.[67] As one report documents: "While 25 per cent and 75 per cent of witnesses at the ICTY and the ICTR respectively were provided protection, 95 per cent of SCSL witnesses are provided some form of protection."[68] Although striking at first, the fact that 95 percent of witnesses are accorded protection says nothing of the level of protection they received or the threats faced and warded off through such protection.[69]

Rule 75 of the Rules of Procedure and Evidence provides that a Judge or Chamber may order appropriate measures to safeguard witnesses and victims "provided that the measures are consistent with the rights of the accused."[70] A Judge or a Chamber is permitted to hold in camera proceedings to determine what measures are appropriate.[71] Rule 78 of the Rules of Procedure and Evidence (RPE) provides that all proceedings shall be held in public, unless otherwise provided.[72] Rule 79 provides for the rather controversial method of protection of witnesses – closed sessions – which are appropriate based on concerns for the following: (1) national security; (2) protection of the privacy, security and identity of a witness or victim; and (3) interests of justice.[73] The Chamber shall make public the reasons for its order to hold court in closed session, and finally, the Chamber should, if appropriate, permit representatives of monitoring agencies to remain and access the transcripts of the closed sessions.[74]

Closed sessions have been heavily debated and in fact, the Chambers have elaborated on the legal standards in a way that suggests a stricter adherence and dedication to holding a public trial than originally foreseen in the Rule. Rather than focus on the primary reasons set forth in Rule 79, the Taylor Trial Chamber outlined three prerequisite conditions that must be satisfied before closed sessions can be justified: (1) there must be a "real and specific risk to the witness and/or his family"; (2) the rights of the accused outlined in Article 17(2) – fair and public trial – are not violated; and (3) no less-restrictive protective measures can adequately deal with the witness's legitimate concerns.[75]

The Taylor Chamber has strictly applied this test, permitting four closed sessions and denying thirteen,[76] in one instance denying a Prosecution request for closed sessions on the basis that the Prosecution failed to elaborate how the less-restrictive protective measures

---

[66] SCSL Statute art. 17(2).

[67] Chris Mahoney, *The Justice Sector Afterthought: Witness Protection in Africa*, 78 Institute for Security Studies (2010).

[68] *Id.*

[69] *Id.* ("there has yet to be an incident of serious consequence for the security of a witness").

[70] Rule 75(A), RPE.

[71] Rule 75(B), RPE.

[72] Rule 78, RPE.

[73] Rule 79(A), RPE.

[74] Rule 79(B) and (C), RPE.

[75] Jennifer Easterday, U.C. Berkeley War Crimes Studies Center, *The Trial of Charles Taylor Part I: Prosecuting Persons Who Bear the Greatest Responsibility* 25 (June 2010).

[76] Easterday, *supra* note 76, and accompanying text.

would not suffice.[77] The Chamber explained that it was "not satisfied that the Prosecution has given full and exhaustive consideration to the use of the less restrictive witness protection measures available."[78]

Another interesting point for consideration is the increasing skepticism regarding closed sessions. Although closed sessions were permitted with some degree of regularity during the first trials at the SCSL, they became rare during the Taylor trial, with only four witnesses permitted to testify in entirely closed sessions.[79] The dearth of closed sessions could be an indication of many different things. Perhaps moving the Court outside of the immediate post-conflict location meant that the Court no longer needed to be victim to an instable environment. It seems likely that the passage of time also contributed to the Chamber's perception that witnesses required less protection and that the environment was safer.

In light of the fact that the SCSL trials relied primarily on eyewitness testimony rather than documentary evidence[80] and in light of the Statute's explicit guarantee that the accused "shall be entitled to a fair and **public** hearing,"[81] the credibility of the Court may be evaluated, at least in part, with reference to whether the Court was able to ensure the live delivery of testimony,[82] especially for Sierra Leoneans watching the trials.[83]

III. THE STRUCTURAL ASPECTS OF WITNESS PROTECTION

A. Location of the Court

As discussed above, witness safety has been expressed in urgent terms at the SCSL. The Court itself evaluated in the 8th Annual Report that "[r]igorous measures are required to ensure that witnesses before international tribunals are able to testify without fear of reprisal and with the confidence to recount their traumatic experiences."[84] The witnesses, too, have expressed concern for their families and dependents.[85] Concerns for witness safety and protection have been voiced with special urgency by NGOs based on the experiences of the ICTR and ICTY where, according to one Human Rights Watch Report, witnesses "face serious security, psychological, and physical challenges related to their appearance in court."[86]

---

[77] Prosecutor v. Taylor, Case No. SCSL 03–01-T-427, Decision on Confidential Prosecution Motion SCSL-03–01-T-372 and SCSL-03–01-T-385 for the Testimonies of Witnesses to Be Held in Closed Session (Feb. 26, 2008).

[78] *Id.* at 6.

[79] Easterday, *supra* note 76, at 24–25 (describing "significant departure from other trials at the SCSL"; despite reports that witnesses were receiving death threats, "the Trial Chamber denied a total of thirteen Prosecution requests for witnesses to testify entirely in closed session").

[80] SCSL Eighth Annual Report, *supra* note 48, at 30.

[81] SCSL Statute art. 17(2).

[82] Best-Practice Report, *supra* note 44, Foreword.

[83] Knowles, *supra* note 2, at 403 ("rare and vital opportunity to learn the truth of their civil war from the people involved, testifying before them in person").

[84] SCSL Eighth Annual Report, *supra* note 48, at 30.

[85] Human Rights Watch, *Bringing Justice: The Special Court for Sierra Leone; Accomplishments, Shortcomings, and Needed Support* 29 (2004), http://www.hrw.org/en/reports/2004/09/07/bringing-justice-special-court-sierra-leone (last visited Apr. 10, 2012) [hereinafter HRW Bringing Justice].

[86] *Id.*

This is even more so at the SCSL, where the trials being held in situ may present additional security problems[87] and challenges to witness security.[88] In the Court's First Annual Report, the President of the Court, Justice Geoffrey Robertson, offered his concern that "[a] war crimes court in a war torn country so soon after the war's end carries obvious risks."[89] Human Rights Watch surmised that the threat of an otherwise protected and anonymous witness being identified or located "is obviously much greater" in Freetown.[90] Moreover, where hostilities have not fully ceased, the presence of the SCSL may endanger witnesses, victims, and their families.[91] Sierra Leone's history of political instability and arguably deficient police and local security contributed to the concern that the Court's location could undermine the SCSL's security and operations.[92] It was also feared that the Court could be vulnerable to manipulation by "disgruntled belligerents."[93] Despite these concerns, "the advantages of delivering justice when and where it matters – where it can be seen to be done by those who need it – are very important."[94] The location enabled the SCSL to be closer to the witnesses, victims, and conflict, and built the foundation for a more credible justice. Thus, the Court sat in Freetown, at least for most of its existence.

However, in contemplation of the potential risks, the Agreement concluded between the United Nations and the government of Sierra Leone included a provision for the Court to meet away from its seat if necessary for the efficient exercise of its functions.[95] It was perhaps this very perception of safety concerns that led the Taylor trial to be moved from Freetown to The Hague.[96] Almost immediately upon Taylor's transfer to Freetown, the President of the SCSL, Judge Raja N. Fernando, requested the government of the Netherlands and the President of the International Criminal Court to facilitate the trial in The Hague.[97] The President Judge repeatedly expressed a view that it was "necessary for the efficient exercise" of the Court's function for the Taylor trial to be moved *outside* of West Africa.[98] The transfer raised questions of the Court's credibility as the Defense questioned whether this was a "premature" request that could "raise a real risk of the appearance of unfairness," but

[87] International Crisis Group (ICG), The Special Court for Sierra Leone: Promises and Pitfalls of a "New Model" (Aug. 4, 2003), Afr. Briefing, 1–2 [hereinafter ICG Promises and Pitfalls].

[88] Knowles, *supra* note 2, at 400 ("The ICTR and ICTY are not *in situ* and so direct comparison of approaches may not be appropriate in regards to the exceptional nature of application").

[89] President of the Special Court for Sierra Leone, *First Annual Report of the President of the Special Court for Sierra Leone* 3 (Dec. 1, 2003) [hereinafter SCSL First Annual Report].

[90] HRW Bringing Justice, *supra* note 86, at 29.

[91] Charles Chernor Jalloh, *The Contribution of the Special Court for Sierra Leone to the Development of International Law*, 15 AFR. J. INT'L COMP. L. No. 2, 174 (Sept. 2007).

[92] HRW Bringing Justice, *supra* note 86, at 31.

[93] *Id.* at 174.

[94] SCSL First Annual Report, *supra* note 90, foreword by President Justice Geoffrey Robertson, at 3.

[95] Agreement between the United Nations and the Government of Sierra Leone on the Establishment of a Special Court for Sierra Leone, art. 10, Jan. 16, 2002, 2178 U.N.T.S. 138.

[96] U.N. News Centre, Former Liberian President Taylor pleads not guilty at trial (Apr. 3, 2006), http://www.un.org/apps/news/story.asp?NewsID=18045&Cr=Taylor&Cr1=court# (last visited Apr. 17, 2012).

[97] Press Release, SCSL, Special Court President Requests Charles Taylor to be Tried in The Hague (Mar. 30, 2006).

[98] Prosecutor v. Taylor, Case No. SCSL-03-01-PT, Decision of the President on Defense Motion for Reconsideration of Order Changing Venue of Proceedings (Mar. 12, 2007).

nonetheless, the trial was ultimately moved.[99] Although the government of Sierra Leone initially unequivocally stated it did not share security fears and in fact, argued for the trial to be held in the country to be closer to those for whom the Court was to be rendering justice,[100] apparently later, both Liberia and Sierra Leone also voiced concerns about destabilization and security problems.[101] And according to the UN Security Council, "the continued presence of former President Taylor in the sub-region is an impediment to stability and a threat to the peace of Liberia and of Sierra Leone and to international peace and security in the region."[102]

Although the Freetown site of the Court had led to the perception of additional risk in some instances, in a number of other ways the location of the court facilitated better support and protection of witnesses.[103] Logically, the SCSL was better-positioned, physically, to provide outreach, to investigate, and to produce witnesses than the ICTR, ICTY, or ICC, or the SCSL itself during its time in The Hague.[104] The location of the Court enables better investigations and it facilitates the collection of evidence.[105] Moreover, it was much easier for the parties to identify and connect with witnesses.[106] For instance, the proximity enabled Prosecutor David Crane to meet with his "client," that is, "the people of Sierra Leone" by traveling for months to town hall meetings throughout the country where he would listen to their stories of the past decade.[107] In that sense, the Court's physical location lends itself to gathering more evidence and connecting directly with witnesses, and ultimately, to delivering a more credible justice directly to the people.[108]

By contrast, in moving the Taylor trial to The Hague, the SCSL suffered a number of arguably unavoidable disadvantages for witnesses.[109] For one, the SCSL Outreach efforts lagged and required more resources.[110] Also, in contrast to trials in Freetown, where Sierra Leoneon people could "witness their tormentors facing justice," in The Hague, people would undoubtedly be disconnected from the Court.[111] These difficulties will be discussed more critically in greater detail in Section D.

---

[99] Charles Jalloh, *The Law and Politics of the Charles Taylor Case*, CCIL Web Exclusive (Apr. 2006).

[100] *Id.*

[101] Mark A. Drumbl, *Charles Taylor and the Special Court for Sierra Leone*, 10 ASIL INSIGHTS 9 (Apr. 12, 2006).

[102] U.N. S.C. Res. 1688, preambulatory para. 14, U.N. DOC. S/Res/1688 (June 16, 2006).

[103] Cassese, *supra* note 50, at paras. 238–242 (in which he discusses the associated witness protection and other witness issues that arose as a result of pulling the trial out of Freetown).

[104] Lindsey Raub, *Positioning Hybrid Tribunals in International Criminal Justice*, 41 N.Y.U. J. INT'L L. & POL. 1014 (2009) (arguing that local trials present advantages over international tribunals including that a tribunal's remote location may create difficulties with conducting investigations and producing witnesses).

[105] Jalloh, *supra* note 92, at 174.

[106] *Id.* at 174.

[107] Crane, *supra* note 29, at 6.

[108] ICG Promises and Pitfalls, *supra* note 88, at 13 (explaining that apart from the location's security difficulties, it gives an opportunity to make a "direct and lasting impact on the society").

[109] When first considering whether relocation would be possible for the SCSL, the founders considered proximity and access to the witnesses, but threatened a biased approach when in stating, "Such proximity and easy access will greatly facilitate the work of the Prosecutor." U.N. DOC. S/2000/915, *supra* note 17, at para. 54.

[110] Cassese, *supra* note 50, at paras. 238–242 and Easterday, *supra* note 76, at 8 (explaining that moving the trial was seen to impose considerable burden on witnesses and victims).

[111] Jalloh, *supra* note 92, at 174 ("it is settled that establishing an international criminal court away from the affected country may limit or undermine its contribution to post-conflict healing and reconciliation").

B. *The Prosecution and Defense Roles in Witness Protection and Support*

The parties to international criminal proceedings play a pivotal role in providing support and protection to victims and witnesses. Undoubtedly, in certain circumstances, one of the parties – not the WVS – is the first court entity to actually reach out to the potential witness as part of the investigation. Moreover, the prosecution invariably relies on numerous witnesses and substantial amounts of testimony in order to meet its heavy burden and prove the elements of its case. Likewise, the defense relies on witnesses to disprove the prosecution's case, both through adversarial cross-examination and the presentation of its own witnesses who tell a different story from that of the prosecution.

The defense and prosecution strategies – in particular, the decisions with regard to which witness to call, how to question that witness, and how to seek or challenge protective measures for that witness – impact the credibility of the process. The parties frequently raise allegations regarding risks to victims, both actual and perceived. In some instances these allegations are found to be disruptive,[112] and in others, they were sometimes critiqued for elongating the process.[113]

However, it is important to recall the rights and interests of victims and witnesses as were discussed previously and are well-established in human rights law. Litigation regarding the protection of a witness may interrupt and slow down the trial, but such concerns for efficiency are naturally outweighed, in many cases, by interests of security and safety. Moreover, the Taylor trial was in the limelight, and it seems reasonable to take extra time to decide matters of great importance, especially when they are going to be closely reviewed by the international community.[114] Finally, the Chamber faced substantially more motions and decisions, which undoubtedly contributed to the disruption and perceived inefficiencies. In other words, the issues of inefficiency are slightly concerning, but are nuanced issues that without a deeper look into the context should not substantially detract from the assessment of the Court's success in protecting witnesses.

In addition to possibly "disrupting" the process, the parties' decisions to call certain witnesses, to enable them to testify, and to persuade them to testify undoubtedly implicate the credibility of the record. The Judgment of the Trial Chamber in the Taylor case explicitly sets out considerations of the "IV. EVALUATION OF THE EVIDENCE,"[115] a framework and review of the law application to evidentiary assessments (in part A),[116] forms of evidence under review (in part B),[117] credibility assessment of specific witnesses (in part

---

[112] Prosecutor v. Taylor, Case No. SCSL 03–01-T, Transcript, 26–27 (Nov. 13, 2007) (bringing to light Prosecution letter to Defense that alleges defense interference with witnesses, Chamber refuses to consider matter).

[113] Easterday, *supra* note 76, at 30–31 n.271 (critiquing the Taylor chamber for having "shown considerable delay in rendering important decisions on motions"; and drawing attention to, inter alia, decisions regarding witnesses and evidence), 61 *et seq.* (charting the amount of time required for each decision of the Court, see references to SCSL-03–01-T-318, Decision on Confidential Prosecution Motion to Rescind and Augment Protective Measures for Witnesses (July 16, 2007)(2 months 13 days to decide); SCSL-03–01-T-348, Decision on Prosecution Motion to Rescind Protective Measures for Witnesses (Oct. 3, 2007)(2 months 8 days to decide); etc.).

[114] *Id.* at 31–32.

[115] Taylor Judgment, *supra* note 19, at para. 156 *et seq.*

[116] *Id.* at paras. 156–160.

[117] *Id.* at paras. 161–211.

C),[118] and finally, authenticity assessment of specific documents (in part D).[119] With regard to the forms of evidence under review, the Judgment first addresses witness testimony.[120] According to the Trial Chamber when looking at "Accomplice Evidence," the Chamber considers "whether or not the accomplice has an ulterior motive to testify as he did."[121] With regard to "Financial Incentives," in assessing credibility the Chamber "has therefore taken into account information about witness payments made both by the WVS and by the Prosecution, and has considered any cross-examination of the witness in relation to these payments" and in particular, on a case-by-case basis, considers whether payments and benefits went beyond that which is reasonably required, and finally, the cost of living in West Africa.[122] The Chamber's assessment of witness evidence takes into account, according to the Judgment, any promises of relocation or actual relocation, and the possible effects that might have had on the witnesses' testimony and the opportunity of the Defense to cross-examine on these issues.[123] Finally, "in assessing witness credibility, the Trial Chamber has also taken into account other incentives that may have been offered to witnesses, including indemnity letters provided to witnesses by the Prosecution, and offers to release witnesses from prison."[124] By addressing the potential biases and other taints of the record from the forefront (i.e., in the first hundred pages of the over two-thousand page Judgment), the Trial Chamber recognizes many of the nuances and challenges of creating a credible record from viva voce testimony of witnesses who undoubtedly have vested interests in the trial.

One of the major challenges in creating the credible record, as is hinted above, is incentivized testimony. As is discussed in greater detail in Jennifer Easterday's chapter,[125] the financial support of witnesses has been under attack as a method of "buying" testimony. This threatens to undermine the legal process, as was argued in the Taylor trial on numerous occasions,[126] and may negatively impact the legacy and local perceptions of justice in Sierra Leone.[127] The Taylor defense team was acutely aware of these problems[128] and, according to the Appeals Chamber, "consistently made the issue of improper payments and inducements to witnesses or potential witnesses and sources, a live issue."[129] The Taylor Judgment indicates the Chamber's deliberate approach to this problem whereby the Chamber's assessment

---

[118] *Id.* at paras. 212–380.

[119] *Id.* at paras. 381–397.

[120] *Id.* at paras. 163 *et seq.*

[121] *Id.* at paras. 182–183; *see, e.g.,* assessment of credibility of TF1–362, paras. 244–253; Joseph "Zigzag" Marzah, paras. 263–268; Isaac Mongor, paras. 269–274; Alimamy Bobson Sesay, paras. 285–289.

[122] *Id.* at para. 195.

[123] *Id.* at paras. 196–197.

[124] *Id.* at para. 198 (internal citations omitted).

[125] See Jennifer Easterday's critical discussion of this issue in this volume.

[126] Prosecutor v. Taylor, Case No. SCSL-03-01-T-1119, Decision on Public with Confidential Annexes A-D Defense Motion for Admission of Documents and Drawing of an Adverse Inference Relating to the Alleged Death of Johnny Paul Koroma (Nov. 11, 2010).

[127] For further discussion of this issue, see Easterday, *supra* note 126.

[128] See, for example, the defense cross-examination of former President Moses Zeh Blah as to the payments he received from the Prosecution including $5,000 for medical bills. Prosecutor v. Taylor, Case No. SCSL 03-01-T, Transcript, 10114 (May 19, 2008).

[129] Prosecutor v. Taylor, Case No. SCSL-03-01-T-1168, Decision on Defense Appeal Regarding the Decision on the Defense Motion for Admission of Documents and Drawing of an Adverse Inference Relating to the Alleged Death of Johnny Paul Koroma, para. 47 (Jan. 25, 2011).

of credibility takes into account whether witnesses were promised benefits and actually received benefits, and the effects this could have on their testimony.[130]

The parties' ability to seek or challenge witness protective measures undoubtedly informed their decisions of whom to call and ultimately, whose testimony forms the record at the SCSL. One concern is that the Defense was disadvantaged by its position, by its inability to compel witnesses on its behalf, and by the shroud protecting the secrecy of the prosecution case. One defense team argued that its potential witnesses would be at great risk if they were to come forward, which they were unwilling to do because they feared they would face international sanctions or consequences.[131] The Chambers stated it would deal with the issue once it faced a tangible motion.[132] Based on only that brief reference, it is impossible to evaluate whether protective mechanisms at the SCSL fell short in that the Defense was powerless to protect and call some of its witnesses as ostensibly guaranteed under the Statute.[133] However, by raising the challenge in the abstraction, the Defense introduces a question of concern of whether the SCSL or any court operating in the international system, for that matter, truly has resources to protect defense witnesses.[134]

In addition to challenging access to its own witnesses, the Defense also challenged the inadequacy of its access to OTP witnesses. The Taylor Judgment identified, "In addition to denying responsibility for crimes committed, the Defense also maintains that: … (vi) much of the Prosecution's case has in large measure been 'shrouded in secrecy' as some insider witnesses have testified with protective measures" and also "(viii) some of the Prosecution's witnesses, particularly linkage witnesses, were so lacking in credibility that the Trial Chamber should completely put aside several Prosecution witnesses altogether."[135] However, as discussed previously, the Chamber took a deliberate approach to its evaluation of the evidence, and in so doing, it altogether avoided addressing the inflammatory characterizations of the OTP case. Scholars, the international community, and local Sierra Leoneans are left with the question of the credibility and completeness of the record.

One scholar questioned the OTP's efforts to seek protective measures for insider witnesses.[136] The policy may have been justified by the unique risks and threats upon insider witnesses.[137] Nonetheless, the policy led to a dichotomy by which the "more sympathetic victim testimony" was completely open to the public but the controversial, "less sympathetic

---

[130] Taylor Judgment, *supra* note 19, at paras. 195–198.

[131] Prosecutor v. Taylor, Case No. SCSL 03–01-T, Transcript, 24–25 (May 7, 2007) (Defense noting at Pretrial Conference its intention to seek protective measures, the difficulties of protecting witnesses, and completing its investigation: "Now, the difficulty for the Defence is numerous individuals, and affidavits are being obtained by my friends, are unwilling to speak to the Defence and their stated reason is that they are petrified of having travel bans imposed upon them and having their assets from by the Security Council because they are associated to the defence of Charles Taylor.").

[132] Prosecutor v. Taylor, Case No. SCSL 03–01-T, Transcript, 25 (May 7, 2007).

[133] Article 17(4)(e), Statute.

[134] By contrast, see Taylor Judgment, *supra* note 19, at para. 240 (Foday Lansana testified under the belief that the Prosecution promised to work for his release from prison, where he feared for his safety; the Trial Chamber found that promise of early release was for protective reasons and the support he received (in excess of $USD 6000) did not influence his testimony.).

[135] *Id.* at para. 17(vi), (viii).

[136] Cockayne, *supra* note 6, at 673.

[137] HRW Bringing Justice, *supra* note 86, at 31 (describing an instance in 2004 when a key inside witness in the AFRC case was nearly beaten to death after ignoring admonishments to stay in the safe house).

insider testimony" was often given in closed-session and unavailable to the public.[138] The policy was criticized on many grounds; for instance, one scholar expresses concern that it discouraged certain witnesses who disagreed with the victim-witnesses' stories from coming forward and thus contributed to an "imbalanced history."[139] Moreover, the strategy might have exacerbated the unfortunate perception that the Prosecution and Court were indistinguishable, and that outreach produced witnesses for the Prosecution but not the Defense.[140]

When the Prosecution sought to deliver evidence and testimony by document rather than live testimony with regard to fact-based witnesses,[141] the Defense voiced objections and requested to cross-examine numerous of these witnesses. Although the testimony appeared relatively uncontroversial in the sense that it was largely fact-based accounts of the crimes and conflicts and had very little, if any, material relevance to the specific determination of guilt for Charles Taylor, the Court nonetheless granted the Defense the opportunity to challenge the testimony. In fact, the Defense had explained on the record during a status conference "at first sight we are unable to see the relevance of crime based witnesses, and it's an aspect of the case I would like to examine carefully in collaboration with my learned friends both for the Defense and the Prosecution with a view to seeing if we can avoid calling any such witness, save where the evidence of such a witness might impact on other aspects of the case … it seems to us at first blush that none of such evidence really needs to trouble this Court."[142] Nonetheless, failure to reach stipulations as to facts made this impossible, and many witnesses were inevitably called.[143]

These strategic decisions, made by both parties, impacted the credibility of justice. As noted previously, these witnesses were not, for the most part, significant to the ultimate determination of guilt.[144] Nonetheless, they were deemed significant enough to be subjected to the difficult process of testifying. One scholar opined that the Prosecution likely "sought to conclude with the maximum emotional impact … remind the Court of the human face

---

[138] *Id.*

[139] Knowles, *supra* note 2, at 403 (warning that if insiders' testimonies are withheld from the public, "then the majority of the public testimony is that of victims providing one-sided interpretation of the civil war. It constructs an imbalanced history and creates specific prejudice against the accused because it denies the possibility of witnesses coming forward after hearing testimony with which they disagree.").

[140] Cockayne, *supra* note 6, at 673 ("The blanket use of protection measures for insider witnesses also exacerbates this tendency, since it leads to challengeable and less sympathetic insider testimony occurring in closed hearings out of public earshot, while more sympathetic victim testimony occurs in public, skewing the public perception of the judicial record.").

[141] Prosecutor v. Taylor, Case No. SCSL 03–01-T, Transcript, 431 (Aug. 20, 2007) (at Status Conference, prosecution explained "you will note that we had approximately 76 witnesses we considered crime base witnesses and we intended to call only 10 witnesses live. So we do not believe that we have to put all of them on live, nor do we believe that we have an obligation to provide this Court with only a paper case of the victims of the crimes that have occasioned this trial in the first place.").

[142] *Id.* at 422–23.

[143] Prosecutor v. Taylor, Case No. SCSL 03–01-T, Transcript, 432 (Aug. 20, 2007) (at Status Conference, Prosecution explained "So we do believe we would have a right to present at least some witnesses live, but we would also have a right, if there were stipulations, to present written statements or prior testimony so that your Honours would have the benefit of the facts and circumstances surrounding the commission of the crimes which bring us all here into court today.").

[144] Jennifer Easterday, UC Berkeley War Crimes Studies Center, *Charles Taylor Trial Report* 3 (Dec. 1, 2008 – Feb. 28, 2009) [hereinafter February Taylor Trial Report] (noting Prosecution's tendency to highlight the horrific events and effects on victims rather than focusing on evidence of Taylor's involvement).

of the injuries suffered."[145] As with any witness called to testify before the Court in The Hague, each witness's life was interrupted by this process, and numerous additional costs were incurred on his or behalf to enable the person to fly to The Hague and to testify. These witnesses were arguably used to dramatize the trial,[146] such as when the Prosecution asked how the crimes committed had affected their lives.[147]

In defense of the presentation of such testimony, one might argue that the SCSL must give witnesses the opportunity to tell their stories so that the people of Sierra Leone know what really happened and to provide background to the trial.[148] The testimony of any and all witnesses contributes to the Court's record of the conflict, regardless of the testimony's relevance to the particular accused.

The use of legal process for purposes other than the determination of the guilt or non-guilt of the accused is troubling, but certainly, a recurring danger of international criminal trials. The presentation of seemingly irrelevant fact-based crime evidence might be overlooked as a mere byproduct of a politically charged trial. On the other hand, perhaps these witnesses were put through unnecessary inconvenience, risk, and potentially, re-traumatization. This evidence does not meaningfully supplement the record because the testimony went in unchallenged and untested (because of its irrelevance to the case) and as such, has not been determined to be a credible account of what really happened and thus, actually detracts from the Court's record. The presentation and examination of witnesses undoubtedly engenders concerns of protection and support of vulnerable witnesses, but, having considered both sides of the argument, it is difficult for us to gauge whether the tactical decisions in this instance actually discredited the Court.

In the adversarial proceedings of the SCSL, the Prosecution and Defense heavily relied on witnesses to support their arguments and advocacy. As demonstrated by the previous examples, the parties' decisions engendered concerns for witness protection and support.

C. The WVS at the SCSL

The WVS, established to protect victims and witnesses and ensure their safety,[149] identifies itself as the primary body responsible for the protection of witnesses. For that reason, it is useful to look at a few key aspects of its operations that impact the support and protection of witnesses as they relate to the credibility of trial.

First, the WVS was originally located, physically, in the same place as the Prosecution.[150] This blurred lines and responsibilities between the WVS and the Prosecution, which

---

[145] *See* February Taylor Trial Report, *supra* note 145, at 2–3.

[146] *Id.* at 3 (noting disappointment that at the close of the Prosecution's case, rather than highlight its evidence against the accused, OTP "simply reiterat[ed] the same emotionally charged rhetoric about victims."); Easterday, *supra* note 76, at 43.

[147] Easterday, *supra* note 76, at 42.

[148] Prosecution strategy in the Taylor trial to focus on events outside of the literal scope of criminal indictment attempts to provide the "context" and "background" and has thus been found relevant, although contested by Defense. *Id.*

[149] SCSL Statute art. 16(4).

[150] *See also* HRW Bringing Justice, *supra* note 86, at 30 (expressing other concerns with regard to location, in particular that witness security is undermined by the fact of a common entrance to the courthouse utilized by not just WVS but also Prosecution and Defense).

disrupted the Defense's access to the services to which it (and its witnesses) were entitled. The blurring is obviously problematic; it reinforced other stereotypes of Court bias (i.e., lack of credibility) by suggesting that the registry was skewed toward the Prosecution.[151] And it may have also led to the dangerous perception that the Prosecution and the Court were indistinguishable.[152]

Second, the ability of the WVS to adequately support and protect witnesses was constrained by the "shoestring budget" of the Court.[153] The WVS lacked the resources and skilled staff to ensure that witnesses received what they are entitled to under the SCSL Rules, that is, the "relevant support, counseling and other appropriate assistance, including medical assistance, physical and psychological rehabilitation, especially in cases of rape, sexual assault, and crimes against children."[154]

Third, we look to the WVS's self-assessment. In 2007, the WVS commissioned Simon Charters,[155] Rebecca Horn,[156] and Saleem Vahidy[157] to perform an internal, research-based evaluation of the WVS[158] in order first, to assess the effectiveness of the WVS, and second, to identify best practices "which contribute to witnesses being able to testify in an international war crimes tribunal without experiencing any negative consequences."[159] Notably, the primary purpose of that evaluation (to evaluate the effectiveness of the WVS) seemingly coincides with the objective of the present chapter – to evaluate the successes of the WVS in protecting witnesses. The report includes data collected through structured interviews with 200 witnesses who had testified before the Court[160] and analysis of that data.

In 2008, von Hebel, the Registrar of the SCSL, reflected, apparently based on the report, that the WVS was "a success."[161] Indeed, witnesses were highly satisfied with the pre-testimony preparation, and the vast majority of witnesses chose to stay in WVS care for weeks up to and during their testimony, living in a secure SCSL accommodation where their needs were taken care of.[162] Although the report addressed a few specific concerns (for instance, that SGBV victims should have been seen by female, not male nurse[163]), it offered little critique or analysis of the specific WVS practices. Instead, it focused on the witnesses' experiences and feelings.

Based on this report, it appears that witnesses were least satisfied with post-testimony services provided by the WVS based on "a sense that the WVS paid insufficient visits to check on their security, and witnesses being unaware that assistance with security concerns was available."[164] Perhaps it is unrealistic for WVS to maintain post-testimony contact with

---

[151] Cockayne, *supra* note 6, at 673 ("The unverified implication is that Outreach may produce more Prosecution than Defense witnesses").

[152] *Id.*

[153] HRW Bringing Justice, *supra* note 86, at 29–30; Cockayne, *supra* note 6.

[154] HRW Bringing Justice, *supra* note 86, at 29–30.

[155] Managed the Witness Evaluation and Legacy Project at the SCSL in the implementation of this report.

[156] WVS psychologist who designed methodology for report, analyzed the data, and implemented the recommendations.

[157] Chief of the WVS from 2003; prior to that, he held a role at the ICTR.

[158] Best-Practice Report, *supra* note 39.

[159] *Id.* at 1.

[160] *Id.* at 1.

[161] *Id.* at Foreword.

[162] *Id.* at 14.

[163] *Id.* at 14–15.

[164] *Id.* at 18.

all witnesses or to provide financial assistance to the extent witnesses would like.[165] It is important that expectations for witnesses involve, "clearly setting, and continuously reinforcing, realistic expectations regarding what witnesses can expect from their contact with the court ... this will not be an easy task, since some witnesses see their contact with the court as an opportunity to benefit materially."[166]

Witnesses need to feel safe; it is a basic human need, and it is crucial to their overall sense of well-being and could impact social and psychological well-being if not met.[167] Although testifying is made out to be a traumatic and difficult experience, contrary to what one might expect, the witnesses were not particularly negative about their experiences on cross-examination.[168] The authors explain[169]:

> This does not support the claims of other researchers that cross-examination is an overwhelmingly distressing event for witnesses. However, the experience of cross-examination is important: those who have a positive cross-examination experience also tend to rate their overall experience of testifying as positive, and vice versa.

The research surrounding the experiences of the ICTY suggests witnesses might be expected to feel more insecure when they return home after testifying.[170] However, there was no significant difference between witness ratings of their security pre-testimony and post-testimony at the SCSL.[171] Interestingly, at the SCSL, witnesses' sense of security was not significantly impacted by their testifying.[172] The report surmises that "it is possible that the presence of the SCSL (and in particular the WVS protection and support services) in the home country of the witnesses was beneficial for their feelings of post-testimony security."[173] Additionally, the report indicated that witnesses who did not have problems in their communities had less security issues.[174]

The WVS report has offered interesting insight into the effectiveness of the section. First, based on the report and the forgoing discussion, the dangers or risks that accompany (or are perceived to accompany) giving testimony and cross-examination at the SCSL are beyond the control of the WVS. As noted, there are a number of deep-seated issues that affect witnesses and are particularly resistant to intervention from the WVS or others: that it would be painful to talk about experiences again, that witnesses would not want to be away from home so long again, and that witnesses would fear reprisals.[175]

---

[165] *Id.* at 19–20.

[166] *Id.* at 20.

[167] *Id.*

[168] *Id.* at 17. On a scale of (1) "very good" to (5) "very bad" examination in chief m=2.0, sd=1.13 cross-examination m=2.68 sd=1.39.

[169] *Id.* at 17.

[170] *Id.* at 20.

[171] *Id.* at 21.

[172] *Id.* at 17.

[173] *Id.* at 21.

[174] *Id.*

[175] The report identified individual factors that significantly contributed to feelings of insecurity: those living in poverty and/or SGBV survivors reported feeling less secure; those whose communities were aware of the witness's status as a witness felt less secure; also, the witness's confidence that the WVS would respond to a request for help. *Id.* at 22–23.

Second, the report emphasizes its recommendation that the WVS needed better under-standing, training, and communication skills with regard to the services offered by the sec-tion. By implication (if not directly) the report also suggests that somewhere through the course of contact between the witness and the SCSL, there is a failure to reach a meeting of the minds between SCSL staff and witnesses who have different expectations of the role and services to be provided to witnesses.

When asked what more could have improved their care during the testimony period, witnesses gave responses relating to financial concerns.[176] The report addressed this as a problem of communication rather than an actual inadequacy of the WVS services (or a reflection on the shoestring budget[177]), asserting that WVS should "explain clearly what the witness can expect, and then deliver on what is promised."[178] The report emphasized that we must be aware that witnesses sometimes have unrealistic expectations about the services available and the rights of witnesses to those services.[179] "There is a fine line between a rea-sonable level of recompense to ensure witnesses are not disadvantaged by testifying and services beyond this, which could constitute an inducement to testify."[180]

The report emphasized the importance of setting clear expectations: "WVS staff (as well as investigators and legal teams) can help to set expectations from their first contact with witnesses by clearly explaining what they should and should not expect."[181] However, it found that the WVS did not provide clear guidelines as to the services and benefits wit-nesses are entitled to post-testimony. The lack of clarity may have contributed to the witness disappointment with post-testimony services.[182]

The fact that there is no complete menu of services available is a reflection on the WVS's ability to provide services. The report agreed that this was a serious oversight that needed to be fixed. The lack of a complete menu has serious implications for witness protection. At first contact with a witness, a staff member of the WVS is unable to openly and clearly com-municate with the witness as to the role of the WVS and the services available and protec-tion offered. At best, the staff member might tell the potential witness the duty of the WVS under the Statute and Rules.

D. Critical Concerns with regard to Location and Relocation

Unfortunately, the move to The Hague also hindered the mechanics of witness protection in some unexpected ways as well.[183] One Berkeley War Crimes Study Center report describes

---

[176] *Id.* at 15 (Family members should be fully provided for (43 percent); financial allowances should be increased (39 percent); communication with family should be ensured, and wanted to talk to a member of WVS about concerns (about 25 percent each); "SCSL staff should not make 'false promises' to witnesses"(19 percent)).

[177] Cockayne, *supra* note 6.

[178] Best-Practice Report, *supra* note 39, at 15.

[179] *Id.* at 19.

[180] *Id.*

[181] *Id.*

[182] *Id.* at 20.

[183] Cassese, *supra* note 50, at para. 217 (moving trial "has had serious repercussions for the future of the Special Court. The transfer of the trial deprives the Special Court of one of its main features: its location in the terri-tory where the crimes were perpetrated. It also creates a complicated – and expensive – logistical situation," requiring, inter alia, the transfer of witnesses.).

how procedures became less transparent in The Hague with regard to closed sessions.[184] When the Presiding Justice Doherty ordered the public gallery to remain open for testimony with the witness shielded from view and no sound or audio feed to the public gallery, problems arose. Presiding Justice Doherty had merely been following Freetown protocol[185] where the public was permitted to watch the proceedings silently, "mitigating some of the loss of transparency caused by the closed sessions." However, at the ICC, there is no procedure for keeping the public gallery open during closed sessions, and no modification to ICC practice was made. The public gallery was thus closed and those who wished to watch had to remain outside until the Court went back into regular session.[186]

The *credibility* of justice was undoubtedly hindered by the trying protocols of calling witnesses to the new location. When witnesses were taken to The Hague, the protocol was that a witness protection officer would accompany five witnesses at a time, who would travel as a group from Freetown to The Hague.[187] After traveling together, the witnesses were then accommodated together in The Hague, thus raising concerns about witnesses talking to each other about the case and their testimony.[188] Multiple scholars have drawn attention to the difficulty of preventing such communications once the witnesses are housed in The Hague together.[189] In fact, the Taylor defense team used cross-examination to attempt to discredit witnesses and demonstrate that the witnesses changed their stories based on subsequent knowledge of the events; similarities in witnesses' testimony made clear that they had been either coached or had spoken to each other despite the fact that such communication is generally disfavored.[190]

This issue did come through in the Judgment although it apparently had little effect on the disposition. For instance, with regard to Joseph "Zigzag" Marzah, the Chamber explained that he had approached the Prosecution to avoid being prosecuted for the crimes he had committed and "as soon as he completed his testimony, Marzah phoned another Prosecution witness whom he had introduced to the Prosecution."[191] This, along with other inconsistencies and implausibilities led the Chamber to conclude that Marzah's evidence "must be considered with caution."[192] With regard to Perry Kamara, the Chamber averred that "Kamara's evidence was influenced by his subsequent knowledge of the events that unfolded and that he added detail to events he recalled with the benefits of hindsight" but nonetheless, the Chamber "did not consider that Kamara's general credibility is adversely affected thereby,"[193] except with regard to specific events, where the Trial Chamber viewed his testimony as influenced by subsequent knowledge of events and thus did not rely on his account.[194] The Defense also challenged TF1–539's testimony on the basis that certain testimony "was manufactured to match the testimony of witnesses who testified before him,"

---

[184] Easterday, *supra* note 76, at n.203.
[185] *Id.*; also, testimony of TF1–371, Prosecutor v. Taylor, Case No. SCSL 03–01-T, Transcript (May 23, 2008).
[186] *Id.*
[187] Cassese, *supra* note 50, at para. 238.
[188] *Id.* at para. 239.
[189] *Id.* at para. 239; Easterday, *supra* note 76, at 44.
[190] Easterday, *supra* note 76, at 44.
[191] Taylor Judgment, *supra* note 19, at para. 264.
[192] *Id.* at para. 268.
[193] Taylor Judgment, *supra* note 19, at para. 229.
[194] *Id.* at paras. 293–294.

and the Chamber, although it refrained from commenting on this coaching, did note its finding that the witness's testimony was unreliable in certain instances and "must be considered with caution and cannot be relied upon without corroboration."[195] With regard to other witnesses, the Chamber did make the suggestion that a witness, TF1–375, provided testimony at trial and late in interviews that he had not previously mentioned and that corroborated other previous prosecution witnesses who testified before him "without providing acceptable explanations."[196] But in another instance, the Chamber openly rejected as "unfounded" the Defense's allegation that evidence of a witness, TF1–585, could have been unduly influenced by the Prosecution and others.[197] These examples demonstrate that the Chamber was willing to consider the inconsistencies and possibility of coaching, but refrained, generally, from referring to it in harsh terms. Moreover, the criticism, if there was any, was lodged more at the witnesses for failing to provide acceptable explanations, or for engaging in unacceptable conduct.

There is no question that the location in The Hague affected the costliness of justice.[198] Witnesses had to travel back and forth from The Hague to give testimony,[199] not only a burden for the witness but also for the budget of the Court. The Prosecution had suggested that each witness who had to make the journey to The Hague to testify should be accompanied by a family member.[200]

In sum, the experiences in The Hague bring to light some of the shortcomings with regard to the protocols for the protection and support of witnesses, which ultimately might have tarnished the credibility of the Court. Perhaps such provisions as suggested by the Prosecution – that witnesses should have traveled with family members – would have better ensured the credibility of the trial record in that the record would not have been unduly influenced by communications among witnesses. However, implementation of such measures was constrained by a tight budget. The international community appeared to be financially committed to protecting witnesses, but such commitment did not necessarily contemplate the preservation of their unbiased testimony as a precursor to the credibility of the Court.[201] By contrast, the location in Freetown enabled the possibility of more efficient, effective, and affordable investigations without putting great strain on the budget of the Court. However, locating trials in Freetown was not a panacea for the difficult and complex problems of witness protection. As the concluding section will show, witness support and protection at the SCSL undoubtedly suffered numerous shortcomings in both locations, many of which were a product of the poor design and planning.

---

[195] *Id.* at paras. 297–303.

[196] *Id.* at paras. 303–312.

[197] *Id.* at para. 331.

[198] Drumbl, *supra* note 102 (noting that "additional resources required to move witnesses to The Hague, although this may come with the benefit of ensuring their safety").

[199] U.N. Doc. S/PV.6163, *supra* note 20, at 5.

[200] Cassese, *supra* note 50, at para. 239.

[201] For the sentiment that the international community was not as critical of the shortcomings of locating the trial in The Hague, consider the view expressed at the Security Council that Resolution 1688 [U.N. Doc. S/Res/1688, *supra* note 103] facilitated conduct of trials away from the seat of SCSL in the interests of regional security, and witnesses "were able personally to bear witness in this historic proceeding because their presence in the Netherlands was made possible by the Security Council." U.N. Doc. S/PV.6163, *supra* note 20, at 5.

IV. CONCLUSION

Based on the foregoing, it is clear that witness protection is a complex concern of international criminal justice that involves multiple aspects of the process. The SCSL system has furthered some of the general purposes of witness protection, while at the same time furthering the credibility of the process. The trials have become progressively more in tune with the interests of public trials, which may have improved the quality of justice by making it more accessible to the public. Likewise, the location of the Court (at least for the first three trials) was a welcome step in the right direction toward giving witnesses better support and enabling more testimony.

It is less clear how well the SCSL has guaranteed and protected the security of the witnesses. Although the region is relatively stable compared to when the Court first was established, there is no way of measuring how individual witnesses have been impacted by their testimony. Additionally, the concerns for safety have at some times made it difficult for the public to access justice. When the Taylor trial moved to The Hague to protect the safety, security, and stability of the sub-region, it had unfortunate consequences for witnesses. It became more difficult for witnesses to testify, and the move created additional barriers to the credibility of the process. Although there have been a number of progressive steps with regard to the protection of witnesses, the structural support and overlap between the WVS and prosecution unit's extending support to witnesses have seriously undercut the success of the Court.

23

The Consequences of Witness Payments at the Special Court for Sierra Leone

Jennifer Easterday[*]

Judge Thompson: *But wouldn't it be contrary to public policy and to the administration of justice for a court to place itself in that position where, by implication, it becomes an inducer in terms of procuring witnesses to come and testify for consideration?*
Wayne Jordash, Counsel for Accused Issa Sesay: *But are we to deny it if it is the fact?*[1]

I. INTRODUCTION

The Special Court for Sierra Leone (SCSL), created in 2002 as the ten-year civil war in Sierra Leone was just coming to an end, faced a tremendous task: investigate and try those who bear the greatest responsibility for serious crimes committed during the conflict.[2] The Court was created to do all of this on a limited "shoe-string" budget under a relatively new "hybrid" institutional structure, intended to allow Sierra Leoneans to participate in and watch the SCSL's justice processes unfold.[3] The first Prosecutor, David Crane, interpreted the "greatest responsibility" mandate very narrowly[4] and focused his indictments on only a few perpetrators: a total of thirteen persons were indicted by the SCSL.[5] These were considered the top commanders of the various warring factions: the Civil Defense Forces (CDF), the Revolutionary United Front (RUF) and the Armed Forces Revolutionary Council (AFRC), and Charles Taylor, the alleged mastermind behind the conflict and then-President of Liberia. However, although narrow in scope with respect to who was charged, the range of the substantive charges and modes of liability were incredibly broad. The Prosecutor

---

[*] PhD Researcher at the Grotius Centre for International Legal Studies, Leiden University, and formerly Senior Researcher and Trial Monitor for the *Charles Taylor* Trial, War Crimes Studies Center, University of California (Berkeley).

[1] Trial Transcript, Prosecutor v. Sesay et al. (RUF) (SCSL-04–15-T), Trial Chamber I, at 68 (lines 4–9) (Mar. 3, 2006).

[2] Art. 1 SCSL Statute. See, for a discussion of this limited mandate, the keynote speech by former SCSL Prosecutor Stephen Rapp and Professor Charles Jalloh's chapter in this volume.

[3] *See, e.g.,* A. McDonald, *Sierra Leone's Shoestring Special Court*, 84 Int'l Rev. of the Red Cross 121 (2002); S. Rapp, *The Compact Model in International Criminal Justice: The Special Court for Sierra Leone*, 57 Drake L. Rev. 11, 20–21 (2008).

[4] *See* D. Crane, *Dancing with the Devil: Prosecuting West Africa's Warlords: Building Initial Prosecutorial Strategy for an International Tribunal after Third World Conflicts*, 37 Case W. Res. J. Int'l L. 4 (2005–2006); C. Jalloh, *Special Court for Sierra Leone: Achieving Justice?*, 32 Mich. J. Int'l L. 395, 413 (2011).

[5] Only ten people were ultimately tried. Information available on SCSL website, www.sc-sl.org.

charged those accused with a comprehensive range of crimes committed throughout the country and during the full range of the Court's temporal jurisdiction.[6]

The Prosecution thus had an immense evidentiary challenge to meet. This required a large number of "crime-base" witnesses who could testify that the crimes were in fact committed, and "linkage evidence," or evidence that could link the accused to the specific crimes. The Prosecution principally used victims as crime-base witnesses and insiders from the various armed factions as linkage witnesses. Testimony from such crime-base and linkage witnesses formed the bulk of the Prosecution's evidence before the SCSL.[7] Therefore, the veracity of the witnesses' testimony is of utmost importance, as it almost exclusively determined the guilt or innocence of the accused before the SCSL.

The manner in which the Court interacts with these witnesses has the potential to influence the accuracy and truth of their testimony. Other scholars have investigated how this interaction can undermine the quality of evidence relied on by judges in their determinations of the guilt or innocence of the accused.[8] Although there are many different ways the SCSL can interact with witnesses, this chapter will focus on the Office of the Prosecutor's (OTP's) provision of financial benefits to witnesses through its Witness Management Unit. It will address the serious allegations made by Defense counsel that these benefits were in fact bribes used to "buy" testimony, and how the Trial Chambers have dealt with this issue. Finally, it will explore the possible impact this interaction could have on the SCSL's legacy and local perceptions of justice in Sierra Leone.

II. OTP WITNESS PAYMENTS

Terry Munyard, Taylor Co-Counsel: *Reimbursing witnesses for genuine expenses is entirely legitimate. [...] Some people have approached us offering to give evidence for the defence if we will pay them more than they are being offered by the Prosecution. Frankly, this corrodes the whole system of justice that the international tribunals are supposed to be upholding.*

Former SCSL Prosecutor Stephen Rapp: *[L]isten, we are talking about reimbursement of expenses here. Nobody is being enriched through testifying. [...] The principle is that nobody should be worse off as a result of testifying.*[9]

There are two official bodies that provide assistance to witnesses, the OTP's Witness Management Unit (OTPWMU) and the Registry's Witness and Victims Section (WVS). This chapter explores payments made by the OTPWMU. The debate over payments to witnesses

---

[6] Indictment, Prosecutor v. Norman et al. (CDF) (SCSL-03-14-I), Trial Chamber I (Feb. 5, 2004); Corrected Amended Consolidated Indictment, RUF (SCSL-04-15-PT), Trial Chamber I (Aug. 2, 2006); Further Amended Consolidated Indictment, Prosecutor v. Kamara et al. (AFRC) (SCSL-04-16-PT) (Feb. 18, 2005); Prosecutor's Second Amended Indictment, Prosecutor v. Taylor (SCSL-03-01-PT) (May 29, 2007).

[7] N. COMBS, FACT FINDING WITHOUT FACTS: THE UNCERTAIN EVIDENTIARY FOUNDATIONS OF INTERNATIONAL CRIMINAL CONVICTIONS 12–14 (2010).

[8] *See, e.g.,* COMBS, *supra* note 7, at 44–62 (arguing that difficulties arising from the witness's culture, the manner of courtroom questioning, and educational or linguistic differences can "create tremendous uncertainty about even the most basic aspects of the criminal activities at issue in international trials."); T. KELSALL, CULTURE UNDER CROSS-EXAMINATION: INTERNATIONAL JUSTICE AND THE SPECIAL COURT FOR SIERRA LEONE 171–224 (2009) (arguing that social and cultural contexts made SCSL fact-finding difficult).

[9] J. Silverman, *Money Troubles at Trial of First African Leader to Face a War Crimes Court,* TIMES ONLINE (Apr. 22, 2008), *available at* http://business.timesonline.co.uk/tol/business/law/article3785508.ece.

by the OTPWMU was a persistent issue in SCSL trials. The quotes above demonstrate the positions taken by the Defense and Prosecution in this debate. Defense teams claim that the practice as a whole is unjust, and threatens to leave a negative legacy in Sierra Leone. The Prosecution sees the issue as fair and necessary to the administration of justice. The following sections will attempt to explain the most contentious issues about the payments: the structure, funding, and function of the OTPWMU; Defense allegations of inducement and impropriety; and the Chambers' general lack of engagement with the issue.

A. Source of Payments: Structure, Funding, and Function of the OTPWMU

One source of the debate over witness payments at the SCSL is their origin from within the OTP. This section will provide greater detail on the structure, funding, and function of the OTPWMU. In particular, it will discuss problems associated with the location of the section within the investigative arm of the OTP and the OTP's lack of standard operating procedures (SOPs) for investigations.

1. Structure: Location within the Investigative Arm of OTP

The OTPWMU is situated in the investigations arm of the OTP organizational structure, under the supervision of the Chief of Investigations, who reports directly to the Prosecutor.[10] In conducting its investigation, the Prosecution will first contact potential witnesses or other persons who can provide information and possible leads during an investigation. These persons are not yet considered "witnesses" in the technical sense. They are, when approached during investigation, only potential witnesses or sources of information. The OTPWMU "provides critical confirmation of witness evidence and provides support for persons required to give evidence."[11] However, the OTPWMU maintains contact with the witnesses after their testimony, especially those who will testify in more than one trial.[12]

Once the Prosecution has determined that it will call an individual as a witness, that person falls under the purview of the WVS. That unit, part of the neutral Registry, is mandated to provide, "in consultation with the Office of the Prosecutor, protective measures and security arrangements, counseling and other appropriate assistance for witnesses, victims who appear before the Court and others who are at risk on account of testimony given by such witnesses."[13] The OTPWMU and WVS are designed to operate separately and have separate oversight, protocols, and budgets. According to the Court, the "functions of [the OTPWMU] are complementary rather than duplicative" of WVS functions.[14]

The location of the OTPWMU within the investigation section of the OTP does not comport with best practices recommendations made by the United Nations for witness protection.[15] A UN report from the UN Office on Drugs and Crime acknowledges the need

---

[10] *Special Court for Sierra Leone Budget 2007–2009*, Special Court for Sierra Leone, at 22 (Apr. 5, 2007) [hereinafter *Budget 2007–2009*].

[11] *Id.*

[12] *Id.*

[13] SCSL Statute art. 16(4).

[14] *Budget 2007–2009, supra* note 10, at 22.

[15] *See generally UN Report on Witness Protection, infra* note 21.

for providing "moderate financial assistance" and other measures[16] to victim witnesses, in an effort to allow vulnerable witnesses to testify securely and to avoid re-traumatization.[17] It emphasizes the need for a neutral body to manage all witness assistance, support, and security concerns. Specifically, the UN report notes that witness assistance should be "administered and delivered by professionals who are independent from the investigation and prosecution services."[18] The role of the investigator should be limited to assessing the security risks a witness might face and to making "recommendations to the designated authority on proposed action."[19] The UN report thus specifically envisages witness assistance being managed by a separate body even during the investigation phase.[20]

In addition to witness assistance being separated, the UN report notes that witness protection schemes should also be separated from the investigation to "ensure objectivity and minimize the risk that admission to the programme unwittingly may become an incentive for witnesses to give false testimony that they believe the police or prosecution wants or needs."[21] Where the program is located within the police department, the report suggests that it is of paramount importance to keep the program organizationally, administratively, and operationally isolated and autonomous from the rest of the police force and the investigation.[22]

The UN report recommends that witness protection programs, especially when they are located within a police department, go to "great lengths to ensure that admittance to the programme is not seen as a reward for cooperation."[23] To this end, financial support[24] during any witness protection program should be of limited duration so as not to appear as compensation.[25] In order to safeguard neutrality, programs should also ensure that witnesses are clearly aware that witness protection is not a reward for cooperating.[26] Important for the SCSL context, the UN recommends that witness programs only provide benefits to witnesses "no greater than their legal earnings before admission to the program."[27]

In addition to the location within the investigative arm of the OTP, the practice of the OTPWMU does not reflect the UN recommendations about the duration of assistance, demonstrated by the long-running payments that are greater than the legal earnings of the witnesses who are paid. These issues will be illustrated later in the chapter.

---

[16] Such as "transportation, accommodation and childcare" which should be "administered and delivered by professionals who are independent from the investigation and prosecution services." *Id.* at 28.

[17] *Id.* at 21.

[18] *Id.* at 28.

[19] *Id.* at 30.

[20] *Id.* at 30. However, it also notes that schemes to provide initial support to persons who are later admitted to a witness protection program could be administered by an authority different from the body organizing the witness protection program, because the logistical issues and risks involved are very different. *Id.* at 30–31.

[21] United Nations Office on Drugs and Crime, *Good Practices for the Protection of Witnesses in Criminal Proceedings Involving Organized Crime*, 45 (Feb. 13, 2008) [hereinafter *UN Report on Witness Protection*].

[22] *Id.* at 45–46.

[23] *Id.* at 55.

[24] The report suggests providing witnesses in witness protection programs with assistance in finding a new job, including education, job training, or even low-interest loans. *Id.* at 61.

[25] *Id.* at 56.

[26] *Id.*

[27] *Id.* at 56–57.

2. Function: Opacity of Investigative Procedures

Although there is some limited public information about the structure and funding of the OTPWMU, less is known about how the unit operates. Indeed, the entire investigative process lacks transparency.[28]

Prosecution investigations are regulated by Rule 39 of the Rules of Procedure and Evidence (RPE), which provides the prosecution incredibly broad discretion when conducting investigations – it is allowed to take all measures necessary for the investigation, including any special measures deemed necessary for the assistance of potential witnesses.[29] There is no provision for oversight of this process or requirement of consultation with the Registry or other Court body. As discussed below, the SCSL Trial Chambers were hesitant to impinge on this discretion, and granted the Prosecutor wide latitude in investigative procedures.

Former Chief Prosecutor Stephen Rapp has explained that witness compensation from the OTP is individualized and is determined by a witness's circumstances.[30] This implies that OTP officers make subjective judgments about the needs of a witness based on his or her circumstances. It also implies that more savvy witnesses can negotiate a better "deal" from the Prosecution, asking for more benefits or assistance than others might. When asked about its practices relating to witness payments, the OTP consistently refuses to provide detailed answers to questions relating to internal protocol, organizational structure, or criteria for providing funds to witnesses.[31] The Prosecution maintains that the Prosecutor oversees the OTPWMU, and that all internal protocols are protected by the disclosure privilege granted under Rule 70(A) of the RPE.[32] It cites Rule 39(ii) as allowing it to take "any special measures to provide for the safety, the support and assistance of potential witnesses and sources."[33]

According to Rapp, there were no internal OTP protocols for dealing with witness payments.[34] The first Prosecutor, David Crane, did not consider that such protocols were necessary.[35] Indeed, Crane provided only cursory training to professionals hired from domestic jurisdictions with no experience working in an international setting.[36] Rapp, who came into office toward the end of the SCSL's mandate, did not consider it worth the OTP's limited resources to develop and implement SOPs during his tenure.[37]

---

[28] P. Van Tuyl, *Effective, Efficient and Fair? An Inquiry into the Investigative Practices of the Office of the Prosecutor at the Special Court for Sierra Leone*, UC Berkeley War Crimes Studies Center, at 36 (Sept. 2008) (noting that "negotiation protocol with insider witnesses and covert sources remains largely impenetrable to outside observers and opposing counsel alike").

[29] Rule 39(ii) SCSLRPE.

[30] Interview with Stephen Rapp (Feb. 9, 2009).

[31] *See, e.g.*, Motion to Request Trial Chamber to Hear Evidence concerning the Prosecution Witness Management Unit and Its Payment to Witnesses, Prosecutor v. Sesay et al. (RUF)(SCSL-04-15-T), Trial Chamber I (May 30, 2008) [hereinafter RUF Motion regarding Witness Payments], Annex E (Letter from Mr. Jordash to Mr. Harrison, dated Dec. 1, 2007 and reply from Mr. Rapp, dated Dec. 18, 2007). The OTP gave this same type of reply to the author in response to questions about the OTPWMU and WVS.

[32] Rule 70(A) SCSLRPE.

[33] Rule 39(ii) SCSLRPE.

[34] Interview with Stephen Rapp (Feb. 9, 2009).

[35] Van Tuyl, *supra* note 28, at 39.

[36] *Id.* at 39–42.

[37] *Id.* at 39.

The Prosecution argues that it has disclosed all witness payments to the Defense, which has the information and power to question witnesses about those payments, and that witness credibility is an issue for the Trial Chamber alone to decide.[38] However, the Prosecution's disclosures (at least those publicly available) are limited to line item descriptions of the reason and amount of the payment. There is no explanation of how the amount is calculated or what the terms used in the reports mean. Several lump sum payments were made for "meals," "transport," and "time wasted."[39] There were large payments for "property" related to temporary protective measures,[40] "maintenance,"[41] and "miscellaneous."[42] The OTP would not elaborate on the specifics of these payments, and additional information about what they were used for was available only through cross-examination.

The opacity of Prosecution investigative processes is exacerbated by what could simply be poor recordkeeping. However, the Prosecution has not explained its policies or procedures, even where informal. The only public information about OTP investigations, described during a rare voir dire during the RUF trial, raises questions about the propriety of the OTP investigative unit, where the WMU is based.[43] Beyond the voir dire, there is little in the public record about the inner function of the investigations unit and WMU.

The voir dire exposed that Trial Chamber I considered that statements made by accused Issa Sesay during prosecution investigations were not made voluntarily because the Prosecution held out "promises and inducements" to the Accused, which the Chamber considered bordering on "a semblance of arm twisting."[44] Notably, Trial Chamber I found that Sesay's statements were made as the result of "fear of prejudice and the hope of advantage" held out to him by the Prosecution, and that the "advantage of […] financial assistance for his family […] were and must have been significant to the Accused […] [and] the statements were not made voluntarily."[45] The Chamber's acknowledgement of the ill effects of promised financial assistance and their inappropriate use as an investigative tool makes it even more surprising that the same analysis was not undertaken after similar allegations regarding other witnesses.

---

[38] *See, e.g.*, RUF Motion regarding Witness Payments, Annex E (Letter from Mr. Jordash to Mr. Harrison, dated Dec. 1, 2007 and reply from Mr.Rapp, dated Dec. 18, 2007); Prosecution Response to Sesay Request to Hear Evidence concerning the Prosecution's Witness Management Unit, RUF (SCSL-04–15-T), Trial Chamber I (June 5, 2008).

[39] See RUF Motion regarding Witness Payments, *supra* note 31. The Prosecution contends that "time wasted" is a Sierra Leonean term that refers to lost earnings. Prosecution Response to Sesay Request to Hear Evidence concerning the Prosecution's Witness Management Unit, RUF (SCSL-04–15-T), Trial Chamber I, para. 27 (June 5, 2008).

[40] RUF Motion regarding Witness Payments, at Annex C (noting payments of $3,000 (TFI-371)).

[41] *Id.* (noting payments for $250 (TFI-046)).

[42] Taylor Witness TFI-375. This witness admitted that the "miscellaneous" payment of nearly $9,000 was in part for computer classes he took in Freetown. Trial Transcript, Taylor (SCSL-03–01-T), Trial Chamber II, at 37–39 (Aug. 27, 2008).

[43] *See generally* Van Tuyl, *supra* note 28.

[44] Written Reasons – Decision on the Admissibility of Certain Prior Statements of the Accused Given to the Prosecution, RUF (SCSL-04–15-T), para. 51 (June 30, 2008).

[45] *Id.* at para. 52.

B. Defense Allegations of False Testimony

Although there may be many reasons for witnesses to lie in court,[46] financial benefits are a particularly compelling incentive.[47] In an impoverished country such as Sierra Leone,[48] it is hard to imagine that potential witnesses would not be motivated to testify and to cooperate with the Court in exchange for financial support, even if modest. There is no question that testifying before an international tribunal can be considered, and in fact can be, lucrative for the witness.[49] However, motivation to cooperate with the SCSL is distinct from motivation to lie under oath. According to defense teams at the Court, the witness payments provided by the OTPWMU incentivized witnesses to lie during interviews and during testimony, thereby tainting the evidentiary record.

As an example of how the debate permeated SCSL trials, this chapter will discuss how the Taylor defense team raised the issue during the last SCSL trial. The Defense alleged that the OTPWMU had impermissibly paid witnesses to testify in the *Taylor* trial, suggesting that their testimony was "bought" by the Prosecution. This, the Defense contended, made these witnesses' testimony unreliable. The Taylor defense alleged that witnesses profited from the payments and claimed that such payments would inevitably influence witnesses to feel obligated toward the party paying them. This, the Defense submitted during closing arguments, was demonstrated by what it characterized as "unique" facts appearing in witness testimony that were not corroborated by other witnesses.[50] This argumentation reflects similar positions taken by other defense teams. For example, the Sesay defense raised an issue during cross-examination concerning the lack of transparency and confusion surrounding payments made by the OTP and WVS to witnesses. They suggested the money from the OTP might have motivated the witness to give testimony against the Accused, and that, in some cases, individuals volunteer to be witnesses in return for payment.[51] The Sesay defense argued that "survival [in Sierra Leone] is a number one priority," and pecuniary motivation undermines the integrity of the witnesses and the judicial process.[52]

Only limited information about the payments is available in public transcripts from defense cross-examinations. Requests made by the author to the Court for public exhibits detailing the payments were denied on the basis that such information might someday be reclassified as confidential. Much of the information about specific payments included in public court documents has been redacted. Therefore, the information presented next is

---

[46] For example, in the Sierra Leone context, these could include ethnic or tribal loyalties, immunity from prosecution, personal animosity, revenge, or threats to the witness's security. COMBS, *supra* note 7, at 136–38.

[47] COMBS, *supra* note 7, at 138.

[48] Sierra Leone ranks 180 out of 187 countries in the Human Development Index Rankings. Data *available at* http://hdr.undp.org/en/statistics/ (last visited Mar. 10, 2012).

[49] COMBS, *supra* note 7, at 139, 141. *See also* E. STOVER, THE WITNESSES: WAR CRIMES AND THE PROMISE OF JUSTICE IN THE HAGUE 78–81 (2005) (describing negotiations among witnesses, local authorities, and ICTY prosecutors and investigators).

[50] Trial Transcript, Taylor (SCSL-03-01-T), Trial Chamber II, at 20 (lines 21–25) (Mar. 10, 2011).

[51] Trial Transcript, RUF (SCSL-04-15-T), Trial Chamber I, at 15 (lines 12–20), at 20 (lines 23–24) (Apr. 11, 2005).

[52] *Id.* at 16 (lines 23–24).

based on open session cross-examinations and public filings, and is a small sample of an issue that was raised time and again during trial.[53]

Witness testimony demonstrates that in some cases, payment totals appear to be quite significant, given the general income level in Sierra Leone. DCT-097, once a potential prosecution witness, said he was paid an estimated $30,000 by the Prosecution from 2004 to 2006, at least in part for "general upkeep." The Defense submitted that it had received copies of seventeen MoneyGram receipts showing payments from five different prosecution employees to the witness in sums such ranging from $800 to $2,000.[54] Witness TF1–375 admitted that a "miscellaneous" payment of nearly $9,000 was in part for computer classes he took in Freetown.[55] Other persons who the Prosecution considered calling as witnesses, but who ultimately never took the stand, also purportedly benefited from large payments of approximately $100,000 each.[56]

The payments apparently did not always comport with expenses incurred by the witness, were unnecessary, or were not paid for the reasons supplied by the OTP. For example, Jabaty Jaward testified that he had received approximately $1,350 from the Prosecution. He was also allegedly paid $100 on one occasion for lost wages and transport and $50 on another for lost wages when he had not been interviewed. He was also given money for medical treatment that he said he could have afforded himself.[57] Suwandi Camara testified that he was given $100 a month for several months for "security," although he could not specify what security measures it paid for. He said some of the money was to put a fence around his orchard, which he had started but not completed when he came to The Hague.[58] Isaac Mongor testified that he received money for lost wages even though he admitted he did not tell the Prosecution the amount he would normally earn or the days he was not working, and was given money for lost wages on days he did not work.[59] TF1–337 received payments for lost wages in excess of what he normally earned or would spend on daily expenses for his family, and received funds for his children's school fees because of "problems" in his family.[60]

Testimony also suggests that payments between the OTPWMU and WVS overlapped, even though the organizations are not supposed to be duplicative and the OTP payments should have ended once the WVS took over. For example, Jaward testified that after he

[53] Further empirical research is needed to thoroughly analyze the amounts and reasons for the witness payments. These examples are meant to be indicative of problems associated with the payments.

[54] For a complete list of the receipts the Defense claims it has on file, see Defense Motion for Disclosure of Statement and prosecution Payments Made to DCT-097, Taylor (SCSL-03–01-T), Trial Chamber II, Annex F (Aug. 4, 2010) [hereinafter Defense Motion for DCT-097 Disclosures].

[55] Trial Transcript, Taylor (SCSL-03–01-T), Trial Chamber II, at 37–39 (Aug. 27, 2008).

[56] A. Stavrianou, *Interview with Lead Defense Counsel Courtenay Griffiths QC in The Hague*, Centre for Accountability and Rule of Law, *available at* http://www.carl-sl.org/home/reports/367-interview-with-taylors-lead-counsel-courtenay-griffiths-qc-in-the-hague (last visited Feb. 5, 2012).

[57] Trial Transcript, Taylor (SCSL-03–01-T), Trial Chamber II, at 9 (July 15, 2008).

[58] Trial Transcript, Taylor (SCSL-03–01-T), Trial Chamber II, at 92–94 (Feb. 13, 2008).

[59] RUF Motion regarding Witness Payments, para. 30.xiii, citing Trial Transcript, Taylor (SCSL-03–01-T), Trial Chamber II, at 95, 102 (Apr. 1, 2008); para 30.xiv, citing Trial Transcript, Taylor (SCSL-03–01-T), Trial Chamber II, at 6705 (Apr. 7, 2008).

[60] RUF Motion regarding Witness Payments, paras. 30.xi–30.xii, citing Trial Transcript, Taylor (SCSL-03–01-T), Trial Chamber II, at 37–42, 63 (Mar. 7, 2008).

had been brought into the care of the WVS, he continued to receive money from the OTP.[61] In addition, the Defense noted, from August 2006 until May 2008, TF1–375 was simultaneously under the care of the Prosecution and the Registry's WVS, during which time he received assistance of approximately $10,000.[62]

It is also apparent from witness testimony that the Prosecution was not always clear about what the funds were for, or there was a misunderstanding on the part of the witness. For example, Mongor testified that the Prosecution never told him he was being reimbursed for what he would lose working, and said that if that was what they were paying him for, they would have asked him what he was losing when coming to testify.[63] When asked whether he expected to receive additional funds, Camara said "at the beginning they told me that all this matter was on a voluntary basis, so if I receive money from them it will be a kind of surprise."[64] Jaward claimed the OTP would give him $50 each time he had an interview, which they told him was for lost wages. He said the OTP explicitly told him this was not a bribe, but admitted that the OTP must have thought he would think the $50 was paid to influence his testimony.[65]

Perhaps most problematically, some witnesses testified that they had received payments as consideration or "rewards" for their cooperation with the OTP. For example, TF1–548 said that he had been given money "as a reward for coming to be interviewed" and as "compensation for the efforts" he made to see the Prosecution.[66] Witness TF1–375 testified that the OTP suggested that he have a medical procedure, which they subsequently paid for, and that this encouraged him to work with them.[67] TFI-375 further testified that he received a payment of $100 as a "gift" after he took a trip,[68] whereas Blah testified that he has been sick for nearly twenty years and "capable of paying my bills," but that the medical bill was a "goodwill gesture [...] to assist" the OTP.[69] Camara testified, "I am the one helping the Special Court. So in that case any assistance I render in that framework – I mean, it is as a compensation."[70] He went on to say that that the money was given to him "as an assistance," and admitted that in West Africa, assistance means financial support.[71] Although these could be simply miscommunications or the result of translation, such statements indicate the possibility that the payments did influence or motivate witnesses to work with the OTP.

---

[61] Trial Transcript, Taylor (SCSL-03–01-T), Trial Chamber II, at 9 (July 15, 2008).

[62] Trial Transcript, Taylor (SCSL-03–01-T), Trial Chamber II (Aug. 27, 2008).

[63] Trial Transcript, Taylor (SCSL-03–01-T), Trial Chamber II, at 107 (Mar. 31, 2008). He testified:
They gave me money which I told you about yesterday, that I received money, but I was not told that it was because of what I had lost. If that was the case they were not supposed to decide for me. They would have asked me, "What is your lost wage?," and then I would have made the estimate. They were not to decide for me and I did not say so, so I cannot say they gave me lost wages.
Trial Transcript, Taylor (SCSL-03–01-T), Trial Chamber II, at 92 lines 9–15 (Apr. 1, 2008); *see also id.* at 101.

[64] Trial Transcript, Taylor (SCSL-03–01-T), Trial Chamber II, at 98, lines 20–22 Feb. 13, 2008.

[65] Trial Transcript, Taylor (SCSL-03–01-T), Trial Chamber II, at 9, lines 5–23 July 15, 2008

[66] RUF Motion regarding Witness Payments, para. 30. xv, citing Trial Transcript, Taylor (SCSL-03–01-T), Trial Chamber II, at 65 (Feb. 13, 2008).

[67] Trial Transcript, Taylor (SCSL-03–01-T), Trial Chamber II, at 33–34 (lines 13–29, 1–5) (Aug. 27, 2008).

[68] *Id.* at 13–14 (lines 25–29, 1–5).

[69] Trial Transcript, Taylor (SCSL-03–01-T), Trial Chamber II, at 28 (line 24); at 29 (lines 13, 18) (May 19, 2008).

[70] Trial Transcript, Taylor (SCSL-03–01-T), Trial Chamber II, at 94, lines 1–3 (Feb. 13, 2008).

[71] *Id.* at 95.

C. Judicial Engagement

In court, the payments are treated as a matter of witness credibility to be determined by the Judges in the final judgment. The general position taken by the SCSL Trial Chambers is that the Prosecution must disclose information about witness payments, which the Defense can then raise on cross-examination in attempts to discredit witnesses. However, as explained below, neither Trial Chamber addressed the issue directly in the RUF and AFRC judgments in their discussions of credibility. In fact, at least until the *Taylor* trial, in their judgments, the Chambers missed the essence of the defense arguments, focusing on the payments by WVS, and not by the OTPWMU. Even if the defense allegations are unsubstantiated, as serious and repeated allegations concerning fair trial rights, they deserved more attention and consideration from the SCSL Judges than they received. This section will describe the approaches of Trial Chambers I and II during trial and in the *RUF*, *AFRC* and *Taylor* judgments.

1. Trial Chamber I: *RUF* Trial

During the *RUF* trial, Trial Chamber I demonstrated a general confusion on the issue of witness payments. The Trial Chamber took a very narrow view of the issue, and did not permit the Defense to address inferences of motivation or impropriety when cross-examining witnesses on benefits they received.

During one trial session, the Judges interrupted a cross-examination of a Prosecution witness about payments from the OTP. Judge Boutet noted that during the investigative process the OTP pays some expenses that are later paid by the witness protection unit, but admitted: "In my own mind there is certainly confusion as to who is paying what, where and when."[72] He noted the difference between a witness admitting he had received a certain sum and inferring that the witness testified because of the incentive for payment.[73] He eventually remarked to the Defense counsel: "I don't know where you want us to place ourselves with this sort of evidence."[74] However, the Chamber did not seek clarification from the OTP on the issue. The Presiding Judge, Benjamin Itoe, considered that the OTP had broad discretion to conduct its investigations and case as it deemed appropriate, noting "There are no hard and fast rules for this [...]."[75]

The Court considered that the defense argument about the impropriety of the payments amounted to an accusation that the "entire judicial process is tainted."[76] The Presiding Judge permitted the defense counsel to continue cross-examination of the witness but instructed that although he may inquire about the expenses or allowances the witness received, the defense counsel could not ask "any question that raises some imputations that you are in fact impeaching the order of this Court or any statute or practice direction in that regard."[77]

The Judges thus indirectly acknowledged the seriousness of the allegations, but did not take steps to clarify or address the issue. Even though the Judges themselves admitted that

---

[72] Trial Transcript, RUF (SCSL-04–15-T), Trial Chamber I, at 9 (lines 3–4) (Apr. 11, 2005).

[73] *Id.* at 17–18 (lines 25–29, 1–7).

[74] *Id.* at 20 (lines 15–17).

[75] *Id.* at 22 (lines 3–8).

[76] *Id.* at 14 (lines 2–7) and 16 (lines 1–3, 6).

[77] *Id.* at 23 (lines 10–12).

they did not clearly understand the differences in who paid the witnesses what and when, and acknowledged that there were no clear rules about it, they nevertheless limited defense questioning and then ignored the distinction in their final trial judgment. The entire substance of the defense argument – which focused on the relative poverty of Sierra Leoneans and possible incentives to testify when offered payments from the OTP – was lost on this Trial Chamber, who considered the suggestion an affront on the judicial process itself and therefore forbidden territory in cross-examination.

Later in the case when the Defense raised witness payments again, the Court took issue with the temporality of the defense arguments. When defense counsel was questioning a witness about whether he was motivated to testify in court because of payments he had received, the Chamber stopped the line of questioning, telling the Defense it could raise the issue "in due course,"[78] concluding that "this is not the time to raise these arguments [...]."[79] Toward the end of the trial, the Sesay defense submitted a motion to hear evidence on OTPWMU payments. However, in spite of repeated contentious arguments about these issues,[80] the Trial Chamber dismissed the motion. The Chamber held that the defense motion was not raised at the "earliest opportunity."[81] The Chamber's approach effectively silenced the Defense: it could not raise the issue on cross-examination because it was not the right time, but later the Chamber refused to hear evidence on the issue because it was untimely. This essentially meant the Defense was not permitted to introduce important evidence relating to the credibility of witnesses relied on to convict the Accused.

The Chamber's confusion over the issue – or reticence to discuss the OTP side of the equation – is also apparent in the final judgment. In the judgment, the Chamber did not address the distinction between payments made by the OTPWMU and payments made by WVS. Instead, it focused its discussion entirely on payments made by the WVS – missing the central defense allegations about the OTPWMU – and concluded that there is nothing to suggest that WVS payments affect the credibility of witness testimony.[82] It drew no negative inferences from the fact that witnesses received compensation.[83] The Chamber

---

[78] Trial Transcript, RUF (SCSL-04–15-T), Trial Chamber I, at 67 (line 4) (Mar. 3, 2006). *See also* A. Thompson, *Special Court Monitoring Program Update #72*, UC Berkeley War Crimes Studies Center (Mar. 2006), *available at* http://socrates.berkeley.edu/~warcrime/documents/Report72_000.pdf.

[79] Trial Transcript, RUF (SCSL-04–15-T), Trial Chamber I, at 66 (line 24) (Mar. 3, 2006).

[80] *See, e.g.*, Motion to Request the Trial Chamber to Hear Evidence concerning the Prosecution's Witness Management Unit and Its Payment to Witnesses, RUF (SCSL-04–15-T), Trial Chamber I (May 30, 2008); *see also* Kallon Defense Response to Motion to Request the Trial Chamber to Hear Evidence concerning the Prosecution's Witness Management Unit and Its Payment to Witnesses, RUF (SCSL-04–15-T), Trial Chamber I (June 3, 2008); Gbao-Notice of Support to Sesay Motion Requesting the Trial Chamber to Hear Evidence concerning the Prosecution's Witness Management Unit and Its Payment to Witnesses, RUF (SCSL-04–15-T), Trial Chamber I (June 3, 2008); Trial Transcript RUF (SCSL-04–15-T), Trial Chamber I, at 15, 71 (Apr. 19, 2005); Trial Transcript, RUF (SCSL-04–15-T), Trial Chamber I, at 49 (July 6, 2006); Trial Transcript, RUF (SCSL-04–15-T), Trial Chamber I, at 164 (Oct. 5, 2004); Trial Transcript RUF (SCSL-04–15-T), Trial Chamber I, at 9–11 (Oct. 6, 2004); Sesay Final Trial Brief, RUF (SCSL-04–15-T), Trial Chamber I, para. 8; Kallon Final Trial Brief, RUF (SCSL-04–15-T), Trial Chamber I, paras. 10, 185, 187–88, 362, 406, 407, 482; Gbao Final Trial Brief, RUF (SCSL-04–15-T), Trial Chamber I, paras. 505, 933.

[81] Decision on Sesay Motion to Request the Trial Chamber to Hear Evidence concerning the Prosecution's Witness Management Unit and Its Payments to Witnesses, RUF (SCSL-04–15-T), Trial Chamber I, at 2 (June 25, 2008).

[82] Judgment, RUF (SCSL-04–15-T), Trial Chamber I, paras. 523–526 (Feb. 25, 2009).

[83] *Id.* at paras. 525, 526.

concluded that it "does not consider such compensation relevant in assessing the credibility of any particular witness."[84]

2. Trial Chamber II: *AFRC* and *Taylor* Trials

Trial Chamber II's treatment of witness payments differed between the *AFRC* and *Taylor* Trials. In the *AFRC* case, the Court held that allegations of inappropriate payments were without merit, as the Chamber was satisfied that the payments had been made in a "transparent way and in accordance with the applicable Practice Direction."[85] Accordingly, the Trial Chamber opted not to give "undue weight" to the alleged "incentives" when assessing witness credibility.[86] However, this also seems to miss the crux of the issue, as the Practice Direction pertains only to WVS payments.

Trial Chamber II did engage with the issue more during the *Taylor* trial. During the *Taylor* trial, a motion by the Defense requesting contempt proceedings against the OTP for abuse of process for, inter alia, improper witness payments,[87] provided an opportunity for the Trial Chamber to address accusations of impropriety related to the witness payments in the *Taylor* case.[88]

The Trial Chamber denied the motion on technical grounds: it was untimely[89] and did not fall within the ambit of Rule 77 of the RPE.[90] The Judges considered that allegations of the impropriety of witness payments fell under Rule 39(ii) as an issue of discretionary payments, which the Judges said they would consider during final deliberations based on evidence adduced at trial.[91] However, given the seriousness of the allegations of contempt, the Court considered that it was in the interests of justice to review the individual allegations of misconduct on the merits. The Chamber considered the issue a question of whether the OTP had abused its discretion under Rule 39(ii) "in that the payments might not have been necessary for the safety, support or assistance of the potential witnesses and sources."[92] The Court found that allegations of misconduct were not based on credible sources, and therefore did not meet the relatively low standard of "reason to believe" that contempt may have been committed by members of the OTP.[93] There was nothing inappropriate in providing payments related to security, and there was nothing to suggest the payments were excessive or improper, the Chamber considered.[94] The Court, however, stated that it would make a

---

[84] *Id.* at para. 525.

[85] Judgment, AFRC (SCSL-04–16-T), Trial Chamber II, at para. 128 (June 20, 2007).

[86] *Id.* at para. 130.

[87] Rule 77(A)(iv) SCSLRPE; Rule 77(C)(iii) SCSLRPE.

[88] Defense Motion Requesting an Investigation into Contempt of Court by the Office of the Prosecution and Its Investigators, Taylor (SCSL-03–01-T), Trial Chamber II, at paras. 57, 60, 104, 127 (Sept. 24, 2010) [hereinafter Defense Contempt Motion]. *See also* J. Easterday, Charles Taylor Monthly Report (August 1, 2010–September 30, 2010), UC Berkeley War Crimes Studies Center 13–14 (2010); J. Easterday, Charles Taylor Monthly Report (October–November 2010), UC Berkeley War Crimes Studies Center (2011).

[89] Decision on Public with Confidential Annexes A-J and Public Annexes K-O Defense Motion Requesting an Investigation into Contempt of Court by the Office of the Prosecutor and Its Investigators, Taylor (SCSL-03–01-T), Trial Chamber II, at para. 24 (Nov. 11, 2010) [hereinafter Decision on Contempt].

[90] *Id.* at paras. 27–31.

[91] *Id.* at para. 40.

[92] *Id.*

[93] *Id.* at para. 150.

[94] *Id.* at para. 78. For example, bimonthly payments of $300 made to a potential witness's guards in response to security threats to the potential witness were acceptable to the Court. *Id.* at para. 82. In the case of another

determination on whether these payments had influenced witnesses when it assessed their credibility and the veracity of their testimony during final deliberations.[95]

In the judgment, the Trial Chamber specifically considered "any motivations to lie" as a factor in determining witness credibility.[96] The Chamber took into account information about witness payments made by both WVS and OTPWMU as well as cross-examination of witnesses about the payments. The Chamber said it had reviewed whether payments went beyond what was reasonably necessary for witness management on a case-by-case basis, taking into account the cost of living in West Africa and the particular life circumstances of the witnesses receiving the payments.[97]

In the discussion on credibility, the Chamber did not find that the payments undermined any witness testimony. The Judges reasoned, for example, that payments made for medical expenses for a witness and his family members, school fees and other expenses did not undermine the credibility of that witness. They noted that "although the witness received some financial benefits from the prosecution, the nature of the information that he provided to the prosecution throughout the interview process was consistent and does not appear to have been tailored in favor of the prosecution as a result of those benefits."[98] Related to Isaac Mongor, the Chamber found that although he received payments for transportation, food, and lost wages that were in excess of what he actually spent, it accepted his testimony that he did not testify for financial gain.[99] The Chamber found that Alimamy Bobson Sesay had received payments from the Prosecution, including for meals and transportation costs when there were no interviews, as well as simultaneous payments from WVS for meals and accommodation. However, the Chamber did not consider these payments to be unreasonable or that there was evidence they influenced his testimony.[100] Moreover, the Judges found that the witness was "forthright and candid when asked about the payments he received from the prosecution."[101] They went on to find that he had no motivations to lie.[102] Generally, when the Chamber found that a witness was not credible and would not rely on that person's evidence without corroboration, the Chamber did not discuss witness payments as a factor influencing that consideration.[103]

---

potential witness, the Court found that OTP offers of money, housing, and overall security protection fell under the ambit of Rule 39 and was therefore a discretionary matter for the OTP, and the allegation that these were inducements to get him to provide false testimony were "highly speculative." *Id.* at paras. 101, 104. The Chamber considered that the "alleged payments would fall under the ambit of Rule 39(ii) as they are legitimate measures to protect the witness's safety and security." *Id.*

[95] *Id.* at para. 148.

[96] Judgment, Taylor (SCSL-03–01-T-1281), Trial Chamber II, para. 165 (May 18, 2012). This is a departure from factors considered by this Chamber in the *AFRC* judgment. Judgment, Prosecutor v. Brima et al. (SCSL-04–16-T), Trial Chamber II, para. 108 (June 20, 2007). Motivation to lie was also a factor considered by Trial Chamber I in the *RUF* judgment. Judgment, RUF (SCSL-04-15-T), para. 486 (Mar. 2, 2009).

[97] Judgment, Taylor (SCSL-03–01-T-1281), Trial Chamber II, para.195 (May 18, 2012).

[98] *Id.* at para. 260.

[99] *Id.* at para. 271.

[100] *Id.* at para. 287.

[101] *Id.*

[102] *Id.* at 289.

[103] *See, e.g., id.* at paras. 263–268 (Joseph "Zigzag" Marzah); 296–303 (Witness TF1–539); 308–12 (TF1–375). Witness TF1–579 was an exception. The Chamber found that his testimony must be considered with caution and needed corroboration. However, in discussing payments made to the witness, including repeated

The Chamber recognized the defense position that the OTPWMU made "large payments on a systematic basis to prosecution witnesses, and that this taints the overall credibility of prosecution evidence and amounts to an abuse of the prosecution's discretion pursuant to Rule 39(ii)."[104] However, although the Court did consider witness payments in some of its case-by-case assessments of witness credibility, it did not discuss or make any findings on the other larger allegations about the payments.[105]

III. CONSEQUENCES FOR THE SCSL'S LEGACY

This chapter does not purport to evaluate the veracity of the positions taken by parties to this debate. It is true that the Prosecution has made payments, in some cases large payments, for the support and assistance of its witnesses. Whether this means that this caused these witnesses to lie in court is not clear. There is also no direct evidence that this has had a negative impact on how Sierra Leoneans view the Court. However, this chapter posits that the manner in which these payments were handled by the Chambers and OTP risks detracting from the legitimacy and legacy of the SCSL, in particular, with regard to the Court's demonstration effect.

Hybrid tribunals are seen as mechanisms that can foster fundamental changes to societies where they operate,[106] and these changes form legacies that are left by the court when it closes down. A court's legacy has been defined as "a hybrid court's lasting impact on bolstering the rule of law in a particular society, by conducting effective trials to contribute to ending impunity, while also strengthening domestic judicial capacity."[107] Legacies can take many forms, and the legacy of the SCSL has been widely debated elsewhere, including in this volume.[108] A key aspect of a tribunal's legacy focuses on "how" the court demonstrates its messages in addition to "what" message the court is imparting. "Demonstration effects" are the messages conveyed about justice to audiences of the court,[109] including the people

---

or overlapping payments for security, transportation, lost wages, and communication, the Chamber "note[d] the questions about these payments," but did not "accept that they improperly influenced the witness in his testimony." *Id.* at paras. 344–345.

[104] *Id.* at para. 185.

[105] The Prosecution did not make any submissions on this issue in its final brief. *Id.* at para. 189.

[106] *See, e.g.,* L. Fletcher, *From Indifference to Engagement: Bystanders and International Criminal Justice,* 26 MICH. J. INT'L L. 1013, 1092 (Summer 2005); D. Cohen, *Hybrid Justice in East Timor, Sierra Leone, and Cambodia: Lessons Learned and Prospects for the Future,* 43 STAN. J. INT'L L. 1, 6 (2007).

[107] OHCHR, *Rule of Law Tools for Post-Conflict States, Maximizing the Legacy of Hybrid Courts,* HR/PUB/08/2, at 4–5 (New York and Geneva 2008) [hereinafter *Maximizing Legacy*].

[108] *See, e.g.,* R. Kerr & J. Lincoln, *The Special Court for Sierra Leone Outreach, Legacy and Impact Final Report,* King's College of London War Crimes Research Group (2008); Open Society Justice Initiative, *Legacy: Completing the Work of the Special Court for Sierra Leone* (2011); V. Nmehielle & C. Jalloh, *The Legacy of the Special Court for Sierra Leone,* 30 FLETCHER F. WORLD AFF. 107 (2006).

[109] T. Cruvellier, *From the Taylor Trial to a Lasting Legacy: Putting the Special Court Model to the Test,* International Center for Transitional Justice and Sierra Leone Court Monitoring Programme 28 (2009) (Noting that "It is fully accepted that a hybrid court cannot by itself rebuild a legal system, but it can still act as a catalyst to impact certain areas, including demonstrating the value of trials for the rule of law through outreach and other strategies (the 'demonstration effect')."); J. Stromseth, *Justice on the Ground: Can International Criminal Courts Strengthen Domestic Rule of Law in Post-Conflict Societies?,* 1 HAGUE J. ON RULE L. 87, 92 (2009) [hereinafter *Justice on the Ground*]. *See also* J. Stromseth, *Pursuing Accountability for Atrocities after Conflict: What Impact on Building the Rule of Law?,* 38 GEO. J. INT'L L. 251 (2007) (arguing that "diffusion" of democratic

of Sierra Leone. This was one of the primary goals for creating a hybrid tribunal located in Freetown – so that the victims of the crimes could "see justice being done."[110]

Legacy-related studies have concluded that the work of the SCSL has resulted in "demonstration effects" or messages about justice conveyed to Sierra Leoneans.[111] However, in acknowledging that the presence of the SCSL in Sierra Leone has an effect on local perceptions of justice and the rule of law, it should also be considered that the SCSL could have a negative local impact. In some ways, the Court could inadvertently be leaving a negative legacy through unintended adverse demonstration effects. Messages conveyed by the court can:

> either build or undermine public confidence in fair justice. [...] [T]rials for atrocity crimes aim to demonstrate and to reassure people that justice can be fair – both procedurally in terms of due process and, substantively, in terms of evenhanded treatment of comparable actions regardless of who committed them.[112]

Trials can have negative effects if they are widely viewed as biased, or if direct perpetrators face no justice or accountability proceedings of any kind.[113] "How" the Chambers addressed issues of equality of arms, fair trial rights, and serious allegations about payments that could undermine the judicial truth-telling function could be a problematic legacy. "What" the OTP said – or did not say – about these issues is also a potential source of a negative legacy. Later in the chapter I discuss how potential (unintended) messages about witness payments could map onto preexisting cultural dynamics in Sierra Leone and thereby increase the risk that the SCSL has demonstrated to Sierra Leoneans that justice systems involve negotiated benefits for those who participate as witnesses. I highlight some of the possible negative consequences of the SCSL in Sierra Leone and raise issues for future empirical study by highlighting some aspects of Sierra Leonean culture that might be related to the witness payment issue.

A. *Importance of Transparency and Accountability*

The impact of witness payments and their possible impact on the legacy of the SCSL are discussed in this section in relation to the importance of transparency and accountability from the OTP and a thorough exploration of the issue by the Chambers. According to the OHCHR:

> A hybrid institution must be perceived as accessible and transparent to be successful. Access to senior officials of the court and to clear information will have a positive effect on how the court is perceived, setting realistic expectations on what the court can achieve.

---

processes can also effect rule of law development); A. Magen, *The Rule of Law and Its Promotion Abroad*, 45 Stan. J. Int'l L. 51, 113–14 (2009).

[110] *See, e.g.*, Nmehielle & Jalloh, *supra* note 108, at 109; *Third Annual Report of the Special Court for Sierra Leone, 2005–2006*, at 28 (noting "The SCSL has always recognized, not only the critical importance of leaving a legacy for the people of Sierra Leone but also the unprecedented opportunity to contribute to the restoration of the rule of law.").

[111] *See, e.g.*, Kerr & Lincoln, *supra* note 108, at 27; R. Shaw, *Memory Frictions: Localizing the Truth and Reconciliation Commission in Sierra Leone*, 1 Int'l J. Transitional Justice 4, 22 (2007).

[112] *Justice on the Ground*, *supra* note 109, at 92; *see also Post-Conflict Rule of Law*, *infra* note 120.

[113] *Justice on the Ground*, *supra* note 109, at 92.

Financial propriety is also an important consideration, as are standards of professional ethics and codes of conduct.[114]

Moreover, the United Nations also suggests that witness protection programs be held accountable for financial disbursements, as "transparency is a basic principle of good governance."[115]

The SCSL OTP's lack of transparency with regard to the WMU does not seem to have followed these recommendations. There are three areas where the OTPWMU could have improved its operations: better recordkeeping, implementation of standard SOPs, and increased transparency about the witness payments.

Based on available information, it seems that how the payments are processed administratively could have been improved, by providing more accurate details about the payments and avoiding lump payments under vague categories such as "miscellaneous."[116] More accurate and detailed records of the payments would help the Judges and parties determine whether payments were legitimate and would contribute to a better understanding of the issue by the SCSL's audience.

The OTP has conceded that information about WMU payments is subject to disclosure and has, it claims, disclosed all such information to the Defense. However, OTP protocol on negotiation with insider witnesses and details about OTPWMU operations remains unavailable. In spite of the Prosecutor's apparent reliance on the professionalism of his staff, there is a clear need for SOPs for OTP operations.[117] Clear SOPs would help reduce questionable instances of witness handling, and would reduce the likelihood of "negotiated" assistance and support for insider witnesses. SOPs could further improve the recordkeeping protocol of the OTPWMU, and would therefore make records about witness payments more clear and transparent, facilitating open debate and communication about the purpose and role of the payments. Indeed, according to the Prosecution's rationale for the payments, SOPs and clear records could help improve witness protection programs in national and international jurisdictions by providing information on what security concerns exist for witnesses during the investigation stage, before they come under the protection of the Registry's WVS.

If the payments were made in good faith, as the Prosecution claims, then no harm can be done by disclosing this information and making information about the payments public, as long as sensitive identifying information is redacted. The Prosecution's lack of transparency, especially considering their role as "ministers of justice assisting in the administration of justice"[118] and evidence about other instances of investigatory misconduct related to inducing testimony[119] raises questions about the confidence the Prosecution had in the proper conduct of investigations with regard to witness payments.

---

[114] *Maximizing Legacy, supra* note 107, at 18.

[115] *UN Report on Witness Protection, supra* note 21, at 56–57.

[116] On one rare occasion, the Prosecution noted that payments were always made in combined amounts not for only lost wages, but for lost wages, transportation, and meals. Trial Transcript, Taylor (SCSL-03–01-T), Trial Chamber II, at 95–100 (Oct. 16, 2008).

[117] *See, e.g.*, Van Tuyl, *supra* note 28, at 36–37.

[118] Prosecutor's Request for Review of Reconsideration, Barayagwiza v. Prosecutor, Decision (ICTR-97–19-AR72), Appeals Chamber (Mar. 31, 2000), Separate Opinion of Judge Shahabuddeen, para. 68.

[119] Written Reasons – Decision on the Admissibility of Certain Prior Statements of the Accused Given to the Prosecution, RUF (SCSL-04–15-T-1188), paras. 51, 68 (June 30, 2008) (finding that the Prosecutor's conduct in the investigation and questioning of Issa Sesay "borders on a semblance of arm-twisting and holding out

The lack of transparency and accountability regarding the OTPWMU is problematic and could have negative repercussions for the SCSL's legacy. Greater transparency could have offset possible negative demonstration effects about the fair trial rights of defendants and the role and responsibilities of prosecutors and could have set clearer expectations about the relationship between the OTP and its witnesses. As an intervener in Sierra Leonean post-conflict society, the SCSL should increase its transparency and accountability – and the perception of this in Sierra Leone – in order to avoid undermining its own efforts to promote justice and accountability.[120]

The OTP's lack of transparency was exacerbated by the Chambers' failure to adequately address the problem. As discussed previously, the Trial Chambers failed to address serious allegations about the effect and consequences of the payments, taking a narrow view of what could amount to serious violations of fair trial rights. An important part of the defense arguments related to witness payments is that they were inherently unjust, and detracted from the judicial process. Beyond a simple evaluation of whether the witnesses lied, the Defense contended that the payments may have affected the reliability of the evidence or influenced its content in ways that shaded or distorted the truth. This is a contention the Chambers should have dealt with in the course of the trials and final judgments, but did not. The search for the truth is a fundamental tenet of a fair judicial process, and should have been a primary concern of the Chambers at the SCSL. Although there is some evidence that Judges grasped the gravity of the issue,[121] there was no direct engagement with these serious concerns in judicial decisions. The Chambers, to the extent the OTP payments were discussed at all, framed the issue as narrowly as possible. The Trial Chambers had an obligation to thoroughly assess the weight and credibility of witness testimony, and in so doing, should have considered any motivations to lie and the witness's responses during cross-examination, which was not done in the *RUF* and *AFRC* trials.[122]

This problem is not unique to the SCSL. Trial Chambers at the ICTR were also faced with the issue of OTP witness payments in evaluating the credibility of witness testimony. However, at that tribunal, the Chambers engaged directly with the issue and recognized its seriousness with regard to the administration of justice. Moreover, Chambers there have requested the OTP to provide the Court ex parte detailed statements of expenses so the Judges could evaluate all payments and determine which payments would be exculpatory.[123] The ICTR Chambers have also engaged more with the nuance of the argument,

promises and inducements to the Accused in the course of the interrogation and particularly during the un-recorded conversations in the course of the break in order to sustain the Accused's cooperation with the prosecution," and were therefore excluded as "involuntary having been so obtained out of 'fear of prejudice and the hope of advantage.'"). *See also* Van Tuyl, *supra* note 28.

[120] J. Stromseth, *Post-Conflict Rule of Law Building: The Need for a Multi-Layered, Synergistic Approach*, 49 WM. & MARY L. REV. 1443, 1455 (2008) [hereinafter *Post-Conflict Rule of Law*].

[121] *See, e.g.*, Trial Transcript, RUF (SCSL-04–15-T), Trial Chamber I, at 68 (lines 4–9) (Mar. 3, 2006).

[122] *See, e.g.*, Appeals Judgment, Nahimana, Barayagwiza and Ngeze v. Prosecutor (ICTR-99–52-A), Appeals Chamber, para. 194 (Nov. 28, 2007).

[123] Decision on Prosper Mugiraneza's Motion for Records of All Payments Made Directly or Indirectly to Witness D, Prosecutor v. Bizimungu et al. (ICTR-99–50-T), Trial Chamber II, para. 6 (Feb. 18, 2008); Decision on Joseph Nzirorera's Motion for Reconsideration of Oral Decision on Motion to Compel Full Disclosure of ICTR Payments for the Benefit of Witnesses G and T and Motion for Admission of Exhibit: Payments Made for the Benefit of Witness G, Prosecutor v. Karemera et al. (ICTR-98–44-T), Trial Chamber III, para. 16 (May 29, 2008).

acknowledging that the issue of witness payments could be used as a bargaining tool and could undermine the legitimacy of the ICTR as an institution. For example, one Trial Chamber recognized that an "unfortunate side-effect of the necessary practice of providing benefits to witnesses who agree to testify for the prosecution may be that their testimony is sometimes influenced to some degree by such payments."[124] The Chamber stated that it accordingly took what it considered to be excessive payments into consideration as an "integral part" of its assessment of the weight afforded to their testimony.[125] However, although the Chamber directly noted in the judgment that some witnesses had received "extensive benefits, financial and otherwise, from the prosecution in exchange for [their] testimony," the Chamber nevertheless relied on these witnesses in its findings.[126]

The ICTR Trial Chambers' acknowledgement of the excessive nature of the payments and their possible impact on the veracity of the witnesses testimony is more than the SCSL Chambers engaged with the issue in all cases except the last. Unlike at the SCSL, notwithstanding the fact that the Chambers relied on these witnesses in their final judgments, they engaged with the issue during trial and evaluated the payments themselves ex parte. They acknowledged that witnesses who have been paid or who are suspected of testifying in exchange for money should be approached with caution. This was the approach of both Trial and Appeals Chambers.[127] This approach is more transparent and thus less problematic for the demonstration effects of the ICTR.

A careful examination of such issues is especially important when, as in these cases, the witnesses are accomplice witnesses. According to the ICTR Appeals Chamber, a Chamber is "bound [...] to carefully consider the totality of circumstances in which [evidence] was tendered."[128] The totality of the circumstances – which included payments by the OTP – was not considered in the *RUF* and *AFRC* trials. In the *Taylor* judgment, the Trial Chamber stated that its main consideration in evaluating the evidence of accomplice witnesses was whether there was an ulterior motive to lie. This is less restrictive than a requirement to consider the totality of the circumstances of an accomplice's testimony, which would suggest an evaluation of the broader arguments about the threat to the judicial process and administration of justice.[129] Although a Chamber is not required to set forth every step of

---

[124] Decision on Joseph Nzirorera's Motion to Dismiss for Abuse of Process: Payments to Prosecution Witnesses and 'Requete de Mathieu Ngirumpatse en Retrait de l'Act d'Accusation,' Karemera et al. (ICTR-98–44-T), Trial Chamber III, para. 7 (Oct. 27, 2008). *See also* Decision on Prosecution's Motion to Permit Limited Disclosure of Information Regarding Payments and Benefits Provided to Witness ADE and His Family, Rules 66(C) and 68(D) of the Rules of Procedure and Evidence, Karemera et al. (ICTR-98–44-T), Trial Chamber III (June 21, 2006).

[125] Decision on Joseph Nzirorera's Motion to Dismiss for Abuse of Process: Payments to Prosecution Witnesses and 'Requete de Mathieu Ngirumpatse en Retrait de l'Act d'Accusation,' Karemera et al. (ICTR-98–44-T), Trial Chamber III, paras. 7, 9 (Oct. 27, 2008).

[126] *See, e.g.,* Judgment and Sentence, Karemera et al. (ICTR-98–44-T), Trial Chamber III, paras. 175, 178, 194 (Feb. 2, 2012).

[127] Appeals Judgment, Nahimana et al. v. Prosecutor (ICTR-99–52-A), Appeals Chamber, para. 545 (Nov. 28, 2007). Noting that "[E]ven if the [evidence is] insufficient to establish with certainty that Witness AFX was paid for his testimony [...], it is nonetheless difficult to ignore this possibility, which undeniably casts doubt on the credibility of this witness." *See also* Trial Judgment, Prosecutor v. Zigiranyirazo (ICTR-01–73-T), Trial Chamber III, paras. 139–40 (Dec. 18, 2008).

[128] Appeals Judgment, Muvunyi v. Prosecution (ICTR-2000–55A-A), Appeals Chamber, para. 128 (Aug. 29, 2008).

[129] Judgment, Taylor (SCSL-03–01-T-1281), Trial Chamber II, para. 183 (May 18, 2012).

its reasoning,[130] the judicial position on such fair trial rights will be an integral part of the SCSL's legacy, and this lacuna is a potential area where there could be a "negative" legacy for the Court.

B. Demonstration Effects in the Local Context

In Sierra Leone, there are complex relationships between power/authority and responsibility/legitimacy, cultural dynamics that very likely influence local impressions of the SCSL.[131] This, combined with other cultural dynamics and the reality of living in an impoverished post-conflict society, could increase the possibility that the Court leaves a legacy of "negotiated justice" as a result of its treatment of witness payments. The specific risk is that the practice of witness payments could lead to the idea that justice is a "pay to play" process, and could foster sentiments of injustice, as direct perpetrators benefit from the SCSL while victims receive nothing.

The particular issue of payment to insider witnesses is especially important given the patron-client dimensions of Sierra Leonean culture described in anthropological literature. In patron-client relationships, "big men" accumulate power that is balanced by generosity and benevolence to their supporters and dependents.[132] According to Kelsall:

> [P]atrons (who may be elders, chiefs, or "big men") provide resources, opportunities and services (for example, land, employment, protection) to their clients (who may be descendants, followers or slaves), who provide tribute, services and allegiance [...], in return, while helping to buy off or coerce potential opponents and dissenters.[133]

Such relationships are reciprocal: "big persons are responsible for the needs of their dependents, and their dependents rely on them for resources, support, and opportunities."[134] Patrimonialism has deep roots in Sierra Leone,[135] where patron-client relationships are a norm.[136] Indeed, this norm structured the rebel forces during the conflict,[137] and we can assume that insider witnesses testifying in SCSL trials are familiar with patrimonialism and patron-clientism.

In many ways, the SCSL – or the OTP in particular – could be considered a "big person"[138] that would thus be expected to provide its clients with necessary resources.[139] The clients,

---

[130] Appeals Judgment, Seromba v. Prosecutor (ICTR-2001–66-A), Appeals Chamber, para. 94, (Mar. 12, 2008); Appeals Judgment, Simba v. Prosecutor (ICTR-01–76-A), Appeals Chamber, para. 143 (Nov. 27, 2007), Appeals Judgment, Gacumbitsi v. Prosecutor (ICTR-2001–64-A), Appeals Chamber, para. 115 (July 7, 2006).

[131] *See, e.g.*, G. Millar, *Between Western Theory and Local Practice*, 29 CONFLICT RESOLUTION Q. 177, 188 (2011).

[132] R. Shaw, MEMORIES OF THE SLAVE TRADE: RITUAL AND THE HISTORICAL IMAGINATION IN SIERRA LEONE 256 (2002).

[133] KELSALL, *supra* note 8, at 76 (internal citations omitted).

[134] Millar, *supra* note 131, at 188.

[135] KELSALL, *supra* note 8, at 77.

[136] Millar, *supra* note 131, at 187. *See also* KELSALL, *supra* note 8, at 74–80.

[137] KELSALL, *supra* note 8, at 79, 154.

[138] For example, Millar writes that "The TRC, as a U.N.-organized and primarily white, European-run operation, was recognized as a patron by Sierra Leoneans." Millar, *supra* note 131, at 187.

[139] Millar, *supra* note 131, at 187. *See also* KELSALL, *supra* note 8, at 233 (writing about how defense lawyers in the *RUF* trial had "expected that the power of the U.N. tribunal would make the witnesses fearful of not telling the truth," "but in fact [it had] the opposite effect.").

or witnesses in this case, would be interested in ensuring that they can maintain the beneficial relationship with the court – and could therefore be motivated to tell lies or embellish
the truth in a manner inconsistent with the goals of judicial fact-finding in the courtroom.
Witnesses might also feel as though they should tell the Prosecution what it wants to hear,
if they see the Prosecution as a benefactor or boss-like figure and the Defense as an oppo-
nent or dissenter.[140] They could fear that if they do not tell the Prosecution what it wants to
hear, they will stop receiving funds or will not be invited to further interviews.[141] This might
extend to the courtroom, given the promise of continued support for security measures
after the trial. If they do a "good job," witnesses might consider that they would be in a better
bargaining position for future assistance.

Although admittedly scant, there is some evidence that the Court is being perceived as
a "pay to play" organization.[142] For example, the Taylor defense contends that it has been
asked during SCSL outreach events why the Defense does not pay its witnesses more
than the OTP to ensure witness participation.[143] This has been echoed by RUF defense
counsel.[144] Moreover, some related research has been done on this regarding the Sierra
Leone Truth and Reconciliation Commission (TRC), whose relationship with the SCSL
is discussed by Alpha Sesay in this volume. One anthropologist noted that "a substantial portion of the victims and survivors who testified had done so in the hope that this
would give them access to economic assistance."[145] Most persons who gave statements
to the TRC viewed the statement giving as "part of an exchange that would bring them
material benefit."[146] The TRC was viewed as a source of resources, similar to the "patron"
in a patron-client relationship.[147] Some refused to give statements because they realized
they would get no material benefit and were angry and felt insulted that the TRC, with
its relatively significant funding,[148] would not compensate them for a public statement of
their memories.[149]

For those that did testify before the TRC, the lack of compensation was a painful reality.[150] Shaw's research on the TRC shows that a patron-client-like reciprocal relationship and
expectations of benefits motivated persons testifying before the TRC:

> For [Adama], telling her story before an audience [...] was neither an act of remember-
> ing for its own sake, nor a pre-existing "need," but part of what she hoped would become

[140] Kelsall, *supra* note 8, at 35.
[141] This was what one potential Prosecution witness said happened. Decision on Defense Motion for Disclosure of Statement and Prosecution Payments Made to DCT-097, Taylor (SCSL-03-1-T), Trial Chamber II, at 23 (Sept. 8, 2010) (noting the defense submission that DCT-097 was interviewed and paid by the Prosecution until the Prosecution told him "they were not getting what they needed from him" and ceased payments).
[142] *See, e.g.*, Trial Transcript, RUF (SCSL-04-15), Trial Chamber I, at 70 (lines 13–17) (Mar. 3, 2006) (one defense counsel noted, "I have people knocking on my office door daily looking for benefit.") (lines 16–17).
[143] Trial Transcript, *Taylor* (SCSL-03-01-T), Trial Chamber II, at 9 (lines 1–8) (Mar. 10, 2011).
[144] Trial Transcript, RUF (SCSL-04-15-T), Trial Chamber I, at 68 (lines 4–9) (Mar. 3, 2006).
[145] Shaw, *supra* note 111, at 2.
[146] *Id.* at 15.
[147] *Id.*
[148] From the perspective of an ordinary person in Sierra Leone. The TRC actually operated on a relatively slim budget and faced considerable budgetary problems. B. Dougherty, *Searching for Answers: Sierra Leone's Truth and Reconciliation Commission*, 8 African Studies Q. 39, 43 (2004).
[149] Shaw, *supra* note 111, at 16.
[150] *Id.* at 22. It should be noted that the TRC did not provide reimbursement for lost wages, which the SCSL did provide to all witnesses.

a reciprocal relationship. By participating in this national and international forum, she had hoped to become part of a circuit connecting her to the national and international resources that would help her rebuild her life and raise her children.[151]

Shaw's research suggests that Sierra Leoneans might have also been motivated to testify before the SCSL for material gain with expectations of entering into a reciprocal give/take relationship. The existing patron-client dynamic in Sierra Leonean culture may have created expectations of such a relationship with the OTP, generating the incentive for witnesses to prolong such a relationship.

Compounding this patron-client dynamic are attitudes about truth telling. Millar writes that clients, who are "very explicitly not the equals of their patrons," do not take an equal role in spreading knowledge and truth.[152] Indeed, "[i]n Sierra Leone the control and communication of knowledge is far more involved in the management of power and influence [and] authority."[153] Tim Kelsall writes about the difficulty of communication between lawyers and witnesses in the SCSL trials, and notes the importance of ambivalence in Sierra Leonean culture.[154] Kelsall hypothesizes that:

> [W]itnesses viewed court staff with circumspection. In some cases this led them to not tell the full truth in their pre-trial statements; in others it led to them not telling the full truth in court, problems that became particularly acute under questioning by hostile lawyers from the opposite team. During these moments [...] witnesses fell back on a repertoire of culturally prized linguistic strategies designed to protect them from the possibly malefic intentions of potential adversaries. They hedged, they qualified, they equivocated, they evaded, and in many cases they ran rings around the lawyers, problems compounded by a slipshod investigation and a witness protection regime that provided witnesses incentives to lie.[155]

This circumspect attitude about the Court staff, defense counsel, and truth increases the risk of a possible negative demonstration effect of the Court's treatment of the witness payments. If the Court is viewed suspiciously, as a "patron" with clients who are insider witnesses, the value of its truth-telling function could be compromised.

The OTP practice of providing insider witnesses with benefits and support also exacerbates a problem that has plagued the SCSL since its inception: perceptions of injustice arising out of OTP discretion in charging only a few high-ranking individuals. The payments to insider witnesses raise ethical issues if Sierra Leoneans see this as a reward for their crimes or relationship with the accused.[156] One of the negative local perceptions of the SCSL is that insider witnesses who testified before the court are considered to bear the "greatest responsibility."[157] OTPWMU witness payments risk undermining the legitimacy of the organization: they raise the question of whether some of these "second-tier" perpetrators may have benefited financially from the Court in exchange for serving as prosecution

---

[151] *Id.* at 23.

[152] Millar, *supra* note 131, at 189.

[153] *Id.* at 192.

[154] KELSALL, *supra* note 8, at 232, 175 ("Indirectness, obliqueness, dissembling and circumspection are practiced arts that function then to protect individuals from the possibly malign intentions of others.").

[155] *Id.* at 35.

[156] Such ethical issues are not necessarily restricted to the Sierra Leone conflict, and would likely arise in other justice systems, international or national.

[157] S. Horovitz, *Sierra Leone: Interaction between International and National Responses to the Mass Atrocities*, 45–46 DOMAC (2009).

witnesses. Because there are no SOPs and the Prosecution has not divulged much about its internal decisions, perceptions of injustice cannot be debated with clear and accurate information.[158]

IV. CONCLUSION

As a "hybrid" tribunal designed to allow victims to see justice being done, the SCSL was meant to demonstrate to Sierra Leoneans what the rule of law looked like and how justice operated. This chapter examined one aspect of the demonstration effect of the SCSL: the possible consequences of payments made by the Court to witnesses for their security, assistance, and support. Whether and how the practices of hybrid courts have a *negative* impact in the countries where they operate because of complex cultural dynamics might not be readily seen or anticipated by outside interveners. Although examples of this potentially "negative legacy" are anecdotal, this chapter contends that this issue is serious enough to warrant further study among academics exploring legacy and impact issues and discussion among policymakers working on international justice issues. It is doubtful that this problem would be limited to the Sierra Leone context, and could be manifested in other situations where international organizations intervene in post-conflict or developing nations.

---

[158] *See, e.g.,* Kerr & Lincoln, *supra* note 108, at 20; *see also* Shaw, *supra* note 111, at 16 (noting that civilians were angry at the expense of the TRC while they received no material benefit for participating and had no jobs).

24

SCSL Practice on Cooperation with the Host State and Third States: A Contribution to Africa and International Criminal Justice

Shakiratu Sanusi[*]

I. INTRODUCTION

The operationalization of the conceptual ideal of a hybrid international tribunal created by bilateral agreement between a government and the United Nations, located in the country in which the atrocities took place and being a significant leitmotif of the restoration of peace and security domestically and regionally, was an additional symbol[1] of the commitment of the international community to the burgeoning fight against impunity. It also illustrated pointedly the interdependence of economies and societies and the increasing importance of international cooperation in a global world.

International cooperation is a core purpose of the United Nations. Article 1, Chapter 1: Purposes and Principles of the United Nations states, inter alia:

> The purposes of the United Nations are: To maintain international peace and security, and to that end: to take effective collective measures for the prevention and removal of threats to the peace, and for the suppression of acts of aggression or other breaches of the peace, and to bring about by peaceful means, and in conformity with the principles of justice and international law, adjustment or settlement of international disputes or situations which might lead to a breach of the peace;
>
> ...
>
> To achieve international co-operation in solving international problems of an economic, social, cultural, or humanitarian character, and in promoting and encouraging respect for human rights and for fundamental freedoms for all without distinction as to race, sex, language, or religion; ....

Fundamental to the operation and success of the Special Court as an institution was the will on the part of the member states of the United Nations to manifest their commitment to international cooperation, financially and politically, in fulfillment of one of the purposes and principles of the UN Charter.

---

[*] Formerly Legal Adviser and Senior Legal Adviser to the Registrar, Special Court for Sierra Leone.
[1] With regard to international tribunals, the ICTY and ICTR were earlier institutional manifestations of international justice and international cooperation necessitating cooperation in the arrest, transfer, trial, and subsequent detention of alleged perpetrators of war crimes. Both were also established in third countries with the attendant arrangements necessary for the successful discharge of the mandate of each.

II. BACKGROUND

The creation and subsequent establishment of the Special Court for Sierra Leone (hereinafter SCSL or "Court") as set out in UN Security Council Resolution 1315 of 2000[2] was predicated on international cooperation for its success both operationally and politically. It required political will on the part of the United Nations and its member states to enter into an agreement with the government of Sierra Leone. In noting the negative impact of the existing security situation on the administration of justice in Sierra Leone, the resolution recognized the urgency of international cooperation in strengthening the judicial system of Sierra Leone. In this regard the resolution observed the contribution that could be made by qualified persons from West African states, the Commonwealth, other member states of the United Nations, and international organizations to expedite the process of bringing justice and reconciliation to Sierra Leone and the region. It was therefore a model that, from inception, noted and based itself on international cooperation as a necessity for its operation and consequent success.[3]

Specifically the Secretary-General was tasked, in the resolution, to report and make recommendations on key aspects of the establishment of a special court that relied heavily on international cooperation from the international community. The recommendations were to cover consideration of any additional agreements that may be required for the provision of international assistance necessary for the establishment and functioning of the court, and the level of participation, support, and technical assistance of qualified persons from UN member states, Economic Community of West African States (ECOWAS) member states, and the Commonwealth necessary for the efficient, independent, and impartial functioning of the court, and the amount of voluntary contributions in the form of funds, equipment, and services including the offer of expert personnel that may be needed as well as whether it was feasible for the court to receive expertise and advice from the existing international criminal tribunals.

It is notable that regional cooperation, through ECOWAS, contributed significantly to the establishment of national and regional security – a precursor to regional stability that provided the groundswell for the establishment of the court. ECOWAS, as the regional organization directly concerned, took the lead in trying to bring about the return of the democratically elected government of Sierra Leone,[4] including through the imposition of sanctions.

III. OPERATIONAL POINTS

Although the Court is established by agreement between the government of Sierra Leone and the United Nations, practical arrangements for its establishment and operation are

---

[2] Adopted by the Security Council at its 4186th meeting on August 14, 2000.

[3] See further *Fifth Report of the Secretary-General on the United Nations Mission in Sierra Leone*, S/2000/751, para. 9ff (July 31, 2000).

[4] See further U.N. Security Council documents S/1997/777, S/1997/776, S/1997/499, S/1997/646, and S/1997/695. *The Final Communique of the Summit of the Economic Community of West African States*, held at Abuja on August 28 and 29, 1997, S/1997/695, paras. 19 to 28, deals with regional peace and security and sets out heads of states and governments' objectives in relation to Sierra Leone; namely (1) the early reinstatement of the legitimate government of President Tejan Kabbah, (2) the return of peace and security; and (3) the resolution of the issues of refugees and displaced persons.

dependent on third parties such as member states, intergovernmental organizations, and nongovernmental organizations in terms of financial contributions, and contributions of personnel, equipment, and services. The government of Sierra Leone was to furnish the land on which the premises of the Court were eventually established.[5] All other requirements were primarily met by the voluntary contribution of third parties – financial, personnel, or otherwise in the spirit of international cooperation. Additional contributions from Sierra Leone were the provision of prison staff and police officers seconded to the court, and there was in place agreements with the fire service, for example, to provide services to the Court.

Operationally, the Court has benefited from the provision of services of seconded personnel from many countries and agencies, unfunded international interns, funded Sierra Leonean interns,[6] and, over the years, staff on-loan from various international tribunals such as the International Criminal Court (ICC) and the International Criminal Tribunal for Rwanda (ICTR). Pro bono lawyers have also assisted with the provision of legal advice on aspects of the Court's work.

IV. FINANCIAL COOPERATION

Despite reservations expressed in the Secretary-General's Report, as discussed in Sara Kendall's chapter in this volume, the proposed funding mechanism of voluntary contributions[7] was selected. In the report, the Secretary-General wrote:

A financial mechanism based entirely on voluntary contributions will not provide the assured and continuous source of funding which would be required to appoint the judges,

---

[5] This requirement for the government of Sierra Leone was set out in the Article 5 of the Agreement between the United Nations and the Government of Sierra Leone on the Establishment of a Special Court for Sierra Leone of January 16, 2002. The government shall assist in the provision of premises for the Special Court and such utilities, facilities, and other services as may be necessary for its operation. *See also Headquarters Agreement between the Republic of Sierra Leone and the Special Court for Sierra Leone of October 21, 2003*, at http://www.sc-sl.org/LinkClick.aspx?fileticket=z8NhRqbTE3g%3d&tabid=176 (last visited Nov. 28, 2011).

[6] For example, in the *Eighth Annual Report of the President of the Special Court for Sierra Leone* [hereinafter *Eighth Annual Report*], it is stated on page 31 that during the relevant period of July 2010 to March 2011:

two funded Sierra Leonean interns were recruited for the Sub-Office in The Hague to perform duties within the Outreach, Section, [t]wo funded National Professional Interns were recruited for professional services in the Office of the Prosecutor and the Court Management Section in Freetown, sixteen funded Sierra Leonean interns were … recruited to perform tasks within the Registry and the Office of the Prosecutor, … and forty-seven unfunded international interns worked at the Special Court for Sierra Leone in both Freetown and The Hague.
Available at http://www.sc-sl.org/LinkClick.aspx?fileticket=kK8RBeHGowQ%3d&tabid=53 (last visited Nov. 29, 2011).

[7] Article 6 of the Agreement between the United Nations and the Government of Sierra Leone:

Expenses of the Special Court
The expenses of the Special Court shall be borne by voluntary contributions from the international community. It is understood that the Secretary-General will commence the process of establishing the Court when he has sufficient contributions in hand to finance the establishment of the Court and 12 months of its operations plus pledges equal to the anticipated expenses of the following 24 months of the Court's operation. It is further understood that the Secretary-General will continue to seek contributions equal to the anticipated expenses of the Court beyond its first three years of operation.

the Prosecutor and the Registrar, to contract the services of all administrative and support staff and to purchase the necessary equipment. The risks associated with the establishment of an operation of this kind with insufficient funds, or without long-term assurances of continuous availability of funds, are very high, in terms of both moral responsibility and loss of credibility of the Organization, and its exposure to legal liability.[8]

Responsibility for fund-raising falls to the Management Committee assisting the Secretary-General of the United Nations.[9]

The requirement to secure funding has taken up a large chunk of the Court's administrators' time.[10] As recently as October 6, 2011, the UN Secretary-General wrote[11] to the President of the Security Council appealing for assessed funding until the completion of the Court's work as there was insufficient voluntary contributions. Consequently, the General Assembly authorized the Secretary-General exceptionally to provide up to 9.9 million USD to supplement voluntary contributions. Further funds were likely to be required for the Court's budget in 2012.[12]

The Court's convicted persons are serving their sentences in Rwanda pursuant to an amended agreement on enforcement of sentence between the SCSL and the Republic of Rwanda of March 18, 2009. On August 13 and October 26, 2009, the President of the Special Court designated Rwanda as the state where SCSL's convicted persons would serve their sentences. The Court's convicted persons were transferred to Rwanda on October 31, 2009.[13] Given the Court's voluntary funding regime, funding for the duration of the enforcement of

---

Should voluntary contributions be insufficient for the Court to implement its mandate, the Secretary-General and the Security Council shall explore alternate means of financing the Special Court.

[8] *Report of the Secretary-General on the Establishment of a Special Court for Sierra Leone*, S/2000/915, at 13 (Oct.4, 2000).

[9] Article 7 of the Agreement between the United Nations and the Government of Sierra Leone states:

Management Committee
It is the understanding of the Parties that interested States will establish a management committee to assist the Secretary-General in obtaining adequate funding, and provide advice and policy direction on all non-judicial aspects of the operation of the Court, including questions of efficiency, and to perform other functions as agreed by interested States. The management committee shall consist of important contributors to the Special Court. The Government of Sierra Leone and the Secretary-General will also participate in the management committee.

[10] See the *Eighth Annual Repor tand Ninth Annual Report* from page 38ff and page 20ff, respectively, for the most recent efforts required to raise funds. This level of fund-raising has always been a significant part of the role of the Court's administrators.

[11] Letter dated October 6, 2010 from the Secretary-General addressed to the President of the Security Council, S/2010/560 (Oct. 29, 2010).

[12] The *Eighth Annual Report* of the SCSL states that a subvention grant of $2,356,750 may be authorized by the United Nations for the Court's budget for 2012, page 35.It is confirmed in the *Ninth Annual Report* at page 30 that a subvention grant of $9,066,400 was granted to the Special Court on the condition that fundraising efforts are intensified with a total of 222 fundraising letters sent out in the 12 months prior to the *Ninth Annual Report*.

[13] Article 22 of the Court's Statute provides:

Enforcement of sentences
1. Imprisonment shall be served in Sierra Leone. If circumstances so require, imprisonment may also be served in any of the States which have concluded with the International Criminal Tribunal for Rwanda or the International Criminal Tribunal for the former Yugoslavia an agreement for the enforcement of sentences, and which have indicated to the Registrar of the Special Court their willingness to accept

sentences –Issa Sesay was handed down the longest prison sentence of fifty-two years – will be required.

A consideration of the diplomatic and fund-raising meetings set out in the SCSL's Eighth and Ninth Annual Reports[14] gives an indication of the extent of international cooperation in its work. Not only does this provide a flavor of the amount of fund-raising required, it allows us to take a view of the extent of cooperation required to manage the work of the Court, substantively and operationally. Following his arrest and transfer to the Court, the last trial, *Prosecutor v. Charles Taylor*,[15] is now being held in the premises of the Special

convicted persons. The Special Court may conclude similar agreements for the enforcement of sentences with other States.2. Conditions of imprisonment, whether in Sierra Leone or in a third State, shall be governed by the law of the State of enforcement subject to the supervision of the Special Court. The State of enforcement shall be bound by the duration of the sentence, subject to article 23 of the present Statute.A number of sentence enforcement agreements were signed with various countries, for example, Finland, Sweden, and United Kingdom. *See further* http://www.sc-sl.org/DOCUMENTS/tabid/176/Default.aspx.

[14] *See further Eighth Annual Report*, Annex I, at 52. The *Ninth Annual Report* provides an overview of similar efforts.

African Union (Office of the Legal Counsel, Office of the Permanent Observer of the African Union to the United Nations), **Australia** (Department of Foreign Affairs and Trade, Agency for International Development), **Austria** (Permanent Representation of Austria to the European Union), **Belgium** (Ministry of Foreign Affairs), **Canada** (Department of Foreign Affairs and International Trade Permanent Mission of Canada to the United Nations, Embassy of Canada to the Netherlands), **China** (Embassy of China to Sierra Leone), **Czech Republic** (Permanent Representation of Czech Republic to the European Union), **Denmark** (Ministry of Foreign Affairs), **European Union** (High Representative of the Union for Foreign Affairs and Security Policy, European Commission, European Union Delegation to Sierra Leone Working Group on Africa (CO AFR Working Group)), **Finland** (Ministry of Foreign Affairs, Embassy of Finland to Ghana), **Germany** (Embassy of the Federal Republic of Germany to Sierra Leone, Embassy of Germany to Belgium), **Ghana** (Permanent Mission of Ghana to the United Nations), **Ireland** (Ministry of Foreign Affairs, Permanent Representation of Ireland to the European Union), **Israel**Ministry of Foreign Affairs, Permanent Mission of Israel to the United Nations), **Liberia** (Permanent Mission of the Republic of Liberia to the United Nations), **Mongolia** (Ministry of Defence), **The Netherlands** (Ministry of Foreign Affairs, Permanent Mission of the Kingdom of the Netherlands to the United Nations), **Nigeria** (Federal Ministry of Justice), **Norway** (Ministry of Foreign Affairs, Permanent Mission of Norway to the United Nations), **Rwanda** (Ministry of Foreign Affairs, Ministry of Justice, National Prison Services) **Sierra Leone** (Government of Sierra Leone, Permanent Mission of Sierra Leone to the United Nations, Embassy of Sierra Leone in Brussels), **Slovenia** (Permanent Representation of Slovenia to the European Union), **South Africa** (Ministry of Foreign Affairs), **Spain** (Embassy of Spain to Liberia), **Sweden** (Ministry of Foreign Affairs, Permanent Representation of Sweden to the European Union), **Turkey** (Ministry of Foreign Affairs), **United Kingdom** (Foreign & Commonwealth Office, British High Commission in Sierra Leone, Permanent Mission of the United Kingdom to the United Nations, Permanent Representation of the UK to the European Union), Embassy of the United Kingdom to the Netherlands, **United Nations** (Office of the Secretary-General, Office of Legal Affairs, Advisory Committee on Administrative and Budgetary Questions, Department of Peacekeeping Operations, Office on Drugs and Crime (UNO DC), Peacebuilding Commission Peacebuilding Mission in Sierra Leone (UNIPSIL), Peacekeeping Mission in Liberia (UNMIL)), **United States** (State Department, United States Embassy in Sierra Leone, United States Embassy in Liberia, United States Mission to the United Nations), **International Tribunals and Courts** (Extraordinary Chambers in the Courts of Cambodia, International Court of Justice, International Criminal Court International Criminal Tribunal for the former Yugoslavia, International Criminal Tribunal for Rwanda Special Tribunal for Lebanon), **International Organizations** (International Committee for the Red Cross, Pan African Parliament), **Foundations** (Gordon Foundation, MacArthur Foundation, Open Society Institute).

[15] Charles Taylor, the former president of Liberia, was indicted under seal on March 7, 2003. The indictment was announced on June 4, 2003, on his first trip outside of Liberia. In August 2003 Charles Taylor resigned as

Tribunal for Lebanon (STL), although it was previously held in the premises of the ICC until that Court's requirement for more court space precluded the continued provision of court space and administrative services to the SCSL. The transfer of the Taylor trial was possible only with agreement of the host state, the Netherlands. The ICC's detention center holds Mr. Taylor, the government of the Netherlands facilitates the movement of witnesses to allow them to give evidence in The Hague from not only Sierra Leone but also Liberia and other countries, the Court's convicted persons are serving their sentences in Rwanda under an enforcement of sentences agreement, there are agreements in place for the protection of witnesses, and security has been provided by Nigerian and most latterly Mongolian forces under the aegis of the UN peacekeeping troops from Liberia pursuant to a number of UN Security Council resolutions.[16] It is evident that international cooperation is key. The meetings with the various foundations point to fund-raising for legacy projects, an important part of the work of the Court.

V. INTERNATIONAL COOPERATION AND THE PROVISION OF ADMINISTRATIVE, SECURITY, AND RELATED SUPPORT

In requesting UN assistance to establish a special court, the security of the court, its premises, equipment, personnel and that of the accused was the government's main concern.[17]

In Resolution 1400 (2002), the Security Council "endorses UNAMSIL's[18] providing, without prejudice to its capabilities to perform its specified mandate, administrative and related support to the Special Court on a cost-reimbursable basis." The Agreement between the government of Sierra Leone and the United Nations provides for a relationship between UNAMSIL and the SCSL. Article 16 of the Statute states,

> Recognizing the responsibility of the Government under international law to ensure the security, safety and protection of persons referred to in this Agreement and its present incapacity to do so pending the restructuring and rebuilding of its security forces, it is agreed that the United Nations Mission in Sierra Leone shall provide the necessary security to premises and personnel of the Special Court, subject to an appropriate mandate by the Security Council and within its capabilities.

When it came time to draw down UNAMSIL's forces,[19] the need for arrangements to be put in place for providing security to the SCSL on its termination was apparent.[20] SC Resolution 1620 (2005)[21] established the United Nations Integrated Office in Sierra Leone

---

president and went into exile in Nigeria. He was transferred to the Special Court on March 29, 2006. Because of concerns about regional security should the trial be held in Sierra Leone, the Special Court arranged for the trial to be held at The Hague in the Netherlands. Charles Taylor was transferred to The Hague on June 30, 2006.

[16] *See further* S.C. Res. 1626 (2005), 1638 (2005), and 1712.

[17] *Agreement between the Government of Sierra Leone and the United Nations*, para. 11.

[18] United Nations Mission in Sierra Leone.

[19] *See* S.C. Res. 1537 (2004).

[20] S.C. Res. 1610 (2005). "Specifically, the Security Council underline[d] also the importance of providing effective security for the Special Court for Sierra Leone after UNAMSIL has withdrawn, and requests the Secretary-General to make recommendations on this to the Security Council as soon as possible."

[21] August 31, 2005.

(UNIOSIL), which was tasked with several objectives including "coordinat[ing] with the Special Court for Sierra Leone." On the termination of UNAMSIL's mandate on December 31, 2005, UNIOSIL, the United Nations Integrated Office in Sierra Leone, took over on January 1, 2006 and continued to provide administrative and related support to the Special Court on a cost-reimbursable basis.

In addition to administrative, logistical, and other support, security support was another element from which the Court benefitted by way of international cooperation. The United Nations Mission in Liberia, UNMIL, established by Security Council Resolution 1509 of September 19, 2003, among other things was mandated to support the implementation of the cease-fire agreement and the peace process, protect civilians, and support humanitarian and human rights activities, as well as assist in national security reform, including national police training and the formation of a new, restructured military and restoration of democratic governance through popular election. On September 19, 2005, the UN Security Council adopted Resolution 1626 authorizing UNMIL to deploy UN military personnel to Sierra Leone to provide security for the SCSL. As noted previously, the United Nations Integrated Office in Sierra Leone (UNIOSIL) was established on January 1, 2006 pursuant to United Nations Security Council Resolution 1620 and assigned, amongst other mandated responsibilities, the key task to coordinate and provide support to the SCSL.[22]

The provision of security to the Court, under the terms of the relevant Security Council resolutions, required the consent of the troop-contributing countries to a UN mission in a different neighboring country. It also necessitated the increase in UNMIL's personnel to ensure that the provision of troops to Sierra Leone did not reduce UNMIL's capabilities in Liberia, required the planning of a contingency for the evacuation of UNMIL personnel deployed to Sierra Leone as well as officials of the Court in the event of a serious security crisis affecting those personnel and the Court, and the provision of logistical support during the deployment of security personnel.[23]

---

[22] S.C. Res. 1793 (2008) extended the mandate of UNIOSIL until September 30, 2008.

After September 30, 2008, the Security Council explained that:
UNIOSIL should be replaced by a United Nations integrated political office to focus on carrying forward the peacebuilding process, mobilizing international donor support, supporting the work of the Peacebuilding Commission and Fund, and completing any residual tasks left over from UNIOSIL's mandate, in particular promoting national reconciliation and supporting the constitutional reform process.

[23] S.C. Res. 1626 (2005) states,

5. *Authorizes* UNMIL, subject to the consent of the troop-contributing countries concerned and the Government of Sierra Leone, to deploy from November 2005 up to 250 United Nations military personnel to Sierra Leone to provide security for the Special Court for Sierra Leone, as recommended in paragraphs 90 to 94 of the Secretary-General's report of September 1, 2005 (S/2005/560);
6. *Authorizes* a temporary increase in UNMIL's personnel ceiling, to a total of 15,250 United Nations military personnel, for the period from November 15, 2005 to March 31, 2006 in order to ensure that the support provided to the Court does not reduce UNMIL's capabilities in Liberia during its political transition period;
7. *Further authorizes* UNMIL, subject to the consent of troop-contributing countries concerned and of the Government of Sierra Leone, to deploy an adequate number of military personnel to Sierra Leone, if and when needed, to evacuate UNMIL military personnel deployed to Sierra Leone pursuant to paragraph 5 of this resolution and officials of the Special Court for Sierra Leone in the event of a serious security crisis affecting those personnel and the Court;

Acting under Chapter VII, UNMIL's mandate was expanded in Resolution 1638 of 2005[24] to include the apprehension and detention of former president Charles Taylor in the event of a return to Liberia and to transfer him or facilitate his transfer to Sierra Leone for prosecution before the SCSL, and to keep the Liberian government, the Sierra Leonean government, and the Council fully informed.

By Security Council Resolution 1712 (2006), a drawdown of the UNMIL contingent was being considered and special arrangements were made for the continued security to the Court. In addition to securing the premises of the Court, the UN peacekeeping troops (Nigerian until 2006 and Mongolians subsequently) provided security during the movement of detainees and prisoners within and outside of Sierra Leone. In February 2011, the UN peacekeepers of the Court's Mongolian Guard Force completed their mandate and formally handed over security responsibility for the SCSL to the Sierra Leone police.[25]

Resolution 1688 (2006) concerns the transfer of Charles Taylor to the ICC based on a Memorandum of Understanding between the Court and the ICC dated April 13, 2006. In paragraph 4, the Security Council urged all states to assist with proceedings in The Hague:

> [The Security Council requests] all States to cooperate to this end, in particular to ensure the appearance of former President Taylor in the Netherlands for purposes of his trial by the Special Court, and encourages all States as well to ensure that any evidence or witnesses are, upon the request of the Special Court, promptly made available to the Special Court for this purpose.

An important element that cannot be overstated in assuring cooperation in the successful discharge of the Court's mandate and its operation is the support of the United Nations and the leverage it brought to bear in ensuring that its member states cooperated with the work of the Court in several key elements.

VI. INTERNATIONAL COOPERATION AND THE FACILITATION OF TESTIMONY BEFORE THE COURT

An illustration of international cooperation going to the heart of the court's operation is that of the operational requirements necessary to present evidence, be it of the accused or prosecution witnesses, before the Court.

The primacy of the SCSL is limited to national courts in Sierra Leone and does not extend to third states. Although the Court is an international tribunal with the capacity to enter into agreements, it lacks the power to request the surrender of an accused from any third state and to ensure compliance with any such request it may make. This lack of power became relevant when it came to taking steps to surrender Charles Taylor to the jurisdiction of the Court.[26] The Security Council was obliged to pass a resolution to ensure the transfer

---

[24] U.N. Doc. S/RES/1638 (Nov. 11, 2005).

[25] *Eighth Annual Report*, SCSL.

[26] *See further Report of the Secretary-General on the Establishment of a Special Court for Sierra Leone*, S/2000/915 (Oct. 4, 2000). The report states:

> The primacy of the Special Court has concurrent jurisdiction with and primacy over Sierra Leonean courts. Consequently, it has the power to request at any stage of the proceedings that any national Sierra Leonean court defers to its jurisdiction (article 8, para. 2 of the Statute). The primacy of the Special

of the former Liberian leader Taylor to the Court upon his apprehension.[27] In paragraph 4, the Council made clear that all states should assist with proceedings in The Hague:

> [The Security Council requests] all States to cooperate to this end, in particular to ensure the appearance of former President Taylor in the Netherlands for purposes of his trial by the Special Court, and encourages all States as well to ensure that any evidence or witnesses are, upon the request of the Special Court, promptly made available to the Special Court for this purpose.

The Registrar has responsibility to develop long- and short-term plans for the protection of witnesses and victims encompassing protective measures, security arrangements, and relevant support including medical, physical, and psychological support as necessary.[28] In discharge of its mandate, particularly in the *Taylor* trial, the Court needed extensive cooperation with regard to the transit of witnesses while maintaining standards of segregation in compliance with the rules of procedure on witness standards. Operating procedures were required to be implemented to ensure frameworks that the Registrar, and the Court, discharged their functions.[29] Necessary frameworks and operating procedures took account

> Court, however, is limited to the national courts of Sierra Leone and does not extend to the courts of third States. Lacking the power to assert its primacy over national courts in third States in connection with the crimes committed in Sierra Leone, it also lacks the power to request the surrender of an accused from any third State and to induce the compliance of its authorities with any such request. In examining measures to enhance the deterrent powers of the Special Court, the Security Council may wish to consider endowing it with Chapter VII powers for the specific purpose of requesting the surrender of an accused from outside the jurisdiction of the Court.

[27] S.C. Res. 1688 (2006) concerns the transfer of Charles Taylor to the International Criminal Court based on a Memorandum of Understanding between the Special Court and the International Criminal Court dated April 13, 2006.

[28] *Rules of Procedure and EvidenceSection (amended May 29, 2004)*

Rule 34: Witnesses and Victims

(A) The Registrar shall set up a Witnesses and Victims Section which, in accordance with the Statute, the Agreement and the Rules, and in consultation with the Office of the Prosecutor, for Prosecution witnesses, and the Defence Office, for Defence witnesses, shall, amongst other things, perform the following functions with respect to all witnesses, victims who appear before the Special Court, and others who are at risk on account of testimony given by such witnesses, in accordance with their particular needs and circumstances:

  (i) Recommend to the Special Court the adoption of protective and security measures for them;

  (ii) Provide them with adequate protective measures and security arrangements and develop long- and short-term plans for their protection and support;

  (iii) Ensure that they receive relevant support, counselling and other appropriate assistance, including medical assistance, physical and psychological rehabilitation, especially in cases of rape, sexual assault and crimes against children.

(B) he Section personnel shall include experts in trauma, including trauma related to crimes of sexual violence and violence against children. Where appropriate the Section shall cooperate with nongovernmental and intergovernmental organizations.

The Court is also obliged to comply with its own "Best-Practice Recommendations for the Protection & Support of Witnesses" of June 19, 2008.

[29] *See further Eighth Annual Report.* It states, at page 30,

> ... across the Court's four trials, the Witness and Victims' Section, WVS, facilitated the appearance of 557 witnesses before the Court. The Taylor Defence team concluded its case in November 2010, calling a total of 21 witnesses including the accused Charles Taylor, who remained on the stand for 8 months in his defence. During the reporting period the Defence called one of the Court's convicted persons, IssaSesay, to testify. WVS provided all necessary assistance to transfer him from Rwanda to The Hague

of multiple considerations not limited to practical arrangements. It was necessary to consider the possible operation of existing international obligations in various territories on the applicability of universal jurisdiction, domestic immigration border control, and existing sanctions regime. The provision of visas for witnesses transiting through Benelux countries was informed by regional agreements such as the Schengen visa scheme, and multiple domestic agencies were of necessity involved in aspects of the cooperation the Court required in achieving its mandate.

A. Sanctions Regime

An important tool in the arsenal of international campaigning is that of seeking sanctions against regimes to bring pressure to bear to achieve democratic change and as a valuable tool for lasting peace and security. In the context of the operation of the Court, where travel restrictions existed as part of the sanctions imposed against a country or named individuals, it was obliged to consider and make applications for a lifting of the travel restriction to enable testimony to be heard from those who were required as witnesses by either party to the proceedings.

For instance, paragraph 5 of UN Security Council Resolution 1171 (1198)[30] concerning Sierra Leone imposed travel restrictions on certain named persons.[31] For those persons who may or may not have been required to testify, it was imperative to obtain the granting of temporary waivers of the travel ban to enable them to travel internationally to testify at the trial of Charles Taylor. A further UN Security Council Resolution facilitated the cooperation of states in obtaining the necessary testimony of witnesses in the Taylor trial.[32] UN Security Council Resolution 1793 of 2007 exempted witnesses whose presence was required

> to give his testimony, with the cooperation of the Governments of the Netherlands and Rwanda, the International Criminal Tribunal for Rwanda and the International Criminal Court. Further WVS managed the appearance of three high-profile witnesses called by the Prosecution in August 2010. The significant media interest generated by their testimony required additional security and witness protection measures. The Court's obligation to its witnesses does not end with the final judgment of the Court. If the Court fails to respond adequately to ongoing threats against witnesses, the Court would put its witnesses and the credibility of the international criminal justice system at risk. WVS is preparing for the transfer of witness protection responsibilities to the Residual Special Court. In particular, the Registry is beginning discussions with organizations that could host the small Freetown office of the Residual Special Court that would house its two witness protection staff.

[30] Paragraph 5 states:

> Decides that all States shall prevent the entry into or transit through their territories of leading members of the former military junta and of the Revolutionary United Front (RUF), as designated by the Committee established by resolution 1132 (1997), provided that the entry into or transit through a particular State of any such person may be authorized by the same Committee, and provided that nothing in this paragraph shall oblige a State to refuse entry to its territory to its own nationals.

[31] The original list of persons affected by the measures was issued by the Sanctions Committee on Jan. 8, 1998, and was subsequently published in Press Releases SC/6472, SC/6808 and SC/8192, http://www.un.org/sc/committees/1132/tblist.shtml. *See also*http://www.un.org/sc/committees/1132/pdf/6472e.html for the list of names, Press Release SC/6472 (last visited Nov. 28, 2011).

[32] Paragraph 8 S.C. Res. 1793 (2007) states,

> *Acting* under Chapter VII of the Charter of the United Nations, *decides* to exempt from the measures imposed by paragraph 5 of resolution 1171 (1998) the travel of any witnesses whose presence at trial before the Special Court for Sierra Leone is required.

in trials before the Special Court from the measures imposed in Resolution 1171. The delisting procedure is set out in S/Res/1730 (2006).

Additionally, the Court is obliged to also comply with any protective measures[33] handed down by the Trial Chamber. Any applications for a waiver of travel restrictions for a protected witness were required to be made in compliance with any existing protective measures; it was also required that the party to which the request was being made complied also or faced contempt of court.

[33] Rules of Procedure and Evidence of the Special Court for Sierra Leone:

Rule 75: Measures for the Protection of Victims and Witnesses (*amended May 14, 2005*)

(A) A Judge or a Chamber may, on its own motion, or at the request of either party, or of the victim or witness concerned, or of the Witnesses and Victims Section, order appropriate measures to safeguard the privacy and security of victims and witnesses, provided that the measures are consistent with the rights of the accused.

(B) A Judge or a Chamber may hold an *in camera* proceeding to determine whether to order:
  (i) Measures to prevent disclosure to the public or the media of the identity or whereabouts of a victim or a witness, or of persons related to or associated with him by such means as:
    (a) Expunging names and identifying information from the Special Court's public records;
    (b) Non-disclosure to the public of any records identifying the victim or witness;
    (c) Giving of testimony through image- or voice-altering devices or closed circuit television, video link or other similar technologies; and
    (d) Assignment of a pseudonym;
  (ii) Closed sessions, in accordance with Rule 79;
  (iii) Appropriate measures to facilitate the testimony of vulnerable victims and witnesses, such as one-way closed circuit television.

(C) A Judge or a Chamber shall control the manner of questioning to avoid any harassment or intimidation.

(D) The Witnesses and Victims Section shall ensure that the witness has been informed before giving evidence that his or her testimony and his or her identity may be disclosed at a later date in another case, pursuant to Rule 75(F).

(E) When making an order under Sub-Rule (A) above, a Judge or Chamber shall wherever appropriate state in the order whether the transcript of those proceedings relating to the evidence of the witness to whom the measures relate shall be made available for use in other proceedings before the Special Court.

(F) Once protective measures have been ordered in respect of a witness or victim in any proceedings before the Special Court (the "first proceedings"), such protective measures:
  (i) shall continue to have effect mutatis mutandis in any other proceedings before the Special Court (the "second proceedings") unless and until they are rescinded, varied or augmented in accordance with the procedure set out in this Rule; but;
  (ii) shall not prevent the Prosecutor from discharging any disclosure obligation under the Rules in the second proceedings, provided that the Prosecutor notifies the Defence to whom the disclosure is being made of the nature of the protective measures ordered in the first proceedings.

(G) A party to the second proceedings seeking to rescind, vary or augment protective measures ordered in the first proceedings shall apply to the Chamber seized of the second proceedings.

(H) Before determining an application under Sub-Rule (G) above, if the effect of the change serves to decrease the protective measures granted to the victim or witness by the Chamber in the first proceedings, the Chamber seized of the second proceedings shall obtain all relevant information from the first proceedings, and may consult with any Judge who ordered the protective measures in the first proceedings, or the relevant Chamber.

(I) An application to a Chamber to rescind, vary or augment protective measures in respect of a victim or witness may be dealt with either by the Chamber or by a Judge of that Chamber, and any reference in this Rule to "a Chamber" shall include a reference to "a Judge of that Chamber."

(J) If the Chamber seized of the second proceedings rescinds, varies or augments the protective measures ordered in the first proceedings, these changes shall apply only with regard to the second proceedings.

The SCSL was always balancing legal, procedural, and financial obligations with its operational requirements on a daily basis to ensure the credibility of the legal process.

VII. CONTINUING AND FUTURE COOPERATION

Once the Court has completed its proceedings, there will remain continuing obligations.[34] All of these will invariably necessitate continuing international cooperation given the constitutive framework of the Court and any Residual Court. The Special Court continues to use the STL's courtroom and office space and the ICC's detention facilities until the conclusion of the Taylor trial. The government of the Netherlands continues to facilitate the requirements of the SCSL as the host government under the Host Country Agreement. The originals of the SCSL's archives were transferred to The Hague in December 2010 and are stored by the government of the Netherlands in the Dutch National Archives with copies in Freetown.[35] Arrangements in place for the SCSL's residual issues and residual mechanism indicate that continued international cooperation and assistance remain key to the success of the discharge of the Court's mandate, not least in the enforcement of the sentences handed down that are being served in Rwanda by the convicted persons.

The SCSL operated – and continues to operate – in a very challenging physical and operational environment given its funding regime. Certainly the United Nations, as a party to the Agreement establishing the Court, possessed sufficient influence in facilitating the provision of substantive and operational support through its neighboring missions. Nonetheless, the willingness of many a member state to provide financial support – directly and indirectly through seconded staff, expertise, and furniture – demonstrates the manifestation of demonstrable political will to end the fight against impunity and to uphold a core purpose of the Charter, which can only bode well for the future of international criminal justice generally and international criminal justice in Africa.

Much debate has taken place during the life of the SCSL as to whether its lack of Chapter VII powers constituted a hindrance to its work, especially considering its bilateral legal basis between the United Nations and the government of Sierra Leone. As this chapter has shown, despite its distinctive legal basis vis-à-vis the twin UN tribunals for Rwanda and the former Yugoslavia, one of the legacies of the Court was to show that states both in Africa and elsewhere are willing to cooperate as necessary to give effect to the mandate of such an institution. To that extent, the experiences and practice of the SCSL constitutes a valuable contribution to international criminal practice.

---

[34] *See* Binta Mansaray & Shakiratu Sanusi, *Residual Matters of Ad Hoc Courts and Tribunals: The SCSL Experience*, 36(3) COMMONWEALTH L. BULL. 593–605 (2010) and *Eighth Annual Report of the Special Court*, at 51. An Agreement on the Establishment of a Residual Special Court for Sierra Leone to fulfill the Court's obligations after the completion of its mandate was signed by the United Nations and the government of Sierra Leone in August 2010.

[35] *See further Eighth Annual Report*, at 51ff.

25

To Compete or to Complement? Assessing the Relationship between the Sierra Leone Special Court and the Truth and Reconciliation Commission

Alpha Sesay[*]

I. INTRODUCTION

After over a decade of conflict that saw the commission of grave human rights violations in Sierra Leone, two transitional justice mechanisms were instituted as a response to numerous calls for accountability, and to ensure justice for the numerous victims of the more than decade-long conflict in the country. In 1999, the government of Sierra Leone and the Revolutionary United Front (RUF)[1] signed a peace agreement[2] that provided for the establishment of a Truth and Reconciliation Commission (TRC or "the Commission") in Sierra Leone. In 2000, the government of Sierra Leone and the United Nations entered negotiations for the establishment of the Special Court for Sierra Leone (SCSL) that would try those bearing the greatest responsibility for atrocities committed during the conflict in Sierra Leone.[3]

Both the SCSL and the TRC started operations at about the same time in 2002. This was a precedent that attracted much debate as to what relationship should exist between the two institutions. Key questions included whether one had primacy over the other, whether they should share information and under what circumstances, and whether they should both operate the same or separate witness protection mechanisms. Once the two institutions started their respective operations, no formal relationship was established between them, and this raised several questions as to how they could complement each other while operating as two independent institutions.

This chapter examines the simultaneous existence of these distinct but related transitional justice mechanisms as they operated in Sierra Leone, the ways in which they sought to answer the numerous questions that arose prior to their establishment, and the viability of this parallel model of transitional justice. It concludes with suggestions as to the extent

---

[*] LL.B. (University of Sierra Leone), LL.M. (Notre Dame, USA); Legal Officer, Open Society Justice Initiative, The Hague and Charles Taylor Trial Monitor at charlestaylortrial.org; formerly cofounder and national director, Sierra Leone Court Monitoring Program.

[1] The Revolutionary United Front, led by Corporal Foday S. Sankoh, waged a rebel war in Sierra Leone on March 23, 1991. The war lasted for another eleven years until it was declared over on January 18, 2002.

[2] Peace Agreement between the Government of Sierra Leone and the Revolutionary United Front of Sierra Leone, Lomé (July 7, 1999) [hereinafter Lomé Peace Agreement].

[3] Agreement between the United Nations and the Government of the Republic of Sierra Leone on the Establishment of a Special Court for Sierra Leone, Freetown (Jan. 16, 2002).

of interrelationships that could exist between them in case the model is replicated in other jurisdictions around the world.

II. BACKGROUND TO THE SIERRA LEONE TRC

The original discussions for the establishment of a transitional justice mechanism in Sierra Leone centered on the establishment of a Truth, Justice and Reconciliation Commission as a measure to promote accountability for gross human rights violations committed during the country's civil conflict.[4] These discussions later formed the basis for the inclusion of transitional justice measures in negotiations between the RUF and the government of Sierra Leone during the 1999 peace talks in the Togolese capital, Lomé.[5] In the peace agreement that was signed in July 1999, the two parties agreed to establish a TRC that would address impunity, provide a forum for victims and perpetrators alike to tell their stories, break the cycle of violence, facilitate healing and reconciliation, provide a historical account of the conflict, and make recommendations for the rehabilitation of victims.[6] Former attorney general and vice president of Sierra Leone, Solomon Berewa, explained the fundamental function of the TRC by aptly mentioning that "the main purpose of the Truth and Reconciliation Commission is to heal the wounds of the nation. Thus, far from being fault-finding and punitive, it is to serve as the most legitimate and credible forum for victims to reclaim their human worth; and a channel for the perpetrators of atrocities to expiate their guilt, and chasten their consciences. The process has been likened to a national catharsis, involving truth telling, respectful listening and above all, compensation for victims in deserving cases."[7]

In what proved to be a highly controversial provision, which Professor Leila Sadat discusses in detail in her chapter for this volume, the Lomé Peace Agreement granted absolute pardon and reprieve to all rebels and their collaborators for all crimes they had committed in pursuant of their objectives.[8] However, the Special Representative of the UN Secretary-General entered a caveat to the Lomé Agreement indicating that "The United Nations holds the understanding that the amnesty provisions of the Agreement shall not apply to international crimes of genocide, crimes against humanity, war crimes and other serious violations of international humanitarian law."[9] This provision indicated that amnesty was granted to fighting forces without prejudice to the right of the United Nations to take appropriate measures to ensure accountability for such grave human rights violations. Accordingly, shortly after the SCSL was established, the Appeals Chamber of the Court dismissed applications

---

[4] *See* Richard Bennett, *The Evolution of the Sierra Leone Truth and Reconciliation Commission, in* TRUTH AND RECONCILIATION COMMISSION IN SIERRA LEONE 37–51 (2001).

[5] *Id.*

[6] Lomé Peace Agreement art. XXVI.

[7] Solomon E. Berewa, *Addressing Impunity Using Divergent Approaches: The Commission and the Special Court, in* TRUTH AND RECONCILIATION COMMISSION IN SIERRA LEONE, *supra* note 4 at 55.

[8] Lomé Peace Agreement art. IX.

[9] Cited from the *Sierra Leone TRC Report*, n.23, vol. 3b, ch. 6, at 1. The statement by the U.N. SRSG does not appear in the text of the Agreement as it was published by the United Nations (U.N. DOC. S/1999/777). The Commission is quoted as having seen a copy of the agreement that had appended a disclaimer in handwriting.

by accused persons that the Trial Chamber lacked jurisdiction to try them because of the amnesty guarantee in the Lomé Accord.[10]

On February 22, 2000, the Sierra Leone Parliament enacted the Truth and Reconciliation Commission (TRC) Act, which incorporated the TRC provision in the Lomé Agreement into domestic law.[11] However, disruptions in the peace process in May 2000 hindered the progress toward the establishment of the TRC.[12] The actions of the RUF during this time led to a request by Sierra Leone's president, Ahmed Tejan Kabbah, to the UN Security Council (UNSC) for the establishment of a court that would prosecute "those members of the Revolutionary United Front (RUF) and their accomplices responsible for committing crimes against the people of Sierra Leone and for the taking of United Nations peacekeepers as hostage."[13] President Kabbah's request was for the leadership of the RUF and those "most responsible" to be prosecuted for the commission of serious crimes. However, as Professor Charles Jalloh discusses in his chapter for this volume, once a Statute was enacted for the proposed court, it introduced a language that the court would "prosecute persons who bear the greatest responsibility" for the commission of serious crimes in Sierra Leone starting from November 30, 1996. This had an impact on initial plans for the establishment of the TRC as all discussions now had to be done with the establishment of an alternate accountability mechanism in perspective.

The TRC began its work in December 2002 and by the end of its hearings in August 2003, a total of 500 persons had testified before the Commission – a majority of them being victims, although many among these could be considered as victim–perpetrators.[14] On October 5, 2004, the Commission formally presented its report to the president of Sierra Leone. The report made several recommendations primarily to be undertaken by the government in relation to addressing the plight of victims through a reparations program, and institutional and legal reform to prevent the causes of war in the future.[15] On August 8, 2005, the TRC launched its report to the Sierra Leonean citizenry in several public ceremonies across the country.[16] Many portions of the report, including those dealing with reparations for victims, are yet to be implemented.

III. RELATIONSHIP BETWEEN THE SIERRA LEONE TRC AND THE SCSL

When the TRC was first established in 2000, the country did not anticipate a Special Court. The TRC was already in place when the court was established but delays in getting the

---

[10] *See* Decision on Challenge to Jurisdiction: Lomé Accord Amnesty, Prosecutor v. Morris Kallon (Case No. SCSL–2004–15–AR72(E)), Brima Bazzy Kamara (Case No. SCSL-2004–16-AR72(E)), Appeals Chamber (Mar. 13, 2004).

[11] Truth and Reconciliation Commission Act 2000 (the TRC Act), Supplement to the Sierra Leone Gazette, vol. CXXXI, No. 9.

[12] In early May 2000, the RUF rebels took several UN peacekeepers hostage in northern Sierra Leone, shot at civilian demonstrators in Freetown, and threatened to unseat the government.

[13] Letter dated Aug. 9, 2000 from the Permanent Representative of Sierra Leone to the United Nations addressed to the President of the United Nations Security Council, U.N. Doc. S/2000/786.

[14] E-mail exchange with former TRC Researcher (Nov. 10, 2005) (on file with author).

[15] *See Final Report of the Sierra Leone Truth and Reconciliation Commission*, vol. 2, chap. 3.

[16] The TRC, with support from the Open Society Initiative for West Africa (OSIWA), recently launched a new website from which a full report of the Commission can be obtained: www.sierraleonetrc.org (last visited on Aug. 6, 2012) [hereinafter TRC Report].

TRC's work started made it possible for both institutions to start their respective work simultaneously. Although the legal instruments establishing both institutions made no reference to each other, it became apparent in the eyes of many that their relationship had to be determined in order to avoid any potential conflict. As Avril MacDonald noted, "[i]t is the first time that an international court, even a quasi one such as the Special Court, will function simultaneously with such an institution, and offers an interesting experiment on how criminal prosecutions can complement other processes aimed at providing justice and promoting reconciliation and peace-building."[17]

Sierra Leone therefore faced a unique situation of operating two separate but related transitional justice mechanisms to achieve the same goal of peace, justice, and reconciliation. The Chairman of the TRC, Bishop J.C. Humper, cogently described the process as "going to the promised land, but by different roads."[18] In view of the fact that both institutions were going to operate simultaneously, discussions on their respective tasks started taking place in and out of Sierra Leone. As early as October 2000, the United States Institute for Peace, the International Human Rights Law Group, and experts from the International Center for Transitional Justice held discussions on how the Court and the Commission should relate with each other.[19] In November 2000, the UN Mission in Sierra Leone together with the UN Office of High Commissioner for Human Rights (OHCHR) also proposed that consultations be held on how the two institutions should work together.[20] The UN Secretary- General also suggested the preparation of guidelines to regulate the relationship between the two institutions. The OHCHR and the Office of Legal Affairs convened another meeting in New York in December 2001 that sought to define the relationship between the two institutions and how certain key issues, including information sharing and the exercise of powers, should be handled. The participants at this meeting suggested that the two institutions should "perform complementary roles in ensuring accountability, deterrence, a story-telling mechanism for both victims and perpetrators, national reconciliation, reparation and restorative justice for the people of Sierra Leone."[21] They further recommended that an agreement be developed so as to institutionalize "the modalities for cooperation" between the two institutions and that they should both respect each other's independence and mandate.[22]

Several proposals were made by other nongovernmental organizations (NGOs) for the establishment of a formal relationship or the development of guidelines to regulate the relationship between the two institutions.[23] In a January 2001 letter to the UN Security

---

[17] Avril MacDonald, *Sierra Leone's Shoestring Special Court*, 84 INT'L REV. RED CROSS 121, 122 (2002).

[18] William A. Schabas, *The Sierra Leone Truth and Reconciliation Commission, in* ROADS TO RECONCILIATION 129, 144 (Elin Skaar, Siri Gloppen & Astri Suhkri eds., 2005).

[19] Bennett, *supra* note 4.

[20] *Situation of Human Rights in Sierra Leone*, U.N. DOC. E/CN.4/2001/35, at 12–13 (Aug. 9, 2001).

[21] U.N. DOC. E/CN.4/2002/3, para. 70.

[22] *Id.*

[23] International Center for Transitional Justice and Human Rights Watch were two leading NGOs that submitted briefing papers/reports with suggestions on how the two institutions should interact with each other. *See* Marieke Wierda, Priscilla Hayner & Paul van Zyl, *Exploring the Relationship between the Special Court and the Sierra Leone Truth and Reconciliation Commission*, International Center for Transitional Justice (ICTJ) (June 24, 2002), *available at* http://www.ictj.org/sites/default/files/ICTJ-SierraLeone-Court-TRC-2002-English.pdf (last visited Aug. 5, 2012) and Human Rights Watch, *The Interrelationship between the Sierra Leone Special Court and Truth and Reconciliation Commission* (Apr. 18, 2002), *available at*

Council, the Secretary-General cautioned that "care must be taken to ensure that the Special Court for Sierra Leone and the Truth and Reconciliation Commission will operate in a complementary and mutually supportive manner, fully respectful of their distinct but related functions."[24] In early 2002, the United Nations sent a Planning Mission to Sierra Leone to make preparations for the Court's work. In its report, the mission noted that both institutions were to "perform complementary roles ... mutually supportive and in full respect for each other's mandate."[25] However, as indicated by former TRC Commissioner and renowned academic Professor William A. Schabas, "although much intellectual and political energy was expended by the United Nations and by international and national NGOs ... most of the discussion and ensuing proposals did not prove to be particularly helpful,"[26] as the two institutions did not establish any formal agreement to regulate their relationship. This notwithstanding, the two institutions operated mostly unhindered. As discussed later in the chapter, tensions arose only at the end of the TRC's work when there was dispute over the Commission's access to detainees in the custody of the Court.

IV. LEGAL INSTRUMENTS OF THE SCSL AND TRC: WHO HAD MORE POWERS?

Upon establishment of the SCSL and the TRC, questions arose about the legal relationship between the two institutions, especially as they relate to issues of primacy and confidentiality. Despite the fact that the SCSL was established long after the TRC Act had been enacted, its implementing legislations[27] made no reference to the TRC.[28] This is somewhat surprising considering that the two institutions would operate concurrently. Perhaps this reflected the feelings of the government and the United Nations that the two were independent institutional processes, with each having its own place in Sierra Leonean law and society. However, specific provisions in the legislation governing both institutions certainly generated discussions on what legal relationship should have existed between them, and some commentators suggested that these legislations gave the SCSL broader powers over the TRC.[29] This related specifically to the issues of primacy and access to confidential information. Article 21(2) of the Special Court Agreement (Ratification) Act 2002 provides that "Notwithstanding any other law, every natural person, corporation, or other body created by or under Sierra Leone law shall comply with any direction specified in an order of the

---

http://www.hrw.org/news/2002/04/18/interrelationship-between-sierra-leone-special-court-and-truth-and-reconciliation-co (last visited Aug. 5, 2012).

[24] Letter dated Jan. 12, 2001 from the Secretary-General addressed to the President of the Security Council, U.N. Doc. S/2001/40 para. 9.

[25] Report of the Planning Mission on the Establishment of the Special Court for Sierra Leone, U.N. Doc. S/2002/246, paras. 49, 53.

[26] William A. Schabas, *A Synergistic Relationship: The Sierra Leone Truth and Reconciliation Commission and the Special Court for Sierra Leone*, 15 CRIM. L.F. 3, 29 (2004).

[27] Statute of the Special Court for Sierra Leone (SCSL Statute), *available at* http://www.sc-sl.org/LinkClick.aspx?fileticket=uClnd1MJeEw%3d&tabid=176, and the Special Court Ratification Act, Supplement to the Sierra Leone Gazette, vol. CXXXIII, No. 2.

[28] Article 15 of the Statute of the SCSL however refers to the use of "truth and reconciliation mechanisms" in the case of juvenile perpetrators. This provision, however, makes no specific reference to an existing truth and reconciliation mechanism in the country.

[29] *See* Wierda et al., *supra* note 23, at 5.

Special Court." According to some commentators, this provision by implication compelled the TRC to cooperate with the SCSL whenever it was required to do so, and if this was the case, it could have had potential legal consequences for the Commission in the conduct of its work.[30] The TRC Act on the other hand provided in section 7(3) that "any person shall be permitted to provide information to the Commission on a confidential basis and the Commission shall not be compelled to disclose any information given to it in confidence." Although this clause granted powers to the Commission, it also imposed an obligation on it to give full respect to confidentiality.[31]

These two provisions apparently drew clear lines for conflict because the Commission might be in possession of information required by the Court, and the Court might use its powers under Section 21 of the Special Court Agreement (Ratification) Act to request such information. The Commission on the other hand might use Section 7 of the TRC Act to protect such information. In such a case, the debate was centered on which provision would prevail in case of conflict. The TRC's position was made clear on this when at a 2002 event in Freetown to launch a report by the Post Conflict Reintegration Initiative for Development and Empowerment (PRIDE), one of the international commissioners at the TRC said publicly that the commissioners would respect their confidentiality obligation and no one (including the SCSL) would compel them to disclose such confidential information.[32] Section 21, however, provides that "Notwithstanding any other law ... any body created by or under Sierra Leone law" must comply with directions from the SCSL. This clause, in the eyes of some experts, suggested that the SCSL's power to order compliance with its demands superseded that of the TRC Act.[33] TRC Commissioners, however, disagreed that the Court had such powers over the Commission.[34] Inasmuch as Article 21 was not legislated explicitly for the Commission, it could however be read as being binding on the Commission and giving the Court greater powers over it. Despite the inclusion of foreign personnel including the Commissioners, it should also be noted that the TRC was a domestic institution, making it solely an entity of the government of Sierra Leone.

Part IV of the Special Court Agreement (Ratification) Act, which provides for the obligations of the government, required it to cooperate and comply with the Court's requests. It seems that the government interpreted its obligations under Part IV of the Court's Ratification Act as including a potential request for the TRC to cooperate with the SCSL. In January 2002 therefore, the government prepared a discussion paper in which it stated that: "The legal relationship between the Special Court and the Truth and Reconciliation Commission is clear. The Special Court is an international judicial body whose requests and orders require no less than full compliance by the Truth and Reconciliation Commission, as by all Sierra Leonean national institutions, in accordance to [sic] the international obligations agreed to by Sierra Leone."[35] This discussion paper does not amount to an act of

---

[30] *Id.* at 4.
[31] *Id.* at 5.
[32] Personal observation of author who was present at the event in Freetown on September 12, 2002.
[33] *See* Wierda et al., *supra* note 23, at 5.
[34] Schabas, *supra* note 26, at 31.
[35] Office of the Attorney General and Ministry of Justice Special Court Task Force, *Briefing Paper on the Relationship between the Special Court and the Truth and Reconciliation Commission, Legal Analysis and*

parliament such as the enacting legislations for both institutions, but it explains explicitly what the government's position was on how the various legislations would be implemented and the powers that the SCSL could enjoy over the TRC. If the Court ever decided to use such powers, then it would have had severe implications on the Commission's relationship with persons who testified before it in confidence. Wierda, Hayner, and van Zyn noted that "The relationship between the Special Court and the Commission is therefore dictated by the broad powers of the Special Court ... it is not resolved to satisfaction and that the legal framework leaves room for an agreement to be concluded which better accommodates the various public interests at stake."[36]

Other commentators, for example, Professor Schabas have contested the correctness of the suggestion that the Commission was somehow legally subordinate to the Court. Schabas argues that the question of primacy as enacted in the Court's statute could apply only "between courts with concurrent jurisdiction" and that this was in no way relevant to the relationship between the Commission and the Court.[37] He further states that in addition to very many statements by the United Nations that the Court and the Commission were to be "mutually supportive and complementary," the fact that the SCSL legislations made no reference to the Commission, which he says was "a body independent of the Government of Sierra Leone," meant that the Court's primacy powers could not apply to the Commission.[38] Schabas called suggestions that the Court could use the powers granted it under Section 21 of its Ratification Act to compel the TRC to release confidential information as "far-fetched and manifestly incorrect."[39] It is however good that the potential legal conflict between both institutions on a request for information by the SCSL never arose in practice as any potential conflict on this issue was eased in September 2002 when the first Prosecutor of the SCSL, David Crane, made a public pronouncement that he did not intend to seek any information or evidence in possession of the TRC.[40] There was therefore no way to legally test whether the Court indeed had powers over the Commission.

V. PREOPERATIONAL DEBATE

Prior to both institutions commencing their respective operations, concerns about their relationship focused mainly on issues such as information sharing, witness protection, public perception of the entire process, and the possibility of a formal relationship between the institutions. A survey by PRIDE in 2002 established that many ex-combatants initially had fears about such a relationship, suspecting that their testimonies before the TRC might be

---

Policy Considerations of the Government of Sierra Leone for the Special Court Planning Mission 9 (Jan. 7–18, 2002).

[36] Wierda et al., *supra* note 23.

[37] Schabas, *supra* note 26, at 36.

[38] *Id.*

[39] *Id.* at 37.

[40] Thierry Cruvellier & Marieke Wierda, *The Special Court for Sierra Leone: The First Eighteen Months* 12, International Center for Transitional Justice (ICTJ) Case Study Series (Mar. 2004), *available at* http://www.ictj.org/sites/default/files/ICTJ-SierraLeone-Special-Court-2004-English.pdf (last visited Aug. 6, 2012).

used against them or their commanders at the SCSL.[41] These preoperational debates focused on these specific issues:

A. Information Sharing

Information sharing was a very complicated issue in the discussions preceding the commencement of the work of both institutions. These discussions occupied experts in and out of Sierra Leone in order to create an atmosphere for cooperation between the institutions. The general question was whether the TRC should share information given to it with the SCSL. Many thought that although the Court had powers to request information in possession of the TRC, if it did, it would have affected the letter and spirit of the TRC Act, which assures confidentiality for certain information. The International Center for Transitional Justice discussed the following options for information sharing by both institutions:[42]

a. *The "Fire wall" Model:* This model proposed that there would be no information sharing between the Commission and the Court. Commentators believed that such a model would enable the Commission to effectively gather testimony from perpetrators, which would be crucial to its fulfilling its required mandate.[43] ICTJ noted that such a model would have potential pitfalls as the TRC might be in possession of information that might be of help to the Court in preventing some miscarriage of justice or that would be indispensable to either the Prosecution or the Defense.[44] This might be the case if such information was necessary to prove the guilt or innocence of an Accused or that of a witness who had earlier testified before the TRC and then gave completely different testimony before the SCSL. The Court might therefore need such information to prove a prior inconsistent statement. Indeed, during proceedings at the SCSL, it sometimes became necessary for witnesses to be confronted with questions about statements that they had made before the TRC, and that became necessary to establish their credibility as witnesses before the Court.[45]

b. *The "Free Access" Model:* This model was the complete opposite of the "fire wall" model wherein the Court would have "unconditional access" to any information that came before the Commission, irrespective of whether such information was confidential.[46]

---

[41] See Post Conflict Reintegration Initiative for Development and Empowerment (PRIDE), in partnership with the International Center for Transitional Justice (ICTJ), *Ex-Combatant Views of the Truth and Reconciliation Commission and the Special Court for Sierra Leone* 7 (Sept. 12, 2002), *available at* http://www.ictj.org/sites/default/files/ICTJ-SierraLeone-Combatants-TRC-2002-English.pdf (last visited Aug. 6, 2012) [hereinafter PRIDE and ICTJ Report].

[42] *See* Wierda et al., *supra* note 23, at 10–15.

[43] *Id.* at 8.

[44] *Id.* at 9.

[45] Personal observation by author during SCSL proceedings. For example, Sam Kolleh, a defense witness who testified for former Liberian president Charles Taylor in November 2010, was confronted under cross-examination by the Prosecution that he had used a different name and presented different facts about issues when he testified at the TRC.

[46] *See* Wierda et al., *supra* note 23, at 8.

The advantage of this model was said to be that the Court and the Commission would not have contradictory records of the conflict. This would help both institutions get a single joint account of the civil war in the country.[47] However, a case for both institutions to present the same account of the conflict should not be a reason for employing this model as the two entities had completely different mandates. Whereas the TRC was supposed to make historical findings and document what happened in Sierra Leone during the conflict, the Court had a very narrow and focused mandate geared at dishing out criminal responsibility to individuals involved in the commission of crimes during the conflict. The TRC, unlike the SCSL, was not a guilt-finding institution. At the end of the day, the two institutions provided a generally common narrative of the conflict, but given their different mandates, the TRC's narrative was more holistic than that of the SCSL. In response to suggestions to use this model of information sharing, PRIDE in its report noted that many perpetrators would have viewed the Commission as an investigative arm of the court and would therefore have been reluctant to testify before it.[48] Another disadvantage of this model was that perpetrators might only have given testimonies before the Commission that they knew would not expose them to trial by the Court and this might have deprived the Commission of much-needed information. Commentators therefore suggested that both "absolutist approaches represented by the "fire wall" and the "free access" models should be put aside in favor of a compromise."[49]

c. *The "Conditional Sharing" Model*: This model suggested that the TRC could share information with the Court only if certain conditions were met. The ICTJ stated that all public and expert testimonies as well as those contained in public documents could be shared with the Court.[50] The problem could arise in situations when the information provided to the TRC was confidential. Such conditional sharing could be divided into inculpatory evidence –one that is essential to proving the guilt of the accused, and exculpatory evidence – one that is essential to establishing the innocence of the accused person.

There were suggestions that such conditional sharing must take note of policy considerations.[51] These included that the information should be very important to the Court's ability to do justice, as well as whether such information may only be obtained from the Commission rather than somewhere else.[52] It was also suggested that the Commission must warn its witnesses that their information might be shared with the Court and that it must assure such persons that their statements will not be used against them in any criminal proceedings.[53]

This model posed the best option for both institutions as it required no amendment to existing legislation and the Commission's work would not be hindered by its information being used by the court. Yet despite these proposals, once the two institutions commenced

---

[47] *Id.*
[48] *See* PRIDE and ICTJ Report, *supra* note 41, at 19.
[49] *See* Wierda et al., *supra* note 23, at 19.
[50] *Id.*
[51] *Id.* at 11.
[52] *Id.*
[53] *Id.* at 13.

their respective task, no formal discussions took place between them on how to handle the issue of information sharing. The potential tension on this issue was eased when the first Prosecutor made it clear that he would not use information in possession of the Commission. However, this guarantee did not completely wipe away fears among perpetrators who still believed that the Commission would be an investigative arm of the court.

PRIDE noted in a 2002 letter to the ICTJ that many former combatants remained concerned that the TRC was an investigative arm of the SCSL and that statements made to the Commission might be used against them or might make them potential targets as witnesses against rebel commanders who were being prosecuted at the SCSL.[54] Schabas notes, however, that such fear did not stop perpetrators from testifying before the TRC as many told their stories and asked for forgiveness.[55] The concern that statements made by perpetrators could be used against them at the SCSL even became moot when persons already in the custody of the Court indicated their willingness to testify publicly before the TRC.[56]

It was also suggested that once the Commission finished its work, its final report should be made available to the Court.[57] This would pose no special threat as the Commission was bound by law to make its final report available to the public. Indeed as seen in several filings in the various cases before the Court, excerpts of the TRC report were presented as exhibits by parties to the proceedings.[58]

B. Operational Collaboration

There were suggestions for some form of operational collaboration between the TRC and the Court. Sierra Leone's Justice Ministry suggested that although it was acknowledged that the two institutions were different in terms of mandate, budget, and time line, there was still a possibility that they could share resources.[59] Such resources would include undertaking joint investigations, shared translation resources, joint witness protection mechanisms, joint public awareness, and trainings for personnel of both institutions. It was suggested that such collaboration would greatly help cut down resources needed for both institutions and that there would be consistency in their respective works. It was anticipated that joint public awareness would also help to convey a common message to the public about the respective tasks of the two institutions and would greatly reduce confusion among the general public.

As attractive as such collaboration might have been, it also had the tendency to affect the work of either or both institutions. For example, whereas the TRC investigators should be

---

[54] Letter from PRIDE to ICTJ (Feb. 2, 2002), *cited in* Wierda et al., *supra* note 23, at 8.

[55] Schabas, *supra* note 26, at 30.

[56] *Id.* In August and September 2003, three accused persons in the custody of the SCSL (Sam Hinga Norman, Augustine Gbao, and Issa Sesay) expressed their willingness to testify publicly before the Commission.

[57] *See* Wierda et al., *supra* note 23, at 16.

[58] Examples included Exhibit D-12: TF1–362 – Witness to Truth: Report of the Sierra Leone TRC, vol. 2 (cover pg., title pg., p. 44); Exhibit D-26: TF1–334 – Appendix 2 Submissions to the SL TRC – Sierra Leone Gov't Statement by Alhaji Dr. Ahmad Tejan Kabbah before the TRC (Aug. 5, 2003); Exhibit D-30: TF1–334 – Witness to Truth: Report of the SL TRC, vol. 2 (Names of the AFRC Leadership); Exhibit D-31: TF1–334 – Appendix 2 Submissions to the SL TRC – Letter from the Director of Prisons to the Commissioner of the TRC (July 12, 2003).

[59] *See* Office of the Attorney General and Ministry of Justice Special Court Task Force, *supra* note 35.

more concerned about gathering information on a broad pattern of abuse relating to the entire conflict, the Court's investigators would be concerned only about information pertaining to specific events that would prove the charges before the Court. Such distinction would therefore have made it unnecessary for any joint investigation.

Collaboration on joint trainings would have been necessary especially on issues of statement taking and witness protection mechanisms. There would have been a risk on the issue of sharing translation resources as this might have created the danger of information sharing, even if accidentally.[60] Proposals for joint public awareness made great sense as the public would have been able to know the distinct nature of both institutions without any contradiction.[61] This goal was not achieved, however, as both institutions ended up operating distinct public information and outreach programs.

Although such collaboration was important on certain issues, it should have been done with a view of complementing the efforts of both institutions and helping the public get a proper understanding of the two processes rather than striving to save resources. A war-torn nation such as Sierra Leone obviously had challenges in getting resources for its transitional justice mechanisms. The TRC especially faced huge challenges in raising funds to reach the original budget set for its work. One can therefore sympathize with concerns by the government that there was a need to save resources. However, a better way to proceed would have been to employ more robust efforts to raise funds and ensure that both institutions had enough resources to undertake their respective mandates. A desire to reduce resources should not have been used to compromise the work of the two institutions.

C. Witness Protection

Commentators noted that a strong witness protection mechanism would be an incentive for people to cooperate with the Commission even if its information would be shared with the Court.[62] Such protection would include protecting the identity of such witnesses. For example, if the Commission shared confidential information with the Court, the Court should have considered such protective measures as use of pseudonyms and closed sessions for such witnesses when they testified. However, it was suggested that having separate witness protection regimes for the two institutions was a better thing to do.[63] As they both started their respective operations, the TRC established a separate Witness Protection Unit (WPU) as one of six operational units of the Commission[64] while the SCSL established its own Witness and Victims Support (WVS) program.

D. Establishing a Formal Relationship

It was suggested that despite their differences in functions and modes of operation, there was a need for the two institutions to establish a formal relationship even before they

---

[60] Wierda et al., *supra* note 23, at 17.
[61] *Id.*
[62] *Id.* at 15.
[63] *Id.* at 16.
[64] The WPU and Reconciliation were merged into one unit. The other operational units of the Commission included Media and Public Education, Research, Investigation, Legal Affairs, and Finance.

got into the operational phase of their respective tasks. The ICTJ suggested that the two institutions should sign an agreement in the form of a memorandum of understanding and orders before the commencement of their operations. Annexed to its briefing paper on the relationship between the TRC and the Special Court, the ICTJ submitted a model "Memorandum of Understanding between the Truth and Reconciliation Commission and the Special Court for Sierra Leone" and "Orders for the Disclosure of Information to the Truth and Reconciliation Commission."[65] Human Rights Watch also suggested in its policy document that a guideline should be developed to regulate the relationship between the Court and the Commission.[66]

Despite these suggestions no such relationship was ever established between the two institutions and therefore many of these issues remained unresolved. In its final report, the Commission indicted other actors for failure to establish such a relationship with the SCSL. The TRC report notes that "it might have been helpful for the United Nations and the Government of Sierra Leone to lay down guidelines for the simultaneous conduct of the two organizations. The Commission finds further that the two institutions themselves, the Commission and the Special Court, might have given more consideration to an arrangement or memorandum of understanding to regulate their relationship."[67]

A major lesson learned from the Sierra Leone experience and which could be considered in future situations is to have such a relationship agreement between the two institutions in order to address many issues that remained unresolved in Sierra Leone.

VI. OPERATIONAL RELATIONSHIP

The SCSL and the TRC started full operations at exactly the same time in 2002. The TRC Commissioners were inaugurated in July 2002, coinciding with the appointment of the judges of the Court. The Prosecutor and Registrar of the Court arrived in Freetown in August 2002, coinciding with the time the TRC started its recruitment phase. The hearing phase of the TRC also coincided with the arrest and detention of indictees by the court. It therefore became apparent that their operations would run simultaneously with the TRC having a shorter life span. The numerous debates that preceded their respective operations and the failure of the two institutions to establish formal ties later had some impact on their operational relationship. This is discussed with respect to the following:

A. *Information Sharing*

Though there was no agreement between the two institutions on this subject, hence leaving it more amenable for debate, it was to a large extent clarified when the Prosecutor of the Special Court announced that he would not seek any information from the TRC. When both institutions started their respective operations, the SCSL Prosecutor's pronouncement was re-echoed by the Chief Investigator of the Court when he asserted that they (the Court)

---

[65] Wierda et al., *supra* note 23, Annex A and Attachment A.
[66] Human Rights Watch, *supra* note 23.
[67] *See* TRC Report, *supra* note 16, vol. 3B, ch. 6.

... strongly support the TRC. We are on record saying that we do not plan to use any information at all from the TRC. We do want to encourage people to come and tell their story so the nation can begin the healing process. We will not concern ourselves if you come before the TRC. Nor do we necessarily want to know who comes before the TRC. It is a separate and distinct operation, and it should be. We do not plan on asking the TRC for any information whatsoever.[68]

However, because such pronouncements and assurances were not institutionalized, there still remained distrust among members of the public. Such distrust was supported by the myth that an underground tunnel linked the two institutions as they were both located just about 200 meters from each other along Jomo Kenyatta Road in Freetown.[69]

This suspicion was also heightened by the fact that some staff members of the TRC accepted appointments to the SCSL. In a particular scenario, a senior investigator at the TRC was granted a more lucrative appointment at the Special Court. Although there were discussions between both institutions that the investigator would not work on cases at the Special Court that he had already worked on at the Commission, this agreement was not respected. There were claims that the same investigator was made to work on the CDF case at the Court, when he had earlier interviewed CDF witnesses on behalf of the TRC at a CDF military base.[70] This particular case created a lot of suspicion about the relationship between the two institutions in relation to information sharing. During proceedings at the SCSL, defense counsel sought to establish that some witnesses had already testified before the TRC. Some witnesses indeed agreed that they had done so.[71] These instances raised questions among members of the public as to whether indeed information was not shared between the two institutions.

At an institutional level, there was no proof of information sharing, and no proof exists that the SCSL ever used its powers to request information from the Commission. However, because of informal interactions between staff of both institutions and peripheral staff members of the Commission, especially investigators and translators being later recruited by the Court, there is a likelihood of informal information moving from the TRC to the Court.

With the launching of the TRC report, defense counsel at the SCSL used it to establish responsibility in the rank and file of the CDF.[72] Prosecution lawyers also used the report to question the credibility of a defense witness in the Charles Taylor trial.

B. *Conflict between the TRC and the SCSL: TRC Access to SCSL Detainees*

During the debate on the operational relationship between the TRC and the SCSL, very little was said about the potential conflict that would arise if the TRC sought to have access to detainees or indicted persons in the Court's custody. In order to fulfill its mandate, the Commission envisaged that it would need to interview key people who had played central

---

[68] All Africa News, *Sierra Leone's Special Court: Will It Hinder or Help? Interview with Special Court Chief Investigator Allan White* (Nov. 12, 2002), *available at* http://allafrica.com/stories/200211210289.html (last visited Aug. 5, 2012).

[69] *See* MacDonald, *supra* note 17, at 151.

[70] *See* TRC Report, *supra* note 16, vol. 3B, ch. 6, at 8.

[71] Personal observation of author while he worked at the Defense Office of the Special Court in 2007.

[72] Interview with former Special Court Defense Counsel in the CDF case, Feb. 20, 2008. *See also supra* note 58.

roles in the conflict. This meant key commanders in the various fighting factions. This was evident in the Commission's request for key government officials such as former Sierra Leonean president Alhaji Ahmed Tejan Kabbah and other government officials to testify in front of the Commission. Former President Kabbah did indeed testify before the Commission. The Court's mandate on the other hand was to try those bearing the greatest responsibility, which could mean the same people that the Commission envisaged would make a vital contribution to the fulfillment of its mandate.

Also during the TRC public hearings, many victims and perpetrators mentioned the names of individuals who were in the custody of the Sierra Leone government on treason charges and those already indicted by the SCSL. The TRC had no problems seeking testimony from persons who were in the custody of the government. But when it came to getting such testimony from those persons in the custody of the Court, the most prominent conflict between the two institutions arose.[73]

The ICTJ had earlier on suggested that "in the case of persons indicted by the Special Court, the TRC should decline to interview them altogether until the proceedings against them are concluded."[74] In the months of May and June 2003, the Commission made a request to hear the testimony of persons in the custody of the Court during the Commission's public hearings.[75]

In a letter dated June 17, 2003, defense counsel for one of those in the Court's custody, Chief Samuel Hinga Norman, wrote a letter to the Registrar of the Court notifying him that counsel considered it inappropriate for his client to appear before the TRC while he remained an indictee before the Court. This view was also expressed by the other indictees, and the Registrar is said to have transmitted this information to the Commission.[76]

However, in August 2003, the indictees changed their initial positions and now expressed the view that they intended to testify before the Commission. On August 26, 2003, Norman wrote a letter to his defense counsel expressing that he "would prefer to be heard by the people of Sierra Leone and also be recorded for posterity."[77] This was followed by a request from Augustine Gbao and Issa Sesay, both former commanders of the RUF, that they also wished to testify before the TRC. The Commission welcomed this request and immediately wrote a letter to the Registrar of the SCSL dated September 3, 2003, requesting a private interview with Norman to be held the following day.

The Court then came up with a mechanism to regulate such an interview in the form of a "Practice Direction," which provided, among other things, that a detainee who agreed to grant an interview to the Commission had to signify his agreement in writing, confirmed by a lawyer who had advised him about it; that he had to be provided with a list of written

---

[73] *See* Decision on the Request by the Truth and Reconciliation Commission of Sierra Leone to Conduct a Public Hearing with Samuel Hinga Norman, The Prosecutor v. Samuel Hinga Norman (SCSL-2003–08-PT (3257–3264)), Trial Chamber (Oct. 29, 2003) and Decision on Appeal by the Truth and Reconciliation Commission for Sierra Leone ("TRC" or "The Commission") and Chief Samuel Hinga Norman JP against the Decision of His Lordship, Mr. Justice Bankole Thompson Delivered on October 30, 2003 to Deny the TRC's Request to Hold a Public Hearing with Chief Samuel Hinga Norman JP, The Prosecutor v. Samuel Hinga Norman (SCSL-2003–08-PT), Appeals Chamber (Nov. 28, 2003).

[74] Wierda et al., *supra* note 23, at 18.

[75] *See* TRC Report, *supra* note 16, at 11.

[76] *Id.*

[77] *Id.*

questions and told that he was not obliged to answer them; that he had to be informed that his answers might be used against him by the Prosecution and that no finding by the Commission about him would sway the Court; and that any interview had to be supervised by a lawyer appointed by the Registrar of the Court and that it had to be held in the presence of the indictee's counsel.[78]

The TRC objected to the provisions of the Practice Direction on the grounds that it would infringe its powers to take a witness's evidence in confidence, a power granted to it by Section 7 of the TRC Act. The two institutions exchanged correspondence on the issue, and because of continued objections by the Commission, on October 4, 2003, amendments were made to the Practice Directions, permitting the Commission to make an application to a Presiding Judge of the Court, who had the authority to reject such application if such "refusal is necessary in the interests of justice or to maintain the integrity of the proceedings of the Special Court."[79]

Based on this, on October 9, 2003, the TRC, joining Norman, filed a "Request to Conduct a Public Hearing with Chief Samuel Hinga Norman." In this motion, the TRC requested at least two days of public hearing with the Accused, accompanied by a live radio broadcast, and with highlights to be shown on television news programs.[80] The Prosecution on their part opposed such an application on grounds that such hearing would "undermine the integrity of the court, imperil the security situation in the country and could serve to intimidate witnesses."[81] On October 29, 2003, Justice Bankole Thompson, Presiding Judge of the Trial Chamber, turned down the TRC's application on the grounds that it was not in the interest of justice to allow such a public hearing to take place.[82] He determined that the TRC by stating in its motion that Norman "played a central role" in the conflict had already described the Accused as a perpetrator and that if the Court agreed to such hearing, it would be accepting that Norman was already a perpetrator, thereby violating the presumption of innocence and fair trial rights of an accused person.[83]

The TRC appealed this decision to the President of the Court, Justice Geoffrey Robertson, who on November 28, 2003, affirmed the Presiding Judge's decision, but made some recommendations that would create a compromise between the two institutions. Justice Robertson recommended that Norman be made to give evidence to the Commission "in writing (with the benefit of legal advice) and sworn in the form of an affidavit … that if he wishes to take this course, the Registrar should arrange for the swearing of the affidavit within the Detention Unit in the presence of a TRC official, and permit the original affidavit to be handed over to the TRC, on condition that it gives an undertaking not to bring or assist any

---

[78] *See* Practice Direction on the Procedure to Take Statements from a Person in the Custody of the Special Court for Sierra Leone (Sept. 9, 2003).

[79] *See* Practice Direction on the Procedure following a Request by a State, the Truth and Reconciliation Commission, or other legitimate authority to take a statement from a person in the custody of the Special Court for Sierra Leone, adopted Sept. 9, 2003, amended Oct. 4, 2003, at para. 5, *available at* http://www.sc-sl.org/LinkClick.aspx?fileticket=8km93ZzghVU%3d&tabid=176 (last visited Aug. 6, 2012).

[80] Found in Decision on Appeal by the Truth and Reconciliation Commission for Sierra Leone, *supra* note 73, at 15, para. 24.

[81] *Id.* at 17, para. 26.

[82] *See* Trial Chamber Decision, *supra* note 73, at paras. 9–16.

[83] *Id.*

other person or agency to bring a prosecution for perjury under Section 9(2) of its Act."[84] Justice Robertson took the view that if an accused person before the Court were allowed to testify in a public hearing before the TRC, he would use it as a political platform and that this would affect the public's perception of the integrity of the Court. Justice Robertson concluded that the TRC was free to make an application for the process discussed earlier in this paragraph or for a confidential hearing, but that no public hearing would be held with an indictee in the custody of the court.[85] The TRC did not pursue the matter further, stating that it no longer had time to make a fresh application as it had barely four weeks before its mandate would expire.

On December 4, 2003, the Registrar of the SCSL wrote a letter to the TRC that a procedure to obtain statements from the Accused in line with the decision of Justice Robertson would be put in place quickly, but the TRC maintained that this procedure would not meet the TRC's confidential requirements.[86]

In the final analysis, the TRC could not obtain any statements from the detainees in the custody of the Court, and this turned out to be the divisive issue in the relationship between the two institutions.[87] Several people including members of the international community frowned at the Special Court's refusal to allow the TRC access to the detainees.[88] The Working Group on the TRC, which was a network of Sierra Leonean civil society groups supporting the work of the Commission, condemned the refusal to hear Norman's testimony before the Commission, stating in a press release that this created a "high risk of incomplete historical memory and denial of Right to Truth."[89] During the 2004 national victims' commemoration conferences that were organized by the Outreach Section of the SCSL, members of local communities, especially in the southern part of the country where Norman had a huge support base, expressed distaste that Norman was not made to testify before the TRC.[90] The TRC on its part issued a statement that the Court's action "dealt a serious blow to the cause of truth and reconciliation in Sierra Leone."[91] It was unfortunate that the relationship between the TRC and the SCSL, which Schabas aptly describes as "otherwise been a cordial and uneventful," had to end in this manner.

In a way therefore, the SCSL tended to affect the work of the TRC. Because the Commission could not obtain testimonies from key players in Sierra Leone's conflict who were in the custody of the Court, the Commission was deprived of vital information that could have been important in the fulfillment of its mandate. Critics argue that this left the Commission's report with a vacuum that could have been filled had it obtained statements

---

[84] Appeals Chamber Decision, *supra* note 73, at para. 41.

[85] *Id.* at para. 42.

[86] Beth K. Dougherty, *Searching for Answers: Sierra Leone's Truth and Reconciliation Commission*, 8 AFR. STUD. Q., No. 1, 39, 45 (Fall 2004).

[87] ICTJ, *supra* note 40, at 13.

[88] Dougherty, *supra* note 86.

[89] Nov. 4, 2003 Standard Times publication on allafrica.com: http://allafrica.com/stories/200311050809.html (last visited Aug. 3, 2012).

[90] Personal observation of author during the Victims Commemoration Conferences. *See also* Marieke Wierda, *National Victims Commemoration Conference in Sierra Leone* (Oct. 14, 2009), *available at* http://www.carl-sl.org/home/reports/269-national-victim-commemorations-conference-in-sierra-leone (last visited July 30, 2012).

[91] Press Release, Truth and Reconciliation Commission, Freetown, Sierra Leone (Dec. 1, 2003).

from these detainees. It is hard to say whether this statement is true as no adverse effect has been identified in the TRC report based on the absence of testimony from certain individuals. Some have argued that it would be misleading to read too much into the statement or interpret it as though it defined the relationship that existed between the two institutions.[92] By all accounts, this was the only significant incident of disagreement that ever came up between the Court and the Commission and this, as a matter of fact, happened only at the very end of the Commission's work.

VII. CONCLUSION

There have been mixed sentiments among commentators and civil society actors as to the successes of this model of transitional justice employed in Sierra Leone. Although the process has not been regarded as a failure, it is still believed that both institutions would have done more if they had a more determined relationship. The Court and the Commission both worked within their required mandates without one being significantly hampered by the other. The fact that the TRC could not obtain statements from people in detention at the court did little or nothing to change the content of its report.[93] There is so much that could be gained from this model especially if the lessons learned or some of the concerns that were discussed in the Sierra Leonean context are addressed. These issues relate mainly to collaboration between the two institutions, discussions around primacy or exercise of powers, information sharing, witness protection, the Commission's access to detainees in the custody of the Court, and the establishment of an institutional relationship.

A. Collaboration on Investigations, Public Outreach, Use of Translators

The Commission and the Court could collaborate on certain issues in order to complement each other's efforts. However, such collaboration needs to be done with caution so that one institution does not jeopardize the work of the other. Because the nature of investigations is different in both institutions, it could be necessary for each institution to carry out its investigation separately. However, during such investigations, if one institution comes in contact with information that will be of assistance to the other, it should consider sharing such information in order to help the other achieve its objectives, but only if sharing such information will not be detrimental to the first institution's own task.[94]

Both institutions should avoid using the same translators and investigators as this will lead to a risk of sharing sensitive information and might also affect the credibility of both institutions in the eyes of the public. Individuals such as investigators and translators who have worked with one institution could be employed by the other institution, but they should ensure their employment upholds the integrity of the respective institutions and poses no real threat to the other's work.

---

[92] Michael Nesbitt, *Lessons from the Sam Hinga Norman Decision of the Special Court for Sierra Leone: How Trials and Truth Commissions Can Co-Exist,* 8 GERMAN L.J. 977, 1004 (2007).

[93] Interview with Marieke Wierda (Apr. 21, 2006).

[94] *See* Wierda et al., *supra* note 23, at 23 and Human Rights Watch, *supra* note 23, at 23.

In certain cases, both institutions could be made to undertake joint outreach activities. There is a risk that the public might perceive both institutions as working together, but such joint outreach activity can help to clarify issues to the public and also help achieve consistency in the messages conveyed by both institutions.[95]

B. *Primacy/Exercise of Powers*

Both the TRC Act and the Statute of the Court gave subpoena powers to the respective institutions. These statutes do not state expressly which institution has more powers or whether there are any limitations to the use of such powers. There is therefore a potential for conflict. In order to avoid any problems, both institutions must be clear that one would not use its powers against the other. Such a position will enhance cooperation between both institutions and will save both institutions valuable time and resources.[96] The Court should not compel the Commission to disclose confidential information, and the Commission on the other hand cannot withhold information unreasonably, especially if such information is necessary in the interest of justice at the Court. Staff members of the Commission, such as Commissioners or investigators, should not be compelled to serve as witnesses at the Court while they remain in employment with the Commission. However, once the Commission has finished its work, they can do so in relation to their work and the content of the report once it is in the public domain. The Commissioners themselves can serve as expert witnesses for the Court.[97] The Commission on the other hand should not use its subpoena powers to compel staff members of the Court to give testimony before it.[98]

C. *Information Sharing*

In order to make both institutions more complementary to each other, it is necessary to have a mechanism in place for possible information sharing. Care must be taken to ensure that such information sharing does not position the Commission as an investigative arm of the Court. Rather, it should be a case where both institutions can operate without frustrating their respective mandates. Information given in public can pose no real threat when shared with either institution. The problem arises when the information is confidential. In such cases, it is recommended that there should be a "conditional information sharing model."[99] With this model, the Commission can only disclose information to the Court in limited circumstances. These limited circumstances could include:

- When the information is vital to the fair determination of a case before the court such as inculpatory or exculpatory evidence[100];
- When it is established that such information cannot be solicited from any other source except from the TRC.[101] Additionally, the following should also be considered:

---

[95] *Id.*
[96] *See* Human Rights Watch, *supra* note 23, at 2.
[97] *Supra* note 93.
[98] Human Rights Watch, *supra* note 23.
[99] Wierda et al., *supra* note 23, at 10.
[100] *Report of the Planning Mission on the Establishment of the Special Court for Sierra Leone*, U.N. Doc. S/2002/246 at 55.
[101] Wierda et al., *supra* note 23, at 10.

- The application for the use of such information should be made to a judge of the Trial Chamber of the Court[102];
- Such application should only be made during trials before the Court and not during investigations[103];
- The Trial Chamber Judge should also consider the impact such information sharing would have on the work of the TRC[104];
- The decision must consider the safety of the person who made the statement or persons whose names are mentioned in the statement;
- Such information sharing should be done with the person who provided the information being fully informed that such will be the case[105];
- Such person must be assured that his/her information will not be used as evidence against him/her in any judicial proceedings.[106]

The Commission must also be encouraged to volunteer information without any request from the Court if such information serves the purpose of exculpatory evidence to determine the innocence of an accused person before the court. If the prosecutor of the Court is in possession of information that is essential to the functions of the TRC, he/she should volunteer such information without any application by the Commission.[107]

D. Access to Detainees in Custody of the Court

As a general rule, the Commission should not have access to detainees in the custody of the Court. However, if excluding such testimony might create a vacuum in the report of the Commission or might affect the Commission's revelation of the truth, then the Commission must be allowed to have access to such detainees. It might be more reasonable to allow such detainees to only make confidential instead of public statements in order to ensure that the Court's work is not affected and that the detainees do not use the Commission as a podium to undermine the cause of justice.

In preparing its final report, the Commission must be careful not to put information that would indicate a statement made by a detainee, if such statement would jeopardize the proceedings before the court.

E. Witness Protection

Both institutions could collaborate on issues relating to witness protection.[108] If somebody who has given confidential testimony/testified with protective measures before the Commission is required to testify at the Court, the Court should make sure that the person's identity is protected from the public.[109] The Court should consider going into closed sessions for such witnesses, using pseudonyms, or regulating questions asked by lawyers so

---

[102] *Id.*
[103] *Id.*
[104] Human Rights Watch, *supra* note 23, at 2.
[105] *Id.* at 3; *see also* Wierda et al., *supra* note 23, at 13.
[106] *Id.*
[107] Human Rights Watch, *supra* note 23, at 4.
[108] *Id.* at 6.
[109] *Id.*

that the public does not identify an incident with a witness. The Commission should inform such witnesses adequately that their information might be shared with the Court.

F. *Establishing an Institutional Relationship*

It is extremely necessary that both institutions establish a formal relationship before they start their respective operations.[110] This would help answer all questions that might arise relating to exercise of powers, information sharing, and witness protection. The institutions should therefore sign a Memorandum of Understanding and Orders for the Disclosure of information as recommended by the ICTJ.[111]

In conclusion, lessons from this model of transitional justice in Sierra Leone indicate that it is possible for truth commissions to operate alongside criminal tribunals without creating trouble. Both institutions can operate with full autonomy while complementing instead of competing with each other. What has been established in Sierra Leone is that the relationship between the two institutions should be cordial and well-defined. Senior staff members of both institutions should meet regularly to discuss any matters arising and evaluate the success of their relationship. Regular updates should be given to the public on how their respective mandates are being implemented and how they are complementing each other's efforts while maintaining their independence of each other.

It must also be noted that there can be no definite proposition as to a preferred model to be adopted in other countries in transition. Each situation should be looked at with its own unique peculiarities. There may be compelling reasons for the establishment of either of these institutions or a combined establishment of both. The goal of both the Truth Commissions and Prosecution Tribunals having a significant impact on a post-conflict society should be kept in mind. A well-structured approach to having these systems complement rather than compete with each other could enhance a "reasonable balance between the conflicting principles of individual criminal responsibility on the one hand, and national reconciliation."[112] The two institutions must be mutually cooperative with each other and complement each other's effort. Without such an interrelationship, the two institutions may offer different and competing narratives of the conflict.[113]

It must be noted that although there is a need to address impunity after violent conflicts, criminal tribunals alone cannot offer the truth of what really happened. As Martha Minow puts it, "the task of making a full account of what happened, in light of the evidence obtained, requires a process of sifting and drafting that usually does not accompany a trial."[114] The limit to what prosecution tribunals can sometimes do was aptly stated by Judges at the International Criminal Tribunal for Rwanda in a December 2008 judgment that "the process of a criminal trial cannot depict the entire picture of what happened ... even in a

---

[110] *Id.* at 1; *see also* Planning Mission Report, *supra* note 23, at 100, and Wierda et al., *supra* note 23, referencing Annex A and Attachment A.

[111] *Id.*

[112] Carsten Stahn, *United Nations Peace-Building, Amnesties and Alternative Forms of Justice: A Change in Practice?*, 84 INT'L REV. RED CROSS 191, 203 (2002).

[113] Dougherty, *supra* note 86, at 51.

[114] MARTHA MINNOW, BETWEEN VENGEANCE AND FORGIVENESS: FACING HISTORY AFTER GENOCIDE AND MASS VIOLENCE 59 (1998).

case of this magnitude. The Chamber's task is narrowed by exacting standards of proof and procedure as well as its focus on the four Accused and the specific evidence placed before it in this case."[115] Truth commissions and prosecution tribunals operating in parallel provide an opportunity for peace and justice efforts to complement each other. They are both in a position to help victims regain their human worth, although from diverging points of view. As Schabas puts it, "the real lesson of the Sierra Leone experiment is that truth commissions and courts can work productively together, even if they only work in parallel. This complementary relationship may have a synergistic effect on the search for post conflict justice as part of the struggle against impunity."[116] In the words of Justice Richard Goldstone, "The works of truth commissions ... share with criminal prosecutions the ability to bring significant satisfaction to victims. If that satisfaction is sufficiently widespread within a community, it can have a soothing effect upon a whole society."[117]

---

[115] The Prosecutor v. Théoneste Bagosoro, Gratien Kabiligi, Aloys Ntabakuze, Anatole Nsengiyumva (ICTR-98–41-T), Trial Chamber, Judgment and Sentence, at 1, para. 5 (Dec. 18, 2008).

[116] Schabas, *supra* note 26, at 6.

[117] Richard J. Goldstone, *Justice as a Tool for Peace-Making: Truth Commissions and International Criminal Tribunals*, 28 N.Y.U. J. INT'L L. & POL. 485, 491 (1995–1996).

PART VI

Institutional Innovations in the Practice of the Special Court for Sierra Leone

26

How Special Is the Special Court's Outreach Section?

Stuart Ford[*]

I. INTRODUCTION

This chapter evaluates the work of the Outreach Section of the Special Court for Sierra Leone (SCSL or "the Court"). In it, I try to answer two questions: (1) how innovative was the Outreach Section?, and (2) has the Outreach Section been successful? In contrast to earlier commentators, I try to answer these questions using a quantitative approach, including examining Sierra Leonean attitudes toward and knowledge about the Court as measured in various public opinion surveys. I conclude that the Outreach Section has been modestly innovative, but that it has largely failed in its primary goal of educating Sierra Leoneans about the SCSL – although virtually all Sierra Leoneans are aware of the existence of the Court, very few have a good understanding of what it does.

II. A BRIEF HISTORY OF THE OUTREACH SECTION[1]

The SCSL was established by joint agreement of the United Nations and the government of Sierra Leone in January 2002.[2] Much of the structure of the SCSL is outlined in the Court's statute, which describes the SCSL as being composed of three principal organs: the Chambers, the Prosecutor's office, and the Registry.[3] Neither the Statute nor the Agreement makes any mention of the Outreach Section.

---

[*] Assistant Professor of Law at the John Marshall Law School in Chicago, Illinois, USA. Professor Ford was formerly an Assistant Prosecutor at the Extraordinary Chambers in the Courts of Cambodia. This chapter was greatly improved by the comments of those who read earlier versions, including Professors Jenia Iontcheva Turner, Margaret Kwoka, and Charles Jalloh. Cristina Headley provided assistance with editing and proofreading.

[1] Numerous descriptions of the Outreach Section's activities appear in the literature, including among others: V. Nmehielle & C. Jalloh, *The Legacy of the Special Court for Sierra Leone*, 30 FLETCHER F. WORLD AFF. 107, 114–16 (2006); J. Pham, *A Viable Model for International Criminal Justice: The Special Court for Sierra Leone*, 19 N.Y. INT'L L. REV. 37, 104–06 (2006); D. Cohen, *"Hybrid" Justice in East Timor, Sierra Leone and Cambodia: "Lessons Learned" and Prospects for the Future*, 43 STAN J. INT'L L. 1, 21–22 (2007); V. Hussain, *Sustaining Judicial Rescues: The Role of Outreach and Capacity-Building Efforts in War Crimes Tribunals*, 45 VA. J. INT'L L. 547, 572–78 (2005); J. Clark, *International War Crimes Tribunals and the Challenge of Outreach*, 9 INT'L CRIM. L. REV. 99, 106–08 (2009). Consequently, I will not attempt to provide an exhaustive history.

[2] Agreement between the United Nations and the Government of Sierra Leone on the Establishment of a Special Court for Sierra Leone, The Special Court for Sierra Leone (Jan. 16, 2002), *available at* http://www.sc-sl.org/LinkClick.aspx?fileticket=CLk1rMQtCHg%3d&tabid=176 (last visited Mar. 7, 2012) [hereinafter the SCSL Agreement].

[3] SCSL Statute art. 11 [hereinafter the SCSL Statute].

A reference to the existence of an "ambitious outreach programme" appears in the SCSL's First Annual Report.[4] This description, however, elides over a somewhat rocky start for the Outreach Section. The first outreach officers were employed by the Office of the Prosecutor (OTP), where they supported the Prosecutor's outreach efforts, including a series of town hall meetings that were held throughout Sierra Leone during 2002.[5] This was problematic, as one could not reasonably expect these outreach personnel to do impartial outreach on behalf of the Chambers or the defense teams. It was not until January 2003 that outreach activities were moved to the Registry and placed within the newly created Outreach Section.[6]

By mid-2003, the Outreach Section had developed a Mission Statement that identified its goals as "promoting understanding of the Special Court" in Sierra Leone, "foster[ing] an environment of two-way communication between the People of Sierra Leone and the Special Court," and promoting "respect for human rights and the rule of law."[7] It targeted both the general population and specific groups with an interest in the Court, including students and members of the police and armed forces.[8] The activities it engaged in included town hall meetings at the district and chiefdom level, regular meetings with civil society organizations (CSOs), radio programs, and print publications.[9] By the end of 2003, the Outreach Section had ten staff members, five located in Freetown and five located at district offices.[10] However, money was tight and the SCSL admitted that the Outreach Section did not have sufficient resources to fulfill its mandate without additional outside funding.[11]

---

[4] The Special Court for Sierra Leone, First Annual Report of the President of the Special Court for Sierra Leone for the Period December 2, 2002–December 1, 2003, at 6 [hereinafter First Annual Report of the SCSL]. The SCSL has produced a series of annual reports from the President of the SCSL to the Secretary-General of the United Nations and the government of Sierra Leone, pursuant to Article 25 of the SCSL Statute. The reports are available from the website of the Special Court at http://www.sc-sl.org (last visited Dec. 14, 2011).

[5] *Id.* at 16, 26.

[6] *Id.* at 26. This made sense, as the Registry is tasked with those functions that "support the Court process as a whole" and had been identified as being responsible for communication on behalf of the SCSL. *Id.* at 18. *See also* Rule 33(A) of the SCSL's Rules of Procedure and Evidence, which states that the Registry serves as the Court's "channel of communication."

[7] Outreach Section's Mission Statement (2003) (copy on file with the author). *See also* First Annual Report of the SCSL, *supra* note 4, at 6, 26; Clark, *supra* note 1, at 107; Hussain, *supra* note 1, at 571.

[8] First Annual Report of the SCSL, *supra* note 4, at 26.

[9] *Id.*

[10] *Id.*

[11] *Id.* Throughout the Outreach Section's existence it has received additional outside funding, which has largely been provided by the European Commission. *See, e.g.,* The Special Court for Sierra Leone, Second Annual Report of the President of the Special Court for Sierra Leone for the Period January 1, 2004–January 17, 2005, at 35 [hereinafter Second Annual Report of the SCSL]; The Special Court for Sierra Leone, Third Annual Report of the President of the Special Court for Sierra Leone, January 2005–January 2006, at 38 [hereinafter Third Annual Report of the SCSL]; The Special Court for Sierra Leone, Fourth Annual Report of the President of the Special Court for Sierra Leone, January 2006–May 2007, at 54 [hereinafter Fourth Annual Report of the SCSL]; The Special Court for Sierra Leone, Fifth Annual Report of the President of the Special Court for Sierra Leone, June 2007–May 2008, at 52 [hereinafter Fifth Annual Report of the SCSL]; The Special Court for Sierra Leone, Seventh Annual Report of the President of the Special Court for Sierra Leone, June 2009–May 2010, at 43 [hereinafter Seventh Annual Report of the SCSL]; The Special Court for Sierra Leone, Eighth Annual Report of the President of the Special Court for Sierra Leone, June 2010–May 2011, at 43 [hereinafter Eighth Annual Report of the SCSL].

By 2004, the Outreach Section had mostly established a nationwide network of outreach officers located at district offices throughout the country and had conducted outreach meetings in more than 450 communities.[12] At the same time, it expanded the targets of its outreach to include programs directed at women, children, people with disabilities, and religious leaders.[13] In 2005, the Outreach Section organized the Victims Commemoration Conference, which brought together delegates from all over Sierra Leone to identify actions that could be undertaken to help victims of the conflict.[14] It also continued its prior activities, including video screenings of trial excerpts, radio programs about the court, and town hall meetings throughout the country.[15]

In 2006, there were two major developments. First, the Outreach Section expanded its operations to include outreach activities in Liberia in conjunction with Liberian CSOs.[16] This resulted, in large part, from the arrest and transfer of Charles Taylor, the former president of Liberia, to the SCSL in March 2006.[17] With the former Liberian head of state in custody, the Outreach Section had to increasingly focus on outreach in Liberia. Second, the Outreach Section retained an outside consultant to assess how Sierra Leoneans perceived the Court and the work of the Outreach Section.[18] The consultant conducted a survey that is discussed in Section V(B)(1).

In 2008, the Outreach Section merged with the Press and Public Affairs Office to create the Outreach and Public Affairs Section.[19] The resulting organization is described as being "responsible for bringing the work of the Court to the public."[20] In 2009, the Outreach and Public Affairs Section concentrated on outreach related to the trial of Charles Taylor, particularly the evidence produced by the Taylor defense team and the issue of fair trial rights for the accused.[21] The emphasis on the Charles Taylor trial continued in 2010 and 2011.[22]

The SCSL is slowly winding down its operations in Freetown,[23] and the Outreach and Public Affairs Section is reducing its staff[24] in anticipation of a completion of all court activities in late 2013.[25] Although there will be a "residual mechanism" for the Court, it has no

---

[12] Second Annual Report of the SCSL, *supra* note 11, at 33–34.

[13] *Id.* at 34.

[14] Third Annual Report of the SCSL, *supra* note 11, at 37.

[15] *Id.* at 37–38.

[16] Fourth Annual Report of the SCSL, *supra* note 11, at 54.

[17] M. Drumbl, *Charles Taylor and the Special Court for Sierra Leone*, 10 ASIL INSIGHTS, No. 9 (Apr. 12, 2006), *available at* http://www.asil.org/insights060412.cfm (last visited Mar. 7, 2012).

[18] Fourth Annual Report of the SCSL, *supra* note 11, at 53.

[19] The Special Court for Sierra Leone, Sixth Annual Report of the President of the Special Court for Sierra Leone, June 2008–May 2009, at 41 [hereinafter Sixth Annual Report of the SCSL]. The Press and Public Affairs Office had been responsible for providing information to local and international media, organizations, academics, and governments. First Annual Report of the SCSL, *supra* note 4, at 18, 27.

[20] Sixth Annual Report of the SCSL, *supra* note 19, at 41.

[21] Seventh Annual Report of the SCSL, *supra* note 11, at 43.

[22] Eighth Annual Report of the SCSL, *supra* note 11, at 43.

[23] *Id.* at 34.

[24] *Id.* at 31.

[25] The date on which the court will finish its work has been a moving target, but the most recent annual report predicts that the court will complete its work in September 2013 with the issuance of the appeals judgement in the Charles Taylor case. The Special Court for Sierra Leone, Ninth Annual Report of the President of the Special Court for Sierra Leone, June 2011–May 2012, at 27 [hereinafter Ninth Annual Report of the SCSL].

mandate for outreach;[26] therefore it appears the Outreach and Public Affairs Section will cease to exist at the same time the SCSL completes its work.[27]

III. WHAT HAS THE OUTREACH SECTION DONE?

A. Methods and Accomplishments

The Outreach Section seeks to accomplish its goals of communicating with and educating Sierra Leoneans through a number of methods, including: (1) video screenings of trial excerpts; (2) town hall meetings; (3) visits to schools by outreach officers; (4) organized visits by the public and CSO representatives to the Court itself; (5) radio programs about the SCSL; and (6) public lectures by court officers about various aspects of the Court's work. Particularly recently, the court has been keen to highlight the number of events the Outreach Section has organized. The published figures are reproduced in Table 26.1 below.

The first thing to note is that the Outreach Section has organized thousands of outreach activities for Sierra Leoneans and, to a lesser extent, Liberians. It has conducted more than 5,000 screenings of trial excerpts (and possibly much more[28]), more than 3,000 town hall meetings, and almost 3,000 school visits. In many cases, this means that the Outreach Section was conducting activities at different locations on the same day. For example, from June 2008 to May 2009, the Outreach Section averaged more than five video screenings, nearly four town hall meetings, and slightly more than three-and-a half school visits every single day. This volume of activity was made possible by a network of district outreach officers employed by the SCSL.[29]

In addition, the Outreach Section has printed and distributed tens of thousands of copies of an informational booklet about the Court, and tens of thousands of copies of an informational booklet about international humanitarian law.[30] It has also made a concerted effort to work with local CSOs, and more than sixty such groups attend monthly briefings held by the Outreach Section.[31] This collaboration has strengthened and empowered local CSOs.[32]

The Outreach Section has also had a number of accomplishments that are not easily reduced to numbers. For example, in 2004, it was instrumental in establishing "Accountability Now Clubs" at eight Sierra Leonean universities, and provided training

---

[26] Eighth Annual Report of the SCSL, *supra* note 11, at 51.

[27] *Cf.* Nmehielle & Jalloh, *supra* note 1, at 107 (suggesting that many legacy activities should build upon initiatives begun by the Outreach Section).

[28] Because the Annual Reports did not contain exact numbers until the later years, the figures discussed here are minimums. It is likely that the actual figures are significantly higher.

[29] Sixth Annual Report of the SCSL, *supra* note 19, at 37 (noting that a "nationwide network of Outreach Officers, some of whom reach many communities by motorbike, is supported by a central office in Freetown").

[30] *Id.* at 42 (noting that the Outreach Section distributed twenty thousand booklets on international humanitarian law and fifteen thousand booklets about the court called *The Special Court Made Simple*); Seventh Annual Report of the SCSL, *supra* note 11, at 45 (noting that the Special Court produced and distributed twenty thousand copies of the *Special Court Made Simple* handbook and twenty thousand copies of the international humanitarian law handbook during 2009 and 2010).

[31] *Id.* at 43. The Outreach Section also works with 20 CSOs in Liberia. *Id.*

[32] J. Stromseth, *Strengthening Demand for the Rule of Law in Post-Conflict Societies*, 18 MINN. J. INT'L LAW 415, 423 (2009). *See also* Nmehielle & Jalloh, *supra* note 1, at 115.

TABLE 26.1 *Outreach Activities*

Year[a]	Video Screenings	Town Hall Meetings	School Visits	Court Visits	Public Lectures
2002–2003	–	–	–	–	–
2004	–	–	–	–	–
2005	–	450	–	–	–
2006–2007	–	–	–	–	–
2007–2008	1873	1377	1300	68	70
2008–2009	1892	1400	1322	50	–
2009–2010	864	–	170	17	61
2010–2011	855	10	165	15	65
Total	**5484**	**3237**	**2957**	**150**	**196**

[a] Each row in this column corresponds with one of the Annual Report periods. The information in the cells was collected from the corresponding Annual Report. The Annual Reports, particularly the earlier ones, do not always contain information on the number of events that were held.

to the club members.[33] The role of the clubs is to involve students in promoting justice, human rights, the rule of law, transparency, and accountability.[34] By 2010, Accountability Now Clubs were active at fourteen universities in Sierra Leone and seven universities in Liberia.[35] Moreover, the Outreach Section has worked hard to ensure that the clubs will be able to continue operating after the SCSL is shut down.[36] The Accountability Now Clubs have been viewed by commentators as a significant accomplishment of the Court.[37]

The Outreach Section also coordinated a series of regional Victims' Commemoration Conferences in 2004 that were attended by hundreds of participants and ultimately culminated in a national conference held in Freetown in February 2005.[38] The national conference resulted in identifying fifty activities that the court and civil society organizations could undertake to help victims of the conflict.[39]

B. *Staffing and Cost*

Initially, there were three outreach officers based in the OTP.[40] However, by the end of 2003, the Outreach Section had moved to the Registry, and staffing had increased to five members at the Court's headquarters in Freetown and five district outreach officers located in the countryside.[41] The Outreach Section continued to grow until it eventually employed eighteen district outreach officers.[42] However, starting in 2009, the section began eliminating

[33] Second Annual Report of the SCSL, *supra* note 11, at 34.
[34] Eighth Annual Report of the SCSL, *supra* note 11, at 44.
[35] Seventh Annual Report of the SCSL, *supra* note 11, at 44. *See also* Fourth Annual Report of the SCSL, *supra* note 11, at 53.
[36] Seventh Annual Report of the SCSL, *supra* note 11, at 44; Eighth Annual Report of the SCSL, *supra* note 11, at 44.
[37] *See, e.g.*, Stromseth, *supra* note 33, at 423.
[38] Second Annual Report of the SCSL, *supra* note 11, at 35.
[39] *Id.* at 25; Third Annual Report of the SCSL, *supra* note 11, at 37.
[40] First Annual Report of the SCSL, *supra* note 4, at 26.
[41] *Id.* at 26.
[42] Sixth Annual Report of the SCSL, *supra* note 19, at 41.

positions in anticipation of its eventual closing. Two posts were eliminated in early 2009, a further two posts were eliminated in late 2009, and seven posts were eliminated in 2010 and early 2011.[43]

It has been difficult to ascertain how much the Outreach Section has cost. Early Annual Reports did not produce any breakdown on how money was spent at the SCSL.[44] Later Annual Reports produced spending levels for the Registry, but failed to break down spending within the Registry.[45] Nevertheless, it has been possible to ascertain some funding amounts from outside sources. For example, Human Rights Watch reported that in 2003, the SCSL had budgeted $600,000 for outreach, but that this was cut by the management committee.[46] The European Union (EU) subsequently contributed €500,000.[47] The EU has continued to fund the Court's outreach programs through a program called the European Instrument for Democracy and Human Rights (EIDHR). Research into EIDHR funding documents indicates the EU provided €800,000 in 2004, €692,000 in 2005, €594,000 in 2007, €600,000 in 2008, and €1,000,000 in 2009.[48]

If these figures are converted to U.S. dollars using the average annual exchange rate for each year, this translates into funding of slightly more than $5.5M (not adjusted for inflation).[49] However, this figure is almost certainly too low, as I could not find funding figures for 2006, 2010, or 2011, despite acknowledgment by the SCSL that it received funding for outreach from the EU during these years.[50] If one assumes that funding during the missing years was roughly commensurate with funding in the closest available years for which information is available, this implies that total funding for the Outreach Section is somewhere between $7M and $10M over the lifetime of the Court. This number may seem large, but it represents just a few percent of the total amount spent on the SCSL as a whole.[51]

[43] *See id.* at 30; Seventh Annual Report of the SCSL, *supra* note 11, at 33; Eighth Annual Report of the SCSL, *supra* note 11, at 31. *See also* note 25 (noting that the court and the Outreach Section will shut down in late 2013).

[44] *See, e.g.,* First Annual Report of the SCSL, *supra* note 4, at 36, Annex III.

[45] *See* Sixth Annual Report of the SCSL, *supra* note 19, at 34–35; Seventh Annual Report of the SCSL, *supra* note 11, at 37–38; Eighth Annual Report of the SCSL, *supra* note 11, at 36–37. The Outreach Section has regularly received additional outside funding, *see* note 11, but the amount of this funding has not been disclosed by the Court.

[46] Human Rights Watch, *Bringing Justice: The Special Court for Sierra Leone: Accomplishments, Shortcomings and Needed Support* 34 (2004), *available at* http://www.hrw.org/reports/2004/09/07/bringing-justice-special-court-sierra-leone (last visited Mar. 7, 2012).

[47] *Id.*

[48] *See* European Initiative for Democracy and Human Rights, *Promoting Democracy and Human Rights Worldwide 2000–2006*, at 306, *available at* http://www.eidhr.eu/files/dmfile/EIDHRInitiativeCompendium-14-07-10.pdf (last visited Mar. 9, 2012) (indicating a contribution of €800,000 in 2004); *id.* at 302 (indicating a contribution of €695,244 in 2005); European Instrument for Democracy and Human Rights, *Compendium 2007–2010*, at 138, *available at* http://www.eidhr.eu/files/dmfile/EUAID_EIDHR_Compendium_LR_20110609.pdf (last visited Mar. 9, 2012) (indicating a contribution of €600,000 in 2008); European Instrument for Democracy and Human Rights, *2008 Annual Action Programme in Favour of Sierra Leone, Annex 3: Action Fiche Legacy Project-Special Court Sierra Leone* 2, *available at* http://ec.europa.eu/europeaid/documents/aap/2008/af_aap_2008_sle.pdf (last visited Mar. 6, 2012) (indicating a contribution of €1,000,000 in 2009).

[49] Historical exchange rates were obtained from www.oanda.com.

[50] *See, e.g.,* Eighth Annual Report of the SCSL, *supra* note 11, at 43 (indicating that the outreach program received funding from the "EC and Macarthur Foundation" during 2010 and 2011).

[51] *See* S. Ford, *How Leadership in International Criminal Law Is Shifting from the United States to Europe and Asia: An Analysis of Spending On and Contributions to International Criminal Courts*, 55 ST. LOUIS U. L.J. 953, 975 (2011) (estimating that the SCSL would cost more than $257M over its lifetime).

C. Obstacles

In the early years, the Outreach Section "suffered from the lack of the requisite financial support for its programs."[52] This was the product of a deliberate decision by the Court's Management Committee to try to fund outreach activities from outside sources rather than from the Court's regular budget.[53] That decision, while it seems myopic, has to be viewed in the context of the extreme financial difficulties the SCSL faced in its early years. For example, the SCSL was nearly shut down because of insufficient funds in 2004, and had to be rescued by the United Nations.[54] The Outreach Section has also been hampered by the large number of small and isolated communities in Sierra Leone as well as a limited communications infrastructure.[55] Finally, many different languages are in use in Sierra Leone and literacy rates are low,[56] which has made it a challenge to communicate effectively with Sierra Leoneans.[57]

D. The Effect of the Outreach Section on Other Tribunals

Outreach programs are now viewed as an essential component of the work of international criminal tribunals.[58] After a late start, the International Criminal Tribunal for the former Yugoslavia's (ICTY) outreach program is now a relatively robust one.[59] The International Criminal Tribunal for Rwanda (ICTR) also has an outreach program, although it is apparently quite anemic and (like the ICTY's program) arrived late in the process.[60] The Extraordinary Chambers in the Courts of Cambodia (ECCC)[61] and the International Criminal Court (ICC)[62] both have an extensive outreach program. The fact that all international criminal courts today have an outreach program appears, at least in part, to be the result of the perceived success of the SCSL's Outreach Section.

---

[52] First Annual Report of the SCSL, *supra* note 4, at 27. This was partially mitigated by securing outside funding. *Id.*

[53] *See* C. Sriram, *Wrong-Sizing International Justice? The Hybrid Tribunal in Sierra Leone*, 29 FORDHAM INT'L L.J. 472, 496 (2006). *See also supra* note 47.

[54] *See* Ford, *supra* note 52, at 993.

[55] Second Annual Report of the SCSL, *supra* note 11, at 33.

[56] English is the official language of Sierra Leone but is spoken by only a relatively small portion of the population. Other common languages include Mende, Temne, and Krio. Krio is the first language of only 10 percent of the population, but is understood by most Sierra Leoneans. Approximately 35 percent of the population is literate. *See* Central Intelligence Agency, *The World Factbook: Sierra Leone, People and Society, available at* https://www.cia.gov/library/publications/the-world-factbook/geos/sl.html (last visited Mar. 3, 2012).

[57] Second Annual Report of the SCSL, *supra* note 11, at 33.

[58] *See, e.g.,* D. Crane, *White Man's Justice: Applying International Justice after Regional Third World Conflicts*, 27 CARDOZO L. REV. 1683, 1684 (2006) (arguing that one of the "essential mandates" for an international criminal court must be a robust outreach program).

[59] *See* Clark, *supra* note 1, at 101–06. The ICTY conducts "hundreds of public events every year" and operates regional offices in Bosnia and Herzegovina, Serbia, Croatia and Kosovo. *See* International Criminal Tribunal for the Former Yugoslavia, *Outreach Activities, available at* http://www.icty.org/sections/Outreach/OutreachActivities (last visited Dec. 16, 2011).

[60] Hussain, *supra* note 1, at 564–65.

[61] *See* S. Ford, *A Social Psychology Model of the Perceived Legitimacy of International Criminal Courts: Implications for the Success of Transitional Justice Mechanisms*, 45 VAND. J. TRANSNAT'L L. 405, 438 (2012).

[62] *See* Clark, *supra* note 1, at 112–15. The ICC's outreach program is also described in more detail on its website. The International Criminal Court, *Outreach, available at* http://www.icc-cpi.int/Menus/ICC/Structure+of+the+Court/Outreach/ (last visited Jan. 27, 2012).

IV. HOW INNOVATIVE WAS THE OUTREACH SECTION?

Commentators often describe the SCSL's outreach program as innovative,[63] but there is some reason to question claims about the Outreach Section's innovation. First, the SCSL was not the first international criminal court to engage in outreach. Rather, the ICTY pioneered the use of outreach programs. The ICTY first became aware of the need for outreach efforts in 1997 and proposed the creation of a formal Outreach Program within the Registry in 1998.[64] It held its first outreach activity in late 1999 with a conference for journalists from the former Yugoslavia.[65] It then had eighteen outreach activities in 2000[66] and more than seventy outreach activities in 2001.[67] All of this occurred before the SCSL began work in early 2002.

Second, beginning at least in 2000, the ICTY was criticized for failing to do effective outreach in the former Yugoslavia.[68] With this criticism in mind, scholars writing about the creation of the SCSL urged the establishment of some sort of outreach capacity.[69] Reflecting this academic critique, the Secretary-General called for "a broad public information and education campaign … as an integral part of the Court's activities."[70] Therefore, it is perhaps somewhat surprising that outreach was not made a formal part of either the SCSL Statute or Agreement. On the other hand, the constituent documents of international criminal tribunals do not generally include much detail on the structure of the Registry.[71]

Third, the SCSL's early efforts at outreach showed a lack of thoughtful planning, with outreach initially located in the OTP.[72] This lack of planning may have adversely affected the

---

[63] *See, e.g.*, Cohen, *supra* note 1, at 21; Stromseth, *supra* note 33, at 422.

[64] *See* The Human Rights Center et al., *Report: Justice, Accountability and Social Reconstruction: An Interview Study of Bosnian Judges and Prosecutors*, 18 Berkeley J. Int'l L. 102, 110–11 (2000).

[65] *See* International Criminal Tribunal for the Former Yugoslavia, *ICTY Outreach Activities – 1999, available at* http://www.icty.org/sid/10110 (last visited Dec. 16, 2011).

[66] *See* International Criminal Tribunal for the Former Yugoslavia, *ICTY Outreach Activities – 2000, available at* http://www.icty.org/sid/10109 (last visited Dec. 16, 2011).

[67] *See* International Criminal Tribunal for the Former Yugoslavia, *ICTY Outreach Activities – 2001, available at* http://www.icty.org/sid/10111 (last visited Dec. 16, 2011).

[68] *See, e.g.*, The Human Rights Center et al., *supra* note 65, at 140, 153 (attributing negative attitudes toward the ICTY among judges in the former Yugoslavia in part to lack of knowledge about the ICTY and urging support for a formal outreach program).

[69] *See* C. Shocken, *The Special Court for Sierra Leone: Overview and Recommendations*, 20 Berkeley J. Int'l L. 436, 460 (2002) (urging the creation of a "public relations bureau" to help Sierra Leoneans understand what is happening at the Court); A. Tejan-Cole, *The Special Court for Sierra Leone: Conceptual Concerns and Alternatives*, 1 Afr. Hum. Rts. J. 107, 119, 125–26 (2001) (urging the TRC and the Court to engage in joint "public awareness and education campaigns"). It is also true that not all articles stressed the importance of outreach efforts. *See, e.g.*, M. Frulli, *The Special Court for Sierra Leone: Some Preliminary Comments*, 11 Eur. J. Int'l L. 857 (2000).

[70] Report of the Secretary-General on the Establishment of a Special Court for Sierra Leone, § 7, at 2, U.N. Doc. S/2000/915 (Oct. 4, 2000).

[71] For example, the Rome Statute of the International Criminal Court simply states that the Registry is responsible for "non-judicial aspects of the administration and servicing of the court." ICC Statute art. 4(1). The only subunit within the Registry that the Rome Statute explicitly requires is a Victims and Witnesses Unit. ICC Statute art. 43(6). Yet, the ICC has an outreach program. *See supra* note 63.

[72] *See* notes 5–6 (noting that outreach efforts were initially organized by the OTP, which created an appearance of partiality, and that only later was an Outreach Section created within the Registry to centralize the Court's outreach efforts and separate it from the work of the OTP).

Outreach Section.[73] In addition, the Management Committee's decision to cut funding for outreach reflects an early failure to prioritize outreach work at the SCSL.[74]

Nevertheless, this was the first court to engage in a comprehensive countrywide outreach effort organized through a network of district offices, and the size of the SCSL's outreach efforts appears to have been significantly larger than that of contemporary programs at the ICTY. In 2007–2008, the SCSL reports having engaged in more than 4,600 outreach activities.[75] At roughly the same time, the ICTY reports having engaged in approximately 170 outreach activities in the former Yugoslavia.[76] The resulting comparison is imprecise,[77] but it appears reasonably certain that the frequency of SCSL outreach activities in 2007 exceeded ICTY outreach activities by at least an order of magnitude.[78] Consequently, it does seem fair to characterize the Outreach Section's work as moderately innovative. In my view, the Outreach Section's innovation lies in the geographic scope and number of its outreach activities.

V. HAS THE OUTREACH SECTION BEEN SUCCESSFUL?

A. Previous Assessments

Assessments of the work of the Outreach Section have generally been positive. For example, Antonio Cassese, in his role as an Independent Expert appointed by the Secretary-General of the United Nations to review the operation of the Court, described the Outreach Section as the "crown jewel of the Special Court."[79] He went on to conclude that the Outreach Section's work was "exceedingly effective" and recommended that it serve as a "model for future international courts."[80] Former Prosecutor David Crane has argued that the SCSL's outreach efforts were "an absolute key to success" and that his town hall meetings around the country were critical in establishing a rapport with the local population.[81]

Academics have also been convinced of the Outreach Section's merit. Professors Nmehielle and Jalloh concluded that the Court's outreach program "probably exceed[ed]" that of any other international criminal court.[82] Professor Stromseth described the Outreach

---

[73] *See* Sriram, *supra* note 54, at 496 (arguing that the legacy of having outreach initially conducted by the OTP led people to identify the views of the Prosecution as those of the Court).

[74] *See id.*; Cohen, *supra* note 1, at 21–22 (noting that the initial budget for the SCSL did not include funding for outreach but that the Registrar sought outside funding for it).

[75] *See supra* Table 1. This represents one calendar year of outreach activities (June 2007–May 2008).

[76] *See* International Criminal Tribunal for the Former Yugoslavia, *ICTY Outreach Activities – 2007*, *available at* http://www.icty.org/sid/10128 (last visited Jan. 30, 2012) (containing list of ICTY outreach activities for 2007).

[77] There are difficulties in directly comparing the number of outreach activities at the ICTY and the SCSL. One cannot simply count the number of entries on the ICTY's list as it often lumps together as a single entry multiple activities that would be counted separately in the SCSL's list. For example, I counted the entry for "Conclusion of youth workshops on the ICTY" that took place in June in Belgrade as thirty activities because it was described as comprising "30 workshops for high school students on the Tribunal's work."

[78] *See also* notes 28–29 (describing the pace of outreach activities at the SCSL).

[79] Report on the Special Court for Sierra Leone, Submitted by the Independent Expert Antonio Cassese 59, Dec. 12, 2006, *available at* http://www.sc-sl.org/LinkClick.aspx?fileticket=VTDHyrHasLc=&tabid=176 (last visited Mar. 8, 2012).

[80] *Id.* at 9, § 30.

[81] *See* Crane, *supra* note 59, at 809–11.

[82] Nmehielle & Jalloh, *supra* note 1, at 121.

Section's efforts as an "innovative effort to strengthen domestic awareness of, and capacity for, the rule of law."[83] Others have been similarly positive.[84] Even those who have criticized the Court's outreach efforts on various points have nonetheless acknowledged that it was extensive, timely, and "impressive."[85]

B. Assessing the Outreach Section Using Empirical Evidence

Although commentators have generally been quite positive in their assessments of the Outreach Section, the vast majority of assessments of the Outreach Section's work appears to be based primarily on two evaluation methods: (1) evaluations of the program's success based on interviews with Outreach Section staff and CSO representatives; and/or (2) evaluations based on the number of outreach activities undertaken. Neither is an ideal method of evaluating the program's success. The first method relies too heavily on anecdotal evidence, particularly anecdotal evidence provided by sources that have an interest in the success of the Outreach Section. The second method assumes that the more outreach activities a program conducts, the more successful it will be. For the reasons discussed later in the chapter, I do not believe such an assumption is warranted. Perhaps more important, neither method directly measures success. If the goal is educating Sierra Leoneans about the Court, then the thing one would most like to measure is whether Sierra Leoneans have learned much about the SCSL.

In this section, I try to measure the success of the Outreach Section in meeting the goals it set for itself in its Mission Statement using empirical evidence. This approach is made possible, in part, by the fact that there have been a number of attitude surveys conducted in Sierra Leone during the lifetime of the court. This allows me to test claims of the Outreach Section's success with data. The goals of the Outreach Section as described in its Mission Statement are: (1) communicate information about the SCSL to the people of Sierra Leone; (2) communicate information from the people of Sierra Leone to the Court; and (3) promote the rule of law and human rights in Sierra Leone.[86] The Outreach Section's success in reaching each goal will be evaluated separately.

1. Educating Sierra Leoneans about the SCSL

The Outreach Section's first goal (communicating information about the Court to the people of Sierra Leone) is its most important one,[87] and the easiest of the goals to evaluate. In fact, several surveys have attempted to measure how well Sierra Leoneans understand

---

[83] Stromseth, *supra* note 33, at 422.

[84] *See* Pham, *supra* note at 1, at 106 (arguing that the Special Court's outreach efforts have strengthened civil society and fostered a sense of participation and ownership in the judicial process); Cohen, *supra* note 1, at 21 (describing the court's outreach efforts as "innovative" and "effective").

[85] Sriram, *supra* note 54, at 495. *See also* Hussain, *supra* note 1, at 577.

[86] *See supra* note 7. These goals were, in practice, expanded to include outreach to people in Liberia. *See supra* notes 16–17, 21–22.

[87] There is no formal hierarchy among the goals listed in the Outreach Section's Mission Statement. Nevertheless, the most common definition of outreach is "to reach out." *See, e.g.*, RANDOM HOUSE WEBSTER'S COLLEGE DICTIONARY (1992); THE AMERICAN HERITAGE DICTIONARY (4th ed. 2000); NEW OXFORD AMERICAN DICTIONARY (3d ed. 2010). Therefore, it seems reasonable to conclude that this is the Outreach Section's most important function.

the SCSL. Of course, one cannot simply assume that everything Sierra Leoneans know about the Court is a result of the work of the Outreach Section. Sierra Leoneans receive information from a number of sources.[88] Radio is by far the most common source of information, and the source that is trusted the most. Only 12 percent of Sierra Leoneans identified "community meetings" as a main source of information about what is happening in Sierra Leone, despite the fact that the largest number of outreach activities (including the town hall meetings and the video screenings) would probably fall into this category.[89] This suggests that these were not the main source of Sierra Leoneans' knowledge about the court.

In June and July 2007, the BBC World Service Trust carried out a detailed survey of attitudes toward transitional justice institutions in Sierra Leone (hereinafter the "BBC Survey").[90] The results shed some light on the question of how effective the Outreach Section has been at educating Sierra Leoneans about the work of the Court. To begin with, virtually everyone in Sierra Leone was aware[91] of the existence of the SCSL.[92] However, knowledge of how the Court works was very low, with just 7 percent of the respondents indicating they knew "a lot" about the court.[93] The vast majority of Sierra Leoneans know little about how the court operates.[94] Other surveys of Sierra Leonean attitudes toward the SCSL have made similar findings. For example, in their survey, Sawyer and Kelsall found that only 15 percent of respondents had a "good" understanding of the Court.[95] At the same time, a combined 60 percent of those surveyed by the BBC said that the SCSL had been either "very successful" (11 percent) or "quite successful" (49 percent) at communicating its work to the people of Sierra Leone.[96] The result is somewhat odd. Virtually all Sierra Leoneans know the court

---

[88] *See* BBC World Service Trust, International Center for Transitional Justice, Search for Common Ground, *Peace, Justice and Reconciliation in Sierra Leone: A Survey of Knowledge and Attitudes towards Transitional Institutions in Post-Conflict Sierra Leone* 24, fig.13 (Aug. 2008), *available at* http://www.communicatingjustice. org/files/content/file/SIERRA%20LEONE%20REPORT.pdf (last visited Mar. 8, 2012) [hereinafter the BBC Survey].

[89] *Id.* at 24 figs.13 and 14.

[90] The BBC surveyed more than 1,700 Sierra Leoneans in nine districts across the country. Within each district, certain towns were selected for surveying so as to reflect the overall diversity within the population. Then, within each town, households were selected at random for surveying. *Id.* at 12.

[91] Throughout this chapter, I distinguish between awareness and knowledge. People are described as being aware of the SCSL if they know the SCSL exists. People are described as having knowledge of the SCSL if they know what the SCSL is supposed to accomplish or how it works. As will become clear, almost all Sierra Leoneans are aware of the SCSL, but very few know how it works, even at the most superficial level.

[92] BBC Survey, *supra* note 89, at 59 (finding that 96 percent of Sierra Leoneans were aware of the Special Court).

[93] *Id.* at 60. Ninety-three percent of respondents indicated they knew "a bit" about the Court. There were only two possible responses to the question. In addition, knowledge was self-assessed, meaning that it is difficult to know what level of understanding those who said they knew "a lot" actually had. A survey that tried to objectively assess knowledge about the Special Court suggests that even those who claim to know "a lot" probably have a relatively unsophisticated understanding of the Court. *See infra* note 96.

[94] BBC Survey, *supra* note 89, at 60.

[95] *See* E. Sawyer & T. Kelsall, *Truth vs. Justice? Popular Views on the Truth and Reconciliation Commission and the Special Court for Sierra Leone*, 7 ONLINE J. PEACE & CONFLICT RESOL. 36, 41, 44 (2007). Notably, respondents were coded as having a "good" understanding of the Court if they responded with "some variation on the theme" that it would prosecute those who bore the most responsibility, "even if their interpretation was not completely accurate." *Id.* This is not a particularly sophisticated understanding of the Court's operation.

[96] BBC Survey, *supra* note 89, at 61.

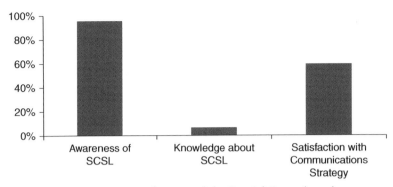

FIGURE 26.1 Attitudes toward the Special Court (2007).

exists, and a majority think its communications strategy has been a success even though actual knowledge levels are quite low.[97] The results are summarized in Figure 26.1.

One possible interpretation of this data is that even though the Outreach Section was unsuccessful in educating Sierra Leoneans about what the Court does, it was successful in making Sierra Leoneans aware of the existence of the SCSL. However, even this more limited claim of success seems open to doubt. The BBC Survey also found that almost 90 percent of Sierra Leoneans were aware of the Truth and Reconciliation Commission (TRC),[98] despite the fact that the TRC had a very limited and largely informal outreach program.[99] In other words, awareness of the TRC was almost as high as awareness of the SCSL despite the fact that the TRC did very little formal outreach.

If one compares awareness levels at other courts, the results are about the same. Awareness of the ICTY in 2002 in the former Yugoslavia was virtually universal despite what had been criticized at the time as an ineffective and anemic outreach program.[100] This casts doubt on the hypothesis that high rates of awareness of the SCSL are a result of the work of the Outreach Section. Rather, it appears that no outreach is necessary to make domestic populations aware of the existence of international criminal courts. If this is true, then the Outreach Section did not succeed in educating Sierra Leoneans about what the Court does and was not responsible for making them aware of the existence of the Court.

It is probably not fair to blame the Outreach Section personnel for this failure, however, because there are good theoretical reasons to believe that outreach programs will not be effective at educating populations about international criminal courts. International

---

[97] This has been noted by other researchers. *See, e.g.,* R. Kerr & J. Lincoln, *The Special Court for Sierra Leone: Outreach, Legacy and Impact, Final Report* at 14, War Crimes Research Group, Department of War Studies, Kings' College London (Feb. 2008), *available at* http://www.kcl.ac.uk/sspp/departments/warstudies/research/groups/wc/slfinalreport.pdf (last visited Mar. 8, 2012) ("general knowledge was high but depth of understanding was poor").

[98] BBC Survey, *supra* note 89, at 26. *See also* Sawyer & Kelsall, *supra* note 96, at 41 (making a similar finding).

[99] *See* B. Dougherty, *Searching for Answers: Sierra Leone's Truth and Reconciliation Commission*, 8 AFR. STUD. Q. 39, 46 (2004) (describing efforts by local and international NGOs to raise public awareness of the TRC).

[100] *See* South Eastern Europe Democratic Support, *Public Agenda Survey: ICTY (The Hague Tribunal): Awareness vs. Trust*, International Institute for Democracy and Electoral Assistance, *available at* http://archive.idea.int/balkans/survey_summary_intl_inst.htm (last visited Mar. 8, 2012) (describing percentage of respondents in the former Yugoslavia aware of the ICTY). For criticism of the ICTY's outreach efforts in the late 1990s and early 2000s, see *supra* note 69.

criminal courts are complicated undertakings that are difficult even for experts to understand and evaluate. The vast majority of people in any given population will not have the
time, inclination, or expertise to understand them.[101] As a consequence, people are likely to
know about and have attitudes toward these courts despite knowing very little about what
they actually do.[102] I am unaware of any tribunals that have been successful at educating
more than a small fraction of the population about what they do, with or without a formal
outreach program.[103] (See Figure 26.3 below.) Nor is this problem limited to international
criminal courts. In one survey of public opinion in the United States about the Supreme
Court, only about a quarter of the respondents had any understanding of the court's role
and operation.[104] Most international criminal courts, which are almost always only a temporary part of the domestic political landscape, probably cannot hope to achieve even this
level of knowledge among their affected populations.

At this point, I must discuss the Outreach Section's own survey of its effectiveness. In late
2006, a survey of perceptions of the Court was undertaken for the Outreach Section by an
outside consultant. This resulted in the Nationwide Survey Report on Public Perceptions of
the Special Court for Sierra Leone.[105] It surveyed more than eight thousand Sierra Leoneans
across all districts.[106] The results of this survey are strikingly different from the results of
the other surveys that have been conducted in Sierra Leone, even though they were done at
roughly the same time.[107]

The Outreach Section's survey duplicates the finding in the BBC Survey and the Sawyer
and Kelsall survey that virtually everyone in Sierra Leone has heard of the Court.[108]
However, it found that 79 percent of those surveyed correctly understood the role of the
SCSL in Sierra Leone.[109] This is a dramatically better result than the equivalent questions
in either the BBC Survey (7 percent) or the Sawyer and Kelsall survey (15 percent). The
results of the three surveys are presented in Figure 26.2. At the same time, the Outreach
Section's survey found that 90 percent of respondents were specifically aware of the existence of the Outreach Section and that 88 percent of respondents said that outreach programs had reached their community.[110] Perhaps more striking, 85 percent of respondents
said that the Outreach Section had provided them with sufficient information about the

---

[101] *Cf.* D. Kahan, *The Cognitively Illiberal State*, 60 STANFORD L. REV. 115, 119 (2007); D. Kahan & D. Braman, *More Statistics, Less Persuasion: A Cultural Theory of Gun-Risk Perceptions*, 151 U. PA. L. REV. 1291, 1312 (2003).

[102] *See* Ford, *supra* note 62, at Section II(B)(2) (arguing that most of the time populations affected by violence form attitudes toward international criminal courts despite not knowing how they operate).

[103] *Id.* n.102 (noting that the vast majority of the population in Rwanda, the former Yugoslavia, and Cambodia had very little knowledge of their respective courts).

[104] Walter F. Murphy & Joseph Tanenhaus, *Public Opinion and the United States Supreme Court*, 2 LAW & SOC'Y REV. 357, 360 (1968). *But see* J. Gibson & G. Caldeira, *Knowing the Supreme Court? A Reconsideration of Public Ignorance of the High Court*, 71 J. POL. 429 (2009).

[105] The report was prepared by a Sierra Leonean researcher for and in partnership with the Outreach Section. It was paid for by the European Union. *See* M. Baby Pratt, *Nationwide Survey Report on Public Perceptions of the Special Court for Sierra Leone*, Special Court for Sierra Leone, at 5–8 (Mar. 2007) (copy on file with author) [hereinafter the Outreach Section Survey].

[106] *Id.* at 15. Fourteen hundred "opinion leaders" were also surveyed. *Id.*

[107] The Outreach Section Survey was conducted in late 2006. The BBC Survey took place in June 2007. The Sawyer and Kelsall survey was conducted in August 2005.

[108] Outreach Section Survey, *supra* note 106, at 30 (99 percent of respondents were aware of the Special Court).

[109] *Id.* at 28.

[110] *Id.* at 30.

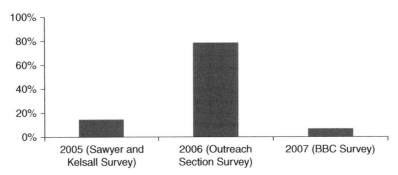

FIGURE 26.2 Knowledge about the SCSL as measured on three different surveys.

Court, and 88 percent of respondents said the Outreach Section was doing a "great job." Only 3 percent thought it was not doing a great job. If these results are taken at face value, the Outreach Section has been extremely successful at its primary goal of educating Sierra Leoneans about the court.

Unfortunately, there are reasons to doubt the results of the Outreach Section's survey. First, its finding about knowledge levels among Sierra Leoneans is at odds with the two other surveys that were conducted around the same time. It would be exceedingly strange for knowledge levels to be low in 2005 at the time of the Sawyer and Kelsall survey, increase dramatically by late 2006 at the time of the Outreach Section survey, and then plummet again by mid-2007 at the time of the BBC survey. This discrepancy is highlighted in Figure 26.2. Moreover, if true, knowledge levels about the SCSL would be dramatically higher than knowledge levels about any of the other international criminal courts.[111] This is illustrated in Figure 26.3.[112] In addition, there are theoretical reasons to believe that it is very difficult, if not impossible, to attain such high knowledge levels in a general population.[113]

Second, the questions asked by the Outreach Section during its survey are troubling. For example, questions 3.3 and 3.9 are non-neutral and leading. Question 3.3 asks "[a]re you aware that the Special Court has an Outreach Programme?" Question 3.9 asks "[d]o you think the Outreach Teams are doing a great job?" Both questions are phrased as yes/no questions, and both contain in the question a suggestion of the preferred answer (yes, in both cases). This is known to bias the results,[114] and may well have affected the results of the Outreach Section's survey.[115]

---

[111] *See supra* note 104.

[112] The figures for other courts shown in Figure 2 come from Ford, *supra* note 62 n.102.

[113] *See supra* notes 101–05.

[114] R. Lawless, J. Robbennolt & T. Ulen, Empirical Methods in Law 75 (2010). A better version of Question 3.9 might have been "How would you evaluate the work of the Outreach Section?" followed by a range of options that included both positive and negative appraisals of varying degrees. *Id. See also* G. Iarossi, The Power of Survey Design: A User's Guide for Managing Surveys, Interpreting Results, and Influencing Respondents 27–37 (2006).

[115] Sawyer and Kelsall found that, in their survey, providing a prompt rather than asking open-ended questions appeared to improve understanding of the Court significantly. However, this seems to be because when given yes/no prompts, their respondents often guessed the answer and usually chose "yes." Sawyer & Kelsall, *supra* note 96, at 43 n.26.

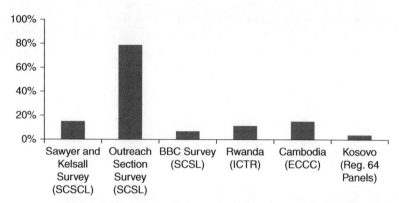

FIGURE 26.3 Knowledge at the SCSL compared with knowledge at other courts.

Others have raised similar concerns about the Outreach Section's survey. For example, Kerr and Lincoln concluded that it is of "limited utility" and raises "methodological concerns."[116] They specifically identify Question 3.9 as being problematic.[117] Finally, Kerr and Lincoln present anecdotal evidence that some of the CSOs involved in administering the survey may have deliberately manipulated the results to improve their prospects of future funding from the Court.[118]

In the end, I believe that the results of the Outreach Section's Survey should be discounted. Instead, the work of the Outreach Section should be evaluated based on the surveys conducted by the BBC and by Sawyer and Kelsall. According to those surveys: (1) the SCSL is nearly universally recognized in Sierra Leone; (2) a majority of Sierra Leoneans are generally happy with the communications strategy of the Court; and (3) knowledge levels about the SCSL are very low. However, it is not clear that the universal awareness of the SCSL has much to do with the work of the Outreach Section. Awareness was equally high for the TRC and even courts that have been criticized for ineffective outreach efforts (such as the ICTY) have had nearly universal awareness. What we are left with then is that people are generally happy with the work of the Outreach Section despite the fact that actual knowledge levels about the Court remain very low. Ultimately, the Outreach Section has not succeeded in its primary goal of educating Sierra Leoneans about the Court.

2. Communicating Information from Sierra Leoneans to the Court

If we look at the other goals of the Outreach Section, it becomes more difficult to evaluate success empirically. The Section's second goal is to communicate information from Sierra Leoneans to the Court. Unfortunately, I have been unable to identify any criteria by which to evaluate success in achieving this goal. In the absence of objective criteria, I think it is reasonable to defer to qualitative evaluations of the Court's success.[119]

---

[116] Kerr & Lincoln, *supra* note 98, at 13.

[117] *Id.* at 13 n.10.

[118] *Id.* at 13.

[119] Moreover, with respect to this goal, qualitative evaluations based on interviews with CSOs are measuring success more directly than for the other two goals. Thus relying on qualitative evaluations seems more appropriate.

The most obvious example of the Outreach Section's efforts to achieve its second goal is the Victims Commemoration Conference, which resulted in a list of recommendations formulated by the victims and presented to the Court about ways in which the Court could respond to the needs of the victims.[120] The Outreach Section has also maintained relationships with local CSOs designed to provide for two-way communication between the Court and those CSOs about the Court's work.[121] Both of these initiatives have generally been viewed as successful by those who have undertaken qualitative analyses.[122] Alison Smith's chapter in this volume also addresses the relationship between the Court and local CSOs and concludes that it was largely successful.

3. Promoting the Rule of Law and Human Rights in Sierra Leone

The Outreach Section's third goal is to promote respect for the rule of law and human rights in Sierra Leone. The Outreach Section's principal contribution to the rule of law and human rights in Sierra Leone appears to be the Accountability Now Clubs (ANCs).[123] Commentators have generally viewed the ANCs as a significant accomplishment.[124] In addition, some commentators have credited the Outreach Section with strengthening CSOs in Sierra Leone,[125] which might be expected to have some impact on the rule of law and human rights. And, of course, it is hoped that the SCSL's work, as a whole, will have some effect on accountability and the rule of law in Sierra Leone,[126] although this is not relevant to an evaluation of the success of the Outreach Section.

It is very difficult, however, to identify any concrete effect of the Outreach Section's efforts on respect for the rule of law and human rights in Sierra Leone, largely because of problems of attribution. Essentially, this inquiry can be decomposed into two parts: (1) has there been any change in respect for human rights and the rule of law in Sierra Leone?; and (2) if so, how much of that change is attributable to the Outreach Section's work? It is possible to answer the first question with empirical evidence. The second question is virtually impossible to answer.

There are various indexes that attempt to measure respect for the rule of law, and some of them contain data on Sierra Leone that covers the lifetime of the SCSL. For example, the World Bank compiles the Worldwide Governance Indicators, which include an indicator for the rule of law.[127] The results are shown in Figure 26.4. According to this indicator, respect for the rule of law in Sierra Leone has been increasing slowly over time, although it remains very low.[128]

---

[120] *See supra* notes 38–39.

[121] *See supra* notes 31–32.

[122] *See supra* Section V(A). *See also supra* note 33; U.C. Berkeley War Crimes Studies Center, *Interim Report on the Special Court for Sierra Leone* 33–34 (Apr. 2005).

[123] *See supra* notes 33–36.

[124] *See supra* note 38.

[125] *See supra* note 33.

[126] *See* U.C. Berkeley War Crimes Studies Center, *Second Interim Report on the Special Court for Sierra Leone* 22–23 (Apr. 2006). *But see id.* (noting that financial and political constraints imposed on the court as a whole make it likely that its effect on the rule of law will be "extremely limited").

[127] Information about the Worldwide Governance Indicators Project as well as the data that is used in Figure 4 can be downloaded from the project's website. The World Bank Group, *The Worldwide Governance Indicators, 2011 Update* (2011), *available at* http://info.worldbank.org/governance/wgi/index.asp (last visited Feb. 2, 2012).

[128] Scores on the WGI indicators range from -2.5 (weak) to 2.5 (strong). Sierra Leone's scores in 2002 placed it somewhere in the 0–10th percentile among states included in the project. The score for 2010 places Sierra

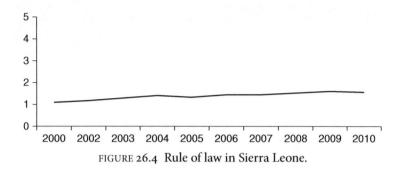

FIGURE 26.4 Rule of law in Sierra Leone.

Another way to measure the rule of law is through the prevalence of corruption. As respect for the rule of law increases, corruption should decrease, and vice versa.[129] Nevertheless, it is difficult to show that there has been any meaningful change in perceived corruption in Sierra Leone over the lifetime of the Court. According to Transparency International's Perceptions of Corruption Index, there has been virtually no trend in the perception of corruption in recent years. See Figure 26.5.[130]

It is also possible to find empirical data on human rights in Sierra Leone. For example, Freedom House has been collecting country-level information on civil and political rights since the 1970s. This information is released annually in the Freedom in the World report.[131] According to their data, respect for civil and political rights has gradually improved during the lifetime of the court, although Sierra Leone has been ranked as only "partly free" for the entire period of the court's existence.[132] See Figure 26.6.[133]

On the other hand, some other human rights datasets show a gradual decline in respect for human rights in Sierra Leone. For example, the CIRI Human Rights Dataset,[134] which

Leone in the 10th–25th percentile. For purposes of Figure 4, 2.5 was added to each of the WGI scores to make all scores positive. As a result, the scale in Figure 4 runs from 0 to 5.

129 *See, e.g.,* T. Herzfeld & C. Weiss, *Corruption and Legal (In)effectiveness: An Empirical Investigation,* 19 Eur. J. Pol. Econ. 621, 625 (2003) (finding that a "broader acceptance of established juridical institutions significantly reduces the perceived level of corruption" and that "a higher level of corruption significantly reduces the acceptance of established institutions and undermines the quality of the judicial system").

130 The results in Figure 5 come from Transparency International's Perceptions of Corruption Index for the years 2003 to 2011. The underlying data is available from Transparency International's Corruption Perceptions Index. Transparency International, *Corruption Perceptions Index* (2003–2011), *available at* http://www.transparency.org/policy_research/surveys_indices/cpi (last visited Jan. 31, 2012). The possible values of this variable run from 0 to 10.

131 Further information about the report and the source data is available. Freedom House, *Freedom in the World* (2012), *available at* http://www.freedomhouse.org/report-types/freedom-world (last visited Feb. 2, 2012). The data points in Figure 6 are an average of Sierra Leone's scores for "political rights" and "civil liberties" for each year. This was done to make the graph easier to read.

132 Freedom House ranks countries on a scale of 1 to 7, where 1 is free and 7 is not free. Scores of 3 to 5 indicate a country is partly free. Sierra Leone has consistently been described by Freedom House during the lifetime of the SCSL as "partly free."

133 In order to have the direction of change in this figure match that in the other figures (i.e., higher is better), the Freedom House Scores were subtracted from 7.

134 CIRI Human Rights Data Project, *available at* http://ciri.binghamton.edu/index.asp (last visited Mar. 9, 2009). A description of the variables and how they are coded is available. D. Cingranelli & D. Richards, *Short Variable Descriptions for Indicators in the Cingranelli-Richards Dataset,* CIRI Human Rights Data Project (Nov. 22, 2010), *available at* http://ciri.binghamton.edu/documentation/ciri_variables_short_descriptions.pdf (last visited Mar. 9, 2012).

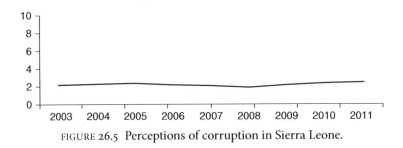

FIGURE 26.5 Perceptions of corruption in Sierra Leone.

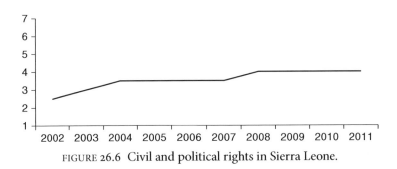

FIGURE 26.6 Civil and political rights in Sierra Leone.

relies on the U.S. State Department's annual Country Reports and reports by Amnesty International, shows a more or less flat trajectory on "physical integrity" rights such as freedom from torture, extrajudicial killing, political imprisonment, and disappearance. See Figure 26.7.[135] However, it shows a gradual decline in respect for "empowerment rights" such as freedom of speech, freedom of movement, freedom of assembly, voting rights, workers' rights, and freedom of religion. See Figure 26.8.[136]

Finally, at the same time it is worth noting that Sierra Leone has shown slow improvement on the United Nations' Human Development Index, which measures the health, wealth, and education of the Sierra Leonean population.[137] See Figure 26.9. Nevertheless, Sierra Leone still ranks 180th out of 187 countries in the 2011 Human Development Index, and its neighbors have similar rankings and similar HDI trends.[138]

Ultimately, the picture in Sierra Leone is mixed. Respect for the rule of law seems to be improving slowly, although it remains weak. Corruption on the other hand, does not seem to have improved. Sierra Leone is slowly becoming healthier, wealthier, and better

[135] This figure relies on the data for the "physical integrity" variable (PHYSINT). The possible values for this variable run from 0 to 8.

[136] This figure relies on the data from the "empowerment rights" variable (NEW_EMPINX). The possible values for this variable run from 0 to 14.

[137] Information about the Human Development Index can be found at, and the data used to create Figure 9 can be downloaded from the U.N. Human Development Programme Human Development Reports. *International Human Development Indicators*, U.N. Human Development Programme Human Development Reports, *available at* http://hdr.undp.org/en/statistics/ (last visited Mar. 8, 2012). The possible values for this variable run from 0 to 1.

[138] Liberia ranks 182nd on the 2011 HDI, while Guinea ranks 178th. Over the period 2005 to 2011, Sierra Leone's HDI score improved by .03. Liberia had almost exactly the same improvement (.029), while Guinea only improved by .018.

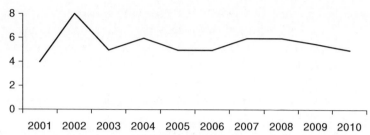

FIGURE 26.7 Protection from torture, extrajudicial killing, political imprisonment, and disappearance.

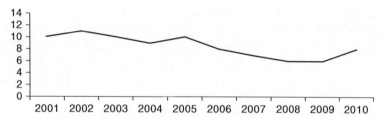

FIGURE 26.8 Respect for freedom of movement, freedom of speech, freedom of assembly, workers' rights, voting rights, and freedom of religion.

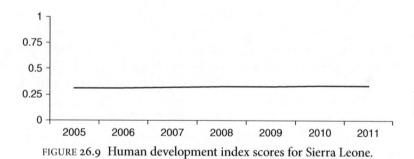

FIGURE 26.9 Human development index scores for Sierra Leone.

educated, but its improvement is similar to that of its neighbors, and it still ranks near the bottom among the nations of the world. Depending on what indexes one looks at, respect for human rights is either getting slightly better or slightly worse.[139] In both indices it remains relatively low in an absolute sense.

More important, I have not been able to identity a way to attribute any part of this change to the work of the Outreach Section. According to data from the World Bank, Sierra Leone has been receiving between $340 and $450 million in economic assistance and development

[139] In this respect, Human Rights Watch concluded that in 2010, "the government of President Ernest Bai Koroma made meaningful progress in addressing endemic corruption and improving access to justice and key economic rights, notably health care and education." Human Rights Watch, *World Report 2011: Sierra Leone, Events of 2010* (2011), *available at* http://www.hrw.org/world-report-2011/sierra-leone (last visited Feb. 2, 2012). Amnesty International was less positive. *See* Amnesty International, *Annual Report 2011 – Sierra Leone* (2011), *available at* http://www.amnesty.org/en/region/sierra-leone/report-2011 (last visited Mar. 8, 2012).

aid per year since at least the mid-2000s.[140] This equates to between 20 percent and 25 percent of GDP per year in aid. Much of this money has been spent on programs aimed at improving the rule of law and respect for human rights.[141] In contrast, the Outreach Section's budget was somewhere between $7M and $10M over the lifetime of the Court.[142] In effect, the Outreach Section's funding was just a drop in the bucket of what the international community has been spending to improve respect for human rights and the rule of law in Sierra Leone.

As a result, even if it were clear that human rights and the rule of law were dramatically improving in Sierra Leone, it would still be virtually impossible to determine objectively what contribution, if any, the Outreach Section's work has made to the trend. For these reasons, I am unable to conclude that the Outreach Section has been successful in its goal of promoting respect for human rights and the rule of law. For the same reasons, I am not able to definitively conclude that it has failed in this goal either. However, given the size of the Outreach Section's budget compared to the amount of money that has been spent on human rights and the rule of law in Sierra Leone, apparently with relatively little success, I am skeptical of claims that the Outreach Section has succeeded in achieving its third goal.

VI. CONCLUSION

In this chapter, I have tried to measure the Outreach Section's success against the goals it set for itself in its 2003 Mission Statement. The results are mixed. For one of the goals (communicating information from Sierra Leoneans to the Court), I was unable to find any objective criteria by which to measure success. For another goal (promoting respect for the rule of law and human rights), the analysis was inconclusive because of attribution problems. Of course, this does not mean that the Outreach Section has not had any success in attaining these two goals, and, indeed, a number of scholars have argued that the Outreach Section has been at least partially successful in achieving them.[143] Nevertheless, claims of success on these two goals do not appear to be based on empirical evidence.

I was, however, able to measure the Outreach Section's success in achieving its most important goal: educating the people of Sierra Leone about the SCSL. On that score, the Outreach Section has not achieved its goal. Awareness of the Court is nearly universal. However, that probably cannot be attributed to the work of the Outreach Section. At the

---

[140] *See* The World Bank Group, *Sierra Leone Country Data Profile 2000–2010, available at* http://ddp-ext.worldbank. org/ext/ddpreports/ViewSharedReport?&CF=&REPORT_ID=9147&REQUEST_TYPE=VIEWADVANCED (last visited Mar. 8, 2012) (showing that Sierra Leone received $340 million in 2005, $379 million in 2008, and $450 million in 2009).

[141] *See, e.g.*, Country Programme Action Plan (CPAP) 2011–2012 entered into between the Government of Sierra Leone and the United Nations Development Programme. The Government of Sierra Leone and the United Nations Development Programme, *Country Programme Action Plan (CPAP) 2011–2012, available at* http://www.sl.undp.org/4_media/publications/CPAP_08–10_appraisal_wkshop.pdf (last visited Mar. 8, 2008) (describing various UNDP programs to improve the rule of law and human rights in Sierra Leone); Human Rights Watch, *World Report 2011: Sierra Leone, supra* note 140 (noting that projects led by the U.K. government, UNDP, and the national government of Sierra Leone were contributing to improvements in the rule of law). *See also* U.C. Berkeley War Crimes Studies Center, *supra* note 127, at 22 (noting that the British government was funding a $50-million-dollar Justice Sector Reform Programme in Sierra Leone).

[142] *See supra* notes 44–51.

[143] *See supra* Section V(A).

same time, objective measures of how well Sierra Leoneans actually understand the Court's work show that only a very small number of Sierra Leoneans understand what the Court does. This is not necessarily an indication that the outreach personnel employed by the Court were incompetent. Rather, it probably reflects the fact that the goal of educating the population about the Court was unattainable from the start.[144]

There are obvious limits to an empirical approach, as evidenced by my inability to offer firm conclusions with respect to two of the Outreach Section's goals. And there are some questions that may be better suited to a qualitative evaluation.[145] Nevertheless, the contrast between an empirical evaluation of the Outreach Section's success in educating Sierra Leoneans about the Court and the conclusions of those who have evaluated the Outreach Section qualitatively is illuminating. My conclusions are very different from most others, including the Secretary-General's Independent Expert, Antonio Cassese, who described the Outreach Section as "exceedingly effective." This suggests that empirical methods can act as a useful complement to, and reality check on, qualitative results.

Another thing my research shows is that one cannot assume that the number of outreach activities conducted correlates positively with the success of the outreach program. There may be particular situations or goals where this correlation does exist, but it does not appear to be true with respect to educating people about what an international court does. Sierra Leoneans do not know more about the Court than people in the Balkans or Rwanda know about their respective courts, despite the fact that the Outreach Section conducted vastly more outreach activities than the courts in those locations. This is important as a number of commentators have implicitly equated the volume of outreach activities with the success of those activities. This has tended to make evaluations of the Outreach Section too optimistic.

Given that the Outreach Section has been viewed as a successful model for other courts,[146] it seems appropriate to ask what implications my findings have for outreach programs more generally. My conclusions are quite negative.[147] If all one wants is awareness of the court among the affected population, a formal outreach program is not needed. On the other hand, it will probably be very difficult for an outreach program to educate the affected population about what the court actually does. Moreover, it seems unlikely that an outreach program the size of the SCSL's Outreach Section can have a measurable impact on the rule of law or human rights in a country.

One other "goal" sometimes attributed to outreach programs by academics is to improve perceptions of the legitimacy of the court among the members of the affected population.[148] This is based on the assumption that negative perceptions of the court are caused by lack of knowledge about what the court does. However, as I have argued at length elsewhere, in most situations people's attitudes toward the court are driven largely by who it prosecutes.[149]

---

[144] *See supra* notes 102–05.

[145] *See supra* Section V(B)(2).

[146] *See supra* Section V(A).

[147] Initially, I was reluctant to be so negative. My belief, based on participating in and speaking at a number of outreach events during my time working at the ECCC, had been that outreach efforts helped the affected population understand the Court. It has been impossible to maintain that belief in the face of the evidence presented in this chapter.

[148] *See* Ford, *supra* note 62, at 405–09.

[149] *See generally id.*

Outreach activities are unlikely to be able to overcome the effect of prosecution strategy on how the court is perceived, particularly for individuals who identify with one of the sides in the conflict that led to the involvement of the court.

So, is there anything that outreach programs can do? There do appear to be some areas where outreach programs can make a difference – such as strengthening local CSOs. And it is possible that careful study can identify other goals that a well-designed outreach program can accomplish. In this regard, it is worth noting that 60 percent of the respondents in the BBC Survey were satisfied with the court's communication strategy, which suggests that the court's outreach program was having some effect, even if it is not clear what that effect was. However, there is good reason to believe that outreach programs cannot accomplish what is usually their principle goal – educating the population about what the court does. Before we spend millions or tens of millions of dollars on future outreach programs, we need to think carefully about what it is we want them to do, and whether the things they can accomplish are worth what they will cost.

27

The Defense Office of the Special Court for Sierra Leone: A Watershed in Realizing the Rights of Accused Persons in International Criminal Justice

Vincent O. Nmehielle[*]

I. INTRODUCTION

Issues around the defense of suspects and accused persons remain important matters that must be debated continuously in this day and age; an age in which international criminal justice is gaining more ground as a way of dealing with mass atrocities and egregious violations of human rights, particularly in Africa. As a general observation, my submission is that, since Nuremberg,[1] the importance attached to the defense of accused persons in the administration of international criminal justice mechanisms has not been remarkable irrespective of elaborate provisions in the various constitutive documents of international criminal tribunals on the rights of accused persons.

One of the difficulties in this regard is that when such institutions are established, the mind-set is always one of ensuring strict accountability without any serious evaluation that justice does not just mean "Just Convict Everyone (JCE)"[2] but providing for and enabling the highest level of due process from the conception of an accountability mechanism. Thus, in creating international criminal justice mechanisms, the tradition, until recently with the important exception of the Special Tribunal for Lebanon (STL), was the nonsimultaneous creation with the Prosecution and the Registry of an institutional mechanism within the tribunals to deal with defense issues. In the case of the SCSL, as well as the two tribunals that preceded it (the ICTY and the ICTR) and the globe's permanent criminal court (the ICC), issues relating to the Defense were an afterthought to be dealt with in the Rules or Regulations of the tribunals rather than in the main statute. As such, the Defense in these mechanisms operates within the ambit of the Registrar's administrative and authoritative oversight even though the Registrar, as head of the registry, is supposedly a neutral

---

[*] Professor and Head of the Wits Programme on Law, Justice & Development in Africa, School of Law, University of the Witwatersrand, Johannesburg, South Africa and formerly the Principal Defender, Special Court for Sierra Leone. I am grateful to the Anderson Cappelli Fund administered by the office of the Deputy Vice Chancellor (Academic) of the University of the Witwatersrand, Johannesburg for a research grant for my six-month sabbatical leave (August 2011–January 2012) that enabled me to conduct research for this piece, among others.

[1] Referring to the Nuremberg trials after World War II and subsequent other trials such ase the Tokyo trials of the post–World War II era.

[2] "*Just Convict Everyone (JCE)*" is used here to make fun of the controversial Joint Criminal Enterprise doctrine that insiders at the tribunals and critics of the doctrine have associated with the mind-set of activist prosecution of accused persons before the tribunals.

party, whose function in terms of the SCSL is "the administration and servicing of the Special Court."[3] Accordingly, one would be right to interpret the function of the Registrar as largely to service the parties to the judicial process – the Chamber, the Prosecution, and the Defense.[4]

The SCSL, however, broke new ground in international criminal justice by endowing its Defense Office, which is also referred to as the Office of the Principal Defender (OPD), with an overall mandate to ensure "the rights of suspects and accused" persons[5] in the spirit of the prescription of the Court's constitutive instrument – the Statute of the Court.[6]

Taking the above context as a point of departure, this chapter seeks to evaluate or assess the phenomenon of the Defense Office of the Court regarding its contributions to the SCSL's obligation to achieve fair trials as an international criminal justice mechanism. An important aspect of this evaluation is the extent to which the contributions of the OPD can be said to have impacted contemporary international criminal justice mechanisms. Also inherent in this evaluation are the limitations in the Court's Defense Office as established to fully carry out its actual mandate and the expectations that followed its creation as the first of its kind in international justice. I, as one-time Principal Defender and a close observer of the tribunal's work in this area, will also venture into lessons learned from the experience of the SCSL's OPD.

The chapter is divided into six sections. Besides this introductory section, Section II sets the scene and contextualizes the creation of the SCSL within the background of the decade-long conflict that engulfed Sierra Leone, which eventually necessitated the creation of the Court to address the atrocities resulting from the conflict. Section III examines the establishment of the Defense Office relative to other organs of the SCSL against the background of the "Practical Arrangements" for the takeoff of the Court under the Agreement between the United Nations and the government of Sierra Leone that established the tribunal. The section makes it clear that from the "practical arrangements," the Defense Office of the SCSL was clearly an afterthought. I argue that this led to the haphazard operationalization of the office, which in turn had consequences for the eventual status of the Defense Office that emerged. Section IV deals with the OPD's mandate and functions as an office entrusted with the nebulous duty of ensuring "the rights of suspects and accused" persons with a mix of limited substantive legal representational functions and administrative duties that oftentimes created a complex relationship between the Defense Office and assigned counsel on the one hand and between the Defense Office and the Registry on the other. Section V highlights the challenges faced by the Defense Office in carrying out its mandate. The section articulates the clash between the OPD serving as an organ to ensure the rights of accused

---

[3] Statute of the Special Court for Sierra Leone art. 16(1) [hereinafter SCSL Statute].

[4] *See* Separate and Concurring Opinion of Justice George Gelaga King on Brima-Kamara Defense Appeal Motion against Trial Chamber II Majority Decision on Extremely Urgent Confidential Joint Motion for the Reappointment of Kevin Metzger and Wilbert Harris as Lead Counsel for Alex Tamba Brima and Brima Bazzy Kamara (Prosecutor v. Alex Tamba Brima, Brima Bazzy Kamara & Santigie Kanu, Case No. SCSL-04–16-AR73), 16956–57 (Nov. 8, 2005).

[5] Rules of Evidence and Procedure of the Special Court for Sierra Leone, Rule 45.

[6] SCSL Statute, Article 17 enumerates "rights of the accused" in a manner reminiscent of the provisions of Article 14 of the International Covenant on Civil and Political Rights, U.N. Doc. A/6316 (1966).

persons and its lack of organic independence from the Registry that had implication for resources and facilities available for the Defense, among others. Section VI concludes the chapter by highlighting lessons learned.

The chapter echoes the point that irrespective of its lack of organic independence, the SCSL Defense Office blazed the trail for defense issues and elevated the defense of accused persons to heights unknown to international criminal justice administration. This had led to the emergence of other mechanisms such as the Defense Office of the STL that drew lessons from the organic shortfall of the SCSL Defense Office. As part of lessons learned from the SCSL, the author suggests the possibility of rethinking the defense of accused persons in international criminal justice accountability mechanisms by proposing the establishment of an in-house defense organ in future tribunals.

II. BRIEF BACKGROUND ON THE ESTABLISHMENT OF THE SPECIAL COURT FOR SIERRA LEONE

The period between 1991 and 2002 was a decade of political instability, misrule, and bad governance that culminated in a brutal civil war in which ordinary Sierra Leoneans, particularly women and children, bore the greatest brunt. According to one commentator, "around 100,000 people were killed. An estimated 2 million were displaced or forced to seek refuge abroad. An unquantifiable number of women and girls were raped, forcibly 'married' or taken into sexual servitude. Over 10,000 children were conscripted. Several had their arms or limbs amputated."[7] Three factions were involved in the decade-long war: the government of Sierra Leone on whose side the Civil Defense Forces (CDF), which comprised of a militia of traditional hunters and loyal remnants of the national army fought; the Revolutionary United Front (RUF), a rebel movement; and the Armed Forces Revolutionary Council (AFRC), a reengaged faction of the national army that overthrew the elected government of President Ahmed Tejan Kabbah in 1997.[8] Strictly speaking, there were actually two main factions in the war – the government forces and the RUF/AFRC, as the latter were actually in alliance from the time the soldiers that formed the AFRC overthrew the government and invited the RUF to join them.[9]

Various efforts to end the conflict failed, resulting in military intervention by the Economic Community of West African States (ECOWAS) through its Monitoring Group (ECOMOG), which intervention restored President Kabbah to power in March 1998.[10]

---

[7] Abdul Tejan-Cole, *Sierra Leone's "Not So" Special Court, in* PEACE VERSUS JUSTICE: THE DILEMMA OF TRANSITIONAL JUSTICE IN AFRICA 233, 233 (Chandra L. Siriam & Suresh Pillay eds., 2009) [hereinafter Tejan-Cole, *Sierra Leone's "Not So" Special Court*]. *See also* Abdul Tejan-Cole, *Human Rights under the Armed Forces Revolutionary Council: A Catalogue of Abuses*, 10 RADIC 481 (1998) [hereinafter Tejan-Cole, *Human Rights under the Armed Forces Revolutionary Council*]; and PRISCILLA HAYNER, NEGOTIATING PEACE IN SIERRA LEONE: CONFRONTING THE JUSTICE CHALLENGE (Center for Humanitarian Dialogue/International Center for Transitional Justice Report, Dec. 2007). For a detailed and more accurate representation of violations and displacements during the decade-long Sierra Leone civil war, see 2 WITNESS TO TRUTH: REPORT OF THE SIERRA LEONE TRUTH AND RECONCILIATION COMMISSION (2004).

[8] *See generally id.*; Tejan-Cole, *Sierra Leone's "Not So" Special Court, supra* note 7, at 223; Charles Jalloh, *The Contributions of the Special Court for Sierra Leone to the Development of International Law*, 15 RADIC 165, 168–70 (2007).

[9] Tejan-Cole, *Human Rights Under the Armed Forces Revolutionary Council, supra* note 7, at 482.

[10] *Id.* at 483; Jalloh, *supra* note 8, at 169.

He then embarked on peace negotiations with the rebels under the watch of ECOWAS. The negotiations resulted in a peace agreement signed in Lomé, Togo (Lomé Peace Agreement) on July 7, 1999.[11] The Lomé Peace Agreement granted free and complete "pardon and amnesty" to the leaders and foot soldiers of the rebel RUF and their allies in the AFRC as well as to the CDF and the former government forces "in order to bring peace to Sierra Leone" and "to consolidate the peace and promote the cause of national reconciliation."[12] As a result, a Government of National Unity (GNU) was formed bringing all the warring parties into government and assigning various portfolios to their leaders.[13]

The formation of a GNU in practical terms did not result in or guarantee lasting peace, as the RUF reengaged in war, attacking and killing civilians, and took some United Nations (UN) peacekeepers hostage.[14] This provided some impetus for the government of President Kabbah, presumably under pressure from some members of the international community through the diplomatic corps in Freetown,[15] to conclude that "the RUF had violated the ceasefire and other key terms in the Lomé Peace Agreement."[16] The result was the arrest of Foday Sankoh, the leader of the RUF, and President Kabbah sought an accountability measure against the rebels by asking for the creation of a court.[17]

In this regard, President Kabbah in June 2000 wrote a letter to the UN Secretary-General requesting the establishment of a "special court for Sierra Leone" whose "purpose" would be "to try and bring to credible justice those members of the Revolutionary United Front (RUF) and their accomplices responsible for committing crimes against the people of Sierra Leone and for the taking of United Nations peacekeepers as hostages."[18] In the ensuing two months, the UN Security Council adopted Resolution 1315 on August 14, 2000, requesting "the Secretary-General to negotiate an agreement with the Government of Sierra Leone to create an independent special court."[19] The Secretary-General followed through and negotiated an agreement (Special Court Agreement) with the government of Sierra Leone.[20] Annexed to the agreement was the Statute of the Court,[21] the execution of which symbolized a commitment in principle by the parties on January 16, 2002, to

---

[11] Peace Agreement between the Government of Sierra Leone and the Revolutionary United Front (July 7, 1999) signed in Lomé, Togo [hereinafter Lomé Peace Agreement] (on file with author). *See also* www.sierra-leone.org/lomeaccord.htm (last visited Jan. 15, 2012).

[12] *See* Lomé Peace Agreement, *supra* note 11, at art. IX.

[13] Tejan-Cole, *Sierra Leone's "Not So" Special Court*, *supra* note 7, at 223.

[14] *Id.* at 225.

[15] *Id.* At an International Conference on Assessing the Contributions and Legacy of the Special Court for Sierra Leone to Africa and International Criminal Justice that was held at the University of Pittsburgh School of Law from April 19–21, 2012, The former High Commissioner of the United Kingdom to Sierra Leone during the crucial period of the conflict, Ambassador Peter Penfold, from his knowledge of events at the time, described and confirmed the existence of this pressure from the international community at the time solutions were being sort on the conflict.

[16] Jalloh, *supra* note 8, at 170.

[17] *Id.*; Tejan-Cole, *Sierra Leone's "Not So" Special Court*, *supra* note 7, at 225.

[18] *See* Letter of June 12, 2000 to Kofi Annan, U.N. Secretary-General by President Tejan Kabbah, U.N. Doc. S/2000/786 (Aug. 10, 2000) (on file with author). *See also id.*, and C. Jalloh, *Special Court for Sierra Leone: Achieving Justice?*, 32 Mich. J. Int'l L. 395, 413 (2011).

[19] S/RES/1315 (2000), adopted by the Security Council at the 4186th Meeting on Aug. 14, 2000.

[20] Agreement between the United Nations and the Government of Sierra Leone on the Establishment of the Special Court for Sierra Leone of Jan. 16, 2002 (on file with author).

[21] SCSL Statute.

the formal establishment of the SCSL after the earlier endorsement of the UN Security Council in July 2001.[22]

With the establishment of the Special Court in 2002, the stage was set for what would be another decade in Sierra Leone's recent history in which an international justice account-ability mechanism would operate in its territory to provide a measure of redress for victims against atrocities that were committed toward the latter part of a decade-long war. Under the Special Court Agreement, the Court was established "to prosecute persons who bear the greatest responsibility for serious violations of international humanitarian law and Sierra Leonean law committed in the territory of Sierra Leone since November 30, 2006."[23] In elaborating the jurisdiction of the Court with the task of prosecuting the "persons who bear the greatest responsibility" the Statute of the Court grants it jurisdiction for crimes against humanity,[24] violations of common Article 3 to the Geneva Conventions and Additional Protocol II,[25] other serious violations of international humanitarian law,[26] and specific crimes under Sierra Leonean law.[27]

To give effect to the requirements of the Agreement and Statute, the first Prosecutor of the Court, David Crane, in the exercise of prosecutorial discretion, indicted thirteen individu-als representing different factions of the war as those that "bear the greatest responsibility" for the crimes committed during the war within the temporal jurisdiction of the Court – from November 30, 2006. In the RUF faction, the Prosecutor indicted Foday Sankoh,[28] Sam Bockarie,[29] Issa Sesay, Morris Kallon, and Augustine Gbao.[30] Within the RUF catchment, the Prosecutor also indicted President Charles Taylor of Liberia separately, not as a member of the RUF but rather as its supporter and a major role player in the conflict.[31] The AFRC faction had Johnny Paul Koroma, the leader of the AFRC;[32] Alex Tamba Brima, Brima Bazzy

---

[22] *See* Tejan-Cole, *Sierra Leone's "Not So" Special Court, supra* note 7, at 225, and Jalloh, *supra* note 8, at 170.

[23] The Special Court Agreement art. 1(1).

[24] SCSL Statute art. 2.

[25] *Id.* at art. 3.

[26] *Id.* at art. 4.

[27] *Id.* at art. 5.

[28] *See* The Prosecutor v. Foday Saybana Sankoh, Case No. SCSL-2003–02–1001A, Indictment (Mar. 7, 2003). The indictment against Sankoh would later be withdrawn following his death in the custody of the Special Court. *See* Decision on the Withdrawal of Indictment, The Prosecutor v. Foday Saybana Sankoh, Case No. SCSL-2003–02-PT (Dec. 8, 2003).

[29] *See* The Prosecutor v. Sam Bockarie, Case No. SCSL-2003–04-I, Indictment (Mar. 7, 2003). Upon the confir-mation of his death, just like Sankoh, the indictment against Bockarie was also withdrawn. *See* Decision on Withdrawal of Bockarie's Indictment, Case No. SCSL-2003–04-PT (Dec. 8, 2003).

[30] Having previously been indicted separately in 2003, the Prosecutor later issued a joint indictment against Sesay, Kallon, and Gbao. *See* The Prosecutor v. Issa Hassan Sesay, Morris Kallon and Augustine Gbao, Case No. SCSL-2004–15-PT-005 (Feb. 5, 2004), which was further corrected and consolidated on Aug. 2, 2006 as Case No. SCSL-04-15-T-619.

[31] *See* Prosecutor v. Charles Ghankay Taylor, Case No. SCSL-2003–01-I-001, Indictment (Mar. 7, 2003). The indictment was later amended. *See* Prosecutor v. Charles Ghankay Taylor, Case No. SCSL-2003–01-I-75, Amended Indictment (Mar. 17, 2006). The SCSCL Trial Chamber II recently found Taylor guilty of aiding and abetting the RUF and of planning with the RUF. *See* Judgment of Trial Chamber II (May 18, 2012) in Prosecutor v. Charles Ghankay Taylor, Case No. SCSL-03–01T. The Trial Chamber sentenced him to fifty years' imprisonment. *See* Sentencing Judgment of Trial Chamber II (May 30, 2012), Prosecutor v. Charles Ghankay Taylor, Case No. SCSL-03–01-T.

[32] *See* Prosecutor v. Jonny Paul Koroma, Case No. SCSL-2003–03–01-I, Indictment (Mar. 7, 2003). Jonny Paul Koroma is currently at large and not in the custody of the Special Court. Rumor abounds that he may be deceased, which has not been confirmed by the Special Court.

Kamara, and Santigie Borbor Kanu as indicted persons.[33] In the CDF, Chief Samuel Hinga Norman, Moinina Fofana, and Allieu Kondewa were indicted.[34] Thus, the SCSL entered into business to bring the accused persons to justice.

III. ESTABLISHMENT OF THE DEFENSE OFFICE

Before delving into the establishment of the Defense Office, it may be necessary to examine a preliminary issue against the background of what the Special Court's Agreement refers to as "Practical Arrangements" in its Article 19. This is in furtherance of my earlier assertion that contemporary international criminal justice accountability mechanisms from Nuremberg up to the SCSL did not think of defense issues as needing upfront attention. Under Article 19 of the Agreement, the Court adopted "a phased-in approach" in operationalizing the Court in order to save cost and to promote efficiency.[35] Further, this had to be done based on what the negotiators considered to be "in accordance with chronological order of the legal process."[36] Thus, that order required the Prosecutor, and his investigative and prosecutorial staff as well as the Registrar and his team to be the first appointments as officials of the SCSL that should be made.[37] The Trial and Appeal Chambers would be required on an ad hoc basis within the initial period for "organizational matters."[38] Close to the end of the completion of the investigation process, the Trial Chamber would be operationalized fully on a permanent basis while the Appeal Chamber would take a permanent sit at the completion of the first trial.[39] In other words, the Appeal Chamber would operate on a part-time basis at the initial stage but would be empanelled on a full-time basis after the first trial was completed.

In the elaborate provisions of Article 19, it appears that no one cared enough to consider the need for initial practical arrangements for the defense of accused persons or suspects who would be arrested and investigated as the Agreement envisaged the investigation "of those already in custody."[40] Thus, in the initial stages of the Court's operations, defense was not part of the "chronological order of the legal process"; neither was there an upfront determination of where it fitted in the order outlined by the negotiators of the founding instruments. In keeping with the chronological order set forth in Article 19 of the Agreement, the

---

[33] See Prosecutor v. Alex Tamba Brima, Brima Bazzy Kamara and Santigie Borbor Kanu, Case No. SCSL-2004–16-PT-006, Indictment (Feb. 5, 2004). The indictment was later consolidated and amended in Prosecutor v. Alex Tamba Brima, Brima Bazzy Kamara and Santigie Borbor Kanu, Case No. SCSL-2004–16-PT-147.

[34] Chief Norman was indicted separately on March 7, 2003, whereas Kondewa and Fofana were both indicted on June 24, 2003 but also separately. However, their indictment was consolidated in 2004. See Prosecutor v. Samuel Hinga Norman, Monina Fofana and Allieu Kondewa, Case No. SCSL-2004–14-PT-003 (Feb. 4, 2004). Chief Norman died in the custody of the Special Court in 2007 while awaiting judgment of the Trial Chamber after the close of his case. Accordingly, on confirmation of the death of Chief Norman, the Special Court terminated his trial. See Prosecutor v. Samuel Hinga Norman, Monina Fofana and Allieu Kondewa, Case No. SCSL-04–14-T-776, Decision on Registrar's Submission of Evidence Death of Accused Samuel Hinga Norman and Consequential Issues (May 21, 2007).

[35] The Special Court Agreement art. 1(1).

[36] Id.

[37] Id. at art. 1(2).

[38] Id. at art. 1(3).

[39] Id. at art. 1(4).

[40] Id. at art. 1(2).

first Chief Prosecutor of the Court, David Crane, was appointed in 2002 by the Secretary-General of the United Nations. Crane commenced work almost immediately, traversing the entire country carrying out investigations. Similarly, the first Registrar of the Court – the late Robin Vincent – was also appointed in 2002. The first Principal Defender of the Special Court would later be appointed in April 2004, "a week before the opening ceremony of the Court."[41]

From this brief background, it is clear that the Defense Office was not a creation of the Statute of the Special Court. Its substantive origins lie in the Rules of Procedure and Evidence (RPE) of the Special Court (as an afterthought), later formalized by an amendment of the Rules in 2005.[42] More directly, Rule 45 of the RPE created an obligation for the Registrar of the Court to "establish, maintain, and develop a Defense Office, for the purpose of ensuring the rights of suspects and accused." The same Rule 45 created the office of the Principal Defender as the head of the Defense Office. Although the Defense Office was given legal impetus in the Rules in 2005, it would be correct to observe that the idea of an institutional mechanism to cater to the defense needs of accused persons was an issue that had bothered the Judges of the Court as far back as 2003 in the face of criticisms by external observers that the SCSL did not seem to make "proper provision for defence."[43] The Judges were also concerned about avoiding the perpetration of inequality of arms between the Prosecution and the Defense in the mold of Nuremberg, which was also the criticism leveled against the ICTR and ICTY by defense counsel.[44]

The Defense Office was envisaged, at least by some, as a Public Defender Office with full responsibility and the necessary competent professional defense counsel to defend all of the accused persons – a "fourth pillar" where the Principal Defender would stand in structural counterbalance to the Office of the Prosecutor – an innovation in international criminal justice accountability mechanisms.[45] One of the reasons for this proposed configuration was to make the process "cost-effective" while at the same time being "competence-effective" relative to the Prosecution.[46] The thinking was that even though Article 17(d) of the Court's Statute guarantees the right of an accused person *"to defend himself or herself in person or through legal assistance of his or her own choosing"* (emphasis added), that right needed to

---

[41] Rupert Skilbeck, *Building the Fourth Pillar: Defence Rights at the Special Court for Sierra Leone*, 1 ESSEX HUM. RTS. REV. 66, 80 (2004).

[42] Rules of Procedure and Evidence of the Special Court for Sierra Leone (RPE), as amended. The latest amendment is that of November 16, 2011.

[43] *See Note for Management Committee: Public Defender Proposal* (Feb. 7, 2003) by Justice Geoffrey Robertson [hereinafter *Justice Robertson's Proposal*], the first President of the Special Court for Sierra Leone and annexed as Appendix to the Separate and Concurring Opinion of Justice Robertson on the Decision on Brima-Kamara Defense Appeal Motion against Trial Chamber II Majority Decision on Extremely Urgent Confidential Joint Motion for the Re-appointment of Kevin Metzger and Wilbert Harris as Lead Counsel for Alex Tamba Brima and Brima Bazzy Kamara in Prosecutor v. Alex Tamba Brima, Brima Bazzy Kamara and Santigie Borbor Kanu, Case No. SCSL-2004-16-PT-446, 17117-21, at 17120 (Dec. 14, 2005) (also on file with author).

[44] *Id.* at 17117.

[45] ROBIN VINCENT, AN ADMINISTRATIVE PRACTICES MANUAL FOR INTERNATIONALLY ASSISTED CRIMINAL JUSTICE INSTITUTIONS 127 (2007).

[46] *Justice Robertson's Proposal, supra* note 43, at 17119. *See also* Jalloh, *supra* note 8, at 180; Skilbeck, *supra* note 41, at 79; VINCENT, *supra* note 45, at 130; and generally, John R.W.D. Jones et al., *The Special Court for Sierra Leone: A Defence Perspective*, 2 J. INT'L. CRIM. JUST. 211 (2004).

be balanced against a component of that right which is to "have legal assistance assigned to him or her, in any case where the interests of justice so require, and without payment by him or her in any such case if he or she does not have the sufficient means to pay for it."[47] In other words, where the Court would provide legal counsel for an accused, there is nothing in Article 17 that requires that the accused must choose the counsel as he would if he were paying for it; instead the obligation that the court has toward an indigent accused is to provide him or her "a competent lawyer," which may or may not be acceptable to the accused.[48] Thus, as observed by Robin Vincent, the first Registrar of the SCSL "where the majority of defendants are indigent, there is an argument (to be made) that salaried defense lawyers could fulfil an effective role beyond that of ... representing defendants immediately after arrest and charge until fee paid lawyers can be identified and appointed."[49]

As it happened, the fully fledged Public Defender model was not adopted, based on a number of concerns ranging from conflict of interest because of the commonality of the charges against most of the accused persons[50] and questions around independence and impartiality[51] as the most serious. Thus, in 2003 the Management Committee of the Special Court endorsed the proposal for a Defense Office to be headed by a Principal Defender with a complement of professional lawyers to serve as advisors, legal officers, and duty counsel to deal with defense issues arising from the imminent arrest, detention, and arraignment of the accused persons before the Court[52] in preparation for an eventual takeover by private assigned counsel appointed by the Principal Defender under a legal services contract. Thereafter the Defense Office would work alongside the private defense teams in ensuring the rights of accused persons.

It must be noted that presumably because of the initial poor planning or no planning around defense issues at the Court, the Defense Office was constituted in a haphazard manner that may have ultimately affected the robust and more effective development of the office that was attempted subsequently in the midlife of the Court by its two substantive Principal Defenders. As indicated earlier, the first substantive Principal Defender was appointed in April 2004.[53] Prior to her appointment, two Sierra Leonean Duty Counsel were appointed in February 2003 at quite a low level and a third one in March 2003 at the same level.[54] An Acting Chief of the Defense Office was brought in and worked from April–June 2003[55] as a consultant, and a Defense Advisor arrived in February 2004 and left in August of the same year[56]; there was later to be an Acting Principal Defender.[57] But the office of the Prosecutor

---

[47] *Justice Robertson's Proposal, supra* note 43, at 17119.

[48] *Id.*

[49] Vincent, *supra* note 45, at 131.

[50] Jones et al., *supra* note 46, at 213–14; Skilbeck, *supra* note 41, at 79.

[51] Vincent, *supra* note 45, at 131.

[52] Skilbeck, *supra* note 41, at 79; Jones et al., *supra* note 46, at 213–14.

[53] Simone Monasebian of the United States was the first substantive Principal Defender and served for only one year from April 2004 to March 2005.

[54] Skilbeck, *supra* note 41, at 79.

[55] John R.W.D. Jones of the United Kingdom acted as Chief of the Defense Office for three months. *See* Jones et al., *supra* note 46, at 211.

[56] Rupert Skilbeck also of the United Kingdom was Defense Advisor within the period. *See* Skilbeck, *supra* note 41, at 66.

[57] Sylvan Roy of Canada acted as Principal Defender for a brief period until the arrival of the first substantive Principal Defender Simone Monasebian.

began operation in 2002 with enormous resources and attracted the best prosecutorial staff he could personally choose and vouch for in taking the mandate of his office forward. In the same vein, the best thing would have been to appoint the Principal Defender at the same time with the Prosecutor for an effective and more robust planning around defense issues and to enable the Principal Defender to personally determine the level of professional legal staff required to advance the fair trial interests of accused persons as well as settling the parameters for the experience and level of private defense counsel to compose defense teams.

Be the foregoing as it may, indeed and as I have observed elsewhere, "the OPD at the SCSL [was] a watershed in the history of the Defense vis-à-vis the rights of accused persons in international criminal tribunals."[58] The watershed moment of the Defense Office phenomenon at the SCSL lies in the mandate of the Defense Office and the Principal Defender under the SCSL RPE. It also rests on the fact that it was the first time in the history of international criminal justice that a mechanism designed to watch out for the defense and to act in the interest of accused persons in ensuring the preservation of their fair trial rights as part and parcel of a tribunal was put in place. This extends over and above the inherent duty and obligation of the judges of the Court to do justice and to protect the rights of the accused. More so, the two tribunals – the ICTY and the ICTR – that were created prior to the SCSL did not boast of any such specific organic mechanism within their structure. The ICTY Rules of Procedure and Evidence of July 2002 relative to the defense provided only for "the appointment, qualifications and duties of defense counsel" in Rule 44 and the assignment of counsel to indigent accused persons by the Registrar under Rule 45. In the same vein, Rule 44 of the ICTR 2002 Rules mirrored the ICTY Rules by providing for "the appointment and qualifications of counsel." Rule 44*bis* introduced the concept of duty counsel whereby under Rule 44*bis*(A) "a list of duty counsel who speak one or both working languages of the Tribunal and have indicated their willingness to be assigned pursuant to this Rule shall be kept by the Registrar." The duty counsel, under the RPE, were required to stay within "reasonable proximity to the detention facility and the seat of the tribunal" in order to "attend the detention facility," among other things, should they be summoned by the Registrar. Finally, the ICTR Rules also provided for assignment of counsel to indigent accused by the Registrar under Rule 45.

The point is that the provisions of the ICTY and ICTR Rules mentioned above were in relation to outside counsel and not to the notion of the Defense Office as configured by the SCSL. Accordingly, the SCSL mechanism was bound to inform the constitutive instruments of future tribunals to provide for an organic defense mechanism as part of the tribunal from the start and an improved substantive functioning of such a mechanism, as the experience in the STL shows. The constitutive instruments of the STL make provisions for a Defense Office as an organ of the tribunal, headed by the Head of the Defense Office in the same manner as the Chamber, Prosecution, and Registry.[59] Under Article 13 of the STL's

---

[58] Vincent O. Nmehielle, The Office Counsel for the Defense at the International Criminal Court: Sharing the Experience of the Office of the Principal Defender of the Special Court for Sierra Leone, Paper delivered at the Seminar on Defense Counsel Issues at the International Criminal Court, The Hague, The Netherlands, May 31, 2006 (on file with author).

[59] *See* Agreement between the United Nations and the Lebanese Republic on the Establishment of a Special Tribunal for Lebanon, art. 1(2) and the Statute of the Special Tribunal for Lebanon, art. 7(d) – all annexed to U.N. S.C. Res. S/RES/1757 (May 30, 2007).

Statute, the Head of the Defense Office is appointed by the UN Secretary-General in consultation with the President of the tribunal. The provision also grants total independence to the Head of the Defense Office regarding staff members of the office and in constituting defense teams:

1. The Secretary-General, in consultation with the President of the Special Tribunal, shall appoint an independent Head of the Defense Office, who shall be responsible for the appointment of the Office staff and the drawing up of a list of Defense counsel.

2. The Defense Office, which may also include one or more public defenders, shall protect the rights of the Defense, provide support and assistance to Defense counsel and to the persons entitled to legal assistance, including, where appropriate, legal research, collection of evidence and advice, and appearing before the Pre-Trial Judge or a Chamber in respect of specific issues.[60]

There is absolutely no doubt in my mind that this feature of the STL was a direct influence of the SCSL experience, particularly because of the involvement of Robin Vincent – the first Registrar of the SCSL – as a consultant in the setting up of the STL based on the wide consultation and fact-finding he undertook on what a future Defense Office should look like.[61] Thus, the phenomenon of the Defense Office of the SCSL created that turning point for international criminal justice mechanisms to begin to look at the defense as an integral part of holistic justice. More important, the mandate set out for the Defense Office created hope for the future and became the point of departure in further envisioning the impact of an effective defense in international criminal justice. The importance of this in the wider scheme of things relative to the rule of law and fair trials cannot be overemphasized as has been recognized by the UN Secretary-General in his report on rule of law and transitional justice.[62]

IV. MANDATE AND FUNCTIONS OF THE DEFENSE OFFICE

A. *Mandate of the SCSL Defense Office*

The mandate or "purpose" of the SCSL Defense Office, as has been previously noted, is articulated formally in Rule 45 of the SCSL RPE, which mandates the OPD to ensure "the rights of suspects and accused" persons before the Court. It is important to note that this overall mandate of the Defense Office can be said to be somewhat distinct from the role of the office. There is of course a very close relationship between that mandate as loosely understood and the role that the office performs in that the office carries out its mandate by performing certain duties, roles, or functions as articulated in the RPE. Before specifically

---

[60] The Statute of the Special Tribunal for Lebanon arts. 13(1) and (2).

[61] The late Mr. Vincent interviewed me in 2006 as Principal Defender of the SCSL on his recommendations about the features of a Defense Office in a future international criminal tribunal. I was categorical in stating that based on the experience of the SCSL and of myself as the Principal Defender, a future Defense Office must be an independent organ of a tribunal and must be included in the founding instrument of such a tribunal.

[62] See generally *Report of the Secretary-General to the Security Council on the Rule of Law and Transitional Justice in Conflict and Post-Conflict Societies*, S/2004/616 (Aug. 23, 2004).

discussing and assessing the role of the SCSL Defense Office in carrying out its mandate, it may be necessary to interrogate the meaning of "ensuring the rights of suspects and accused" persons as the mandate or purpose of the SCSL Defense Office. What exactly does the phrase mean? There is nothing in the RPE that clearly defines the meaning of the phrase. In actual terms, one is tempted to ask the question whether the SCSL Defense Office could really ensure the rights of suspects and accused persons. If one examines the phrase more closely and ponders on the weight of the mandate, one is likely to come up with the conclusion that it is rather the Court or the Judges that are ultimately endowed with actual authority to really ensure the rights of suspects and accused persons. This conclusion is supported by the fact that Article 17 of the SCSL Statute that enumerates the rights of the accused lends itself more to judicial enforcement than anything else. It does, however, follow that the role or duties enumerated in Rule 45 of the RPE were one way of giving practical expression to how the rights of suspects and accused persons were going to be ensured from an organic perspective in addition to the responsibility of the Judges to give ultimate judicial protection to those rights.

The lack of clarity and precision on the meaning of the OPDs mandate meant that it depended on the Principal Defender as the head of the Defense Office, and as possibly allowed by the Registrar, to define the operational meaning of his or her office's mandate. The ability of the Principal Defender to effectively do this depended on another factor – the personality and character of the Principal Defender himself or herself. A strong and activist-minded Principal Defender would possibly push the envelope in furthering the interests of accused persons, whereas a weak or establishment-minded Principal Defender would be more hesitant, particularly because of the lack of institutional independence of the office from the Court's Registry. Of course, the Registrar appointed the Principal Defender, who therefore reported to him. The Registrar conducted the Principal Defender's annual performance evaluation and review, a particularly tricky position for an activist-minded Principal Defender to be in.

As Principal Defender, I was activist-minded and saw my mandate and that of my staff as a guardian of the Article 17 rights of the accused persons at the SCSL. Thus, I felt that I should act independently in the realization of those rights relative to both the Court as an institution and assigned counsel who from time to time had differences with the accused on a number of issues. The strong personality of the Principal Defender was, however, bound to lead to sharp disagreements and contentions between the Defense Office and a number of structures at the SCSL. This will be further elaborated in the section that deals with the challenges that the Defense Office faced.

B. The Functions and Roles of the Defense Office

Having articulated the broad and nebulous mandate of the Defense Office, Rule 45 of the RPE goes further to state three specific roles for the Defense Office: (1) the provision of "advice"; (2) the provision of "assistance"; and (3) the provision of "representation" to persons under the jurisdiction of the SCSL either as "suspects being questioned by . . . the Court or its agents under Rule 42, including non-custodial questioning," or as "accused persons."[63]

---

[63] See SCSL RPE, Rule 45(A)(i) and (ii), *available at* http://www.sc-sl.org/LinkClick.aspx?fileticket=Psp%2bFho%2bwSI%3d&tabid=176 (last visited Oct. 1, 2012).

Thus, the activities of the Defense Office largely gravitated around these three areas from which specific functions were crafted under the Rule 45(B) of the RPE relating to the:

(i)   Provision of "initial legal advice by duty counsel who shall be situated within a reasonable proximity to the Detention Facility and the seat of the Special Court and shall be available as far as practicable to attend the Detention Facility in the event of being summoned."[64]

(ii) Provision of "legal assistance as ordered by the Special Court in accordance with Rule 61, if the accused does not have sufficient means to pay for it, as the interest of justice may so require."[65]

(iii) Provision of adequate facilities for counsel in the preparation of the defence.[66]

From the above, the role and functions of the Defense Office were quite varied. First, the Defense Office through Duty Counsel, which included the Principal Defender, acted as counsel at the initial stages – when accused persons were arrested and detained and during initial appearance of the accused under Rule 61 of the RPE in order for them to formally plead to the charges in the indictment if they did not have a legal counsel of their own, or if one had not been assigned to them.[67] Where accused persons have their own legal counsel or had one assigned to them prior to the initial appearance, such counsel represented the accused person at the Rule 61 initial appearance.[68] The most recent performance of the initial advisory and legal representation function of the Defense Office at the initial hearing was that of former president Charles Taylor of Liberia in April 2006 by the Principal Defender and all Duty Counsel in the Defense Office.[69]

The extent to which the OPD gave advice, provided assistance, or represented accused persons as "suspects" being questioned by the SCSL or its agents during "non-custodial questioning" as recognized in Rule 45(i) is indeed arguable. In fact, it does not appear that the Defense Office offered any assistance to "suspects" undergoing "non-custodial questioning" as envisaged in that sub-rule, as only the Prosecutor was aware of who was a suspect as part of his investigations. The Prosecutor was not known to share any information with the Defense Office as to whom he was investigating as a possible suspect until a formal indictment was issued, arrest made, and the suspect detained. In fact, at the time the Prosecutor was carrying out his investigations, the Defense Office was not in existence; it was only an afterthought as initially indicated. In other words, the suspects had to be in custody somehow as a form of provisional detention under Rule 40*bis* of the RPE.[70] Thus, it is doubtful how the rights of suspects under investigation within the meaning of Rule 42 of the RPE

---

[64] *Id.* Rule 42(B)(i).

[65] *Id.* Rule 42(B)(ii).

[66] *Id.* Rule 42(B)(iii).

[67] The Defense Office represented Foday Sankoh, Chief Hinga Norman, Issa Sesay, Morris Kallon, and Brima Kama who were the earlier accused persons to make their initial appearance, as well as Santigie Borbor Kanu. *See* Jones et al., *supra* note 46, at 213–16.

[68] Augustine Gbao had assigned counsel at his initial appearance, while Ibrahim Kamara had joint representation provided by a counsel and the Defense Office. *See id.* at 216.

[69] *See specifically* Transcript of the Hearing for the Initial Appearance of Charles Taylor of April 3, 2006 in Prosecutor v. Charles Ghankay Taylor, Case No. SCSL-2003–01-PT.

[70] Thus, as suspects under provisional custody within Rule 40*bis*, Augustine Gbao, Monina Fofana, and Allieu Kondewa were represented by the Defense Office in the Rule 40*bis*(J) hearing in which the Defense Office argued against the legality of their arrest and detention. *See id.*

were protected. This leads to the question as to how the Defense Office can ensure the rights of "suspects" who are being investigated and not yet indicted, charged, or detained within the purview of the RPE.

In addition to providing advice, assistance, and representation during the initial stages of the process at the SCSL, the OPD was required by Rule 45 (B)(i) to be in a position to attend to the detention needs of accused person and also to be in a position to represent an accused person if assigned counsel is not available, such as where a counsel has withdrawn based on "exceptional circumstance" under Rule 45(E) of the RPE. With regard to attending to the detention needs of the accused, it proved to be a very effective function of the Defense Office in dealing with various detention issues, such as visiting the accused persons, liaising with the Chief of Detention and detention officers on the welfare of the accused, and handling their detention complaints within the necessary administrative channels in the Court. The role of the Defense Office in this regard was a stabilizing factor in the course of the proceedings at the SCSL, as it helped to reduce any serious altercation between the accused persons themselves, between them and their lawyers, or between them and the detention officers, that would have seriously affected the progress of the proceedings. The importance of this role needs to be evaluated from the unique position of the SCSL within whose premises the accused persons were detained and the fact that assigned counsel were not always within the court's premises or Sierra Leone for that matter, as many of them were foreign. The existence of a mechanism within the Court to play this role was invaluable in aiding a smooth court process, as many issues that would have affected the pace of proceedings were dealt with by the intervention of the Defense Office.

Unfortunately, the role played by the Defense Office in this regard was often vilified by some defense counsel who felt that the OPD was meddling in affairs between them and accused persons. But these defense counsel appear to forget that on numerous occasions, the Defense Office mediated between them and the accused persons when differences arose, and even when some defense counsel in a defense team sabotaged each other using the accused person. A few examples among many on the intervention of the Defense Office would suffice.

First, the Defense Office persuaded the late Sam Hinga Norman to cooperate with the Court and his defense team and to attend the court proceedings. Similarly, the Defense Office talked Issa Sesay out of his threat to dismiss his defense team on its failure to appoint a Sierra Leonean as part of the team as required in defense team configuration. In the same manner, the OPD counseled Alex Tamba Brima and Brima Bazzy Kamara, two AFRC accused persons, against further destabilizing their defense teams after the withdrawal of their earlier counsel. The Augustine Gbao defense team suffered from internal intrigues in which a cocounsel used the accused person to undermine his lead counsel and to supplant him with a promise of accepting whomever the accused would choose to work with if the cocounsel were chosen as lead counsel to replace the initial lead counsel. The Defense Office made efforts to properly address and resolve this matter; its efforts were, however, misconstrued by the initial lead counsel and defense counsel in other teams until when the initial Gbao lead counsel was replaced by his cocounsel with the blessing of the Court.[71]

---

[71] *See* Decision on Application of Third Accused to Dispense with the Mandate of the Court Appointed Counsel, Mr. Andreas O'Shea (Prosecutor v. Issa Hassan Sesay, Morris Kallon and Augustine Gbao, Case No. SCSL-04–15-T (July 2, 2007)).

Unfortunately, the Court was not careful to understand the situation the Defence Office was faced with in the matter. Finally, the Defense Office was instrumental in making Charles Taylor effectively participate in the court process after he dismissed his initial counsel.

Regarding substantive legal representation role by the Defense Office beyond the initial stages of the judicial process, the Rules envisaged two situations. First, where assigned counsel is unavailable (say because of exceptional circumstances withdrawal) in which case the Principal Defender could exercise discretion to assign a Duty Counsel in his office to represent the accused.[72] Second is where the Defense Office's Duty Counsel who is part of the Principal Defender's list of competent counsel is assigned to represent an accused person.[73] In terms of the former, which was what prevailed at the SCSL, the withdrawal of counsel could be by the counsel himself or herself, by the Principal Defender, or by the termination of the counsel's services, in which case Article 25(A) of the Directive on Assignment of Counsel (DAC) requires the Defense Office to provide legal representation to the accused.[74] Under this scenario, Defense Office Staff have served as counsel on both a permanent and an interim basis. When Chief Hinga Norman sacked his lawyers, a Duty Counsel in the Defense Office was mandated to represent Norman.[75] Similarly, when Taylor terminated the services of his lawyers during the opening of the Prosecution's case, the Trial Chamber applied the Rule and the DAC to order Duty Counsel in the Defense Office to represent him on an interim basis until the Principal Defender assigned new defense counsel to Taylor.[76]

Apart from these specific Rule and DAC-mandated roles, there is a representation role that emerged out of the practical exigencies of the situation at the SCSL – a tribunal situated in the country where the conflict took place, but where quite a number of defense counsel were not resident. It became necessary to have Duty Counsel, who acted as a professional link between defense counsel and the Defense Office on the one hand and between accused persons and the Defense Office on the other, to readily step in when defense counsel were not available, but with specific instructions from assigned counsel. A direct legal representation role by the Defense Office, no matter how innovative, was frowned upon by the Trial Chambers on the grounds that the Defense Office/Principal Defender lacked *locus standi* to do so. The Defense Office's attempt, with the agreement of defense teams, to challenge the installation of surveillance cameras in the detention center, which had an impact on consultations between defense counsel and accused persons, was struck down by the Trial Chamber on this ground.[77]

---

[72] SCSL RPE, Rule 45(E).

[73] SCSL RPE, Rule 45(C).

[74] Directive on Assignment of Counsel, art. 25(A), requires the Duty Counsel or the Principal Defender himself or herself to provide representation to the accused until new counsel is assigned where the Principal Defender withdraws as counsel, or where a counsel's services is terminated.

[75] Ibrahim Yilla, as Duty Counsel, was mandated to take over the defense of Norman until Yilla left the SCSL to join the International Criminal Court whereupon the Principal Defender sought an order to the Trial Chamber to appoint another counsel to replace him.

[76] Pursuant to Trial Chamber II's oral decision of June 25, 2007, Charles Jalloh, as Duty Counsel in the OPD in The Hague for the Taylor trial, was ordered to "represent the Accused in the interim." *See* Decision on Defense Office Application to Suspend All Time Limits Pending the Resolution of Issues Surrounding the Termination of Mr. Karim Khan by Mr. Charles Ghankay Taylor before the Prosecution Opening Statement (June 4, 2007), Prosecutor v. Charles Ghankay Taylor, SCSL-03–1-T-311, at 11238.

[77] *See* Decision on the Principal Defender's Motion for a Review of the Registrar's Decision to Install Surveillance Cameras in the Detention Facility of (Apr. 2006) in Prosecutor v. Monina Fofana, Allieu Kondewa and Samuel

Another very important legal representative role played by the Defense Office was its participation in the twice-yearly Judges Plenary where major decisions that had bearing on the judicial process were taken, including the amendment of the RPE and other constitutive instruments and directives. The input of the Defense Office was quite instrumental in ensuring that issues having an impact on the Defense were also examined from a defense perspective. Apart from direct inputs made by the Defense Office, prior to the plenary sessions the Defense Office would often circulate notice of the plenary to defense teams to request proposals that they might want included in the Rules. In addition, the Office would circulate prosecution plenary proposals for changes to the Rules and other amendments to give defense teams an opportunity to offer their comments and suggestions, which were then later presented at the plenary.

The SCSL has shown that the importance of such legal representation provided by the Defense Office – a unit of an international criminal tribunal – cannot be underestimated. Unfortunately, legal representation by the Defense Office at the SCSL was still too limited, which made the office essentially more of an administrative unit of the Court that administratively coordinated defense issues. As a former Principal Defender of the SCSL, I believe that there should be a leaning toward endowing Defense Offices in international criminal tribunals with more legal representation powers for indigent accused persons than is currently allowed. This issue will be examined later in the section on lessons learned.

Second, the Defense Office also functioned as the manager of the SCSL legal aid system. Rule 45(C) states that "the Principal Defender, shall in providing effective defence maintain a list of highly qualified criminal defense counsel whom he believes are appropriate to act as duty counsel or to lead the defense or appeal of an accused." Thus, the Defense Office invited lawyers across the world who met the qualifications listed in the Rules and the DAC[78] to be included in a list of counsel kept by the Office, and the Principal Defender assigned counsel to accused persons in accordance with the DAC, the Statute, and the Rules based on a determination of the indigence of an accused person pursuant to a "declaration of means," or in the interest of justice. An assigned counsel would enter into a Legal Services Contract (LSC) to provide legal representation services to an accused person. Through the LSC, the Principal Defender monitored the work of defense counsel and remunerated them for their work based on a legal taxing system as required – an often very challenging aspect of the Defense Office's function, as will be discussed in the next section on challenges.

One element of the Court's legal aid system was the determination of the means of an accused person in order to be satisfied that the accused person qualified for legal assistance. Under the DAC, the Principal Defender is empowered to make a decision in this regard on the basis of proved indigence, partial indigence, or in the interest of justice irrespective of whether a determination of means has been done.[79] However, one tricky aspect of the legal aid system was the need for the Defense Office to investigate the means of the accused persons

---

Hinga Norman, Case No. SCSL-04–14–T and Prosecutor v. Issa Hassan Sesay, Morris Kallon and Augustine Gbao, Case No. SCSL-04–15T, at 15160.

[78] SCSL RPE, Rule 45(C)(i)-(iv) and DAC, art. 13. These provisions require a minimum of seven years of "relevant" legal experience as counsel.

[79] *See* DAC arts. 5, 6, 7 and 9. *See* http://www.sc-sl.org/LinkClick.aspx?fileticket=1FClI7mri4k%3d&tabid=176 (last visited Oct. 1, 2012).

that sought legal representation on the basis of being indigent.[80] This proved to be a very diffi-cult task at the SCSL, as the OPD was not equipped to carry out such an investigation. Again, it created a somewhat unhealthy situation in which the same office that is designed to ensure the rights of accused persons was also required to investigate them regarding their means relative to their qualification for free legal representation. Although it may be reasonable to expect proof that a person seeking legal assistance qualifies for it, it was practically impossible for the Principal Defender to embark on that process before making a decision on whether or not an accused person qualified for legal assistance. The interest of justice basis for assign-ment of counsel under Article 10 of the DAC was the overriding factor for me as Principal Defender in pursuit of an accused's right to speedy trial notwithstanding the non-verification or investigation of the means of an accused over and above what was contained in his affidavit of means. There was no doubt that the SCSL was cash strapped. It was therefore clear that the OPD should perform the means verification function in the expectation that it would save the Court money. But the Office did not have the requisite resources to do so. The OPD did not have professional financial investigators or fee assessors, and because of the small size of its staff could not be expected to adequately perform that particular function.

Third, Rule 45(B)(iii) made it a function of the Defense Office to provide "adequate facili-ties for counsel in preparation of the defence." Unfortunately, the OPD did not have its own specific resources; rather it would annually motivate a budget to the Registry under which the Defense Office institutionally and administratively operated to ensure that adequate human and other support resources were available for a formidable defense of the accused persons. This was indeed one critical area where, compared to the Prosecution, it cannot be said that the hallowed principle of equality of arms was fully observed. The disparity in the resources available to the Prosecution and the Defense was gapingly glaring. This created a lot of tension between the Defense Office and the Registry on the one hand, and between the Defense Office and defense counsel on the other.

As part of adequate facilities, the Defense Office provided logistical and administrative support services to defense counsel such as liaising with the responsible units within the court for the travel arrangements of counsel, land transportation to the hinterland for pur-poses of investigations, provision of office spaces and equipment, recruitment of local inves-tigators, etc. The services afforded to defense counsel in this regard could be better than was provided when compared with the facilities that were available to the Prosecution.[81] Unfortunately, some defense counsel blamed the Defense Office for this. This, in my view, is a misplacement of responsibility taking into account the clear fact that the Defense Office was administratively under the tight policing of the Registry and not independent. The Principal Defender literally had to fight for everything with the Registry. The inadequacy of resources provided to defense counsel should be clearly the responsibility of the Registry under the Registrar, which threatened the Defense Office and the Principal Defender with the fact that they functioned under the Registrar's authority. This issue played out in the additional resources motion filed by defense counsel in which the Defense Office was named as a respondent with the Registrar.[82] Despite drafting a separate response that

---

[80] *Id.* at art. 8.

[81] *See* Skilbeck, *supra* note 41, at 82–83.

[82] *See* Decision of Trial Chamber II on Sesay Defense Application I – Logistical Resources (Jan. 24, 2007) and Decision of Decision of Trial Chamber II on Sesay Defense Application II (Feb. 28, 2007).

identified with defense counsel's position, the Registry literally bullied the Defense Office, using the authority of the Registrar, to require the Office to sign on to the Registry's submissions for a joint filing, which diluted the OPD's position. Despite this rather humiliating episode for the Principal Defender, during the oral argument of the motion, he requested the Trial Chamber to find out from the Registrar why the adequate resources were not provided to the defense. The lesson from this episode would later play out in the Taylor case where the Principal Defender and the Defense Office took the risk to break free from the apparent suffocation by the Registrar.

Finally, the Defense Office functioned in a number of other areas that were not specifically mandated in the RPE or any other instrument, such as bolstering the Court's outreach activities from defense perspectives as a tribunal that was situated in the country where the conflict took place. The Defense Office engaged and challenged the Outreach Section of the Court to be more defense-sensitive rather than the initial prosecution-minded outreach that the SCSL started out with. With time, defense outreach became increasingly popular across Sierra Leone, bringing about some balanced view of the trials, as there was a particularly high level of bias against accused persons and the defense in the general society. The Defense Office also contributed to the legacy of the SCSL by interfacing with the Judiciary of Sierra Leone, the Ministry of Justice, the Sierra Leonean Bar Association, and the SCSL on the need for a national office of a Public Defender;[83] recruiting national legal defense counsel, legal assistants, and interns as well as investigators. The Office organized trainings for the national investigators, legal assistants, and interns.

Although the SCSL Defense Office was an afterthought and fell far short of being the "fourth pillar" that it was envisioned to be, it did set the stage for what was to come in international criminal justice accountability mechanisms. The mandate and role of the Defense Office were therefore an experiment from which important lessons would follow. These lessons, however, could only be learned from the performance of the functions that the Defense Office was entrusted with, which in turn could only be gauged by examining the challenges faced in carrying out the mandate of the office.

V. CHALLENGES THAT THE SCSL DEFENSE OFFICE FACED

As argued in the beginning of this chapter, the OPD headed by a Principal Defender at the SCSL is truly an innovation in international criminal justice accountability mechanisms and was thus a welcome development that added to the credibility and integrity of the judicial process at the SCSL. However, as the first such mechanism within an international tribunal, the SCSL Defense Office did face some challenges, which on occasions led my staff, and I, as the Principal Defender to lament that we were handed the proverbial "poisoned chalice." Although the challenges alluded to here may point at the SCSL, they would readily apply to the other existing tribunals relative to defense counsel issues and to the defense as an organic unit where that unit is not statutorily independent. The challenges need to be understood from organic and functional perspectives, which though generally are not mutually exclusive (because there is an interplay between them), need such articulation for a better understanding of the issues.

---

[83] *See* Vincent O. Nmehielle & Charles Jalloh, *The Legacy of the Special Court for Sierra Leone*, 30(2) FLETCHER F. WORLD AFF. 107, 119 (2006).

From an organic perspective, there were three major challenges. First, the lack of recognition of the Defense Office as an organ during the design of the SCSL mechanism and the drawing up of its constitutive instruments proved to be a major challenge that impacted the status and functioning of the Defense Office when it was eventually established. This made it impossible for a Principal Defender to be appointed at the same time that the Prosecutor was appointed, leading to a lack of checks (at least by the mere presence of formidable defense interest) on the investigative tactics of the Prosecutor. It also had a serious impact on the operationalization of the Defense Office in terms of the staff, office space, and other resources needed to constitute the Office from the start of the SCSL. Efforts that were made by the first and second Principal Defenders to eventually actualize this organic status of the SCSL Defense Office came to nothing.[84] The lack of the autonomy and independence of the Defense Office was of serious concern, which motivated the first substantive Principal Defender, Simone Monasebian, to seek amendments to the constitutive instruments of the Court to achieve organic and institutional independence from the Registry. Unfortunately, not much success came out of her efforts before she left the Court. As Principal Defender, I carried on the mission of achieving autonomy for the defense by engaging with the Management Committee through a position paper presented to the Committee in that regard.[85] However, the Management Committee did not give any serious attention to the position paper and the quest for the autonomy and independence of the Defense Office died a natural death. This reinforced the position of the Registrar in continuing to subjugate the Defense Office to the control of the Registry. It is, therefore, gratifying that the STL from the beginning dealt with the organic status of its Defense Office. Hopefully, when its functioning is evaluated, the impact of its organic status will be meaningful.

Second, despite the elevation of the Defense and defense issues to a new level, the Defense Office was ultimately an administrative unit within the Registry, thereby lacking the vital autonomy needed to fulfil its mandate effectively. In theory and depending on who occupied the office of the Registrar at the time, there was some recognition of the need for the Office to act "with as much autonomy as it is feasible for it to be given in the circumstances."[86] As the custodian of the rights of suspects/accused persons, the Principal Defender (or such designations in other tribunals) must act independently of the Registry and other organs of the Court in the interests of justice in order to realize the fair trial rights of accused persons that are entrenched in the Statute and Rules.

In the SCSL experience, it was not uncommon that in acting as an institutional guardian of the rights of accused persons, the Defense Office and by extension the Principal Defender, found itself at odds with the Registry on certain issues that impacted more on the accused's fair trial rights than just mere administrative concerns. Unfortunately, some of the challenges to the Registrar's decisions and authority were not perceived as the Principal Defender and the Defense Office performing their independent professional duty as mandated by the Court's instruments but were rather taken personally by some in the Registry. This resulted in an emotionally charged and personality-driven working relationship by a

---

[84] *See* Charles Jalloh, *Special Court for Sierra Leone: Achieving Justice?*, 32 Mich. J. Int'l L. 395, 438–39 (2010–2011).

[85] Vincent O. Nmehielle, Position Paper on the Independence of the Office of the Principal Defender at the Special Court for Sierra Leone (on file with author).

[86] Vincent, *supra* note 45, at 127.

particular Registrar who came in the midlife of the SCSL from another tribunal without the Defense Office–type mechanism and who failed to learn about the SCSL mechanism and its peculiarities. The debacle of June 4, 2007 whereby the opening of the Taylor trial that was designed akin to a movie premier, but woefully failed when Taylor not only failed to appear but also dismissed his counsel, was arguably a direct result of the undue undermining of the work of the SCSL Defense Office and the Principal Defender by the Registrar of that era.[87] The Registrar refused to allow the Principal Defender to travel to The Hague to consult with Taylor to sort out the defense issues that Duty Counsel Jallohhad initially brought to the attention of the Principal Defender and the judges and which the Trial Chamber had directed the Registry to resolve.[88] The result was a serious delay to the start of the Taylor Trial, after Taylor terminated his counsel, which the Trial Chamber recognized as the "responsibility of the Registry for failure to address the concerns of Mr. Taylor as and when they arose."[89] The Trial Chamber, however, issued two orders to the Registrar as follows:

> The Registrar is directed to immediately facilitate the Principal Defender to travel to The Hague for the purpose of speaking with Mr. Taylor and sorting out his defense problems. The Registrar is further directed to ensure that logistically the accused has adequate facilities, in accordance with Article 17 of the Statute, without further delay.[90]

In this regard, the Defense Office rose to the occasion and prepared a report to the Trial Chamber addressing the Taylor resources and facilities issues after the Principal Defender had consulted with Taylor. This led to the constitution of a robust defense team for Taylor that was led by a senior and experienced counsel.

Third, from an organic perspective the allocation of resources to the defense was meagre. Although the funding structure of the Court on "voluntary contributions" was a problem of its own, as Sara Kendall shows in her contribution to this volume, budgetary allocation to the Defense Office for the provision of adequate facilities to defense counsel to conduct the defense of accused persons was an item within the overall Registry budget, unlike that of the Office of the Prosecutor, which was treated as independent. Thus, no matter the strength of the Principal Defender's budgetary motivation for the defense, it was within the remit of the Registrar and his budgetary staff to slash it as he wanted without any objection even from the Management Committee. The prosecution-mindedness of institutions such as the SCSL following the commission of mass atrocities plays out in the funding available to the prosecution as against the defense. At the SCSL, there were extra-budgetary donations and allocations to the Office of the Prosecutor from donor states and organizations that enhanced its investigative activities, the hiring of consultants, informants, and other services over and above those provided by the court. There was no such corresponding donation or allocation to the Defense Office. In fact, in one case, a donation was made to the Court with a condition that it should not be used for the defense. One is left to wonder aloud as to how accused persons can be said to be formidably defended with this kind of skewed funding of the defense relative to the Prosecution. It was therefore always a struggle

---

[87] *See* Richard J. Wilson, *"Emaciated" Defense or a Trend to Independence and Equality of Arms in Internationalized Criminal Tribunals*, 15(2) Hum. Rts. Brief 6, 7 (2008).

[88] *See* Transcript of the Opening of the Prosecution's Case against Charles Taylor, at 1–21 (June 4, 2007).

[89] *Id.* at 91–92.

[90] *Id.* at 99.

between the Defense Office and the Registry regarding adequate funding for the Defense. For the Registry, the mind-set appeared to be that as long as defense counsel were paid their legal fees, it was taken that accused persons were being adequately provided with facilities for their defense. The OPD believed that there should be much more to adequate facilities than just paying defense lawyers' fees. The Taylor case is one example where it was clearly evident that the Defense Office was just too tired of being suffocated by the Registry in the performance of its role in furthering the interest of the accused persons in the realization of their fair trial rights.

In terms of the organic challenges that the Defense Office faced relative to the general workings of the Registry, one was left to feel that the Defense had to grapple with almost a reversed presumption standard – at least, administratively – to the effect that an accused person was assumed guilty until he or she proved himself or herself innocent. I make this observation not necessarily in relation to the judicial determination process, but in the whole process of international criminal justice administration where national and international public opinion appear to be that accused persons are guilty of the crimes charged as displayed among the administrative staff of the tribunal. This no doubt impacts the quality of services as well as the timing of services that are rendered to the Defense. In essence, the *realpolitik* of international criminal justice presents an overwhelming challenge to the work of the Defense.

From the functional perspective, I would highlight three further challenges that the Defense Office faced at the SCSL. The first of such challenge is the nebulous mandate of the OPD that created a situation in which professional lawyers in the Defense Office served as Duty Counsel in the initial stages up to the initial appearance of accused persons until counsel was assigned to the Accused. The inherent challenge here related to the counsel–client relationship between the OPD and the accused persons that would later be taken over by assigned counsel.[91] The situation was further complicated by the fact that Duty Counsel and the Principal Defender still had a role to play in ensuring the rights of the accused person within the Rules despite the assignment of private counsel. This created a tense atmosphere in terms of the Defense Office having an interest in how defense counsel performed relative to the interest of the Accused and the mandate of the OPD, which the Principal Defender believed was continuous irrespective of the assignment of private counsel.[92]

Second, the legal aid functions of the Defense Office proved challenging in a number of ways. Although the listing and assignment of counsel were relatively easy, often the Defense Office was at odds with assigned counsel who would want to constitute a legal team with a cocounsel that did not meet the experience requirement of the Rules and the DAC, or a satisfaction of the exceptional circumstances requiring him or her to have such a counsel on the team. From a monetary perspective, it made sense for a defense team to bring into the team a less-qualified counsel in order to save some money, as less-qualified counsel would demand less pay. The Defense Office resisted this practice, one example of which was the case of Andrew Iannuzi, whom a defense team sought to make a cocounsel despite not meeting the minimum prescribed legal practice experience of seven years under Rule 45(C)(iii) of the SCSL Rules and Article 13 of the DAC, or the five years under the discretionary

---

[91] Jalloh, *supra* note 8, at 182–83.
[92] *Id.*

"exceptional circumstances" determination of the Principal Defender under Rule 45(F). Similarly, the management of assigned counsel's LSCs, which required the taxing of legal fees and the assessment of other counsel payment requests, was challenging. As with all issues related to money, it elicited "tension between the support role of" the Defense Office "and the administrative supervisory role" over the work of assigned defense counsel.[93] Defense counsel detested the taxing of legal bills and often engaged in altercations with OPD staff that were responsible for that duty. This did not promote a very healthy working relationship between staff of the Defense Office and some defense counsel, and appeared to pit the OPD as "enemies" of defense counsel and vice versa.

Third, the day-to-day dealings with the accused persons in detention in ensuring their rights were equally challenging. The accused persons would make all manner of requests relative to their welfare and their relationship with assigned counsel, which as Principal Defender or other representative of the Defense Office one was required to pursue with strict objectivity. Where such requests were assessed as not sustainable, the accused persons looked at one as being not really interested in their rights despite whatever successes that may have been achieved on their behalf in the past. At times they would conclude that all organs of the SCSL were in a conspiracy to make sure that they were convicted; after all, just like the Prosecution and the Judges, defense staff were all staff members of the Court.

As with any other human endeavor, there were bound to be challenges in the work of the Defense Office at the SCSL particularly because of the novelty of the mechanism. As Jalloh has rightly observed:

> the Defence Office ... helped to elevate the fundamental rights of the accused in the SCSL, and by extension international criminal justice administration, to a new level by offering itself as a possible model for other international criminal courts from the ICC to the Cambodian and Lebanon tribunals, and to that extent, it represents a good contribution to the development of international law.[94]

Indeed the experience of the SCSL formed the building block for the other tribunals that came after it. The ICC, the Office of the Public Counsel for the Defense (OPCD), and the Extraordinary Chamber in the Courts of Cambodia adopted a somewhat similar structure as the Defense Office with the Principal Defender or a similar characterization as its head but without the preferred organic status that was also lacking in the SCSL. However, the STL Defense Office is a culmination of the organic and structural yearnings of the SCSL OPD but with similar administrative roles as the SCSL Defense Office.

VI. CONCLUSION AND LESSONS LEARNED

There is no doubt that the Defense Office at the SCSL was a watershed in the history of the Defense vis-à-vis the rights of accused persons in international criminal tribunals. This development must be preserved in modern international criminal justice administration. Yet although the innovation of the SCSL set a high standard, it did not go far enough in according the Defense equal organic status with the Prosecution and other organs of an international

---

[93] *Id.* at 183.
[94] *Id.*

tribunal. The achievement of the STL in this regard is quite promising, but it is only an ad hoc tribunal. The ICC, as a permanent international criminal tribunal, needs to take the stage set by the STL after the SCSL to another level as it consolidates the OPCD. The OPCD should grow to become an organ of the ICC if member states of the Rome Statute have an open mind toward autonomy of the Defense and if international human rights and accountability movements come to the party in this regard. After all, the rights of accused persons to adequate and formidable defense are also human rights and go to test the holistic commitment of the international community and international civil society to human rights and the rule of law.

From the lessons of the SCSL Defense Office, one question remains in my mind: how should the Defense in international criminal justice administration be organized in the future? Despite the organic step taken regarding the Defense at the STL, its mandate and operation have still not answered this question. Unfortunately, I may not definitively answer this question, as any particular answer may be controversial. I can, however, proffer some suggestions based on my experience at the SCSL. I strongly believe that in order to effectively realize the rights of accused persons in the international criminal process as provided for in the constitutive instruments of such tribunals and human rights instruments at large, the Defense should enjoy the same structural status and profile as the Prosecution, Chambers, and the Registry. It is imperative that the Defense should be autonomous so that it can act wholly to represent the welfare and legal rights of the accused persons and persons under investigations as well as structurally organize itself for adequate and formidable representation of accused persons in the same manner as the Prosecution.

Despite the controversy this issue may generate, it may also be necessary to begin to think of a full-time in-house defense organ in the international criminal process equipped with professional staff defense counsel who would function just like the various levels of prosecution trial lawyers. The organ should be headed by a Principal Defender, Principal Counsel, Chief Defender, or Chief Defense Counsel (whatever designation may seem appropriate) who should be equal in status with the Chief Prosecutor. There is usually the question of how to deal with issues of conflict of interest, the interest and right of accused persons in choosing their own counsel, etc. On the issue of conflict, the Principal Defender, Principal Counsel, Chief Defender, or Chief Defense Counsel should be in a position to handle all matters of conflict when and if they arise. One way of preventing Defense Office conflict of interests would be for the court or tribunal to have individual or single-accused trials rather than joint trials. Issues of conflict will be minimized when in-house defense teams deal with single-accused trials than in joint trials where one accused person may implicate another. In addition, the head of the Defense should be in a position to recruit external consultants for purposes of dealing with conflicts that are foreseeable. Regarding the right of accused persons to choose their own counsel, it may be important to observe that the right is not absolute when accused persons are provided free legal assistance by the Court because they do not have sufficient means to pay for their defense. That is why there are various shades of appointment of counsel for accused persons – court-appointed counsel, standby counsel, etc. – under certain circumstances that may not be with the agreement of the accused person.[95] The model being suggested should be one that attracts the best staff defense counsel

---

[95] On the various shades of legal representation for accused persons and particularly in international criminal justice, *see generally,* Charles Jalloh, *Does Living by the Sword Mean Dying by the Sword?,* 117 Penn St. L. Rev. 707 (2013)., *available at* http://ssrn.com/abstract=2027121 (last visited June 5, 2012).

just like the Prosecution that seeks to attract the best trial lawyers. This will eliminate the fear that in-house counsel will be mediocre and will not be in a position to render an effective and formidable defense. It will also lead to proper utilization of resources.

I am not oblivious of the fact that the above suggestion would not be acceptable to bar associations around the world. However, my experience at the SCSL shows that a fully fledged in-house defense organ within a tribunal would ensure speedy trial and proper consolidation of resources for the benefit of accused persons. Such a defense organ would also leave a legacy that will impact domestic criminal systems, particularly in developing countries, which in most cases, because of the politics of international criminal justice, are likely to be where most accused persons that would face international criminal justice would come from. More important, if it is accepted that accountability for international crimes will increasingly lie in domestic justice systems in view of the principle of complementarity envisaged by the Rome Statute of the ICC as a permanent international criminal tribunal, it becomes more instructive to begin to give serious attention to the public defender systems in dealing with these trials.

Whatever happens henceforth, we would all agree that the work of institutions such as the SCSL Defense Office and an army of defense counsel that have worked and continue to work in the various international tribunals with the conviction of the need for true justice and the fair trial of accused persons have only but elevated and will continue to elevate the fair trial rights of accused persons to new heights in international criminal justice.

28

The Naked Defense Office: How an Unclear Mandate, Poor Staffing, and Registry Disinterest Stripped the Office of the Principal Defender

Sareta Ashraph[*]

At the outset there was a fervent desire for the Office of the Principal Defender (OPD)[1] to be a success. For those focused on fair trial rights, the OPD represented a new stage in the protection of defense rights and an unequivocal rebuttal to the charge that post-conflict trials delivered "victor's justice."[2] The very existence of the Defense Office became integral to conversations about the legitimacy of the trials.[3] For those concerned with finances, the creation of an in-house unit that would support the defense teams was seen as a most efficient use of the Court's limited funds. For defense counsel, the OPD offered the opportunity for a level of institutional support that had been lacking in the ad hoc tribunals.

Assessments of the Defense Office, particularly in its early years, tended to celebrate the Office as an "innovative model" for future tribunals.[4] The focus tended to be on what it was hoped it would do, rather than what it did.[5] Where critical assessments were made of the Office's substantive work, most linked its shortcomings to the Court's inadequate funding.[6] Although, as this chapter acknowledges, the Defense Office was underfunded – both as a result of the SCSL's general lack of funding and the Registry's lack of prioritization of the OPD – a critical examination of whether it had foundational problems unrelated to its poor

---

[*] Sareta Ashraph was Co-Counsel on the Sesay Defense team in the RUF trial from November 2003 to October 2009. During 2010 and 2011, she worked as a Legal Adviser in the Office of the Public Counsel for the Defense at the International Criminal Court. She thanks Professors Nancy Coombs and Jenia Turner, as well as Chantal Refahi and Daniel Eyre, for their comments.

[1] Hereinafter, "the Defense Office" or "Office."

[2] See Rupert Skilbeck, *Building the Fourth Pillar: Defence Rights at the Special Court*, 1 Essex Human Rights Rev. 66, 71–77 for a history of defense rights, and defense offices, at international and internationalized tribunals.

[3] Among them, Charles C. Jalloh, *Special Court for Sierra Leone: Achieving Justice?*, 32 Mich. J. Int'l L. 395, 413 (2011), who writes (at 437) "the credibility and integrity of the SCSL depends, at least partially, on the accused party's access to fair trial rights."

[4] In fact, the Defense Office was not really as innovative as others have suggested. The internationalized courts in Kosovo, also known as "Regulation 64 panels," had by May 2001 their own Criminal Defense Resource Center set up to assist defense lawyers.

[5] For example, Human Rights Watch, *Bringing Justice: The Special Court for Sierra Leone – Accomplishments, Shortcomings, and Needed Support* (Sept. 2004); International Center for Transitional Justice, *The Special Court for Sierra Leone under Scrutiny* (Mar. 2006); W.A. Schabas, The UN International Criminal Tribunals: The Former Yugoslavia, Rwanda and Sierra Leone 615 (2005).

[6] See Jalloh, *supra* note 3, at 413, 429, 437–44, in which he discusses "how the shoestring funding of the SCSL translated into limited support for the Defence Office."

funding, and whether it made good use of the funds that it did receive, are questions that have largely gone unasked.

I. THE LAST-MINUTE CREATION OF THE DEFENSE OFFICE

While the Defense Office was later heralded as an innovation in defense rights, there was little mention of it at the time of the Court's creation. Neither the Agreement between the United Nations and Government of Sierra Leone on the Establishment of a Special Court for Sierra Leone,[7] nor the Statute (annexed to the Agreement) mentioned an office specifically dedicated to protecting defense rights. Article 17 of the Statute of the SCSL set out recognized fair trial guarantees, but none of the Court's founding documents envisaged how those rights would be realized within the institutional framework.[8] The decision to include a Defense Office in the Court's structure appears to have been made in early 2003, prompted by a realization that the first arrests were likely weeks away and that the detainees would require representation.

The belated push for a defense office, in some form, came from three separate impulses. The first was ideological in nature: the evolution of defense rights demanded an office within the institution specifically dedicated to ensuring the rights of the accused. Those committed to defense rights recalled the "first generation" of the post–World War II international tribunals in Nuremberg and Tokyo, where "except for guaranteeing a right to counsel … they paid very little attention to the rights of the accused."[9] Although the International Criminal Tribunal for the former Yugoslavia (ICTY) had the Lawyers and Detention Facility Management Section, and the International Criminal Tribunal for Rwanda (ICTR) the Defense Counsel Management Section, these creations had come about in response to reports of fee-splitting and inflated fees and did not fulfill the role of providing legal support to defense counsel. A Defense Office within the Court therefore suggested a serious commitment to ensuring defense rights.

The second impulse came from those concerned with the perception of the SCSL and the damage that would be done to its legitimacy by the absence of a unit charged with protecting defense rights. For the Court, this was seen as particularly pressing as the trials – unlike the trials of the ICTY and ICTR – would take place in the country where the conflict had occurred. The OPD would be a tangible reminder of the Court's adherence to the presumption of innocence. It would also signal that the accused from the pro-government Civil Defense Forces militias (CDF) – which a vocal part of the population believed to be, if not innocent, then heroes – would be provided with a vigorous defense by the Court.

The third, and arguably the most powerful, impulse was financial. The SCSL was to operate inexpensively and, following the realization that a Defense Office was needed, there was an immediate concern about its cost. Funding the defense at the ad hoc tribunals had become unfeasibly expensive, with a 2003 report finding that the cost of one defense team at

---

[7] *Available at* www.sc-sl.org/documents.html ("the Agreement").

[8] In contrast, the same documents detailed the roles of the Prosecution, the Registry, and the Judicial Chambers.

[9] Kenneth Gallant, *Politics, Theory and Institutions: Three Reasons Why International Criminal Defence Is Hard and What Might Be Done about One of Them*, 14 CRIM. L.F. 317, 318 (2003).

the ICTY exceeded USD 360,000 a year.[10] A 2001 UN report had found evidence of overbilling and fee-splitting at the ICTY and ICTR, underlining the need to assess and supervise the payments to defense teams.[11] The Court could not afford to spend large amounts on the defense teams, and a Defense Office would assist in keeping costs down in two ways. First, the legal support provided by the Defense Office would justify the capped payments provided to the defense teams. Second, the Office could also supervise and assess the bills of the defense teams and reduce them when necessary.

II. DEVELOPING THE FORM OF THE DEFENSE OFFICE: JUSTICE ROBERTSON'S "PUBLIC DEFENDER" MODEL VERSUS REGISTRAR VINCENT'S "DEFENSE SUPPORT" MODEL

In early February 2003, just over a month before the Court's first arrests took place, discussions about the form of the Defense Office began in earnest. Two models were put forward: the first was Justice Robertson's "public defender" model;[12] the second was a "defense support" model favored by the Registrar, Robin Vincent.

Justice Robertson, then President of the Court, interpreted Article 17 as indicating that an accused had the right to choose his own counsel only where the accused retained counsel privately or where counsel agreed to act pro bono. An indigent accused, therefore, had no right to select his own counsel but was obliged to accept counsel provided to him by the SCSL. Justice Robertson's vision of the Defense Office was one in which defense counsel for indigent defendants were employed as staff by the Court. It would be headed by a Principal Defender who would be "an experienced trial lawyer with a reputation for able and fearless defense, and some proven administrative ability."[13] The defense counsel, as SCSL staff, would reside full-time in Sierra Leone and would have to represent "one or at the most two" indigent defendants.[14] If the Principal Defender judged there to be a conflict of interest, he or she could arrange for a defendant to have "outside" counsel. The Defense Office would also provide support for privately retained and pro bono counsel.

Justice Robertson's proposal failed to address a number of evident concerns. It was unlikely, for example, that experienced defense counsel would be willing to leave a more lucrative independent practice to be employed by the Court. More glaring, perhaps, was the ease with which Justice Robertson suggested that conflicts of interest could be resolved by bringing in "outside" counsel. Given the likelihood of conflicts of interest in joint trials of accused charged with the same crimes, and the fact that such conflicts may arise without warning, the hiring of "outside" counsel would have likely delayed trials. Where multiple conflicts arose, bringing in a number of "outside" counsel would soon have had the same financial consequences as contracting independent counsel.

---

[10] Comprehensive Report on the Progress made by the International Criminal Tribunal for the Former Yugoslavia in Reforming its Legal Aid System, U.N. Doc. A/58/288, para. 31 (Aug. 12, 2003), cited in Sylvia de Bertadano, *What Price Defence? Resourcing the Defence at the ICTY*, 2 J. INT'L CRIM. JUST. 503–04 (2004).

[11] Report of the Office of Internal Oversight Services on the Investigation into Possible Fee-Splitting Arrangements between Defense Counsel and Indigent Detainees at the ICTY and ICTR, U.N. Doc. A/55/759 (Feb. 1, 2001).

[12] Justice Robertson, Public Defender Proposal (copy in author's possession).

[13] *Id.* at 2.

[14] *Id.*

Registrar Vincent preferred a model in which the Court would retain the services of independent defense counsel through a contract. The OPD would support the work of these contracted defense counsel through the provision of legal research and administrative services. His vision of the Principal Defender (and thus, the Defense Office) was "more as a behind the scenes administrator who would mediate between the defense teams, organize and facilitate the drafting of legal research and motions common to the defense, and who would have more of a limited advocacy within the Court's Outreach Program."[15]

It was the Registrar's vision of a Defense Office that was ultimately put into practice. The form of the OPD became thus: lawyers employed by the OPD stood in as "duty counsel" until defense counsel were assigned to each accused. Defense counsel were not staff but provided their services as per the terms of a Legal Services Contract.[16] For all the defense teams, save for the Charles Taylor defense team, the contract allowed a quarterly lump sum to cover the fees of the entire legal team, and flights and associated travel costs, as well as the living allowances and insurance costs normally provided to Court staff in addition to their salaries. While the Contract proposed hourly rates for defense counsel and legal assistants, the quarterly lump sum formed a cap on the amount that could be paid to a defense team, unless a "special considerations" clause was activated.

The "defence support" model may have prevailed for pragmatic reasons. Justice Robertson's proposal was dated February 7, 2003 and with the first arrests taking place on March 10, 2003, there was no time to recruit and employ defense counsel to be primary trial counsel for the indigent accused. Although the Registrar had rejected the "public defender" model, the Registry had no choice but to recruit duty counsel for the OPD: there were indictments to be challenged and first appearances to be had before it was possible to contract independent counsel to represent the defendants. There were also sound financial reasons: having duty counsel to provide support to defense teams through legal research would decrease the work of the individual teams and so lower costs.

Recruitment of in-house counsel happened rapidly, with the Defense Office becoming "functional" on February 17, 2003.[17] This swift recruitment, which installed duty counsel in the OPD for the duration of the trials, was a dangerous gamble to take and, in most instances, did not pay off.

III. AN ACCEPTABLE CRITIQUE: THE INADEQUATE FUNDING OF THE SPECIAL COURT

As virtually all commentators have recognized, one cannot critically assess the successes and failures of the Court without addressing its inadequate funding. Within a year of its operating, the spin about the SCSL being "leaner and meaner"[18] collapsed; instead the Court

---

[15] Sara Kendall & Michelle Staggs, *Interim Report on the Special Court for Sierra Leone: The Special Court as a Model for "Hybrid Justice,"* War Crimes Studies Center, UC Berkeley, 2005, at 19.

[16] Hereinafter, the "Contract."

[17] Position Paper on the Independence of the Office of the Principal Defender at the Special Court for Sierra Leone [hereinafter OPCD Position Paper"], at 1 (copy in author's possession). The first Acting Principal Defender was not appointed until April 2003, six weeks after the Defense Office started to function.

[18] Human Rights Watch, *supra* note 5, at 2.

was "so lean it was anorexic";[19] one commentator called it an example of "shoestring justice,"[20] while another noted that the shoestring was "fraying."[21] They are right: the essential question that the SCSL must surely raise is whether we should seek justice and raise expectations in traumatized societies if there is no commitment to pay what is required to do it properly.

The creation of the Court came at time of intense frustration with the spiraling costs and slow progress of the ad hoc tribunals. A 2004 UN Report indicated that the ICTY and ICTR had more than 2,000 job posts and a combined annual budget of a quarter of a billion dollars – more than 15 percent of the UN's budget.[22] The Report noted that "although trying complex cases of this nature would be expensive for any legal system and the tribunal's impact and performance cannot be measured in financial numbers alone, the stark differential between cost and the number of cases processed does raise important questions."[23] The most important of these questions appears to have been "how can international criminal justice be made less costly?"

It is important to appreciate that what was being considered was not a more cost-effective model but simply a cheaper one. Although the Court is – in the world of international criminal tribunals – relatively inexpensive, this is because of the limited number of cases it has tried. In fact, in an analysis conducted by Charles Jalloh, "even though [the SCSL's] total budget is much lower, given the relatively low number of persons it ultimately prosecuted over nine years, the Court turns out to not be significantly more cost effective" than the ad hoc tribunals.[24] The overriding preoccupation, following on from the costly experiences of the ICTY and ICTR, was whether future models for ad hoc international criminal tribunals fitted within a limited budget, not whether they provided value for money.

For the SCSL, the principal means chosen to reduce costs was to devise new, more limited means through which funding was sourced. Whereas the ICTY and ICTR received funding through the UN budget, the Court had to rely on voluntary donations by UN member states for its funding.[25] Its original budget had initially been set at USD 114.6 million over three years (then the expected life span) but was reduced, following pressure from the Security Council, to USD 56 million.[26]

The UN Secretary-General highlighted the risks of funding the Court through voluntary contributions, stating "[a] special court based on voluntary contributions would be neither viable nor sustainable."[27] In a worrying portent, member states proved unwilling

[19] Registrar Robin Vincent, cited in Dougherty, *Right-Sizing International Criminal Justice: The Hybrid Experiment at the Special Court for Sierra Leone*, 80(2) INT'L AFFAIRS 326 (2004).

[20] AVRIL MCDONALD, SIERRA LEONE'S SHOESTRING SPECIAL COURT 84 IRRC 121 (2002).

[21] James Cockayne, *The Fraying Shoestring: Thinking Hybrid War Crimes Tribunals*, 28 FORDHAM INT'L L.J. 616 (2004).

[22] The Rule of Law and Transitional Justice in Conflict and Post-Conflict Societies: Report of the Secretary-General, U.N. SCOR 59th Session, U.N. DOC. S/2004/616 (2004).

[23] *Id.*

[24] Jalloh, *supra* note 3, at 432. In his "Independent Expert Report on the Special Court," Dec. 12, 2006, Justice Antonio Cassese reached similar conclusions. At para. 5, Cassese concluded that the overall level of efficiency of the SCSL trials "is not a significant improvement on the record of the ICTR and ICTY."

[25] Article 6, Agreement.

[26] Skilbeck, *supra* note 2, at 70.

[27] Report of the Secretary-General on the Establishment of a Special Court for Sierra Leone, U.N. SCOR, 55th Sess., 915th mtg., U.N. DOC. S/2000/915, para. 70 (2000).

to contribute funds for even the reduced budget. Before any trials had commenced, a 2003 audit noted that the Court had not received sufficient contributions to cover its future operations.[28] It was an open secret, particularly in the later years of the SCSL, that because of lack of funds it teetered on the edge of not being able to continue.

The inadequate funds and the emphasis on being in budget rather than being cost-effective had a most adverse impact on the Defense Office, which struggled for adequate funding throughout its lifetime. Undoubtedly, it suffered by virtue of being a sub-office of the Registry. Unlike the Office of the Prosecutor, which was an independent organ of the Court, the OPD had no budget of its own. Rather it had to fight for funds along with the other Registry sub-offices, and often lacked the funding to provide resources, such as experts and international investigators, that the defense teams required.

IV. PRIVATELY ACKNOWLEDGED, PUBLICLY OMITTED: OTHER FOUNDATIONAL PROBLEMS OF THE DEFENSE OFFICE

A. An Unclear Mandate

On January 18, 2006, a dispute between the Defense Office and defense counsel erupted before Trial Chamber I during the CDF Status Conference.[29] The OPD representative requested that the then-Principal Defender, Dr. Vincent Nmehielle, the author of the previous chapter in this volume, be allowed to make "an opening statement" at the start of defense cases of the three CDF Accused.[30] The Trial Chamber indicated that it had already received a written application from Dr. Nmehielle to this effect.

While the Judges were on notice, the request caught defense counsel by surprise. Mr. Johnson, Counsel for the 2nd Accused Kondewa, objected, saying, "this is the first we've heard of an opening statement by the Principal Defender." Mr. Pestman, Counsel for the 3rd Accused Fofana, was more direct:

> I would like to state for the record that we object to the Principal Defender giving an opening statement. We do not see any reason why he should do so and there is also no provision in the rules to do so. And I certainly don't want the Principal Defender to speak on behalf of my client, whatever his intention is.[31]

A copy of the intended statement was later given to defense counsel and, judging it anodyne, they withdrew their objections. Nevertheless, the Trial Chamber denied the request, signaling that the Principal Defender and other Defense Office staff were not in a position to address the Court on behalf of the accused, particularly without the prior knowledge and consent of the counsel assigned to represent them. The OPD subsequently issued the statement as a press release.[32]

---

[28] Shauket A. Fakie, Summary Report of the Auditor (Mar. 24, 2004) (submitted to the Management Committee of the Special Court for Sierra Leone), *available at* www.sc-sl.org/documents.html.

[29] Although the Accused were tried as individuals albeit in joint trials, the division of the trials along the lines of the fighting groups led to them being referred to as the CDF, RUF, and AFRC trials.

[30] SCSL Transcript, Prosecutor v. Norman et al., Status Conference, at 54 (Jan. 18, 2006).

[31] *Id.* at 55.

[32] Press Release, SCSL, Statement Issued by the Principal Defender at the Beginning of the Defense Case in the CDF Trial (Jan. 19, 2006).

The incident brought to light, not for the first time, the contradictory understandings of the mandate of the Defense Office. Though the varying conceptions in this instance were between the OPD and defense counsel, it had already become apparent that the Defense Office's view of itself was shared by neither the Trial nor the Appeals Chamber. Rupert Skilbeck, a Special Adviser to the Defense Office from February to August 2004, stated that one of the entrenched difficulties faced was that there was no clear, well-defined view of what the Office's role was and where the limits of its independence lay.[33]

What quickly becomes apparent is this: to discuss the lack of clarity inherent in the OPD's mandate is to return to the differing conceptions of the Defense Office being offered by Justice Robertson and Registrar Vincent in early 2003. The debate about whether the OPD can advocate directly on behalf of the accused or whether this is the purview of defense counsel, as well as whether the Defense Office is an autonomous "fourth pillar" or merely a sub-office of the Registry are, in their essence, the same debate about the merits of the "public defender" and "defence support" models.

In Justice Robertson's model, counsel employed as staff would have advocated on behalf of indigent accused in the courtroom, barring any conflict of interests. The Defense Office would, in effect, have the same status as the Office of the Prosecutor, which of course had employed attorneys appearing in the courtroom as the prosecuting counsel. In this conception of the OPD, it would have been natural for it to be an autonomous "pillar" of the Court, in control of its own budget, just as the Office of the Prosecutor was.

Registrar Vincent's view was that the Defense Office was there to support the defense counsel who would have primary responsibility for representing the accused to whom they had been assigned. The OPD, although it might have had a role in representing the accused prior to the defense counsel being assigned, would then take on a secondary, supportive role. The Registrar did not therefore envisage the Defense Office continuing to have an active role in the courtroom once counsel were assigned. Registrar Vincent's vision did not rule out the OPD as a "fourth pillar," but it is clear that the arguments for it being an autonomous unit were far weaker under this model. It may be that, given the emphasis on the administrative support role of the Defense Office in the Registrar's model, it was felt that it would be more appropriate for it to be a Registry sub-office, more akin to the Victims and Witnesses Unit than to the Office of the Prosecutor.

The unclear mandate of the Office was a direct result of its rushed entry into the institutional framework of the Court. With the discussion about which of the two models to follow occurring only in February 2003, there was insufficient time to have a full, transparent debate of the merits of each approach and, more important, to ensure that the Rules of Procedure and Evidence reflected the choice made as to its final form. The murkiness as to the role of the Defense Office also appears to be attributable, in part, to Justice Robertson's continuing to champion his vision of the Office, even after it was apparent that this was not the structure that had been created.

1. The Role of the Defense Office as Defined by Rule 45

The mandate of the Defense Office, set out in Rule 45, directs the Registrar to "establish, maintain and develop a Defence Office, for the purpose of ensuring the rights of suspects

---

[33] Interview with Rupert Skilbeck (Jan. 25, 2012).

and accused." The OPD was to fulfill its functions by providing advice, assistance, and representation to suspects being questioned and the accused; initial legal advice and assistance by duty counsel who would remain reasonably close to the detention center; legal assistance for indigent accused as ordered by the Court in the interests of justice; and adequate facilities for counsel in the preparation of the defense.

The wording of Rule 45 owes more to Justice's Robertson's model, with Rule 45(A) and (B) arguably foreseeing an ongoing direct relationship between the accused and the duty counsel. This, however, put it at odds with the assignment of defense counsel to the accused and development of a relationship of privilege and confidence between them.

Rule 45 provided scope, therefore, for different interpretations on the part of the various Principal Defenders. What this meant in practice was that each Principal Defender determined the extent to which the Defense Office's role overlapped with the role of defense counsel. The two Principal Defenders who had experience as counsel before international tribunals, John R.W.D. Jones and Simone Monasebian, recognized the potential pitfalls of ongoing communication between the Defense Office and the accused. Mr. Jones, the first Acting Principal Defender, stated his view was that once defense counsel had been assigned, the OPD's primary relationship should be with the defense counsel, and contact with the accused ought to be only with the counsel's permission.[34] Ms. Monasebian, the first Principal Defender, emphasized while in office that the communications with the accused should be restricted to detention issues and that counsel should be kept informed of communications between the accused and duty counsel.

In contrast, Dr. Nmehielle, Principal Defender from May 2005 to May 2008, informed Alison Thompson and Michelle Staggs that he "interprets this Rule [Rule 45] as establishing that he leads the defense of the accused persons in front of the SCSL."[35] This view appeared to be informed by Dr. Nmehielle's belief that the OPD formed a "fourth pillar" of the Court and that he, therefore, occupied the same role as the Prosecutor, who gave the opening speeches on behalf of the Prosecution.

It was clear, however, that the Principal Defender did not have a role equivalent to that of the Prosecutor, as the Prosecutor was the head of a team of lawyers presenting one central case. The Principal Defender, in contrast, stood outside of a privileged relationship with any of the accused and had no access to the instructions, case strategy, or substance of the accused's intended defense cases. It was inevitable that the surprise attempt to make an opening speech, and Dr. Nmehielle's subsequent comments to Thompson and Staggs, would further inflame the relationship between the Defense Office and defense counsel.

Fewer than six weeks after the January 2006 CDF Status Conference, the Principal Defender was summoned before the same Trial Chamber to explain a far more serious trespass on the relationship between defense counsel and accused, this time in the RUF trial. This incident, detailed below, would lead the Trial Chamber to issue a written ruling in which it declared,

> The institutional role of the Defence Office, once Defence Counsel have been assigned or appointed to an Accused person, is essentially to provide legal research as well as fiscal,

---

[34] Interview with John R.W.D. Jones, Acting Principal Defender (April–June 2003) (Jan. 23, 2012).
[35] Alison Thompson & Michelle Staggs, *The Defence Office at the Special Court for Sierra Leone: A Critical Perspective*, War Crimes Studies Center, UC Berkeley, Apr. 2007, at 37.

logistical and related support services to Counsel assigned to defend the rights of suspects and . . . accused. . . . In our view, Rule 45 has not created, or did not contemplate the creation of a two-tiered parallel mechanism for the effective representation and defence of suspects and accused within the Court system.[36]

2. The Limits of Its Independence: Fourth Pillar or Sub-Office?

Early on in the Defense Office's life, there was support within the Court, principally originating from Justice Robertson, that the OPD form the "fourth pillar" of the SCSL, after the Prosecution, Registry, and Judicial Chambers. In the Court's First Annual Report, the OPD was described as a "fourth pillar," which would provide "a counterbalance to the Prosecution."[37] At the time the Annual Report was published, however, it was already clear that this was not the case: the Defense Office had been set up within the Registry, in the same manner as the Detention or Outreach Units. Justice Robertson's vision, as set out in the First Annual Report, did not reflect the aspirational nature of what was being described. This description of the Defense Office as a "fourth pillar" was repeated in the Court's Second Annual Report.[38]

Ms. Monasebian, during whose tenure as Principal Defender the Second Annual Report was published, attempted to amend the Statute and Rules to formalize the Defense Office as an independent organ of the Court.[39] Ms. Monasebian's draft amendments were approved by the Plenary of Judges, the Government of Sierra Leone, and the Management Committee. Although the UN Office of Legal Affairs agreed in principle, Ralph Zacklin, the UN Assistant Secretary-General for Legal Affairs, determined that there was "insufficient motivation" for the change in status.[40]

On December 8, 2005, the Appeals Chamber issued a Decision that set out its understanding of the Defense Office's place within the Court's structure. The Decision had been prompted by what Trial Chamber II viewed as the OPD's unwillingness to follow the Registry's instructions to appoint new counsel for two of the Accused in the AFRC trial, the Trial Chamber having authorized the withdrawal of the previous defense counsel.[41] The Appeals Chamber stated

> it results from the Statute and Rules that the Defence Office is not an independent organ of the Special Court, as Chambers, the Office of the Prosecutor and Registry are. . . . As a creation of the Registry, the Defence Office and at its head, the Principal Defender, remain under the administrative authority of the Registrar.[42]

In March 2006, however, Dr. Nmehielle raised before the Management Committee the issue of the Defense Office being made an independent organ.[43]

---

[36] Prosecutor v. Sesay et al., SCSL-04-15-T-584, §§ 41–43 (June 19, 2006).

[37] The First Annual Report of the President of the Special Court for Sierra Leone: For the Period of December 2, 2002–December 1, 2003.

[38] The Second Annual Report of the President of the Special Court for Sierra Leone: For the Period of January 1, 2004–January 17, 2005.

[39] *See* Thompson & Staggs, *supra* note 35, at 32 for a summary of the various draft amendments.

[40] OPCD Position Paper, at 1. *See also* Thompson & Staggs, *supra* note 35, at 32.

[41] Prosecutor v. Brima et al. (SCSL-4-16-T), § 11 (June 9, 2005).

[42] Prosecutor v. Brima et al. (SCSL-4-16-AR73), § 83 (Dec. 8, 2005).

[43] Thompson & Staggs, *supra* note 35, at 32.

Shortly afterward, the Principal Defender was required to attend court in relation to allegations of the OPD's trespass on the relationship between defense counsel and an Accused in the RUF trial. Trial Chamber I stated that it believed the incident to have arisen out of a misconception on the part of the Defense Office as to its role and, on March 28, 2006, questioned Dr. Nmehielle as to what he saw that role as being. In response, Dr. Nmehielle referred to the OPD as a "fourth pillar" and was interrupted by the Presiding Judge, who stated "I don't see anything that says this in this Rule [Rule 45] … the Appeals Chamber has clearly stated in a recent decision that your office comes under the Registrar, as such, the Registrar being the third pillar of the Court."[44] In its Written Reasons, the Trial Chamber held:

> the language of Rule 45 is clear, precise and explicit in providing for the creation of the entire machinery of the Defence Office. Accordingly, giving the Rules and its various sub-rules their plain and ordinary meaning, in terms of its purpose and context, the inference is irresistible, and so we hold, that the Defence Office does not enjoy institutional autonomy and independence as a separate organ of the Court.[45]

Despite the "irresistible inference," there had been an undeniable shift in the attitude of the Registry, Office of the Prosecutor, and Judicial Chambers as to the question of whether the Defense Office should become an independent organ of the Court.[46] It remains unclear what prompted this change. Despite the rulings of the Appeals and Trial Chambers, however, the Principal Defender continued to refer to the OPD as the "fourth pillar" on the Court's website, in press releases, and in interviews.[47]

B. Poor Staffing

One of the most significant and least-examined deficiencies of the Defense Office was its poor staffing, as a result of which it provided woefully inadequate support to the defense teams in relation to its duties under Rule 45(B). In some notable instances, described in the next subsections, the OPD made the work of defense teams significantly harder. Given the low level of funding enjoyed by the Court, there should have been periodic assessments of whether the Defense Office provided support effectively or whether the limited funds dedicated to it could have been better used to assist the defense teams.

1. Lack of Legal Research Facilities
Recruitment of the duty counsel happened rapidly in the weeks prior to the March 10, 2003 arrests. None of the duty counsel employed had any background in international criminal law or procedure, and no training was ever provided to them by the Registry. The charges in indictments against all Accused were based solely on international law.

---

[44] SCSL Transcript, Prosecutor v. Sesay et al., at §§ 40–41 (Mar. 28, 2006).

[45] Prosecutor v. Sesay et al. (SCSL-04–15-T-584), § 40 (June 19, 2006).

[46] As noted by Thompson and Staggs, in 2005, both Registrar Vincent and the first Prosecutor, David Crane, had earlier stated their support for an independent Defense Office, but in 2006, Registrar Herman von Hebel took the position that the Defense Office was under his purview while the then Prosecutor Stephen Rapp indicated that his Office opposed even the reference to the Defense Office as a "fourth pillar" and stated he did not know "what is even implied by the phrase." Thompson & Staggs, *supra* note 35, at 33.

[47] Thompson & Staggs, *supra* note 35, at 34.

The duty counsels' lack of understanding of the relevant law proved devastating. Duty counsel had no knowledge of the jurisprudence of the ad hoc tribunals and were unfamiliar with legal databases and search engines. In this way the lack of commitment to defense rights again became visible: it was unthinkable lawyers with no experience in international criminal law would have been hired to provide legal research support to the prosecution trial teams.

The situation could, however, have been remedied: in the course of a six-year trial, it would have been possible – and should have been unavoidable – to gain the needed experience. Indeed, one duty counsel who supported the CDF defense teams subsequently left the Defense Office to take up a position with the Office of the Prosecutor at the ICTR. Other duty counsel did not attempt to fill the gaps in their knowledge and so remained largely ineffective in relation to the provision of legal research. In this there was a failure of the Principal Defender and the Registrar who had duties of supervision, and who ought to have taken steps to ensure that those employed as duty counsel and paid to provide legal support were able to do so.

There was no proactive legal research undertaken by the duty counsel. Despite the mandate, the clear vision of the first Registrar and indeed the view of Trial Chamber I that the Defense Office was there "essentially to provide legal research ... services to Counsel assigned to defend the rights of suspects,"[48] the OPD, in written comments to Thompson and Staggs in September 2006, stated "it only engages in research work when specifically asked, as the main responsibility for this falls on the team themselves and the Office does not wish to be perceived as interfering."[49] Thompson and Staggs made suggestions as to the proactive research that could be done by the Defense Office, including summarizing the law being created at the SCSL and providing legal updates of decisions from other tribunals, and noted "these services would likely benefit the defense teams, though undoubtedly would require the staff of the Defence Office to devote considerably larger amount of time to assisting the teams with legal research than they do currently."[50] None of these suggestions, which mirrored the long-standing requests of defense counsel, were ever taken up by the OPD.

Duty counsel initially engaged in legal research on request but the number of requests declined as it became apparent to many of the defense teams that the work was of such poor quality that it was of limited usefulness. The defense teams therefore had to conduct legal research that should have been undertaken by the Defense Office. This put additional pressure on the teams and often meant this research had to be completed pro bono, the capped limits of the budget having been exceeded. As James Cockayne observed,

> [g]iven that the envisioned research support provided by the Office was cited as a key justification for the strict control over team budgets, the reality that substantial support has generally not been forthcoming has meant that the teams are often either (i) not carrying out the research or (ii) relying on underpaid interns or *pro bono* services to undertake it for them.[51]

---

[48] Prosecutor v. Sesay et al., SCSL-04–15-T-584, §§ 41–43 (June 19, 2006).
[49] Thompson & Staggs, *supra* note 35, at 51.
[50] *Id.* at 52.
[51] Cockayne, *supra* note 21, at 672.

For defense counsel who worked alongside the OPD and then later with the ICC's OPCD and the ECCC's Defense Support Section (DSS), the difference was stark. Unlike the Defense Office, the OPCD keeps statistics of the work it produces for the ICC defense teams. From January 2009 to January 2011, the OPCD provided approximately 1205 pieces of legal research for defense teams.[52] This includes a significant amount of proactive research including, for example, a "Pre-Confirmation Briefing Manual"; a document summarizing the oral decisions made by the various Pre-Trial, Trial, and Appeals Chambers; and a variety of memoranda on topics such as jurisdictional challenges and interlocutory appeals. The OPCD also produced over 242 briefs and memoranda yearly in response to specific requests by defense counsel. The Defense Office kept (and keeps) no such statistics, and indeed the amount of legal research conducted by its duty counsel is negligible compared to the legal support provided by the OPCD.[53]

One legal assistant who worked on an AFRC defense team before the Court and then as a Legal Consultant to a defense team before the ECCC stated:

> the DSS had already done a lot of research on specific topics before the defence team had ever got on the ground. Examples of this include a briefing note about the conflict and a memorandum on criminal trials in civil law system, as most of the team had not worked in a civil law system before. The DSS lawyers also did a lot of research for our team on French procedural law which was very helpful. At the SCSL no such expertise was ever present, and we never received substantive support from the Defence Office there.[54]

The defense team representing the Accused Fofana in the CDF trial, now representing the Defendant Nuon Chea in Trial No. 2 before the ECCC, described the comparative experience:

> where the Defence Office was largely characterized by bureaucratic waste, professional ineptitude, and, at times, malicious obstruction, the DSS proved a world apart. Directed by experienced and creative practitioners and staffed with a range of helpful and enthusiastic assistants, the office functioned as a well-oiled litigation-support unit delivering appropriate levels of assistance at various stages of our case. If the Defence Office clearly (and sadly) represents a failure of leadership and vision, the DSS tells another story: the United Nations, with the right individuals in positions of authority, may in fact be capable of delivering legal models worth replicating elsewhere.[55]

Defense teams at the SCSL received little support despite, for example, multiple requests to put together a library of jurisprudence that defense counsel could draw upon.[56] When

---

[52] Statistics provided to the author by the OPCD. The OPCD also provided for statistics showing that for 2010 alone, the OPCD provided 742 instances of legal support to the defense teams.

[53] Interviews with Wayne Jordash, Chantal Refahi, Sesay Defense team, RUF trial; Michel Pestman, Victor Koppe, and Andrew Ianuzzi, Fofana Defense, CDF trial; Karlijn van der Voort, Kanu Defense, AFRC trial.

[54] E-mail correspondence with Karlijn van der Voort, Senior Legal Assistant to the Kanu Defense team (AFRC trial) before the Special Court for Sierra Leone (2005–2008) and Legal Consultant to the Ieng Thirith defense team before the ECCC (April 8, 2012).

[55] E-mail correspondence with Michel Pestman, Victor Koppe, and Andrew Ianuzzi (Apr. 12, 2012).

[56] In *Prosecutor v. Sesay et al.* (SCSL-04-T-672) (Jan. 9, 2007), the team indicated "The Defence Office … does not – and has not – provided *any* assistance as regards other aspects of substantive defence preparation including legal research, evidential collation or any other aspects of case management." Although the Court had a library on its premises, this was a library where people could conduct their own research by looking through books and articles; it was not a resource where defense teams could obtain analysis of jurisprudence.

legal research was requested, the work product was generally unusable either because the legal point had been missed or because the research was so incomplete that it was inaccurate. Eventually, requests for legal research were passed on from duty counsel to Defense Office interns or to universities with which the defense teams or the OPD had developed a relationship. Although this proved to be sounder than relying on duty counsel, it raised the question of why the Court's funds were being used to employ full-time staff when the legal research was being completed by volunteers.

The frustration felt by the defense teams was palpable. The justification for not being provided with additional funds was the fact that the Defense Office existed to provide legal support to the defense teams. That the duty counsel were either incapable or unwilling to do so prompted no response from the Principal Defender, the Registry, or the Management Committee, all of whom received complaints from defense counsel. The result was that defense teams worked long hours, many of which were pro bono (the cap on their paid hours being exceeded) while duty counsel left promptly at 5:30 PM, without it being entirely clear what their work on any particular day entailed.

2. Lack of Assistance in Securing Resources

As detailed later in the chapter, the under-resourcing of the defense teams was not the fault of the Defense Office; if fault were to be apportioned it would likely fall on the Registry, which controlled the OPD's budget, its decisions taken in the context of generally inadequate funding for the Court. Where the Defense Office failed was in its equivocation in supporting defense teams' efforts to secure those resources for themselves, against a background of OPD staff being better resourced than the defense teams that they were meant to be supporting.

In late 2006, in the months preceding the opening of its defense case, the Sesay defense team requested additional resources[57] from the Defense Office, and once this was declined, then to the Registry. When the Registry also declined the request, the defense team put the matter before Trial Chamber I "seeking an order ... to compel the Defence Office and/or Registry to provide specified resources to ensure an effective defence and a fair trial pursuant to Article 17."[58] The team – which, with five members, an office measuring 15 meters by 7 meters, and only one networked computer – noted not only the office space and computers allocated to the Prosecution, but also that allocated to the OPD. Specifically it noted that the Principal Defender's office, for his sole use, was twice the size of each defense team's office and that each Defense Office staff member – and intern – had his or her own computer.[59] The defense team further noted it was difficult to conduct investigations because of the lack of available vehicles and the absence of an experienced investigator, and that the lack of space afforded to the team meant it was not possible for all of the defense team to fit in its office at the same time with the consequence that, by necessity, work on confidential and privileged material took place in public spaces and on personal laptops.[60]

---

[57] The additional resources requested were more office space, a second computer, a vehicle dedicated to defense investigations, a witness management office, and one investigator with international experience.

[58] Prosecutor v. Sesay et al. (SCSL-04-T-672) (Jan. 9, 2007).

[59] "The fact that interns in the Defence Office have more space than Counsel and their Legal Assistants is inexplicable"; Prosecutor v. Sesay et al. (SCSL-04-T-690), § .17 (Jan. 23, 2007).

[60] *Id.*

The OPD joined with the Registry in opposing the defense team's application for the requested resources. In their Joint Response, the Defense Office and Registry failed to engage with whether the resources were adequate to properly prepare a defense but argued that they had provided more resources than they were obliged to under the Legal Services Contract and noted that "the office space and equipment of Staff Members of the Defence Office is in full compliance with the established regulations and policies of the Special Court."[61] Trial Chamber I granted the defense team's request for a second office, a second computer, a vehicle dedicated to investigations, and a witness management officer, but denied the request for an international investigator at that stage, noting that the Principal Defender had undertaken to secure resources for such an investigator.[62]

In 2007, the Sesay defense team sought to activate the "special consideration" clause of the Contract, providing data to show that, as a result of defending the first Accused, they conducted longer cross-examinations, filed more motions, and were preparing for and would conduct a significantly larger defense case as compared to the other defense teams in the RUF, while having the same budget. The Defense Office joined with the Registry and, while accepting the statistics put forward by the defense team, refused to activate the clause, saying that "the case of Issa Sesay is neither large enough nor complex enough to be treated as of an exceptional nature."[63] The matter went before an independent arbitrator.

The arbitrator sought to ascertain what situation would amount to a "special consideration" case. The Principal Defender, representing both the Defense Office and the Registry, responded:

> [n]ow, the work of an exceptional nature I would define, depending on what the parameters are for you to determine them as an Arbitrator, which is over and above what a lawyer would do in the normal course of legal defence which, in this case, is very difficult to say, to come to say that my case is much larger or more larger than every other case because I will be calling, say, 300 witnesses.[64]

The independent arbitrator found that the services provided by the Sesay defense team were of an exceptional nature and so fell within the "special considerations" clause.

Responsibility for the under-resourcing of the defense teams cannot be laid at the door of the Defense Office. Nevertheless the Office's failure to explicitly support defense teams in applications to receive additional resources is difficult to fathom and added to the general distrust of the OPD by many of the defense teams.

3. Interference with Defense Counsel–Accused Relationship

The foundation for interference in the privileged relationship between the accused and his counsel was the unclear mandate set out in Rule 45. Rule 45(A) states that the "The Defence Office shall, in accordance with the Statute and the Rules, provide advice, assistance and representation to: (i) suspects being questioned by the Special Court or its agents ... including non-custodial questioning; (ii) accused persons before the Special Court."

---

[61] Prosecutor v. Sesay et al. (SCSL-04-T-15–688) (Jan. 22, 2007).
[62] Prosecutor v. Sesay et al. (SCSL-04-T-15–691) (Jan. 24, 2007).
[63] Defense Office and Registry position as quoted in the Judgment of the Independent Arbitrator, June 26, 2007 (copy in author's possession).
[64] Judgment of the Independent Arbitrator (June 26, 2007).

The ambiguity contained within Rule 45(A) comes into focus when comparing it with the equivalent Regulation of the ICC, Regulation 77(4) and (5) setting out the role of the OPCD.[65] Although the OPCD's mandate drew a clear delineation between its direct relationship with the accused "during the initial stages of the investigation" and its role as providing support and assistance to defense counsel once they are assigned, the Defense Office's did not. Furthermore, lawyers employed by the OPCD are also bound by the ICC's Code of Professional Conduct for Counsel, Article 28 of which states, "Counsel shall not address directly the client of another counsel except through or with the permission of that counsel." The OPCD confirmed that they are so bound and, once counsel for an accused is assigned, the office may only have contact with an accused with the express permission of his or her defense counsel.[66]

In the context of the SCSL, however, there was a failure to address in the Rules what the relationship between the Defense Office and the accused ought to have been after defense counsel were assigned. While there is no clear basis for it in the Rules, a belief and a practice developed that the OPD was responsible for detention issues that collectively affected the accused.[67] Another reason given for the ongoing unsupervised contact between the Defense Office and the accused was that this was necessary as defense counsel were not always in Freetown. This was not particularly compelling as legal assistants on the defense teams, not to mention local investigators, were based in Freetown and available to the accused.

In practice, throughout the trials, the duty counsel visited the accused in the detention center regularly and spoke to them by telephone often. Counsel were not informed of when these visits or conversations occurred, what their substance was, or what advice was given.[68] The duty counsel did not keep regular notes of what occurred during conversations with the accused and did not consider it necessary to apprise counsel of the communications, unless specifically asked. One defense counsel recalled voicing concern to one of the duty counsel that the counsel was providing unrecorded advice to his client and was told that she was not advising the accused "as a lawyer, but was speaking to him as a friend."[69]

It was a regular occurrence, therefore, that soon after any dispute between an accused and his counsel, the duty counsel would inform defense counsel that she had spoken to the accused and "calmed him down." While this constant communication with the accused, the content of which was rarely relayed to defense counsel, was viewed by the Defense

---

[65] Regulation 77(4) and (5) of the Regulations of the ICC state,(4) The tasks of the Office for the Public Counsel for the Defence shall include representing and protecting the rights of the defence during the initial stages of the investigation …; (5) The Office for the Public Counsel for the Defence shall also provide support and assistance to defence counsel and to the person entitled to legal assistance, including, where appropriate a) legal research and advice; and b) appearing before a Chamber in respect of specific issues.

[66] Interview with Melinda Taylor, OPCD Senior Legal Officer (Apr. 10, 2012).

[67] It is clear that defense counsel implicitly consented to the Defense Office communicating with the accused about detention conditions that affected them collectively as, for example, defense counsel did not object to the Defense Office's two motions relating to detention conditions. The concern was that the Defense Office lawyers were speaking to the accused about a range of issues, including the accused's relationship with counsel, which as – as discussed above – was the case.

[68] After a logbook was introduced for legal visits at the SCSL Detention Centre in 2005, it was possible for Defense Counsel, belatedly, to see how often duty counsel visited the various accused. It was impossible to verify what the content of the conversations were. In respect of telephone conversations, it was impossible to verify either the frequency or the content of the calls.

[69] E-mail correspondence with Wayne Jordash, Lead Counsel, Sesay Defense team (Apr. 14, 2012).

Office as being helpful – and indeed, in the very short-term, may have been helpful – the OPD failed to appreciate how detrimental it was to the long-term relationship between the accused and his defense counsel. The ongoing contact between the Defense Office and accused meant that the relationship between defense counsel and accused failed to solidify, with several defense counsel citing this as the primary reason their relationship with the accused before the Court remained fragile, as compared with their relationships with clients who stood accused before other tribunals.[70] Further duty counsel did not appreciate – and in some instances, did not accept – that they were not in a privileged relationship with the accused and that they therefore could be compelled to give evidence about the content of conversations.

The OPD's interference in the relationship between defense counsel and accused was brought into public view on March 27 and 28, 2006, when Professor Andreas O'Shea, Lead Counsel for 3rd Accused Gbao in the RUF trial, made an oral application to withdraw from the case before Trial Chamber I. After prompting from the Chamber, Professor O'Shea stated that the Defense Office had facilitated a visit to his client on March 4, 2006, by outside counsel, Mr. Shears-Moses, and that the duty counsel, Ms. Kah-Jallow, had been present at the visit, which had taken place without his knowledge or consent. He further stated that duty counsel had repeated a confidential conversation that Professor O'Shea had with her about a concern about fee-splitting to his client, again without Professor O'Shea's knowledge or consent. The accused, Gbao, subsequently requested that Mr. Shears-Moses represent him, and that Professor O'Shea withdraw from the case.

The following day the Principal Defender and duty counsel were summoned before the Trial Chamber to provide an explanation of what had occurred. Dr. Nmehielle stated the OPD had indeed facilitated a visit between a lawyer, Mr. Shears-Moses, and the Accused Gbao and had failed to inform Professor O'Shea about the request or obtain his consent for the visit. He stated that the accused had requested the visit and that the Defense Office did not know that Mr. Shears-Moses was a lawyer until the time of the visit, and also did not know that the accused intended to discuss legal representation with Mr. Shears-Moses until the visit was underway.[71]

This version of events – which the Trial Chamber declined to accept[72] – was unlikely on a number of levels. First, any accused who wanted to arrange a visitor had no need of the assistance of the Defense Office as there existed the facility of "social" visits, occurring at least four times a week. To enter under a social visit, people had to go through a screening

---

[70] Professor Andreas O'Shea stated, before Trial Chamber I in the course of his application to withdraw from the case, that the deteriorating relationship with his client, Augustine Gbao, the 3rd Accused in the RUF trial, was attributable in part to the inappropriate interference of the Defense Office with that relationship – interference that Professor O'Shea said had "contributed to a total breakdown in communication with the Accused," SCSL Transcript, Prosecutor v. Sesay et al. (Mar. 27, 2006). *See also* Thompson & Staggs, *supra* note 35, at 49.

[71] The Principal Defender stated that although, in a letter dated February 24, 2006, addressed to the Trial Chamber (before the relevant facilitated visit) he recommended the inclusion of a Sierra Leonean lawyer on the Gbao defense team as Co-Lead Counsel with Professor O'Shea, he did not suggest a particular lawyer or Mr. Shears-Moses in particular. The Presiding Judge intervened, however, stating, "Mr. Principal Defender, you may not have [named Mr. Shears-Moses] in that letter, but certainly in our discussion and communication the name was very clear.... Maybe your letter does not make reference to it, but there was absolutely no doubt between you and I that when we were talking of a Sierra Leonean at that time we were talking of Shears Moses, nobody else." SCSL Transcript, Prosecutor v. Sesay et al., at 11–12 (Mar. 28, 2006).

[72] Prosecutor v. Sesay et al., § 35 (June 19, 2006).

process, which would have identified Mr. Shears-Moses as neither a friend nor a family member, but someone being invited to provide legal services, which would have led to the request being denied. As the OPD facilitated the meeting as a "legal" visit, Mr. Shears-Moses could enter in his capacity as a lawyer, avoiding security checks.[73] Second, it was unthinkable that the duty counsel did not take steps to ascertain who Mr. Shears-Moses was, if indeed she did not know. One would hope the OPD was not in the habit of waiving security requirements by escorting unknown visitors through the "legal visits" procedure at the request of an accused. If Ms. Kah-Jallow did not know who Mr. Shears-Moses was, then it was incumbent on her and indeed the Principal Defender to make those inquiries – and inform defense counsel of the request – before facilitating it.

Ms. Kah-Jallow indicated to the Trial Chamber that she became aware that Mr. Shears-Moses was a lawyer only when he arrived at the Court "straight from Court [accompanied by] his legal assistants."[74] She claimed, however, that she did not realize, as she escorted Mr. Shears-Moses and one of his assistants into the detention center under the guise of "legal visit," that "there was any intention on [Gbao's] part to have him in the legal team."[75] She stated that it was only in the meeting, which carried on for just under forty-five minutes, that she learned that the accused's intention was to have Mr. Shears-Moses on his team and that she "vigorously opposed any substantive discussions into Mr. Gbao's case ... [and] defended Professor O'Shea against the numerous allegations that Mr. Gbao catalogued in the hearing of Mr. Moses."[76] Ms. Kah-Jallow admitted that she had admonished Mr. Gbao about the allegation of fee-splitting – itself an example of communication that fell outside of the duty counsel's role – but did not say this concern had been raised with her by Professor O'Shea.

In declining Professor O'Shea's application to withdraw, the Trial Chamber was moved, in its Written Reasons, to state "[o]nce a Defence Team is put in place by the Principal Defender, he can no longer, and should not interfere in the conduct of the Defence of the Accused which henceforth is exclusively under the control of the Defence Team he has put in place."[77] The Registry, which has a supervisory role in respect of the Defense Office, did not investigate or address the actions of the OPD, despite the Trial Chamber stating explicitly that it did not accept the version of events proffered by the Defense Office.

4. Lack of Communication with Counsel
The level of communication between the OPD and defense counsel in relation to the work of the Defense Office and how it represented the interests of the defense teams varied immensely between Principal Defenders. While there was little difference in the work of the OPD – there was still little legal support being provided, for example – when there was communication with defense counsel about negotiations with the Registry over resources,

---

[73] The question of why the Defense Office did not suggest the Mr. Shears-Moses go through the procedure for social visits was raised by Professor O'Shea before the Trial Chamber, but neither the Principal Defender nor the duty counsel engaged with this question. *See* SCSL Transcript, Prosecutor v. Sesay et al., at 55 (Mar. 28, 2006).

[74] *Id.* at 57.

[75] *Id.*

[76] *Id.* at 42–43.

[77] Prosecutor v. Sesay et al., §§ 41–43 (June 19, 2006).

it had a soothing effect on the relationship between the Defense Office and the defense teams.

During the tenure of the Principal Defenders that were employed following Ms. Monasebian's departure in 2005 – Dr. Nmehielle, Ms. Nahamya (previously Deputy Principal Defender), and Ms. Carlton-Hanciles (previously one of the duty counsel) – there were far fewer meetings between the OPD and defense counsel. Filings placed before the Trial Chamber later demonstrated that the Defense Office had been making representations to the Registry on behalf of the defense teams in relation to the provision of resources.[78] The problem, in part, was not that the OPD necessarily failed to represent the defense teams within the structure of the Court, but that it did not communicate what it was doing to the teams and, moreover, did not appear to recognize a need to communicate with the teams.

There was also, in the later years of the Defense Office, a failure to seek input from defense counsel about the needs of the defense teams at particular junctures in the cases. Such was the situation in respect to the 2005–2006 budget, which saw a 15 percent increase in the budget for OPD staffing, with a corresponding 74 percent cut in the money available to defense teams for defense team staffing, international investigators, and experts. This budget came at a time when the defense teams were either in or about to start their defense cases and was agreed by the Defense Office without consulting defense teams as to what resources they needed and whether an increase in OPD staff would be of service. By early 2007, the Defense Office had bloated to thirteen staff members, a stark contrast to the OPCD's five staff members who provide support for cases for twenty-seven accused in fifteen cases or the DSS in the ECCC, where a staff of three supported the defense teams for six accused across two trials.

There was concern from external commentators about the lack of input sought from the defense teams as to the need for more Defense Office staff and about the absence of any discussion as to why the work of these new positions could not be carried out by the under-employed duty counsel .[79] As noted by Thompson and Staggs "as one of the Defence Office's key roles is to provide counsel with adequate facilities for the preparation of the Defence, further consultation with regard to the extent to which hiring of these staff would assist with them [the defence teams] with their work seems warranted."[80]

Coming at a time where the Defense Office had accepted a 74 percent cut in the allocation to contractual services and against a tense background between the OPD and defense counsel (contributed to by some of the incidents described above), the increase in staffing positions by the Defense Office was viewed as little more than empire-building motivated by the OPD's campaign to elevate its status to that of a "fourth pillar."

---

[78] See, for example, copies of correspondence to the Registry and other Registry sub-offices annexed to *Prosecutor v. Sesay et al.* (SCSL-04-15-T-688) (Jan. 22, 2007).

[79] Written Comments from a defense team to Thompson and Staggs:

> While this [the hiring of a Defence Witness Liaison] was done to assist the teams, there was no discussion with the teams beforehand as to neither what support the team required nor why specialist members of the [Defence Office] needed to be hired as opposed to Duty Counsel liaising with the established Outreach and Witnesses Sections of the Court. That is not to say that the Counsel would necessarily have opposed such hirings in the event of a discussion, but rather the lack of communication added to a generally tense relationship.
> Thompson & Staggs, *supra* note 35, at 50.

[80] *Id.*

C. Registry Disinterest

Although the Defense Office made repeated efforts to become an independent organ of the Court, it remained a sub-office of the Registry. Such an understanding was confirmed by the Appeals Chamber in 2005, and the Trial Chamber in 2006. It was the Registry's obligation, therefore, to ensure that the OPD was sufficiently funded to be able to properly carry out its duties under Rule 45, and to supervise whether its staff members were working effectively. The two concerns were related as the Registry was spending a significant amount of its financial resources, particularly after 2006, on Defense Office staff. It was part of the Registrar's duties to ask whether those limited funds could have been spent more effectively to better ensure the rights of the defense.

1. Failure to Adequately Fund the Defense Office

That the defense teams before the SCSL, with the exception of the Taylor defense team, lacked resources is well-known. In September 2004, Human Rights Watch warned

> [w]hile fairness does not require a dollar for dollar match between the resources available to the OTP and to the defence, the extent of the disproportionate allocation of such resources at the Special Court could contribute to the perception that the trials are unfair and that equality of arms is not upheld.[81]

The poor resourcing of the defense teams stemmed primarily from the belated creation of the Defense Office and the consequent lack of funds allocated to it in the Court's initial budget. The limited funding, and lack of consideration of resources needed, can be seen in the terms of the Contract, which the defense counsel signed without the possibility of negotiation. The Contract presupposed that there would be one defense room per trial, shared by three defense teams. In order to protect confidentiality of documents, each team received a three-drawer filing cabinet. There was no shelving, and the teams were expected to use the photocopier in the Court Management Section, which was shared with both the other Registry sub-offices and the Judicial Chambers.[82]

That the Contract was drafted by a lawyer with little experience of criminal law was evident. The resources to be provided would have not only been impractical but would have likely put defense counsel in breach of their professional ethics. With three defense teams to a room and such limited storage space, it was impossible to have confidential meetings or to house the confidential and often privileged material, which in the course of the trials spiraled to over 150,000 pages. Although the Contract was never amended, it was clear from early on it was not possible to run a defense with such resources. By late 2004, each team had its own office, measuring 15 meters by 7 meters, with one networked computer available for each team. A photocopier, not suitable for large-scale photocopying, was provided to the OPD.

Aside from office space and physical assets, there was also a lack of support services specifically allocated to the defense teams. Whereas the Prosecution relied on skilled investigators, most with significant experience at the ad hoc tribunals, each defense team was

---

[81] Human Rights Watch, *supra* note 5, at 6.
[82] *See id.* at 23–24. The Office of the Prosecutor had two of its own photocopiers.

permitted, under the Contract, funding (at the rate of USD 600 per month) for a Sierra Leonean investigator, a job description that required only a background in policing.

The lack of resources had a particularly detrimental effect on defense investigations. Whereas the Prosecution had investigators, drivers, interpreters, vehicles and satellite phones on hand, a defense team had to apply for those resources and obtain them in competition not only with the other nine defense teams, but also with the other Registry sub-offices including the Outreach Section, which often needed these resources for events in rural Sierra Leone.[83] Whereas professional prosecution investigators traveled into the provinces in white four-wheel drive SUVs, the local defense investigator together with legal assistants would climb into *poda-podas* of dubious roadworthiness and rumble along Sierra Leone's poorly maintained roads.[84] The anger that this state of affairs generated was not only because of the inequality of arms, but also because of the lack of care shown by the Court as to the issue of safety of members of the defense teams.

In the context of court preparation and drafting, there were similar problems. Each prosecuting lawyer, and indeed their interns, had his or her own computer and sufficient office space. Although equality of arms does not require a "dollar for dollar" match, concerns should have been raised when defense teams, not able to fit into their offices, began using the Court's canteen as a secondary office. CaseMap, a case management system, was in use by the Prosecution, but for budgetary reasons was only purchased for the defense teams in 2006.[85] In the monthly stationery supplies, defense team members were allocated one pen each and three to four binders. Sitting in a sea of prosecution and defense papers, and needing to make copies of the papers for the accused and for general team use, defense counsel who lived abroad began printing and binding papers and flying in with them.

Even while recognizing the generally inadequate funding of the Court and the difficulties this created for the Registry in determining the internal budgets of its sub-offices, there was still a failure to ensure the defense teams had sufficient facilities and services to allow them to properly conduct the defense of the accused. In failing to provide adequate funds for the running of the Defense, and in particular defense investigations, the Registry failed to ensure an equality of arms within the SCSL.

2. Failure to Supervise Defense Office in Order to Ensure Effective Use of Funds
The Registry's approach to the Defense Office mirrored, in many ways, the attitude of the international community toward the Court – which is to say, there were sound political reasons to have it, but it needed to be as cheap as possible. Although the OPD, like the Court, was relatively inexpensive, it was not cost-effective.

The distinction between an institution being cheap and it being cost-effective is significant. To be cheap requires only a minimum of funds be spent, which in the case of the Court and the Defense Office was precisely the amount budgeted. To be cost-effective demands

---

[83] *See* Cockayne, *supra* note 21, at 671–72; Jalloh, *supra* note 3, at 441.

[84] The term "podas podas" is used in Sierra Leone to described minibuses that operate as private taxis, usually along set routes in the capital or between provincial towns.

[85] It was then very difficult to use CaseMap in 2006 as it would have required returning to the start of the trials in 2004 (for RUF and CDF) and 2005 (for AFRC) and inputting information from transcripts and exhibits. Coming right before the start of the defense cases, it was judged by many of the defense teams to be an ineffective use of defense team time and resources to start using CaseMap at that point.

an examination of whether one is getting value for the money spent. This requires care and a commitment to the quality of the product being provided. In respect of the OPD, the Registry, preoccupied with fund-raising and keeping its various offices within budget, failed to properly examine whether the Defense Office operated effectively.

Through its lifetime, there were clear indications that the OPD was not performing as it should or could have. There were numerous complaints from defense counsel, not to mention the various incidents before the Trial Chambers. The Registry never undertook an exploration of the incidents where the Trial Chambers voiced concern over inappropriate conduct of the Defense Office. There was also never an internal review in which the views of the primary users, the defense counsel, were sought.

The Registry's failure to ensure a properly functioning OPD demonstrated a lack of commitment to protecting the rights of the accused. The justification for the more limited funding provided to the defense – which translated into smaller, less-experienced teams assigned to represent accused charged with multiple counts of crimes against humanity and war crimes, and who were facing extended prison sentences if convicted – was the Defense Office. Where the OPD worked ineffectively or, in some cases created tensions between the accused and his counsel, the people who ultimately suffered were those in the detention center. In not reviewing the work of the Defense Office – and in particular the lack of legal research support being provided to the defense teams – the Registry failed to ensure that the funds being spent to ensure the rights of the defense were being spent to good effect.

In this, the Registry's failure to critically assess the work of the OPD was aided by many of the external commentators who, having confused criticizing the Defense Office with criticizing the sound ideas behind having a defense office, largely restricted their public criticisms of the Defense Office to its lack of proper funding. This resulted in a situation where individual staff members in different units of the Court, including the Registry, and external commentators privately acknowledged that the OPD was not providing the support it should have, and in many cases recognized that the duty counsel did not have sufficient skills or experience to do their mandated jobs, but refused to offer these observations up to public view. The failure to publicly acknowledge the deficiencies of the Office and the Registry's supervision of it was undoubtedly one of the reasons that the deficiencies remained unaddressed.

V. CONCLUSION

Defense rights at the Court suffered from a distinct lack of commitment at the outset from the SCSL's founders, and then throughout its life, from the Registry. The need for a Defense Office was overlooked during the SCSL's creation, only to be remembered in early 2003, weeks before the initial arrests. Having suddenly realized that challenges to the indictment and the initial appearances could not be left to the Registry, there was a rush to assemble an OPD.

The hasty creation of the Defense Office – the initial recruitment for which took place less than a month before the indictments were handed down – led to the Office being saddled with an unclear mandate and with legal staff who had no experience in international criminal law or procedure. These factors were the foundation of a relationship of friction with many of the defense teams. One human rights advocate, who followed the Court closely throughout its lifetime, stated that when she visited the SCSL in 2006, she found the relationship between the Defense Office and many of the defense teams across all three ongoing trials "so irretrievably broken down" that it raised serious questions as to the viability of this model for defense offices at future tribunals, despite such offices' theoretical advantages.[86]

The OPD suffered greatly from Registry disinterest. The Registry, which did not prioritize the budgeting needs of the Defense Office over any of its other sub-offices, was far more concerned with whether the OPD was within budget rather than whether it was using the funds effectively. There was a distinct lack of supervision of the Defense Office's ability to fulfill its mandate, and in particular, there was a failure to examine whether the funds being spent on its staff were translating into effective legal assistance to defense teams.

Many of the lessons from the SCSL's Defense Office have already been learned: make the office part of the initial plans for the Court, determine its mandate clearly, and fund it appropriately. The question of whether the OPD, or defense offices as a whole, would be more effective if they were independent organs of these courts is still a matter of discussion. There are clear advantages to this, particularly in respect of it controlling its own budget. Being a "fourth pillar," however, should not be made synonymous with being an effective office. Neither the ICC's OPCD nor the ECCC's DSS are independent organs of those tribunals, although both are widely credited by defense counsel as being effective. Similarly, it is unlikely the Defense Office, by virtue of gaining "fourth pillar" status, would have been transformed into an office that represented an effective use of the money allocated to it.

There is no substitute for the recruitment and training of staff with relevant skills and experience, and following the recruitment, appropriate supervision of this staff and how they contribute to the work of the defense teams. For the most part, critical assessments of the OPD chose to avoid addressing this and other thorny issues for which there was no easy means of resolution. As noted by Thompson and Staggs, the "challenges [faced by the Defence Office] have largely been subsumed in public discourse by general praise for the idea behind the Defence Office."[87] Many commentators appeared to believe that to criticize the OPD as having ingrained problems – rather than merely challenges that could be resolved through, for example, more funding, a proactive approach to conducting legal research and the purchase of a heavy-duty photocopier – was somehow tantamount to suggesting that the Defense Office ought never to have existed.

To find the Defense Office to have failed in important respects seemed to be viewed as indistinguishable, for reasons that are not entirely clear, from an attack on the very idea of a need for the OPD and, thus, on the creation of future defense offices in other tribunals. Indeed although the shortcomings explored in this chapter have been privately recognized by many commentators, they have shied away from making them public criticisms. There has always been something of "the emperor has no clothes" about the discussions of the Defense Office, with a focus on what we wanted it to look like, rather than what it unfortunately was. Perhaps with the Court finally closing and the OPD shutting its doors, it is finally time to tell it like we saw it?

---

[86] Interview with human rights advocate (Jan. 23, 2012).
[87] Thompson & Staggs, *supra* note 35, at 11.

29

Addressing the Democratic Deficit in International Criminal Law and Procedure: Defense Participation in Lawmaking

Kenneth S. Gallant[*]

I. INTRODUCTION

All international criminal courts and tribunals make law. This lawmaking authority is an underappreciated aspect of their operations. Lawmaking in International Criminal Courts and Tribunals (ICC&Ts) is not limited to making judicial decisions that might later be used in interpreting and applying the substantive and procedural law of the court.[1] ICC&Ts are not simply "courts" resolving specific cases.[2]

The basic criminal law and procedure applicable in these courts is outlined in their respective Statutes, the organic documents creating them. However, these are not the only documents in which law is made in any of the ICC&Ts, and the rights and responsibilities of both substantive and procedural criminal law often appear in the other documents. The courts must also have legislation setting forth how they work, and must have some enforcement authority. An effective criminal court cannot exist without these elements of

[*] Professor, University of Arkansas at Little Rock, William H. Bowen School of Law; Representative of Counsel, International Criminal Court Advisory Committee on Legal Texts (completing second and final term at the time of this writing). This chapter draws upon my experience with the ICC Advisory Committee on Legal Texts.

This chapter is an expansion of remarks made at the International Conference Assessing the Contributions and Legacy of the Special Court for Sierra Leone to Africa and International Criminal Justice, University of Pittsburgh School of Law, USA, April 21, 2012, panel on the Defense and Outreach. My remarks were transmitted by Skype videolink from the Max Planck Institute for Foreign and Comparative Criminal Law in Freiburg, Germany, and I appreciate the technology wizards at MPI, University of Pittsburgh, and Skype who made this possible. The research and writing of this chapter were supported by a grant from the University of Arkansas at Little Rock William H. Bowen School of Law.

The views expressed in this chapter are my own, and do not reflect those of any organization with which I am associated.

[1] For the doctrine that international criminal courts may use their prior decisions, ICC Statute art. 21(2) ("The Court may apply principles and rules of law as interpreted in its previous decisions"); Prosecutor v. Aleksovski (Judgment), IT-95-14/1-T, App. ch. [107–09] (Mar. 24, 2000); Kambanda v. Prosecutor (Judgment), ICTR 97-23-A, App. ch. [15–34], [49–95] (Oct. 19, 2000) (ICTR Appeals Chamber accepted prior reasoning of ICTY Appeals Chamber on issues of waiver and of validity of guilty plea).

[2] For a discussion of this issue and collection of many sources on the functions of international courts, not limited to criminal courts and tribunals, see generally Armin von Bogdandy & Ingo Venzke, *On the Functions of International Courts: An Appraisal in Light of their Burgeoning Public Authority*, Amsterdam Center for Int'l L., Research Paper No. 2012–10, finalized June 12, 2012, *available at* http://ssrn.com/abstract=2084079.

governmental authority. In other words, substantive and procedural criminal lawmaking is not confined to the drafting, by political authorities, of the Statutes and other organic documents creating the ICC&Ts.

Substantive international criminal law includes matters of universal jurisdiction. The law and procedure of ICC&Ts is a matter of the law governing every person in the world.[3]

ICC&Ts share a so-called democratic deficit with International Organizations (IOs) generally.[4] As with most IOs, there is no direct democratic participation in the creation of these courts and tribunals and the making of their laws. No substitute device has generally ensured that the interests of all people whose conduct may be regulated by international criminal law and courts are taken into account in the lawmaking process.

In most ICC&Ts, there is no entity having the sole duty of protecting individual human rights, both the criminal procedure rights generally thought of as "defense rights" and the right to be free from unjust substantive criminal law and procedure generally. In other words, the Statutes or the Rules of Procedure and Evidence (RPE) of these entities systematically cut the Defense out of the lawmaking process, while systematically allowing prosecution participation in the same process. To use Melinda Taylor's phrase, the Defense is denied "a seat at the table" during the lawmaking process.[5]

The Special Court for Sierra Leone (SCSL), the subject of this volume, created a Defense Office that was given a greater voice in lawmaking – as discussed by Vincent Nmehielle in his chapter contribution to this volume. This led the way toward a major change at the Special Tribunal for Lebanon (STL): the creation of a Defense Office as a full organ of the Court with status and rights equivalent to that of the Prosecution. This progress, however, has not been duplicated at the ICC or at the new residual Mechanism for International Criminal Tribunals (MICT), recently established to complete the work of the International Criminal Tribunals for the Former Yugoslavia (ICTY) and for Rwanda (ICTR). This chapter will make suggestions to build on the progress begun at the SCSL concerning defense representation in the lawmaking process, and take lessons from the issues raised by the experience of the SCSL.[6]

---

[3] *See* Section II(A).

[4] The literature on the idea of a democratic deficit in IOs generally is large. However, that focused on ICC&Ts in particular is much smaller. *E.g.*, Madeline Morris, *The Democratic Dilemma of the International Criminal Court*, 5 BUFF. CRIM. L. REV. 591 (2002); Diane Marie Amann, *The Only Thing Left Is Justice*, in THE THEORY AND PRACTICE OF INTERNATIONAL CRIMINAL LAW 365, 368, 372 (Michael P. Scharf & Leila N. Sadat eds., 2008).

[5] Remarks of Melinda Taylor, a member of the Office of Public Counsel for the Defense at the International Criminal Court, at the same panel of this Conference. Between the time of this Symposium and the time this Comment was finalized, Melinda Taylor went to Libya to meet with her client, Saif al-Islam Gaddhafi, who is facing charges in the International Criminal Court. She was detained, with three other ICC Staff Members, for nearly a month by the Zintan Brigade, a paramilitary entity that had Mr. Gaddhafi in its custody, on the basis of alleged information that was obtained in violation of the right of Mr. Gaddhafi to counsel "with whom he can communicate freely and confidentially" under the Arab Charter of Human Rights, art. 16(3), done May 22, 2004, *entered into force* Mar. 15, 2008, *reprinted in* 12 INT'L HUM. RTS. REP. 893 (2005), to which Libya is a party. *See also* ICC Statute art. 48, and the Agreement on Privileges and Immunities of the Court, arts. 16 and 18 (on privileges and immunities of Counsel and the Court), both of which applied to Libya and those acting for it through United Nations Security Council Resolution 1970. As I understand the matter from press reports, she admirably demonstrated the independence of the defense by maintaining her client's confidences, in the face of pressure to reveal professional secrets.

[6] *See* Section IV.

Taylor and others who discuss the Defense on this panel have argued for a Defense Organ in these institutions, seeing it as necessary to both the independence and equality of the Defense, particularly in budgetary matters.[7] In the jargon of IO law, an "organ" (sometimes capitalized) is one of the principal structural units of an IO, usually with a distinct function. In most of the ICC&Ts the organs are the Chambers, the Office of the Prosecutor, and the Registry.[8]

I agree that the creation of a Defense Organ is necessary in order to promote both the independence and equality of the Defense in international criminal justice. These two sets of issues are extremely important, and in my view would alone justify creating a Defense Organ. Those particular issues will be omitted from discussion here solely because they are addressed by the contributions of Vincent Nmehielle and Sareta Ashraph.[9]

This chapter will consider a number of factors. First, it will examine the democratic deficit as an important reason for having an independent Defense Organ in international criminal institutions. An independent Defence Organ can provide the missing voice for individual civil rights concerns in the lawmaking and other processes of international criminal justice. Giving an effective voice for all concerned interests does not eliminate the democratic deficit in IOs, but it can mitigate the ill effects of the deficit. Second, it will suggest that an independent Bar is necessary as well. An independent Bar, established for the Courts of almost all democratic states, would represent the interests of Counsel in the many ways in which this is necessary in all court systems.[10] This paper will also address a recent development at the ICC: the ability of essentially anyone to make a "suggestion" concerning substantive criminal law or procedure to an Advisory Committee on Legal Texts (ACLT). This provides an IO analogue, limited though it is, to the ability of citizens to petition lawmakers in national governments.[11]

II. THE DEMOCRATIC DEFICIT AND THE NEED FOR AN EQUAL DEFENSE VOICE IN THE LAWMAKING PROCESS

A. *Criminal Law for the Entire World: The Need for Civil Rights and Rights of the Defense in the Structure of International Criminal Justice*

A few introductory words on the meaning of "Civil Rights" and "Rights of the Defence": I include here all of the substantive and procedural rights of accused persons, suspects, and persons who might become accused persons and suspects. That is, I include those rights that protect persons from being entangled in the criminal law process – for example, the right to protection from arbitrary arrest and detention or from retroactively created crimes. These rights protect all persons, whether or not currently facing any criminal charges.

The claim that all persons are impacted by international criminal law and procedure needs a bit of justification. This law seems so far away from most individuals living in normal

---

[7] See Vincent O. Nmehielle's and Sareta Ashraph's chapters in this volume. These two chapters agree on the need for a Defense Organ, even if they disagree on certain other points.

[8] The ICC also has a Presidency, made up of three Judges elected from the Chambers.

[9] Nmehielle, *supra* note 7; Ashraph, *supra* note 7.

[10] Bars exist in nondemocratic states as well, although in some their actual independence can be questioned.

[11] *See* Section IV(A).

circumstances. Moreover, some have asked: what is important about having the Defense represented in the lawmaking function? Is there an interest in giving a voice in this process to the alleged perpetrators of mass atrocity? The answer lies in the nature of the criminal process. It is a power arrangement that can, for very good reasons, deprive persons of their liberty. In most of the ICC&Ts, this can be a deprivation of liberty for one's entire life.[12]

Any criminal justice system that is strong enough to deter serious crime is strong enough, if erroneously or wrongfully used, to deprive innocent persons of their liberty. This is an unfortunate fact of human nature. This is not to say that any specific actor in any of these courts has been oppressive. It is only to admit that any criminal justice system that continues for a long enough time will likely see this type of problem.[13]

In other words, the substantive and procedural rights of the Defense are of importance to us all. In all ICC&Ts, lawmaking documents help define these rights. All of us have an interest in their fairness, just as all of us have an interest in national criminal law and procedure – in case we are ever stopped, searched, wiretapped, arrested, or charged with crime. In terms of substance, the core international criminal law crimes – genocide, crimes against humanity and war crimes – are offenses over which there is universal jurisdiction. Thus, any person anywhere who commits these crimes is subject to punishment.

In the ICC, for example, the Elements of Crimes are interpretive tools defining more specifically the conduct prohibited by the Rome Statute. Put differently, they are one of the tools that make substantive international criminal law. The Elements of Crimes are equally important to the Prosecution and the Defense. Yet the Prosecution has the ability to propose changes to these Elements as a matter of right,[14] but the Defense does not.

Even if the ICC does not have automatic universal jurisdiction, its normal jurisdiction covers crimes committed in over 120 states parties to the ICC Statute, or by nationals of those 120 states anywhere.[15] Through Security Council referrals and submission by non-party states to its jurisdiction, it potentially has jurisdiction over crimes anywhere.[16] The decisions of the ICC&Ts affect criminal law and the rights of people around the world.

Other substantive rights that can be affected by law in international criminal courts (including so-called rules of procedure) include the right not to be subject to substantive criminal law that violates the human rights to free expression, freedom of association, or freedom of religion and conscience; the right to be free from torture or cruel, inhumane, or degrading treatment; the right to be free from arbitrary arrest or detention; the right to be free from discrimination on the bases of race, sex, and religion; the right to be subject only to non-retroactive criminal law, and so on.[17]

---

[12] Even in the Special Court for Sierra Leone, where life sentences are not authorized, a sentence to a term of years may reasonably be expected to exceed the life of some convicts. *See* Prosecutor v. Taylor (Sentencing Judgment), SCSL-03-01-T, Tr. Ch. II (May 30, 2012) (fifty-year sentence for a sixty-four-year-old man).

[13] For an argument that there have already been cases of abuse, see Diane Marie Amann, *Impartiality Deficit and International Criminal Judging, in* ATROCITIES AND INTERNATIONAL ACCOUNTABILITY 208 (Adel Hughes, William A. Schabas & Ramesh Thakur eds., 2007).

[14] ICC Statute art. 9.

[15] ICC Statute art. 12.

[16] ICC Statute arts. 12, 13.

[17] *See* Kenneth S. Gallant, *Individual Human Rights in a New International Organization: The Rome Statute of the International Criminal Court, in* 3 INTERNATIONAL CRIMINAL LAW 693 ("Enforcement") (M. Cherif Bassiouni ed., 2d ed. 1999).

Here is an example of how the substantive law of ICC&Ts purports to bind the entire world: the case of criminal contempt of court in the ICTY. There have been several convictions of journalists and others for contempt of court for publishing information deemed secret by the ICTY. The Tribunal found the existence of the crime of contempt in general principles of international law. In at least one case, it has found notice of punishability of a particular act of contempt (in that case, witness tampering) on its placement in the Tribunal's Rules of Procedure and Evidence (RPE).[18] The punishment – currently, up to seven years' imprisonment and a fine of up to 100,000 Euros – and the specific authorization to prosecute were found in the RPE.[19] Effectively, the ICTY is claiming a right to control certain publications by anyone, anywhere in the world.[20] Whether or not one agrees with the specific convictions entered by the ICTY on these grounds, it is easy to see how this power could be abused to the detriment of human rights.

Freedom of expression is just an example of the rights of all persons in the international community that can be affected by international criminal proceedings. These rights either define or (in the case of criminal procedure rights) protect the freedom of all. In the operations of a criminal court, their protection falls most heavily on those who exercise the defense function. Their clients are the ones who, in the criminal system, face loss of liberty. Where prosecutors are overzealous or biased, or the criminal law is unclear, or witnesses are unreliable, it is the Defense that must stand for these individual civil rights. Yet the Defense, which plays the institutional role of protecting these rights, does not have an equal voice in most ICC&Ts with the Prosecution in the lawmaking function.

The criminal procedure law of these courts and tribunals can broadly affect individuals. This broad claim to obedience requires an equally broad responsibility to individual human rights in criminal procedure. The right to counsel and the ability of counsel to conduct an independent and complete investigation and defense on both fact and law are major parts of the rights of the Defense, but they do not exhaust the procedural rights with which the defense is concerned. These procedural rights are generally set out in one or more articles of the Statutes of these Courts and Tribunals. They are usually developed from the procedural rights found in documents such as the International Covenant on Civil and Political Rights.[21]

In any event, purely procedural and evidentiary rules are vitally important to suspects and the accused, as well as to the prosecution. For example, the question of what evidence in the possession of the court or prosecutorial officials must be turned over to the defense is an issue that arises in almost every legal system. The general rules on this issue are at least as important to the Defense as to the Prosecution, and yet only the Prosecution, as a matter of right, has the ability to propose changes to the rules.[22] If the Prosecutors in these

---

[18] Prosecutor v. Tadic (Vujin) (Judgment on Contempt), IT-94-1-A-R77, ICTY App. ch. [19–24] (Feb. 27, 2001) (prohibition put in RPE in 1995; contemptuous acts began in 1997).

[19] ICTY RPE, Rule 77; Prosecutor v. Marijacic, IT-95-14-R77.2, ICTY App. ch. (Mar. 10, 2006) (first journalist case in Appeals Chamber); Prosecutor v. Tadic (Vujin) (Judgment on Contempt), IT-94-1-A-R77, ICTY App. ch. [19–24] (Feb. 27, 2001) (first contempt case in Appeals Chamber).

[20] *See* William A. Schabas, *The UN International Criminal Tribunals: The Former Yugoslavia, Rwanda and Sierra Leone* (2006) 129–32 (suggesting that the ICTY's claim of contempt authority goes beyond its territorial jurisdiction).

[21] *See* International Covenant on Civil and Political Rights, arts. 14, 15, Dec. 16, 1966, 999 U.N.T.S. 171.

[22] ICC Statute art. 51(2).

courts and tribunals properly do their work of presenting their legitimate interests, there is a danger that, without increased Defense participation, the rules will become unbalanced in favor of the Prosecution. The danger is much greater if there were to come a time when a Prosecutor would seek improper advantage through the rules – a possibility that cannot be dismissed over the long term.

For these reasons, a voice for these interests is vital in the lawmaking process for the protection of liberty as a whole. The question about a voice for "alleged perpetrators of mass atrocity" should not be the focus. The liberties protected by the defense in the lawmaking process protect all.

B. Democratic States versus International Organizations

The difference between criminal courts in national jurisdictions and in IOs explains the need for a full defense voice inside criminal courts or tribunals that are, or are associated with, IOs. Within democratic states,[23] civil society – including both individuals and non-government organizations – will generally have within itself strong elements representing civil liberties and rights of the defense. These persons and organizations take part in the democratic process, both in terms of election advocacy and development of policy by legislators and others.

By contrast, IOs have no such direct democratic controls. They are ultimately controlled by states, and their lawmaking functions are given either to the member states, the Judges, or some combination of the two. For example, in the ICC, the RPE and Elements of Crimes are both enacted by the ASP, and the Regulations of the Court are enacted by the Judges, with oversight by the ASP.[24] In other courts and tribunals, the Judges amend the RPEs, whether or not there are Advisory Committees including other voices.[25] There is no independently acting constituency within the ICTY, ICTR, MICT, or ICC that has the same interests in civil rights as civil society in a democratic state, or a full voice in the lawmaking process.

Unfortunately, one cannot equate the participation of civil society in these international institutions with its participation in democratic states. The persons who make up civil society in states are their citizens. The same persons are not the equivalent of "citizens" of international organizations. Membership of the relevant IOs generally consists of states. The SCSL and the STL are IOs, which were created by treaties between the United Nations and Sierra Leone and Lebanon, respectively. These states (and the United Nations as an international organization, in the ICTY, ICTR, MICT, SCSL, and STL) are the real constituents of the Courts, not the individuals and groups of individuals[26] who make up civil society in states.

---

[23] The problems of undemocratic states cannot be addressed here, except to say that they need not be taken as models for international criminal justice.

[24] ICC Statute arts. 51, 52.

[25] *See* Section III(A)(3).

[26] Organized civil society indeed had a tremendous influence in the creation of the International Criminal Court. It is unlikely the ICC would exist today without the advocacy and activism of many organizations throughout the world. Through the Coalition for the International Criminal Court (CICC), these organizations continue to play important roles, both as supporters and watchdogs of the ICC.

One can also say that "representation of interests" in an IO is not the same as true democratic participation. Clearly, this criticism is correct. However, at this point, direct democratic decision making in IOs, especially ICC&Ts, seems unobtainable. Representation of interests, then, may be the best that can be done. If the interests of all in civil rights are to be represented fairly and equally, there must be a device within each Court as an IO to ensure this.

III. DEFENSE VOICES IN THE CURRENT LAWMAKING PROCESSES OF ICC&TS

A. Voices in Lawmaking in the ICTY, ICTR, and ICC: Structural Omission of the Defense, and Remedial Measures

The Prosecution was systematically given a lawmaking voice as to these documents in the ICC Statute – a voice that was not given to the Defense.[27] In the ICTY, ICTR, and their successor, the MICT, the same result was achieved in the RPE.[28]

The SCSL, the subject of this volume, and the STL have made significant progress here. The hope is that the ICC, the MICT, and other institutions will follow.

1. The Lawmaking Documents

The most important lawmaking document in the modern ICC&Ts is usually the institution's Rules of Procedure and Evidence (RPE).[29] These general prescribe rules of procedure for the parties (the Prosecution and the Defense) and for the Judges and the Registry in the handling of cases. Often these texts provide the specific implementations for the procedural rights protected in the Statutes of the court or tribunal. Until now, they have not contained an equivalent of an Evidence Code or a set of Rules of Evidence. At some point, however, the ICC or another international criminal tribunal might wish to do so.

The RPE creates laws for suspects, accused persons, victims, witnesses, and others. Although most of the law is procedural, much of it is substantive. The example of contempt in the ICTY shows that the acts deemed contemptuous of the Tribunal are defined in part by the RPE. The possible sentence is defined by the RPE as well. Both the substantive crime of contempt and punishment are defined through the RPE.

The ICC has two other important lawmaking documents, the Elements of Crimes and the Regulations of the Court. The Elements of Crimes is designed to "assist the Court in the interpretation and application of articles 6, 7 and 8 [defining crimes in the ICC's jurisdiction]." These articles, and their accompanying Elements of Crimes, essentially set out the "special part" of the substantive criminal law of the ICC.[30] The Elements as written today

---

[27] ICC Statute arts. 9, 51, 52, discussed in Section II(B)(2).

[28] ICTY RPE, Rule 6; ICTR RPE, Rule 6; MICT RPE, Rule 6.

[29] ICC Statute art. 51, ICTY Statute art. 15; ICTR Statute art. 14; SCSL Statute art. 14; STL Statute art. 28.

[30] "Special part" is used in many criminal law systems to denote the definitions of specific crimes in the system, as opposed to the "general part" of criminal law, containing general principles of liability and defenses available in the system. In most civil law countries, the general part precedes the special part in the Criminal Code. In most common law countries, the terms "general" and "special" parts of criminal law are mostly used by academics, but most judges, lawyers, and law students will recognize that certain principles (e.g., existence of "physical" and "mental" elements in almost all crimes) exist across criminal law, while some apply only to a single crime or group of crimes (e.g., the specific definition of "malice aforethought" in the law of murder and the distinction between murder and other homicides).

generally cover the required elements for actual commission of the various types of war crimes, crimes against humanity, and genocide under the ICC Statute. They do not generally concern the elements that might make one criminally responsible for these acts under other theories of commission, but they might be amended to do so in the future. The second of these documents is the Regulations of the Court, which are generally more procedural and technical than the Rules of Procedure and Evidence. However, they do cover extremely important matters.

Each Tribunal has other lawmaking documents, covering matters such as detention, conduct of counsel, operations of the Registry, etc. Those documents are too diverse to be covered in detail here, but they may affect both the substantive rights of persons (e.g., places and conditions of imprisonment and pretrial detention[31]) as well as procedural rights (e.g., proceedings before the Registry[32]). They also define legal ethics for Defense Counsel and, in the ICC, Legal Representatives of Victims.[33]

2. Who Makes and Changes This Law – Official Omission of the Defense and Counsel

In the ICTY, ICTR, and MICT, the Judges make and amend the RPE.[34] In the ICC, the ASP, made up of representatives from each state party to the ICC Statute, adopts and amends the RPE and Elements of Crimes.[35] The Judges adopt the Regulations of the Court, subject to review by the ASP.[36]

This is, however, not the whole story. The class of people who can make official proposals to make law here is very limited. It includes the Prosecution, but not the Defense.

A Judge, the Prosecutor, and the Registrar in each respective court may make official Proposals for changes to the RPE in the ICTY,[37] the ICTR,[38] and the MICT.[39] No one associated with the Defense has these rights in the Statute or RPEs of these Tribunals.[40]

In the ICC, only the Judges (acting by a majority), the Prosecutor, or a State Party may make proposals to change the RPEs and Elements of Crimes to the ASP.[41] The ICC Prosecutor and Registrar must be consulted on proposals to change the Regulations of the Court.[42] A democratic deficit is created whereby persons with specific interests in civil rights and the Defense are systematically excluded from the lawmaking process.

---

[31] *E.g.*, SCSL Rules of Detention.
[32] *E.g.*, ICC Regulations of the Registry.
[33] *E.g.*, ICC Code of Conduct for Counsel.
[34] ICTY RPE, Rule 6; ICTR RPE, Rule 6; MICT RPE, Rule 6.
[35] ICC Statute arts. 9, 51.
[36] ICC Statute art. 52.
[37] ICTY RPE, Rule 6(1) (a Judge, the Prosecutor, or the Registrar may propose).
[38] ICTR RPE, Rule 6(A) (a Judge, the Prosecutor, or the Registrar may propose).
[39] MICT RPE, Rule 6(A) (a Judge, the Prosecutor, or the Registrar may propose).
[40] The ICTY Practice Direction on Procedure for the Proposal, Consideration of and Publication of Amendments to the Rules of Procedure and Evidence of the International Tribunal, IT/143/Rev. 2, para. 1(a), (2002), indicates that proposals might come from "other groups" without further specifications. Because this document is subsidiary to the RPEs themselves, it cannot expand the list of persons who can make official Proposals.
[41] ICC Statute, arts. 9, 51 (a State Party to the Statute, the Judges acting by a majority, or the Prosecutor may propose).
[42] *See* ICTY Practice Direction on Procedure for the Proposal, Consideration of and Publication of Amendments to the Rules of Procedure and Evidence of the International Tribunal, IT/143/Rev. 2 (2002).

3. Advisory Committees Including a Defense Voice – and a New Mechanism for Petitioning an IO

At the creation of the first modern international criminal tribunal, the ICTY, there was a complete exclusion of the Defense from the lawmaking process. As time went on, ICC&Ts attempted to deal with this official exclusion of the Defense from the lawmaking process. They have created advisory bodies that include a defense voice. Two will be considered here: the ICTY Rules Committee,[43] and the ICC's roughly analogous Advisory Committee on Legal Texts (ACLT). Focus will be on the ACLT, largely because I have been a Member of that Committee,[44] but also because it has two features that mark it as a further advance in representation of interests in an IO. These Committees advise on official proposals that have been made, and in some circumstances might consider suggestions from other sources. They are both advisory, and do not bind anyone.

In 2002, the ICTY added three members to its Rules Committee, which had previously been made up solely of Judges. The current Rules Committee is made up of three Judges and three nonvoting members (from the Prosecution, the Registry, and the Defense).[45] However, as established from the very beginning the Prosecutor and the Registry had the right to make official Proposals to change the RPEs, whereas the Defense did not, and still does not. This group advises the Plenary of Judges on the Proposals submitted to it. The ICTY also has an independent group, the Association of Defense Counsel Practicing in the International Criminal Tribunal for the Former Yugoslavia (ADC-ICTY), which acts roughly as the Bar of the Court, able to discuss matters of interest to Counsel with appropriate Court officials.

The ICC's ACLT has a mandate to consider and give advice to the Plenary of Judges[46] on proposals to amend the RPE, Elements of Crimes, and the Regulations of the Court. It may also consider and provide advice concerning certain proposed agreements between the Court and intergovernmental organizations or states not party to the ICC Statute, if referred to it by the Presidency, and may consider and provide advice on other matters referred by the Presidency. None of its decisions are binding on the Plenary of Judges, the Presidency, or the ASP. The ACLT cannot prohibit any proposal (including proposals of the Prosecutor) for changes in the RPE and Elements of Crimes from being presented to the Assembly of States Parties (ASP).

(a) Full Voice for the Representative of Counsel in the ICC's Advisory Committee on Legal Texts

The ACLT has six voting members, one Judge each from the Pre-Trial, Trial, and Appeals Chambers, a member of the Prosecutor's Office, a Member from the Registry, and a Member who is the Representative of Counsel from the List of Counsel maintained by the Registry.[47] The Chair must be one of the Judges.

---

[43] *See* ICC Regulations of the Court, Reg. 4.

[44] I am completing my second and final term on the ICC ACLT.

[45] *Compare* ICTY Practice Direction on Procedure for the Proposal, Consideration of and Publication of Amendments to the Rules of Procedure and Evidence of the International Tribunal, IT/143/Rev. 2 (2002), *with id.* Rev. 1 (2001), and *id.* [original] (1998).

[46] The body consisting of all ICC Judges.

[47] ICC Regulations of the Court, Regs. 4, 107. For information on the makeup of the Registry's List of Counsel, see ICC Regulations of the Court, Regs. 67–72.

The Representative of Counsel participates fully in the work and debates of the Committee, and in advising the Plenary of Judges on Proposals, and the Presidency on other matters. In this sense, it is an important advance over the ICTY's Rules Committee, where the Representative of Counsel has no vote.

Two aspects of full participation in the ACLT are of prime importance. The first is the ability to discuss issues and points of view, which are of an interest to the Court, and are not otherwise represented. These include the interests of both Defense Counsel and Legal Representatives of Victims. Even more important is the ability to bring the interests of suspects, accused persons, and victims (i.e., the clients of Counsel) to the table.

The second aspect of full participation is the ability to suggest amendments to proposals and referrals. That is, in advising the Plenary of Judges or the Presidency on what might be done with proposals and referrals, the Representative of Counsel has the same ability to suggest amendments to proposed or referred texts as any other Member of the ACLT. This is particularly important because of the limitations of the ICC Statute,[48] which prohibit the Representative of Counsel (and the Member from the Registry) from making official proposals concerning changes to the RPE and Elements of Crimes.

As the Representative of Counsel on the ACLT, my views, as well as the views of my constituents, have always been treated with the upmost respect by other members of the ACLT.[49] My suggestions for changes to proposals or referrals were always treated seriously and discussed fairly.[50] I am convinced that my views were heard not just within the Committee, but within the Plenary of Judges, through ACLT Reports.

Structural issues, however, create problems for using the ACLT as the principal means of having a defense voice in the process of writing and amending lawmaking documents in the ICC. These issues will face any successor of mine on the ACLT, and go beyond the formal inability to make official Proposals.

First, unlike in the ICTY, "Counsel" in the ICC refers to a group broader than Defense Counsel. This is because persons claiming to be victims of crimes within the jurisdiction of the ICC have a right to participate in ICC proceedings and to be represented in the ICC.[51] Members of the List of Counsel may be either Defense Counsel who represent suspected or accused persons or Legal Representatives of Victims. They may take on each of these different roles in different cases. Prosecutors, however, are not included in the category of "Counsel." Thus, as Representative of Counsel, my mandate was not to focus solely on the procedural "rights of the defence" or the substantive interests of liberty. My constituents were representatives who might represent accused persons, victims, or both. One can easily imagine that the interests of victims and accused persons are not always the same in the making of substantive and procedural criminal law, and that a single Representative of Counsel might find it difficult to represent both sets of interests at the same time.

Second, a person titled Representative of Counsel is just that – someone who represents the interests of lawyers. Although lawyers generally hope that we place the interests of our clients first, we must admit that we are sometimes driven by self-interest (often legitimate)

---

[48] ICC Statute arts. 9, 51.

[49] Because our discussions of issues are confidential, see Rules of Procedure of the Advisory Committee on Legal Texts, Rule 8, I will not give specific examples.

[50] *See id.*

[51] ICC Statute art. 68(3).

as well. Therefore, no Representative of Counsel, including myself, can be a pure advocate for civil rights and the rights of the Defense.

Third, the ACLT speaks to constituencies within the Court, especially the Plenary of Judges and the Presidency. It does not speak directly to the ASP, which has ultimate responsibility for changes to the RPE, the Elements of Crimes, and (through the ability to veto them) the Regulations of the Court.

Fourth, the mandate of the ACLT encompasses a very important, but limited, range of the lawmaking documents of the ICC. There are all sorts of lawmaking documents, such as the Code of Conduct for Counsel, Regulations of the Registry, Detention Rules, etc., which simply are not within the remit of ACLT.

The ICC's ACLT (building on the ICTY Rules Committee) is a very important improvement on the complete exclusion of the Defense from the lawmaking process at the beginning of the modern era of ICC&Ts. However, it does not eliminate the democratic deficit in the lawmaking processes in the ICC.

(b) "Suggestions" in the ACLT – Opening up to Petitions from the World's Citizenry
Because all persons may be affected by the law of ICC&Ts, all persons have an interest in the creation and modification of that law. This is a reasonably clear deduction from standard democratic theories.

The ACLT has devised one innovation to allow for some true outside participation in the lawmaking process, open to all. It will receive "suggestions" for changes to the RPE or the Elements of Crimes. Essentially anyone may make a "suggestion."[52]

Effectively, anyone who wishes to may suggest amendments to the ICC RPE and Elements of Crimes. This essentially creates an ability to petition the ICC as an IO for changes in these lawmaking documents. No limitation is placed on who may do so, because the core criminal law of mass violence (genocide, crimes against humanity, war crimes) binds everyone.

This is indeed merely an ability to make limited suggestions and permits only suggestions concerning the RPE and Elements of Crimes in the ICC, and does not extend to other lawmaking documents in the ICC or to the ICC Statute itself. It does not guarantee that

---

[52] Rules of Procedure of the Advisory Committee on Legal Texts, Rules 11, 12 (Rev. 2, Mar. 4, 2011), which state:**11. Procedure for submission of proposals, referrals or suggestions to the ACLT**11.1 The following items:(i) Proposals for amendments to the Rules of Procedure and Evidence and the Elements of Crimes by the Judges and the Prosecutor … ;(ii) Referrals from the Presidency … ;(iii) Proposals for amendments to the Regulations of the Court … ;(iv) Suggestions for amendments to the Rules of Procedure and Evidence and the Elements of Crimes, accompanied by explanatory material and presented in writing in at least one of the working languages of the Court;shall be marked by the sender with the requested level of confidentiality and urgency and shall either be sent by email to the ACLT email address, ACLT@icc-cpi.int, the inbox of which shall be accessible to the Chairperson and persons designated by him or her, or by post to:"The Advisory Committee on Legal TextsInternational Criminal CourtPO Box 195192500 CM, The HagueThe Netherlands".11.2 Upon receipt of a proposal, referral or suggestion, as described in rule 11.1, the Chairperson shall send an acknowledgement of receipt to the sender.**12. The ACLT work plan**12.1 The Chairperson shall circulate proposals, referrals or suggestions received in accordance with rule 11 to the members at intervals determined to be appropriate by him or her and may, if he or she considers it appropriate, provide a summary thereof. The Chairperson shall also indicate whether, in his or her view, a matter is urgent.12.2 The Chairperson shall prepare a work plan detailing how the ACLT shall consider and report on proposals and referrals and how it shall consider suggestions. This process may include one or more rounds of written comments and one or more meetings,unless the Chairperson concludes that a matter can be finalised by way of a written procedure.

the suggestion will ever become an official proposal. This procedure in the ACLT cannot expand the ICC Statute's limitations on who may make such proposals.[53]

Nonetheless, this procedure does recognize some interest of all of society in the criminal laws and procedures that bind all. It is a step toward recognizing and remedying the democratic deficit in international criminal law.

B. *Contribution of the SCSL and Further Advancement (and Retreat) in the STL*

The SCSL has made important contributions in structural advancement of the lawmaking opportunities of the Defense. The SCSL RPE is made and amended by the Judges. Its RPEs allow both the Principal Defender and the Bar Association of Sierra Leone to make proposals to amend the rules as a matter of right.[54] This allows participation in the process both by the Defense directly, and by the Bar of Sierra Leone as a separate institution representing domestic counsel. It is not quite the same thing as having a true independent Defense Organ, or a true independent Bar of the Court, but it is an important step in that direction. The rules also allow the President of the Court to invite other persons to make proposals.[55]

The division between the SCSL Defense Office and the Bar of Sierra Leone offers a solution for the problem of differing interests of lawyers and citizens affected by international criminal law. Assume a situation where both of these institutions exist, and are truly independent, and have the ability to participate in the lawmaking process. Here, the Defense Office can concentrate on the interests of those affected by criminal law and procedure (i.e., the interests of the citizenry), whereas the Bar can protect the interests of counsel, as is true in most national systems. Unfortunately, this model did not come to pass at the SCSL,[56] as the Bar of Sierra Leone did not serve as the Bar of the SCSL. It raises the question whether a true independent Bar of the SCSL might have helped resolve some of the conflicts that arose in that Court.

The STL has followed up on some of these advances. It is the first international criminal tribunal with a Defense Office as an independent Organ,[57] which Vincent Nmehielle has argued in his chapter are attributable to the SCSL's innovation in this area. The Head of Defense Office may propose amendments to the Rules of Procedure and Evidence, on equal terms with the Prosecutor.[58] As a member of the Senior Management Team of the Tribunal, the Head of Defense Office also has the opportunity to participate, on an equal footing with the Prosecutor, in making decisions concerning all other aspects of Court operations. As a matter of status, the Head of Defense Office is the equal of the Prosecutor in the law of IOs generally, and the law of the STL, an independent IO, particularly.[59]

The STL does not, however, recognize a Bar as an independent lawmaking voice in the system. It also provides no vote for the Prosecutor, the Defense Office, or the Registrar in

---

[53] ICC Statute arts. 9, 51.

[54] SCSL RPE, Rule 6(A).

[55] *Id.*

[56] *See* Nmehielle, *supra* note 7; Ashraph, *supra* note 7.

[57] STL Statute arts. 7, 13.

[58] STL RPE, Rule 5(A) (a Judge, the Prosecutor, the Head of Defense Office, or the Registrar may propose).

[59] Because of space limitations, this chapter will not address the internal organization of the STL Defense Office, which may provide a model for the future.

its Rules Committee.[60] It sees actual lawmaking through the RPE, then, as centered on the Judiciary, with limited participation from outside, even at the stage of giving advice.

V. A DEFENSE ORGAN, AN INDEPENDENT BAR, AND SECOND-BEST OPTIONS FOR THE FUTURE

One might be tempted to see the story told in Section IV as an evolution. When the ICTY was created in 1993, the Defense was completely shut out of the formal lawmaking process in the court. With the creation of the STL and its Defense Office as an organ of the Tribunal, there is now formal defense equality with the prosecution in the lawmaking process and other aspects of court operations.

Unfortunately, the ICC, the one Court intended to be permanent, does not have a Defense Office on the model of the STL. Neither does the newly created MICT, taking over from the ICTY and ICTR. Given that residual matters from the ICTY and ICTR (such as issues regarding clemency, conditions of imprisonment, and release of documents) could last for decades, the MICT may also be the second longest-term institution of the ICC&Ts.

In terms of lawmaking, the Defense and its interests do not receive equal treatment with the Prosecution, in either the ICC or the MICT.[61] The ICC and MICT do not have a Bar either.[62]

A Defense Organ (whether or not called a Defense Office) has as its sole duty promotion of the interests of the defense. This would be true in the legal aid administration process, the provisions of legal research and support, and the budgetary process, as well as in the lawmaking process. This would take the Registry out of the no-win position in which it – unfairly in my view – has been put: being a neutral Organ for all parties and interests, while being asked to "promote" the interests of the Defense. A Defense Organ does not wholly eliminate the possibility of conflicts about the Defense,[63] but it eliminates a great deal of conflict seen in the ICTY, ICTR, and ICC between the Registry and defense counsel. Most importantly it makes the overall structure of the Court much fairer.

In terms of creation of a true independent Defense Organ, things are much easier in the MICT than in the ICC. The Security Council could, and in my view should, create a Defense Office as an organ of the MICT on the model of the STL – that is, including both the Defense Legal Aid function and the Defense Support function. This could be done through an amendment to the MICT Statute. Such an organ should be given equal status in lawmaking authority with the Prosecutor, again on the model of the STL. It should also be treated as equal with the Prosecutor in terms of voice in the budgeting process and management process of the Tribunal as a whole, again on the model of the STL.

The creation of a Defense Organ in the ICC will be much more difficult. This is because the ICC Statute is in fact a treaty among over 120 or so nations as of this writing. Its amendment provisions are complex. The ASP could amend the Statute to create a Defense Organ

---

[60] STL RPE, Rule 5 (no mention of Bar; votes only for Judges).

[61] *See* Section III(A).

[62] As of September 2012, the MICT website www.unmict.org does not give any indication that the ADC-ICTY will maintain its status in the Mechanism.

[63] The Defense Office of the SCSL was not an independent organ of the Court. However, compare Nmehielle and Ashraph for a description of conflicts concerning legal aid and legal research.

on its own only if this were treated as an amendment of an "exclusively institutional nature."[64] If it is not treated that way by the Assembly, the amendment would require ratification of seven-eighths of the state parties,[65] an extremely difficult percentage to achieve.

Moreover, there was agreement among Nmehielle, Ashraph, Taylor, and myself at the underlying conference on the subject of the SCSL that creation of a Defense Organ for the ICC is necessary – for the reasons that Nmehielle and Ashraph have stated, as well as those I have suggested in this chapter. The legacy of the SCSL includes agreement on this point, even among some who strongly disagree on other matters. However, I want to make clear that, outside of this conference, a very small percentage of the people who matter agree with us. In general, criminal courts are created because people perceive a problem with crime – in this case impunity for criminal acts of mass violence – and not because they want to protect defendants.[66] The task of getting agreement that the interests represented by the defense are so important that they need to be represented by a separate organ will be difficult.

I am committed to the idea that an independent Defense Organ in the ICC is necessary. Nonetheless, I recognize the difficulties of creating such an organ in the near future. Therefore, like Vincent Nmehielle in the conclusion to his chapter, I feel it necessary to suggest secondary options for promoting equality of the defense in lawmaking and other aspects of ICC operations.

The first option would be the creation of a Defense Office at the ICC, which would be on the model of that of the SCSL, along with the creation or recognition of a Bar. That is, the Defense Office would not be an independent organ, but would be guaranteed functional independence from the Registry in the performance of its defense duties. These duties would include the administration of legal aid for the Defense (today performed by the Registry) and the legal research and advice functions of the OPCD. The fact that the OPCD has been functionally independent in its research and advice function bodes well for the possibility that a larger Defense Office would be independent as well.

The structural inequality in the ICC Statute concerning the Defense in the lawmaking process poses a problem here, and this proposed solution is only second-best. Given the Statute, the Judges, acting by an absolute majority, and the Prosecutor are the only entities from within the Court who can make official proposals to the ASP on amending the RPE and the Elements of Crimes. I would therefore suggest the ASP should adopt an internal procedure that would allow the Defense Office that I have suggested to bring before the ASP documents that might be called something other than a proposal – let us say (following the current ACLT procedure) a "suggestion." A Defense Office suggestion could be circulated to the state parties like other communications, available for any state parties who wish to pick it up and turn it into a proposal. I would also suggest that the Defense Office, if created, be given a place on the ACLT so that its suggestions could be given the same careful analysis and comment now given to proposals from Judges and the Prosecutor.

As to the many other lawmaking documents in the ICC, the situation is much easier. The Statute generally does not define who may participate in the creation of these documents.

---

[64] ICC Statute art. 122. This would depend on whether the list of "institutional" provisions in article 122 is considered exclusive.

[65] ICC Statute art. 121.

[66] One interesting exception to this rule is the movement over the past hundred years or so to create quasi-criminal juvenile courts to encourage rehabilitation of young offenders.

Therefore, it is possible for the Court, through its Regulations, or the ASP, through the RPE, to grant the Defense Office the same rights in the lawmaking process as the Prosecution.

To avoid the conflicts that arose between the Defense Office at the SCSL and defense counsel, which have been described in the earlier chapters in Part VI of this volume, the ICC could – and should – create or recognize a Bar. One of the chief functions of independent Bars, particularly, but not exclusively in civil law systems, is addressing this sort of conflict with Court entities and personnel. This can help to depersonalize the conflict, while at the same time providing an entity that can support the interests of Counsel and their clients. (Indeed, even if an independent Defense Organ could be created, a Bar would be necessary, for the same reason.) The Bar could be created within the ICC as an IO by authorization of the ASP on the model of the "staff representative body" of the ICC.[67] That is, it would be an independent, self-governing group, separate from the organs of the Court.

Another model for the Bar would be that of the ADC-ICTY. It was created under national law (the law of the Netherlands), but recognized by the ICTY as the functional equivalent of a Bar. Now I must disclose my own interest in this matter: I am an active member of the International Criminal Bar (ICB), a representative body of counsel and associations of counsel from around the world, organized under the law of the Netherlands, that some of us, including myself, believe might serve this purpose.

Whatever form is chosen for a Bar, the point is to create an independent, self-governing, representative group that can truly perform the functions of a Bar in the ICC. Because the interests of Counsel are not always identical with those of their clients, a representative of the Bar should take over the current position of the Representative of Counsel on the ACLT – even if the proposed Defense Office has a seat there.

The second option for structuring the defense so as to allow its representation in the lawmaking process would involve something a bit less tested in the ICC&Ts. This would be to use the U.K. model of a board of legal aid commissioners to administer defense legal aid. Additionally, these commissioners would be responsible for supervising staff and providing the research and support currently provided by the OPCD. Finally, they would have the lawmaking functions described for the Defense Office suggested in option one. There are legal aid commissioners in the ICC now, who help resolve conflicts over legal aid between the Registry and Counsel.[68] Their functions would be greatly expanded in this model. The creation or recognition of a Bar would be an important element of this plan, as of the plan described previously. This option has the advantage that legal aid commissioners can be drawn from various legal traditions and systems. It has the disadvantage in that an Office with a single head can sometimes be more efficient.

None of these proposals eliminate the democratic deficit in ICC&Ts. All of them at best ameliorate the deficit, by providing representation of vital omitted interests in the lawmaking process of the Court. Where amelioration of a problem is the best that can be done, it should be done.

---

[67] *See* ICC Staff Regulations, Reg. 8.1, ICC-ASP/2/10 (2003). This idea is not original with me, but the person who suggested it to me prefers not to be identified.

[68] ICC Regulations of the Registry, Reg. 136.

PART VII

Special Challenges Facing the Sierra Leone Tribunal

30

Prosecuting Those Bearing "Greatest Responsibility": The Contributions of the Special Court for Sierra Leone

Charles Chernor Jalloh[*]

I. INTRODUCTION

The Special Court for Sierra Leone ("SCSL" or "the Court") was established through a bilateral treaty between the United Nations (UN) and the government of Sierra Leone signed on January 16, 2002.[1] The SCSL's *jurisdiction ratione materiae*[2] included crimes against humanity, war crimes, other serious violations of international humanitarian law, as well as various offenses under Sierra Leonean law prohibiting the abuse of underage girls, wanton destruction of property, and arson.[3] Although the Sierra Leonean conflict started in March 1991,[4] the jurisdiction *ratione temporis*[5] only covers the crimes perpetrated after November 30, 1996.[6] This means that, over the objections of the national authorities, the international community, as represented by the UN, only supported prosecution of the atrocities committed during the second half of the conflict.[7] With respect to *ratione loci* jurisdiction,[8] the Court was authorized to prosecute the crimes that occurred within the territory of Sierra Leone.[9]

Given the SCSL's limited subject matter, temporal, and territorial jurisdiction,[10] it is evident that the UN's goal was to establish an ad hoc tribunal with a narrower and more focused mandate compared to the International Criminal Tribunals for the former Yugoslavia and Rwanda (ICTY and ICTR). The ICTY and ICTR were created by the Security Council ("UNSC" or "the Council") in 1993 and 1994, respectively, partly as ways of addressing the

---

[*] Assistant Professor, University of Pittsburgh School of Law, Pittsburgh, Pennsylvania, USA. I thank Erika de Wet (Pretoria), Harmen van der Wilt (Amsterdam) and David J. Scheffer (Northwestern) for their excellent feedback on an earlier draft of this chapter. All opinions, and errors, are mine alone.
[1] Agreement Between the United Nations and the Government of Sierra Leone on the Establishment of a Special Court for Sierra Leone, U.N.-Sierra Leone, Jan. 16, 2002, 2178 U.N.T.S. 137 [hereinafter U.N.-Sierra Leone Agreement].
[2] BLACK'S LAW DICTIONARY 930 (9th ed. 2009) (directing reader from *jurisdiction ratione materiae* to *subject-matter jurisdiction*).
[3] Statute of the Special Court for Sierra Leone arts. 2–5, Jan. 16, 2002, 2178 U.N.T.S. 145 [hereinafter SCSL Statute].
[4] U.N. Secretary-General, *Report on the Establishment of a Special Court for Sierra Leone*, ¶ 25, U.N. Doc. S/2000/915 (Oct. 4, 2000) [hereinafter Secretary-General, *Report on SCSL*].
[5] BLACK'S LAW DICTIONARY 930 (9th ed. 2009) (directing reader from *jurisdiction ratione temporis* to *temporal jurisdiction*).
[6] U.N.-Sierra Leone Agreement, *supra* note 1, art. 1(1); Secretary-General, *Report on SCSL*, *supra* note 4, ¶ 25.
[7] *See* SCSL Statute, *supra* note 3, art. 1(1).
[8] *See* BLACK'S LAW DICTIONARY 1377 (9th ed. 2009) ("By reason of place.").
[9] U.N.-Sierra Leone Agreement, *supra* note 1, art. 1(1).
[10] Secretary-General, *Report on SCSL*, *supra* note 4, ¶¶ 1, 12, 27.

threats to international peace and security caused by genocide in the Balkans and in East Africa.[11]

Article 1(1) of the UN-Sierra Leone Agreement, and its annexed statute, defined the Court's *ratione personae* jurisdiction – that is, the "power to bring a person into its adjudicative process."[12] It gave the SCSL competence in the following terms: "to prosecute persons who bear the *greatest responsibility* for serious violations of international humanitarian law and Sierra Leonean law ... including those leaders who, in committing such crimes, have threatened the establishment of and implementation of the peace process in Sierra Leone."[13]

A. *Greatest Responsibility Jurisdiction and Its Significance*

There is no aspect of the Court's jurisdiction that was more controversial than the notion that it should prosecute only those persons bearing "the greatest responsibility" for what happened in Sierra Leone during the second half of that country's notoriously brutal conflict. Indeed, the idea of greatest responsibility had been controversial from the moment the UNSC proposed the phrase to the UN Secretary-General (UNSG) as a way to define the SCSL's personal jurisdiction in the resolution that it requested him to negotiate with the Sierra Leonean government to establish the Court.[14] Several factors explain why this qualified personal jurisdiction was contentious, which in turn, make the issue worthy of further study in this chapter.

First, while both the UN-Sierra Leone Agreement and the SCSL Statute included the phrase, neither specified what it meant.[15] Yet, both instruments gave prominence to the idea as each mentioned the phrase at least twice: first, in the personal jurisdiction provision in Article 1(1),[16] and second, in the clause setting out the powers of the Prosecutor in Article 15 of the Statute.[17] Although the framers appeared to have included these two provisions to underscore the Court's narrow jurisdiction and to ensure that the prosecutions would stay within the strict boundaries that they had demarcated, Article 1 and Article 15, when taken separately but also when considered together, sent two apparently contradictory messages.

When taken separately, the provisions in Article 1 suggested, at least to the defense counsel, that the greatest responsibility phrase established a jurisdictional requirement that the

---

[11] S.C. Res. 827, U.N. Doc. S/RES/827 (May 25, 1993); S.C. Res. 955, U.N. Doc. S/RES/955 (Nov. 8, 1994).

[12] Black's Law Dictionary 930 (9th ed. 2009).

[13] SCSL Statute, *supra* note 3, art. 1 (emphasis added). The Agreement between the United Nations and Sierra Leone also provided, in Article 1, as follows:

    (1) There is hereby established a Special Court for Sierra Leone to prosecute persons who bear the greatest responsibility for serious violations of international humanitarian law and Sierra Leonean law committed in the territory of Sierra Leone since 30 November 1996.

    (2) The Special Court shall function in accordance with the Statute of the Special Court for Sierra Leone. The Statute is annexed to this Agreement and forms an integral part thereof.U.N.-Sierra Leone Agreement, *supra* note 1, art. 1.

[14] *See* S.C. Res. 1315, ¶ 3, U.N. Doc. S/RES/1315 (Aug. 14, 2000). For an account of the controversy, see *Report on SCSL*, *supra* note 4, ¶¶ 29–31.

[15] Charles Chernor Jalloh, *Special Court for Sierra Leone: Achieving Justice?*, 32 Mich. J. Int'l L. 395, 413 (2011).

[16] SCSL Statute, *supra* note 3, art. 1(1); U.N.-Sierra Leone Agreement, *supra* note 1, art. 1.

[17] SCSL Statute, *supra* note 3, art. 15(1).

Prosecution must fulfill.[18] A failure to do so meant that the Defense could challenge the non-compliance before the judges. If successful, the defendants would not be prosecutable by the Tribunal. When taken together, Article 15 and Article 1 gave rise to a debate about the actual mandate and function of the Prosecutor, in particular, the extent and limits of his discretion in deciding whom to prosecute. Effectively, the defendants sought to take advantage of the vagueness of the greatest responsibility formulation in both provisions, attempting to further curb the scope of the prosecutorial power by suggesting that the Prosecutor had acted beyond his competence in seeking to prosecute them instead of others.[19] The problem is that the Prosecution's fight to keep its turf tended to exaggerate the broad scope of its authority and further masked the real nature of greatest responsibility jurisdiction.

Second, although the UNSC, the UNSG, and the government of Sierra Leone purportedly agreed on the meaning of "greatest responsibility" in the letters that they exchanged during the negotiations of the Court's founding instruments,[20] the correspondence was marked by sharp disagreement and ultimately left a measure of ambiguity regarding the actual purpose but more importantly the implications of the phrase.[21] So, once the Tribunal was established and became operational, it would only take a matter of time for the issue to boil to the surface and for the judges to be asked to give their rulings on the subject.

Third, starting with the International Military Tribunal at Nuremberg ("IMT" or "Nuremberg Tribunal") continuing through the ad hoc ICTY and ICTR and the permanent International Criminal Court (ICC), the thrust of international criminal law has been to focus on prosecuting the top leaders and architects of mass atrocities.[22] However, this was the first time that the language mandating the prosecution of only those bearing *greatest responsibility* was introduced into the statute of an ad hoc, international, penal tribunal.[23] Though on one level this could be argued to be an innovation in the SCSL, the reality is that, as this chapter will show, the vague greatest responsibility phrase was more of an explicit limitation on the Court's jurisdiction in terms of the number of people that it would eventually prosecute.[24]

While the SCSL's work is nearing completion, with appeals judgment outstanding solely in the case involving former Liberian President Charles Taylor as of this writing,[25] the debate

---

[18] Jalloh, *supra* note 15, at 414–15.

[19] *See* discussion *infra* Part III.B–C.

[20] U.N. President of the S.C., Letter dated Jan. 31, 2001 from the President of the Security Council addressed to the Secretary-General, para. 1, U.N. Doc. S/2001/95 (Jan. 31, 2001) [hereinafter Letter dated Jan. 31, 2001 from Pres. of S.C.].

[21] Yet, undoubtedly because of awareness of the controversies that dogged this phrase in Sierra Leone, the draft statute for the Special Tribunal for Kenya, which ultimately failed to obtain sufficient support in that country's Parliament, at least attempted to provide a definition. *See* Special Tribunal for Kenya Bill, pt. I, § 2 (Jan. 28, 2009), *available at* http://www.kenyalaw.org/Downloads/Bills/2009/The_Special_Tribunal_for_Kenya_Statute_2009.pdf.

[22] *See* discussion *infra* Part II.A–B.

[23] *See* SCSL Statute, *supra* note 3, art. 1(1).

[24] *See infra* Part II.B. In fact, the President of the Special Court later presented the uniquely structured personal jurisdiction as an "innovation in the structure of international courts and tribunals." GEOFFREY ROBERTSON, FIRST ANNUAL REPORT OF THE PRESIDENT OF THE SPECIAL COURT FOR SIERRA LEONE (2002–2003), *available at* http://www.sc-sl.org/LinkClick.aspx?fileticket=NRhDcbHrcSs%3d&tabid=176.

[25] Oral hearing of the appeal commenced at 10:00 a.m. on Jan. 22, 2013. Prosecutor v. Taylor, Case No. SCSL-03-01-A, Decision on Urgent Motion for Reconsideration or Review of "Scheduling Order," (Dec. 5, 2012), *available at* http://www.sc-sl.org/LinkClick.aspx?fileticket=%2fE4wpxbRJr8%3d&tabid=191; Jennifer Easterday, *Parties In Taylor Trial Make Appeals Submissions*, THE TRIAL OF CHARLES TAYLOR (Jan. 22, 2013), http://www.charlestaylortrial.org/2013/01/22/parties-in-taylor-trial-make-appeals-submissions/.

about the nature and scope of greatest responsibility is important for a proper assessment of the jurisprudential legacy of the Court. More significantly, it seems crucial because it might offer useful lessons for future formulations of personal jurisdiction in other international criminal courts. In fact, while both the ICTY and ICTR were endowed with personal jurisdiction to investigate and prosecute "persons responsible," since the establishment of the SCSL, it appears that the "greatest responsibility" threshold has become the gold standard for the framing of *ratione personae* jurisdiction in contemporary international criminal tribunals.

Surprisingly, although a decade-long controversy persisted over the meaning of greatest responsibility at the Court, the question of what exactly the phrase means and the benchmark, if any, that the prosecutors in time-limited ad hoc international criminal courts should use to select those persons most deserving of prosecution inside their own courtrooms, as opposed to domestic ones, seems to have escaped the attention of legal scholars.[26] Perhaps the general feeling outside the Defense Bar at the SCSL was that resolving this question would not change the outcome in the concrete cases brought by the Prosecution, or that, as David Cohen has argued, this type of narrow personal jurisdiction essentially relieved the Court of the burden of deciding whether to prosecute any middle or lower ranking perpetrators.[27] Or it may be that, as William Schabas has suggested, academic lawyers recognized greatest responsibility as a rather vacuous concept that said more about donor generosity in the first court, which would be funded entirely by donations from states, than something with "any autonomous legal meaning."[28]

Yet, the practical dangers of glossing over "greatest responsibility" jurisdiction will remain for time and resource constrained international criminal tribunals. The SCSL's attempt to grasp this proverbial nettle appears to, therefore, have wider significance for other penal courts tasked with a similar mandate. This is all the more so because states increasingly resort to the greatest responsibility formula popularized by the Court to indicate the attitude that the expensive work of international criminal tribunals should generally be limited to trials of only a handful of top leaders instead of a large number of perpetrators, including lower ranked suspects.[29]

It is against this backdrop that this chapter, which seeks to fill the current gap in the literature, will attempt to discern the meaning of "greatest responsibility" personal jurisdiction. Its general aims are twofold. First, to determine and expose how that phrase was developed, interpreted, and road tested for the first time in international criminal law at the SCSL. Essentially, even as the Court introduced this phrase to our lexicon, I will examine whether the judges advanced our understanding of this type of narrow way of setting out personal jurisdiction, and, if so, how and if not, why not. Second, the chapter will aim to situate the SCSL's experience within the broader normative evolution of

---

[26] Although a Westlaw TP-ALL database search of the phrase "those who bear the greatest responsibility" returned approximately 120 results, only one article seems to have taken up the issue. *See* Sean Morrison, *Extraordinary Language in the Courts of Cambodia: Interpreting the Limiting Language and Personal Jurisdiction of the Cambodian Tribunal*, 37 CAP. U. L. REV. 583, 610–14 (2009).

[27] David Cohen, *"Hybrid" Justice in East Timor, Sierra Leone, and Cambodia: "Lessons Learned" and Prospects for the Future*, 43 STAN. J. INT'L L. 1, 11 (2007) (discussing the creation of the SCSL).

[28] W.A. Schabas, *Genocide Trials and Gacaca Courts*, 3 J. INT'L CRIM. JUST. 879, 882 n.11 (2005).

[29] *See infra* notes 75–79 and accompanying text.

international criminal justice. The idea is to identify, to the extent possible, the types of lessons that could be learned for future courts created with an expressly limited mandate of bringing only the architects of the core crimes to justice. Finally, besides the moral difficulties inherent in effectively conferring impunity on some perpetrators through their non-prosecution, while prosecuting a few others, it is important to determine whether the SCSL devised a principled approach to greatest responsibility. This would at least serve as a starting point for considerations of who should be the targets for internationally supported prosecutions from among a mass of perpetrators in other situation countries in Africa and other parts of the world.

Overall, while contending that the UN in particular the Council, made some problematic jurisdictional choices that ultimately resulted in the SCSL conducting an inadequate number of prosecutions compared to the ICTY and the ICTR, I will argue that the Court's jurisprudence on this question has offered international criminal justice a helpful point of departure regarding how to determine who it is that may be said to bear *greatest responsibility* for the purposes of prosecution in an international criminal court. That said, perhaps understandably, I will show that the interpretation preferred by the majority of the SCSL judges focused more on ensuring that those before the Court would actually be tried. They did not generally engage the broader and more systemic issue about how international penal courts might best distinguish between those that have greater versus lesser degrees of individual criminal responsibility for the international crimes committed in a given armed conflict.

B. Structure of the Chapter and Main Arguments

The chapter is organized as follows. Section II provides a brief overview of the way that personal jurisdiction has been framed in international criminal courts from the watershed Nuremberg International Military Tribunal to the present. By reviewing the personal jurisdiction clauses of prior ad hoc courts, this part of the chapter will demonstrate that the focus of such tribunals has generally been to punish only a limited group of persons in high-ranking leadership positions. The tendency to emphasize the so-called big fish, instead of small fish, continued as a general matter with the modern ICTY and ICTR, and because of a variety of factors, including concerns about costs and speed, reached its apex by the time the SCSL was formally established.

In Section III, I examine the fierce disagreement regarding the meaning of "greatest responsibility," which, driven by the challenges made by some defense counsel, arose between the judges of the two trial chambers at the SCSL. I will show that Trial Chamber I correctly determined that greatest responsibility as expressed in the Tribunal Statute was intended to be both a jurisdictional requirement and a guideline for the exercise of prosecutorial discretion, whereas Trial Chamber II incorrectly interpreted it solely as a type of guidance for the exercise of prosecutorial discretion. Although the Appeals Chamber weighed in to endorse what I respectfully submit was the wrong interpretation, thereby weakening the value of the Court's case law on this particular issue, there was sufficient common ground among the majority of the SCSL judges. We can therefore discern a clear jurisprudential path holding that the greatest responsibility phrase should be understood to include both those in leadership and high ranking positions as well as their most cruel underlings, whose conduct was so outrageous and beyond the pale that it merited international, rather than domestic, investigation and prosecution.

Section IV uses established methods of treaty interpretation in an attempt to locate the ordinary meaning of the phrase "to prosecute persons who bear the greatest responsibility" in light of the text, object and purpose of the SCSL Statute and the drafting history of that provision, as well as the Tribunal's practice. In this regard, I assess the extent to which the solution proffered by the appeals court judges was consistent, or inconsistent, with the apparent intention behind the greatest responsibility language articulated in Article 1. I submit that had the Appeals Chamber adopted a different reading of the law, it would still have been able to dispense justice – contrary to what it implied in its judgment – and in that way, would have made a better contribution to the Court's ultimate jurisprudential legacy for the still fledgling international criminal justice system.

Section V draws conclusions. As a theoretical matter, I prefer broader and more inclusive grants of personal jurisdiction for ad hoc international criminal courts. However, given the reality that such a preference contradicts the current narrower approach among the time and cost conscious states, I will attempt to offer preliminary reflections on ways treaty drafters might in the future alleviate some of the challenges inherent in deploying the greatest responsibility standard as the statutory mandate for the investigation and prosecution of some of the world's worst crimes.

II. PERSONAL JURISDICTION IN INTERNATIONAL CRIMINAL LAW FROM NUREMBERG TO FREETOWN

A. *The Nuremberg and Tokyo Tribunals Had Limited Personal Jurisdiction*

Although unique in its statutory terminology, the SCSL is not alone in having a restricted personal jurisdiction.[30] In fact, there is a discernible trend to limit international tribunal prosecutions to a relatively small group of political and military leaders deemed most responsible for the widespread violence.[31] This doctrinal attitude dates back to the origins of modern international criminal law.[32] It is predicated on the arguably pragmatic recognition that individual accountability at the international level, when compared to domestic legal systems, can only be meted out swiftly and efficiently in relation to a small group of perpetrators. Thus, by circumscribing the scope of international trials in the hope of deterring the top brass, rather than all of them together with their subordinates, international penal law also carves out an informal division of labor between national and international criminal jurisdictions.

---

[30] *See generally* Morrison, *supra* note 26, at 605–15 (discussing the limiting language in personal jurisdiction statutes of ad hoc and hybrid tribunals, as well as the manner in which that language has been interpreted).

[31] *See* Morrison, *supra* note 26, at 588. *See generally* Cohen, *supra* note 27.

[32] *See* Charter of the International Military Tribunal art. 6, Aug. 8, 1945, 59 Stat. 1544, 82 U.N.T.S. 279 [hereinafter IMT Charter]; *see also* Memorandum to President Roosevelt from the Secretaries of State and War and Attorney General, § III (Jan. 22, 1945), *available at* http://avalon.law.yale.edu/imt/jack01.asp (noting that the "outstanding offenders are, of course, those leaders of the Nazi Party and German Reich who since January 30, 1933, have been in control of formulating and executing Nazi policies").

One way it increasingly does this is to devise institutional mechanisms to ensure that the planners, leaders and others responsible for fomenting heinous international crimes are prosecuted at the international level wherever the relevant national jurisdictions are unable or unwilling to prosecute.[33] This arrangement anticipates that the middle and lower ranking suspects would be investigated and prosecuted in domestic courts so that there is no impunity gap.[34] This general approach finds expression in the prior personal jurisdiction clauses of international criminal courts and in their practice.[35]

Article 1 of the IMT Charter declared as its purpose "the just and prompt trial and punishment of the *major* war criminals of the European Axis."[36] Under the heading "Jurisdiction and General Principles," Article 6 specified that the tribunal "shall have the power to try and punish persons who ... whether as individuals or as members of organizations, committed ... crimes against peace[,] ... war crimes[,] ... [and] crimes against humanity."[37] In a provision that seems to be more about the modes of participation in international crimes than about personal jurisdiction as such, Article 6 spelled out the types of individuals that were envisaged to fall within the personal jurisdiction as those "[l]eaders, organisers, instigators and accomplices participating in the formulation or execution of a common plan or conspiracy to commit any of the foregoing crimes" and, moreover, placed responsibility on these individuals "for all acts performed by any persons in execution of such plan."[38] The Tokyo Tribunal essentially reflected an identical position in Articles 1 and 5 of its statute,[39] although its geographic focus was on the "major war criminals in the Far East,"[40] whereas the IMT addressed those who masterminded the atrocities committed in the European theatre.[41]

Despite some criticisms of those tribunals as "victor's justice,"[42] it is undisputed that as part of their achievements, they did prosecute and convict high-ranking government officials associated with the German and Japanese wartime regimes. In the Nuremberg

---

[33] *See, e.g.,* ICC-OTP, *Prosecutorial Strategy 2009–2012,* para. 19 (Feb. 1, 2010) [hereinafter *Prosecutorial Strategy*]; Office of the Prosecutor, *Report on Prosecutorial Strategy,* pt. II, ICC (Sept. 14, 2006) [hereinafter *Report on Prosecutorial Strategy*].

[34] *See, e.g., Prosecutorial Strategy, supra* note 33, para. 19; *Report on Prosecutorial Strategy, supra* note 33, pt. II.a.

[35] *See* SCSL Statute, *supra* note 3, art. 1(1); Agreement Between the United Nations and the Royal Government of Cambodia Concerning the Prosecution Under Cambodian Law of Crimes Committed During the Period of Democratic Kampuchea, U.N.-Cambodia, art. 1, June 6, 2003, 2329 U.N.T.S. 117 [hereinafter U.N.-Cambodian Agreement]; U.N.-Sierra Leone Agreement, *supra* note 1, art. 1(1); Morrison, *supra* note 26, at 587–88.

[36] IMT Charter, *supra* note 31, art. 1 (emphasis added).

[37] *Id.* art. 6.

[38] *Id.*

[39] *Id.* art. 1–6; *cf.* International Military Tribunal for the Far East arts. 1–5, Jan. 19, 1946, 4 U.S.T. 20, T.I.A.S. No. 1589 [hereinafter IMTFE Charter], *available at* http://www.jus.uio.no/english/services/library/treaties/04/4–06/military-tribunal-far-east.xml.

[40] IMTFE Charter, *supra* note 39, art. 1.

[41] IMT Charter, *supra* note 32, art. 1.

[42] William A. Schabas, *Victor's Justice: Selecting "Situations" at the International Criminal Court,* 43 J. MARSHALL L. REV. 535, 537 (2010) quoting Prosecutor v. Tadic, Case No. IT-94-1-T, Decision on Prosecutor's Motion Requesting Protective Measures for Victims and Witnesses, ¶ 21 (Int'l Crim. Trib. for the Former Yugoslavia Aug. 10, 1995).

Tribunal, these ranged from Herman Goering, the "Successor Designate"[43] to Adolf Hitler, to the commander-in-chief of the Germany Navy, Admiral Karl Doenitz, who later replaced the *Fuehrer* after he committed suicide, and to a number of other highly ranked military and civilian officials.[44] Those prosecutions set the stage for the subsequent American and other Allied national prosecutions of World War II offenses within their respective zones of occupation under Control Council Law 10.[45] Even in the setting of allied country prosecutions, it was, at least initially, mainly senior military officers who were tried.[46] These officers spanned from lieutenant colonels to majors, captains, and generals, as exemplified by, for instance, the *United States v. Pohl* case.[47]

Similarly, at the International Military Tribunal for the Far East (IMTFE), twenty-eight of the eighty initially detained "Class A war criminals" were prosecuted, eighteen of whom were military officers.[48] United States Army General Douglas McArthur effectively shielded Japanese Emperor Hirohito from prosecution.[49] However, the list of others put on trial included four former Japanese premiers, six generals, several former ministers, going through ranking ambassadors, and other important advisers on matters of state.[50]

This brief summary appears sufficient to confirm that, although not employing the "greatest responsibility" language to frame the contours of their personal jurisdiction, from the genesis of international criminal justice, the focus of cases in the ad hoc international courts has not been to prosecute everyone who might have committed a crime. Rather, the objective has been to prosecute a smaller number of leaders, architects, and planners of the mass atrocities. As with national criminal law, the assumption, although not yet empirically proven, seems to be that this will deter specific individuals as well as others generally, who might otherwise emulate them in their repugnant conduct. Indeed, the persons tried, both at Nuremberg and at Tokyo, were those who largely held important political and military posts in the government hierarchy. For the most part, these were not direct perpetrators, but people who used, or rather abused, their positions of authority to order, instigate, or encourage subordinates to commit reprehensible crimes.[51] The convicted perpetrators

---

[43] International Military Tribunal, *Indictment*, app. A, *in* 1 Trial of the Major War Criminals Before the International Military Tribunal 27 (Oct. 6, 1945) [hereinafter IMT, *Indictment*, app. A], *available at* http://avalon.law.yale.edu/imt/counta.asp.

[44] *Id.*

[45] Nuremberg Trials Final Report app. D (Dec. 20, 1945) (Control Council, Law No. 10, art. III), *available at* http://avalon.law.yale.edu/imt/imt10.asp.

[46] *See id.* art. 2; IMT, *Indictment*, app. A, *supra* note 43.

[47] United States v. Pohl, Indictment of the International Military Tribunal, Trials of the War Criminals Before the Nuremberg Military Tribunals Under Control Council Law No. 10, vol. 5 (Jan. 13, 1947), *available at* http://avalon.law.yale.edu/imt/indict4.asp.

[48] United States v. Araki, Indictment of the International Military Tribunal for the Far East, app. E (1946), *reprinted in* Documents on the Tokyo International Military Tribunal: Charter, Indictment, and Judgments 63–69 (Neil Boister & Robert Cryer eds., 2008) [hereinafter *Araki* Indictment]; *see also* Timothy P. Maga, Judgment at Tokyo: The Japanese War Crimes Trials 2 (2001) (noting that the eighty indicted men classified as "Class A war criminal suspects" including, "war ministers, former generals, economic and financial leaders, an imperial advisor, an admiral, and a colonel … were accused of plotting and carrying out a war of conquest; murdering, maiming, and ill-treating civilians and prisoners of war; plunder; rape; and 'other barbaric cruelties").

[49] Herbert P. Bix, Hirohito and the Making of Modern Japan 587 (2000).

[50] *Araki* Indictment, *supra* note 48, app. E.

[51] *See supra* notes 43, 47 and accompanying text.

were deemed more culpable than their junior partners and enforcers who actually imple-mented their orders.[52] In any event, in the other instances where the actual perpetrators of the crimes were prosecuted through national-level prosecutions, the gravity, brutality, and scale of their crimes generally served as ample justification for their investigation, prosecu-tion, and punishment.

B. Contemporary International Tribunals Also Have Only Limited Personal Jurisdiction

The ICTY and ICTR Statutes adopted similar ways of defining their personal jurisdictions as the IMT and IMTFE immediately after World War II. The context of their establishment suggested that they were also created to bring the top perpetrators of international crimes to justice. Perhaps reflecting what may have been the golden age of international criminal jus-tice, and its perceived high potential to assist in solving the intractable problems of impu-nity in post-conflict situations, in their respective jurisdictional provisions, the constitutive documents of the UN twin tribunals both provided in their Article 1 that they "shall have the power to *prosecute persons responsible* for serious violations of international humani-tarian law."[53] This was notably distinct from the formulation used in the later Sierra Leone court conferring on the Tribunal "the power to prosecute persons who bear the greatest responsibility" for the serious international humanitarian and Sierra Leonean law viola-tions that took place in the context of that country's conflict.[54]

It is true that in the resolutions preceding the creation of the ICTY and ICTR, the UNSC repeatedly emphasized its determination to bring to justice all those persons responsible for the commission of international crimes.[55] But those decisions should be understood in context. They were taken at a time when the international community was faced with bitter and ongoing conflicts characterized by atrocity crimes and a climate of ongoing hostilities in which stopping the further commission of heinous offenses was an obvious international policy goal.[56] They were thus worded in a way that exaggeratingly suggested that more than a limited group of perpetrators would be prosecuted and punished by each of those insti-tutions. This emphasis made sense given the clear deterrent goal of international criminal law.

The reality proved to be different, however, although far more than the IMT and IMTFE, the UN tribunals have also succeeded in prosecuting a large part of the middle management

---

[52] *See generally* IMT, *Indictment, supra* note 43, app. A (referring to misuse of high-ranking positions, personal influence, and intimate connections in the statement of responsibility for individuals indicted).

[53] *See* S.C. Res. 955, *supra* note 11, Annex I, art. 1 (emphasis added); U.N. Secretary-General, *Report of the Secretary-General Pursuant to Paragraph 2 of Security Council Resolution 808* (1993), U.N. Doc. S/25704, Annex I, art. 1 (May 3, 1993) [hereinafter ICTY Statute] (emphasis added). Articles 6 and 5 of the ICTY and ICTR Statutes, respectively, clarify that the jurisdiction of the Tribunal only applies to natural persons. ICTY statute, *supra*, art. 6; S.C. Res. 955, *supra* note 11, Annex I, art. 5. Under Articles 15(1) and 16(1), the prose-cutor's role is to prosecute "persons responsible" for the serious violations of IHL committed in the former Yugoslavia. S.C. Res. 955, *supra* note 11, Annex I, art. 15(1); ICTY statute, *supra*, art. 16(1). U.N.S.C. Res. 808 and Res. 955 decided on February 22, 1993, and November 8, 1994, respectively, to establish the Tribunal to prosecute "persons responsible." S.C. Res. 808, U.N. Doc. S/RES/808, ¶ 1 (Feb. 22, 1993); S.C. Res. 955, *supra* note 11, art. 1.

[54] *See* SCSL Statute, *supra* note 3, art. 1.

[55] S.C. Res. 827, *supra* note 11, ¶ 2; S.C. Res. 955, *supra* note 11, ¶ 1.

[56] S.C. Res. 827, *supra* note 11; S.C. Res. 955, *supra* note 11.

of the atrocities in the former Yugoslavia and Rwanda respectively. Sometimes, for various pragmatic reasons, such as the need to show concrete results in the early days, those ad hoc tribunals even ended up with prosecutions of otherwise insignificant perpetrators, such as Dusko Tadic and Jean-Paul Akayesu, who were not necessarily the most culpable persons in the grand scheme of things – at least when it comes to their official ranks. In other words, even though those individuals were important, they were ultimately minor players; they were not the brains behind the massive offenses committed in the tragic Balkans and African conflicts during the early 1990s.

The problem is that the initial enthusiasm for international criminal justice, which coincided with the end of the Cold War and a new era of East–West cooperation in the Council, did not last. In the intervening years between the creation of the ICTY and ICTR tribunals in 1993 and 1994,[57] and the Sierra Leone court in 2002,[58] there had been much discussion among the powerful countries (especially the United States) about the viability of the ad hoc Chapter VII tribunal model.[59] The so-called "[t]ribunal fatigue,"[60] driven primarily by concerns about the slow pace of the international trials and the spiraling costs of those UN courts,[61] is said to have taken hold of the UNSC and the United States government in particular.[62] It therefore seems like a deliberate decision, in a move to what was perceived to be a more financially viable and a more politically acceptable model, to limit the jurisdiction of future courts, such as the SCSL, to prosecuting only a handful of persons in leadership positions deemed to bear greatest responsibility for the serious international humanitarian law violations committed during the West African nation's brutal war.

Interestingly, although the phrasing of the personal jurisdiction clause that granted the SCSL authority was a departure from the equivalent personal jurisdiction language in the statutes for the UN Chapter VII tribunals,[63] the ICTY and ICTR, in their respective Rules of Procedure and Evidence,[64] jurisprudence,[65] and Completion Strategies,[66] now use similar language expressing the greatest responsibility limitation.[67] They seem to have adjusted to

---

[57] S.C. Res. 827, *supra* note 11; S.C. Res. 955, *supra* note 11.

[58] U.N.-Sierra Leone Agreement, *supra* note 1, art. 1(1), (23).

[59] David J. Scheffer, Remarks, *Challenges Confronting International Justice Issues*, 4 New Eng. Int'l & Comp. L. Ann. 1, 4–6 (1998).

[60] Scheffer, *supra* note 59, at 1.

[61] Morrison, *supra* note 26, at 587–88; Sean D. Murphy, Contemporary Practice of the United States Relating to International Law, *State Department Views on the Future of War Crimes Tribunals*, 96 Am. J. Int'l L. 482, 483 (2002).

[62] Scheffer, *supra* note 59, at 2.

[63] *Compare* SCSL Statute, *supra* note 3, art. 1(1) ("greatest responsibility"), *with* S.C. Res. 955, *supra* note 11, art. 1, *and* S.C. Res. 827, *supra* note 11, art. 2 ("persons responsible").

[64] International Tribunal for the Former Yugoslavia, Rules of Procedure and Evidence, Rule 11 *bis*, 28, U.N. Doc. IT/32/Rev. 45 (Dec. 8, 2010); International Tribunal for Rwanda, Rules of Procedure and Evidence, U.N. Doc. ITR/3/REV.1 (June 29, 1995).

[65] Prosecutor v. Luckic, Case No. IT-98-32/1-PT, Decision on the Referral of Case Pursuant to Rule 11 *bis* with Confidential Annex A and Annex B, ¶¶ 28, 30 (Int'l Crim. Trib. for the Former Yugoslavia Apr. 5, 2007); Prosecutor v. Todović, Case No. IT-97-25/1-AR11*bis*.1, Decision on Savo Todović's Appeal Against Decision on Referral under Rule 11 *bis*, ¶¶ 19–22 (Int'l Crim. Trib. for the Former Yugoslavia Sept. 4, 2006).

[66] S.C. Res. 1503, U.N. Doc. S/RES/1503 (Aug. 28, 2003); Completion Strategy for the International Criminal Tribunal for Rwanda, transmitted by letter dated Oct. 3, 2003 from the Secretary-General addressed to the President of the Security Council, U.N. Doc. S/2003/946, para. 6 (Oct. 6, 2003).

[67] *See supra* notes 63–66.

the political environment in which they function, in light of the high cost and slow pace of trials. As the tribunals came under increased pressure from the Council to wrap up their work, the Prosecutors have pragmatically had to make a policy choice to identify the top layer deemed most responsible and most appropriate for trial within their jurisdiction.[68] They justify this by arguing that they had no choice but to leave it to the willing national jurisdictions to pursue the remainder of the fugitives, either through independently initiated prosecutions of lower ranked suspects or voluntary acceptance of transferred cases of the alleged middle level perpetrators to national courts.[69]

Similarly, in the other ad hoc criminal court negotiated by the UN with one of its member states around the same time period as the SCSL, the Extraordinary Chambers in the Courts of Cambodia (ECCC or Cambodia Tribunal), the international community adopted a similarly worded jurisdictional provision.[70] This lends further credence to the idea of tribunal exhaustion taking hold at the level of UN member states, although a different set of factors were admittedly at play in the Cambodia context. These included a government that was not necessarily acting in good faith, when compared to the Sierra Leone negotiations with the UN, which demonstrated strong national–political will to deal with accountability for the international crimes experienced during the conflict.

Be that as it may, Article 1 of the ECCC Law empowered it to prosecute the "*senior leaders* of Democratic Kampuchea and those who were *most responsible* for the crimes."[71] Much like the Sierra Leone court, which was also territorially and temporally confined in its ability to prosecute compared to the ICTY and ICTR, the Cambodia Tribunal was intended to carry out only a limited number of prosecutions of senior leaders along with those apparently deemed to possess the greatest level of individual responsibility for committing heinous offenses.[72] Both tribunals' jurisdiction clauses therefore reflect the fiscally conservative spirit informing the late 1990s ad hoc court models.

In the similar vein, although having a distinctive multilateral treaty basis, vis-à-vis the ad hoc tribunals, Article 1 of the Rome Statute of the permanent Hague-based International Criminal Court (ICC) defines the competence of the global penal court as the power to "exercise its jurisdiction over *persons* for the most serious crimes of international concern."[73] There is plainly no explicit limitation on the ICC's personal jurisdiction. Indeed, in

---

[68] Murphy, *supra* note 61, at 483 (on U.S. encouragement of ad hoc tribunal completion strategies); Pierre-Richard Prosper & Michael A. Newton, *The Bush Administration View of International Accountability*, 36 New Eng. L. Rev. 891, 897 (2002) (on U.S. support for the greatest responsibility limitation).

[69] Prosper & Newton, *supra* note 68, at 896–97.

[70] Law on the Establishment of Extraordinary Chambers in the Courts of Cambodia for the Prosecution of Crimes Committed During the Period of Democratic Kampuchea, *as amended*, Reach Kram., No. NS/RKM/1004/006, Oct. 27, 2004 (Cambodia) [hereinafter ECCC Law], *available at* http://www.eccc.gov.kh/sites/default/files/legal–documents/KR_Law_as_amended_27_Oct_2004_Eng.pdf and http://www.eccc.gov.kh/sites/default/files/legal–documents/Kram_and_KR_Law_amendments_27_Oct_2004_--_Eng.pdf (unofficial translation).

[71] ECCC Law, *supra* note 70, art. 1; U.N.-Cambodian Agreement, *supra* note 35, art. 1.

[72] ECCC Law, *supra* note 70; U.N.-Cambodian Agreement, *supra* note 35, art. 1. even though it is expected to only prosecute a handful of people, Article (1) of the Statute of the Lebanon Tribunal has, perhaps as a reflection of a lesson learned by the Secretary-General about the controversies of greatest responsibility, returned to use of the phrase "to prosecute persons responsible." S.C. Res. 1757, Annex, art. 1, U.N. Doc. S/RES/1757 (May 30, 2007).

[73] Rome Statute of the International Criminal Court art. 1, July 17, 1998, 2187 U.N.T.S. 90 (emphasis added).

contrast to the ad hoc courts, it appears that many states were clearly interested in having a broad personal jurisdiction for the permanent international tribunal than a narrower one.[74] On the other hand, the concern about framing jurisdiction in a very narrow way was less of an issue in the ICC setting since various restrictions were already inbuilt into the permanent court's statutory framework through the several carefully negotiated substantive provisions that gave the first bite at the apple of prosecution to willing and able states.

However, rather interestingly for the argument advanced by this chapter, the ICC Prosecutor has in her policy papers, strategy documents and emerging practice interpreted this reference to personal jurisdiction as mandating a focus only on those "who bear the greatest responsibility."[75] Put differently, though not textually required to endorse and follow the greatest responsibility standard in the Rome Statute, the key official deciding on the scope of the ICC's investigations has adopted this same threshold. This has an expressive function by signaling to states that the permanent tribunal too will play its part to limit its costs while at the same time endorsing the prevailing belief in the necessity of limiting the possible situations that could come within the permanent court's jurisdiction. The foregoing brief review suggests that, as states and tribunal authorities have developed more experience designing, interacting with and or managing international criminal tribunals, they increasingly seem to prefer to confer a relatively narrow type of personal jurisdiction – at least when it comes to the more prominent, situation-specific ad hoc international criminal courts. In the ICC, this captures the SCSL trend in terms of limiting who can be prosecuted in specific situation countries. Much of this concern, from the point of view of states, is about the various ways of controlling costs and keeping the international justice project on the cheap.

This international environment helps to explain why the UN, and in particular the Council, introduced the problematic "greatest responsibility" personal jurisdiction into international criminal law's lexicon through the SCSL Statute. It therefore suggests reasons to be cautious in celebrating the addition of this phrase into our vocabulary because of what it seems to imply. The phrase effectively signals the reduced political will amongst states to ensure the broadest possible investigations and prosecutions of perpetrators of serious international offenses that reach beneath the top layer to uncover others, perhaps of a lesser rank, who should also be held accountable for mass atrocity crimes. But it may be countered that settling on a particular and more realistic phraseology for personal jurisdiction is part of the necessary evolution or maturing of international criminal tribunals. Such

---

[74] *See id.*, Rome Statute of the International Criminal Court, art. 1 & pmbl.

[75] *See* ICC-OTP, *Paper on Some Policy Issues Before the Office of the Prosecutor* 7 (Sept. 2003), *available at* http://www.icc-cpi.int/nr/rdonlyres/1fa7c4c6-de5f-42b7-8b25-60aa962ed8b6/143594/030905_policy_paper.pdf (stating that the Office of the Prosecutor will "focus its investigative and prosecutorial efforts and resources on those who bear the greatest responsibility, such as the leaders of the State or organization allegedly responsible for those crimes" (emphasis omitted)); *see also Prosecutorial Strategy, supra* note 35, para. 19 ("In accordance with this statutory scheme, the Office consolidated a policy of focused investigations and prosecutions, meaning it will investigate and prosecute those who bear the greatest responsibility for the most serious crimes, based on the evidence that emerges in the course of an investigation." (emphasis omitted)); *Report on Prosecutorial Strategy, supra* note 35, para. 2(b); Luis Moreno-Ocampo, *The International Criminal Court: Seeking Global Justice*, 40 Case W. Res. J. Int'l L. 215, 221 (2008) (stating that "[m]y role is to prosecute those bearing the greatest responsibility for the most serious crimes").

jurisdiction can also be seen as a way to manage the currently high expectations about what these courts can realistically contribute in societies torn apart by brutal conflict.

At the end of the day, more than any other factor, the UNSC's decision to limit the jurisdiction of the SCSL to those with greatest responsibility was driven by pragmatic, political, economic, and other *realpolitik* considerations. This in turn affected the mandate that the Court was given – essentially, to investigate and prosecute a handful of persons in leadership positions based on a strict personal, temporal, and territorial jurisdiction,[76] which would help to ensure, it was hoped at the time, that all the trials would be completed within three years.[77]

III. THE JUDICIAL DEBATE REGARDING THE MEANING OF GREATEST RESPONSIBILITY IN THE SPECIAL COURT FOR SIERRA LEONE

A. *Approaches to Interpretation of Greatest Responsibility*

Once indictments were issued and suspects were arrested, some of the defense counsel at the SCSL immediately filed motions asking the judges to clarify the exact scope of Article 1(1) of the SCSL Statute, which is entitled "Competence of the Special Court."[78] As the provision is key to the analysis in this chapter, and was reproduced in essentially the same form in Article 1(1) of the UN-Sierra Leone Agreement, to which the Statute was an annex, it is worth setting out in full, as follows:

> The Special Court shall, except as provided in subparagraph (2), have the power *to prosecute persons who bear the greatest responsibility* for serious violations of international humanitarian law and Sierra Leonean law committed in the territory of Sierra Leone since 30 November 1996, including those leaders who, in committing such crimes, have threatened the establishment of and implementation of the peace process in Sierra Leone.[79]

In construing this clause, honing in for now on the italicized portion, we can discern at least three possible interpretations.[80]

The first is that Article 1(1) required the prosecution of the persons deemed most responsible or most culpable for the serious crimes perpetrated in Sierra Leone. On this view, a key criterion for selection could be the rank or position held by the persons in this category and whether they were the movers and shakers behind the conflict and the widespread

---

[76] *See* SCSL Statute, *supra* note 3, art. 1(1).

[77] As I have argued elsewhere, the number of persons that it was expected would be prosecuted by the SCSL reportedly totaled between two to three dozen. *See* Jalloh, *supra* note 15, at 420–22. Unfortunately, the Tribunal, partly because of this constrained greatest responsibility mandate and a conservative prosecutorial interpretation of that language, only successfully completed about nine cases. *Id.* For a court that operated for over ten years, this meant that the tribunal averaged less than one case per year. *Id.* (criticizing the "extremely small number of trials" ultimately carried out).

[78] SCSL Statute, *supra* note 3, art. 1; *see, e.g.*, Prosecutor v. Norman, Case No. SCSL-04–14-PT, Decision on the Preliminary Defence Motion on the Lack of Personal Jurisdiction Filed on Behalf of Accused Fofana, ¶¶ 1–2 (Mar. 3, 2004).

[79] SCSL Statute, *supra* note 3, art. 1(1) (emphasis added); *See* U.N.-Sierra Leone Agreement, *supra* note 1, art. 1.

[80] Further on in this chapter, I will examine the second part of that phrase reading as follows: including those leaders who, in committing such crimes, have threatened the establishment of and implementation of the peace process in Sierra Leone.

commission of the crimes. This interpretation, which as we shall see later the Prosecution seemed to prefer,[81] would emphasize the leadership status of the suspect and whether the suspect had the capacity to impact the general course of events over the years of the war, but failed to prevent or punish the wrongful conduct of the perpetrators as Stephen Rapp suggested in his chapter in this volume. The thrust would effectively be on the top political and or military leaders who committed, planned, instigated, ordered, or otherwise aided and abetted the heinous international crimes that were perpetrated by the combatants under their command, control and supervision. For convenience, in this chapter, we may call this the political military leader category.

A second interpretation implied by the greatest responsibility language in the above provision was that the Prosecutor could scour the lower rank and file of the thousands of persons who perpetrated the various crimes within the SCSL's jurisdiction and select from among them those who did not necessarily hold high ranking positions in the military or political structures of the various parties to the conflict. Instead, he would choose those who were most cruel and most notorious for the brutality and depravity of their crimes. In other words, the jurisdiction mentioned in Article 1(1) could be read as a directive to pursue the worst persons, killers, or ordinary combatants whose criminal acts caused the most harm, to the most victims, in the most brutal way during the period falling within the SCSL's temporal jurisdiction. We can refer to this group of prospective suspects bearing greatest responsibility as the killer perpetrator category.

Irrespective of which of the above two categories a particular defendant falls into, it is likely that he would argue that he fell outside the jurisdiction of the Court because he was merely a foot soldier, rather than a political or military leader, and vice versa. But many lawyers might perhaps agree more with the third plausible interpretation of the first part of Article 1(1). In this view, asserting that the Tribunal has power to prosecute those bearing greatest responsibility would indicate that individuals from either, or better yet, both the political military leadership and the killer perpetrator categories are prosecutable. The latter interpretation of the clause and its drafting history,[82] as well as the SCSL's practice seems to confirm that the last is ultimately the better and more flexible way to construe the greatest responsibility personal jurisdiction – at least from a prosecutorial and, perhaps, even an interest-of-justice perspective.

The simplicity with which these three plausible interpretations of Article 1(1) of the SCSL Statute are suggested here belies the fierce discord among the judges of Trial Chambers I and II on how best to construe this phrase. It also masks the fact that the Prosecution faced a steady stream of challenges from the Defense, throughout some of the trials, claiming that a particular accused should not be prosecuted because that person was not among those envisaged to fall within the jurisdiction of the Tribunal. Indeed, so much time and energy was wasted by lawyers and judges debating the meaning of greatest responsibility that it might even have had a chilling effect on the Prosecutor's decision not to pursue additional suspects for the crimes apparently committed in Sierra Leone. Rapp's chapter, at the beginning of this volume, confirms this point.

---

[81] *See* discussion *infra* Part III.C.
[82] *See* discussion *infra* Section IV.B.

Nonetheless, despite curiously reaching divergent legal conclusions as to whether Article 1(1) was a jurisdictional requirement (Trial Chamber I)[83] or a mere guideline for prosecutorial strategy (Trial Chamber II),[84] the SCSL judges were in general agreement that the phrase mandating the prosecution of those bearing the greatest responsibility contained in the Tribunal Statute implicitly included what I have characterized as the political-military leadership and killer perpetrator categories.[85] Put differently, even though the phrase "greatest responsibility" was highly divisive when debated during the Freetown trials,[86] a key lesson from the SCSL case law is that the greatest responsibility phrase should, as a *prima facie* matter, be interpreted as a broad jurisdictional grant capable of covering both different types of actors and different types of conduct in a given armed conflict.[87]

That said, as I will endeavor to show shortly, a review of the relevant case law demonstrates that there was conflation of several important questions that muddied the greatest responsibility waters even further. For analytical purposes, these could be broken down into the following sub-issues: (1) whether the phrase to prosecute persons bearing greatest responsibility established a jurisdictional threshold or was a type of guidance for the Prosecutor's determination of whom to prosecute; (2) if so, the timing or stage of the proceedings during which an accused should raise the objection that the Tribunal lacks authority to try him because he did not bear greatest responsibility; (3) the evidentiary burden that the Defense would have to discharge if they chose to raise the issue (and the nature of the Prosecution's burden to counter it); (4) the role of the evidence and judges in the assessment of greatest responsibility; and, finally, (5) the consequences of positive or negative findings on jurisdiction for the defendant, the Prosecutor, and the Tribunal itself. For space reasons, the next part of this chapter will only take up analysis of the first of these five issues.

B. Greatest Responsibility as a Jurisdictional Requirement

In the first defense motion to raise the argument that the SCSL was not entitled to try a particular defendant because it lacked the legal capacity or power to do so, the assigned counsel for Moinina Fofana[88] filed a preliminary jurisdictional challenge before Trial Chamber I on November 17, 2003.[89] The counsel submitted that the Court did not have personal jurisdiction over Fofana because the suspect fell outside the category of persons who bore "the

---

[83] *Norman*, Case No. SCSL-04–14-PT, Decision on the Preliminary Defence Motion, ¶ 27.

[84] Prosecutor v. Brima, Case No. SCSL-04–16-T, Judgment, ¶ 653 (July 20, 2007).

[85] *Compare Norman*, Case No. SCSL-04–14-PT, Decision on the Preliminary Defence Motion, ¶¶ 23–27, *with Brima*, Case No. SCSL-04–16-T, Decision on Defence Motion for Judgment of Acquittal Pursuant to Rule 98, ¶¶ 30–34 (Mar. 31, 2006).

[86] *See, e.g., Brima*, Case No. SCSL-04–16-T, Decision on Defence Motion, ¶¶ 28–29.

[87] *Id.* ¶¶ 34–35.

[88] Moinina Fofana held the rank as the National Director of War of the CDF, the armed state-supported militia faction involved in the Sierra Leone conflict. *See Norman*, Case No. SCSL-04–14-PT, Decision on the Preliminary Defence Motion, ¶ 42; Prosecutor v. Fofana, Case No. SCSL-03–11-PT, Preliminary Defence Motion on the Lack of Personal Jurisdiction, ¶ 14 (Nov. 17, 2003), *available at* http://www.sc-sl.org/scsl/Public/SCSL-03–11-Fofana/SCSL-03–11-PT-062.pdf.

[89] *Fofana*, Case No. SCSL-03–11-PT, Preliminary Defence Motion.

greatest responsibility" for the alleged serious international humanitarian law violations contained in his indictment.[90]

The Defense asserted that the personal jurisdiction discussed in Article 1(1) of the Tribunal Statute could be interpreted in only one of two ways.[91] First, it could be taken as a reference to the leaders of the parties or states bearing the greatest responsibility for the Sierra Leonean armed conflict, including those who had threatened the peace process.[92] Second, and alternatively, it could be seen as a way of referring to those individuals responsible for most of the crimes committed during the armed conflict.[93] According to the Defense, neither Fofana's indictment nor the subsequent prosecution disclosure of evidence supported the view that Fofana belonged to the latter class of persons.[94] Indeed, under neither interpretation could he be deemed among those bearing greatest responsibility and therefore properly within the Court's personal jurisdiction.

The Prosecution responded that the documents forming the context for the establishment of the SCSL amply showed that the question whether a particular person is one of those who bore the greatest responsibility was a matter of prosecutorial discretion based on the evidence collected during the investigations.[95] To justify judicial review of the exercise of that discretion, the defendant needed to demonstrate that the Prosecutor unlawfully exercised his power or acted based on improper or impermissible discriminatory motives.[96] The Accused had failed to adduce any proof establishing such intentions.[97] According to the Prosecution, although defense counsel had suggested that Fofana was associated with the Civil Defense Forces (CDF) militia that was known more for its work in attempting to restore peace in Sierra Leone, rather than the commission of international crimes, this was not substantiation that he might not ultimately be found after the conclusion of the trial as among those bearing greatest responsibility.[98] Fofana was, in any event, a leader fitting that description since he had been the second in command of the CDF organization, as had been alleged in his indictment.[99]

In its unanimous ruling, Trial Chamber I reviewed the drafting history of the provision and correspondence between the UN Secretary-General and the Council discussing

---

[90] *Id.* ¶ 2. Rule 72B of the Rules of Procedure and Evidence provides:

> Preliminary motions by the accused are (i) objections based on lack of jurisdiction; (ii) objections based on defects in the form of the indictment; (iii) applications for severance of crimes joined in one indictment Rule 49, or for separate trials under Rule 82(B); (iv) objections based on the denial of request for assignment of counsel; or (v) objections based on abuse of process.
>
> Special Court for Sierra Leone, Rules of Procedure and Evidence (amended Mar. 7, 2003), *available at* http://www.sc-sl.org/LinkClick.aspx?fileticket=1YNrqhd4L5s%3D&tabid=70. The Rules further provide that "[o]bjections based on lack of jurisdiction or to the form of the indictment, including an amended indictment, shall be raised by a party in one motion only, unless otherwise allowed by the Trial Chamber." *Id.* at 72C.

[91] *Norman*, Case No. SCSL-04–14-PT, Decision on the Preliminary Defence Motion, ¶ 2.

[92] *Id.* ¶ 2(a).

[93] *Id.* ¶ 2(b).

[94] *Id.* ¶ 2.

[95] *Id.* ¶ 5; *see also Fofana*, Case No. SCSL-03–11-PT, Prosecution Response to the Defence Preliminary Motion on Lack of Personal Jurisdiction, ¶ 6 (Nov. 26, 2003), *available at* http://www.sc-sl.org/scsl/Public/SCSL-03–11-Fofana/SCSL-03–11-PT-074/SCSL-03–11-PT-074-I.pdf.

[96] *Fofana*, Case No. SCSL-03–11-PT, Prosecution Response, ¶ 12–14.

[97] *Norman*, Case No. SCSL-04–14-PT, Decision on the Preliminary Defence Motion, ¶ 7.

[98] *Id.* ¶ 8.

[99] *Id.* ¶ 10.

"greatest responsibility" and the former's proposed alternative to use those "most respon-sible"[100] instead. The judges rightly pointed out that the UNSC's preference was to limit the jurisdiction of the SCSL primarily to the prosecution of those who had played a leadership role.[101] But the UNSG had insisted that the greatest responsibility clause should not be taken to imply that personal jurisdiction would be limited only to the political and military lead-ers.[102] He argued that it would also extend to others on the basis of the scale or severity of their crimes.[103] After this review, Trial Chamber I unanimously concluded that "the issue of personal jurisdiction is a jurisdictional requirement, and while it does of course guide the prosecutorial strategy, it does not exclusively articulate prosecutorial discretion, as the prosecution has submitted."[104]

Having essentially determined that Article 1(1) established a jurisdictional threshold, which the Prosecution ought to show it could fulfill, the judges ruled that the Prosecution had discharged that burden in the context of that particular case.[105] They were satisfied that Fofana *appeared* to fall within the court's personal jurisdiction because there was sufficient *prima facie* evidence tending to show that he held a leadership position as the number two person in the CDF – one of the main parties in Sierra Leone's armed conflict.[106] They under-scored, however, that whether or not he could be found to be among those holding greatest responsibility is a factual and "an evidentiary matter to be determined at the trial stage."[107] The Chamber clarified that, at the stage of the Defense's preliminary motion, it was merely concerned with basic allegations.[108] It therefore correctly underscored that it was not, in reaching this finding, pronouncing Fofana's final guilt or innocence, which would only be adjudged after the conclusion of his case.[109]

In their judgment on the merits, which followed several years later, Trial Chamber I reit-erated its initial holding that Article 1(1) created a jurisdictional requirement.[110] However, although the judges had (at the preliminary motions stage) deferred the question of whether in actuality Fofana could be one of those bearing greatest responsibility until the end of the trial because such assessment could only follow after hearing all the evidence against the Accused, it appeared to sidestep the issue. It reasoned that the personal jurisdiction requirement did not constitute a legal or material ingredient of the crimes. It followed that to secure a conviction, the Prosecutor did not need to prove beyond a reasonable doubt that Fofana was one of those in fact bearing greatest responsibility. Put differently, at the judg-ment stage when it decided Fofana was actually guilty, the Trial Chamber implied that it had accepted the Prosecutor's conclusion that the defendant was one of those that, in fact, bore greatest responsibility for the events and crimes in Sierra Leone. This suggests that the

---

[100] *Id.* ¶ 40.
[101] *Norman*, Case No. SCSL-04–14-PT, Decision on the Preliminary Defence Motion, ¶ 40.
[102] U.N. Secretary-General, Letter dated Jan. 12, 2001 from the Secretary-General addressed to the President of the Security Council, para. 2, U.N. Doc. S/2001/40 (Jan. 12, 2001) [hereinafter Letter dated Jan. 12, 2001 from Secretary-General].
[103] *Id.* paras. 2–3.
[104] *Norman*, Case No. SCSL-04–14-PT, Decision on the Preliminary Defence Motion, ¶ 27.
[105] *Id.* ¶ 45.
[106] *Id.* ¶ 42.
[107] *Id.* ¶ 44.
[108] *Id.*
[109] *Id.* ¶ 47.
[110] Prosecutor v. Fofana, Case No. SCSL-04–14-T, Judgement, ¶¶ 91–92 (Aug. 2, 2007).

judges saw the assessment of whether personal jurisdiction existed to try Fofana as being only a relevant question for consideration at the indictment review stage on a *prima facie* basis to believe, as opposed to a matter to be put to prosecutorial proof beyond a reasonable doubt during or at the completion of the trial.

Two other observations seem pertinent about Trial Chamber I's analysis of the greatest responsibility in Article 1(1). First, the Chamber helpfully clarified that the clause should essentially be understood as expressing two separate, if closely related, ideas. To begin with, the phrase confirmed that the prosecution of persons who bear the greatest responsibility constituted a personal jurisdictional requirement before the Court and that it is the Prosecutor's function in carrying out the mandate that is then prescribed in Article 15.[111] This showed that the Prosecution must establish that a particular suspect fulfilled this criterion by tendering evidence, assessed at the low reasonable basis to believe indictment review threshold, that the person was a *leader* (whether military or political) *appearing* to be one of those bearing greatest responsibility. If the Prosecution meets the burden – which would not be difficult because the threshold is very low – of having reasonable grounds to believe that the suspect in question committed the crime charged, then the Chamber can properly try the defendant. Conversely, if the Prosecution failed to prove even a *prima facie* case against the suspect, showing that the Court has jurisdiction over him covering particular crimes on a given territory during an appropriate time period, then the Chamber would have to dismiss the case. The Court's logic was likely that the suspect did not need to endure an unnecessary trial when the SCSL lacked the basic personal, temporal and subject matter jurisdiction to try him. This seems sensible as there would be no point in subjecting the indictee to the hassle of an unnecessary trial when the Tribunal actually lacked the personal jurisdiction to commit him to trial.

A related point is that, unlike the first part of Article 1(1) of the SCSL Statute, the Chamber implied that the second part of the same sentence, "including those leaders who, in committing such crimes, have threatened the establishment of and implementation of the peace process in Sierra Leone[,]" was not an element of the crime.[112] Rather, it was intended to serve as a type of guideline to the Prosecutor in his determination of his strategy regarding whom to prosecute.[113] The judges illustrated that the practical focus of who the Tribunal ought to investigate and try, from the perspective of the Council during the negotiations, were the important political and military leaders;[114] whereas, from Secretary-General Annan's perspective, it would include the top leaders plus anyone else that was found to be among those who carried out the worst of the crimes perpetrated in Sierra Leone.[115]

Second, Trial Chamber I essentially confirmed the interpretation that the phrase those "who bear the greatest responsibility" was sufficiently flexible phraseology to capture all those (1) who held high ranking positions and (2) those whose crimes were so cruel that they would be among the worst perpetrators of the mayhem during the Sierra Leone Civil War.[116] The caveat, of course, was that the judges unanimously, and correctly in my view, determined that the UNSC clearly stated preference for the "greatest responsibility"

---

[111] *Norman*, Case No. SCSL-04-14-PT, Decision on the Preliminary Defence Motion, ¶¶ 21, 26, 27.
[112] *Id.* ¶ 38.
[113] *Id.* ¶¶ 24–25, 27.
[114] *Id.* ¶¶ 22–25.
[115] Letter dated Jan. 12, 2001 from Secretary-General, *supra* note 102, para. 2.
[116] *See Norman*, Case No. SCSL-04-14-PT, Decision on the Preliminary Defence Motion, ¶ 39.

language signaled that the leadership role of the suspect should be the primary consideration with the severity of a crime and its massive nature bearing only secondary importance to the decision as to whom to charge and prosecute.[117]

Overall, when assessed using the language of the three-part interpretive scheme suggested above, the Trial Chamber I judges concluded that Fofana fell within the political military leader category instead of the killer perpetrator category, the former being the main criterion that presumably guided his indictment by the Prosecutor. In fact, in its judgment on the merits, Trial Chamber I found that Fofana was one of the top three men in the so-called Holy Trinity of the CDF organization. It underscored, much like the founders of the SCSL did during the negotiations of the constitutive founding instruments, that greatest responsibility should, at least partly, be understood as a reflection of rank or position of the suspect in the organization(s) that perpetrated the crimes within the subject matter jurisdiction of the international tribunal.[118] This did not however preclude the trials of others, whose responsibility maybe based not on their leadership status but their cruelty. These deductions, therefore, seem to be helpful clarifications to the jurisprudence and eventual literature on the scope of personal jurisdiction in international criminal courts.

C. Greatest Responsibility as a Guideline for Exercise of Prosecutorial Discretion

The Armed Forces Revolutionary Council (AFRC) Case, which was heard by the judges of Trial Chamber II, involved three mutinying soldiers from the Sierra Leone Army who organized a coup d'etat that unseated the democratically elected Kabbah government.[119] Once they assumed power, the three suspects directed others within their command and control to commit some of the most brutal acts witnessed during the Sierra Leone conflict.[120] Unlike the *Fofana* case, none of the three defense teams in the AFRC joint trial filed preliminary challenges objecting to the Court's assertion of personal jurisdiction over their clients during the limited twenty-one day period following the release of the prosecution disclosure under the SCSL Rules of Procedure and Evidence.[121] It is unclear whether this was just an oversight or a deliberate defense strategy. However, at the halfway point of the trial when the Prosecution had rested its case-in-chief, the defendants addressed the issue as part of their no case to answer or motion for judgment of acquittal submissions.[122]

For example, Brima contended that the references in Article 1(1) and 15 of the SCSL Statute *to persons who bear the greatest responsibility* was a "limitation on the Court's jurisdiction as to which persons may or may not be prosecuted and creates an evidentiary burden to be satisfied by the Prosecution."[123] According to the Defense, the Prosecutor had not discharged his burden because its witnesses instead showed that other more prominent military leaders higher in rank, not their accused clients who were only *lower ranked non-*

---

[117] *Norman*, Case No. SCSL-04-14-PT, Decision on the Preliminary Defence Motion, ¶ 40.

[118] *See id.* ¶¶ 38–40.

[119] Prosecutor v. Brima, Case No. SCSL-04-16-T, Judgment, ¶¶ 4, 316, 432, 507 (June 20, 2007).

[120] *See, e.g., id.* ¶¶ 233–39.

[121] *Norman*, Case No. SCSL-04-14-PT, Decision on the Preliminary Defence Motion; Rules of Procedure and Evidence Rule 72(A), *supra* note 90.

[122] *Brima*, Case No. SCSL-04-16-T, Joint Legal Part Defence Motion for Judgment of Acquittal Under Rule 98, ¶¶ 1–2 (Dec. 13, 2005).

[123] *Brima*, Case No. SCSL-04-16-T, Decision on Defence Motion for Judgment of Acquittal Pursuant to Rule 98, ¶ 28 (March 31, 2006).

commissioned officers, bore greatest responsibility for the heinous offenses perpetrated in Sierra Leone.[124] In its response, the Prosecution made a two-pronged argument. First, there was no jurisdictional threshold that had to be met under Article 1(1). Second, the question of whether an accused is among those who bears greatest responsibility ought to only be determined after the conclusion of the trial.[125] Alternatively, and in any event, based on the evidence presented up to that point in the trial, a reasonable trier of fact could find the Accused to fall within the Court's personal jurisdiction.[126]

In its judgment, Trial Chamber II reviewed the documents discussing the history of the personal jurisdiction provision; in particular, it examined two letters exchanged between the UNSG and the Council in 2001.[127] The Chamber observed that in the January 12, 2001 letter, the UNSC rejected Annan's preferred "most responsible" personal jurisdiction language in favor or retaining its own "'greatest responsibility' formulation."[128] The Secretary-General had insisted on clarifying that the greatest responsibility wording should not be taken to mean that the Court's personal jurisdiction was limited to "political and military leaders" only, a position which the Council subsequently appeared to approve in its January 31, 2001 reply.[129] This SCSL chamber found that "greatest responsibility" jurisdiction in Article 1(1) "*solely purports to streamline the focus of prosecutorial strategy.*"[130] The judges then went on to observe that the phrase, understood in its ordinary sense, was meant to include, at a minimum, two groups of perpetrators, at the top of which were the political and military leaders of the parties to the conflict.[131] They emphasized, nevertheless, that the broad language used in the clause implied that an even wider range of individuals, presumably including ordinary combatants whose conduct might have been very egregious, were all potentially prosecutable before the Court.[132]

It seems apparent but perhaps surprising that, in reaching two divergent conclusions, the two sets of judges in each of the SCSL trial chambers examined the same drafting history and historical documents. While they agreed on the importance of those documents and relied on the analysis contained therein, each chamber's legal reasoning towards their respective conclusions differed.[133] The question is, why? Two reasons seem to stand out. First, it would appear that the Trial Chamber II judges did not read in their entirety either the drafting history of Article 1(1) and the subsequent correspondence between Secretary-General Annan and the Council. After the Secretary-General's January 12, 2001 letter proposing that the Council switch from its preferred, but apparently narrower, "greatest responsibility" formulation to his alternative and purportedly wider "most responsible" standard for personal jurisdiction, he conceded that, in rejecting his alternative proposal, the Council was thus

---

[124] *Brima*, Case No. SCSL-04-16-T, Decision on Defence Motion for Judgment of Acquittal Pursuant to Rule 98, ¶ 28 (March 31, 2006).

[125] *Id.* ¶ 29.

[126] *Id.*

[127] *Id.* ¶¶ 32–33.

[128] *Id.* ¶ 32.

[129] *Id.* ¶¶ 33–34.

[130] *Brima*, Case No. SCSL-04-16-T, Judgment, ¶ 653 (June 20, 2007) (emphasis added).

[131] *Brima*, Case No. SCSL-04-16-T, Decision on Defence Motion, ¶¶ 34–35.

[132] *See id.* ¶ 35.

[133] *Compare id.* ¶¶ 32–34, *with* Prosecutor v. Norman, Case No. SCSL-04-14-PT, Decision on the Preliminary Defence Motion on the Lack of Personal Jurisdiction Filed on Behalf of Accused Fofana, ¶¶ 22–25 (Mar. 3, 2004).

"limiting the focus of the Special Court to those who played a leadership role."[134] He pled, however, that the phrase should not be construed to "mean that the personal jurisdiction is limited to the political and military leaders only."[135] Indeed, in his view, this determination in a concrete case would initially have to be made by the Prosecutor and, ultimately, by the Court itself. The President of the Council, in a somewhat ambiguous, subsequent reply, stated that the UNSC shared in the Secretary-General's "analysis of the importance and role of the phrase 'persons who bear the greatest responsibility.'"[136]

Second, Trial Chamber I introduced a nuance when it reached the conclusion that greatest responsibility was both a jurisdictional requirement in Article 1(1) and also a description of the prosecutorial duty as fleshed out in Article 15. This group of judges emphasized the second part of the January 12, 2001 letter from the Secretary-General to the Council, in which it accepted that the particular reference made in the second sentence of Article 1(1) would then explicitly encompass "those leaders who, in committing such crimes, have threatened the establishment of and implementation of the peace process in Sierra Leone."[137] Secretary-General Annan understood the second sentence to serve as "guidance to the Prosecutor in determining his or her prosecutorial strategy."[138] The UNSC, in a subsequent reply to him, also endorsed the clarification that the words in the second sentence of Article 1(1), following the comma, were intended as a type of guideline to frame the prosecutorial strategy.[139] This gave credence to the later Trial Chamber I position that the effect of that preference for the greatest responsibility, instead of the people most responsible language, meant that leadership, instead of severity of the crime, ought to be the primary consideration when determining which suspect to prosecute.[140]

In other words, even though the two trial chambers used two different routes and Trial Chamber I correctly felt that leadership, as a criterion was intended to have primacy over severity, the judges from both chambers were on essentially the same page that greatest responsibility as phrased in the Statute meant that both political military leaders as well as killer-perpetrators could be prosecuted. They had effectively reached the same outcome, but using different analytical routes. The difference is that Trial Chamber I correctly distinguished between the first sentence of Article 1(1) (which it read as outlining the personal jurisdiction) and the second sentence of the same clause (which put in place the criteria – later explicitly developed in Article 15 – that would serve to guide or circumscribe prosecutorial discretion towards a particular class of individuals obstructionists towards the peace).[141] Whereas, for its part, Trial Chamber II interpreted the second part of the phrase in Article 1(1) as being subsumed by the first and reasoned that both elements, taken as one, did not establish a jurisdictional requirement, but rather, it functioned as additional guidance for the prosecutor's strategy.[142] To the latter group of judges then, Article 1(1) was not so much a jurisdictional

---

[134] Letter dated Jan. 12, 2001 from Secretary-General, *supra* note 102, para. 2; *see also* Secretary-General, *Report on SCSL*, *supra* note 4, ¶¶ 30–31.

[135] Letter dated Jan. 12, 2001 from Secretary-General, *supra* note 102, para. 2.

[136] Letter dated Jan. 31, 2001 from Pres. of S.C., *supra* note 20, para. 1.

[137] *Norman*, Case No. SCSL-04–14-PT, Decision on the Preliminary Defence Motion, ¶¶ 38, 40.

[138] Letter dated Jan. 31, 2001 from Pres. of S.C., *supra* note 20, para. 1.

[139] *Id.*

[140] *Norman*, Case No. SCSL-04–14-PT, Decision on the Preliminary Defence Motion, ¶¶ 39–40.

[141] *Id.*

[142] Prosecutor v. Brima, Case No. SCSL-04–16-T, Judgment, ¶ 653 (June 20, 2007).

clause as much as it was a guidance clause. However, the Trial Chamber II reasoning appears hard to reconcile with the fact that the rest of the elements in Article 1(1) of the Statute explicitly referred to matters of (geographic, territorial, and temporal) jurisdiction only. Their decision in the AFRC trial also seemingly failed to confront the question why the same "greatest responsibility" language separately found its way into Article 15, which stated the functions of the Prosecutor. One way of possibly reconciling the Trial Chamber II ruling would be to say that the judges saw the provision enumerating the prosecutorial power (Article 15) as doing the same job as the clause explaining the Tribunal's jurisdictional competence (Article 1(1)). Under this reading, both articles point the Prosecutor to make the choice of whom to pursue from those in leadership roles as well as those in lower ranks because they could prove to bear "greatest responsibility" for the crimes committed in Sierra Leone.

As we will see presently, when the Appeals Chamber confronted this same issue, it adopted lock-stock-and-barrel the Trial Chamber II reasoning that greatest responsibility, as worded in Article 1(1) of the SCSL Statute, was solely a guideline to the prosecutor for the exercise of his discretion instead of a jurisdictional requirement. It is submitted that this conclusion, which effectively endorsed the faulty prosecution and Trial Chamber II reasoning, was not necessarily borne out by the *travaux préparatoires*[143] of the SCSL's founding instruments.

D. *The Appeals Chamber Weighs In*

Because the two trial chambers of the Court had fiercely disagreed on the interpretation of "greatest responsibility" in separate decisions, it naturally fell to the Appeals Chamber to break the tie and furnish an authoritative interpretation of the clause once and for all. Santigie Borbor Kanu, the third defendant in the *Brima* trial, raised greatest responsibility as his first ground in the appeal of his conviction. He claimed that the trial court erred when it failed to establish its proper jurisdiction over him pursuant to Article 1(1).[144] In assessing his plea, the Appeals Chamber first distinguished separation of power issues relating to the competence of the Court, its organizational structure, and the role of the Prosecutor as set out in the SCSL Statute vis-à-vis the chambers from issues pertaining to jurisdiction.[145]

To begin, it assessed the role of the Prosecutor set out in Article 15.[146] It then observed that, flowing from that rule, he is mandated to act as "a separate organ" and is therefore barred from seeking or receiving instructions from any government or from any other source.[147] Accordingly, the Appeals Chamber concluded, "[i]t is evident that it is the Prosecutor who has the responsibility and competence to determine who are to be prosecuted as a result of investigation undertaken by him."[148] It is then up to the chambers, as the adjudicative organ, to "try such persons who the prosecutor has consequently brought before it as persons who

---

[143] *See Norman*, Case No. SCSL-04-14-PT, Decision on the Preliminary Defence Motion, ¶ 40.

[144] *Brima*, Case No. SCSL-04-16-A, Kanu's Submissions to Grounds of Appeal, ¶¶ 1.1–.30 (Sept. 13, 2007), *available at* http://www.sc-sl.org/scsl/Public/SCSL-04-16%20AFRC%20APPEAL%20DOCS/SCSL-04-16-A-647%20A. pdf.

[145] *Brima*, Case No. SCSL-04-16-A, Judgement, ¶¶ 280–81.

[146] *Id.*

[147] *Id.* ¶ 280 (emphasis omitted).

[148] *Id.* ¶ 281.

bear the greatest responsibility."[149] Put more succinctly, the decision as to whether someone bears greatest responsibility is made by the Prosecutor, during his investigations, and is not one for the judges whose sole function it is to adjudicate the individual cases brought before them.

This position is correct insofar as it demarcates the sharp division of responsibilities between the prosecutorial and judicial organs of the Court. For example, Trial Chamber II had similarly reasoned that, because of the separation of the prosecutorial and judicial roles in the Tribunal's founding instrument, Article 15 of the Statute implied that even the exercise of prosecutorial discretion in bringing a case against a particular accused was not reviewable by the court.[150] This was a broader finding than even the Prosecutor would have expected. In fact, he had conceded in the briefing process, both at trial and during the appeal, that a discretionary decision in choosing whom to prosecute is reviewable by the judges if exercised in a manifestly unreasonable manner, for instance, by violating the rights of the accused through abuse of process or exercising the power for impermissible or discriminatory motives.[151]

However, there appears to be errors in the judicial reasoning. Both the Appeals Chamber and Trial Chamber II's interpretation of Article 1(1), as a whole, was that the language delineated the outer boundaries of how far the Prosecutor can go when exercising her discretion. There are obvious difficulties with this conclusion, which the judges did not address in either the trial or appellate decisions. Among other issues, this stance ignores why a traditional jurisdictional provision setting out the competence of an ad hoc international criminal court would be adopted by the framers of a statute only to be reduced to a simple guideline for prosecutorial policy at a later time. A related concern is that the judges did not speak to the obvious link between Article 1(1), which usually enumerates the personal jurisdiction of the Tribunal, with Article 15(1), which defined the power of the Prosecutor, when it provided that he or she shall be responsible for the investigation and prosecution of persons who bear the greatest responsibility for the crimes committed in Sierra Leone after November 30, 1996. In other words, why would the drafters adopt Article 15(1) if Article 1(1) serves essentially the same purpose? Conversely, why would they include Article 1(1) if Article 15(1) sufficiently described both the Court's jurisdiction and the mandate of the Prosecutor? The answer is that they adopted each of these separate provisions because each played a distinctive role in the statute: the former setting out the jurisdiction of the Tribunal, and the latter, expressly outlining the functions (and limitations) imposed on the Prosecutor and her exercise of her power.

In Kanu's appeal, the Prosecution had further argued that the Appeals Chamber should not hold the phrase "persons who bear the greatest responsibility" as a test criterion or a distinct jurisdictional threshold.[152] To do so, according to them, would lead to an "absurd interpretation"[153] requiring a factual determination at the pre-trial stage that there is no

---

[149] *Brima*, Case No. SCSL-04–16-A, Judgement, ¶¶ 281.

[150] *Brima*, Case No. SCSL-04–16-T, Judgement, ¶ 654.

[151] *Id.* ¶ 643; *Brima*, Case No. SCSL-04–16-T, Decision on Defence Motion for Judgment of Acquittal Pursuant to Rule 98, ¶ 29 (Mar. 31, 2006); Prosecutor v. Norman, Case No. SCSL-04–14-PT, Decision on the Preliminary Defence Motion on the Lack of Personal Jurisdiction Filed on Behalf of Accused Fofana, ¶ 7 (Mar. 3, 2004).

[152] *Brima*, Case No. SCSL-04–16-A, Judgement, ¶¶ 274–75.

[153] *Id.* ¶ 274.

person who has been indicted who bears greater responsibility than the particular accused when it would be impossible to determine the precise scope of criminal liability before the trial concludes. Yet, at the same time, it would be "unworkable to suggest that this determination should be made by the Trial or Appeals Chamber at the end of the trial."[154] By analogy to Article 1 of the ICTY and ICTR Statutes, which provide for prosecution of "persons responsible," the Prosecution submitted that construing "greatest responsibility" as a jurisdictional requirement would imply that those other tribunals could prosecute only those who are actually guilty.[155]

Adopting this line of argument, the Appeals Chamber, in a crucial statement that betrayed the real concern underpinning their conclusion, ruled as follows:

> [I]t is inconceivable that after a long and expensive trial the Trial Chamber could conclude that although the commission of serious crimes has been established beyond reasonable doubt against the accused, the indictment ought to be struck out on the ground that it has not been proved that the accused was not one of those who bore the greatest responsibility.[156]

With respect, the Appeals Chamber, like Trial Chamber II that first accepted this prosecutorial argument, should have queried this submission. For one thing, the argument assumes that a determination that greatest responsibility was a personal jurisdiction requirement implied that the judges might not have found at the pre-trial stage, that there is possibly no other person that bore greater responsibility than the particular accused before the Court. For another thing, without referring to the prosecution evidence, it implicitly suggests that the case would not necessarily have been proved beyond a reasonable doubt. Both these propositions seem untenable.

The better view appears to be that advanced by Trial Chamber I judges, which held in their *Fofana* preliminary decision that an assessment of whether someone can be said to bear greatest responsibility should be handled differently by assessing, during the indictment review stage, whether the prosecution had made out a *prima facie* case that a particular suspect appears to be one of the individuals bearing greatest responsibility for what happened in a particular armed conflict.[157] If there is basic evidence supporting the prosecution's case, then the trial would proceed, much like it would with respect to the other jurisdictional criteria that had to be met, for example, persuading the judges that the suspect appears to have committed crimes within the jurisdiction of the SCSL.[158] Another possibility is for the greatest responsibility issue to be considered at the Rule 98 (no case to answer) stage, when the judges would have heard all the evidence from the prosecution. They could then decide, on the standard reflecting that stage of the process, if there was substantial evidence that – if believed – would appear to support the charges in the indict-

---

[154] *Brima*, Case No. SCSL-04–16-A, Judgement, ¶¶ 274.

[155] *Id.*

[156] *Id.* ¶ 283.

[157] Prosecutor v. Fofana, Case No. SCSL-04–14-T, Judgement, ¶¶ 91–92 (Aug. 2, 2007).

[158] Prosecutor v. Norman, Case No. SCSL-04–14-PT, Decision on the Preliminary Defence Motion on the Lack of Personal Jurisdiction Filed on Behalf of Accused Fofana, ¶¶ 28–45 (Mar. 3, 2004).

ment such as to put the defendant to answer the Prosecution case made up to that point of the trial.

But, even more fundamentally, the Appeals Chamber, in endorsing the Prosecutor's argument, did not distinguish the SCSL from the ICTY and the ICTR. Yet, the UN twin tribunals were differently situated vis-à-vis the SCSL for several reasons. First, the personal jurisdiction provision is simply framed differently. Second, the debate that arose in the Court did not arise in the UN twin tribunals as a consequence of the wider formulation of their jurisdiction compared to the narrower one of the SCSL. The latter was not only saddled with explicit limitations on its jurisdiction, it was also saddled with specific directives narrowing down the powers of the Prosecutor. In other words, it seems like a false analogy to treat as equal the circumscribed Sierra Leone Tribunal jurisdiction and the broader jurisdiction clauses of the Yugoslav and Rwanda Tribunals.

Be that as it may, the crucial question arises whether the drafting history of the Statute of the SCSL reflected the position taken by the Appeals Chamber and Trial Chamber II. In the next part of this chapter, I will argue that the appellate judges misconstrued Article 1 of the Statute. I submit that, clouded by their concern for the practicalities of finding differently on the personal jurisdiction provision for the concrete cases before them, the appeals court misinterpreted the provision. I will contend that Trial Chamber I, which methodically reviewed the greatest responsibility formula with closer and more complete reference to the drafting history, more accurately reflected the intention of the drafters of the SCSL Statute. For clarity, that intention was that Article 1(1) would establish the personal jurisdiction of the Court, while Article 15(1) would further circumscribe the discretion of the Prosecutor to pursue only a limited class of suspects deemed to bear greatest responsibility. Ultimately, as I will hopefully show, despite their various differences, the overall conclusion to draw from the Sierra Leone court case law seems to be that the greatest responsibility language was controversial but was sufficiently broad to ensure that the Tribunal could prosecute individuals from both the political-leader and the killer-perpetrator groups. That much agreement existed between all of the judges, even if their reasoning towards that conclusion differed.

IV. DISCERNING THE ACTUAL MEANING OF "GREATEST RESPONSIBILITY"

The drafting history of Article 1(1) in the Statute of the SCSL supports the argument that at least part of the provision was initially intended as a jurisdictional requirement, while another part of the provision was intended as a sort of redline not to cross or guideline to limit the prosecutorial strategy. An examination of the ordinary textual meaning of the provisions, in accordance with Article 31 of the Vienna Convention on the Law of Treaties demonstrates this theory. Article 31, in relevant part, provides that:

1. A treaty shall be interpreted in good faith in accordance with the *ordinary meaning* to be given to the terms of the treaty in their context and in the light of its object and purpose. [Emphasis added].
2. The context for the purpose of the interpretation of a treaty shall comprise, in addition to the text, including its preamble and annexes ...

3. There shall be taken into account, together with the context ...

4. [Any] special meaning given to a term if it is established that the parties so intended.[159]

As the agreement between the UN and the Sierra Leone government constitutes a bilateral treaty,[160] Article 31 of the Vienna Convention on the Law of Treaties (VCLT) is applicable.[161] The Statute of the Tribunal, which of course contains the identical provision on personal jurisdiction, is an annex to the UN-Sierra Leone Agreement and therefore forms an integral part of the treaty.[162] The ordinary meaning of the phrase "to prosecute persons who bear the greatest responsibility" in Article 1(1) of those two instruments can therefore be read in light of the context; as well as the preamble, object, and purpose of the provision and the statute; the Court's intended role to ensure accountability for international crimes committed in Sierra Leone; and the special meaning accorded to the term by the founders of the SCSL as well as in light of the Tribunal's practice.

A. *The Ordinary Meaning of "Persons Who Bear the Greatest Responsibility"*

Let us examine, using a standard English dictionary, each of the terms in the phrase "to prosecute persons who bear the greatest responsibility." The *Oxford English Dictionary* defines "person" in various ways. For our purposes the most relevant is the following: "an individual human being; a man, woman or child;" and, as used in a technical legal sense, as "[a] human being (natural person) or body corporate or corporation (artificial person), having rights and duties recognized by the law."[163] It is clear from even the ordinary dictionary meaning that the term "person" refers most likely to a natural person. So far, all the SCSL prosecutions have related to natural persons, although there is nothing to foreclose trials of legal persons. That said, in the context of this particular chapter, this issue does not appear to have a major bearing on the argument so it need not detain us.

The noun "who" is used "[a]s the ordinary interrogative pronoun, in the nominative singular or plural, used of a person or persons: corresponding to *what* of things."[164] More specifically, it is "[a]s compound relative in the nominative in general or indefinite sense: Any one that ...."[165]

The term "bear," which is the root word for "bearing," means "to carry; to sustain; to thrust, press; to bring forth."[166] Bearing is therefore "the action of carrying or conveying" or "[t]he carrying of oneself (with reference to the manner); carriage, deportment; behaviour, demeanour."[167]

---

[159] Vienna Convention on the Law of Treaties art. 31, May 23, 1969, 1155 U.N.T.S. 331 [hereinafter Vienna Convention] (emphasis added).

[160] *See* Secretary-General, *Report on SCSL, supra* note 4, ¶ 9.

[161] Vienna Convention, *supra* note 159, art. 1.

[162] SCSL Statute, *supra* note 3, art. 1(1); U.N.-Sierra Leone Agreement, *supra* note 1, art. 1.

[163] 11 OXFORD ENGLISH DICTIONARY 597 (2nd ed. 1989) (emphasis omitted).

[164] 20 OXFORD ENGLISH DICTIONARY 288–89 (2nd ed. 1989).

[165] *Id.* at 289.

[166] 2 OXFORD ENGLISH DICTIONARY 20 (2nd ed. 1989).

[167] *Id.* at 26.

Of course, "the" is a definite article. As used in Article 1(1) of the SCSL Statute outlining personal jurisdiction, it modifies or rather particularizes the superlative "greatest" as a way of connoting that about which the Tribunal *is* or *should be most concerned*. It thus essentially captures the notion of individuals who belong to a class or group of persons bearing relatively greater responsibility, although, admittedly, the idea of those with which it should be most concerned does not necessarily imply exclusivity.

"Greatest" is, of course, the "superlative of great in various senses."[168] As used ordinarily, "the greatest" is a reference to "[t]hat which is great; great things, aspects, qualities, etc. collectively; also, great quantity, large amount."[169] When used to describe persons who bear the qualities of "being great," the *Oxford English Dictionary* clarifies that it is an allusion to persons "[e]minent by reason of birth, rank, wealth, power, or position; of high social or official position; of eminent rank or place."[170] Greatest is, more helpfully in our context, an additional way of denoting "conditions, actions, or occurrences; with reference to degree or extent .... [and of] things, actions, [or] events ... [o]f more than ordinary importance, weight, or distinction; important, weighty; distinguished, prominent; famous, renowned."[171]

As to "responsibility," it is defined as "[t]he state or fact of being responsible ... *for* ... [a] charge, trust, or duty, for which one is responsible."[172]

From the above, we can distill from the ordinary dictionary meaning of each of the words when combined together and viewed in their context, that the phrase "persons who bear the greatest responsibility" is a description of two separate but not entirely distinct ideas. First, it describes a person of high rank, position, or power who carries out certain actions and brings forth events or conditions of more than ordinary importance, and who, given the core purpose of the SCSL to administer justice, should be investigated and prosecuted.

Second, and flowing from these definitions, we can also see that the ordinary meaning of the phrase is also a reference to the degree or amount of something or event that a person engages upon as part of a certain type of behavior – in this case, the commission of crimes during the course of the Sierra Leone armed conflict. Individual criminal liability was rightly deemed necessary for those actions or events. It also reveals the state or fact of being in charge of or of having a duty or obligation towards a person or thing, which was then breached by those persons. A reference to the drafting history will demonstrate that these two ordinary definitions of the personal jurisdiction provision were also expressed during the negotiations of the agreement creating the SCSL.

As argued previously, and as will be further detailed in the next section, focusing specifically on the drafting history, the category of persons over which the Court was to have jurisdiction was always going to be limited. The Council's preference was evidently that the leadership role or command authority of a suspect should be the principal criterion for the application of the greatest responsibility formulation.[173] Whereas, the Secretary-General's

---

[168] 6 OXFORD ENGLISH DICTIONARY 801 (2nd ed. 1989).

[169] *Id.* at 800 (footnote omitted).

[170] *Id.* at 797.

[171] *Id.* (formatting omitted).

[172] 13 OXFORD ENGLISH DICTIONARY 742 (2nd ed. 1989).

[173] U.N. President of the S.C., Letter dated Dec. 22, 2000 from the President of the Security Council addressed to the Secretary-General, para. 1, U.N. Doc. S/2000/1234 (Dec. 22, 2000) [hereinafter Letter dated Dec. 22, 2000 from Pres. of S.C.].

view was that the gravity, scale or massive nature of the crime should also be taken into account, if not the main consideration, in the exercise of personal jurisdiction.[174] Bear in mind that although the former seemingly endorsed the juxtaposition of these two separate ideas, according to Trial Chamber I, the Council ultimately saw the scale or gravity of a particular crime as being of secondary, instead of primary, importance vis-à-vis the leadership or functional positions held by the suspects.[175]

B. *The Drafting History of "Persons Who Bear the Greatest Responsibility"*

Under Article 31(2) of the VCLT, in addition to the preamble and annexes, the context for a treaty is additionally comprised of any subsequent agreements relating to the treaty made between all the parties in connection with the conclusion of the treaty.[176]

The four paragraphs of the preamble to the UN-Sierra Leone Agreement refer to Council Resolution 1315, adopted on August 14, 2000, in which the UNSC expressed deep concern at the very serious crimes committed within the "territory of Sierra Leone against the people of Sierra Leone and United Nations and associated personnel and at the prevailing situation of impunity."[177] It therefore asked the Secretary-General to negotiate an agreement with the Sierra Leone government to "create an independent special court to prosecute persons who bear the greatest responsibility" for the commission of the serious international and Sierra Leonean law violations committed.[178]

The same language contained in the resolution was reiterated verbatim in Article 1(1) of the SCSL Statute, which prescribed the competence of the Court and delimited its core jurisdictional components.[179] In the Statute, as opposed to Agreement, however, a clarification was added to the effect of "including those leaders who, in committing such crimes, have threatened the establishment of and implementation of the peace process in Sierra Leone."[180] Besides the text of those two instruments, the *travaux préparatoires*[181] reveal a subsequent discussion between, on the one hand, internal organs of the UN (the Council and the Secretary-General), and on the other hand, the UN as a single entity vis-à-vis the other party (Sierra Leone).

In Resolution 1315, the UNSC directed the Secretary-General that the personal jurisdiction of the Tribunal shall cover only "persons who bear the greatest responsibility for the commission of crimes" in Sierra Leone.[182] As the UNSG later tried to explain, the Council intended that phrase to mean two things, which also appear to coincide with the ordinary dictionary meaning discerned in the previous section.[183]

---

[174] *See* Secretary-General, *Report on SCSL, supra* note 4, ¶ 30.

[175] Prosecutor v. Norman, Case No. SCSL-04-14-PT, Decision on the Preliminary Defence Motion on the Lack of Personal Jurisdiction Filed on Behalf of Accused Fofana, ¶ 40 (Mar. 3, 2004).

[176] Vienna Convention, *supra* note 159, art. 31(2).

[177] S.C. Res. 1315, *supra* note 14, pmbl.; *see also* U.N.-Sierra Leone Agreement, *supra* note 1, pmbl.

[178] S.C. Res. 1315, *supra* note 14, ¶ 1; *see also* U.N.-Sierra Leone Agreement, *supra* note 1, pmbl.

[179] SCSL Statute, *supra* note 3, art. 1(1); S.C. Res. 1315, *supra* note 14, ¶ 3.

[180] *Compare* SCSL Statute, *supra* note 3, art. 1(1), *with* U.N.-Sierra Leone Agreement, *supra* note 1, art. 1(1).

[181] *See supra* note 140 and accompanying text.

[182] S.C. Res. 1315, *supra* note 14, ¶ 3.

[183] Secretary-General, *Report on SCSL, supra* note 4, ¶ 30; *see also* Letter dated Jan. 12, 2001 from Secretary-General, *supra* note 102, paras. 2–3.

In his Report to the Council explaining the steps he had taken to implement Resolution 1315, the Secretary-General suggested that an alternative phrase, "persons most responsible," replace "greatest responsibility."[184] Annan rationalized this suggestion as follows:

> While those "most responsible" obviously include the political or military leadership, others in command authority down the chain of command may also be regarded "most responsible" judging by the severity of the crime or its massive scale. "Most responsible[,]" therefore, denotes either a leadership or authority position of the accused, and a sense of the gravity, seriousness or massive scale of the crime. It must be seen, however, not as a test criterion or a distinct jurisdictional threshold, but as guidance to the Prosecutor in the adoption of a prosecution strategy and in making decisions to prosecute in individual cases.[185]

However, the UNSC did not endorse that proposal because, for one thing, it implicitly disagreed that the phrase "those most responsible" was broader than the phrase those "bearing greatest responsibility."[186] The President of the Council, in a December 22, 2000 letter, rejected the Secretary-General's proposed modification to the personal jurisdiction provision.[187] The Council reiterated its preference contained in Resolution 1315 that jurisdiction should extend to only those persons who bear the greatest responsibility for the commission of crimes under national and international law.[188] The President put it as follows: "The members of the Security Council believe that, by thus limiting the focus of the Special Court to those who played a leadership role, the simpler and more general formulations suggested in the appended draft will be appropriate."[189] It seems apparent enough, then, that the Council's main interest was to hone in on those holding a leadership role, as the judges of Trial Chamber I and the SCSL Prosecution have also confirmed.

In the Secretary-General's response to the President of the UNSC, which followed about three weeks later (January 12, 2001), Annan canvassed the difference between the two positions.[190] He then tried to reframe his argument to again reassert the relevance of the gravity, scale and severity of the crimes – a point he had initially made when he suggested that "the term 'most responsible' would not necessarily exclude children between 15 and 18 years of age" from possible responsibility for crimes within the SCSL jurisdiction.[191] The question surrounding the responsibility of child soldiers, who had been some of the most notorious perpetrators of atrocities during the war, was one of the thorniest issues for the Sierra Leonean negotiators.[192] So the UNSG effectively used that issue as a trump card to emphasize why the gravity of the crimes is a vital consideration in addition to the functional (leadership) position held by the suspect. He wrote in his report, as follows:

> While it is inconceivable that children could be in a political or military leadership position (although in Sierra Leone the rank of "Brigadier" was often granted to children as young

---

[184] Secretary-General, *Report on SCSL, supra* note 4, ¶¶ 29–31.
[185] *Id.* ¶ 30.
[186] *See* Letter dated Dec. 22, 2000 from Pres. of S.C., *supra* note 173.
[187] *Id.*
[188] *Id.* para. 1; *see* S.C. Res. 1315, *supra* note 14, ¶ 3.
[189] Letter dated Dec. 22, 2000 from Pres. of S.C., *supra* note 173, para. 1.
[190] Letter dated Jan. 12, 2001 from Secretary-General, *supra* note 102, para. 1–2.
[191] Secretary-General, *Report on SCSL, supra* note 4, ¶ 31.
[192] *Id.* ¶ 34.

as 11 years), the gravity and seriousness of the crimes they have allegedly committed would allow for their inclusion within the jurisdiction of the Court.[193]

With hindsight, we know that the evidence that came out of the trials never supported this contention about child brigadiers. However, the foregoing extract does indicate that at least one of the negotiators, the UNSG, intended the gravity of the conduct to be a crucial element of greatest responsibility personal jurisdiction. The above accepts that the Council's purpose in framing jurisdiction this way was to limit the prosecutorial investigations to those in leadership or authority positions. Going by the reasoning of Trial Chamber I, which again discerned this singular thrust that leadership was or should be the determinative criterion for prosecutorial decisions, the massive nature of the crime could and should also be taken into account – albeit as a secondary factor. If this deduction is correct, and it does seem not only correct but also reasonable, it would permit the prosecution of either, or both, of the lower ranked perpetrators in addition to leaders in the same jurisdiction.

In fact, in the same report, one might also recall, Secretary-General Annan had claimed that the wording of Article 1(1) of the draft statute, as the Council had proposed it, did "not mean [to limit] personal jurisdiction... to the political and military leaders only."[194] Almost as a tie breaker in case the powers that be in the UNSC continued to disagree with him, he observed that the determination of the meaning of the term "persons who bear the greatest responsibility in any given case falls initially to the Prosecutor, and ultimately to the SLSC itself."[195] This seems obvious in the sense that part of the initial determination of whom to prosecute falls within prosecutorial discretion.

Using this language, the Secretary-General adopted a negotiating tactic in an attempt to have his way, although he did not later clarify whether his position that the "most responsible" language should not require proof beyond a reasonable doubt,[196] which was ultimately rejected,[197] was also equally applicable to the "greatest responsibility" formulation. It reasonably could be read as being equally applicable. We might thus speculate as to the omission. One explanation is that he left some ambiguity on the point in the hope that it would help bolster his reading, which invoked Sierra Leone's concerns as well, to caution the UNSC that it would be up to the Prosecutor and judiciary to settle on the final position as to what greatest responsibility jurisdiction ultimately entailed. Essentially, it is an argument that says to the Council the limits of how much it could realistically expect from the Statute, considering that the Court could independently diverge from that expectation. He also, by framing things in this way, sent a message to the future Prosecutor that s/he still enjoyed a measure of discretion, despite the prescriptive greatest responsibility language contained in the Agreement and Statute. If this analysis is correct, it would seem that great weight can

---

[193] *Id.* ¶ 31.

[194] Letter dated Jan. 12, 2001 from Secretary-General, *supra* note 102, para. 2.

[195] *Id.* (internal quotation marks omitted).

[196] *See* U.N. Secretary-General, Letter dated July 12, 2001 from the Secretary-General addressed to the President of the Security Council, U.N. Doc. S/2001/693 (July 12, 2001) [hereinafter Letter dated July 12, 2001 from Secretary-General] (indicating acceptance of the agreement by the parties with no subsequent mention of the "most responsible" and "greatest responsibility" language).

[197] *See* SCSL Statute, *supra* note 3, art. 1(1) (containing the language "persons who bear the greatest responsibly"); U.N.-Sierra Leone Agreement, *supra* note 1, art. 1(1) (containing the language "persons who bear the greatest responsibility").

therefore be attached to the Tribunal's practice in line with that Annan position as well as the VCLT principles.

It is this context that informs the Secretary-General's letter, which then stated, with explicit reference to the second half of Article 1(1):

> Among those who bear the greatest responsibility for the crimes falling within the juris-diction of the Special Court, particular mention is made of "those leaders who, in commit-ting such crimes, have threatened the establishment of and implementation of the peace process in Sierra Leone." *It is my understanding that, following from paragraph 2 above, the words "those leaders who … threaten the establishment of and implementation of the peace process" do not describe an element of the crime but rather provide guidance to the prosecutor in determining his or her prosecutorial strategy.* Consequently, the commission of any of the statutory crimes without necessarily threatening the establishment and implementation of the peace process would not detract from the international criminal responsibility other-wise entailed for the accused.[198]

The President of the Council's response to the Secretary-General, appeared to endorse Annan's preferred ways of interpreting Article 1(1) in the following terms:

> The members of the Council share your analysis of the *importance* and *role* of the phrase "persons who bear the greatest responsibility[."] The members of the Council, moreover, share your view that the words beginning with "those leaders who …." are intended as guidance to the Prosecutor in determining his or her prosecutorial strategy.[199]

This language was vague in that the reference to the "importance" and "role" of Article 1(1) provision does not entirely specify whether the UNSC felt that the personal jurisdic-tion phrase is (1) limited to leaders alone, or (2) not necessarily limited to leaders alone because it will include those whose actions were so grave that they merited prosecutions (even if they did not functionally hold high-ranking positions). As to the second sentence of the clause, and arguably by implication not the first sentence, it appears evident that the Council agreed with Annan that Article 1(1) does constitute a guideline for the Prosecutor's exercise of his or her discretion without necessarily serving as a legal ingredient or legal requirement of the crimes that ought to be proven beyond a reasonable doubt.

Thus, consistent with the finding of this chapter as shown in Section III, Article 1(1) offered two separate meanings: the first part of the sentence being a personal jurisdictional threshold; and the second part, especially when read together with Article 15(1) outlining the powers of the Prosecutor, establishing a limitation for the prosecutorial application of her discretion without necessarily foreclosing the extension of the jurisdiction to the polit-ical leaders and the killer perpetrators.

In his last publicly available letter on the greatest responsibility issue, dated July 12, 2001, Annan notified the Council that the exchange of letters led to modifications of the text in both the draft UN-Sierra Leone Agreement and the Statute annexed to it.[200] As this back and forth communication had been an internal conversation between two U.N. organs, he confirmed that "[t]he Government of Sierra Leone was consulted on these changes and

---

[198] Letter dated Jan. 12, 2001 from Secretary-General, *supra* note 102, para. 3 (emphasis added).
[199] Letter dated Jan. 31, 2001 from Pres. of S.C., *supra* note 20, para. 1.
[200] Letter dated July 12, 2001 from Secretary-General, *supra* note 196.

by letter of 9 February 2001 to the Legal Counsel expressed its willingness to accept the texts."[201] This fact, therefore, made the communication a subsequent agreement among all the parties in connection with the conclusion of the treaty in the Article 31(2) VCLT sense.

In *Fofana*, Trial Chamber I, after meticulously reviewing this drafting history, had also ruled that the "agreed text resulted in the adoption of the phrase" on personal jurisdiction as articulated in Article 1(1) of the Statute with the specific duties of the prosecutor in that regard prescribed in accordance with Article 15(1).[202] It was on this basis that the Chamber concluded that "the issue of personal jurisdiction is a jurisdictional requirement, and while it does of course guide the prosecutorial strategy, it does not exclusively articulate prosecutorial discretion, as the Prosecution has submitted."[203]

Upon closer examination, it is clear that Trial Chamber I believed, correctly in my view, that personal jurisdiction created a jurisdictional threshold. However, the nuance in the language is that this group of judges did not say that "greatest responsibility" was a jurisdictional requirement in the entirety of the provision. Rather, they felt that the "*issue* of personal jurisdiction" also contained language purporting to guide the Prosecutor on how she should use her power. It follows that it is correct that Article 1(1) was neither exclusively jurisdictional nor exclusively directed at demarcating the contours of prosecutorial discretion. In contrast, Trial Chamber II, for its part, was critical of the judicial colleagues in the other chamber and explicitly determined that the "greatest responsibility" did not create a jurisdictional requirement because it only limited to a small category the number of persons that were to be prosecuted.[204] Significantly, the above reading that the two ideas were encompassed in the same phrase, as well as in that clause enumerating the Prosecutors duties, appears to be confirmed by the contents of the July 12, 2001, letter to the Council, in which the Secretary-General explained as follows:

> Members of the Council reiterated their understanding that, without prejudice to the independence of the prosecutor, the *personal jurisdiction* of the Special Court *remains limited to the few who bear the greatest responsibility* for the crimes committed.[205]

In the Cambodia Tribunal, which has the closest personal jurisdiction wording to that of the Sierra Leone court, an identical concern arose as to the meaning of Article 1(1) of the ECCC Law, which provided for the trial of "senior leaders of Democratic Kampuchea and those who were most responsible for the crimes."[206] This phrase is in one way an improvement on what was used in Sierra Leone in the sense that the first part of the phrase specifically identifies senior leaders while the second part mentions those most responsible. In that way, the ECCC approach apparently adequately addresses the policy concerns of Secretary-General Annan in the Sierra Leone situation: that the leaders, architects, or planners of the mass crimes as well as their followers responsible for grave crimes should all as a *prima facie*

---

[201] Letter dated July 12, 2001 from Secretary-General, *supra* note 197.

[202] Prosecutor v. Norman, Case No. SCSL-04–14-PT, Decision on the Preliminary Defence Motion on the Lack of Personal Jurisdiction Filed on Behalf of Accused Fofana, ¶ 26 (Mar. 3, 2004).

[203] *Id.* ¶ 27.

[204] *See* Prosecutor v. Brima, Case No. SCSL-04–16-T, Judgment, ¶ 653 (June 20, 2007).

[205] Letter dated July 12, 2001 from Secretary-General, *supra* note 196 (emphasis added).

[206] U.N.-Cambodian Agreement, *supra* note 35; *see also* G.A. Res. 57/228, ¶ 1, U.N. Doc. A/RES/57/228 B (May 13, 2003) (approving draft of ECCC Agreement).

matter be deemed prosecutable.[207] The legal framework must be clear and accommodating, but the Prosecutor should ultimately make the final choice. The Cambodia formulation also reflects the general purpose behind internationally supported criminal prosecutions which, as we saw in our historical review starting with the Nuremberg Tribunal, had always aimed to ensure the prosecution of leaders for their crimes.

The only difficulty is that even the ECCC phrase is still somewhat ambiguous. The second part of the sentence, speaking to those most responsible, suggests a focus on the persons to be tried for the depravity or severity of their acts. Unsurprisingly, taking a cue from the developments respecting their brethren at the SCSL, the defense counsel litigated that issue arguing, at the close of the first trial, that the Cambodia Tribunal lacked jurisdiction over the first defendant Duch.[208] The Chamber, drawing on the reasoning of the Sierra Leone jurisprudence, determined that the accused, as a senior leader, fell within its personal jurisdiction as one of those most responsible.[209] That conclusion was unsuccessfully challenged on appeal.[210]

V. CONCLUSION: KEY CONTRIBUTIONS OF THE SCSL

In taking up previously uncharted terrain, outside the confines of the debates in the trials in Sierra Leone, this chapter hopes to have shown that it is imperative for the creators of international criminal tribunals to properly delineate their personal jurisdiction. The greatest responsibility formula used at the SCSL was politically convenient for the Council, which was keen to establish a relatively cheap and time limited ad hoc court that would prosecute only a small group of people in Sierra Leone. But, as I have shown through this original contribution to the literature, without further specificity, such general statements of personal jurisdiction in practice raise serious issues of interpretation and application in concrete cases. Vagueness, it seems, is hardly a positive factor in a criminal tribunal instrument.

With respect to the contributions and lessons learned from Sierra Leone, it maybe too early to draw final conclusions as to whether the SCSL jurisprudence will be found well-reasoned enough to be followed by other courts. That said, the following tentative observations may still be offered regarding the case law it has bequeathed us on this particular issue.

First, the type of "greatest responsibility" clause found in Article 1(1) of the SCSL Statute setting out personal jurisdiction should be avoided at all cost. Failing that, if such language needs to be used, it is important to at least attempt to define what the phrase means to say that a court shall prosecute those bearing greatest responsibility. There is helpful precedent, in this area, as this is in fact what the draft statute of the Special Tribunal for Kenya attempted to do. Again, in that instance, the same logic of focusing on leaders in positions of authority and influence as well as those most vicious in committing the crimes was already evident in the relatively more precise definition that was offered.[211] The drafters of

---

[207] Secretary-General, *Report on SCSL*, *supra* note 4, ¶¶ 29–30.

[208] Prosecutor v. Duch, Case No. 001/18–07–2007/ECCC/TC, Judgment, ¶ 14 (July 26, 2010).

[209] *Id.* ¶ 24–25.

[210] *Duch*, Case No. 001/18–07–2007-ECCC/SC, Appeal Judgment, ¶ 79 (Feb. 3, 2012).

[211] Special Tribunal for Kenya Bill, *supra* note 21, pt. I § 2. The Bill offers the following definition:

> "[P]ersons bearing the greatest responsibility" means a person or persons who were knowingly responsible for any or all of the following acts: planning, instigating, inciting, funding, ordering or providing other logistics which directly or indirectly facilitated the commission of crimes falling within the

that clause clearly knew of the SCSL experience, since they attempted to resolve some of the thorny issues that led to much ink being spilled by counsel and judges during the Sierra Leone Tribunal's decade-long life. Regrettably, because the Kenya hybrid tribunal never saw the light of day, as the bill failed to obtain sufficient support for passage into law in the Kenyan Parliament,[212] there was a missed opportunity to see whether that relatively clearer phrase would have fared better during the trials of the suspects allegedly responsible for the post-election violence which rocked that country in December 2007.

Second, future ad hoc tribunal statutes should explicitly state whether such a phrase is or is not a jurisdictional requirement that must be proved beyond a reasonable doubt as an element of the crime. It seems obvious that it should not be treated as a jurisdictional requirement, because it would otherwise make prosecutions of concrete cases both procedurally cumbersome and difficult. This is the lesson of the Sierra Leone Court, which struggled throughout its trials to repeatedly make the simple point to defendants and their defense counsel that the focus of prosecution of persons in leadership positions did not mean that those of lower rank, in effective control, could not also simultaneously or alternatively be pursued by an international court with "greatest responsibility language" as the center of its personal jurisdiction. Instead, as we have seen, attempts to judicially settle the issue led to more challenges, in different cases, at different stages of the trial process (pre-trial, trial, and appeal).

Third, and closely related to the second point, if greatest responsibility is to be used to delineate the boundaries of the power that the Tribunal prosecutors enjoy, that purpose should be stated explicitly. Although it seems unlikely, if there is another purpose for employing such language going beyond limiting prosecutorial wiggle room, that purpose too would ideally be stated. Indeed, it may be wise to include a provision discussing the relationship and link between the personal jurisdiction article and the limitations to the prosecutorial mandate. This would help to avoid unnecessary hurdles during trials of the suspects and arguments that the prosecution lacks the power to make choices as to whom to prosecute from among a wide range of potential perpetrators. The obviousness of that position did not make the task of the SCSL prosecutors any less challenging. At the least, these points and intersections should be discussed in the founding documents and a clear position taken to guide the later interpreters of the text.

Fourth, though not discussed in this chapter *per se*, to put the matter beyond any doubt, consideration should also be given to clarifying that the judges have *ex proprio motu*[213] power to review whether the prosecution has fulfilled the personal jurisdiction and other requirements when making a *prima facie* case. It is the duty of the judges to ensure fair trials that respect the rights of the accused take place in a given criminal case. It is therefore

---

jurisdiction of the Tribunal; *in determining whether a person or persons falls within this category, the Tribunal shall have regard to factors including the leadership role or level of authority or decision making power or influence of the person concerned and the gravity, severity, seriousness or scale of the crime committed.*

Id. (emphasis added).

[212] *Kenya: Quorum Stops the Bill on the Establishment of the Special Tribunal to Try Violence*, AFRICAN PRESS INT'L (Fed. 6, 2009), http://africanpress.me/2009/02/06/kenya-quorum-stops-the-bill-on-the-establishment-of-the-special-tribunal-to-try-violence/.

[213] "Of one's own accord." BLACK'S LAW DICTIONARY 662 (9th ed. 2009).

not enough for them to abdicate this function of deciding who falls within the jurisdiction solely to the prosecution, as one chamber effectively did at the SCSL, by holding that the judges were not empowered to review the choices made by the prosecutorial organ. This wrongly implied that the chamber was simply there to rubber stamp the prosecutorial *allegations* in an indictment that someone is among those bearing greatest responsibility for the atrocities committed during a particular conflict.

Fifth, the drafters of statutes, especially at the United Nations Office of Legal Affairs, should explicitly consider stating the consequences of a finding that personal jurisdictional requirements had either been fulfilled or not. What standard should apply to determine that it had been fulfilled, and at what stages of the trials? If the threshold is not fulfilled, what should happen? Would the tribunal have to release the defendant, and if so, should this be with or without prejudice to the prosecution? Given the Sierra Leone experience, it may also be helpful to indicate whether any such determinations require factual assessments of evidence or are purely legal questions to be considered by the judges even before the Prosecution calls any witnesses. If factual assessments are required, then the stage of the trial at which the point should be considered should be delineated keeping in mind the appropriate standard of proof. If it is a legal assessment, that too should guide how the claims can be made, using what evidentiary burden, before reaching the legal conclusion. These fundamental concerns need some answers. While they cannot always be addressed in the statute, as a practical matter, they could form part of the drafting history of the relevant tribunal's instruments.

Finally, while this chapter has observed that the ICC Prosecutor has adopted the "greatest responsibility" standard to guide his prosecutorial policy, it may be worth noting that the concern about personal jurisdiction does not arise there in the same way as it did at the SCSL. Although the structure and content of the Rome Statute makes this rather difficult, it may be only a matter of time for a creative defendant to argue that he should not be prosecuted because he is not among those bearing greatest responsibility for what happened in a given conflict. Fortunately, the phrase "greatest responsibility," though widely used in ICC prosecutorial practice, is not included in the ICC statute in the same way it was in the founding document of the SCSL. Its use in the permanent tribunal is therefore purely a function of prosecutorial policy, which, although logical, could also be changed at any time without requiring any amendments to the Rome Statute. Consequently, as a prosecutorial policy, defendants should not be able to rely on the phrase to mount a jurisdictional challenge, at least one that would cause the same type of difficulties for the Court as occurred in Sierra Leone. If a defendant did, it would presumably be relatively easy for the pre-trial or trial chambers to resolve the issue on the ground that the prosecutorial policy is mere policy, rather than a statutory requirement.

31

The Civil Defense Forces Trial: Limit to International Justice?

Lansana Gberie[*]

On June 3, 2004, the UN-created Special Court for Sierra Leone began prosecution of those it alleged bore "greatest responsibility"[1] for war crimes, violations of humanitarian law, and related offenses during Sierra Leone's decade-long dirty war. It was a "solemn occasion," said the Court's American prosecutor, David Crane, whose many shortcomings surely did not include modesty or understatement. Evoking the Nuremberg trials at the end of World War II, Crane summoned all of mankind to "once again [assemble] before an international tribunal to begin the sober and steady climb upwards toward the towering summit of justice." He continued:

> The path will be strewn with the bones of the dead, the moans of the mutilated, the cries of agony of the tortured, echoing down into the valley of death below. Horrors beyond the imagination will slide into this hallowed hall as this trek upward comes to a most certain and just conclusion. The long dark shadows of war are retreating. The pain, agony, the destruction and the uncertainty are fading. The light of truth, the fresh breeze of justice moves freely about this beaten and broken land. The rule of the law marches out of the camps of the downtrodden onward under the banners of "never again" and "no more."

[*] The author is a writer and historian and the author of *A Dirty War in Sierra Leone: The RUF and the Destruction of Sierra Leone* (Univ. of Indiana Press 2005). He is writing a book on War, Memory and Justice in West Africa for Hurst, London. He is grateful to Peter Penfold, Stephen Ellis, Ismail Rashid, Kingsley Lington, and Danny Hoffman for very helpful comments on parts of the initial draft of this chapter.

[1] Ralph Zacklin, the UN's lawyer who negotiated the SCSL with the Sierra Leone government, took some trouble to try to persuade the Security Council to modify this curious phrase and adopt the "most responsible" standard:

> While those "most responsible" obviously include the political or military leadership, others in command authority down the chain of command may also be regarded "most responsible" judging by the severity of the crime or its massive scale. "Most responsible," therefore, denotes both a leadership or authority position of the accused, and a sense of the gravity, seriousness or massive scale of the crime. It must be seen, however, not as a test criterion or a distinct jurisdictional threshold, but as a guidance to the Prosecutor in the adoption of a prosecution strategy and in making decisions to prosecute in individual cases. Within the meaning attributed to it in the present Statute, the term "most responsible" would not necessarily exclude children between 15 and 18 years of age. While it is inconceivable that children could be in a political or military leadership position (although in Sierra Leone the rank of "Brigadier" was often granted to children as young as 11 years), the gravity and seriousness of the crimes they have allegedly committed would allow for their inclusion within the jurisdiction of the Court.

> See *Report of the Secretary-General on the Establishment of a Special Court for Sierra Leone*, U.N. DOC. S/2000/915 (Oct. 4, 2000).

A people have stood firm, shoulder to shoulder, staring down the beast, the beast of impunity. The jackals of death, destruction, and inhumanity are caged behind bars of hope and reconciliation. The light of this new day-today-and the many tomorrows ahead are a beginning of the end to the life of that beast of impunity, which howls in frustration and shrinks from the bright and shining specter of the law. The jackals whimper in their cages certain of their impending demise. The law has returned to Sierra Leone and it stands with all Sierra Leoneans against those who seek their destruction.[2]

The high-flown rhetoric, so unsettling coming from a prosecutor, was perhaps meant to convey moral outrage at the atrocities that marked the Sierra Leone rebel war, but the pathos of it would not have been lost on onlookers: what inspired Crane's demagogic eloquence was not the leaders of the so-called Revolutionary United Front (RUF), whose campaign of terror had brought Sierra Leone down on its knees and killed tens of thousands of its citizens. Instead, Crane was hyperventilating at the opening of the trial of the putative leaders of the Civil Defense Force (CDF), a group of civilians who organized to liberate villages overrun by the RUF, keep the bloodthirsty rebel force in check, and restore a democratically elected government that had been overthrown by the rebels and rogue government soldiers. He had perversely chosen to open his "momentous" trials with Chief Samuel Hinga Norman, Moinina Fofana, and Allieu Kondewa, rather than the already-indicted RUF leaders in the dock. This obvious lack of sensitivity to historical context was deliberate: it was a signal that the SCSL was not there to serve the interests and needs of the people of Sierra Leone, and would even trample those interests in favor of an inchoate notion of "international humanitarian justice." This chapter will show just how successful the Court has been in this respect by examining the trial of the CDF leaders.

It is important to first review the war that led to the setting up of the SCSL in the first place. Before doing so, I should make an important disclaimer. I followed the war closely as a journalist from the time it started in 1991 to its end in 2002, and have written extensively about it, but I am not a lawyer or legal scholar. I am primarily a historian and journalist. The views I express in this chapter are not legal judgments, although I will be citing several legal opinions. I examine the evidence presented in the Court against my knowledge of the war and the findings of other scholars, mainly the anthropologists Danny Hoffman and Tim Kelsall, both of whom have written very insightfully of the CDF trial, and with whom I have engaged with this issue for many years now.

I. THE SIERRA LEONE WAR 1991–2002

Sierra Leone's war started in March 1991 when Foday Saybanah Sankoh, a self-adoring former army corporal, led a petty army from territories controlled by then insurgent leader, Charles Taylor, in Liberia into southern and eastern Sierra Leone.[3] Like Taylor, Sankoh had

---

[2] Transcripts of SCSL Trial (June 3, 2004), http://www.sc-sl.org/LinkClick.aspx?fileticket=S5UdSAv95zk%3d&t abid=154.

[3] For more on the war, see PAUL RICHARDS, FIGHTING FOR THE RAINFOREST: WAR, RESOURCES AND YOUTH IN SIERRA LEONE (1996); LANSANA GBERIE, A DIRTY WAR IN WEST AFRICA: THE RUF AND THE DESTRUCTION OF SIERRA LEONE (2005); DAVID KEEN, CONFLICT AND COLLUSION IN SIERRA LEONE (2005); the Sierra Leone Truth and Reconciliation (TRC) report, WITNESS TO TRUTH (2004); and BETWEEN DEMOCRACY AND TERROR: THE SIERRA LEONE CIVIL WAR (Ibrahim Abdullah ed., 2004).

trained in Libya and, according to the trial judgment in the case of Taylor delivered on April 26, 2012, met Taylor there. The trial judges, however, rejected the Prosecution's over-drawn argument that Taylor and Sankoh "made common cause" in Libya to wage wars in West Africa. The 2493-page trial judgment, including annexes of maps, sources, and a long table of authorities, found "beyond reasonable doubt" that Taylor was the principal foreign supporter and mentor of the RUF. The judges wrote that he knew about the RUF's atroc-ities while playing that role. Diamonds mined or stolen at gunpoint by the RUF in Sierra Leone were taken to Taylor in Liberia for "safekeeping" – or in exchange for weapons. The Chamber unanimously found that Taylor's support for the RUF was driven by pillage not politics.[4]

The judgment accepted the Prosecution's submission that Taylor facilitated the training of RUF recruits in Liberia and helped launched the RUF's war, noting that Taylor's National Patriotic Front of Liberia (NPFL) forces "actively participated" in the rebels' initial invasion in March 1991. The Court, presided over by Samoan Judge Richard Lussick, had on April 26, 2012 found Taylor guilty of five counts of crimes against humanity, five counts of war crimes, and one count of other serious violations of international humanitarian law perpe-trated by Sierra Leone's RUF rebels. Taylor was convicted as planner, aider, and abettor of murder, rape, other inhumane acts, acts of terrorism, pillage, outrages upon personal dig-nity, and conscripting or enlisting children under fifteen years. However, striking a balance between the Prosecution's claim that Taylor "effectively controlled" and led the RUF at this point, and Taylor's claim that only former NPFL members joined Sankoh, and that he had nothing to do with the RUF after the Sierra Leone invasion, the judgment delicately noted that the Prosecution did not prove beyond reasonable doubt that Sankoh took orders from Taylor – or that Taylor participated in the planning of the invasion.

There is no dispute, however, that Sankoh spent considerable time with Taylor's NPFL forces in Liberia at the initial stages of Liberia's civil war (from 1989 to 1991) and that he recruited and trained most of his initial RUF fighting force under Taylor's patronage in territory controlled by the NPFL in Liberia.[5] This is of particular interest because the SCSL Prosecutors have charged that Taylor and Sankoh made "common cause" to launch a war in Sierra Leone from their time in Libya as well as in Taylor's territory in Liberia at about this time. The Prosecutors charge that this was in furtherance of a "joint criminal enterprise" (JCE) to loot Sierra Leone's mineral resources, mainly diamonds, as Simon Meisenberg, Wayne Jordash, and Scott Martin discuss in their chapter contributions to this volume. Although Trial Chamber II has ruled unanimously that Taylor was a planner, aider, and abettor of the RUF in Sierra Leone, the Judges have determined that the two men supported each other because of the confluence of mutual interests and, in what some are arguing was a loss for the Prosecution, they dismissed the JCE charges.

SCSL trial transcripts[6] show that all the so-called Vanguards – the fighters who con-stituted the original invading RUF force from Liberia – were trained at Camp Naama in Taylor's occupied territory in Liberia by Isaac Mongor, a Liberian NPFL who had been a

---

[4] Trial Chamber II of the Special Court for Sierra Leone, Judgment in Prosecutor v. Charles Taylor (Apr. 26, 2012) (SCSL website last visited on July 14, 2012).

[5] See 3A WITNESS TO TRUTH: REPORT OF SIERRA LEONE'S TRUTH AND RECONCILIATION COMMISSION, at para. 126 (2004).

[6] The trial transcripts from the SCSL's website, http://www.sc-sl.org (last visited Nov. 1, 2011).

guard at Monrovia's Executive Mansion (the presidential palace). These included future leaders of the RUF: Issa Sesay, Sam Bockarie, and Morris Kallon. Sankoh was clearly now leader of the RUF; Rashid Mansaray was battlefront commander (and No. 2 in the RUF hierarchy), and Mohamed Tarawalie was battlefield commander (No. 3). All three had trained in Libya, and were known as Special Forces. The Prosecution's argument that Taylor "created and effectively controlled the RUF" is based on these allegations, as well as on the evidence that the majority of the original RUF fighters who entered Sierra Leone in 1991 were Liberians who were members of Taylor's NPFL.[7] Trial transcripts show several witnesses testifying that many of the Sierra Leoneans who were recruited into the RUF at that point were already prisoners held by Taylor's forces, and almost certainly would have been executed had they not joined Sankoh's RUF.

On this, even Taylor's defense conceded, noting in its final brief that

> Recruitment into the RUF was accomplished in part by deceit and blackmail; and many were … reluctant volunteers preferring the relative safety of joining the RUF to the prospect of indefinite detention in a NPFL camp. The Sierra Leoneans recruited by Sankoh were predominantly expatriate Sierra Leoneans from Liberia and Ivory Coast.[8]

But the lawyers noted, in defense of their client's claim that he never entered into a pact with the Sankoh before the launch of the RUF war, that only "former members of the NPFL and some ordinary citizens of Liberia chose to throw in their lot with the RUF."[9] Even Issa Sesay testified that he was forced to join the RUF on threat of death. A key prosecution witness testified that the RUF's plan to attack Sierra Leone was drawn at Voinjama between Taylor and Sankoh.[10]

Witness to Truth, the report of the Truth and Reconciliation Commission (TRC) in 2004, estimated that as many as 1,600 NPFL fighters were involved in the early phase of the Sierra Leonean war,[11] or about 80 percent of the RUF forces. This grew to 2,000 within a few months of the invasion. The report called the original RUF recruits in Liberia "detainee-turned-vanguards," noting that:

> Sankoh personally accompanied members of NPFL "hit squads" who visited some of the detention facilities, apparently for the sole purpose of enlisting the men and women he wanted to make into his first revolutionary commandos … Sankoh's favored means of recruitment depended on convincing people that their lives lay squarely in his hands and that if they refused to join him, they would be responsible for their own fate – effectively, he blackmailed them into becoming members of the RUF. Many of those enlisted by this means were acutely aware of what Sankoh was doing, but were equally powerless to prevent it in view of the all-pervading dangers at that time of being a Sierra Leonean in Liberia.[12]

The war's impact on the course of Sierra Leone's history was almost immediately dramatic. A year after it started, disgruntled young soldiers fighting the RUF in the eastern part of the country descended on the capital, Freetown, and overthrew the feckless one-party state

---

[7] *Prosecution Final Trial Brief: Public Version* (SCSL's website), at 22 (Jan. 17, 2011).

[8] *Defence Final Brief: Public Version* (on SCSL's website) (May 23, 2011).

[9] *Defence Final Brief: Public Version* (on SCSL's website) (May 23, 2011).

[10] *Prosecution Final Trial Brief: Public Version*, *supra* note 7.

[11] Witness to Truth: Report of Sierra Leone's Truth and Reconciliation Commission, *supra* note 5.

[12] *Id.*

government of President (formerly Major General) Joseph Saidu Momoh. The soldiers instituted what they were pleased to call the National Provisional Ruling Council (NPRC) junta. The NPRC hired mercenary forces to help them fight the RUF and, failing to defeat the group, was forced to organize elections, which Tejan Kabbah, a former UN civil servant leading the Sierra Leone Peoples Party (SLPP) won in 1996. Before the elections, the NPRC, convinced that it could not win the war militarily, and disabled by its own disloyal soldiers, had initiated direct talks with the RUF leadership aimed at forging a peaceful resolution of the conflict.

The conflict was characterized by vandalism and terror, and soon enough, it became evident that pillage – of mainly the country's forest resources and diamond mines – was a far greater motivation than politics. Sierra Leone's feeble and corrupt army almost imploded, with a large number of its members collaborating with the RUF. Hundreds of thousands of the country's rural population were displaced by the fighting. It was out of this dreary displacement that various civil defense forces, including the Kamajors, the Gbenthis, Tamaboros, Donsos, and Kapras, emerged. The Kamajors, which became the most important of these civil defense militias, mobilized mainly from makeshift displaced peoples' camps, drew on the traditional coherence and resources of a putative hunters' guild, and organized to fight back the rebels and reclaim their lost villages and towns. They soon became the only bulwark against the complete overrunning of the country by the RUF.

Danny Hoffman's very penetrating account of the CDF[13] has traced its origins as early as April 1991 (a month after the war started) to the pioneering effort of Captain Prince Benjamin Hirsch's in Segbwema, eastern Sierra Leone. The idea spread after Hirsch was killed in suspicious circumstances: "Fearing the military as much as the rebels," Hoffman writes, "many communities organized civil defense committees or civil defense units, mostly groups of local youth manning roadblocks, interrogating strangers, or conducting defensive patrols." These early efforts "lacked a central command and fixed organizational structure." This started to change as the war spread, and as it became clear after the NPRC coup that some army officers who remained loyal to the overthrown All Peoples Congress (APC) government were actively sabotaging the NPRC's war efforts by collaborating with the RUF at various levels (the *Sobel* phenomenon). Dr. Alpha Lavalie organized EREDCOM in Kenema, which was "one of the largest and most successful of these civil defense efforts." Lavalie, too, was murdered, undoubtedly by the Sobels.

For the purposes of the trials, however, the SCSL asserted that the CDF "fought between November 1996 and December 1999." November 1996 was when the first substantive peace agreement (Abidjan Accord) between the Sierra Leone government and the RUF was signed, and it was chosen as the starting point for the Court's temporal jurisdiction because, in the words of Ralph Zacklin, the senior UN lawyer who negotiated the setting up of the Court with the Sierra Leone government, this "would have the benefit of putting the Sierra Leone conflict in perspective without unnecessarily extending the temporal jurisdiction of the Special Court."[14] In the view of the SCSL, the CDF was most active after the overthrow of Kabbah – who had negotiated the Abidjan Accord – in May 1997 to the end of 1999, after

---

[13] Danny Hoffman, The War Machines: Young Men and Violence in Sierra Leone and Liberia (2011).
[14] *Report of the Secretary-General on the Establishment of a Special Court for Sierra Leone*, U.N. Doc. S/2000/915 (Oct. 4, 2000).

which thousands of UN troops were brought to the country to disarm all combatants and help establish normative order. Calling itself the Armed Forces Ruling Council (AFRC), the junta, which unseated Kabbah, turned out to be nothing more than bloody chaos. The AFRC was unseated in 1998 by West African troops led by Nigeria and significantly backed by the CDF. Kabbah was reinstated, but the rebels resurged and attacked Freetown once again in January 1999. Once again the CDF helped to push back the rebels, but only after they had killed over five thousand people in a scorched earth campaign of terror against civilians, and after crudely amputating and maiming nearly a thousand. These atrocities finally led to the creation of the UN mission (UNAMSIL) that brought in thousands of troops as peacekeepers.

As Hoffman has insightfully noted, it was the CDF's role in the reinstatement of Kabbah, and in defending Freetown in January–February 1999, that warranted the indictment of its leaders by the SCSL:

> The CDF moved from defending rural communities to fighting to reinstate an elected government, and to protecting that government from a military that had proven itself to be uncooperative, it grew much harder to construe the force as a grassroots mobilization of society against the state. The Black December operation and the other efforts by the CDF to restore the SLPP shifted the "defensive" role of the militia from one of defending rural communities to defending the state – albeit in the form of the SLPP party and a certain fantasy of democratic governance. The militia grew more predatory and more abusive toward the population it was ostensibly meant to defend (though it never approached the thoroughly paranoid, necropolitical mode of violent authority exercised by the AFRC and RUF).[15]

It is important to note that in its final report – after collecting thousands of testimonies and holding many public hearings – the TRC concluded that overall the RUF committed 60.5 percent of the atrocities committed during the war in Sierra Leone; the AFRC 9.8 percent; the Sierra Leone Army 6.8 percent; the CDF (mainly Kamajors) 6 percent; and ECOMOG, the Nigerian-led West African intervention force, 1 percent.

II. WHY CHARGE THE CDF?

Of all the questions relating to the SCSL trial of the CDF, the most mysterious remains the one regarding who prompted, or influenced, the Prosecutor's decision to put the civil defense group on trial in the first place. The SCSL Prosecutor was given wide discretionary powers by the statute setting up the court, so his indicting the CDF leaders does not raise legal issues: it was within his rights to do so. Still the decision, given the historic role of the CDF in the war, was hugely perplexing. The apparent fanaticism of Crane – he believed that everyone in Sierra Leone was compromised by the war, and that all the factions were equally culpable in atrocities, despite all the evidence – was clearly a factor.[16] Crane had the

---

[15] Hoffman discusses this transition in the enormously interesting ch. 3 of THE WAR MACHINES, *supra* note 13, at 88–123.

[16] Crane told the former U.K. High Commissioner to Sierra Leone, Peter Penfold, that he indicted the leaders because he wanted to be "evenhanded": in other words, he feared being seen as having anti-RUF bias if he had indicted only the RUF and its rogue military accomplices (author's interview with Penfold, Apr. 12, 2012). It is hard to take such a prosecutor seriously. Never one to shy away from expressing his strongly held views, Crane has made pretty much the same points in several of his publications on his role as Prosecutor.

powers to indict even the president, not to mention senior ministers in the sitting govern-ment whose guest he was – he spoke often of following the evidence "wherever it leads." But it is hard to imagine him going against the wishes of the government, a crucially important partner of the SCSL, without clear signals from President Kabbah himself. In his memoir, *Coming from the Brink*, Kabbah largely skirts the issue of his own responsibility for the Court's decision in this particular respect, and instead resorts to legalese, rather than intro-spection or a proper analysis of the Court's impact, to account for his dealings with the tribunal.[17]

This is a very telling omission, as the records show that Kabbah's government was intensely involved in all the key decisions relating to the setting up of the Court, includ-ing its mandate, temporal jurisdiction, and the category of persons who could be indicted. Kabbah's government, for example, showed itself interested in such details as whether the Court should indict children, in a meeting with a critical UN Security Council mission, led by the U.K.'s Permanent Representative Jeremy Greenstock (who visited Sierra Leone in October 2000). In the mission's report, we read (rather chillingly, one might add):

> The possibility that children could be prosecuted by the Special Court was the subject of animated debate in Sierra Leone and there appeared to be no prevailing view. In the view of the Government of Sierra Leone, the Court should prosecute those child combatants who freely and willingly committed indictable crimes. On the other hand, non-governmental organizations and United Nations agencies, especially those engaged in the protection of children, favoured excluding those under the age of 18 years. In Lungi, the mission heard a passionate appeal from a 14-year-old ex-combatant, on behalf of his fellows, not to try any children. Members of the mission made it publicly clear that the purpose was to indict only those persons who bore the greatest responsibility.[18]

Also, Zacklin noted in his report issued the same month the same sentiments: "The Government of Sierra Leone and representatives of Sierra Leone civil society clearly wish to see a process of judicial accountability for child combatants presumed responsible for the crimes falling within the jurisdiction of the Court." However, he noted:

> It was said that the people of Sierra Leone would not look kindly upon a court which failed to bring to justice children who committed crimes of that nature and spared them the judi-cial process of accountability. The international non-governmental organizations respon-sible for childcare and rehabilitation programmes, together with some of their national counterparts, however, were unanimous in their objection to any kind of judicial account-ability for children below 18 years of age for fear that such a process would place at risk the entire rehabilitation programme so painstakingly achieved.[19]

In none of these reports, however, is there any hint that the pro-government CDF would be a subject of serious investigation, let alone indictment, by the SCSL. Crane's indictment of the CDF, therefore, came as something of a surprise to many people in Sierra Leone, more

---

See *Dancing with the Devil: Prosecuting West Africa's Warlords: Building Initial Prosecutorial Strategy for an International Tribunal after Third World Armed Conflicts*, 37 CASE W. RES. J. INT'L L. 1. (2005).

[17] AHMED TEJAN KABBAH, COMING FROM THE BRINK: A MEMOIR (2011).

[18] *Report of Security Council Mission to Sierra Leone* (S/2000/992) (Oct. 16, 2000).

[19] *Report of the Secretary-General on the Establishment of a Special Court for Sierra Leone*, U.N. DOC. S/2000/915 (Oct. 4, 2000).

so as he opened the SCSL trial with it. The indictment described the CDF as a fighting force that believed it could be made immune to bullets through "cultish rituals"; that wilfully destroyed villages and towns; and that committed cannibalism, mutilation, and evisceration on alleged rebels and collaborators.

Crane's charge-sheet was long. The first part of the Indictment was largely forensic or rhetorical: it described, in colorful details, the conditions and ideas that supposedly guided the activities of the CDF. The purpose of the CDF, it said, was "to use any means necessary to defeat the RUF and AFRC forces and to gain and exercise control over Sierra Leone territory." The CDF sought to do this by the "complete elimination of the RUF/AFRC, its supporters, sympathizers, and anyone who did not actively resist the RUF/AFRC occupation of Sierra Leone." Specific acts of war crimes are all limited to about the end of 1997 to about April 1998 – when the fighting against the rebel forces was at its most intense – and they are alleged to have included "practices of elimination" of the RUF/AFRC in Tongo Field, Kenema, Bo, and Koribondo. These included "human sacrifices and cannibalism." There was also the conscription of children below the age of fifteen, as well as "multiple attacks on Tongo Field and the surrounding area and towns, during which the Kamajors unlawfully killed or inflicted serious bodily harm and serious physical suffering on an unknown number of civilians and captured enemy combatants." The CDF was accused of killing of "collaborators," including "an unknown number of police officers" in Kenema by the Kamajors on February 15, 1998; and of the so-called Black December operation, in which the Kamajors allegedly killed "an unknown number of civilians" in 1997.

The theatrical Crane declared, his voice rising:

> Mankind has stepped back from the brink of chaos several times in the past 59 years. In 1945, civilization gasped in horror at its capacity to cause suffering. Again in the early 1990s, reacting to the horrors of Rwanda and Yugoslavia, the world joined in a further step away from the abyss and now in West Africa, in Sierra Leone, another bold and noble step has been taken away from the grim jaws of the beast[20]

He alleged that Norman, Kondewa, and Fofana:

> Tragically failed in that duty [to protect civilians and the government] by being unable to push the other organized armed factions out, and in their frustration turned on their own – their fellow citizens – the Mende people whom they declared to be collaborators of the RUF or AFRC in such districts and places as Bonthe, Pujehun, Bo, Kenema, Moyamba, the killing field of Tongo, and the black hole of Base Zero.[21]

Then the inevitable disclaimer: "The issues ... are not, cannot be, political. We have not charged political crimes. The court of law, this Chamber, must focus on the alleged criminal acts of these jointly charged indictees. Politics must remain barred from the proceedings."

> Now defending one's nation is a just cause. It is accomplished by an honoured and necessary profession – the profession of arms – which for centuries has adhered to the laws of armed conflict. The just cause of a civil defense force in Sierra Leone, set up to defend a nation became perverted and was twisted beyond measure by Norman, Kondewa, and Fofana. Under their leadership these accused war criminals turned what should have been

---

[20] Transcript of SCSL CDF Trial (June 3, 2004), *supra* note 2.
[21] *Id.*

a just cause into an unjust effect –serious breaches of the laws designed to protect humanity. These so-called defenders of the nation were really offenders of the nation looking out
for their own self-interests.[22]

Crane noted that the CDF leaders transformed what began as a noble civil defense organization into a JCE that was driven by "greed and avarice." In fact, there was considerable
shock in Sierra Leone when Crane's indictments of leaders of the CDF, especially the popular war hero, Norman. Widely regarded in Sierra Leone as "one of those most responsible for restoring peace and democracy" to the country, according to Peter Penfold, British
Commissioner to Sierra Leone at the time, Norman's indictment and arrest nearly led to violence. Thousands of former CDF fighters mobilized in Liberia and southern Sierra Leone,
but Norman "sent word to his supporters to stay calm and let the judicial process play
its course."[23] In Liberia, the National Transitional Government of Gyude Bryant worked
quickly with the UN forces to diffuse the situation by bringing together leaders of the Sierra
Leonean ex-CDF at a meeting during which they were told about Norman's message to keep
calm; later some of these CDF were arrested and deported to Sierra Leone.[24]

III. THE TRIAL

Hinga Norman was indicted on March 3, 2003, and was unnecessarily brusquely arrested
that same day in his office in Freetown. Public humiliation appeared to have been a key
objective: Crane was determined to show that holding political office in Sierra Leone was
of no consequence to the Court. The SCSL did not at the time have a detention facility, so
Norman was flown to Bonthe Island in southern Sierra Leone, and detained at a former
holding facility for enslaved Africans before being shipped to the Americas. There, he
appeared before a special sitting of the SCSL on March 15, 17, and 21, 2003 where he pleaded
"not guilty" to all the charges in the Indictment. Fofana and Kondewa were both arrested
on May 29, 2003, and both also pleaded "not guilty" at an initial appearance at the Bonthe
detention facility on July 1, 2003. On February 5, 2004, the charges against the CDF leaders,
now detained at the SCSL facility in Freetown, were consolidated following a "joinder" of
the proceedings – by which the three were to be tried together, as the charges against all of
them were essentially the same.

The CDF were tried before Trial Chamber I, comprised of Benjamin Itoe (Cameroon),
Pierre Boutet (Canada), and Bankole Thompson (Sierra Leone), as Case No. SCSL-2004–
14-T, opening with Crane's colorful statement of June 3, 2004 cited in Section II. It closed
on October 18, 2006, after the appearance of 75 prosecution witnesses (including a couple
of "experts") over 131 trial days, and 44 defense witnesses (including Hoffman as an expert)
over 112 trial days. The closing arguments were heard on November 28, 29, and 30, 2006.
Of the three indicted CDF leaders, only Norman chose to take the witness stand; the final
judgment in the case would note this point, but with mock-delicacy, implying that this may

---

[22] Transcripts of SCSL CDF Trial (June 3, 2004), http://www.sc-sl.org/LinkClick.aspx?fileticket=S5UdSAv95zk%
3d&tabid=154.

[23] Peter Penfold, *The Special Court for Sierra Leone: A Critical Analysis, in* LANSANA GBERIE, RESCUING A
FRAGILE STATE: SIERRA LEONE 2002–2008 (2009).

[24] Author's interview with Bryant (now in retirement) in Monrovia (Dec. 11, 2009).

well have been because Norman is the acknowledged leader of the group. In fact, the two other leaders, Kondewa and Fofana, were both illiterate, and were completely lost in the Olympian setting of the SCSL.

The Prosecution made great use, both during the trial proceedings and in the Final Brief, of the testimony of one Colonel Richard Mortimer Iron, a British officer supplied to the SCSL prosecutors by the U.K. Ministry of Defense, as an "expert" on the CDF as a military organization; as it happened, the same approach was taken by the Judges in their trial judgment in the case. But until he was selected by the Prosecution as an expert witness, Iron had never been to Sierra Leone, and probably had not heard about the CDF. He was engaged with NATO trying to develop a doctrine for land operations – as far away from the unconventional field in which the CDF fought as could be imagined. He interviewed seven people (whose names were supplied by the SCSL Prosecutors) for his report, and gallantly reported that he supplemented this impressive rooster by visitingKoribondu, Bo, and a few minor battlefield sites, as well as a few villages and locations from which these battles were supposedly launched. Informing this simple methodology were four questions Iron was interested in. First, did the CDF have a military hierarchy and structure? Second, did it exhibit the characteristics of a military organization? Third, were its strategic aims transferred to tactical activity on the ground during the course of its operations? Finally, was its command effective? In evaluating the CDF's command structure, he focused on the group's decision making, leadership, and control.

Iron's conclusion was that the CDF had a recognizable hierarchy and structure, with the first Accused, Norman, performing throughout the conflict the role of commander-in-chief. Norman was surrounded by supporting staff officers, Iron stated, and there were a large number of hierarchically structured CDF units based in Talia, the CDF's supposed headquarters. This command, he said, was highly effective at strategic and operational levels. He noted, however, that command was less effective at a tactical level because of the inexperience and lack of training of many junior commanders. Communication as well was not particularly good, he wrote, as the CDF had few radios, and in some cases commanders communicated by use of runners or fighters on motor bikes.

It appeared that Iron had worked all this out even before he started his "research," as he noted very early in the report that:

> The *nature* of conflict is regardless of the *type* of conflict. General war and insurgency, whether today or two thousand years ago, have more in common with each other than any other kind of non-warlike activity. It should be no surprise, therefore, that military organizations tend to have recognizable hierarchies and structures.

When he took the witness stand on June 14, 2005, Iron repeated the same arguments, calling the CDF a proper military organization – although, he added loftily, "not a very good one."[25]

This picture was later countered by Hoffman as an expert for the Defense. Hoffman, an American scholar of extraordinary resourcefulness and sensitivity, had studied for his PhD the various militias that made up the CDF, in particular the Kamajors, in Sierra Leone and

---

[25] Cited in Danny Hoffman, *The Meaning of a Militia: Understanding the Civil Defence Forces of Sierra Leone*, 106 Afr. Aff. (425): 639–62 (2007).

Liberia, in the course of which he met and interviewed hundreds of Kamajors as well as countless other people involved in the war. In his brief, Hoffman noted that the CDF is better understood as "the militarization of a web of social relations," and not a military outfit to begin with. This was not simply a matter of awkward linguistic parsing; the characterization goes to the heart of the Court's indictment of Norman, Fofana, and Kondewa, who were deemed to have "individual criminal responsibility" as leaders of a military organization in which they "exercised authority, command, and control over all subordinate members of the CDF." "The Kamajors' very identity is predicated on the protection of [their] villages" rather than as a military force with capacity for both offensive and defensive actions, Hoffman noted.[26] According to him, different units of the CDF operated in different parts of the country more or less independently, getting directives, when at all, from "all kinds of authorities based on all kinds of contingencies," and the CDF simply lack the communication capacity to centrally coordinate movements across the country.

The British scholar Tim Kelsall has provided a most insightful detailed examination of the CDF in *Culture under Cross-Examination: International Justice and the Special Court for Sierra Leone* (2009).[27] Kelsall examined the evidence of both experts, as well as testimony by dozens of key players, and concluded that "confusion or contradiction in the chain of command, a lack of ability to discipline [wayward] Kamajors, and problems in mobilising them too" made the idea of command and control within the CDF largely illusory.[28]

The Prosecution's most important "insider-witness," however, was Albert Nallo. Nallo had risen to the rank National Deputy Director of Operations for the CDF, and was also the CDF's Regional Director of Operations for the Southern Region. He claimed to have been inferior in rank to Moinina Fofana, who was – at least on paper – the substantive Director of War for the CDF. But, unlike Fofana, Nallo, a former mission worker, was educated, meaning he could read and write. His testimony was recorded on tape – so dramatic were his disclosures that the Prosecutors persuaded him to testify openly. The video recording shows a heavy-set middle-aged man with a wry, unreliable smile, his face often vacant or grimacing, alternating between vapidity and latent viciousness. He calmly describes participating in at least three ritual murders, the massacre of at least fifteen villagers (on the orders of Norman, he said), and the slicing off of the ears of one Joseph Lansana, whose mother he also threw into a raging fire. He testified that Norman had on occasion intervened to prevent the punishment of Kamajors who had acted murderously.[29]

Kelsall examines the crucial evidence of Nallo with respect to the chain of command of the CDF placing Norman at the top. Though the Chamber in its judgment in the trial "expressed doubt about the effectiveness of the chain of command for the majority of the CDF's alleged crimes," Kelsall writes, the Judges perplexingly accepted the "single testimony" of Nallo in the important respect of tying Norman to the crimes of the CDF. When asked about his role as National Deputy Director of Operations for the CDF, Nallo responded that he was "taking instructions from Hinga Norman, general and specific, and I transmitted to the war front people." He also claimed to have "sat with Moinina Fofana" (allegedly

---

[26] *Id.*

[27] Tim Kelsall, Culture under Cross-Examination: International Justice and the Special Court for Sierra Leone (2009).

[28] *Id.* at 93.

[29] *See id.* at 46–47.

appointed by Norman as Director of War) to "plan strategies for war operations" and that he wrote down these strategies and passed it to others to implement, because Fofana was illiterate. To this, Kelsall comments: "Aside from the fact that there were good reasons to doubt the credibility of Nallo ... do we really get from this testimony proof that Nallo was under Fofana's effective command? If anything, Fofana's illiteracy and corresponding dependence on Nallo ... suggest that Nallo was the dominant party in this relationship."[30]

More shockingly still, Kelsall shows how the presiding judge in the trial chamber, Judge Benjamin Itoe, put words in Nallo's mouth during the testimony, and these words later appeared verbatim in the Trial Chamber's final judgment. When questioned pointedly about who constituted the War Council of the CDF, Nallo, Kelsall writes, "utters 'Err,'" and then, "visibly chortling," Judge Itoe came to Nallo's rescue with the immortal phrase "the Holy Trinity," to which Nallo answered, "Yes, My Lord. It's the trinity." Kelsall comments:

> In this exchange Nallo appears to be momentarily floundering, perhaps unable to give a precise description of the relations at the apex of the CDF. He thus begins to speak in metaphors. Surprisingly, he is assisted in this diversion by Judge Itoe, who heartily helps him along. In the final judgment, this metaphorical and metaphysical notion of command responsibility appears without commentary: "Norman, Fofana and Kondewa were regarded as the "Holy trinity." Norman was the God ... Fofana was the Son, and Kondewa was the Holy Spirit." The three of them were the key and essential elements of the leadership structure of the organization and were the executive of the Kamajor society.[31]

IV. NORMAN TESTIMONY

It is important to note that for a large part of the period of the Indictment, Norman was in Liberia as a guest of the Nigerian-led ECOMOG force coordinating support for the disparate groups of pro-Kabbah militias who had, by fiat in Conakry, been tagged as the CDF leader. When, on January 25, 2006, Norman was questioned in court about his activities at the time by his lead counsel Bubuakei Jabbi, the SCSL's transcripts recorded these exchanges:

Jabbi: Your own interaction with ECOMOG?

Norman: Well, I have called that interaction co-ordination.

Jabbi: Yes.

Norman: My task was to receive whatever that was a support, whether in the form of arms, ammunition, food, medicine, transport, from ECOMOG and then have it delivered to the men on the ground through their commanders and this was done between myself and the one appointment that had been made in the person of Mr. MS Kallon as administrator. He received and then delivered to the commanders. Sometimes I went there and made sure these deliveries were actually done so they could not be deceived, like especially arms and ammunition and food.

Jabbi: What about the interaction between the hunters and ECOMOG?

Norman: That was strictly between themselves and the commanders of hunters. I linked up with the chief of staff. The chief of staff had his various officers in the field who were

---

[30] *Id.* at 99.
[31] *Id.* at 220–21.

to link up with the commanders of the hunters as they went further into the hinterland of Sierra Leone.

Jabbi: Was that interaction under your personal purview?

Norman: The interaction between myself and ECOMOG –

Jabbi: No.

Norman: Was the interaction between the hunters and commanders and commanders were in their own area of command.

Jabbi: That was outside your own responsibility?

Norman: That was definitely, My Lord.[32]

I spent an hour with Norman in his cell, a room in a small house with a curiously domestic atmosphere, at the Court a day before his testimony. He seemed untroubled by the charges against him – he spoke in sadness, more than in anger, about the cruel turn of events that got him into the cell. In Crane's Indictment, Norman is described as the principal force in establishing, organizing, providing logistical support, and promoting the CDF. What the Indictment does not say is that Norman had been appointed to this putative position by Kabbah in Guinea,[33] and in the presence – and with the endorsement – of the diplomatic representatives of the United States (Ambassador John Hirsch), United Kingdom (High Commissioner Peter Penfold), Nigeria (High Commissioner Alhaji Abu Bakar), and the United Nations (Berkhanu Dinka.) The four diplomats had made it clear to Norman that this was the only way to sustain the resistance against the AFRC and reinstate the democratically elected government.

Of the four, only Penfold, retired by his government a few years before, testified on behalf of Norman. He called Norman "a true hero" who should never have been charged by the Court. Probably through Penfold's encouragement, General David Richards, the British commander (he later headed the NATO forces in Afghanistan) whose intervention helped save the faltering UN mission in 2000, also took the witness stand in favor of Norman. General Richards had observed the CDF in action in Freetown in 1999, and thereafter interacted intimately with Norman for about three months in Sierra Leone. On February 21, 2006, he took the witness stand. He spoke warmly of Norman ("He had military acumen. He was very determined.... But I suppose I had already formed the opinion on my first visit that he was a very effective minister. He was dynamic. He took decisions and had the courage of his convictions, if you like."). On the crucial matter whether the CDF was an organized, hierarchical military force, General Richards said that he had spent a total of fourteen days observing the CDF prepare for battle, "watching how the overall command and control of government forces functioned."

> **General Richards:** So although I take the point about only observing a battle once, of course I'm forming, as a professional soldier, a view of them all the time from all the other activities that an army of any kind manifests. My view remains that ... they were a very brave and, at a low level, effective fighting force. They exhibited what to me could best be described as a

---

[32] SCSL trial transcripts, *at* www.sc-sl.org (last visited Nov. 10, 2011).

[33] Penfold had suggested the appointment to Kabbah after Kabbah confided in the British diplomat that he feared Norman was a "loose cannon." If that's what he is, Penfold advised, then make him coordinator of the new CDF, and that way he would report to you directly, and he'll be busy doing what he had a passion for (author's interview with Penfold, Apr. 12, 2012).

militia force. Some were well trained, others came along for a few weeks and then would go away again, which I know frustrated their commanders ... there were those that were, if you like, mainstream CDF and those that appeared to me to be on the periphery of the organisation that, nevertheless, were described as CDF and I never really could quite – I never really knew which was which except some clearly were more cohesive in their approach. What I do know is that they were vital to the defence of Freetown in January '99. I observed very little fighting in February '99, but we already discussed with the President [Tejan Kabbah] the idea that they ought to be brought into the mainstream of government defence forces, which of course happened, I think, in 2000 – some time later. But there was a clear desire to bring them in to the mainstream to ensure they acted in line with the government's intentions and could be part of a coherent defence force. I think that's probably enough.[34]

Norman's defense cleverly tried to push this line, which appears to completely undermine the Court's expert testimony – a highly significant development, as Colonel Iron was entirely inferior in every respect (rank and knowledge of the CDF and of Sierra Leone) to the distinguished General Richards.

> **Jabbi:** Thank you very much. Finally, General, do you know one Colonel Iron?
>
> **GeneralRichards:** I do.
>
> **Jabbi:** Would it surprise you to learn that he depicted the –

At this point, Prosecutor Desmond de Silva, a friend and former senior colleague of Tejan Kabbah who had been seconded to the Court by the Sierra Leone government, sensing the danger intervened and stopped the questioning. The grounds of his objection are as absurd as the trial itself: "Colonel Iron was an expert witness whose expert report was laid before the Court," de Silva said, the parody of the moment so appositive of the entire trial.

> What my learned friend Mr. Jabbi is now trying to do is to get this very distinguished senior officer, General Richard, to comment on an expert whom the Court has already heard about. This was the very thing that I have been trying to avoid. In our respectful submission, it is quite wrong that expert evidence should be dealt with in this....[35]

It is a testament to the awe that this very experienced lawyer held over the defense team that even Jabbi meekly submitted to his bullying on every substantive point throughout the trial. Needless to say, there was an awful mismatch – in experience, talent and resources – between the Prosecution and the Defense, making our ordinary conception of justice unlikely from the very start.

As it happened, on February 22, 2007, Norman died after a botched operation on his hips in Senegal. He had been taken there while in the detention of the Court, so there was no verdict in his case.[36] But the judgment convicting Fofana and Kondewa on August 2, 2007 made clear that had he not died, Norman would also have been convicted. The judges wrote:

> ... it was not a trial of the CDF organisation itself but, rather, a trial of three individuals alleged to be its top leaders. Samuel Hinga Norman was the national coordinator of the CDF; Moinina Fofana was its Director of War and Allieu Kondewa waits High Priest.

---

[34] *Id.*

[35] *Id.*

[36] The Special Court claimed that Norman had suffered heart failure during "post-operative care." *See* Special Court Press Release (Feb. 22, 2007).

The CDF was a security force comprised mainly of Kamajors, traditional hunters normally serving in the employ of local chiefs to defend villages in the rural parts of the country. The CDF fought in the conflict in Sierra Leone between November 25, 1996 and December 1999. In general terms it can be said that the CDF supported the elected government of Sierra Leone in its fight against the Revolutionary United Forces, the RUF, and Armed Forces Revolutionary Council, the AFRC. Leaving aside the motives behind the conflict, that atrocities of all sorts were committed by members of all the parties to the conflict. Each of the three accused was charged with eight counts of war crimes, crimes against humanity and other serious violations of International Humanitarian Law relating to atrocities allegedly committed by them during the conflict. The charges included murder of civilians, violence of life, health and physical and mental well-being, inhumane acts, cruel treatment, pillage, acts of terrorism, collective punishments and enlisting children under the age of 15 years, or using them to participate actively in hostilities.[37]

The Judges ruled out the question of JCE as it related to the CDF leaders, as "the evidence led by the Prosecution in this case to show a joint criminal enterprise [is] insufficient to prove its existence against those named persons beyond reasonable doubt." They also ruled that "without finding the existence of a widespread or systematic attack directed primarily against the civilian population, neither of the accused can be held responsible for the crimes against humanity as alleged in the indictment." Thus, "the Chamber dismissed count 1, murder as a crime against humanity and count 3, other inhumane acts as a crime against humanity." They, however, found Fofana and Kondewa guilty of "violence to life, health and physical or mental well-being of persons, in particular murder and cruel treatment respectively." Kondewa was additionally found guilty of "enlisting children under the age of 15 years into an armed group and/or using them to participate actively in hostilities." The Prosecutors asked for thirty years' imprisonment for both, but the trial judges demurred on the ground that:

> A manifestly repressive sentence, rather than providing the deterrent objective which it is meant to achieve, will be counterproductive to the Sierra Leonean society in that it will neither be consonant with nor will it be in the overall interests and ultimate aims and objectives of justice, peace and reconciliation that this court is mandated by the U.N. Security Council Resolution 1315 to achieve.

The Judges helpfully added that the fact that CDF leaders had fought "to reinstate democracy, and the prevailing circumstances in which their crimes were committed" had to be taken into account. They accordingly sentenced Kondewa to eight years' imprisonment and Fofana to six years.

The Prosecutors were incensed. Stephen Rapp, the chief prosecutor at the time, described the Judges' approach to the issue as "formulistic," and appealed. On May 28, 2008, the Appeals Chamber overturned convictions of both defendants on the collective punishments charge as well as Kondewa's conviction for the use of child soldiers. But the Chamber curiously entered new convictions against both Kondewa and Fofana for murder and inhumane acts as "crimes against humanity." Using the new convictions, it then enhanced the

---

[37] Trial Chamber I Judgment, Prosecutor v. Fofana and Kondewa, SCSL-04-14-T, Judgment on the Sentencing of Moinina Fofana and Allieu Kondewa (Oct. 9, 2007), *at* www.sc-sl.org (last visited Nov. 10, 2011) [hereinafter CDF Sentencing Judgment].

sentences against the two: Kondewa was now to serve twenty years and Fofana fifteen years. The CDF leaders were in late 2009 flown to Rwanda to serve their jail times there – the first time in the history of postcolonial Sierra Leone that its citizens have been taken out of the country to serve convictions imposed in the country.

In the Trial Chamber I decision, the Judges concurred with the Prosecutors, including their expert, Colonel Iron, that the CDF had a command structure "largely as it operated out of Talia, also known as Base Zero, since this was the location where the High Command established its headquarters for the CDF." They noted that the "meetings, speeches and other events occurring there, and the accused's [sic] involvement in them, [impacted] upon their liability for crimes" committed during the war. At this camp, Fofana, "in his capacity as Director of War at Base Zero, planned and executed the war strategies and received frontline reports from commanders. In executing these functions he was largely assisted by Nallo[38] and, on occasion, Fofana passed on his responsibilities to Nallo. Fofana selected commanders to go to battle and could, on occasion, issue direct orders to these commanders. Fofana was responsible for the receipt and provision of ammunitions at Base Zero to the commanders upon the instructions of Norman. Fofana was seen as having power and authority at Base Zero and was the overall boss of the commanders in Base Zero." For his part, Kondewa, "in his capacity as High Priest, was in charge of initiations at Base Zero and, after time, was a head of all process of initiation and immunisation would make them bullet-proof."

According to the Court:

> The Kamajors looked up to Kondewa and admired him for such powers. They believed he was capable of transferring his powers to them to protect them. By virtue of these powers, Kondewa had command over the Kamajors in the country. He never went to the war front himself but, whenever a Kamajor was going to war, Kondewa would give his advice and blessings as well as the medicines which the Kamajors believed would protect them against bullets. No Kamajor would go to war without these blessings. Kondewa attended passing out parades at Base Zero, which signified that the Kamajors had passed their training and could present their skills. He, along with Norman, and Mbogba, signed a training certificate which each trainee received after the training.[39]

A very different picture, however, emerges of Kondewa from those who actually knew him and who spoke to him and his colleagues during the trial. In what other war crimes dock can you find the likeness of this man?:

> I was born in Sierra Leone. No one sent me to school. No one taught me a trade. I simply lived in my village in Yawbeko Chiefdom, Bonthe District, until the war came.
>
> Many people died when the war reached Yawbeko. My father was killed. My brother Kafu was killed. My mother was killed. My wife ... was injured, and our child starved when we were in the bush running from the rebels....

---

[38] Nallo was the key witness for the Prosecution; the Prosecution made a deal with him to testify against his former comrades in exchange for immunity against his own likely prosecution. During his testimony, Nallo confessed to having committed several murders, and was caught lying on many important points. The SCSL Judges, however, accepted his highly jaundiced and compromised testimony, and used it extensively in their ruling.

[39] Trial Chamber I Judgment, Prosecutor v. Fofana and Kondewa, SCSL-04-14-T.

It was there in the bush that I had my dream. I saw my father and my mother. They came to me with three people I did not know. "Alieu," my father said, "we have come to see you." We have come with them so that you will not be afraid.[40]

The first of the three figures was a man, and he spoke to me about his death and the death of his wife and children. "We have come," he explained, "so that you ... can stop the killing. We have come to bring you an herb [tifa] that you can use to stop this violence."[41]

On the conviction of Kondewa on grounds of recruiting child solders, Kelsall's mordant comment, which could be applied to all the elements of Kondewa's trial and conviction, deserves to be quoted:

Only "an unyielding universalist," he writes, "could believe that locking up men for acts they did not know were wrong should be a solution, or that making examples of such would be the most humane way to reform the practices of a culture ... kondewa ... was convicted on this charge without regard to moral guilt .... And if this is not enough to make international lawyers think that there is something wrong with the way this case was brought, they should consider that the wider ambitions of transitional justice surely require that judicial decisions make sense to the communities in which they are made."[42]

Justice Thompson, the only Sierra Leonean on the bench, disagreed with the Trial Chamber judgment, writing in his dissenting opinion the following:

The safety of the State of Sierra Leone, as the supreme law, became for the CDF and the Kamajors the categorical imperative and paramount obligation in their military efforts to restore democracy to the country. I entertain more than serious doubts whether in the context ... a tribunal should hold liable persons who volunteered to take up arms and risk their lives and those of their families to prevent anarchy and tyranny from taking a firm hold in their society.[43]

As noted above, Thompson's colleagues had no apparent issue with this viewpoint. In the judgment they readily admitted that:

There is nothing in the evidence which demonstrates that either Fofana or Kondewa joined the conflict in Sierra Leone for selfish reasons. In fact, we have found that both Fofana and Kondewa were among those who stepped forward in the efforts to restore democracy to Sierra Leone, and, for the main part, they acted from a sense of civic duty rather than for personal aggrandizement or gain.

They were merely keen on punishing Kondewa and Fofana for violations that they had committed in serving what the Judges admitted was a noble cause. Was there a defense of "necessity" in international law for those violations, they asked? Certainly "validating the defense of Necessity in International Criminal Law would create a justification for what offenders may term and plead as a 'just cause' or a 'just war' even though serious violations of International Humanitarian Law would have been committed," they copiously argued. But to do so in the CDF cases would "negate the resolve and determination of the

---

[40] Kondewa quoted in Hoffman, *supra* note 13, at 232–33.

[41] Hoffman, *supra* note 13, at 232–33.

[42] Kelsall, *supra* note 27, at 170.

[43] Trial Chamber I Judgment, Prosecutor v. Fofana and Kondewa, SCSL-04–14-T, Judgment on the Sentencing of Moinina Fofana and Allieu Kondewa (Oct. 9, 2007).

International Community to combat" the "heinous, gruesome or degrading" crimes against innocent victims whom international humanitarian law intends to protect.

V. CONCLUSION

It is clear from the foregoing that I consider the trial of the CDF to have been a gross perversion: its attempt to criminalize legitimate and necessary civilian defense against armed and highly predatory and criminal elements was both an attempt to distort the collective memory of the people of Sierra Leone and to besmirch the reputation of its national heroes. It should never have been allowed to happen. I also concur with Hoffman in arguing that the trial may have serious implications for the future of Sierra Leone. Hoffman has written:

> The Court's approach to the CDF leaves no room to envision an acceptable mode of civilian defensive mobilization. This is a legacy that would have to be on the minds of regional or local authorities (governmental or non-governmental) organizing against future excesses by the military or by the ruling party. Certainly any political party in power in Sierra Leone will be able to draw upon the precedent set by the Court to crack down on what it perceives to be (or simply labels as) mobilizations of community defence bodies.
>
> And it seems increasingly likely that such circumstances will arise. There are two key reasons. First, such violent mobilizations are woven into the logic of postcolonial African democracies. And second, there is an ever greater push on the part of external forces, notably the United States, to militarize social networks as a form of community defence.

Hoffman adds:

> [t]he possibility that communities, particularly in the rural areas, will be required to mobilize themselves for their own security against the forces of the State or against forces the State is in no position to defeat [remains immense]. Such mobilizations may be as limited as gathering intelligence or as expansive as violent, armed resistance. Whatever form such community defence initiatives take, they will no doubt be part of a more general conversation about the rights and responsibilities of citizenship in Africa today; and ... that is a project made vastly more complex in the aftermath of Sierra Leone's Special Court.[44]

Throughout the trial of the CDF leaders, the SCSL Prosecutors staunchly rejected any idea that politics may be injected into the trial – they plainly meant by this that the political context did not matter, as crimes were crimes. The SCSL, however, was a geopolitical mechanism, and although the fetish of the law as blind and equal is all very well, the same Chamber had erroneously excused President Kabbah from testifying – even though his testimony would have been of immense material and symbolic importance. This seems consistent with the view of Chacha Murungu who has examined that decision in his contribution to this volume. In other words, the Chamber implied that there were limits to how far the Prosecutors could go. The SCSL had to be selective, and clearly the choice of the CDF leaders for prosecution was singularly wrongheaded, and, as Hoffman has noted, could well be inimical to the wider interests of Sierra Leoneans in the future.

---

[44] Danny Hoffman, *Citizens and Soldiers: Community Defence in Sierra Leone before and after the Special Court*, *in* LANSANA GBERIE, *supra* note 23.

32

Lessons from the Trial of Charles Taylor at the Special Court for Sierra Leone

Annie Gell[*]

I. INTRODUCTION

On April 26, 2012, Charles Taylor became the first former head of state since the Nuremberg trials to face a verdict before an international or hybrid international–national court on charges of serious crimes committed in violation of international law.[1] Although it has been a long road, Taylor's trial and the issuance of a judgment at the end of a credible judicial process sends a strong signal that the world has become a less hospitable place for the highest-level leaders accused of committing the gravest crimes.

Trials of the highest-level leaders can be complex, lengthy, and fraught proceedings. The Taylor trial progressed against a backdrop of criticism and concern over the viability of trying the highest-level leaders before international or hybrid war crimes courts following the trial of former Serbian president Slobodan Milosevic before the International Criminal Tribunal for the former Yugoslavia. Milosevic's trial was notable for its sometimes chaotic atmosphere and the death of the accused almost seven years after his indictment but before a judgment could be issued.

The purpose of this chapter is to draw lessons from the Taylor trial to promote the best possible trials in the future of the highest-level suspects who are accused of serious crimes in violation of international law. This chapter is neither a chronological account of the trial nor an examination of the legal arguments, but an analysis of notable aspects of the trial's practice. Section II provides a brief background on Taylor, including his political career, indictment by the Special Court, and surrender, and basic facts regarding his trial. Section III examines the conduct of the Taylor trial, including issues related to efficiency, fairness, and the Defense, and interaction with witnesses, potential witnesses, and sources. Section IV suggests lessons from the Taylor trial that should be considered in future trials of the highest-level leaders.

---

[*] B.A. (Columbia University), J.D. (Columbia University School of Law). Sandler Fellow in the International Justice Program of Human Rights Watch. The author would like to thank the many colleagues who provided their critical input, feedback, and review of this material, especially Elise Keppler, Corinne Dufka, and Richard Dicker.

[1] This chapter draws from the Human Rights Watch report, *"Even a 'Big Man' Must Face Justice": Lessons from the Trial of Charles Taylor* (2012), of which I was the principal author. Further information on the methodology used to prepare that report is included in that document.

II. CHARLES TAYLOR

A. Background

From 1989 to 1997 Taylor led a rebel group, the National Patriotic Front of Liberia (NPFL), which sought to unseat Liberia's then-president, Samuel Doe. Forces under Taylor's command were implicated in widespread abuses committed against civilians, including summary executions, numerous massacres, systematic rape, mutilation, torture, large-scale forced conscription, and the use of child soldiers.[2]

The conflict ended on August 2, 1997, when Taylor was sworn in as president.[3] Taylor's presidency, which lasted until 2003, was characterized by significant human rights violations in Liberia, including the repression of civil society, journalists, and anyone deemed opposing his government.[4] By 1999, Taylor's widespread abuses had fueled a rebellion to unseat him.

During the armed conflict in neighboring Sierra Leone, Taylor supported the rebel Revolutionary United Front (RUF) and the RUF/Armed Forces Revolutionary Council (AFRC) alliance, whose fighters killed, raped, and cut off the limbs of tens of thousands of people and forcibly recruited thousands of child soldiers.[5] Among other methods of support, Taylor traded arms to the rebels for diamonds mined in Sierra Leone, prompting UN sanctions and embargoes on his government.[6] Taylor was also implicated in destabilizing the wider West African sub-region, including neighboring Guinea and Côte d'Ivoire.[7]

---

[2] *See, e.g.*, Human Rights Watch, *Liberia – Emerging from Destruction* (Nov. 17, 1997), *available at* http://www.hrw.org/en/reports/1997/11/17/emerging-destruction (last visited June 15, 2012) [hereinafter Human Rights Watch, *Emerging from Destruction*]; Human Rights Watch, *Youth, Poverty and Blood: The Lethal Legacy of West Africa's Regional Warriors* (Mar. 2005), *available at* http://www.hrw.org/sites/default/files/reports/westafrica0405.pdf (last visited June 15, 2012).

[3] Taylor was elected president after elections that were held under an implicit threat that he would resume the war in Liberia unless he was elected. Human Rights Watch, *Emerging from Destruction*, *supra* note 2. *See also* Helene Cooper, *Recalling Horrors in Liberia Wrought by Taylor*, N.Y. TIMES (Apr. 26, 2012), *available at* http://www.nytimes.com/2012/04/27/world/africa/recalling-horrors-in-liberia-wrought-by-taylor.html?_r=1&pagewanted=all (last visited May 2, 2012).

[4] Press Release, Human Rights Watch, HRW Calls on Liberian President to Cease Harassment of Civil Society (Oct. 24, 1998), *available at* http://www.hrw.org/news/1998/10/23/hrw-calls-liberian-president-cease-harassment-civil-society (last visited June 15, 2012); Letter from Human Rights Watch to Charles Taylor, President of Liberia, *Intimidation of Human Rights Defenders: Offices of the Centre for Democratic Empowerment Stormed* (Dec. 12, 2000), *available at* http://www.hrw.org/news/2000/12/11/letter-liberian-president-charles-taylor-intimidation-human-rights-defenders (last visited June 15, 2012); Press Release, Human Rights Watch, Leading Liberian Rights Lawyer Tortured by Police (Apr. 27, 2002), *available at* http://www.hrw.org/news/2002/04/26/leading-liberian-rights-lawyer-tortured-police (last visited June 15, 2012).

[5] Judgment Summary, Prosecutor v. Charles Ghankay Taylor (SCSL-03-1-T), Trial Chamber II, at 5–12, 13–33 (Apr. 26, 2012).

[6] *See Report of the Panel of Experts Appointed Pursuant to Security Council Resolution 1306*, U.N. DOC. S/2000/1195, §§ 180–193 (Dec. 2000). The United Nations imposed an embargo on the importation of Liberian diamonds and a travel ban on Taylor, his family, and members of his government in 2001. S.C. Res. 1343, §§ 6–7 (2001), Judgment Summary, Prosecutor v. Charles Ghankay Taylor (SCSL-03-1-T), Trial Chamber II, at 15, 18–19, 21–22, 24–26, 29, 39 (Apr. 26, 2012).

[7] Press Release, Human Rights Watch, The Human Rights and Humanitarian Situation in the Mano River Union (May 22, 2002), *available at* http://www.hrw.org/news/2002/05/21/human-rights-and-humanitarian-situation-mano-river-union (last visited June 15, 2012); Press Release, Human Rights Watch, Côte d'Ivoire: Liberian Fighters Attack Civilians (Apr. 15, 2003), *available at* http://www.hrw.org/news/2003/04/14/c-te-d-ivoire-liberian-fighters-attack-civilians (last visited June 15, 2012).

B. *The Issuance of the Indictment*

The Special Court for Sierra Leone[8] issued a sealed Indictment for Taylor on March 7, 2003 for war crimes and crimes against humanity committed during the second half of Sierra Leone's armed conflict.[9] The underlying offenses constituting these crimes include murder, pillage, outrages upon personal dignity, cruel treatment, terrorization of civilians, mutilation, rape, enslavement, sexual slavery, and use of child soldiers. The Indictment covers a multitude of locations across Sierra Leone where crimes were committed over the course of a five-year period, involving six of Sierra Leone's thirteen districts.

The Indictment alleges that Taylor is individually criminally responsible for these crimes based on three theories. The first theory is that Taylor "planned, instigated, ordered, committed or ... aided and abetted" in the "planning, preparation, or execution" of the crimes.[10] The second theory is that he participated in a joint criminal enterprise involving the alleged crimes or in which the crimes were "a reasonably foreseeable consequence."[11] The final theory is that he held a position "of superior responsibility and exercis[ed] command and control over subordinate[s]" who directly committed the atrocities, namely the RUF, AFRC, RUF/AFRC alliance, and Liberian fighters.[12]

The Indictment does not allege that Taylor entered Sierra Leone during the time in question, but rather that he is responsible for the crimes "from the outside ... through his participation, involvement, concerted action with and command over the criminal conduct."[13] The Indictment alleges that Taylor's support of the RUF and later RUF/AFRC alliance took many forms, including strategic instruction, direction, and guidance; provision of arms, ammunition, and manpower; training of fighters; creation and maintenance of a commu-

---

[8] Following the end of the conflict in Sierra Leone, the domestic justice system lacked the capacity to hold perpetrators of war-related crimes accountable. Prompted by a request from then Sierra Leone president Tejan Kabbah to the United Nations, the Special Court for Sierra Leone was established in 2002. The Sierra Leone government and the United Nations agreed to prosecute serious crimes committed during the war based on "international standards of justice, fairness, and due process of law." *See* Human Rights Watch, *Bringing Justice: The Special Court for Sierra Leone* 1, 10 (Sept. 2004), *available at* http://www.hrw. org/reports/2004/09/08/bringing-justice-special-court-sierra-leone (last visited June 15, 2012); Letter from President of Sierra Leone to the Secretary-General (2000), Annex S/2000/786; Agreement between the United Nations and the Government of Sierra Leone on the Establishment of a Special Court for Sierra Leone (2000), Annex S/2000/915; S.C. Res. 1315 (2000). The court is the first stand-alone international–national war crimes tribunal – often referred to as a "hybrid" or "mixed" tribunal – that is not a part of a domestic justice system and is located in the country where the crimes were committed. The Special Court has jurisdiction over "serious violations of international humanitarian law and Sierra Leonean law committed in the territory of Sierra Leone since 30 November 1996." The court's jurisdiction notably excludes crimes committed during the first five years of Sierra Leone's armed conflict. Its mandate also is limited to prosecuting those who "bear the greatest responsibility" for the crimes. SCSL Statute art. 1(1).

[9] Taylor was initially indicted on seventeen counts, but an amended Indictment was approved in March 2006, which reduced the counts to eleven. *See* Indictment, Prosecutor v. Charles Ghankay Taylor (SCSL-03-01-I-001) (Mar. 7, 2003); Amended Indictment, Prosecutor v. Charles Ghankay Taylor (SCSL-03-01-I-75) (Mar. 16, 2006). *See also* Second Amended Indictment, Prosecutor v. Charles Ghankay Taylor (SCSL-03-01-PT) (May 29, 2007).

[10] Second Amended Indictment, *Prosecutor v. Charles Ghankay Taylor*, *supra* note 9, §§ 33–34.

[11] *Id.*

[12] *Id.*

[13] Prosecution Final Trial Brief, Prosecutor v. Charles Ghankay Taylor (SCSL-03-01-T), § 48 (Apr. 8, 2011).

nications network; provision of a safe haven for fighters; financial support; and medical support.[14]

C. *Taylor's Surrender*

The Special Court "unsealed" its Indictment against Taylor, still president of Liberia, on June 4, 2003 while he was attending peace talks in Ghana with officials from rebel groups fighting to oust him from Liberia. The Ghanaian government declined to detain Taylor and provided him a presidential plane to promptly return to Liberia. As rebel forces moved on the Liberian capital, Monrovia, in August 2003, Taylor stepped down as president and accepted an offer of safe haven in Nigeria.[15]

For nearly three years after the unsealing of Taylor's Indictment, he lived in comfortable exile in Nigeria, still a player in West African politics. In March 2006, newly elected Liberian president Ellen Johnson-Sirleaf made a request to the Nigerian government that Taylor be surrendered. On March 25, 2006, then-president Olusegun Obasanjo of Nigeria stated that Liberia was "free to take former President Charles Taylor into its custody," but he remained at liberty in Nigeria.[16] Within forty-eight hours, Taylor disappeared. On March 29, 2006, Nigerian police arrested and detained Taylor near Nigeria's border with Cameroon. He was then sent back to Liberia, where he was taken into UN custody and transferred to the Special Court in Freetown.[17]

D. *The Trial*

Over the course of Taylor's trial, the Trial Chamber heard a total of 115 witnesses, admitted 1,522 exhibits into evidence, and issued 281 written decisions.[18] By the close of the case, there were almost fifty thousand pages of trial records.[19] The court sat for 420 days over the course

---

[14] *Id.* § 49.

[15] The precise terms of Nigerian President Obasanjo's offer to Taylor have never been disclosed. Human Rights Watch, *Sierra Leone – Trying Charles Taylor in The Hague: Making Justice Accessible to Those Most Affected*, 15 (June 2006), *available at* http://www.hrw.org/reports/2006/06/21/trying-charles-taylor-hague (last visited June 15, 2012); *Nigeria Would Shield Taylor from Trial*, CNN WORLD (July 9, 2003), *available at* http://articles.cnn.com/2003-07-09/world/liberia_1_liberian-politics-charles-taylor-nigerian-president-olusegun-obasanjo?_s=PM:WORLD (last visited June 15, 2012).

[16] *Statement by the Federal Government of Nigeria – Former President Taylor to Be Transferred to the Custody of the Government of Liberia* (Mar. 25, 2006), *available at* http://jurist.law.pitt.edu/gazette/2006/03/charles-taylor-transfer-statement.php (last visited Dec. 16, 2011).

[17] In November 2005, the UN peacekeeping force in Liberia had been given authority to detain and transfer Taylor to the Special Court for prosecution if he were to enter Liberian territory. S.C. Res. 1638 (2005). The day after Taylor's surrender, the President of the Special Court submitted requests to the Netherlands and the International Criminal Court (ICC) that Taylor's trial be relocated to The Hague, citing concerns about the stability of the West African sub-region if Taylor were tried in Freetown. Special Court for Sierra Leone Press Release, *Special Court President Requests Charles Taylor Be Tried in The Hague* (Mar. 30, 2006), *available at* http://www.sc-sl.org/LinkClick.aspx?fileticket=gR%2BYCtzTfKg%3D&tabid=111 (last visited Jan. 25, 2012). Taylor was transferred to The Hague on June 30, 2006. Prosecutor v. Charles Ghankay Taylor, *Special Court for Sierra Leone: Cases, available at* http://www.sc-sl.org/CASES/ProsecutorvsCharlesTaylor/tabid/107/Default.aspx (last visited Feb. 27, 2012).

[18] Judgment Summary, Prosecutor v. Charles Ghankay Taylor (SCSL-03–1-T), Trial Chamber II, § 8 (Apr. 26, 2012).

[19] *Id.*

of three years and ten months from the Prosecutor's opening statement to the closing arguments on final trial briefs.[20]

The Prosecution's case began on June 4, 2007, closed on February 27, 2009, and reopened briefly in August 2010. In total, the Prosecution presented testimony from ninety-four witnesses who fell into three categories: three experts; fifty-nine "crime-base" witnesses[21]; and thirty-two "linkage witnesses."[22] The Prosecution relied heavily on "insider" witnesses – often themselves suspected of or having admitted to serious crimes – in its attempt to adequately link Taylor to the perpetration of crimes.

The defense's case began on July 13, 2009 and closed on November 12, 2010. Twenty-one witnesses testified for the Defense, including Taylor and former leaders and fighters from the RUF and NPFL. Their testimony challenged the allegations that Taylor controlled, supported, or assisted the RUF or RUF/AFRC alliance. Taylor's examination-in-chief lasted approximately thirteen weeks, an exceptionally long testimony by an accused before an international or hybrid trial.[23] Taylor's cross-examination lasted almost nine weeks, resulting in a total of approximately six months on the stand.

E. *Verdict and Sentencing*

On April 26, 2012, Taylor was found guilty beyond a reasonable doubt on all eleven counts of the Indictment on the theory that he aided and abetted the commission of the crimes. He was also found guilty of planning attacks on the districts of Kono and Makeni and the invasion of Freetown in which war crimes and crimes against humanity were committed.

The Judges found that the Prosecution failed to prove beyond a reasonable doubt that Taylor held positions of superior responsibility or exercised command and control over subordinate fighters, or that he participated in a joint criminal enterprise. Both Prosecution and Defense indicated they plan to appeal the verdict, and subsequently, proceeded to do so.[24]

On May 18, 2012, the Court released the written judgment, totaling over 2,500 pages. On May 30, Taylor was sentenced to fifty years in prison, which he will begin to serve concurrently with any appeals process. The Appeals Chamber judgment is expected before the end of 2013.

---

[20] *Id.* The Prosecutor's opening statement was delivered on June 4, 2007. The trial phase officially concluded on March 11, 2011.

[21] Individuals who testified to the underlying crimes committed.

[22] Individuals who testified to links between Taylor and the underlying crimes.

[23] Human Rights Watch interview with member of prosecution team, New York (Sept. 13, 2011); Human Rights Watch interview with former member of prosecution team, Washington, DC (Nov. 2, 2011); Human Rights Watch interview with member of prosecution team, Leidschendam (Nov. 8, 2011).

[24] Special Court for Sierra Leone Office of the Principal Defender Press Release, *Morris Anyah Named Lead Defence Counsel for Taylor Appeal* (May 4, 2012), *available at* http://www.sc-sl.org/LinkClick.aspx?fileticket=d%2fs%2ba5HqB9Q%3d&tabid=53 (last visited May 17, 2012); *Sierra Leone: Taylor's Appeal Judgement Due Next Year*, HERITAGE (MONROVIA) (June 13, 2012), *available at* http://allafrica.com/stories/201206130287.html (last visited June 14, 2012).

III. THE CONDUCT OF THE TAYLOR TRIAL

A. *The Indictment: A Complicated Balance*

Having charges that are representative, but not exhaustive, of the most serious crimes committed should be a fundamental objective of a prosecutor in trials of the highest-level leaders. This reflects the balancing of two central goals: first, to provide a thorough account of an individual's alleged role in the crimes; and second, to encourage a trial that can be concluded in a reasonable time period, especially taking account of the reality of limited resources. At the same time, indictments should be specific enough to provide sufficient notice of the nature and cause of the charges to protect the accused's fundamental rights.[25]

The Milošević trial showed the significant risks of highly detailed indictments that include a large number of charges and crimes scenes: The counts of the Milošević indictments totaled sixty-six and referenced hundreds, if not thousands, of crime scenes. This contributed to a long trial with delays in the proceedings.[26]

The Taylor prosecution employed a different approach than that of Milošević, using a technique called "notice pleading" – providing a short and plain statement of the charges to give the defendant notice, while omitting substantial detail.[27] The Indictment, and accompanying case summary, provides more general geographic areas and time periods of crimes rather than specific crime scenes and identification of individual victims.[28] The Taylor Indictment also includes a limited list of charges, totaling eleven.

The Prosecutor's efforts to provide an indictment in the Taylor case unencumbered by excessive details with a limited number of counts alleged appear to have contributed to avoiding some of the pitfalls of the Milošević trial. Notice pleading had never been expressly used in international or hybrid tribunals prior to the Special Court.[29]

However, defense counsel and some observers have raised questions about the adequacy of the notice provided in the Indictment and accompanying case summary. They have argued that the lack of specificity in these materials meant that the Indictment did not provide adequate notice to the Accused.[30]

---

[25] The Statute of the SCSL enshrines the accused's fundamental right "to be informed promptly and in detail in a language which he or she understands of the nature and cause of the charge against him or her." SCSL Statute art. 17(4)(a). *See also* art. 14, International Covenant on Civil and Political Rights (ICCPR).

[26] Human Rights Watch, *The Balkans – Weighing the Evidence: Lessons from the Slobodan Milosevic Trial* 52–57 (Dec. 2006), *available at* http://www.hrw.org/reports/2006/12/13/weighing-evidence-0 (last visited June 15, 2012) [hereinafter Human Rights Watch, *Weighing the Evidence*].

[27] The SCSL Rules require that the indictment be accompanied by a case summary that should set forth allegations that "if proven, amount to the crime or crimes as particularised in the indictment." Rule 47(E)(ii) SCSL RPE.

[28] Human Rights Watch e-mail correspondence with Office of the Prosecutor former staff, New York (Mar. 26, 2012).

[29] *Id.*; Human Rights Watch e-mail correspondence with former SCSL defense counsel, The Hague (May 9, 2012). *See also* Th. Cruvellier & M. Wierda, *The Special Court for Sierra Leone: The First Eighteen Months*, Int'l Center for Transitional Justice (ICTJ) Case Study Series 5 (Mar. 2004), *available at* http://ictj.org/publication/special-court-sierra-leone-first-eighteen-months (last visited May 21, 2012). *But see also* Wayne Jordash & John Coughlin, *The Right to Be Informed of the Nature and Cause of the Charges: A Potentially Formidable Jurisprudential Legacy*, Judicial Creativity at the International Criminal Tribunals, February 2010, which discusses the limited detail provided in early indictments at the ad hoc tribunals.

[30] Human Rights Watch interview with member of Taylor defense team, London (Nov. 9, 2011); Human Rights Watch interview with member of Taylor defense team, London (Nov. 10, 2011); Human Rights Watch telephone

The sufficiency of Taylor's Indictment was affirmed by a designated judge as required by the Special Court Rules and in more limited decisions on aspects of the pleadings by the Judges.[31] Yet the requirements for indictments before international and hybrid tribunals remain an area of evolving jurisprudence. Notably, the ad hoc tribunals have over time required greater specificity in their indictments in order to ensure adequate notice to the accused.[32]

The crafting of indictments that are representative of the crimes committed, but not burdened with an unmanageable number of charges or excessive detail, is desirable. However, achieving expeditious and fair proceedings will necessitate carefully balancing considerations of efficiency and manageability with the imperative of providing sufficient information to ensure adequate notice to the accused.

B. Trial Management

1. Taylor's Representation by Counsel

Taylor agreed to be represented by counsel in the proceedings and was generally cooperative during the trial.[33] Sources interviewed by Human Rights Watch were unanimous in their assessment that Taylor's representation by counsel contributed in a significantly positive way to the generally respectful and organized tenor of the courtroom and facilitated focus by the Court on the key substantive legal work before it.[34] According to some observers, Milošević's decision to represent himself was the single largest problem with his trial.[35]

2. The Courtroom Calendar and Rulings on Motions

The Trial Chamber set an ambitious trial calendar during the Taylor proceedings: it sat for consistently long hours, did not allow excessive breaks, and often compensated for lost

interview with SCSL former staff (Nov. 28, 2011). *See also* Decision on "Defence Notice of Appeal and Submissions regarding the Majority Decision Concerning the Pleading of JCE in the Second Amended Indictment," Prosecutor v. Charles Ghankay Taylor (SCSL-03–01-T-775), Appeals Chamber, §§ 2–6 (May 1, 2009).

[31] Rule 47 SCSL RPE; Decision on Public Urgent Defense Motion regarding a Fatal Defect in the Prosecution's Second Amended Indictment Relating to the Pleading of JCE, Prosecutor v. Charles Ghankay Taylor (SCSL-03–01-T-752), Trial Chamber II (Feb. 27, 2009); Decision on "Defence Notice of Appeal and Submissions Regarding the Majority Decision Concerning the Pleading of JCE in the Second Amended Indictment," Prosecutor v. Charles Ghankay Taylor (SCSL-03–01-T-775), Appeals Chamber (May 1, 2009).

[32] Human Rights Watch interview with former SCSL defense counsel, Pittsburgh (Apr. 20, 2012); Human Rights Watch telephone interview with former SCSL staff (May 23, 2012).

[33] At the opening of the trial, Taylor's first attorney, Karim Khan, told the Court that Taylor had fired Khan and intended to represent himself. However, this decision was short-lived and by June 25, 2007, Taylor indicated to the principal defender that he would agree to court-appointed representation provided the team had adequate resources. The Chamber proceeded to appoint Charles Jalloh, as temporary defense counsel, until the Office of the Principal Defender found and assigned Courtenay Griffiths as permanent counsel. Trial Transcript, Prosecutor v. Charles Ghankay Taylor (SCSL-2003–01-T), at 344–45 (June 25, 2007). Taylor's acceptance of legal representation is in stark contrast to Slobodan Milošević, who refused representation and often behaved in an obstructionist manner during his trial. Human Rights Watch, *supra* note 26, at 70. For further analysis of the SCSL's approach to Taylor's assertion of the right of self-representation, see Charles C. Jalloh, *Does Living by the Sword Mean Dying by the Sword?*, 117 PENN ST. L. REV. 707, 735–37 (2013).

[34] Human Rights Watch interview with member of Taylor defense team, The Hague (Nov. 7, 2011); Human Rights Watch interview with civil society member, The Hague (Nov. 7, 2011); Human Rights Watch interview with Office of the Prosecutor former staff, London (Nov. 10, 2011); Human Rights Watch interview with Registry staff, New York (Dec. 6, 2011); Human Rights Watch interview with Office of the Principal Defender staff, Freetown (Jan. 17, 2012).

[35] Human Rights Watch, *supra* note 26, at 70. The ICCPR provides that in the determination of any criminal charge against him, everyone has the right "to defend himself in person." Art. 14(3)(d) ICCPR.

time by reconvening earlier than scheduled and by sitting for extra sessions on Friday afternoons.[36] The long courtroom hours helped keep the trial moving forward. However, they left little time for the Trial Chamber to deal with important matters outside the courtroom that also needed to be addressed, namely motions.

The Trial Chamber issued many rulings on motions in a relatively timely manner. However, a number of decisions took more than 90 days and at least four decisions took more than 180 days.[37] It is notable that the Trial Chamber became significantly faster at issuing decisions over time: from March 2009 until the recess for deliberations, most, if not all, decisions were rendered in approximately two months or less. More timely rendering of decisions overall, however, can make an important contribution to the efficiency of the process.

3. Delay in Decision on Pleading of Joint Criminal Enterprise (JCE)

Extended delays in the delivery of decisions on motions raise particular concerns when fair trial issues are implicated, such as the Trial Chamber's decision on the defense's motion challenging the pleading of joint criminal enterprise (JCE). The pleading of JCE in the Taylor trial was a highly contested issue: defense team members and trial observers have argued that the Prosecution submitted an Indictment that does not adequately identify the elements of the JCE, and then used a shifting conception of "common purpose," a key element, throughout its case.[38]

The Defense submitted a motion for clarification of the pleading of JCE before the start of the Prosecution's case.[39] The Trial Chamber took over ten months from the date of the parties' final submissions on the issue to deliver its decision dismissing the Defense's motion and affirming the Prosecution's pleading of JCE as sufficient, which it announced on the

---

[36] Human Rights Watch interview with member of Taylor defense team, The Hague (Nov. 7, 2011); Human Rights Watch interview with member of prosecution team, Leidschendam (Nov. 9, 2011); Human Rights Watch telephone interview with SCSL former staff (Nov. 28, 2011). *See also* Jennifer Easterday, *The Trial of Charles Taylor Part I: Prosecuting "Persons Who Bear the Greatest Responsibility,"* U.C. Berkeley War Crimes Study Center 30 (June 2010).

[37] Human Rights Watch conducted an informal review of the approximate time measured from the filing date of the last submission by parties to the issuance of a ruling on the motion for public decisions available on the Court website for the Taylor trial as of March 2012. The analysis – which does not capture confidential motions or any other motions that were not posted on the Court's website – is on file with Human Rights Watch.

[38] Human Rights Watch interview with civil society member, The Hague (Nov. 7, 2011); Human Rights Watch interview with member of Taylor defense team, The Hague (Nov. 7, 2011); Human Rights Watch interview with member of Taylor defense team, Leidschendam (Nov. 8, 2011); Human Rights Watch interview with member of Taylor defense team, Leidschendam (Nov. 9, 2011); Human Rights Watch interview with member of Taylor defense team, London (Nov. 10, 2011). *See also* Wayne Jordash & Penelope Van Tuyl, *Failure to Carry the Burden of Proof: How Joint Criminal Enterprise Lost Its Way at the Special Court for Sierra Leone*, 8(2) J. Int'l Crim. Just. 2 (2010) and the chapters on JCE by Wayne Jordash, Scott Martin, and Simon Meisenberg in this volume.

[39] The Defense's motion was submitted December 14, 2007. *See* Decision on Urgent Defense Motion Regarding a Fatal Defect in the Prosecution's Second Amended Indictment Relating to the Pleading of JCE, Prosecutor v. Charles Ghankay Taylor (SCSL-03–01-T-752), Trial Chamber II (Feb. 27, 2009). It was known at the time of the Defense's submission that the SCSL Appeals Chamber would be deciding the same issue in the context of the AFRC case. Handing down its decision in late February 2008, the Appeals Chamber found that the Prosecution's formulation of JCE, which mirrored that of the Taylor prosecution, was proper. Judgment, Prosecutor v. Brima, Kamara, and Kanu (SCSL-04–16-T), Appeals Chamber, §§ 84–86 (Feb. 22, 2008). After the appellate decision, parties in the Taylor trial were permitted to submit responses to the Appellate Chamber's decision in the AFRC case.

same day the Taylor prosecution rested.[40] The Appeals Chamber affirmed the decision of the Trial Chamber.[41]

Defense team members claim that they did not have adequate notice of the charges they were defending against during the Prosecution's case and suffered "irremediable prejudice" as a result of the Trial Chamber's delay in rendering a decision.[42] While the Judges disagreed with this claim,[43] allegations of prejudice to the Accused likely could have been avoided if the Trial Chamber had rendered its decision in a more reasonable time.

In addition, although Taylor was ultimately found not guilty by the Trial Chamber of participating in a JCE, the not-guilty verdict on the basis of JCE is expected to be an issue appealed by the Prosecution.[44]

4. Two Major Confrontations Stalled Court Proceedings

The Taylor trial was bracketed by two significant delays: the appointment and preparation of a new defense team after the first team ceased representation, and a dispute over the Defense's submission of its final trial brief. In both instances, the Court seemed to prioritize the trial moving ahead over flexibility in engaging with defense requests. This approach ultimately created longer delays than if the Trial Chamber had agreed to the Defense's requests or potentially than if the Trial Chamber had more actively sought compromise solutions. This reality points to the difficult balancing act judges must engage in during proceedings to implement methods that should promote efficiency, while remaining flexible enough to amend practices where such methods prove counterproductive.

Taylor's first lead defense lawyer, Karim Khan, left the case after indicating on the opening day of the trial that Taylor had terminated his representation because of what Khan and Taylor saw as insufficient resources to put forward a vigorous defense.[45] Khan had previously made requests to the Court for a five-month postponement of the trial start date, additional staff, and increased legal support, but the Court denied these requests.[46] Sources

---

[40] "Prosecution Response to the Defence's Consequential Submissions Regarding the Pleading of JCE" was filed on April 10, 2008 and "Defence Reply to the Prosecution Response to the Defence's Consequential Submission regarding the Pleading of JCE" was filed on April 15, 2008. *See* Decision on Public Urgent Defense Motion regarding a Fatal Defect in the Prosecution's Second Amended Indictment Relating to the Pleading of JCE, Prosecutor v. Charles Ghankay Taylor (SCSL-03–01-T-752), Trial Chamber II (Feb. 27, 2009).

[41] Decision on "Defence Notice of Appeal and Submissions Regarding the Majority Decision Concerning the Pleading of JCE in the Second Amended Indictment," Prosecutor v. Charles Ghankay Taylor (SCSL-03–01-T-775), Appeals Chamber (May 1, 2009).

[42] Human Rights Watch interview with member of Taylor defense team, The Hague (Nov. 7, 2011); Human Rights Watch interview with member of Taylor defense team, Leidschendam (Nov. 8, 2011); Human Rights Watch interview with member of Taylor defense team, London (Nov. 9, 2011); Human Rights Watch interview with member of Taylor defense team, London (Nov. 10, 2011); Defense Final Trial Brief, Prosecutor v. Charles Ghankay Taylor (SCSL-03–01-T), § 52 (May 23, 2011).

[43] Judgment, Prosecutor v. Charles Ghankay Taylor (SCSL-03–1-T-1281), Trial Chamber II, §§ 141–147 (May 18, 2012).

[44] Human Rights Watch informal discussion with former members of prosecution team, Leidschendam (Apr. 26, 2012).

[45] Trial Transcript, Prosecutor v. Charles Ghankay Taylor (SCSL-2003–01-T), at 250, 259, 267 (June 4, 2007).

[46] *See* Decision on Defense Application for Leave to Appeal "Joint Decision on Defence Motions on Adequate Facilities and Adequate Time for the Preparation of Mr. Taylor's Defence" dated Jan. 23, 2007, Prosecutor v. Charles Ghankay Taylor (SCSL-03–1-PT), Trial Chamber II, Feb. 15, 2007; Human Rights Watch interview with former member of Taylor defense team, The Hague (Nov. 8, 2011); Human Rights Watch interview with former member of prosecution team, The Hague (Nov. 8, 2011).

suggest that the Court's limited willingness to engage with the Defense was at least partly because of a sense that any further postponements would create perceptions that the trial was not proceeding efficiently.[47] However, the approach actually led to a nine-month delay in proceedings while a new defense team was appointed and given time to prepare. The trial restarted on January 7, 2008.

The Trial Chamber and the Defense had a second major confrontation when the defense team filed a motion on January 10, 2011 for an extension of the January 14 deadline to submit its final trial brief.[48] The Defense requested an extension of one month or until outstanding motions were resolved, on the basis that they "significantly impacted on the Accused's ability to present a conclusive and well-reasoned Final Trial brief."[49] The Trial Chamber denied the request on January 12, 2011, but noted that it would entertain applications to subsequently supplement the final briefs.[50] The Defense did not meet the final trial brief deadline and sought to submit its brief on February 3, 2011, which the Trial Chamber by a majority opinion declined to accept.[51]

Defense appealed the decision and the Appeals Chamber ruled on March 3, 2011 that the Trial Chamber must accept the brief, stating that Taylor had not given an adequate waiver of his fundamental rights to be heard and to put on a defense.[52] In the end, the standoff between the Defense and the Trial Chamber created a two-month delay as opposed to the one-month delay the Defense originally requested.

5. Witness Testimony: Largely Unlimited in Scope and Duration

Under the SCSL Rules, the Trial Chamber "may admit any relevant evidence" but must balance this with the imperative to "avoid the wasting of time."[53] In the Taylor trial, the Trial Chamber took a noninterventionist approach to witness testimony: the judges did not set limits on the length of witness testimony or actively interrupt prosecution or defense counsel during examinations except to clarify details.[54]

---

[47] Human Rights Watch interview with civil society member, The Hague (Nov. 7, 2011); Human Rights Watch interview with former member of Taylor defense team, The Hague (Nov. 8, 2011).

[48] Urgent and Public Defense Motion for a Stay of Proceedings Pending Resolution of Outstanding Issues, Prosecutor v. Charles Ghankay Taylor (SCSL-03–01-T-1144) (Jan. 10, 2011).

[49] Confidential with Annexes A–C Defense Final Brief, Prosecutor v. Charles Ghankay Taylor (SCSL-03–01-T-1186) (Feb. 3, 2011).

[50] Decision on Defense Request for a Status Conference Pursuant to Rule 65*bis* and Defense Motion for Stay of Proceedings Pending Resolution of Outstanding Issues, Prosecutor v. Charles Ghankay Taylor (SCSL-03–01-T-1154), Trial Chamber II, at 3–4 (Jan. 12, 2011).

[51] Decision on Late Filing of Defense Trial Brief, Prosecutor v. Charles Ghankay Taylor (SCSL-03–01-T-1191), Trial Chamber II, at 3 (Feb. 7, 2011).

[52] Decision on Defense Notice of Appeal and Submissions regarding the Decision on Late Filing of Defense Final Trial Brief, Prosecutor v. Charles Ghankay Taylor (SCSL-03–01-T-1223), Appeals Chamber, §§ 48, 65 (Mar. 3, 2011).

[53] Rule 89(C) SCSL RPE; Rule 90(F)(ii) SCSL RPE.

[54] Human Rights Watch interview with civil society member, The Hague (Nov. 7, 2011); Human Rights Watch interview with member of prosecution team, Leidschendam (Nov. 8, 2011); Human Rights Watch interview with member of Taylor defense team, London (Nov. 9, 2011). *See also* U.C. Berkeley War Crimes Studies Center, *Charles Taylor on the Stand: An Overview of His Examination-in-Chief* (Jan. 4, 2010), http://www.charlestaylortrial.org/2010/01/04/charles-taylor-on-the-stand-an-overview-of-his-examination-in-chief-by-u-c-berkeley-monitors/ (last visited May 21, 2012).

The impact of the Trial Chamber's approach was seen most significantly during Taylor's direct testimony, which lasted thirteen weeks. During the testimony, the Trial Chamber allowed Taylor to cover a range of topics that went beyond the Court's temporal and geographic jurisdiction, although they were arguably related to it. More specifically, observers noted that Taylor and his defense team used his time on the stand to discuss at length issues such as his rise to power, general West African politics, and alleged international support for the RUF, along with providing Taylor's reaction to the testimony of the Prosecution's witnesses, among other subjects.[55] The Prosecution also enjoyed latitude regarding the scope of the evidence it presented. As highlighted in the Defense's final trial brief, for example, prosecution witnesses testified to crimes perpetrated in areas not included in the Indictment, despite defense objections.[56]

This approach has its merits in that neither side is likely to claim that it was not given the time it needed in the presentation of its case.[57] However, more active management of examinations by the bench and attempts to focus and limit testimony likely would have contributed to more expeditious proceedings without compromising international fair trial standards. Specifically, an interventionist style can have positive contributions by setting a tone of efficiency in which proceedings are pushed forward and counsel are held accountable.[58]

Some trials, including the Milošević trial, have employed time limits on examinations.[59] However, strict time limits may not always be the most sensible or desirable option. Instead, active and regular intervention by the Judges during examinations to keep them as bounded and relevant as possible can serve as a valuable alternative by balancing the need for flexibility and a full hearing of the parties with the need for an efficient presentation of evidence.

6. Lengthy Presentation of Crime-Base Evidence

To prove Taylor guilty of any of the counts alleged, the Prosecution had the burden of demonstrating beyond a reasonable doubt two issues: first, the alleged crimes had actually occurred; and second, Taylor was linked to the crimes in such a way as to make him individually criminally responsible for them. The Defense in the Taylor trial repeatedly stated in court and elsewhere that it did not contest that widespread atrocities were committed in Sierra Leone during the war.[60] The RUF and AFRC trials at the SCSL also already extensively explored and established the underlying crimes of the armed conflict in Sierra Leone. This opened up the possibility that the Prosecution's case would focus largely on evidence linking Taylor to the crimes.

---

[55] U.C. Berkeley War Crimes Studies Center, *supra* note 54.

[56] *See, e.g.,* Trial Transcript, Prosecutor v. Charles Ghankay Taylor (SCSL-2003–01-T), at 8054 (Apr. 18, 2008); Defense Final Trial Brief, Prosecutor v. Charles Ghankay Taylor (SCSL-03–01-T), at § 40 (May 23, 2011).

[57] Human Rights Watch interview with civil society member, The Hague (Nov. 7, 2011); Human Rights Watch interview with member of prosecution team, Leidschendam (Nov. 8, 2011); Human Rights Watch interview with member of Taylor defense team, London (Nov. 9, 2011); Human Rights Watch interview with member of prosecution team, London (Nov. 9, 2011).

[58] *See* Human Rights Watch, *Justice in Motion: The Trial Phase of the Special Court for Sierra Leone* 12 (Nov. 2005), *available at* http://www.hrw.org/reports/2005/11/01/justice-motion-0 (last visited June 15, 2012).

[59] *See* Human Rights Watch, *supra* note 26, at 62–63.

[60] Human Rights Watch interview with member of Taylor defense team, London (Nov. 9, 2011); Trial Transcript, Prosecutor v. Charles Ghankay Taylor (SCSL-2003–01-T), at 24295–24296 (July 13, 2009).

The Prosecution and Defense engaged in negotiations on limiting the number of witnesses presenting evidence of the underlying crimes ("crime-base" evidence) given that the fact of the crimes' commission was in theory not at issue.[61] However, agreement on almost any facts related to the crime-base could not be found.[62] One reason for this was because the defense team concluded that many of the witnesses the Prosecution identified as crime-base witnesses might also present linkage evidence.[63]

Some presentation of crime-base evidence, even where the crimes themselves are not at issue, is important because one fundamental purpose of a trial is to provide a forum in which victims' voices can be heard. In addition, crime-base evidence could be a powerful tool for the Prosecution to emphasize the gravity and extent of the underlying crimes, and the Defense is under no obligation to stipulate to crime-base evidence. At the same time, the extent of presentation of crime-base evidence should be balanced with the need for an efficient proceeding in which the Prosecution sufficiently focuses on key evidence to meet its burden of proof, which in the Taylor case was the linkage between the Accused and the crimes.

Ultimately, fifty-nine witnesses testified to the crime-base evidence, roughly twice as many as those who testified concerning Taylor's alleged links to the crimes. The Trial Chamber, for its part, did not significantly intervene to narrow the number of witnesses, either through status conferences or its ability to take judicial notice of adjudicated facts or documentary evidence from previous SCSL trials.[64] The use of such tools by the Trial Chamber might have helped promote further efficiencies without negative implications for fair trial rights.

7. A Delayed Judgment

Over thirteen months passed between the close of arguments on March 11, 2011, and the announcement of a verdict and judgment summary on April 26, 2012. During that time, the Court formally and informally indicated an estimated date for the judgment's release several times, only to reschedule it. In December 2011, a court staff member told the media that the Court had intended to deliver its verdict in September 2011. However, the Court pushed the date to October 2011 and then December 2011. The staff member said that the verdict might be delivered in January 2012 but there were no guarantees.[65]

---

[61] Human Rights Watch interview with member of prosecution team, New York (Sept. 13, 2011); Human Rights Watch interview with former member of prosecution team, Washington, DC (Nov. 2, 2011); Human Rights Watch interview with civil society member, The Hague (Nov. 7, 2011).

[62] Joint Filing by the Prosecution and Defense, Admitted Facts & Law, Prosecutor v. Charles Ghankay Taylor (SCSL-03–01-PT-227) (Apr. 26, 2007).

[63] Human Rights Watch interview with civil society member, The Hague (Nov. 7, 2011); Human Rights Watch interview with member of Taylor defense team, The Hague (Nov. 7, 2011); Human Rights Watch interview with member of Taylor defense team, Leidschendam (Nov. 8, 2011); Human Rights Watch interview with member of prosecution team, Leidschendam (Nov. 8, 2011); Human Rights Watch interview with member of Taylor defense team, London (Nov. 10, 2011).

[64] Rule 65*bis* SCSL RPE; Rule 94(b) SCSL RPE. International criminal law expert Patricia Wald has noted the need for judges to allow for summaries of evidence for the crime-base, limit the number of crime-base witnesses, or even have an investigative judge or truth and reconciliation commission make determinations on crime-base facts. Patricia Wald, *Tyrants on Trial: Keeping Order in the Courtroom* (2009), Open Society Justice Initiative, at 25–26.

[65] The Eighth Annual Report of the Special Court covering the period ending May 2011 stated that the Court's latest completion strategy "envisaged that the Trial Judgment in the Charles Taylor case would be delivered

One factor that undoubtedly contributed to the long period during which the judgment was prepared is the judgment's length, which totals over 2,500 pages. However, another factor was turnover in staff, especially the loss of legal officers in the Trial Chamber who had worked on the trial since its beginning.[66]

Although no individual is irreplaceable, new staff can be expected to need far more time to perform tasks – especially sensitive responsibilities such as judgment drafting – than staff who had been at the Court throughout the trial. Finding new legal officers who could take up such a difficult position on short notice was also resource-intensive.[67]

The Special Court offered financial incentives for staff to stay through the judgment-writing phase.[68] However, more effective communication of accurate projections of the Court's time line and greater consultation with key staff on adequate terms for continued employment might have enhanced the prospects for greater retention.

As a tribunal with a limited mandate conducting its last anticipated trial, the Special Court has been winding down operations for some time. Staff who continued to work on the trial through the delivery of judgment could be expected to need to find new employment shortly thereafter. As a result, uncertainty over when the judgment would be issued may have fueled decisions by staff to leave for positions that were available prior to the end of the drafting of the judgment as opposed to risking a period of unemployment.

8. A Challenge for the Judges

The Judges did not have an easy job at the Taylor trial. In the relatively nascent system of international criminal justice, there is limited jurisprudence and practice in comparison to more developed national judicial systems. Trials of the highest-level leaders are moreover heavily scrutinized affairs involving a tremendous amount of evidence and complex charges. In addition, as is common at international and hybrid tribunals, the Judges of the Special Court are drawn from a variety of judicial traditions, which can create further challenges for effective operations.

Experience has shown that the appointment of judges with prior experience in complex criminal proceedings whether as judges, prosecutors, or defense attorneys can help maximize efficient trial management.[69] The Judges of Trial Chamber II, although experienced jurists, largely did not join the Special Court with extensive experience in managing complex criminal trials.[70] Such experience likely would have proven valuable in assisting the Judges in managing the multiple, changing, and sometimes conflicting factors at play in

---

in June 2011." *Eighth Annual Report of the Special Court for Sierra Leone: June 2010 to May 2011*, at 5; Othello B. Garblah, *Taylor's Verdict Due Next Month?*, New Dawn Liberia (Dec. 2, 2011), *available at* http://www.thenewdawnliberia.com/index.php?option=com_content&view=article&id=4790:taylors-verdict-due-next-month&catid=25:politics&Itemid=59 (last visited May 4, 2012). On March 1, 2012, the Trial Chamber issued a scheduling order announcing that the verdict would be released on April 26, 2012.

[66] Human Rights Watch interview with Registry staff, Leidschendam (Nov. 9, 2011).

[67] *Id.*

[68] *Id.*

[69] *See* Human Rights Watch, *Courting History: The Landmark International Criminal Court's First Years*, 10 (July 12, 2008), *available at* http://www.hrw.org/reports/2008/07/10/courting-history (last visited June 15, 2012).

[70] *See* biographies of Trial Chamber II Judges, *available at* http://www.sc-sl.org/ABOUT/CourtOrganization/Chambers/TrialChamberII/tabid/89/Default.aspx (last visited May 17, 2012).

the courtroom described throughout this section, such as: the use of methods that generally promote efficiency, flexibility in making exceptions to these practices that will actually promote efficiency, and provision of adequate opportunities for case presentation while not allowing the trial to drag on and become unmanageable.

C. *The Defense*

1. Defense Teams

A vigorous defense with adequate support is a key component to ensuring fair, credible judicial proceedings. As discussed previously in the chapter, the assembly of a defense team acceptable to Taylor was not without its hiccups.

On the opening day of the proceedings on June 4, 2007, Taylor boycotted the trial and his first defense lawyer, Karim Khan, told the Court that Taylor had withdrawn permission to have Khan represent him.[71] Khan read a letter from Taylor in which Taylor stated that, because of the inadequate time and facilities provided to his one court-appointed lawyer to prepare a case, he believed he would not receive a fair trial.[72] Despite Taylor's letter terminating Khan's representation, the Court ordered Khan to stay and represent Taylor through the first day of the trial.[73] However, Khan said he no longer had Taylor's authority and left the courtroom.[74]

Following Khan's firing and walkout, the Judges noted in court on June 25, 2007 that defense concerns over resources and time to prepare "has been known to the Acting Registrar in general and the Principal Defender in particular since early March 2007 and nothing practical seems to have been done to address the problems."[75]

On July 6, 2007, the Registry almost doubled the defense budget to $70,000 per month.[76] With additional funds allocated for the senior investigator and office space for the defense team included, the budget for Taylor's defense team amounted to approximately $100,000 per month.[77] In addition, the principal defender compiled a list of candidates and approved the hiring of a second defense team of highly experienced lawyers, including what is referred to as a Queen's Counsel in the British legal system and two eminent co-counsels, who began their work on July 17.[78]

---

[71] Trial Transcript, *supra* note 45, at 250.

[72] *Id.* at 248–50; Letter from Charles Taylor to the Special Court for Sierra Leone (June 1, 2007), *available at* http://charlestaylortrial.files.wordpress.com/2007/06/taylor_l.pdf (last visited June 15, 2012).

[73] Trial Transcript, *supra* note 45, at 259.

[74] *Id.* at 266–67.

[75] Trial Transcript, *supra* note 33, at 382.

[76] Marlise Simons, *Liberian Ex-Leader's War Crimes Trial Is Stalled*, N.Y. TIMES (Aug. 27, 2007), *available at* http://www.nytimes.com/2007/08/27/world/africa/27taylor.html?pagewanted=1&_r=1&adxnnl=1&adxnnlx=1338394327-Bt7aa2OFKHLqogLLqxEG1g (last visited May 30, 2012); Eric Witte, *Acting Registrar Agrees to Increased Funding for Taylor Trial*, Open Society Justice Initiative (July 6, 2007), *available at* http://www.charlestaylortrial.org/2007/07/06/acting-registrar-agrees-to-increase-funding-for-taylor-trial/ (last visited May 4, 2012).

[77] *Id.*

[78] *See* Eric Witte, *Principal Defender Assigns Taylor New Counsel*, Open Society Justice Initiative (July 18, 2007), *available at* http://www.charlestaylortrial.org/2007/07/18/principal-defender-assigns-taylor-new-counsel/ (last visited May 21, 2012).

2. Office of the Principal Defender

At the time of its creation, the SCSL's Office of the Principal Defender (OPD) within the Registry represented a potentially pioneering step toward promoting the rights of the accused at an international or hybrid tribunal. In addition to administrative functions, such as payment of counsel fees, the OPD has the authority to advocate on behalf of the interests of the accused vis-à-vis other court actors, such as the Registrar or Judges.[79] The rules also authorize the OPD to provide legal support to the Accused.[80]

In practice, the OPD's functioning at the SCSL has faced criticism.[81] In particular, several defense counsel – including those representing Taylor – have stated that the legal assistance provided by the OPD to defense teams was weak.[82] OPD staff also expressed the view that the OPD model is not suitable for the provision of legal support to semiautonomous defense teams, in part due to confidentiality issues.[83] In the Taylor case, defense counsel indicated that they preferred to rely on their own team members to perform substantive legal work and suggested that providing greater financial support directly to defense teams to carry out tasks such as legal research is preferable to an OPD with a dual administrative–legal assistance role.[84]

At the same time, the OPD provided some important contributions, particularly during times of crisis or transition in the case. For example, after the termination of the first defense team, the principal defender and other OPD staff consulted with Taylor to advise him of his legal rights and the best course forward, spearheaded the effort to create a new defense team, and appeared in court on behalf of Taylor.[85] OPD staff also worked to ensure that the contracts of key defense team members were extended during the deliberations phase, enabling them to better prepare for potential sentencing and appeal briefs and to address any potential issues with Taylor's detention during this period.[86]

D. Witnesses and Sources

1. Management of Witnesses

The Witness and Victims Section (WVS), which is located in the Court's Registry, did a commendable job handling the formidable challenges of witness management. Witnesses

---

[79] Rule 45 SCSL RPE; "Directive on the Assignment of Counsel," Special Court for Sierra Leone, adopted Oct. 1, 2003.

[80] *Id.* However, the Special Court's rules and directives do not provide guidance on the extent to which OPD should act independently of the Registry or the relationship between the Office of the Principal Defender and the accused after the assignment of defense counsel, which appears to be a contributing factor to difficulties it has faced.

[81] For a more detailed discussion of the Office of the Principal Defender, see Human Rights Watch, *supra* note 8, at 21–28; Human Rights Watch, *supra* note 58, at 3–5, 14–16.

[82] Human Rights Watch interview with member of Taylor defense team, The Hague (Nov. 7, 2011); Human Rights Watch interview with member of Taylor defense team, London (Nov. 10, 2011); Human Rights Watch interview with former SCSL defense counsel (Apr. 20, 2012).

[83] OPD staff stated that legal research tasks for Taylor's defense would often necessarily involve sensitive and confidential issues related to defense strategy and therefore could not be performed by individuals outside of Taylor's defense team. Human Rights Watch interview with Office of the Principal Defender staff, Freetown (Jan. 17, 2012).

[84] Human Rights Watch interview with member of Taylor defense team, London (Nov. 10, 2011).

[85] Human Rights Watch interview with Office of the Principal Defender staff, Freetown (Jan. 17, 2012). *See* Trial Transcript, *supra* note 33; Trial Transcript, July 3, 2007; Witte, *supra* note 78.

[86] Human Rights Watch telephone interview with Registry staff (May 4, 2012).

testifying in the Taylor trial included individuals who had never before left West Africa, insider witnesses who had admitted to extensive criminal activity, and victims who had suffered severe trauma. Many witnesses had to be transported from West Africa to the Netherlands, which involved numerous logistical demands.[87] Witnesses also had to be kept safe and secure in both locations, requiring the maintenance of safe houses with constant supervision.[88] In addition, WVS provided psychosocial support to witnesses both on and off the stand, allowing witnesses to successfully testify.[89]

By various accounts, the bench, Prosecution, and Defense generally treated witnesses respectfully during their testimony. However, there were isolated incidents where victim witnesses were treated harshly by the bench or Defense, such as insensitive questioning of witnesses who testified to the atrocities they or their loved ones suffered.[90] It is critical that when witnesses come forward to testify, often at great risk to themselves and their families, they are treated with dignity and respect. This is a matter of principle and pragmatism, as ill-treatment of witnesses will have a chilling effect on witness cooperation with the court and will undermine the very principles on which trials for serious crimes are pursued.

2. Prosecution's Provision of Funds to Potential Witnesses and Sources

Under the SCSL rules, for the purpose of its investigation, the Prosecution "may take … special measures to provide for the safety, support and assistance of potential witnesses and sources."[91] Funds for such purposes are handled by the Witness Management Unit (WMU), which is a unit within the Office of the Prosecutor. No such funds are available for use by the Defense for potential witnesses and sources, partly because it is the Prosecution that bears the burden of proof in the case.

The situation for potential witnesses and sources is different than that of witnesses who take the stand. Witnesses who testify, whether for the Prosecution or the Defense, are eligible to receive funds provided by the Registry through Witness and Victims Services (WVS).[92] In addition, whereas funds provided to witnesses by the Registry are determined on the basis of guidelines, no transparent guidelines exist for the provision of support by the Prosecution to potential witnesses and sources.[93]

---

[87] Human Rights Watch interview with Witness and Victims Services former staff, Leidschendam (Nov. 8, 2011); Human Rights Watch interview with Registry staff, Leidschendam (Nov. 9, 2011); Human Rights Watch interview with Registry staff, New York (Dec. 6, 2011); Human Rights Watch interview with Witness and Victims Services staff, Freetown (Jan. 17, 2012).

[88] Human Rights Watch interview with Witness and Victims Services staff, Freetown (Jan. 17, 2012).

[89] Human Rights Watch interview with Witness and Victims Services former staff, Leidschendam (Nov. 8, 2011); Human Rights Watch interview with Registry staff, New York (Dec. 6, 2011); Human Rights Watch interview with Witness and Victims Services staff, Freetown (Jan. 17, 2012).

[90] For example, defense counsel harshly questioned a prosecution witness about her continued allegiance to the RUF after her small child had been allegedly buried alive by an RUF commander. Trial Transcript, at 12302–309 (June 19, 2008). The bench made witnesses who had suffered obvious injuries such as amputations show their injuries to the Court. Trial Transcript, at 18607–608 (Oct. 17, 2008). *See also* Human Rights Watch interview with civil society member, The Hague (Nov. 7, 2011); Human Rights Watch interview with member of Taylor defense team, London (Nov. 10, 2011).

[91] Rule 39 SCSL RPE.

[92] WVS provides support and assistance to witnesses in the form of monetary allowances, rehabilitation, and counseling, among others. Rule 34 SCSL RPE.

[93] "Practice Direction on Allowances for Witnesses and Expert Witnesses Testifying in The Hague," Special Court for Sierra Leone, adopted June 8, 2007.

During the Taylor trial, the Prosecution's support and assistance to potential witnesses and sources gave rise to a number of disagreements between the parties. First, the Defense alleged that payments to the Prosecution's potential witnesses and sources created inappropriate incentives for those who were later selected as witnesses to give favorable testimony to the Prosecution.[94] Second, the Prosecution and Defense disagreed over whether payments made through the WMU rose to the level of "exculpatory evidence," which must be disclosed to the Defense.[95]

Finally, the parties disagreed over whether the Prosecution's disclosure obligations extended to individuals who received funds from the Prosecution in the course of its investigation, but who were ultimately called as defense witnesses. For example, the Defense made a motion for the disclosure of prosecution payments estimated at $30,000 to witness DCT-097, which the Prosecution opposed on the grounds that DCT-097 was called as a defense witness. The Trial Chamber ruled that the Prosecution was obligated to disclose the payments.[96]

The provision of funds to witnesses, potential witnesses, and sources is a controversial issue for international and hybrid courts, especially when these institutions are engaging with impoverished and war-torn areas, and where insiders – who are themselves implicated in crimes – may be crucial witnesses or sources. The provision of resources by the Prosecution to potential witnesses and sources may be unavoidable in conducting a criminal investigation and building a case. However, increased transparency where possible and clear guidelines for prosecution funds provided to potential witnesses and sources may be helpful to avoid distraction and unnecessary suspicion in future tribunals.

IV. LESSONS LEARNED

Drawing from the above analysis, the trial of Charles Taylor provides a number of important lessons that may be useful for similar types of trials involving the highest-level suspects. These are:

- The appointment of judges with substantial complex criminal trial experience can make important contributions to effective courtroom management.
- Measures aimed at increasing efficiency – such as a schedule that does not provide significant hours outside the courtroom – should be periodically assessed for their actual effect and amended as necessary to achieve desired outcomes.

---

[94] Human Rights Watch interview with civil society member, The Hague (Nov. 7, 2011); Human Rights Watch interview with member of Taylor defense team, The Hague (Nov. 7, 2011); Human Rights Watch interview with member of Taylor defense team, Leidschendam (Nov. 8, 2011); Human Rights Watch interview with member of Taylor defense team, London (Nov. 9, 2011); Human Rights Watch interview with member of Taylor defense team, London (Nov. 10, 2011).

[95] The SCSL rules state that the Prosecution is required to disclose any evidence "which in any way tends to suggest the innocence or mitigate the guilt of the accused or may affect the credibility of prosecution evidence." Rule 68 SCSL RPE. Human Rights Watch interview with member of prosecution team, New York (Sept. 13, 2011); Human Rights Watch interview with former member of prosecution team, Washington, DC (Nov. 2, 2011); Human Rights Watch interview with member of prosecution team, Leidschendam (Nov. 8, 2011); Human Rights Watch interview with member of Taylor defense team, Leidschendam (Nov. 8, 2011); Human Rights Watch interview with member of Taylor defense team, London (Nov. 9, 2011); Human Rights Watch interview with member of Taylor defense team, London (Nov. 10, 2011).

[96] Decision on Defense Motion for Disclosure of Statements and Prosecution Payments to DCT-097, Prosecutor v. Charles Ghankay Taylor (SCSL-03–01-T-1084), Trial Chamber II (Sept. 23, 2010).

- Active engagement by Judges and Registry staff with the Defense regarding concerns about resources and time to prepare in the lead-up to trials may be important to avoid disruptions in proceedings and ensure the promotion of international fair trial rights.
- Decisions on motions should be rendered in a timely manner to avoid inefficiency and negative implications for ensuring the fairness of proceedings.
- The development of guidelines for payments to potential witnesses and sources by prosecution offices during investigations, and greater transparency regarding these payments, can assist in minimizing concerns over potential inappropriate use of such funds.
- Providing adequate psychosocial support to witnesses as was done in the Taylor trial should be a priority in trials concerning serious crimes.
- It is critical that when witnesses come forward to testify, often at great risk to themselves and their families, that they be treated with dignity and respect by all court actors.
- Ensuring communities most affected by the crimes receive timely and accessible information about proceedings should be a priority for future trials, as was demonstrated by the Taylor trial model.
- Transparent projection of accurate time lines, along with active consultation with key staff with substantive knowledge, may promote greater staff retention during judgment drafting.
- Transparency in decisions on the location of the trial, especially when the trial will be held far from the scenes of the crimes, can minimize misunderstanding and frustration within affected communities.

PART VIII

The Impact and Legacy of the Sierra Leone Tribunal

33

Legacies in the Making: Assessing the Institutionalized Legacy Endeavor of the Special Court for Sierra Leone

Viviane E. Dittrich[*]

And it is essential that, from the moment any future international or hybrid tribunal is established, consideration be given, as a priority, to the ultimate exit strategy and intended legacy in the country concerned.[1]

I. INTRODUCTION

The pending closure of the Special Court for Sierra Leone (SCSL or "Court") represents a critical moment for the Court, but also for the so-called international criminal law regime as a whole. After completion of all appeals proceedings in the case of former Liberian president Charles Taylor, the SCSL will be the first contemporary war crimes tribunal to ceremonially close in the near future.[2] Within the next few years, the United Nations (UN) twin tribunals, the International Criminal Tribunal for the former Yugoslavia (ICTY) and the International Criminal Tribunal for Rwanda (ICTR), will also conclude their work and close down.[3] The imminent closure of these temporary tribunals will fundamentally alter the international criminal justice and tribunal landscape. Talk about their closure and legacy is all pervasive. Often, however, stakeholders neglected to recognize that serious

[*] Postgraduate Researcher, Department of International Relations, London School of Economics and Political Science (LSE), London, U.K. Email: v.dittrich@lse.ac.uk. I am grateful to Chris Brown, Mark Hoffman, Charles Jalloh, Jens Meierhenrich, and Valerie Oosterveld for their valuable comments on previous drafts and our stimulating discussions, as well as to Goodenough College and the LSE for providing an inspiring research environment in London. Special thanks go to the interviewees for being so generous with their time. All staff and former staff from the SCSL and other officials, quoted anonymously here, have made their comments in their personal capacity, and their remarks do not necessarily represent the views of the SCSL, other tribunals, or the United Nations.

[1] Report of the Secretary-General on the Rule of Law and Transitional Justice in Conflict and Post-Conflict Societies, U.N. Doc. S/2004/616, Aug. 23, 2004, § 46, at 16 [hereinafter Report of the Secretary-General].

[2] The Special Panels for Serious Crimes in East Timor and Serious Crimes Unit closed in 2005, however, generally are classified as hybrid process within the national court system, whereas the SCSL is classified with the international criminal tribunals. See International Center for Transitional Justice, *Prosecutions of Crimes against Humanity in Timor Leste: A Case Analysis*, Briefing, June 2011, *available at* http://ictj.org/sites/default/files/ICTJ-TimorLeste-Maubuti-Prosecutions-2011-English.pdf (last visited June 15, 2012); Open Society Justice Initiative, *Legacy: Completing the Work of the Special Court for Sierra Leone*, Nov. 2011, *available at* http://www.soros.org/initiatives/justice/articles_publications/publications/scsl-legacy-20111101 (last visited June 15, 2012).

[3] For further analysis of the legal basis, authority, and operations of these tribunals, see W. SCHABAS, THE U.N. INTERNATIONAL CRIMINAL TRIBUNALS: THE FORMER YUGOSLAVIA, RWANDA AND SIERRA LEONE (2006).

attention to a tribunal's legacy should begin at its very creation, not just once it closes.[4] As argued here, the SCSL appears to be the precursor among the tribunals showcasing considerable institutional innovation in its legacy efforts and its own role in legacy production, recording, and enforcement. It is timely to engage in much-needed introspection and critical analysis to theoretically accompany the important contemporary developments in international law. In order to fully understand the significance and dynamics of legacies as a phenomenon and resource for politics, a systematic examination of their construction appears indispensable.

Based on field research, this chapter contributes to a new conceptualization of the legacies of the SCSL. The focus of this ongoing research is on assessing the SCSL's legacy efforts against the backdrop of theorizing the construction of legacies in contrast to other attempts of empirical stocktaking or assessment. That said, nothing in this chapter is either intended or expressed to detract from the notable achievements of the Court. A rigorous analytical approach should not be understood as dwarfing its important work but rather be seen as an attempt to analyze legacy as a dynamic construct, and in particular the role of the SCSL in that legacy. Therefore examination of the development and relevance of legacies provides the often-missing but much-needed meta-perspective. Drawn on insights from constructivist scholarship in International Relations theory, an analytical framework for explaining and understanding the construction process of legacies is presented here. By so doing, the proverbial black box of legacy is opened in order to more systematically examine legacies. Serious attention is focused on unfolding the dynamic and multifaceted legacy construction process and on the SCSL as a central, albeit solely one of a panoply of actors. Furthermore, in taking such a process-oriented perspective, the exactitude of viewing legacy primarily or solely as the Court's own institutionalized endeavor and object of intended and deliberate planning needs rethinking because realized legacies, as argued here, are ultimately above and beyond the control of the Court.

This chapter is divided into three parts. First, after briefly exploring the language of legacy, the proposed framework is introduced in order to conceive of legacies in light of their dynamic process of construction. The importance of actors is emphasized and, ideal-typically, five legacy actors are distinguished. Second, the SCSL is analyzed as a legacy leaver through the prism of the increasing institutionalization of legacy. Third, the diverse legacy actor landscape is briefly outlined, and key dynamics and tensions regarding the creation, contestation, and control of legacies in light of their ongoing construction are critically highlighted.

II. THEORIZING LEGACY CONSTRUCTION

The topic of legacy construction seems of great significance today as it resonates with the politics of meaning and memory. Legacies are a political construct and contest for influence over remembrance, a deliberate selective use of the past according to the demands of the present. It is hence important to appreciate the politics, power, and pathologies behind and

---

[4] See Report of the Secretary-General, *supra* note 1, § 46, at 16.

beyond such construction.[5] Here it is proposed to heed calls to study international criminal tribunals not solely in the sense of abstract institutions but as complex social processes.[6] International legal scholarship has produced invaluable insights into the *legal lives* of the tribunals but has sidelined their *social lives*.[7] The multifaceted social process underpinning the development of legacies has to date been given scant attention. The omnipresence of talk about legacy seems highly relevant in light of the burgeoning constructivist literature on the role of norms and social processes in International Relations theory.[8] Countering the dearth of preoccupation with the actual process of constructing legacies, this chapter sketches the contours of a new framework outlining a notional legacy process with the social construction of legacies at the center of the analysis.

A. Language of Legacy

In anticipation of their closure, we have witnessed what might be called the "legacy turn" in the realm of the temporary international criminal tribunals. A whole host of activities, projects, and debates under the seemingly ever-growing "legacy" chapeau have mushroomed. This does not seem coincidental as the ad hoc tribunals, first established in the early 1990s, are now in the throes of their respective completion strategies under which they will, in a few years, all have shut down – save, of course, for what has become known as the "residual mechanisms" that will have to necessarily remain.[9] Furthermore, the "legacy turn" may be seen as a result of changes taking place in international relations since the end of the Cold War toward an increased emphasis on international law and criminal trials as a post-conflict justice mechanism and an increased number of states actively embedded in the expanding international criminal justice endeavor. It appears that one of the earliest, if not the first, article discussing the legal developments of the Nuremburg war crimes trials under the explicit heading of *The Legacies of Nuremberg* was published in 1987.[10]

---

[5] *See* M. Barnett & M. Finnemore, *The Politics, Power and Pathologies of International Organizations*, 53(4) INT'L ORG. 699 (1999).

[6] PATHS TO INTERNATIONAL JUSTICE: SOCIAL AND LEGAL PERSPECTIVES 8 (M-B. Dembour & T. Kelly eds., 2007).

[7] J. Meierhenrich, *The UN International Criminal Tribunals: The Former Yugoslavia, Rwanda and Sierra Leone by William A. Schabas*, 102(3) AM. J. INT'L L. 696 (2008) (book review).

[8] *See, e.g.*, J.T. Checkel, *International Institutions and Socialization in Europe: Introduction and Framework*, 59(4) INT'L ORG. 801 (2005); J.T. Checkel, *Review Article: The Constructivist Turn in International Relations Theory*, 50(2) WORLD POL. 324 (1998); M. Finnemore, *International Organizations as Teachers of Norms: The United Nations Educational, Scientific and Cultural Organization and Science Policy*, 47(4) INT'L ORG. 565 (1993); M. Finnemore & K. Sikkink, *The Constructivist Research Program in International Relations and Comparative Politics*, 4 ANN. REV. POL. SCI. 391 (2001); A.I. Johnston, *Treating International Institutions as Social Environments*, 45 INT'L STUD. Q. 487 (2001); A.I. JOHNSTON, SOCIAL STATES. CHINA IN INTERNATIONAL INSTITUTIONS: 1980–2000 (2008); S. PARK & A. VETTERLEIN, OWNING DEVELOPMENT. CREATING POLICY NORMS IN THE IMF AND THE WORLD BANK (2010).

[9] *See* Mechanism for International Criminal Tribunals Statute and S.C. Res. 1966, December 22, 2010. *See also* Agreement on the Establishment of a Residual Special Court for Sierra Leone, August 2010, and Residual Special Court for Sierra Leone Agreement (Ratification) Act 2011, enacted on February 1, 2012.

[10] D. Luban, *The Legacies of Nuremberg*, 54(4) SOC. RES. 779 (1987). Of course, the significance and impact of the so-called Nuremburg Principles have been discussed ever since the early 1950s.

Leaving a legacy is not a novel idea or practice. Legacy building has ostensibly become a social and political expectation and responsibility mirrored in the ubiquitous question "What will be your legacy?" This expectation has also increasingly become prominent for the tribunals both in terms of costs and expected deliverables. This is because of the sheer expense of the tribunals and a fundamental realization in recent years by the international community that simply convicting a number of alleged perpetrators may not be sufficient to impact more broadly post-conflict countries transitioning to societal stability, peace, and reconciliation.[11] Hence, pressure on the tribunals grew to demonstrate successes and lasting contributions also "outside the narrow confines of the courtroom."[12] The SCSL will have by far been the least-expensive court compared to the ICTY and ICTR, nonetheless, given its creation in situ, hybrid nature, and voluntary funding scheme, it seems that it has arguably faced the highest expectations in terms of contributions and legacy. Talk about legacy often arises in a valedictory setting when reflecting upon accomplishments and the meaning of being. In the face of mortality, the idea of making a difference in the world and leaving a legacy takes on a particular salience and urgency.[13] Similarly, a parallel can be drawn to the SCSL and all ad hoc tribunals that have a finite lifespan and face imminent institutional closure, a kind of symbolic "death."[14]

Etymologically, the term "legacy" in the English language today (Middle English *legacie*) can be traced to the Medieval Latin *legatia,* Latin *legatus*, and Old French *legacie*. The *Oxford English Dictionary* defines legacy in its current usage as "a sum of money, or a specified article, given to another by will" (1514) or, figuratively speaking, "anything handed down by an ancestor or predecessor" (1595).[15] Historically, the term legacy has known different meanings, yet a rather technical, mechanical element is visible in the lexical definitions. What is strikingly absent is an emphasis on the process behind and politics surrounding legacies, that is, addressing how, why, and when legacies come into being as well as the meaning or effort vested in their creation, promotion, and maintenance over time. In the context of the tribunals defining legacy as a formal bequest by will seems not the most apposite. Such institutions do not leave legacies per legally executable will, even if they leave legal legacies pertaining to the law, jurisprudential value, or modelling components of these tribunals. Two other conceptualizations have figured most prominently against the backdrop of criminal tribunals, namely legacies as remains and as lessons.

No uniform or single definition seems to exist across all tribunals. The SCSL refers to legacy as a "lasting impact on bolstering the rule of law … by conducting effective trials to contribute to ending impunity, while also strengthening domestic judicial capacity."[16] This definition was introduced by the UN publication *Maximizing the Legacy of Hybrid*

---

[11] *See* V.O. Nmehielle & C.C. Jalloh, *The Legacy of the Special Court for Sierra Leone*, 30(2) Fletcher F. World Aff. 107 (2006).

[12] *Id.* at 110–11.

[13] *See* E.G. Hunter & G.D. Rowles, *Leaving a Legacy: Toward a Typology*, 19 J. Aging Stud. 327 (2005).

[14] Using a metaphorical term such as "death" should not be mistaken for attempts to anthropomorphize the institution.

[15] Oxford English Dictionary (2d ed. 1989), online version June 2012, *available at* http://www.oed.com/view/Entry/107006 (last visited June 15, 2012).

[16] Eighth Annual Report of the President of the Special Court for Sierra Leone (2010–2011), at 47.

Courts.[17] A number of publications have taken up this definition making it the most common definition for hybrid courts as well as the one the SCSL explicitly adopted.[18] It seems, however, that it is unnecessarily limited to a very narrow, albeit perhaps practical, conceptualization. It ultimately neglects to encapsulate the spectrum of possible legacies of a hybrid court. Moreover, it contrasts with a broader conceptualization of legacy as "that which the Tribunal will hand down to successors and others" used by the ICTY.[19] Similarly, the 2006 Independent Expert Report by Antonio Cassese introduced legacy in broad terms as remains: "This is the question of a tribunal's legacy: tribunals must leave something useful behind."[20]

The nexus between legacies and lessons has also been prominently featured in the context of the tribunals.[21] The issue of learning has risen to the fore because of a commitment to participate and contribute to the ever-expanding international criminal law regime and perpetuate the developed legal practices and procedures from one court to the next. Turning to the past and resorting to historical analogies or "lessons" for dealing with the present is common practice among policy makers and has been carefully discussed before.[22] Learning lessons in the context of a collective, such as an organization, appears highly complex and constitutes no automatism as the reverse experience of lessons not learned reveals.

Conceptually, the term "legacy" remains largely uncharted terrain. Its general appeal as well as casual usage warrants further examination, summarized here in three brief observations: First, the term is often used in the singular, which seems problematic and misleading. A plural conceptualization of legacy is advocated here in order to pinpoint to the construction of multiple legacies instead of a single objective legacy. The legal dimension (i.e., legal legacy) seems privileged both inside and outside of the tribunals.[23] This, on one level, may not be all that surprising because lawyers, who are the most prominent actors

---

[17] OHCHR (UN Office of the High Commissioner for Human Rights), *Rule-of-Law Tools for Post-conflict States: Maximizing the Legacy of Hybrid Courts* 4–5 (2008), *available at* http://www.ohchr.org/Documents/Publications/HybridCourts.pdf (last visited June 15, 2012).

[18] *See, e.g.,* T. Cruvellier, *From the Taylor Trial to a Lasting Legacy: Putting the Special Court Model to the Test,* International Center for Transitional Justice and Sierra Leone Monitoring Programme, 2009, *available at* http://ictj.org/sites/default/files/ICTJ-SierraLeone-Taylor-Trial-2009-English.pdf (last visited June 15, 2012); OSJI, *supra* note 2; C. Reiger, *Where to From Here for International Tribunals? Considering Legacy and Residual Issues,* ICTJ Briefing, Sept. 2009, *available at* http://ictj.org/sites/default/files/ICTJ-Global-Legacy-Tribunal-2009-English.pdf (last visited June 15, 2012); M. Wierda, H. Nassar & L. Maalouf, *Early Reflections on Local Perceptions, Legitimacy and Legacy of the Special Tribunal for Lebanon,* 5 INT'L CRIM. JUST. 1065 (2007).

[19] http://www.icty.org/sid/10293 (last visited June 15, 2012).

[20] Report on the Special Court for Sierra Leone submitted by the Independent Expert Antonio Cassese, Dec. 12, 2006, § 76, at 61.

[21] Examples include Human Rights Watch, *Even a "Big Man" Must Face Justice: Lessons from the Trial of Charles Taylor* (July 2012), *available at* www.hrw.org/sites/default/files/reports/sierraLeone0712ForUpload.pdf (last visited July 30, 2012), OHCHR, *supra* note 17 (whose English title reads *Maximising the Legacy of Hybrid Courts* whereas the French title reads *Valorisation des enseignements tirés de l'expérience des tribunaux mixtes* (literal translation: Maximizing the Lessons of Hybrid Courts (emphasis added)) and the "Lessons and Legacies I–VIII" conferences on the Nuremburg trials.

[22] *E.g.,* Y.F. Khong, ANALOGIES AT WAR. KOREA, MUNICH, DIEN BIEN PHU, AND THE VIETNAM DECISIONS OF 1965 (1992); E.R. MAY, "LESSONS" OF THE PAST. THE USE AND MISUSE OF HISTORY IN AMERICAN FOREIGN POLICY (1973).

[23] There has been some focus on legacy beyond the legal or jurisprudential legacies of tribunals in recent years, for example in the case of the ICTR; see A. Dieng, *Capacity-Building Efforts at the ICTR: A Different Kind of Legacy,* 9(3) NW. J. INT'L HUM. RTS. 403 (2011); N. Eltringham, *"A War Crimes Community?": The Legacy of the International Criminal Tribunal for Rwanda beyond Jurisprudence,* 14 NEW ENG. J. INT'L & COMP. L. 309 (2008).

working within the tribunals and those commenting from outside, approach the institutions from the vantage point of the law and as first and foremost criminal courts. Still, such one-sided or single-discipline focus may bear a risk of distorting the overall SCSL legacy picture. Here it is argued that the common concept of legacy is too simplistic and one-dimensional. Often, based on a loose understanding of the term "legacy," it is not uncommon that even the singular term implies various meanings or legacies. However, this chapter aims to expose the various legacy constructions in parallel at a given point in time and legacies over time. To avoid reification and usage of a grossly perfunctory catchphrase it seems most appropriate to speak of legacies instead of legacy, thus reflecting the semantic and pragmatic differences. The notion of multiple legacies[24] in turn raises the question of how these may be logically connected, complementary, competing, or even conflicting as explored below.

Second, most often only marginal attention is paid to the issue of leaving a legacy as a social process. In the official tribunal discourse the legacy is generally presented as a product of intent and deliberation. The underlying assumption is that its legacy is highly malleable by the Court itself. Such an approach to legacy construction not only neglects the social dynamics of leaving a legacy as a constructive process but also underestimates the crucial role of various stakeholders and narratives and thus overestimates the tribunals' own influence. Such neglect raises a serious concern with regard to a possible conceptual misperception of legacy and the political dimension of legacy building by the tribunals. Alternatively, it suggests a reduction of legacy to discreet concrete projects that may be conceptualized and implemented by the Court.

Third, especially at the outset of the emerging discourse, "legacy" has been used as an imprecise umbrella term. There still seems to be some confusion between residual functions and legacy. One SCSL official pointedly observed, "The discourse has improved. At the beginning everything was legacy, it was confusing and inaccurate."[25] Although legacy may temporally overlap both with completion and residual or post-completion issues, it is very important to clearly distinguish between these interrelated but separate matters in order to minimize conceptual confusion.[26]

The success of any buzzword, such as the term "legacy" today, calls for vigilance. Going forward it is important to bear in mind the conceptual confusion, vagueness, and malleability outlined. Yet simply calling for the abandonment or replacement of the term seems beyond the point. Rather, the question of how and why legacies come into being requires to be addressed. In the following the importance of opening the proverbial black box of legacy and of proposing a new theoretical framework that places the social construction center stage is highlighted.

---

[24] Few publications use the plural "legacies"; *see* K. Campbell & S. Wastell, *Legacies of the International Criminal Tribunal for the Former Yugoslavia*, Consultation Report, Jan. 2008, *available at* http://jupiter.gold.ac.uk/media/Legacies_Consultation_Report.pdf (last visited June 15, 2012); Luban, *supra* note 10.

[25] Author interview, The Hague (June 2011).

[26] Completion issues refer to completion of the mandate and all work prior to the actual closing. The residual functions such as trials of fugitives, reviewing of sentences, and management of the archives will be continued by the residual mechanisms created (see *supra* note 10). Legacy issues encompass what the tribunals will leave behind and what the tribunals are doing to promote their own legacies.

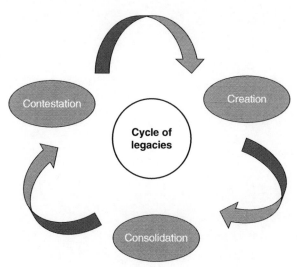

FIGURE 33.1 Phases of the cycle of legacies.

B. Social Construction of Legacies

Adopting a constructivist lens enables a "focus on the role of ideas, norms, knowledge, culture and argument in politics, stressing in particular the role of collectively held 'intersubjective' ideas and understandings of social life."[27] Legacies as collective mental representations are an interesting example of the prevalence of creating intersubjective rather than idiosyncratic constructs of meaning. Similarly, the focus is less on their material reality and more on their value as "social facts."[28] Here a cyclical perspective is adopted to capture the continuous (re)construction of legacies. Such a perspective allows legacies to be examined at every stage in the cycle, thereby emphasizing a point often neglected: there is no definitive starting or end point of legacy construction, as highlighted in Figure 33.1.[29]

Three phases in the cycle (see Figure 33.1) are identified here: creation, consolidation, and contestation. Actors project their own understanding of reality and thereby (re)construct legacies. Consolidation occurs when legacies are increasingly legitimized and institutionalized. Legacies that acquire considerable emotional baggage and become invested with meaning and power may become sites of contestation. The cycle described is best considered a heuristic device for examining how and why certain legacies or legacy interpretations come to the fore.

C. Legacy Actors

The presence and role of different actors have to date been given inadequate consideration. This oversight is problematic for two reasons. First, it turns a blind eye to the

---

[27] Finnemore & Sikkink, *supra* note 8, at 392.
[28] J. SEARLE, THE CONSTRUCTION OF SOCIAL REALITY (1995).
[29] *See* norm circle in PARK & VETTERLEIN, *supra* note 8, at 20.

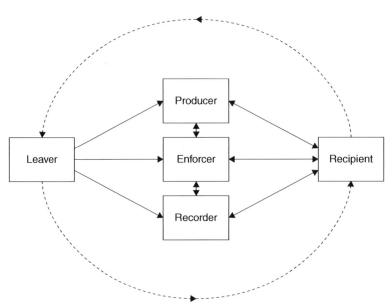

FIGURE 33.2 Ideal typical interaction between main legacy actors.

construction of legacies and the interplay of intentionality and non-intentionality. A focus on the latter puts paid to the common assumption that legacies somehow simply happen or emerge organically. Second, such oversight ignores actor diversity. Not all actors are given equal weight, recognition, and standing by those both inside and outside of the legacy process. Different legacy actors can have different motivations, interests, stakes, tools, and legacy visions that may be complementary, competing, or even conflicting. Legacies therefore may become sites of debate, contestation, and struggle. In this sense, at a given time different actors may perceive different phases in the cycle of legacies as most salient.

Five ideal types of actors, indicative and reflective of the actor diversity, are distinguished here: legacy leavers, producers, enforcers, recorders, and recipients (see Figure 33.2).

First, the type of actors generally given the most attention are the legacy leavers, also called legators, without whom there would be no legacies. Many leavers actively attempt to shape their legacies and how they want to be remembered. It seems nearness to death rather than age per se influences the individual impulse for legacy creation.[30] Planning presumably helps legacy leavers gain a sense of control over their lives and thereby face (or fail to face) mortality.

Second, legacy producers actively attempt to construct or respectively deconstruct and reconstruct legacies. Legacies do not simply emerge, but are made and created; in other words, they are produced. Not all producers, be they legal or political experts or the media, are granted the same authority. Two different producers appear in opposition: positive and negative legacy producers. The idea of production moreover illuminates that legacies may be subject to the logic of branding and marketing and even exploitation.

---

[30] Hunter & Rowles, *supra* note 13.

Third, legacy enforcers attempt to establish and safeguard certain legacies or visions. They are concerned with securing a certain desired content and form of remembrance, thus first and foremost they attempt to claim and gain the privilege of interpretation of legacies. The struggle for the privilege of interpretation is the centerpiece of legacy contestation. Different legacy enforcers can be opposed over the meaning and appropriation of a certain legacy vision, yet even a shared vision is not homogeneous or static.

Fourth, legacy recorders document, preserve, and store legacies for posterity. Recordings may take different forms – academic, practitioner, and popular – which encompass, but are not limited to, biographies, monographs, articles, policy documents, archives, audiovisual media, and museum exhibitions.

Fifth, as a counterpart to the leavers, legacy recipients, also called legatees, receive legacies. Recipients can be designated by a leaver or receive legacies voluntarily. Legatees can be individuals, but also groups, a community or society, an entire generation, or humanity as a whole in the case of legacies that are not bequeathed monopolistically to a single named recipient.

The dyad between legator and legatee frames every legacy process. Legacies are transmitted, or often bestowed, from a leaver to the recipient(s). Their interaction is not solely unidirectional, however, as legatees can act upon legacies and are not solely passive consumers. Reception and (re)interpretation shape their meaning and value anew. The legacy process remains ongoing as recipients take on an active role in continuous (re)production, enforcement, and recording of legacies received as well as those they themselves will hand down to future legatees. A certain legacy cycle becomes discernible with no definite end point or starting point. The actor types developed above are not static or mutually exclusive. The continuous interaction among the different actors is multifaceted and highly dynamic. Legacies do not emerge in a singular fashion as the construction of legacies is an inherently social process involving discussion, negotiation, and contestation. The actor constellation may vary according to the respective stage in the legacy cycle, that is, creation, consolidation, or contestation (see Figure 33.1).

All five types of actors engage in forms of legacy building, as argued here. The question arises as to how much importance may be accorded to agency and deliberation in the process over time. With regard to agency the question of intentionality is an important issue. It is crucial to appreciate the interplay between intended and unintended legacies, but, equally, between realized and unrealized legacies.[31] Any legacy construction, be it intentional strategic legacy "engineering" or more unintentional contingent legacy building, ultimately shapes certain versions of history and creates a particular image of reality or a purported truth. Hence, the politics of legacy construction deserve more attention than they generally are accorded. In the remainder of this chapter the above-sketched framework will be selectively applied to particularly salient dynamics and key actors in the legacy construction, especially of the Court itself. For our purposes here, the SCSL is considered primarily as a single institutional actor. The Court's life span is shortly coming to an end – however not at a particularly old age. As institutional legacy leaver the SCSL has increasingly engaged in so-called deliberate legacy planning.[32]

---

[31] As elaborated in Section IV(C) below (see Figure 33.4).
[32] Nmehielle & Jalloh, *supra* note 11, at 120.

III. INSTITUTIONALIZING LEGACY AT THE SCSL

As an institution the SCSL portrayed itself early on as a proactive and deliberate legacy leaver. The Court's approach to legacy planning seemingly has focused on maximizing its activities and impact beyond its core judicial work. The SCSL appears to be a precursor pioneering many developments in efforts to institutionalize a legacy focus within the institution. Three main steps toward institutionalization are discernible. First, rhetorically, legacy is recognized as an issue, and a formal legacy vision is developed. Second, structurally, institutional bodies or working groups and professional positions devoted to legacy are created. Third, practically, efforts of designing, fund-raising for, and implementing concrete legacy projects and activities are intensified. These three steps did not occur strictly consecutively at the SCSL; however, for analytical purposes, they will be considered in turn. The SCSL has showcased considerable institutional innovation in its legacy efforts and its own role in legacy production, enforcement, and recording.

A. *Developing a Legacy Vision*

Leaving an indelible legacy has purportedly been an institutional concern since the SCSL's creation, and has become a visible institutionalized endeavor. Since 2002 the Court gradually specified its legacy vision. The SCSL Annual Reports, the Court's own regular public legacy recordings, depict the significant legacy developments. The First Annual Report (2003) already "consider[s] the important issue of the legacy the Court will leave behind,"[33] which the Court considers both an opportunity and a challenge, and devotes a special section to legacy. In a critical evaluation one might consider that from the start legacy was a rhetorical and a fund-raising device or even public relations tool to bolster the support for the Court given that it was funded entirely by donations from UN member states.[34]

The year 2004–2005 seems to have been pivotal for more weighty efforts and a concretized SCSL legacy vision. By March 2005 three out of four cases were underway.[35] In addition, the National Victims Commemoration Conference organized by the Court in Freetown in 2005 appears to have foreshadowed that the issue of legacy may be or become a bone of contention for some Sierra Leoneans and the institution itself.[36] Going forward the Court began to take the challenge of leaving a lasting legacy for Sierra Leoneans increasingly seriously and the institutionalization of legacy really made headway.[37] By 2005 references to the term "legacy" tripled in the SCSL Annual Reports. Ever since, however, the frequency of using the term has remained relatively stable, as depicted in Figure 33.3.

---

[33] First Annual Report of the President of the Special Court for Sierra Leone (2002–2003), at 4 and 28. All annual reports cited below are available at http://www.sc-sl.org (last visited June 15, 2012).

[34] *See* Nmehielle & Jalloh, *supra* note 11.

[35] The Civil Defense Forces (CDF) case began on June 3, 2004, the Revolutionary United Front (RUF) case began on July 5, 2004, and the Armed Forces Revolutionary Council (AFRC) case began on March 7, 2005.

[36] *See* M. Wierda, *Report on the National Victims Commemoration Conference*, Oct. 2009, *available at* http://www.carl-sl.org/home/reports/269-national-victim-commemorations-conference-in-sierra-leone (last visited June 15, 2012); *see also* author interviews, The Hague (June 2011).

[37] *See* Second Annual Report of the President of the Special Court for Sierra Leone (2004–2005).

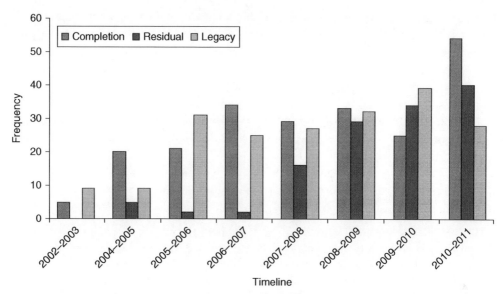

FIGURE 33.3 Frequency of the terms "completion," "residual," and "legacy" appearing in the SCSL Annual Reports (2002–2011).

It would not be surprising to find a contrary trend, namely a steady increase in the official use of "legacy" until closure to strengthen the impact (in line with the findings for the terms "completion" and "residual"). How this trend continues and whether it is indicative of the intensity and effectiveness of the Court's legacy work remains to be seen. The SCSL certainly remains under increasing pressure especially by local civil society actors to engage in effective legacy planning with rapid strides leaving a legacy that is strong and worthwhile in the eye of the respective beholder.

The legacy leaver's vision was first formally expressed in the so-called Initial Legacy White Paper of 2005. This is an important document in the form of a strategic legacy preview. Four thematic areas were identified therein to ensure continuity after the SCSL's closure, namely promoting (1) the rule of law and accountability, (2) human rights and international humanitarian law, (3) civil society in the justice sector, and (4) capacity building of legal professionals in Sierra Leone.[38] The Initial White Paper has never been available to the public. It appears the Legacy White Paper was written as an internal document to prompt court-wide discussions on legacy. Every institution may have internal working documents considering sensitivity of information, funding pressures, sensibilities of stakeholders, and importance of managing expectations. There seems to have been legitimate reasons not to publicize it because if projects go unrealized (because of lack of funding for instance, which, given the precariousness of its overall voluntary funding scheme, seems not an unrealistic concern), the Court's position or performance may be viewed as compromised in the public eye. However, it is noteworthy that the Court did not make available a publicly redacted version or an official statement, although it did publish a booklet entitled "A Commitment to Legacy." There seems to still be a paradox here: as legacy producer, recorder, and enforcer

---

[38] Nmehielle & Jalloh, *supra* note 11, at 113.

the Court seems to be acting, at least in part, behind the scenes of the public sphere where ultimately the reception and eventual contestation of legacies occurs. In the light of ever-greater demands for transparency and accountability in modern governance this practice seems to raise questions about the Court's claims of inclusiveness and accountability as a public institution in situ. With regard to legacy this discrepancy between the goals expressed and the unintended, often inefficient communication policy seemingly illustrates the "pathologies of international organizations" – that is the unanticipated and unintended goal-shifting compared to the agreed aims of the international community at the time of creation of the organization.[39]

By 2005, a third so-called legacy phase was officially envisaged by the Court, following the completion and post-completion phase to focus on the long-term impact of the Court's presence in Sierra Leone. It appears that:

> The central thrust of the Legacy Phase is to address the concerns of the many Sierra Leoneans who feel that the restoration of the national judiciary, civil society, and the rule of law are critical.... In that sense, the Legacy Phase may be said to reflect the popular will of Sierra Leoneans, which did not explicitly make it into the points for negotiation between the UN and Sierra Leone preceding the establishment of the courts and its founding instruments.[40]

On November 23, 2006, the SCSL Judges adopted a resolution noting the importance of the issue of legacy, especially the future use of the court site and archiving.[41] Repeatedly, the SCSL President has underscored that legacy "must be one of the Court's top priorities" and "continues to be one of the Court's topmost priorities."[42] Moreover, the outreach work can be viewed in light of the Court's overall legacy planning as outreach is a certain legacy promotion, a certain form of marketing and proactive legacy production. Similarly to outreach, legacy work also is not funded by the Court's core budget but required separate fundraising. The SCSL has become increasingly proactive in laying the foundations for leaving its desired legacy and has engaged in legacy production, recording, and enforcement to varying degrees. The growing legacy awareness has also become reflected in a professionalization of legacy within the Court.

B. *Professionalizing Legacy*

Through creating specific institutional bodies dedicated to legacy, the SCSL skillfully enhanced the visibility of its own endeavor. This represented a first in international criminal tribunals. The first SCSL Registrar, Robin Vincent, initiated a so-called Legacy Working Group, which was established in 2005.[43] Given the recognition of a need for greater input

[39] *See* Barnett & Finnemore, *supra* note 5.
[40] Nmehielle & Jalloh, *supra* note 11, at 111.
[41] Third Annual Report of the President of the Special Court for Sierra Leone (2005–2006), at 11.
[42] Fourth Annual Report of the President of the Special Court for Sierra Leone (2006–2007), at 6; Seventh Annual Report of the President of the Special Court for Sierra Leone (2009–2010), at 6.
[43] *See id.* Detailed information regarding the Legacy Working Group is not publicly available; hence the information following in this same paragraph is based on Nmehielle & Jalloh, *supra* note 11. Established in 2005 the group comprised eight members drawn from various sections of the Court and comprised mainly of Sierra Leoneans. According to Nmehielle & Jalloh, *supra* note 11, at 123, the composition of the LWG, cochaired by

and ownership of the process by Sierra Leoneans themselves, the working group's objective was to identify and implement projects aimed at contributing to a lasting legacy for Sierra Leone. Its main focus was on the initial Legacy White Paper identifying possible legacy projects, and then implementing and securing funding for them. A year following the creation of the group, the SCSL Plenary set up a Legacy Committee headed by Justice Benjamin Mutanga Itoe in 2006. This committee was tasked with overseeing legacy projects, archiving, preserving records, and the future use of the Court site in Freetown.[44]

Another important step toward institutionalization was the creation of the post of legacy officer in 2007. This professional position within the Court Management Section was initially tasked with coordinating the development and implementation of the SCSL archival policy.[45] The Court's archives are viewed as the Court Management Section's "most important legacy."[46] Keeping in mind the trying environment of institutional downsizing, the eventual abolition of the legacy officer post as well as the dormant working group and committee prima facie may reflect an obvious de-institutionalization or neglect of legacy at the SCSL. Rather, it seems that once specific legacy projects started to gain momentum, project-specific working groups and management boards were established instead of solely focusing on one internal centralized legacy management body.[47] The focal point of the Court's ongoing legacy work today is the Registry.

Three tasks of these new institutional structures can be identified: affirmation of the importance of legacy, internal coordination across organs, and identification and implementation of potential projects. Also, fund-raising for legacy activities has become part of the portfolio as legacy is considered an extra-budgetary activity compared to the Court's core budget. In 2007 the SCSL established a Special Project Fund for the legacy program administered by the Rockefeller Philanthropy Advisors.[48] Given the increasingly ambitious legacy projects, the limited funding secured at present does not seem sufficient to fully implement the projects, and hence the Court continuously seeks funding.[49]

C. Implementing Legacy Projects

The conceptualization and ongoing implementation of specific so-called legacy projects has further institutionalized legacy at the SCSL. Above and beyond being a producer of jurisprudential legacies the Court has also turned to promoting legacies in areas such as capacity building, best practices, promotion of the rule of law, and physical infrastructure. Specific initiatives such as the internship program that provided funding for Sierra Leoneans can be

---

the Completion Strategy Coordinator and the Project Officer responsible for legacy, seems as follows: Chief of Outreach; Deputy Chief of Press and Public Affairs; Trial Attorney, Office of the Prosecutor; Senior Defense Advisor, Defense Office; Senior Secretary to the Registrar; and a representative from Staff Council.

[44] Fourth Annual Report, *supra* note 42, at 6.

[45] Memunatu Pratt, a Sierra Leonean, served as first and only legacy officer from September 2007 to December 2009. In light of the completion strategy and downsizing dynamics, the post of legacy officer was downgraded from P4 to P3 (see Sixth Annual Report of the President of the Special Court for Sierra Leone (2008–2009), at 30) and eventually was downsized.

[46] Fifth Annual Report of the President of the Special Court for Sierra Leone, at 49 (2007–2008).

[47] Author interview (March 2012).

[48] Fifth Annual Report, *supra* note 46, at 6, 11, and 37.

[49] *See* "Legacy" SCSL information sheet (2010), copy obtained in June 2011 (on file with the author).

viewed as an early internal legacy initiative even if it was not explicitly framed as such externally. Legacy has seemingly evolved from a concern of primarily the Registry to an area of debate and activity across all court organs.[50] The two notable legacy projects of the Office of the Prosecutor include the Sierra Leone Legal Information Institute (SierraLII)[51] and a "Best Practices" manual. On the one hand, the fact that the concept of legacy permeated all organs of the tribunal shows the pervasiveness of the concept and the shared responsibility, input, and creativity in relation to considering what legacy to leave and how. On the other hand, the organ-specific initiatives may be an expression of a limited overarching policy direction and a reflection of the fragmentation already in existence in the Court's legacies.

The SCSL legacy projects have continuously developed.[52] At first glance it may seem that the Court was active on legacy especially in 2005 and then did not follow up on the early initiatives. Yet it seems important to fully appreciate that identifying, preparing, and implementing projects involves considerable behind-the-scenes work (and legacy enforcement), including drafting proposals, obtaining funding, and working with donors and partners. Table 33.1 illustrates the evolution of legacy planning at the SCSL.

Paradoxically, immediately prior to the closure, at a time when new legacy efforts could be anticipated to peak, it seems that in light of the completion strategy the Court does not have more time and resources dedicated to legacy work. Within the Court it has been observed that the scope for legacy-type work has decreased given recent staff attrition and loss of expert skills.[53] Nonetheless there is still a strong focus today on the successful implementation of ongoing legacy projects. Vis-à-vis its pending closure and the advanced implementation, the SCSL as legacy leaver seems to be moving toward legacy consolidation in the cycle of legacies. Time pressure is acknowledged as "only a limited time remains for the Court to transfer its skills, knowledge and resources to national partners."[54] Currently six big legacy projects are ongoing, as detailed in Table 33.2.

The Peace Museum will be exemplarily described here in some detail as it is commonly referred to by court staff as a showcase project and seems to draw a wide gamut of stakeholders inside and outside Sierra Leone.[55] Its origins are deeply connected to the Site Project looking into future uses of the court site. When it transpired that the Sierra Leonean government could not afford to exclusively run the facility to house the Supreme Court, alternative multipurpose uses of the site including international fund-raising were discussed. Possibly the Peace Museum project could be more easily fund-raised as it has the soft value component for it to obtain broader support than to fund-raise exclusively for Sierra Leonean courts to move into the facility. The SCSL obtained $195,000 from the UN Peacebuilding Fund in

---

[50] Whose respective projects were reported separately in the Seventh Annual Report, *supra* note 42 (see Table 1).

[51] http://www.sierralii.org (last visited June 15, 2012).

[52] Three initial projects were identified in the Legacy White Paper: (1) Site Project (transfer of the Court's 11.5-acre site to Sierra Leone), (2) Radio Justice (radio program with focus on SCSL proceedings and information on justice and rule of law), and (3) Legal Resources Development Project (transfer of SCSL's specialized library to domestic courts). *See* C.C. Jalloh, *The Contribution of the Special Court for Sierra Leone to International Law*, 15 RADIC 165 (2007); Nmehielle & Jalloh, *supra* note 11.

[53] Author interview (Feb. 2012).

[54] "Legacy" SCSL information sheet, *supra* note 48, at 1.

[55] This project was referred to as "one of the most important tangible legacies" in author interviews, The Hague, June 2011. The information following in this paragraph was confirmed in author interviews, March 2012.

TABLE 33.1 *Overview of legacy projects and developments as reported in the SCSL Annual Reports (2002–2011)*

Year	Legacy Projects mentioned	Legacy Developments
1: 2002–03	-Development of international court site -Development of SL staff -Internship program for SL	
2: 2004–05	-Transfer of court site -Four two-day regional conferences	-Legacy Phase envisaged
3: 2005–06	-Number of legacy-oriented outreach projects:Grass Roots Campaign; rule-of-law stakeholder forums; Accountability Now Clubs; booklets on IHL; developing national SCSL staff; national internships; assisting national judicial monitoring -Site Project -Radio Justice -Virtual Tribunal Project	-Legacy Working Group -Legacy Booklet
4: 2006–07	-Communicating Justice in the Mano River Union -Site Project -Witness Evaluation and Legacy Project -Sierra Leone Rule of Law and Capacity Building Project	-Legacy Committee -Trips by SCSL officials to raise profile of its legacy program -Resolution by SCSL judges
5: 2007–08	-Communicating Justice Project i. Grassroots Awareness Campaign ii. Strengthened Media Coverage Project -Strengthening the Capacity of SCSL employees -Witness Evaluation and Legacy Project -Site Project	-Special Project Fund for legacy program
6: 2008–09	**Registry:** -Site Project -Witness Evaluation and Legacy Project -Communicating Justice -Archiving Project -Capacity Building for legal associates and interns	
7: 2009–10	**Registry:** -Site Project -Witness Evaluation and Legacy Project -Communicating Justice -Archiving Project -Capacity Building for legal associates and interns **Prosecution:** -Training the Police Prosecutors -Archival and Records Management Training -Sierra Leone Legal Information Institute -Training workshop on IHL **Chambers:** -Site Project meeting -Transfer of detention facility to the government -Commission of Inquiry into allegations of rape and sexual abuse -Juvenile Justice training program -Training for war-affected women	-Detention facility handover to the government -Courtesy calls by SCSL President to major donor states

TABLE **33.1** (*cont.*)

Year	Legacy Projects mentioned	Legacy Developments
8: 2010–11	**Registry:** -Transfer of Court's records to The Hague -National Witness Protection Unit in SL police -Professional development -Conference on Forced Marriage in Conflict Situations -Site Project	-Peace Museum preview exhibition

TABLE 33.2 *Overview of the six biggest ongoing SCSL legacy projects*

Projects	Estimated project costs (in $)
1. Site Project	Not available (European Commission (EC):~ $89,000)
2. Peace Museum	$600,000 (UN Peacebuilding Fund: $195,000)
3. National Witness Protection Program	$1,605,000 and $ 60,000 (EC: ~ $70,000)
4. Archives Development Program	$1,500,000 (EC: $270,000)
5. Capacity Building: Professional Development Program	$150,000 (EC: $55,000)
6. Improving Detention Standards and Access to Justice for Women and Juveniles	$100,000

Note: Latest figures available from 2010.

December 2010, and the project management team formed in January 2011. The envisaged Peace Museum contains, to be registered as company of guarantee, three components: first, the archives, including the public records of the SCSL, Truth and Reconciliation Commission, and National Commission for Disarmament, Demobilisation and Reintegration, as well as a list of 150 records on the conflict; second, an exhibition including artifacts relating to the conflict and peace process; and third, a memorial to be established on the converted car park. The project has been promoted through several activities. An open public design competition for the memorial was launched on March 1, 2011, and the winning entry chosen in summer 2012. Also, a three-day preview of the exhibition was held as part of the festivities marking Sierra Leone's 50th Independence Anniversary and a sponsored "Walk for Peace" converging at the museum was organized on November 26, 2011.[56] The museum project has become increasingly ambitious and is an example of legacy production, recording, and enforcement in parallel. It is anticipated to benefit both Sierra Leoneans and non–Sierra Leoneans, for instance researchers and tourists, as all future museum visitors represent the manifold legacy recipients. Some Sierra Leoneans from outside Freetown feel alienated given that the museum is located in the capital so again outside their reach, on the premises of the SCSL whose physical site was controversial since the beginning.[57]

[56] http://www.sierraexpressmedia.com/archives/23194, http://www.sierraexpressmedia.com/archives/32364, and http://www.sierraexpressmedia.com/archives/32758 (last visited June 15, 2012).
[57] Author interview (March 2012).

In terms of innovation, two other developments are worth mentioning here. First, the SCSL is exploring multimedia avenues for promoting its legacy. A new "Legacy" section has been added to its existing website briefly presenting the six ongoing legacy projects. The Court is also planning and designing its own legacy website.[58] Second, the Court has been involved with preparations for a legacy survey seeking to establish the impact of the SCSL. The survey was conducted independently through the administration of questionnaires in Sierra Leone and Liberia during summer 2012 by the Brussels-based nongovernmental organization (NGO), No Peace Without Justice, in partnership with the local NGOs Manifesto 99, the Coalition for Justice and Accountability, the Sierra Leone Institute of International Law, and the Liberian NGO network. This represents an impressive first-of-its-kind legacy recording exercise and ultimately legacy production in the immediate wake of the Taylor trial judgment.[59]

From this it is clear that the SCSL has showcased considerable institutional innovation with regard to legacy as well as institutional legacy recording and production.[60] Given the constellation of its location in the country where the crimes were committed, its mixed subject-matter jurisdiction and composition, and the ailing domestic legal system in Sierra Leone, the SCSL has engaged in unprecedented deliberate legacy planning.[61] Not surprisingly, what is currently fueling legacy planning is the Court's quasi-imminent closure. In the lifecycle of the tribunals, it would appear that the current institutional focus on legacy is an attempt to face institutional decline by transcending and (re)constructing "The End."[62] One interviewee echoed this: "I would like to see the SCSL remembered for its legacy programmes.... If we invest in legacy programmes, we will invest in life after death."[63] However, it seems that planned legacies and realized legacies do not necessarily coincide as multiple actors and social dynamics are involved in the construction of legacies.

IV. THE MAKING OF LEGACIES

The SCSL certainly is a central actor, albeit only one among many legacy actors inside and outside Sierra Leone. Ultimately, legacy is what the Court makes of it, but also what all other actors make of it, too.[64] Prior to closure, the SCSL's legacies have already become sites of debate and struggle over the Court's definitive meaning for post-conflict Sierra Leone, Africa, and international criminal justice. It appears no tribunal can build its own authoritative legacies as collective interaction and multiplicity of voices are part and parcel of the construction of legacies. There have been calls for viewing the hybrid court "not as a driver but as a catalyst for motivating a broader set of actors or initiatives that may contribute to

---

[58] *See* author interview, The Hague (June 2011).

[59] Delivered on April 26, 2012 and published on May 18, 2012. Judgment, Taylor (SCSL-033–01-T), Trial Chamber II (May 18, 2012).

[60] Other tribunals have also demonstrated institutional innovation; for example, the ICTY organized two legacy conferences in February 2010 and November 2011, and the ICTR also has a legacy committee.

[61] *See* Jalloh, *supra* note 52.

[62] In this context, see F. Pocar, *Completion or Continuation Strategy, Appraising Problems and Possible Development in Building the Legacy of the ICTY*, 6 J. INT'L CRIM. JUST. 655 (2008).

[63] Author interview, The Hague (June 2011).

[64] *See* A. Wendt, *Anarchy Is What States Make of It: The Social Construction of Power Politics*, 46(2) INT'L ORG. 391 (1992).

legacy"[65] and feeling vested in the legacy process. It has been moreover suggested that "effective legacy must be a result not just of the policies and actions of the tribunals themselves but of a multiplicity of actors that seek to ensure that the tribunals have a lasting impact."[66] Although such perspectives recognize the multiplicity of actors, the underlying assumption of the homogeneity and convergence of actor interests and legacy visions is problematic. The diversity of actors and social dynamics involved in legacy construction has hitherto been largely overlooked.[67] The following section seeks to foreshadow the broader legacy actor landscape by selectively applying the actors' framework developed previously and to highlight selected important dynamics and tensions in terms of meaning and control of the multiple legacies in the making.

A. *Legacy Actor Landscape*

A plethora of legacy recipients are to be recognized, both locally and globally – including victims, witnesses, defendants, court staff, various professionals, civil society, local courts, the Sierra Leonean government, other tribunals, the UN, and the international community. It may appear that a balance is being attempted between leaving legacies for internationals and for Sierra Leoneans. In the context of a hybrid court, the question of the addressee or recipient is particularly germane. The issue of to whom the legacies are being bequeathed is complex and ultimately linked to the much debated question "justice for whom?"[68] Concluding that the SCSL was caught between high and wide-ranging expectations both by Sierra Leoneans and the international community seems to the point.[69] The importance of managing expectations of diverse actors in regard to the objectives but also legacies of the tribunals is stressed repeatedly in this context.[70] At the formal opening of the Courthouse on March 10, 2004, former Sierra Leonean president Ahmad Tejan Kabbah highlighted the bifurcation of the Court's purpose and constituents as follows:

> This is a Special Court for Sierra Leone, a symbol of the rule of law and an essential element in the pursuit of peace, justice and national reconciliation for the people of Sierra Leone. It is also a Special Court for the international community, a symbol of the rule of

---

[65] OHCHR, *supra* note 17, at 6; *see also* Report of the Secretary-General, *supra* note 1, § 17.

[66] Reiger, *supra* note 18, at 4.

[67] Such a dynamic view has recently been supported by a preliminary description of legacy as a collection of narratives of different actors; *see* F. Mégret, *The Legacy of the ICTY as Seen Through Some of Its Actors and Observers*, 3 Goettingen J. Int'l L. 1011 (2011).

[68] *See* C. Sriram, *Justice for Whom? Assessing Hybrid Approaches to Accountability in Sierra Leone, in* Security, Reconciliation, and Reconstruction: When the Wars End 145 (M. Ndula ed., 2007).

[69] ICTJ & UNDP, *The "Legacy" of the Special Court for Sierra Leone*, Draft Discussion Paper, Sept. 29, 2003, *available at* http://www.unrol.org/files/LegacyReport.pdf (last visited June 15, 2012); J. Lincoln, Transitional Justice, Peace and Accountability. Outreach and the Role of International Courts after Conflict (2011).

[70] *See* R. Byrne, *Promises of Peace and Reconciliation: Previewing the Legacy of the International Criminal Tribunal for Rwanda*, 14(4) Eur. Rev. 485 (2006); R. Kerr & J. Lincoln, *The Special Court for Sierra Leone. Outreach, Impact and Legacy*, War Crimes Research Group, King's College London, February 2008, *available at* http://www.kcl.ac.uk/content/1/c6/04/95/60/SCSLOutreachLegacyandImpactFinalReport.pdf (last visited June 15, 2012); OHCHR, *supra* note 17.

international law ... the Special Court is good for Sierra Leone. It is also good for the world today.[71]

It would seem erroneous to assume a monolithic Sierra Leonean perspective on legacy. Indeed, Sierra Leonean civil society, political and legal professionals, defendants, victims, members of the general public, and the government may have very different perceptions of the Court as well as its legacies. These different perceptions depend on various factors, in particular the respective knowledge level, exposure to the Court, expectations, and assessments as well as the underlying interests of actors engaged in legacy production, recording, and enforcement.[72] It seems central to give members of the affected communities a voice and role in the Court's legacy work. If the SCSL was established to bring justice to victims of the conflict, it would seem shortsighted if legacies solely revolve around the issue of value for money based on an international interest to justify public expenditure by pointing to investment longevity in the form of legacies.[73] From a Sierra Leonean point of view, in essence, "it is also about creating a legacy for the victims. Victims who survived can tell their story. Victims who perished can be remembered."[74] The widely distributed leaflet *Wetin Na Di Speshal Kot?* concludes: "The Special Court is the people's Court. It exists for the good of all Sierra Leoneans."[75]

Promoting sustainable and positive legacies for Sierra Leone is a leitmotif in the Court's public discourse. The SCSL attempted to engage in a regular dialogue with the Sierra Leonean public, for instance via its outreach program and the National Victims Commemoration Conference in 2005.[76] The establishment of the so-called Special Court Interactive Forum, a forum for exchange between NGOs and tribunal officials, can be seen as noteworthy steps in this direction. Some civil society actors however lament a perceived one-way communication.[77] There was a sense of feeling to "become patronized" by the SCSL who decided top-down what were the best legacy projects and what the ultimate legacy for Sierra Leone would or should be. A Sierra Leonean opined that "one of the biggest issues ..., without

---

[71] A.T. Kabbah, Statement of Alhaji Dr. Ahmad Tejan Kabbah, President of the Republic of Sierra Leone, at the Formal Opening of the Courthouse for the Special Court for Sierra Leone, *available at* http://www.sierra-leone.org/Speeches/kabbah-031004.html (last visited June 15, 2012).

[72] Accordingly, the above-mentioned post-Taylor judgment legacy survey was administered to specific target groups, including political actors, security sector, civil society, and legal professionals as well as randomly selected members of the general public (http://www.npwj.org/node/3991 (last visited June 15, 2012)).

[73] This was echoed by one SCSL official:

> Because something should stay. If you work for something like eight years, you would regret that a lot of money has been spent and nothing stays.... It was very soon that we started to come up with training programmes. A little selfish maybe, if we have better prosecutors, we have better results, but it was the right direction, give something lasting.
> (Author interview, Aug. 2011).

[74] J.F. Kamara, Preserving the Legacy of the Special Court for Sierra Leone: Challenges and Lessons Learned in Prosecuting Grave Crimes in Sierra Leone, Address delivered as part of the Supranational Criminal Law Lecture Series organized by the Coalition for the International Criminal Court 24, T.M.C. Asser Institute, *available at* http://www.iccnow.org/documents/Presrving_the_Legacy_of_the_Special_Court_-Grotius_lecture.pdf (last visited June 15, 2012).

[75] See *Wetin Na Di Speshal Kot? (What Is the Special Court?*, in Krio; title in English version: *The Special Court Made Simple)*, SCSL outreach leaflet (undated) (on file with the author).

[76] See, for more on outreach and the role of civil society, Stuart Ford (Chapter 26) and Alison Smith (Chapter 2) in this volume.

[77] *Id.*

being xenophobic, was that internationals were discussing legacy. For all the time it had and legacy it could have shared, the Special Court has not done well … especially if it was hoping to deliver justice to those who lost limbs, loved ones and property."[78]

Discussions about legacy that resemble a top-down monologue rather than a dialogue obfuscate an important dimension in legacy leaving: the active reception of legacies. A recent one-day legacy symposium is a case in point.[79] At least two separate discussions on legacy seem to have emerged, one within the Court and one within Sierra Leone. A gaping divide between modest or practical claims for legacy made mainly by the international (donor) community and stronger demands mirrored in national expectations of the SCSL as a panacea for legal, sociopolitical, or economic ills in Sierra Leone is striking. The sense of alienation resonates with a powerful critique advanced that the SCSL, in the conduct of its actual trials such as the CDF case, failed to appreciate, if not adjust, to the local culture.[80] This seemingly heightened the confusion and tension between the SCSL and local civil society and legal professionals. Such confusion, tension, or contestation among legacy leavers and recipients however represents not an unusual facet of legacy construction (see Figure 33.1). Contrary to conventional depiction, the recipients, as elaborated above, take on an active role in legacy construction, which is an ongoing process.

There seems to be a macro-level interest of the government of Sierra Leone in preserving and promoting the Court's legacies and engaging in legacy production, recording, and enforcement. Ernest Bai Koroma, president of Sierra Leone, enthusiastically noted on February 20, 2008, "Around 2010, when the Special Court is expected to complete its mandate, it will leave behind for posterity and generations yet unborn this magnificent and imposing legacy."[81] In 2004, then-president Kabbah already eagerly anticipated that "at the end of its mandate the Special Court will leave a legacy in the annals of the administration of justice in Sierra Leone and in the international community. It will also bequeath to the people of Sierra Leone a citadel of justice in the form of this beautiful courthouse."[82] The government has taken direct interest in the legacies of the SCSL it seems as part of an effort as a modern African state to showcase commitment to accountability, the rule of law, justice and peace, cooperation with the international community and political will to be viewed as a post-conflict "success story." Nowadays, it is noticeable that countries take a firsthand approach to the perception of their image. In the case of Sierra Leone, former president Kabbah emphasized that the brutal acts committed had "tarnished the image of Sierra Leone, a small but peaceful, friendly and enlightened nation."[83] The self-interest of the state's cooperation with the Court might well be perceived as an example of nation branding in Africa. The Peace Museum project is a good case in point, demonstrating, on the one hand, an official Sierra Leonean commitment to peace and coming to terms with

[78] Author interview (March 2012).
[79] E. Kalloon, *Lumpa Community Gets Knowledge on the Legacy of the Special Court*, *available at* http://www.awoko.org/2012/02/15/lumpa-community-gets-knowledge-on-the-legacy-of-special-court (last visited June 15, 2012).
[80] T. Kelsall, Culture under Cross-examination: International Justice and the Special Court for Sierra Leone (2009).
[81] Cited in Fifth Annual Report, *supra* note 46, at 39.
[82] Kabbah, *supra* note 71.
[83] *Id.*

the past, and on the other hand, openness toward international exchange and tourism. The government is involved in the decision-making process and thus in legacy production also with respect to other SCSL projects such as the Site Project.

Legacy producers, recorders, and enforcers active inside and outside Sierra Leone are diverse and numerous. The SCSL as legacy leaver and the recipients have taken on different roles in production, recording, and enforcement. Various actors have engaged in positive and negative legacy production since the establishment of the Court. There have also been numerous legacy recorders ranging from journalists, civil society actors, policy makers, artists, institutions, and ordinary citizens to academics.[84] Hopes and expectations regarding the Court's achievements and legacy were high from the outset.[85] Several themes figured prominently in legacy recordings, which formed the basis of positive or negative legacy production, for instance, the Court's hybrid nature,[86] unique opportunity to leave a lasting legacy,[87] outreach program,[88] staff composition,[89] establishment and indictments,[90] jurisprudence,[91] and cultural appropriateness.[92] A recent publication and legacy recording including a Best Practice Guide explicitly aimed at "bridging the gap" and "ensuring the lasting legacy" of the SCSL and the Truth and Reconciliation Commission in Sierra Leone.[93] Actors stressing the need to ensure and safeguard a legacy appear to be taking on the role of legacy enforcers promoting and protecting a certain desired content or interpretation. Legacy enforcers may for instance be NGOs that also produce and record legacies respectively. Sierra Leonean NGOs carefully following the work of the SCSL include the Centre for Accountability and the Rule of Law in Sierra Leone, Coalition for Justice and Accountability, and Manifesto

---

[84] Until this volume, no book-length legacy account of the SCSL has been published, unlike the case of the ICTY: *see* Assessing the Legacy of the ICTY (R.H. Steinberg ed., 2011); The Legacy of the International Criminal Tribunal for the Former Yugoslavia (B. Swart, A. Zahar & G. Sluiter eds., 2011).

[85] ICTJ & UNDP, *supra* note 69.

[86] *See, e.g.*, B.K. Dogherty, *Right-Sizing International Justice: The Hybrid Experiment at the Special Court for Sierra Leone*, 80(2) Int'l Aff. 311 (2004); C.L. Sriram, *Wrong-Sizing International Justice? The Hybrid Tribunal in Sierra Leone*, 29(3) Fordham Int'l L.J. 472 (2006); J. Stromseth, D. Wippman & D. Brooks, Can Might Make Rights? Building the Rule of Law after Military Interventions (2006).

[87] *See, e.g.*, L.A. Dickinson, *The Promise of Hybrid Courts*, 97(2) Am. J. Int'l L. 295 (2003); Human Rights Watch, *Justice in Motion. The Trial Phase of the Special Court for Sierra Leone* (June 2005), *available at* http://www.hrw.org/fr/reports/2005/11/02/justice-motion (last visited June 15, 2012); Kelsall, *supra* note 80; Nmehielle & Jalloh, *supra* note 11; OHCHR, *supra* note 17; M. Staggs, *Bringing Justice and Ensuring Lasting Peace: Some Reflections on the Trial Phase at the Special Court for Sierra Leone, Second Interim Report on the Special Court for Sierra Leone* (War Crimes Studies Center, Univ. of California, Berkeley Mar. 2006).

[88] *E.g.*, Cruvellier, *supra* note 18; Ford, *supra* note 76; Lincoln, *supra* note 69.

[89] *E.g.*, Cruvellier, *supra* note 18; D. Keen, Conflict and Collusion in Sierra Leone (2005). One Sierra Leonean highlighted this aspect of legacy: "The point is, I see myself as a product of legacy. I am Sierra Leonean, I have acquired skills at the Special Court, working with civil society I am taking these into domestic practice.... I look at myself as a legacy of the Special Court." Author interview, The Hague (June 2011).

[90] *E.g.*, P. Penfold, *What Legacy? The Special Court*, 486 New African 20 (2009).

[91] *E.g.*, C.C. Jalloh, *Special Court for Sierra Leone: Achieving Justice?*, 32 Mich. J. Int'l L. 395 (2011); V. Oosterveld, *The Gender Jurisprudence of the Special Court for Sierra Leone: Progress in the Revolutionary United Front Judgments*, 44 Cornell Int'l L.J. 49 (2011).

[92] *E.g.*, D.M. Crane, *White Man's Justice: Applying International Justice after Regional Third World Conflicts*, 27(4) Cardozo L. Rev. 1683 (2006); Kelsall, *supra* note 80.

[93] University of Nottingham Human Rights Law Centre, *Bridging the Gap: Ensuring Lasting Legacy of the Truth and Reconciliation Commission and the Special Court for Sierra Leone* 1 (2012), *available at* http://www.nottingham.ac.uk/hrlc/projects/bridging-the-gap–ensuring-lasting-legacy-of-the-truth-and-reconciliation-commission-and-the-special-court-for-sierra-leone.aspx (last visited June 15, 2012).

99. Also some international NGOs offered numerous recommendations to maximize legacy, for example by intensifying engagement with national courts and coordinating legacy efforts within the Court, drawing more upon its unique strengths as a hybrid court, and more substantially including Sierra Leoneans and pursuing ongoing outreach and collective protection of the legacy. Most recently an Open Society Justice Initiative Report published in November 2011 issued a warning that more serious attention needs to be paid to seven pressing issues, concluding with an appeal to all stakeholders to "act quickly to safeguard the Court's legacy."[94]

Legacy financiers are rarely included in any analysis. Yet, their enabling function for legacy production, enforcement, and recording should not be underestimated. Legacy financiers of the SCSL include the government of Canada, European Commission, Ford Foundation, MacArthur Foundation, Oak Foundation, Open Society Institute, Rockefeller Foundation, and UN Peacebuilding Fund. Inadequate funding seems to be an endemic challenge for legacy efforts at international tribunals generally.[95] Legacy projects require resources in terms of time and money that do not exist in overabundance at an organization that is winding down. The Court's precarious funding situation, which is discussed by Sara Kendall in her contribution to this volume, exists not just for its legacy work but also its core work; thus "the decision to use donations to fund this important justice initiative proved to be a bane to the operations and ultimate legacy of the SCSL."[96] All legacy actors inside and outside of Sierra Leone are involved in the continuous construction of legacies.

B. *Legacies under Construction*

High and conflicting expectations exist regarding what the legacies of an international criminal tribunal or hybrid court are and should be. A key factor of confusion and tension between different actors has been identified in the lack of clarity about what the legacy actually is.[97] Put simply, legacy means different things to different actors inside and outside the tribunals. This is another reason to advocate the notion of plural legacies to obviate that actors talk past one another despite allegedly using the same language. Legacy construction is an ongoing process and has sparked some controversy. A SCSL official conceded, "You are never going to have uncontroversial legacies.... You are going to have supporters and opponents of these institutions."[98] Indeed, ultimately debates about the tribunals' legacies are both a reflection and a sideshow of broader debates about the tribunals' raison d'être, the international community's involvement in post-conflict peacebuilding, and the meanings of justice.

There is an ongoing controversy, inside and outside the tribunals, over whether legacy work should be part of a tribunal's mandate and agenda at all.[99] This debate exposes different legacy visions and perspectives on the purpose of these institutions. On the one hand, it can be suggested that only a core judicial mandate is appropriate for criminal courts, and

---

[94] OSJI, *supra* note 2, at 14.

[95] *See* LINCOLN, *supra* note 69; Nmehielle & Jalloh, *supra* note 11.

[96] Jalloh, *supra* note 91, at 402.

[97] *See id.*

[98] Author interview, The Hague (June 2011).

[99] *See* OHCHR, *supra* note 17.

that legacies can be sustainable even if not explicitly mandated. On the other hand, it can be argued that these institutions can aspire to affect more than prosecute and conduct legal proceedings for a few individuals. Without an explicit mandate though there may be only weak political and financial support for legacy if considered a distraction or side project. The Court's founding documents do not contain any explicit mention of the term "legacy"; however they refer to wider aims such as "dealing with impunity" and "developing respect for the rule of law." The Court has come to see legacy as a core commitment in line with its mandate.[100] According to SCSL Judge Renate Winter, "the Court has, since its inception, understood the creation of a durable legacy as a significant component of its mandate" and "the court's desire to plan and leave a solid legacy in Sierra Leone ... is consistent with its mandate."[101]

Within the Court uniform interest and support of the various legacy projects seems difficult to perceive. An appropriation of legacy, real or perceived, occurred under the aegis of the Registry, which is now seen as the section of expertise and responsibility. Legacy thereby risks not being viewed as the spin-off of the quotidian work across all sections of the Court but as a grand specific task carried out by an institutional focal point through specific projects (i.e., a division of labor and distinct self-understandings becoming visible within the SCSL).[102] In contrast to the legacy approach prevalent in the Registry, a view that has been repeated in Chambers reveals skepticism toward legacy as a specific task of a criminal court. It seems to reflect a strict understanding of a court as an exclusively judicial institution that should consequently not attempt to perform advocacy or policy work in parallel. Two SCSL staff members in Chambers described their impressions as follows: "Is legacy our task? No. The Special Court was supposed to deliver 'cheap, fast, effective, fair' justice.... It is a criminal court which is often forgotten, not a legacy institution" and "The Legacy of Nuremburg emerged, they did not have a peace museum, archives project etc."[103] In addition, they seemingly distanced themselves from what they perceive as the Court's official legacy work. These statements should not be mistaken for a display of indifference, however – some interviewees simply did not see legacy as their task. In a similar vein regarding the jurisprudential legacy, a SCSL high official in Chambers noted:

> I don't sense there is a fascination with the legal legacy, it seems to be only about buildings, archives. I cannot interfere there; I have no competence and no interest. Our work is to give a fair trial in a reasonable amount of time. What comes after that, I don't take any interest in, it is not my focus. I do my work as best as I can.[104]

---

[100] *See* S.C. Res. 1315, Aug. 14, 2000; *Report of the Secretary-General on the Establishment of the Special Court for Sierra Leone*, U.N. Doc. S/2000/915, Oct. 4, 2000, § 7; *A Commitment to Legacy*, SCSL legacy booklet, 2005 (on file with the author).

[101] R. Winter, *The Special Court for Sierra Leone and the Work of the Judges*, in Völkerstrafrecht, Rechtsschutz und Rule of Law: Das Individuum als Herausforderung für das Völkerrecht. Beiträge zum 34. österreichischen Völkerrechtstag 2009, at 119 (W. Schroeder & J. Mayr-Singer eds., 2011); and Nmehielle & Jalloh, *supra* note 11, at 111.

[102] Interestingly, when asked whether they see an explicit link between their work and legacy, many staff members were hesitant and regarded Registry officials directly working on legacy projects as solely competent and authorized to speak on the topic. For example: "We do not work on legacy, we are not the right people to speak to. You should speak to the Registry and outreach people." Author interviews, The Hague (June 2011).

[103] Author interviews, The Hague (June 2011).

[104] Author interview, The Hague (June 2011).

The question arises whether there is a lack of communication or coordination among court organs or a fundamental conflict of interest between a narrow and a broad understanding of the objectives and self-understanding of the Court.

Viewing legacy as a secondary luxury for a criminal court has been particularly advocated by key political and financial actors. The SCSL Management Committee, which advises the Court on nonjudicial matters and oversees financial issues, purportedly did not provide full support of its legacy work from the start. The view that legacy building, put crudely, was a secondary luxury that the Court could not afford to consider prior to completion of its judicial core work was seemingly reflected within the committee in order to keep the fund-raising required for the core budget as low as possible. Originally this view stemmed from early discussions within the Security Council and interested states regarding the first voluntary budget projections and is reflected through until the most recent budget discussions.[105] Until all indictees are apprehended and prosecuted, and judicial proceedings are completed, donors seem reluctant to finance what they considered a side project. From within the SCSL it has been observed:

> in defence of the tribunal, in phases "creation" and "operation," donors don't want to hear about legacy. They want to hear about how many cases you are prosecuting. When a prosecutor is prosecuting a case, they cannot work on legacy. If you want a legitimate legacy from the start, give money to staff that are not involved in core mandate stuff.[106]

In this sense, the role of the Management Committee could be significant for legacy production, recording, and enforcement, provided that the Court is backed politically, financially, and rhetorically in its legacy efforts, constructively monitored, and encouraged by the major supporters early on.

Importantly, there seems an obvious gap between the ambitious expectations and objectives created for the Court and ultimate resources or tools invested to contribute to the wider goals of justice, peace, and reconciliation in Sierra Leone as advertised. The perception of legacy as a "plus" to be added at the whim of the donors and the tribunals themselves depending on resources and capacity has generated considerable criticism. Abdul Tejan-Cole, former member of the Office of the Prosecutor and former Head of the Anti-Corruption Commission in Sierra Leone, remarked, "I think the hybrid concept is excellent. But you don't just start legacy when you are about to end. It has to be from the start."[107] Overall, "legacy does not seem to have ever been a full priority."[108] However, although legacy is not explicitly incorporated into the SCSL mandate reflected in the core budget, it is not necessarily to be seen as incidental. Many Sierra Leoneans apparently regard lack of resources as a poor and unconvincing excuse for not "doing more."[109] In their eyes the SCSL seems a comparatively wealthy internationally funded institution, showcased in its state-of-the-art courthouse, much praised and endowed with ambitious objectives. Consequently, many believed that the Court could achieve more than it was ultimately given the tools to do, and certain constructions of legacy are colored by disenchantment.

---

[105] ICTJ & UNDP, *supra* note 69, at 7; Lincoln, *supra* note 69.
[106] Author interview, The Hague (June 2011).
[107] Cited in Cruvellier, *supra* note 18, at 36.
[108] *Id.* at 44.
[109] LINCOLN, *supra* note 69.

The fundamental basis of the Court's legacies is its core work as a judicial institution – that is, investigations, trials, and judgments. Constructing legacy as a secondary luxury and not as a task of a criminal court strictly speaking suggests an artificial divorce between the Court's judicial core work and its legacies. If the term "legacy" is restricted as a label to specific projects or identified solely with the work of the Registry for example, such a narrow perspective may distort the overall legacy picture of the Court. One tribunal staff member insisted that "almost everything we do is legacy. The judicial work is our biggest legacy; it is not a special project, but our everyday work."[110] Criticisms that what the SCSL is doing today is "too little too late" need to be reviewed in this light. How opposing narratives are already constructed in the courtroom was explored recently by examining the discourses of the Prosecution and the Defense in the case of Charles Taylor.[111] Different constructions of legitimacy are underpinned by conflicting discourses about one's own self-understanding, the trial, defendant, Court, and Sierra Leonean conflict.[112]

Contestation surrounding different legacies of the SCSL is not novel or a recent phenomenon. Debates have nonetheless intensified in light of the pending closure. The physical legacy is a case in point that illuminates different narratives from the outset. Symbolically, the physical site and state-of-the-art courthouse of the SCSL and thus its physical legacy is controversial in and of itself. Some Sierra Leoneans do not relate to the court site, or negatively relate to it as an alien empty shell, a spaceship structure with stringent security measures. Hence, "this very visual beacon of justice for many is seen as a symbol of injustice."[113] Given the fact that the government stated it cannot maintain the site alone after closure of the SCSL seems to confirm to critics that the choice and design of the site was an internationally driven project ill-fitted to the local context. The impact of this contention may amount to alienation also with regard to other legacies of the SCSL. For instance opening the Peace Museum on the Court's site in Freetown has not unsurprisingly seen critical voices resurface.

What is at play ultimately are conflicting claims over constructions of truth and the power of interpretation. Given the constructed nature of legacies, the vantage point of the actor is paramount. The same event or outcome may be viewed and promoted positively by one actor and negatively by another; thus different legacies may transpire underpinned by positive or negative legacy production. Constructions of legitimacy, effectiveness, and purpose are also indicative of possible different constructions of legacy. Identifying legacies that are being threatened or undermined reveals a normative position favoring a particular conception of the Court and its achievements. Threats to legacy within the control of the Court (including ignorance, lack of ownership, perceived bias, lack of access, and false expectations) and threats outside its control (inadequate funding) have been distinguished.[114] This bipartite distinction between threats within and beyond the SCSL's control seems a stark dichotomization suggesting far greater power of control than any court seemingly has. From

---

[110] Author interview, The Hague (July 2011).

[111] M. Glasius & T. Meijers, *Constructions of Legitimacy: The Charles Taylor Trial*, 6 INT'L J. TRANSITIONAL J. 229 (2012).

[112] For a documentary portrayal of different narratives surrounding SCSL legal proceedings in the trial of Issa Sesay, see the film *War Don Don* (2010), directed by Rebecca Richman Cohen.

[113] Kerr & Lincoln, *supra* note 70, at 29; *see also* Cruvellier, *supra* note 18; Author interviews, The Hague (June–July 2011).

[114] Nmehielle & Jalloh, *supra* note 11.

a static or linear legacy approach some issues such as counter-narratives and unwillingness to cooperate may be identified as legacy threats. So-called legacy threats may alternatively be viewed as alternative constructions of legacy, attempts of negotiation, contestation, and recreation as integral part of any cycle of legacies (see Figure 33.1). Legacy outcomes need to be viewed as highly uncertain and constantly "in the making" in light of a framework of social construction.

C. Limits to the Control over Legacies

The interpretation of legacies intimately entwines with the attribution of meaning to the past, present, and future that itself changes over time. Indeed, the so-called Nuremberg legacy "is often mentioned but its meaning has never been coherent, changing from time to time, context to context."[115] If the ongoing debates over the legacies of the Nuremberg and Tokyo International Military Tribunals are any indication, it is certainly doubtful that legacies of the SCSL constructed and disputed today will be the same as those in ten, twenty, or fifty years. In the popular imagination legacy is often linked to a linear conception of time relating to the life cycle of the legacy leaver. Legacies however seem to involve a certain disruption of a linear temporality.[116] Time performs the role of a prism "refracting unpredictable meanings and purposes. Emphasizing what remains after one leaves and the fragility and uncertainty about how actions will be understood underscores the importance of humility in transmitting a legacy."[117] With the new conceptualization of legacy presented here it is explicitly acknowledged that legacies evolve over time and are intrinsically linked to shifts in meaning and power of interpretation.

International criminal tribunals do not operate in a political vacuum; thus struggles over the power of interpretation and editorial control over their legacies are inevitable. It has been noted with concern, "there is a great deal of controversy about who controls the Special Court legacy ... an abstract concept, [which is] to the detriment of actual action."[118] The notion of "framing"[119] seems to capture well the highly constructible and constructed nature of legacies. Framing relates to content as well as forms of remembrance and legacy enforcement.[120] This highlights the volatility of legacy constructions and the importance of understanding meanings and power dynamics over time. A discrepancy exists between the power a legacy leaver may wish to wield and effectively has given the multitude of actors and dynamics shaping legacies. On an abstract level, the SCSL has recognized that the judgment on legacy is out of its hands, acknowledging "history will judge how successful these initiatives have been, but the foundation for leaving behind a legacy of accountability and contributing to legal reform efforts in Sierra Leone are being laid."[121] Nonetheless legacy

---

[115] M. Futamura, War Crimes Tribunals and Transitional Justice: The Tokyo Trial and the Nuremburg Legacy 14 (2008).

[116] See analysis of "trauma time" by J. Edkins, Trauma and the Memory of Politics (2003).

[117] P. Dobel, *Managerial Leadership and the Ethical Importance of Legacy*, 8(2) Int'l Pub. Mgmt. J. 225, 237 (2004).

[118] Cited in Lincoln, *supra* note 69, at 125.

[119] E. Goffman, Frame Analysis: An Essay on the Organization of Experience (1986).

[120] *See also* I. Irwin-Zarecka, Frames of Remembrance: The Dynamics of Collective Memory (1994).

[121] First Annual Report, *supra* note 33, at 28.

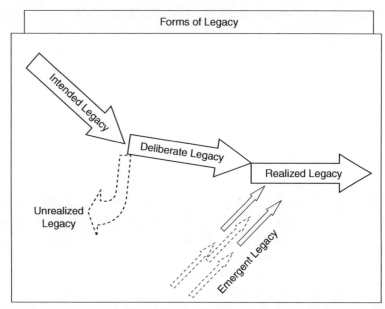

FIGURE 33.4 Forms of legacy as a dynamic process over time. *Adapted from* H. Mintzberg & J.A. Waters, *Of Strategies, Deliberate and Emergent*, 6 STRATEGIC MGMT. J. 257 (1985).

planning as well as the long-term sustainability of legacy projects seems an acute institutional concern for the SCSL and other tribunals.

In light of the proliferation of legacy assessments, a paradox appears at first glance. Indeed, "in theory, the verdict on legacy should still be out ... at least until all of the Tribunals' verdicts are in. In practice, conclusions proliferate on the impact of the ad hoc international criminal tribunals, from the conventional to the extreme."[122] On the surface, legacy "previews" seem premature and oxymoronic, yet they merit attention for the underlying assumptions and claims about the objectives and expectations of international criminal justice. A distinction has been made for instance between the "potential for legacy" and the actual legacy,[123] or legacy and the purportedly "real legacy."[124] Contrary to claims about the realness and objectivity of a tribunal's legacy assessable only after final closure, here it is argued that a distinction between intended and realized legacies as well as a cyclical approach to legacies seem heuristically more valuable to capture the ongoing legacy construction, as illustrated in Figures 33.1 and 33.4.

A focus on intended legacy[125] and planning in this regard seems to suggest attempts toward maximizing control and possibly enforcing a certain legacy vision. There is however no strict linearity between intended legacy and realized legacies, as illustrated in Figure 33.4. Two

---

[122] Byrne, *supra* note 70, at 486.

[123] *E.g.*, T. Perriello & M. Wierda, *The Special Court for Sierra Leone under Scrutiny*. ICTJ Prosecutions Case Studies Series (Mar. 2006), *available at* http://ictj.org/publication/special-court-sierra-leone-under-scrutiny (last visited June 15, 2012).

[124] *E.g.*, M. Swart, *Tadic Revisited: Some Critical Comments on the Legacy and the Legitimacy of the ICTY*, 3 GOETTINGEN J. INT'L L. 985 (2011).

[125] Report of the Secretary-General, *supra* note 1.

further legacy variants may be distinguished: deliberate legacies act as a bridge for intentions to be realized, and emergent legacies develop in the absence of intentions or despite them. A pure version of deliberate and emergent legacies can be considered rare as most realized legacies seem part of a continuum. The underlying assumptions of deliberate legacy planning seem to be twofold: that legacies are highly malleable, and that the more intended, deliberate, and sophisticated the planning is, the more one actually shapes and controls legacies. In anticipation of final closure there are attempts to consolidate the legacies. One SCSL official noted, "in fairness, this institution looked at legacy a long time ago, because it was in contact with civil society, but now there is a consolidation approach everywhere, inside and outside."[126] The consolidation approach has certainly been colored by the Court's pending closure. Indeed, despite its rather technocratic and bureaucratic approach to legacy, inadequate planning has been referenced as the main impediment to the Court's realization of its legacy vision.[127] The common solution proposed to maximize the legacy is more planning.[128] Given the limits to planning and controlling legacies, advocating more planning seems to suggest a myopic panacea ignoring the social and political facets of legacy constructions.

Legacies can acquire significance and meaning beyond the original intent and emphasis. They constantly shift and are both a movable and moving target. In other words, no legacy actor controls their definite meaning. Legacy actors significantly shape legacies; thus the tendency to overestimate what the legacy leaver has achieved needs to be carefully balanced, as experience suggests a measure of humility. In this vein, Joseph Kamara, former SCSL Deputy Prosecutor and current President of the Anti-Corruption Commission in Sierra Leone, noted:

> one is however, cognizant of the fact that setting an example is very different to actually ensuring that the example is acted upon.... The recognition of the Rule of Law is a bastion of the Special Court. The question I will leave for stakeholders is whether there is a political will prepared to emulate the set standards?[129]

Ultimately, the actual realization of legacies and their interpretation and (re)construction over time appears outside the control of the Court – although that may be influenced by the extent of success of self-promoted legacy projects. Despite meticulous and admirable legacy planning, realized legacies are not all amenable to planning and control. Such an observation does not advocate apathy or disengagement vis-à-vis legacies or dwarf legacy planning efforts as such. It is rather hoped that illuminating the multifaceted and complex construction process involving diverse actors will foster a greater appreciation that legacies are not bestowed authoritatively, that unintended and unrealized legacies exist, and that legacy constructions may inevitably result in cacophony rather than concordant harmony.

V. CONCLUSION

The legacies of the SCSL remain in the making. Critically examining the key actors and social and political dynamics involved in the creation, contestation, and control of legacies

---

[126] Author interview, The Hague (June 2011).
[127] Cruvellier, *supra* note 18, at 3.
[128] OHCHR, *supra* note 17.
[129] Kamara, *supra* note 7, at 74.

therefore needs to take center stage. First, the concept of legacy and the process of leaving legacies require more systematic conceptualization. The notion of plural legacies advocated recognizes the multiplicity of meanings of legacy and the variety of contributions of the Court as viewed by different actors. The contours of a new framework depicting a notional legacy process were outlined in this chapter, highlighting the cycle of legacies and actor diversity. A focus on legacy actors has been markedly absent to date. It is important to distinguish five actor types: legacy leavers, producers, recorders, enforcers, and recipients. All the other actors are as crucial as the legacy leavers in constructing legacies. Second, the Court's own self-understanding as legacy leaver and engagement in legacy building calls for greater scrutiny. The institutionalization of legacy at the Court itself can be traced rhetorically, structurally, and practically. The SCSL has showcased considerable institutional innovation and demonstrated a forward-looking, proactive approach. Finally, analysis of the broader actor landscape and the social and political dynamics underlying legacy construction is indispensable. Different actors have different interests, resources, and legacy visions. The existence of both complementary and conflicting perceptions and definitions of legacy result in a complex interplay of multiple legacy constructions. Efforts aimed at legacy production, recording, and enforcement are proliferating, which demonstrates that the legacies of the Court have been married with considerable ambition. Certain limits inherent to intended and deliberate legacy planning in general and the institutionalized legacy endeavor of the SCSL need to be acknowledged against the backdrop of struggles over the power of interpretation and control of legacies. By shedding light on the otherwise little-illuminated actor diversity as well as certain dynamics and tensions of multiple legacy constructions, it has been shown here that the SCSL has a central, albeit limited role.

The SCSL has taken on a pioneering role and championed many firsts, not least as the first criminal court to develop its own legacy approach and ceremonially close down leaving multiple legacies under construction. The Court is however not the first criminal court ever to be closed down. Notable historical precedents include the Nuremberg and Tokyo International Military Tribunals. Above and beyond differences between the respective tribunal generations, closing a tribunal that has been in existence for roughly one or two years or rather ten (as the SCSL) or twenty years (as the ICTY and ICTR) is an undertaking of quite a different caliber given the considerable differences in context. A recent development of the last decade is the novel explicit interest of the Court in proactively shaping, developing, and leaving a legacy. This is discernible as a broader trend across all international criminal tribunals where leaving a lasting legacy has, to varying degrees, become an institutionalized endeavor.

It is time to more thoroughly inquire into the role and relevance of legacies in the case of the SCSL and for international criminal justice more broadly. The concept of legacy that has become so central in debates and activities surrounding the tribunals seems to be engulfed in a paradoxical situation: it is understudied, yet rhetorically overused. Hence, as proposed here, a more systematic conceptualization is essential to foster understanding of the complexities of the development of legacies. All future developments need to be accompanied by a rigorous interrogation as the issue of the creation, consolidation, and contestation as well as control of legacies examined here will certainly remain topical for some time to come.

34

Delivering International Criminal Justice at the Special Court for Sierra Leone: How Much Is Enough?

Mohamed A. Bangura[*]

I. INTRODUCTION

Although the great strides made by the Special Court in delivering international criminal justice to the people of Sierra Leone appear to have muted criticism about its establishment over the years,[1] the debate about the rationale for its creation has never quite been swept aside.[2]

Much of the criticism surrounding this debate is economic. Critics have argued that the huge sums of money so far expended in delivering justice at the international level could have been better utilized addressing other important postwar nation-building imperatives such as reducing unemployment, alleviating poverty, improving health care, strengthening the education system or generally building a more efficient

---

[*] LL.B. (Hons) (Fourah Bay College, University of Sierra Leone), LL.M. (London), M.Sc. South Bank University London; Member of the Taylor prosecution team in the Office of the Prosecutor, Special Court for Sierra Leone, The Hague, and former Trial Attorney in the CDF and RUF Cases, Freetown.

[1] Antonio Cassese, Independent Expert Report on the Special Court for Sierra Leone § 34 (Dec. 12, 2006), a report commissioned by the U.N. Secretary-General "to review the efficiency of the Special Court." It highlights achievements of the SCSL up to the date of its publication, discusses difficulties in achieving its mandate, and makes recommendations. At para. 34 it states, "The Special Court has in some respects made much headway, establishing a new benchmark for international criminal justice. On the other hand the court has also experienced a number of challenges and setbacks ...." [hereinafter Independent Expert]; *cited also by* Charles C. Jalloh, *Special Court for Sierra Leone: Achieving Justice?*, 32 Mich. J. Int'l L. 395, 396 (2011).

[2] Lansana Gberie et al., *Charles Taylor, Why Me?*, 45 New African (May 2006). Contains sixteen pages of special coverage published shortly after the arrest and transfer of Charles Taylor to the SCSL. The article, a three-part series, states,

> The UN Special Court in Sierra Leone began work nearly four years ago. It has since spent more than $80m. This is mainly as salary to its mainly expatriate staff amounting to $16m a year – more than that for the entire Sierra Leonean civil service .... Four years of its ponderous work, the court had clearly satisfied nobody's sense of justice, reconciled no one to the brutal past, and left many people plainly angry or bemused – until Taylor was flown in by helicopter ....

social infrastructure,[3] or better still, delivering justice at a substantially reduced cost domestically.[4]

This argument has hardly impressed the minds of the promoters of peace and justice the world over, notwithstanding its apparent appeal. Their desire to ensure accountability for the atrocious crimes committed in Sierra Leone during the war, to put an end to impunity, and to lay solid foundations for application of the rule of law and respect for human rights, remains uncompromised.[5]

The case against Charles Taylor in The Hague, being the last of four trials held by the Court,[6] has contributed in no small measure in reigniting arguments about the need for establishment of the Court, given the comparatively bigger slice this case commands of the

---

[3] Population 5.696 Million, GDP per capita $341, GDP growth 4.0%, Life Expectancy 48, Income Level Low, Poverty Ratio 70.2 %, *available at* http://web.worldbank.org/WBSITE/EXTERNAL/COUNTRIES/AFRICAEXT/SIERRALEONEEXTN/0,,menuPK:367829~pagePK:141159~piPK:141110~theSiteP K:367809,00.html (last visited May 7, 2012); *see also* William Reno, Countries at the Crossroads, at 9, unpublished, *available at* http://unpan1.un.org/intradoc/groups/public/documents/nispacee/unpan016206.pdf (last visited May 10, 2012); *see also* David Mathews, *Courting Disaster in Sierra Leone: The £75m Bureaucratic Farce,* Mail Online, Mar. 28, 2008, *available at* http://www.dailymail.co.uk/home/moslive/article-548161/Courting-disaster-Sierra-Leone-The-75m-bureaucratic-farce.html (last visited June 4, 2012).

[4] Lydia Apori Nkansah, "Justice within the Arrangement of the Special Court for Sierra Leone Verses Local Perceptions of Justice: A Contradiction or Harmonious?" – Paper presented at the American Political Science Annual Conference, 2011, held at Seattle, Washington from September 1 to 4, 2011 under the Panel on "Promise Effects and Limits of the Rule of Law under National, International and Transitional Setting," at 23, *available at* Social Science Research Network website, at http://papers.ssrn.com/sol3/papers.cfm?abstract_id=1901113 (last visited Aug. 17, 2012); *see also* Rachael Kerr & Jessica Lincoln, The Special Court for Sierra Leone: Outreach, Legacy and Impact, War Crimes Research Group, Department of War Studies, King's College London, University of London, Final Report, February 2008, at 20; *see also* Jalloh, *supra* note 1, at 433–35 – Jalloh examines the argument for domestic trials in Sierra Leone as a cost-saving method versus an international trial, but roundly dismisses the argument from its various perspectives. He concludes that generally, the quality of justice produced domestically would fail to meet international standards.

[5] S.C. Res. 1315, U.N. Doc. S/RES/1315 (Aug. 14, 2000) – The preamble to the Special Court Agreement that this document gives rise to mentions the Council's concern about the "prevailing situation of impunity in Sierra Leone"; *see also* S.C. Doc. S/PRST/2007/23 (June 28, 2007), "Statement by the President of the Security Council – At the 5708th meeting of the Security Council, held on June 28, 2007," in connection with the Council's consideration of the item entitled "The situation in Sierra Leone," the President of the Security Council, in his statement, congratulated the Outreach Section of the Court for its effort in bringing the judicial work of the court to the people of Sierra Leone, "... thereby contributing to the restoration of the rule of law throughout the country and region"; also Human Rights Watch Report, Sierra Leone: Getting Away with Murder, Mutilation, Rape – New Testimony from Sierra Leone, July 1999, vol. 11 No. 3(A): Recommendations: "We call on the Government of Sierra Leone to ... thoroughly investigate and prosecute in full compliance with international law, individuals responsible for grave breaches of humanitarian law. Where combatants have committed abuses against civilians, they should be held accountable in a court of law." To the International community, the Report states, "[We] ... Oppose a general amnesty that would apply to those who have committed gross violations of human rights and humanitarian law and insist on the need for the cycle of impunity to be broken if peace is to be restored to Sierra Leone," *available online at* http://www.hrw.org/legacy/reports/1999/sierra/SIERLE99–01.htm#P84_19258 (last visited Aug. 18, 2012).

[6] *Prosecutor v. Sam Hinga Norman, Moinina Fofana and Allieu Kondewa* (SCSL-2004–14), also called "The CDF Case" (Later, *The Prosecutor v. Moinina Fofana and Allieu Kondewa*) – three persons initially indicted, one died of natural causes before judgment – the other two were convicted – appeals completed in May 2008; *Prosecutor v. Alex Tamba Brima, Ibrahim Bazzy Kamara and Santigie Borbor Kanu* (SCSL-2004–16), also called "The AFRC Case" – three persons indicted, tried and convicted – appeals completed in February 2008; *The Prosecutor v. Issa Hassan Sesay, Morris Kallon and Augustine Gbao* (SCSL-2004–15), also called "The RUF Case" – three persons indicted, tried, and convicted – appeals completed in October 2009.

SCSL budget, relative to each of the other three completed cases.[7] The thrust of the argument is again economic, although other reasons have been canvassed. One such example is the moribund argument about supremacy of a sovereign's authority above the authority of the courts.[8] As the SCSL is now at an advanced stage of completing its mandate, appeals in the Taylor Case being the only issue now pending, the case for beginning a process of stocktaking of its achievements over the past eleven years is no longer premature.

The issue of legacy was, for instance, a major preoccupation on the minds of the founders of the court from its inception.[9] It then grew to become a central theme even as the Court worked to complete its first trials. As early as October 2004, even before judgment on the first of the trials was delivered, the Court had started its planning for the completion of its mandate. Its first Completion Strategy Paper was approved by the Management Committee,[10] necessarily also stimulating discussion about its legacy. Since then, not only has the Court been scaling down its operations and staffing pursuant to a draw down policy, it has also outlined and started implementing projects and activities intended to leave behind a lasting legacy in Sierra Leone.[11] This is in addition to the legacy most symbolic of

---

[7] Alfred Sam Foray, *Charles Taylor and the Fallacy of the Special Court*, Patriotic Vanguard Sierra Leone News Portal, May 11, 2012:

> The enormous cost of running the court – over two hundred million United States dollars in the case of Sierra Leone – which could better have been used to improve the lives of the living rather than avenging the dead is another compelling reason against the establishment of such a court. And what did Sierra Leoneans get for two hundred million dollars spent in their name? A divided nation, a set of ramshackled buildings along Jomo Kenyatta Road in Freetown and ten convictions at the cost of $20 million per person all held outside Sierra Leone. For a country with the highest infant and maternal mortality rate in the world, we could have built ten universities or ten hospitals for women, infants and children.
>
> *Available at* http://www.thepatrioticvanguard.com/spip.php?article6500 (last visited Aug. 17, 2012).

[8] The argument of sovereign immunity has lost its appeal in modern day accountability principles in international criminal law. Taylor's jurisdictional challenge to his indictment on the basis of head-of-state or sovereign immunity was dismissed, as such immunity was inapplicable to the authority of an international court or tribunal – see Decision on Immunity from Jurisdiction, Prosecutor v. Charles Ghankay Taylor, SCSL-03-01-I-059, Appeals Chamber, paras. 52–53 (May 31, 2004).

[9] *First Annual Report of the President of the Special Court to the United Nations* [hereinafter First Annual Report] March 2004, at 28, reads:

> History will judge how successful these initiatives have been, but the foundations for leaving behind a legacy of accountability and contributing to legal reform in Sierra Leone are being laid. More globally, it is hoped that the legacy of the Special Court will also serve as a template for ensuring accountability for violations of international humanitarian law in other post-conflict situations.
>
> *Available at* http://www.sc-sl.org/LinkClick.aspx?fileticket=NRhDcbHrcSs%3d&tabid=176 (last visited Aug. 17, 2012).

[10] The First Version of the Completion Strategy Paper was adopted by the Management Committee on October 6, 2004, with a Draft Personnel policy approved on October 19, 2005 – U.N. Doc. A/59/816-S/2005/350, updated on May 18, 2005. Subsequent updates have included, SCSL/IC/2006/008/ of March 22, 2006 – SCSL Completion Strategy – Personnel Policy, approved by the Management Committee on October 19, 2005, but published to staff on March 22, 2006, expressed to take effect retroactively, on November 1, 2005. This was superseded by SCSL/IC/2008/030 – SCSL Completion Strategy – Revised Personnel policy, dated October 28, 2008.

[11] *Fourth Annual Report of the President of the Special Court to the United Nations*, January 2006–May 2007, at 41 [hereinafter Fourth Annual Report]:

> In seeking to leave a tangible legacy, the Special Court is motivated by several factors. As a Court operating in a context such as Sierra Leone, the prosecution of individuals must be pursued along with other transitional justice strategies, such as the development of national judicial institutions, in order to achieve the desired objective of strengthening the rule of law and maintaining peace and security in Sierra Leone.

its physical presence in the country – the sprawling complex situated in the west end of Freetown, with its iconic courthouse.[12]

The legacy initiatives have included training of Sierra Leone police personnel seconded to the Office of the Prosecutor as investigators, and officers who prosecute the bulk of criminal cases in the magistrate's court in the national system, assisting in the development of a national witness protection program that will fully take over SCSL witnesses still in post-testimony protection, establishing a museum to memorialize ten years of war in Sierra Leone, and creating an online legal research database that will store all SCSL and related ad hoc tribunal jurisprudence, international legal instruments, and Sierra Leone legislation and jurisprudence.[13] Although none of these activities forms part of the core mandate of the SCSL, they are *incidental* to the Court's core business or could *be conveniently combined* with that core activity to achieve the Court's objectives. Alternatively, it can be said that they are reasonably necessary for the effective implementation of the Court's mandate, or are reasonably expected outcomes of its core activities and operations.[14]

On the eve of completing such an important mandate at a huge budget cost of U.S. $220 million and counting,[15] it is worth examining in depth the value of the work of the SCSL not just to its beneficiaries, the people of Sierra Leone, but also its benefactors, the international community, as to whether their expectations of justice at the international level, focused on putting an end to impunity and laying foundations for the rule of law and respect for human rights as enshrined in S.C. Res. 1315 (2000), have been met. Additionally, it is important to evaluate whether the injustices of the conflict have, through the establishment of the Court, been addressed. More important, we should also consider whether and to what extent the legacy projects so far embarked upon by the Court make a meaningful contribution in addressing the quest for justice brought about by the conflict, and if not, the reasons therefore.

Critics of the Court whose perception of achievement is measured only in tangible, physical terms will continue to raise the economic argument, supported with examples of missed alternatives – such as good roads, clean water, electricity, education, and health care. However, it is by the values of the largely intangible, metaphysical achievements – such as deterrence, which justice fosters – that the court's work will be judged.

As part of a continuing effort to assess the value of SCSL's achievements, this chapter will examine and evaluate several achievements with which the Court is thus far credited, both within and outside the framework of its mandate. As a first step, the evaluation will crucially entail a discussion of the various possible interpretations that the mandate is open to,

---

– Excerpt of Speech by President Justice George Gelaga King (2006–2007) to the United Nations Peacebuilding Commission, Feb. 28, 2007, *available at* http://www.sc-sl.org/LinkClick.aspx?fileticket= NRhDcbHrcSs%3d&tabid=176 (last visited Aug. 17, 2012).

[12] "The Special Court currently sits on an 11.5 acre site that includes a state-of-the-art courthouse, detention facility, 200 containerized office blocks, security building, etc.," excerpt of speech by President Justice Gelaga King (2006–2007) to the United Nations Peacebuilding Commission, Feb. 28, 2007.

[13] See Legacy page on the SCSL website, *available at* http://www.sc-sl.org/LEGACY/tabid/224/Default.aspx (last visited Aug. 17, 2012).

[14] It is typical in the insurance industry to have clauses that seek to distinguish between core activities and non-core activities, with exceptional rules for incorporating certain noncore activities. This distinction used to be important also in discerning the object clauses of a company in its memorandum of association before the ultra vires rule lost its significance.

[15] Jalloh, *supra* note 1, at 447–48, in particular fn. 253 gives a breakdown.

reasonable expectations that it generates, and a determination as to whether all of these are achievable. Alongside successes, the work will also consider the shortcomings, if any, of the various projects the Court has, or intends to undertake, and whether and why any alternative options will work better.

Further, the author will assess the extent to which the implementation of other transitional justice mechanisms alongside SCSL's work may have contributed to, or hindered effort, at achieving its mandate. Additionally, it will discuss the impunity gap created, seemingly inadvertently, by the Court's Statute in providing for complementary jurisdiction over the conduct of foreign peacekeepers,[16] and also, by the grant of an amnesty to perpetrators by the government of Sierra Leone in the Lomé peace agreement.[17] Although these acts may not have restrained or inhibited exercise of the Court's mandate, they clearly denied the people of Sierra Leone a full measure of the justice they deserve. Finally, the chapter will consider whether the national legal system benefitted from the presence of the Special Court in Sierra Leone to boost justice delivery. In particular, the involvement of Sierra Leonean professionals in the work of the Court and the anticipated transfer of knowledge and skills toward building capacity in the justice sector will be critically assessed to determine the degree of success, if any, that has been achieved.

II. DEFINING THE SCOPE OF SCSL'S WORK

A. *Origins of Its Mandate*

At its establishment, the scope of the work of the SCSL was clearly defined in its Statute, and in *travaux préparatoires* that preceded its creation.[18] Those critical defining statements of its creation were key to determining the height of its success at adulthood. Overambitious and highfalutin objectives, for instance, were bound to be a recipe for underachievement or failure. In many respects, the mandate of the Court as outlined in the Statute could reasonably be described as measured and achievable.[19] If anything, concerns have been expressed more about the limiting effect of the mandate on the Court's potentialities for achieving even greater success in the fight against impunity.[20]

---

[16] SCSL Statute art. 1(1) and art. 1(3) – these provisions enable the Special Court to exercise jurisdiction over foreign peacekeeping forces who committed crimes covered by the Statute only where the sending state is unwilling or unable to carry out investigations or prosecute its own forces.

[17] Lomé Peace Agreement, July 7, 1999, Article IX – Pardon and Amnesty.

[18] Jalloh, *supra*, note 1, at 398–401; *see also* Decision on the Preliminary Defense Motion on the lack of personal jurisdiction filed on behalf of the Accused Fofana, Prosecutor v. Norman, Fofana & Kondewa, SCSL-04-PT-026, paras. 21–27 and 40 (Mar. 3, 2004) [hereinafter *Prosecutor v. Norman, Fofana & Kondewa*, SCSL-04-PT-026].

[19] David M. Crane, *The Take Down: Case Studies regarding "Lawfare" in International Criminal Justice: The West African Experience*, 33 CASE W. RES. J. INT'L L. 201, at 204 (2010).

[20] SCSL Statute art. 1(1): "The Special Court shall, except as provided in subparagraph (2), have the power to prosecute *persons who bear the greatest responsibility* (emphasis added) for serious violations of international humanitarian law and Sierra Leonean law committed in the territory of Sierra Leone since November 30, 1996, including those leaders who, in committing such crimes, have threatened the establishment of and implementation of the peace process in Sierra Leone."; Jalloh, *supra* note 1, at 412–28. Discussing the topic, "Some Limitations of the Special Court for Sierra Leone," Jalloh critically examines factors responsible for the narrowness with which the Prosecutor's mandate was exercised, some he attributes to the prosecutor's deliberate judgment or "discretion," others to factors outside his powers. In effect, he makes the point that,

The founding stakeholders of the Court were clear in their vision as to the type of justice that they were seeking to achieve for Sierra Leone. President Ahmed Tejan Kabbah, perhaps owing to his background as a lawyer and long experience as a UN civil servant, was unequivocal in his request to the UN Security Council about the type of justice the people of Sierra Leone needed. He envisioned "a court that will meet international standards for the trial of criminals while at the same time having a mandate to administer a blend of international and domestic law on Sierra Leonean soil."[21] The Security Council in its response through the Secretary-General was equally unequivocal about the scope of the Court's mandate.[22] The drafters of the Statute had no doubt given effect accurately to the desires and intentions of the parties, regarding the scope of work that this newly created justice body should undertake. The same message was conveyed to the world on January 16, 2002, by the UN Under-Secretary for Legal Affairs Hans Corell, when he signed the SCSL agreement in Freetown.[23] If in the implementation of this mandate, gaps emerged between expectation and reality, it can hardly be said that this arose from some ambiguity in defining the objectives that this institution was designed to undertake. Even if, as some have argued, President Kabbah's true motivation for requesting the Court's establishment was driven not by a genuine desire for peace, but rather politics,[24] the message that his, and the actions of other key actors conveyed, was clear and unambiguous.

Once established however, the challenges to the Court's success lay in the efficient management of its affairs. As a judicial entity, its core responsibility to fairly try those deemed to bear greatest responsibility for the crimes committed in Sierra Leone, which in fact was the raison d'etre for its creation and existence, rested on the Office of the Prosecutor (OTP), one of three main organs of the court, headed by the Prosecutor.[25] The extent to which the OTP interpreted and executed the Court's legal mandate, with the support and collaboration of the other two organs, largely determined the degree of success that the Court was to achieve. The OTP, by such interpretation of its legal mandate, became the key driver of events in the life of the Court. In effect, the OTP has been and remains the mover and shaker of the Court's principal business. This interpretation and execution practically translates into two principal considerations – operations and staffing. In turn, these cascade into budgeting, logistical, personnel, communication and technology, public affairs and security needs, all of which are serviced by the Registry. Filling these needs is essentially what gives flesh and blood to the day-to-day existence of the Court as an entity. This analysis underlines the central role of the OTP in assessing the Court's achievements.

prosecutorial discretion aside, many more perpetrators of crimes could have been charged and prosecuted by the SCSL, but for the "circumscribed" nature of the mandate given to the Prosecutor.

[21] Jalloh, *supra* note 1, at 399.

[22] See, for more on this, Chapter 30 of this volume where Charles Jalloh discusses the Court's personal jurisdiction.

[23] *Sierra Leone News*, Jan. 2002, *available at* http://www.sierra-leone.org/Archives/slnews0102.html (last visited June 21, 2012).

[24] Tom Perriello & Marieke Wierda, *The Special Court for Sierra Leone under Scrutiny*, ICTJ Prosecution Case Studies Series, March 2006, under the rubric, "Establishment of the Court: sub, (B) National Political Context," at 12–13, *available at* http://www.ictj.org/sites/default/files/ICTJ-SierraLeone-Special-Court-2006-English.pdf (last visited Aug. 17, 2012); *see also* Jalloh, *supra* note 1, at 426.

[25] SCSL Statute art. 15, "The Prosecutor" – this article discusses the Office of the Prosecutor, including his role and functions.

B. *Interpretation and Execution of the Court's Mandate*

The statutory mandate of the Court is stated in plain language,[26] but its interpretation has been open to a wide range of notions, some legal and others not. On the legal front, interpretation of the SCSL mandate has necessarily involved the Prosecutor, at his/her sole discretion,[27] making such decisions as to which persons to investigate, indict, or prosecute; how to conduct investigations, including who to use as sources or witnesses; which witnesses to call in support of the Prosecution's case; and which material are considered relevant as exhibits, and where necessary, seeking orders for their seizure from an accused person. Also included is whether and which authorities of state or foreign entities the Prosecution seeks cooperation from in furtherance of its mandate, and above all in the event of a conviction, an entitlement to request of the Judges a quantum of punishment commensurate to the crimes committed.

The exercise of this discretion is not however, uncurbed. It has been argued variously that the Trial Chamber should have oversight responsibility to check the improper exercise of discretion by the Prosecutor, particularly where decisions are driven by motives that may not be purely legal but rather partial, or are contrary to the interest of justice.[28] In the CDF case, it was argued that the Trial Chamber lacked personal jurisdiction over Fofana, on the basis that the Accused was not one of those falling within the category of "those who bear the greatest responsibility" deserving of prosecution.[29] In the RUF Case, the Defense argued a motion for disclosure by the Prosecution regarding an alleged relationship between governmental agencies of the United States, in particular, the Federal Bureau of Investigation, and the Office of the Prosecutor. The alleged link between the two bodies, they argued, amounted to a breach of the Prosecutor's obligation to maintain his independence under Article 15 of the Statute. The Trial Chamber held that no such links had been established, and it was for the Defense to specifically identify material in the possession of the Prosecution that allegedly established such connection.[30] Similarly, in the Taylor case the Defense argued that the Prosecution was selective in its indictment of Taylor, and that it lacked independence and impartiality.[31] It has even been argued that prosecutorial discretion equates to a

---

[26] SCSL Statute art. 1(1), *supra* note 20.

[27] The OTP operates a Prosecutions and an Investigations section with qualified and experienced personnel whose duties assist in the judicious exercise of the Prosecutor's discretion.

[28] Daniel D. Ntanda Nsereko, Prosecutorial Discretion before National Courts and International Tribunals, University of Botswana, unpublished, *available at* http://www.isrcl.org/Papers/Nsereko.pdf (last visited July 3, 2012); also Nkansah, *supra* note 4, at 17:

> The Government was perceived to have requested for the SCSL in pursuit of his political objectives. Some participants believed that the Government of Sierra Leone engaged the SCSL largely to get rid of the RUF which had metamorphosed into a political party. They also maintained that the government wanted to get rid of its political opponents in the party notably Hinga Norman.

[29] *Prosecutor v. Norman, Fofana & Kondewa*, SCSL-04-PT-026, *supra* note 18, § 2.

[30] Decision on Sesay – Motion Seeking Disclosure of the Relationship between Governmental Relationship of the United States of America and the Office of Prosecutor, Prosecutor v. Issa Sesay, Morris Kallon & Augustine Gbao, SCSL-04-15-T, paras. 65–67 (May 2, 2005).

[31] Prosecutor v. Taylor, SCSL-03-01-T-1174, Decision on Urgent and Public with Annexes A–N Defense Motion for Disclosure and/or Investigations of United States Government Sources within Trial Chamber, Prosecution and the Registry based on Leaked USG Cables, at 7 (Jan. 28, 2011); *see also* Public with Confidential Annex Defense Corrected and Amended Final Trial Brief Defense, Prosecutor v. Charles Ghankay Taylor, SCSL-03-I-T, Mar. 9, 2011, "Selective Prosecution," at 34962–967 and paras. 9–22.

failure by the Prosecutor to fairly exercise that mandate. Nonetheless, in none of these cases has the Trial Chamber agreed with the Defense about ineffective or improper interpretation of the mandate so as to warrant the Chamber's intervention.[32] In its recent judgment in the Taylor Case, the Trial Chamber "[found] that the accused [Taylor] has not been singled out for selective prosecution."[33]

On the nonlegal front, the main allegation mounted against the Prosecution's interpretation of its mandate is that it is underpinned by a political motivation at the behest of the United Nations, intended to shield President Kabbah, the Commander-in-Chief of the Sierra Leone Armed Forces,[34] and also members of the Nigeria-led Economic Community of West African States Monitoring Group (ECOMOG) peacekeeping troops, widely accused of overstepping their peacekeeping mandate, becoming partisan, and inevitably sharing responsibility for some of the crimes committed against civilians.[35]

C. Interpretation and Execution of the Court's Mandate – Wider Expectations

The reasons that propelled the outbreak of conflict in Sierra Leone are well documented.[36] Among them are corruption, nepotism, bad governance, political exclusion, a breakdown of the social infrastructure, and a dysfunctional legal system.[37] Thus after the war was declared over and the SCSL was set up to try war criminals, there were reasonably legitimate expectations on the part of Sierra Leoneans that this newly created justice-dispensing body would address chronic problems associated with the justice system in the country. Although the SCSL was expressly tasked to investigate and prosecute perpetrators of crimes in the conflict, expectations lingered, some might say naively, that this new international court operating on home soil would serve as a model for the local judiciary. Issues of proper observance of due process, delays at trial, delivery of fair and impartial decisions, bribery and corruption of court officials, were all vices in the domestic criminal justice process. Those expectations, it should be admitted, are not far-fetched.[38]

---

[32] Judgment, Prosecutor v. Charles Ghankay Taylor, SCSL-03–01-T, May 18, 2012, "Selective Prosecution," at 40631–635, paras. 71–84; also Corrigendum to Judgment Filed on May 18, 2012, Prosecutor v. Charles Ghankay Taylor, SCSL-03–01-T, May 30, 2012; *Prosecutor v. Norman, Fofana & Kondewa*, SCSL-04-PT-026, *supra* note 18, paras. 27, 28, 48, and 49.

[33] Judgment, Taylor Case, *id.*

[34] Kerr & Lincoln, *supra* note 4, at 9 – encapsulating the perceptions of Sierra Leoneans about exercise of the Court's mandate vis-à-vis President Kabbah and Vice-President Berewa, from a research survey conducted by the writers; Nkansah, *supra* note 4, at 12 and 17.

[35] Human Rights Watch Report Sierra Leone, July 1999, *supra* note 5, V. *Human Rights Abuses Committed by ECOMOG, Sierra Leonean Defence Forces and Police: Summary Executions:*Human Rights Watch has taken the testimonies of witnesses to over 180 summary executions of rebel prisoners and their suspected collaborators, mostly by ECOMOG forces but also by members of the Civil Defense Forces (CDF), and the Special Security Division (SSD) of the Sierra Leonean Police (who when on combat operations are under ECOMOG command). While the victims were overwhelmingly young men, witnesses confirm the execution of some women, and children as young as eight.

[36] *See TRC Report*, vol. I, Introduction, § 11 – Causes of the Conflict.

[37] Sigall Horowitz, *Sierra Leone: Interaction between International and National Responses to Mass Atrocities*, DOMAC/Dec. 3, 2009, at 12, cites the Human Rights Commission of Sierra Leone, as stating in its First Annual Report, 2007 that "[b]ad governance, endemic corruption and the denial of human rights together with their attendant consequences made conflict inevitable."

[38] TRC Report, *Supra*, note 36.; Michelle Gehrig, International Courts and The Domestic Judiciary In Africa –

Second, given the huge capacity gap at the local level that the Special Court experienced initially, especially of professionals in the field of international criminal law and practice, expectations grew that Sierra Leonean lawyers recruited into the process would build up knowledge and experience in this emerging field and, in due course, be able and willing to apply that knowledge and experience to improving standards in the national legal system.[39] The same feelings applied in respect of specialists from nonlegal areas, such as personnel from the national police (SLP) assisting the OTP as investigators, some of very senior rank; and court administrators, including recorders and translators, stenographers, and specialists in courtroom technology.

Third, it is fair to say that the establishment of the Court created hope or expectation that other institutions of state, whether associated with the justice process directly or indirectly, would reflect this new spirit of respect for the rule of law and human rights, and imbibe the fresh resolve around the world to discourage impunity. Coming into existence just as the final signatures to the Rome Statute were opening the way for commencement of operations of the International Criminal Court in The Hague,[40] the SCSL must surely have imbued the people of Sierra Leone and beyond with this new feeling of hope being ushered around the world – hope that impunity, especially that associated with the activities of greedy, ruthless, power-hungry political leaders and warlords, would no longer be tolerated.

D. *Interpretation and Execution of the Court's Mandate – Peace Expectations*

An immediate initial objective at the time of the Court's commencement of operations was the hope or expectation that the indictment and arrest of high-level officials in an erstwhile volatile society would bring a certain level of calm and deterrence among the still-restive members of disarmed and demobilized factions, pending the trials.[41] This was only an immediate short-term objective of the wider overarching goal of achieving peace through justice. At the international level, the realization of this smaller objective fueled expectations that by the end of the process not only would impunity in all its forms be addressed, wherefrom and howsoever arising, but it would lay solid foundations for the rebirth of a fair, just, and law-abiding society based on respect for human rights and the

---

With jurisdiction over both national and international crimes and a mixture of national and international staff the international community had high expectations of what the Special Court could do in the rebuilding of the post conflict Sierra Leonean justice system. Purely, its location and structure as a hybrid court gave it an advantage in transferring knowledge, building infrastructure and rebuilding judicial institutions.
– Jan. 19, 2012, unpublished, *available at* website of e-International Relations, http://www.e-ir. info/2012/01/19/international-courts-and-the-domestic-judiciary-in-africa/ (last visited May 15, 2012); *see also* Reno, *supra* note 3, at 1; *see also* Horowitz, *supra* note 37, at 22.

[39] Independent Expert, *supra* note 1, § 288; *see also* First Annual Report, *supra* note 9, at 3: Forward of the Court President, Justice Robertson, "… It will provide a legacy for this recovering nation not merely by building and leaving behind an impressive, modern courthouse and by providing training and experience for local lawyers, investigators and administrators, but more importantly, by encouraging respect for the rule of law."

[40] United Nations Treaty Collection Databases, Rome Statute of the International Criminal Court, Rome July 17, 1998, Entry into Force: July 1, 2002, in Accordance with Article 126, Status as at 16.06.2012, 10.04.06. EDT – Sierra Leone: Signed Oct. 17, 1998, Ratified Sept. 15, 2000, *available at* http://treaties.un.org/Pages/ViewDetails.aspx?src=TREATY&mtdsg_no=XVIII-10&chapter=18&lang=en (last visited Aug. 17, 2012).

[41] Reno, *supra* note 3, at 8.

rule of law.[42] In the view of many, the amount of money being spent to fix the problem in Sierra Leone should not be applied to the fight against impunity associated with international humanitarian law violations alone, but at its core, the elimination of impunity in all its forms.

The responsibility for restoring peace and rebalancing society after such bloody conflicts is a core UN responsibility,[43] not to be left to chance to the core functions of a hybrid international criminal tribunal more focused on investigating and prosecuting war crimes perpetrators. The United Nations Department for Peace Keeping Operations (UN DKPO), under whose auspices the UN Assistance Mission for Sierra Leone (UNAMSIL) had been established and was functioning, therefore had primary responsibility over this restoring and rebalancing. To this extent, efforts by the SCSL to fulfill some of that role, which at best can be described as incidental, ought not be a basis for measuring its own success. But perhaps out of eager desperation, it can be argued, these expectations lingered.

E. Interpretation and Execution of the Court's Mandate: Should Reparation Be a Legitimate Expectation?

In spite of the important role victims have played as witnesses in the successful prosecution of crimes committed during the conflict, they seem to have attracted very little attention materially. Yet indeed, from the Court's interaction with victims through its Witnesses and Victims Section (WVS) and the OTP's Witnesses and Management Unit (WMU), the urgent need to address some of their very basic needs such as food, housing, health care and education could not have been accentuated more. Victims of amputation, of single or both limbs, are in more acute need, as they also require regular physical support and assistance for performing even the most basic tasks of life. Often, children have to play such a supportive role, at the expense of their education. The lack of access to these basics means that amputees often resort to street begging, a phenomenon very common in the capital, and in other major cities in the provinces.[44]

SCSL through WVS and WMU provides limited support to the handful of victim witnesses who assist the Court, to the extent of their assessed needs.[45] Beyond this, any other assistance or support to victims has come from benevolent gestures of individual staff.[46]

---

[42] First Annual Report, *supra* note 9; *see also Third Annual Report of the President of the Special Court to the United Nations, January 2005–January 2006* [hereinafter Third Annual Report]; Legacy: "The Special Court has always recognized, not only the critical importance of leaving a legacy for the people of Sierra Leone, but also the unprecedented opportunity to contribute to the restoration of the rule of law.", at 28, *available at* http://www.sc-sl.org/LinkClick.aspx?fileticket=S7DTFHKKRRg%3d&tabid=176 (last visited Aug. 17, 2012).

[43] Chapters VI and VII U.N. Charter – The Charter gives the UN Security Council primary responsibility for the maintenance of international peace and security. In fulfilling this responsibility, the Council may adopt a range of measures, including the establishment of a UN peacekeeping operation – see "Mandates and the Legal Basis for Peacekeeping," *at* http://www.un.org/en/peacekeeping/operations/pkmandates.shtml (last visited May 18, 2012); also Nkansah, *supra* note 4, at 18, citing ICTJ (2004, 2006) – discusses the size and justification for the UN peacekeeping mission in Sierra Leone.

[44] Global Times Online, OPINION: *Street Begging A Cause for Concern*, by Alhaji Saidu Kamara, *available at* http://www.globaltimes-sl.org/news1896.html (last visited July 2, 2012).

[45] Special Court for Sierra Leone Practice Direction on Allowances for Witnesses and Expert Witnesses – adopted on July 16, 2004; Special Court for Sierra Leone Practice Direction on Allowances for Witnesses and Expert Witnesses Testifying in The Hague – adopted on June 8, 2007.

[46] OTP staff members for instance make an annual Christmas presentation of basic food and educational material to the Amputee Association located at Murray Town in Freetown. A similar annual cash donation is made

Thus in a situation where there is hardly any form of regular or sustained state support,[47] and largely uncoordinated NGO support,[48] expectations are bound to arise that in addition to its core functions, the Court will also be addressing issues of reparation. At Court outreach events, when members of the public inquire about long-term plans for victims of the conflict, they are often met with disappointment. The Court's mandate and available resources do not extend to addressing reparation issues. This inevitably triggers the economic argument that begs rationalization: should such huge sums be spent prosecuting so few while the very many – their victims – continue to languish in abject conditions forced upon them by the conduct of these same perpetrators?

F. Interpretation of the Court's Mandate – The Role of the TRC, a Limiting Factor?

An accolade that Sierra Leone earned itself in its postwar transitional drive is the distinction of being the first country to concurrently pursue two major transitional justice processes: a restorative justice process, in the form of a truth-telling commission, and an accountability justice process, in the form of a war crimes tribunal.[49] Given the different processes with completely different outcomes,[50] as Alpha Sesay explains in his chapter in this volume, one might be tempted to think that pursuing both concurrently was not just a contradiction in terms, but a somewhat bewildering adventure. However, barring minor misunderstandings

---

to the Milton Margai School for the Blind, also located in Freetown, although these are not necessarily war victims.

[47] The Lomé Peace Agreement, art. XXIX: Special Fund for War Victims: "The Government, with the support of the International Community, shall design and implement a program for the rehabilitation of war victims. For this purpose, a special fund shall be set up." In spite of calls by many including the TRC in its Final Report – 2006 for implementation of this provision, hardly much has been done. In 2009, the National Commission for Social Action (NaCsa) a state institution with designated responsibility for handling the reparation program, received U.S. $3 million from the UN Peace Building Fund in Sierra Leone. From its own reports, NaCsa made a one-off payment of Le 300,000/00 (three hundred thousand Leones) to each of the three thousand recorded victims, the equivalent of U.S. $85. To date for lack of funding, no further payments or assistance in another form has been provided by NaCsa.

[48] Modern Ghana, Opinion December 3, 2011 – *Amputees' Life. After Sierra Leone's 11 Years Civil War* – by Daily Guide, *available at* http://www.modernghana.com/news/364730/1/amputees-life-after-sierra-leones-11-years-civil-w.html (last visited Aug. 17, 2012).

[49] Priscilla Hayner, Negotiating Peace in Sierra Leone: Confronting the Challenge, ICTJ Report Dec. 2007, at 7: "The simultaneous operation of the TRC and the Special Court for Sierra Leone revealed the complementarities of the two institutions, but also several difficulties and confusions," *available at* http://www.ictj.org/sites/default/files/ICTJ-CHD-SierraLeone-Negotiating-Peace-2007-English_0.pdf (last visited Aug. 17, 2012).

[50] SCSL Statute art. 1, Competence of the Special Court: 1. The Special Court shall, except as provided in subparagraph (2), have the power to prosecute persons who bear the greatest responsibility for serious violations of international humanitarian law and Sierra Leonean law committed in the territory of Sierra Leone since November 30, 1996, including those leaders who, in committing such crimes, have threatened the establishment of and implementation of the peace process in Sierra Leone; The Truth and Reconciliation Commission Act 2000 (TRC Act 2000), Part III – Functions of Commission: 6.(1) The object for which the Commission is established is to create an impartial historical record of violations and abuses of human rights and international humanitarian law related to the armed conflict in Sierra Leone, from the beginning of the Conflict in 1991 to the signing of the Lomé Peace Agreement; to address impunity, to respond to the needs of the victims, to promote healing and reconciliation and to prevent a repetition of the violations and abuses suffered.

and confusion,[51] both processes were successfully undertaken,[52] a testimony to the high level of professionalism demonstrated by the staff of the two institutions and the supportive role of civil society.[53]

By the nature of their activities and the ultimate goal of these two processes, it was inevitable that some interaction would occur in their operations, and from that, possible frictions. Whereas the Truth and Reconciliation Commission (TRC) focused on restoring peace in society through a truth-telling process that was largely voluntary, the SCSL's focus was on achieving peace through justice, in the form of retribution and deterrence. Considering that the primary focus of both processes was to achieve justice for victims of the conflict, in the one case by getting perpetrators to come face-to-face with their victims, publicly confess their crimes, and ask for forgiveness if need be; and in the other, by prosecuting and punishing perpetrators, it was inevitable that both sides would seek to work with victims and perpetrators for purposes of investigating crimes, gathering evidence, and giving testimony. Furthermore, given the range of crimes covered by both institutions, which overlap in many areas,[54] and that the events from which the crimes arose were the same conflict; same perpetrators; same crime locations; same town, village, or district, etc. – not only did the potential for confusion exist, but the risk of having victims relive their trauma many times over as they gave, corrected, or confirmed their statements threatened to undermine efficacy.

Indeed, such was the threat to efficacy that matters came to the fore in public discussions about the likelihood of conflict in the exercise of authority between the two bodies. First, by their constitutive instruments, both institutions were empowered if need be to use coercive powers to summon persons or to obtain information from any person/institution/authority of interest in Sierra Leone, not excluding state functionaries or institutions.[55] Additionally, the SCSL had powers of arrest.[56] The SCSL's ability and coercive power to request information from the TRC, was publicly and widely debated. The work of both institutions kicking off around the same period did not help either.[57] Within a short time of commencing work,

---

[51] Paul James Allen, Sheku B. S. Lahai & Jamie O'Connell, *Sierra Leone's Truth & Reconciliation Commission and Special Court: A Citizen's Handbook*; for National Forum for Human Rights (Freetown) and ITCJ (New York), 2003, "Relationship between the TRC and the Special Court," at 50; *see also* A study by PRIDE in partnership with the ITCJ, "*Ex-Combatant Views of Truth and Reconciliation Commission and the Special Court in Sierra Leone*," Freetown, Sept. 12, 2002, at 4 – Introduction: "PRIDE, in partnership with the International Centre for Transitional Justice (ICTJ) has completed a two month survey assessing ex-combatants' awareness of and views on the Special Court (SC) and Truth and Reconciliation Commission (TRC). Through the survey and subsequent focus groups, we investigated ex-combatants' views about the possible relationship between these two accountability institutions, namely models of information sharing, and how these models would impact their decision to provide testimony to the TRC," *available at* http://www.ictj.org/sites/default/files/ICTJ-SierraLeone-Combatants-TRC-2002-English.pdf (last visited Aug. 17, 2012).

[52] Hayner, *supra* note 49, at 25–27.

[53] Press Release, Office of the Prosecutor, TRC Chairman and Special Court Prosecutor Join Hands to Fight Impunity (Dec. 10, 2002).

[54] Statute of the Special Court for Sierra Leone, art. 1, Competence of the Special Court, *supra* note 50; The TRC Act 2000, Part III – Functions of Commission: 6.(1), *supra* note 50.

[55] The TRC Act 2000, S.8(1)(a, g, h) & 8(2); Special Court Ratification Act 2002, S.21(2).

[56] Rule 54 SCSL RPE empowers the Trial Chamber to issue "such orders, summonses, subpoenas, warrants and transfer orders as may be necessary for the purposes of an investigation or for preparation of the conduct of a trial" at the instance of either of the parties before it.

[57] Allen et al., *supra* note 51, at 35–40.

teams of interviewers from the TRC as well as investigators from the SCSL were traversing Sierra Leone to investigate incidents, obtain statements, make follow-up calls, and set up meetings for victims and witnesses living in remote inaccessible areas, in bigger nearby towns. Somehow, the two institutions initially managed to avoid the potential for conflict by staying above the minutiae. They made public statements intended to allay public concern and anxiety, promising to stay clear of each other's paths.[58] Essentially, an unwritten code developed whereby SCSL investigators and TRC statement takers would avoid talking to the same persons at the same time. In practice, SCSL investigators, to the extent possible, avoided dealing with persons who had previously given a statement to the TRC as witnesses. Confused and marginally enlightened country folks eager to narrate their experience managed to play along, although often finding it difficult to distinguish between one set of visitors and another, especially where teams consisted of a *waite man*,[59] as was often the case.

The SCSL's image was also not helped when it started issuing indictments and making arrests, particularly the arrest of Chief Hinga Norman, seen largely as a national hero, and not in the category of other bad guys from the RUF and AFRC. Uncertainty over the scope of the Prosecutor's intended interpretation of his legal mandate also sparked fears and concern among many former combatants, some of whom had already made statements to the TRC. Would their statements, being a truthful account of their role in the conflict, and possibly containing incriminating information, be turned over to the SCSL and used as a basis for their indictment and arrest?[60] It is not clear how this affected cooperation with the TRC, particularly from middle-level former commanders, but in the case of the SCSL, although it dissuaded many potential witnesses, victims were still committed to conveying the truth.[61]

In Hinga Norman's situation, matters came to a head after his indictment and detention, when the TRC filed a request to the SCSL for his attendance at the Commission to give public testimony about his role in the conflict. Justice Bankole Thomson, a Trial Chamber I judge sitting on the substantive case against Norman, but specially designated to give a determination on the application pursuant to a practice direction, denied the request.[62] His decision was appealed to the President of the court, who in principle, recognized Norman's right to make a statement to the TRC, but in the interest of protecting the principle of presumption of innocence, the interests of his codefendants and other indictees, and the court's integrity, considered that Norman should exercise this right by a sworn written affidavit made privately, with the possibility of further affidavits to respond to follow-up questions, or by an unsworn statement made to commissioners in private. The essence of these

---

[58] Press Release, Office of the Prosecutor, Special Court Prosecutor Addresses Seminar Participants; Encourages Perpetrators to Talk to the TRC (Feb. 27, 2003).

[59] Krio word in Sierra Leone for a white person, literally translated "white man." A white person visiting a town or village is not an event that is easily forgotten.

[60] *Ex-Combatant Views of Truth and Reconciliation Commission and the Special Court in Sierra Leone, supra* note 51, at 4–6.

[61] *Id.*

[62] Prosecutor v. Samuel Hinga Norman, SCSL-2003–08-PT, Decision on the Request by the Truth and Reconciliation Commission of Sierra Leone to conduct a public hearing with Sam Hinga Norman, para. 16 (Oct. 29, 2003).

restrictions was to protect against the dangers of his self-incrimination.[63] In the end, the TRC, which seemed more interested in a public hearing, chose not to take up the offer. To this extent it could be said that the SCSL had exercised its overriding powers over the TRC. The downside however, is the obvious limitations that this situation placed on the Prosecutor's reach in the interpretation of his mandate, not so much over the decision about who to indict, but how much evidence he could muster in proof of charges against particular indicted persons.[64]

G. Interpretation of the Court's Mandate – The July 1999 Lomé Peace Agreement, How Limiting?

Eight years into the bloody conflict in Sierra Leone with no end in sight, three changes of government,[65] two major peace deals scuppered,[66] the country at its knees with the machinery of state at a standstill, massive displacement of the population, the countryside lying in complete waste, and in the wake of the January 1999 invasion of the capital Freetown, city residents were still reeling from shock and bewilderment over the trail of destruction and atrocities. This was the grim situation in which Sierra Leone found itself on the eve of the signing of the July 7, 1999 "Lomé Peace Agreement," more than enough battering for its people to come to the realization, particularly the government,[67] that to bite the bullet and take another chance at peace with the rebels, the AFRC/RUF forces, was going to be the best – perhaps the only – way forward.

The Lomé Peace Agreement that followed was not ideally what many Sierra Leoneans would have wanted. Its terms were dictated largely by the military situation on the ground, which did not favor the government or its allied forces.[68] War-wearied and unwilling to leave its fortunes in the hands of a foreign peace-enforcing ECOMOG force, the government negotiated a deal. Notably disappointing on its terms was the blanket amnesty from prosecution that it granted former combatants for all atrocities they had committed from the beginning of the conflict in March 1991, the bulk of whom were rebels of the RUF. It was an undeservedly high price that Sierra Leoneans were being asked to pay – after all those years of atrocities and destruction, peace to the rebels on a platter? The United Nations,

---

[63] Decision on Appeal by the Truth and Reconciliation Commission of Sierra Leone ("TRC" or "The Commission") and Chief Sam Hinga Norman JP, against the Decision of His Lordship Mr. Justice Bankole Thompson delivered on October 30, 2003, to hold a public hearing with Chief Samuel Hinga Norman JP, Prosecutor v. Samuel Hinga Norman, SCSL-2003–08-PT-122, paras. 41–42 (Nov. 28, 2003).

[64] *Ex-Combatant Views of Truth and Reconciliation Commission and the Special Court in Sierra Leone, supra* note 51, at 16–17.

[65] See the *TRC Report*: "The Military and Political History of the Conflict," at 6–7, §§ 23–28.

[66] "Peace Agreement between the Government of the Republic of Sierra Leone and the Revolutionary United Front of Sierra Leone ("Abidjan Accord"), Nov. 30, 1996," and "ECOWAS Six-month Peace Plan for Sierra Leone ("Conakry Accord"), Oct. 23, 1997."

[67] Hayner, *supra* note 49, at 6; *also see* Nkansah, *supra* note 4, at 6, citing Campaign for Good Governance 2002 & Hirsch 2001, states that both sides to the conflict, not just the government side as canvassed above, had become war wearied. It must be stressed however, that the government side with an elective mandate and a constitutional responsibility, was in a more anxious position to end the carnage.

[68] Nigerian soldiers under ECOMOG command & Sierra Leone Civil Defense Forces (CDF), predominantly, the Kamajors; see Hayner, *supra*, note 49, at 6.

which was present as a moral guarantor, appended its signature with a disclaimer that the amnesty would not apply to crimes that violate International Humanitarian Law.[69] In spite of the government's high commitment to peace, it would take another two years for the guns to finally fall silent.[70]

A number of accused persons sought to challenge the lawfulness of their indictment and prosecution before the Special Court, but the Appeals Chamber was unequivocal about the limitations of the amnesty granted, and its non-applicability to international crimes.[71] This created the theoretical possibility of the indictment and prosecution of any and all perpetrators of crimes falling within the Court's mandate, but the reality was different. For many, although the UN's disclaimer to the amnesty and its subsequent action jointly with the government to establish a mechanism of accountability for crimes was applauded, disappointment loomed over the limited nature in which the Prosecutor eventually chose to interpret his mandate as pertaining to the number of persons indicted. Such narrow interpretation, given the amount of money spent so far in trying so few, is not only perplexing, but has led some to believe that the Court's efficacy in addressing issues of accountability for crimes committed during the conflict is negligible.[72] Undoubtedly, a huge impunity gap relating to the conduct of a large number of mid-level commanders and actual perpetrators exists, which may never be addressed by the Court. To this end, it is fair to say that the manner of interpretation of the Court's mandate by the Prosecutor did not meet the expectation of many, given the continuation of this huge impunity gap.

H. Conclusion

In sum, many factors exist that make it almost impossible to conclude that the Special Court has truly fulfilled its mandate. From the perspective of the narrow interpretation of its legal mandate, and given resource constraints, one might be inclined to agree that a high degree of success has been achieved, judging from the number and position in the hierarchy of persons now successfully prosecuted, the impressive jurisprudence developed, and the outstanding success of the Court's outreach program. However, even on this front, there is extensive comparative factual data suggesting that both in terms of cost and time, the SCSL as an example of a new model of international criminal justice has not significantly outclassed the ICTY and the ICTR as had been expected.[73]

---

[69] S.C. Res. 1315 (2000), adopted by the Security Council at its 4186th meeting on August 14, 2000 – S/Res/1315 (2000): *see also* ICTJ Report December 2007; Hayner, *supra* note 49, at 5. Further, SCSL Statute art. 10 states: "An amnesty granted to any person falling within the jurisdiction of the Special Court in respect of crimes referred to in Articles 2–4 of the present statute shall not be a bar to prosecution."

[70] Sierra Leone News, Jan. 18, 2002, *available at* http://www.sierra-leone.org/Archives/slnews0102.html (last visited Aug. 17, 2012).

[71] Decision on Challenge to Jurisdiction: Lomé Accord, Prosecutor v. Morris Kallon, SCSL-2004-15-AR-72(E), Appeals Chamber (Mar. 13, 2004), and Prosecutor v. Brima Bazzy Kamara, SCSL-2004-16-AR-72(E), Appeals Chamber, paras. 69, 72 and 86–90 (Mar. 13, 2004); *see also* Nkansah, *supra* note 4, at 14–15.

[72] Nkansah, *supra* note 4, at 8; *see also* Perriello & Wierda, *supra* note 24, at 43.

[73] Independent Expert, *supra* note 1, § 66 – after reviewing SCSL's time lines and cost implications in relation to the then-ongoing trials, CDF, RUF, and AFRC, Cassese concluded:

> As demonstrated in Annex D page 10, these timelines are similar to those for multi-accused trials at the ICTY and ICTR. In fact, the Special Court's trials have taken longer than many of the ICTR and

As to wider expectations from the Court's exercise of its mandate, there is hardly a sufficient basis to conclude that it has successfully met those expectations or will meet them, primarily because these are built-on, falling outside the Court's core mandate. Although the Court by its activities has sought not to restrict itself solely to its core mandate, but has been making efforts to meet some of these expectations, the fact remains that the expectations outstrip its capacity, especially from the point of view of the resource constraints it endures. As Justice Cassese puts it:

> At this stage, I do not think that it is realistic to expect that the Court's legacy will directly: (a) ensure greater respect for the rule of law in Sierra Leone; (b) promote or inspire substantive law reforms; (c) improve the conditions of service and remuneration of judges in Sierra Leone; or (d) alleviate corruption allegedly existing in the judiciary. The Court may contribute to these goals, but they will only materialize as an indirect effect, in the long run, and thanks to other concomitant factors.[74]

III. COUNTING SUCCESS AT THE SCSL: SOME NOTE OF ACHIEVEMENT?

The Special Court has been credited with many successes thus far. In analyzing these achievements it helps to categorize them into two: those resulting from the exercise of its core mandate, and those outside its mandate, built on from wider expectations. Although fulfillment of its core mandate should be the basis for measuring success, fulfilling wider expectations such as providing training, helping build national capacity, strengthening the rule of law, bolstering respect for human rights, and addressing reparation issues also have the potential to earn the Court accolades and enhance its image.

A. Core Mandate Successes

Although successful completion of all its four trials is in and of itself a mark of great achievement, the Court's pioneering effort in developing new jurisprudence in areas where none existed has propelled its image even higher in the field of international criminal law.

First, the Court became the first tribunal to enter convictions for the crime of recruitment of child soldiers in international law, which Cecile Aptel and Noah Novogdrosky discuss in-depth in their chapters in this volume.[75] Before the SCSL Indictments, no international

---

ICTY multi-accused cases. Even the AFRC case, which ran continuously before Trial Chamber II, does not show a significant improvement over the length of trials at the other tribunals. Jalloh, *supra* note 1, at 428–37.

[74] Independent Expert, *supra* note 1, § 279.

[75] Prosecutor v. Moinina Fofana and Allieu Kondewa, SCSL-14-T, Judgment, paras. 970 and 971 (Aug. 2, 2007); also Centre for Accountability and Rule of Law (CARL), Interview with Joseph Kamara Former Acting Prosecutor for the Special Court for Sierra Leone:

> As far as International Law, the list of key precedents established by the Court is truly impressive: the world's first recognitions of the use of child soldiers and of forced marriage as crimes under international humanitarian law, and the first ever convictions on these charges; the first-ever convictions on the charge of Attacks on UN Peacekeepers. These rulings have the potential to help protect civilians and soldiers alike in the conflict zones of the world.

court had charged this crime as an offense, partly because of its late development as a crime under international law and partly because it was not a phenomenon that featured prominently in the conduct of the warring factions in either the Balkans in the early 1990s or Rwanda in the mid 1990s.[76] Before the advent of these two ad hoc international tribunals, the only previous opportunity to have charged any such offense was during the Nuremberg and Tokyo trials following WWII, but even at those times, we were dealing with established regular armies that respected rules about protecting children in war, including restrictions on the age of recruitment.[77] The customary practice of protecting children in war and prohibitions against their recruitment in the armed forces or their use in combat was already widely recognized among some of the highly advanced nations, including the key perpetrators of crimes then, Germany and Japan, although no internationally accepted age for recruitment existed.[78]

Second, Trial Chamber I recorded groundbreaking jurisprudence when it convicted the three accused persons in the RUF case of the offense of attack against peacekeepers – as Alhagi Marong discusses in his chapter in this volume. Until its inclusion in the statute of the Special Court as an "Other Serious Violations of International Humanitarian Law,"[79] this offense had never been developed as a crime under international law, although the practice had been previously condemned by many states and organizations, including the United Nations. Also, it was later outlawed in a 1994 Convention,[80] which established a framework for state parties to criminalize the practice domestically. However, this did not bring the issue of prosecuting it as an international crime to the fore until it was first included in the statute of the SCSL, then charged, and successfully prosecuted. Previously, such attacks could have been treated as an attack against unarmed civilians under customary international law, depending on the mandate of the peacekeeping mission and their rules of engagement.[81]

Third, the Special Court's jurisprudence established a new separate offense in the category of sexual violence crimes called "forced marriage" – as Michael Scharf, Sidney Thompson, and Valerie Oosterveld make clear in their respective chapters for this book. The phenomenon of forced marriage itself was not new, although introduced as a separate

---

Dec. 9, 2009, by Angela Stavrianou, *available at* http://www.carl-sl.org/home/reports/384-interview-with-joseph-kamara-former-acting-prosecutor-for-the-special-court-for-sierra-leone- (last visited Aug. 17, 2012).

[76] Neither the Statute of the ICTY available at (http://www.icls.de/dokumente/icty_statut.pdf) nor the Statute of the ICTR available at (http://www.icls.de/dokumente/ictr_statute.pdf) lists an offense relating to recruitment or enlistment or use of children in hostilities as a crime over which the Court could exercise jurisdiction.

[77] Jean-Marie Henckaerts & Louise Doswald-Beck, Customary International Humanitarian Law, Volume I: Rules 479–86 (2009). These pages cover rules relating to respect and protection of children in war (p. 479), prohibition of recruitment of children into armed forces or armed groups (p. 482), and prohibition on allowing children to participate in hostilities (p. 485). In all of these cases, Germany is cited as one of several states where these prohibitions are stated to be contained in military manuals that are applicable to both international and non-international conflicts (p. 480, fn.38 and p. 483, fn.57).

[78] Prosecutor v. Norman, Fofana and Kondewa, SCSL-04-14-AR72 (E)-131-7398, Appeals Chamber, Decision on Preliminary Motion Based on Lack of Jurisdiction (Child Recruitment), paras. 49–51 (May 31, 2004).

[79] SCSL Statute art. 4.

[80] Convention on the Safety of U.N. and Associated Personnel.

[81] For a discussion on the historical and legal development of this crime, see Mohamed A. Bangura, *Prosecuting the Crime of Attack on Peacekeepers: A Prosecutor's Challenge*, 23 Leiden J. Int'l L. 165–81 (2010).

new offense in the AFRC and RUF indictments at a late stage, following a Trial Chamber order allowing an amendment. The Prosecution had argued that to the extent the practice involves acts that go beyond the elements of sexual slavery, it should be treated as a separate offense, falling under the category of, "Other inhumane acts" and not simply another strand of sexual violence offenses. The Judges in the AFRC trial, Trial Chamber II, did not in their final judgment convict under this new count, but the Appeals Chamber in reviewing that Chamber's decision agreed with the Prosecution that the elements of forced marriage went beyond the scope of sexual slavery and were sufficiently distinctive to constitute a separate sexual violence offense as a crime against humanity. The appellate judges did not however enter a conviction for the offence. It was the Trial Chamber in the RUF Case that entered the first-ever conviction for the offense, as "Other Inhumane Acts," in its judgment that was delivered subsequently.[82]

The RUF Trial decision, which effectively created a new offense under crimes against humanity, has attracted extensive commentary reflecting a generally favorable reaction among jurists.[83] However, Trial Chamber II in the recent Taylor Judgment, took the liberty of revisiting the forced marriage issue in its consideration of the applicable law on sexual violence Offenses, in particular sexual slavery, even though the Taylor Prosecution had not charged forced marriage. In its opinion, obiter, the Chamber sought to reinforce its views reflected in the AFRC Judgment, which were judicially muted after it delivered judgment in that case and became *functus officio*. The Judges, in the Taylor Judgment stated that the term "Forced Marriage" is a misnomer for "forced conjugal association," a situation imposed on women and girls in circumstances of armed conflict, which involved both sexual slavery and forced labor,[84] but to which the nomenclature of marriage does not fit, to amount to a separate offense of forced marriage. The Chamber considered that part of the confusion created by the Prosecution's charge of "forced marriage" was its presentation of the offense as the conceptualization of a new crime, when conjugal slavery is better conceptualized as a distinct form of sexual slavery, with additionally the component described by the Appeals Chamber.[85] In effect, this later judicial foray into the subject of forced marriage leaves the issue of a new offense not only questionable, but rather baffling. Was the Trial Chamber seeking to drive a coach and horses through an Appellate Chamber's settled position on the law, or was this just judicial intellectualism simply overstretched?

Finally, as Micaela Frulli and Annie Gell show in their two chapters on immunity and the Taylor trial respectively, the handing down of judgment in the Taylor case[86] marks another

---

[82] Prosecutor v. Issa Sesay, Morris Kallon, Augustine Gbao, SCSL-04-15-T, Judgment, paras. 2150, 2151, 2168, 2306, 2307, and 2168 (Mar. 2, 2009).

[83] Valerie Oosterveld, *The Gender Jurisprudence of the Special Court for Sierra Leone: Progress of the United Revolutionary Front Judgments*, CORNELL INT'L L.J. 64–68, Gender Jurisprudence of the SCSL (2011); Amy Palmer, *An Evolutionary Analysis of Gender-Based War Crimes and Continued Tolerance of Forced Marriage*, 7 Nw. U. J. INT'L HUMAN RIGHTS §§ 44–72 and 82–85 (Spring 2007).

[84] Judgment, *Prosecutor v. Charles Ghankay Taylor*, supra note 32, at paras. 425 and 426. Paragraph 426 states: "... The Trial Chamber does not consider the nomenclature of 'marriage' to be helpful in describing what happened to the victims of this forced conjugal association and finds it inappropriate to refer to their perpetrators as 'husbands.'"

[85] *Id.* § 429.

[86] A summary of the Trial Chamber's Final Judgment was delivered orally on April 26, 2012, followed by the filing of the full written version on May 18, 2012, and a Corrigendum filed on May 30, 2012.

unprecedented achievement for the Court, being the first international tribunal to indict a sitting head of state, then successfully trying and convicting him for war crimes, crimes against humanity, and other violations of international humanitarian law committed during his leadership.[87] The significance and implications of this conviction are far-reaching globally and have attracted wide commentary. In an age where increasing vigilance is being shown by the world community in spotting and stamping out impunity, especially arising from the conduct of high state officials, the precedent laid by Charles Taylor's conviction could not have come at a more propitious time.

B. Achievements Outside the Mandate

The bulk of the Special Court's activities away from the courtroom fall outside its core mandate. Necessarily, these activities are undertaken to complement its image as an institution created to also address some of the underlying problems of justice delivery in Sierra Leone. Thus the effort to execute its core mandate has always been inextricably tied to considerations of its legacy to the people of Sierra Leone. As noted earlier, it was recognized even by the funders and creators of the Court from the outset that simply indicting and prosecuting those who bear the greatest responsibility for the atrocious crimes committed during the conflict would not be sufficient to end impunity.

The Court's outreach program is usually the vehicle through which its legacy activities are articulated. For this purpose, it is important to distinguish between outreach events that basically provide information and update on progress with the Court's core mandate (trial proceedings, etc.), and events that promote its legacy initiatives (training, knowledge, and skills transfer, etc.).[88] The focus is on the latter, but these initiatives are undertaken by various sections of the Court, with outreach playing only a facilitating and awareness raising role.

Up until 2005, there was little demonstration of a coordinated effort at streamlining legacy initiatives undertaken by various organs of the Court, despite expressed commitment to advance the Court's legacy aspirations. The updated Completion Strategy Paper of 2006, which included broad ideas about the Court's legacy strategy, followed by the appointment of a Legacy Coordinator under the supervision of the Registrar,[89] and perhaps coupled with

---

[87] Other heads of state have been indicted while in office, but never successfully tried or convicted. Serbian leader Milošević is an example. The President of Sudan, Omar El-Bshir, has also since been indicted while in office; so also was the Leader of the then Libyan Arab Jamahiriyya Republic, Colonel Muammar Ghadaffi, before his demise.

[88] Currently the Court's website lists the following activities as ongoing projects in its legacy program: Site Project, Peace Museum, National Witness Protection Programme, Archives Development Programme, Improving Detention Standards, and Professional Development Programme, *available at* http://www.sc-sl.org/LEGACY/tabid/224/Default.aspx (last visited Aug 17, 2012).

[89] Third Annual Report, *supra* note 42, at 28, under "Legacy," it reads:

> The Special Court has always recognized, not only the critical importance of leaving a legacy for the people of Sierra Leone, but also the unprecedented opportunity to contribute to the restoration of the rule of law. With this in mind and as part of the Completion Strategy, the Special Court created a Legacy Working Group in 2005 comprised mainly of Sierra Leoneans. The Working Group's objective is to identify and implement a range of projects which will contribute to the Special Court's lasting legacy.

recommendations from the Cassese Expert Report, did initiate some focused changes in the way the Court pursued its legacy objectives.[90]

IV. CASE-SPECIFIC LEGACY ACTIVITIES AND THEIR IMPACT

A. *Professional Training, Knowledge, and Skills Transfer: Thinking behind the Concept*

Of the legacy activities so far discussed, the involvement of Sierra Leoneans in the work of the Court at professional and nonprofessional levels holds the greatest chances for a more enduring benefit for the country.[91] From an outsider's perspective, the recruitment of nationals and their exposure to attainment of the highest standards possible may be viewed simply as an end in itself – the utilization of local knowledge and skills of a lucky few whose services are handsomely remunerated. To the extent the knowledge and skills developed prove useful to national advancement, this simply is an added benefit, purely incidental. However, court founders and administrators view the situation differently: not just as a personal benefit that develops individual capacity, but part of a continuum, an adjunct to the process of restoring the rule of law and respect for human rights, and strengthening national capacity. These are the building blocks to getting Sierra Leone back on its feet on law, order, and justice. The credit for any success on this score should therefore accrue to the Court as part fulfillment of its mandate.

B. *Professional Training, Knowledge, and Skills Transfer: How Adequate?*

Legacy objectives aimed at developing local capacity through training and knowledge transfer always remained a recurring theme in SCSL official statements, releases, and publications during its early years, but with little being done to put it into reality.[92]

Quite significant effort was made in the early period of the Court's life in the area of capacity building. Sierra Leonean lawyers, judges, and investigators (Sierra Leone police officers) received training mainly geared toward building knowledge of the principles of international criminal law and procedure, and improving investigations skills and techniques.[93]

See also *Fifth Annual Report*, June 2007–May 2008, at 48, *available at* http://www.sc-sl.org/LinkClick. aspx?fileticket=hopZSuXjicg%3d&tabid=176.

[90] Fourth Annual Report, *supra* note 11, Extract from Judge King's Foreword, on legacy:

The Special Court is slated to complete its operations by December 2009. With that in mind, and in order to leave the legacy of the Court for posterity, the Plenary has set up a Legacy Committee headed by Hon. Justice Benjamin Mutanga Itoe to take charge of legacy projects, archiving, the preservation of records and maintenance and future use of the Court site. Several international bodies are assisting in legacy projects, which I opine must be one of the Court's top priorities.

[91] Fourth Annual Report, *supra* note 11, Judge Gelaga King's Foreword.

[92] Gehrig, *supra* note 38 n.18, "The focus of legacy for the first two years was solely on bringing cases to trial. While it engaged in some capacity building for institutions that promote accountability, these initiatives were conducted more as an afterthought than through careful planning" – citing Mohamed Suma, *The Charles Taylor Trial and the Legacy of the Special Court for Sierra Leone* 2 (Briefing Paper, ICTJ 2009).

[93] Press Release, SCSL, Canadian Government, Train Police Investigators in Sierra Leone (Nov. 7, 2005), *available at* http://www.sc-sl.org/LinkClick.aspx?fileticket=LXmX%2b7Ykdys%3d&tabid=112 (last visited Aug. 17, 2012); *see also* Press Release, SCSL, Freetown, Sierra Leone, Defence Office Holds Seminar to Train

The Witnesses and Victims Section (WVS) provided training for their staff on witness management issues, a relatively uncharted area in Sierra Leone's justice delivery process.[94] Additionally, Sierra Leone prison officers seconded to the Court received in-house training from their expatriate colleagues at the Detention Unit in various skills relating to handling and movement of detainees.[95] In the Security Section locally recruited security officers also benefited from training from their expatriate colleagues.[96]

However, much of this early laudable effort was uncoordinated and therefore remained unsustainable.[97] Legacy at this time, mainly a matter of rhetoric, had no allocation in the SCSL's "shoestring budget."[98] Most of these early training activities were made possible through extra-budgetary sources, sometimes from individuals or groups rather than institutional effort. Justice Geoffrey Robertson, the Court's first president, providing commentary on the difficult challenges of legacy at the time, had this to say:

> Whilst the combination of the Court's limited funding and three year mandate serves to provide a more than significant challenge in itself, the importance of leaving a legacy for the Government and people of Sierra Leone also presents both a challenge and an opportunity.[99]

Following the publication of the Court's Completion Strategy paper in October 2004, and ensuing discussions around legacy, a more structured central approach began to emerge. From a funding point of view, although legacy projects remained funded from external funds, a coordinated and centralized approach to harnessing and managing legacy activities and funding began to be taken.

In the succeeding years since 2005, much more effort has been devoted to providing additional training to Sierra Leoneans, by way of knowledge and skills transfer, especially as the Court approaches completion of its mandate. Again, Sierra Leone police officers have benefited from training programs, although given the limitedness of resources, the depth of treatment of some of the programs leaves questions about their utilitarian value. Nonetheless, in a rolling series, the OTP has conducted five training sessions in basic prosecutorial skills for SLP prosecutors in the national system.[100] Further, a National Witness Protection Training Programme has been launched, intended to train SLP officers, as part of a projected longer-term effort to continue protection after the closure of

---

Investigators (Nov. 9, 2005), *available at* http://www.sc-sl.org/LinkClick.aspx?fileticket=LXmX%2b7Ykdys%3d&tabid=112 (last visited Aug. 17, 2012).

[94] Special Court Monthly Newsletter vol. XVIII, *Special Court Launches Witness Protection Training Programme*, Dec. 2009, *at* http://www.sc-sl.org/LinkClick.aspx?fileticket=UQSFbb43cqk%3d&tabid=186.

[95] Press Release, SCSL, Freetown, Sierra Leone, Former Detention Staff Members Honoured (Aug. 26, 2005), *available at* http://www.sc-sl.org/LinkClick.aspx?fileticket=LXmX%2b7Ykdys%3d&tabid=112 (last visited Aug. 17, 2012); *see also* Press Release, SCSL, Freetown, Sierra Leone, Prison Officers Recognized by Special Court (Feb. 4, 2008), *available at* http://www.sc-sl.org/LinkClick.aspx?fileticket=LXmX%2b7Ykdys%3d&tabid=112 (last visited Aug. 17, 2012).

[96] First Annual Report, *supra* note 9, at 22.

[97] Gehrig, *supra* note 38 n.17, citing Thierry Cruveiller, *From the Taylor Trial to a Lasting Legacy: Putting the Special Court Model to the Test* 37 (ICTJ 2007).

[98] Independent Expert, *supra* note 1, § 293; *see also* Jalloh, *supra* note 1, at 428.

[99] First Annual Report, *supra* note 9, at 28.

[100] The writer has himself participated in two of these training sessions, as a trainer/facilitator, October 2010 in Bo, Southern Sierra Leone, May 2011, Hastings Police Training School, Western Area and May 2013, Police Officers Mess Kingtom, Freetown, Western Area.

the Court.[101] In January 2004, the Court also introduced a funded internship program for young Sierra Leonean professionals.

Other activities not directly involving training have been embarked upon, all in an effort to build capacity. These include public discussion programs for the Sierra Leonean public by Outreach, intended to stimulate debate about SCSL's justice delivery process, ending impunity, and engendering respect for the rule of law.[102] Also, "Accountability Now" clubs have been established in schools and university to help sow the seeds of a culture of respect for human rights and the rule of law in Sierra Leone's future leaders.[103]

C. Sierra Leonean Staff Profile at the SCSL: Early Missteps and a Turnaround

Statistics at various periods in the life of the Court show a staff structure of international composition with a Sierra Leonean majority,[104] many of whom fall in the lower rung of the ladder in terms of position, authority, influence, pay, and allowances. In effect, numerical advantage has not necessarily matched positions of authority and influence, particularly during the early years of the Court's life. It took up to three years of the Court's existence before any noticeable changes in staff structure and mobility were realized.

The Court's fair and transparent process of recruitment coupled with higher-than-average national rates of remuneration attracted extremely highly qualified and experienced nationals in all cadres. Admittedly, many became exposed to new systems and ethics of work and needed to go through a learning process especially in the use of appropriate technology applicable in their duties. But they were soon able to catch up and match the task, requiring little or no supervision with assigned duties. Nevertheless, the perception of the Court in those early years and for a significant period afterward continued to be non–Sierra Leonean, an issue that ultimately drew strong criticism from both within and outside the Court.[105]

---

[101] Press Release, SCSL, Freetown, Sierra Leone, Special Court Launches Witness Protection Training Programme (Nov. 6, 2009): The Special Court for Sierra Leone this week launched a month-long witness training programme for Sierra Leone police officers which, it is hoped, will lead to a national witness protection programme in the country, *available at* http://www.sc-sl.org/LinkClick.aspx?fileticket=kJuoOgoLU2E%3d&tabid=214 (last visited Aug. 17, 2012).

[102] Second Annual Report, *supra* note 9, Legacy, at 25–26.

[103] Second Annual Report, *supra* note 9, at 34; *also* Third Annual Report, *supra* note 42, at 29.

[104] First Annual Report, *supra* note 9, at 20 – personnel statistics as at December 2003: Sierra Leone Nationals – 149, International staff – 106, Total – 255; Second Annual Report, *supra* note 9, at 28 – personnel statistics as of January 17, 2005: Sierra Leone Nationals 162, International staff – 127, Total – 287; Third Annual Report, *supra* note 42, at 33 – personnel statistics as at December 2005: Sierra Leone Nationals – 179, International staff – 136, Total – 315; Fourth Annual Report, *supra* note 11, at 46, – personnel statistics as at December 31, 2006: Sierra Leone National staff – 176, International staff – 130, Total – 306.

[105] Independent Expert, *supra* note 1, §§ 206, 208, 265, and 266; *see also* Perriello & Wierda, *supra* note 24, at 2, "Summary of Conclusions – Legitimacy": "The legitimacy of the Special Court at the local level is partly affected by the perception that it is an international court, a perception the Court has cultivated through its jurisprudence and presentation. There are almost no Sierra Leoneans in the most senior positions at the Court"; also at p. 21, under the rubric, The Office of the Prosecutor, it reads:

At the height of its operations, the Office of the Prosecutor (OTP) had a professional staff of approximately 65. Sierra Leoneans comprise more than one-third of the professional staff, the largest

Across the main organs of the Court, Chambers (Judges excepting), OTP, and Registry, Sierra Leonean professionals filled quite a number of positions but hardly made it to supervisory level. As an almost unspoken rule, the Outreach Section that falls under the Registry excepted,[106] no position in the Court at a supervisory level was manned by a Sierra Leonean until after the first three years.[107] Similarly, there was hardly any representation of Sierra Leoneans in any of the key committees established by the Registrar to assist him in day-to-day administration.[108] The Registry, comprising several sections that carry out administrative support functions of the Court, and having the lion's share of the Court's workforce, reflected this situation worse than the other organs. Whereas the OTP and Chambers, and exceptionally the Defense Office,[109] were staffed largely by legally qualified personnel holding positions at a professional level, and giving at least a semblance of an even picture,[110] the Registry's Personnel, Finance, Court Management Section (CMS), Communication and Information Technology Section (CITS), Transport, Witnesses and Victims Section (WVS), Public Affairs, General Services, Security and Detention Sections/Units, were staffed by hundreds of nationals possessing varying qualifications, skills, and experience, largely in nonprofessional categories.[111]

It was obvious that this trend was not going to score the Court any credits in its effort to develop local knowledge and skills and build capacity. A change in direction, perhaps partly engendered by outside criticisms,[112] and partly by the 2006 Cassese Expert Report,[113] brought about a rethinking in personnel policy. For an institution initially set up to last only three years, which but for the arrest and transfer of Charles Taylor for trial in The Hague between March and June 2006, would have been closing its doors by about late 2009 in any event,[114] the Special Court was already on the verge of missing out on one of its most important legacy targets.

> percentage by nationality. Nearly half the professional posts and almost every one of the senior ones are occupied by people from the Global North (mostly Americans and Canadians).
> Further at p. 25, under the Rubric, The Registry, the report again reads,
> Virtually all of the leadership positions in the Registry are occupied by internationals, including all chiefs of sections, with the exception of Outreach and Information Technology.... Although the Court has a majority of Sierra Leoneans, at about 60 percent, many national staff members are in nonprofessional posts (drivers, close protection officers, cleaners, etc.) all chiefs of sections, with the exception of Outreach and Information Technology.

[106] This section was headed by a Sierra Leonean Binta Mansaray, since its creation.

[107] In the UN system, professional staffs are in two categories, P Category and D Category. In the lower P category, the highest rank P-5 generally is considered supervisory.

[108] Advisory Committee on Personnel Questions (ACPQ); also ad hoc committees are created to deal with specific administrative issues as they arise.

[109] The Defense Office fell under the Registry for administrative purposes, but largely exercised professional independence from the Registry.

[110] Many were in the UN's professional staff category.

[111] *Supra* note 107. The nonprofessional categories according to UN recruitment policy are the Field Staff and National Staff categories.

[112] *Supra* note 107.

[113] Independent Expert, *supra* note 1, § 12, wrote: "Finally, with regard to the Completion Strategy and the Court's Legacy, I consider that the Court should begin to focus more on its Sierra Leonean staff. I am recommending some strategies to enhance the enduring impact of the Special Court on the Sierra Leonean legal system....."; also §§ 267 & 269.

[114] Projections in Annual Report 2005/2006; Appeal Judgment in the last of the first three trials, Issa Sesay et al., came out on October 26, 2009.

The changes that have occurred since have seen Sierra Leonean nationals heading sections and units of the Court and being involved in decision making at various levels. In the Registry, there is currently a Sierra Leonean Registrar, who became first, Deputy Registrar, and before that the first team leader of the Outreach Section, at Level P-5 (Supervisory).[115] At the OTP there has been one outstanding case of upward mobility. From recruitment as an Associate Trial Attorney at Level P-3, this staff member rose through Levels P-4 and P-5, to become Senior Trial Attorney and Team Leader (Supervisory). Then, following an appointment by the government of Sierra Leone, he became Deputy Prosecutor, and subsequently Acting Prosecutor, by an appointment by the UN Secretary-General.[116] He fell short of being appointed substantively as Prosecutor, when appointment for the position came up in January-February 2010, while in an Acting capacity. In the Defense Office, a Sierra Leonean now holds the position of Principal Defender, having started out her career with the SCSL in the Defense Office as an Associate Legal Officer, P-2.[117] Across other sections, Sierra Leonean nationals or Sierra Leone–born foreign nationals now sit either as principals or are in decision-making positions as officers in charge.[118] Similarly, committees assisting the Registrar's day-to-day administrative duties now reflect increased Sierra Leonean participation.

A positive trend that developed at the OTP over the years is the Prosecutor's decision to share the podium with Sierra Leonean professionals in presenting the Prosecution's Opening Statement in each of the trials.[119] Symbolic as this gesture may seem, and probably intended largely to appease Sierra Leonean professionals in the face of earlier criticisms, the practice was maintained and became evidence of increasing confidence in their ability to take on the task. This was further demonstrated by their increasing levels of participation in courtroom work as the trials progressed.

Some may be quick to argue that the depth of these changes was possible only because the Court had started discussing its completion strategy in 2005, before Taylor's arrest, and had set tentative time lines for winding up. And as it did so, many expatriate staff who, otherwise might have been considered more suited for these positions began to leave for greener pastures, ultimately leaving the Court with no better option than to look to its local staff, as though they were a reserve lot. This view is likely reinforced by the fact that in recent times, the Court has been affected by its own personnel policy on draw down, which is making it difficult to attract or retain the best qualified on a long-term basis. For instance, faced with continuing prospects of much higher staff attrition before the core functions of the Court are completed, a recent rethinking of policy now assures staff members a continuation of their employment until the Court's core duties are completed, impliedly, when the Taylor appeals are over.[120]

---

[115] Binta Mansaray, *see profile available at* http://www.scsl.org/PRESSROOM/CourtPrincipals/tabid/98/Default.aspx (last visited Aug. 17, 2012).

[116] Joseph Fitzgerald Kamara.

[117] Claire Carlton-Hanciles.

[118] Sierra Leoneans are principals at CITS and CMS, and they occupy second-tier positions in Finance, Personnel, General Services, and Public Affairs and Outreach.

[119] CDF Trial, June 3, 2004 – David Crane and Joseph Kamara; RUF Trial, July 5, 2004 – David Crane and Abdul Tejan-Cole; AFRC Trial, Mar. 7, 2005 – David Crane and Boi-Tia Stevens; Charles Taylor Trial, June 4, 2007 – Stephen Rapp and Mohamed A. Bangura.

[120] Oral statement by Registrar to SCSL staff at a general staff meeting in Freetown, December 2011.

Conversely, the Court can point to these changes simply as a fulfillment of its commitment to build local capacity, unaffected by any criticisms or a boomerang of its personnel policies. The question perhaps is: why must the initiation be delayed? If Taylor's trial had not come along, this legacy objective would certainly have merited negative assessment from critics.

D. Benefits to the National System – Justice Delivery Process

It is beyond question that the exposure Sierra Leoneans and Sierra Leone–born foreign nationals have had holds great potential for building the country's domestic capacity in justice delivery. Various categories of staff have acquired knowledge and skills directly useful for strengthening the domestic process. These include judges, lawyers, in both prosecution and defense roles, crime investigators, and Court support staff in various areas, including interpreting/translation, court reporting, court filing and archiving, witness protection, witness support, courtroom technology, security management relating to the detention facility, and movement of high-profile detainees.

The expected benefit from the involvement of nationals in SCSL's work is a contribution to the overall improvement in quality in the dispensation of justice at a domestic level, ranging from ending chronic delays to ensuring fairness of the process, and from respecting due process rights of accused persons to eliminating corrupt practices. These vices, which were partly responsible for the loss of confidence by citizens in the judicial process, led to a breakdown of the rule of law and the reign of impunity in the country that followed. SCSL personnel, in particular lawyers and judges with professional training and a better understanding of the judicial process, are obviously looked upon to spearhead the articulation of these changes. However, given the relatively small number of participators and the paucity of their return to the national system, expectations of any quick changes from their contribution will take long to be realized.

In more specific terms, the national system is expected to benefit substantively and procedurally from the SCSL's existence in a handful of areas. Substantively, it is expected that the content of SCSL's Statute that creates jurisdiction for mass atrocity crimes committed against civilians in conflict and non-conflict situations would engender a domestication of the ICC's Rome Statute to which Sierra Leone is a signatory.[121] As the SCSL is only ad hoc, a system of international norms that will remain applicable to permanently deal with any future recurrence of such crimes is that provided in the ICC Statute, but to make them applicable nationally, they have to be domesticated.[122]

From a procedural standpoint, it is expected that the national system can benefit from the application of procedures and practices that help to streamline and expedite trials, ensure their fair and efficient management, and bring about judicial economy. The hallmarks of

---

[121] *Supra* note 40.

[122] The Sierra Leone Constitution, Act No. 6 of 1991, Section 40(4)(d) provides that international treaties, agreements, or conventions executed by or under the authority of the President, relating to matters within the legislative competence of parliament, or which alter the law of Sierra Leone, or imposes a charge or authorizes expenses from the Consolidated Revenue Fund, and any declaration of war, must be subject to ratification by Parliament either by an enactment or by a resolution supported by the votes of not less than one half of the members of parliament.

an efficient judicial process should, with some modification, help to instill confidence in a country's judicial system. Therefore, adopting rules of procedure and practice in the domestic system that reflect these values should hold great benefit for the process. Additionally, rules relating to pretrial disclosure by the parties,[123] and those that enable a less restrictive system for admitting evidence are invaluable, and subject to appropriate modification, can be adopted.[124] Equally useful for expeditiousness and ensuring adequate trial preparation, are rules that enable speedy judicial determination of pretrial issues on the basis of the parties' written submissions only,[125] and a more proactive approach to judicial monitoring of the trial preparation process through status conferences.[126]

E. Developing Local Capacity: Some Challenges

As already noted, expectations that the national system will benefit from transfer of knowledge, experience, and skills may not be fully realized given the paucity of personnel return to the national system. Further, unless that knowledge, experience, and skill are harnessed in a coordinated way to collectively benefit the national system, success will be limited, as isolated individual contributions will only have piecemeal and unsustained impact. In addition, a number of other factors militate against the full realization of the benefits to the national system.

The first major shortcoming is a failure thus far by the national judicial authorities to establish a process for harnessing the benefits of the SCSL's work in Sierra Leone. This could be achieved by setting up a project or an SCSL desk under the supervision of the Chief Justice or some senior judicial officer to monitor, retrieve, and absorb everything useful from the SCSL's work. Everything of relevance should be garnered and assessed for its usefulness, in particular, the Court's Statute, its legislative enactments, protocols, directives, rules, practice directions, and jurisprudence. Also, maintaining an interest in its human resource, such as establishing a database of nationals involved in the process, and facilitating contact and coordination between and among them, should hold great benefits. Such contact can include meetings and discussions focused on laying a blueprint for the eventual implementation of anything useful from the Court's work and existence.

Second, as international and national law operate on two different planes, and Sierra Leone practices the dualist approach to internalizing international norms, the improved processes and procedures, as well as jurisprudence produced by the SCSL cannot just be transplanted into the domestic system without an enabling legislative framework.[127] To cite or use the jurisprudence of the SCSL in national proceedings or apply it in a local decision without such legislative basis would amount to introducing international law into Sierra Leone's domestic system, a major constitutional flaw that could invalidate such proceedings. Part XII, Section 170(1) of the Sierra Leone Constitution specifically sets out the Laws of Sierra Leone. International law is not a listed source of the Laws of Sierra Leone. Thus, to

---

[123] With appropriate modification, Rules 66–SCSL RPE.
[124] With appropriate modification, Rule 89(c) SCSL RPE.
[125] With appropriate modification, Rule 73(a) & (b) SCSL RPE.
[126] With appropriate modification, Rules 73*bis* & 73*ter* SCSL RPE.
[127] *Supra* note 123.

enable the application of its jurisprudence domestically, some amendment would be necessary to Section 170(1) of the constitution, specifically stipulating that jurisprudence from
the Special Court shall to the extent applicable, be considered part of the laws of Sierra
Leone, or by a specific enabling enactment. Nonetheless, it should be appropriate jurispru-
dentially to cite SCSL decisions as having persuasive authority in relevant situations before
Sierra Leonean courts.

A third hurdle in using the jurisprudence of the SCSL in Sierra Leonean courts is the fact
that, being international in character, the norms and decisions of the SCSL reflect a blend of
both common law and civil law principles. Sierra Leone's legal system on the other hand is
based on the common law system, a legacy of British colonial rule.[128] For example, the previous suggestion about introducing some relaxation of rules of evidence is borne from the fact
that the common law rules of evidence, which Sierra Leone practices, are almost inflexible
on the issue of admission of documentary evidence in criminal trials. They demand very
tight foundational requirements, more especially the production of originals or a reasonable explanation for their unavailability, where absent.[129] The rules of admission of evidence
in international tribunals on the other hand, including the SCSL, are more flexible and do
not require meeting such stringent foundational requirement, if the evidence is shown to
be relevant.[130] The focus of this civil law principle is to get to the truth. Similarly, the SCSL
and other international tribunals admit hearsay evidence, again under a flexible approach
to admission of evidence applying the same principle. On the other hand, restriction on the
use of hearsay evidence, especially its unsafeness to base a conviction on, is a hallmark of
the common law system. The downside to this rigidity is its potential for producing glaring
miscarriages of justice from the exclusion of cogent evidence.[131]

V. WIDER IMPACT OF THE SPECIAL COURT'S LEGACY

A. Developing a Culture of Compliance with International Legal Obligations

Apart from a direct impact on justice delivery within the domestic system, the establishment of the SCSL situated in Sierra Leone where the crimes were committed has other positive influences on the country's attitude toward compliance with its legal obligations under
international instruments that it enters into.

Until international attention came to be focused on Sierra Leone, during, but more
intensively, after the war, records show that there had been scant effort by successive governments to take necessary steps to ratify and/or domesticate international legal instruments that they signed. In effect, particularly in the area of observance of human rights,
due process, civil and political rights, local laws were either nonexistent, or where they
existed, were outdated and in need of reform, or simply a culture of low compliance
prevailed.

---

[128] BANKOLE THOMPSON, THE CONSTITUTIONAL HISTORY AND LAW OF SIERRA LEONE (1961–1995), at 1–11 (1996)
(Chapter One – Constitutional Development (1787–1960): The Period of Colonial Tutelage).

[129] *Application 26766/05 and 22228/06, AL-Khawaja and Tahery (Applicants) v. The United Kingdom (Respondent
Government)*, Third Party Intervention submitted by JUSTICE (2010), §§ 14–16.

[130] Rule 89(c) SCSL RPE.

[131] *Al-Khawaja* case, *supra*, note 129.

Of the key bilateral and multilateral international instruments signed, entered, or acceded to by Sierra Leone since independence in April 1961, a significant number still remained un-ratified, or not internalized by about 2000.[132] Further, there has been little if any compliance with periodic reporting as required under certain instruments.[133] On the eve of the establishment of the Special Court and the TRC, the two transitional justice mechanisms set up to address issues of violations of human rights and impunity, Sierra Leone's position in terms of compliance with these obligations was extremely low and hardly supportive of the new environment being ushered in requiring local norms that obligate respect for and observance of these values.

For instance, in drafting the Indictments at SCSL, it was necessary for the Prosecutor to ascertain whether Sierra Leone was a signatory to the Geneva Convention and its Additional Protocols to counter any possible argument that the offenses of war crimes charged in violation of the Convention were inapplicable in Sierra Leone.

Furthermore, for the purpose of determining whether the practice of protecting children below the age of fifteen years from conscription, recruitment, or use in armed conflict had attained universal recognition as a crime under customary international law by about a certain date, prior to the coming into force of the Convention on the Rights of the Child (CRC),[134] it was not only necessary to ascertain that Sierra Leone had signed or acceded to the convention itself, but also, the extent of state practice the country had had, if any, in affording such protection before the Convention came into force.[135]

Similarly, pursuant to Article 19(1) of the Statute of the SCSL, the Trial Chamber is enjoined, upon a conviction of an Accused, to have recourse to the sentencing practice of the ICTR and the national courts of Sierra Leone. The absence of well-developed and consistent principles, laws, or code on sentencing in Sierra Leone's judicial system has often made it difficult for the parties to make submissions in all of the cases for consideration of a distinct Sierra Leonean principle on sentencing.[136]

---

[132] "*Is it in Force*" – A compilation of key international treaties in Sierra Leone, by the Justice Sector Development Programme (JSDP), July 2006, *available at* http://www.britishcouncil.org/is_it_in_force.pdf (last visited Aug. 18, 2012).

[133] International Covenant on Civil and Political Rights, acceded to by Sierra Leone on August 23, 1996.

[134] Convention on the Rights of the Child, date of entry into force: September 2, 1990. Sierra Leone signed the Convention on February 13, 1990, and ratified same on June 18, 1990, *available at* http://treaties.un.org/doc/Publication/MTDSG/Volume%20I/Chapter%20IV/IV-11.en.pdf (last visited Aug. 18, 2012).

[135] The Child Rights Act No. 7 of 2007 is described in its short title as follows:

> Being an Act to provide for the promotion of the rights of the child compatible with the Convention on the Rights of the Child, adopted by the General Assembly of the United Nations on 20th November, 1989, and its Optional Protocols of 8th September, 2000; and the African Charter on the Rights and Welfare of the Child, and for other related matters.
> Section 141 lists a number of legislations dealing with children's rights in Sierra Leone, which it amends to streamline pre-existing law and practice with international standards. These include: Protection of Women and Girls Act, Cap. 30; Prevention of Cruelty to Children Act, Cap 31; Children and Young Persons Act, Cap 44; Muslim Marriage Act, Cap 96; Armed Forces of Sierra Leone Act, 1961 (Act No. 34 of 1961); Interpretation Act, 1971 (Act No. 8 of 1971), *available at* http://www.sierra-leone.org/Laws/2007–7p.pdf (last visited Aug. 18, 2012); essentially, these amendments adjust age limits for various purposes/activities regulated by law in Sierra Leone, to reflect international standards.

[136] Although the Article 19(1) of the Statute directs the Court to consider, when appropriate, the sentencing practices of Sierra Leonean national courts, often the excuse for not adopting or following any of the local principles is because there is nothing consistent to follow. Part of the reason put forward in the Taylor Sentencing

Since the end of the conflict and the establishment of the two transitional justice institutions, an improved atmosphere appears to be emerging reflecting stronger inclination toward upgrading its position both in the realm of compliance with its international obligations on human rights and in the promotion of those rights on the domestic scene. This has been achieved through the creation of national oversight institutions with quasi-judicial monitoring functions,[137] coupled with the enactment of appropriate laws.[138]

Critics might argue that this changed atmosphere was brought about by the specific recommendations of the TRC in its Final Report, necessitated by one of the provisions in the Lomé Peace Agreement.[139] Nonetheless, it has to be conceded that the SCSL as an international judicial institution, empowered by its constitutive instruments to apply both international law and Sierra Leone law,[140] must have contributed very positively in ushering in this changing environment of greater respect and compliance with international legal obligations and their domestic application.

B. *Regional, Continental, and Global Impact*

The ultimate goal of the Special Court in implementing its legal mandate is to end impunity in Sierra Leone, following years of mindless destructive violence. There is an expectation

Judgment is that such a move would not be appropriate as no offense was charged under Article 5 of the Statute, which provides for the charging of offenses under Sierra Leonean Law. However, it must be said that the same Judgment went on to consider the position under Sierra Leonean law, whereby a convicted accomplice is held equally culpable and is punishable as a principal felon; see Sentencing Prosecutor v. Charles Ghankay Taylor, SCSL-03-01-T, Judgment, para. 37 (May 30, 2012). Other reasons that have been cited for not relying on Sierra Leonean jurisprudence include that Sierra Leonean law still imposes the death penalty, and sentences for life, none of which exists within the Statute; see CDF Sentencing Judgment, § 43.

[137] The Human Rights Commission of Sierra Leone Act No. 9 of 2004 – BEING AN ACT to establish a commission for the protection and promotion of human rights in Sierra Leone and to provide for other related matters, *available at* http://www.sierra-leone.org/Laws/2004-9p.pdf (last visited Aug. 18, 2012); also there is a Parliamentary Committee on Human Rights with oversight responsibility in this area, created pursuant to Section 93(1)(h) of the Sierra Leone Constitution, Act No. 6 of 1991, *available at* http://www.sierra-leone.org/Laws/constitution1991.pdf (last visited Aug. 18, 2012).

[138] "The Sierra Leone Citizenship (Amendment) Act No. 11 of 2006 – BEING AN ACT to amend the Sierra Leone Citizenship Act, 1973 so as to grant the right of dual citizenship and citizenship by birth directly through the mother"; "Child Rights Act No. 7 of 2007," *id.*; "The Domestic Violence Act No. 20 of 2007 – BEING AN ACT to suppress domestic violence, to provide protection for the victims of domestic violence and to provide for other related matters"; "The Devolution of Estates Act No. 21 of 2007 – BEING AN ACT to provide for surviving spouses, children, parents, relatives and other dependents of testate and intestate persons and to provide for other related matters"; "The Registration of Customary Marriage and Divorce Act No. 1 of 2009 – BEING AN ACT to provide for the registration of customary marriages and divorces and for other related matters"; "Persons with Disability Act No. 3 of 2011 – BEING AN ACT to establish the National Commission for Persons with Disability, to prohibit discrimination against persons with disability, achieve equalization of opportunities for persons with disability and to provide for other related matters."

[139] "Peace Agreement between the Government of the Republic of Sierra Leone and the Revolutionary United Front of Sierra Leone (RUF/SL)," Article XXIV: Guarantee and Promotion of Human Rights & Article XXV: Human Rights Commission – (1). "The Parties pledge to strengthen the existing machinery for addressing grievances of the people in respect of alleged violations of their basic human rights by the creation, as a matter of urgency and not later than 90 days after the signing of the present Agreement, of an autonomous quasi-judicial national Human Rights Commission"; *see also* Report of the TRC, vol. Two, ch. 3, under the Rubric, Recommendations, subheading, Human Rights Commission, at 136–37.

[140] SCSL Statute arts. 2–5.

also that this effort by the international community will send a strong message that reso-nates globally that impunity in all its forms will never be tolerated. It bears much greater significance for countries in the West African sub-region, particularly those in the Mano River basin,[141] embroiled either directly or indirectly in internal conflicts of one kind or the other.

The position in hierarchy or status of perpetrators actually put on trial undermines that significance and renders the message ineffective, if only, at the low- or mid-level. Obviously, the higher up perpetrators are in the hierarchy, the more sobering the message. But for the arrest and trial of Liberia's ex-president Charles Taylor, many observers would have viewed much of the AFRC, RUF, and CDF now-convicted persons as not carrying enough weight to convey that message strongly. Taylor's indictment, arrest, trial, and conviction no doubt added big clout in strengthening the message about impunity.

Earlier assessments of public opinion about issues of legitimacy of the Special Court and the effective implementation of its mandate indicated a very negative picture among Sierra Leoneans. Many felt that the Court had not lived up to its expectations, in terms of the number and level of authority of those being tried. However, this perception soon changed with the arrest and transfer of Charles Taylor to The Hague for trial.

VI. CONCLUSION

In this work, I have endeavored to highlight activities of the Special Court that can argu-ably be considered part of its legacy. These activities derive from the Court's effort to fulfill its mandate. I have distinguished between activities that derive from the exercise of its core mandate and those that necessarily and reasonably derive from efforts associated with ful-fillment of that mandate.

Also, I have attempted to justify the activities that constitute the SCSL's legacy, which are largely borne out of the hopes and expectations of the international community and the people of Sierra Leone, as to the role, purpose, and function that the Court should serve. The expectations of the two groups as shown do not necessarily coincide, just as in life gen-erally, people's perceptions of justice almost always vary significantly. But no matter how wide the variations, these expectations remain central to the achievement of the Court's core mandate, or are reasonably associated with the fulfillment of that purpose.

Space considerations has not permitted an exhaustive discourse of the merits and demer-its of each activity. However, I have endeavored to analyze those identified from the point of view of whether, and to what extent, the Court has worked to fulfill them. As the record will conclude, some of these expectations have been met whereas for others it is a value judgment call.

The indictment of arguably all the key members of all the factions in the conflict, plus a sitting head of state of a neighboring country, who in many ways was the mastermind behind the conflict, and the successful trial and conviction of those surviving, is undoubt-edly a great achievement in fulfilling the Court's core mandate, especially in the face of a funding situation that put severe constraints on the management of its work. With these

---

[141] Geographically, Guinea, Liberia, and Sierra Leone, and on political consideration, now includes Ivory Coast.

convictions and long sentences, it is to be hoped that the issue of impunity as it relates to mass atrocity crimes has been given deserved attention. Any person wanting to foment trouble of that kind in Sierra Leone, or even Liberia and beyond, will think twice about it today, no matter what that person's grievance. Impunity as it affects people's daily lives and the law compliance culture in Sierra Leone remain quite a challenge, but on a different plain. Further, the fact cannot be denied that an excellent and appreciable effort has been made by the Court to achieve the other ambit of its core mandate, which is to restore the rule of law. This being an effort that requires extensive rebuilding of capacity nationally, credit should be given for the numerous training programs and activities that have been provided mostly outside the Court's core budget in developing individual and institutional capacity, alongside working on the Court's core mandate. The fruits of some of these efforts will only be realized over time.

The reparation of war victims is a difficult expectation to meet. Besides the huge budgetary challenge that it poses, the magnitude of which this Court might never aspire toward, it is simply an activity that falls outside its core judicial functions. Although there are provisions within the Court's rules that give it a role in reparation issues, these are strictly limited to legal procedural processes than the actual provision of practical assistance.[142] Nonetheless, the expectation lingers on. At outreach events by the Court in recent times, one question that is frequently asked is about provision, if any, that the SCSL has for war victims.

On a final note, as the jurists, critics, and readers continue to churn through the big prize trophy of the court, the Taylor Judgment on conviction pending appeals,[143] scope still remain for determining the extent of the full value of this decision, and indeed the overall activities of the Court in meeting the quest for justice by the international community and the people of Sierra Leone. Whether and to what extent the Court has fulfilled this quest will only be fully determined over time. One thing that should stand out in everyone's mind though, no matter what that final assessment will be, is the incredible effort and contribution that has been made by everyone involved with the Court in making these things happen. Across board and without prejudice to whether they were foreign or local, Sierra Leonean or non–Sierra Leonean, every person has shown true dedication and professionalism for which they richly deserve this tribute. In many ways the Special Court has been an experiment that exceeded expectations. This would not have been possible without such high level of dedication.

Words about the Court's achievements and its legacy in the First Annual Report of the President to the United Nations are pertinent in this regard:

---

[142] SCSL RPE – Rule 88(B) and Rule 104 deal with forfeiture of property respectively. Rule 105 deals with and compensation to victims. Although Rule 88(B) empowers the Court to "order forfeiture of property, proceeds and any asset acquired unlawfully or by criminal conduct" if it finds the Accused guilty of a crime (necessarily a crime relating to property), Rule 104 lays the procedure for the process of the forfeiture, which involves a hearing and may include possible third parties intervening. Rule 105 provides for the Registrar to transmit to the competent authorities of the state the Judgment finding the Accused guilty, and it is for the state authorities, through relevant national legislation to enable victims of crime to claim compensation in national courts for an injury they have suffered. The rule provides that any finding of guilt by the Special Court shall be final and binding as regards the criminal responsibility of the convicted person for any such injury.

[143] The Judgment spans over 2,500 pages.

History will judge how successful these initiatives have been, but the foundations for leaving behind a legacy of accountability and contributing to legal reform in Sierra Leone are being laid. More globally, it is hoped that the legacy of the Special Court will also serve as a template for ensuring accountability for violations of international humanitarian law in other post-conflict situations.[144]

---

[144] First Annual Report, *supra* note 9.

35

International Judicial Trials, Truth Commissions, and Gacaca: Developing a Framework for Transitional Justice from the Experiences in Sierra Leone and Rwanda

Linda E. Carter[*]

Both Sierra Leone and Rwanda invoked multiple forms of post-conflict processes.[1] In the case of Sierra Leone, there were parallel international judicial proceedings and a truth commission. For Rwanda, an international criminal tribunal was created and "Gacaca" tribunals were established in villages throughout the country. The use of multiple procedures in these two situations provides us with an opportunity to learn from these experiences and to formulate ways in which to structure how decisions about post-conflict processes should be made in the future.

In both cases, a court was created that had an international focus, although there are significant differences between the two courts. Among the differences are the appointment process for the judges and the locations of the courts. For Rwanda, the United Nations Security Council established the International Criminal Tribunal for Rwanda (ICTR) in 1994. The ICTR comprises internationally drawn judges and is located outside Rwanda, in Arusha, Tanzania. For Sierra Leone, the United Nations entered into an agreement in 2002 with the government of Sierra Leone to create the Special Court for Sierra Leone (SCSL), which is composed of both internationally drawn and Sierra Leone (appointed) judges. The SCSL also differs from the ICTR in that the SCSL sits in-country in Freetown, Sierra Leone.[2]

[*] Professor of Law and Co-Director, Global Center, University of the Pacific, McGeorge School of Law. I would like to thank Professor Charles Jalloh and the University of Pittsburgh School of Law for the opportunity to present the ideas in this chapter at the April 2012 conference on "Assessing the Contributions and Legacy of the Special Court for Sierra Leone to Africa and International Criminal Justice." I would also like to express my appreciation to my research assistants on this project, Michael Youril and Andrew Ducart.

[1] In this chapter, I discuss only the international tribunals and one local process for each country, the Truth and Reconciliation Commission in Sierra Leone and the Gacaca trials in Rwanda. My goal is to compare two different international tribunals and two different alternatives to traditional judicial proceedings. In each country, however, other processes were also put in place. For a description of other processes, see Christopher W. Mullins, *The International Criminal Court, in* The Pursuit of International Criminal Justice: A World Study on Conflicts, Victimization, and Post-Conflict Justice 399, 402 (M. Cherif Bassiouni ed., 2010) (describing various entities in Rwanda, including the National Unity and Reconciliation Commission); Mark A. Drumbl, Atrocity, Punishment, and International Law 73–85 (2007) (commenting on national and military prosecutions in Rwanda and prosecutions in foreign national courts); M. Cherif Bassiouni, *Mixed Models of International Criminal Justice, in* The Pursuit of International Criminal Justice: A World Study on Conflicts, Victimization, and Post-Conflict Justice 423, 441–44 (M. Cherif Bassiouni ed., 2010) (describing the DDR program and traditional reconciliation ceremonies in Sierra Leone).

[2] The only exception is the trial of Charles Taylor, which because of security concerns, occurred in The Hague.

The more striking differences, however, occur with the additional process that was set up in each situation. In Sierra Leone, a truth and reconciliation commission was established to create an impartial historical record ... ; to address impunity, to respond to the needs of the victims, to promote healing and reconciliation and to prevent a repetition of the violations and abuses suffered.[3] Testimony was taken from many individuals to create a record of the events and harms. In Rwanda, in addition to some prosecutions in the national court system, Gacaca tribunals were created throughout the country. In contrast to the single entity of the Commission in Sierra Leone, 12,000 Gacaca jurisdictions were established in Rwanda. Of these, 1,545 were trial level and 1,545 were appellate level. The approximately nine thousand other Gacacas were an investigative level. The Gacaca process combined a goal of punishment (up to life imprisonment) with a conciliatory purpose. The Gacaca law reflects the dual purposes, stating that the goal is "to eradicate forever the culture of impunity in order to achieve justice and reconciliation in Rwanda."[4] The Gacaca trials began in 2005 and concluded in June 2012. These tribunals will have tried approximately 1.9 million individuals through this process.[5]

Lessons can be learned from each situation, both positive and negative. In the case of Rwanda, a concern with a victor's justice effect has been raised regarding both the ICTR and Gacaca. Another critique is the distance of the ICTR, sitting in Tanzania, from Rwanda. Gacaca is also criticized for conducting trials without basic due process protections. On the other hand, an innovative process was created in Gacaca to adjudicate accountability on a large scale, something that cannot be done in an international criminal tribunal.[6] In the case of Sierra Leone, the relationship between the Commission and the Court has been critiqued for not resolving in advance issues such as information sharing, but the Commission is also commended for providing a nonjudicial complement to the Court.[7] In general, lessons from both Sierra Leone and Rwanda include the significance of accountability, justice,[8] reconciliation, and reparations in post-conflict societies. In both situations, the international and national communities considered it important to take steps and to work toward achieving these goals.

From both the criticism and the praise, it should be useful to distill principles and factors that will help formulate even more workable combinations of responses in the future. One

---

[3] The Truth and Reconciliation Commission Act of 2000 (2000), *available at* http://www.sierraleonetrc.org/downloads/legalresources/trc_act_2000.pdf (Sierra Leone) [hereinafter TRC Act].

[4] Organic Law No. 16/2004, *available at* http://www.inkiko-gacaca.gov.rw/pdf/newlaw1.pdf [hereinafter 2004 Organic Law].

[5] GACACA COURTS, SUMMARY OF THE REPORT PRESENTED AT THE CLOSING OF GACACA COURTS ACTIVITIES 10, 15 (2012), *available at* http://inkiko-gacaca.gov.rw/English/wp-content/uploads/2012/06/Gacaca-Report-Summary.pdf (reporting that as of June 18, 2012, the official closure date of the Gacaca courts, exactly 1,958,634 cases have been tried).

[6] See discussion of strengths and weaknesses of Gacaca in Linda E. Carter, *Justice and Reconciliation on Trial: Gacaca Proceedings in Rwanda*, 14 NEW ENG. J. INT'L & COMP. L. 41 (2007).

[7] See also the interesting insights into whether "truth" is necessary for reconciliation in Tim Kelsall, *Truth, Lies, Ritual: Preliminary Reflections on the Truth and Reconciliation Commission in Sierra Leone*, 27 HUM. RTS. Q. 361 (2005).

[8] As used in this chapter, "justice" refers to retributive justice, punishment for the crimes committed. As Prof. Jeremy Sarkin and others have pointed out, "justice" in a broad sense can also include restorative and transitional justice. *See* Jeremy Sarkin, *The Role of the International Criminal Court (ICC) in Reducing Massive Human Rights Violations Such as Enforced Disappearances in Africa: Towards Developing Transitional Justice Strategies*, 11 STUD. ETHNICITY & NATIONALISM 130, 138 (2011).

significant principle is that there is no one perfect approach – in other words, this is not a "one size fits all" field. Every situation may not call for both a court and a truth commission. In the same vein, a Gacaca system may not be workable in other countries. A more particularized application of the general principle is that no one form of a specific procedure is best for all situations. For example, truth commissions can be designed with or without amnesty, or with amnesty for all crimes, or only for some crimes. Judicial trials can occur on an international level in The Hague or Arusha, or can occur within the country involved. The critical inquiry is what factors should be considered in making these decisions.

This chapter explores the experience of both Sierra Leone and Rwanda with the combination of an international court and a nonjudicial or quasi-judicial process. The first two sections describe the combination used for each country, including commentary on how well the processes worked and some lessons that can be learned from those experiences. The third section identifies the benefits of a combination of processes and considers what general factors can be distilled to assist in deciding which processes should be invoked in post-conflict situations that are likely to be very different from one another.

I. THE EXPERIENCE OF SIERRA LEONE

A. *The Special Court for Sierra Leone (SCSL)*

Sierra Leone was engulfed in a brutal civil war for eleven years from 1991 to 2002. As described in other commentary,[9] this conflict devastated the country on both human and infrastructure levels. The SCSL came into existence pursuant to an agreement entered into between the United Nations and the government of Sierra Leone in January 2002.[10] Unlike the earlier International Criminal Tribunals for the former Yugoslavia (ICTY) and for Rwanda (ICTR), which were located outside the countries affected, the SCSL was situated within the country, and facilities were built in Freetown. The Special Court had two Trial Chambers and one Appeals Chamber. For both types of chambers, the composition included both Sierra Leonean and international judges, with the latter appointees constituting the majority in each instance. The Sierra Leonean judges were appointed by the national government, and the international judges were appointed by the UN Secretary-General.[11] As of September 2012, the SCSL is still in existence as the appeal of the final case, involving Charles Taylor, is pending; the other cases are completed. With the conviction of Taylor, the Court has adjudicated cases involving nine individuals, all of whom were found guilty.[12]

---

[9] *See, e.g.,* Jennifer Moore, Humanitarian Law in Action within Africa 241–53 (2012); Charles C. Jalloh, *Special Court for Sierra Leone: Achieving Justice?*, 32 Mich. J. Int'l L. 395, 398–99 (2011); Rosalind Shaw, *Memory Frictions: Localizing the Truth and Reconciliation Commission in Sierra Leone*, 1 Int'l J. Transitional J. 183, 185–86 (2007); Daniel J. Macaluso, *Absolute and Free Pardon: The Effect of the Amnesty Provision in the Lome Peace Agreement on the Jurisdiction of the Special Court for Sierra Leone*, 27 Brook. J. Int'l L. 347, 349–51 (2001).

[10] Jalloh, *supra* note 9, at 401.

[11] *About: Court Organization: Chambers*, Special Ct. for Sierra Leone, http://www.sc-sl.org/ABOUT/CourtOrganization/Chambers/tabid/86/Default.aspx (last visited Aug. 18, 2012).

[12] See description of indictments and convictions on the website for the Special Court, *Cases*, Special Ct. for Sierra Leone, http://www.sc-sl.org/CASES/tabid/71/Default.aspx.

The purposes for creating the Special Court included justice, accountability, reconciliation, and peace. The UN Resolution stated that the purposes were to: "[e]nd impunity, provide redress for atrocities committed, provide public awareness of the crimes committed and the perpetrators (legal and social accountability), contribute to the process of national reconciliation, and the restoration and maintenance of peace and legal order."[13]

B. Truth and Reconciliation Commission (TRC)

The Truth and Reconciliation Commission was authorized by the Lomé Peace Accord in 1999,[14] and enacted into law in Sierra Leone in 2000.[15] There were seven commissioners, four Sierra Leoneans, and three international members. The TRC held hearings in many locales throughout the country, ultimately interviewing about 7,000 individuals. The work of the TRC lasted from 2002 to 2004.[16] The purpose of the TRC was defined by the legislation as:

> The object for which the Commission is established is to create an impartial historical record of violations and abuses of human rights and international humanitarian law related to the armed conflict in Sierra Leone, from the beginning of the Conflict in 1991 to the signing of the Lomé Peace Agreement; to address impunity, to respond to the needs of the victims, to promote healing and reconciliation and to prevent a repetition of the violations and abuses suffered.[17]

The Commission did not have the authority to grant amnesty, unlike the South African truth and reconciliation commission, which had that capacity.[18] However, a blanket amnesty had been granted in the Lomé Agreement.[19]

The comprehensive report of the TRC[20] fulfilled several significant purposes. The Commission researched and documented the history preceding the conflict and the major causes of the conflict, thus creating a historical record going back before the conflict. The report also systematically documented information about the types of violations committed, the perpetrators, and the victims. Particular attention was paid in the analysis to women and children. The appendices to the report contain data that will be helpful both to Sierra Leone and to research into other post-conflict situations. The importance of the

---

[13] U.N. S.C. Res. 1315, pmbl., para. 7.

[14] Peace Agreement between the Government of Sierra Leone and the Revolutionary United Front of Sierra Leone, art. VI (May 18, 1999), *available at* http://www.sierra-leone.org/lomeaccord.html [hereinafter Lomé Agreement].

[15] TRC Act, *supra* note 3.

[16] MOORE, *supra* note 9, at 259; William A. Schabas, *Conjoined Twins of Transitional Justice? The Sierra Leone Truth and Reconciliation Commission and the Special Court*, 2 J. INT'L CRIM. L. 1082, 1084 (2004).

[17] TRC Act, *supra* note 3, at 6(1). The Act further specified that the Commission's work should include, inter alia, investigating and reporting on the causes of the conflict, violations, and who was responsible for the violations, and promoting human dignity and reconciliation. *Id.* at 6(2).

[18] William A. Schabas, *Truth Commissions and Courts Working in Parallel: The Sierra Leone Experience*, 98 AM. SOC'Y INT'L L. PROC. 189, 191 (2004).

[19] Lomé Agreement, *supra* note 14, at art. IX.

[20] SIERRA LEONE TRUTH & RECONCILIATION COMM'N, WITNESS TO TRUTH: REPORT OF THE SIERRA LEONE TRUTH & RECONCILIATION COMMISSION (2004), *available at* http://www.sierra-leone.org/TRCDocuments. html.

TRC did not end with their report. The TRC made recommendations[21] that the government of Sierra Leone is bound to implement. Among the many recommendations is one requiring the government to set up a reparations program for the victims. This is occurring today through the National Commission for Social Action.[22] Among the other recommendations were ones related to protecting human rights, improvements to government, anti-corruption measures, programs for women and children, and reconciliation approaches. Of particular relevance here, the TRC also made suggestions for the international community, based on the experience in Sierra Leone, regarding future combinations of an international court and a truth commission.

C. Commentary and Lessons

The insights of the Commission on how best to coordinate two parallel processes largely mirror issues raised in academic commentary. The Commission recommends taking measures at the outset to establish shared objectives and fundamental principles regarding the rights of individuals vis à vis each body.[23] This reflects the experience from the incident that arose when Hinga Norman, who was in the custody of the Special Court, wanted to testify in public before the Commission. The President of the Special Court ultimately found that, although Hinga Norman could make a statement, it could not be in public.[24] Professor William Schabas, a member of the TRC, has noted the dissatisfaction of the TRC with the decision against a public hearing, but also has noted that the SCSL's decision was an attempt to accommodate the work of both processes.[25] The Commission further recommended a binding dispute resolution mechanism to resolve conflicts between organizations.[26]

Based again on experience of the Commission, there is a recommendation that an international tribunal provide use immunity for testimony provided in a TRC. Some individuals were hesitant to testify before the TRC out of a fear, real or perceived, that they could be prosecuted based on what they stated.[27] Reflecting a growing theme in the academic commentary, the Commission further recommends that there should be a "major investment in the national justice system instead of, or in addition to establishing international tribunals

---

[21] *See* Sierra Leone Truth & Reconciliation Comm'n, Witness to Truth: Report of the Sierra Leone Truth & Reconciliation Commission Vol. 2, at 116–28 (2004), *available at* http://www.sierra-leone.org/Other-Conflict/TRCVolume2.pdf [hereinafter TRC Report Vol. 2].

[22] *See generally*, National Commission for Social Action, http://www.nacsa.gov.sl/index.html (last visited Aug. 18, 2012).

[23] TRC Report Vol. 2, *supra* note 21, at 191.

[24] Prosecutor v. Norman, Case No. SCSL-2003–08-PT, Decision on Appeal by the Truth and Reconciliation Commission for Sierra Leone and Chief Samuel Hinga Norman JP against the Decision of his Lordship, Mr. Justice Bankole Thompson, *available at* http://www.sc-sl.org/Documents/SCSL-03–08-PT-122-II.pdf.

[25] Schabas, *supra* note 16, at 1098.

[26] *See* Elizabeth M. Evenson, Note, *Truth and Justice in Sierra Leone: Coordination between Commission and Court*, 104 Colum. L. Rev. 730 (2004) (commenting on need for coordination between processes, such as the TRC and SCSL in Sierra Leone).

[27] Schabas, *supra* note 16, at 1091–92 (noting that it is difficult to know why individuals did not testify before the TRC, but also suggesting that use immunity be considered); Rosalind Shaw, *Linking Justice with Reintegration?: Ex-Combatants and the Sierra Leone Experiment*, in Localizing Transitional Justice: Interventions and Priorities after Mass Violence 111, 120 (Rosalind Shaw et al. eds., 2010).

to investigate and prosecute violations of human rights."[28] The Commission additionally notes that foreign legal professionals could be enlisted to assist, all with an eye toward building national capacity.

Additional commentary on the Special Court and the TRC provide further insight into strengths and weaknesses that are helpful lessons for the future. The need for voluntary contributions to fund the SCSL and the TRC is roundly criticized as undermining the operation of each entity.[29] Without guaranteed funding, the two entities were placed in the awkward position of soliciting funds for their operation at the same time that they were trying to move forward in a professional and impartial manner. The parallel situation of the Special Court and the TRC on funding also put them in an unintended, but unfortunate, competition with each other.[30] The unstable funding is additionally criticized as having an impact on the fairness of the trials because the Defense was under-resourced.[31]

Another point in the commentary relates to advance planning to make decisions on information sharing between a Court and a TRC. Whether the decision is to share some, all, or none of the information between entities, most commentators advocate having this issue clarified at the outset.[32] In the case of Sierra Leone, a de facto "firewall" approach was implemented because the SCSL Prosecutor declared that the Prosecution would not use information from the TRC.[33] The concern is that, without clarity, there will be confusion over what can happen if one testifies in the TRC. Some commentators have noted that many Sierra Leoneans, in general, were confused about the precise roles of the TRC and the SCSL.[34] This confusion probably contributed to another point that is made by some

---

[28] TRC REPORT VOL. 2, *supra* note 21, at 192; *see also* Judge Renate Winter, *The Special Court for Sierra Leone*, *in* THE PURSUIT OF INTERNATIONAL CRIMINAL JUSTICE: A WORLD STUDY ON CONFLICTS, VICTIMIZATION, AND POST-CONFLICT JUSTICE 155, 156–58 (M. Cherif Bassiouni ed., 2010) (advocating for an increased role in prosecutions by the national courts of Sierra Leone and an increased coordination and cooperation between the international tribunal's prosecutors and national prosecutors).

[29] TOM PERRIELLO & MARIEKE WIERDA, INT'L CTR. FOR TRANSITIONAL JUST., THE SPECIAL COURT FOR SIERRA LEONE UNDER SCRUTINY 31–32 (2006); Sara Kendall, Chapter 20 in this volume; Jalloh, *supra* note 9; Schabas, *supra* note 18, at 191; Eric Wiebelhaus-Brahm, *Truth Commissions and Other Investigative Bodies*, *in* THE PURSUIT OF INTERNATIONAL CRIMINAL JUSTICE: A WORLD STUDY ON CONFLICTS, VICTIMIZATION, AND POST-CONFLICT JUSTICE 477, 562 (M. Cherif Bassiouni ed., 2010).

[30] Schabas, *supra* note 16, at 1088–90.

[31] Funding inadequacies and unequal status within the Court for the Defense are criticized. *See* Jalloh, *supra* note 9, at 437–44. For general commentary on issues related to defense counsel at the SCSL, *see* Vincent O. Nmehielle, Chapter 27 in this volume and Sareta Ashraph, Chapter 28 in this volume.

[32] *See* Marieke Wierda et al., Int'l Ctr. Transitional Just., *Exploring the Relationship between the Special Court and the Truth and Reconciliation Commission of Sierra Leone* (2002) (describing "firewall," "free access," and "conditional sharing" approaches; suggesting a limited sharing approach, balancing the interests of the Special Court and the TRC); Matiangai Sirleaf, *Regional Approach to Transitional Justice?: Examining the Special Court for Sierra Leone and the Truth & Reconciliation Commission for Liberia*, 21 FLA. J. INT'L L. 209, 251–56 (2009) (describing approaches and arguing for resolution of the approach at the outset); Evenson, *supra* note 26, at 763–66 (suggesting the "firewall" approach and that decisions should be made at the initial establishment of the entities).

[33] Evenson, *supra* note 26, at 763; Sirleaf, *supra* note 32, at 251.

[34] *See, e.g.*, Shaw et al., *supra* note 27, at 121 (noting the confusion about the SCSL, the TRC, and the DDR); Donna E. Arzt, *Views on the Ground: The Local Perception of International Criminal Tribunals in the Former Yugoslavia and Sierra Leone*, 603 ANNALS AM. ACAD. POL. & SOC. SCI. 226, 234 (2006) (noting the confusion between the SCSL and the TRC).

commentators that the truth about occurrences and roles in atrocities was not forthcoming in the TRC.[35] It is interesting to note, though, that Professors Rosalind Shaw and Tim Kelsall suggest that reconciliation may occur even if the full truth is not revealed.[36] This, too, may prove to be valuable insight, gained from the Sierra Leonean experience, for future post-conflict processes. Yet another common thread in the commentary relates to the expectations and need for economic assistance.[37] Although the TRC recommended reparations, there was no immediate response from the SCSL or the TRC to provide those who were witnesses or who gave statements with any form of economic assistance. This point is important in terms of the communication of the purposes of the processes as well as how relief is structured.

In addition to the critical analysis, positive aspects of the Special Court and the TRC are also identified. Through its prosecutions, the Special Court is commended for ensuring a lack of impunity for major figures in the war.[38] The location of the Court in Sierra Leone is considered an advantage for visibility and access to the tribunal. The TRC is viewed as instrumental in creating an accurate factual description of the causes of the conflict[39] and also in reintegrating ex-combatants into their communities.[40] Moreover, despite various issues, the Sierra Leonean experience demonstrated that parallel processes, with different goals, can coexist and serve the needs of the population and the international community.

II. THE EXPERIENCE OF RWANDA

A. ICTR

In 1994, Rwanda experienced a devastating conflict that resulted in the deaths of about 800,000 Tutsi and moderate Hutu individuals within 100 days. The causes and circumstances of this genocide are described in many articles and books.[41] In the aftermath of

---

[35] Shaw et al., *supra* note 27, at 127 (commenting that ex-combatants did not acknowledge individual responsibility for atrocities). *But see* Schabas, *supra* note 18, at 191–92 (suggesting that the threat of criminal prosecution did not deeply impact the decisions of some perpetrators who declined to make public admissions before the TRC).

[36] Shaw et al., *supra* note 27, at 129 (further commenting that the assumption that truth-telling is necessary for reconciliation may not be the model in many societies); Kelsall, *supra* note 7.

[37] Shaw, *supra* note 9, at 184; Moore, *supra* note 9, at 266–68 (describing the need for and efforts toward reparations); Naomi Roht-Arriaza, *Reparations in International Law and Practice, in* The Pursuit of International Criminal Justice: A World Study on Conflicts, Victimization, and Post-Conflict Justice 655, 674 (M. Cherif Bassiouni ed., 2010) (describing reparations efforts, but limited results, in Sierra Leone).

[38] *See, e.g.*, Jalloh, *supra* note 9, at 456–60 (describing both achievements and problems with the Special Court).

[39] *See* Schabas, *supra* note 16, at 1084–86.

[40] *See* The Post-Conflict Reintegration Initiative for Development and Empowerment, Ex-Combatant Views of the Truth and Reconciliation Commission and the Special Court in Sierra Leone 11–15 (2002) (explaining the important role the TRC plays in the reintegration of ex-combatants into their communities, and ex-combatant perceptions of the TRC).

[41] *See, e.g.*, Samantha Power, A Problem from Hell: America and the Age of Genocide (2007); Roméo Dallaire, Shake Hands with the Devil: The Failure of Humanity in Rwanda (2004); Mahmood Mamdani, When Victims Become Killers: Colonialism, Nativism, and the Genocide in Rwanda (2001); Jose Doria et al., *Africa, in* 2 The Pursuit of International Criminal Justice: A World Study on Conflicts, Victimization, and Post-Conflict Justice 357, 398–402 (M. Cherif Bassiouni ed., 2010);

the genocide, the UN Security Council established the ICTR.[42] The ICTR was situated in Arusha, Tanzania, rather than in Rwanda. Initially, there were two trial chambers and an appeals chamber that is shared with the ICTY.[43] Subsequently, a third trial chamber was added.[44] The judges are elected by General Assembly of the United Nations and come from the international community. Unlike the SCSL, no national judges are included in the complement in chambers. Thus, not only is the ICTR located outside of Rwanda, there is also no Rwandan participation in the judiciary of the tribunal.[45] As of August 10, 2012, cases involving seventy-four individuals had been adjudicated.[46]

The purpose of the ICTR is "to put an end to [genocide and other serious violations of international humanitarian law] and to take effective measures to bring to justice the persons who are responsible for them" with the goal that "the prosecution of persons responsible for serious violations of international humanitarian law would enable this aim [of justice] to be achieved and would contribute to the process of national reconciliation and to the restoration and maintenance of peace ...."[47] As with the SCSL, the initial statement of the purposes included justice, reconciliation, and peace.

B. *Gacaca*

The Gacaca jurisdictions were created pursuant to a 2001 law that has subsequently been amended in some particulars.[48] In establishing Gacaca, Rwanda combined objectives of justice and reconciliation. The 2004 Organic Law states the following factors were considered in setting up Gacaca:[49]

> Considering the necessity to eradicate forever the culture of impunity in order to achieve justice and reconciliation in Rwanda, and thus to adopt provisions enabling rapid prosecutions and trials of perpetrators and accomplices of genocide, not only with the aim of pro-

---

Megan M. Westberg, *Rwanda's Use of Transitional Justice after Genocide: The Gacaca Courts and the ICTR*, 59 U. KAN. L. REV. 331, 333–36 (2011).

[42] S.C. Res. 955, U.N. DOC. S/RES/955 (Nov. 4, 1994).

[43] *About ICTR: ICTR Structure: The Chambers*, INT'L CRIMINAL TRIBUNAL FOR RWANDA, http://www.unictr.org/tabid/103/Default.aspx (last visited Aug. 19, 2012); Jose Doria et al., *supra* note 41, at 405.

[44] *About ICTR: ICTR Structure: The Chambers*, INT'L CRIMINAL TRIBUNAL FOR RWANDA, http://www.unictr.org/tabid/103/Default.aspx (last visited Aug. 19, 2012).

[45] Mark A. Drumbl, *Law and Atrocity: Settling Accounts in Rwanda*, 31 OHIO N.U. L. REV. 41, 46 (2005). Apparently, there was a concern about at least the appearance of neutrality. *See id.* (noting that Rwandans were excluded from the ICTR judiciary out of concerns for neutrality and impartiality).

[46] The cases resulted in forty-eight convictions complete through appeal, sixteen convictions pending appeal, and ten acquittals. Status of Cases, INT'L CRIMINAL TRIBUNAL FOR RWANDA, http://www.unictr.org/Cases/tabid/204/Default.aspx (last visited Aug. 19, 2012). One case is currently in trial. *Id.*

[47] S.C. Res. 955, U.N. DOC. S/RES/955 (Nov. 4, 1994).

[48] Organic Law No. 40/2000, *available at* http://www.inkiko-gacaca.gov.rw/pdf/Law.pdf. Note that this was created in 2000 and passed in 2001. *Id.* The Organic Law has been amended on multiple occasions: 2004, 2006, 2007, and 2008. For the 2004 amendments see 2004 Organic Law, *supra* note 4. For the 2006 amendments see Organic Law No. 28/2006, *available at* http://www.geneva-academy.ch/RULAC/pdf_state/2006-Gacaca-Organic-Law-28–2006.pdf. For the 2007 amendments see Organic Law No. 10/2007, *available at* http://www.geneva-academy.ch/RULAC/pdf_state/2007-Gacaca-Crts-Organic-Law-10–2007–3-languages-.pdf. For the 2008 amendments see Organic Law No. 13/2008, *available at* http://www.geneva-academy.ch/RULAC/pdf_state/2008-Gacaca-Courts-Organic-Law-13.2008.pdf.

[49] 2004 Organic Law, *supra* note 4.

viding punishment, but also reconstituting the Rwandan Society that had been destroyed by bad leaders who incited the population into exterminating part of the Society;

Considering the necessity for the Rwandan Society to find by itself, solutions to the genocide problems and its consequences;

Considering that it is important to provide for penalties allowing convicted persons to amend themselves and to favour their reintegration into the Rwandan Society without jeopardizing the people's normal life ...

The official Rwandan government website on Gacaca states these objectives and also lists discovery of the truth as a goal.[50] The Gacaca jurisdictions were within communities throughout Rwanda. As mentioned at the outset, there were about 12,000 Gacaca jurisdictions, approximately 3,000 of which were trial- and appellate-level proceedings.[51] Through this process, about 1.9 million cases were processed with sentences ranging up to life imprisonment. Many individuals were also released through this process, performed community service, and were reintegrated into communities. Although prosecuting individuals for genocide, Gacaca trials were unusual in that there were no attorneys involved, either for the prosecution or the defense, and the judges were elected from the community and were not legally trained.[52]

C. *Commentary and Lessons*

There is very little commentary about the combination of the ICTR and Gacaca. For the most part, the two processes are written about separately. In part, this may be because there was little overlap between them. The individuals prosecuted by the ICTR were not brought on charges before Gacaca. The Court and Gacaca were not competing for funds as with the SCSL and the Commission. The ICTR was funded by the United Nations whereas Gacaca was a national endeavor. Some overlap occurred when witnesses before Gacaca were also witnesses before the ICTR. In particular, the use of prior inconsistent statements by witnesses was brought up by the Defense at the ICTR.[53] This was not a conflict, however; rather it was an evidentiary matter at the ICTR.

Moreover, the transfer of cases to Rwanda has been to the national court system,[54] not to Gacaca, which avoided any potential problems with Gacaca as a system without some

---

[50] National Service of Gacaca Jurisdictions, *The Objectives of the Gacaca Courts*, http://www.inkiko-gacaca.gov.rw/En/EnObjectives.htm (last visited Aug. 19, 2012). Five objectives are stated:

1) To reveal the truth about what has happened
2) To speed up the genocide trials
3) To eradicate the culture of impunity
4) To reconcile the Rwandans and reinforce their unity
5) To prove that the Rwandan society has the capacity to settle its own problems through a system of justice based on the Rwandan custom. *Id.*

[51] National Service of Gacaca Jurisdictions, *Gacaca FAQs*, http://inkiko-gacaca.gov.rw/English/?page_id=464 (last visited Aug. 19, 2012); Maya Sosnov, *The Adjudication of Genocide: Gacaca and the Road to Reconciliation in Rwanda*, 36 Denv. J. Int'l L. & Pol'y 125, 135 (2008); Sarah L. Wells, *Gender, Sexual Violence and Prospects for Justice at the Gacaca Courts in Rwanda*, 14 S. Cal. Rev. L. & Women's Stud. 167, 174 (2005).

[52] Carter, *supra* note 6, at 45–47; Drumbl, *supra* note 45, at 55–59.

[53] *See, e.g.,* Prosecutor v. Kanyabashi, Case No. ICTR-96-15-T, Decision on Kanyabashi's Motion to Re-Open His Case and to Recall Prosecution Witness QA, para. 10 (July 2, 2008).

[54] *Cases: Case Transferred to National Jurisdiction*, Int'l Criminal Tribunal for Rwanda, http://www.unictr.org/Cases/tabid/77/Default.aspx?id=7&mnid=7 (last visited Aug. 19, 2012) (listing the cases transferred from the ICTR to Rwanda's domestic courts). For an example of how a referral from the ICTR to the Rwandan

of the traditional due process protections. To the extent there is commentary that relates to both the ICTR and Gacaca, it is usually with regard to Gacaca filling the need to prosecute all *genocidaires* whereas the ICTR could only prosecute relatively few, but high-level individuals.[55] In other words, the overlap relates largely to the reasons for establishing the Gacaca courts.

The lack of commentary on the combination of the ICTR and Gacaca may also reflect the lack of coordination or planning related to the two processes. The ICTR was well underway as its own entity before Gacaca was established. Further, there may have been less overlap than in Sierra Leone because the ICTR is in Tanzania whereas Gacaca is within Rwanda. Because both processes were prosecuting individuals for genocide, there also may have been less confusion about the purposes of each tribunal than occurred in Sierra Leone.

Regardless of commentary specifically on the overlap of the two processes, much can be learned from the experiences and commentary on each process. Like the International Criminal Tribunal for the former Yugoslavia (ICTY), the ICTR was a pioneer in international criminal justice. Similarly, Gacaca was a process that was innovative and unique, providing us with new information about how to construct transitional justice mechanisms. In 2012, we know much more than we did in 1994 (when the ICTR was established) or 2005 (when Gacaca commenced).

One theme from the Rwanda experience relates to the conduct of the proceedings. Part of this theme is the need to avoid as much as possible a "victor's justice" situation. Both the ICTR and Gacaca have been criticized as prosecuting only one side of the conflict.[56] This undermines the legitimacy of the proceedings. A second part to the theme of the conduct of the proceedings specifically concerns Gacaca. Some commentators have questioned whether Gacaca was effective in achieving its goals of finding truth, imposing justice, and furthering reconciliation.[57] Some have commented that, unlike what is expected in a truth commission, the accused in Gacaca did not have a strong motivation to tell the truth; instead, the motivation was to avoid imprisonment or to be released.[58] The criticism with regard to justice relates primarily to the lack of some of the basic due process guarantees,

---

national court system works, *see* Uwinkindi v. Prosecutor, Case No. ICTR-01-75-AR11*bis*, Decision on Uwinkindi's Appeal against the Referral of His Case to Rwanda and Related Motions (Dec. 16, 2011), http://www.unictr.org/Portals/0/Case/English/Uwinkindi/decisions/111216.pdf.

[55] *See* Coel Kirkby, *Rwanda's Gacaca Courts: A Preliminary Critique*, 50 J. Afr. L. 94, 99–100 (2006); Sarkin, *supra* note 8, at 158–59.

[56] Lars Waldorf, *"Like Jews Waiting for Jesus": Posthumous Justice in Post-Genocide Rwanda*, in Localizing Transitional Justice: Interventions and Priorities after Mass Violence 183, 193 (Rosalind Shaw et al. eds., 2010); Max Rettig, *Gacaca, Truth, Justice, and Reconciliation in Postconflict Rwanda?*, 51 Afr. Stud. Rev. 25, 40 (2008) (noting that Rwandans interviewed complained about the lack of prosecution of RPA soldiers).

[57] Rettig, *supra* note 56, at 26 (listing a number of challenges Gacaca faced in trying to achieve these goals, including the lack of protections for the accused, the fear of reprisal by victims for testifying, and the lack of motivation by the public to participate).

[58] *See* Waldorf, *supra* note 56, at 193 (describing false accusations in Gacaca); Sosnov, *supra* note 51, at 136–40 (commenting on problems with truth telling in Gacaca); Carter, *supra* note 6 (noting the partial admissions in Gacaca); Rettig, *supra* note 56, at 39 (noting that confessions in Gacaca are often challenged as inaccurate or incomplete); Lars Waldorf, *Mass Justice for Mass Atrocity: Rethinking Local Justice as Transitional Justice*, 79 Temp. L. Rev. 1, 70–74 (2006) (describing reasons that truth was not forthcoming in Gacaca).

especially defense counsel.[59] Although there has been some debate about whether Gacaca was the best that could be constructed if all *genocidaires* are to be prosecuted, Rwanda is a party to the International Covenant on Civil and Political Rights[60] and the African Charter on Human and Peoples' Rights,[61] both of which guarantee basic due process rights to an accused.[62]

Reconciliation is more elusive to measure. Some believe that Gacaca has worked well to allow reconciliation, at least in the form of reintegrating individuals into communities.[63] Others believe that Gacaca did little to further reconciliation.[64]

Other themes relate to the location of the ICTR and to the lack of reparations for survivors. Although there were security and infrastructure concerns that led to locating the ICTR in Arusha,[65] many experts believe that a better approach, wherever possible, is to situate an international tribunal in the country affected, as was done with the SCSL.[66] The lack of reparations for survivors is the same issue raised with regard to Sierra Leone. In the case of Rwanda, compensation was part of the plan for Gacaca, but because of a lack of funds it has been hard to effectuate the reparations.[67]

Other lessons from Rwanda are positive ones. The attempt to add Gacaca to the ICTR process was a strong statement about the need for accountability. Gacaca was also a process designed by Rwanda for its own situation. Moreover, multiple goals were identified as desired and a process was constructed to try to achieve those goals. The ICTR has prosecuted the highest-level military and political leaders who were responsible for the genocide. This is an achievement that should not be overlooked for either Rwanda or Sierra Leone. The fact that there was accountability for international crimes is a significant message for the people of Rwanda and Sierra Leone as well as for the whole international community. The fact that these goals, or others, were not fully realized is helpful in constructing transitional justice mechanisms for the future.

---

[59] *See, e.g.,* Erin Daly, *Between Punitive and Reconstructive Justice: The Gacaca Courts in Rwanda*, 34 N.Y.U. J. Int'l L. & Pol. 355, 382 (2002); Westberg, *supra* note 41, at 355–56.

[60] International Covenant on Civil and Political Rights art. 14, Dec. 16, 1966, 999 U.N.T.S. 171.

[61] African Charter on Human and Peoples' Rights art. 7, June 27, 1981, 21 I.L.M. 58 (listing the rights of an accused).

[62] As I have suggested elsewhere, Gacaca could have been constructed using a plea bargain model through which the accused waived his or her rights in exchange for the speedier, less punitive Gacaca process. This would have allowed for Gacaca proceedings in accord with international norms. Carter, *supra* note 6.

[63] Drumbl, *supra* note 45, at 53–59; *see also* Westberg, *supra* note 41, at 348–53. *But see* Christina Cacioppo, Report on Education and Reintegration of Former Prisoners in Rwanda: The Attempt of Ingando and Viewing Reconciliation as a Duty Instead of a Choice 5–6 (2005), *available at* http://www.christinacacioppo.com/content/publications/EducationAndReintegrationOfFormerPrisoners.pdf (claiming that the reintegration process has marginalized many participating perpetrators within their communities).

[64] Drumbl, *supra* note 1, at 94–99 (commenting on reasons Gacaca has not achieved fully its restorative and reconciliatory goals); Rettig, *supra* note 56, at 42–44 (commenting on problems with reconciliation).

[65] *International Criminal Tribunal for Rwanda (ICTR)*, Project on Int'l Cts. & Tribunals, http://www.pict-pcti.org/courts/ICTR.html (last visited Aug. 19, 2012).

[66] *See, e.g.,* the statement of the UN Secretary-General in *The Rule of Law and Transitional Justice in Conflict and Post-Conflict Societies: Rep. of the Secretary-General*, U.N. Doc. S/2004/616, para. 44 (Aug. 23, 2004), *available at* http://daccess-ods.un.org/TMP/5551286.93580627.html; Winter, *supra* note 28, at 160.

[67] Sosnov, *supra* note 51, at 152; Waldorf, *supra* note 58, at 56–59; Roht-Arriaza, *supra* note 37, at 673–74 (describing efforts, with limited success, in Rwanda).

III. COMBINATIONS OF PROCESSES: THE BENEFITS AND FACTORS TO CONSIDER

A. *The Benefits of a Combination of Processes*

From the praise for and criticism of the Sierra Leonean and Rwandan experiences, two points regarding a combination of processes are worth noting. First, a combination can be valuable because multiple goals can be pursued and achieved. Instead of choosing justice over reconciliation, or a trial over a historical record (or vice versa), all of these goals conceivably can be accommodated. Other combinations, such as having both international and national judicial proceedings, or prosecutions and healing ceremonies, could similarly advance multiple goals.[68]

Second, but less obviously, using a combination of processes can assist in defining realistic expectations for each process, rather than unrealistic expectations undermining the legitimacy of a process. For example, the international courts have been criticized for trying very few cases, for not providing reparations, and for not yielding a full historical record. Although the points are true and the aspirational language in the documents creating the courts includes these multiple objectives, the criticism does not reflect what we should realistically expect from an international court. International courts, such as the SCSL and the ICTR, are not designed to try a large number of cases. Instead, they were created in order to try those most responsible, those at the highest political and military levels, for the crimes. Moreover, any judicial proceeding is not likely to be the best avenue for creating a full historical record. Trials are always constrained by rules that restrict what evidence is relevant and admissible. Similarly, reparations could be made through a court, but again, that is likely to be only a subsidiary function of a judicial proceeding, which is designed to decide guilt or innocence and to impose a sentence on the guilty. If there is a second process that can be designed to achieve the goals that are not prominent in a judicial proceeding, we are one step closer to having realistic expectations for both processes. A TRC, for instance, will usually be designed to create a historical record of causes of the conflict and the events. National prosecutions could fill the void of too-few cases in the international courts. A reparations system can be designed through either a TRC or an independent body.

Communication is key to the success of any combination. It is important to communicate and explain the purposes of each process, what one can expect from each one, and how other goals can be achieved through other processes or agencies. It is also essential to explain the timing of any process. If concerns are raised about reparations, for example, it is imperative to explain from which entity those will issue and when one can expect them.[69] If multiple proceedings are sequential, then that timing, too, should be explained.

---

[68] As Professor Sarkin has so aptly described it, there is a "complex mosaic" of needs and processes in a post-conflict situation. Sarkin, *supra* note 8, at 138.

[69] It is worth noting that, in the evolution process of international justice, the more recently established International Criminal Court has a better-defined reparations program. Article 75 of the Rome Statute provides that "[t]he Court shall establish principles relating to reparations to, or in respect of, victims, including restitution, compensation and rehabilitation" and that reparations may be ordered directly against the convicted person or from a Trust Fund that was established. As of September 2012, the Trial Chamber in the Lubanga case is in the process of applying the reparations provisions for the first time. *See* Prosecutor v. Lubanga, Case No. ICC-01/04–01/06–2904, Decision Establishing the Principles and Procedures to Be Applied to Reparations (Aug. 7, 2012).

B. Factors to Consider in Deciding on Processes

Given the benefits of a combination of processes, what factors should be considered or questions asked when deciding upon the combination that will best serve a particular post-conflict situation? This subsection explores the sources and inquiries that might assist in the decision-making process.

1. Studies and Guides on Post-Conflict Processes

Post-conflict, or transitional, justice efforts in all parts of the world have been studied by numerous organizations and academic writers. One cannot do justice to all of the sources in this short chapter,[70] but three sources will be highlighted here. The framing of the issues and the studies conducted in these sources are strong foundation and guidance for the factors suggested here.

One highly comprehensive study was organized by Professor Cherif Bassiouni.[71] The study considered 313 conflicts throughout the world from World War II to 2008. The data is analyzed both thematically and by regions of the world. The starting point for this work is the Chicago Principles on Post-Conflict Justice. The principles are used to evaluate the mechanisms used after a conflict. Those principles reflect the goals of prosecution, truth, the needs of and remedies for victims, vetting, memorialization and education, traditional local approaches, and institutional reform.[72] These are essential in any consideration of multiple processes.

In the two-volume work, there is commentary on each principle, elaborating on both purpose and implementation. Among many important points made, the study identifies the desirability of multiple post-conflict processes, the importance of domestic prosecutions, the need to consider funding for the processes, the importance of national consultations on processes, the consideration of the nature of the conflict, and the necessity of reparations.[73] These important points are incorporated into the factors suggested later in this subsection.

---

[70] Among many other very useful commentaries, *see* Winter, *supra* note 28, at 160 (recommending courts be situated in-country; provision of assistance to national judiciaries; outreach to population; establishment of a legacy of jurisprudence; and provision of a basis of remedies to victims).

[71] THE PURSUIT OF INTERNATIONAL CRIMINAL JUSTICE: A WORLD STUDY ON CONFLICTS, VICTIMIZATION, AND POST-CONFLICT JUSTICE (M. Cherif Bassiouni ed., 2010).

[72] *International Guidelines on Post-Conflict Justice: The Chicago Principles, in* THE PURSUIT OF INTERNATIONAL CRIMINAL JUSTICE: A WORLD STUDY ON CONFLICTS, VICTIMIZATION, AND POST-CONFLICT JUSTICE 41 (M. Cherif Bassiouni ed., 2010). The Principles are:

> Principle 1: States shall prosecute alleged perpetrators of gross violations of human rights and humanitarian law.
> Principle 2: States shall respect the right to truth and encourage formal investigations of past violations by truth commissions or other bodies.
> Principle 3: States shall acknowledge the special status of victims, ensure access to justice, and develop remedies and reparations.
> Principle 4: States should implement vetting policies, sanctions, and administrative measures.
> Principle 5: States should support official programs and popular initiatives to memorialize victims, educate society regarding past political violence, and preserve historical memory.
> Principle 6: States should support and respect traditional, indigenous, and religious approaches regarding past violations.
> Principle 7: States shall engage in institutional reform to support the rule of law, restore public trust, promote fundamental rights, and support good governance. *Id.* at 43–44.

[73] *See id.* at 41–65.

Another major source comes from the International Centre for Transitional Justice (ICTJ), which has conducted studies and prepared reports on many different post-conflict situations. Among the many contributions of these materials, there are five themes from the ICTJ work that are particularly helpful in designing factors here.[74] One of the primary themes is what victims have a right to expect. As ICTJ has noted, two of the important normative works promulgated by the United Nations are the Updated Set of Principles to Combat Impunity[75] and the Basic Principles on Reparation.[76] The Principles to Combat Impunity identify three rights of victims: the right to know, which includes a right to truth; a right to justice; and a right to reparation, which includes guarantees of nonrecurrence.

A second theme is how to coordinate processes. In a 2011 briefing, the ICTJ called for a greater integration of transitional justice into the core work of the UN Human Rights Council.[77] A third theme is the impartial examination of issues. This can be especially difficult in post-conflict situations in which one "side" has prevailed. The fourth and fifth themes distilled from ICTJ's work identify a need to consult all stakeholders and the importance of accountability.

Another source of frameworks comes from the United Nations. The Secretary-General of the United Nations submitted reports in 2004 and 2011 to the Security Council on "the rule of law and transitional justice in conflict and post-conflict societies."[78] There are also annual reports to the Security Council on strengthening rule-of-law activities. In addition, the UN Office of the High Commissioner for Human Rights (OHCHR) has promulgated a series of guides called "Rule of Law Tools for Post-Conflict States."[79] These reports and

---

[74] INT'L CTR. FOR TRANSITIONAL JUSTICE, *Transitional Justice in the United Nations Human Rights Council* (2011), *available at* http://ictj.org/sites/default/files/ICTJ-Global-TJ-In-HRC-2011-English.pdf [hereinafter ICTJ 2011 Report].

[75] *Updated Set of Principles for the Protection and Promotion of Human Rights through Action to Combat Impunity*, Econ. & Soc. Council, E/Cn.4/2005/102/Add.1 (Feb. 8, 2005) (by Diane Orentlicher).

[76] G.A. Res. 60/147, U.N. DOC. A/RES/60/147 (Mar. 21, 2006).

[77] ICTJ 2011 Report, *supra* note 74, at 1.

[78] U.N. Secretary-General, *The Rule of Law and Transitional Justice in Conflict and Post-Conflict Societies: Rep. of the Secretary-General*, U.N. DOC. S/2004/616 (Aug. 23, 2004); U.N. Secretary-General, *The Rule of Law and Transitional Justice in Conflict and Post-Conflict Societies: Rep. of the Secretary-General*, U.N. DOC. S/2011/634 (Oct. 12, 2011) [hereinafter 2011 U.N. Secretary-General Report].

[79] There are eight different reports in this series: OFFICE OF THE UNITED NATIONS HIGH COMM'R FOR HUM. RTS., RULE-OF-LAW TOOLS FOR POST-CONFLICT STATES: AMNESTIES (2009), *available at* http://www.ohchr. org/Documents/Publications/Amnesties_en.pdf; OFFICE OF THE UNITED NATIONS HIGH COMM'R FOR HUM. RTS., RULE-OF-LAW TOOLS FOR POST-CONFLICT STATES: NATIONAL CONSULTATIONS ON TRANSITIONAL JUSTICE (2009), *available at* http://www.unrol.org/files/Tool_National_Consultations_final_web.pdf [hereinafter OHCHR TOOLS: NATIONAL CONSULTATIONS]; OFFICE OF THE UNITED NATIONS HIGH COMM'R FOR HUM. RTS., RULE-OF-LAW TOOLS FOR POST-CONFLICT STATES: MAXIMIZING THE LEGACY OF HYBRID COURTS (2008), *available at* http://www.unrol.org/files/HybridCourts.pdf [hereinafter OHCHR TOOLS: LEGACY]; OFFICE OF THE UNITED NATIONS HIGH COMM'R FOR HUM. RTS., RULE-OF-LAW TOOLS FOR POST-CONFLICT STATES: REPARATIONS PROGRAMMES (2008), *available at* http://www.unrol.org/files/ReparationsProgrammes[1].pdf [hereinafter OHCHR TOOLS: REPARATIONS]; OFFICE OF THE UNITED NATIONS HIGH COMM'R FOR HUM. RTS., RULE-OF-LAW TOOLS FOR POST-CONFLICT STATES: MONITORING LEGAL SYSTEMS (2006), *available at* http://www.unrol.org/files/RoL%20Tools%20for%20Post%20Conflict%20States_Monitoring%20Legal%20 Systems.pdf; OFFICE OF THE UNITED NATIONS HIGH COMM'R FOR HUM. RTS., RULE-OF-LAW TOOLS FOR POST-CONFLICT STATES: TRUTH COMMISSIONS (2006), *available at* http://www.ohchr.org/Documents/ Publications/RuleoflawTruthCommissionsen.pdf; OFFICE OF THE UNITED NATIONS HIGH COMM'R FOR HUM. RTS., RULE-OF-LAW TOOLS FOR POST-CONFLICT STATES: MAPPING THE JUSTICE SECTOR (2006),

guides provide a significant body of materials on establishing and maintaining transitional justice mechanisms. The 2011 report of the Secretary-General, for example, emphasizes the need for a coordinated and comprehensive effort to create and maintain a rule of law, with input from all stakeholders through national consultations. The report recognizes that there are multiple possible mechanisms:

> Transitional justice initiatives may encompass both judicial and non-judicial mechanisms, including individual prosecutions, reparations, truth-seeking, institutional reform, vetting and dismissals.[80]

Among the many important points in the report, a special note is made that there needs to be follow-up after a truth commission to be sure that the recommendations are implemented.[81] Reparations are recognized as an important part of the process of reconciliation and maintaining peace.[82] There is also recognition of the importance of assisting and developing the capacity of national judicial institutions.[83] A special emphasis is placed on seeking justice for women.[84]

The OHCHR Rule of Law series covers many topics, all of which are pertinent here.[85] The report on "National consultations on transitional justice" in particular is helpful in considering how to make decisions about processes. Two of the major reasons for national consultations on post-conflict processes are based on highly important considerations. One is to involve all stakeholders in voicing their views and feeling invested in whatever processes are created. The second is to allow for tailoring of the processes to the needs and concerns of those most affected by the conflict.[86] The guide further elaborates on the key stakeholders, such as victims, including women and children; witnesses; those outside the country; civil society groups; traditional and religious leaders; political representatives; former combatants; and many other segments of a national society ranging from the business community to academics.[87] Among the other reports, the one on reparations[88] lays out steps for a successful program, and the one on legacy of hybrid courts[89] has a thorough discussion of how to assist in building national capacity.

2. Preliminary Efforts toward a Framework of Factors

From the sources described above, it is clear that there will be multiple goals in a post-conflict situation, a need to take into account the views of all stakeholders, and some method

---

available at http://www.unrol.org/files/RoL%20Tools%20for%20Post%20Conflict%20States_Mapping%20 the%20Justice%20Sector.pdf; Office of the United Nations High Comm'r for Hum. Rts., Rule-of-Law Tools for Post-Conflict States: Vetting: An Operational Framework (2006), *available at* http:// www.ohchr.org/Documents/Publications/RuleoflawVettingen.pdf.

[80] 2011 U.N. Secretary-General Report, *supra* note 78, at para. 17.

[81] *Id.* at para. 24.

[82] *Id.* at para. 26; *see* G.A. Res. 60/147, U.N. Doc. A/RES/60/147 (Mar. 21, 2006).

[83] 2011 U.N. Secretary-General Report, *supra* note 78, at paras. 32–40.

[84] *Id.* at paras. 41–46.

[85] The subjects covered include issues related to amnesty, reparations programs, truth commissions, and the monitoring of domestic legal systems in post-conflict states, among other topics. See *supra* note 79 for a list of all the reports in this series and the topics they cover.

[86] OHCHR Tools: National Consultations, *supra* note 79, at 2.

[87] *Id.* at 20–23.

[88] OHCHR Tools: Reparations, *supra* note 79.

[89] OHCHR Tools: Legacy, *supra* note 79.

for tailoring the responses to a specific culture and society. In an effort to draw together this body of resources, and to create a framework of factors to consider in making decisions on combinations of post-conflict processes, in this subsection I propose that ten factors be evaluated in any design for post-conflict processes.

They are:

1. *Purpose:* What purpose(s) is (are) to be achieved? Justice? Reconciliation? Historical record? Reparations? Reintegration of perpetrators? Rebuilding the national judiciary? What are the expectations of the affected population? What are the expectations of the national government and the international community?

2. *Proceeding:* What type of proceeding is best designed for the purpose(s) and for the particular culture and society? Judicial, truth commission, other? If a judicial proceeding is chosen, how will decisions be made on who will be prosecuted? Should only those considered the most responsible be prosecuted? What about those bearing lesser responsibility? Who will be responsible for prosecuting them? Is there a way for those decisions to be reviewed, and if so, how? If a truth commission is chosen, will it include recommendations and, if so, how will the implementation be monitored? If reparations are part of the design, how will they be administered – through a court? A truth commission? An independent body such as a reparations commission?

3. *National infrastructure:* What is the capacity of the national judiciary? Would it be able to handle cases of international crimes? How will the fairness of the trials or other proceeding be ensured? Will there be equality of arms for the defense? Is there a local, nonjudicial dispute resolution process? Is it widely accepted, or only accepted by part of the population? Depending on the answer, what are the implications for the success of the process, in terms of its legitimacy and its consistency with the rule of law?

4. *Level and location:* What should be the level and location of the process? Local? National? Sub-regional? Regional? International? Foreign national court? Or should there be a combination of these?

5. *Political and security situation:* Will the current government(s) be supportive or tolerant of prosecutions, including of their own members? If they are not, what will be the impact on the various objectives? Is there a peace process ongoing? If so, what is the relationship between the judicial and nonjudicial proceedings and the peace process? What are the security concerns in situating judicial or nonjudicial processes in-country? Are neighboring countries involved in the conflict? If so, are they included in the decisions on setting up the processes? Will any such involvement potentially affect the mechanisms chosen, and if so, do those reflect the interests of those states or the country affected by the conflict?

6. *Coordination and timing:* Should multiple processes (e.g., judicial proceedings and a truth commission) occur simultaneously? Sequentially? What issues could be resolved in advance to promote coordination of multiple proceedings? What kind of information sharing will occur between proceedings?

7. *Communication:* How will information about the processes be disseminated in the country? How can misunderstandings be avoided? How will information be disseminated to the international community, especially to neighboring countries?

8. *Funding:* How will the processes be funded? Will competition between types of processes be avoided in the funding mechanisms?

9. *Interactions with other international and national entities:* What are the possible relationships between the processes set up and the International Criminal Court? Will conflicts in jurisdiction or goals arise (e.g., if amnesty is offered on a national level, is there a possibility of a prosecution in the ICC)? Can the international processes assist in national capacity building?

10. *Decision process:* Who will make the decisions on which procedures to use? How will the views of women and children be considered? The views of minority or marginalized groups?

Purpose. Each of the factors, in turn, requires its own more nuanced analysis, often in combination with other factors. The starting point, however, is the first factor that asks what purposes are the goals. This decision will be important to the decisions on the rest of the factors. It will also help frame the expectations for any particular process. For example, if retributive justice is a goal, then most likely a judicial process will be necessary. This question, however, is important for distilling multiple purposes that inevitably should exist in a post-conflict situation. Identification of the purposes makes it more feasible to design appropriate proceedings and to avoid some of the unrealistic expectations that have tended to be raised in current post-conflict situations. It is clear that each situation may call for prioritizing different purposes.

For instance, Sierra Leone opted for both a retributive justice goal with the Special Court and a historical record and reconciliation goal with the TRC. In the case of Rwanda, the ICTR was designed for retributive justice as the dominant goal. The Gacaca proceedings also had a justice goal with punishment as a result. However, the Gacaca proceedings combined a goal of reconciliation into the same process. From the experiences of Sierra Leone and Rwanda, it would appear that the goal of reparations should have been better identified at the outset in order to provide for an adequate process and funding. It is important to think through all the purposes before proceeding further with setting up any mechanisms.

Proceedings. The nature of the proceedings is intertwined with the purposes. For example, one might conclude that both justice, in the sense of retributive punishment, and reconciliation are desirable purposes. Although one could then conclude that a court and a truth commission are the best proceedings, one might also consider that judicial trials bring some level of reconciliation, and that truth commissions may bring some level of accountability. A further evaluation is needed to determine whether, in a given situation, two proceedings are needed, or whether one proceeding may be sufficient to achieve both purposes.[90]

Similarly, if a historical record is a dominant goal, then a process other than a judicial trial is probably going to allow for a more complete examination of what occurred as evidence in trials will necessarily be limited by relevancy to the actual charges. However, there may be problems in creating a historical record through a truth commission if amnesty is not offered, or perpetrators feel disinclined to participate. The experiences in Sierra Leone

---

[90] Also of interest on this point, Professor Sarkin suggests that the International Criminal Court should be more involved in aspects of transitional justice. Sarkin, *supra* note 8, at 131.

and Rwanda demonstrate the problems that may arise in obtaining truthful accounts. One might conclude that the more limited historical record created through a judicial trial is preferable and will be more likely to be perceived as impartial.[91] In each instance, the circumstances of the specific situation, the culture and society involved, and the resources available will be important in making these decisions as to the particular case.

National infrastructure. The existing national infrastructure, both judicial and nonjudicial, is important to several decisions. Again, taking into account the purposes, the state of the national infrastructure needs to be assessed to determine how much can be handled nationally. For example, in Sierra Leone and Rwanda, it would have been difficult for the national judiciary to handle the cases involving the atrocities and levels of responsibility of the perpetrators immediately after the conflicts. Often a country will not have laws that cover international crimes, and judicial institutions will need time to rebuild. In most post-conflict situations, there is also a concern with at least the appearance of impartiality. In order to avoid allegations of victor's justice, it may be better not to have the national judiciary handle the most serious cases.

On the other hand, if a strong goal is to rebuild the national judiciary, then it may be worthwhile to work within the national setting instead of an international one, or to combine those efforts. The mixed court in Sierra Leone stands as one way in which to help rebuild the national judiciary while still having international expertise infused into the process.[92] Another important issue is whether there are alternatives to a traditional judicial process. Rwanda's adoption of the Gacaca trials is an example of an attempt to use a modified form of a national infrastructure within the country to adjudicate cases. Similarly, local dispute resolution processes, such as a healing ceremony[93] or mediation, can be essential to a number of purposes, especially reconciliation, but also a form of accountability.

Level and location; Political and security situation. The next two factors, level and location, and political and security situation, are related to each other, and to purposes and national infrastructure. The level and location of any tribunals may depend, in part, on whether they are judicial proceedings, truth commissions, or mediation processes. Judicial proceedings are the most likely to involve an option of location within or outside a particular country. The reasons for the location, in turn, are multifaceted, involving issues of the character of the judicial proceeding (e.g., international or combination of international and national judges), security issues, and available infrastructure.

---

[91] *See* Charles Michael Dennis Byron, *The International Criminal Tribunal for Rwanda, in* THE PURSUIT OF INTERNATIONAL CRIMINAL JUSTICE: A WORLD STUDY ON CONFLICTS, VICTIMIZATION, AND POST-CONFLICT JUSTICE 146, 147–48 (M. Cherif Bassiouni ed., 2010) (commenting on the significant role of the ICTR in documenting the historical record).

[92] Assisting the development of national capacity has also been a focus of the ICTR's efforts. *See id.* at 148 (noting the important priority of capacity building of the Rwandan national judiciary); Hassan Jallow, *The International Criminal Tribunal for Rwanda, in* THE PURSUIT OF INTERNATIONAL CRIMINAL JUSTICE: A WORLD STUDY ON CONFLICTS, VICTIMIZATION, AND POST-CONFLICT JUSTICE 149, 151, 154 (M. Cherif Bassiouni ed., 2010) (commenting on the importance of national prosecutions).

[93] For example, the work of Fambul Tok International in Sierra Leone facilitates "family talk" bonfire ceremonies in villages; such ceremonies are designed to foster community-based reconciliation and assist in the development of sustainable community activities. *See* MOORE, *supra* note 9, at 270 (describing the goals of Fambul Tok as social and historical justice); *see generally* FAMBUL TOK INT'L, FAMBUL TOK (2011).

For example, the ICTR was located in Arusha, in part out of concerns for security and infrastructure issues in the immediate aftermath of the genocide in Rwanda. The decision to have an international court, whether in-country or elsewhere, is likely to be determined by the goal of prosecuting high-level perpetrators, the question whether a national judiciary can handle such cases, and the question whether the trials would have security issues.

Issues may also arise related to the current government's political positions on the trials. In Sierra Leone, the Special Court was able to prosecute individuals on multiple sides of the conflict, including those associated with the current government.[94] The ICTR, on the other hand, encountered resistance to the prosecution of military personnel related to the current government.[95] The receptivity of a post-conflict government to accountability for all crimes, whoever committed them, may affect both the level and the location of a court. Even without concerns about the political and security situation, the level and location of a court are important considerations.

There are many advantages to locating a court within the affected country. Communication about and access to the court for the people within the country is far easier. In his interesting comparison of Sierra Leone and Rwanda on "restoration of the security, legal systems and administrative structures," Mba Chidi Nmaju concludes that there were clear advantages in Sierra Leone from locating the SCSL in Freetown compared with locating the ICTR in Arusha.[96] He does not find fault with the ICTR's location, given the circumstances post-genocide,[97] but his documentation of the feasibility of communication and training in Sierra Leone is strong support for situating post-conflict processes in-country if possible.[98] Sierra Leone is also an example where the location and composition of the Court within the country should make it easier to build the capacity of the national judiciary. Moreover, the physical facilities will remain as part of Sierra Leone's infrastructure after the Court closes. A TRC is likely to be more easily placed within a country than is a court structure. It is crucial to take into account the purposes that are desired. If prosecution is the goal, then the level and location of the court may be highly dependent upon the state of the national

---

[94] There is some criticism of the decision to prosecute the government-supported forces, the CDF. *See* Lansana Gberie's chapter in this volume. However, the fact that it was possible to prosecute any side of the conflict remains an important point. Note, though, that even prosecuting all sides may have fairness, political, and stability implications. In Sierra Leone, the prosecution particularly of Hinga Norman has been criticized. There is also criticism of under-inclusion and over-inclusion in prosecutorial decisions. *See* Jalloh, *supra* note 9, at 420–25.

[95] *See, e.g.*, Sigall Horovitz, *The Impact of the International Criminal Tribunal for Rwanda and the Special Court for Sierra Leone on Impunity in Rwanda and Sierra Leone*, *in* Africa and the Future of International Justice 15, 21–22 (Vincent O. Nmehielle ed., 2012) (describing the investigation of four RPF officers at the ICTR, the decision not to indict them at the ICTR, and their subsequent trial in Rwanda).

[96] Mba Chidi Nmaju, *The Role of Judicial Institutions in the Restoration of Post-Conflict Societies: The Cases of Rwanda and Sierra Leone*, 16 J. Conflict & Security L. 357, 384 (2011).

[97] *Id.* at 383.

[98] *See* Tim Gallimore, Int'l Criminal Tribunal for Rwanda, The ICTR Outreach Program: Integrating Justice and Reconciliation (2006), *available at* http://www.unictr.org/Portals/0/English/News/events/Nov2006/gallimore.pdf (detailing the efforts of the ICTR Outreach Program in Rwanda); *Legacy*, Special Ct. for Sierra Leone, http://www.sc-sl.org/LEGACY/tabid/224/Default.aspx (last visited Aug. 20, 2012) (detailing the various legacy and outreach projects of the SCSL, such as a peace museum, a national witness protection program, and a professional development program); Horovitz, *supra* note 95, at 45–49 (explaining the current activities of the SCSL's legacy projects); OHCHR Tools: Legacy, *supra* note 79 (setting forth ways in which hybrid courts can have a lasting effect on national infrastructure).

infrastructure. If a goal is to localize the process as much as possible, such as with Gacaca, then it is essential to locate the processes in communities.

Coordination and timing; Communication. The coordination and timing of multiple types of proceedings is an area that needs more attention. For example, with Sierra Leone, the issue that arose with regard to detainees of the Court testifying before the truth commission might have been avoided if the truth commission had come after the judicial trials.[99] On the other hand, the judicial trials may take years, and it may not be advisable to wait before commencing a truth commission. The point is that the advantages and disadvantages of the timing should be taken into account. The experience of Sierra Leone with parallel judicial and TRC proceedings also has brought attention to the need to decide on an information-sharing policy in advance of operations. Whether processes are sequential or concurrent, coordination of efforts, including communication are important to consider. Coordination also includes efforts to ensure support for each process so that backing of one mechanism, financial or otherwise, does not undermine the efforts of another process.[100]

In Sierra Leone, there was confusion about the role of the Special Court and the role of the TRC. In hindsight, there may have been ways in which to coordinate communication efforts that would have better explained what each process was intended to do, who would be subject to each process, and what to expect as results from each. In Rwanda, Gacaca was very apparent to the population because the proceedings were occurring in every com-munity. The ICTR, however, was not as well understood, at least at the outset.[101] As the ICTR stepped up its outreach programs, greater information was disseminated throughout Rwanda. The lesson, however, is to contemplate how best to coordinate multiple processes and to communicate the necessary information about each process.[102] These are especially important issues when multiple processes are occurring simultaneously.

Funding. Funding of the processes is a crucial question to ask when setting up post-conflict mechanisms. The experience of Sierra Leone has taught us that a court's work is hindered if that court has to seek its own funding, compared with the ICTR that received funding from the United Nations.[103] Moreover, Sierra Leone has taught us that multiple processes should not have to compete for funding.[104] Although the competition was not intended, this issue arose because the TRC had to seek funding, just like the Court did. The

---

[99] *See Norman, supra* note 24.

[100] In Sierra Leone, for example, there appears to have been greater support within the international community for the tribunal than for the truth commission. *See* Jalloh, *supra* note 9, at 436.

[101] Drumbl, *supra* note 45, at 47 (noting that, as of 2005, many Rwandans were unaware of the ICTR's work, viewing it as a foreign tribunal; but as more Rwandans learn of the ICTR's work, the more inclined they are to view it favorably); *see also* GALLIMORE, *supra* note 98 (explaining the increased outreach efforts on the part of the ICTR to educate the Rwandan population of its work, including increased use of media, such as domestic radio broadcasts of hearings, and informational seminars).

[102] Communication and education go hand in hand. One issue that is often raised, both by affected populations and by commentators, is the expensive nature of international criminal justice. Although the debate over choices will still remain, communication and education about the goals and choices made (and how those choices were made) could assist in better understanding and acceptance of the processes.

[103] *See* Kendall, *supra* note 29 (criticizing the SCSL's voluntary funding mechanism's detrimental effect on the Court's political and institutional structure).

[104] *See* William A. Schabas, *The Relationship between Truth Commissions and International Courts: The Case of Sierra Leone*, 25 HUM. RTS. Q. 1035, 1040 (2003) (stating that both the SCSL and the TRC were funded by con-tributions from international donors and the SCSL's budget had been reduced by almost half over the course of three years); Schabas, *supra* note 18, at 191 (stating that the TRC "suffered terribly from poor funding").

purposes of post-conflict processes are undermined if there is a constant concern about the adequacy of the funding.

Interactions with other international and national entities. Another potential conflict and benefit that should be considered at the outset is interactions with other international and national entities. In the cases of the ICTR and SCSL, the courts did not have conflicts with other international entities because both are international courts. However, issues in the future may arise based on the relationship of national proceedings and the ICC. For instance, if amnesty is granted on a local level, as it was in Sierra Leone in an effort to achieve peace, how would that affect prosecutions in the ICC? What if the ICC does not recognize the amnesty as legitimate under international law?[105] Would a prosecution in the ICC undermine the national efforts? Would the national amnesty undermine the international justice of the ICC? This could impact a process such as a TRC and how it is constructed. Although the TRC in Sierra Leone did not have authority to grant amnesty, if such authority exists in another TRC in a future location, the issue may arise. The interaction of international and national entities is also a potential benefit that should be factored into the decisions. If, for example, capacity building in the judicial system, human rights bodies, or other parts of the national system are goals, then coordination of those efforts should be considered at the outset.

Decision process. The final factor proposed is the decision process. Who should make all of these decisions on each factor? Should it be the international community, through the Security Council or another entity? Should it be the national government? Should it be the local populations? If it is desirable to include all of these constituencies in the process of deciding on proceedings, how should that be coordinated, and who should do it?[106] Yet another issue regarding this factor is what to do if there are disagreements about what to do. For instance, what should happen if some want a truth commission or healing process while others want judicial trials? In the OHCHR publication on national consultations, they suggest that an independent expert should be used to do the consultations, but in conjunction with national initiatives.[107] Thus, the OHCHR is not suggesting that independent experts be in the position of dictating any particular process; rather, experts are providing an impartial survey based on the needs of the particular national situation. There still remains an issue of who makes the final determinations. Perhaps another form of assistance from an impartial expert or entity would be to set up in advance a process by which decisions will be made if there is a conflict. In that way, if for instance, the national government wants trials and the local population wants a traditional healing ceremony, there would be a procedure that could be followed to determine the best solution or combinations. This type of procedure would allow more voices to be considered, not only in the consultation, but in the decision

[105] *See* Prosecutor v. Kallon & Kamara, Case No. SCSL-2004-15-AR72(E), Decision on Challenge to Jurisdiction: Lome Accord Amnesty (Mar. 13, 2004), http://www.sc-sl.org/LinkClick.aspx?fileticket=Ft%2FRoiLzl3U%3D &tabid=197; *see* discussion of the issues in Leila Nadya Sadat, *Exile, Amnesty, and International Law,* 81 NOTRE DAME L. REV. 955 (2006).

[106] *See* Harvey M. Weinstein et al., *Stay the Hand of Justice, in* LOCALIZING TRANSITIONAL JUSTICE: INTERVENTIONS AND PRIORITIES AFTER MASS VIOLENCE 27, 47 (Rosalind Shaw et al. eds., 2010) (discussing the need to carefully evaluate the priorities of people in each situation).

[107] OHCHR TOOLS: NATIONAL CONSULTATIONS, *supra* note 79, at 18–19.

process. As the OHCHR guide indicates, one of the goals of the consultation process is to get "a strong sense of local ownership" and to "promote stakeholder participation."[108]

One key aspect that underlies an analysis of these factors is a realistic assessment of what purposes can be achieved by any one type of proceeding. There especially needs to be a more accurate understanding that international criminal courts are not designed to try large numbers of cases. From the experiences of Sierra Leone and Rwanda, it is clear that expectations and the reality of the courts and other tribunals were not always synchronized. For instance, the expectations for the SCSL and the ICTR included justice, reconciliation, and peace.[109] It is highly unlikely that all of these expectations can be met by any one proceeding. There needs to be a realignment of what can be achieved through a judicial proceeding and, consequently, when it should be invoked, and how we define success. Similarly, there needs to be a realistic statement of what can be achieved through a truth commission or any other process. There is also a further need to manage expectations by articulating only realistic goals.

The need to coordinate multiple types of proceedings is also essential to best achieve objectives in post-conflict justice. In the future, planning should include coordination and harmonization of multiple approaches. In this way, achieving multiple goals can be maximized to the benefit of the people affected by the conflict and the international community.

IV. CONCLUSION

The framework of factors identified in this chapter is intended as a starting point for further discussion. The experiences of Sierra Leone and Rwanda in pioneering combinations of post-conflict processes are highly instructive for the future. Significant documentation and commentary exists on the perceived strengths and weaknesses of the courts, the TRC, and Gacaca. The rich body of literature on other post-conflict processes and on general guidelines is also highly valuable insight and information. However the broad factors are ultimately framed, it is clear that considerable flexibility is needed. It is important to consider the views of all stakeholders, to take into account the particular culture and society, and to develop post-conflict processes that are designed to meet the specific needs of each situation.

---

[108] *Id.* at V.

[109] For a thoughtful commentary on the mixed result for the Special Court in achieving justice, peace, and reconciliation, *see* Jalloh, *supra* note 9. Other goals for international criminal courts have included an even longer list: ending impunity, accountability, justice for victims, deterrence or prevention of future crimes, creation of a historical record, reconciliation, restoration of society, development of the law, and consistency of jurisprudence. *See, e.g.,* discussions in Gregory McClelland, *A Non-Adversary Approach to International Criminal Tribunals,* 26 SUFFOLK TRANSNAT'L L. REV. 1, 21–29; Mirjan Damaška, *The Competing Visions of Fairness: The Basic Choice for International Criminal Tribunals,* 36 N.C. J. INT'L LAW AND COM. REG. 365, 376–78 (2011).

36

Assessing the Special Court's Contribution to Achieving Transitional Justice

Theresa M. Clark[*]

Post-settlement societies,[1] such as Sierra Leone, face magnanimous tasks in a context of severe economic, political, and social detriment. One pressing issue facing these societies concerns how to address the violations of human rights and international criminal law to achieve transitional justice.[2] Sierra Leone uniquely employed several mechanisms for transitional justice simultaneously: an amnesty, a hybrid international criminal tribunal, a truth and reconciliation commission, and a reparations fund. Historically, transitional justice practitioners and scholars understood and evaluated these mechanisms as conflicting alternatives. However, they are increasingly taking a more comprehensive approach to transitional justice issues, recognizing the mechanisms as functioning more in complement than in competition.[3]

Drawing on this emerging trend, this chapter seeks to place the Special Court's work into the broader narratives of peace- and democracy-building and transitional justice as a goal of those processes. It does not focus on the Court's contributions to international criminal law or international criminal process, as other chapters in this volume address those issues in detail. Rather, this chapter investigates the contribution made by the Special Court to achieving transitional justice by first, establishing a clear conceptualization of transitional justice, and second, analyzing the Special Court's contribution to achieving that goal. The methodology employed is interdisciplinary, holistic, and purposive, and relies on the

---

[*] Associate Professor, Villanova Law School, USA.

[1] The term "post-settlement" is adopted to indicate societies that have achieved negative peace (a cessation of hostilities), and that are working to prevent a relapse into war and to construct a self-sustaining peace. Traditionally, the term "post-conflict" is used. However, in the interest of clarity and consistency, the more accurate term of "post-settlement societies" is adopted. For a detailed discussion on the entrenched misnomer, see L. REYCHLER & T. PAFFENHOLZ, PEACE-BUILDING: A FIELD GUIDE 188–89 (2001).

[2] S. Parmentier, *Global Justice in the Aftermath of Mass Violence. The Role of the International Criminal Court in Dealing with Political Crimes*, 41, 1–2 INT'L ANNALS OF CRIMINOLOGY, INT'L SOCIETY FOR CRIMINOLOGY 203, 204–05 (2003).

[3] This trend is emerging in transitional justice scholarship. *See* M. MINOW, BETWEEN VENGEANCE AND FORGIVENESS – FACING HISTORY AFTER GENOCIDE AND MASS VIOLENCE (1998); POST-CONFLICT JUSTICE (M.C. Bassiouni ed., 2002); R. TEITEL, TRANSITIONAL JUSTICE (2000); Parmentier, *supra* note 2. It is also emerging in transitional justice practice. *See* S. Katzenstein, *Hybrid Tribunals: Searching for Justice in East Timor*, 16 HARV. HUM. RTS. J. 245 (2003); W. Schabas, *The Relationship between Truth Commissions and International Courts: The Case of Sierra Leone*, 25 HUM. RTS. Q. 1035 (2003); C. Sriram, *Globalising Justice: From Universal Jurisdiction to Mixed Tribunals*, 22 NETHERLANDS Q. HUM. RTS. 7 (2004). For an excellent articulation of the need for a comprehensive and holistic approach to transitional justice, see N. Kritz, *Progress and Humility: The Ongoing Search for Post-Conflict Justice*, in Bassiouni, *supra*, 55, at 55–60.

current legal scholarship in the area of transitional justice augmented by philosophical, political science, and sociological erudition.

I. DEFINING TRANSITIONAL JUSTICE: A COMPREHENSIVE AND PURPOSE-DRIVEN APPROACH

A. *The Context: Transitional Justice in the Landscape of Peace-, Democracy- and Justice-Building Efforts in Post-Settlement Societies*

Although considered one of the worst civil conflicts in recent history, the war, destruction, and violence suffered in Sierra Leone are not unique. The sixty-seven years following World War II witnessed unrivalled conflict, mostly of a non-international character, and mass atrocities by repressive regimes resulting in over 170 million civilian deaths.[4] Societies transitioning from such atrocities ultimately seek to achieve sustainable peace[5] and to move toward a consolidated democracy.[6] The United Nations, in its work on peacebuilding, and scholars have identified the framework for post-settlement peacebuilding as the attempt to address three interlinked deficit areas in post-settlement societies: political/constitutional incapacity, economic/social debilitation, and psycho/social trauma.[7]

Justice is a necessary element to decreasing the deficits existing in each of these areas.[8] Justice in the post-settlement context, as defined by Rama Mani,[9] has three interrelated and interdependent dimensions: legal justice, which refers to the national rule of law and mechanisms of legal redress in a society; distributive justice, which refers to the structural and systemic injustices such as political and economic discrimination and inequality; and

---

[4] Richard Goldstone, *Fifty-Years after Nuremberg: A New International Criminal Tribunal for Human Rights Criminals*, *in* CONTEMPORARY GENOCIDES: CAUSES, CASES, CONSEQUENCES 215 (A. Jongman ed., 1996). In 2002, it was estimated that in that time more than 250 conflicts had occurred, resulting in an estimated 86 million casualties. M.C. Bassiouni, *Accountability for Violations of International Humanitarian Law and Other Serious Violations of Human Rights*, *in* Bassiouni, *supra* note 3, at 6 and sources cited therein.

[5] According to peace and conflict resolution scholarship, the following characteristics are required to achieve sustainable peace: (1) the absence of physical violence; (2) the elimination of unacceptable political, economic, and cultural forms of discrimination; (3) self-sustainability; (4) a high level of internal and external legitimacy or approval; and (5) a propensity to enhance the constructive transformation of conflict. L. REYCHLER, DEMOCRATIC PEACE-BUILDING AND CONFLICT PREVENTION: THE DEVIL IS IN THE TRANSITION 23 (1999). Post-settlement peacebuilding efforts seek to achieve sustainable peace. These efforts must incorporate both the negative tasks of preventing a relapse into overt violence and the positive tasks of aiding national recovery and expediting the eventual removal of the underlying causes of internal war. *See* REYCHLER & PAFFENHOLZ, *supra* note 1, at 187–88; R. MANI, BEYOND RETRIBUTION: SEEKING JUSTICE IN THE SHADOWS OF WAR 12–17 (2002).

[6] The term "consolidated democracy" indicates the final stage in the development of democracies and requires five basic conditions: (1) a free and lively civil society; (2) an autonomous political society; (3) effective rule of law, including application to political actors; (4) a functioning state bureaucracy usable by the new democratic government; and (5) an institutionalized economic society. For an in-depth discussion of these conditions, see J. Linz & A. Stepan, *Toward Consolidated Democracies*, 7(2) J. DEMOCRACY 14 (1996).

[7] REYCHLER & PAFFENHOLZ, *supra* note 1, at 191.

[8] MANI, *supra* note 5, at 17.

[9] Contemporary philosophers have not paid significant or comprehensive attention to conceptualizing justice in the post-settlement context. Thus, it remains largely undefined, and efforts to restore justice in these societies are not grounded in the necessary comprehensive understanding of the goal. MANI, *supra* note 5, at 4–5. Because of this gap in erudition, the author relies heavily on Mani's three-dimensional conception of justice.

transitional justice,[10] which refers to the question of dealing with injustice in terms of the gross violations of human rights, international criminal law, and international humanitarian law suffered by the people during the conflict.[11] All three dimensions of justice correlate to the deficits identified above.[12] For example, rebuilding legal justice or the rule of law is an essential component of political/constitutional reconstruction; distributive justice, or rather injustice, is the raison d'être of the socioeconomic programs implemented; and transitional justice is a crucial component to psycho/social rehabilitation.[13] As such, seeking to achieve or restore justice is necessarily linked with and contributes to achieving the goals of sustainable peace and consolidating democracy.[14]

Issues of transitional justice receive significant and often exclusive attention from both practitioners and academics in virtually every discipline. Achieving transitional justice is a crucial and urgent task. However, it is neither the only task, nor is it the most important. Developing a sustainable peace, transitioning to a consolidated democracy, and achieving justice in these post-settlement societies require that the new governments, the international community, and civil society acknowledge and tackle these goals with a comprehensive conceptualization at the fore. Attempt these tasks without a clear conceptualization, one that incorporates a holistic view of the requirements necessary to achieve these goals from all dimensions, and none of them will be obtained to the optimal extent. The goals and requirements for achieving sustainable peace, consolidated democracy, and transitional justice are interrelated, interdependent, and sometimes overlapping or even potentially conflicting. The international community has been particularly guilty of acting without understanding or accounting for the immense complexity of the situations faced by what are often low-income, war-torn nations in their attempts to transition to peace and democracy.[15] However, in order to achieve lasting, sustainable results, all aspects of each goal must be acknowledged, addressed, and strived for in a synchronized manner.

This chapter focuses on one very narrow, but important, aspect of achieving or restoring justice following mass atrocities, transitional justice, and within that context, specifically, the Special Court for Sierra Leone's contribution to achieving transitional justice. However, it is essential to remain cognizant of the other equally important dimensions to the goal of achieving or restoring justice in this context, as well as its implications for sustaining peace and consolidating democracy.

---

[10] The term "transitional justice" is adopted here to indicate the issues Mani discusses under the reparative justice dimension to avoid undue attention on the reparations aspect of transitional justice. MANI, *supra* note 5, at 5. Reparations are just one of the four building blocks necessary for achieving transitional justice. *See infra* notes 50–61 and accompanying text.

[11] MANI, *supra* note 5, at 4–5.

[12] *Id.* at 17.

[13] *Id.*

[14] *Id.*

[15] *See* MANI, *supra* note 5, at 16. This critique is not intended to negate or to discredit the hard work and significant efforts made both at a national and international level in the efforts to achieve peace, justice, and respect for human rights, and to build democracies. The concepts and practice of peace- and democracy-building have developed rapidly in the last twenty years, and a range of actors, from UN agencies and departments to innumerable regional, bilateral and nongovernmental organizations, have undertaken its various tasks. These criticisms merely indicate the inevitable difficulties of translating into practice evolving and ambitious concepts. However, this does not change the reality that to date these efforts have fallen short largely because of short-cited and disconnected approaches to all three endeavors.

B. A Comprehensive Definition of Transitional Justice

The concept of transitional justice, although frequently invoked, is seldom defined.[16] Before investigating the effect of a mechanism employed to achieve it, it is necessary to precisely define the concept and its functions. The necessity of a clear conceptual basis manifests in both the practical and academic arenas. First, prospectively, if the governments and the international community working to achieve transitional justice possess a clear understanding of what it is they are seeking to achieve, then they will be better equipped to evaluate the costs and benefits of the array of transitional mechanisms available. Second, retrospectively, a clear conceptual basis of transitional justice is necessary for academics analyzing and evaluating the choices made and effectiveness of the collection of transitional justice mechanisms.

If we draw on the emerging comprehensive approach to transitional justice issues,[17] transitional justice is defined from a comprehensive, purpose-driven, and relationship-driven perspective. It is comprehensive because it accounts for the effect and influence of diverse disciplines and disciplinary subspecialties, contexts, goals, and mechanisms contributing to the field of transitional justice.[18] It is purpose-driven in its conceptual approaches, defining transitional justice in terms of its goals.[19] Finally, it is relationship-driven, because it focuses on the potential for interrelated, interdependent, and complementary relationships between the key objectives and mechanisms, rather than understanding them as competitive alternatives.

Utilizing Parmentier's TARR heuristic model[20] (Figure 36.1), the concept of transitional justice adopted here has both contextual and substantive limits. First, transitional justice is contextually limited to situations where societies are transitioning from periods marked by gross violations of international human rights, international humanitarian law, and international criminal law.[21] Second, in these societies, all the dimensions of justice are seriously debilitated or have essentially broken down and must be restored or achieved.[22] In substance, transitional justice is understood as a purposive concept, consisting of four essential goals: truth, accountability, reparation, and reconciliation.[23] There are copious lists enumerating the basic functions of transitional justice. However, ultimately each of those functions can be distilled down to these four goals, their interaction and combination, and how this combination contributes to the post-settlement society's transition to peace and democracy. Further, transitional justice is conceived as a continuum, rather than a binary concept.[24] Thus, transitional justice in post-settlement societies is the final result of the interaction

---

[16] TEITEL, *supra* note 3, at 3.

[17] *See supra* note 5 and accompanying text.

[18] *Id.* TEITEL, *supra* note 3.

[19] Parmentier, *supra* note 2, at 204–08; Miriam J. Aukerman, *Extraordinary Evil, Ordinary Crime: A Framework for Understanding Transitional Justice*, 15 HARV. HUM. RTS. J. 39, 91–95 (2002).

[20] *See* Parmentier, *supra* note 2, at 204–09.

[21] Parmentier, *supra* note 2; MANI, *supra* note 5, at 4–11.

[22] MANI, *supra* note 5, at 4–5.

[23] Parmentier, *supra* note 2, at 208 (identifying truth, accountability, reparations, and reconciliation as the key issues of transitional justice).

[24] *Id.*

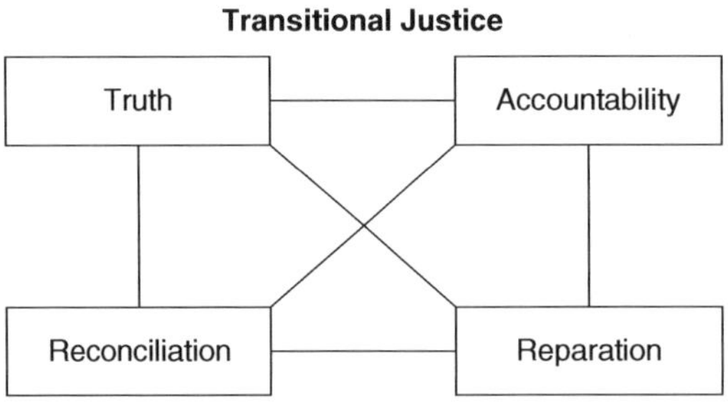

Transitional Justice

FIGURE 36.1 TARR model of key issues in the search for transitional justice.[25]

between these four goals.[26] Because of the unique contextual circumstances faced by every post-settlement society, and because of the differences in every society, community, and individuals' culture and self-identity, post-settlement societies will ascribe varying values to these four objectives of transitional justice. This means that a given post-settlement society will achieve more or less justice, as opposed to justice or no justice, depending on the interaction between these four goals and the effectiveness of the mechanisms employed to achieve them.[27]

In sum, transitional justice is an element of the justice needed and sought after by societies emerging from a period marked by large-scale violations of international human rights, international humanitarian law, and international criminal law, in order to help that society transition to a sustainable peace. Specifically, transitional justice seeks to ascertain the truth at all levels of society about the violations committed during the period in question; to hold the perpetrators of these crimes accountable for the atrocities; to reconcile individuals, communities, and societies after the commission of these large-scale atrocities; and to provide reparations for the atrocities committed at the individual, community, and societal level.

C. Defining the Four Goals of Transitional Justice

1. Truth

Truth as a goal of transitional justice is both an ultimate objective and a process that encompasses identifying and distilling the facts surrounding the mass atrocities committed. It entails establishing an accurate and comprehensive account of the atrocities committed in a given post-settlement society, their causes, and the context in which they occurred, as well as arriving at a consensus and memorializing controversial and complex events. Its forms include: (1) factual or forensic truth; (2) personal or narrative truth; and (3) social or dialogue truth.[28] Factual or forensic truth includes the evidence

---

[25] *Id.* at 204–09.
[26] *Id.*
[27] *Id.*
[28] Truth and Reconciliation Commission of South Africa, 1 Truth and Reconciliation Commission of South Africa Report 110 (1998), *available at* http://www.justice.gov.za/trc/report/index.htm (last visited May 3, 2012) [hereinafter TRC Report]. *See also* D. Crocker, *Truth Commissions, Transitional Justice, and Civil Society, in* Truth v. Justice: The Morality of Truth Commissions 100, 100–01 (R. Rotberg & D. Thompson eds., 2000). The South African Truth and Reconciliation Commission's Report included a fourth

obtained and corroborated through reliable procedures.[29] This truth affects all levels of society. On the communal and national level, this truth relates to compiling the evidence and data to determine the context, the causes, and the patterns of violations.[30] On an individual level this truth establishes who the victims were, what happened to them, when it happened, and who participated.[31] Personal truth is truth through the eyes and narrative of the individuals who lived through the atrocities.[32] This truth accounts for the fact that there is never just one truth.[33] Every person has his or her own distinct memories, and they may contradict another's.[34] The third dimension of truth, the social or dialogue truth, is the "truth of experience that is established through interaction, discussion and debate."[35]

Establishing the truth in post-settlement societies is vital to transitional justice. However, it is important to reiterate that the value and priority given to truth may vary from society to society. Truth in and of itself is important on an individual level, for the victims and their survivors, and on a societal level.[36] Some scholars and human rights activists refer to this as the right to truth.[37] Additionally, at the societal, communal, and individual level constructing a collective memory is important in and of itself.

2. Accountability

Accountability as a goal of transitional justice encompasses the idea of holding responsible those who have committed gross violations of human rights, international humanitarian law, and international criminal law. Accountability is taking action to right the wrongs committed by affirming that it violated agreed standards of national and international law, and as such, is wrong and warrants response and condemnation.[38] However, accountability can come in several different forms, may apply to different types of offenders, and potentially serves a variety of important functions. The forms of accountability include: legal accountability via criminal prosecutions or civil law suits; administrative accountability via lustrations; political accountability via economic or diplomatic sanctions; and social accountability through some form of public reprimand, stigmatization, or shaming.[39] Further, post-settlement societies may seek to hold many different types of offenders accountable, ranging from those who orchestrated the atrocities to those who executed

---

dimension of truth: healing or restorative truth. TRC REPORT, *supra*, at 114–15. This dimension is not included here because it fits more accurately as a form of reparation, such as public acknowledgment and condemnation of the events, or as a contribution to achieving reconciliation. *See infra* notes 50–66 and accompanying text.

[29] *Id.*

[30] TRC REPORT, *supra* note 28, at 111.

[31] *Id.*

[32] TRC REPORT, *supra* note 28, at 112–13.

[33] PRICILLA B. HAYNER, UNSPEAKABLE TRUTHS: CONFRONTING STATE TERROR AND ATROCITY 163 (2001).

[34] *Id.*

[35] TRC REPORT, *supra* note 28, at 113.

[36] Jane E. Stromseth, *Introduction: Goals and Challenges in the Pursuit of Accountability, in* ACCOUNTABILITY FOR ATROCITIES: NATIONAL AND INTERNATIONAL RESPONSES 1, 8 (J. Stromseth ed., 2003).

[37] *See Independent Study on Best Practices, Including Recommendations, to Assist States in Strengthening Their Domestic Capacity to Combat All Aspects of Impunity,* U.N. DOC. E/CN.4/2004/88, Feb. 27, 2004, at 6–10.

[38] Stromseth, *supra* note 36, at 7.

[39] N. Kritz, *The Dilemmas of Transitional Justice, in* I TRANSITIONAL JUSTICE xix, at xix–xxx (Neil J. Kritz ed., 1995).

the orders to those who carried out the orders and even possibly bystanders who benefited from the actions or failed to intervene.[40]

Providing accountability in post-settlement societies is vital to transitional justice. First, accountability in the context of transitional justice seeks to achieve the societal goals of prevention and deterrence.[41] It also contributes to breaking the cycle of violence for two reasons: first, to some extent it satisfies victims' desires for justice, which decreases the risk of vigilante violence; and second, it individualizes guilt, which can contribute to reconciling deep ethnic divides.[42] Further, from a cathartic perspective, public accountability aids in the healing process of victims and society.[43] Additionally, from a moral perspective, accountability may contribute to reestablishing the moral order of the society.[44] Moreover, legal accountability seeks to reaffirm the rule of law and human rights.[45] This is important because failure to hold perpetrators accountable vitiates the authority of the rule of law and depletes its power to deter proscribed conduct.[46] Further, from a political perspective, legal accountability advances the nation's transition to sustainable peace and consolidated democracy, because it fosters a respect for democratic institutions deepening the democratic culture, and it affirms the supremacy of publicly accountable civilian institutions over military might.[47] Finally, the specific aims of criminal accountability also include punishment, rehabilitation, and incapacitation.[48] It is important to note that many legal scholars consider criminal accountability to be, not only advantageous, but to be required by law – at least with respect to the core international crimes of genocide, crimes against humanity, and war crimes.[49]

3. Reparations

Reparations as a goal of transitional justice is a broad term that encompasses a wide range of measures taken to redress past wrongs – that is, to repair the victims of the atrocities.[50] In this context, it encompasses the term not only from the strictly legal perspective of compensation for injuries or wrongs,[51] but also the psychosocial perspective of contributing to the cathartic process.[52] Further, in the post-settlement context reparations encompass efforts to compensate and repair the injuries and wrongs at both the individual level and the societal level. As such, there are two general forms of reparations, *material reparations*, which

---

[40] Parmentier, *supra* note 2, at 206.

[41] Bassiouni, *supra* note 4, at 9.

[42] L. Huyse, Justice, in Reconciliation after Violent Conflict: A Handbook 97, 97–98 (D. Bloomfield, T. Barnes & L. Huyse eds., 2003).

[43] TRC Report, *supra* note 28, at 114.

[44] Parmentier, *supra* note 2, at 206.

[45] *Id.*

[46] D. Orentlicher, *Settling Accounts: The Duty to Prosecute Human Rights Violations of a Prior Regime*, 100 Yale L.J. 2537, 2542–44 (1991).

[47] *Id.*

[48] Bassiouni, *supra* note 4, at 9.

[49] *Id.* at 10–26.

[50] Hayner, *supra* note 33, at 170–71; Mani, *supra* note 5, at 173–74; Minow, *supra* note 3, at 91–117. *See also* Black's Law Dictionary 1301 (B. Garner ed., 7th ed. 1999).

[51] Garner, *supra* note 50.

[52] For a detailed discussion about the two disciplines' perspectives on reparation and the merging and inclusion of the concepts in post-settlement societies' attempts to achieve transitional justice *see* Mani, *supra* note 5, at 173–74.

include restitution of goods, financial compensation, and declaratory judgments; and *social reparations*, which include rehabilitation through social and medical measures, symbolic measures, education, and guarantees of non-repetition of the alleged acts.[53] Restitution seeks to reestablish the situation that existed before to the extent it is possible and includes the return of property; the restoration of liberty, citizenship, and other legal rights; and the return to place of residence or the restoration of employment.[54] Financial compensation is provided to recognize the wrong and to recompense the losses suffered.[55] It encompasses nominal damages, pecuniary damages, moral damages, and punitive damages.[56] Symbolic measures may include commemorations, symbolic redress, acknowledgment and condemnation of the violations, and apologies.[57] Guarantees of non-repetition relate to measures taken to prevent the recurrence of these violations in the future, such as reform of norms and institutions relating to the independence of the judiciary, and civilian control of the military and security forces.[58] As such, reparations may be individual and collective, financial and nonfinancial, commemorative and reformative.[59]

Reparations are important on an individual and societal level because they reaffirm the individual worth and equality of each victim. Further, at the societal level, they contribute to the creation of a culture of respect for human rights because they acknowledge the harm done, that it was wrong, and seek to repair that harm. Finally, it is important to note that some forms of reparation stem from a legal right to reparations either under national or international law.[60] Additionally, some scholars argue that a corresponding duty exists for the offending state to provide reparations.[61]

4. Reconciliation

Reconciliation as a goal of transitional justice is the development of peaceful coexistence, trust, understanding, and empathy between former enemies.[62] Thus, reconciliation is both a process and a goal, which can occur at many levels: (1) the individual level; (2) the interpersonal level between specific victims and perpetrators; (3) the community level addressing the conflicts within local communities and between them; and (4) the national level between the state institutions as well as with non-state institutions.[63] At each level, reconciliation requires acknowledgement of the harm committed, acknowledgment of responsibility on the part of the wrongdoer,[64] apology for the harm committed,[65] and a letting

---

[53] Hayner, *supra* note 33, at 170–71.

[54] *Id.*

[55] *Id.*

[56] S. Vandeginste, *Reparation*, *in* Bloomfield, *supra* note 42, at 145.

[57] Hayner, *supra* note 33, at 170–71.

[58] *Id.*

[59] Vandeginste, *supra* note 56, at 146–47.

[60] Bassiouni, *supra* note 4, at 37–39.

[61] *Id.*

[62] Parmentier, *supra* note 2, at 207.

[63] TRC Report, *supra* note 28, at 107.

[64] Partially Dissenting Opinion of Honorable Justice Renate Winter, Fofana and Kondewa ("CDF Appeal") (SCSL-04-14-A), Appeals Chamber, May 28, 2008, § 93 [hereinafter Winter Dissent].

[65] J. Quinn, *Introduction*, *in* Reconciliation(s): Transitional Justice in Postconflict Societies 3, at 5 (J. Quinn ed., 2009).

go of and moving forward from the harm committed.[66] However, it is essential to remain cognizant of the approach to transitional justice outlined. Reconciliation is a goal achieved on a continuum. It is not binary. Thus, for example, it is possible to achieve some degree of reconciliation without fully moving past the harm committed or forgiving the wrongdoer. Reconciliation is important for post-settlement societies because positive working relationships must exist at all levels of society to achieve justice, sustainable peace, and consolidated democracies.

D. *Mechanisms for Achieving Transitional Justice*

Within the quest for transitional justice, a plethora of mechanisms exist that seek to achieve it, each possessing its own unique goals and characteristics.[67] These transitional justice mechanisms include: amnesties, criminal prosecution, commissions of inquiry, reparations programmes, and noncriminal sanctions. Traditionally, practitioners and scholars evaluate these mechanisms in isolation from one another.[68] Additionally, often this spectrum was and continues to be considered a hierarchy ranging from the most effective and desirable response to the least effective and desirable response. Moreover, each mechanism was designed to focus particularly on one goal of transitional justice at the expense of achieving the other necessary goals – for example, criminal prosecutions focus primarily on accountability and deterrence, and commissions of inquiry focus primarily on truth telling. However, as noted, a trend is emerging that recognizes not only the goals of transitional justice, but also the mechanisms employed to achieve it, as functioning more in complement than in competition.

This trend evidenced in Sierra Leone's efforts to achieve transitional justice. The decisions regarding which transitional justice mechanisms to adopt were integral to Sierra Leone's efforts to achieve sustainable peace and consolidated democracy. Struggling with these difficult decisions while in the throes of violent conflict, the government of Sierra Leone, with the aid of the international community, uniquely combined the historically alternative mechanisms of amnesty, truth and reconciliation commission, criminal prosecution, and reparations program.[69] Assessing in detail whether this combination on the whole increased the degree of transitional justice achieved in Sierra Leone is beyond the scope of this chapter. However, it is worth noting that each mechanism was uniquely positioned to contribute more to one of the four goals of transitional justice, for example the Truth and Reconciliation Commission likely contributed more to the goal of truth than the Special Court because of its mode of operation, structure, and character. As such, it is likely that the combination overall enhanced the degree to which each goal was achieved.

---

[66] This requirement is understood by some as forgiveness or an aspect of forgiveness. The inclusion of forgiveness is controversial because of its religious underpinnings and multiple definitions. B. Hamber & G. Kelly, *Beyond Coexistence: Towards a Working Definition of Reconciliation, in* Quinn, *supra* note 65, at 286, 287–90. However, the understanding that reconciliation requires the ability to accept and move beyond the harm committed is not controversial. It is understood by most commentators as necessary. *Id.*

[67] Minow, *supra* note 3.

[68] Parmentier, *supra* note 2, at 207.

[69] A. Tejan-Cole, *Note from the Field: The Complementary and Conflicting Relationship between the Special Court for Sierra Leone and the Truth and Reconciliation Commission,* 6 Yale Hum. Rts. & Dev. L.J. 139, 141 (2003).

II. ASSESSING THE SPECIAL COURT'S CONTRIBUTION TO TRANSITIONAL JUSTICE

A. *The Assessment Framework*

A clear assessment framework is required to determine the SCSL's contribution to achieving transition justice in Sierra Leone. The degree of transitional justice achieved varies in relation to the degree that each goal of transitional justice is achieved in a given post-settlement society. Further, each transitional justice mechanism's contribution to each goal varies. Thus, to determine the degree of transitional justice achieved, one must evaluate the contributions made to each goal by the mechanism. This section relies on three factors to determine the Court's contribution to the four goals of transitional justice: the Court's mode of operation and structure; the Court's jurisdiction; and the Court's judgments. The following subparts assess each factor's contribution to the different forms of each goal and the credibility of the contributions made to each goal.

B. *Assessing the Special Court's Contribution to the Truth*

Establishing the truth about the mass atrocities in Sierra Leone was not an express goal of the Court.[70] The main objective of the Court was to criminally prosecute persons who bore the greatest responsibility for the atrocities committed during the civil war.[71] Specifically, according to Security Council Resolution 1315, the Court was to provide a "credible system of justice and accountability" in order to end impunity, and contribute to "national reconciliation and to the restoration and maintenance of peace."[72] Further, the Special Court was expected to reaffirm international humanitarian law and to contribute to strengthening the national judicial system of Sierra Leone.[73] Thus, truth, as a necessary component of justice, was an underlying goal of the Court.[74] To assess the Court's contribution to establishing the truth, this section examines the extent that each factor contributes to the different types of truth and the credibility of the truth.

1. Mode of Operation and Structure

The Special Court's mode of operation and structure on the whole contributed to credibly establishing the three forms of truth. The Court's mode of operation contributed significantly to the forensic truth established. Factual or forensic truth includes the evidence obtained and corroborated through reliable procedures.[75] The Court's Statute and Rules of

---

[70] Agreement between the United Nations and the Government of Sierra Leone on the Establishment of a Special Court for Sierra Leone, art. 1(1), Jan. 16, 2002, 21 U.N.T.S. 137 [hereinafter SCSL Agreement].

[71] *Id.*

[72] S.C. Res. 1315 (2000), preamble, §§ 5–6; Report of the Secretary-General on the establishment of a Special Court for Sierra Leone, U.N. Doc. S/2000/915, Oct. 4, 2000, § 23 [hereinafter S-G Report].

[73] *Id.*

[74] Debate exists among scholars and practitioners about the role of courts with respect to establishing the truth. *Compare* A. Cassese, *Reflections on International Criminal Justice*, 61 Mod. L. Rev. (1998), *with* J. Alvarez, *Rush to Closure: Lessons of the* Tadic *Judgment*, 96 Mich. L. Rev. 2031, 2085–87 (1998).

[75] TRC Report, *supra* note 28.

Procedure and Evidence (RPE) provided the necessary reliable procedures for the Court to credibly determine this individual and communal forensic truth.[76]

The broad investigatory powers granted by the Court's RPE to the Office of the Prosecutor (OTP) contributed to the Court's establishment of the forensic truth at the individual and communal levels. Specifically, the OTP possessed the power to gather any information it considered relevant, from any source, including national and international individuals, governments, and organizations, by any means deemed appropriate, and the Court possessed the power to compel its production when necessary via orders, summonses, subpoenas, warrants, and transfer orders.[77]

However, the nature of the adversarial process also limited the Court's contribution to forensic truth at both levels. First, the Court's Statute necessarily protected the rights of the Accused, which limited the Court's contribution to the truth.[78] The Court ultimately did not render a judgment in three cases because of the death of the Accused while in custody, citing the rights of the Accused and a cessation of personal jurisdiction.[79] Moreover, the defense attorneys' duties included asserting legal arguments designed to challenge and exclude information that was relevant to establishing a comprehensive understanding of the atrocities.[80]

Second, the adversarial process limited the extent that the Court contributed to establishing narrative and social truth. The adversarial system in a criminal trial is not designed for establishing narrative truth. Rather, it is designed to determine guilt or innocence of a particular accused person who is alleged to have committed crimes. Thus, the Special Court was not a forum for witnesses, and in particular victims, to explain the truth about the atrocities as seen through their eyes. These witnesses were subject to direct examination and cross-examination, which is not conducive to establishing this form of truth. Further, the adversarial process is not particularly well suited for establishing social or dialogue truth. Following a period marked by gross violations, there is often denial and controversy surrounding the events. Arriving at a collective social consensus about what actually occurred is a vital aspect of truth as a goal of transitional justice. Although it may act as a catalyst for the development of this form of truth, the adversarial process is not an adequate forum for the dialogue necessary to achieve this type of truth.

Moreover, the Court's structure indirectly detracted from its ability to contribute to the establishment of forensic truth at the individual and communal levels. The Court's insecure and inadequate funding is partially responsible for the OTP's decision to indict only

---

[76] SCSL RPE.

[77] *Id.* at Rules 39–40, 54.

[78] SCSL Statute art. 17.

[79] Decision on Registrar's Submission of Evidence of Death of Accused Samuel Hinga Norman and Consequential Issues, Norman, Fofana, and Kondewa (SCSL-04–14-T-776), Trial Chamber I, May 21, 2007, § 12; Withdrawal of Indictment, Sankoh (SCSL-2003–02-PT-054), Trial Chamber, Dec. 8, 2003; Withdrawal of Indictment, Bockarie (SCSL-03–04-I-022), Trial Chamber, Dec. 8, 2003.

[80] For example in the CDF case, the Norman defense succeeded in excluding the exploration of the incident referred to as "Operation Black December." Decision on Joint Motion of the First and Second Accused to Clarify the Decision on Motions for Judgment of Acquittal Pursuant to Rule 98, Norman, Fofana, and Kondewa ("CDF") (SCSL-04–14-T-550), Trial Chamber I, Feb. 3, 2006.

thirteen individuals.[81] As a result, the Court's contribution to establishing the truth was limited.

The Court's mode of operation lent credibility to the information asserted as truth, which is essential for any institution seeking to contribute to truth as a goal of transitional justice. The Court's Statute and RPE comported with the internationally recognized standards of due process. Thus, the RPE functioned to ensure accuracy of information and to protect the rights of the Accused.[82] Particularly, the Court's ability to administer oaths, to compel testimony, to protect witnesses, and to punish individuals providing false testimony or engaging in witness tampering afforded credibility to the facts established.[83] Accordingly, the evidence presented to the Court possessed a high degree of credibility.

The structure and character of the Special Court also increased credibility. First, the Court was a "treaty-based *sui generis* court of mixed jurisdiction and composition."[84] Thus, the role of the United Nations and the Court's international components lent it the credibility of the United Nations and the international community and reduced the risk of coercion or intimidation by the Sierra Leonean government or others.[85] Further, transparency was a necessary component of the Court's work. It submitted annual reports both to the UN Secretary-General and to the government of Sierra Leone summarizing its operation and activities.[86] However, the Court's reliance on voluntary funding led to questions about the Court's independence and impartiality by some defendants.[87] Second, the Court was an entirely separate institution from the Sierra Leonean judicial system, and exercised primacy over it.[88] This distance, separation, and power over the national court system enhanced the Court's credibility, and as such, any facts it established, because the national judiciary was severely crippled by the war and the people lacked confidence and trust in the rule of law because of its abuse by the NPRC and AFRC.[89]

---

[81] C. Jalloh, *Special Court for Sierra Leone: Achieving Justice?*, 32 Mich. J. Int'l L. 395, 421–22, 428–29 (2011).

[82] Aukerman, *supra* note 19, at 74.

[83] Rules 75, 77, 90, 91 SCSL RPE; *cf.* N. Combs, Fact-Finding without Facts: The Uncertain Evidentiary Foundations of International Criminal Convictions (2010) (questioning the credibility of witness testimony in the international criminal context).

[84] S-G Report, *supra* note 72, § 9.

[85] A. Haines, *Accountability in Sierra Leone: The Role of the Special Court, in* Stromseth, *supra* note 36, at 210.

[86] SCSL Statute art. 25.

[87] Decision on the Urgent and Public with Annexes A-C Defense Motion to Re-open Its Case in Order to Seek Admission of Documents Relating to the Relationship between the United States Government and the Prosecution of Charles Taylor, Taylor (SCSL-03–01-T-1171), Trial Chamber II, Jan. 27, 2011 (granting defense motion to reopen to introduce evidence alleged to indicate a lack of judicial and prosecutorial independence and impartiality); Decision on the Urgent and Public with Annexes A-N Defense Motion for Disclosure and/or Investigation of United States Government Sources within the Trial Chamber, the Prosecution, and the Registry Based on Leaked USG Cables, Taylor (SCSL-03–1-T-1174), Trial Chamber II, Jan. 27, 2011 (dismissing the motion for failure to establish prima facie evidence of interference with the independence or impartiality of the court); Decision on Sesay Motion Seeking Disclosure of the Relationship between Governmental Agencies of the United States of America and the Office of the Prosecutor, Sesay, Kallon, and Gbao (SCSL-04–15-T-363), Trial Chamber I, May 2, 2005.

[88] SCSL Statute art. 8.

[89] For a detailed analysis of the state of the national judiciary in Sierra Leone at the end of the conflict, see N. Thompson, *In Pursuit of Justice: A Report on the Judiciary of Sierra Leone*, Commonwealth Human Rights Commission (2002), *available at* http://www.humanrightsinitiative.org/publications/ffm/sierra_leone_report.pdf (last visited May 11, 2012).

Third, the Court's composition lent credibility to the truth established. The Court was composed of international and national judges: two international judges and one Sierra Leonean judge presided over the Trial Chamber; and three international judges and two Sierra Leonean judges presided over the Appellate Chamber.[90] The Court rendered its decisions by majority, requiring the agreement of one international judge, furthering the credibility of the Court as an independent and impartial body.[91] However, it is important to note that the dissents of two Sierra Leonean justices in the CDF trial and appellate judgments detracted from the local perceptions of fairness and the court's credibility, and raised questions of bias.[92]

Fourth, the Court's location and connection to civil society augmented credibility. With the exception of the Taylor trial, the Special Court sat in the capital of Sierra Leone, Freetown.[93] Moreover, the Court created the Outreach and Public Affairs Office (OPA)[94] to specifically target the general population and specific groups "to foster two-way communication between Sierra Leoneans and the Special Court."[95] This combination increased the connection of the Sierra Leonean people to the process and results.[96] However, the effectiveness of the OPA has drawn criticism,[97] particularly with respect to the Taylor trial.[98] Creating this sense of ownership was vital to the credibility of the truth the Court established.

2. Jurisdiction

Despite its narrow mandate, the Court's jurisdiction overall enhanced the Special Court's contribution to the types of truth and the credibility of truth. The Court's personal jurisdiction narrowly, but significantly, permitted the Court to contribute to the forensic and social truth about the atrocities committed at the individual and communal levels. The Special Court's personal jurisdiction required the Court to focus on those "who [bore] the greatest responsibility" for the crimes covered by the Court's statute.[99] Thus, the OTP focused on trying the individual high-level directors, planners, and implementers of the atrocities, as Stephen Rapp and Charles Jalloh discussed in the respective contributions to this

---

[90] SCSL Statute art. 12.

[91] *Id.* at art. 18.

[92] T. Cruvellier, *From the Taylor Trial to a Lasting Legacy: Putting the Special Court Model to the Test*, International Center for Transitional Justice and Sierra Leone Court Monitoring Programme, 25–27, Jan. 1, 2009, *available at* http://ictj.org/publication/taylor-trial-lasting-legacy-putting-special-court-model-test (last visited May 3, 2012).

[93] SCSL Agreement, *supra* note 70, at art. 10.

[94] The Court merged the Press Office and Public Affairs and Outreach Offices in 2008. See announcement, *available at* http://www.sc-sl.org/ABOUT/CourtOrganization/TheRegistry/OutreachandPublicAffairs/tabid/83/ Default.aspx (last visited Apr. 5, 2012).

[95] A summary of the role of the Office of Outreach and Public Affairs is available at http://www.sc-sl.org/ ABOUT/CourtOrganization/TheRegistry/OutreachandPublicAffairs/tabid/83/Default.aspx (last visited Apr. 5, 2012).

[96] J. Easterday, *The Trial of Charles Taylor Part I: Prosecuting "Persons Who Bear the Greatest Responsibility,"* UC Berkley War Crimes Studies Center, June 2010, *available at* http://socrates.berkeley.edu/~warcrime/ SL-Reports/Prosecuting_persons_who_bear_the_greatest_responsibility.pdf, at 10–13.

[97] See S. Ford's chapter in this volume.

[98] A. Sesay, *Reaching Out: The Successes and Failures of the Special Court for Sierra Leone*, Open Space on International Criminal Justice, at 68–69, *available at* http://www.osisa.org/sites/default/files/reaching_out-alpha_sesay.pdf (last visited May 3, 2012).

[99] SCSL Statute art. 1(1).

volume. The OTP indicted only thirteen individuals, and only nine were convicted.[100] This high-level focus broadened the horizon of the Court's investigation and countered to some extent the limitations imposed by the necessary focus on individual perpetrators' crimes. However, the failure of the OTP to even indict some known leaders, such as John Kargbo, Rashid Mansaray, Patrick Lamin,[101] Hassan K. Conteh, James Max-Kanga,[102] and Solomon A. J. Musa[103] limited its contributions to establishing the truth.

Additionally, the OTP's narrow interpretation of this jurisdictional mandate limited the scope of individuals indicted, and thus, the Court's contribution to establishing the truth. The OTP focused on individuals holding formal leadership positions. However, there were several individuals who arguably bore the "greatest responsibility" because of their excessive brutality.[104] Those individuals were not indicted.

Finally, juveniles under the age of fifteen were outside the Court's competence, which limited its contribution to forensic and social truth,[105] and although permitted by the Court's Statute,[106] the OTP did not indict any individuals who were between the ages of fifteen and eighteen at the time of the commission of the alleged crime.[107] As a result, overall the Court's personal jurisdiction contributed in a very limited, but important way to its ability to establish forensic truth at the individual and communal levels.

Similarly, the Court's subject-matter jurisdiction also narrowly, but significantly, permitted the Court to contribute to the forensic and social truth established at the individual and communal levels with respect to the specific international crimes within its jurisdiction: crimes against humanity, violations of common Article 3 of the Geneva Conventions and Article 4 of Additional Protocol II, and other serious violations of international humanitarian law.[108] The Statute also included offenses under Sierra Leonean law relating to the abuse

---

[100] Judgment, Taylor (SCSL-03-1-T) Trial Chamber II, May 18, 2012, § 6994; Judgment, Sesay, Kallon, Gbao ("RUF") (SCSL-04-15-A), Appeals Chamber, Oct. 26, 2009, at 477–81 [hereinafter RUF Appeal]; Judgment, Sesay, Kallon, Gbao ("RUF") (SCSL-04-15-T), Trial Chamber I, Mar. 2, 2009, at 677–87 [hereinafter RUF Trial]; Judgment, Fofana and Kondewa ("CDF") (SCSL-04-14-A), Appeals Chamber, May 28, 2008, at 189–94 [hereinafter CDF Appeal]; Judgment, Brima, Kamara, and Kanu ("AFRC") (SCSL-04-16-A), Appeals Chamber, Feb. 20, 2008, at 105–106 [hereinafter AFRC Appeal]; Judgment, Fofana and Kondewa ("CDF") (SCSL-04-14-T) Trial Chamber I, Aug. 2, 2007, at 290–92 [hereinafter CDF Trial]; Judgment, Brima, Kamara, and Kanu ("AFRC") (SCSL-04-16-T) Trial Chamber II, June 20, 2007, §§ 2112–2123 [hereinafter AFRC Trial].

[101] Sierra Leone Truth and Reconciliation Commission, 2 Witness to Truth: Report of the Sierra Leone Truth and Reconciliation Commission, at 48 (2004) [hereinafter SL TRC Report].

[102] *Id.* at 54.

[103] *Id.* at 63.

[104] Human Rights Watch, *Bringing Justice: The Special Court for Sierra Leone: Accomplishments, Shortcomings, and Needed Support*, at 5, Sept. 8, 2004, *available at* http://www.unhcr.org/refworld/docid/45d45b862.html (last visited May 3, 2012).

[105] Over 5,000 children under the age of 18 participated in the war, and were recruited by all sides to the conflict. Over half of those killed during the conflict were children. As a result of the widespread use of child soldiers, children committed many of the atrocities. Haines, *supra* note 85, at 222. *See also* M. DRUMBL, REIMAGINING CHILD SOLDIERS IN INTERNATIONAL LAW AND POLICY (2012).

[106] SCSL Statute art. 7.

[107] Prosecution's Second Amended Indictment, Taylor (SCSL-03–01-PT) May 29, 2007; Corrected Amended Consolidated Indictment, Sesay, Kallon, Gbao ("RUF") (SCSL-2004–15-PT) Aug. 2, 2006; Further Amended Consolidated Indictment, Brima, Kamara, and Kanu ("AFRC") (SCSL-2004–16-PT) Feb. 18, 2005; Indictment, Norman, Fofana, and Kondewa ("CDF") (SCSL-03–14-I) Feb. 5, 2004.

[108] SCSL Statute arts. 2–4. Ultimately, nine defendants were convicted of crimes in violation of Articles 2, 3, and 4. *See supra* note 100.

of girls under the Prevention of Cruelty to Children Act (1926) and offenses relating to the wanton destruction of property under the Malicious Damage Act (1861).[109] This subject-matter jurisdiction permitted the Court to contribute significantly to the forensic and social truth uncovered. However, the OTP investigated the facts and circumstances surrounding the commission of these crimes only to the extent that the individual perpetrators indicted played a role, necessarily limiting the number of violations investigated and the extent of the contributions made to elucidating even forensic truth.

The Court's temporal and territorial jurisdiction significantly limited its contribution to establishing both forensic and social truth. The jurisdiction encompassed crimes committed from November 30, 1996 onward only in the territory of Sierra Leone.[110] The conflict began in March 1991.[111] The Sierra Leone Truth and Reconciliation Commission estimates that the RUF, SLA, and CDF combined committed 14,625 violations of human rights from 1991 to 1995.[112] The NPRC military junta controlled Sierra Leone from 1992 to 1996, but the NPRC leaders, and the atrocities they orchestrated, fell outside the Court's competence.[113] This necessarily limited the Court's contribution to forensic and social truth surrounding the conflict. Finally, the Court's territorial jurisdiction limited its contribution to establishing the truth as well. The Court's jurisdiction extended only to those crimes committed in the territory of Sierra Leone. Because of the regional dimension to the war, crimes committed outside the territory of Sierra Leone in connection to the civil war were not investigated. In particular, the crimes committed against the Sierra Leonean refugees in Guinea did not fall within the Court's competence.[114] Additionally, crimes committed in Liberia fell outside the Court's jurisdiction.[115]

The Court's jurisdictional limits also detracted from the credibility of the truth established. The limited number of perpetrators and instances of abuse investigated negatively impacted its credibility. However, the Court's strong commitment to engaging civil society and society's awareness about the reasoned and required limits counteracted this concern to some extent.

3. Judgments

The Court's judgments on the whole increased the degree of truth provided in Sierra Leone by credibly establishing limited forensic and social truth. Criminal prosecutions seek to determine the real facts surrounding a given case in order to assess an individual's guilt or innocence in the context of reliable procedures.[116] Thus, on an individual level with

---

[109] SCSL Statute art. 5.

[110] SCSL Statute art. 1(1).

[111] Tejan-Cole, *supra* note 69, at 141–44.

[112] SL TRC Report, *supra* note 101, at 39.

[113] *Id.* at 56. During the NPRC's rule, government soldiers terrorized villages, participated in deliberate amputations, tortured suspects, committed extrajudicial killings, and were responsible for disappearances. *See* United States Department of State, *Sierra Leone Country Report on Human Rights Practices for 1996*, 1997, *available at* http://www.state.gov/www/global/human_rights/1996_hrp_report/sierrale.html (last visited May 3, 2012).

[114] Enormous numbers of refugees fled to Guinea during the war. Haines, *supra* note 85, at 220–21. Guinean President Conte accused the refugees of harboring rebels, and mob violence by civilian militias, police, and soldiers against the refugees ensued, including beatings, rapes, looting, and arbitrary arrests. *Id.*

[115] SL TRC Report, *supra* note 101, at 85.

[116] *See* S. Uglow, Criminal Justice 1 (1st ed. 1995).

respect to the roles played in committing, planning, and participating in the crimes, the Court contributed significantly to credibly establishing the forensic truth surrounding the crimes committed by the nine convicted individuals.[117] The Special Court's trials culminated in a determination of the guilt or innocence of the Accused and written judgments by the Court. These judgments were rendered by a majority of the judges, requiring at least one international judge to concur, and provided the court's supporting rationale. Thus, they serve as written proclamations of the truth with respect to each perpetrator's guilt and his role in the atrocities. The judgments are considered conclusive pronouncements of the facts, circumstances, and guilt. This public and official sanctioning of the truth acts as a credible confirmation to dissuade any doubt and end any controversy surrounding the particular incidents under review; thus, they establish beyond a reasonable doubt the forensic truth.

At the communal level, the Court's judgments significantly enhanced the forensic and social truth provided because the judgments contributed to the development of a coherent, contextual account of the war's context, causes, and patterns of violence.[118] Each written judgment contains a section devoted to outlining in detail the context of the war and the commission of the crimes at issue in that case.[119] Additionally, the judgments, the records of the proceedings, and the evidence gathered created a documentary archive, which helped establish both forensic and social truth.

However, there were limits to the forensic and social truth provided. For example, in the AFRC case, the Appeals Chamber refused to adjudicate the OTP's ground for appeal with respect to the commission of crimes in the Port Loko District.[120] The Court reasoned that the defendants were sentenced to forty-five and fifty years imprisonment for the commission of other crimes committed in Bombali and the Western area, and as such, further adjudication on the minute details raised by the OTP's appeal would be a pointless academic exercise.[121] This decision necessarily limited the Court's contribution to establishing the truth.

Finally, the judgments did not contribute to establishing the narrative truth. First, the judgments do not articulate what happened through the eyes of the victims and perpetrators, and do not invite social dialogue to establish the truth. Second, the Court's decision to limit defendants' participation in the work of the Truth and Reconciliation Commission restricted that institution's ability to establish both narrative and social truth.[122]

---

[117] *See supra* note 100.

[118] *Id.*

[119] RUF Trial, *supra* note 100, §§ 7–46; CDF Trial, *supra* note 100, §§ 50–86; AFRC Trial, *supra* note 100, §§ 55–209.

[120] AFRC Appeal, *supra* note 100, §§ 168–169.

[121] *Id.*

[122] Decision on Appeal by the Truth and Reconciliation Commission ("TRC" or "the Commission") and Chief Samuel Hinga Norman JP against the Decision of his Lordship, Mr. Justice Bankole Thompson Delivered on Oct. 30, 2003 to Deny the TRC's Request to Hold a Public Hearing with Chief Samuel Hinga Norman JP, Norman (SCSL-2003-08-PT-122) Appeals Chamber, Nov. 28, 2003; Decision on Appeal by the Truth and Reconciliation Commission ("TRC") and Accused against the Decision of Judge Bankole Thompson Delivered on Nov. 3, 2003 to Deny the TRC's Request to Hold a Public Hearing with Augustine Gbao, Gbao (SCSL-04-15-PT-109) Appeals Chamber, May 7, 2004.

C. Assessing the Special Court's Contribution to Accountability

Achieving legal and social accountability were express goals of the Special Court. Indeed, the Court's primary purpose was to provide Sierra Leone with "a credible system of justice and accountability" to reaffirm "that persons who commit or authorize serious violations of international humanitarian law are individually responsible and accountable for those violations and that … every effort [will be] exert[ed] to bring those responsible to justice in accordance with international standards of justice, fairness and due process of law."[123] To assess the Special Court's contribution to accountability, this section analyses the extent that each factor contributed to each type of accountability.

1. Mode of Operation and Structure

The Special Court's mode of operation and structure on the whole enhanced its contribution to credible legal and social accountability. The Court's mode of operation and structure contributed to credibility in the same manner noted previously regarding truth. Thus, the analysis will not be repeated here. Clearly, the adversarial process is particularly well designed for credibly providing legal accountability. However, there are limits to that contribution.

The Court's mode of operation limited its contribution to providing legal or social accountability, but the Court's structure enhanced the social accountability provided. First, the rights of the Accused limited the Court's contribution to both legal and social accountability. As noted above, three of the indicted individuals died before the Court rendered judgment in their cases.[124] Thus, they will never be held formally accountable. Moreover, in the CDF case, the Trial Chamber refused to allow the OTP to amend its Indictment to include the crimes of rape as a crime against humanity, forced marriage the crime against humanity of other inhumane acts, and the war crime of outrages upon personal dignity, citing the prejudice to the defendants' rights to a fair and expeditious trial.[125] Second, many practical issues also limited the Court's contribution to accountability. The ability to apprehend indicted individuals,[126] the sheer volume of perpetrators; the amount of time required to try each individual,[127] and the evidentiary issues posed by the nature of the conflict and the lapse of time since the commission of the crimes all limited the number of individuals the Court held accountable and the types of crimes those individuals were held accountable for committing. Finally, however, the Court's structure and character did enhance the social accountability provided because of its location in Freetown and its public outreach campaign.[128]

---

[123] S.C. Res. 1315 (2009), preamble, §§ 6–7.

[124] *See supra* note 79 and accompanying text.

[125] See V. Oosterveld's chapter in this volume.

[126] Johnny Paul Koroma, indicted on March 7, 2003, remains at large. Prosecutor v. Koroma, Indictment, SCSL-2003–03-I and summary, *available at* http://www.sc-sl.org/CASES/JohnnyPaulKoroma/tabid/188/Default.aspx (last visited Apr. 6, 2012). Additionally, the court was unable to secure the arrest and detention of Charles Taylor, being harbored by Nigeria, until March 29, 2006, two years and nine months after his indictment. Taylor case summary, Special Court for Sierra Leone website, *available at* http://www.sc-sl.org/CASES/ProsecutorvsCharlesTaylor/tabid/107/Default.aspx (last visited Apr. 6, 2012).

[127] A. Cassese, Report on the Special Court for Sierra Leone available December 12, 2006, at 4, *available at* http://www.sc-sl.org/LinkClick.aspx?fileticket=VTDHyrHasLc=&tabid=176 (last visited May 3, 2012).

[128] *See supra* notes 93–98 and accompanying text.

2. Jurisdiction

The Court's jurisdiction directly impacted the types and credibility of its contribution to accountability. The boundaries of the Court's contributions to accountability essentially track those established with respect to establishing the truth. This section will address in detail only those issues particular to accountability. The Court's personal jurisdiction necessarily limited the extent that it could hold individuals socially and legally accountable. The Court lacked the jurisdiction and practical ability to try all individuals responsible for the atrocities carried out during the war, nor was it intended to do so. Moreover, the Court did not hold any child soldiers accountable for their crimes, although because of the widespread use of child soldiers in the conflict, children perpetrated many of the atrocities. Thus, the Court's narrow personal jurisdiction necessarily limited the extent that the Court contributed to social or legal accountability.

The clearly defined selectivity of the Court's personal jurisdiction enhanced the credibility of the Court's efforts to contribute to accountability. Selectivity is a prime criticism of prosecutions in the post-settlement context, which hinders the efficacy of a court's efforts to achieve credible accountability.[129] Often because of political and practical difficulties criminal prosecutions try only a few, often low-level, perpetrators. This random selectivity endangers the efficacy of the prosecutions because it appears unfair, sends the message that the powerful are above the law, and may make martyrs out of the individuals who are prosecuted.[130] Sierra Leone's precise personal jurisdiction limited the reach of the Court in a reasoned and calculated manner, thus diffusing the negative impact of this criticism. The Secretary-General recognized this fact in his report to the Security Council on the establishment of the Special Court, highlighting that "while the number of persons prosecuted before the Special Court will be limited, it [will] not be [indiscriminately] selective or otherwise discriminatory."[131] However, the OTP's exercise of prosecutorial discretion and the Court's abdication of its ability to review this exercise raised some selectivity concerns.[132]

The Court's subject matter jurisdiction made a limited, but significant, contribution to legal and social accountability. As noted previously, the Court's subject-matter jurisdiction was restricted to select international crimes,[133] and offenses under Sierra Leonean law relating to the abuse of girls and to the wanton destruction of property under the Malicious Damage Act, 1861.[134] Thus, the Court only had the potential to hold individuals accountable for a narrow subset of crimes. Moreover, ultimately, the Court only convicted individuals of international crimes.[135] The Court's subject-matter jurisdiction also prohibited it from holding individuals accountable for the illegal mining and sale of diamonds, although

---

[129] Minow, *supra* note 3, at 25–51.
[130] *Id.*
[131] S-G Report, *supra* note 72, § 7.
[132] The Appellate Chamber of the Court held that the OTP's decisions regarding which individuals bore the "greatest responsibility" were not reviewable. AFRC Appeal, *supra* note 100, §§ 281–283. For an in-depth analysis of the impact of these decisions, see Jalloh, *supra* note 81, at 413–28.
[133] SCSL Statute arts. 2–4.
[134] *Id.* at art. 5.
[135] Taylor Judgment, AFRC Appeal, AFRC Trial, RUF Appeal, RUF Trial, CDF Appeal, CDF Trial, *supra* note 100.

the diamond industry played a significant role in funding and fueling the Sierra Leonean conflict.[136]

Additionally, the amnesty restricted the Court's ability to hold individuals legally and socially accountable. The denial of the amnesty's legal effect extended only to the international crimes within the Court's subject-matter jurisdiction.[137] Thus, the perpetration of the national crime of abusing girls and abducting them for immoral purposes when those crimes occurred from November 30, 1996 to July 7, 1999 was outside the Court's competence, unless those crimes also fell within the umbrella of the international crimes.

Finally, the Court's temporal and territorial jurisdiction significantly limited its contribution to accountability. The Court could not hold accountable any perpetrators of atrocities committed in the first five years of the war.[138] Moreover, the Court lacked jurisdiction over crimes committed outside the territory of Sierra Leone.[139] However, the United Nations and the Sierra Leonean government did ensure that regional instigators, "those leaders who, in committing such crimes, have threatened the establishment and implementation of the peace process in Sierra Leone,"[140] fell within the Court's personal jurisdiction, as Charles Jalloh has also argued in his contribution.[141]

3. Judgments

The Court's judgments directly impacted its contribution to accountability. These judgments did not contribute to political or administrative accountability. However, they provided a high degree of legal and social accountability with respect to the convicted individuals. Ultimately, the Court convicted nine individuals for engaging in crimes against humanity and war crimes.[142] The Court's judgments were rendered by a majority of the Judges and announced publicly, with the Court's written opinions providing the legal support and underlying rationale for each decision. These public and official judgments are not only legal pronouncements of the individuals' responsibility, but are also social pronouncements and public condemnation of their actions. They send the strong message that the Accused's actions violated agreed standards of national and international law, that such violations are profoundly wrong, and that the perpetrator must accept the consequences. These judgments are a determination "beyond a reasonable doubt" of the Accused's guilt, resulting in imprisonment. Finally, the Court's judgments enhanced the credibility of the accountability provided. The public, written, and reasoned explanation and pronouncement of each individual's guilt or innocence afforded transparency to the accountability process, thus enhancing its credibility.

---

[136] I. Abdullah & P. Muana, *The Revolutionary United Front of Sierra Leone: A Revolt of the Lumpenproletariat, in* African Guerillas 177, 179 (C. Clapham ed., 1998).

[137] S-G Report, *supra* note 72, at para. 24.

[138] *See supra* notes 110–12 and accompanying text.

[139] *Id.*

[140] SCSL Statute art. 1(1).

[141] *See* Haines, *supra* note 85, at 221. The Special Court relied on this language to indict Charles Taylor. *See* Indictment, Taylor (SCSL-03-01-I) Mar. 7, 2003.

[142] Judgment, Taylor (SCSL-03-1-T) Trial Chamber II, May 18, 2012; Sentencing Judgment, Sesay, Kallon, Gbao ("RUF") (SCSL-04-15-T-1251) Trial Chamber I, Apr. 8, 2009 [hereinafter RUF Sentencing Judgment] on the Sentencing of Moinina Fofana and Allieu Kondewa, Fofana and Kondewa (SCSL-04-14-T-796) Trial Chamber I, Oct. 9, 2007 [hereinafter CDF Sentencing Judgment]; Sentencing Judgment, Brima, Kamara, Kanu (SCSL-04-16-T-624) Trial Chamber II, July 19, 2007 [hereinafter AFRC Sentencing Judgment].

D. Assessing the Special Court's Contribution to Reparations

Reparations were not an express goal of the Court. However, reparations are a necessary goal of transitional justice. To assess the Special Court's contribution to providing reparations, this section examines the extent that each factor contributed to the different types of reparations at the individual and societal levels.

1. Mode of Operation, Structure, and Jurisdiction

The Special Court's mode of operation, structure, and jurisdiction did not contribute to providing victims with reparations. The Special Court's statute did not specifically provide for reparations.[143] Article 19(3) permitted the Court to order the "forfeiture of the property, proceeds and any assets acquired unlawfully or by criminal conduct, and their return to their rightful owner or to the State of Sierra Leone";[144] however, the Court did not exercise this ability.[145] Additionally, as previously noted, the diamond industry funded and fueled this controversy, but the OTP did not indict any businessmen who benefited from the crimes committed and who arguably possessed funds that could provide reparations to the victims.[146]

Moreover, the financial cost of operating the Court detracted from the goal of providing reparations. The total cost of the Court's work exceeded $222 million total – approximately $23 million per Accused.[147] The Court was funded primarily through voluntary donations.[148] The National Commission for Social Action and the Special Fund for War Victims is a reparations fund distinct from the Court; it also is funded by voluntary contributions. Not surprisingly, the Commission suffered from chronic underfunding.[149] According to the United Nations Peacebuilding Fund, functioning with a budget of $4.4 million dollars, this fund registered more than 32,000 war victims, paid first installments of micro-grants and educational activities that benefitted 20,000 victims, provided assistance to 235 sexual violence victims, and began work on 40 community symbolic reparations.[150] Although no donors have expressly named their contributions to the Court as the reason for the paltry support of the reparations program, it is not unreasonable to assume that the cost of the court depleted the international resources available for reparations, thus directly detracting from the reparations provided to Sierra Leonean victims.

2. Judgments

The Court's judgments did not provide material reparations to any victims, but did make a small contribution to social reparations. Despite the Court's arguable ability to do so,

---

[143] *Passim* SCSL Statute. *Compare* Rome Statute for the International Criminal Court, art. 75.

[144] SCSL Statute art. 19(3).

[145] Judgment, Taylor (SCSL-03-1-T) Trial Chamber II, May 18, 2012, § 6994; RUF Sentencing Judgment, *supra* note 142; CDF Sentencing Judgment, *supra* note 142; AFRC Sentencing Judgment, *supra* note 142.

[146] Cruvellier, *supra* note 92, at 20.

[147] Jalloh, *supra* note 81, at 395 n.253.

[148] SCSL Agreement, *supra* note 70, at art. 6.

[149] *No Signs of Victim Compensation in Sierra Leone*, THE HAGUE JUSTICE PORTAL (Nov. 18, 2010), *available at* http://www.haguejusticeportal.net/index.php?id=12284 (last visited May 3, 2012).

[150] United Nations Peacebuilding Fund, Sierra Leone Overview, *available at* www.unpbf.org/countries/sierra-leone/.

none of the convicted defendants was ordered to pay compensation to his identified victims in any form.[151] Thus, the Court's judgments did not provide any material reparations to the victims. However, the Court's judgments did contribute to social reparations through acknowledgement of the commission of the atrocities by the defendants. Public acknowledgment of the harm and suffering of the victims and their families is a form of social reparation, and it contributes to reconciliation. Establishing the forensic truth via criminal trial contributes to the necessary acknowledgment that the atrocities were committed. This public acknowledgment is a form of reparation.[152] Additionally, acknowledging and holding responsible those individuals who committed the atrocities contributes to social reparations.[153] Thus, the Court's credible and public pronouncements in court and in writing on the facts surrounding the conflict and the Accuseds' guilt contributed to social reparations via acknowledgement.

E. Assessing the Special Court's Contribution to Reconciliation

Unlike truth, reconciliation was an express goal of the Court as previously noted.[154] To assess the Special Court's contribution to reconciliation, this section examines the extent that each factor contributed to the requirements of reconciliation at all levels.

1. Mode of Operation, Structure, and Jurisdiction

The Court's mode of operation, structure, and jurisdiction did not contribute directly to reconciliation at any level. The adversarial nature of criminal trials reinforces the divide between the perpetrators and the victims.[155] Trials alienate perpetrators because they take a defensive stance. Additionally, the necessity of cross-examination alienates the victims.[156] As such, the Court's work did not contribute to individual, interpersonal reconciliation. Moreover, at the community and national levels, trials exclude bystanders, beneficiaries, and populations structurally affected by the war,[157] because of the necessary focus on proving the guilt or innocence of the accused. Thus, the Court's mode of operation and structure by its very nature did not contribute significantly to community or national reconciliation.

However, the Court's mode of operation and jurisdiction did contribute to acknowledging the harm and those who were responsible, which are necessary requirements of reconciliation. As recognized in the section on truth, the Court's mode of operation and structure contributed to establishing in part credible forensic truth about the atrocities committed. As such, at least with respect to the crimes investigated, the Court's mode of operation and jurisdiction enhanced the Court's contribution to acknowledgement.

---

[151] RUF Sentencing Judgment, *supra* note 142; CDF Sentencing Judgment, *supra* note 142; AFRC Sentencing Judgment, *supra* note 142; Sentencing Judgment, Taylor (SCSL-03-1-T) Trial Chamber II, May 30, 2012.

[152] N. Roht-Arriaza, *Reparations in the Aftermath of Repression and Mass Violence, in* MY NEIGHBOR, MY ENEMY: JUSTICE AND COMMUNITY IN THE AFTERMATH OF MASS ATROCITY 121, 122–23 (E. Stover & H. Weinstein eds., 2004).

[153] *Id.*

[154] *See supra* note 72 and accompanying text.

[155] H. COBBAN, AMNESTY AFTER ATROCITY? HEALING NATIONS AFTER GENOCIDE AND WAR CRIMES 211 (2007).

[156] *Id.*

[157] *Id.*

2. Judgments

The Court's judgments impacted its contribution to reconciliation at all levels. First, as noted, truth contributes to acknowledging that the atrocities occurred and identifying the perpetrators. Second, accountability contributes to acknowledgment by holding those perpetrators responsible. Thus, the Court's credible and public pronouncements in court and in writing on the facts surrounding the conflict and the Accuseds' guilt contributed to acknowledging the atrocities committed and who were responsible for their commission. Thereby, the convictions of the nine high-level offenders indirectly contributed to the reconciliation process at the individual, community, and national level by providing some degree of the underlying requirement of acknowledgment by the Court itself.

However, this accountability lacked acknowledgement, remorse, and apology on the part of the perpetrators. As a result, the Court's contribution to acknowledgment is limited. Only one of the nine defendants expressed genuine remorse, apologized to the victims, and acknowledged directly his crimes.[158] This significantly minimized the contribution the Court made toward achieving reconciliation.

Moreover, the CDF Trial Chamber's decision, and the Appellate Chamber's affirmation of that decision, to recognize the defendants' statements in that case as sincere indications of remorse and apology detracted from the degree of reconciliation achieved.[159] The majority decision in the CDF appeal affirmed the trial court's recognition that the convicted individuals expressed sincere remorse, and accepted those expressions as a mitigating factor in their sentences.[160] These decisions on the whole detracted from the goal of reconciliation. As recognized by Justice Renate Winter in her partially dissenting opinion, the defendants' did not acknowledge their responsibility, did not express real and sincere remorse for the crimes committed, and did not indicate a desire to further reconciliation.[161] Defendant Fofana did not address the court directly.[162] His attorney spoke on his behalf and stated only that:

> Mr. Fofana accepts that crimes were committed by the CDF during the conflict in Sierra Leone. Indeed, at least one [defence] witness ... accept[ed] and attest[ed] to crimes committed by the CDF. Mr. Fofana deeply regrets all the unnecessary suffering that has occurred in his country.[163]

Defendant Kondewa simply said, "Sierra Leoneans, those of you who lost your relations within the war, I plead for mercy today, and remorse, and even for yourselves."[164] Fofana's statement expressed no regret for the suffering of the victims.[165] The statement merely indicated regret for the general situation, that some CDF committed crimes, and for the general

---

[158] RUF Sentencing Judgment, *supra* note 142, at paras. 88–89; AFRC Sentencing Judgment, *supra* note 142, at §§ 67, 139; Winter Dissent, *supra* note 64, §§ 98–105.

[159] CDF Appeal, *supra* note 100, §§ 478–490; CDF Sentencing Judgment, *supra* note 142, §§ 63–65.

[160] *Id.*

[161] Winter Dissent, *supra* note 64, §§ 98–105.

[162] CDF Sentencing Judgment, *supra* note 142, § 63.

[163] Winter Dissent, *supra* note 64, § 99. *Compare* RUF Sentencing Judgment, *supra* note 142, §§ 88–89 (Morris Kallon made a personal statement where he acknowledged his guilt, expressed remorse, and apologized to the victims).

[164] Winter Dissent, *supra* note 64, § 101.

[165] *Id.* § 100.

suffering in Sierra Leone. These statements appear to be nothing more than self-serving requests for mercy and leniency, made only after convictions of guilt.[166]

III. CONCLUSION

In sum, the Special Court for Sierra Leone contributed significantly, but limitedly, to achieving transitional justice. Primarily, the Court's work enhanced the degree of truth and accountability. Nevertheless, on the whole, its work detracted from the goal of reparations and added little to the goal of reconciliation. First, the Court was particularly well designed for establishing the forensic truth surrounding the role played by the individuals who bore the greatest responsibility, and as such, meaningfully contributed to credibly establishing this type of truth. However, the Court's mode of operation, structure, and jurisdiction restricted its contribution. Additionally, the Court's judgments contributed to the social truth established, but the difficulties of communicating this truth to civil society constrained its contribution. Moreover, although it made small contributions to establishing narrative truth by virtue of witness testimony, the Court's procedures were not designed to contribute to this type of truth.

Second, the Court provided considerable legal and social accountability by affirming that the atrocities occurred, condemning their commission, and punishing those most responsible. The Court's mode of operation and structure, jurisdiction, and judgments overall enhanced the legal and social accountability achieved. Particularly, the Court's focus on those bearing the greatest responsibility for the atrocities committed in Sierra Leone was a magnanimous contribution to accountability in Sierra Leone. Moreover, the Court's mode of operation and structure, jurisdiction, and judgments all served to shore up the Court's contributions to accountability by lending great credibility to its efforts. However, there were significant limitations as well. Most poignantly, the Court only served to hold accountable nine individuals. This small number pales in comparison to the thousands of perpetrators and atrocities committed throughout the war. Further, the Court's jurisdictional limitations prevented it from providing accountability for the atrocities committed throughout the entire first half of the conflict. However, despite these limitations, overall the Court significantly and credibly contributed to legal and social accountability for the atrocities committed.

Third, the Court did contribute to social reparations in a very limited form through its convictions of the nine high-level offenders, and through its pronouncements on their crimes; their roles in the conflict; and the context, causes, and patterns of violence of the war. However, the Court provided no material reparations to the identified victims. Moreover, the Court's significant cost likely impaired Sierra Leone's ability to raise money for its independent Special Fund for War Victims.

Finally, the Court's potential to contribute to reconciliation was limited at best despite the fact that it was lauded as an express goal of the institution. On the whole, the Court's mode of operation and structure were not designed to foster reconciliation at the individual level because the adversarial nature of criminal prosecutions is divisive. The Court's work contributed to a limited acknowledgement of the harms committed and

---

[166] *Id.* § 103.

acknowledgement of perpetrators of those harms. However, the failure of the majority of the defendants to personally acknowledge their roles or to directly apologize to the victims detracted from the Court's contributions. Moreover, the Court's acceptance of the CDF defendants' statements as meaningful articulations of remorse detracted from the Court's contributions.

Conclusion

A Positive (Not Perfect) Legacy

Charles Chernor Jalloh

As noted in the Introduction to this volume, the primary goal of this book was to assess the legacy and contributions of the Special Court for Sierra Leone (SCSL) to international criminal law and practice. We saw that "legacy", as used in this volume, was defined as a specific reference to the legal rules, principles, practices and norms that the SCSL is expected to leave behind for current and future generations of international, internationalized and national courts charged with the responsibility to prosecute the same or similar international crimes.

On one level, much like Justice Robert Jackson argued in relation to the International Military Tribunal at Nuremberg (IMT) in 1946, as discussed in the Introduction to this volume, it can be argued that it is too early to appreciate the full impact and legacy of the SCSL and its contributions to international criminal law and practice. History proved Justice Jackson right. And although he had presciently observed that it was possible that the Nuremberg trials would become the biggest moral and legal advance from World War II, humanity only felt the full reverberations of the IMT's legacy several decades later. In fact, it took until the early 1990s for the Nuremberg Legacy to be realized after the United Nations invoked the post–World War II trials to create the International Criminal Tribunal for the Former Yugoslavia (ICTY) and the subsequent international criminal courts that followed in its wake, including the International Criminal Tribunal for Rwanda (ICTR) and the SCSL.

Yet, as the experience with the IMT, the recent books assessing the legacy of the ICTY, and the thirty-six substantive chapters assembled in this volume attest, the right question may no longer be whether it is useful to begin to assess the SCSL's legacy. It unquestionably is. Indeed, even if we accept for the sake of argument that it is somewhat premature to identify the whole legacy of the SCSL, it is also true that it is never too early to start to observe what its likely long-term impact will be. In any event, much as was the case with the IMT and since then the UN ad hoc tribunals, not all of a tribunal's entire legacy is necessarily indeterminate. Some aspects are relatively more determinate and may therefore already be discernable. Others are less determinate and may remain hidden for a while, taking years if not decades to come out of the shadows. Such is no doubt the case with the expectation which was floated when the Sierra Leone court was created that it might help lead to national reconciliation through its prosecutions. Reconciliation is both a goal and a process. As a goal, it signifies an end point, after forgiveness. As a process, it implies movement on a spectrum, towards forgiveness. Both can occur, in individuals, and to entire societies. Both will require time.

But not all parts of the legacy require a considerable passage of time to be identified or fairly evaluated. For instance, if we judge the Court by Justice Jackson's standard of whether the tribunal has achieved what it was primarily set up to do, that is to prosecute those bearing greatest responsibility for the serious crimes within its jurisdiction (in fair trials that comport with the requirements of international human rights law), then we are able to conclude that it has. Indeed, the SCSL made an important contribution to the people of Sierra Leone by prosecuting a total of nine military/political leaders found to be among those most responsible for what happened in that country. It did so through the investigations and prosecutions in the AFRC, CDF, RUF, and Taylor cases – all of which are summarized in the Introduction to this book.

Although it is legitimate to ask whether nine trials constituted enough justice, especially given the scale of the widespread atrocities experienced during a terrible eleven-year conflict and the millions of dollars expended in the prosecutions, those trials constitute at least *some measure of* justice. Some justice seems better than no justice. This is all the more so considering the reality that with the Sierra Leonean government's endorsement of the much derided amnesty clause included in the 1999 peace accord, which helped to end the hostilities by conferring impunity to all the killers, it seems that but for the creation of the SCSL, no justice might have been meted out by the Sierra Leonean domestic courts for the heinous offenses committed during the latter part of that country's infamous civil war. Indeed, today, many known middle and lower ranking associates of the perpetrators of the vile acts prosecuted by the SCSL today roam the streets of Freetown, the Sierra Leonean capital, seemingly secure in the knowledge that they will never be prosecuted. And we have not even mentioned the apparent lack of legal and institutional capacity to prosecute international offenses in the largely troubled national justice system.

In the end then, if nothing else, the legacy of the Court might stand more as a *symbol* of justice rather than *actual* justice. After a decade of mayhem, the SCSL's achievements, as meager as they may at first seem, imply that the international community and a concerned state can, where there is political will, successfully join forces to fight against impunity. Some justice was dispensed on behalf of some of the victims, leaving little if any space for denial that horrific crimes were committed against innocents. The result is far from perfect, but a common narrative of justice in the name of the people and for the people has emerged. Even more importantly, the guns have fallen silent, and peace and a measure of rule of law have replaced the rule of the gun in Sierra Leone. And while the Court cannot realistically claim credit for all those developments, it can justifiably claim credit for making some small contributions towards the achievement of the current post-conflict stability.

Overall, the individual and collective works of the scholars, practitioners and scholar-practitioners assembled in this book constitute important additions to the legal literature on the SCSL and the impact of international criminal tribunals more broadly. As a general matter, the contributing authors to this volume have advanced two principal types of arguments about the Court's legacy. First, the overwhelming majority of the authors, who focused on assessments of the legal legacy as found in the Statute and jurisprudence of the Tribunal, generally conclude that the SCSL made some useful contributions to the emerging system of international criminal justice. Of course, this is not to imply that the Court did not face challenges or that it was not criticized by many of the scholarly chapters in this work, where the authors felt that such criticism was deserved.

Second, the relatively fewer authors who examined the SCSL's practice with respect to more institutional matters, such as the creation of the Defense Office and the Outreach Section, also generally concur that the Court added some value to the architecture of international criminal law institutions. In other words, the trials, guilty verdicts, reasoned judgments, and factual findings bequeathed to the people of Sierra Leone are in many ways the SCSL's primary legacy. But by also fleshing out the international criminal law and applying it to new factual situations, as well as innovating new institutional structures and road testing them, the SCSL has offered both positive (what to do) and negative legacies (what not to do) for international criminal justice. It follows that, in big picture terms, the right question is no longer whether the SCSL contributed in a range of areas, it is how much it did contribute, and with the benefit of hindsight, how much more it could have contributed to Sierra Leone, Africa and international criminal justice.

In terms of the positive lessons, among others, the Court's approach to amnesties, treatment of head-of-state immunity, child recruitment, forced marriage, and the war crime of attacks against UN peacekeepers will likely be among its most significant jurisprudential legacies. These legal contributions are the ones likely to be consulted by other courts looking for helpful precedents in future trials. This has already occurred in several cases at several tribunals, including the International Criminal Court (ICC), where for instance, the Sierra Leone jurisprudence on the war crime of child recruitment has served as important precedent in the seminal Thomas Lubanga case.

Regarding its practice, the Court's laudable attempt to experiment with the creation of a Defense Office, to engage in extensive outreach, and to deliberately plan its legacy will all likely be remembered for adding some significant value to the *corpus juris* of the international criminal law process. Here too, the impact of the Sierra Leone court can already be felt elsewhere. For example, the institutional defense innovation from the SCSL served as inspiration for the first such autonomous office in the history of international criminal law at the Special Tribunal for Lebanon. In the same vein, the Court's outreach activities *in situ* has provided a compelling model for the work of the ICC, which has in some cases hired former SCSL staff members to lead its outreach efforts in some situation countries in East Africa.

If we turn to the other types of lessons from the SCSL, the negative lessons so to speak, that is those that may not be worth replicating elsewhere or that at least bear closer examination before we do so, there appears to be some lessons yet to be retrieved from an assessment of the Court's legacy. That said, the contributors to this volume appear to have unearthed the majority of them. Two examples will suffice to make the point. Firstly, the UN's practice, which started with Sierra Leone, to create ad hoc tribunals with limited personal jurisdiction over a few persons bearing greatest responsibility is probably worth reconsidering in the future. That much appears to flow from the keynote speech by a former chief prosecutor of the tribunal and the chapter contribution of the editor of this volume. Secondly is the always controversial Joint Criminal Enterprise (JCE) doctrine, which is discussed by two chapters in this book. While I do not necessarily subscribe to all the authors' analysis of JCE, it seems fair to conclude that the Court's interpretation and application of the third variant of the JCE mode of liability stands out. Not only was it highly controversial during the trials, it continues to remain so, and might therefore need to be carefully re-examined if not completely abandoned by future tribunals and judges. Contrary to what seems implied by the contributors to this volume, I would not go so far as to suggest that the perpetrators of the wartime atrocities convicted by the SCSL judges using JCE III were unjustly treated or that they were only found guilty by association.

Another lesson is this. As a structural matter, the SCSL experiment suggests that states should not set up such justice institutions, which generate super-high expectations in local victim and international advocacy communities as to the quality and quantity of justice that they will deliver, only to then starve them of the requisite financial means to succeed. The states should certainly not subject these institutions to the vagaries of donations-based funding. Indeed, in my humble view, if there is a single lesson that we can draw for the international community from the SCSL, it will have to be this: international criminal tribunals should never be funded primarily or solely by voluntary contributions from states. That the SCSL struggled throughout its life to secure the most basic funding to do its work was an open secret and bad enough.

But, perhaps even worse, is that as it winds down towards closure, the SCSL today subsists on the subvention grant handouts from the United Nations. It is a court literally functioning on welfare. This raises separate concerns as to whether the Tribunal should confidently expect to secure the basic funds required to establish its important residual mechanism. If, between the affected state (Sierra Leone) and the international community (as represented by the United Nations) the political will does not exist to find the necessary funding for the primary trials of suspects to take place, how will the residual court obtain the money to carry out its inevitable functions such as reviews of defendant sentences and conditions of detention?

Going forward, for future ad hoc tribunals, the implication seems clear enough. If funding has to be voluntary instead of assessed, as was the case for the UN twin tribunals, then serious consideration should be given to alternatives means of dispensing justice such as the creation of special panels or an international crimes division within the national courts of the concerned jurisdiction. So, the experiments with creating hybrids in Bosnia, Kosovo, East Timor and even Uganda might need to be taken more seriously than has so far been the case. Depending on the specific factors at play in the given situation, such as whether this could lead to possible bias in prosecutions, a mixed court that offers more in the way of technical legal assistance for an existing national justice system could prove to be more cost effective. At least when compared to the creation of an entirely autonomous and therefore relatively more expensive institution such as the SCSL. Another benefit is that, if done well, such efforts might help build or supplement local capacity to prosecute international crimes, a benefit that was hoped for but that hardly materialized in Sierra Leone.

In closing, this book is meant to spark a conversation about the SCSL and its legacy to Africa and international criminal law. It is therefore intended to be the first of hopefully many scholarly works that will in the future engage in analysis of the impact of that tribunal from the perspective of lawyers as well as non-lawyers, using diverse disciplinary and other approaches, from the legal to the empirical and theoretical and beyond. My goal will be achieved if this work succeeds in achieving this modest objective.

By convening a group of eminent scholars on the Court today, and the leading ones of tomorrow, to engage in this first substantive assessment of the legal legacy and impact of the

SCSL, the third UN-sponsored ad hoc international criminal court, it is my sincere hope that this volume, taken as a whole, will constitute a major contribution to existing knowledge regarding the achievements, and shortcomings, of one of the more significant internationally supported anti-impunity initiatives in post–Cold War era Africa.

Index